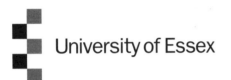

University of Essex   Library

Date Due Back

Books may be renewed online (or telephone 01206 873187)
Unless they have been recalled.

Form No. L.43 April 2004

Company Law

Robert R Pennington LLD

Solicitor, Professor of Commercial Law at the
University of Birmingham, formerly Adviser on
Company Law to the Commission of the
European Communities

Sixth edition

Butterworths
London, Dublin and Edinburgh
1990

United Kingdom	Butterworth & Co (Publishers) Ltd, 88 Kingsway, LONDON WC2B 6AB and 4 Hill Street, EDINBURGH EH2 3JZ
Australia	Butterworths Pty Ltd, SYDNEY, MELBOURNE, BRISBANE, ADELAIDE, PERTH, CANBERRA and HOBART
Canada	Butterworths Canada Ltd, TORONTO and VANCOUVER
Ireland	Butterworth (Ireland) Ltd, DUBLIN
Malaysia	Malayan Law Journal Sdn Bhd, KUALA LUMPUR
New Zealand	Butterworths of New Zealand Ltd, WELLINGTON and AUCKLAND
Puerto Rico	Equity de Puerto Rico, Inc, HATO REY
Singapore	Malayan Law Journal Pte Ltd, SINGAPORE
USA	Butterworth Legal Publishers, AUSTIN, Texas; BOSTON, Massachusetts; CLEARWATER, Florida (D & S Publishers); ORFORD, New Hampshire (Equity Publishing); ST PAUL, Minnesota; and SEATTLE, Washington

A CIP Catalogue record for this book is available from the British Library.

ISBN 0 406 51041 5

Typeset, printed and bound in Great Britain by William Clowes Limited, Beccles and London

Preface

The increasing complexity and volume of company legislation, which was commented on in the preface to the fifth edition of this book, has not abated since its publication in 1985. The Financial Services Act 1986, as well as providing a statutory framework for the regulation of investment business, has completely recast the law governing the marketing of companies' shares and other securities; the Insolvency Act 1986 has substantially revised the law governing company liquidations and receiverships, and has introduced alternative proceedings to deal with insolvent companies in the form of the administration order and voluntary arrangements assented by a majority of creditors. More recently, the Companies Act 1989 has altered and supplemented the existing legislation in many ways, particularly in respect of the contents of companies' annual accounts and group accounts, and the rules relating to the eligibility of appropriately qualified accountants for appointments as auditors of companies and their tenure of office; the registration of charges created by companies over their assets at the Companies Registry; and the reversal of the external effect of the ultra vires rule on the validity of companies' contracts. At the same time, the 1989 Act has simplified many of the procedural requirements imposed on private companies with regard to the filing of their annual accounts and other matters, or at least has made it possible for them to do so by adopting the so-called elective régime.

While company legislation has grown in quantity and intricacy, the flow of decisions by the courts elaborating the statutory rules and applying equitable principles in company situations (particularly in respect of directors' obligations and the protection of minority shareholders) has kept pace. Probably the most notable development in this respect has been the growing body of case law in respect of petitions for relief presented by minority shareholders of private companies who complain of the unfairly prejudicial conduct of their companies' affairs in ways which affect their interests adversely. The courts have shed their earlier inhibitions about applying the relevant legislation (the Companies Act 1985, ss 459–461, as amended) in situations where minority shareholders have been treated in a cavalier fashion, or where their legitimate expectations have been frustrated, and there has been established a fairly consistent pattern of typical situations where the court will give relief because it is equitable to do so. The most used remedy in these situations has been an order of the court that the petitioner's shares shall be bought out by the respondents who were responsible for the matters complained of, and that the price to be paid shall be calculated on the basis of an equitable apportionment of the company's net worth without any discount from that value because the petitioner's interest is a minority one.

The substantial growth in the volume of company law has inevitably led academic lawyers and practitioners in the field to treat what has traditionally been considered a single subject as naturally dividing itself into three divisions which, because of their size and importance, are each in the course of becoming subjects in their own right. The three components of company law which are now seen to be distinct are: (1) the law relating to the formation and operation of companies (including the law governing the raising of share and loan capital and the marketing of company securities, a topic which is itself becoming a subject in its own right); (2) the law governing insolvent companies, covering liquidations, administration orders, arrangements with creditors and receiverships; and (3) the law governing mergers and acquisitions of companies (including takeovers, management buy-outs and buy-ins), reconstructions of companies and corporate acquisitions and participations with an international element. The courses provided for law degree and professional examinations already reflect this accepted division, and although undergraduate courses as yet rarely cover more than the first two components mentioned above, they are usually taught as separate courses because of the physical impossibility of teaching them adequately in a single course. The third component is generally regarded as appropriate only for postgraduate taught courses and thesis work, but of necessity it does figure to varying degrees in courses for the different professional qualifications in law, accountancy, banking and the securities industry.

In previous editions of this book it has been possible to give an account of all the matters traditionally comprised in company law in sufficient detail, and this it is hoped has met the needs of both students and practitioners. However, this had been at the cost of increasing the size of the book in successive editions. In view of the general acceptance of the necessity to treat company law as now comprising three, if not more than three, components, and because a single book dealing with all of them would be too large if it were to deal with all the material adequately, the author and publisher have decided that the new edition of this book should be confined to the first component mentioned above, namely the company as a going concern. It is hoped that this will ensure that the subject matter can be presented in a logical and progressive manner and in sufficient detail, with appropriate brief references to the other components of company law with which the book does not deal. It is intended to follow the publication of this new edition with the publication in a year or so of a companion volume on insolvency law, which will deal with corporate insolvency and insolvency proceedings with a similar attention to detail and completeness as this book.

Company law will inevitably become more complex and voluminous as time passes. The issue of additional harmonisation directives by the Council of Ministers of the European Communities will ensure that new company legislation, in the form of Acts of Parliament or delegated legislation, will be a perennial occurrence. Also new practices in the corporate field, changes in the structure of company management, new forms of company securities and the opening of new markets for company securities will call for corresponding legislation. At the same time, the interpretative work of the court and the application by it of existing principles of law and equity in new corporate situations will result in an expanding volume of case law. Company law has never been a simple subject. Its prospect for the future, despite its continuing growth and increasing intricacy, is that it can be successfully moulded by the legislature and the courts so as to provide effective protection for investors whilst leaving management free to employ its talents more widely and more profitably, subject only to those restrictions which are necessary to ensure the honest and competent conduct of companies' affairs.

The law is stated in this book as it stood on 1 June 1990. The Companies Act 1989 is treated as though it had been brought wholly into operation by that date, although in fact it will not be completely in force until the end of 1990. Where the detailed operation of any of its provisions is dependent on the making of delegated legislation in the future, the fact that the relevant legislation is as yet incomplete is indicated.

University of Birmingham   ROBERT R PENNINGTON
June 1990

Table of statutes

References in this Table to *Statutes* are to Halsbury's Statutes of England (Fourth Edition) showing the volume and page at which the annotated text of the Act may be found.

Table of cases

B

PAGE

O

P

PART 1

Corporate personality, rights and liabilities

CHAPTER 1

Formation of a company

CLASSIFICATION OF COMPANIES AND INCORPORATION PROCEDURE

Companies registered under the Companies Act 1985, or the earlier Companies Acts, are divided into two main categories, namely, public companies and private companies. A public company is defined as a company limited by shares, or limited by guarantee and having a share capital, whose memorandum of association states that it is to be a public company,[1] and which complies with the provisions of the Companies Act 1985, as to its name[2] and the amount of its nominal share capital,[3] and which has a certificate of incorporation stating that it is a public company.[4] All other companies registered under the Companies Acts are private companies, and they comprise private companies limited by shares, companies limited by guarantee and unlimited companies.[5]

Whether a company is a public or private company, it is incorporated by the Registrar of Companies issuing a certificate of incorporation.[6] To obtain this certificate, the persons who form the company must deliver to the Registrar a number of documents, the most important of which are the memorandum and articles of association.

MEMORANDUM OF ASSOCIATION

The memorandum of association contains the fundamental provisions of the company's constitution. It must provide for certain matters (such as the activities which the company may pursue, and the company's share capital), and it may provide for any additional matter which could be dealt with in the articles of association. Specimen forms of memorandum of association for a public company and for the different kinds of private companies are set out in Tables B, C, D and E in the Schedule to regulations made by the Secretary of State for Trade and Industry;[7] these regulations were made under the Companies Act 1985, and like it, came into operation on 1 July 1985.[8] So far as possible, the memorandum of a company to be incorporated must be in the form set out in Table B, C, D, E or F, whichever is appropriate, or as near thereto as circumstances admit.[9] However, this does not mean that the contents of the memorandum and articles, as distinct

1 Companies Act 1985, s 1 (3). But since 22 December 1980 no new company may be registered as one limited by shares and by guarantee (s 1 (4)).
2 Companies Act 1985, s 25 (1) (see p 4, post).
3 Ibid, s 11 and s 118 (1) (see p 9, post).
4 Ibid, s 13 (6) (see p 27, post).
5 Ibid, s 1 (2) and (3).
6 Ibid, s 13 (1) and (3).
7 The Companies (Tables A to F) Regulations 1985, (SI 1985/805), para 2 and Schedule.
8 Ibid; Companies Act 1985, s 746.
9 Companies Act 1985, s 3 (1).

from their arrangement, must be similar to the models in the regulations; their contents are valid even though they differ radically from those of the models, or even conflict with them.[10] When printed, the memorandum must be signed by at least two persons,[11] and if the company has a share capital there must be shown against the name of each subscriber the number of shares he agrees to take,[12] so that when the company is incorporated the subscribers will become its first members,[13] and the signature of each subscriber must be attested.[14] The memoranda of companies incorporated before August 1970 had to be stamped 10s,[15] but the duty has been abolished in respect of memoranda executed since then.[16]

The matters for which the memorandum must make provision are six in number for a public company, and five for a private company other than an unlimited one. They will now be dealt with in detail.

Name

The first clause of the memorandum states the name of the company.[17] If the company is a public company, its name must conclude with the words 'public limited company' or the contraction 'plc',[18] and if the company is a private one, and the liability of the company's members is limited by shares or guarantee, the last word of the name must be 'limited' or the contraction 'ltd'.[19] The name is chosen by the promoters; it may comprise the name of the owner of the business the company is formed to acquire, or it may describe the kind of activities the company will carry on, or it may comprise an invented word, or be decided upon in any other way. There is no general legal requirement that the name should be approved by any public authority before it is chosen, but the founders' freedom of choice is seriously restricted in three ways, namely, by special statutory provisions, by restrictions imposed by the Companies Act 1985, and by the common law in respect of the tort of passing off.

Special statutory restrictions

Statute has prohibited the use of certain names which have an association with recognised charitable organisations in order to prevent private individuals from profiting by the public goodwill which attaches to them. Thus, a company's name may not comprise the words 'Red Cross' or 'Geneva Cross' without the authority of the Army Council,[20] nor the word 'Anzac' without the authority of the Secretary of State for Foreign and Commonwealth Affairs,[21] nor may the company's name consist of or imitate the names of certain organisations incorporated by royal charter.[1]

10 *Gaiman v National Association for Mental Health* [1971] Ch 317, [1970] 2 All ER 362.
11 Companies Act 1985, s 1 (1).
12 Ibid, s 2 (5).
13 Ibid, s 22 (1).
14 Ibid, s 2 (6).
15 Companies Act 1948, s 3 and Stamp Act 1891, 1st Sch, Deed (32 Halsbury's Statutes (3rd Edn) 137).
16 Finance Act 1970, s 32 and Sch 7, para 1 (2) (41 Halsbury's Statutes (4th Edn) 302).
17 Companies Act 1985, s 2 (1).
18 Ibid, s 25 (1) and s 27 (1) and (4).
19 Ibid, s 25 (2) and s 27 (1) and (4).
20 Geneva Convention Act 1957, s 6 (10 Halsbury's Statutes (4th Edn) 461).
21 Anzac (Restriction on Trade Use of Word) Act 1916, s 1 (48 Halsbury's Statutes (4th Edn) 40). The word 'Anzac' consists of the initial letters of the name of the Australian and New Zealand Army Corps, which earned fame by its heroism at Gallipoli in 1915 during the First World War.
1 Chartered Associations (Protection of Names and Uniforms) Act 1926, s 1 (48 Halsbury's Statutes (4th Edn) 41). These protected organisations at present comprise the Boy Scouts and Girl Guides Associations, the Order of St John of Jerusalem, and the Royal Life Saving Society.

It is a criminal offence for a company to use any name or to describe itself or its business in a way which indicates that it is a bank or carries on a banking business, unless it is an institution authorised by the Bank of England to carry on a deposit taking business under the Banking Act 1987.[2] The Registrar of Companies will refuse to register a company whose name includes the word 'bank' or any cognate word despite the repeal of his explicit statutory power to do so,[3] on the ground that the inevitable publication of the company's name would constitute a criminal offence.[4]

Restrictions imposed by the Companies Acts

A company cannot be registered with a name which includes the words 'limited', 'unlimited' or 'public limited company' or contractions of those words, unless those words or contractions of them appear at the end of its name and are appropriate for a company of its status.[5] Nor can a company be registered with the same name as one which is already entered in an index kept by the Registrar of Companies of the names of all companies registered under the Companies Act 1985, or the earlier Companies Acts, of all overseas companies which have delivered particulars of themselves to the Companies Registry on establishing a place of business in Great Britain[6] or Northern Ireland,[7] of all unregistered companies to which certain of the provisions of the Companies Act 1985 apply,[8] and of all registered limited partnerships.[9] To fall within the prohibition the name must be the same as, and not merely similar to, that of an existing company or limited partnership whose name is included in the index kept by the Registrar; for this purpose certain minor and purely formal differences between names are disregarded and are insufficient to prevent the name of a company being treated as the same as that of an existing company.[10]

Furthermore, a company will not be registered with a name which the Secretary of State for Trade and Industry considers offensive, or if the Secretary considers that the use of that name would involve a criminal offence (eg by infringing the exclusive right conferred by the statutes mentioned above to the use of certain names).[11] Finally, unless the Secretary of State for Trade and Industry gives his approval, a company may not be registered with a name which suggests a connection with HM Government or with a local authority, nor without such approval may a company be registered with a name which includes words or expressions specified in regulations made by the Secretary of State.[12] The regulations may specify a Government or other body whose opinion on, and possible objections to, the proposed name of the company must be sought before

2 Banking Act 1987, s 67 (1) (4 Halsbury's Statutes (4th Edn) 600).
3 The statutory power to reject the name was conferred by the Banking Act 1979, s 36 (10), which was repealed by the Companies Act 1981, s 119 (5) and Sch 4.
4 Companies Act 1985, s 26 (1) (*d*). The Registrar acted on the opinion of the Secretary of State for Trade and Industry to this effect.
5 Companies Act 1985, s 26 (1) (*a*) and (*b*).
6 Ibid, s 691.
7 Companies (Index of Names) (Variation) Order 1982 (SI 1982/1654), para 2.
8 Companies Act 1985, s 718.
9 Ibid, s 26 (1) (*c*) and s 714 (1).
10 Ibid, s 26 (3). These minor and formal differences which are disregarded are:—(i) the inclusion or omission of the definite article as the first word of a company's name; (ii) the terminal words 'company', 'and company', 'company limited', 'and company limited', 'limited', 'unlimited', 'public limited company' or their Welsh equivalents; (iii) abbreviations of any of the words listed in (ii); (iv) type and case of letters (capitals or small), spaces between letters, accents and punctuation marks; and (v) the word 'and' and the ampersand sign.
11 Companies Act 1985, s 26 (1) (*d*) and (*e*).
12 Ibid, s 26 (2) and s 29 (1).

the papers to lead to its incorporation are delivered to the Registrar of Companies, and the person who makes the statutory declaration of compliance with the requirements of the Companies Act 1985,[13] must also make a statement that this opinion has been sought, and the statement and a copy of the response of the Government or other body must be delivered to the Registrar.[14] The regulations made by the Secretary of State list certain words or groups of words, such as 'British', 'Charitable', 'Chamber of Commerce', 'Chartered', 'European', 'Foundation', 'Holding', 'Insurance', 'International', 'Registered', 'Royal', 'Trade Union' and 'United Kingdom', which may be included in a company's name only with the approval of the Secretary of State for Trade and Industry, and the regulations also specify against certain such words or groups of words the Government or other bodies whose possible objections to their inclusion in a company's name must be sought.[15]

Common law: passing off

It is a tort for one person to represent his business to be that of another or to mislead the public into believing that it is, because the person guilty of the deception thereby profits illegitimately from the goodwill which attaches to the other's business. The commonest means by which this deception is practised is by the adoption of a business name which is calculated to cause the public to confuse the spurious business with the genuine one. If the spurious business is conducted by a company incorporated with a name likely to cause such confusion, the owner of the genuine business may obtain an injunction to restrain the company from trading in its own name, or even from continuing to have its own name.[16] If the injunction takes this latter form, the company must either change its name or be wound up.

A passing off action lies, however, only when the company carries on the same kind of business as the plaintiff,[17] or where business transactions are likely to come to the company because the public will believe that it is in some way connected with the plaintiff.[18] Consequently, where a company was incorporated to carry on the business of motor vehicle insurance in a name similar to that of a motor dealers' trade protection association, the court refused an injunction to the association, because the difference between the activities of the company and the association precluded any possibility of confusion.[19]

The law is jealous to preserve the right of an individual to trade in his own name, even if confusion may thereby be caused between his business and that of another person with the same name. Likewise, the court will not restrain a company from using a name which comprises the name of the individual from whom it bought its

13 See p 27, post.
14 Companies Act 1985, s 29 (2) and (3).
15 The Company and Business Names Regulations 1981 (SI 1981/1685), paras 3 to 5 and Schedule; The Company and Business Names (Amendment) Regulations 1982, (SI 1982/1653), para 3. The regulations are continued in force by the Companies Consolidation (Consequential Provisions) Act 1985, s 31 (2).
16 *North Cheshire and Manchester Brewery Co v Manchester Brewery Co* [1899] AC 83; *Anciens Etablissements SA des Panhard et Levassor v Panhard Levassor Motor Co Ltd* [1901] 2 Ch 513; *Exxon Corpn v Exxon Insurance Consultants International Ltd* [1982] Ch 119, [1981] 2 All ER 495.
17 *North Cheshire and Manchester Brewery Co v Manchester Brewery Co* (supra); *Standard Bank of South Africa Ltd v Standard Bank Ltd* (1909) 25 TLR 420.
18 *Ewing v Buttercup Margarine Co Ltd* [1917] 2 Ch 1; *Exxon Corpn v Exxon Insurance Consultants International Ltd* (supra).
19 *Society of Motor Manufacturers and Traders Ltd v Motor Manufacturers' and Traders' Mutual Insurance Co Ltd* [1925] Ch 675.

business, despite the risk of confusion of its business with that of a third person.[20] But the law will not go farther than this, and so if a company's name merely comprises the name of one of its directors or shareholders, the court will restrain the company from using that name if there is any such risk of confusion.[1]

There are no facilities for reserving a name for a company while its memorandum and articles and the other documents leading to its incorporation are being prepared. Consequently, even if a proposed name is unobjectionable when the promoters of the company search the index of companies' names before having its memorandum or articles printed, or when the promoters obtain the approval of the Secretary of State for the proposed name of the company (if this is required), the Registrar is bound to reject it when the memorandum and articles are delivered to him if it has by then become objectionable, in particular, by another company having meanwhile been registered with the same name. To overcome this difficulty the Jenkins Committee recommended that the Registrar should have power to reserve a name for a proposed company for up to 30 days on payment of a fee;[2] it would not then be possible for him to refuse to register the company with that name if the memorandum and articles were delivered to him within that time, and no other company would be registered with the same or a similar name in the meantime. This recommendation has not been adopted.

Dispensation with the word 'limited'

A private company limited by guarantee whose objects are the promotion of commerce, art, science, education, religion or charity, or any profession and anything incidental or conducive to those objects, and whose memorandum or articles of association require the company's profits or other income to be applied exclusively in promoting its objects and not in making distributions to its members, and also require its net assets in a winding up to be transferred to another body with similar objects, may dispense with the word 'limited' as the last word of its name.[3] Such a company may not alter its memorandum or articles of association in a way which would disqualify it from dispensing with the word 'limited' as part of its name without adding that word at the end of its name.[4] If such a company carries on any business other than the promotion of any of the objects which entitle it to dispense with the word 'limited' as part of its name, or if it applies any of its income otherwise than in promoting such objects, or if it pays a dividend to its members, the Secretary of State for Trade and Industry may direct the company to change its name to one terminating with the word 'limited' within a period specified by the Secretary of State, and the company may not thereafter be re-registered with a name which omits the word 'limited' unless the Secretary of State approves.[5]

A private company which conforms to the conditions mentioned in the preceding paragraph may omit the word 'limited' from its name without the need to obtain special permission from a Government authority.[3] Formerly this could be done only if the Department of Trade issued a licence for the purpose before the registration of the company, or subsequently on the company altering its name.[6]

---

20 *Tussaud v Tussaud* (1890) 44 ChD 678.
1 *Fine Cotton Spinners and Doublers' Association Ltd and John Cash & Sons Ltd v Harwood Cash & Co Ltd* [1907] 2 Ch 184; *Kingston, Miller & Co Ltd v T Kingston & Co Ltd* [1912] 1 Ch 575.
2 Report of the Company Law Committee (Cmnd 1749), paras 450 and 456 (*k*).
3 Companies Act 1985, s 30 (1) to (3).
4 Ibid, s 31 (1).
5 Ibid, s 31 (2) and (3).
6 Companies Act 1948, s 19 (1) and (2).

Companies which obtained such a licence before the need for it was abolished[7] may continue to omit the word 'limited' from their name, but only as long as their memoranda and articles contain the provisions required for a newly formed company to do so,[3] and the Secretary of State for Trade and Industry may direct such a company to add the word 'limited' to its name in the same circumstances as a newly registered company.[5] The only advantage which a company incorporated under the former law has in this respect, therefore, is that it may be limited by shares instead of by guarantee.

Publicity in respect of the company's name

A company, other than a private company entitled to dispense with the word 'limited' as the last word of its name,[8] must exhibit its name outside every place where its business is carried on, must have its name legibly engraved on its common seal unless it dispenses with such a seal,[9] and must mention its name in all business letters and publications and in all bills of exchange, cheques, promissory notes, orders for money or goods, receipts and invoices signed or issued on its behalf.[10] In the case of a private company, it suffices that the word 'limited' as part of the company's name appears in the contracted form, 'Ltd' or, possibly, 'Ld',[11] but the omission of the word 'limited'[12] or of any other word forming part of the company's name[13] results in an infringement of the Companies Act. In the case of a public company the terminal words 'public limited company' or the contraction 'plc', must similarly be included in the statement of the company's name.[14] The word 'company' forming part of the company's name may be legitimately contracted to 'Co', but must be included in either its full or its contracted form.[15]

The rule requiring publicity in respect of a company's name is enforced by criminal sanctions against the company and its officers,[16] and additionally an officer or agent of the company who signs or authorises the signature of a bill of exchange, cheque, promissory note or order for money or goods on its behalf which does not contain its name is liable on the instrument to the holder of it if the company does not satisfy the obligation which it embodies.[17] An instrument is not invalid if the company's name is not fully or correctly set out in it, however, provided that there is no likelihood of another company or firm being mistaken for the one which is intended by the instrument.[18] This also applies to documents connected with litigation.[19] Consequently, if a company carries on business in a

---

7 By the Companies Act 1981, s 119 (5) and Sch 4.
8 Companies Act 1985, s 30 (1) to (3).
9 A company may have a separate facsimile of its common seal with the addition of the word 'Securities' for the purpose of sealing documents creating or evidencing title to shares, debentures and debenture stock issued by it, and the provisions of the Companies Act 1985, relating to the use of the company's common seal in that connection apply to the securities seal (Companies Act 1985, s 40, as amended by Companies Act 1989, s 130 (7) and Sch 17, para 3).
10 Companies Act 1985, s 36A (3), s 348 (1), s 349 (1) and s 350 (1), as amended by Companies Act 1989, s 130 (7) and Sch 17, para 7. Section 36A was inserted by the Companies Act 1989, s 130 (2).
11 Companies Act 1985, s 27 (1) and (4). The contraction 'Ld' was held sufficient under the former Companies Acts (*Stacey & Co Ltd v Wallis* (1912) 106 LT 544).
12 *Penrose v Martyr* (1858) EB & E 499; *British Airways Board v Parish* [1979] 2 Lloyd's Rep 361.
13 *Atkins & Co v Wardle* (1889) 58 LJQB 377; affd 5 TLR 734; *Durham Fancy Goods Ltd v Michael Jackson (Fancy Goods) Ltd* [1968] 2 QB 839, [1968] 2 All ER 987.
14 Companies Act 1985, s 27 (1) and (4).
15 *Banque de l'Indochine et de Suez SA v Euroseas Group Finance Co Ltd* [1981] 3 All ER 198.
16 Companies Act 1985, s 348 (2), s 349 (2) to (4) and s 350 (2).
17 Ibid, s 349 (4).
18 *Lynne Regis Corpn Case* (1612) 10 Co Rep 120a at 122b; *Croydon Hospital v Farley* (1816) 6 Taunt 467; *F Goldsmith (Sicklesmere) Ltd v Baxter* [1970] Ch 85, [1969] 3 All ER 733.
19 *Whittam v W J Daniel & Co Ltd* [1962] 1 QB 271, [1961] 3 All ER 796.

name different from its corporate name, an action brought against it in its business name will not be invalid and the court will not set aside the action, even after judgment has been entered against the company in default of notice of its intention to defend, if the company was aware that the action had been brought against it and failed to apply to the court to set the proceedings aside within a reasonable time.[20]

Business names

A company can lawfully carry on a business in a name other than its corporate name[1] if it does not contravene the special statutory provisions protecting certain designated names, or the statutory prohibition on persons other than authorised deposit taking institutions using business names which indicate that they are banks or carry on a banking business.[2] However, a company may not without the approval of the Secretary of State for Trade and Industry carry on business in a name which suggests that the business is connected with HM Government or a local authority, nor without such approval may a company carry on business in a name which includes a word or expression specified in regulations made by the Secretary of State.[3] Before such approval is given the company must seek the opinion of the relevant Government or other body specified in the regulations and deliver to the Secretary of State a statement that this has been done and a copy of its response, setting out any objections it has to the proposed business name.[4] The words and expressions which may be included in a business name only with the approval of the Secretary of State are the same as those whose inclusion in a company's name requires his approval.[5] Finally, a company which carries on business in a name which is the same as or similar to that of another existing business may be enjoined from using that name in a passing off action brought by the proprietor of that existing business.[6]

A company which carries on business in a name other than its corporate name, must state its corporate name in all business letters, written orders for goods or services, invoices, receipts and written demands for the payment of debts sent out in connection with the business, and must display its corporate name on all premises where the business is carried on and to which its customers or suppliers of goods or services have access.[7] If the company fails to do this, it and its directors commit a criminal offence.[8] Furthermore, if the company brings an action to enforce a contract made in the course of a business in respect of which it is in default in stating or displaying its corporate name, the court will dismiss the proceedings if the defendant proves that he has a claim against the company under the contract which he has been unable to pursue because of the company's default, or that he has suffered financial loss as a result of the company's default, but the court may

20 *Singh v Atombrook Ltd* [1989] 1 All ER 385, [1989] 1 WLR 810, CA.
 1 The commonest reasons for a company doing this are that the business was acquired from another person and the company continues to carry it on in its former name, or that the company carries on several businesses of different kinds.
 2 See p 5, ante.
 3 Business Names Act 1985, s 2 (1) and s 3 (1).
 4 Ibid, s 3 (2); the Company and Business Names Regulations (SI 1981/1685), paras 4 and 5 and Schedule; the Company and Business Names (Amendment) Regulations 1982 (SI 1982/1653), para 2. These regulations are continued in force by the Companies Consolidation (Consequential Provisions) Act 1985, s 31 (2).
 5 Companies Act 1985, s 29 (1); the Company and Business Names Regulations 1981, para 3 and Schedule; the Company and Business Names (Amendment) Regulations 1982, para 2.
 6 See p 6, ante.
 7 Business Names Act 1985, s 4 (1).
 8 Ibid, s 4 (6) and s 7 (4).

nevertheless allow the company's action to proceed if it is just and equitable to do so.[9] A defendant who seeks the dismissal of the company's action because of its default in stating or displaying its corporate name, must obviously satisfy the court that he did not know its name or know that it was the proprietor of the business in question at any material time, and if the defendant alleges that he has suffered financial loss as a result of the company's default, he must also prove that he would not have contracted with the company if he had known its identity. It is difficult to see how the court could permit the company to enforce the contract if these matters are proved by the defendant, except possibly to the extent that he has obtained benefits from the company's performance of its part of the contract, and even then allowance would have to be made for the loss which the defendant has suffered in consequence of the company's default.

Formerly, a company which carried on business in a name other than its corporate name had to register particulars of the business and of itself with the Registrar of Business Names,[10] and the registered particulars were open to public inspection.[11] The legislation governing the registration of business names has now been repealed[12] and the registered particulars are no longer open to public inspection. Nevertheless, if a company registered a business name before the repeal took effect,[13] it may continue to use that name without the need to obtain the approval of the Secretary of State for Trade and Industry, even though the name includes a word or expression specified in regulations made by him as requiring his approval.[14]

Category of company

The second clause of the memorandum of association of a public company must state that it is to be a public company.[15] There is no corresponding clause in the memorandum of a private company stating that it will be a private company or the kind of private company it will be.

Registered office

The next clause of the memorandum of association states that the registered office of the company will be situated in England and Wales, or in Wales or Scotland, as the case may be.[16] If the registered office is to be in England or Wales, the papers to lead to incorporation will be delivered to the Registrar of Companies for England and Wales, and he will issue the certificate of incorporation; if the registered office is to be in Scotland, those functions are fulfilled by the Registrar of Companies for Scotland.[17] If a company's memorandum of association states that its registered office will be situated in Wales, its memorandum and articles may be in Welsh;[18] whether those documents are in Welsh or English, if it is a public company, its name may terminate with the words 'cwmni cyfyngedig cyhoeddus' or the contraction 'ccc' instead of the English equivalents, and if it is a private

9 Ibid, s 5 (1).
10 Registration of Business Names Act 1916, s 7 (d), Companies Act 1947, s 58 (1) (37 Halsbury's Statutes (3rd Edn) 867).
11 Registration of Business Names Act 1916, s 16.
12 By the Companies Act 1981, s 119 (5) and Sch 4.
13 On 26 February 1982 (Companies Act 1981 (Commencement No 3) Order 1982 (SI 1982/103), para 2.
14 Business Names Act 1985, s 2 (3).
15 Companies Act 1985, s 1 (3).
16 Ibid, s 2 (1), and (2).
17 Ibid, s 704 (1) and (5).
18 Ibid, s 21 (1). The originals in Welsh must be accompanied by certified translations into English.

limited company, the termination of its name may be 'cyfyngedig' or 'cyf' instead of 'limited' or 'ltd'.[19] Alterations subsequently made to a memorandum or articles in Welsh must also be in Welsh.[20] A company whose registered office is in Wales may also comply with any requirement in the Companies Act 1985 for the delivery of a document to the Registrar of Companies by delivering the document in Welsh accompanied by a certified translation into English.[1]

The statement in the memorandum that the company's registered office will be in England, Wales, or Scotland fixes its nationality as British,[2] and its domicil as English or Scottish, as the case may be.[3] Its residence, however, depends on where the central control and management of its business is exercised,[4] and this may be in two or more different countries if control of the different parts of its business is divided.[5] The determination of a company's residence depends on where the acts of management by those who control it are in fact carried out, and so it is immaterial that those acts are in defiance of the terms of its constitution or are transacted elsewhere than where its constitution permits.[6] The residence of a company is primarily important in connection with taxation; a company is only liable to pay corporation tax on the whole of its profits, wherever arising, if it is resident in the United Kingdom.[7] However, every company incorporated in the United Kingdom on or after 15 March 1988 is to be conclusively treated as resident there for the purposes of corporation tax and income tax.[8]

A company must at all times have a registered office at a particular address to which all communications and notices may be addressed to it.[9] Also it must in all its business letters and order forms state whether it is registered in England, Wales or Scotland, the registration number assigned to it (as given in its certificate of incorporation) and the address of its registered office.[10] If a public or private limited company whose registered office is in Wales has the termination of its name in Welsh, it must also state in English in all its business letters and order forms and in a notice displayed at every place where it carries on business that it is a public limited company, or if it is a private company, that it is a limited company.[11] A company is required to keep a variety of registers and records at its registered office,[12] but in some cases the registers may be kept elsewhere in England or Wales,

19 Companies Act 1985, s 25 (1) and (2).
20 Ibid, s 21 (4).
1 Ibid, s 21 (3).
2 *Janson v Driefontein Mines Ltd* [1902] AC 484.
3 *Gasque v IRC* [1940] 2 KB 80. In private international law the legal effect of the incorporation of a company, and the rights, powers and duties of its members and directors, are determined by the law of its domicil. (See Cheshire and North, *Private International Law* (11th edn) p 177; Dicey and Morris, *Conflict of Laws* (11th edn) p 1130.)
4 *Swedish Central Rly Co Ltd v Thompson* [1925] AC 495.
5 *Union Corpn Ltd v IRC* [1952] 1 All ER 646; affd [1953] AC 482, [1953] 1 All ER 729.
6 *Unit Construction Co Ltd v Bullock* [1960] AC 351, [1959] 3 All ER 831. In that case the company's articles conferred the powers of management on the directors, but prohibited them from holding board meetings in the United Kingdom; the company's affairs were in fact directed from England by a holding company which owned all its shares; it was held that the company was resident in England.
7 Income and Corporation Taxes Act 1988, s 8 (1) and s 11 (1) (44 Halsbury's Statutes (4th Edn) 33 and 36).
8 Finance Act 1988, s 66 (1) and Sch 7, para 7 (43 Halsbury's Statutes (4th Edn) 1519, 1585).
9 Companies Act 1985, s 287 (1), as re-enacted by Companies Act 1989, s 136.
10 Ibid, s 351 (1).
11 Ibid, s 351 (3) and (4).
12 The registers which must be so kept are: (a) of members (Companies Act 1985, s 352); (b) of debenture holders (s 190); (c) of mortgages and charges (s 411); (d) of directors and secretaries (s 288); and (e) of directors' and substantial shareholders' share and debenture holdings (ss 211 and 325). Additionally minutes of general meetings of members of the company (s 382) and copies of directors' service contracts (s 318) must be kept at the registered office.

or in the case of a Scottish company, in Scotland, if the Registrar of Companies is notified where they are kept.[13]

Any document (including a document connected with litigation) may be served on a company by leaving it at or sending it by registered or unregistered post[14] to its registered office.[15] If a document sent by post is not correctly addressed to the company's registered office but is nevertheless delivered there, it will have been left at its registered office by the sender, and so will have been validly served.[16] It has been held that if the company has no registered office, the court will give leave to serve writs and summonses on it by serving any director, or, possibly, even the secretary.[17] However, it would appear that it is now impossible for a company not to have a registered office at all times, because its registered office on its incorporation will be at the address specified in the statement delivered to the Registrar of Companies with the papers to lead to the company's incorporation,[18] and it will cease to have that address as its registered office only on delivering to the Registrar a notice of a new address which will become its registered office on such delivery being made.[19] Moreover, the service of documents on a company by delivery at, or sending by post to, its registered office is permissive only, and so it would seem possible in any case to serve a document on a company by leaving it with its directors or managing director, or if the purpose of service is merely to bring the matters set out in the document to the company's notice, by leaving it with any of its directors or its secretary.[20] A writ or summons cannot be served on a defendant outside England without leave of the court,[1] but if the defendant is a Scottish company which carries on business in England, it may be served by leaving the writ or summons at, or posting it to, the company's principal place of business in England, and at the same time a copy of the writ or summons must be sent by post to the company's registered office in Scotland.[2]

Objects

The next and most important clause of the memorandum is the objects clause.[3] In this clause there is set out the purpose which the company is formed to achieve or the kind of activities or business which it is to carry on. The contents of the clause set the outer limits of the company's legitimate activities, so that if it attempts to do anything beyond those limits it is exceeding its legitimate functions and is acting ultra vires. The courts keep a company within its legitimate field of activity by allowing any of its members to sue for an injunction to restrain it from going

---

13 These registers are the register of members (Companies Act 1985, s 353 (1)) and the register of debenture holders (s 190 (3)). If the register of members is kept elsewhere than at the registered office, the register of directors' and substantial shareholders' holdings may be kept with it (s 211 (8) and s 325 (5) and Sch 13, para 25). Copies of directors' service contracts may be kept at the same place as the register of members or at the company's principal place of business in England or Scotland (s 318 (1) and (3)).
14 *TO Supplies (London) Ltd v Jerry Creighton Ltd* [1952] 1 KB 42, [1951] 2 All ER 992.
15 Companies Act 1985, s 725 (1).
16 *Stylo Shoes Ltd v Prices Tailors Ltd* [1960] Ch 396, [1959] 3 All ER 901.
17 *Gaskell v Chambers* (1858) 26 Beav 252.
18 Companies Act 1985, s 287 (2), substituted by Companies Act 1989, s 136 (see p 27, post).
19 Ibid, s 287(3) and (4), substituted by Companies Act 1989, s 136.
20 *Houghton Co v Nothard, Lowe and Wills Ltd* [1928] AC 1; *Singh v Atombrook Ltd* [1989] 1 All ER 385, [1989] 1 WLR 810, CA.
1 RSC Ord 11, r 1.
2 Companies Act 1985, s 725 (2) and (3).
3 Ibid, s 2 (1).

outside, and until the rule was modified by statutory provisions,[4] the courts also treated as void any transaction between the company and another person which was ultra vires the company, and this was so whether or not the other person was aware of the irregularity. Because of this serious sanction of invalidity behind the ultra vires rule and because of the personal liability which directors incur if they act outside the company's objects,[5] draftsmen were and still are careful to include in the objects clauses of memoranda of association the most comprehensive list of powers which the company might in any conceivable circumstances wish to exercise. Thus, in practice the ultra vires rule has been shorn of most of its terrors, but only at the expense of excessively long objects clauses, most of the paragraphs of which are in a stereotyped form and vary little whatever may be the business which the company is really formed to carry on.

Objects and powers

There is, of course, a difference between the objects of the company and the powers given to it to achieve those objects. If a company is formed to manufacture motor vehicles, that is its object; if it is given powers to hold land, build factories and workshops, acquire machinery and materials, engage and pay for labour, have a bank account and institute litigation, these powers are clearly only incidental or ancillary to its object, and are given to it solely to enable it to manufacture motor vehicles. There is therefore a strong argument against the inclusion of lists of powers in the objects clauses of memoranda of association. This argument was expressed strongly by Lord Wrenbury in *Cotman v Brougham*.[6] After distinguishing between objects and powers, and observing that the specimen form of memorandum in the Companies Act[7] contains a short objects clause, confined strictly to setting out the company's authorised business without the enumeration of incidental powers, and that the Act requires this specimen form to be adhered to as closely as possible,[8] he said:[9]

> 'There has grown up a pernicious practice of registering memoranda of association which, under the clause relating to objects, contain paragraph after paragraph not specifying or delimiting the proposed trade or purpose, but confusing power with purpose and indicating every class of act which the corporation is to have power to do. The practice is not one of recent growth ... It has arrived now at a point at which the fact is that the function of the memorandum is taken to be, not to specify, not to disclose, but to bury beneath a mass of words the real object or objects of the company with the intent that every conceivable form of activity shall be found included somewhere within its terms ... Such a memorandum is not, I think, a compliance with the Act.'

But despite Lord Wrenbury's opinion, which was concurred in by the other members of the House of Lords, the Registrar has continued to accept memoranda which do confuse objects with powers. The existence of the ultra vires rule makes it inevitable that memoranda should be drafted in this way. There is, it seems, a serious divergence between the requirement of the Companies Act 1985, that the objects clause should state objects and not powers, and the ultra vires rule, by which

---

4 European Communities Act 1972, s 9 (1) re-enacted by Companies Act 1985, s 35. These provisions are now superseded by the wider validating provisions of Companies Act 1985, ss 35, 35A and 35B as substituted for the original s 35 by Companies Act 1989, s 108 (see p 96, post).
5 See p 583, post.
6 [1918] AC 514.
7 At that time the Companies (Consolidation) Act 1908, Sch 3, Form A, now the Companies (Table A to F) Regulations 1985 (SI 1985/805), para 2 and Schedule, Table B.
8 Companies Act 1985, s 3 (1).
9 [1918] AC 514 at 523.

the omission of powers may hamper the company in achieving its objects. The reason for this divergence must now be explained.

Implied powers

The intention of the legislature was undoubtedly that the court should assist the company to achieve its expressed objects by implying all powers necessary for it to do so, and the House of Lords has held that the company is impliedly granted such necessary and incidental powers when it is incorporated.[10] In theory the combination of the company's expressed objects and its implied powers should enable it to enter into any transaction or do any thing it legitimately wishes.

On the whole, the courts have been liberal in implying powers. Thus, powers have been implied to do acts obviously appropriate to the carrying on of any business, such as appointing agents and engaging employees,[11] borrowing money and giving security for loans,[12] selling the company's property,[13] entering into partnership or joint venture agreements for carrying on the kind of business it may itself carry on,[14] paying gratuities to employees,[15] paying pensions to former officers and employees or their dependants,[16] and instituting, defending and compromising legal proceedings.[17] The Companies Act 1948 formerly added to this list by conferring a power on every company to hold land, subject to a restriction on the amount of land which charitable and similar companies might hold.[18] Since the repeal of this provision in 1960,[19] a company will only have an implied power to hold land if it is necessary or appropriate to enable the company to achieve its expressed objects, but the court will readily hold such a power to be necessary or appropriate in the case of a trading company.[20]

In addition to powers which are required to carry on any business, powers have been implied by the court because of the particular nature of the company's business or undertaking. Thus, a company formed to manufacture coal gas, which had power to manufacture, convert and sell by-products, was held to have power to convert a by-product, naphthalene, into marketable naphthol by running a plant and purchasing quantities of caustic soda which were mixed with the naphthalene for the purpose.[1] A large company formed to manufacture chemicals was held to have power to make grants to universities and scientific institutions to facilitate scientific research and the training of scientists, although the company might not obtain any immediate financial benefit in consequence.[2] Finally, an insurance company which had issued fire policies which excluded liability for loss caused by explosion, was held entitled to make ex gratia payments to persons who

---

10 *A-G v Great Eastern Rly Co* (1880) 5 App Cas 473.
11 *Ferguson v Wilson* (1866) 2 Ch App 77 at 89.
12 *General Auction Estate and Monetary Co v Smith* [1891] 3 Ch 432.
13 *Re Kingsbury Collieries Ltd and Moore's Contract* [1907] 2 Ch 259.
14 *Newstead (Inspector of Taxes) v Frost* [1979] 2 All ER 129 at 137, [1978] 1 WLR 1441 at 1449, per Buckley LJ; affd [1980] 1 All ER 363, [1980] 1 WLR 135.
15 *Hampson v Price's Patent Candle Co* (1876) 45 LJ Ch 437.
16 *Henderson v Bank of Australasia* (1888) 40 ChD 170.
17 *Re Norwich Provident Insurance Society, Bath's Case* (1878) 8 ChD 334.
18 Companies Act 1948, s 14 (1).
19 By the Charities Act 1960, ss 38 (1) and 48 (2) (5 Halsbury's Statutes (4th Edn) 855 and 861). It is uncertain whether the repeal of s 14 divested existing companies of the power they had hitherto enjoyed of holding land. If it did, the holding of land which they had already lawfully acquired might become ultra vires ex post facto, which would be absurd.
20 *Johns v Balfour* (1889) 5 TLR 389.
1 *Deuchar v Gas Light and Coke Co* [1925] AC 691.
2 *Evans v Brunner, Mond & Co* [1921] 1 Ch 359.

had suffered loss in that way, because such payments were reasonably incidental to carrying on the business of insurance.[3]

Before implying a power, however, the court has always insisted on two conditions being satisfied, namely, (a) that there must be some reasonable connection between the company's objects and the power it seeks to exercise, it being insufficient for the company merely to show that it will benefit in some way by the exercise of the power;[4] and (b) that the company will in fact benefit in some way, even though remote, from the exercise of the power.[5] Thus, it has been held that there was no connection between the power sought and the company's objects when a trading company wished to sell its whole undertaking,[6] or to subscribe for shares in another company or amalgamate with another company,[7] or to guarantee the share capital of another company which it had been instrumental in forming,[8] or to purchase the undertaking of another company when it had been formed to purchase and carry on only one particular business.[9] Moreover, when a company was being wound up, or when it had disposed of its undertaking and merely held the proceeds of sale but had no business to manage, it was held before statute intervened that the company could not pay gratuities to its officers and employees, although such payments were normally within its powers, because the payment could now reflect no benefit on the company.[10] However, statute now provides that every company has power to make financial or other provision for the benefit of employees or former employees of itself or its subsidiaries in connection with the cessation or transfer of the whole or any part of its or their undertakings, and this power cannot be excluded by the company's memorandum or articles, although conditions may be imposed on its exercise.[11] Generosity which has no commercial motivation is also beyond the powers of a company when the beneficiary is another company in the same group. Thus a subsidiary company was held to have acted ultra vires when it borrowed from its holding company, not in order to satisfy its own business needs, but merely in order to enable it to pay a large fraction of its profits to the holding company in lieu of interest on the loan.[12]

From the foregoing it is clear that, ideally, there should be no need to insert powers in the objects clause of a company's memorandum, because the law will imply them, and therefore, again ideally, there is no lacuna in the Companies Act 1985, in not providing for the inclusion of powers in the objects clause. In reality, however, the inclusion of powers is necessary for two reasons. In the first place a company often needs powers which the court has ruled cannot be implied, and the only way it can obtain them is by having them in its memorandum. Were it not for the practice of conferring express power on companies to acquire shares in other companies, for example, it would not be possible for one company to be the holding company of another, and holding companies are not only undoubtedly lawful,[13] but are expressly recognised and regulated by the Companies Act 1985.[14] In the second place, there are many powers required by companies upon which the court

3 *Taunton v Royal Insurance Co* (1864) 2 Hem & M 135.
4 *Evans v Brunner Mond & Co* supra, at 368.
5 *Hutton v West Cork Rly Co* (1883) 23 ChD 654.
6 *Simpson v Westminster Palace Hotel Co* (1860) 8 HL Cas 712.
7 *Re European Society Arbitration Acts* (1878) 8 ChD 679.
8 *Colman v Eastern Counties Rly Co* (1846) 10 Beav 1.
9 *Ernest v Nicholls* (1857) 6 HL Cas 401.
10 *Hall Parke v Daily News Ltd* [1961] 1 All ER 695, [1961] 1 WLR 493; *Parke v Daily News Ltd* [1962] Ch 927, [1962] 2 All ER 929.
11 Companies Act 1985, s 719 (1), re-enacting Companies Act 1980, s 74 (1) (see p 585, post).
12 *Ridge Securities Ltd v IRC* [1964] 1 All ER 275 at 287–8, [1964] 1 WLR 479 at 494.
13 *Re Barned's Banking Co, ex p Contract Corpn* (1867) 3 Ch App 105.
14 See Chapter 18.

has not yet pronounced, so that it is doubtful whether they would be implied or not; to avoid uncertainty and the expense of litigation the draftsman plays safe by inserting them expressly in the memorandum. The Jenkins Committee, which recommended many reforms in company law in 1962, sought to avoid the need for the enunciation of ancillary powers in the objects clause by proposing that the Companies Act should itself set out a list of common form powers which would be impliedly incorporated into the objects clause of every company, unless expressly excluded.[15] Unfortunately, no such comprehensive catalogue of incidental implied powers has yet been enacted; if this were done it would be desirable for the Secretary of State for Trade and Industry to be empowered to amend and supplement the list by regulations so as to meet changing needs arising in practice.[16]

Limitations imposed by the courts on expressed powers

Faced with objects clauses of excessive length conferring a universal range of powers on companies, the courts have sought some standard of interpretation which would enable them to prevent companies from having power to do anything and everything, thus making nugatory the requirement of the Companies Acts that objects should be defined and limited.[17] The courts have devised such a standard by notionally dividing the objects clause into two parts. The first part comprises those paragraphs which state the business or activities which the company is really formed to carry on; these activities the court calls its main objects. The second part consists of the remaining paragraphs, which the court treats as conferring merely incidental and ancillary powers to enable the main objects to be achieved; these paragraphs are construed by reference to the main objects, and their meaning is limited thereby. The result is that a paragraph of the objects clause which appears, when read in isolation, to give the company power to carry on an independent business, is found, when read together with the main objects, to confer merely a power to do a limited class of acts with a view to carrying out the company's main objects.

Thus, where a company's objects were stated to be the acquisition of mines or mineral properties in New Zealand or elsewhere, and more particularly to carry out a specified contract to purchase a named gold mine, it was held that its main object was the acquisition and working of that particular mine, and that it could acquire and work other mines only for the purpose of working that mine more effectively.[18] Likewise, where a company's objects were (a) to purchase and carry on the undertaking of a named gold mining company in India, and (b) to acquire gold or other mines in that part of India or elsewhere, and to acquire the undertaking of any person or company carrying on any business which the company was authorised to carry on, it was held that (a) alone was the main object, and so the company could not acquire a mine outside India, the ancillary power (b) having been given to it only in order that it might work the named undertaking which it was formed to acquire more effectively.[19] The inclination of the court to treat a specific, limited purpose as the company's sole main object can, however, be stultifying. A company may quite unobjectionably be formed not only to work a particular mine, but to engage in mining generally. The court has recognised this,

---

15 Report of the Company Law Committee (Cmnd 1749), paras 43 and 54 (a).
16 Such lists of corporate powers implied by law have been enacted in Australia, New Zealand, Canada, South Africa, Singapore and Malaysia.
17 Vaughan Williams LJ, stated in *Re Amalgamated Syndicate* [1897] 2 Ch 600 at 604, that this was the court's purpose.
18 *Re Haven Gold Mining Co* (1882) 20 ChD 151.
19 *Stephens v Mysore Reefs (Kangundy) Mining Co Ltd* [1902] 1 Ch 745.

and in two cases where the objects were in practically the same form as in the last example, it was held that the company might purchase and work a mine quite remote from the one mentioned in the objects clause, and even though the acquisition of the new mine would involve abandoning the original one.[20] Similarly, when a company was formed (a) to acquire and carry on a particular engineering business, and (b) to carry on the business of general engineering, it was held that both objects were main ones, and on the sale of the original business the company had power to acquire and run a new engineering business in its place.[1]

Where the objects clause begins by empowering the company to carry on a certain kind of business, however, the court is reluctant to hold that a later paragraph which empowers it to carry on a different kind of business, contains a main object, and this is particularly so if the later paragraph is separated from the main object stated at the beginning of the objects clause by several other paragraphs which undoubtedly set out merely incidental or ancillary powers. Thus, a company whose objects clause began by enabling it to act as a bank and continued by enabling it to invest in securities and land and to underwrite issues of securities, was held not entitled to abandon its banking business and confine itself to investment and financial speculation.[2] Again, a company formed to promote entertainments in connection with Queen Victoria's Diamond Jubilee was held not entitled to engage in investing in securities and promoting other companies after the Jubilee, even though its memorandum empowered it to do these things.[3] But it is not impossible for a company to have as its main objects the carrying on of two or more different kinds of business. Thus, where a company's memorandum empowered it to operate a telegraph undertaking and also to sell its undertaking to another company for shares or debentures therein, it was held, after it had sold its undertaking, that holding such securities and acting as a holding company was equally a main object of the company as operating the telegraph undertaking.[4]

Attempts to evade the restrictive interpretation of objects clauses

To mitigate the restrictive effect of the interpretations which the court puts upon objects clauses, draftsmen began to add concluding paragraphs to the clause expressed in general terms. Their hope was that these concluding paragraphs would induce the court to treat the contents of each of the paragraphs of the clause as main objects, or at least to interpret them in a more liberal way. Two such concluding paragraphs have been construed by the courts.

The first empowers the company

'to do all such other things as are incidental or conducive to the attainment of the above objects or any of them.'

This paragraph could be interpreted to mean that the company may do anything which is incidental to carrying out the powers contained in the earlier paragraphs regarded as ends in themselves, thus making those powers main objects. The court has rejected this interpretation. It has held that the powers in the earlier paragraphs are not thereby made main objects, and as powers, they are still limited in scope to

20 *Pedlar v Road Block Gold Mines of India Ltd* [1905] 2 Ch 427; *Butler v Northern Territories Mines of Australia Ltd* (1906) 96 LT 41.
1 *Re Kitson & Co Ltd* [1946] 1 All ER 435.
2 *Re Crown Bank* (1890) 44 ChD 634.
3 *Re Amalgamated Syndicate* [1897] 2 Ch 600.
4 *Re Eastern Telegraph Co Ltd* [1947] 2 All ER 104.

enabling the real main objects to be carried out.[5] But it has also been held that the concluding paragraph may have the effect of widening the meaning of the earlier paragraphs, so that they not only confer ancillary powers, but also themselves create subsidiary and associated objects.[6] In the case where the Court of Appeal so ruled, the company had been formed to carry on the business of general, civil and engineering contractors, and in particular to build houses, and it had power by its memorandum 'to carry on any other trade or business whatsoever which can in the opinion of the board of directors, be advantageously carried on by the company in connection with . . . the general business of the company', and 'to do all such other things as are incidental or conducive to the above objects or any of them.' It was held that the company could lawfully contract for a fee to procure loans to other concerns from sources of finance to which it had itself resorted in the past. Such contracts were incidental to its business of building, since increased contacts with financiers would help to cement good relations with them, which would be valuable when the company required finance for its building operations in the future. Entering into such contracts to procure finance was also a subsidiary business which the directors might well consider it advantageous to combine with the company's main business. The test was whether the directors could in good faith conclude that undertaking the subsidiary business was advantageous; the court would not substitute its own opinion for the directors', unless bad faith or some improper motive on their part was shown.

The other concluding paragraph is in the following form:

> 'The objects set out in any paragraph of this clause shall not be in any way limited by reference to or inference from the terms of any other paragraph, or by the name of the company. None of such paragraphs or the objects therein specified or the powers thereby conferred shall be deemed subsidiary or auxiliary to the objects mentioned in the first paragraph, and each paragraph shall be deemed to contain a separate main object of the company.'

At first it was held that this paragraph did not alter the way in which the court should interpret the objects clause,[7] but it was later conceded reluctantly by the House of Lords that such a paragraph can make the contents of each paragraph of the objects clause a separate main object, which may be independently pursued.[8] It has since been held, however, that under such a direction in the objects clause a paragraph of the objects clause may not be read in isolation, as though it were the company's only main object, if its wording shows that it is really dependent on or ancillary to an activity expressed in another part of the clause.[9] Consequently, a paragraph which enables the company to borrow and to give security for loans made to it will always be read as ancillary to its main objects, because money is never borrowed for its own sake, but only to finance the carrying out of some other activity.[9] Similarly, a power in the objects clause of a memorandum for the company to do all such other things as may be deemed incidental or conducive to the attainment of the . . . objects' expressed earlier in that clause cannot be elevated into a main object of the company by the objects clause concluding with a paragraph in the form set out above.[10] On the other hand, it has been held that if the objects clause empowers the company to grant pensions to employees and

---

5 *Evans v Brunner, Mond & Co* [1921] 1 Ch 359 at 364.
6 *Bell Houses Ltd v City Wall Properties Ltd* [1966] 2 QB 656, [1966] 2 All ER 674.
7 *Stephens v Mysore Reefs (Kangundy) Mining Co Ltd*, supra.
8 *Cotman v Brougham* [1918] AC 514.
9 *Re Introductions Ltd, Introductions Ltd v National Provincial Bank Ltd* [1968] 2 All ER 1221; affd [1970] Ch 199, [1969] 1 All ER 887.
10 *Brady v Brady* [1988] BCLC 20 at 34 and 39, per Croom-Johnson and Nourse LJJ; revsd on other grounds [1989] AC 755, [1988] 2 All ER 617, [1988] BCLC 579, HL.

directors and their dependants and to assist in the promotion of charitable, benevolent or public purposes, the presence of a direction in the above form in the objects clause makes the procurement of a pension for a retiring director a main object of the company, since the pursuit of the purposes mentioned was possible as an independent main object.[11] Moreover, a company may dispose of its assets without receiving any consideration if its objects clause expressly empowers it to do so and each separate provision of that clause is expressed by it to contain a main object, but the company would not be able to make gratuitous dispositions so as to defeat the rights of its creditors.[12] A direction in the objects clause in the above form can therefore only elevate authorised activities into a main object if the activity in question can be pursued for its own sake as a distinct business purpose or activity.

A direction in a memorandum that each paragraph of the objects clause shall be construed independently does not stand high in judicial favour. In one case the court refused to approve the alteration of an objects clause by inserting such a paragraph,[13] and in another case such an alteration was approved only because all the other paragraphs conferred powers which were similar in nature, so that the addition of the concluding paragraph would not enable the company to pursue any new activity as an end in itself.[14] But since the House of Lords' decision that such a concluding paragraph is legitimate, there can be no doubt about the validity of the paragraph if originally included in the memorandum, or if inserted by way of an alteration which is not challenged within the period limited for doing so.[15]

General commercial objects

In order to encourage companies to be formed with simplified and generalised objects (and to remove any doubt as to the lawfulness of their doing so), the Companies Act 1989 provides that where a company's object is stated to be 'to carry on business as a general commercial company', the object of the company shall be to carry on any trade or business whatsoever, and the company has power to do all things which are incidental or conducive to the carrying on of any trade or business by it.[16] This provision is expressed as an interpretative one by which the abbreviated form of object: 'to carry on business as a general commercial company', is given a statutory meaning, but the real significance of the provision is that it legitimises the conferment on a company of power to carry on any number of different businesses or commercial activities, whether related to one another or not, and to engage in new businesses or commercial activities in addition to, or in place of, those already carried on by it. If a company's memorandum employs the statutory formula, there is no need for it also to specify any particular businesses or activities which the company is formed to carry on, and it would seem that if such a particular business or businesses are specified, the company's power to carry on any other business or commercial activity, whether related or not, is in no way diminished. The weakness of the provisions, however, lies in the fact that they limit the company's incidental and ancillary powers in carrying on any trade or business it chooses, to those which are in fact incidental or conducive to the business or commercial activities which it is carrying on. This means that it will not be sufficient for the company or its board of directors to consider that a proposed act

11 *Re Horsley & Weight Ltd* [1982] Ch 442, [1982] 3 All ER 1045.
12 *Brady v Brady* [1989] AC 755, [1988] 2 All ER 617, [1988] BCLC 579, HL.
13 *Re John Brown & Co Ltd* (1914) 84 LJ Ch 245.
14 *Re E K Cole Ltd* [1945] 1 All ER 521 n.
15 See p 68, post.
16 Companies Act 1985, s 3A, inserted by Companies Act 1989, s 110(1).

or transaction will be incidental or conducive to carrying on that business or activity, and it will be for the court to determine whether the act or transaction qualifies as incidental or conducive if its legality is challenged by a member of the company.

Limitation of liability

After the objects clause, the next following clause of the memorandum of association of a public company or of a private company limited by shares or guarantee states that the liability of its members is limited.[17] This clause must appear even though the company is entitled to omit the word, 'limited', from its name. If the company is limited by guarantee, the clause is followed by one setting out the terms of the guarantee, which consists of an undertaking by each member to contribute a specified sum toward payment of the company's liabilities and the cost of winding up if the company is wound up while he is a member or within one year thereafter.[18] Before the Companies Act 1980 came into force on 22 December 1980[19] a company could be formed as one limited by guarantee with a share capital,[20] but this is no longer possible,[1] and so such companies are now confined to those existing at that date. More recently formed companies limited by guarantee are therefore unavoidably private companies.[2]

Capital

The next following clause of the memorandum of association of a company limited by shares, states the share capital with which the company proposes to be registered and the nominal value of each of the shares into which the share capital is to be divided.[3] A company limited by guarantee need not have a share capital, however, and such a company incorporated since the Companies Act 1980 came into force cannot do so; even before that time companies limited by guarantee were not often formed to carry on business activities and so rarely needed to have a share capital. No minimum nominal capital is prescribed by law for a private company limited by shares, but a public company must have a nominal capital of not less than £50,000.[4]

The share capital stated in the company's memorandum is its nominal capital, that is, the total of the nominal values of the shares it is authorised to issue. A company's nominal capital fixes the maximum amount of share capital it may issue, and so if it purports to issue shares in excess of its nominal capital, the issue is void, and the subscribers can claim the return of the money which they have paid to the company as money paid for a consideration which has wholly failed.[5] It does not follow, however, that a company will issue the whole of its nominal capital immediately it is formed. The founders of the company may fix the nominal capital at a sum which will enable the company to issue enough shares to pay for the business which it is to acquire and to provide it with working capital, but which

---

17 Companies Act 1985, s 2 (3).
18 Ibid, s 2 (4).
19 Companies Act 1980, s 90 (3); Companies Act 1980 (Commencement No 2) Order 1980 (SI 1980/ 1785), para 2.
20 Companies Act 1948, s 1 (2) and s 2 (4).
 1 Companies Act 1985, s 1 (4), re-enacting Companies Act 1980, s 1 (2).
 2 Ibid, s 1 (3).
 3 Ibid, s 2 (5).
 4 Companies Act 1985, s 11 and s 118 (1). The minimum may be altered from time to time by orders made by the Secretary of State for Trade and Industry (s 118 (1)).
 5 *Bank of Hindustan, China and Japan Ltd v Alison* (1871) LR 6 CP 222.

will still leave some shares available for issue in case the directors later require to raise further money, or to acquire further assets in return for an issue of shares. However, it is unnecessary to have a nominal capital much in excess of the company's immediate requirements, because if a company finds that it needs to issue shares in excess of its original capital, it can always increase its nominal capital by altering its memorandum.[6] On the other hand, a public company must issue at least £50,000 of its nominal capital soon after its incorporation in order to become entitled to carry on its business and to borrow,[7] but in practice this puts no pressure on it to raise capital which it does not need since it is unlikely that a company would be formed as a public company if its initial assets were less than £50,000.

The capital clause of the memorandum must state the nominal value of each share into which the nominal capital is divided. The following are examples of capital clauses:

'The share capital of the company is one million pounds divided into one million shares of one pound each.'

or

'The share capital of the company is one million pounds divided into two million eight hundred thousand ordinary shares of twenty five pence each and three hundred thousand preference shares of one pound each.'

The nominal value of the company's shares is left to the founders' discretion, but it is rare for the nominal value to be more than £1, because shares of a greater nominal value tend to be less saleable, and it is not uncommon to find shares with a nominal value of 50p, 25p or even 5p. Moreover, it is possible for a company to express its nominal capital and the nominal value of its shares in the currency of a foreign or Commonwealth country, provided that in the case of a public company the nominal capital with which it is registered includes at least £50,000 sterling and that part of its capital is divided into shares with a nominal value expressed in sterling.[8]

The requirement that shares should have a nominal value prevents companies from issuing shares of no par value such as are issued by American, Canadian and Belgian companies.[9] The advantages of such shares are that dividends must be declared as a certain sum of money per share instead of being expressed as a percentage of the nominal value of the share, which is misleading;[10] the artificial

---

6 Companies Act 1985, s 121 (1) and (2). (See p 170, post.)
7 Companies Act 1985, s 117 (1) and (2) and s 118 (1) (see p 30, post). The figure of £50,000 may be altered by order of the Secretary of State for Trade and Industry (s 118 (1)).
8 *Re Scandinavian Bank Group plc* [1988] Ch 87, [1987] 2 All ER 70. It would appear, however, that a company's capital cannot be expressed in a notional currency which is used in international transactions merely as a currency of account (eg the European Unit of Account or European Currency Unit and Special Drawing Rights issued by the International Monetary Fund).
9 In 1954 a committee appointed by the Board of Trade under the chairmanship of Mr Montague Gedge reported in favour of permitting the issue of ordinary shares of no par value (Cmd 9112). The Jenkins Committee endorsed this proposal, and would have extended it to preference shares (Report of the Company Law Committee (Cmnd 1749), paras 32 to 34).
10 It is misleading because the dividend does not represent the same percentage of the amount which the shareholder paid for the share, or of the current market value of the share. For example, if X bought a £1 share in the market for £2, and the share is now worth £4, a dividend of 20 per cent represents a return to X of only 10 per cent on the price he paid, and a yield on the current market value of only 5 per cent. Of course, there is nothing to prevent a company from declaring a dividend in the form of a certain sum per share. In the above example, the company could declare a dividend of 20p per share instead of a dividend of 20 per cent.

prohibition on the issue of shares at a discount is done away with;[11] and the reduction of capital when the company suffers a loss of assets is simplified.[12] In fact, the no par value share concentrates attention on the total amount the company has received for all its issued shares, at whatever varying prices they have from time to time been issued, instead of on the nominal value, which is merely the amount subscribed for the company's first issue of shares, and not even that if they were issued at a premium.

Before 1901 it was possible for an English company to issue shares of no par value by being incorporated as a company limited by guarantee.[13] This is not possible in the case of a company which is incorporated after 1900, because a provision in the memorandum or articles of such a company limited by guarantee purporting to divide its undertaking into shares or interests, is deemed to be a provision for the creation of a share capital,[14] and consequently the shares had to be given a nominal value. The statutory prohibition does not apply to a company limited by guarantee which was incorporated before 1901, and so such a company could still issue no par value shares after 1901 and can still do so.[15] Such shares are not considered to constitute share capital, however, and so the provisions of the Companies Act 1985, which relate to companies with a share capital (eg the provisions authorising the increase, reduction or re-division of share capital) do not apply to such no par value shares. There appears to be nothing to prevent an unlimited company, whenever incorporated, from issuing shares of no par value,[16] but the loss of limited liability is a disproportionate price to pay for this facility. The observation above that no par value shares issued by a company limited by guarantee do not constitute share capital would seem to apply equally to no par value shares issued by an unlimited company, but this is of little importance since the provisions of the Companies Act 1985, which authorise the increase, reduction or re-division of share capital, do not apply to unlimited companies.

Additional clauses

The memorandum of association of a company may additionally contain provisions which would normally be found in its articles of association. The additional clauses most commonly found provide for the special rights of different classes of shareholders. The value of inserting additional matters in the memorandum is that they can thereby be protected against subsequent alteration, whereas if they are included in the articles they can be altered by a special resolution passed by a general meeting of the company despite any provision to the contrary in the memorandum or articles.[17]

Association clause

The memorandum of association of a company, whatever kind it may be, concludes with an association clause by which the two or more subscribers state that they are desirous of being formed into a company in pursuance of the memorandum, and if

11 See p 142, post.
12 See p 177, post.
13 *Malleson v General Mineral Patents Syndicate Ltd* [1894] 3 Ch 538.
14 Companies Act 1985, s 15 (2) (re-enacting Companies Act 1900, s 27 and Companies Act 1948, s 21 (2)).
15 Companies Consolidation (Consequential Provisions) Act 1985, s 10.
16 Ibid, s 7 (2), which requires the share capital of an unlimited company to be stated in its articles of association, but does not require its division into shares of a fixed nominal value.
17 Companies Act 1985, s 9 (1) (see p 75, post).

the company has a share capital, that they respectively agree to take the number of shares in the capital of the company set opposite their respective names.[18] There then follows the attested signatures of the subscribers, and if the company has a share capital, the number of shares for which they subscribe. The association clause is the foundation for the so-called statutory contract between the members of the company and the company itself when incorporated.[19]

ARTICLES OF ASSOCIATION

Every company, except a public company or a private company limited by shares, must have its own articles of association; public and private companies limited by shares may do so,[20] and public companies always do have their own articles in practice. If a public company or a private company limited by shares is incorporated under the Companies Act 1985, with no articles of its own, the regulations contained in Table A of regulations made by the Secretary of State for Trade and Industry constitute its articles.[1] Companies limited by shares which were incorporated without special articles of their own before 1 July 1985 (when the Companies Act 1985 came into operation) have the regulations contained in Table A of the First Schedule to the Companies Act 1948 (as amended by the Companies Acts 1967, 1976, 1980 and 1981), or of the earlier Companies Act in force at the time of the companies' registration as their articles of association.[2] Formerly, Table A was divided into two parts, Part I comprising a model set of articles for a public company and Part II incorporating most of Part I and adding further provisions which were necessary for a private company. Private companies are no longer defined by the restrictions imposed on them by their articles,[3] and so Part II of Table A has been repealed, although it will continue to apply to private companies incorporated before 22 December 1980 whose articles incorporated it by reference.[4] Unless otherwise stated, references to Table A in this book are to Table A in the Schedule to the regulations made in 1985 by the Secretary of State.[5]

If the company is to be a partnership company, ie a company limited by shares, whose shares are intended to be held to a substantial extent by or on behalf of its employees, it may adopt as its articles the whole or any part of the articles set out in Table G of the Regulations yet to be made by the Secretary of State for Trade and Industry.[6] Although this speaks of the company adopting such articles, which would be literally possible only by the company resolving that the whole or part of Table G shall be its articles in place of those with which it was incorporated, there is no reason why a partnership company should not be incorporated with articles which expressly incorporate Table G.

The articles of companies limited by guarantee and unlimited companies must

18 Ibid, s 3 (1); Companies (Tables A to F) Regulations 1985, para 2 and Schedule, Tables B to F.
19 Companies Act 1985, s 14 (1) (see p 52, post).
20 Ibid, s 7 (1).
1 Ibid, s 8 (1) and (2); Companies (Tables A to F) Regulations 1985, para 2 and Schedule, Table A.
2 Companies Consolidation (Consequential Provisions) Act 1985, s 31 (8) (*b*).
3 Companies Act 1948, s 28 (1) (repealed by Companies Act 1980, s 88 (2) and Sch 4).
4 Companies Act 1980, s 88 (2) and (4) and Sch 4; Companies Consolidation (Consequential Provisions) Act 1985, s 31 (8).
5 The Companies (Tables A to F) Regulations 1985.
6 Companies Act 1985, s 8A (1) and (2), inserted by Companies Act 1989, s 128.

follow as closely as possible the specimen forms set out in Tables C, D or E of the regulations made by the Secretary of State.[7]

All articles of association must be signed by the same two or more subscribers who signed the memorandum, and their signatures must be attested.[8] The articles of companies incorporated before August 1970 had to be stamped 10*s*,[9] but the duty has been abolished in respect of articles executed since then.[10]

Contents

The articles regulate the manner in which the company's affairs will be managed. The memorandum defines the company's objects and confers powers on it; the articles determine how those objects shall be achieved and those powers exercised. But the Companies Act 1985 does not require the articles to provide for certain specified matters as a minimum in the same way as it requires the memorandum to do. Consequently, the contents of the articles of different companies may vary substantially, and the utmost flexibility is allowed to the persons who form the company to organise its management as they wish.

Articles of association always provide for certain matters in practice. They define the rights of different classes of shareholders (unless these rights are specified in the memorandum) or, at least, they empower the directors or a general meeting of the company to define these rights when the shares are issued; they provide for calling and holding meetings of members and determine their voting rights; they provide for the appointment of a board of directors to manage the company's business and they specify the powers which the directors may exercise in the company's name; and finally, they provide that the company may exercise certain powers in respect of its share capital which the Companies Act 1985 enables it to exercise only if the articles permit.[11]

Interpretation

The articles of association are subordinate to the memorandum, so that if there is any inconsistency between them, the memorandum prevails, and the articles are void to the extent of the conflict. Thus, where a company's memorandum stated that its objects were the development of land in Ireland and activities incidental thereto, it was held that a provision in its articles was void by which part of its capital was to be invested so that the income might be used as a guarantee fund for the payment of dividends on its preference shares; the intention of the memorandum was that the whole of the company's capital should be employed in achieving its objects of land development; and the establishment of a guarantee fund was inconsistent with that.[12] Moreover, the articles are void to the extent of the conflict, even though the provision in the memorandum with which they conflict is not required by law to be there. Thus, where a company's memorandum set out the class rights of its preference shareholders, a conflicting provision in the articles was held to be void.[13]

Subject to the rule that the memorandum prevails in the event of a conflict, the

---

7 Companies Act 1985, s 8 (4); Companies (Tables A to F) Regulations 1985, para 2 and Schedule, Tables C, D and E.
8 Ibid, s 7 (3).
9 Companies Act 1948, s 9 and Stamp Act 1891, 1st Sch, Deed (21 Halsbury's Statutes (2nd Edn) 671).
10 Finance Act 1970, s 32 and Sch 7, para 1 (2) (41 Halsbury's Statutes (4th Edn) 461).
11 See Chapter 6.
12 *Guinness v Land Corpn of Ireland Ltd* (1882) 22 ChD 349.
13 *Ashbury v Watson* (1885) 30 ChD 376.

memorandum and the articles, as contemporaneous documents, must be read together, and so any ambiguity or uncertainty in the one may be removed by reference to the other. Thus, where the memorandum was silent as to whether the company's shares were to be all of one class or might be of different classes, it was held that a power given by the articles to issue shares of different classes resolved the uncertainty and enabled the company to do so.[14] Where the memorandum of a trading company empowered it to do all things incidental to achieving its objects, it was held that a provision in the articles empowering the company to lend money merely exemplified the general words of the memorandum, and the company was therefore entitled to lend money to its employees.[15] Again, where the memorandum empowered the company to borrow on the security of its assets or credit, and the articles provided that it might mortgage its uncalled capital, it was held that the articles merely made specific the general words of the memorandum, and so the company did have power to mortgage its uncalled capital.[16] But the memorandum and articles can be read together only to remove an ambiguity or uncertainty. If the memorandum is perfectly clear, a doubt as to its meaning cannot be raised by reference to the articles; in such a case the articles are simply inconsistent with the memorandum and are disregarded. Thus, where the memorandum exhaustively defined the rights of the company's preference shareholders, and the articles provided that on a winding up the company's surplus assets, after paying all its debts and repaying share capital, should be distributed among all its shareholders, it was held that the preference shareholders were not entitled to share in surplus assets, because their rights were to be ascertained from the memorandum alone, and the memorandum did not confer a right to participate on them.[17]

In one respect, however, the articles may not be resorted to to assist in the interpretation of the memorandum. This is where the provision of the memorandum concerned is one which the law requires to be there, such as the objects clause.[18] In that case the memorandum must be interpreted solely by reference to its own wording. But in relation to the objects clause, it again becomes important to distinguish objects from powers, because powers are not required to be inserted in the memorandum by law, and in determining the meaning of powers conferred by the memorandum, as distinct from delimiting the scope of the company's objects, it is therefore legitimate to refer to the articles.[19]

If a company limited by shares has its own articles, the regulations contained in Table A still govern it, except so far as its own articles do not exclude or modify those regulations.[20] The company's articles and Table A must therefore be read together, and Table A is excluded only so far as the articles are inconsistent with it. The mere fact that the articles deal expressly with the matter in question does not necessarily exclude Table A. Thus, where the articles provided that the company's profits available for dividend should be applied in a certain order amongst the different classes of its shareholders, it was held that the directors could nevertheless set aside reserves out of profits before paying any dividends at all, relying on the power to do so given by Table A in force when the company was incorporated.[1] If

14 *Re South Durham Brewery Co* (1885) 31 ChD 261.
15 *Rainford v James Keith and Blackman Co Ltd* [1905] 2 Ch 147.
16 *Re Pyle Works (No 2)* [1891] 1 Ch 173.
17 *Re Duncan Gilmour & Co Ltd* [1952] 2 All ER 871. This decision was undoubtedly influenced by the general law relating to preference shareholders' rights (see p 212, post).
18 *Guinness v Land Corpn of Ireland*, supra; *Re Southern Brazilian Rio Grande do Sul Rly Co Ltd* [1905] 2 Ch 78.
19 *Re Pyle Works (No 2)* [1891] 1 Ch 173; *Re Southern Brazilian Rio Grande do Sul Rly Co Ltd*, supra.
20 Companies Act 1985, s 8 (2).
1 *Fisher v Black and White Publishing Co* [1901] 1 Ch 174. The Table A referred to was Table A of the Companies Act 1862, art 74, which also appeared in Table A of the Companies Act 1948, art 117, but is omitted from the present Table A.

the company is to be governed exclusively by its own articles, therefore, they should commence by providing that no part of Table A shall deemed to be incorporated therein.

Companies formed under the earlier Companies Acts

Companies which were formed under the earlier Companies Acts[2] are all now governed by the Companies Act 1985,[3] and the earlier Acts have been repealed.[4] But the repeal does not affect the respective Tables A[5] of the earlier Acts so far as they apply to companies limited by shares which were formed thereunder.[6] It follows, therefore, that a company formed under the Companies Act 1862 is still governed by Table A of the First Schedule to that Act so far as its own articles do not otherwise provide, and such a company formed under the Companies (Consolidation) Act 1908, or the Companies Act 1929 or 1948, is likewise governed by the Table A of the Act under which it was formed. This is a matter of some importance, because the old Tables A are in many respects different from the Table A in the regulations made by the Secretary of State for Trade and Industry which are currently in force under the Companies Act 1985. Likewise private companies registered under the Companies Acts 1948 to 1976 before 22 December 1980 whose articles incorporate Table A, Part II of the 1948 Act are still governed by that Part II, despite its repeal as regards companies incorporated since that date.[7]

It should be remembered, however, that if there is anything in the articles of a company formed under the earlier Companies Acts which is inconsistent with the provisions of the Companies Act 1985, other than Table A, the articles are void to the extent of the conflict.[8] So far as substantive law is concerned (as distinct from their articles of association) all companies incorporated since 1856 are now governed by the Companies Act 1985, irrespective of the dates of their incorporation.

Provision of copies

Any member of a company may require it to supply him with a copy of its memorandum and articles of association for a fee not exceeding 5p.[9]

ADDITIONAL DOCUMENTS REQUIRED TO LEAD TO INCORPORATION

In addition to the memorandum and articles of association, the following documents must be filed with the Registrar of Companies in order to obtain the incorporation of a company:

2 These Acts are the Joint Stock Companies Act 1856, the Joint Stock Banking Companies Act 1857, the Companies Act 1862, the Companies (Consolidation) Act 1908, the Companies Act 1929 and the Companies Acts 1948 to 1983.

3 By reason of the definitions of 'company' and 'existing company' in the Companies Act 1985, s 735 (1).

4 Each major Companies Act has repealed its predecessor. The Companies Acts 1948 to 1983 were repealed by the Companies Consolidation (Consequential Provisions) Act 1985, s 29 and Sch 1.

5 Table B in the Joint Stock Companies Act 1856.

6 Companies Act 1985, s 8 (3) and s 744; Companies Consolidation (Consequential Provisions) Act 1985, s 31 (8) (*b*).

7 Companies Act 1980, s 88 (2) and (4) and Sch 4.

8 An example of this is the requirement in the articles of companies formed under the earlier Acts that proxies appointed to vote on behalf of members at meetings of the company must themselves be members. The Companies Act 1862, Sch 1, Table A, art 49, and the Companies (Consolidation) Act 1908, Sch 1, Table A, art 65, imposed this requirement. All such provisions are now void (Companies Act 1985, s 372 (1)).

9 Companies Act 1985, s 19 (1).

(1) A statement of the address of the intended registered office of the company signed by the subscribers of the memorandum of association;[10] this address becomes the registered office of the company on the company's incorporation;[11]

(2) A statement signed by the subscribers of the memorandum setting out the names of the first directors and the first secretary or secretaries of the company and containing the information in respect of them required to be inserted in a company's register of directors and secretaries,[12] together with the signed consents of the persons named to act in those capacities;[13]

(3) A statutory declaration by the solicitor engaged in forming the company, or by a director or secretary named as such in the statement signed by the subscribers under (2) above, that all the requirements of the Companies Act 1985 in respect of registration of the company have been complied with.[14]

A registration fee of £50 must be paid to the Registrar of Companies on the presentation of the documents to lead to its incorporation.[15]

CERTIFICATE OF INCORPORATION

The Registrar of Companies examines the documents filed, and after satisfying himself that they are formally in order, that the company's name is unobjectionable and that its objects are lawful, and if the company is to be incorporated as a public company, that its nominal capital is not less than £50,000, he issues a certificate under his signature or official seal which certifies that the company is incorporated, that the company is a public company (if that is so), and if it is a company limited by shares or guarantee, that the company is limited.[16] If the conditions laid down in the Companies Act 1985 have been complied with, the Registrar must issue the certificate of incorporation, and if he refuses to do so, the court will compel him to do so by an order of mandamus on an application for judicial review of his refusal.[17] After issuing a certificate of incorporation, the Registrar must publish a notice in the London Gazette that it has been issued.[18] At the time of issuing the certificate of incorporation the Registrar must allocate a distinguishing number to the company, which may include a letter indicating the kind of company it is.[19] This number is shown in the company's certificate of incorporation, and must also be stated by the company in all its business letters and order forms.[20]

The certificate of incorporation is conclusive evidence that all the requirements

---

10 Ibid, s 10 (6).
11 Ibid, s 287 (2), inserted by Companies Act 1989, s 136.
12 See p 553, post.
13 Companies Act 1985, s 10 (2) and (3) and Sch 1, as amended by Companies Act 1989, s 145 and Sch 19, para 7.
14 Companies Act 1985, s 12 (3).
15 Ibid, s 708 (1); Companies (Fees) Regulations 1988 (SI 1988/887), reg 3 and Schedule.
16 Companies Act 1985, s 11, s 12 (1), s 13 (1) and (2) and s 118 (1).
17 *R v Registrar of Companies, ex p Bowen* [1914] 3 KB 1161. Proceedings for judicial review are brought in the Queen's Bench Division of the High Court under RSC Ord 53, r 7. An application is made by originating motion (r 5 (2)).
18 Companies Act 1985, s 711 (1) (*a*).
19 Ibid, s 705 (1) and (2), substituted by Companies Act 1989, s 145 and Sch 19, para 14.
20 Ibid, s 351 (1).

of the Companies Act 1985 in respect of registration and matters precedent and incidental thereto have been complied with, that the company is a company authorised to be registered and duly registered under the Act, and if the certificate states that the company is a public company, that it is in fact such a company.[1] The certificate, therefore, is not only the company's birth certificate, evidencing the fact that it has been created a legal person; it is also conclusive evidence that the company was rightfully born after the proper ante-natal procedure had been followed.[2] If there has been any procedural irregularity in the incorporation of the company, it is irrelevant in determining whether the company exists as a legal person. Consequently, where the memorandum and articles of a company were altered after signature by the subscribers but before registration, the company was nevertheless held to be validly incorporated with its memorandum and articles in the altered form.[3] Furthermore, the Companies Act 1985, provides that the company shall be incorporated from the date mentioned in the certificate of incorporation.[4] Consequently, where by error the certificate bore a date some few days earlier than the date on which it was signed by the Registrar, it was held that the company was validly incorporated on the date mentioned in the certificate, and so a contract made in the company's name on the following day was binding on the company and the other party, even though at that time the certificate had not actually been issued.[5]

The certificate of incorporation is also conclusive evidence that the company is authorised to be registered.[1] Consequently, the company is validly incorporated even though some of its objects are unlawful,[6] or even though it ought not to be registered under the Act at all.[7] To this there is only one exception; a trade union[8] may not be registered as a company under the Companies Act 1985, and any such registration is void and ineffective to incorporate the trade union.[9]

The issue of a certificate of incorporation does not, of course, make lawful any activity by the company which is unlawful under the general law, or validate any provision of the company's memorandum or articles which conflicts with the general law, eg a mandatory provision of the Companies Act 1985.[10] Furthermore, a company incorporated with unlawful objects may be ordered by the court to be wound up on the petition of a creditor or member,[11] or on the petition of the Secretary of State for Trade and Industry after appointing an inspector to investigate the company's affairs who reports adversely on the legality of the

1 Ibid, s 13 (7).
2 Consequently all English companies are corporations de jure. Unlike the laws of France, Belgium and some of the states of the USA, United Kingdom law does not have a hierarchy of companies whose incorporation is defective to a small or greater extent, and which are consequently classified as companies de facto or companies merely by estoppel.
3 *Re Barned's Banking Co, Peel's Case* (1867) 2 Ch App 674; *Oakes v Turquand and Harding* (1867) LR 2 HL 325.
4 Companies Act 1985, s 13 (3).
5 *Jubilee Cotton Mills Ltd v Lewis* [1924] AC 958.
6 *Princess of Reuss v Bos* (1871) LR 5 HL 176.
7 *Hammond v Prentice Bros Ltd* [1920] 1 Ch 201.
8 Trade unions are defined by the Trade Union and Labour Relations Act 1974, s 28 (1) (16 Halsbury's Statutes (4th Edn) 271).
9 Trade Union and Labour Relations Act 1974, s 2 (2) and (4). An exception is made for organisations of workers which were incorporated under the Companies Acts before August 5 1971, and were registered in the special register kept under the Industrial Relations Act 1971, s 84 while it was in force.
10 *Ayre v Skelsey's Adamant Cement Co Ltd* (1904) 20 TLR 587; affd (1905) 21 TLR 464; *Gaiman v National Association for Mental Health* [1971] Ch 317, [1970] 2 All ER 362.
11 *Princess of Reuss v Bos*, supra. The ground for the petition is that it is just and equitable that the company should be wound up: Insolvency Act 1986, s 122 (1) (g) (4 Halsbury's Statutes (4th Edn) 800).

purposes for which it was formed.[12] Additionally, it has been suggested that the Attorney General can either apply to the Queen's Bench Division for an order of certiorari or judicial review to cancel the certificate of incorporation because it was improperly issued,[13] or may give his fiat for the issue of a writ of scire facias out of the Queen's Bench Division so that the company's incorporation may be revoked,[14] but also the opinion has been expressed that the only way by which the company may be dissolved is by winding it up under the Companies Act 1985.[15] On the other hand, it has been held that the court cannot cancel a certificate issued by the Registrar of Companies on an application by an interested person (other than the Attorney General) for judicial review, when the Companies Act 1985 provides that the issue of the certificate shall be conclusive evidence that all the necessary conditions for the issue of the certificate have been fulfilled,[16] and this appears to apply to a certificate of incorporation. If the remedies of cancellation of the certificate of incorporation or revocation of the company's incorporation are available on an application by or in the name of the Attorney General, it would be preferable, in the interests of persons to whom the company has incurred liabilities, that the Attorney General should proceed by way of scire facias for revocation. Cancellation would annul the certificate of incorporation as though it had never been issued, and the company would be deemed never to have owned any property or incurred any debts or obligations, so that none of the property in its apparent ownership would be available to satisfy the liabilities incurred in its name. Judgment on a scire facias, however, merely dissolves the company from the time it is pronounced, and the company's property would be applicable to meeting its liabilities before the residue passed to the Crown as bona vacantia[17] in the same way as in a winding up of the company.

The First Directive for the harmonisation of the company laws of the member states of the European Communities which was issued by the Council of Ministers in March 1968[18] contained provisions requiring national legislatures to enact certain rules as to the consequences of the judicial annulment of a defectively formed company.[19] In particular, these rules would ensure that annulment brought about the winding up of the company under the ordinary provisions of national law governing liquidations; that contracts, debts and liabilities of the company would not be invalidated or terminated by the annulment; and that members would remain liable for the capital unpaid on their shares.[20] These rules have not yet been enacted in the United Kingdom, although it may be that they apply in any case, since the United Kingdom is bound by its Treaty of Accession to the European Communities to give effect to them. The question remains, however, whether proceedings for the cancellation of a company's certificate of incorporation or the revocation of its incorporation are to be equated with proceedings for annulment within the meaning of the directive; it would seem that they are.

---

12 Companies Act 1985, s 432 (1) and (2) (*b*) and Insolvency Act 1986, s 124A (1), inserted by Companies Act 1989, s 60 (3).
13 *Bowman v Secular Society Ltd* [1917] AC 406 at 439; *R v Registrar of Companies, ex p Central Bank of India* [1986] QB 1114 at 1169, 1177, per Lawton and Slade LJJ, [1986] 1 All ER 105 at 117, 123. This has actually been done in one unreported case, *R v Registrar of Companies, ex p A-G* 17 December 1980, unreported (Divisional Court of the Queen's Bench Division).
14 *Salomon v Salomon & Co* [1897] AC 22 at 30.
15 *Princess of Reuss v Bos*, supra.
16 *R v Registrar of Companies, ex p Central Bank of India*, supra.
17 *Naylor v Brown* (1673) Cas temp Finch 83.
18 Official Journal of the European Communities for 1968, No L 65/8.
19 First Directive, arts 11 and 12.
20 Ibid, art 12 (2), (3) and (5).

COMMENCEMENT OF BUSINESS

A private company may enter into contracts, borrow money and carry on business immediately it is incorporated, but a public company may not do these things until it has satisfied certain conditions and obtained a certificate from the Registrar of Companies that it is entitled to do business.[1] This certificate is commonly known by the same name as its precursor under the Companies Act 1948, the certificate of a public company's entitlement to commence business;[2] both certificates are known as the company's trading certificate, although that term is not employed by the Companies Act 1985. When issued, the certificate is conclusive evidence that the company is entitled to do business.[3] The Registrar must publish in the London Gazette the fact that a statutory declaration has been delivered to him in connection with an application for a certificate that a public company is entitled to do business.[4]

In practice trading certificates are not frequently met with. This is because public companies are usually incorporated initially as private companies, and are converted into public companies by being re-registered later when their directors are ready to offer their shares to the public, or their controlling shareholders wish to sell part of their holdings to the public, or the company seeks the admission of its shares to dealing on the Stock Exchange. As companies initially incorporated as private companies, they can commence business on incorporation, and they do not need trading certificates when they are later converted into public companies.

Before the Registrar may issue a certificate of entitlement to do business in respect of a public company, he must be satisfied that the company has allotted shares whose nominal value amounts to not less than £50,000, and there must have been delivered to the Registrar a statutory declaration by a director or the secretary of the company stating that this is so and setting out the amount paid up on the allotted shares, the amount of the preliminary expenses of forming the company and of allotting share capital and putting the company in a position to do business, together with particulars of the persons by whom those expenses have been paid or are payable, and the statutory declaration must also set out the amount of any benefits given or intended to be given to the company's promoters and the consideration for those benefits.[5] The minimum amount which must have been paid up on the shares which the company has allotted is one quarter of their nominal value plus the whole of any share premium in respect of them (ie the excess of the price at which they are issued over their nominal value).[6] Consequently, if the company wishes to raise the minimum amount of capital necessary before applying for a certificate of entitlement to do business, it will allot £50,000 in nominal value of shares at par and receive in cash or kind at least £12,500 from the allottees. This is the same minimum as the amount which must be paid up on any other allotment of any shares by a public company, with the exception of shares issued under an employees' share scheme;[7] the exception does not apply to the first allotment of a public company's shares, however, and so if shares have been allotted under such a scheme for the purpose of obtaining a certificate of entitlement to do business, their nominal value counts toward the

1 Companies Act 1985, s 117 (1).
2 Companies Act 1948, s 109.
3 Companies Act 1985, s 117 (6).
4 Ibid, s 711 (1)(g).
5 Companies Act 1985, s 117 (2) and (3) and s 118 (1).
6 Ibid, s 101 (1).
7 Ibid, s 101 (2). An employees' share scheme is defined by the Companies Act 1985, s 743 (see p 247, post).

minimum allotted capital of the company and the amount paid up on them counts toward the minimum paid up share capital only if at least one quarter of their nominal value has been paid up.[8]

The failure by a company to obtain a certificate of entitlement to do business before entering into any transaction for the purpose of the business it was incorporated to carry on, or any other business, entails the criminal liability of the company and any director or officer who is in default,[9] but it does not affect the validity of any such transaction entered into by the company or any loan made to it,[10] and so the rights and obligations of the company and the other party are fully enforceable.[11] However, the other party may require the company to fulfil its obligations under the transaction and if it fails to do so within 21 days thereafter, its directors become jointly and severally liable to indemnify the other party against any loss or damage he suffers in consequence of the company's failure to fulfil its obligations.[10] It is uncertain whether the other party may make such a demand before the company's obligations have fallen due for fulfilment under the terms of the transaction. If the company does fail to perform its obligations under the transaction, it is also uncertain whether the other party may recover from its directors the same amount of damages as those for which he could sue the company, or whether his claim against the directors is limited to the damages the other party would actually have been able to recover out of the company's assets if it had raised the minimum amount of capital to entitle it to a certificate of entitlement to do business. If the latter interpretation is correct, it would be necessary to take all other similar transactions by the company into account in quantifying the claim of the other party against the company's directors.

8 Companies Act 1985, s 117 (4).
9 Ibid, s 117 (7).
10 Ibid, s 117 (8). This provision is badly drafted. The 'obligations' referred to could be construed as meaning the obligation to obtain a certificate of entitlement to do business before the company commences to do business. It is submitted that this is not the correct meaning of the word because obtaining such a certificate is not an obligation, but merely a condition precedent to the company becoming entitled to do business.
11 Under the Companies Act 1948, s 109 contracts made by a public company before obtaining its trading certificate were provisional only and became binding on the company only when the certificate was issued.

CHAPTER 2

Corporate personality

THE SEPARATE LEGAL PERSONALITY OF THE COMPANY

A company is a corporation, and is therefore a person in the eyes of the law quite distinct from the individuals who are its members. As a distinct person the company can own property, have rights and be subject to liabilities, and it does not hold its property merely as an agent or trustee for its members,[1] and they cannot sue individually or collectively to enforce its rights otherwise than in exceptional circumstances,[2] nor can they be sued in respect of its liabilities.[3] The case which clearly established the independent legal personality of the company, *Salomon v A Salomon & Co Ltd*,[4] is of such importance to an understanding of this branch of the law that it is now proposed to deal with it at some length.

Salomon v A Salomon & Co Ltd

Aron Salomon had for some years carried on business as a leather merchant and boot manufacturer. He decided to form a limited company to purchase his business, but he wished to retain control over the conduct of the business, and so his plan was that the shareholders of the company should be restricted to himself and members of his family. The company was formed, and he and six other members of his family subscribed its memorandum for one share each, and he and two of his sons were appointed directors. A contract for the sale of his business to the company was then entered into. The purchase price was £38,782, and was apportioned amongst the various assets which made up the business so that the price of the assets was the same as their respective values as shown in a balance sheet prepared by Salmon's accountant, save that the price of some of the assets was fixed at figures exceeding their balance sheet value by a total of approximately £8,000. The purchase price was to be paid in cash, except for £16,000 which the company might satisfy in cash or by issuing debentures secured by a charge over the assets of the company at its option. The company's nominal capital was £40,000 in £1 shares, and except for seven shares issued to the subscribers of the memorandum, the only shares it issued were 20,000 to Salomon, which he alleged were fully paid by the company retaining £20,000 out of the purchase price for his business. The business was transferred to the company, and it issued debentures for £10,000 to Salomon and paid him £8,782 in cash in satisfaction of the balance of the purchase price.

The business did not prosper, and when it was wound up a year later its liabilities (including the debenture debt) exceeded its assets by £7,733. The liquidator

---

1 *Macaura v Northern Assurance Co Ltd* [1925] AC 619 at 626; *Short v Treasury Comrs* [1948] AC 534 at 545, [1948] 2 All ER 509, 512; *R v Arnaud* (1846) 9 QB 806 at 817; *Hood-Barrs v IRC* [1946] 2 All ER 768 at 775.
2 *Foss v Harbottle* (1843) 2 Hare 461.
3 *Daimler Co Ltd v Continental Tyre and Rubber Co (Great Britain) Ltd* [1916] 2 AC 307, per Lord Parker of Waddington, at 338.
4 [1897] AC 22, reversing the judgments of Vaughan Williams J, and the Court of Appeal sub nom *Broderip v Salomon* [1895] 2 Ch 323.

(representing the unsecured trade creditors of the company) claimed that the company's business was in reality still Salomon's, the company being merely a sham designed to limit Salomon's liability for debts incurred in carrying it on, and therefore Salomon should be ordered to indemnify the company against its debts, and payment of the debenture debt to him should be postponed until the company's other creditors were satisfied.

Judgments of Vaughan Williams J, and the Court of Appeal

The trial judge, Vaughan Williams J, agreed with the liquidator. He held that the subscribers of the memorandum, other than Salomon, held their shares as mere nominees for him, and Salomon's sole purpose in forming the company was to use it as an agent to run his business for him. Vaughan Williams J, said:[5]

'It seems to me, however, that when one considers the fact that these shareholders were mere nominees of Mr Salomon's, that he took the whole of the profits, and that his intention was to take the profits without running the risk of the debts and expenses, one must also consider the position of the unsecured trading creditors, whose debts amount to some £11,000. As I have said, the company was a mere nominee of Mr Salomon's . . . and therefore I wish, if I can, to deal with this case exactly on the basis that I should do if the nominee, instead of being a company, had been some servant or agent of Mr Salomon's to whom he had purported to sell his business.'

The Court of Appeal reached the same conclusion as Vaughan Williams J, but for different reasons. They held that the Companies Acts were intended to confer the privilege of limited liability only on genuine, independent shareholders who had combined their capital to enable an enterprise to be started, and not upon a man who was really the sole owner of a business and who merely found six nominees to join with him in going through the formalities of incorporating a company. In the words of Lopes LJ:[6]

'It never was intended that the company to be constituted should consist of one substantial person and six mere dummies, the nominees of that person, without any real interest in the company. The Act contemplated the incorporation of seven independent bona fide members, who had a mind and a will of their own, and were not the mere puppets of an individual who, adopting the machinery of the Act, carried on his old business in the same way as before, when he was a sole trader.'

Consequently, Salomon had incorporated his company for an unlawful purpose. The court could not hold the incorporation void, because the issue of its certificate of incorporation was conclusive evidence that it had been incorporated,[7] but it could give relief to the company's creditors by requiring Salomon to indemnify the company against its liabilities and to contribute to the company's assets a sum sufficient to enable it to meet its liabilities in full. Lindley LJ, said:[8]

'I do not go so far as to say that the creditors of the company could sue him [Salomon]. In my opinion, they can only reach him through the company. Moreover, Mr Aron Salomon's liability to indemnify the company in this case is, in my view, the legal consequence of the formation of the company in order to attain a result not permitted by law. The liability does not arise simply from the fact that he holds nearly all the shares of the company. . . . His liability rests on the purpose for which he formed the company, on the way he formed it, and the use which he made of it.'

5 [1895] 2 Ch 323.
6 Ibid, at 341.
7 See p 27, ante.
8 [1895] 2 Ch 323 at 338.

Judgment of the House of Lords

The House of Lords unanimously reversed Vaughan Williams J, and the Court of Appeal, and held that Salomon was under no liability to the company or its creditors, that his debentures were validly issued, and the security created by them over the company's assets was effective against the company and its other creditors. The Court of Appeal's reasoning was quickly demolished. Lord Halsbury LC, said:[9]

'I must pause here to point out that the statute enacts nothing as to the extent or degree of interest which may be held by each of the seven [subscribers of the memorandum] or as to the proportion of influence possessed by one or the majority of the shareholders over the others. One share is enough. Still less is it possible to contend that the motive of becoming shareholders or of making them shareholders is a field of enquiry which the statute itself recognises as legitimate. If they are shareholders, they are shareholders for all purposes; and even if the statute was silent as to the recognition of trusts, I should be prepared to hold that if six of them were the cestuis que trust of the seventh,[10] whatever might be their rights inter se, the statute would have made them shareholders to all intents and purposes with their respective rights and liabilities, and, dealing with them in their relation to the company, the only relations which I believe the law would sanction would be that they were corporators of the body corporate.'

As there was nothing improper, therefore, in the purpose for which, and the manner in which, the company was formed, the reasons of the Court of Appeal for holding Salomon liable to indemnify the company fell to the ground.

Vaughan Williams J's hypothesis, that the company must be treated as Salomon's agent appointed to run his business for him, was equally found without merit. Lord Halsbury LC, remarked in his usual trenchant manner:[11]

'I confess it seems to me that that very learned judge becomes involved by this argument in a very singular contradiction. Either the company was a legal entity or it was not. If it was, the business belonged to it and not Mr Salomon. If it was not, there was no person and no thing to be an agent at all.'

Lord Herschell observed, more generally:[12]

In a popular sense, a company may in every case be said to carry on business for and on behalf of its shareholders; but this certainly does not in point of law constitute the relation of principal and agent between them or render the shareholders liable to indemnify the company against the debts which it incurs.'

And Lord Macnaughten added:[13]

'The company is at law a different person altogether from the subscribers to the memorandum; and, though it may be that after incorporation the business is precisely the same as it was before, and the same persons are managers, and the same hands receive the profits, the company is not in law the agent of the subscribers or a trustee for them. Nor are the subscribers as members liable, in any shape or form, except to the extent and in the manner provided by the Act.'

Subsequent cases

The principle of the company's separate legal personality has on the whole been fully applied by the courts since *Salomon's* case. This has not only been done in cases

---

9 [1897] AC 22.
10 His lordship appears to mean 'trustees for the seventh'.
11 [1897] AC 22 at 31.
12 Ibid, at 43.
13 [1897] AC 22 at 51.

where the principal question before the court was one of company law, and in some situations where the corporate personality of the company involved was really of secondary importance, the application of the principle has worked hardship and injustice. There have been only a few cases where the court has disregarded the company's corporate personality and paid attention to where the real control and beneficial ownership of the company's undertaking lay. When it has done this, the court has relied either on a principle of public policy, or on the principle that devices used to perpetrate frauds or evade obligations will be treated as nullities, or on a presumption of agency or trusteeship which at first sight *Salomon's* case seems to prohibit. These cases will be dealt with later in this chapter. At present we are concerned to see how the principle of the company's separate personality has been affirmatively applied.

Property

A company is the beneficial owner of its own property; it does not hold it as a trustee for its members, and they have no legal or equitable interest therein.[14] Consequently, when a local authority purchased compulsorily some land, the freehold in which belonged to the plaintiff subject to a lease to a company in which she was the majority shareholder, it was held that the compensation payable to her was restricted to the value of her freehold reversion, and could not extend to the diminution in the value of her shares resulting from the company having to move its business elsewhere.[15] Likewise, where the plaintiff was the tenant of a shop and flat above, and a business was carried on in the shop by a company of which he was the managing director and majority shareholder, he was held not entitled to apply to the court for a renewal of his tenancy under statutory provisions for the protection of business tenants, because he was not 'the occupier of a shop under a tenancy' as required by the statute.[16] The company occupied the shop, but only as a licensee of the plaintiff and not as a sub-tenant, so that it, too, was disabled from seeking a renewed tenancy. Evershed MR, and Jenkins LJ,[17] did concede, however, that if the plaintiff had owned all, or substantially all, the shares of the company, so that he was the only person really interested in its business, they would have held that he occupied the shop himself. In another case,[18] the owner of a house formed a company in which he became the sole shareholder, and the company purported to let the house to one of its employees; it was held that the tenant was not protected by the Rent Acts against the owner recovering possession, because the company which granted the tenancy had no title to do so, and apparently the owner, who controlled the company, was not estopped from relying on this. Again, it has been held that a landlord's insistence on granting tenancies of residential accommodation to companies of which the individual occupiers of the accommodation are the sole or controlling shareholders will be given full legal effect, even though the purpose of doing so instead of granting tenancies to the occupiers individually is to prevent them from enjoying the protection of Rent Acts.[19]

Because a shareholder has no legal or equitable interest in the company's

---

14 See cases cited supra, p 32, footnote 1.
15 *Roberts v Coventry Corpn* [1947] 1 All ER 308.
16 *Pegler v Craven* [1952] 2 QB 69, [1952] 1 All ER 685. The statute was the Leasehold Property (Temporary Provisions) Act 1951, now replaced by the Landlord and Tenant Act 1954, Part II of which is to the same effect (23 Halsbury's Statutes (4th Edn) 144).
17 [1952] 2 QB 69 at 79, 74 [1952] 1 All ER 685 at 690, 687–8.
18 *Torbett v Faulkner* [1952] 2 TLR 659.
19 *Hilton v Plustitle Ltd* [1988] 3 All ER 1051, [1989] 1 WLR 149.

property, he cannot insure it,[20] but a policy taken out by a shareholder to insure the success of a venture in which a company is engaged has been held to be valid.[1] At first sight this latter decision seems to conflict with the principal rule, because if a company's property belongs to it alone, so does a business venture in which it is engaged, and its shareholders have no insurable interest in either. The distinction between the two cases appears to lie in the fact that in the case in which the shareholder was held to have an insurable interest, the policy contained an 'agreed value' clause, which provided that the insured property 'for so much as concerns the assured, by agreement between the assured and the assurers, in this policy [is] and shall be valued at £200 on the [adventure concerned], value, say on twenty shares [in the company], valued at £10 per share.' What the shareholder was really insuring against was a fall in the value of his shares in consequence of the failure of the company's venture, and a shareholder has an insurable interest in the maintenance of the value of his shares, which are, of course, his own property. Unlike a shareholder, a debenture holder can insure the property of the company on which his debenture is secured,[2] and he now has a statutory power to insure that property against loss by fire.[3] The difference in the debenture holder's position is logically justifiable, because as a secured creditor he has an interest in the company's property, which the shareholder does not. But the rule does work a practical hardship on the shareholder. He ranks for repayment of his capital in a winding up of the company only after the debenture debt has been fully repaid, so that his risk of loss and need to insure are consequently the greater. Yet the only insurance which the law will permit him to make is against a diminution in the value of his shares, and unless the policy effecting such an insurance contains a provision for calculating the amount of the diminution, it will be exceptionally difficult for him to prove that his shares have fallen in value in consequence of a loss or depreciation of the company's assets which is not serious enough to cause it to be wound up.

Contracts and torts

A shareholder cannot enforce a contract made by his company; he is neither a party to the contract, nor entitled to the benefit of it under the rule that in certain circumstances parties to a contract are taken to have contracted as trustees for third persons,[4] for a company is not a trustee for its shareholders. Likewise, a shareholder cannot be sued on contracts made by his company,[5] nor can the court compel a shareholder to vote at a general meeting of the company in a way which will ensure that the company will fulfil its contractual obligations, or prohibit him from voting in any other way.[6] The distinction between a company and its members is not confined to the rules of privity, however; it permeates the whole law of contract. Thus, if a director fails to disclose a breach of his duties to his company, and in consequence a shareholder is induced to enter into a contract with the director which he would not have entered into had there been disclosure, the shareholder cannot rescind the contract; the duty of disclosure is owed to the company alone,

20 *Macaura v Northern Assurance Co* [1925] AC 619.
1 *Wilson v Jones* (1866) LR 1 Exch 193.
2 *Westminster Fire Office v Glasgow Provident Investment Society* (1888) 13 App Cas 699.
3 Law of Property Act 1925, s 101 (1) (ii) (37 Halsbury's Statutes (4th Edn) 223). But the statutory power may not be available to a debenture holder secured by a floating charge, if the court's decision that the statutory powers of a mortgagee are not exercisable by a creditor secured by a floating charge (*Blaker v Herts and Essex Waterworks Co* (1889) 41 ChD 399) is correct.
4 *Chitty on Contracts* (26th edn), p 668 et seq.
5 *Daimler Co Ltd v Continental Tyre and Rubber Co (Great Britain) Ltd* [1916] 2 AC 307 at 338, per Lord Parker of Waddington.
6 *Northern Counties Securities Ltd v Jackson and Steeple Ltd* [1974] 2 All ER 625, [1974] 1 WLR 1133.

and the shareholder cannot, because of it, treat the contract he has entered into as one uberrimae fidei.[7] Again, if a shareholder undertakes to pay a judgment debt owed by his company in order to induce the judgment creditor not to levy execution on the company's property, the agreement, as a contract of guarantee, is unenforceable unless it is evidenced by a written memorandum signed by the shareholder.[8] If the shareholder had a legal or equitable interest in the company's property (as he would if he had agreed to buy it),[9] the memorandum would be unnecessary, because the main purpose of the agreement would then be to relieve the property from the risk of seizure and sale, and not to guarantee the payment of a debt owed by the company. However, the shareholder has no such interest in the company's property, and the written memorandum is therefore necessary. Again, in another case[10] it was held that, despite the rule that a mortgagee cannot exercise his power of sale by selling the mortgaged property to himself or to a trustee for himself, he may sell it to a company which he promotes and of which he is the controlling shareholder, because the company is neither his agent nor his trustee. However, the court will scrutinise a sale carefully if the purchaser from the mortgagee is a company which he controls, and the sale will be rescinded in equity if the price paid by the company is less than the full market value of the property.[11]

A member of a company cannot sue in respect of torts committed against it, nor can he be sued for torts committed by it.[12] So anxious are the courts to preserve the distinct legal personality of the company, that it has been held that proof of the commission of a tort by a company does not automatically prove that the directors who manage its affairs are guilty of that tort as well.[12] If the directors are to be made liable, it must be shown that they actively participated in committing the tort or that they authorised or directed its commission, and the court will not infer that they did this merely because the act complained of was one which would normally be done only on the authority of the directors.[12]

Holding and subsidiary companies

A holding company is one which owns sufficient shares in its subsidiary company to determine who shall be its directors and how its affairs shall be conducted.[13] Often the holding company controls a number of subsidiaries, and the respective businesses of the companies within the group are managed as an integrated whole, as though they were merely departments of one large undertaking owned by the holding company. The law, however, is not concerned with the functional organisation of the group; in its eyes the holding company is merely a large shareholder of each subsidiary, so that the rule which distinguishes the legal personality of a company from that of its shareholders also separates the holding company from its subsidiaries. Consequently, a holding company cannot sue to enforce rights which belong to its subsidiary,[14] nor is it liable for its subsidiary's

7 *Bell v Lever Bros Ltd* [1932] AC 161 at 228, [1931] All ER Rep 1 at 32, per Lord Atkin.
8 *Harburg India Rubber Comb Co v Martin* [1902] 1 KB 778. The written memorandum is required by the Statute of Frauds (1677), s 4 (11 Halsbury's Statutes (4th Edn) 205).
9 *Fitzgerald v Dressler* (1859) 7 CBNS 374.
10 *Farrar v Farrars Ltd* (1888) 40 ChD 395.
11 *Tse Kwong Lam v Wong Chit Sen* [1983] 3 All ER 54, [1983] 1 WLR 1349.
12 *Rainham Chemical Works Ltd (in liquidation) v Belvedere Fish Guano Co Ltd* [1921] 2 AC 465 at 475–6 per Lord Buckmaster; *British Thomson-Houston Co v Sterling Accessories Ltd* [1924] 2 Ch 33; *Performing Rights Society v Ciryl Theatrical Syndicate Ltd* [1924] 1 KB 1; *C Evans & Sons Ltd v Spritebrand Ltd* [1985] 2 All ER 415, [1985] 1 WLR 317; *Mancetter Development Ltd v Garmanson Ltd* [1986] QB 1212, [1986] 1 All ER 449.
13 The subject of holding and subsidiary companies is more fully dealt with in Chapter 18.
14 *Bell v Lever Bros Ltd* [1932] AC 161 at 228.

breaches of contract and torts,[15] and conversely, a subsidiary cannot sue to enforce rights belonging to its holding company or recover damages for wrongs done to it.[16]

This insulation can often work to the holding company's advantage. For example, if the subsidiary is resident in a foreign country where it carries on business, the United Kingdom holding company will in principle not have to pay corporation tax on the subsidiary's profits earned overseas,[17] but only on distributions of those profits made by the subsidiary to the holding company.[18] Likewise, if a holding company sells some of its machinery to its subsidiary, the subsidiary will be entitled to a depreciation allowance for tax purposes based on the price it paid, even though the value of the machinery in the holding company's books at the date of the sale was less than that price.[19] But equally the rule can work to the holding company's disadvantage. Thus, where a holding company formed a subsidiary solely for the purpose of being the nominal owner of the holding company's barges, and the holding company managed the subsidiary's business as part of its own, it was held that the holding company could not be treated as the owner of the barges for the purposes of the Merchant Shipping Act 1894,[20] and therefore could not claim the statutory immunity of an owner from liability for more than a limited amount of damages when one of its own employees caused damage to property by negligently navigating a barge vested in the subsidiary.[1]

EXCEPTIONS TO THE RULE OF SEPARATE LEGAL PERSONALITY

Four inroads have been made by the law on the principle of the separate legal personality of companies. By far the most extensive of these has been made by legislation imposing taxation. The Government, naturally enough, does not willingly suffer schemes for the avoidance of taxation which depend for their success on the employment of the principle of separate legal personality, and in fact legislation has gone so far that in certain circumstances taxation can be heavier if companies are employed by the taxpayer in an attempt to minimise his tax liability than if he uses other means to give effect to his wishes.[2] Taxation of companies is a complex subject, and is outside the scope of this book. The reader who wishes to pursue the subject is referred to the many standard text books on Corporation Tax, Income Tax, Capital Gains Tax and Inheritance Tax.

15 *Ebbw Vale UDC v South Wales Traffic Licensing Authority* [1951] 2 KB 366, [1951] 1 All ER 806.
16 *Lindgren v L & P Estates Ltd* [1968] Ch 572, [1968] 1 All ER 917.
17 *Kodak Ltd v Clark* [1902] 2 KB 450.
18 Nevertheless, the tax avoidance provisions of the Income and Corporation Taxes Act 1988, ss 707 to 709 (44 Halsbury's Statutes (4th Edn) 817 to 827) may result in the whole of the subsidiary's overseas profits becoming taxable in the hands of the holding company. Moreover, if a holding company fails to ensure that its overseas subsidiaries distribute at least half their available profits after overseas taxation, they may be liable for corporation tax as if a fraction of the subsidiaries' profits proportionate to the holding company's shareholdings in them had been earned by the holding company itself (Income and Corporation Taxes Act 1988, ss 747 to 752 and Schs 24 and 25 (44 Halsbury's Statutes (4th Edn) 871 to 878 and 1113 to 1128).
19 *Pioneer Laundry and Dry Cleaners Ltd v Minister of National Revenue* [1940] AC 127, [1939] 4 All ER 254.
20 39 Halsbury's Statutes (4th Edn) 424.
 1 *William Cory & Son Ltd v Dorman Long & Co Ltd* [1936] 2 All ER 386.
 2 See in particular the Income and Corporation Taxes Act 1988, ss 703 to 709 (44 Halsbury's Statutes (4th Edn) 817 to 827), which enable the Inland Revenue to counteract tax advantages obtained through certain transactions in securities.

The other inroads on the principle of separate corporate personality have been made by five sections of the Companies Act 1985, the Company Directors Disqualification Act 1986 and the Insolvency Act 1986, by judicial disregard of the principle where the protection of public interests is of paramount importance or where the company has been formed to evade obligations imposed by the law, and by the courts implying in certain cases that a company is an agent or trustee for its members.

Companies Act 1985 and related statutes

Liability of a sole member for a company's debts

If a company carries on business without having at least two members for more than six months, any person who is the one remaining member of the company during any period thereafter and who knows that the company is carrying on business with himself as its only member, is liable jointly and severally with the company for its debts contracted during that period.[3] This situation may be brought about either by the death of members, for personal representatives do not became members in place of a deceased shareholder until they are entered on the register of members,[4] or by shareholders transferring all their shares to one of their own number. The situation may also come about if a company has another company as a member of it, and that other company becomes the sole member of the first company, or is itself dissolved leaving only one other member of the company. The statutory liability imposed on the one remaining member may easily be avoided, however, except in cases where the articles impose restrictions on the transferability of members' shares. Liability does not attach until the membership has remained below the statutory minimum for six months, and it attaches only in respect of debts contracted after that time; the sole shareholder may therefore escape personal liability by transferring some of his shares, or in the case of a corporate shareholder some of its shares during the six months to nominees or trustees for himself or itself, so that the number of members is restored to the statutory minimum before the six months expire.

A member is liable under this provision only in respect of debts contracted by the company, and not in respect of claims for damages against it for breach of contract or tort or in respect of statutory claims against the company, whether liquidated or not (eg taxation, claims by employees for redundancy payments or compensation for unfair dismissal).[5] Furthermore, a member is personally liable only if he was the only member of the company at the time the debt in question was contracted (not when it fell due) and he was aware of the fact at that time. If a member is liable to a creditor, he may be sued personally, and it is not necessary for the creditor to procure the winding up of the company in order to enforce the member's liability. Moreover, the member is liable without limit to pay the debts for which he is personally responsible under the provision; his liability is not limited, as it normally is, to the amount unpaid on his shares. If a member is compelled to satisfy a debt as the sole member of a company, he may demand an

---

3 Companies Act 1985, s 24.
4 *Re Bowling and Welby's Contract* [1895] 1 Ch 663.
5 The sole member will not incur personal liability merely because the claimant has obtained judgment against the company. The amount payable under the judgment is a species of debt, but it is not contracted by the company as required by the Companies Act 1985, s 24.

indemnity from the company, because the debt is still primarily the company's liability.[6]

Holding companies are under a statutory liability to pay the debts of their wholly-owned subsidiaries (ie subsidiaries all of whose shares are owned beneficially by the holding company) if all the shares issued by the subsidiaries are registered in the name of the holding company for more than six months and the debts are contracted after that time.[7] A holding company can easily avoid this liability, however, by having a few of each subsidiary's shares registered in the names of nominees for itself, so that the membership of the subsidiary is at least two persons. It should not therefore be readily assumed that because a company is described as the wholly-owned subsidiary of another, the holding company is liable for its debts. In practice holding companies do take care to protect themselves from liability by employing the device of nominee holdings.

Liability of a disqualified person for a company's debts

If a person is a director of a company or is concerned, directly or indirectly, in the management of a company while he is an undischarged bankrupt, or while an order of the court disqualifying him from being or acting as a director of any company or in certain other capacities is in force, and in either case the court has not given him leave to do so,[8] he is personally liable for the debts of the company which are incurred while he is a director of it or is concerned in its management. The liability may be enforced against him by the creditors to whom such debts are owed either by suing him alone or jointly with the company and any other persons who are similarly liable.[9] A person is similarly liable for the debts of a company incurred while he is concerned in the management of the company and acts, or is willing to act, on instructions given without leave of the court by a person whom he knows to be an undischarged bankrupt or the subject of an order of the court disqualifying that person from being or acting as a director of the company or in certain other capacities,[8] which is currently in force.[9] In this connection, a person who has acted on the instructions of someone whom he knew to be an undischarged bankrupt, or to be subject to disqualification from being or acting as a director, is assumed, unless the contrary is shown, to continue at any time thereafter to be willing to act on such instructions.[10]

Many of the comments made above in connection with the personal liability of a sole member of a company, in respect of debts contracted by it while he is such a member, apply also to personal liability incurred under the present provisions, including the right of a person who satisfies a debt of the company to recover an indemnity from the company itself.[11] In one respect, however, the liability of a person under the present provisions is wider than that of a sole member. The liability under the present provisions extends to debts incurred by the company during the relevant period, and not merely to debts contracted by it, so that a person is liable under the present provision both for contractual debts and for debts and liquidated sums for which the company is statutorily liable.

---

6 The member could recover his indemnity by suing for money paid to the use of the company. This action lies whenever statute requires one person to satisfy a debt or obligation which is primarily the liability of another (*Brook's Wharf and Bull Wharf Ltd v Goodman Bros* [1937] 1 KB 534, [1936] 3 All ER 696).

7 Companies Act 1985, s 24.

8 For the disqualification by the court of directors and other persons from being or acting as directors or in certain other capacities, see p 535, post.

9 Company Directors Disqualification Act 1986, s 11 (1) and s 15 (1) to (4).

10 Ibid, s 15 (4).

11 *Brook's Wharf and Bull Wharf Ltd v Goodman Bros*, supra.

Liability for the use of prohibited names

The Insolvency Act 1986 makes it an offence for a person who has been a director of a company within 12 months before it goes into an insolvent liquidation, to be a director of, or to be concerned, directly or indirectly, in the promotion, formation or management of another company without leave of the court within five years after the original company went into liquidation, if the other company is known by a name which is the same as one by which the original company was known at any time within 12 months before it went into liquidation, or by a name which is so similar to such a name by which the original company was known that it suggests an association between the original and the new companies.[12] It is also an offence for such a director of the original company without leave of the court within the same five year period to be concerned in the management of a business carried on otherwise than by a company, if the business is known by such a prohibited name.[13] All the prohibitions in the present provisions apply also to a person who has within 12 months before it went into insolvent liquidation been a shadow director of the original company (ie a person in accordance with whose directions or instructions the directors of the original company were accustomed to act).[14] The purpose of these provisions is to prevent the setting up of so-called 'phoenix companies', whose directors and controllers are the same persons as the directors and controllers of another company or companies which previously carried on business under the same or a similar name before going into insolvent liquidation, so making it appear that the successor company is the same as, or at least connected with, the original one and is responsible for its debts and liabilities.

If a person is a director of, or involved in the management of, a successor company in contravention of the prohibitions mentioned above, or if such a person acts, or is willing to act, on instructions given without leave of the court by a person whom he knows to be in contravention of any of those prohibitions, that person is personally liable for the debts and other liabilities of the successor company which are incurred during the period while he is a director of it or so involved in its management, or while he so acts or is willing to act on such instructions.[15] The same rules apply as to the liability of a person subject to these provisions, both individually and jointly with the successor company, and as to the presumed continuance of the willingness of a person to act on the instructions of another person, as apply when an undischarged bankrupt or a person disqualified from acting as a director is sought to be made liable for the debts of a company in whose management he is involved.[16] The liability imposed by the present provisions goes further than that of such an undischarged bankrupt or disqualified person, because it extends not only to debts incurred by the successor company, but also to the other liabilities of that company incurred during the relevant period, including liabilities for unliquidated damages for breach of contract or tort.[17] It would not seem, however, that the liability would extend to equitable obligations of the company to make restoration of money or property, or to indemnify sureties or other persons, or to pay compensation.

Fraudulent trading

If when a company is wound up it appears that its business has been carried on with intent to defraud its creditors or the creditors of another person, or for any

12 Insolvency Act 1986, s 216 (1) to (4).
13 Ibid, s 216 (3) (*c*).
14 Ibid, s 216 (1) and s 251.
15 Ibid, s 217 (1) and (4).
16 Ibid, s 217 (2) and (5).
17 Ibid, s 217 (3).

fraudulent purpose, the court may on the application of the liquidator order that any persons who were knowingly parties to carrying on its business in that way shall be liable to make such contributions to the company's assets as the court thinks proper.[18] The court may charge the amount which such a person is directed to contribute on any debt due from the company to him, or on any mortgage or charge on the company's assets to which he is entitled; the amount ordered to be paid may also be charged on any debt due from the company or on any mortgage or charge on its assets if the debt, mortgage or charge is vested in a trustee for the person against whom the order is made, or in anyone in whose favour it was created on the direction of that person, or if it is vested in or is held in trust for an assignee (other than an assignee for money or money's worth) from the person against whom the order is made or from his trustee or a person so nominated by him.[19] The primary purpose of this complex supplementary provision is to enable the court to charge debentures or debenture stock with payment of the amount of the order if they were issued to the person against whom the order is made, or were issued or transferred at his direction to nominees for himself.

The court cannot make an order under the statutory provision simply because the company is insolvent, or because the company was formed to enable the shareholders to escape personal liability for the debts incurred in carrying on a business. An order could not be made in the circumstances of *Salomon's* case, for example. It is only where the persons responsible for managing the company's business have been guilty of dishonesty that personal liability may be imposed on them,[20] but a single act of dishonesty which they commit or in which they participate suffices for an order to be made against them.[1] The dishonest intentions of the respondents may be apparent from the circumstances in which the company's business was carried on. Thus, in a case where a company was insolvent, but its directors continued to carry on its business and purchased further goods on credit, Maugham J, declaring one of them personally liable for the price of those goods, said:[2]

'. . . if a company continues to carry on business and to incur debts at a time when there is to the knowledge of the directors no reasonable prospect of the creditors ever receiving payment of those debts, it is, in general, a proper inference that the company is carrying on business with intent to defraud.'

Too much emphasis should not be placed on the word 'ever' in this passage. A person is guilty of fraudulent trading if he has no reason to believe that the company will be able to pay its creditors in full by the dates when their respective debts become due or within a short time thereafter.[3] On the other hand, the mere fact that directors in the course of disposing of the company's assets with a view to its ultimate winding up have made a payment which would be voidable as a fraudulent preference in the winding up,[4] does not necessarily mean that they have carried on its business with intent to defraud its other creditors.[5]

---

18 Insolvency Act 1986, s 213 (1) and (2).
19 Ibid, s 215 (2) and (3).
20 *Re Patrick and Lyon Ltd* [1933] Ch 786, [1933] All ER Rep 590; *R v Cox and Hodges* (1982) 75 Cr App Rep 291, [1983] BCLC 169.
 1 *Re Gerald Cooper Chemicals Ltd* [1978] Ch 262, [1978] 2 All ER 49.
 2 *Re William C Leitch Bros Ltd* [1932] 2 Ch 71 at 77, [1932] All ER Rep 892 at 895.
 3 *R v Grantham* [1984] QB 675, [1984] 3 All ER 166.
 4 That is, a fraudulent preference, voidable in the insolvent winding up of the company under the Companies Act 1985, s 615(1), which is now repealed and replaced by the Insolvency Act 1986, s 239 as to preferences made or given by a company within a limited period before the onset of its insolvency.
 5 *Re Sarflax Ltd* [1979] Ch 592, [1979] 1 All ER 529.

A person is not a party to carrying on a company's business with intent to defraud its creditors unless he actively participates in its management. If he merely fails to warn its directors that it is insolvent and that no further debts should be incurred on its behalf, he cannot be made liable under the statutory provision, even though he is guilty of negligence in failing to give that advice, and could be sued by the company for breach of duty as an officer of the company or for breach of a contract to advise it properly.[6] Furthermore, a shareholder cannot be made personally liable for a company's debts by an order of the court, however large his holding, merely because he was in a position to influence the conduct of its affairs, or merely because he nominated or procured the appointment of directors who are guilty of fraudulent trading. To impose liability on a shareholder it must be shown that he took part in making management decisions which were intended to defraud creditors or were known to be likely to cause them loss, or that he gave instructions to the directors which he knew would produce such results and to which the directors submitted. Moreover, the directors of the company or the persons who manage its affairs must have acted fraudulently themselves, and so no liability can be imposed by the court on a parent or holding company which undertakes informally to give the necessary financial support to enable a loss-making subsidiary to continue trading, if the directors of the subsidiary honestly believe that the parent company intends to give that financial support and is capable of doing so.[7] But a third person who knowingly participates in an act of fraudulent trading committed by a company's directors (for example, a creditor of the company who accepts payment of his debt out of money which he knows its directors have obtained by fraud), may be compelled personally to repay the amount so applied to the liquidator of the company.[8] For liability to be imposed on a third person it is essential that he personally should have acted fraudulently, and so even if the directors of a company have carried on its business with knowledge of its insolvency, the court cannot impose liability for its debts on its parent company, which has given a temporary informal undertaking to support its current trading activities at a time when the parent company was financially able to do so, if the parent company declines to extend the undertaking when the subsidiary later becomes insolvent.[7]

Although an order by the court imposing personal liability on an individual who has knowingly participated in the fraudulent carrying on of a company's business takes away the protection afforded to directors and shareholders by the company's separate legal personality, it does not entirely disregard the company's existence. The effect of the order is not to make the person subject to it personally liable to a creditor of the company who has been defrauded; instead, he must pay the sum ordered by the court to the liquidator, who will apply it with the other funds of the company in paying all its creditors rateably, and the creditors who have been defrauded have no preferential claim to the sum ordered to be paid.[9] Similarly, if the court charges the sum ordered to be paid on any mortgage of the company's assets held by or on behalf of the person in default, the sole effect is to destroy his priority as a secured creditor to that extent, and no defrauded creditor of the company is thereby subrogated to his rights as a mortgagee.

On the other hand, it has been held under the former provisions of the Companies Act relating to fraudulent trading[10] that if a creditor of the company obtains

6 *Re Maidstone Building Provisions Ltd* [1971] 3 All ER 363, [1971] 1 WLR 1085.
7 *Re Augustus Barnett & Son Ltd* [1986] BCLC 170, (1986) 2 BCC 98, 904.
8 *Re Gerald Cooper Chemicals Ltd*, supra.
9 *Re William C Leitch Bros Ltd (No 2)* [1933] Ch 261, [1932] All ER Rep 897.
10 The decision was given under the Companies Act 1948, s 332(1), which was re-enacted by the now repealed Companies Act 1985, s 630(1) and (2).

payment of his debt from directors out of their own resources by threatening to take proceedings against them for an order making them personally liable, the payment is not impressed with a trust in favour of the company's creditors as a whole, and so the liquidator cannot require the recipient to account for it to him.[11] In the same case Denning MR said obiter that in making an order under the statutory provision, the court may direct that payment of the sum ordered to be paid by the directors shall be made to the defrauded creditors individually for their own exclusive benefit, instead of to the liquidator for the benefit of the creditors generally; and that although the amount ordered to be paid will never exceed the company's indebtedness outstanding during the period of fraudulent trading, the court does have jurisdiction to make a punitive order requiring the directors to pay debts incurred by the company before that period began as well as debts incurred during it.[12] The court later held under the same legislation in a case where a defrauded creditor sought an order imposing liability on a company's directors and others who had participated in their fraud, that the court did indeed have power to make an order for payment by the respondents directly to the defrauded creditor.[13] Such an order in favour of a particular creditor cannot now be made under the provisions of the present legislation, which confine the court to making orders imposing liability on persons responsible for fraudulent trading to make such contributions to the company's assets as the court thinks fit, and an application for such an order can be made only by the company's liquidator.[14]

A person who is a party to carrying on a company's business with intent to defraud its or another person's creditors, or for any other fraudulent purpose, is guilty of a criminal offence.[15] A prosecution may be brought for the offence, whether the company is being or has been wound up or not.[15] The offence is committed if the accused carries on a company's business with intent to defraud its customers, who are potential creditors of the company for the claims they will have against it for reparation in respect of the fraud.[16]

Wrongful trading

If, in the winding up of a company which has gone into insolvent liquidation, it appears that a person, who was a director or shadow director[17] of the company at some time before the commencement of the winding up, knew or ought to have concluded that there was no reasonable prospect that the company would avoid such an insolvent liquidation, the court may on the application of the liquidator order that person to contribute such amount to the assets of the company as the court thinks fit.[18] The court may not make such an order, however, if the director or shadow director satisfies it that after he first realised or should have concluded that the company would inevitably be wound up in an insolvent condition, he took every step to minimise the potential loss to the company's creditors which he ought to have taken.[19]

The court may make an order for a contribution by a director or shadow director in circumstances where it cannot be proved that he knowingly and fraudulently carried on the company's business with intent to defraud the company's creditors,

11 *Re Cyona Distributions Ltd* [1967] Ch 889, [1967] 1 All ER 281.
12 Ibid, [1967] Ch 889 at 902, [1967] 1 All ER 281 at 284.
13 *Re Gerald Cooper Chemicals Ltd*, supra.
14 Insolvency Act 1986, s 213 (1) and (2).
15 Companies Act 1985, s 458.
16 *R v Kemp* [1988] QB 645, [1988] BCLC 217, (1988) 4 BCC 203.
17 For shadow directors, see p 41, ante and p 531, post.
18 Insolvency Act 1986, s 214 (1), (2) and (7).
19 Ibid, s 214 (3).

and that he was therefore guilty of fraudulent trading; liability for wrongful trading can be imposed if it is proved that the respondent ought by the exercise of proper skill and care to have concluded that the company's insolvent liquidation could not be avoided. Once that is established, however, the respondent can escape having an order to contribute made against him only by showing that he took every possible step which he reasonably believed to be appropriate, or which he ought to have concluded was appropriate, to minimise the loss suffered by the company's creditors. To determine whether the respondent ought to have concluded that the company's insolvent liquidation was inevitable and whether he then took every step to minimise loss to creditors, the following will be considered: the facts which the respondent should have known or ascertained, the conclusions which he should have reached, and the steps which he should have taken, as compared with those which would be known, ascertained, reached or taken by a reasonably diligent person who had the general knowledge, skill and experience which may reasonably be expected of a person carrying out the respondent's functions in relation to the company, together with any additional knowledge and experience which the respondent actually had.[20] The respondent's functions in relation to the company include those which were entrusted to him, even if he did not carry them out personally (eg functions which he delegated) or at all.[1]

The standard of awareness, perspicacity and diligence required of a director or shadow director if he is to resist an application for an order to contribute is therefore that of a person who is competent to fulfil the functions he was appointed to fulfil (eg as a director responsible for a particular sector of the company's operations and activities, as well as a member of the board responsible for supervising the management of the company's affairs) and who manifests appropriate skill and care in doing so. It will be no defence to show that the respondent lacked the skills and abilities requisite for fulfilling those functions properly, or that his level of intelligence was below that required for appreciating the company's commercial and financial condition and the steps which were necessary to prevent it becoming insolvent, or to minimise the loss suffered by its creditors. On the other hand, if the respondent had a higher level of intelligence or ability than would normally be expected of a director or shadow director in his position, the standard of performance required of him is correspondingly higher (eg a finance director who is a professionally qualified accountant, or a production director who is a qualified and experienced engineer). The nature, size and circumstances of the company will be relevant in determining the standard of performance required of its directors; directors of companies engaged in complex, expensive or risky business activities and directors of companies with high turnover or large scale operations (particularly if they are correspondingly well remunerated) will be expected to manifest an appropriately enhanced degree of skill and care.

In the one case on liability for wrongful trading which has so far been reported,[2] Knox J held that where directors were aware that their company had made losses in successive years, that its turnover was contracting and that it was likely that its liabilities exceeded its assets, an order requiring them to contribute to the company's assets in its subsequent liquidation should be made when they had continued to carry on the company's business and incur further liabilities on the company's behalf, and this is so even though it was not until later that the company's insolvency was revealed by its audited annual accounts. This decision shows that the court will make orders imposing liability for wrongful trading even though

---

20 Ibid, s 214 (4).
1 Ibid, s 214 (5).
2 *Re Produce Marketing Consortium Ltd* (1989) 5 BCC 569.

there is no suspicion of dishonesty on the part of directors, and that the standard of attentiveness to the company's financial condition required of them is a high one. In the same case, Knox J held that the amount of the contribution ordered to be paid by directors guilty of wrongful trading should be measured by the indebtedness of the company outstanding during the period of wrongful trading, in the same way as the contribution ordered to be paid by directors guilty of fraudulent trading.[3] The contributions recovered by the liquidator will be applied as part of the assets of the company in paying equal dividends to its creditors generally, and as in the situation where liability for fraudulent trading is established, the contribution will not be applied primarily in satisfying creditors whose debts were incurred during the period of wrongful trading.[3]

The court which orders the payment of contributions by directors or shadow directors who are guilty of wrongful trading may charge the contribution ordered on any debt owed by the company to the respondent or his nominee, trustee or assignee, or on any mortgage or charge on assets of the company held by the respondent or such a person, in the same way as the court may do when it orders the payment of contributions by persons guilty of fraudulent trading.[4]

Paramount public interest

In a few cases the court has disregarded the separate legal personality of a company and has investigated the personal qualities of its shareholders or the persons in control of it because there was an overriding public interest to be served by doing so. All these cases involved questions of nationality, and all of them, except one, were decided in wartime when the nationalities involved were those of enemy aliens.

In the first of these cases[5] an action was brought during the 1914–18 War by a company incorporated in England all of whose shares, except one, were held by German nationals, and all of whose directors were German nationals resident in Germany. The defendant contended that the company was an alien enemy, and that it was therefore unable to sue unless licensed to do so by the Crown. The House of Lords upheld this contention. Their lordships disregarded the fact that the company had British nationality by being incorporated in England, and concentrated on where control of the company's business and assets lay in determining the company's status. Lord Parker of Waddington said:[6]

'It would seem, therefore, logically to follow that, in transferring the application of the rule against trading with the enemy from natural to artificial persons, something more than the mere place or country of registration or incorporation must be looked at. My Lords, I think the analogy is to be found in control, an area which, if not very familiar in law, is of capital importance and is well understood in commerce and finance. The acts of a company's organs, its directors, managers, secretary, and so forth, functioning within the scope of their authority, are the company's acts and may invest it definitively with enemy character. It seems to me that similarly the character of those who can make and unmake those officers, dictate their conduct mediately or immediately, prescribe their duties and call them to account, may also be material in a question of the enemy character of the company.'

In another case[7] a local authority during the 1914–18 War refused to renew a cinematograph licence held by a company incorporated in England because a

3 See p 44, ante.
4 See p 42, ante.
5 *Daimler Co Ltd v Continental Tyre and Rubber Co (Great Britain) Ltd* [1916] 2 AC 307.
6 Ibid, at 339–340.
7 *R v LCC, ex p London and Provincial Electric Theatres Ltd* [1915] 2 KB 466.

substantial majority of its shares was held by German nationals and three of its six directors were Germans. The court upheld the refusal, holding that the control or, at least, influence which enemy nationals might exert over the activities of the company in exhibiting films was a relevant matter which the local authority might take into account.

By the Merchant Shipping Act 1894, s 1[8] a ship is deemed to be a British ship if it is owned by a corporation which is established under the laws of some part of Her Majesty's dominions and has its principal place of business in those dominions. It has long been established that a ship owned by a company incorporated in Great Britain is a British ship, even though the majority of the company's shares are held by aliens,[9] but it has been doubted whether this would be so if all its shares were so held.[10] In determining where the company's principal place of business is situate, however, the court does not confine itself to discovering the locality of the company's registered office; instead, it enquires where control over the company's affairs is exercised, either by the use of powers vested in the directors or by the exercise of voting power belonging to the company's shareholders, and if the place where such control is located is outside British territory, the company's ship is not British.[11]

In the one case where the nationality involved was not an enemy one,[12] the company was incorporated in England to enable films produced in its name to qualify as British under the Cinematograph Films Act 1938. The company was promoted by an American company, two of its three directors were English, the third being the president of the American company, and the American director held ninety of the company's hundred issued shares. The English company contracted with its American parent to make the film in question, but the money for the purpose was to be found by the American parent, and in fact all contracts and arrangements for making the film were made by the American parent in the name of the English company. The court held that the film did not qualify as British, because it had not been made by the English company at all; what little the English company did, it did as a mere nominee of the American company.

Evasion of obligations imposed by law

There are only two decided cases where the court has disregarded the separate legal personality of a company because it was formed or used to facilitate the evasion of legal obligations.[13] In the first of these cases[14] the defendant had been employed by the plaintiff company and had entered into a valid agreement not to solicit the plaintiff's customers or to compete with it for a certain time after leaving its employment. After ceasing to be employed by the plaintiff the defendant formed a company which carried on a competing business, and caused the whole of its shares to be allotted to his wife and an employee of the company, who were appointed to be its directors. It was held that since the defendant in fact controlled the company, its formation was a mere 'cloak or sham' to enable him to break his agreement with the plaintiff, and an injunction was issued against him and against the company he had formed restraining them from soliciting the plaintiff's

8 39 Halsbury's Statutes (4th Edn) 424.
9 *R v Arnaud* (1846) 9 QB 806.
10 *The Tommi* [1914] P 251 at 263.
11 *The Polzeath* [1916] P 241.
12 *Re F G (Films) Ltd* [1953] 1 All ER 615, [1953] 1 WLR 483.
13 But see also the judgment of Denning MR, in *Wallersteiner v Moir* [1974] 3 All ER 217, [1974] 1 WLR 991.
14 *Gilford Motor Co Ltd v Horne* [1933] Ch 935, [1933] All ER Rep 109.

customers. In the second case[15] a vendor of land sought to evade specific performance of a contract for sale by conveying the land to a company which he 'bought' for the purpose. The company had been formed by third parties, and the vendor purchased the whole of its shares from them, had the shares registered in the name of himself and a nominee, and had himself and the nominee appointed directors. It was held again that the acquisition of the company and the conveyance of the land to it was a mere 'cloak or sham' for the evasion of the contract of sale, and specific performance of the contract was therefore ordered against the vendor and the company which he had acquired.

The American courts have been far readier to disregard a company's separate legal personality when it was clearly formed or acquired to facilitate a breach of the general law[16] or of a contractual obligation.[17] Their attitude is summed up in the words of Sanborn J, in a passage which further litigation in this country will probably show represents English law too.[18]

'... A corporation will be looked upon as a legal entity as a general rule ... but when the notion of legal entity is used to defeat public convenience, justify wrong, protect fraud, or defend crime, the law will regard the corporation as an association of persons.'

Implied agency and trusteeship

The courts have made an inroad on the principle of a company's separate legal personality by implying in some cases that the company was acting as an agent for its shareholders, or that the company held its property as a trustee for its shareholers. It is impossible in the present state of the law to determine when the court will imply such an agency or trusteeship. It is noteworthy, however, that the court is more ready to do so when the strict application of the principle of separate personality would result in an anomaly or an injustice, but it is far from true to say that an anomaly or injustice will always induce the court to depart from the strict rule, as the examples given earlier in this chapter show.

In one such case[19] Atkinson J attempted to catalogue the matters which the court will take into account in determining whether a subsidiary company is carrying on its business as an agent of its holding company. He said:[20]

'... I find six points which were deemed relevant.... The first point was: were the profits treated as the profits of the company?—when I say "the company" I mean the parent company—secondly, were the persons conducting the business appointed by the parent company? Thirdly, was the company the head and brain of the trading venture? Fourthly, did the company govern the adventure, decide what should be done and what capital should be embarked on the venture? Fifthly, did the company make the profits by its skill and direction? Sixthly, was the company in effectual and constant control?'

In that case Atkinson J held that a holding company was in occupation of premises, and was consequently entitled to compensation for the disturbance of its business on the compulsory purchase of the premises by a local authority, even though the business was carried on at the premises in the name of a subsidiary. The subsidiary had been formed simply in order to separate formally the business carried on in its

15 *Jones v Lipman* [1962] 1 All ER 442, [1962] 1 WLR 832.
16 *United States v Milwaukee Refrigerator Transit Co* 142 Fed 247 (1905) (where a company which despatched goods by rail was convicted of receiving illegal rebates on the charges made by the railway company when the rebates were paid to a subsidiary company formed by the consignor company for the purpose).
17 *Artic Dairy Co v Winans* (1934) 267 Mich 80.
18 *United States v Milwaukee Refrigerator Transit Co*, supra at 255.
19 *Smith, Stone and Knight Ltd v Birmingham Corpn* [1939] 4 All ER 116.
20 Ibid, at 121.

name from another business carried on by the holding company. The freehold in the premises and the assets of the business carried on in the subsidiary's name were never transferred by the holding company to the subsidiary. All the subsidiary's shares were held by or in trust for the holding company, and the subsidiary's directors were all directors of the holding company. Accounts in respect of the business carried on in the subsidiary's name were kept as part of the holding company's accounts, and the subsidiary's profits were dealt with as though they had been earned by the holding company. It is difficult to imagine a more complete identification of a holding company with its subsidiary, and it would have been a clear denial of justice to refuse the holding company compensation for loss suffered in respect of a business which in substance was its own. But in a business sense the identification of the holding company with its subsidiary was equally as close in *William Cory & Son Ltd v Dorman Long & Co*,[1] and yet the court there refused to treat the subsidiary as the holding company's agent so that the holding company might be deemed the owner of the vessel vested in the subsidiary. Nevertheless, Atkinson J's decision represents the modern tendency, as the Court of Appeal held in a later case,[2] where the facts were similar to those in *Smith, Stone & Knight Ltd v Birmingham Corpn*, except that the freehold of the premises where the holding company carried on its business was vested in its wholly-owned subsidiary. In compulsory purchase cases where a holding company claims compensation for the disturbance of a business carried on by it or its wholly-owned subsidiary, the group will be treated in law as being the single unit which it is commercially, and the holding company or subsidiary will not be deprived of compensation for disturbance merely because the freehold of the premises where the business is carried on or any other assets of the business are vested in another company belonging to the same group.

It is in revenue cases that the court shows the strongest inclination to treat subsidiaries as agents of their holding companies, so that the holding companies may be taxed in respect of the subsidiaries' profits. For example, in an early case[3] an English company was held liable for income tax on the profits of its wholly-owned American subsidary earned in the United States. The English company had agreed to buy the assets and business of the American company as well as the whole of its share capital, and the assets were left vested in the American company only as a matter of convenience. The American company was managed by directors appointed by the English company, but they acted as the board of the English company instructed them. It was clear that the English company was carrying on the business of the American company as much as if the assets of the business were vested in itself. But mere ownership of all, or substantially all, of the subsidiary's shares does not entitle the court to infer that the subsidiary is the holding company's agent. Thus, in a similar case[4] where an English company held 98 per cent of the shares of an American company, the court refused to find that the American subsidiary carried on its business as the English company's agent, so as to make the English company liable for tax on the subsidiary's profits. Phillimore J said:[5]

'A company may control another company; but it does not necessarily follow because an individual controls the company, or the company controls the individual, that the business carried on by the person or company controlled is necessarily a business carried on by the controller; and particularly is that the case when the machinery of companies is used and the controller is a company.'

1 [1936] 2 All ER 386 (see p 38, ante).
2 *DHN Food Distributors Ltd v London Borough of Tower Hamlets* [1976] 3 All ER 462, [1976] 1 WLR 852.
3 *Apthorpe v Peter Schoenhofen Brewing Co Ltd* (1899) 4 TC 41.
4 *Kodak Ltd v Clark* [1902] 2 KB 450.
5 Ibid, at 459.

A more recent revenue case[6] goes a great deal farther than the earlier decisions in inferring the existence of an agency. In that case an American company formed a wholly-owned subsidiary in England to manufacture and sell its brand of vehicle tyres in Europe. The American company negotiated agreements with European distributors under which they would place orders with the American company, which the English subsidiary would fulfil. In practice the distributors sent their orders directly to the subsidiary, and the orders were met without the American company being consulted. The subsidiary received payment for the tyres sold to the distributors, and after deducting its operating expenses plus 5 per cent of the payments received, it forwarded the balance to the American company. All the directors of the subsidiary (except one who was also the president of the American company) resided in England, and they managed the subsidiary's business free from day to day control by the American company. The Court of Appeal and the House of Lords held on these facts that the American company was carrying on business in England through its English subsidiary acting as its agent, and it was consequently liable to pay United Kingdom income tax on the profits made by the subsidiary's operations and activities. In the Court of Appeal Evershed MR indicated the matters which led him to find that the English subsidiary acted as its holding company's agent. He said:[7]

> 'My conclusion does not involve the proposition that [the subsidiary], instead of being an independent legal entity, is a mere branch of [the American company]; but [the subsidiary], though a separate entity, is in fact wholly controlled by [the American company], and in the making of what may be described as [the American company's] proprietary branded articles it acts under the close direction of [the American company] in all respects, and in selling those articles to [the American company's] customers it does so on terms fixed by [the American company], so that after allowing [the subsidiary] its costs and a percentage thereon the whole of the profits on the transactions go to [the American company].'

There has been only one case where the court has used the concept of trusteeship to escape from the principle of separate legal personality.[8] In that case a club was incorporated as an industrial and provident society in order to provide recreational facilities for its members. A committee managed the club, and in its name purchased intoxicating liquor, which was sold to the members. The club was prosecuted for selling liquor without a justices' licence. The court acquitted the club, holding that there had been no sale, because the members were in reality the owners of the liquor when it was purchased on their behalf by the managing committee. The legal title to the liquor was, of course, vested in the club because it was purchased in the club's name, and the transfer of title when a member bought liquor therefore looked like a true sale; but the court overcame this difficulty by holding that the club held the liquor as a trustee for its members, so that the beneficial ownership was all along vested in them collectively, and the transfer of the legal title when a member bought liquor was therefore not a sale at all, but a release to that member of the equitable beneficial interests of the other members.

The tenuous evidence from which the court had implied an agency or trusteeship in some of the foregoing cases naturally leads one to question whether the agency or trusteeship is not merely a convenient legal fiction used by the court to enable it to give decisions which it thinks just. The description of the subsidiary as the holding company's agent or trustee often appears to be merely an epithet used to

---

6 *Firestone Tyre and Rubber Co Ltd v Lewellin* [1956] 1 All ER 693, [1956] 1 WLR 352; affd [1957] 1 All ER 561, [1957] 1 WLR 464, HL.
7 [1956] 1 All ER 693 at 700, [1956] 1 WLR 352 at 367.
8 *Trebanog Working Men's Club and Institute Ltd v Macdonald* [1940] 1 KB 576, [1940] 1 All ER 454.

indicate the subsidiary's complete subjection to the holding company, and not a statement of their legal relationship at all. For example, in *Smith, Stone and Knight Ltd v Birmingham Corpn*,[9] Atkinson J described the subsidiary company as 'the agent or employee, or tool or simulacrum' of the holding company,[10] words which are obviously intended to be understood in a metaphorical rather than a legal sense. Indeed, in that case it was unnecessary for the court to find that the subsidiary was the holding company's agent in order to reach the decision that the holding company was in occupation of the premises which were compulsorily purchased. The ownership of the premises and the business carried on there was vested in the holding company, and it carried on the business itself; the fact that the business was carried on in the subsidiary's name was of no more significance than if it had been carried on in a fictitious name. This was of course not the situation in the other compulsory purchase case cited above.[11]

It is therefore possible to distinguish *Smith, Stone & Knight v Birmingham Corpn* from *William Cory & Son Ltd v Dorman Long & Co.*[12] In the latter case the property in question, the barge, was vested in the subsidiary and registered in its name, so that there was an impediment in the way of the court holding that the holding company was the owner of it. But it is not so easy to distinguish the *Cory* case from *Apthorpe v Peter Schoenhofen Brewing Co*[13] and a fortiori from *Firestone Tyre and Rubber Co v Lewellin*,[14] and it is impossible to distinguish the *Cory* case from the second compulsory purchase case.[11] In the *Firestone* case integration of the holding company and the subsidiary was far less close than in the *Cory* case, for the subsidiary there did have a separate board of directors with a fair degree of independence in managing its business, which was not so in the *Cory* case. Perhaps the distinction lies in the fact that in the *Peter Schoenhofen* and *Firestone* cases the question which the court had to decide was whether the holding company was carrying on a particular business, an activity which can be performed by an agent, unlike being the owner of property, which was the matter in issue in the *Cory* case. Even so, the court in the *Cory* case could have invoked the concept of trusteeship, as it did in *Trebanog Working Men's Club and Institute Ltd v Macdonald*,[15] but the point was not taken by counsel or the court. Indeed, the trusteeship in the *Trebanog* case seems equally as metaphorical as the agency in *Smith, Stone & Knight Ltd v Birmingham Corpn*,[12] but unlike the agency implied in that case, the trusteeship implied in the *Trebanog* case was essential to the court's decision acquitting the club of selling intoxicants. In *DHN Food Distributors Ltd v London Borough of Tower Hamlets*,[16] however, the concept of trusteeship was not employed, and the court relied entirely on the commercial unity of the group of companies in order to identify the holding company, which carried on the business, with its wholly-owned subsidiary, which owned the premises where the business was carried on. In other words, this decision cannot be reconciled with the *Cory* case at all.

Despite the fancifulness of the agency or trusteeship implied in some of the cases where the separate legal personality of a company has been disregarded, it is submitted that the courts are still not free to imply an agency or trusteeship merely in order to give what they believe to be a just decision. This has been emphasised

---

9 [1939] 4 All ER 116 (see p 48, ante).
10 Ibid, at 121.
11 *DHN Food Distributors Ltd v London Borough of Tower Hamlets* [1976] 3 All ER 462, [1976] 1 WLR 852.
12 [1936] 2 All ER 386 (see p 38, ante).
13 (1899) 4 TC 41 (see p 49, ante).
14 [1956] 1 All ER 693, [1956] 1 WLR 352; affd [1957] 1 All ER 561, [1957] 1 WLR 464 (see p 50, ante).
15 [1940] 1 KB 576, [1940] 1 All ER 454 (see p 50, ante).
16 [1976] 3 All ER 462, [1976] 1 WLR 852.

in two recent cases[17] in which the court has held that a tax avoidance scheme relying on the fact that the participants were companies belonging to the same group could not be defeated by the Revenue showing that the scheme also involved a company outside the group and concluding from this that one of the companies within the group must have acted as its agent. Where an agency has been implied the court has been careful to seek out some of the indicia of a real agency relationship, such as control by the holding company over the management of the subsidiary's business, or the management of the subsidiary's property together with that of the holding company. Undoubtedly the court is influenced toward implying an agency by the holding company owning all, or substantially all, of the subsidiary's shares, and it is then more ready to find the existence of an agency from evidence which would not be sufficient if the holding company held fewer shares. The *Firestone* case is an example of this. The only indicia of agency there were that the subsidiary manufactured and sold a product bearing the holding company's brand to buyers chosen by the holding company, and retained only a fixed sum out of the amount of such sales. The subsidiary was in no different a position in respect of those matters from any other distributor of proprietory goods sold at a standard price, and those matters alone certainly do not make a distributor an agent of the manufacturer.[18] The element which tipped the scales in the *Firestone* case, therefore, was the extent of the holding company's shareholding in the subsidiary. But an agency cannot be implied in such a case merely because the holding company owns all or most of the subsidiary's shares, if there is nothing else at all to indicate the existence of an agency. Such an implication is clearly precluded by the decision of the House of Lords in *Salomon's* case, which therefore sets the limits beyond which this exception to the rule of separate legal personality cannot go. Nevertheless, if the decision of the Court of Appeal in *DHN Food Distributors Ltd v London Borough of Tower Hamlets*[16] sets the pattern for future decisions, the rule of separate legal personality seems destined to be set aside in specific instances, not by resorting to an avoidance technique, such as invoking an agency or trusteeship, but by a direct rejection of the separate personality rule in the circumstances of the particular case.

THE LEGAL RELATIONSHIP BETWEEN THE COMPANY AND ITS MEMBERS

Rights and duties created by the memorandum and articles of association

The Companies Act 1985, provides:[19]

> 'Subject to the provisions of this Act, the memorandum and articles shall, when registered, bind the company and its members to the same extent as if they respectively had been signed and sealed by each member, and contained covenants on the part of each member to observe all the provisions of the memorandum and of the articles.'

17 *Floor v Davis (Inspector of Taxes)* [1978] Ch 295, [1978] 2 All ER 1079; affd [1980] AC 695, [1979] 2 All ER 677; *Burman v Hedges & Butler Ltd* [1979] 1 WLR 160. The decisions in these cases as matters of tax law have, however, probably been superseded by the decision of the House of Lords in *W T Ramsay Ltd v IRC* [1982] AC 300, [1981] 1 All ER 865 and *Furniss (Inspector of Taxes) v Dawson* [1984] AC 474, [1984] 1 All ER 530.

18 *Taddy & Co v Sterious & Co* [1904] 1 Ch 354; *McGruther v Pitcher* [1904] 2 Ch 306; *Re Austin Motor-Car Co Ltd's Agreements* [1958] Ch 61, [1957] 3 All ER 62.

19 Companies Act 1985, s 14 (1).

This section is derived historically from the covenant which appeared at the beginning of the deeds of settlement of unincorporated companies formed at common law. By this covenant all the members, original and future, bound themselves to one another and to trustees for the company to conform to the provisions of the deed of settlement.[20] To ensure that future members were bound, the deed of settlement provided that they should not become members until they had executed it,[1] but it is now unnecessary for members of companies formed under the Companies Acts to execute the memorandum and articles unless they are the original two subscribers, because the Companies Act 1985 itself binds them to conform to the provisions of those documents.[19] Although the Act provides that the company shall be bound by the memorandum and articles, it is not deemed to have executed them, as the members are deemed to have done.[2] This, no doubt, is the result of an oversight in translating the covenant in the old deed of settlement (which could not be entered into by the company because it was unincorporated), into terms of a law for modern, incorporated companies. Nevertheless, it has been held[3] that the company is bound by the memorandum and articles as much as its members, although its obligations under them are treated as arising under a simple contract or by statute, and not under a deed.[2]

Contract between the company and its members

Read literally, the Companies Act 1985, s 14 appears to create a contract between the company and its members to observe all the provisions of the memorandum and articles, whatever they may relate to. However, the section has been construed to create a contract only in respect of the rights and duties of members as such, so that if the memorandum and articles provide for other matters, those provisions do not form part of the contract. In the leading case on the section, Astbury J said:[4]

'. . . no right merely purporting to be given by an article to a person, whether a member or not, in a capacity other than that of a member, as for instance, as solicitor, promoter, director, can be enforced against the company; and . . . [only] articles regulating the rights and obligations of the members generally as such do create rights and obligations between them and the company respectively.'

Thus a member may sue the company to restrain it from excluding him from membership,[5] or to compel it to enter his name on the register of members, or restore his name if it has been wrongfully removed,[6] or to compel the company to allow him to vote at a meeting of members.[7] He may also sue to compel the company to pay him the financial benefits to which he is entitled as a member, whether as a dividend on his shares[8] or as a return of his capital on a winding up.[9] Conversely, a member is contractually bound to the company to pay the unpaid balance of the issue price of the shares which he holds, and a member of a company limited by guarantee is contractually bound to contribute the amount of the

20 For an example of such a covenant, see the precedent of a deed of settlement in Collyer's *A Practical Treatise on the Law of Partnership* (2nd edn 1840), at 879.
1 Ibid, pp 902–3, cll 116 and 123.
2 *Re Compania de Electricidad de la Provincia de Buenos Aires Ltd* [1980] Ch 146, [1978] 3 All ER 668.
3 *Hickman v Kent or Romney Marsh Sheep-breeders' Association* [1915] 1 Ch 881 at 897.
4 Ibid, at 900.
5 *Johnson v Lyttle's Iron Agency* (1877) 5 ChD 687; *Hickman v Kent or Romney Marsh Sheep-breeders' Association*, supra.
6 *Re British Sugar Refining Co* (1857) 3 K & J 408. For the summary procedure now available for rectifying the register of members under the Companies Act 1985, s 359 (see p 337, post).
7 *Pender v Lushington* (1877) 6 ChD 70.
8 *Wood v Odessa Waterworks Co* (1889) 42 ChD 636.
9 *Griffith v Paget* (1877) 5 ChD 894.

guarantee when the company is wound up. The Companies Act 1985 provides that all such moneys payable by members under the memorandum or articles are specialty debts,[10] and so the company may sue to recover them within twelve years after they became due.[11] As part of the statutory contract, the company may also enforce against its members a provision in its articles that a member who wishes to sell his shares must first offer them to the other members before transferring them to an outsider.[12]

On the other hand, a provision in the memorandum or articles which does not relate to the rights and duties of members of the company as such, does not form part of the contract between the company and its members, and a fortiori, no such provision creates a contract between the company and someone who is not a member of it. Thus, where the articles provided that the company should purchase certain property belonging to a member,[13] or that a particular member should be the company's solicitor,[14] there was held to be no contract between the company and the member to that effect. Furthermore, if the articles provide that each director shall hold a certain minimum number of shares in the company, a member who serves the company as a director is not bound as part of the statutory contract to take those shares from it, because the obligation is imposed on him not in his capacity as a member, but in his capacity as a director; consequently, if the company allots those shares to him in the absence of a separate contract for subscription, the allotment is void.[15] Again, because of the limits of the statutory contract, a promoter who was not a member of the company was held not entitled to sue for his promotion remuneration, even though the articles directed such remuneration to be paid,[16] and a director who was not a member was held unable to sue to prevent the company from dismissing him, even though his term of office prescribed by the articles had not expired.[17]

Articles of association sometimes contain a provision that disputes between members, or between members and the company, shall be settled by arbitration. Such a provision is a valid written submission to arbitration for the purpose of the Arbitration Act 1950,[18] but it is only effective in respect of disputes about the rights and duties of members as such,[19] and so it cannot be relied upon when the dispute relates to the rights or duties of a director who also happens to be a member.[20]

Contracts incorporating part of the memorandum or articles

Although a contract is not automatically created by a provision in the memorandum or articles which does not relate to membership of the company, a contract embodying that provision may subsequently be entered into between the company and one of its members, or between the company and a person who is not a member of it. Such a situation may obviously be brought about by the parties expressly agreeing to incorporate part of the memorandum or articles into their contract, but it may also come about by the parties acting in such a way that the court

10 Companies Act 1985, s 14 (2).
11 Limitation Act 1980, s 8 (24 Halsbury's Statutes (4th Edn) 655).
12 *Lyle & Scott Ltd v Scott's Trustees* [1959] AC 763, [1959] 2 All ER 661.
13 *Re Tavarone Mining Co, Pritchard's Case* (1873) 8 Ch App 956.
14 *Eley v Positive Government Security Life Assurance Co* (1875) 1 ExD 20; affd (1876) 1 ExD 88.
15 *Re Wheal Buller Consols* (1888) 38 ChD 42.
16 *Melhado v Porto Alegre Rly Co* (1874) LR 9 CP 503.
17 *Browne v La Trinidad* (1887) 37 ChD 1.
18 *Hickman v Kent or Romney Marsh Sheep-breeders' Association*, supra. For the Arbitration Act 1950, s 32 requiring submission to arbitration to be in writing, see 2 Halsbury's Statutes (4th Edn) 567.
19 *Hickman v Kent or Romney Marsh Sheep-breeders Association*, supra.
20 *Beattie v E and F Beattie Ltd* [1938] Ch 708, [1938] 3 All ER 214.

interprets their conduct as meaning that they have contracted by reference to the memorandum or articles.[1] Thus, where the articles provided that the directors should be paid a certain sum as remuneration each year, and the plaintiff served the company as a director without any express agreement for remuneration, it was held that the provision in the articles was impliedly incorporated into his contract of service, because that was what he and the company intended.[2] Again, in two cases[3] where the articles provided that directors who did not obtain their qualification shares[4] within a month of their appointment should be deemed to have agreed to take those shares from the company, it was held that the provision was impliedly incorporated into the directors' service contracts, so that at the end of the month the company could allot qualification shares to a director who had not obtained them elsewhere meanwhile. These two decisions are distinguishable from *Re Wheal Buller Consols*,[5] because there the articles merely prescribed the directors' share qualification, and gave no express power to the company to allot the shares if the director failed to obtain them by purchase from other shareholders; but it is not easy to reconcile that case with another case[6] where it was held that when the company altered its articles to increase the directors' share qualification, the directors impliedly agreed to take the further shares from the company, because they continued to act and did not obtain the further shares elsewhere within a reasonable time. The implied incorporation of the articles into contracts has not been confined to directors' service contracts. When a company's articles provided that the members should mutually insure each other's ships for the amount entered against each member's name in a register kept by the company, it was held that each member on joining the company impliedly agreed to pay such contributions as were necessary to give effect to the insurance, even though the contributions were in no way connected with the share capital he agreed to subscribe.[7]

The provisions of the articles cannot, of course, be treated as incorporated into a contract which provides expressly for the matters with which the articles deal,[8] but the mere fact that the contract provides for certain of those matters does not prevent the incorporation of the articles in respect of other matters about which the contract is silent.[9] Thus, where a company agreed to employ the plaintiff as its managing director and conferred on him powers in excess of those enjoyed by the other directors, it was held that the duration of his employment was governed by the articles, because his service contract was silent on the point.[9] Furthermore, a contract entered into by reference to a company's articles will be taken to incorporate only so much of the articles as is relevant to its subject matter.

1 In *Browne v La Trinidad* (1887) 37 ChD 1, it was held that a contract could not be implied merely because the parties had acted on the provisions of the articles, but this decision has not been followed in later cases, other than *Newtherapeutics Ltd v Katz* [1990] BCC 362. In *Eley v Positive Government Security Life Assurance Co* (1875) 1 ExD 20; affd (1876) 1 ExD 88, it was held by the court of first instance that a service contract embodying the terms set out in the articles was created by the member serving the company as its solicitor, but the contract was unenforceable, because the articles contemplated his employment for an indefinite time, possibly longer than a year, and there was no written memorandum of the contract signed on behalf of the company to satisfy the requirement of the Statute of Frauds (1677), s 4 then in force.
2 *Re New British Iron Co, ex p Beckwith* [1898] 1 Ch 324.
3 *Re Anglo-Austrian Printing and Publishing Union, Isaacs' Case* [1892] 2 Ch 158; *Salton v New Beeston Cycle Co* [1899] 1 Ch 775.
4 A share qualification is a requirement in the articles that directors should hold a prescribed minimum number of shares in the company, and qualification shares are shares which a director acquires to satisfy the requirement.
5 (1888) 38 ChD 42 (see p 54, ante).
6 *Molineaux v London, Birmingham and Manchester Insurance Co Ltd* [1902] 2 KB 589.
7 *Lion Mutual Marine Insurance Association Ltd v Tucker* (1883) 12 QBD 176.
8 *Nelson v James Nelson & Sons Ltd* [1914] 2 KB 770.
9 *Read v Astoria Garage (Streatham) Ltd* [1952] Ch 637, [1952] 2 All ER 292.

Consequently, when a member of a company served as a director without an express service contract, it was held that a provision in the company's articles that disputes between members and the company should be referred to arbitration was not incorporated into his terms of employment, because the provision related only to disputes with members as such, not to disputes with them in some other capacity.[10]

Contract between the members themselves

It was formerly uncertain whether the provisions of the earlier Companies Acts now re-enacted in the Companies Act 1985, s 14 (1) created a contract between the members of a company themselves, as distinct from a contract between the members and the company. The section does not say with whom the members impliedly covenant to observe the provisions of the memorandum and articles. There were dicta that the precursors of s 14 did create a contract between the members inter se,[11] but on the other hand in one case[12] Lord Herschell expressed the opinion that there was no such contract, and in another case[13] Farwell LJ conceded that contractual rights between members might be created, but thought that the court would rarely enforce them. However, it has now been settled that the members of a company are contractually bound to one another to obey the provisions of its memorandum and articles so far as they relate to their rights and duties as members.[14] In the case which so decided it was held that a member could enforce an obligation imposed by the articles on his fellow members who were directors to purchase his shares from him when he wished to dispose of them. The ruling will apply equally to the common provision in the articles of private companies that a member who wishes to sell his shares must offer them to the other members before selling them to a stranger, and so the other members will have contractual rights of pre-emption against him, which they can enforce individually even if the company does not insist on compliance.

Legal nature of shares

The court has found it extraordinarily difficult to define the legal nature of shares, despite its familiarity with them. Usually, the court has been content to describe them as choses in action,[15] a description which does nothing more than assure us that they are personalty,[16] and are not tangible chattels, which is self-evident.

Originally the court seemed inclined to think that companies held their property in trust for their members, so that their shares embodied equitable rights of property.[17] But from early in the last century it has consistently been held that shareholders are not the owners at law or in equity of the company's property,[18] and if the company does hold its property upon a trust, it is simply a trust to

10 *Beattie v E and F Beattie Ltd* [1938] Ch 708, [1938] 3 All ER 214.
11 *Wood v Odessa Waterworks Co* (1889) 42 ChD 636 at 642; *Re Tavarone Mining Co, Pritchard's Case* (1873) 8 Ch App 956 at 960; *Eley v Positive Government Security Life Assurance Co* (1875) 1 ExD 20 at 26 and (1876) 1 ExD 88 at 89.
12 *Welton v Saffery* [1897] AC 299 at 315.
13 *Salmon v Quinn and Axtens Ltd* [1909] 1 Ch 311 at 318.
14 *Rayfield v Hands* [1960] Ch 1, [1958] 2 All ER 194.
15 *Humble v Mitchell* (1839) 11 Ad & El 205; *Colonial Bank v Whinney* (1886) 11 App Cas 426.
16 The Companies Act 1985, s 182 (1), provides that shares are personal estate and not realty, thus setting at rest the doubts raised by early cases as to whether shares in companies formed primarily to hold and manage land were not themselves land.
17 *Child v Hudson's Bay Co* [1723] 2 P Wms 207; *Harrison v Pryse* (1740) Barn Ch 324; *Ashby v Blackwell and Million Bank Co* (1765) Amb 503.
18 *Bligh v Brent* (1837) 2 Y & C Ex 268; *Myers v Perigal* (1851) 2 De G M & G 599.

manage the property in accordance with its constitution, and the members' rights are confined to receiving the profits earned by doing so.[19] A shareholder does not even have an equitable lien on the company's property, similar to a partner's lien, to ensure that it is properly applied in conformity with the company's constitution.[20]

Shareholders' rights were purely contractual at common law and in equity, and a share today is simply the bundle of contractual rights given to the shareholder by the Companies Act 1985, s 14, and the company's memorandum and articles together with the statutory rights conferred on the shareholder by the Companies Acts 1985 and 1989. This was made clear by Farwell J in the following passage:[1]

'A share according to the plaintiff's argument, is a sum of money which is dealt with in a particular manner by what are called for the purpose of argument executory limitations. To my mind it is nothing of the sort. A share is the interest of a shareholder in the company measured by a sum of money, for the purpose of liability in the first place, and of interest in the second, but also consisting of a series of mutual covenants entered into by all the shareholders inter se in accordance with s 16 of the Companies Act 1862 [now s 14 of the Companies Act 1985]. The contract contained in the articles of association is one of the original incidents of the share. A share is not a sum of money settled in the way suggested, but is an interest measured by a sum of money and made up of various rights contained in the contract, including the right to a sum of money of a more or less amount.'

In the light of these observations, Farwell J held that provisions of the memorandum and articles affecting shares, such as restrictions on transfer and pre-emption rights conferred on members when shares are sold, are not subject to the rule against perpetuities, and this would appear still to be so despite subsequent legislation in respect of options and pre-emption rights.[2]

But the contractual rights which make up a share are of a peculiar nature. They were transferable at common law at a time when other choses in action were not legally assignable.[3] Because of this, shares have been called 'property',[4] which is innocuous enough, provided that it is remembered that they do not comprise any proprietary interest in the company's assets. Furthermore, shares are transferable in a manner peculiar to themselves,[5] and possibly the full legal title to them does not pass, as it does in respect of other legal choses in actions, by the transferee merely notifying the company of the transfer.[6] Finally, it is important to remember that many of the most significant rights attached to shares are conferred by the Companies Acts 1985 and 1989, and are not the result of the statutory contract between the company and its members. These rights conferred by legislation include the right to require the directors to call a meeting of members or to put a resolution on the agenda of a meeting the directors have called themselves,[7] and the right to appoint a proxy to represent a member at a meeting of the company.[8] Perhaps the most important statutory rights of members, however, are to be sent

---

19 *Watson v Spratley* (1854) 10 Exch 222.
20 *Ashworth v Munn* (1880) 15 ChD 363.
1 *Borland's Trustee v Steel Bros & Co Ltd* [1901] 1 Ch 279 at 288.
2 Perpetuities and Accumulations Act 1964, s 10 (33 Halsbury's Statutes (4th Edn) 522).
3 *Pinkett v Wright* (1842) 2 Hare 120; *Poole v Middleton* (1861) 29 Beav 646.
4 *Poole v Middleton*, supra; *Birkenhead Lancashire and Cheshire Junction Rly Co v Pilcher* (1851) 5 Exch 114 at 123. Similarly, Lord Maugham in *Carruth v Imperial Chemical Industries Ltd* [1937] AC 707 at 765, [1937] 2 All ER 422 at 459 described shareholders' voting rights as rights of property, merely in order to emphasise that they may be exercised as the shareholder chooses, without regard to the welfare of the company.
5 See Chapter 10.
6 *Ireland v Hart* [1902] 1 Ch 522.
7 See pp 620 and 621, post.
8 See p 627, post.

copies of the company's annual accounts and directors' report[9] and to inspect various registers, records and other documents which the company is required to keep.[10] It is important to distinguish these rights conferred by the Companies Acts 1985 and 1989, from contractual rights arising under the statutory contract, because in general rights conferred by the Act cannot be abridged by agreement, whereas rights under the statutory contract only exist, of course, so far as the memorandum and articles expressly spell them out.

Limited liability

It has already been shown that one of the principal advantages of trading through the medium of a limited company is that the members of the company are only liable to contribute toward payment of its debts to a limited extent. If the company is limited by shares, the shareholder's liability to contribute is measured by the nominal value of the shares he holds, so that once he or someone who held the shares previously has paid that nominal value plus any premium agreed on when the shares were issued, he is no longer liable to contribute anything further towards meeting the company's debts and liabilities.

If a company is unable to pay its debts, its creditors may petition the court to wind it up.[11] If a winding up order is made, a liquidator is appointed to realise the company's assets, and if he realises insufficient to pay its debts and other liabilities by selling its assets, he calls upon its shareholders to make good the deficiency, but, of course, their liability to do so is limited to the balance of capital unpaid on their shares plus unpaid premiums.[12] It may be that some of the shareholders at the date the winding up commences are themselves insolvent and unable to contribute the balance of unpaid capital in respect of their shares. In that case the liquidator can recover the unpaid capital from any person who held the shares in question within a year before the winding up began.[13] A person who transfers partly paid shares, therefore, is in effect a guarantor,[14] that his transferee will pay the amount of unpaid capital if the company is wound up within the following twelve months. In practice he is not often called on to honour this guarantee, because companies nowadays call up the whole of the unpaid capital within a very short time after the shares are issued.[15]

A shareholder is liable to contribute to the payment of his company's debts; he is not liable to pay them himself. A creditor of the company cannot sue him, therefore, even to compel him to pay such part of the debt as is equal to the amount of unpaid capital in respect of his shares. The creditor can obtain payment of his debt out of unpaid capital only by petitioning the court to wind up the company, so that unpaid capital will be paid to the liquidator, who will discharge all the company's debts thereout rateably. This ensures that one creditor cannot, merely

---

9 See p 698, post.

10 See pp 335, 370, 470, post.

11 Insolvency Act 1986, s 122 (1) and s 124 (1).

12 Ibid, s 74 (1) and (2) and s 139.

13 Ibid, s 74 (2).

14 The relationship of the present and former shareholders is not strictly that of principal debtor and surety, however, and so a compromise between the liquidator and the present holder of the shares in respect of the amount unpaid on them does not release the former holder of the shares from liability (*Helbert v Banner* (1871) LR 5 HL 28).

15 This is because partly paid shares are always less saleable on account of the holder's contingent liability for unpaid capital, and because they consequently command a lower price in the market. For this reason in 1957 the commercial banks which are members of the Committee of London Clearing Bankers cancelled the unpaid capital on their shares, and turned them into fully paid shares.

by being the first to sue, obtain payment of his debt in full out of unpaid capital, even though the other creditors go unpaid. It is, of course, possible for a creditor to steal a march on his fellow creditors by suing the company to judgment and levying execution on its assets. But there is no mode of execution available against capital which has not been called up by the directors or otherwise fallen due for payment, though it would seem possible for a garnishee order to be made in respect of capital which has already been called up, or which is already due under the terms of issue of the shares but has not yet been paid.[16]

16 In the United States a judgment creditor may attach uncalled or unpaid capital by applying to the court for the appointment of a receiver (*Hatch v Dana* (1879) 101 US 205).

CHAPTER 3

Alteration of the memorandum and articles of association

The needs and circumstances of a company may change considerably in the course of time. The objects with which it was formed may be found too limited when, after years of successful trading, it has accumulated sufficient resources to expand into new fields. The capital with which it was formed may prove insufficient to enable it to expand its activities, or even to keep its original business going. And even though the nature of its business is still the same, the internal distribution of powers and functions between its shareholders and directors may not be suitable in changed circumstances. It may become desirable to extend or diminish the powers of the directors, to alter the voting rights attached to shares, or to create different classes of shares.

If companies were unable to alter their memoranda and articles of association to give effect to these desired changes, either corporate enterprise would be frustrated, or companies would constantly be transferring their undertakings to new companies promoted solely in order to effect the changes by incorporating them in their memoranda or articles. The Companies Act 1985 avoids these alternatives by giving wide powers to companies to alter their original memoranda and articles by passing resolutions at general meetings of the members. The Act aims to give the utmost flexibility to companies' constitutions which is consistent with honesty and fairness, and it is in substance this criterion which the court applies in testing the validity of alterations which are challenged before it.

When an alteration is made in a company's memorandum or articles, a printed copy of the resolution effecting the alteration must be delivered to the Registrar of Companies within fifteen days after it is passed,[1] and a printed copy of the altered memorandum or articles must be delivered to the Registrar at the same time.[2] The Registrar must advertise the filing of the resolution effecting the alteration in the London Gazette,[3] and until the advertisement is published the alteration is not effective against other persons who at the material time are unaware of it having been made.[4] Other persons in this context seem to comprise all persons other than the company, and therefore shareholders and directors, as well as outsiders, are included. The material time appears to mean the time when a transaction is entered into. However, the fact that the Registrar of Companies has advertised the filing of a resolution altering the company's memorandum or articles in the London Gazette does not mean that third persons are deemed to have knowledge or notice of it in cases where knowledge or notice is material, unless the company can also prove that they actually knew of the alteration.[5]

---

1 Companies Act 1985, s 18 (1).
2 Ibid, s 18 (2).
3 Ibid, s 711 (1) (*b*).
4 Ibid, s 42 (1). The sub-section also provides that the alteration is ineffective against any such person if the material time is within fifteen days after the alteration is advertised and he was unavoidably prevented from knowing that it had been made. This provision is unlikely to be of importance.
5 *Official Custodian of Charities v Parway Estates Developments Ltd* [1985] Ch 151, [1984] 3 All ER 679; Companies Act 1985, s 711A (1), inserted by Companies Act 1989, s 142 (1).

THE MEMORANDUM OF ASSOCIATION

Name

A company may change its name by special resolution,[6] and the change takes effect from the date on which the Registrar of Companies issues a new certificate of incorporation after entering the company's changed name in the register of companies.[7] The same restrictions apply to the alteration of a company's name as to the choice of its original name.[8] Consequently, the altered name must not be the same as one included in the index of names of companies, corporations and other bodies kept by the Registrar of Companies, and the altered name will not be registered if in the opinion of the Secretary of State for Trade and Industry it is offensive, or its use would constitute a criminal offence, or it would give the impression that the company is connected with HM Government or a local authority.[9] Furthermore, certain words and expressions listed in regulations made by the Secretary of State may only be included in the altered name if the Secretary of State approves after the company has obtained the opinion of the appropriate Government or other body specified in the regulations and submitted it to the Secretary of State with the company's application for his approval.[10]

The company is the same legal person after its change of name as before, and statute provides that the change shall not affect the company's rights or obligations or any legal proceedings already brought by or against the company, and any legal proceedings which might have been continued or commenced against it in its former name may be commenced or continued against it in its new name.[11] A director or agent of the company who enters into a contract on its behalf or in its altered name before the Registrar has issued a new certificate of incorporation does not incur personal liability by statute under the contract merely because of that fact,[12] but if he signs a bill of exchange, promissory note, cheque or order for money or goods in the company's altered name without mentioning its former registered name, he may do so.[13] The Registrar must publish the issue of the new certificate of incorporation in the London Gazette,[14] and it would appear that proceedings brought against the company in its old name before this is done are fully effective if the persons initiating them were unaware of the change.[15]

If a company is originally registered with a name which is the same as[16] or, in the opinion of the Secretary of State for Trade and Industry, too like that of another

---

6 A special resolution is one passed by a three quarters' majority of the members voting at a meeting of the company of which not less than 21 days' notice has been given to members (Companies Act 1985, s 378 (2)).

7 Companies Act 1985, s 28 (1) and (6). A fee of £40 is payable on the change of name being registered (Companies Act 1985, s 708 (1) and Companies (Fees) Regulations 1988 (SI 1988/887), reg 3 and Schedule).

8 See p 4, ante.

9 Companies Act 1985, s 26 (1) and (2).

10 Ibid, s 26 (2) and s 29 (1) to (3) (see p 5, ante).

11 Ibid, s 28 (7).

12 The liability in question is that imposed by the Companies Act 1985, s 36(4) where a contract is entered into in the name on behalf of a company before it has been incorporated (see p 90, post).

13 *Oshkosh B'gosh Inc v Dan Marbel Inc Ltd* [1989] BCLC 507. The statutory liability is imposed by the Companies Act 1985, s 108 (4) (see p 107, post).

14 Companies Act 1985, s 711 (1) (a).

15 Ibid, s 42 (1). In civil proceedings the name of the defendant company must be amended when the plaintiff learns of the change of name, but it appears that he may make the amendment as of right, and in cases where leave of the court is necessary, leave will be given as of course (see *Mitchell v Harris Engineering Co Ltd* [1967] 2 QB 703, [1967] 2 All ER 682).

16 For the formal differences which are disregarded in determining whether a company's name is the same as that of another company, see the Companies Act 1985, s 26 (3) (p 5, ante).

company, corporation or body whose name is either already included or should have been included in the index of names kept by the Registrar of Companies,[17] the Secretary of State may within twelve months of the company's incorporation require it to change its name, and it is guilty of an offence if it does not do so within a period specified by the Secretary of State, which he may extend one or more times before the current period expires.[18] There is no right of appeal to the court against the Secretary of State's requirement. The Secretary of State may likewise within twelve months after a company has changed its name require it to change its name again if the first change of name is to one which is the same as or too like that of another company, corporation or other body which is included or should have been included in the index kept by the Registrar, and the company must then change its name again within the period specified by the Secretary of State or an extension thereof.[18] A company whose original or altered name is too like that of another company may, of course, change its name voluntarily for that reason at any time. The Companies Act 1985 does not state whether alterations of a company's name required by the Secretary of State because its existing name is the same as or too like that of another concern need be effected by special resolution, or whether an ordinary resolution[19] suffices. The official view is that the first subsection of s 28 of the Act (which gives the general power to alter the company's name by special resolution) governs the whole section, so that a special resolution is necessary in this particular case. It is arguable, however, that s 28 (2) (which enables a company to alter its name for the specific reason of identity or similarity) is intended to add to s 28 (1), and does not merely give an example of an alteration already permitted by it. If this argument is correct, alterations under s 28 (2) may be effected by ordinary resolution, in accordance with the principle that whenever a company is entitled to do an act but no special method is prescribed for doing it, the act may be done by an ordinary resolution passed by the members.

If the Secretary of State for Trade and Industry considers that misleading information has been provided for the purpose of procuring the registration of a company by a particular name, whether on its incorporation or when it later changes its name, or that undertakings or assurances have been given for that purpose which have not been fulfilled, the Secretary of State may within five years after the company is registered with the name require it to change its name within a period specified by the Secretary of State, and that period may be extended by him before its expiration.[20] This power is particularly useful where a new company is formed by an existing company with a name identical or similar to that of the existing company or its subsidiary, and an undertaking is given that the existing company or its subsidiary will change its name or be wound up. It would seem that although the misleading information or the unfulfilled undertaking or assurance must be given by the company which procures its own registration with a particular name, the Secretary of State may act even if the company has not been incorporated at the time and the name in question is its original name, and it would also seem that whether the name is the original or a changed name, it suffices that the information, undertaking or assurance is given by persons purporting to act on the company's behalf or for its benefit in procuring its registration with that name. Where the Secretary of State requires a company to change its name, it is uncertain whether it must pass a special resolution at a general meeting to do so, or whether

---

17 The index is kept under the Companies Act 1985, s 714 (1) (see p 5, ante).
18 Companies Act 1985, s 28 (2).
19 An ordinary resolution is passed by a simple majority of the members voting at a meeting of the company, and so it is passed if more votes are cast for than against it.
20 Companies Act 1985, s 28 (3).

an ordinary resolution suffices. The reasons for this uncertainty are the same as those which apply when a company is required to change its name because of identity with, or similarity to, the name of another company or concern.

The Secretary of State for Trade and Industry may also require a company to change its name at any time if in the Secretary of State's opinion its existing name 'gives so misleading an indication of the nature of its activities as to be likely to cause harm to the public'.[1] The company must comply within six weeks,[2] but it has a right to appeal to the court within three weeks after the Secretary of State's requirement is notified to it.[3] Again, no indication is given whether the change of name directed by the Secretary of State must be effected by special resolution, or whether an ordinary resolution suffices. A change in a company's name under this provision takes effect from the date when an appropriately altered certificate of incorporation is issued by the Registrar of Companies.[4]

Category of company

It is possible for a private company with a share capital to be re-registered as a public company[5] and for a public company to be re-registered as a private company (other than an unlimited company).[6] It is therefore possible for an unlimited company or a company limited by guarantee to be re-registered as a public company if it has a share capital, but a company limited by guarantee may now have a share capital only if it existed and had a share capital on 22 December 1980.[7]

Conversion of a private company into a public company

A private company limited by shares, or a company limited by guarantee or an unlimited company which has a share capital, may be re-registered as a public company if a general meeting so resolves by a special resolution which alters the company's memorandum to provide that it shall be a public company and makes such other alterations in its memorandum and articles as are necessary for it to be a public company,[8] in particular an increase in its nominal capital to £50,000 or more if it is less than that amount,[9] and a change in the company's name so that it terminates with the words 'public limited company' or the contraction 'plc'.[10] An application for the re-registration of the company as a public company must be signed by a director and the secretary of the company, and must be submitted to the Registrar of Companies together with:[11]

(a) a printed copy of the company's memorandum and articles in their altered form;

(b) a copy of the company's most recent audited balance sheet for a financial

1 Ibid, s 32 (1).
2 Ibid, s 32 (2).
3 Ibid, s 32 (3).
4 Ibid, s 32 (5).
5 Ibid, s 43 (1).
6 Ibid, s 53 (1).
7 Ibid, s 1 (4) (see p 20, ante).
8 Ibid, s 43 (1) and (2) and s 48 (1). An unlimited company cannot be re-registered as a public company if it has previously been registered as a limited company and has already been re-registered as an unlimited company.
9 Companies Act 1985, s 43 (2) and s 118 (1).
10 Ibid, s 25 (1) and s 43 (2). The Welsh equivalents may be used if the memorandum states that the company's registered office is to be in Wales.
11 Companies Act 1985, s 43 (3).

year,[12] or if that year expired more than seven months before the application is submitted, an audited balance sheet made out at a date not earlier than seven months before that time;

(c) a copy of a written statement by the company's auditors that in their opinion the balance sheet submitted shows that the company's net assets were not less than the aggregate of its called up share capital[13] and its undistributable reserves;[14] and

(d) a statutory declaration by a director or the secretary of the company stating that the special resolution for re-registration of the company has been passed; that the statutory conditions for re-registering the company have been satisfied (in particular that the company's issued share capital is not less than £50,000), and that there has been paid up on all shares already allotted at least one quarter of their respective nominal values and the full amount of any premiums at which they were issued;[15] and that there has not been any change in the company's financial position since the date at which the copy balance sheet referred to above was made out resulting in its net assets becoming less than the aggregate of its called up share capital and its undistributable reserves.[16]

The copy of the audited balance sheet submitted with an application for re-registration must be accompanied by an unqualified report thereon by the company's auditors, and for this purpose the report is treated as qualified if it contains any qualification of the auditor's expressed view that the balance sheet conforms to the requirements of the Companies Act 1985, and gives a true and fair view of the company's affairs, unless the auditor also reports that the qualification was not material for determining whether the company's net assets equalled or exceeded its called up capital plus its undistributable reserves.[17] Additionally, if the company has issued shares for a consideration other than cash since the date at which the balance sheet was made out, the consideration must have been valued and reported on by an independent person in the same way as though the company were already a public company.[18]

If the Registrar is satisfied that the application for re-registration of the company as a public company is in order, he issues the company with a new certificate of incorporation stating that it is a public company, and thereupon it becomes a public company and the alterations in its memorandum and articles made in con-nection with the re-registration take effect.[19] The new certificate of incorporation

12 For a company's financial year, see p 696, post.

13 Called up share capital is the aggregate of the company's paid up capital, its unpaid capital which has been called up, and its unpaid capital which has fallen or will fall due on a particular date or dates under the terms of issue (Companies Act 1985, s 737).

14 Undistributable reserves are those reserves of a company which it cannot lawfully distribute as a dividend to its members (Companies Act 1985, s 264 (3) and s 744) (see p 423, post).

15 Companies Act 1985, s 45 (1) and (2), and s 118 (1). The statutory declaration must also state that if the company has issued shares in consideration of a promise to do work or perform services, the promise has been fulfilled or otherwise discharged, and that if the company has issued shares for any other consideration in kind, that the consideration has been provided or the promise to provide it will fall due for performance within 5 years after the special resolution for re-registration is passed (Companies Act 1985, s 43 (3) and (4)). Compare the similar rules relating to the issue of shares by a public company for a consideration in kind (see pp 146 to 148, post).

16 This prevents a private company whose net assets are less than £12,500 from re-registering as a public company.

17 Companies Act 1985, s 46 (1) to (3) and (5), as amended by Companies Act 1989, s 23 and Sch 10, para 7.

18 Companies Act 1985, s 44 (1) and (2). For the valuation of a consideration in kind on the issue of shares by a public company, see p 149, post.

19 Companies Act 1985, s 47 (1).

is conclusive evidence that the company's conversion into a public company has been properly effected and that it is a public company.[20] The Registrar must publish the issue of the new certificate of incorporation in the London Gazette.[1]

Conversion of a public company into a private company

A public company may be re-registered as a private company limited by shares or by guarantee if a general meeting passes a special resolution to that effect deleting the provision of its memorandum of association that the company is to be a public company and making such other alterations to the company's memorandum and articles as are requisite for its change in status,[2] in particular the substitution of the terminal word 'limited' or its contraction 'ltd' in the company's name for 'public limited company' or 'plc'.[3] A public company cannot be re-registered as an unlimited company[4] nor can it be re-registered as a company limited by guarantee with a share capital unless it was in existence as a company limited by guarantee on 22 December 1980 and had a share capital on that date.[5] When the public company's memorandum and articles have been appropriately amended, an application for re-registration must be signed by a director and the secretary of the company and must be submitted to the Registrar accompanied by a printed copy of the altered memorandum and articles,[6] and after the expiration of 28 days from the date of the resolution for re-registration or the later rejection by the court of any applications to cancel it, the Registrar will issue a new certificate of incorporation appropriate to a private company.[7] The company thereupon becomes a private company, and the new certificate of incorporation is conclusive evidence that the conversion of the company has been properly effected and that it is a private company.[8] The Registrar must publish the issue of the new certificate of incorporation in the London Gazette.[9]

Within 28 days after a special resolution is passed to re-register a public company as a private one, an application to the court to cancel the resolution and so prevent the re-registration[10] may be made by one or more persons holding at least 5 per cent of the company's issued share capital or any class of it, or by not less than 50 members of the company, or by any one or more of such shareholders or members who are authorised by the others to do so.[11] On the hearing of the application the

---

20 Ibid, s 47 (5). For the effectiveness of the certificate, see p 28, ante. A fee of £50 is payable to the Registrar (Companies (Fees) Regulations 1988 (SI 1988/887), reg 3 and Schedule).
1 Ibid, s 711 (1)(a).
2 Ibid, s 53 (1) and (2).
3 Ibid, s 25 (1) and s 27 (1) and (3). If the company's memorandum provides that its registered office shall be in Wales, the company's altered name may terminate with the Welsh equivalent (ibid, s 25 (2) and s 27 (1) and (3)).
4 Companies Act 1985, s 53 (3).
5 Ibid, s 1 (4).
6 Ibid, s 53 (1).
7 Ibid, s 53 (1) and s 55 (1).
8 Ibid, s 55 (2) and (3). For the effectiveness of the certificate see p 28, ante. A fee of £50 is payable to the Registrar (Companies (Fees) Regulations 1988 (SI 1988/887), reg 3 and Schedule).
9 Ibid, s 711 (1) (a).
10 The application is made by a petition presented to any court which has jurisdiction to wind up the company (Companies Act 1985, s 54 (1) to (5)). In practice all applications to the court under the Companies Act 1985 are made to the High Court and are assigned to the Chancery Division, a separate department of which, known as the Companies Court, has been established for the purpose. References in the remainder of this book to applications to the court under the Companies Act 1985 are to be understood as meaning applications to the Companies Court, unless otherwise stated. The procedure on petitions under the Companies Act 1985, s 54 is governed by RSC Ord 102, rr 4 (1) and 6 (1) and (2).
11 Companies Act 1985, s 54 (1) to (3).

court may cancel or confirm the resolution for re-registration, or may confirm it on such conditions as the court thinks fit, including the purchase of dissenting members' shares by other members or by third persons who are willing to purchase them or by the company itself, and in the latter case the court may order a corresponding reduction in the company's share capital.[12] Additionally, the court may adjourn the hearing so that arrangements may be made subject to its approval for the purchase of dissenting members' shares.[13] The court may also impose conditions if it cancels the resolution, and it would therefore seem that the court could require the whole or part of the shareholdings of the majority who voted for re-registration to be purchased by the minority shareholders who oppose it or by the company.[13] Whether the court confirms or cancels the resolution for re-registration, it may make such alterations in the memorandum or articles as the court thinks fit, and such alterations take effect as though made by resolution of the company itself,[14] and so are susceptible to further alteration by the company by passing the appropriate resolution. On the other hand, the court may as a condition of confirming or cancelling the resolution for re-registration, require the company not to make any, or any specified, alteration to its memorandum or articles (including any modification of them ordered by the court itself) and the company cannot then do so without leave of the court.[15]

Registered office

The Companies Act 1985 does not empower a company to alter the clause of its memorandum which states that its registered office is situate in England, Wales or Scotland, and the clause is consequently unalterable.[16] A company, therefore, cannot change its nationality or domicile, but it can change its country of residence.[17]

However, there is nothing to prevent a company from changing the address of its registered office, provided that its new registered office is in England or Wales if its memorandum states that its registered office is situate in England and Wales,[18] or in Wales or Scotland respectively if its memorandum states that its registered office is situate in either of those countries. The change need not even be decided upon resolution of the members if the directors are given wide enough powers by the articles to decide on it themselves.[19] A change in the address of the company's registered office takes effect only when notice of the change and of the address of the new registered office has been given by the company to the Registrar of Companies and he has registered the notice.[20] However, until the end of 14 days from the date when the change is registered, any document may be validly served on the company at its previous registered office.[1] The Registrar must advertise the

12 Ibid, s 54 (5) and (6).
13 Ibid, s 54 (5).
14 Ibid, s 54 (5) and (9).
15 Ibid, s 54 (5) and (8).
16 Ibid, s 2 (7).
17 For the country of a company's residence, see p 11, ante.
18 If the company was incorporated under one of the earlier Companies Acts, its memorandum will state that its registered office is to be situate in England or Scotland. If its registered office is stated to be in England, it may change the address of its registered office to one in Wales. This is because the term 'England' in the Companies Act 1948, s 2 (1) includes Wales (Wales and Berwick Act 1746, s 3 (32 Halsbury's Statutes (3rd Edn) 412)).
19 If the company's articles incorporate Table A, the general delegation of the company's powers to the board by art 70 thereof suffices for this purpose.
20 Companies Act 1985, s 287 (3) and (4), as amended by Companies Act 1989, s 136.
 1 Ibid, s 287 (4), as amended by Companies Act 1989, s 136.

change of registered office in the London Gazette,[2] and until this is done the change is not effective against any person who serves a document on the company and is unaware of the change.[3]

Objects

A company may by special resolution alter the provisions of its memorandum with respect to the objects of the company.[4] The power is not confined to the alteration of the company's objects strictly so called; ancillary powers contained in the objects clause may also be altered, and new ancillary powers may be inserted, because, although such powers are not objects, they are part of the provisions of the memorandum with respect to the company's objects.[5] The Companies Act 1985 itself recognised this to be so in its original form, for some of the purposes for which it authorised the alteration of the objects clause could not possibly do anything but add or to extend ancillary powers.[6] But there must be some connection between the proposed alteration and the achievement of the company's objects. Therefore, when the memorandum of a limited company required all its income to be applied in furthering its objects, and provided that if any income were distributed to a member he and the managing committee of the company should become liable for the company's debts without limit, it was held that the deletion of this provision for unlimited liability could not be sanctioned as an alteration of the company's objects, because it was completely unrelated to the pursuit of them.[7] On the other hand, it has been held that if the provision it is sought to alter has been inserted in the objects clause of the memorandum, it must be conclusively deemed an object of the company,[8] even though taken by itself it contains neither an object nor an ancillary power, and so it may be altered by special resolution.[9]

Purposes for which the objects clause may be altered

In its original form, the provision of the Companies Act 1985 which authorised companies to alter their memoranda of association with respect to their objects, specified seven alternative purposes for which they could do so. The widest of these purposes was to enable the company to carry on some business which under existing circumstances might conveniently or advantageously be combined with some other business of the company.[10] The restriction on the company's powers to alter its objects only for one or more of these seven purposes, so that it could not, for example, abandon the whole of its original objects and adopt new objects relating to an entirely different kind of business, or a business completely unconnected with or in conflict with the original objects, was removed by the Companies Act 1989, s 2. Consequently, a company can now reconstruct its objects clause in any way it thinks fit, provided that the reconstructed clause does express objects or purposes which the company is to pursue in the future. The fact that there is no connection, whether logical, historical or commercial, between the original and the new objects is immaterial. Moreover, a company need not change its name so as to indicate the altered character of its future activities, but if the Secretary of State for Trade and

---

2 Companies Act 1985, s 711 (1).
3 Ibid, s 42 (1).
4 Ibid, s 4 (1), as amended by Companies Act 1989, s 110 (2).
5 *Re Scientific Poultry Breeders' Association Ltd* [1933] Ch 227.
6 See Companies Act 1985, s 4 (*a*), (*b*), (*f*) and (*g*) in the original form of the section.
7 *Re Society for Promoting Employment of Women* [1927] WN 145.
8 Because of the Companies Act 1985, s 13 (7) (see p 28, ante).
9 *Re Hampstead Garden Suburb Trust Ltd* [1962] Ch 806 at 825, [1962] 2 All ER 879 at 889.
10 Companies Act 1985, s 4 (*d*), in the original form of the section.

Industry considers that, in view of its altered objects, the company's name gives so misleading an indication of the nature of its activities as to be likely to cause harm to the public, he may require it to change its name.[11] If the alteration of the objects clause results in the company's objects being expressed to be the carrying on of business as a general commercial company, it may after the alteration carry on any trade or business whatsoever, and may do all such things as are incidental or conducive to the carrying on of any trade or business by it.[12]

Procedure to alter the objects clause

The alteration of a company's objects clause appears to take effect as soon as the special resolution for the alteration is passed, but if an application is made to the court to cancel the alteration under the provisions dealt with below, its operation is suspended until the court confirms it.[13]

Within 21 days after the resolution is passed, an application may be made to the court by petition[14] to cancel the alteration of the objects clause.[15] It is, therefore, inadvisable for the company to act on the alteration until the time for applying to the court has expired. The application to the court may be made by the holders of 15 per cent in nominal value of the company's issued share capital, or where the company has two or more classes of shares, by the holders of 15 per cent in nominal value of the issued shares of any class.[16] An application may also be made by the holders of 15 per cent in nominal value of the company's debentures secured by a floating charge which were issued, or form part of a series issued, before December 1 1947.[17] When the meeting of members is called to pass the resolution for the alteration, notice of the meeting must at the same time be sent to debenture holders who are entitled to petition the court to cancel the alteration so that they may be made aware of their rights.[18] Notice must be sent to the individual debenture holders, and not merely to the trustees of the debenture trust deed, even though the latter are empowered to receive notices on behalf of the debenture holders by the terms of the trust deed.[19] Moreover, if the company has issued debenture stock[20] notice must be sent to the individual debenture stockholders, even though the debenture debt is owed in law not to them but to the trustees of the covering trust deed.[1] An application to the court to cancel the alteration may be made on behalf of the requisite fraction of share or debenture holders by one or more of their number appointed by the others in writing,[2] but the written authority must be given[3] and communicated[4] to the petitioners before they present their petition. If they present it without the authority of the requisite fraction of share or debenture

11 Companies Act 1985, s 32 (1) (see p 63, ante).
12 Ibid, s 3A, inserted by Companies Act 1989, s 110 (1) (see p 19, ante).
13 Ibid, s 4 (2).
14 The petition may be presented to any court which has jurisdiction to wind up the company (Companies Act 1985, s 744). The procedure on an application to cancel an alteration of the objects clause is governed by RSC Ord 102, rr 4 (1) and 6 (1) and (3).
15 Companies Act 1985, s 5 (1).
16 Ibid, s 5 (2). If the company is an unlimited company or a company limited by guarantee without a share capital, the application may be made by 15 per cent of its members.
17 Companies Act 1985, s 5 (2) and (8).
18 Ibid, s 5 (8).
19 *Re Hampstead Garden Suburb Trust Ltd* [1962] Ch 806 at 822, [1962] 2 All ER 879 at 888.
20 See p 443, post.
 1 *Re Hampstead Garden Suburb Trust Ltd* [1962] Ch 806 at 821, [1962] 2 All ER 879 at 887.
 2 Companies Act 1985, s 5 (3).
 3 *Re Suburban and Provincial Stores Ltd* [1943] Ch 156, [1943] 1 All ER 342.
 4 *Re Sound City (Films) Ltd* [1947] Ch 169, [1946] 2 All ER 521.

holders, it is not possible for the requisite fraction to ratify their act afterwards, and so validate the petition. On the other hand, if a petition is presented by the holders of more than 15 per cent of the shares of one class together with the holders of less than 15 per cent of the shares of another class, and their combined holdings amount to less than 15 per cent of the company's total issued share capital, the holders of shares of the second class may appear on the hearing in support of the arguments advanced by the holders of shares of the first class, but not in support of arguments which they alone advance.[5]

Unless proceedings are taken to cancel an alteration of the objects clause within 21 days after the resolution is passed, the validity of the alteration cannot thereafter be questioned on the ground that it was not authorised by the Companies Act 1985, either in proceedings to cancel the resolution brought under the Act or otherwise.[6] The only other proceedings which could be brought to challenge the alteration would be an action by a member of the company for an injunction to prevent the alteration taking effect, or to prevent the directors giving effect to it, because it was not authorised by the Act, and was therefore ultra vires. The Act obviously contemplates that such an action may be brought by limiting the period for instituting it, and so it seems that any member, however small his shareholding, may sue for such an injunction, provided he does so within the period of 21 days.[7] Whether creditors can similarly sue for an injunction is doubtful. A creditor can ordinarily sue to restrain an ultra vires or illegal act only if it affects property specifically mortgaged to him, and so a debenture holder secured by only a floating charge,[8] and, a fortiori, an unsecured creditor,[9] cannot sue.

The provision of the Act precluding challenges of the validity of an alteration of a company's objects because the alteration was unauthorised by the Act,[6] was of more significance before the Companies Act 1985 was amended in 1989 so as to enable companies to alter their objects clauses for any purpose whatsoever. It is now obviously impossible to seek invalidation of an alteration because it was not made for an authorised purpose, because all purposes are authorised. Nevertheless, the provision may still be significant in preventing challenges to the validity and effectiveness of an alteration after the expiration of the 21 day period on the ground that the proper procedure for passing the special resolution for the alteration was not followed (eg because proper notice of the proposed resolution was not sent to all the persons to whom it should have been),[10] but this would, of course, not prevent the alteration being challenged at any time on the ground that the resolution making it was not passed by the appropriate majority vote.

If a petition is presented for the cancellation of an alteration of a company's objects or ancillary powers in its memorandum, the court may confirm the alteration in whole or part, and subject to such conditions as it thinks fit, or it may cancel the alteration.[11] Where the court approves a substantial alteration of the business which the company's memorandum empowers it to carry on, the court may require the company to change its name to indicate that the alteration has

---

5 *Re Hampstead Garden Suburb Trust Ltd* [1962] Ch 806 at 819, [1962] 2 All ER 879 at 886.
6 Companies Act 1985, s 6 (4).
7 This is supported by a dictum of Lord Maugham in *Carruth v Imperial Chemical Industries Ltd* [1937] AC 707 at 765, [1937] 2 All ER 422 at 458, that any shareholder may sue for an injunction to restrain an alteration of the articles in respect of class rights, even though the Companies Act 1985, s 127, like s 5, gives a statutory right to a certain fraction of shareholders to petition for the cancellation of the alteration.
8 *Lawrence v West Somerset Mineral Rly Co* [1918] 2 Ch 250.
9 *Mills v Northern Rly of Buenos Aires Co* (1870) 5 Ch App 621.
10 For the invalidation of resolutions because not passed by the requisite majority vote, see p 656, post.
11 Companies Act 1985, s 5 (4).

been made,[12] and in one such case the court required the company to give a floating charge over its undertaking to its existing unsecured debenture holders so that they might be able to realise the money owing to them more easily if need arose.[13] The court may additionally approve arrangements for the purchase of the shares of dissenting members,[11] but not the debentures of debenture holders who oppose the alteration, or the court may make its confirmation of the alteration of the objects conditional on the purchase of dissenting members' shares by the other shareholders or by third persons who are willing to acquire them or by the company itself, and if the company acquires the shares the court may order a corresponding reduction in the company's issued capital.[14] Furthermore, the court may confirm an alteration of the objects clause subject to alterations in the company's memorandum or articles directed by the court, and such alterations take effect as though they had been made by the company itself, and so are susceptible to further alteration by the appropriate procedure.[15] On the other hand, the court may as a condition of confirming the alteration of objects require the company not to make any, or any specified, alterations to its memorandum or articles (including any modification ordered by the court), and the company cannot then do so without leave of the court.[16]

Within 15 days after the expiration of the period for petitioning the court to cancel an alteration of a company's memorandum of association in respect of its objects, or if such a petition is presented, within 15 days after the court disposes of it, the company must deliver to the Registrar of Companies a printed copy of its altered memorandum and a copy of any order made by the court, but it is unnecessary to deliver a copy of the memorandum if the court has cancelled the alteration.[17]

Limited liability

A private company limited by shares or by guarantee (but not a public company) which has not previously been an unlimited company may re-register as an unlimited company with or without a share capital, provided all its members consent and its memorandum and articles are altered so as to conform to those of an unlimited company.[18] The written consent of all the members, a statutory declaration by the directors that the consenting members comprise the whole membership of the company, and copies of the altered memorandum and articles must be delivered to the Registrar of Companies.[19] The Registrar thereupon issues a new certificate of incorporation in the form appropriate for an unlimited company, and the certificate is conclusive evidence that the company has been

---

12 In *Re Governments Stock Investment Co (No 2)* [1892] 1 Ch 597, where the alteration extended the company's objects from investing in British and foreign government securities to investing in the securities of commercial companies as well, the court required the company to change its name by adding the words 'and other' after the word 'Governments'. In *Re Egyptian Delta Land and Investment Co* [1907] WN 16, the court approved an alteration enabling a company which was formed to invest in land in the Nile Delta, to invest also in land in the Sudan, on condition that the company added the words 'and Sudan' after the word 'Delta'.
13 *Re Governments Stock Investment Co (No 2)* (supra).
14 Companies Act 1985, s 5 (4) and (5).
15 Ibid, s 5 (5) and (7). It seems that the court may alter the memorandum or articles whether it confirms or cancels the alteration of the objects clause.
16 Companies Act 1985, s 5 (6).
17 Ibid, s 6 (1). The period of 15 days may be extended by the court (s 6 (2)).
18 Companies Act 1985, s 49 (1) to (3), (5), (6) and (8).
19 Ibid, s 49 (4) and (8).

effectively re-registered as an unlimited company.[20] The Registrar must also publish the issue of the new certificate of incorporation in the London Gazette.[1]

The effect of the conversion is that members of the company become liable when the company is wound up to contribute without limit towards the payment of its debts and liabilities, whether incurred before or after the conversion.[2] But a former member of the company who ceased to be a member within a year before the conversion, and who may therefore be liable in a winding up to contribute towards debts incurred before he ceased to be a member,[3] does not come under any increased liability by reason of the conversion, and so can be compelled to contribute no more than the amount unpaid on the shares he formerly held which cannot be recovered from subsequent holders of the shares, or as the case may be, the amount which all members were liable to contribute under the guarantee clause originally in the company's memorandum[4].

An unlimited company may be re-registered as a private company limited by shares or by guarantee unless it has previously been converted from a limited to an unlimited company,[5] but it cannot be re-registered as a company limited by guarantee with a share capital even if it was in existence and had a share capital on 22 December 1980.[6] The re-registration must be authorised by a special resolution of a general meeting setting out the company's share capital, if it has one, and making the necessary alterations to its memorandum and articles of association for them to conform to those of a limited company; the conversion is then effected by the company delivering copies of its altered memorandum and articles of association to the Registrar of Companies, and the Registrar issuing a new certificate of incorporation, which is conclusive evidence of the effectiveness of the conversion.[7]

The result of the re-registration of an unlimited company as a private company limited by shares or by guarantee is that persons who become members of the company after the date of the company's re-registration are liable to contribute toward the payment of its debts and liabilities when it is wound up only to the extent of the capital unpaid on their shares or, if the company is now limited by guarantee, to the extent of the amount expressed in its memorandum.[8] Members of the company at the date of the re-registration and persons who ceased to be members before the re-registration, however, do not enjoy such limited liability in respect of the contributions they may be required to make in a winding up of the company toward meeting its debts and liabilities incurred before its re-registration.[9] Moreover, the normal rule that a former member does not have to make any contribution in a liquidation if he has ceased to be a member more than one year before the liquidation commences[10] is modified in the case of the re-registration of an unlimited company as a limited one, so that in respect of debts and liabilities incurred before the re-registration, persons who were members at the date of the re-registration but have since ceased to be are liable to contribute if the winding up commences within three years of the re-registration of the company.[11] Persons

---

20 Ibid, s 50 (1) and (3). For the effectiveness of the certificate, see p 28, ante.
1 Ibid, s 711 (1) (*a*).
2 Ibid, s 50 (2) and Insolvency Act 1986, s 74 (1) and (2).
3 Insolvency Act 1986, s 74 (2) (*a*) and (*b*).
4 Ibid, s 78 (1) and (2).
5 Companies Act 1985, s 51 (1), (2) and (6).
6 Ibid, s 1 (4).
7 Ibid, s 51 (1), (3) and (4) and s 52. For the effectiveness of the certificate, see p 28, ante.
8 Insolvency Act 1986, s 74 (2) (*d*) and (3).
9 Ibid, s 77 (1) and (2).
10 Ibid, s 74 (2) (*a*).
11 Ibid, s 77 (2).

who were members of the company at the date of re-registration are liable to contribute to debts and liabilities of the company incurred before the re-registration, even though none of the members of the company at the date of its re-registration are members at the commencement of the winding up.[12] Persons who became members of the company after its re-registration are liable to contribute toward debts and liabilities of the company incurred both before and after the company's re-registration as a limited company but only to the extent of the amount unpaid on their shares or the amount of the guarantee in the company's memorandum, and to the extent that a proper application of their contributions satisfies debts and liabilities of the company incurred before re-registration, the liability of former members of the company at the date of re-registration is reduced.[13]

An unlimited company with a share capital which has not previously been registered as a limited company can be re-registered as a public company by following the same procedure as is prescribed for the re-registration of a private company limited by shares as a public company.[14] The consequences of re-registration (including the liability of present and past members of the company to contribute toward payment of debts and liabilities in its winding up) are the same as when an unlimited company is converted into a private company limited by shares.[15]

When the Registrar of Companies has issued a new certificate of incorporation on the re-registration of an unlimited company as a company limited by shares or by guarantee, he must publish the fact in the London Gazette,[16] and persons who deal with the company before this is done and who are ignorant of the re-registration can treat it as ineffective against themselves.[17] It follows that such persons can enforce their claims against the company and its members as though it were still an unlimited company, and this would appear to mean that if the company is wound up, the liquidator can make unlimited calls on its present members and persons who have been members within one year before the commencement of the liquidation in order to raise sufficient money to discharge in full the claims of persons who dealt with the company in ignorance of its re-registration.[18] Whether such calls would be segregated to meet the claims of such special creditors is doubtful, however, and it would seem that the proceeds of the calls would merely augment the company's assets for the benefit of all its creditors.[19]

On the re-registration of an unlimited company as a private company limited by shares or by guarantee, a fee of £50 must be paid to the Registrar of Companies as on the original registration of a company, but on the re-registration of a private company limited by shares or guarantee as an unlimited company, a reduced fee of £5 only is payable.[20]

Capital and guarantee clauses

A limited company may increase, reduce or reorganise its share capital, but the provisions of the Companies Act 1985 empowering it to do so can only be understood in the context of the other rules relating to share capital, and they are

12 Ibid, s 77 (3).
13 Ibid, s 74 (1) and (2) (d), Helbert v Banner (1871) LR 5 HL 28.
14 Companies Act 1985, ss 43 to 46 and s 48 (see p 63, ante).
15 Insolvency Act 1986, s 77.
16 Companies Act 1985, s 711 (1) (a).
17 Ibid, s 42 (1).
18 Insolvency Act 1986, s 74 (1) and (2) (a).
19 Webb v Whiffin (1872) LR 5 HL 711.
20 Companies (Fees) Regulations 1988 (SI 1988/887), reg 3 and Schedule.

therefore dealt with below in that connection.[1] A company limited by guarantee which has a share capital may make the same alterations of its share capital as a company limited by shares, but a company limited by guarantee, whether it has a share capital or not, cannot alter the amount of the guarantee fixed by its memorandum of association,[2] or eliminate it completely if the company has a share capital.[3] Because a company cannot be registered as one limited by guarantee with a share capital since 22 December 1980,[4] it is now impossible for a company limited by guarantee to alter its memorandum so as to create a nominal share capital, and this is so whether the company seeks to remain a private company or to re-register as a public company. Moreover, the re-registration of a company limited by guarantee as a public company cannot be effected indirectly by the company first being re-registered as an unlimited company with a share capital and then being re-registered again as a public company, for the latter re-registration can be effected only by a company which has not previously been re-registered as an unlimited one.[5]

Additional clauses

Before the Companies Act 1948 was enacted, a company could not alter any provision in its memorandum which could have been originally inserted in its articles, or add any such provision to its memorandum, unless the memorandum expressly empowered it to do so.[6] A power of alteration given by the articles was insufficient, but if the memorandum provided that an alteration could be made to it in accordance with provisions for the purpose contained in the articles, the alteration could then be made, because the power to alter was given by the memorandum, the articles merely containing details of the procedure to be adopted.[7] The Companies Act 1985 (re-enacting a corresponding provision in the 1948 Act) now confers a limited power of alteration of such additional provisions on all companies,[8] but in cases where the statutory provision does not apply, the old law still governs.

A company may by special resolution alter any provision in its memorandum which could lawfully have been contained in its articles,[8] but not if the provision is contained in the objects clause of the company's memorandum, because it is then conclusively deemed to be an object of the company, and so could not be inserted in the articles.[9] The alteration of an additional clause of the memorandum appears to be effective as soon as the resolution to alter it is passed, but within 21 days after the resolution is passed, an application may be made to the court by petition[10] by or on behalf of the holders of 15 per cent in nominal value of the company's issued shares, or, if it has shares of more than one class, the holders of 15 per cent in nominal value of the issued shares of any class, for an order cancelling the alteration, and the alteration is thereupon suspended, and does not take effect

---

1 See pp 169 to 188, post.
2 *Hennessy v National Agricultural and Industrial Development Association* [1947] IR 159.
3 Companies Act 1985, s 2 (7).
4 Ibid, s 1 (4).
5 Ibid, s 43 (1).
6 *Ashbury v Watson* (1885) 30 ChD 376.
7 *Re Welsbach Incandescent Gas Light Co Ltd* [1904] 1 Ch 87.
8 Companies Act 1948, s 17 (1).
9 *Re Hampstead Garden Suburb Trust Ltd* [1962] Ch 806 at 823, [1962] 2 All ER 879 at 889. The provision could, of course, be altered as part of the objects clause under the Companies Act 1985, s 4 (see p 67, ante).
10 RSC Ord 102, r 4 (1).

unless it is confirmed by the court.[11] There is no provision by which debenture holders may apply to have the alteration cancelled, as they may when the objects clause is altered. Probably a shareholder who does not hold enough shares to petition himself may nevertheless sue for an injunction to prevent the alteration from taking effect on the ground that it is unfair and oppressive,[12] and if such an action does lie, it need not be brought within 21 days after the resolution is passed, for the Companies Act 1985 imposes no time limit on proceedings to challenge the alteration other than on petitions under the Act itself. On hearing a petition against the alteration, the court has the same powers as on hearing a petition against an alteration of the objects clause, and so may confirm it in whole or part and on such terms and conditions as it thinks fit, or may approve it subject to dissenting members' shares being purchased at a satisfactory price (including a purchase by the company and a consequent reduction in its capital).[13] Whether the court confirms or cancels the alterations, it may order that alterations shall be made to the company's memorandum or articles, or may direct that the company shall not make any alteration, or any specified alteration, to its memorandum or articles without leave of the court.[13]

The statutory power to alter additional clauses of the memorandum does not apply where the memorandum itself provides for or prohibits the alteration of an additional clause, nor when the additional clause confers special rights on any class of members.[14] It is uncommon to find additional clauses in the memorandum dealing with matters other than the rights of different classes of members, and this consequently reduces the practical significance of the statutory power. Such rights cannot be altered by special resolution under the Companies Act 1985, and they can therefore be altered only if the memorandum so provides and the procedure there laid down is followed, or if a scheme of arrangement is propounded and approved by the court.[15] Other additional clauses may be entrenched against alteration either by the memorandum prohibiting their alteration altogether, or by it providing a method of alteration of its own. If an alteration is effected under such an express provision, no petition may be presented against the alteration by dissenting members under the provisions dealt with above, but they could sue for an injunction to prevent it from taking effect on the ground that it was unfair and oppressive.[16]

Within 15 days after the expiration of the period for petitioning the court to cancel an alteration of an additional clause in a company's memorandum of association in exercise of the power conferred by the Companies Act 1985, or if such a petition is presented, within 15 days after the court disposes of it, the company must deliver to the Registrar of Companies a printed copy of its altered memorandum and a copy of any order made by the court, but it is unnecessary to deliver such a copy of the memorandum if the court has cancelled the alteration.[17]

---

11 Companies Act 1985, s 17 (3). If the company is an unlimited company or a company limited by guarantee and, in either case, has no share capital, the application may be made by 15 per cent of its members.
12 See the dictum of Lord Maugham in *Carruth v Imperial Chemical Industries Ltd* [1937] AC 707 at 765, [1937] 2 All ER 422 at 458.
13 Companies Act 1985, s 17 (3) (applying s 5 (1) to (7)).
14 Ibid, s 17 (2).
15 Variation of class rights is dealt with in detail in Chapter 7 (see pp 219 to 232, post). Schemes of arrangement are governed by Companies Act 1985, ss 425 and 427.
16 See p 232.
17 Companies Act 1985, s 17 (3) (applying s 6 (1)).

Copies of altered memorandum

When a company has altered its memorandum in any respect, all copies of it issued thereafter must embody the alteration.[18]

THE ARTICLES OF ASSOCIATION

A company may by special resolution alter its articles of association.[19] Its power to do so cannot be taken away or limited by any provision in its memorandum or articles,[20] nor can the memorandum or articles enable or require the alteration to be made in any other way than by special resolution.[1] But the articles after the alteration must be consistent with the company's memorandum, and so if there is a conflict between any part of the altered articles and a provision in the memorandum, whether required to be there by the Companies Act 1985, or not, the articles are to that extent void.[2]

It was at one time thought that provisions in the articles could be altered only if they related to the company's management, and that fundamental provisions which formed part of the company's constitution, such as the rights of its shareholders, were unalterable.[3] This division of the provisions of the articles into fundamental and alterable has long been held to be baseless, however.[4] The Companies Act 1985 makes no such distinction, and there is none. Consequently, companies have been held entitled to alter their articles to facilitate the issue of preference shares having priority for both dividend and repayment of capital in a winding up over existing shares,[4] to impose a lien or equitable charge in favour of the company on its existing fully paid shares for debts owed to it by its shareholders (thus turning the debts from unsecured into secured ones),[5] and to alter the voting and other rights given by the articles to a particular class of shareholders,[6] subject to the provisions of the Companies Act 1985 requiring the consent of the class of shareholders affected in certain circumstances.[7]

LIMITATIONS ON THE POWER OF ALTERATION

The alteration must benefit the company as a whole

In *Allen v Gold Reefs of West Africa Ltd*[8] Lindley MR said that the statutory power given to shareholders to amend their company's articles '. . . must be exercised, not only in the manner required by law, but also bona fide for the benefit of the company as a whole'. In that case the criterion was not difficult to apply, because the alteration imposed a lien on the company's shares for debts owed to it by its

---

18 Ibid, s 20 (1).
19 Ibid, s 9 (1).
20 *Walker v London Tramways Co* (1879) 12 ChD 705; *Allen v Gold Reefs of West Africa Ltd* [1900] 1 Ch 656 at 671, 676.
1 *Ayre v Skelsey's Adamant Cement Co Ltd* (1905) 21 TLR 464; *Bushell v Faith* [1969] 2 Ch 438, [1969] 1 All ER 1002; affd [1970] AC 1009, [1970] 1 All ER 53.
2 *Ashbury v Watson* (1885) 30 ChD 376.
3 *Hutton v Scarborough Cliff Hotel Co Ltd B* (1865) 2 Drew & Sm 521.
4 *Andrews v Gas Meter Co* [1897] 1 Ch 361.
5 *Allen v Gold Reef of West Africa Ltd* [1900] 1 Ch 656.
6 *Re Australian Estates and Mortgage Co Ltd* [1910] 1 Ch 414 at 424.
7 Companies Act 1985, s 125 (see p 221, post).
8 [1900] 1 Ch 656 at 671.

shareholders, and this was obviously for the company's benefit, since it facilitated the collection of the debts. Later cases have been more complex, and the criterion of benefit to the company as a whole has been defined more specifically in consequence. All of these later cases relate to alterations of the articles, but the principle is equally applicable to alterations of the objects[9] and capital[10] clauses of the memorandum and, undoubtedly, also to alterations of the other obligatory clauses in the memorandum and of additional clauses in the memorandum which deal with matters which could be provided for in the articles.

The subjective test

In *Shuttleworth v Cox Bros & Co (Maidenheard) Ltd*[11] a company altered its articles to provide that any director should cease to hold office if requested to resign by all the other directors. The original articles did not enable a director to be dismissed for misconduct, and the admitted purpose of the alteration was to facilitate the dismissal of the plaintiff, who was suspected of misconduct by his fellow directors. The court upheld the alteration, but the criterion of benefit to the company as a whole which the court applied was expressed in far more subjective terms than in *Allen's* case, and amounted to little more than a requirement of good faith on the part of the majority who voted for the alteration. Scrutton LJ said:[12]

> 'Now when persons, honestly endeavouring to decide what will be for the benefit of the company and to act accordingly, decide upon a particular course, then, provided there are grounds on which reasonable men could come to the decision, it does not matter whether the court would or would not come to the same or a different decision.... The absence of any reasonable ground for deciding that a certain course of action is conducive to the benefit of the company may be a ground for finding lack of good faith or for finding that the shareholders, with the best motives, have not considered the matters which they ought to have considered.'

According to this interpretation of the principle, the court's function is not to ascertain whether the alteration will be for the company's benefit, nor even whether the belief of those who voted for the alteration that it would be for the company's benefit is a reasonable belief; the court is confined to ensuring that the majority who voted for the alteration acted honestly without improper motives, and the unreasonableness of the alteration is merely evidence, but not conclusive evidence, of an improper motive. In *Shuttleworth's* case it made no difference whether the criterion of benefit to the company were applied objectively, so that the court had to ascertain whether the company would benefit, or subjectively, as it was in fact applied in that case.[13] In the light of *Allen's* case the alteration was clearly for the company's benefit either way. But in other cases, particularly those where the company has taken power to compel a member to sell his shares to other members, the difference of interpretation has been vital.

The objective test

In the most recent leading case on this subject, *Greenhalgh v Arderne Cinemas Ltd,*[14]

---

9   *Re Cyclists' Touring Club* [1907] 1 Ch 269 at 273.
10   *Clemens v Clemens Bros Ltd* [1976] 2 All ER 268.
11   [1927] 2 KB 9.
12   Ibid, at 23.
13   The directors would be able to use the power of dismissal only for the benefit of the company, not for private or personal reasons. This applies to all powers given to directors by the articles (see p 584, post). Consequently the alteration might be read as conferring a power of dismissal on the directors only when it was in the interest of the company to exercise it.
14   [1951] Ch 286, [1950] 2 All ER 1120; see also *Rights and Issues Investment Trust Ltd v Stylo Shoes Ltd* [1965] Ch 250 [1964] 3 All ER 628.

the court re-affirmed the objective interpretation of the criterion, and restated it in more detail. In that case the original articles of a private company required any shareholder who wished to sell his shares to offer them to the other members at a fair price before selling them to an outsider. A group of shareholders who controlled a majority of the votes at meetings of shareholders wished to sell their shares to an outsider, but owing to a quarrel between them and the minority shareholder, they were unable to induce him to forgo his right of pre-emption under the articles. Consequently, they procured the passing of a resolution by which the articles were altered to enable any shareholder to sell his shares to an outsider without first offering them to the other members if the company permitted this by ordinary resolution. The practical consequence of the alteration was obvious. The majority shareholders, who had sufficient voting power to pass a special resolution to alter the articles, would be able to pass an ordinary resolution to sanction the sale of their own shares to the outsider who wished to buy them. The minority shareholder, on the other hand, would still be bound to sell his shares to the other members if they exercised their right of pre-emption, because he did not have sufficient voting power to procure an ordinary resolution to enable him to override it.

Nevertheless, the court held that the alteration was valid. After reviewing the earlier decisions on the criterion of benefit to the company, Evershed MR said:[15]

'Certain principles, I think, can be safely stated as emerging from those authorities. In the first place, I think it is now plain that "bona fide for the benefit of the company as a whole" means not two things but one thing. It means that the shareholder must proceed upon what, in his honest opinion, is for the benefit of the company as a whole. The second thing is that the phrase, "the company as a whole" does not (at any rate in such a case as the present) mean the company as a commercial entity, distinct from the corporators; it means the corporators as a general body. That is to say, the case may be taken of an individual hypothetical member and it may be asked whether what is proposed is, in the honest opinion of those who voted in its favour, for that person's benefit.

I think that the matter can, in practice, be more accurately and precisely stated by looking at the converse and by saying that a special resolution of this kind would be liable to be impeached if the effect of it were to discriminate between the majority shareholders and the minority shareholders, so as to give the former an advantage of which the latter were deprived. When the cases are examined in which the resolution has been successfully attacked, it is on that ground. It is therefore not necessary to require that persons voting for a special resolution should, so to speak, dissociate themselves altogether from their own prospects and consider whether what is thought to be for the benefit of the company as a going concern [sic]. If, as commonly happens, an outside person makes an offer to buy all the shares, prima facie, if the corporators think it a fair offer and vote in favour of the resolution, it is no ground for impeaching the resolution that they are considering their own position as individuals.'

Despite the references in the first of these two paragraphs to the state of mind of the members who vote for the alteration, it is clear from the second paragraph that the court applied the test of benefit to the company itself. Also important is the attention the court pays to the position of the 'individual hypothetical member.' He is not quite a fictitious character, like the man on the top of the Clapham omnibus at whose door responsibility for the whole law of negligence is laid. He is a hypothetical member of the particular company, so that the business and size of the company and the distribution of powers between the directors and different classes of members must be borne in mind, because the effect of the alteration on him will depend largely on these factors. But he is not simply a particular member of the company holding a particular number of shares and having a particular

15 [1951] Ch 286 at 291, [1950] 2 All ER 1120 at 1126.

number of votes as compared with another member or group of members, who may have more shares or more votes. The company's position must be viewed in the long term, because the altered articles will govern the company for the indefinite future, and the validity of the alteration cannot be judged solely by its immediate effect on the present shareholders according to the present distribution of shares and voting power among them. The hypothetical member, then, is someone who may be a member at any time, present or future, who has no particular number of shares or votes, and who is not affected by any particular distribution of shares or voting power among his fellow members. In this light, the alteration of the articles in *Greenhalgh's* case was clearly justifiable, for the hypothetical member might benefit equally with any other member by the extension of his power to sell his shares to strangers.

Criticism of the objective test

The fact that the decision in *Greenhalgh's* case can be rationalised in this way does not mean that the principle underlying it is satisfactory, however, as the later decision of Pennycuick J in *Rights and Issues Investment Trust Ltd v Stylo Shoes Ltd*[16] shows. In that case the plaintiff, as a minority shareholder of the defendant company, challenged the validity of resolutions altering its articles of association so as to double the votes which might be cast in respect of management shares held by directors of the company. The original issued share capital of the defendant consisted of 3,600,000 ordinary shares of 5s. each, carrying one vote per share, and 400,000 management shares of 5s. each, which carried the same rights as the ordinary shares save that each management share carried eight votes. The defendant company successfully negotiated the takeover of another company, W. Barratt & Co Ltd, and under the takeover arrangement 8,400,000 further ordinary shares of the defendant were to be allotted to Barratt shareholders in exchange for their shares. This would increase the number of ordinary shares issued by the defendant company to 12,000,000, and if the voting rights attached to the management shares remained unchanged, would reduce the percentage of votes which their holders could cast from 47 per cent to 21·5 per cent. The resolution to double the voting rights of the management shares would partially restore this proportion to 34·8 per cent. The defendant was a public company with a stock exchange listing for its shares, which were held by many thousands of shareholders, many of whom had comparatively small holdings. Control of one-third of the voting rights in practice sufficed to give the directors effective control over general meetings, having regard to the numerous small shareholders who neither attended nor appointed proxies to represent them; control over little more than one-fifth of the voting rights by the directors might have been too marginal to ensure effective control.

In order to ensure the continuance of their effective voting control before the new shares were issued to the Barratt shareholders, the directors called two shareholders' meetings, namely, a class meeting of ordinary shareholders to consent to the doubling of the voting rights attached to the management shares by passing an extraordinary resolution under the standard variation of rights clause in the articles,[17] and secondly a general meeting to pass a special resolution effecting the necessary alteration of the articles. At neither meeting did holders of management shares vote. The result of the votes were that at the class meeting of ordinary shareholders all but 8 per cent of the votes cast were in favour of doubling the

16 [1965] Ch 250, [1964] 3 All ER 628.
17 The clause was the same as that in the Companies Act 1948, Table A, art 4.

voting rights of the management shares, and at the general meeting all but 10·3 per cent of the votes cast were in favour.

The plaintiff attacked the resolutions on the ground that the alteration to the articles was not in the interests of the members of the company as a whole. Pennycuick J held against the plaintiff. He was satisfied that the resolutions were passed in good faith, that they did not discriminate against the plaintiff in view of the fact that all the ordinary shareholders suffered the same dilution of their voting power, and that the matter was one of business policy on the merits of which it was not the court's function to pronounce. He was undoubtedly greatly influenced by the overwhelming support for the resolutions and by the fact that holders of the management shares had abstained from voting. He cited part of Evershed MR's judgment in *Greenhalgh's* case on the question whether the alteration of articles of association satisfied the test of benefiting the company as a whole, and was constrained to hold that it did.

It might, perhaps, be conceded that where the articles of association originally conferred disproportionate voting rights on one class of shareholders, the other class take their shares on the understanding that they are to be excluded from voting control, and consequently cannot complain if the alteration of the articles merely perpetuates that situation. But Pennycuick J went farther than this, and posed the hypothetical case of a company which originally had a single class of shares carrying equal voting rights and which now alters its articles so as to confer voting control on the holders of a minority of its shares. This case, too, he thought, would be governed by the same considerations as the one before him, and it must be admitted that in the light of the reasoning of Evershed MR, in *Greenhalgh's* case this may well be so. Clearly the test laid down in *Greenhalgh's* case is unsatisfactory if it can be applied in as lax a way as this.

Expropriation of shares and voting rights

The courts have applied the objective test of benefit to the members of a company far more effectively when dealing with alterations of articles empowering the majority shareholders to compel the minority to sell their shares. There have been three such cases. In two of them, *Brown v British Abrasive Wheel Co*[18] and *Dafen Tinplate Co Ltd v Llanelly Steel Co* (1907) *Ltd*[19] the alteration was held to be void. In the third, *Sidebotham v Kershaw, Leese & Co Ltd*,[20] it was held valid.

In *Brown v British Abrasive Wheel Co* the company altered its articles so that the holders of nine-tenths in nominal value of its shares might require any other shareholder to sell his shares to them at par, or at a sum which would be the value of his shares if the average dividend paid during the last three years before the purchase had yielded a return of 12·5 per cent, whichever was greater. All but two per cent of the company's shares were held by two shareholders who were willing to subscribe further capital, which the company badly needed, but only if they were able to acquire the remaining shares held by the other members, and it was for this purpose that they procured the alteration of the articles.

Astbury J held that a power of compulsory acquisition of shares is not void per se, so that, had it been contained in the original articles, it would have bound all the members, because it would be on the footing that it might be exercised against

18 [1919] 1 Ch 290.
19 [1920] 2 Ch 124.
20 [1920] 1 Ch 154.

them that they joined the company.[1] But he held that the addition of such a power to articles which did not originally contain it was void, because:[2]

'... the majority may acquire all the shares and provide further capital. That would be for the benefit of the company as then constituted. But the proposed alteration is not for the present benefit of this company.'

In *Dafen Tinplate Co Ltd v Llanelly Steel Co* (1907) *Ltd*[3] the defendant company was formed to manufacture steel bars, and its members were companies which used steel bars and intended to buy their supplies from the defendant company, although they entered into no contract to do so. After a time the plaintiff company began to buy its supply of steel bars elsewhere. The defendant company thereupon altered its articles to enable the company by ordinary resolution to require any member to sell his shares to the other members at a fair price fixed by the directors, but one member was expressly exempted from being expropriated in this way. The plaintiff company sought a declaration that the alteration of the articles and the pretended expropriation of its shares were void. Peterson J made that declaration. After observing that the power of expropriation was wide enough to reach a member against whom the company had no legitimate complaint, he said.[4]

'It may be for the benefit of the majority of the shareholders to acquire the shares of the minority, but how can it be said to be for the benefit of the company that any shareholder against whom no charge of acting to the detriment of the company can be urged, and who is in every respect a desirable member of the company, and for whose expropriation there is no reason except the will of the majority, should be forced to transfer his shares to the majority or to anyone else?'

With regard to the exemption of one particular member from expropriation, Peterson J added:[5]

'... the power ought in my view to apply to all the shares, unless perhaps it could be established that it is for the benefit of the company that certain shares should be exempt. Prima facie all the shares of the classes affected should be on the same footing; some should not be placed in a position of inferiority or superiority. The majority cannot alter the articles in such a way as to place one or more of the minority in a position of inferiority, ... nor can it in my view confer on one or more of its own number benefits or privileges in which other shareholders of the same class do not participate.'

Some points in *Brown*'s case and the *Dafen Tinplate Co* case call for comment. In the first place, the majority shareholders referred to in both cases were the members who controlled the voting power at shareholders' meetings at the date the alteration was made, so that it seems as though the validity of the alteration was being judged in the light of its immediate effect on the existing minority shareholders. That was undoubtedly what was in the judges' minds, but if the passages quoted above are read as though the minority shareholder were the 'hypothetical member' of *Greenhalgh's* case, and the majority shareholders were any group who at any time held the requisite number of shares to exercise the power of expropriation, the conclusion would be exactly the same. It is impossible for a bare power of expropriation ever to be for the benefit of a hypothetical member, for he must, as the personification of any member of the company, always be subject to the risk of losing his investment without any corresponding gain. The other point is that,

---

1 See also *Borland's Trustee v Steel Bros & Co Ltd* [1901] 1 Ch 279; *Phillips v Manufacturers' Securities Ltd* (1917) 86 LJ Ch 305.
2 [1919] 1 Ch 290.
3 [1920] 2 Ch 124.
4 Ibid, at 141.
5 Ibid, at 143.

although the purport of the second passage quoted from Peterson J's judgment is undoubtedly correct, it does not mean that where the immediate effect of an alteration is to the detriment of a minority of shareholders, the alteration is necessarily void. In the *Dafen Tinplate Co* case the exemption of one member from the effect of the alteration did not result from the size of his shareholding and voting power at the date of the alteration, as in the *Greenhalgh* case, but was written into the articles, so that it would last indefinitely and would permanently discriminate between shareholders of the same class. Such a permanent discrimination cannot benefit the individual hypothetical member, and is therefore void.

In *Sidebotham v Kershaw, Leese & Co Ltd*[6] the alteration of the articles empowered the directors to require any member who carried on a business competing with that of the company, to sell his shares at a fair price to persons nominated by the directors. The company was a private one, and the evidence showed that a competitor who was a member of the company might be able to cause it loss by using information which he obtained as a member.[7] The court held the alteration valid. It was clearly in the interest of the company as a whole and of the 'individual hypothetical member', that the company's trade secrets should not be available to its competitors, and the power of expropriation was merely designed to ensure this. A power of expropriation added to articles will not always be void, therefore; it will be valid if it is calculated to protect the company from an injury which it might otherwise suffer, and is expressly limited to serving that purpose.

The hostility shown by the courts to amendments of articles of association introducing expropriation provisions has been extended exceptionally in one recent case[8] to an alteration of the memorandum of association of a company increasing its nominal capital coupled with resolutions as to the destination of the newly created shares, when the purpose of the majority shareholders who voted in favour of these measures was to deprive a minority shareholder of her power to prevent special resolutions being passed in the future by reducing her proportionate voting power from more than 25 per cent to less than that fraction. This was held to be an oppressive expropriation of the minority shareholders' voting rights, and it is the element of oppression accompanying an expropriation unsupported by special reasons which distinguishes this case from other cases, where in the absence of proved bad faith, the court has held that the diminution of an existing shareholders' voting powers by an alteration of the articles is not necessarily incompatible with the benefit of the members of the company as a whole[9] In the present case the individual hypothetical member to be considered is one who originally has sufficient votes to block special resolutions, but who is deprived of that power by the alteration of the memorandum or articles. Such a hypothetical member can only lose by such an alteration without any possibility of a corresponding gain.

---

6 [1920] 1 Ch 154.

7 At the time the case was decided the Companies (Consolidation) Act 1908 did not require companies to lay annual accounts or directors' reports before the members in general meeting (although the articles of association could require this, as did Table A of the 1908 Act, art 106), and there was no statutory requirement that copies of annual accounts and directors' reports should be delivered to the Registrar of Companies. Under the present law members and outsiders therefore have access to far more information about a company's affairs than in 1920, but in private companies it is still true that members may obtain more detailed information about the company's affairs more speedily than outsiders because of their contact with the directors, and so the basis for the decision in *Sidebotham's* case still holds good today.

8 *Clemens v Clemens Bros Ltd* [1976] 2 All ER 268.

9 Eg *Rights and Issues Investment Trust Ltd v Stylo Shoes Ltd* [1965] Ch 250, [1964] 3 All ER 628.

Conclusions

It will now be useful to summarise the decided cases in the form of a number of propositions.

(1) It is not necessary to prove that any member will derive any particular advantage from an alteration of the memorandum or articles in order to uphold it.

(2) The fact that some members suffer a detriment in consequence of the alteration does not inevitably make it void,[10] but if the alteration literally discriminates between members of the same class by giving a privilege to some, or imposing a detriment on others, it is void.

(3) The alteration must be made in good faith, and the shareholders who vote for it must not be guilty of fraud or oppression toward the minority.[11] But the mere fact that the majority are moved to make the alteration by the special circumstances of one member, and the alteration operates to his disadvantage, is not, by itself, proof of bad faith.[12]

(4) In addition to being made in good faith, the alteration must be for the benefit of any individual hypothetical member, which means that, in the long term, any member must be equally likely to benefit from it or be burdened by it as any other member; the identification of the individual hypothetical member may depend on the kind of alteration which is being made, however, but it will never depend simply on the distribution of shares or voting power at the time of the alteration.[13]

Breach of contract

A company cannot by altering its memorandum or articles alter the terms of a contract which it has already entered into, or escape liability for breach of such a contract.

Remedies for breach of contract by the company

The other party to a contract has his ordinary remedies against the company which breaks it in consequence of an alteration of its memorandum or articles, and it appears that any member who votes for the alteration will also be liable in damages to the other party for inducing the company to break its contract, if the inevitable consequence of the alteration is that the contract will be broken.[14] It seems, however, that the other party cannot obtain an injunction to prevent the alteration of the memorandum or articles from taking effect. In one case[15] a company agreed with the vendor of its business that he and his trustees after his death should have

---

10 Eg *Allen v Gold Reefs of West Africa Ltd* [1990] 1 Ch 656 (impositions of a lien on fully paid shares); *Greenhalgh v Arderne Cinemas Ltd* [1951] Ch 286, [1950] 2 All ER 1120 (loss of right of pre-emption over other members' shares).

11 *Clemens v Clemens Bros Ltd*, supra. Despite the opinion of Evershed MR in *Greenhalgh v Arderne Cinemas Ltd*, supra, it is suggested that this is a separate rule from the following one. It is a principle of general application that the court will restrain acts by majority shareholders which are fraudulent or oppressive of the minority (see p 659, et seq, post), and it is quite possible for an alteration of articles to be valid under rule 4, but nevertheless invalid under the present rules because it is part of a scheme to oppress the present minority shareholders.

12 *Sidebotham v Kershaw, Leese & Co* [1920] 1 Ch 154 at 161. Directors and shareholders are not expected to be clairvoyants and to alter the company's articles before an occasion for the application of the altered articles arises.

13 *Clemens v Clemens Bros Ltd*, supra.

14 *Southern Foundries (1926) Ltd v Shirlaw* [1940] AC 701, [1940] 2 All ER 445.

15 *Punt v Symons & Co Ltd* [1903] 2 Ch 506.

power to appoint and dismiss the company's directors, and that a provision would be inserted in the company's articles accordingly, which the company would not alter. The articles did contain the appropriate provision, but after the vendor's death the company purported to alter the articles by striking it out. The trustees sued the company for an injunction to prevent the alteration from taking effect. The court held that a company cannot deprive itself of its statutory power to alter its articles by contracting not to exercise it, and the trustees' remedy was therefore to sue the company for damages or other relief for breach of its contract to accept their nominees as its directors. The court did not say what other relief could be granted, and it was unnecessary to do so, because it was held, on the facts, that the resolution altering the articles had not been properly passed. But there seems no reason why the trustees should not have obtained an injunction to restrain the company from refusing to accept their nominees as its directors if, acting under the altered articles, the company did in fact reject them.[16]

In a later case where the facts were almost identical, the court did grant an injunction to prevent the articles from being altered,[17] on the ground that the earlier decision had been overruled in the meantime,[18] but this was undoubtedly incorrect. Moreover, there has since been a dictum by Lord Porter[19] supporting the earlier decision. The preponderant judicial opinion at present, therefore, is that the company is free to alter its articles, and must merely face the normal consequences of breaking the contract. This seems to be the preferable opinion, too, for if the other party to the contract is given his normal contractual remedies, he obtains all that the law entitles him to for a breach of the kind of contract in question. An injunction to restrain the alteration of the articles is useful to him only if he cannot obtain an injunction to prevent the contract being broken under the general law,[20] and if an injunction restraining the alteration were issued in those circumstances, the company would be put in a worse position than any other defendant who entered into such a contract would be.

Contracts incorporating part of the articles

A question which has not yet been settled is whether, when a contract is made which impliedly incorporates part of the memorandum or articles of association of a company,[1] the contract is broken or frustrated by the company altering the relevant part of the memorandum or articles, or whether the terms of the contract are automatically altered with the memorandum or articles because that is assumed to have been the original intention of the parties. In *Shuttleworth v Cox Bros & Co (Maidenhead) Ltd*[2] it was held that the contract is automatically altered. Scrutton LJ said:[3]

16 *British Murac Syndicate Ltd v Alperton Rubber Co Ltd* [1915] 2 Ch 186 at 196. Although a director's contract of service will not usually be specifically enforced, there is no reason why a contract giving the right to nominate directors to serve the company should not be enforced by injunction.
17 *British Murac Syndicate Ltd v Alperton Rubber Co Ltd*, supra.
18 By *Baily v British Equitable Assurance Co* [1904] 1 Ch 374, but the only relief sought in that case was a declaration that a company was not entitled to break its contract merely because it had altered its articles.
19 *Southern Foundries (1926) Ltd v Shirlaw* [1940] AC 701 at 741, [1940] 2 All ER 445 at 469. This dictum was affirmed by Scott J in *Cumbrian Newspapers Group Ltd v Cumberland and Westmoreland Herald Newspaper and Printing Co Ltd* [1987] Ch 1 at 24, [1986] 2 All ER 816 at 831.
20 For example, where the contract is for personal services or where damages would be an adequate remedy.
1 See p 54, ante.
2 [1927] 2 KB 9.
3 Ibid, at 22.

'But if a contract is contained in the articles, it must be, as the articles themselves are, subject to alteration in accordance with the power given by [the Companies Act 1985, s 9].'

In that case the articles were altered to enable the company to dismiss its directors for a reason not specified in the original articles, and it was held that the contract of employment of a director who was already serving on the terms of the original articles, was varied accordingly, so that the company committed no breach of contract by dismissing him on the new ground.

The decision in *Shuttleworth's* case must, however, be read subject to a number of reservations. In the first place, it does not apply when the company has broken an express term of a contract, even though other terms of the contract are impliedly incorporated from the memorandum or articles.[4] Secondly, it does not apply if the other party to the contract has an accrued right to insist on performance by the company of an obligation incorporated in the contract from the memorandum or articles. Thus, where directors served the company under articles which provided that their remuneration should be a certain sum, it was held that an alteration of the articles could not deprive them of remuneration for a period which they had already served.[5] Thirdly, it is suggested that the obligations of the other party to a contract cannot be made more onerous by the company altering its memorandum or articles, so that, for example, if the articles appoint a director to serve for a period of years in a part-time capacity, he cannot be compelled to devote his full time to the company's affairs by the company altering its articles so as to require him to do so. And finally, there may be contracts which impliedly incorporate part of the memorandum or articles, but do not also impliedly empower the company to vary the incorporated terms by altering them. The possibility of such contracts has clearly been recognised by the court,[6] and they are especially important in connection with rights conferred upon classes of shareholders by the articles.

Rights of classes of shareholders

If the special rights of a class of shareholders are conferred by the articles, they may be varied by an alteration of the articles,[7] and if such rights are conferred by the memorandum, they may be altered if the memorandum, or in certain situations, the articles so provide.[8] But it is common for the articles to provide that such rights may be varied only with the consent of the holders of a certain fraction of the shares of that class,[9] in which case a variation would undoubtedly be ineffective unless the appropriate consent were given.[10] If the contract between the company and the members of that class impliedly permitted the company to vary the contract by striking the requirement of a class consent out of the articles, however, the protection given to those members against a variation of their rights would be worthless. It is suggested that the company has no such implied contractual power, and that if it does alter its articles in that way, the contractual rights of the members

---

4 *Southern Foundries* (1926) *Ltd v Shirlaw* [1940] AC 701, [1940] 2 All ER 445.
5 *Swabey v Port Darwin Gold Mining Co* (1889) 1 Meg 385.
6 *Allen v Gold Reefs of West Africa Ltd* [1900] 1 Ch 656 at 673 and 679.
7 Companies Act 1985, s 9 (1) (see p 220, post).
8 Ibid, s 125 (4) (see p 221, post).
9 See Companies Act 1948, Table A, art 4. The question of the consent of a class of members to variations of their rights is now governed by the Companies Act 1985, s 125 (see p 221, post).
10 The consent of the class is also required by Companies Act 1985, s 125 (2) to (5) (see p 221, post).

of the class remain what they originally were.[11] Probably Lindley MR had this situation in mind when he said in *Allen v Gold Reefs of West Africa Ltd*:[12]

'I take it to be clear that an application for an allotment of shares on the terms of the company's articles does not exclude the power to alter them nor the application of them, when altered, to the shares so applied for and allotted. To exclude that power or the application of an altered article to particular shares, some clear and distinct agreement for that exclusion must be shewn, or some circumstances must be proved conferring a legal or equitable right on the shareholders to be treated by the company differently from other shareholders.'

That standard variation of rights clause formerly included in articles of association[9] provides uncontrovertible evidence of an agreement excluding the company's power to alter the original contract except in accordance with the clause itself, and the original contract includes the provision making the consent of the class of shareholders a condition precedent to the exercise of the power of alteration.

Increase in members' liability to contribute capital

By the Companies Act 1985, no alteration of the memorandum or articles of a company can impose a liability on members of the company at the date when the alteration is made to take more shares than they already hold, or to contribute more share capital or pay more money to the company than they have already agreed to contribute or pay.[13] The rule applies notwithstanding anything in the memorandum or articles to the contrary.[14] But if a member at the date of the alteration agrees in writing to be bound by it, he becomes individually bound by the terms of the alteration,[14] and it does not seem necessary that he should receive any consideration for his promise to make an additional payment or contribution.

The effect of the rule is to deny power to a company to raise further capital by coercing its members when it cannot raise the capital from them voluntarily. Such coercion might be exerted by a variety of alterations to the memorandum or articles, for example, by an alteration requiring each member to take a certain number of additional shares, or requiring him to take a number of debentures proportionate to his present shareholding, or by an alteration increasing the nominal value or decreasing the paid-up value of the company's issued shares, thereby increasing the amount of unpaid capital which the company could require shareholders to pay up. All such devices are made equally ineffective by the rule. But the section leaves untouched other devices for the compulsory raising of further capital which do not involve an alteration of the company's memorandum or articles. Thus, a company may by a reconstruction[15] increase its members' liability to contribute share capital, and a similar increase may result from a reduction of share capital approved by the court where the paid up value of issued shares is reduced but their nominal value remains the same.[16]

---

11 This is supported by the Companies Act 1985, s 125 (7), which treats the alteration of the provisions of the articles governing the procedure for the variation of the rights of a class of shareholders as equivalent to the variation of those rights themselves (see p 223, post).
12 [1900] 1 Ch 656 at 674.
13 Companies Act 1985, s 16 (1).
14 Ibid, s 16 (2).
15 A reconstruction is an operation by which a company transfers the whole of its assets to a new company in return for that company issuing the whole, or substantially the whole, of its share capital to shareholders of the original company.
16 See p 180, post

The court's power to amend the memorandum and articles

Before the Companies Act 1948, the court had no power to amend the memorandum or articles of a company, even where there was a drafting error which the court would rectify in the case of any other contract.[17] The court now has statutory powers to amend the memorandum or articles in any way it thinks fit on hearing a petition to cancel an alteration of the objects of the company,[18] or to cancel an alteration of a provision in the company's memorandum which could have been included in its articles,[19] or to cancel a resolution for the re-registration of a public company as a private one,[20] or for the giving by a private company of financial assistance for the acquisition of shares in it,[1] or for the purchase by a private company of shares in itself out of its capital,[2] or on a petition by a member for relief from the unfairly prejudicial conduct of the company's affairs.[3] If the court orders the amendment of the memorandum or articles, it may direct that the amendment shall not be further amended or amended in a specified manner without its consent,[4] but subject to such a direction the company may amend or cancel the alteration imposed by the court in the same way as it may amend other provisions in its memorandum or articles.[5] In exercising its powers under these provisions the court may only amend the memorandum or articles in order to give appropriate relief to the petitioners, and so it could not use its powers to correct drafting errors.

Charitable companies

Companies whose objects are wholly charitable in character[6] are subject to two restrictions on altering their memoranda or articles of association which do not apply to other companies.

Any alteration of the objects of a charitable company is ineffective unless the Charity Commissioners have consented in writing to the alteration before it is made, and when a printed copy of the altered memorandum of the company is delivered by it to the Registrar of Companies,[7] a copy of the Charity Commissioners' consent to the altered objects of the company must also be delivered.[8]

Secondly, if a company which is a charity alters its memorandum or articles in a manner which results in it ceasing to be a charity, the alteration is effective if it otherwise complies with the Companies Act, but the alteration does not affect the application in the future of:

(a) any property previously acquired by the company otherwise than for full consideration in money or money's worth (ie donations and purchases by the company at an undervalue) or property representing such property (eg the re-invested proceeds of sale by the company of such property);

(b) any property representing income accruing before the alteration is made (ie re-invested income); or

(c) the income from property falling under (b).[9]

---

17 *Scott v Frank F Scott (London) Ltd* [1940] Ch 794, [1940] 3 All ER 508.
18 Companies Act 1985, s 5 (5) (see p 68, ante).
19 Ibid, s 17 (3) (see p 73, ante).
20 Ibid, s 54 (6) (see p 65, post).
1   Ibid, s 157 (2) and (3) (see p 387, post).
2   Ibid, s 177 (3) (see p 196, post).
3   Ibid, s 461 (1) (see p 666, post).
4   Ibid, s 5 (6), s 17 (3), s 54 (8), s 157 (3), s 177 (4) and s 461 (3).
5   Ibid, s 5 (7), s 17 (3), s 54 (9), s 157 (3), s 177 (5) and s 461 (4).
6   Charities Act 1960, s 45 (1) and s 46 (5 Halsbury's Statutes (4th Edn) 858 and 860). For the meaning of charitable purposes, see 5 Halsbury's Laws (4th edn) paras 501–547.
7   Companies Act 1985, s 6 (1) (see p 74, ante).
8   Ibid, s 30A (2), inserted by Companies Act 1989, s 111 (1).
9   Ibid, s 30A (1), inserted by Companies Act 1989, s 111 (1).

CHAPTER 4

Contracts, torts and crimes

PRE-INCORPORATION CONTRACTS

Company's incapacity to contract before incorporation

A company cannot enter into a contract before it is incorporated, because it does not yet exist as a legal person. Nor, for the same reason, is it bound by contracts made by agents purporting to act on its behalf before its incorporation. By a strict application of this rule, it has been held[1] that a company may not after its incorporation ratify such a contract made on its behalf before it was incorporated. The creation of a contract by ratification presupposes that the only element lacking when the pretended agent purported to make the contract was the actual authority of his principal, but in the case of a company which was not incorporated at that date, actual authority could in no way have been given to the agent, because the company did not yet exist. It makes no difference that the contract limits the fund out of which the other contracting party is to be paid to the company's paid up capital.[2] Such a provision only states what the result of the contract would be if it were binding on the company; it cannot overcome the initial difficulty that the company cannot be bound at all. Nor for the same reason would it make any difference if the contract were expressly made conditional on the company being incorporated.

It was once held[3] that, wholly apart from the common law rules about ratification, a company can in equity adopt a contract made on its behalf before its incorporation, and thereby make itself a party to the contract. This decision has not been overruled, but it has been held in later cases[4] that adoption and ratification are one and the same thing, and are both subject to the common law rules stated above, so that it is not now possible for a company to make itself a party to a pre-incorporation contract by adopting it. The Jenkins Committee in 1962 recommended that companies should be given statutory power to adopt contracts made in their names or on their behalf before incorporation, and that this power should be unilateral and not dependent on the consent of the other party to the contract.[5] This proposal has not yet been embodied in legislation, however.

New contract after incorporation

If a company is to acquire rights or liabilities in consequence of negotiations before it was incorporated, it must be shown that a fresh contract has been made with it since its incorporation. It is not sufficient that the company's memorandum provides that it shall carry out the pre-incorporation contract,[6] nor that the company has

---

1 *Kelner v Baxter* (1866) LR 2 CP 174.
2 *Scott v Lord Ebury* (1867) LR 2 CP 255.
3 *Spiller v Paris Skating Rink Co* (1878) 7 ChD 368.
4 *Natal Land and Colonization Co Ltd v Pauline Colliery and Development Syndicate* [1904] AC 120; *Re National Motor Mail-Coach Co Ltd, Clinton's Claim* [1908] 2 Ch 515.
5 Report of the Company Law Committee (Cmnd 1749), para 54 (*a*).
6 *Melhado v Porto Alegre Rly Co* (1874) LR 9 CP 503.

acquiesced in the other contracting party treating it as liable to him,[7] for example, by sending invoices to the company for amounts owing under the pre-incorporation contract. Only the company's express agreement, or acts done by it which are necessarily referable to the making of a new contract,[8] will be sufficient to bind it. Thus, where a contract had been made before a company's incorporation by which it was to have an option to take a lease of lands thought to be coal bearing, and after its incorporation the company carried out trial borings and on discovering a seam of coal purported to exercise the option, it was held that the company's acts taken by themselves were equivocal and were insufficient for the court to infer the making of a new contract giving the company an option for a lease.[8] It will be particularly difficult to establish a new contract from the company's acts when they are done in performance of another contract made by the company with a third person. Thus, where the plaintiff licensed X or a company to be promoted by him to exploit a patent on certain terms, and X agreed with the company after he had procured its incorporation that it might use the patent on the same terms, it was held that performance of those terms by the company was not evidence of a new contract between the plaintiff and the company, because the company's acts were explicable by the contract between it and X.[9] Furthermore, an act by the company which is necessarily referable to a supposed new contract, does not of itself bring such a contract into existence. It will be interpreted merely as an offer, and unless there is evidence of acceptance by the other party to the pre-incorporation contract, there is no contract.[8] In this respect our courts have been less generous than those of the United States, which have held that a contract made before the company's incorporation takes effect as a continuing offer open for acceptance by the company, so that any act done by the company after its incorporation which is necessarily referable to the offer is an acceptance of it, and not merely an offer made by the company itself.[10]

A company will be bound by a new contract made after its incorporation only if it intended to enter into such a contract. Where it carries out part of the contract made before its incorporation because its directors mistakenly believe that it is bound by that contract, the company's acts are explicable by the mistaken belief; the company has no intention of entering into a new contract, and consequently no new contract is entered into.[11] The explanation of this lenient treatment of the company is not to be found in the rules relating to mistake as an element which invalidates a contract, for the directors' mistake may well be one of law. The reason why there is no contract is that the company had no intention of entering into one, because its directors believed it to be bound by the pre-incorporation contract, and the company is permitted to give evidence of its directors' state of mind to prove this. But whatever the directors' beliefs may be, if the company agrees with the other party to vary the terms of a contract made before its incorporation, the company will be bound by the contract as varied, because it must have had an intention to enter into a contract on the original terms as modified by the variations when it assented to the variations.[12]

---

7 *Scott v Lord Ebury* (1867) LR 2 CP 255.
8 *Natal Land and Colonization Co v Pauline Colliery and Development Syndicate* [1904] AC 120.
9 *Bagot Pneumatic Tyre Co v Clipper Pneumatic Tyre Co* [1902] 1 Ch 146.
10 *Wall v Niagara Mining and Smelting Co*, 20 Utah 474 (1899); *Knox v First Security Bank* (1952) 196 F 2d 112.
11 *Re Northumberland Avenue Hotel Co* (1886) 33 ChD 16; *Bagot Pneumatic Tyre Co v Clipper Pneumatic Tyre Co* [1901] 1 Ch 196.
12 *Howard v Patent Ivory Manufacturing Co* (1888) 38 ChD 156.

Alternative remedies in respect of pre-incorporation contracts

It is clearly unjust that neither the company nor the other party should benefit by the acquisition of property or money or the performance of services under contracts made before the company's incorporation without giving the consideration promised in return. The courts have therefore tried in some cases to give relief to the company or other party on some ground outside the law of contract. Thus, it has been held that where before the company's incorporation its promoters have performed services which have increased the value of the company's property, they can either enforce an equitable claim against that property for the value of their services,[13] or may recover the reasonable value of their services from the company by suing for a quantum meruit.[14] Where under a pre-incorporation contract money has been paid or property has been transferred, it has been held by the Court of Appeal that both the company and the other intended party may recover any money paid under the contract as money paid under a mistake of fact, and may recover any property transferred by the equitable process of restitution, but only if the payment or transfer was made after the company's incorporation.[15] Furthermore, as an alternative to restitution or where it is not possible (eg where the contract was for the performance of services), both the company and the other intended party may recover the value of work done under the contract as a quantum meruit, or, it would seem, the value of goods delivered as a quantum valebant, provided that the work was done or the goods were delivered after the company's incorporation.[15]

Again, it has been held that a person who contracts with the company's promoters purporting to represent it before its incorporation may enforce his claim against the company by being subrogated to the promoters' rights to an indemnity out of the company's assets for the expense of carrying out the contract.[16] This right of subrogation would appear to be of limited value, however, because the promoters are entitled to an indemnity for their expenses only if the company contracts to indemnify them after its incorporation.[17] The principle of subrogation was applied more extensively by Romer LJ in one case[18] where a promoter had entered into a pre-incorporation contract with the plaintiff for the grant of a patent licence to the promoter or a company to be formed by him, and the promoter had then entered into a new contract in identical terms with the company after its incorporation to grant the licence to it for the same consideration; Romer LJ held that the plaintiff was entitled to be subrogated to the promoter's rights under his contract with the company, even though they were not merely rights to be indemnified against the promoter's personal liability to the plaintiff under the first contract.

On the other hand, it has been held by the Court of Appeal in two decisions[19] that a person who has performed services for a company or incurred expense on its behalf before its incorporation has no claim against it or its assets, unless it contracts with him after its incorporation to satisfy his claim. In the present confused state of the decisions, the claimant's remedies are, therefore, very uncertain.

---

13 *Re Hereford and South Wales Waggon and Engineering Co* (1876) 2 ChD 621.
14 *Re Empress Engineering Co* (1880) 16 ChD 125.
15 *Rover International Ltd v Cannon Film Sales Ltd (No 3)* [1989] 3 All ER 423, [1989] 1 WLR 912, CA.
16 *Touche v Metropolitan Railway Warehousing Co* (1871) 6 Ch App 671.
17 *Melhado v Porto Alegre Rly Co* (1874) LR 9 CP 503.
18 *Bagot Pneumatic Tyre Co v Clipper Pneumatic Tyre Co* [1902] 1 Ch 146.
19 *Re English and Colonial Produce Co Ltd* [1906] 2 Ch 435; *Re National Motor Mail-Coach Co Ltd, Clinton's Claim* [1908] 2 Ch 515.

Pre-incorporation contracts bind the persons who make them

Although a contract made before a company's incorporation cannot bind the company, it is not wholly devoid of legal effect, even if all the persons who negotiated the contract are aware that the company has not yet been incorporated.[20] The contract takes effect as a personal contract with the persons who purport to contract on the company's behalf,[1] and they are liable to pay damages for failure to perform the promises made in the company's name or on its behalf; this is so despite the fact that the contract expressly provides that only the company's paid up capital shall be answerable for performance.[2] The persons who make the contract are liable to each other as parties to it, and the person, or persons, who purports to represent the company are not merely liable to pay damages for breach of their implied warranty that they had authority to contract on the company's behalf. This distinction may be of importance when the contract is specifically enforceable (eg a contract for the sale of land to the company), for there seems to be no reason why the vendor should not obtain an order of specific performance against the persons who make the contract instead of suing them for damages. Also because the contract is effective as one made personally by the person who purports to represent the company and the other parties to it, the former can enforce the contract against the latter by suing to recover any damages which he suffers as a result of breaches by the other party, and in appropriate cases he can also sue them for specific performance.

Formerly, these consequences did not ensue when a contract was made in the name of a company before its incorporation by a person who did not purport to contract on its behalf or as its agent, but simply described himself in the offer or acceptance as an officer of the company or as being in some other way connected with it.[3] Such contracts were simply as non-existent as the company in whose name they were made. However, statute now equates such contracts with those expressed to be made on behalf of a company before its incorporation, and they therefore take effect as contracts entered into personally by the persons who make them,[4] and the knowledge or ignorance of those persons of the fact that the company has not yet been incorporated is immaterial.[5]

Practices usually followed by promoters

From the foregoing it is clear that it is purposeless, and even dangerous, to make contracts on behalf of a company in course of formation. The simplest way of avoiding the difficulties created by the law is to incorporate the company first, and then have it enter into the contract. The costs of incorporation are comparatively small, so that even if the other party to the proposed contract refuses to enter into it with the company after they have been incurred, not much is lost. In order to bind the other party morally, if not legally, a draft contract is often approved by him before incorporation, and the objects clause of the company's memorandum is drawn so as to empower it to enter into a contract in the form of the draft. If it is essential that the other party should be contractually bound before incorporation, the promoters may contract with him personally, and then assign the benefit of the

---

20 *Phonogram Ltd v Lane* [1982] QB 938, [1981] 3 All ER 182.
1 *Kelner v Baxter* (1866) LR 2 CP 174; Companies Act 1985, s 36C (1), inserted by the Companies Act 1989, s 130 (4). The provision applies also to deeds executed in the name or on behalf of the company before its incorporation (Companies Act 1985, s 36C (2)).
2 *Scott v Lord Elbury* (1867) LR 2 CP 255.
3 *Newborne v Sensolid (Great Britain) Ltd* [1954] 1 QB 45, [1953] 1 All ER 708.
4 Companies Act 1985, s 36C (1), inserted by Companies Act 1989, s 130 (4).
5 *Phonogram Ltd v Lane*, supra.

contract to the company after it is incorporated. The disadvantage of doing this is that the promoters remain personally liable for the performance of their promises in the contract after the assignment to the company, and an undertaking by the company to indemnify them does not immunise them from liability. For this reason it is desirable, where possible, for the other party to the contract to agree that the promoters shall be released from their obligations if the company is willing to enter into an identical contract with the other party after it has been incorporated. The promoters will usually control the company at this stage, and will be able to ensure that it does offer to enter into an identical contract with the other party so as to procure their own release. If the contract is for the purchase of property or for a lease or hiring of property, and the other party will not agree to release the promoters on the company being willing to contract in their place, the promoters can alternatively protect themselves by taking an option to purchase the property or to take a lease or hire of it. When the company is incorporated they may assign the option to it, and it will then be able to compel the other party to sell, lease or let the property on hire to the company (as the case may be), without the promoters at any stage being exposed to personal liability for the purchase price or other consideration, and their only expenditure will be the consideration paid for the option.

CONTRACTS AND THE DOCTRINE OF ULTRA VIRES

Nature and origin of the doctrine

The classical doctrine of ultra vires is based on the fact that companies and other corporate bodies are formed to fulfil the specific limited purposes or objects stated in the documents constituting them, and are intended by their founders and persons who become members of them, as well as by the state which recognises their corporate status, to achieve those purposes or objects and nothing else. In its full form the doctrine limits the legal capacity of a company or corporate body to fulfilling the purposes or objects for which it was incorporated, and so it may not only be restrained from pursuing other purposes which are ultra vires or beyond its powers, but also any attempt by it to do so is a nullity and produces no legally effective results.

The doctrine of ultra vires had been worked out in some detail by the courts before the earliest Companies Acts were enacted. The doctrine was probably derived from public law, where the courts employed it to explain why, in order to protect private rights, they prevented public authorities from doing acts which were not authorised by the statutes under which they functioned. Traces of the idea that the public has an interest in keeping statutory bodies within the limits of their powers are seen in the early cases where the ultra vires rule was applied to companies.[6] There was justification for this, because many of the early statutory companies (such as railway and canal companies) had power to interfere with private rights for the purposes of their undertakings, and so in that respect they were as much public bodies as departments of the central government. In time, however, the ultra vires rule came to be based on two different theories, neither of which had any connection with public law. The first and older theory was simply that a company had power to do any act which its constitution did not forbid, so that if its constitution was silent as to whether it might do a certain act, it was free

---

6 *East Anglian Rlys Co v Eastern Counties Rly Co* (1851) 11 CB 775; *Taylor v Chichester and Midhurst Rly Co* (1867) LR 2 Exch 356 at 370, per Montague Smith J.

to do it.[7] This theory had much in common with the ultra vires rule in public law in that it treated the rule as imposing limitations on the company's otherwise unlimited capacity to do anything which a natural person could do. The second theory, upon which the law relating to companies incorporated under the Companies Acts has historically been based, equates the company's capacity to act with the sum total of the powers conferred on it by its constitution, and the company is treated as having legal capacity only to do those acts which its memorandum of association empowers it to do, or which are incidental to or consequential on the achievement of its express objects or the exercise of its express powers. By this theory, if the company's constitution is silent as to whether it may do a particular act, it cannot do it unless it is incidental to or consequential on the fulfilment of a stated object of the company or the exercise of an express power, and the ultra vires rule may be invoked to prevent the company from attempting to do the unauthorised act.[8]

It was fairly well settled from an early date that a company could not only be restrained from doing ultra vires acts at the suit of its members, but that any contract entered into by the company beyond its powers was void and could not be enforced against it.[9] The point was finally settled in *Taylor v Chichester and Midhurst Rly Co*,[10] despite a powerful dissenting judgment by Blackburn J who sought to restrict the application of the doctrine to actions brought by members against their company. If the opinion of Blackburn J had prevailed, the subsequent development of the law would have been relieved of much of the complexity and confusion revealed in the following pages, and would certainly have been far more just to persons who entered into contracts with companies. As it is, it has only been in consequence of legislation dating from 1972,[11] which has now been superseded by the provisions of the Companies Act 1989,[12] that the interests of persons dealing with a company, and of the company itself in respect of transactions entered into by it, have been effectively safeguarded from the ravages of the classical ultra vires doctrine. Nevertheless, despite the statutory changes, shareholders and members of companies have retained the preventive remedies which have always been available to them to restrain the managements of their companies from engaging in ultra vires activities.

Ashbury Railway Carriage and Iron Co v Riche

When the first Companies Acts were enacted it was uncertain whether the courts would apply the ultra vires rule to companies formed thereunder in the same way as it had previously been applied to companies incorporated by individual Acts of Parliament. Companies formed under the Companies Acts were corporations created under statute, and so under the theory that the ultra vires rule related to the capacity to act of all corporations (other than those created at common law by

---

7 *Norwich Corpn v Norfolk Rly Co* (1855) 4 E & B 397, per Erle J at 413–419; *Bateman v Ashton-under-Lyne Corpn* (1858) 3 H & N 323 at 335–336, per Martin B.

8 *Colman v Eastern Counties Rly Co* (1846) 10 Beav 1; *Salomons v Laing* (1850) 12 Beav 339; *East Anglian Rly Co v Eastern Counties Rly Co* (1851) 11 CB 775; *Eastern Counties Rly Co v Hawkes* (1855) 5 HL Cas 331; *Shrewsbury and Birmingham Rly Co (Directors) v North-Western Rly Co and Shropshire Union Rlys and Canal Co (Directors)* (1857) 6 HL Cas 113; *A-G v Great Eastern Rly Co* (1880) 5 App Cas 473.

9 *East Anglian Rly Co v Eastern Counties Rly Co*, supra; *Norwich Corpn v Norfolk Rly Co*, supra.

10 (1867) LR 2 Exch 356.

11 European Communities Act 1972, s 9 (1), re-enacted by Companies Act 1985, s 35 (1) and (2).

12 Companies Act 1985, ss 35, 35A and 35B, substituted and inserted by the Companies Act 1989, s 108 (1).

royal charter),[13] the rule should have applied to them. But, historically, the new companies were the successors of the former unincorporated joint stock companies, which were not subject to the ultra vires rule. The objects of these unincorporated companies set out in their deeds of settlement merely limited the authority of their directors to act so far as shareholders were concerned, and did not operate to upset contracts made with third persons who were unaware of the limitation on the directors' authority, or contracts to which the shareholders gave their unanimous consent.[14] Because of their historical origins, it was arguable that the new companies, too, should not be subject to the ultra vires rule, and that the objects clauses of their memoranda of association should not be regarded as lists of statutory powers outside which they could not act, but as merely limiting the kinds of business which they contracted with their members to carry on, the members having power to extend those limits at any time.

The uncertainty was settled by the House of Lords in *Ashbury Rly Carriage and Iron Co v Riche*[15] in favour of the ultra vires rule applying in full to companies formed under the Companies Acts. The company's objects clause was treated as conferring specific statutory powers outside which the company could not act, even with the unanimous consent of its members. Lord Cairns stated the ultra vires rule in terms of the now accepted 'capacity' theory. He said:[16]

'My Lords, this is the first section [now Companies Act 1985, s 1] which speaks of the incorporation of the company; but your Lordships will observe that it does not speak of that incorporation as the creation of a corporation with inherent common law rights, such rights as are by common law possessed by every corporation, and without any other limit than would by common law be assigned to them, but it speaks of the company being incorporated with reference to a memorandum of association; and you are referred thereby to the provisions which subsequently are to be found upon the subject of that memorandum of association.'

and, after referring to the requirement of the Act that the company's objects should be stated in its memorandum, he added:[17]

'... if that is the condition on which the corporation is established—if that is the purpose for which the corporation is established—it is a mode of incorporation which contains in it both that which is affirmative and that which is negative. It states affirmatively the ambit and extent of vitality and power which by law are given to the corporation, and it states, if it is necessary so to state, negatively, that nothing shall be done beyond that ambit, and that no attempt shall be made to use the corporate life for any other purpose than that which is so specified.'

A second reason given by the House of Lords for its decision was that a company is prohibited from altering its memorandum except in the manner authorised by the Act,[18] and if it could pursue activities not authorised by the objects clause of its

---

13 Chartered corporations have always been treated at common law as having the same unlimited capacity to enter into contracts and other transactions as individual persons of full age subject to no disability (*Sutton's Hospital Case* (1612) 10 Co Rep 1a, 23a and 30b; *Baroness Wenlock v River Dee Co* (1883) 36 ChD 675 at 685 per Bowen LJ; *British South Africa Co v De Beers Consolidated Mines Ltd* [1910] 1 Ch 354).

14 *Natusch v Irving* (1824) 2 Coop temp Cott 358; *Re Norwich Yarn Co, ex p Bignold* (1856) 22 Beav 143. These rules are now contained in the Partnership Act 1890, ss 8 and 24 (8) (32 Halsbury's Statutes (4th Edn) 642 and 649).

15 (1875) LR 7 HL 653.

16 Ibid, at 668.

17 Ibid, at 670.

18 Companies Act 1985, s 2 (7). At the date the *Ashbury* case was decided companies had no power to alter their objects clauses. Their present power to do so does not invalidate the argument, however, for the power of alteration which they now have can only be exercised on the terms prescribed by the Companies Act 1985.

memorandum, it would in effect be altering its memorandum in defiance of the Act. Lord Cairns LC linked this with the implied covenant[19] between the company and its members to comply with the conditions in its memorandum and articles. He said:[20]

> 'The covenant, therefore, is not merely that every member will observe the conditions on which the company is established, but that no change shall be made in those conditions; and if there is a covenant that no change shall be made in the objects for which the company is established, I apprehend that that includes within it the engagement that no object shall be pursued by the company, or attempted to be attained by the company in practice, except an object which is mentioned in the memorandum of association.'

Actions by members to restrain ultra vires acts

A member of a company has always had an inherent right to sue for an injunction to restrain the company[1] or its directors[2] from doing an ultra vires act and this right is preserved to members notwithstanding the changes made by the Companies Act 1989 to the legal capacity of a company and the binding effect of transactions entered into by it.[3] Only a member may sue for an injunction, however. A creditor has no title to sue, even though the ultra vires act will diminish the company's resources and make it less able to pay its debts.[4] This is so even if he is a secured creditor, unless the ultra vires act will affect the property on which his debt is secured.[5] A member who sues must, of course, show that the proposed act is ultra vires his own company, and so if his company proposes to enter into a contract with another company, he cannot sue to restrain his own company from contracting merely because the contract is ultra vires the other company.[6] For this reason, in a case where one company had agreed to sell its undertaking to another in consideration of the other allotting its shares to members of the vendor company, a member of the vendor company was held not entitled to sue to restrain the other company from paying an allegedly ultra vires underwriting commission in respect of the shares, even though the payment would diminish the value of the shares in the other company which the plaintiff and his fellow shareholders would eventually take.[7] The parties wanted to have the question settled, however, and the court overcame the difficulty by adding as a second plaintiff someone who had already taken shares in the purchasing company, and who was therefore entitled to sue for an injunction against it.

The invalidity of contracts made for ultra vires purposes at common law

The ultra vires rule at common law was self-executing in that all contracts made by a company which were not relevant to achieving its objects,[8] or authorised by

---

19 Companies Act 1985, s 14 (1).
20 (1875) LR 7 HL 653 at 670.
 1 *Colman v Eastern Counties Rly Co* (1846) 10 Beav 1; *Simpson v Westminster Palace Hotel Co* (1860) 8 HL Cas 712; *Maunsell v Midland Great Western (Ireland) Rly Co* (1863) 1 Hem & M 130; *Hoole v Great Western Rly Co* (1867) 3 Ch App 262.
 2 *Salomons v Laing* (1850) 12 Beav 339; *Spokes v Grosvenor Hotel Co* [1897] 2 QB 124.
 3 Companies Act 1985, s 35(2), substituted by Companies Act 1989, s 108(1).
 4 *Mills v Northern Rly of Buenos Ayres Co* (1870) 5 Ch App 621.
 5 *Lawrence v West Somerset Mineral Rly Co* [1918] 2 Ch 250; *Cross v Imperial Continental Gas Association* [1923] 2 Ch 553.
 6 *Maunsell v Midland Great Western (Ireland) Rly Co*, supra.
 7 *Booth v New Afrikander Gold Mining Co* [1903] 1 Ch 295.
 8 *Ashbury Railway Carriage and Iron Co Ltd v Riche* (1875) LR 7 HL 653.

its memorandum of association, or incidental to or consequential on the carrying out of its objects, were void.[9] Consequently, not only the company itself, but also the other party to the contract could rely on the fact that the contract was ultra vires in order to escape liability under it.[10] But a distinction was drawn between contracts which were patently ultra vires when they were compared with the company's memorandum, and contracts which such a comparison did not show to be necessarily outside the company's powers. The former kind of contract was absolutely void, and was enforceable neither by the company nor by the other party to it,[11] but the latter kind of contract was enforceable by the other party against the company if at the time when the contract was made he did not know and had no reason to believe that the company, or rather its management or the agent who represented it, entered into the contract in order to achieve a result which was ultra vires.[12] For example, if a company which had power to borrow raised a loan in order to use the money for an ultra vires purpose,[13] or guaranteed a loan made to another person for a purpose unconnected with the main objects of the company,[14] or mortgaged or charged its own assets to secure such a guarantee,[15] the lender could recover the loan from the company or enforce his guarantee, mortgage or charge if he was unaware of the purpose which the company sought to achieve when the transaction was entered into, but not if he was aware of that purpose.[16] Again, where a company's main object was the manufacture of women's clothing, but the company in fact manufactured veneered panels and bought a quantity of coke for the purpose, it was held that the coke merchant was disabled from suing for the price of the coke by the fact that he had notice that it was required for the ultra vires business of making veneered panels; if he had been ignorant of the purpose for which it was to be used, his claim would have succeeded.[17]

It was and still is important to distinguish contracts which are ultra vires a company and therefore void at common law, from contracts which are not ultra vires but beyond the powers of the directors or any other representative of the company conferred by or under the company's articles, and from contracts which are intra vires and within the directors' or representative's powers but entered into for an improper purpose, for example, to benefit the directors or the representative personally and not the company. It has always been possible for both of these latter kinds of contract to be confirmed or ratified by a general meeting of members of the company,[18] and in the absence of ratification it has never been possible for the company to rescind or repudiate the second kind of contract, unless the other party to the contract was aware of the improper purpose intended by the directors.[19]

A situation of this latter kind can, of course, only arise if the contract in question falls literally within one of the powers expressly conferred by the objects clause of the company's memorandum, and either the contract could by its nature be entered

9 *A-G v Great Eastern Rly Co* (1880) 5 App Cas 473.
10 *Bell Houses Ltd v City Wall Properties Ltd* [1966] 1 QB 207, [1965] 3 All ER 427; revsd on other grounds [1966] 2 QB 656, [1966] 2 All ER 674.
11 *Ashbury Rly Carriage and Iron Co v Riche* (1875) LR 7 HL 653.
12 *Re David Payne & Co Ltd* [1904] 2 Ch 608; *Rolled Steel Products (Holdings) Ltd v British Steel Corpn* [1982] Ch 478, [1982] 3 All ER 1057, affd on other grounds [1986] Ch 246, [1985] 3 All ER 52.
13 *Re David Payne & Co Ltd*, supra.
14 *Charterbridge Corpn Ltd v Lloyds Bank Ltd* [1970] Ch 62 at 74, [1969] 2 All ER 1185 at 1194; *Rolled Steel Products (Holdings) Ltd v British Steel Corpn.*
15 *Rolled Steel Products (Holdings) Ltd v British Steel Corpn*, supra.
16 *Hill v Manchester and Salford Water Works Co* (1831) 2 B & Ad 544.
17 *Re Jon Beauforte (London) Ltd* [1953] Ch 131, [1953] 1 All ER 634.
18 See pp 575 and 595, post.
19 *Charterbridge Corpn Ltd v Lloyds Bank Ltd* [1970] Ch 62, [1969] 2 All ER 1185.

into for the purpose of pursuing one of the company's main objects, or the objects clause expresses the powers conferred by each of its paragraphs to be independent main objects. For example, where a property development company had power by its objects clause to guarantee loans made to other persons, and it guaranteed a loan made to its holding company for the benefit of that company, it was held that the guarantee could not be ultra vires, because when the company's main objects, the power to give guarantees and the guarantee actually given were looked at, and the directors' motices were left out of account, it could not be said that the guarantee was necessarily inconsistent with the company's main objects.[19] To invalidate the guarantee the company had to rely on the directors' abuse of their powers in giving it, a quite separate cause for avoidance, and to succeed on this ground the company had additionally to prove the lender's knowledge of the directors' improper motives.[19] Similarly, when a company guaranteed the indebtedness of another company in which the first company's controlling shareholder was interested and charged its assets with amounts payable under the guarantee, it was held by the Court of Appeal that the guarantee and charge were not ultra vires, because the first company had power by the objects clause of its memorandum to enter into such transactions, but the guarantee and charge were nevertheless unenforceable by the creditor of the second company to whom they were given, because the motive of the directors of the first company was to benefit its controlling shareholder and the second company, and the creditor was aware of this improper motive.[20] If, of course, the power expressed in the objects clause of the company's memorandum is elevated by it to the status of a main object,[1] any enquiry as to the directors' motives in exercising it is completely excluded in determining whether their act was intra vires, because the pursuit of a purpose which has to be treated as a main object of the company must necessarily be intra vires and lawful.[2]

All the cases cited above[3] where contracts which were latently ultra vires were held unenforceable by the other contracting party if he was aware of the ultra vires purpose intended by the directors, could be subsumed under the present head and the contracts could be treated as unenforceable because of the directors' abuse of their powers in using the contract to achieve the ultra vires purpose. Nevertheless, contracts of this kind do form a distinct category, for a contract is not necessarily entered into for an ultra vires purpose if the directors abuse their powers in making it, and in fact the purpose they intend may be one which is expressly countenanced by the objects clause of the company's memorandum (eg directors contracting to pay one of their number excessive remuneration under a power in the objects clause to fix directors' remuneration). The difference between a contract which is latently ultra vires and one which was an abuse of the directors' powers is that the latter kind of contract can be affirmed by a general meeting of the company, whereas the former could not be ratified by a general meeting and made binding on both parties at common law.

The new dispensation under the Companies Act 1989

The purpose of the new rules enacted by the Companies Act 1989[4] is, subject to certain reservations, to validate transactions entered into by a company, even

---

20 *Rolled Steel Products (Holdings) Ltd v British Steel Corpn* [1986] Ch 246, [1985] 3 All ER 52, affg the
     decision of Vinelott J [1982] Ch 478, [1982] 3 All ER 1057, but rejecting his conclusion that the
     guarantee and charge were ultra vires.
 1 See p 18, ante.
 2 *Re Horsley and Weight Ltd* [1982] Ch 442, [1982] 3 All ER 1045.
 3 See p 95, ante.
 4 Companies Act 1989, ss 108, 109 and 111.

though they are ultra vires or beyond the company's objects and the powers conferred on it by its memorandum and articles of association; at the same time the new rules maintain the personal liability of the company's directors to it for loss caused by them engaging in ultra vires activities,[5] and preserve the right of individual members of the company to obtain injunctive relief to prevent the company and its directors from entering into ultra vires transactions and engaging in ultra vires activities.[6] In other words, the external operation of the ultra vires rule in invalidating transactions entered into by a company beyond its objects and powers is brought to an end, but the internal or disciplinary function of the rules for the protection of members or shareholders of the company is retained.

A company's legal capacity

The Companies Act 1985, as amended, now provides that 'the validity of an act done by a company shall not be called in question on the ground of lack of capacity by reason of anything in the company's memorandum'.[7] This provision is drafted in an oddly oblique manner. The provision does not provide that companies shall have full and unlimited legal capacity, so as to overrule the conclusion reached by the House of Lords in the leading case that their legal capacity was restricted to pursuing the objects expressed in their memorandum and articles of association;[8] instead the provision leaves the legal capacity of companies as it was at common law, but precludes both the company and the other parties to a contract or transaction in which the company is involved from questioning its validity on the ground that it is irrelevant to achieving the company's objects, or that it is outside the company's powers. Likewise, since the provision extends to acts as well as transactions of a company, both the company and any persons affected by its unilateral acts are precluded from disputing the validity or effectiveness of such acts (and their sufficiency to impose responsibilities or liabilities on the company and those other persons) on the ground that the acts are unconnected with the company's objects. Nevertheless, the result of the statutory provision is exactly the same as if it did confer full and unlimited legal capacity on a company so far as the validity and effectiveness of its acts and transactions are concerned, and the probable reason why the provision takes the form it does is to be found in the reservations contained later in the statutory provision where directors exceed their powers to represent the company.

The Companies Act 1989 expressly reserves the right of any member of a company, however small his shareholding or other interest in it, to 'bring proceedings to restrain the doing of an act which but for [the earlier part of the validating provision] would be beyond the company's capacity.[9] However, in order to preserve the unchallengeable character of the company's concluded acts and transactions, despite their ultra vires character, no such restraining proceedings 'shall lie in respect of an act to be done in fulfilment of a legal obligation arising from a previous act of the company',[9] eg an action to restrain the company from performing an ultra vires contract which it has entered into, or paying damages to the other party for not performing the contract.

Furthermore, notwithstanding the statutory provision, 'it remains the duty of the directors [of the company] to observe any limitations on their powers flowing

---

5 See p 98, post.
6 See text, post.
7 Companies Act 1985, s 35 (1), substituted by Companies Act 1989, s 108 (1).
8 *Ashbury Railway Carriage and Iron Co Ltd v Riche* (1875) LR 7 HL 653.
9 Companies Act 1985, s 35 (2), substituted by Companies Act 1989, s 108 (1).

from the company's memorandum',[10] and so if directors cause loss to their company by entering into and carrying out an ultra vires transaction or by doing an ultra vires act, they are liable to compensate the company for the breach of their fiduciary duty. Nevertheless, any act or transaction which is ultra vires the company may be ratified by the company and so made effective against it by a general meeting of the company passing a special resolution to that effect, and by a separate special resolution the company may release a director or any other person from liability to it for such an act.[10] The double resolution procedure is curious. The first resolution does not make the act or transaction in question binding on the company, because it is already conclusively treated as being within the legal capacity of the company by the earlier part of the statutory provision,[7] and any obligation or liability resulting from the act or transaction has already been incurred by the company; the function of the first ratifying resolution is merely to lay a foundation for the second special resolution, which exonerates the director or any other person concerned from liability to the company for a breach of any duty which he owes it to abstain from the act or transaction. It is arguable, however, that the first special resolution does also have a useful function in setting at rest any argument that the directors or other agents of the company were acting in disregard of any limitations on their authority to act on the company's behalf so as to bind it by the ultra vires act or transaction. This matter is dealt with separately below.

It should also be noted that a special resolution ratifying an ultra vires act or transaction can be passed only when the act has been done or the transaction entered into. Neither a special nor an ordinary resolution may authorise directors in advance to do an ultra vires act or to enter into an ultra vires transaction. The proper course by which a company may authorise the act or transaction in advance is for a special resolution to be passed by a general meeting altering the objects clause of the company's memorandum so as to empower the company to engage in the act or transaction before it is done or entered into. When an ultra vires act has already been done, it can be ratified under the statutory provision[10] only by the passing of a special resolution, whereas acts of directors or other officers of a company which are in excess of the powers conferred on them by the company's memorandum or articles but are not ultra vires the company, and acts which merely breach directors' fiduciary duties, can be ratified after the event or authorised in advance by ordinary resolutions passed by a general meeting.[11] The distinction between acts done on behalf of a company which are beyond its own powers, and acts which are within the company's powers but beyond its directors' powers, or which are not done by them in the interests of the company and for its benefit, is therefore still important.

Limitations on the directors' powers

To make ultra vires acts and transactions binding on a company, it was not sufficient for the Companies Act 1989 merely to provide that objections to them could not be taken on the ground that the acts or transactions exceeded the company's legal capacity. A company, unlike an individual, cannot act for itself, but must always act through officers or agents, whose authority, by the nature of their representative status, cannot be unlimited. The limitations imposed by law on their authority are threefold, namely:

10 Companies Act 1985, s 35 (3).
11 *Grant v United Kingdom Switchback Railways Co* (1880) 40 ChD 135; *Re London and New York Investment Corpn* [1895] 2 Ch 860; *Bamford v Bamford* [1970] Ch 212, [1969] 1 All ER 969 (see pp 575 and 595, post).

(1) by implication, they are not authorised to do acts or to enter into transactions on the company's behalf which are not for the purpose of pursuing the company's legitimate objects or exercising the powers conferred on it by its memorandum;

(2) they are not authorised to disregard other limitations, restrictions or conditions imposed on them by the company's memorandum or articles (eg a limitation on the total amount which the board of directors may borrow on the company's behalf, or a requirement that the board must obtain the consent of a general meeting before entering into specified transactions on the company's behalf); and

(3) they are not authorised to disregard instructions properly given to them by the company as to the exercise of their powers or authority.[12]

In order to make these limitations ineffective against persons who deal with a company's directors, officers or other agents in good faith, the Companies Act 1989 provides that 'In favour of a person dealing with a company in good faith, the power of the board of directors to bind the company, or authorise others to do so, shall be deemed to be free of any limitation under the company's constitution'.[13] Nevertheless, there is a provision in the Act similar to that in respect of the right of members to challenge intended acts and transactions on the ground that they are beyond the company's legal capacity.[14] This provision enables any member of a company to bring an action to restrain directors from doing any act which is beyond their powers as defined by the company's memorandum and articles, or by any resolution validly passed by a general or class meeting or by any valid agreement between members of the company or any class of them.[15] However, the provision does not enable a member to obtain an injunction on this ground to prevent the directors from fulfilling any legal obligation of the company or themselves resulting from an act they have already done or a transaction which they have already entered into.[15]

The components of the statutory protection for persons who deal with representatives of a company are complex. A person deals with a company for this purpose 'if he is a party to any transaction or other act to which the company is a party.'[16] The transaction or act which the other party claims to be binding on the company must be entered into with, or done by, the board of directors of the company, or by a person authorised by them,[13] such as an individual director, or two or more directors acting together, or an officer, agent or employee of the company. Where the act or transaction is effected by a person authorised by the board, it is within the powers of the board to authorise any of these persons to act on the company's behalf, and that power is deemed in favour of the other party to be free from any limitations imposed by the company's memorandum or articles;[17] consequently, the other party is not required to examine those documents to see whether they contain any restrictions on the board's power of delegation, or whether they contain any power for the board to delegate its powers at all.[13] The scope of the authority conferred on the delegate is, of course, subject to different considerations.

If the transaction in question is entered into as a result of a resolution of the

---

12 For the effectiveness of instructions as to the exercise of directors' powers given by a general meeting, see p 573, post.

13 Companies Act 1985, s 35A (1), inserted by Companies Act 1985, s 108 (1).

14 Companies Act 1985, s 35 (2).

15 Ibid, s 35A (4).

16 Companies Act 1985, s 35A (2).

17 Ibid, s 35B.

board approving all its terms or if the act of the company is resolved on by the board, the board's powers are in favour of the other party deemed to be unrestricted by anything contained in the company's memorandum and articles or in a resolution passed by a general meeting or an agreement between shareholders, and so if the other party acts in good faith, the transaction or act is inevitably binding on the company. This is not necessarily so where the person representing the company is a director or directors (not comprising the whole board) or an officer, agent or employee of the company. By the board resolution authorising him to act, restrictions may have been imposed on his authority, including restrictions implicit in the description of the transaction he is authorised to engage in. These restrictions will be of concern to the person who deals with him, and that person will be entitled to disregard such restrictions only if he can do so under the rules of agency law, either because the board has held out the authorised person as having a wider authority to act on the company's behalf than the board has given him, or because the authorised person has been appointed to a position in the company (eg managing director, manager) which normally carries the authority which he pretends to have.[18]

The references in the statutory provision to limitations on the board of directors' powers to act on the company's behalf or to authorise others to do so, mean limitations expressed in the company's memorandum or articles (including limitations on the powers of the company itself) and also limitations derived from resolutions passed by general meetings of the company, or by meetings of any class of its shareholders, and from agreements between the members of the company or between the members of a class.[19] For the statutory provision to apply, a limitation need not relate to the substance of the act or transaction in question, but may relate to the procedure by which it is effected (eg prescriptions in the articles as to the manner in which documents shall be executed on behalf of the company or the manner in which contracts or other transactions shall be effected by it).[20] Morever, a limitation may take the form of an express restriction, or it may be part of the affirmative definition of the board of directors' powers, where the powers conferred are less than those of the company itself (eg power for the board to borrow up to a stated amount on the company's behalf when there is no limitation on the company's own borrowing powers, or where the power conferred is subject to a proviso or condition, such as power for the board to act provided the approval of a general meeting is first obtained).[20]

An act or transaction is binding on a company despite failure to observe limitations imposed on the powers of its board of directors to effect it or to authorise any other person to effect it on the company's behalf, but the act or transaction is binding only in favour of a person who deals with the company in good faith.[13] Good faith is presumed on the part of such a person unless the contrary is proved,[16] and a party to a transaction with a company is not bound to inquire whether it is permitted by the company's memorandum, or whether limitations imposed on the powers of its board have been complied with.[1] Consequently, the person so dealing is not treated as having constructive notice of the contents of the company's

18 See p 126, post.
19 Companies Act 1985, s 35A (3).
20 *TCB Ltd v Gray* [1986] Ch 621, [1986] 1 All ER 587, affd [1987] Ch 458, [1987] 1 All ER 108, CA. This case was decided under the more limited protective provisions of the European Communities Act 1972, s 9 (1).
1 Companies Act 1985, s 35B. This makes inapplicable the doctrine of constructive notice applied by the House of Lords in *Ernest v Nicholls* (1857) 6 HL Cas 401. For a more general reversal of the doctrine of constructive notice to the public of company documents delivered by the Companies Registry, see Companies Act 1985, s 711A (1), inserted by Companies Act 1989, s 142 (1).

memorandum and articles because they are available for public inspection at the Companies Registry.[1] Moreover, a person dealing with company is not regarded as acting in bad faith by reason only of his knowing that the act or transaction to which he is a party is beyond the powers of its directors under its constitution.[16] This means that actual knowledge by such a person that the directors have not conformed to limitations on their own or the company's powers in the company's memorandum or articles, or in any shareholders' resolution or agreement, does not prevent him from treating the act or transaction as being valid and enforceable against the company. The company may repudiate the act or transaction, therefore, only if there is some other vitiating element present, such as fraud, misrepresentation, the exercise of undue influence over the company or its directors, the disregard of a fiduciary duty owed to the company by the person dealing with it, or the knowing concurrence by that person in breaches of fiduciary duties by directors, officers or agents of the company. But if such another vitiating element is present, the company may repudiate the act or transaction because of it alone under the general law, and its position is in no way altered by the act or transaction being also in disregard of limitations on its directors' powers.[2]

The statutory provision protecting persons dealing with a company in good faith makes the act or transaction binding and effective as regards the company, but does not expressly make it binding and effective as regards the other party. The question therefore arises whether the other party who acts in good faith can himself challenge the validity of the act or transaction if he later discovers that it was done or entered into in disregard of limitations on the board of directors' powers as defined by the company's memorandum and articles or by relevant shareholders' resolutions or agreements. If the reason why the board acted beyond its powers is that the act or transaction was ultra vires the company, it would appear that the other party cannot contend that the act or transaction is invalid or ineffective, because the provision of the Companies Act 1989, that its validity cannot be called into question on that ground, is objective and general, and applies both to the company and to the other party.[3] Whether the other party may repudiate the act or transaction because, although within the company's objects, it is in excess of the powers of its board of directors, or was done or entered into for an improper purpose or otherwise than for the company's benefit, is not determined by the Companies Act 1989. It would seem, curiously, that the other party could rely on either of these grounds to repudiate the transaction under the relevant principles of common law and equity, unless he affirms the act or transaction after discovering the defect attaching to it (eg by suing the company for its failure to perform its obligations under the transaction), so enabling it to rely upon the other party's breaches of his obligation under it by way of defence or counterclaim.

The scope of the new preclusive provision for the benefit of persons who deal with the board of directors of a company, or with persons to whom the board delegates authority to act on the company's behalf, goes wider than validating ultra vires acts and transactions in favour of persons acting in good faith, and reference to the statutory provision will therefore be made again in later chapters where the limits on directors' powers and the improper exercise of their powers are dealt with.[4] Nevertheless, the statutory provision is of crucial importance when acts or transactions of a company are challenged as being ultra vires, because the affirmation by the Companies Act 1989 of a company's effectively unlimited capacity to engage in acts and transactions is of no help to a person dealing with

2 Companies Act 1985, s 35A (1).
3 Ibid, s 35 (1).
4 See pp 121 and 131, post.

the company if he cannot overcome the first obstacle of making the company responsible for acts or transactions effected by the officers or agents who purported to represent it.

Transactions in which directors are interested

There are special provisions in the Companies Act 1989 which modify the rules discussed above where a director or directors of a company, or its holding or parent company, are interested in an act or transaction of the company which is ultra vires or is entered into or done in disregard of limitations on the powers of its board of directors. These provisions apply if the act is done or the transaction is entered into by the company in disregard of limitations on the powers of its board of directors, and the other party is, or one or more of the parties are, a director or directors of the company or its holding company,[5] or a person connected with such a director, or a company with whom he is associated.[6] A person is connected with a director if (not being himself or itself a director of the company or its holding company), he or it is:

(a) the director's spouse, minor child, adopted child or step child;
(b) a company or body corporate with which the director is associated;
(c) a trustee of a trust under which the director, his spouse or any of his minor children or any company or body corporate with which he is associated are beneficiaries or potential beneficiaries; or
(d) a person who is acting in his capacity as a partner of the director or any person with whom he is connected under the foregoing alternatives.[7]

A director is associated with a company or body corporate if he and persons connected with him are together interested in at least one fifth of the nominal value of the issued equity share capital of the company or body corporate, or if he and persons connected with him are together able to exercise or control the exercise of at least one fifth of the voting rights which are exercisable at a general meeting of the company or body corporate.[8]

Where the special provisions apply because of the interest of a director or a person connected with him or a company associated with him, the act or transaction in question is voidable by the company, but it ceases to be voidable if it is ratified by the company passing a special or ordinary resolution in general meeting (the kind of resolution apparently depending on whether the act or transaction is ultra vires the company or not), or if restitution of the money or other assests which were the subject matter of the act or transaction is no longer possible, or if the company has been indemnified for any loss or damage it has suffered from the act or transaction, or if rights under the act or transaction have been acquired in good faith and for value by a person other than a party to it who had no actual notice that the directors exceeded their powers in entering into or authorising the transaction or effecting the act.[9] Whether the act or transaction is avoided by the company or not, any director who is a party to it and any other person who is connected or associated with such a director, and who cannot prove that when he became a party to the act or transaction he was unaware that the act or transaction was entered into or effected in disregard of any limitations on the directors' powers,

---

5 For the definition of holding company and subsidiary for the purposes of the Companies Acts 1985 to 1989, see p 730, post.
6 Companies Act 1985, s 322A (1) and (8), inserted by Companies Act 1989, s 109 (1).
7 Companies Act 1985, s 346 (1) to (3).
8 Ibid, s 346 (4). For equity share capital, see p 247, post.
9 Companies Act 1985, s 322A (2) and (4).

is liable to account to the company for any gain made by him directly or indirectly from the act or transaction, and is also obliged to indemnify the company against any loss or damage resulting to it from the act or transaction.[10] If the parties to an act or transaction, to which a director or a person connected or associated with him is a party, also include another person or other persons who do not belong to either of those categories and who act in good faith, the act or transaction is not voidable by the company as against any such persons, and they can enforce rights arising under the act or transaction without regard to any limitations on the director's powers which have been exceeded.[11] However, any such person, or the company, may apply to the court either to affirm or to set aside the act or transaction, or to sever it, preserving the parts of it in which they are interested and cancelling the remainder, and the court may do so on such terms and conditions as it thinks just.[11]

Charitable companies

The statutory provisions as to the binding effect on a company of acts and transactions entered into in disregard of limitations on directors' powers apply in the case of companies whose objects are wholly charitable, but only in favour of persons who give full consideration in money or money's worth and do not know at the time of the act or transaction that it is not permitted by the company's memorandum and articles of association, or (as the case may be) that it is beyond the powers of its directors.[12] Such an act or transaction by a company which is a charity is also binding in favour of a person who satisfies the conditions for treating the act or transaction as binding which would apply if it were not a charity, if that person does not know at the time that the company is a charity.[12]

If an interest in property is created or transferred by a charitable company under a transaction which is voidable by it under these provisions, and the property or an interest in it is later acquired by a person for full consideration without actual notice of the circumstances which made the original transaction voidable, that person's title to the property or the interest in it which he acquires is valid and unaffected by the voidability of the original transaction.[13]

Finally, a charitable company can ratify an act or transaction which is ultra vires the company by a special resolution passed by a general meeting in the same way as any other company, but only if the Charity Commissioners give their prior written consent.[14]

Secondary remedies in respect of ultra vires contracts

While the classical ultra vires rule was in full operation at common law, the courts gave relief to a party to a contract or transaction with a company, which was irrelevant to pursuing its objects or was beyond its powers, whenever that party had wholly or partly performed his own obligations under the transaction and was met by the defence that it was ultra vires the company when he sought to enforce its obligations. This was also the case when the party seeking to enforce obligations arising under the transaction was the company itself. The plaintiff could not rely on the contract or transaction as the basis for suing because it was void, but instead the courts made available to the plaintiff a variety of common law and equitable remedies by way of restitution or redress which were not derived from the contract

10 Ibid, s 322A (3).
11 Ibid, s 322A (7).
12 Charities Act 1960, s 30B (1), inserted by Companies Act 1985, s 111 (1).
13 Charities Act 1960, s 30B (2).
14 Ibid, s 30B (4).

or transaction, but from the fact that the plaintiff had given benefits or suffered detriments as a result of carrying it out. These remedies included equitable tracing orders, where a company which lacked power to borrow, or to borrow beyond a certain amount, had received the amount of an unauthorised loan and had mixed it with its other cash resources, or had used the loan to acquire assets which it still owned, or where the company's assets when it was wound up were inflated by the fact that the proceeds of the loan or assets acquired with it must have been included among them.[15] Where an ultra vires loan made to a company was wholly or partly applied by it in discharging its debts, the lender could claim to be subrogated to the rights of the creditors who had been paid, and was treated as though the creditors had assigned the debts to him.[16] If the plaintiff had performed services for the benefit of the company or, possibly, if he had supplied goods to it under an ultra vires contract, he could recover the value of the services or goods by suing at common law for a quantum meruit or a quantum valebant,[17] and if he had paid money to the company and received no performance of its promises in return, he could recover the amount paid as money paid for a consideration which had wholly failed.[18]

Theoretically, these secondary remedies are still available to a plaintiff who has performed his obligations under an ultra vires transaction, but except where the company is insolvent and the remedy sought is of a proprietary character (such as an equitable tracing order), the plaintiff is better served by relying upon his right to enforce the other party's obligations under the terms of the contract, or transaction itself, in reliance on the statutory provisions for his protection which have been dealt with above. It is only in the case of ultra vires transactions entered into with a company by a director of it, or of its holding company, or by a person connected or associated with such a director,[19] or in the case of such transactions with a charitable company where the claimant knew that the company was acting beyond its powers or where he did not give full consideration himself,[20] that the secondary remedies will be the only ones available to the claimant. Because instances of this character will be rare, those remedies are not dealt with in detail here.[1]

THE FORM OF COMPANIES' CONTRACTS

A contract or other transaction must be in the proper form prescribed by law, or at least must conform to any formal requirements imposed by law, if it is to be legally recognised and enforced. Similarly, non-contractual documents, such as certificates of certain facts or authorisations to do certain acts, must by law conform to certain formal requirements. At common law corporations, including companies, were required to observe considerable formalities in this respect, and with certain exceptions, could only enter into contracts or authenticate non-contractual

---

15 *Sinclair v Brougham* [1914] AC 398.
16 *Cunliffe Brooks & Co v Blackburn and District Benefit Building Society* (1884) 9 App Cas 857, HL; *Re Wrexham, Mold and Connah's Quay Rly Co* (1899) 1 Ch 440.
17 *Bell Houses Ltd v City Wall Properties Ltd* [1966] 1 QB 207, [1965] 3 All ER 427, revsd on other grounds [1966] 2 QB 656, [1966] 2 All ER 674, CA.
18 *Re Phoenix Life Assurance Co, Burgess and Stock's Case* (1862) 2 John & H 441.
19 See p 102, ante.
20 See p 103, ante.
 1 For a detailed treatment of the secondary remedies, see the Fifth Edition of this work at pp 115 to 122.

documents by executing instruments in writing under their common seals. This is no longer so.[2]

Companies were formerly required to have a common seal, but this is no longer necessary.[3] If a company has a common seal, it may execute documents which are required by law to be executed as deeds by affixing its common seal,[4] normally, but not necessarily, attested by two of its directors or by a director and the secretary of the company.[5] Whether a company has a common seal or not, a document signed by a director and the secretary of the company, or by two directors, and expressed in any form of words to be executed by the company, now has the same effect as a document executed under its common seal.[6] If the document makes it clear that it is intended to be a deed, it has effect as a deed on its delivery, and it is presumed unless the contrary is shown that the document was delivered upon it being executed.[7]

Contractual and non-contractual documents

Companies formed under the Companies Acts have always been able to make their contracts in the same form as individuals.[8] Consequently, when the contract is one which individuals would have to make by deed (such as a legal conveyance, mortgage or lease of land,) a company, too, must make it by deed; but this does not prevent a verbal contract being enforced against a company when the plaintiff has partly performed his obligations, so that, if the contract were between individuals, equity would give him relief.[9] Again, when the contract is one which the law requires to be in writing, it may be made on behalf of the company in writing signed by a person authorised by it. This provision applies not only to contracts which the law requires to be made in writing, such as contracts for the sale or disposition of land and hire purchase and consumer credit agreements,[10] but also to contracts, such as contracts of guarantee, which are merely required to be evidenced by a written memorandum signed by the defendant,[11] and in this latter case it is not necessary that the memorandum should be prepared as part of the transaction, nor that the person authorised to sign it should be the agent who negotiated the contract.[12] Moreover, the requirement that the contract should be made in writing does not oust the jurisdiction of equity to enforce an oral contract which the plaintiff has partly performed.[9] Finally, if individuals could make the contract in question orally, so may a company, the contract being concluded on its

---

2 *Yarborough v Bank of England* (1812) 16 East 6; but see now Corporate Bodies' Contracts Act 1960, ss 1 and 2 (11 Halsbury's Statutes (4th Edn) 213).
3 Companies Act 1985, s 36A (3), inserted by Companies Act 1989, s 130 (2).
4 Ibid, s 36A (2).
5 Table A, reg 101 provides that the board of directors shall determine who shall attest the affixation of the company's common seal, and unless otherwise determined it shall be attested by a director and the secretary or by two directors.
6 Companies Act 1985, s 36A (4).
7 Ibid, s 36A (5).
8 Companies Act 1985, s 36, substituting Companies Act 1989, s 130 (1). This section re-enacts the provisions of earlier Companies Acts.
9 *Wilson v West Hartlepool Rly Co* (1865) 2 De G J & Sm 475.
10 Law of Property (Miscellaneous Provisions) Act 1989, s 2 (1) to (3) (37S Halsbury's Statutes (4th edn) Real Property 8); Consumer Credit Act 1974, s 61 (1) (11 Halsbury's Statutes (4th Edn) 57).
11 Statute of Frauds (1677), s 4 (11 Halsbury's Statutes (4th Edn) 205); *Beer v London and Paris Hotel Co* (1875) LR 20 Eq 412.
12 *Jones v Victoria Graving Dock Co* (1877) 2 QBD 314 (where the memorandum was a minute of a resolution of the directors that the contract should be entered into; the minute was signed by the chairman of the board of directors under an authority given to him by the articles to authenticate the minutes of board meetings).

behalf by a person authorised by it. These provisions, of course, prescribe minimum formalities. There is nothing to prevent a company from observing greater formalities than the law requires, and so a contract made under its common seal is fully effective, even though the law only requires it to be made or evidenced in writing, or permits it to be made orally.

When a company has to execute an instrument in writing which is not a contract or a written memorandum of a contract, its board of directors may appoint an agent to execute it on the company's behalf by signing, or signing and sealing it, as the case may require.[13] This power is useful when notices have to be given or demands made under the terms of a contract already entered into by the company, as well as in cases where no contract is involved at all. In this connection the Companies Act 1985 provides that a document or proceeding requiring authentication by a company may be signed on its behalf by a director, secretary or other duly authorised officer of the company.[14]

Negotiable instruments

A bill of exchange, cheque or promissory note may be drawn, made, accepted or indorsed on behalf of a company by any person authorised by it signing its name, or signing his own name and adding words showing that he signs on behalf of the company.[15] The usual form of signature is the latter one, of which the following is an example:

For [and on behalf of] XYZ Ltd

AB   Director

CD   Secretary

If the person who draws a bill or cheque signs it with his own name and merely adds words describing himself as an officer of the company, the bill or cheque is issued by him and not by the company, and he is personally liable in respect of it.[16] Likewise, if directors make a promissory note by which 'the directors of the company [naming it] promise to pay' a certain sum, the note is their note and they are liable to pay the sum promised, and it makes no difference that they sign their names at the foot of the note 'for and on behalf of the company'.[17] On the other hand, if directors or other persons acting for a company sign cheques with their personal signatures immediately beneath a printed or typed statement of the company's name and no words are added to show that the signatories sign on the company's behalf, the cheque is the company's cheque and not one issued by the signatories personally, and they are not liable on it if the company does not pay it.[18]

The Bills of Exchange Act 1882[19] provides that 'in determining whether a signature on a bill [cheque or promissory note] is that of the principal or that of the agent by whose hand it is written, the construction most favourable to the validity of the instrument shall be adopted'. Consequently, if a bill is drawn on a company, and the directors accept it by writing their signatures across it with the addition, 'directors of the company [naming it]', the bill is accepted by the company, because if the acceptance were read as that of the directors personally, it

---

13 Law of Property Act 1925, s 74 (2) (37 Halsbury's Statutes (4th Edn) 176).
14 Companies Act 1985, s 41, as amended by Companies Act 1989, s 130 (7) and Sch 17, para 4.
15 Ibid, s 37.
16 *Landes v Marcus and Davids* (1909) 25 TLR 478; *Kettle v Dunster and Wakefield* (1927) 138 LT 158.
17 *Dutton v Marsh* (1871) LR 6 QB 361; *Penkivil v Connell* (1850) 5 Exch 381.
18 *Bondina Ltd v Rollaway Shower Blinds Ltd* [1986] 1 All ER 564, [1986] 1 WLR 517.
19 Bills of Exchange Act 1882, s 26 (2) (5 Halsbury's Statutes (4th Edn) 349).

would be ineffective, as only the person on whom a bill is drawn, here the company, can accept it.[20] For the same reason bills, cheques and promissory notes drawn in favour of a company are validly indorsed on its behalf by the personal signatures of its directors or other agents with an addition describing them as such. There is no conflict with the Companies Act 1985 in this, because the form of signature prescribed by it is merely permissive, and does not exclude other modes of signing negotiable instruments on behalf of a company which are permitted by the general law.

Personal liability of signatories

The requirement of the Companies Act 1985, that a company must have its name mentioned in all its business letters, official publications, bills of exchange, cheques, promissory notes, orders for money or goods, and invoices and receipts, has already been adverted to.[1] If an officer of the company or any person acting on its behalf signs or authorises the signature of a negotiable instrument or order for money or goods which does not mention the company's name in full, he is liable to the holder of the document for the obligation embodied in it if the company does not satisfy that obligation.[2] The word 'holder' is inapposite for an order for the payment of money or delivery of goods to the company, but it has been construed to mean the person to whom the order is addressed and who is to benefit by it.[3] It should be noticed that personal liability attaches not only to the person who signs the irregular document, but also to the person who authorises its signature.[4] However, a person who gives such an authority is personally liable only if he expressly authorises the signature by another of a document which he knows will be irregular, or does so implicitly because he knows the document which the signatory will use is one which is irregular (eg a pre-printed form which does not contain a correct statement of the company's name).[4] The statutory liability imposed on a person who signs or authorises the signature of a document which does not set out the company's name correctly is a secondary or collateral one, and not that of a surety or guarantor. Consequently, the fact that the company's obligations under the document are subsequently varied without the consent of the signatory, or that an extended time is allowed by the holder of the document for performance of the company's obligations, or that the company's obligations are discharged otherwise than by fulfilment, does not release or vary the signatory's statutory liability.[5]

The fact that an officer of the company is liable in respect of a document which should, but does not, set out the company's name in full does not exonerate the company if it is liable in accordance with the rules discussed in this chapter, and if the company is liable, it would appear that the officer or a gent who has been compelled to satisfy the obligation may recover an indemnity from it.[6] The policy behind the imposition of personal liability on the company's officers and agents is to ensure proper publicity of the company's name. It is not an exception to the rule about the company's separate legal responsibility, as is clearly shown by the fact that the company remains liable in respect of the irregular document. It may best be considered as a statutory extension of the personal liability of an agent who

---

20 *Elliott v Bax-Ironside* [1925] 2 KB 301.
1 Companies Act 1985, s 349 (1) (see p 8, ante).
2 Ibid, s 349 (4).
3 *Civil Service Co-operative Society Ltd v Chapman* (1914) 30 TLR 679.
4 *John Wilkes (Footwear) Ltd v Lee International (Footwear) Ltd* [1985] BCLC 444, 1 BCC 99 452.
5 *British Airways Board v Parish* [1979] 2 Lloyd's Rep 361.
6 The officer may recover any money paid by him as money paid to the use of the company (*Brook's Wharf and Bull Wharf Ltd v Goodman Bros* [1937] 1 KB 534, [1936] 3 All ER 696).

contracts with another person without disclosing the fact that he is an agent. For this reason it is a defence to an action brought against the signatory of a document within the provision that the defective statement of the company's name was inserted by the plaintiff himself, because the plaintiff thereby takes responsibility on himself for the correctness of the name.[7] But this defence is a personal one, and would not be available against a subsequent holder in due course of a negotiable instrument in which the company's name is defectively stated.[7] Nor is the defence available if the signatory must have realised that the company's name was not correctly set out in the document when he signed it, for example, because the document mentioned the name under which the company carried on business instead of its corporate name and the two names did not resemble each other.[8] In such circumstances it makes no difference to the defendant's liability that he signed the acceptance of a bill of exchange drawn on the company in an incorrect or incomplete name by writing the company's name in the acceptance in the same manner, because he could properly have signed the acceptance on behalf of the company in its correct name.[9] The personal liability of the signatory of a document in which the company's name is given incompletely or incorrectly cannot be avoided by the signatory seeking to have the document rectified on the ground that both the company and the other party intended that the company, and not the signatory, should be a party to it.[10] Rectification is ordered only when the document signed by or on behalf of the parties fails to express their mutual intentions accurately, which is not so when the company's name is mis-stated, because both parties intended that the company shall be a party to the transaction to which the document relates, and it is such a party, and so there is no mistake to be rectified.[10]

TORTS AND CRIMES

It has been long established that a company, like any other employer, is liable for the torts of its employees committed within the scope of their employment, and this is so even though the tort involves wilful wrongdoing, malice or fraud.[11] Likewise, it is clear that a company may be prosecuted for the crimes of its officers or employees if the statute creating the offence is interpreted as imposing liability on the company or employer as well as on the officer or employee.[12] The court has in the past inclined strongly toward interpreting statutes as imposing criminal liability on companies or employers when the offence was committed while the officer or employee was acting within the scope of his employment,[13] and it has been held immaterial that the offence is one which requires mens rea, which the company, as a legal abstraction, cannot have, and which its board of directors in fact did not have. There is at present a tendency in the opposite direction, however, and in three more recent cases[14] the court has refused to infer that a statute imposes

---

7 *Durham Fancy Goods Ltd v Michael Jackson (Fancy Goods) Ltd* [1968] 2 QB 839, [1968] 2 All ER 987.
8 *Maxform SpA v Mariani & Goodville Ltd* [1979] 2 Lloyd's Rep 385; affd [1981] 2 Lloyd's Rep 54.
9 *Lindholst & Co A/S v Fowler* [1988] BCLC 166, 4 BCC 776.
10 *Blum v OCP Repartition SA* [1988] BCLC 170, (1988) 4 BCC 471.
11 *Barwick v English Joint Stock Bank* (1867) LR 2 Exch 259; *Citizens' Life Assurance Co v Brown* [1904] AC 423.
12 *Pearks Gunston and Tee Ltd v Ward* [1902] 2 KB 1; *Chuter v Freeth and Pocock Ltd* [1911] 2 KB 832; *Mousell Bros Ltd v London and North-Western Rly Co* [1917] 2 KB 836.
13 *Director of Public Prosecutions v Kent and Sussex Contractors Ltd* [1944] KB 146 at 156, [1944] 1 All ER 119 at 124.
14 *Tesco Supermarkets Ltd v Nattrass* [1972] AC 153, [1971] 2 All ER 127; *R v Andrews Weatherfoil Ltd* [1972] 1 All ER 65, [1972] 1 WLR 118; *R v HM Coroner for East Kent, ex p Spooner* (1987) 3 BCC 636.

criminal liability on a company in the absence of active participation in the crime by the person or persons who manage its affairs generally, participation by a senior employee or employees being insufficient. Although the liability of companies for torts and crimes is extensive, it is still based on the concept of the liability of a master for the wrongs of his servants, so that a company is never liable in tort or criminally for the wrongs of its shareholders acting as such, for they are neither employees nor agents of the company and cannot act in its name or on its behalf.

Two problems in respect of the company's liability have not yet been explored in detail by the courts. They are: (a) for what acts of the governing body of the company is the company responsible? and (b) how far is the company liable for wrongful acts done in the course of pursuing objects which are ultra vires the company?

With regard to the first problems it is clear that the company is liable in tort for all wrongful acts and omissions of the persons who control the management of its undertaking when they are acting as such.[15] Those persons may be the directors collectively, or they may be merely those of the directors who in fact manage the company's business,[16] or the organ of management may be a single managing director,[17] or even a manager who is not a director at all.[18] The court is not bound by the formal provisions of the company's memorandum and articles in discovering who controls the management of the company's business; the answer in each case will depend on the way the company's affairs are actually managed at the date the tort is committed. The court has adopted the same rule in criminal cases,[19] and has held that even when a criminal act has been done by a director or a managing director of the company for its benefit or in the course of carrying on its business, the prosecution must still prove that that person or those persons, if two or more of them acted together, controlled the management of the company at the time if the company is to be convicted.[20] This is not to say, of course, that in the circumstances of a particular company one managing or other director may not be found to be in de facto control, and in that case his criminal act in his capacity as managing director would also be the crime of the company. On the other hand, it has been held that a sole director of a company cannot be convicted of conspiring with the company itself; this is because conspiracy requires the participation of two or more active intelligences, and the company, as a legal abstraction, has no active intelligence, its acts being determined by the will of its sole director.[20] The importance of the company's liability for the wrongs of the persons who control its management lies in the fact that the company may be liable even though those persons acted outside the scope of their authority delegated by the company's articles or by a resolution of its board of directors. The company may certainly be criminally liable for the wrongful act of its managing director, even though the act was unconnected with the performance of his duties,[1] and it is practically certain that liability would similarly attach in tort in view of the way the court treats the acts of the company's organ of management as being the acts of the company itself.[2]

The other problem, whether the company is liable for torts and crimes committed

---

15 *Lennard's Carrying Co v Asiatic Petroleum Co Ltd* [1915] AC 705 at 713–14.
16 *Prudential Assurance Co Ltd v Newman Industries Ltd (No 2)* [1981] Ch 257 at 328, [1980] 2 All ER 841 at 878. The court gave no ruling on this point on appeal [1982] Ch 204, [1982] 1 All ER 354.
17 *Rudd v Elder Dempster & Co Ltd* [1933] 1 KB 566 at 594.
18 *Tesco Supermarkets Ltd v Nattrass*, supra.
19 *R v Andrews Weatherfoil Ltd*, supra.
20 *R v McDonnell* [1966] 1 QB 233, [1966] 1 All ER 193.
1 *R v ICR Haulage Ltd* [1944] KB 551 at 559, [1944] 1 All ER 691 at 695.
2 *Lennard's Carrying Co v Asiatic Petroleum Co*, supra.

by its officers or employees in the course of activities which are ultra vires the company, has as yet received scant attention from the courts. It is certain that, although an ordinary employee has implied authority to do acts necessary for the performance of the work he is employed to do, so as to make the company liable if he does them tortiously,[3] an employee has no implied authority to do an act which is ultra vires the company, and the company will not be liable if he does such an act tortiously.[4] On the other hand, it seems that the company will be liable if its organ of management commits or expressly authorises a tort in the course of pursuing an ultra vires object,[5] and it follows from this that the company will be liable for a tort similarly committed by an ordinary employee if its organ of management employs him in carrying on an ultra vires activity. The court has never been called upon to deal with the defence of ultra vires in a criminal prosecution of a company, but presumably the law would be the same as in an action against it in tort. The statutory provisions which protect a person dealing in good faith with a company in connection with a contract or other transaction which is ultra vires the company, or which is entered into in disregard of limitations on the authority of its board of directors[6] are not applicable in determining the tort or criminal liability of the company, because the effect of those provisions is merely to make the contract or transaction binding on the company, and not to impose liability for wrongs resulting from it being carried out, or carried out defectively.

---

3 *Citizens' Life Assurance Co v Brown* [1904] AC 423 at 427.
4 *Poulton v London and South Western Rly Co* (1867) LR 2 QB 534, as explained in *Campbell v Paddington Corpn* [1911] 1 KB 869 at 878, and *Ormiston v Great Western Rly Co* [1917] 1 KB 598 at 602.
5 *Campbell v Paddington Corpn,* supra. This conclusion is amply supported by American decisions (*First National Bank of Carlise v Graham* (1880) 100 US 669; *Nims v Mount Hermon Boys' School* (1893) 160 Mass 177; *Smith v First Bank of Casselton* 268 Fed 780 (1920); affd 254 US 655 (1920)). It is, moreover, logical; the contrary rule would make the company's funds immune from liability for injuries inflicted in the course of carrying on the very activities which they were used to finance.
6 See pp 96 to 101, ante.

CHAPTER 5

The protection of persons dealing with a company

A person who dealt with a company was at common law deemed to have notice of the contents of its memorandum and articles of association when the company's incorporation had been published in the London Gazette,[1] and also had constructive notice of the contents of the other documents which companies were required to deliver and had delivered to the Registrar of Companies, provided they were open to public inspection and had been gazetted where necessary.[2] This is no longer so since an amendment was made in 1989 to the Companies Act 1985, providing that a person shall not be taken to have notice of any matter merely because it is disclosed in a document delivered to the Registrar of Companies and so is available to public inspection, but this does not affect the question whether a person is affected by notice of any matter because he has failed to make such inquiries as ought reasonably to be made,[3] presumably including inspecting documents of the company which have been filed at the Companies Registry. The statutorily modified doctrine of constructive notice may therefore, according to the circumstances, mean that a person will be treated as being aware of the contents of certain documents filed in respect of the company with which he deals. These documents will tell the person who deals with the company what objects it may pursue, how much share capital it has issued and may issue in the future, how much unpaid capital remains to be paid by its shareholders, how its board of directors is constituted, what powers its board of directors and its members in general meeting may respectively exercise, what its net assets and profits or loss were at the end of its most recent complete financial year for which accounts have been filed, and how much of its indebtedness is secured by mortgages and charges created by it over its assets.[4] In theory, therefore, a person who deals with a company cannot complain if a transaction which he enters into with the company is held to be invalid because it patently conflicts with the provisions or requirements of those documents which he could, and should in the circumstances, have inspected, at the Companies Registry.

Even the statutorily modified doctrine of constructive notice of the contents of the documents relating to a company which are available for inspection at the Companies Registry, is operative only in those circumstances where statute has not given an even wider protection to persons dealing in good faith with a company. The most important of these wider protective enactments is that introduced in 1989, by which in favour of a person dealing in good faith with a company the power of its board of directors to bind it by an act or transaction or to authorise other persons to do so is deemed to be free from any limitation imposed by the company's memorandum and articles, or by resolutions passed by a general

---

1 *Ernest v Nicholls* (1857) 6 HL Cas 401; Companies Act 1985, s 42 (1) and s 711.
2 Ibid; *Wilson v Kelland* [1910] 2 Ch 306. These other documents will be dealt with hereafter in connection with the subjects to which they relate.
3 Companies Act 1985, s 711A(1) and (2), inserted by Companies Act 1989, s 142 (1).
4 There are separate special provisions relating to constructive notice of matters disclosed in filed particulars of mortgages and charges created by a company over its assets (Companies Act 1985, s 416 (1) to (3), inserted by Companies Act 1989, s 103 (see p 521, post)).

meeting of the company or a meeting of any class of its shareholders, or by any agreement between its members or any class of its shareholders, and for this purpose a person dealing with the company is regarded as acting in good faith notwithstanding his knowing that an act is beyond the directors' powers.[5] As was shown in the preceding chapter, this provision enables parties to ultra vires transactions with a company, and to transactions which are not ultra vires but beyond the powers of the company's board of directors as defined by its memorandum and articles, to enforce the transactions against the company and to have them treated as valid and binding on it. The protective provision has a wider operation than this, however, but its full extent will only be determined over a period of time by judicial decision.

Apart from statutory protection, the rules of common law established over the last 150 years have already provided extensive protection for persons dealing with a company in good faith where the act or transaction concerning or involving such persons is not ultra vires and beyond the company's powers. This has been achieved by the courts establishing a principle known as the rule in *Royal British Bank v Turquand*,[6] one of the earliest cases in which it was applied. Until the scope of the statutory protection afforded by law to a person dealing with a company in good faith has been determined, the decisions under the rule in *Turquand*'s case will continue to be of importance in determining the minimum protection afforded by law. The rule prescribes that if a person deals in good faith with the board of directors or other representative body of a company which is in fact exercising powers of management and direction of its business and affairs, that person is not affected by defects of procedure within the company or failure to fulfil conditions which are prescribed by the company's memorandum or articles to be fulfilled before the act or transaction in question is effected. The reason for the rule is not simply one of business convenience, although it obviously does reduce the enquiries which a person dealing with a company must make. The legal basis of the rule is that a person dealing with a company has no right to insist on proof by its directors that the provisions of its memorandum or articles have been complied with, and he cannot therefore be deemed to have constructive notice of some failure to comply which he has no means of discovering.[7] Of course, a person dealing with a company will not be able to rely on the rule, and the company may refuse to be bound by the transaction, if he knows that there has been some failure to comply,[8] or if he knows facts which would lead a reasonable man to enquire further and thus to discover the failure to comply,[9] or if he could and should in the circumstances have discovered the defect by inspecting documents filed with the Registrar of Companies which are open to public inspection,[10] provided they have been gazetted where necessary.[11]

The rule in *Royal British Bank v Turquand* is designed to protect persons dealing

---

5 Companies Act 1985, s 35A (1) to (3), inserted by Companies Act 1989, s 108 (1).
6 (1855) 5 E & B 248.
7 *Gloucester County Bank v Rudry Merthyr Steam and House Coal Colliery Co* [1895] 1 Ch 629 at 636 per Lindley LJ.
8 *Howard v Patent Ivory Manufacturing Co* (1888) 38 ChD 156.
9 *Kansen v Rialto (West End) Ltd* [1944] Ch 346, [1944] 1 All ER 751; affd sub nom *Morris v Kanssen* [1946] AC 459, [1946] 1 All ER 586; but contra *Channel Collieries Trust Ltd v Dover, St Margaret's and Martin Mill Light Rly Co* [1914] 2 Ch 506.
10 Including the fact that a document which would have been filed if the transaction had been properly carried out, has not been filed (eg notice of a special resolution having been passed) (*Irvine v Union Bank of Australia* (1877) 2 App Cas 366). But third persons are not treated as having constructive notice of the contents of documents other than those filed at the Companies Registry merely because a filed document makes reference to them (*Wilson v Kelland* [1910] 2 Ch 306).
11 Companies Act 1985, s 42 (1) and (2) and s 711 (1) and (2).

with the company, not to protect the company itself, and so there is no reason why a person who enters into a transaction with a company should not rely on the company's failure to comply with its memorandum or articles as a defence when the company sues him,[12] though, here again, if he knows of the failure to comply when the transaction is entered into and the defect is purely procedural, the court may hold that he has waived his right to object, so that the transaction is binding on both him and the company.[13] However, the fact that a defective transaction has been notified to the Registrar of Companies or gazetted makes no difference when it is the person who deals with a company who contends that the transaction is not binding on him. Registration and gazetting in no way validate acts of the company which are invalid or ineffective.

Closely connected with cases under the rule in *Royal British Bank v Turquand* are cases involving questions about the scope of the apparent authority of directors and other agents of a company to enter into transactions on its behalf. These cases do not really come within the rule at all, although they are often treated as though they do. They are in fact part of the common law of agency, and the rules applicable to them are in some respects different from the rule in *Royal British Bank v Turquand*. Nevertheless, there are some situations where both the rules of agency law and the rule in *Turquand's* case are applicable. Because of this, the cases on the apparent authority of the company's agents are deferred until later in this chapter, and they are dealt with there in conjunction with the statutory protection enacted in 1989 for the protection of persons dealing with the board of directors of a company or with persons whom they have authorised to act.

APPLICATION OF THE RULE IN *ROYAL BRITISH BANK v TURQUAND*

The cases decided under the rule in *Turquand's* case have usually involved one of three kinds of defects, namely, (a) the defective appointment of a director, or a director continuing to act for a company after he has ceased to be a director; (b) failure to hold a properly convened board meeting to authorise the company to enter into a transaction; and (c) a disregard of the limitations imposed on the directors' authority by the memorandum or articles. The cases will be examined under those heads.

Defects in a director's title to office

De facto directors

A leading example of this type of case is *Mahony v East Holyford Mining Co.*[14] There, a company was formed by one Wadge to purchase a mine belonging to him at a price much in excess of its real value. The memorandum and articles were subscribed by two persons. Hoare and Wall (who subsequently joined Wadge in directing the company's affairs), four clerks employed by Wadge at the address which become the company's registered office, and one independent person, McNally. The articles provided that the subscribers of the memorandum should

---

12 *Howbeach Coal Co Ltd v Teague* (1860) 5 H & N 151; *Garden Gully United Quartz Mining Co v McLister* (1875) 1 App Cas 39; *Re Alma Spinning Co, Bottomley's Case* (1880) 16 ChD 681. In all these cases the defendant was a member of the company, but there is no reason why the same principle should not apply when the defendant is an outsider.
13 *Re Home and Foreign Investment and Agency Co Ltd* [1912] 1 Ch 72.
14 (1875) LR 7 HL 869.

appoint the first directors, but in fact none were ever appointed. Instead Wadge, Hoare and Wall managed the company's affairs from its registered office, and issued a prospectus inviting the public to subscribe for the company's shares, in consequence of which they received money from applicants for shares. They paid this money into an account in the company's name at the appellant bank, and to enable them to draw on the account, Wall, purporting to act as the company's secretary although never appointed to that post, wrote to the bank requesting it to honour cheques signed on the company's behalf by any two of its three 'directors', Wadge, Hoare and McNally, in accordance with a resolution passed at a meeting of the 'directors'. The bank acted on this authority, and allowed Wadge, Hoare and Wall to draw on the company's bank account. When the company was subsequently wound up the liquidator sued the bank for the amount thus paid out. His claim was that since Wadge, Hoare and McNally had never been appointed directors of the company, they had no authority to draw on its bank account, and the bank had consequently dissipated the company's money without its authority.

The House of Lords held that the bank was not liable. If it had inspected the articles of the company, it would have seen that the subscribers were entitled to appoint the first directors, and if it had visited the company's office it would have found two of the subscribers, Hoare and Wall, and another person, Wadge, managing the company's affairs with the apparent consent of four of the other subscribers, from which it could reasonably have deduced that Wadge and Hoare had been appointed directors, and that Wall had been appointed secretary. The bank had no right to insist on proof that these conclusions were correct, but since they appeared to be, the rule in *Turquand's* case protected the bank, and it was entitled to treat Wadge, Hoare and Wall as though they had been lawfully appointed to the offices they pretended to hold.

The interesting point in *Mahony v East Holyford Mining Co* is that although the arrangements made by Wadge, Hoare and Wall made it appear that they had been appointed officers of the company, the bank never inquired whether they had been appointed and it did not rely on the appearance that they had; the bank simply accepted Wall's letter and acted on it. This shows clearly that the rule in *Turquand's* case does not depend on estoppel, as do the rules relating to the apparent authority of a company's agents to act in its name.[15] A further problem, however, is whether a person dealing with a company may assume that persons who pretend to act as its directors have been properly appointed in the absence of any evidence to that effect. It appears that this assumption can be made. In one case[16] the proprietor of a business formed a company to carry it on, and he and his wife acted as directors of the company without being appointed by the subscribers of the memorandum, as the articles required, and without those subscribers in any way acquiescing in them so acting, or in any way making it appear that they had been properly appointed. The 'directors' issued a debenture in the company's name to secure a loan made to the company. It was held that the debenture holder was entitled to assume that the 'directors' had been properly appointed from the mere fact that they were in control of the company's business, and consequently the company was bound by the debenture. Likewise, in another case[17] the sole continuing director of an insurance company purported to appoint new directors to fill vacant places on the company's board of directors, although the articles gave him no power to do so, and the 'directors' issued a policy in the company's name to the claimant. Here again there was no evidence that the new directors had been

15 See p 126 et seq, post.
16 *Duck v Tower Galvanising Co* [1901] 2 KB 314.
17 *Re County Life Assurance Co* (1870) 5 Ch App 288.

properly appointed, beyond the fact that they and the director who appointed them were in control of the company's business, but the court held that the company was liable on the policy issued in its name.

Invalid appointments of directors

Some doubt may seem to be cast on the correctness of these last two cases by a later decision of the House of Lords,[18] but it is nevertheless submitted that they still represent the law. In the case before the House of Lords, the appellant contended that he was entitled to treat as valid an allotment of shares made to him by a board of directors to which one member had been validly appointed, another had never been appointed at all (his sole title to act being a minute of a board resolution appointing him forged by the first director, no such resolution having ever been passed), and the third was the appellant himself, who had been 'appointed' to the board by the other two directors before the allotment of shares was made. There was another director who had been validily appointed, but the first two of the trio of directors who had made the allotment had illegally purported to expel him from office before the appellant was appointed to the board. This other director took no part in the allotment of shares to the appellant, and the appellant knew at that time that the other director contested the legality of the board which made the allotment. The articles of the company permitted the board of directors to fill vacancies on the board, and the quorum of directors (ie the minimum number who must attend a board meeting if business is to be transacted) was fixed by the articles at two.

The appellant relied in the court of first instance and the Court of Appeal[19] solely on what is now s 285 of the Companies Act 1985. This section provides that 'the acts of a director or manager shall be valid notwithstanding any defect that may afterwards be discovered in his appointment or qualification'. The House of Lords held that this section did not help the appellant, because it only entitles a person to treat a transaction as binding on the company if it is entered into by directors who were properly appointed in substance, and the defect in their appointment was merely a procedural one. It therefore covers cases where a director is appointed under the articles at a shareholders' meeting or a board meeting which has been irregularly convened, but it does not cover a case where the persons who made the appointment had no power to appoint at all. Consequently, in the present case so far as the appellant was concerned, the appointments of the second director and himself to be the second and third of the three directors who made the allotment of shares were void, and so there was no quorum at the board meeting which made the allotment to the appellant, and the allotment itself was therefore void.

In the House of Lords the appellant also relied on the rule in *Royal British Bank v Turquand*, but the House, while holding that the rule covers much of the ground covered by s 285, held the appellant disentitled to rely on it, because he had assumed the functions of a director at the date of the allotment to him, and was therefore under a duty to see that the company's articles had been complied with in connection with the transaction in which he participated as a director, apparently, even with regard to matters which took place before his pretended appointment. This point is dealt with in more detail hereafter, but the important point to notice at present is that the House of Lords did not exclude the application of the rule in *Turquand's* case entirely, so that if the appellant had not assumed the

---

18 *Morris v Kanssen* [1946] AC 459, [1946] 1 All ER 586.
19 *Kanssen v Rialto (West End) Ltd* [1944] Ch 346, [1944] 1 All ER 751.

functions of a director, the rule would have protected him, and he would have been entitled to treat the allotment of shares to himself as valid. This is in accord with the earlier decisions quoted above, and it is noteworthy that the House of Lords expressed no doubts about their correctness.

To some extent the rule in *Turquand's* case and s 285 of the Companies Act 1985 overlap, and to some extent they differ. Apart from the obvious fact that s 285 entitles a person dealing with the company to disregard a failure to comply with the articles only when it relates to the appointment of directors or their qualification to act,[20] there appear to be these further differences between the section and the rule in *Turquand's* case:

(1) A director may rely on the Companies Act 1985, s 285, even though he cannot rely on the rule in *Turquand's* case because he participated as a director in the transaction in question. Consequently, if a director is allotted shares at a board meeting which he attends, and unknown to him some of the members of the board were irregularly appointed (as distinct from not appointed at all), he can treat the allotment as valid;[1]

(2) The Companies Act 1985, s 285 does not apply when a director continues to act after he has ceased to hold office,[2] for the defect then is not one of appointment, but the rule in *Turquand's* case does apply in such circumstances;[3] and

(3) The company may rely on the Companies Act 1985, s 285 when it seeks to enforce an obligation against its members, such as payment of an instalment of share capital called for by resolution of a board of directors whose appointments were irregular,[4] but the rule in *Turquand's* case only applies when someone is seeking to enforce an obligation against the company.

On the other hand, the Companies Act 1985, s 285 and the rule in *Turquand's* case share the common feature that a person who deals with a company cannot rely on either of them, unless he was unaware of the irregularity in question at the time he entered into the transaction.[5]

Returns of directors' appointments delivered to the Registrar of Companies

The statement giving particulars of the first directors of a company filed with the papers to lead to its incorporation[6] and the notification of any change in a company's directors or the particulars registered in respect of them which the company is required to give to the Registrar of Companies[7] may be relied on by a third party who deals with the persons currently shown as the company's directors in the belief that they were properly appointed and still hold office, but it is

---

20 The defect in a director's qualification which can be disregarded is not confined to his failure to obtain his qualification shares (*Morris v Kanssen* [1946] AC 459, [1946] 1 All ER 586), nor to defects which existed when he was appointed, so that a disqualification for holding office as a director which is subsequently introduced into the article can likewise be disregarded (*Dawson v African Consolidated Land and Trading Co* [1898] 1 Ch 6).
1 *Channel Collieries Trust Ltd v Dover, St Margaret's and Martin Mill Light Rly Co* [1914] 2 Ch 506.
2 *Morris v Kanssen* [1946] AC 459 at 471, [1946] 1 All ER 586 at 590.
3 *Craven-Ellis v Canons Ltd* [1936] 2 KB 403, [1936] 2 All ER 1066.
4 *Dawson v African Consolidated Land and Trading Co*, supra; *British Asbestos Co Ltd v Boyd* [1903] 2 Ch 439. These cases were decided on an article in the same form as Table A, art 92, which is to the same effect as s 285, and also validates the acts of directors even though it is later discovered that any of them was disqualified from holding office (eg by an order of the court (see p 535, post)) or had vacated office or was not entitled to vote.
5 *Kanssen v Rialto (West End) Ltd* [1944] Ch 346, [1944] 1 All ER 751.
6 Companies Act 1985, s 10 (2).
7 Ibid, s 288 (2).

necessary for this purpose that the third party should have inspected the notification in the case of directors other than those appointed on the company's incorporation.[8] The company is bound by the notification under the common law rules of estoppel, which apply when a statement of fact is made on which other persons are intended to rely, and so this is not strictly speaking an application of the rule in *Royal British Bank v Turquand*, but an alternative means of achieving the same result. Whether the appointment of directors or the change in their number has been gazetted or not is, of course, immaterial. It should be noted that when persons who have not been appointed directors, or who have been defectively so appointed, in fact control the management of the company, there is no need for the person who deals with the company to have inspected the notifications of directors' appointments at the Companies Registry. In this situation the rule in *Turquand's* case does apply, and as was shown above, the rule is not based on estoppel by representation. Reliance by a third party on the notifications of directors' appointments filed at the Companies Registry is therefore only of significance in the case of persons appointed as directors who do not consistently or regularly take part in the management of the company when the transaction in question is entered into.

Failure to hold a properly convened board meeting

In the absence of different provisions in a company's memorandum or articles of association, in general its directors can only exercise their powers collectively or collegiately, by resolving at properly convened meetings of the board of directors that acts shall be done in the company's name. They are not like partners, who have authority to represent their firm individually and to enter into transactions on its behalf for the purpose of carrying on its business in the usual way without the concurrence of their fellow partners.[9] The second kind of defect which may affect a transaction entered into by a company, therefore, is that no resolution approving it has been passed at a regularly convened board meeting.

Irregularly convened board meeting

If the board meeting was irregular because proper notice of it was not given in advance to each director, there can be no doubt that the other party to the transaction is not affected by the irregularity if he was unaware of it,[10] and the company is bound by the transaction. The cases which have been decided on this aspect of the rule in *Turquand's* case, however, have been concerned not with notice, but with the attendance of a quorum of directors at the meeting. A quorum is the minimum number of directors prescribed by the articles who must attend the board meeting if business is to be transacted. Often the articles leave the directors to fix their own quorum, and in that case a person dealing with the company may treat a transaction resolved upon at a board meeting as binding on the company even though there was no quorum present, because the outsider has no means of discovering what numbers of directors should attend.[11] Even if the articles fix the number of directors who form a quorum, so that the person dealing with the

---

8 The statement of the company's directors appointed on its incorporation operates to appoint the named directors effectively, even though they are not appointed by or under the provisions of the company's memorandum or articles of association (Companies Act 1985, s 13 (5)).
9 Partnership Act 1890, s 5 (32 Halsbury's Statutes (4th Edn) 641).
10 In *Browne v La Trinidad* (1887) 37 ChD 1, it was held that the court will not interfere with the board's decision, even at the instance of a director, unless the decision is unlawful or oppressive.
11 *Gloucester County Bank v Rudry Merthyr Steam and House Coal Colliery Co* [1895] 1 Ch 629; *Re Bank of Syria, Owen and Ashworth's Claim* [1901] 1 Ch 115; *Montreal and St Lawrence Light and Power Co v Robert* [1906] AC 196; *Re Fireproof Doors Ltd* [1916] 2 Ch 142.

company could discover what that number is by inspecting the articles, he is still not concerned to see that that number of directors in fact attended the board meeting.[12] This is logical, because even though the outsider knows what number of directors should attend, he has no means of ensuring that that number actually did attend.

No board meeting

Far more difficult are cases where an act has been done in a company's name without a board meeting being held at all. If the act is done by someone who is not a director and who has not been appointed by the board to act on the company's behalf, the company is not bound by what has been done in its name, except in the situations dealt with above where the transaction is entered into by persons who are acting as the company's board of directors, even though they have not been appointed to be directors,[13] but are nevertheless in control of the company's business. But if an act has been done by some or all of the directors, whether de jure or de facto, and the outsider assumes that it has been authorised at a board meeting even though no board meeting has been held, the weight of authority supports the conclusion that the outsider is protected, and can treat the company as bound.[14] There is in fact only one early case to the contrary.[15] There the board was empowered to borrow on the company's behalf, and a bond was issued by the secretary with the authority of two of the directors to secure a loan made to the company. The articles fixed the quorum of directors at three, but in fact no board meeting was held, so that the absence of a quorum could not have been the basis of the court's decision. The court held that the lender could not enforce the bond, even though he believed it to have been regularly authorised and executed. It is submitted that the decision was wrong, despite the attempts to distinguish it made in later cases where the rule in *Turquand's* case has been more generously applied.[15] The decisions which protect the outsider in these circumstances are more consistent with the principle underlying *Turquand's* case, because, as in the quorum cases, the outsider has no means to discover whether a board meeting has been properly held. Such cases should, however, be distinguished from those where the outsider knows that he is dealing with a single director or less than all the directors, and also knows that the board has not specifically authorised the transaction entered into. Whether the company is bound by the transaction in that situation depends upon the scope of the authority of the director or directors who negotiate it and, possibly, on the statutory provision protecting persons who deal with a company in good faith;[16] this involves the law of agency, which is dealt with later in this chapter. That situation is quite different from the one at present under discussion, where the outsider believes that the board has resolved that the company shall enter into a particular transaction with him, and that the individual directors with whom he deals are merely carrying out the resolution.

Execution of documents

Many of the cases where there has been a defect in holding a board meeting have been concerned with the effectiveness of a document which purports to have been

---

12 *Prince of Wales Assurance Society v Athenaeum Assurance Society* (1858) 3 CBNS 756n; *Davies v R Bolton & Co* [1894] 3 Ch 678.
13 See p 113, ante.
14 *Bargate v Shortridge* (1885) 5 HL Cas 297; *Davies v R Bolton & Co* [1894] 3 Ch 678; *Duck v Tower Galvanising Co* [1901] 2 KB 314.
15 *D'Arcy v Tamar, Kit Hill and Callington Rly Co* (1867) LR 2 Exch 158.
16 Companies Act 1985, s 35A(1), inserted by Companies Act 1989, s 108 (1).

executed on the company's behalf at such a meeting. Thus, a mortgage executed at a board meeting not attended by a quorum, but which appeared to be properly executed, was held binding on the company in favour of a mortgagee who was unaware of the irregularity.[17] Likewise, a debenture which appeared to be properly executed was held binding on the company even though no board meeting to sanction its issue was held at all.[18] The Law of Property Act 1925 and the Companies Act 1989,[19] assist in this respect by providing that in favour of a purchaser a deed is deemed to have been validly executed by a company if its seal has been affixed in the presence of a director and the secretary of the company, and where persons purporting to be a director and the secretary have attested the execution, the deed is deemed to be validly executed even though they do not in fact hold those offices; and that in favour of a purchaser a document shall be deemed to have been duly executed by a company if it purports to be signed by a director and secretary, or by two directors, of the company, and if the document makes it clear that it is intended to be a deed, it shall be deemed to have been delivered as a deed. However, the statutory provisions can only be relied on by a purchaser, that is a person who in good faith and for valuable consideration acquires an interest in property including a lessee or mortgagee.[20] Consequently, the two provisions will assist a debenture holder whose debenture gives him a charge on the company's property to secure his loan, but not an unsecured debenture holder, who will have to rely on the parallel protection given him by the rule in *Turquand's* case.

Forgeries

The protection afforded by the rule in *Turquand's* case in respect of documents does not extend to forgeries. A company cannot be bound by a forged document, even though the person who took it believed that it was issued under the authority of a board resolution.[1] Thus, where a company's secretary issued a share certificate under the company's seal with his own signature and the signature of a director forged by him in attestation, it was held that the certificate could in no circumstances be binding on the company, even in favour of a person who relied on its apparent genuineness and advanced money on the security of it.[1] More recent cases have extended the category of forgeries to a degree which endangers the protection normally afforded by the rule in *Turquand's* case. Thus, a bill of exchange signed by the manager of a company with his own signature under words stating that he signed on behalf of the company, was held to be a forgery when the bill was drawn in favour of a payee to whom the manager was personally indebted and endorsed by him to a bank which would, but for the forgery, have been a holder in due course.[2] The bill was forged because it purported to be a different document from what it was in fact; it purported to be issued on behalf of the company in payment of its debt, when in fact it was issued in payment of the manager's own debt. In another case[3] a share certificate bearing the company's seal and attested by a director and the secretary of the company was held to be a forgery because the

---

17 *Gloucester County Bank v Rudry Merthyr Steam and House Coal Colliery Co* [1895] 1 Ch 629.
18 *Davies v R Bolton & Co*, supra; *Duck v Tower Galvanising Co*, supra.
19 Law of Property Act 1925, s 74 (1) (37 Halsbury's Statutes (4th Edn) 175); Companies Act 1985, s 36A (6), inserted by Companies Act 1989, s 130 (2).
20 Law of Property Act 1925, s 205 (1) (xxi); (37 Halsbury's Statutes (4th Edn) 331); Companies Act 1985, s 36A (6).
 1 *Ruben v Great Fingall Consolidated* [1906] AC 439.
 2 *Kreditbank Cassel GmbH v Schenkers Ltd* [1927] 1 KB 826.
 3 *South London Greyhound Racecourses Ltd v Wake* [1931] 1 Ch 496.

affixing of the company's seal had not been authorised by a board resolution as required by the articles.

It is submitted that this last decision is wrong. Although a document may be a forgery even though it does not bear a forged signature,[4] it does not follow that the rule in *Turquand's* case may be excluded simply by showing that the document was signed without due authority, and therefore concluding that it must be a forgery. The first question to be asked is whether the person who relied on the document was entitled to assume that the board of directors had authorised its execution. If the document was signed by a director and the only defect alleged is that no proper board meeting was held, the outsider is entitled to make this assumption, and the company cannot contend that the document is a forgery.[5] If, however, the document was not signed by a director but by another person, the outsider must show that the board has held out that person as having authority to sign on behalf of the company, which it may have done by appointing him to a position under the company which in other companies normally carries the power to sign the kind of document in question. The company is then bound by the document, because it was signed by a person who had apparent authority to sign it, and the company is estopped from denying his authority. But if signing the document was not within the apparent authority of the person who signed it, the outsider who relies on it cannot treat it as having been signed on the company's behalf, and if it purports on its face to have been so signed, the company can contend that it is a forgery or a falsified document, because it purports to be a different document from what it really is. Thus understood, the second of the three cases cited above[6] was correctly decided, because the court also found that it was not within the apparent authority of the manager to sign bills of exchange on behalf of the company at all. But the third case[7] was incorrectly decided on this point, for it must be within the apparent authority of a director and the secretary to authenticate share certificates. In that case, however, the evidence showed that the third party was well aware that the director and secretary were not acting for the benefit of the company whose shares they pretended to issue, but for the benefit of another company of which they were also the director and secretary and which was indebted to the third party, the shares in the first company being issued to him as security for the debt. Because of his knowledge of the circumstances, the third party was precluded from relying on the rule in *Turquand's* case anyway.

Documents and transactions

It must, of course, be remembered that the fact that a third party is entitled to treat a document as binding on a company does not necessarily mean that he is also entitled to treat the transaction underlying it as binding. If he is entitled to assume that both the transaction and the execution of the document in connection with it have been authorised by a board resolution, the company is bound by both.[8] But if he knows that the signatory of the document is merely fulfilling the function of authenticating the document (eg the secretary signing a letter containing an offer by the company to enter into a business transaction), it must also appear that the

4 The more recent term adopted judicially for such a document is a falsified document, but it is equally void as a document which bears a forged signature (see *United City Merchants (Investments) Ltd v Royal Bank of Canada* [1982] QB 208, [1981] 3 All ER 142, revsd on other grounds [1983] 1 AC 168, [1982] 2 All ER 729.

5 *Re Land Credit Co of Ireland* (1869) 4 Ch App 460; *Dey v Pullinger Engineering Co* [1921] 1 KB 77.

6 *Kreditbank Cassel GmbH v Schenkers Ltd* [1927] 1 KB 826.

7 *South London Greyhound Racecourses Ltd v Wake* [1931] 1 Ch 496.

8 *Gloucester County Bank v Rudry Merthyr Steam and House Coal Colliery Co* [1895] 1 Ch 629.

transaction itself has been authorised by the board or by a director to whom the board has delegated its powers.[9] If the acts or transaction appears to have been authorised only by the signatory (eg an offer to enter into a business transaction in a letter signed by a director or by the secretary not purporting to act on the board's instructions), the company will not be bound, unless the board or a director, or other officer or agent of the company to whom the board has delegated power to enter into the transaction on the company's behalf, has in fact authorised it.[10]

If the material question is whether a document signed by a director or the secretary by way of authentication is effective against the company, and the company has notified the signatory's appointment as director or secretary to the Registrar of Companies, a third party who inspects or knows of the notification may rely on the effectiveness of the appointment, even though it turns out that it was invalid or defective. This is another application of the common law rule of estoppel mentioned above,[11] but the third party can treat the document as emanating from the company, of course, only if he believes the notification to be correct.

Disregard of limitations on the directors' authority

As was shown in the preceding chapter, the Companies Act 1989 provides that if a company enters into a transaction which has been decided on by its directors, and the transaction infringes a limitation on the powers of the directors contained in the company's memorandum or articles, or a resolution of a general meeting or a meeting of a class of members passed under the memorandum or articles, the other party to the transaction may nevertheless treat the company as bound by it if he entered into it in good faith, which he may do even though he was aware at the time that the transaction was beyond the powers of the directors under its memorandum and articles and such resolutions.[12] The other party is not bound to enquire about limitations on the powers of the directors to bind the company, and he is presumed to have acted in good faith unless the contrary is proved.[13] This statutory provision goes farther than the rule in *Turquand's* case in two respects. Under the latter rule a person dealing with a company is not protected against absolute prohibitions in the company's memorandum or articles, nor against infringements of restrictions on the powers of its directors which the transaction he enters into necessarily involve.[14] Consequently, a third party is unprotected by the rule in *Turquand's* case if he takes a transfer of property of the company which its articles expressly forbid its directors to dispose of, or if he contracts with the directors to subscribe for shares in the company carrying special rights when the company's articles reserve the power to attach such rights to the shareholders in general meeting. In these situations the statutory provision nevertheless enables the person dealing with the company to enforce the contract or to treat the transfer of property as effective, unless he acted in bad faith. Secondly, a person is protected by the rule in *Turquand's* case only if he neither knows nor has cause to suspect that the act or transaction in question is beyond the powers of the directors,[15] whereas the statutory protection applies notwithstanding his knowledge or suspicion that it is beyond their powers.

9 *Dey v Pullinger Engineering Co* [1921] 1 KB 77.
10 *Houghton & Co v Nothard, Lowe & Wills Ltd* [1927] 1 KB 246; affd [1928] AC 1.
11 See p 117, ante.
12 Companies Act 1985, s 35A (1) to (3) (see p 99, ante).
13 Ibid, s 35A (2) and s 35B.
14 *Irvine v Union Bank of Australia* (1877) 2 App Cas 366.
15 *Howard v Patent Ivory Manufacturing Co* (1888) 38 ChD 156.

On the other hand, both the statutory provision and the rule in *Turquand's* case protect an outsider who deals with a company if its directors are empowered by its memorandum or articles to enter into the transaction in question, but only if certain conditions are fulfilled or a specified procedure is followed. For example, the rule in *Turquand's* case applies if directors are empowered to borrow on the company's behalf[16] or to re-issue redeemed debentures,[17] provided the shareholders in general meeting consent, and no such consent is given. Similarly, a lender is protected by the rule if the directors are empowered to borrow not more than a specified total amount on their own initiative, and also to borrow in excess of that amount if a general meeting consents; in such a case the lender may assume that any necessary consent has been given, even if he knows that the directors have already borrowed up to the limit set for them personally.[18] The reason why the rule protects the outsider in these cases is that he has no means of ensuring that the conditions or the procedure prescribed by the memorandum or articles have been adhered to. The statutory provision, on the other hand, treats the conditions or the procedural requirements as a limitation on the directors' powers to enter into any transaction within the company's capacity, and enables the other party to the transaction to disregard them in any event, provided he acts in good faith, which he may do, notwithstanding his knowledge that the directors are acting beyond their powers because they have not in fact obtained the requisite consent.[19] It has been held that the statutory provision also enables an outsider to disregard provisions in the company's memorandum and articles which restrict the manner or form in which the company shall execute documents.[20] Consequently, a company was held bound in favour of a lender by a debenture executed under the company's common seal, whose affixation was attested by the signatures of one director and an attorney acting for another director, when the company's articles provided that the attestation should be by two directors personally.[20]

The statutory provision applies only in respect of acts and transactions effected by the board of directors of a company or by a person or persons authorised by the board.[19] It does not extend to transactions effected on their own initiative by managing or other directors or by other officers or agents of the company, but does extend to acts and transactions by such persons where the board of directors has authorised them to act, or has delegated its own powers to them in excess of the board's power to do so under the company's memorandum and articles. The rule in *Turquand's* case does, however, apply to such acts and transactions effected by managing and other directors or other officers or agents of the company acting on their own initiative, and under the rule an outsider may make the same assumptions about the fulfilment of conditions and procedural requirements when he deals with such persons as when he deals with the board of directors.[1] In that situation, therefore, the only difference in the scope of the protection given to the other party by the rule in *Turquand's* case as compared with the statutory protection which the other party would have if the board had authorised the director, officer or agent to act, is that the other party cannot disregard absolute prohibitions imposed by the memorandum or articles on the managing director or other person with whom he

---

16 *Royal British Bank v Turquand* (1855) 5 E & B 248; affd (1856) 6 E & B 327.
17 *Fountaine v Carmarthen Rly Co* (1868) LR 5 Eq 316.
18 *Re Hampshire Land Co* [1896] 2 Ch 743.
19 Companies Act 1985, s 35A (1) and (2).
20 *TCB Ltd v Gray* [1986] Ch 621, [1986] 1 All ER 587, affd on other grounds [1987] Ch 458n, [1988] 1 All ER 108. This decision was under the original s 35 (1) of the Companies Act 1985 (re-enacting the European Communities Act 1972, s 9 (1)). In this respect s 35A of the Companies Act 1985 (inserted in 1989) is the same as the original s 35 (1).
1 *Dey v Pullinger Engineering Co* [1921] 1 KB 77.

deals, nor can he disregard express reservations of powers to other organs of the company, such as the board of directors or a general meeting, or implied reservations arising from limitations placed on the powers of the persons with whom he deals when the memorandum or articles do not empower any other organ of the company to waive those limitations.[2]

If a managing director or other officer or agent of a company is authorised by its memorandum or articles to enter into a specified transaction only if a general meeting authorises it, there appears to be one situation where an outsider dealing with him cannot assume that the necessary resolution has been passed by a general meeting. This is where the authorisation can be given only by a resolution which is required to be notified to the Registrar of Companies.[3] The requirement of registration appears to put the outsider on enquiry, so that if an appropriate resolution has not been notified, he cannot assume that it has been passed.[4] Thus, if the managing director or other officer is empowered to exceed the borrowing powers conferred on him by the articles only with the consent of the shareholders by special resolution, the lender cannot assume that the resolution has been passed in the absence of its notification to the Registrar, and if the director or other officer is in fact exceeding his borrowing powers, the lender will be able to recover the loan from the company only if he is unaware that this is so, and honestly believes that his loan does not take the company's total borrowing beyond the limit prescribed by the articles. Even in this situation he may be unprotected despite his good faith, however, because the company's total borrowing may be shown to be in excess of the limit prescribed for the managing director or other officer by the particulars of mortgages and charges created by it filed at the Companies Registry,[5] or by the company's most recently filed annual accounts, but the outsider will only be treated as knowing of these matters if he fails to make such inquiries as he ought reasonably to make, or if he takes a mortgage or charge over the company's assets himself.[6]

Insiders and outsiders

The court has often said that the rule in *Turquand's* case is designed to protect third parties dealing with the company from outside, or more shortly, outsiders, against defects and irregularities in the internal management of the company's affairs. It follows that persons who are inside the company and act as insiders cannot rely on the rule. To ascertain who are insiders, however, is not as simple as might appear. A member of a company is not outside the protection of the rule simply because he is a member.[7] Thus, where the articles of a company required members to obtain the consent of the board of directors before transferring their shares, it was held that a member could rely upon a written consent which purported to be given by the board, although, in fact, it was given by the managing director alone, and so after the member had transferred his shares, the company could not restore his name to the register of members.[8]

Directors and persons who assume the functions of directors even though not

2 *Irvine v Union Bank of Australia*, supra.
3 Companies Act 1985, s 380 (1) and (4) (see p 647, post).
4 *Irvine v Union Bank of Australia*, supra.
5 Companies Act 1985, s 397 (2) and s 398 (4), as substituted by Companies Act 1989, ss 94 and 95; and Companies Act 1985, s 226 (3) and Sch 4, paras 48 and 50 (1), as substituted by Companies Act 1989, s 4 (1).
6 Companies Act 1985, s 416 (1) and s 711A, inserted by Companies Act 1989, s 103 and s 142 (1).
7 *Bargate v Shortridge* (1855) 5 HL Cas 297; *Re British Provident Life and Fire Assurance Society, Grady's Case* (1863) 1 De G J & Sm 488.
8 *Bargate v Shortridge*, supra.

properly appointed as such, are insiders if they act as directors in connection with the transaction in question, and are then unable to rely on the rule for their own benefit.[9] It is their duty to ensure that the company's affairs are properly managed, and if they have dealings with the company, they are not entitled to assume that the requirements of its articles have been complied with when in fact they have not because of their own neglect of duty,[9] nor can they pretend not to have notice of matters which it is their duty, as directors, to know.[10] Indeed, a director or a person who has assumed a director's duties, is so far excluded from protection by the rule in *Turquand's* case that he is affected in his dealings with the company by irregularities which took place before his appointment, and over which he therefore had no control.[9] This takes the exclusion of directors farther than is warranted, and discriminates against them in a way which they do not invariably deserve. On the other hand, if a director does not act as such in connection with a transaction between himself and the company, he can rely on the rule in *Turquand's* case.[11] For example, it has been held that a director who lent money to his company's subsidiary and guaranteed loans made to it by other persons, could enforce an agreement to indemnify him given in the company's name by a fellow director who had irregularly assumed the functions of a managing director with the acquiescence of the board.[11] The company was represented in the transaction solely by the fellow director, and the director who made the loan had not therefore disqualified himself from relying on the rule in *Turquand's* case, as had the directors in the other cases cited above,[9,10] who acted on the company's behalf in concluding the transaction as well as on their own account.

Although a member of a company or a director who does not act as such may be entitled to the protection of the rule in *Turquand's* case, he will not be protected in all the circumstances where a complete outsider would be. This is because the member or director has means of obtaining information about the company's affairs which the outsider lacks, such as notice of resolutions proposed at meetings of members or directors which he is entitled to attend,[12] notice of business transacted at members' meetings or board meetings,[13] and notice of the contents of the company's annual accounts laid before a general meeting of shareholders but not yet filed at the Companies Registry.[14] Armed with these means of knowledge, the member or director cannot assume the regularity of matters into which they enable him to enquire. So, for example, a member would not be entitled to assume that a resolution has been passed at a shareholders' meeting enabling the directors to enter into a transaction beyond the powers conferred on them by the articles, nor that a person who claims to have been appointed a director at a shareholders' meeting was properly appointed, if he attended the meeting and therefore knew that the resolution had not been properly passed, or if he was absent from the meeting but could have discovered that the resolution had not been passed by inspecting the minutes. Nevertheless, a member is protected by the statutory provision where the transaction or act of the company which concerns him is

9 *Morris v Kanssen* [1946] AC 459, [1946] 1 All ER 586.
10 *Howard v Patent Ivory Manufacturing Co* (1888) 38 ChD 156.
11 *Hely-Hutchinson v Brayhead Ltd* [1968] 1 QB 549, [1967] 3 All ER 98.
12 Notice of members' meetings must be sent to every member unless the articles otherwise provide (Companies Act 1985, s 370 (2)).
13 A member may inspect the minutes of members' meetings (Companies Act 1985, s 383 (1)). A director may inspect the minutes of board meetings as well (see p 577, post).
14 Copies of the annual accounts, and the directors' and auditors' report accompanying those accounts, must be sent to the members before the meeting of members at which they are to be laid (Companies Act 1985, s 238 (1), as substituted by Companies Act 1989, s 10). Unless the company is an unlimited one, outsiders can also inspect the copy of a company's accounts filed at the Companies Registry (Companies Act 1985, s 709 (1), as substituted by Companies Act 1989, s 126 (2)).

effected in excess of the board of directors' powers, including their powers to authorise other persons to exercise those powers, and the member deals with the company in good faith even though he is aware that the act or transaction is beyond the powers of the board of directors under the company's constitution.[15]

COMPANIES AND THE LAW OF AGENCY

Directors' actual authority

By the general law directors can act on behalf of a company only at board meetings at which their collective decisions are expressed by resolutions.[16] They have no power by law to act individually as agents for the company. This applies equally to the chairman of the board of directors, who is distinguished from the other directors only by the fact that he presides at board meetings.[17] Furthermore, the board may not delegate any of its powers to one or more of its members or to any other person, unless the articles empower it to do so.[18] In practice the articles of companies contain the widest powers of delegation by the board, both to individual directors[19] and to other agents chosen by the board.[20] The prohibition on delegation by the board by the general law in the absence of contrary provisions in the memorandum or articles does not, of course, prevent the board from engaging persons to assist in managing the company's affairs under its direction and control, but the board may not preclude itself by a service contract or a contract of employment from controlling those persons' actions, because if such a provision were valid, it would amount to an irregular delegation of the directors' powers.[1] Nor does the general prohibition on delegation prevent the board from employing any person to do formal or administrative acts, such as signing contracts and cheques, which the board has authorised by resolution. It is not necessary that every document signed on behalf of a company should be signed by a director.

The articles of most companies empower the board of directors to appoint one or more of their number to be a managing director or managing directors, and to delegate to him or them any of their powers either concurrently with or to the exclusion of the board.[2] Unless there is such an express power in the articles, a managing director cannot be appointed.[3] Even if there is an express power to appoint him, the managing director is merely a delegate of the board, and so his powers may be revoked by the board at any time if the company's memorandum or articles contain no contrary provision,[4] and unless a managing director is appointed for a fixed period, his appointment, too, may be revoked by the board at any time. This can only be prevented by the memorandum or articles providing that the managing director shall be appointed for a fixed period and shall exercise

---

15 Companies Act 1985, s 35A (1) and (2), inserted by Companies Act 1989, s 108 (1).
16 *Re Athenaeum Life Insurance Society, ex p Eagle Insurance Co* (1858) 4 K & J 549 at 558; *D'Arcy v Tamar, Kit Hill and Callington Co* (1867) LR 2 Exch 158; *Re Haycraft Gold Reduction and Mining Co* [1900] 2 Ch 230.
17 See, for example, Table A, art 91.
18 *Re County Palatine Loan and Discount Co, Cartmell's Case* (1874) 9 Ch App 691. But see *Freeman & Lockyer (a firm) v Buckhurst Park Properties (Mangal) Ltd* [1964] 2 QB 480, [1964] 1 All ER 630 (p 130, post).
19 Eg, Table A, art 72.
20 Eg, Table A, art 71, by which the directors may give powers of attorney delegating the exercise of any of their powers to any person.
1 *Horn v H Faulder & Co Ltd* (1908) 99 LT 524.
2 Eg, Table A, art 72.
3 *Boschoek Pty Co Ltd v Fuke* [1906] 1 Ch 148.
4 *Harold Holdsworth & Co (Wakefield) Ltd v Caddies* [1955] 1 All ER 725, [1955] 1 WLR 352.

his powers to the exclusion of the board. He is then not a delegate of the board at all, but an independent organ of the company with power in his own right to manage its affairs. It is rare to find such a provision in articles of association, however. Its effect would be to create a two-tier structure of management, under which the managing director or directors would exercise all or most of the powers of managing the company's affairs independently, and the remainder of the directors would merely have the functions of supervising his or their acts, consenting to transactions for which the board's approval was required by the memorandum or articles, and removing a managing director from office if the articles reserved the power of removal to the board.

The secretary

The secretary of a company is its administrative officer. It is his function to give effect to the decisions of the board of directors by drafting and signing contracts, drawing cheques on the company's bank account, conducting correspondence, keeping the company's records and doing all such other acts as are necessary. But the company's secretary has no power to make commercial decisions on the company's behalf, and so he acts outside his authority if he borrows money in the company's name,[5] or negotiates contracts on its behalf,[6] other than contracts necessary for carrying on the administration of the company's organisation, such as contracts for the employment of staff, the acquisition of office equipment or the hiring of transport for customers visiting the company's factory.[7] Apart from such exceptional cases, a company is not bound by contracts entered into by its secretary or by other acts or transactions effected by him. Of course, if the articles empower the directors to delegate any of their powers to any agent they choose, they may delegate to the secretary, and this is not uncommon, especially when the secretary is also a director.

Apparent authority of the company's agents

If a principal appoints an agent of a recognised class, such as a broker, commission agent or commercial representative, he impliedly holds the agent out as having authority to do all acts on his behalf which an agent of that class is ordinarily empowered to do. Consequently, if the principal by express instructions restricts the authority of that agent, a transaction entered into by the agent in defiance of the restrictions, but within the limits of his apparent authority, is nevertheless binding on the principal if the other party to the transaction is unaware of the restrictions on the agent's authority when the transaction is entered into. This applies equally to transactions entered into by agents acting for a company. The terms of the appointment of the agent will usually be unknown to the person who deals with him. They will not appear in the memorandum or articles of the company, and they are not required to be publicly registered, even when they amount to a complete delegation of the powers of the board to a managing director. Consequently, a person who deals with the agent, unaware of restrictions imposed on the scope of his authority, can assume that he has the powers which an agent of that kind normally has, and the company is estopped from denying that this is so. If the agent belongs to a recognised trade or profession, he has the same apparent authority to bind the company as if he were acting for an individual principal. It

---

5 *Re Cleadon Trust Ltd* [1939] Ch 286, [1938] 4 All ER 518.
6 *Barnett v South London Tramways Co* (1887) 18 QBD 815.
7 *Panorama Developments (Guildford) Ltd v Fidelis Furnishing Fabrics Ltd* [1971] 2 QB 711, [1971] 3 All ER 16.

is where the agent is one who can only be employed by a company, such as a director or secretary, that the court has been called upon to determine particularly the scope of his apparent authority.

Managing and other directors and secretary

A managing director is invested with apparent authority to carry on the company's business in the usual way, and to do all acts and enter into all contracts necessary for that purpose. Thus, he may sign cheques and bills of exchange on the company's behalf,[8] even in favour of himself,[9] borrow money on the company's account and give security over the company's property for its repayment,[10] receive payment of debts owed to the company, even by a cheque made payable to him personally,[11] guarantee loans made to the company's subsidiary and agree to indemnify persons who have given such guarantees themselves,[12] and where the company has power to guarantee the payment of debts owned by other persons generally, he may give such guarantees.[13] It has also been held to be within the implied powers of a managing director of a merchant bank to guarantee loans made to a company whose financial affairs it supervises and which it hopes eventually to float as a public company.[12] The apparent authority of a managing director is confined to commercial matters, however,[14] and so he has no apparent authority to approve transfers of shares in the company or to alter its register of members,[14] and undoubtedly he has no authority to sell the company's business, either as a going concern or on a break-up basis.

An ordinary, non-managing director and the secretary have no power to act as agents of the company by virtue of the offices they hold, apart from the limited authority of the secretary to negotiate contracts and do acts necessary for the administration of the company's organisation.[15] Consequently, subject to this reservation, directors, even though appointed to be executive directors, and a secretary are invested with no apparent authority to act on the company's behalf.[14] If a person negotiates a commercial contract with a director or secretary, therefore, he does so at his own risk, because if the board of directors has not validly delegated its power to enter into the contract to the director or secretary, or held him out as having delegated powers, the company will not be bound by the contract.[16] The statutory provision designed to protect persons who deal with the board of directors or a person whom the board has authorised to exercise any of its powers[17] do not apply in this situation, because the director or secretary acts in exercise of powers which he pretends are vested in him under the company's constitution, and not as a delegate or person authorised by the board. A director does have apparent authority to sign documents on behalf of the company, however, and so if the outsider negotiates the contract with the board, or, what is equally good, if he is

8 *Dey v Pullinger Engineering Co* [1921] 1 KB 77.
9 *Bank of New South Wales v Goulburn Valley Butter Co Pty Ltd* [1902] AC 543.
10 *Biggerstaff v Rowatt's Wharf Ltd* [1896] 2 Ch 93.
11 *Clay Hill Brick and Tile Co Ltd v Rawlings* [1938] 4 All ER 100.
12 *Hely-Hutchison v Brayhead Ltd* [1968] 1 QB 549, [1967] 3 All ER 98.
13 *British Thomson-Houston Co Ltd v Federated European Bank Ltd* [1932] 2 KB 176, [1932] All ER Rep 448.
14 *George Whitechurch Ltd v Cavanagh* [1902] AC 117.
15 *Panorama Developments (Guildford) Ltd v Fidelis Furnishing Fabrics Ltd* [1971] 2 QB 711, [1971] 3 All ER 16.
16 *Houghton & Co Nothard, Lowe and Wills Ltd* [1927] 1 KB 246; affd [1928] AC 1; *Rama Corpn Ltd v Proved Tin and General Investments Ltd* [1952] 2 QB 147, [1952] 1 All ER 554, but, contra, *Freeman and Lockyer (a firm) v Buckhurst Park Properties (Mangal) Ltd* [1964] 2 QB 480, [1964] 1 All ER 630.
17 Companies Act 1985, s 35A (1), inserted by Companies Act 1989, s 108 (1).

entitled to assume that the board or its delegate have approved the contract under the rule in *Royal British Bank v Turquand*, the statutory provision[17] protects him against the board having disregarded any limitations on its powers to conclude the contract or to authorise another person to do so, and the contract will be binding on the company if signed by one director.[18]

It seems that a company if affected by notice of all matters known to any of its directors, whether managing or ordinary, executive or non-executive, unless he acquires knowledge of the matter while participating in a transaction in breach of his duties to the company.[19] It seems that a company is also affected by notice of a matter known by a director before he is appointed, if he is under a duty to communicate it to the company, or if it concerns a transaction in which the company becomes interested after his appointment.[20] But it is doubtful whether a company will be deemed to have notice of a matter which a director would have discovered but for his negligence,[1] and it is affected by notice of matters known to its secretary only if he acquired knowledge of them in the course of performing his duties.[2] It would seem, however, that if an outsider gives express notice of a matter to a director or secretary, he can treat the company as affected by it, whether the director fails to inform the board as a result of his negligence, or because he deliberately wishes to conceal the matter from the board.

Notice of irregularity

A person dealing with a company is entitled to rely on the apparent authority of its agent only if he is unaware of the limits on the agent's actual authority, or if nothing has come to his attention which would make a reasonable man suspicious and cause him to make enquiries. Thus, where the board of directors mortgaged the company's property to secure loans made to them personally, it was held that the mortgagee was put on enquiry, because directors cannot normally exercise their powers for their personal benefit; in fact, the mortgage had not been properly authorised, and so it was held not to be binding on the company.[3] Again, where the sole director of a company indorsed cheques payable to the company specially to himself and paid them into his private bank account, it was held that the bank was put on enquiry by the unusual nature of the transaction, and since it had not enquired whether the indorsement was authorised, it was liable to the company for the conversion of the cheque.[4] This decision is distinguishable from those where banks have been held entitled to pay or collect cheques drawn on the company's bank account in favour of directors without particular enquiry.[5] There is nothing unusual in a company making a payment to its directors, unless the amount is exceedingly large and is therefore unlikely to be in respect of directors' fees or salary.[6] But it is unusual for a company to indorse cheques payable to it over to its directors instead of paying them into its own bank account, and the collecting bank is therefore put on enquiry.

A person dealing with a company may be put on enquiry by facts brought to his

18 See pp 112 and 122 ante.
19 *Houghton & Co v Nothard Lowe and Wills Ltd* [1928] AC 1.
20 *Aluminium Industrie Vaassen BV v Romalpa Aluminium Ltd* [1976] 2 All ER 552, [1976] 1 WLR 676.
 1 In *Houghton & Co v Nothard Lowe and Wills Ltd*, supra, Lord Sumner (at p 19) thought that the company would have notice; Lord Dunedin (at p 15) thought that it would not.
 2 Ibid, per Lord Dunedin (at p 14).
 3 *EBM Co Ltd v Dominion Bank* [1937] 3 All ER 555.
 4 *A L Underwood Ltd v Bank of Liverpool and Martins* [1924] 1 KB 775.
 5 *Bank of New South Wales v Goulburn Valley Butter Co Pty* [1902] AC 543; *Corpn Agencies Ltd v Home Bank of Canada* [1927] AC 318.
 6 *Lloyds Bank Ltd v Chartered Bank of India, Australia and China* [1929] 1 KB 40.

attention in connection with the same or similar transactions. Thus, in one case[7] a director warned the company's bank of his suspicion that his fellow director was drawing on the company's bank account for his private purposes, and instructed the bank not to honour cheques in future unless they bore the signatures of both directors, but the bank continued to honour cheques drawn by the suspected director alone without enquiring for what purposes they were drawn. It was held that the bank was put on enquiry by the warning, and was therefore liable to the company for money drawn out by the suspected director and misapplied by him.

The statutory provision[8] which protects persons dealing in good faith with a company's board of directors or a person authorised by it if the board disregards limitations in the company's memorandum or articles on the scope of either the board's powers or on the board's power to authorise other persons to exercise its powers, will not be applicable where a director, secretary, or other agent of the company acts without the authorisation of the board. Moreover, it will not apply in those situations where the director, secretary or other agent acts with the board's authorisation, or appears to be authorised by the board to act so that the apparent authority may be treated as a real one under the rule in *Turquand's* case, where the other party who seeks to enforce rights against the company did not act in good faith because he knew, or had reason to suspect, that the transaction was irregular or improper, and he will not then be within the protection of the statutory provision.[8] The matter known to the other party which does not deprive him of protection under the statutory provision is any limitation in the company's constitution on the board's power to act or to delegate,[8] and knowledge of an irregularity or impropriety in the transaction itself is not knowledge of such a limitation.

Presumed delegation

The preceding section of this chapter is concerned with the effect of acts done by a director, secretary or agent duly appointed by the company when the acts are in excess of the actual authority conferred on him. It is next necessary to discover how far a company may be bound by the acts of a person who was never properly appointed its agent at all. The company will be bound by the acts of such a person only if it is estopped from denying that it conferred on him the authority he appeared to have, and this will be so if it has held him out as having that authority and the other party to the transaction has been misled.[9]

The rule of estoppel

The essence of the other party's case is that he relied on some act or statement of the company representing the existence and extent of the authority of the person he dealt with. Consequently, if the other party negotiates with a director who purports to act on the company's behalf, it is not enough for the other party to show that the company's articles enable the directors to delegate their powers to one of their number, so that they could have delegated power to negotiate the transaction to the director in question.[10] Of course, if before entering into the transaction the other party was unaware that the articles enabled the board to delegate its powers, he cannot say that he relied on the power of delegation at all.[11]

---

7 *B Liggett (Liverpool) Ltd v Barclays Bank Ltd* [1928] 1 KB 48.
8 Companies Act 1985, s 35A (1) and (2), inserted by Companies Act 1989, s 108 (1).
9 *Wilson v West Hartlepool Harbour and Rly Co* (1864) 34 Beav 187.
10 *Houghton & Co v Nothard Lowe and Wills Ltd* (supra); *Kreditbank Cassel GmbH v Schenkers Ltd* [1927] 1 KB 826; *Rama Corpn Ltd v Proved Tin and General Investments Ltd* [1952] 2 QB 147, [1952] 1 All ER 554.
11 *Houghton Co v Nothard, Lowe and Wills* [1927] 1 KB 246 at 267.

But even if he did know of the power of delegation, he is not automatically entitled to assume that the board has exercised it in a way which suits his case. If the director he dealt with was a managing director, a small amount of evidence will warrant the assumption that the board delegated the power in question to the director in addition to his ordinary powers (particularly if the act or transaction in question calls for only a small extension of the managing director's actual powers), but if the director was not a managing director, more convincing evidence of delegation will be necessary.[11]

Although inspection of the articles helps to prove that the other party was entitled to assume that the board had delegated its powers, it is not the only way he may prove that he knew of the power of delegation. If the board has power to delegate by the articles, and it has held out one of the directors as invested with delegated powers, the company is estopped from denying that the powers were properly delegated, even though the other party to the transaction did not inspect the articles, but merely assumed that they contained a power of delegation from the fact that the board pretended to have exercised it.[12] Furthermore, it has been said in two cases[13] that if the board has expressly held out a director as having power to represent the company, or has done so impliedly by acquiescing in him acting on the company's behalf, it is unnecessary that the company's articles should contain a power of delegation. This is inconsistent with the law laid down in earlier cases and is illogical, for if the board can only delegate actual authority when the articles so provide, it surely cannot bind the company by pretending that it has exercised a power of delegation which it does not possess.

If the other party deals with a person who purports to represent the company, and contends that the company has held out that person as its agent, he must show that the agent has been held out by the organ of the company which would have power to appoint him regularly.[14] This will normally be the board of directors, but it could also be a managing director if it is within the scope of his actual or implied authority to make representations about the authority of the company's officers, employees or agents to act on its behalf. Subject to this possibility, it is therefore, not sufficient for the other party to show that one or some of the company's directors have held out the pretended agent as having been regularly appointed and duly authorised; all members of the board must do so, or must at least acquiesce in him being held out by other members of the board as being authorised to act on the company's behalf.[14] Consequently, the other party cannot safely rely on the protestation of the director with whom he deals that the board has delegated the necessary powers to him, because that director has no power to make representations as to the existence and extent of his authority on behalf of the other directors.[15] Nevertheless, if the board has authorised that director to make representations about the existence and extent of his delegated powers, or has held him out as being so authorised, it appears that the company will be bound by the director's representations in the same way as if they had been made by the board.[16]

---

12 *Biggerstaff v Rowatt's Wharf Ltd* [1896] 2 Ch 93; *British Thomson-Houston Co v Federated European Bank Ltd* [1932] 2 KB 176; *Clay Hill Brick and Tile Co Ltd v Rawlings* [1938] 4 All ER 100.
13 *Freeman & Lockyer (a firm) v Buckhurst Park Properties (Mangal) Ltd* [1964] 2 QB 480 at 505–506, [1964] 1 All ER 630 at 645–646; per Diplock LJ; *Hely-Hutchinson v Brayhead Ltd* [1968] 1 QB 549, [1967] 3 All ER 98.
14 This is in accord with the rule that a principal can only be bound by the acts of a person held out to be his agent by himself or by his duly authorised agent (*Fox v Clifton* (1830) 6 Bing 776). An individual director has no authority to appoint an agent for the company, and therefore has no authority to hold anyone out as having been appointed to be such an agent.
15 *Armagas Ltd v Mundogas SA, The Ocean Frost* [1986] AC 717, [1986] 2 All ER 385, HL.
16 *Ebeed v Soplex Wholesale Supplies Ltd* [1985] BCLC 404 at 414, per Browne-Wilkinson LJ.

Inapplicability of the rule in Royal British Bank v Turquand

In a few early cases[17] it was held that a person dealing with one director might assume under the rule in *Turquand's* case that the board had delegated to him the powers which he pretended to possess. If this were the law, the burden of proof on the outsider would be very much lighter than later cases have shown it to be, for he would not have to prove that the board had actually held out the director as having those powers. Later cases[18] have shown, however, that the rule in *Turquand's* case does not apply in this situation. It is difficult to justify the exclusion of the rule in *Turquand's* case logically, because as the early decisions point out, delegation by the board under the articles is a matter of internal management of the company, like the appointment of directors and the holding of board meetings, and so there is no intrinsic reason why an outsider should not be entitled to assume that a delegation essential to the validity of his transaction has been properly effected, in the same way as he may assume that other conditions imposed by the articles have been fulfilled. The reason for the exclusion of the *Turquand* rule, however, is the purely practical one that if it did apply, each director would be invested with apparent authority to enter into transactions on the company's behalf without consulting his fellow directors, and this would be destructive of the system of collective management by the board on which English company law is based. Collective management is the normal system, and everyone dealing with a company must be taken to know that it is. Individual acts of management by directors are, in theory, exceptional, and persons relying on them must therefore be able to show not only that they might have been regular, but also that they either were regular or, at least, that the organ of the company responsible for collective management, the board of directors, held them out to be regular.

Statutory protection

It has recently been held that under the statutory provision for the protection of persons dealing with a director, an outsider who acts in good faith is entitled to treat the resulting transactions as binding on the company if he assumes that the board has a power to delegate its functions to the director, even though in fact it has no such power, or only a restricted power, to delegate according to the company's memorandum and articles.[19] The court held that if the memorandum and articles do not confer a full power for the board to delegate, there would be a limitation on the powers of the board of directors, which does not affect the outsider if he acts in good faith.[19] However, it does not follow that an outsider who deals with a director may also assume that the board has exercised the power of delegation (which the outsider may assume to exist) in favour of that director, unless the board has purported to delegate power to deal with the outsider to that director, or has represented to the outsider that the board has in fact delegated such a power to him, and it is significant that in the case in question all the directors had assented individually to the delegation.[19]

17 *Smith v Hull Glass Co* (1852) 11 CB 897; *Totterdell v Fareham Blue Brick and Co Ltd* (1866) LR 1 CP 674.
18 See cases cited in footnote 10 on p 129, supra.
19 *TCB Ltd v Gray* [1986] Ch 621, [1986] 1 All ER 587, affd on other grounds [1987] Ch 458n, [1988] 1 All ER 108. The case was decided under the European Communities Act 1972, s 9 (1), which was re-enacted by the original s 35 (1) of the Companies Act 1985. The result would appear to be the same under s 35A (1) of the Companies Act 1985, inserted by the Companies Act 1989, s 108 (1).

Effect of transactions which are not binding on the company

If a pretended agent lacks both actual and apparent authority to bind the company for which he claims to act, the other party to the transaction may not sue the company for breach of contract, because there is no contract between them. The company may ratify the acts of the agent, however, and the contract negotiated by him then becomes binding on it, as it would on any other principal who ratifies. The ratification will usually be by the board of directors as the organ of the company which could originally have entered into the contract on its behalf. Ratification may be express, or may be implied from the board carrying out some of the obligations imposed on the company by the contract,[20] or from the board allowing the company to benefit by the other party performing his obligations,[1] or possibly, even from the board allowing the other party to act on the assumption that the contract is binding on the company without warning him that it is not.[2] But if the contract is one which the board could not have entered into itself, it can only be ratified consistently with the company's memorandum and articles if an ordinary resolution is passed by the members in general meeting.

It would appear that ratification of a contract by the board either itself brings about a new transaction between the company and the other party, or if it does not, the ratification is certainly an act done by the board on the company's behalf to which the other party to the contract is a party. Consequently, if the other party acts in good faith, the ratification is binding on the company, even though the transaction or the ratification is beyond the board's powers under the company's memorandum and articles and the other party is aware of this.[3] However, if the contract is irrelevant to achieving the company's objects and so is ultra vires, and the ratification is not to be treated as a transaction in its own right, it would appear that the ratification is valid so as to make the transaction binding on the company only if it is effected or approved by a special resolution passed by a general meeting of the company.[4]

It is rare for a contract which has been wholly or partly carried out to be held not to be binding on the company, for the court is ready to infer that the company has ratified the contract from the performance of part of it by either party. Consequently, ratification resolutions passed by the board of directors or by a general meeting will rarely be necessary. If money is paid or property is transferred without the company ratifying the contract expressly or by implication, however, the court would no doubt restore it to the party from whom it came,[5] and a person who pays money to a company in such a case has the right to be subrogated to creditors of the company whose debts have been discharged with his money, and he would be in the same position as an assignee of those debts.[6]

The rule in Turquand's case in the future

The rule in *Royal British Bank v Turquand* has been one of the most efficacious rules of company law for ensuring that persons who deal with companies in good faith are treated fairly, and the essentially common-sense solutions it produces contrast

---

20 *Reuter v Electric Telegraph Co* (1856) 6 E & B 341.
1 *Smith v Hull Glass Co* (1852) 11 CB 897; *Allard v Bourne* (1863) 15 CB NS 468.
2 *Wilson v West Hartlepool Rly Co* (1865) 2 De G J & Sm 475.
3 Companies Act 1985, s 35A (1) to (3), inserted by Companies Act 1989, s 108 (1).
4 Ibid, s 35 (3), substituted by Companies Act 1989, s 108 (1).
5 Money paid to the company would seem to be recoverable by an action for money paid by mistake or for money paid upon a consideration which has wholly failed, or more widely, as money had and received by the company to the use of the payer.
6 *B Liggett (Liverpool) Ltd v Barclays Bank Ltd* [1928] 1 KB 48.

notably with the injustices formerly worked by the ultra vires rule. The rule is peculiar to English law and the laws of the Commonwealth countries. American law has the same rules of agency law in respect of company transactions, but in only three cases have the American courts gone beyond this and applied the *Turquand* rule in full so as to protect third parties against irregularities other than an agent for a company exceeding his instructions.[7] The countries of Western Europe give no legal protection to innocent third parties if conditions or procedures which the articles of association[8] of the company require to be fulfilled are not complied with, but limit the protection afforded to third parties to preventing the company from treating transactions as invalid on the grounds either that they are ultra vires the company, or that they are in excess of the powers conferred by the articles on the board of directors.

English law is therefore more advantageous to third persons dealing with a company than other legal systems in providing the protection afforded by the rule in *Royal British Bank v Turquand*, but the question remains whether the protection of third parties acting in good faith should be extended further in the future, in particular by treating companies as bound by transactions entered into by individual directors pretending to act on their behalf, even though the board of directors had not delegated the necessary powers to them or held them out as having delegated powers, or even though the board had no power to delegate under the company's memorandum and articles.

In a Court of Appeal decision in 1964,[9] Diplock LJ ruled in effect that this later proposition was already law, subject to one important reservation, and without distinguishing or dissenting from earlier conflicting decisions, he laid down a far wider principle than the rule in *Turquand's* case would seem to warrant. He said:

'... if in the case of a company the board of directors who have "actual" authority under the memorandum and articles of association to manage the company's business permit [an] agent to act in the management or conduct of the company's business, they thereby represent to all persons dealing with such agent that he has authority to enter on behalf of the corporation into contracts of a kind which an agent authorised to do acts of the kind which he is in fact permitted to do usually enters into in the ordinary course of such business. The making of such a representation is itself an act of management of the company's business. Prima facie it falls within the "actual" authority of the board of directors, and unless the memorandum or articles of the company either make such a contract ultra vires the company or prohibit the delegation of such authority to the agent, the company is estopped from denying to anyone who has entered into a contract with the agent in reliance upon such "apparent" authority that the agent had authority to contract on behalf of the company.'

The one important difference between this reading of the law and the proposition mentioned in the last preceding paragraph is that under Diplock LJ's ruling a third party could safely rely on the authority professed by the director he deals with only if the board of directors or the managing director (if the authority were within his competence) has permitted the director to assume or exercise the authority. It would not be necessary for the third party to show that he was aware that the company's articles permitted such delegation, or that the board or the managing

---

7 *Manhattan Hardware Co v Roland* (1889) 128 Pa 119; *Louisville, New Albany and Chicago Rly Co v Louisville Trust Co* (1889) 174 US 552; *Dowdle v Central Brick Co* (1934) 206 Ind 242.
8 The articles of association are generally called the 'statutes' of the company, a dangerous expression for the English lawyer, who is likely to confuse it with legislation.
9 *Freeman & Lockyer (a firm) v Buckhurst Park Properties (Mangal) Ltd* [1964] 2 QB 480 at 505, [1964] 1 All ER 630 at 645–646; followed in *Hely-Hutchinson v Brayhead Ltd* [1968] 1 QB 549, [1967] 3 All ER 98 and *IRC v Ufitec Group Ltd* [1977] 3 All ER 924.

director had held out the director he dealt with as being invested with authority to represent the company. Tolerance of the assumption of functions by the director would be sufficient. In the case in which Diplock LJ gave this ruling it would seem unnecessary for the Court of Appeal to have laid down such a wide principle, because there were only two directors of the company (who were also the only shareholders), and one had held out the other as having been appointed managing director under a power in the articles. For this reason the other two members of the Court of Appeal were content to decide that the transaction was binding on the company on the ground that it came within the normal scope of a managing director's powers.

Nevertheless Diplock LJ's reasoning in this case has been followed in two later cases. In the first of these[10] the company's articles enabled the board to appoint a managing director, and all the directors had acquiesced in one of their number acting in effect as the company's managing director without a formal appointment being made. In the second case[11] the board of directors knew that one of the directors, who was also the controlling shareholder and had power under the company's articles to appoint or remove any member of the board, was negotiating the sale of shares which the company held in another concern, yet did nothing to show its dissent from the sale and allowed a contract for sale to be concluded in the company's name. In both cases the board of directors was considered by its acquiescence to have held out the active director to the person with whom he dealt as having power to represent both the board and the company, despite the fact that that person was not proved to have any knowledge of the contents of the company's articles or of the internal distribution of functions between members of the board. The first of these two cases could have been decided on the narrower ground that the acquiescence of the board of directors in one of their number acting as managing director was the equivalent of an actual appointment of him to that position under the terms of the company's articles, but the second case could certainly not have been decided in that way. There is therefore now substantial authority for Diplock LJ's point of view.

It is true that most such situations will now be covered by the statutory provision which protects persons who deal in good faith with persons authorised by the directors to enter into transactions or to do acts by which the company would be bound if the board effected them itself.[12] The one situation, however, where the statutory protection will not apply is that in the second of the cases mentioned above[11] where the board merely acquiesced in what the individual director had done without its authorisation. Unless authorisation in the statutory provision is held to include acquiescence (which seems unlikely), any protection afforded to the other party will have to be founded on an extended application of the rule in *Turquand's* case. Although this may be desirable from the point of view of a third party dealing with a director, it should be realised that any such extension weakens the principle of collective or collegiate management by a board of directors. This principle was devised in the first half of the last century as a means of protecting the shareholders against hasty, uninformed and ill-considered transactions being entered into by their company. Every extension of the *Turquand* rule inevitably takes away some part of this protection.

10 *Hely-Hutchinson v Brayhead Ltd* [1968] 1 QB 549, [1967] 3 All ER 98.
11 *IRC v Ufitec Group Ltd* [1977] 3 All ER 924.
12 Companies Act 1985, s 35A (1) to (3), inserted by Companies Act 1989, s 108 (1).

PART II

Share and loan capital

CHAPTER 6

Capital

SHARE CAPITAL

Definition

Capital and assets

In the context of the law of trusts capital is conceived to be a fund of money that is invested in assets which may be varied from time to time, but which, so long as they represent the original fund and until they are sold and replaced by new assets, are the property in equity of the beneficiaries of the trust. No distinction is made between the original fund, the capital with which the trust began, and the assets which now represent it, and no distinction need be drawn, because the beneficiaries have exactly the same interests in the present assets as they had in the original fund. The only distinction which need be drawn is between the capital and the income of the trust fund, which may belong in equity to different groups of beneficiaries. With companies a clear distinction must be drawn between the company's assets and the share capital which it has issued or may issue, because, as was shown in Chapter 2,[1] the shareholders are not the equitable owners of the company's assets, which are solely and beneficially owned by the company itself, and the shareholders are not directly responsible for the company's debts and liabilities, but only to contribute the capital unpaid on the shares which they hold. In company law a fundamental distinction must be made between the company's assets and the capital contributed or to be contributed by the shareholders with which the company has acquired or will acquire those assets.

It was also shown in Chapter 2[2] that shares are simply bundles of contractual and statutory rights which the shareholder has against the company. He acquires these rights by paying or agreeing to pay for the shares he takes or by contributing or agreeing to contribute assets which the company agrees shall be treated as having a certain value. The amount of the payments or the agreed value of the contributions he makes becomes part of the company's capital, and this capital is the total of such payments or contributions made by all the shareholders. But the money by which the payments are made and the assets which are contributed become the property of the company immediately they are received or transferred, so that straightaway there is a distinction between the capital contributed and the medium, money or assets, by means of which the contribution is made and which become the company's property. It is tempting to deduce from this that, since the shareholder ceases to have any proprietary interest in the money he pays or the assets he contributes to the company for his shares, the relationship between him and the company is that of creditor and debtor, and that one of the promises contained in the bundle which makes up a share is a promise by the company to repay the money paid by the shareholder or to restore the value of the contribution made by him when the company is wound up. This deduction is encouraged by

1 See p 35, ante, et seq.
2 See p 57, ante.

companies' balance sheets prepared in double columnar form, which show share capital as an item on the liabilities side together with debts owed by the company.[3] The deduction is quite wrong, however. A shareholder is not a creditor of the company for his share capital,[4] although he undoubtedly has a contractual right to share in the company's assets in a winding up after its creditors have been paid, and if the company has accumulated profits, his share will amount to more than the money he originally subscribed or the value of the assets he contributed. The reason why share capital is entered on the liabilities side of the company's double columnar balance sheet is that a balance sheet shows what payments would fall to be made out of the company's assets if it were wound up immediately, and one of these payments is, of course, the repayment of share capital. It does not follow that all such payments are debts of the company; share capital is one of the payments which is not.

Share capital, then, is the amount contributed by the shareholders to the company's resources. The money or assets which are contributed become the company's property forthwith, but the company does not become the shareholder's debtor for its repayment or restoration. The shareholder has a number of contractual and statutory rights against the company, among which are rights to share in its residual assets when it is wound up and to receive dividends out of its profits when duly declared in accordance with the articles,[5] and it is primarily these two rights which give his shares a value and make them saleable.

Nominal value of shares

It was shown in Chapter 1[6] that every share of a limited company must have a nominal value expressed in money terms. There is nothing inherent in the nature of a share which makes this necessary. A system of company law can be based on shares which have no nominal or par value, as has been done in some of the states of the USA, and in Canada and Belgium. Some of the early English companies had shares which had no nominal value, but were merely expressed to be fractions of the whole undertaking, such as one-thousandth shares, or one thousandth shares.[7] It was the coming of limited liability which gave the nominal value of shares the significance it now has. If a company is limited by shares, the measure of its shareholders' liability to contribute toward payment of its debts is the nominal value of the shares they hold, unless they have agreed to pay additional sums, or premiums, for the issue of their shares. Once a shareholder has paid to the company a sum equal to the nominal value of his shares plus any agreed premium, he has discharged his obligation to contribute. If the shareholder has discharged only part of his obligation, his shares are said to be paid up to the extent of the payments he has already made, and the difference between the nominal value and the paid up value of his shares is the amount unpaid, which he can still be called on to contribute. Beyond being the measure of the shareholder's liability, the nominal value of shares is useful in declaring dividends (which are usually expressed as a

3 The interpretation of balance sheets is dealt with in Chapter 17, post.
4 Consequently, before the Companies Act 1981 made specific provision for enforcing redeemable shareholders' rights when the date for the redemption of redeemable preference shares had passed, their holders could not sue the company for the repayment of their capital as creditors, though they could petition for the winding up of the company as shareholders (*Re Holders Investment Trust Ltd* [1971] 2 All ER 289, [1971] 1 WLR 583).
5 See Chapter 11.
6 See p 20, ante.
7 An example of this is the share capital of the former London Stock Exchange. At the time of its conversion in 1948 it consisted of 20,000 shares of no nominal value, but with £36 credited as paid up on each share.

percentage of the nominal value), in determining voting rights at shareholders' meetings,[8] and in the case of preference shares which have priority for repayment of capital, in determining the amount which must be paid to the preference shareholders in a winding up before the company's remaining assets are shared between the ordinary shareholders.[9]

Nominal, issued, paid up, called up and reserve capital

A reference to the capital of a company may be to its nominal capital, its issued capital, or its paid up capital, but if a reference to a company's capital is made in its business letters or order forms, the reference must be to its paid up capital.[10]

The nominal capital of a company is the total of the nominal values of the shares which it may issue, and this is the figure which appears in the capital clause of its memorandum of association if it is a limited company.[11] A company cannot issue shares beyond its nominal capital. If it attempts to do so, the issue is void, and the person to whom the allotment is made may recover any money he has paid to the company as money paid for a consideration which has wholly failed.[12] The nominal capital of a public company must not be less than £50,000 or such other amount as the Secretary of State for Trade and Industry may order from time to time.[13] There is no minimum nominal capital for a private company.

A company's issued capital is the total of the nominal values of the shares which have so far been allotted to shareholders, and it follows, of course, that the difference between the company's nominal and issued capital is its unissued capital. The company's paid up capital is the total amount paid up by shareholders on the shares they have taken, and its called up capital is defined statutorily as its paid up capital plus unpaid capital which the company has called on its members to pay and unpaid capital which will fall due for payment on one or more specified future dates under the terms of issue of shares.[14] The principal significance of called up capital is that a private company cannot be re-registered as a public company unless its auditors certify that its net assets are at least equal to the aggregate of its called up capital and its undistributable reserves,[15] and a public company cannot make a distribution of profits to its members if its net assets after doing so will not be less than the same aggregate amount.[16]

If a company has not received payment of amounts from its shareholders equal to the nominal value of the shares issued to them, the difference is its unpaid capital, and the shareholders are, of course, liable to contribute this unpaid capital when properly called on to do so or when payment becomes due under the terms of issue of the shares. The company has here a source from which it can raise further money to meet the needs of its business. Furthermore, if the company's powers in its memorandum are wide enough, it may raise loans by mortgaging or charging its unpaid capital. In that case, when the capital is paid up, it must be applied first in

8 The articles sometimes make voting rights proportionate to the nominal value of the company's shares, so that if shares of one class have a nominal value of £1, and shares of another class have a nominal value of 50p, each share of the former class carries double the voting rights of a share of the latter class. But this is far from always being the scheme adopted. Table A, art 54 confers one vote for each share held, without regard to its nominal value.
9 See Chapter 7.
10 Companies Act 1985, s 351 (2).
11 Ibid, s 2 (5).
12 *Bank of Hindustan, China and Japan Ltd v Alison* (1871) LR 6 CP 222.
13 Companies Act 1985, s 11 and s 118 (1).
14 Ibid, s 737 (1).
15 Ibid, s 43 (3) (see p 64, ante).
16 Ibid, s 264 (1) (see p 423, post).

paying off the indebtedness secured on it, and if the company is being wound up, its other creditors will rank for payment out of such capital only after the indebtedness secured on it has been discharged.

The members of a limited company may wish to set aside the whole or part of its unpaid capital as a fund for the payment of its unsecured creditors when it is wound up,[17] and so prevent its directors from calling up that unpaid capital or mortgaging or charging it in the meantime. This cannot be done effectively by inserting a provision in the company's memorandum or articles that uncalled capital shall not be called up or charged, because such a provision may subsequently be altered,[18] but it can be done irrevocably by the members passing a special resolution converting any part of the company's uncalled capital[19] into reserve capital.[20] On the conversion of an unlimited company into a public company or into a private company limited by shares[1] the special resolution for the re-registration of the company may similarly provide that any part of the company's uncalled capital shall become reserve capital.[2] Reserve capital cannot be called up until the company is wound up,[20] and any mortgage of it is void;[3] consequently, it serves the desired purpose of providing a fund for the benefit of unsecured creditors in the company's liquidation.

Nominal and real values

From what has already been said, it is clear that the nominal and paid up values of shares merely serve a number of useful purposes, the chief of which are providing a measure of the shareholder's liability to contribute toward payment of the company's debts and calculating the dividend payments to which he is entitled. It should be equally clear that the nominal value provides no measure of the real value of the share, that is, the price which a buyer will pay for it. Company law is not often directly concerned with the real value of shares, but the real value is, of course, the one which is of practical concern to the shareholder, and is the one which underlies many of the rules of company law.

It is impossible to calculate the real value of any share with mathematical precision. The value of a share (ie the price which a willing buyer will pay for it) depends on the number of shares offered by sellers and sought by buyers at any particular time. The amounts so sought and offered change from day to day, and so in consequence does the ruling price. If the shares are listed on a stock exchange, the value of the shares may be said to be the price at which they are currently quoted on that exchange. Even so, it must be remembered that less than one third of the 9,800 public companies registered in Great Britain at the end of March 1989 have shares which are listed on a stock exchange, and the shares of private companies, numbering 968,000 registered in Great Britain at that date, cannot be

---

17 This course was taken by a number of banks during the early 1880s when they converted themselves from unlimited companies into companies limited by shares. The creditors they sought to protect were their depositors. Apart from this, the practice has not often been followed.

18 *Malleson v National Insurance and Guarantee Corpn* [1894] 1 Ch 200. Such a provision in the memorandum would be effective, however, if the memorandum stipulated that it should not be altered (Companies Act 1985, s 17 (1) and (2)).

19 Uncalled and unpaid capital are not exactly the same thing. Uncalled capital is that part of nominal value of the company's issued shares which it has not yet called on the shareholders to pay, but does not include capital which is by the terms of issue of shares payable on fixed dates in the future (Companies Act 1985, s 737(1) and (2)). Unpaid capital also comprises capital which has been called up or which has fallen due for payment on dates which have passed or which will fall due on fixed dates in the future, but which has not been paid to the company.

20 Companies Act 1985, s 120.

1 Ibid, ss 43 and 51 (see pp 71 and 72, ante).

2 Ibid, s 124.

3 *Re Mayfair Property Co* [1898] 2 Ch 28.

listed on a stock exchange at all.[4] The International Stock Exchange of the United Kingdom and the Republic of Ireland, which is based in London and is referred to in this book as the Stock Exchange, publishes daily an official list of bargains done on the exchange in listed securities and in securities dealt in on the Unlisted Securities Market and the Third Market.[5]

It is impossible to list all the factors which influence buyers and sellers in arriving at the price at which they will buy or sell shares. They are as numerous and various as the factors which may influence any human action, and include such obvious things as the current national and international political and economic situations, the state of trade in general and in the industry or business in which the company is engaged, relations with employees, expected government action, changes in the supply and price of the materials which the company uses or the goods in which it deals, and the competitive strength of the company compared with other firms engaged in the same area of business. Four factors do deserve special mention, however. They may be described as internal factors, because they account for any difference between the value of the company's shares and those of any other company which is engaged in the same area of business, is of approximately the same size, and has the same range of business opportunities.[6] These four factors are capital cover, yield, earning capacity and marketability.

Capital cover

Every company aims to have a balance sheet which shows that its assets after paying its debts will be at least sufficient to repay its paid up share capital. The capital will then be adequately covered. In the case of preference shares this is particularly important, because the preference dividend is fixed, and will not be increased however large the company's profits may be,[7] so that the value of the shares is largely dependent on adequate capital cover. It might be though that if a company's net assets are not sufficient to cover its paid up share capital, the shares must inevitably be worth less than their paid up value. This is not necessarily so, for what the shares lose in value by inadequate capital cover, they may more than make up for by the company's earning capacity being better than the average. Such shares are risky investments, however, for their value will fall more rapidly than shares with adequate capital cover if earnings recede, and if the company suffers losses, the inadequate capital cover will weaken the company's ability to absorb them and to survive.

Yield

Yield is the proportion which the dividends paid in respect of shares bear to the price at which they can be bought. Thus, if a company pays a dividend of 10 per cent on its £1 ordinary shares, and the price at which those shares can be bought is £2 each, the yield is 5 per cent. Conversely, if the shares could be bought at 50p each, the yield would be 20 per cent. Other things being equal, the yield on the

---

4 The numbers of companies are as shown in the Report of the Department of Trade and Industry, *Companies in 1988–89*. Of the total number of companies (977,800), 923,500 were registered in England and Wales.
5 Rules of the Stock Exchange, rr 520.1, 520.4, 525.3 and 526.2.
6 These are the factors which the practitioner has principally to bear in mind in agreeing the value of shares not listed on a stock exchange with the revenue authorities for the purposes of inheritance tax and capital gains tax in respect of gifts of shares.
7 See p 210, post. In the case of preference shares and debentures, investors expect the capital of their investments to be covered several times over, three or four times being considered sufficient if the shares or debentures are listed on the Stock Exchange.

shares of companies of similar size engaged in the same kind of business is approximately the same. This means that the income which an investor receives from dividends on shares in one such company bears the same proportion to the price he pays for the shares as the income he would receive from the dividends of another such company bears to the price he would have to pay for its shares. For example, if the yield on the ordinary shares of general engineering companies is 4 per cent, and X plc, which is such a company, pays a dividend of 16 per cent on its £1 ordinary shares, while Y plc, another such company, pays a dividend of only 2 per cent on its £1 ordinary shares, X's shares will be worth approximately £4 each, while Y's shares will be worth approximately 50p each, other things being equal.

The yield on shares depends on the amount paid in dividends, not on the profits earned by the company, so that if the board of a company pursues an over-cautious dividend policy, and recommends that only a small part of the company's profits be distributed as a dividend, the inevitable result is to depress the value of the company's shares. Conversely, the yield on shares and consequently their market value may be increased by a company raising part of the capital it needs by issuing debentures or preference shares, the interest or fixed dividend on which costs less than the profits generated by the capital they represent. For example, if a company needs £5m capital to generate profits of £750,000 and it raises the whole of it by issuing ordinary shares at par, the yield on those shares will be 7·5 per cent if the company retains half of its profits. But if the company raises £2m of the capital by issuing debentures at 12 per cent, its net profits will be £510,000 after paying debenture interest, and if it distributes half of this among ordinary shareholders who have subscribed the other £3m of the capital at par, the yield on their shares will be 8·5 per cent.[8] This beneficial arrangement is known as gearing, and in a well established business can be carried as high as a ratio of equality between loan or preference capital and ordinary share capital, although traditionally British companies seek to ensure that their gearing ratio does not exceed 1:2, in other words that their ordinary share capital is at least twice the amount of their loan and preference share capital combined.

Earnings

If a company is earning higher profits than its competitors proportionately to the capital employed in its business, the value of its shares will tend to rise. This is so even though it does not distribute its extra profits as dividends, provided that the board has good reason for pursuing a conservative dividend policy, for example, in order to provide money for expanding the company's business. It is because of the sound earning capacity of some companies which are in the process of expanding, that their shares, the so-called 'growth stocks', have a comparatively high value even though the present yield is moderate or small.[9] Earning capacity is also an important element in the value of preference shares. Where the preference dividend is adequately covered by earnings, so that there is no risk of profits being insufficient

---

8 These examples do not take taxation into account. If the company's profits after corporation tax at 25 per cent were £750,000 in the first example, they would be £827,500 after corporation tax but before deducting debenture interest in the second, since debenture interest is a deductible charge for corporation tax, and the yield on the ordinary shares would then be 9·79 per cent.

9 Many of these 'growth stocks' are the shares of companies engaged in new industries, such as the manufacture of electronic equipment (particularly computers), electronically operated communications equipment and robot machinery.

to pay it, the shares will command a good price;[10] where the dividend is barely covered, or is not covered at all, the value of the shares will fall considerably.

Before 1965, when companies' profits were taxed only once, to income tax, and the company recouped itself for the tax paid by deducting tax at the standard rate from the dividends it distributed, it was customary to express the yield on shares as the percentage ratio of the gross dividend last paid to the current dealing price of the shares. Now that companies' profits are taxed twice, once to corporation tax in the hands of the company and secondly to income tax on the dividends paid to the shareholders (with a credit given for part of the corporation tax paid by the company), a more useful ratio as a guide to the comparative value of the shares of companies which distribute different fractions of their profits as dividends, is that between the current market price of the shares and the company's profits (after deduction of corporation tax) attributable to the shares. This is known as the price-earnings ratio of the shares, and has in practice replaced yield as a measure of comparative performance. For example, if a company's capital consists of 1,000,000 £1 10 per cent preference shares and 2,000,000 £1 ordinary shares, and its after-tax profits amount to £600,000, £500,000 of those profits are attributable to the ordinary shares; consequently, if the ordinary shares are currently selling at £4 each, their price-earnings ratio is 16 (£4 × 2,000,000: £500,000). The price-earnings ratio, of course, does not take into account the fraction of the company's after-tax profits which is distributed as dividend, nor the fraction of corporation tax which is credited against income tax on dividends. It is possible to construct alternative price-earnings ratios taking this second element into account by assuming either that the company distributes none of its after-tax profits, or that it distributes all of them and that the net rate of corporation tax it pays on its profits is correspondingly reduced.

Marketability

Shares are more readily saleable and command a better price if they are numerous, and if large blocks of them are not held by single persons or groups of persons who are likely to act in concert, such as members of the same family. Investors do not like to hold shares in which there is only a 'narrow' market, that is, where only a few shares out of those issued are regularly offered for sale. Experience shows that when a company with such shares suffers an adversity, the market value of its shares falls far more than if they were regularly dealt in. Furthermore, a 'narrow' market often indicates that some person or group of persons holds sufficient of the company's shares to predominate in voting at shareholders' meetings, so that the voting rights of small shareholders are practically valueless.

Another feature which affects marketability is the denomination or nominal value of shares. If the nominal value is high, say more than £10, the market price is always lower than it would be if the shares were split into multiple shares with a lower nominal value each. Also a disproportion between the market price and the nominal value of shares tends to depress the price. For this reason shares whose market price has risen to four or five times their nominal value are often made 'lighter' by an issue of bonus shares, and after the issue it is found that the aggregate price for an original share and the bonus shares issued in right of it is slightly more than the price of the original share before the issue.

10 The preference dividend should ideally be covered several times by earnings, three or four times usually being considered sufficient.

PAYMENT FOR SHARES

Where shares are allotted by a company without any different method of payment for them being agreed, the shareholder must pay the nominal value or greater issue price of his shares to the company in cash. Nevertheless, it is possible for a company to allot shares which are credited as paid up to an agreed amount for a consideration other than cash. This is put in statutory form by the Companies Act 1985 which provides that shares allotted by a company and any premium over their nominal value payable to the company in respect of them (a share or issue premium) may be paid up in money or money's worth (including goodwill and 'know-how').[11] Thus, a company may agree to purchase a business in consideration of allotting the vendor one million £1 ordinary shares which are credited as fully paid, or two million £1 ordinary shares on which 50p per share is credited as paid. If shares are allotted in this way and, if the company is a public one, a proper valuation of the business is carried out,[12] the shareholder cannot be called on to pay in cash the part of their nominal value which is deemed to have been paid up.

Whether shares are issued for payment in cash or for a consideration other than cash, they cannot be issued at a discount,[13] that is, for a consideration of an agreed value which is less than the nominal value of the shares. Thus, if £1 shares are issued at an issue price of 90p and it is agreed that they shall be credited as fully paid when that amount has been paid to the company,[14] or if a property or business is sold to a company for £1m to be satisfied by the issue of two million £1 shares by the company credited as fully paid,[15] there is a discount of 10p per share in the first case and a discount of £1m in the second.

If shares are in fact issued at a discount, the allottee and any subsequent holder of the shares (other than a purchaser for value without actual notice that the shares had been issued at a discount or a person deriving title under such a purchaser) are liable to pay the company the amount of the discount in cash.[16] For this purpose a subsequent holder of the shares includes a member of the company who is registered as holder of the shares in its register of members and also any other person who has an unconditional right to be so registered or to have an instrument of transfer of the shares executed in his favour.[17] Consequently, a renouncee of a letter of allotment of shares who is entitled to be registered in the company's register of members,[18] an unregistered transferee of shares and a person who has unconditionally contracted to acquire shares may be compelled to pay the amount of the discount to the company.

Because the allotment of shares at a discount is prohibited, an executory contract for such an allotment is void and cannot be enforced by the intended allottee or by the company.[19] For the same reasons, directors who allot shares at a discount are guilty of a breach of duty to the company, and are liable to pay the amount of the discount to it as damages if that amount cannot be recovered from the allottee or a holder of the shares.[20]

11 Companies Act 1985, s 99 (1).
12 Ibid, s 103 (1) (see p 153, post).
13 Ibid, s 100 (1). This section enacts a rule which has long been applied by the courts; the rule was deduced from the statutory liability of shareholders to contribute the unpaid capital on their shares in the company's liquidation.
14 *Ooregum Gold Mining Co of India v Roper* [1892] AC 125.
15 *Re Theatrical Trust Ltd, Chapman's Case* [1895] 1 Ch 771; *Re Wragg Ltd* [1897] 1 Ch 796.
16 Companies Act 1985, s 100 (2) and 112 (1) and (3).
17 Ibid, s 112 (4).
18 See p 313, post.
19 *Re Almada & Tirito Co* (1888) 38 ChD 415.
20 *Hirsche v Sims* [1894] AC 654.

The converse of the allotment of shares at a discount is their allotment at a premium, that is, at a price or for a consideration which exceeds their nominal value. The excess is known as a share premium or an issue premium, and is subject to special rules which treat it in the same way as share capital. Because of the complexity of these rules, an examination of them will be deferred until the rules governing the allotment of shares for cash and for a consideration other than cash have been dealt with.[1]

Allotment of shares for cash

Definition

Shares are obviously allotted for cash when the shareholder agrees to pay their nominal value or higher issue price by legal tender or by a cheque or negotiable instrument on which the company may sue him. Equally, shares are allotted for cash when the company is indebted to the shareholder, and they agree that the debt shall be discharged by crediting the shares as paid up by an equivalent amount. In the words of Sir W M James LJ:[2]

'If it came to this, that there was a debt in money payable immediately by the company to the shareholders, and an equal debt payable immediately by the shareholders to the company [for their shares], and that each was accepted in full payment of the other, the company could have pleaded payment in an action brought against them (sic) and the shareholder could have pleaded payment in cash in a corresponding action brought by the company against him for calls.'

The debt owing from the company which the company and the shareholder agree to treat as cash paid by the shareholder, may arise from any transaction. Thus, a shareholder has been held to have paid for his shares in cash by the agreed cancellation of a debt owing to him as the vendor of property to the company,[3] or as agreed compensation for the variation of another contract he had with the company,[4] including compensation payable to a director for the variation of his service contract.[5] Furthermore, it is not necessary that the debt owed by the company should be owed to the shareholder; if the creditor agrees with the company that his debt shall be paid by crediting the shares of another person as paid up by an equal sum, that person is entitled to have his shares so credited.[6]

Conditions for payment by appropriation of debts owed by the company

Shares will not be considered as paid up in cash by appropriation or cancellation of a debt, unless the company owes a liquidated sum which is immediately payable, and agrees that it shall be appropriated in payment for the shares. The fact that the shareholder would be entitled to set off a debt owing to him from the company if it sued him for unpaid calls or instalments of the issue price of his shares, does not

---

1 See p 161, post.
2 *Re Harmony and Montague Tin and Copper Mining Co, Spargo's Case* (1873) 8 Ch App 407 at 412.
3 *Spargo's Case*, supra, *Re Limehouse Works Co, Coates' Case* (1873) LR 17 Eq 169; *Larocque v Beauchemin* [1897] AC 358.
4 *Re Paraguassu Steam Tramway Co, Adamson's Case* (1874) LR 18 Eq 670.
5 *Re Regent United Service Stores, ex p Bentley* (1879) 12 ChD 850.
6 *Re Paraguassu Steam Tramroad Co, Ferrao's Case* (1874) 9 Ch App 355; *Re Barrow-in-Furness and Northern Counties Land and Investment Co* (1880) 14 ChD 400; *Re Jones, Lloyd & Co* (1889) 41 ChD 159; *North Sydney Investment and Tramway Co v Higgins* [1899] AC 263.

amount to payment of the calls or instalments if the company has not agreed to the debt being appropriated for that purpose.[7] However, if the shareholder successfully pleads the defence of set-off in the company's action, and judgment is entered for the company for the net amount of the calls after deducting the debt owed by it, the calls are deemed to be paid to the extent of the set-off, and the shares are treated as correspondingly paid up.[8] On the other hand, if the company goes into liquidation before judgment is entered in its favour for the net balance of the calls, the shares are not paid up by the amount which the shareholder is entitled to set off in the company's action,[8] and so the liquidator may make a fresh call for the whole amount unpaid on the shares, which the shareholder will have to pay in cash.[9] When a company does agree to appropriate a debt owed to the shareholder in satisfaction of his liability for unpaid capital, its agreement is usually evidenced by entries being made in its accounting records, but it is not essential that this should be done if the company's assent can be proved by other means.[10]

Shares will not be paid up in cash if a person has a mere unliquidated claim for damages against the company, and they agree to compromise the claim by the allotment of shares of a nominal value equal to or less than the amount of the claim.[11] At no point of time is the shareholder entitled to demand payment of a fixed sum of money from the company, and so there is no debt which can be appropriated in payment for the shares. It would, of course, be different if the compromise were for the payment of money by the company, and the shareholder afterwards agreed to take fully paid shares of an equivalent nominal value in satisfaction.

If shares are to be paid for by appropriating a debt owing from the company, the debt must be immediately payable, and so shares cannot be treated as paid for in cash by the company agreeing to set off against their nominal value or higher issue price sums which will become payable by it in the future.[12] On the other hand, if an amount is immediately payable by the company, it may agree to appropriate it in payment of calls made in the future, and if calls are made while the company is a going concern, the shares will be paid up to the extent of the amount payable by the company as and when the calls are made.[13] The same applies if the issue price of the shares is payable by instalments which fall due while the company is a going concern. But if the issue price of the shares has not been fully called up or fallen due for payment before the company is wound up, the shareholder cannot treat further calls made by the liquidator as satisfied by the appropriation of the debt which the company owes to the shareholder, and he must pay the further calls in cash.[14] This is because the shareholder would otherwise obtain a preference over the other creditors of the company, and this would conflict with the rules that in a winding up creditors must be paid equally and rateably

---

7 *Re Government Security Fire Insurance Co, White's Case* (1879) 12 ChD 511 at 517. The earlier decision in
   Re London and Colonial Co, ex p Clark (1869) LR 7 Eq 550, which treated a right of set-off as equivalent
   to payment, is therefore wrong.
8 *Re Hiram Maxim Lamp Co* [1903] 1 Ch 70.
9 *Re Overend, Gurney & Co, Grissell's Case* (1866) 1 Ch App 528; *Re General Works Co, Gill's Case* (1879)
   12 ChD 755.
10 *Re Jones, Lloyd & Co* (1889) 41 ChD 159.
11 *Re Barangah Oil Refining Co, Arnot's Case* (1887) 36 ChD 702.
12 *Re Richmond Hill Hotel Co, Elkington's Case* (1867) 2 Ch App 511; *Re Richmond Hill Hotel Co, Pellat's
    Case* (1867) 2 Ch App 527; *Re Land Development Association, Kent's Case* (1888) 39 ChD 259.
13 *Re Jones, Lloyd & Co*, supra.
14 *Re Paraguassu Steam Tramroad Co, Black & Co's Case* (1872) 8 Ch App 254; *Re Johannesburg Hotel Co,
    ex p Zoutpansberg Prospecting Co* [1891] 1 Ch 119.

and that a debt owed by the company to a shareholder cannot be set off against calls.[15]

Ineffective variations of the obligation to pay cash

Before 1900, while the Companies Act 1867, s 25, was in force, it was held that a shareholder who had taken shares to be paid for in cash could not discharge his liability for the amount unpaid by agreeing with the company that it should take a consideration other than cash in full satisfaction. There were two reasons for this. In the first place, s 25 provided that payment for shares must be made in cash, unless at or before the time the shares were issued a written contract specifying the consideration to be given to the company for them was filed with the Registrar of Companies. Since it was impossible to file such a written contract after the shares had been issued, an agreement to alter the method of payment for shares allotted for payment in cash could never be effective.[16] In the second place, it was held that a shareholder's obligation to pay for his shares is not only contractual, but is also a statutory obligation imposed for the benefit of the company's creditors, and the company therefore cannot agree to its variation by substituting a different obligation.[17] The statutory obligation has not been set out expressly in the Companies Acts (except in the Companies Act 1867, s 25, which was repealed in 1900), but the court has inferred it from the provision that in a winding up a shareholder in a company limited by shares can be called on to contribute only the amount unpaid on his shares,[18] and the court has deduced that he cannot by any agreement with the company be discharged by doing anything other than paying that amount in full.

Since the repeal of the Companies Act 1867, s 25, the first reason for the invalidity of agreements varying the method of paying for shares has gone, but the second reason remains, and the law is undoubtedly still the same. However, an agreement for such a variation of an obligation to pay for shares in cash is not wholly ineffective. If the shareholder actually furnishes the consideration promised, the company becomes indebted to him for an amount equal to the amount unpaid on his shares, and since the company has agreed to appropriate the debt in payment of the amount unpaid on his shares, that amount will be taken as paid up on them in accordance with the principles discussed above.[19] Likewise, if a company issues shares on terms that they shall be paid for out of amounts which will subsequently become payable by the company to the shareholder, the shares are not paid up by those amounts when they are issued,[20] but they will automatically be paid up to the extent of each amount as it becomes due and payable.[19] However, it must be remembered that shares cannot be considered as paid up until calls have been made by the company or instalments of the issue price have become due, and so if calls are not made until after the company is wound up, or if the whole issue price has not become immediately due and payable before the company's winding up commences, the shareholder will have to pay the amount unpaid on the shares in cash, even though the company was already indebted to him before the winding up began.[1]

15 *Re Overend, Gurney & Co, Grissell's Case* (1866) 1 Ch App 528; *Re General Works Co, Gills Case* (1879) 12 ChD 755.
16 *Re Richmond Hill Hotel Co, Pellatt's Case* (1867) 2 Ch App 527.
17 *Ooregum Gold Mining Co of India v Roper* [1892] AC 125.
18 Now Insolvency Act 1986, s 74 (1) and (2) (*d*).
19 *Re Richmond Hill Hotel Co, Pellatt's Case*, supra at 535; *Re Mercantile Trading Co, Schroder's Case* (1870) LR 11 Eq 131; *Re Wragg Ltd* [1897] 1 Ch 796 at 829; *Gardner v Iredale* [1912] 1 Ch 700 at 716.
20 See cases cited in footnote 12 on p 144, ante.
1 See cases cited in footnote 14 on p 144, ante.

Statutory definition of payment for shares in cash

For the purposes of the Companies Act 1985 (but not for the purpose of applying the rules of common law and equity dealt with above), a share in a company is deemed to be paid up in cash if the consideration for the allotment or payment up of the share is cash received by the company, or is a cheque received by the company in good faith which its directors have no reason for suspecting will not be paid, or is the release of a liability of the company for a liquidated sum, or is an undertaking to pay cash to the company at a future date.[2] This statutory definition differs from the accepted meaning of payment for shares in a number of ways. Although the issue price of shares payable in cash is usually paid by cheque and not in currency, a payment by cheque is conditional payment only at common law,[3] and if the cheque is dishonoured on presentation, payment is retrospectively treated as not having been made, and so the shares revert to their former status as nil paid shares or shares paid up to a lesser amount. It would seem that the statutory reference to payment by the release of a liability of the company for a liquidated sum means the same as the agreed cancellation of the shareholder's liability to pay for the shares in consideration of the cancellation of a debt owed by the company, which was mentioned above. Payment in cash by the acceptance of an undertaking to pay cash at a future date would appear to mean that the acceptance of such an undertaking by the company results in the shares being treated as paid up straightaway, but if the undertaking is not fulfilled, it would seem that the shares are immediately and retrospectively treated as not being paid up,[3] so that the company may exercise any power it has in its articles to forfeit the shares, as well as sue the person who gave the undertaking, or as an alternative to doing so.[4]

Allotment of shares for a consideration other than cash

The commonest consideration for the allotment of shares other than the payment of cash is the transfer of property to the company (whether land, buildings or tangible or intangible movable property), but allotments of shares may also be made for any other valuable consideration, such as a licence to use a patent, trade mark or 'know-how'.[5] However, a public company[6] (unlike a private one) cannot allot shares on terms that the whole or part of their nominal value or any premium on their issue shall be paid up by the allottee giving an undertaking that he or another person shall do work or perform services for the company or a third person (eg another company for which the first company has contracted to supply the services).[7] It would seem that this prohibition precludes a public company from remunerating the underwriters of an offer of its shares to the public by issuing fully paid shares to them instead of paying underwriting commission in cash.[8]

When a contract is made for the allotment of shares for a consideration other than cash, it may provide simply that the company shall allot a certain number of shares, which shall be credited as paid up to a certain extent in return for the consideration given or promised by the shareholder.[9] The contract may, on the

---

2 Companies Act 1985, s 738 (1).
3 *Everett v Collins* (1810) 2 Camp 515; *Currie v Misa* (1875) LR 10 Exch 153, affd sub nom *Misa v Currie* (1876) 1 App Cas, HL 554; *Cohen v Hale* (1878) 3 QBD 371.
4 See p 321, post.
5 Companies Act 1985, s 99 (1).
6 Including a private company which has passed a resolution to be re-registered as a public company (Companies Act 1985, s 116) (see p 63, ante).
7 Companies Act 1985, s 99 (2).
8 See p 305, post.
9 *Re Heyford Co, Pell's Case* (1869) 5 Ch App 11; *Re Baglan Hall Colliery Co* (1870) 5 Ch App 346.

other hand, provide that the price payable by the company shall be a certain sum of money to be satisfied by the allotment of so many shares which shall be credited as paid up to an equivalent amount, eg £500,000 to be satisfied by the allotment of 500,000 ordinary shares of £1 each credited as fully paid.[10] If the company's promise takes this latter form, the contract is still a contract to allot shares for a consideration other than cash,[11] for at no point of time can the shareholder require the company to pay him a sum of money under the contract, and so there is never a debt owing from the company which can be appropriated to pay for the shares in cash. The sum of money mentioned in the contract is a mere cipher, and it does not affect the substance of the bargain, which is that shares shall be allotted in return for property or services or the other consideration to be given for them. Whatever the form of the contract, however, a public company[12] may not allot shares as fully or partly paid up in consideration of a promise which is to be performed, or may at the option of the promisor be performed, at a time more than five years after the allotment,[13] nor may it agree to a variation in such a contract which defers, or gives the promisor the right to defer, the performance of his promise to such a time.[14]

It should not be imagined that every contract which fails to qualify as a contract to issue shares in consideration of cash will be a contract to issue them for a consideration other than cash, so as to enable the shareholder to escape from paying the nominal value of his shares in money. A contract by which the shareholder is relieved from liability to pay part of the nominal value of his shares in consideration of agreeing to take them, is not a contract to allot shares for a consideration other than cash, for in reality the shareholder gives nothing for the amount by which his shares are credited as paid up.[15] For the same reason an allotment of shares credited as fully paid in consideration of services previously performed by the shareholder is not an allotment for a consideration other than cash, for past services are no consideration at all.[16] The release by the shareholder of a debt payable only out of the company's future profits, which the company is therefore only contingently liable to pay, is no consideration for the allotment of shares,[17] and probably the release of any debt or liability which is not immediately payable or enforceable, even though it will become payable or enforceable in the future, is no consideration either. A safe guide as to what is consideration for the allotment of shares is found in the words of Farwell LJ:[18]

'Now I apprehend that shares are issued subject to payment either in money or money's worth, by which I understand that there must be something to set on the credit side of the company against the liability for the amount of shares issued. It may be cash; it may be

10 The introduction of a price expressed in money terms resulted from the enactment of the Companies Act 1867, s 25 (repealed in 1900). It gave the contract a spurious appearance of providing for the allotment of shares for cash, but the device rebounded on those who used it when the court held otherwise, and compelled the shareholder to pay cash for his shares if the contract had not been registered.
11 *Re Church and Empire Insurance Co, Pagin and Gill's Case* (1877) 6 ChD 681; *Re Church and Empire Fire Insurance Fund, Andress' Case* (1878) 8 ChD 126; *Re Government Security Fire Insurance Co, White's Case* (1879) 12 ChD 511; *Re Stapleford Colliery Co, Barrow's Case* (1879) 14 ChD 432. In this respect *Gardner v Iredale*, supra, appears to have been wrongly decided.
12 Including a private company which has passed a resolution to be re-registered as a public company (Companies Act 1985, s 116) (see p 63, ante).
13 Companies Act 1985, s 102 (1).
14 Ibid, s 102 (3).
15 *Ooregum Gold Mining Co of India v Roper* [1892] AC 125.
16 *Re Eddystone Marine Insurance Co* [1893] 3 Ch 9.
17 *Bury v Famatina Development Corpn Ltd* [1909] 1 Ch 754; affd sub nom *Famatina Development Corpn Ltd v Bury* [1910] AC 439.
18 *Bury v Famatina Development Corpn* [1909] 1 Ch 754 at 761.

property taken at a valuation in consideration of fully paid shares issued. But here there is nothing. The contract by the company is that it will appropriate in futuro profits, if made, in discharge of certain indebtedness. That is not an asset of the company in any sense at all, nor does it properly appear in the capital account.'

If the consideration given by the shareholder will result in an increase in the company's assets, it is immaterial that it takes the form of a promise (eg a promise to transfer property to or confer benefits on the company in the future).[19] The allotment need not be deferred until the promise is fulfilled, and the shares will be paid up to the extent provided by the contract immediately they are allotted. If the shareholder then fails to perform his promise, the company's remedy is to sue him for damages for breach of contract; it cannot sue him for the nominal value of his shares in cash.[19] Moreover, if in contravention of the Companies Act 1985 a public company allots shares as fully or partly paid up in consideration of a promise to do work or perform services,[20] or in consideration of a promise to provide other benefits within a period which will or may exceed five years after allotment,[1] or if a public company does not receive such other benefits within a period of five years or less after allotment fixed by the contract with the allottee,[2] the allottee and any subsequent holder of the shares[3] are liable to pay the company an amount in cash equal to the nominal value of the shares plus any premium on their issue,[4] but a holder subsequent to the allottee can escape this liability by showing that he purchased the shares for value without notice of the contravention, or that he derives title under such a holder.[5] On the other hand, the fact that there has been such a contravention of the Companies Act 1985 does not prevent the company from enforcing the allottees' promise made in consideration of the allotment.[6] If the allottee in fact performs his promise with the company's concurrence, it would seem that he has a claim against the company for an amount equal to the sum credited as paid up on the shares, and that he may set this off against the company's statutory claim for payment in cash. Whether a subsequent holder of the shares can effect a similar set-off is uncertain, though it would appear that he may be able to do so in equity.[7] It also seems that

19 *Re Theatrical Trust Ltd, Chapman's Case* [1895] 1 Ch 771; *Gardner v Iredale* [1912] 1 Ch 700.
20 Companies Act 1985, s 99 (1).
1 Ibid, s 102 (1).
2 Ibid, s 102 (5).
3 'Holder' is defined as a member of the company who is registered in respect of the shares, or a person who has an unconditional right to be so registered or to have an instrument of transfer of the shares executed in his favour (Companies Act 1985, s 112 (4)). A holder is liable, however, only if he becomes a holder after the contravention occurs (s 112 (1)), and so a transferee of shares which are to be paid up by performance of a promise within five years of allotment falls under the statutory liability only if he becomes a holder after the contractual period for performing the promise has expired (s 112 (5)).
4 It is unlikely that an issue or share premium would be agreed on expressly, but it could arise by the contract between the company and the allottee attributing a money value to the consideration to be given by the allottee which exceeds the nominal value of the shares to be issued to him by the company credited as fully paid.
5 Companies Act 1985, s 112 (3) and (5).
6 Ibid, s 115 (1).
7 This could be achieved by the court holding that the allottee is a trustee for the holder of the claim he has against the company for payment for the services or other consideration he has performed; the holder would then, as equitable owner of this claim, be able to set it off against the company's legal claim for payment of the nominal value of the shares in cash plus any share premium in respect of the shares (*Jones v Mossop* (1844) 3 Hare 568; *Bankes v Jarvis* [1903] 1 KB 549). If the court holds that there is no such trust, however, it would be impossible for the holder of the shares to effect a set-off against the company's claim by relying on a personal claim he has against the allottee for reimbursement of the amount the holder is liable to pay the company and linking it with the allottee's claim against the company; in a tripartite situation where the first party has a claim against the second, the second against the third and the third against the first, the first party cannot set-off against the third the lesser of his own claim against the second and the latter's claim against the third.

the company's statutory right to recover an amount in cash equal to the nominal value of the shares and any premium on their issue is in addition to, and not in substitution for, its right to recover the unpaid nominal value and premium, and so the shares are not to be treated as paid up until the company has received the issue price in full in cash or the holder of the shares is entitled to set off an equal sum, but when this occurs both the company's right to be paid the issue price and the statutory liability of the holder are satisfied.[8]

Value of consideration for allotment of shares

The allotment of shares for a consideration other than cash is open to the obvious abuse that the real value of the consideration may be less than the amount credited as paid up on the shares. In the case of public companies a safeguard against this is now provided by the requirement of an expert valuation of the consideration before the shares are allotted,[9] but this is not so in the case of private companies. The court exercises some control over the abusive over-valuation of consideration in kind whether the company is a public or a private one, but it will not ordinarily interfere to ensure that the consideration is equivalent to the amount credited as paid up on the shares.[10] The court treats the valuation of the consideration as a matter to be negotiated by the company and the allottee of the shares, and declines to limit their freedom to agree what terms they wish. The court has rarely recognised that other shareholders who pay for their shares in cash have an interest in the value of the consideration too. In fact they do have such an interest, because if the consideration in kind is less valuable than the amount credited as paid up on the shares issued in exchange, their own shares will suffer a corresponding diminution in value.[11]

The court's unwillingness to depart from the normal principles of contract law in order to protect shareholders who pay for their shares in cash is all the more surprising when it is realised that usually it is to the company's promoters that shares are allotted in consideration of kind, and it is these very people who are usually also appointed the first directors of the company, and who in that capacity fix the terms on which their shares shall be allotted.[12] The court has shown some solicitude for creditors of the company by reasoning that if shares could be paid up by shareholders giving inadequate consideration, creditors would be defrauded, because when their debts are incurred, they rely for payment partly on the reality of the company's capital, which they quite reasonably expect to be paid up in cash or its equivalent value in kind.[13] But it is the persons who subscribe for shares in cash, and not the company's creditors, who most need protection. A creditor who

---

8 Contrast Companies Act 1985, s 101 (1) and (3) where the minimum amount is not paid up on the allotment of shares for cash by a public company, but the shares are nevertheless deemed to be paid up by that minimum amount (see p 160, post).

9 Companies Act 1985, s 103 (1) and s 108 (1) (see p 153, post).

10 *Ooregum Gold Mining Co of India v Roper* [1892] AC 125; *Re Theatrical Trust Ltd, Chapman's Case* supra; *Re Wragg Ltd* [1897] 1 Ch 796.

11 This is because the assets of the company may not be sufficient to cover the nominal value of the issued shares. For example, if a company acquires a business which is really worth £50,000 in return for the issue of 100,000 £1 shares credited as fully paid, and at the same time issues 100,000 £1 shares at par for cash which is paid to it, its total assets will be worth £150,000, whereas its issued share capital is £200,000. Unless its earning capacity is better than the average, therefore, each £1 share will be worth only about 75p. This practice is graphically called 'stock watering' by the Americans.

12 Stock watering has ceased to be as prevalent as it was at the end of the last century and the beginning of this, largely because of the stricter requirements of legislation and the Stock Exchange in respect of companies' prospectuses (see Chapter 8).

13 *Ooregum Gold Mining Co of India v Roper*, supra.

enquires into the company's resources before allowing it to become indebted to him does not in practice rely on the amount of the company's capital, paid or unpaid, in assessing its creditworthiness.[14] He relies instead on the value of its assets, for it is out of them that he will be paid, and so the inadequacy of the consideration for which shares have been allotted will rarely mislead him.

In a few cases the court will enquire into the true value of the consideration given for shares, and if it is found inadequate, or if the transaction is in some way improper, the court will interfere, with the result that the shareholder will be liable to pay the whole or part of the nominal value of the shares in cash. These cases are following.

Patent inadequacy of the consideration

If on the face of a contract for the issue of shares for a consideration in kind it is clear that the consideration given by the allottee to the company for the shares is worth less than the amount by which they are credited as paid up, the shares will be deemed to be paid up only to an amount equal to the value attributed to the consideration by the contract.[15] Lord Macnaghten gave an example of this kind of contract when he said:[16]

> But I desire to protest against some of the propositions which were advanced in connection with this part of the argument. It was said that if a company limited by shares owes its bankers £1,000, and its shares are at 50 per cent discount, fully paid shares of £2,000 nominal value may be given in discharge of the debt. It was said that a company limited by shares may issue fully paid shares at their market price at the time, however much they may have become depreciated, in exchange for goods having a recognised market value. Speaking for myself, I am not prepared to assent to either of those propositions without further argument.'

A L Smith LJ, gave another example.[17]

> '. . . if in a registered contract a money value less than the face value of the share be placed upon the consideration which the company had agreed to accept as representing in money's worth the nominal value of the share, that share, I should think, would not be fully paid up; for instance, as was put in argument, a contract to supply to a limited company 100 tons of coal valued at 10s per ton, as a consideration for 100 £1 shares in the company—ie a value of £50 worth of coal for 100 £1 shares—these shares would not be, I think, fully paid up.'

In practice such cases are never met with, for whatever the real value of the consideration given for an allotment of fully paid shares may be, the allottee is unlikely to advertise the inadequacy of the consideration by agreeing to show its value in the contract for the allotment as less than the nominal value of the shares.

Failure by the company to assess the money value of the consideration

Although the court does not ordinarily assess the value in cash of the consideration given for shares, it does ensure that the board of directors has made its own assessment of that value in good faith, for without such an assessment no equation of the consideration with the amount credited as paid up on the shares is possible, and the shares cannot be considered to be paid up at all. Thus, where a company

---

14 This is so even when a creditor lends money on the security of the company's unpaid capital. He always takes a charge on the company's assets as well, and it is by reference to their value and the company's earning capacity that he calculates the amount he is willing to lend.
15 *Re Theatrical Trust Ltd, Chapman's Case* [1895] 1 Ch 771 at 774.
16 *Ooregum Gold Mining Co of India v Roper* [1892] AC 125 at 148.
17 *Re Wragg Ltd* [1897] 1 Ch 796 at 836.

allotted shares in consideration of the transfer to it of certain mining leases and of expenditure by the vendor on improving the mines, but the directors had made no assessment of the cash value of the leases and improvements, it was held that the shares were not paid up at all, because 'no attempt had been made to correlate the nominal value of the shares to the value of the payments, property and services'.[18] In that case no contract had been made between the company and the vendor before the allotment. If a contract had been made by which the company agreed to allot the number of shares actually allotted (whether or not the contract stated the cash value of the consideration as a sum equal to the nominal value of the shares), the contract would have been prima facie evidence that the directors had assessed the cash value of the consideration, and unless their assessment was a nullity for one of the reasons given below, the shares would be deemed to be paid up to the extent agreed.

When the directors have assessed the cash value of the consideration, the court will not set their assessment aside unless it was made dishonestly or in bad faith, or unless the facts show that as reasonable men they could not possibly have concluded that the consideration was equal in value to the amount credited as paid up on the shares. In one case,[19] for example, a company acquired a trading concession in exchange for an allotment of shares, and agreed that if at any time it increased its issued share capital, the vendor should be entitled as further consideration to a quarter of the increase in fully paid shares. It was held that the vendor could call for the further shares, but if he did, he would have to pay for them in cash, because the number of further shares to be allotted to him was uncertain when the contract was made, and so the directors could not possibly have equated their nominal value with the value of the concession acquired by the company. Again, where a company accepted deferred creditors' certificates for amounts unpaid on shares held by an insolvent shareholder, and the certificates entitled the company to payment out of the future profits of the shareholder, it was held that the shares were not paid up by the acceptance of the certificates, because the directors could not possibly have considered them equal in value to the amounts unpaid on the shares, and the only reason why the directors accepted them was to obtain something in the shareholder's insolvency.[20]

The acts of the parties may show that the directors did not genuinely believe that the consideration given for the shares was equal to the amount credited as paid up on them. Thus, where vendors contracted to sell property to a company for a certain number of fully paid shares, but agreed to forgo some of the shares on being pressed by other shareholders who had paid for their shares in cash, and the shares given up by the vendors were allotted to the other shareholders instead, it was held that the shares were wholly unpaid, because the concession by the vendors showed that the directors could not have judged the property sold to the company to be worth the number of fully paid shares originally agreed to be allotted to the vendors.[1] But the mere fact that the company pays an extravagant price for property or a service is not sufficient evidence by itself that the directors have failed to make an honest assessment of its value. Nor is the fact that the cash value attributed by the contract to one item of the consideration given by the shareholder is in excess of the value of that item according to a recent professional valuation, for it does not follow that the value of all the items of the consideration taken together is less than the amount credited as paid up on the shares issued in

18 *Tintin Exploration Syndicate Ltd v Sandys* (1947) 177 LT 412 at 418.
19 *Hong Kong and China Gas Co Ltd v Glen* [1914] 1 Ch 527.
20 *Re White Star Line Ltd* [1938] Ch 458, [1938] 1 All ER 607.
 1 *Re Alkaline Reduction Syndicate, Ames' Case* [1896] WN 79.

exchange.[2] The farthest the courts have gone in upholding a transaction where the propriety of the directors' assessment was questionable was in a case[3] where a vendor agreed with promoters to sell a business to a company yet to be formed in consideration of the allotment of fully paid shares with a nominal value of £6,000, and when the company was incorporated the vendor contracted to sell the business to it for fully paid £1 shares of a total nominal value of £25,000, 6,000 of which were to be allotted to him, and the remaining 19,000 of which were to be allotted to the promoters as his nominees so that they might make presents of them to customers who dealt with the company. It is submitted that there was sufficient evidence in this case for the court to conclude that the directors did not make a genuine assessment of the value of the business, and consequently, that none of the shares allotted were paid up at all.

If directors do not make a genuine assessment of the consideration given for the shares they issue, the shares are wholly unpaid and the shareholder must pay their nominal value in cash.[4] Usually the shareholder will be aware that no proper assessment was made, and he cannot therefore complain of the risk which he knowingly runs. But if he is unaware of the facts when he takes the shares, and he has not yet been entered on the company's register of members, he may repudiate the allotment of the shares and so escape liability.[5] Presumably, if his name has been put on the register of members, he may still repudiate the allotment on discovering the irregularity (at least, before the company is wound up), and may apply to the court for the removal of his name from the register.[6] In one case[7] it was held that an allotment of shares is void if the directors have made no assessment of the consideration given for them at all, because it is ultra vires a company for it to make an allotment without proper consideration. It is very doubtful if this is correct. In the case in question the liquidator of the company successfully sought to make the directors liable in damages to the company for the irregular allotment, and it sufficed that the court should hold either that they acted ultra vires the company, or that they had broken their duty to manage its affairs properly.[8] By holding the allotment void because it was ultra vires, the court would also have implicitly released the allottee from his obligation to pay for the shares, and it is most unlikely that this result was intended.

The court has not yet been called on to decide what rights a shareholder has against the company to recover the value of the consideration which he has in fact given for shares allotted to him, if the directors have not properly valued the consideration and the shareholder is compelled to pay the nominal value of the shares in cash. The shareholder cannot require the company to pay him the value attributed to the consideration in the contract, because the contract did not contemplate that he should be paid in cash. Presumably, however, he may sue for a quantum meruit for the value of services he has given, or a quantum valebant for the value of goods or other property he has transferred, and it will be for the court to decide what the real value of the services or property is. If the company is in liquidation the shareholder can prove for the amount of his claim only if he pays the nominal value of the shares he has taken in full,[9] and he

2 *Re Wragg Ltd* [1897] 1 Ch 796.
3 *Re Innes & Co Ltd* [1903] 2 Ch 254.
4 *Re White Star Line Ltd*, supra.
5 *Re Macdonald Sons & Co* [1894] 1 Ch 89.
6 The reasoning in *Re Derham and Allen Ltd* [1946] Ch 31 supports this view.
7 *Tintin Exploration Syndicate Ltd v Sandys*, supra.
8 See pp 583 and 591, post.
9 *Re White Star Line Ltd* [1938] Ch 458, [1938] 1 All ER 607.

cannot set off the amount of his claim against the nominal value of the shares and tender the balance to the liquidator.[10] Consequently, if the company is insolvent he will recover only a fraction of his claim; this is perfectly fair, for if the law were otherwise, the shareholder would have an advantage over the company's other creditors. Moreover, he would also be in a better position than the other shareholders, who if the company is insolvent, will receive no repayment in respect of their shares or the consideration they gave for them, or if the company is solvent but has insufficient assets to repay the capital it has raised in full, will receive back only a fraction of the capital they have contributed.

Where the company is entitled to rescind the transaction

If the company has been induced to accept the consideration for which it allotted shares by a fraudulent misrepresentation,[11] or if the transaction is voidable because of a breach of fiduciary duty owed to the company by a director or promoter,[12] the company may rescind the contract on returning the consideration given by the other party.[13] But the other party does not thereupon automatically cease to be a member of the company, and since his shares are now wholly unpaid in consequence of the rescission, he is under a statutory liability to pay their nominal value in cash if he retains them. If he repudiates the allotment of the shares when the company rescinds the underlying contract, however, it seems that he ceases to be under any liability to pay for them in cash,[14] but such a repudiation is effective only if made immediately after the company rescinds the contract and in any case before the company commences to be wound up.[15]

When contracts for the allotment of shares have been set aside by the court, it has usually been on the ground that the company is entitled to rescind the transaction because the allottee, as a promoter or director of the company, has not properly disclosed his interest in the transaction or the real value of the consideration he gave, or has not obtained the approval of the shareholders for the transaction when this is necessary. In such circumstances the rescission of the underlying contract provides little real protection for the shareholders who have subscribed for their shares in cash, for if the company is to continue, they must either negotiate the purchase of a similar business or property to the one returned to the promoter or director, or must use the cash subscribed by themselves to embark on a different kind of venture. In practice the inevitable consequence of the rescission of an important acquisition of property is that the company goes into liquidation. What is needed to protect cash subscribers for shares is some preventive procedure which will ensure that the consideration given for shares is really the equivalent of their nominal value. This is the purpose of the compulsory valuation of consideration in kind given for shares issued by public companies which is next dealt with.

---

10 *Re Overend, Gurney & Co, Grissell's Case* (1866) 1 Ch App 528.
11 *Re Almada and Tirito Co* (1888) 38 ChD 415 at 423, per Cotton LJ; *Re Wragg Ltd* [1897] 1 Ch 796 at 830, per Lindley LJ.
12 *Re Wedgwood Coal and Iron Co, Anderson's Case* (1877) 7 ChD 75 at 94. For the fiduciary duties of promoters and directors, see Chapters 13 and 14.
13 The company cannot rescind unless it can restore to the other party what he has given. It is this limitation which has often prevented companies from compelling promoters who have watered their shares from paying in cash for the shares they have taken.
14 *Re Wedgwood Coal and Iron Co, Anderson's Case* (1877) 7 ChD 75 at 104, per Jessel MR.
15 *Re Hull and County Bank, Burgess's Case* (1880) 15 ChD 507.

Valuation of consideration in kind on allotment by a public company

When a valuation is required

A public company[16] may not allot shares on terms that the whole or part of their nominal value or any premium on their issue[17] shall be paid up otherwise than in cash, unless the consideration has been valued by an independent expert who has reported to the company on its value within six months before the allotment and a copy of his report has been sent to the allottee before allotment.[18]

No valuation or report is required, however, if a company allots shares in connection with an arrangement (including any agreement, scheme or, it would seem, any offer) under which the company will or may acquire from their holders all or some of the shares issued by another company, or all or some of the shares of a particular class issued by another company, provided that the arrangement is open to all the shareholders of the other company, or all the holders of the class of shares to be acquired,[19] but the arrangement need not extend to shares in the other company held by the offeror company or by another company in the same group as the first company[20] or by nominees of the first company or another company in the same group.[1] The same exception applies if the arrangement is for the allotment of shares by the first company in return for the cancellation of all or some of the shares, or of all or some of the shares of a particular class, issued by another company.[1] It would seem that the arrangement for the acquisition or cancellation of shares may take the form of a direct offer made by the first company to the shareholders of the other company, and that a formal scheme of arrangement approved by a general or class meeting of the other company is not necessary. Consequently, the exception makes a valuation unnecessary when a takeover bid or other general bid is made by a company for the shares of another company, and the offeror company offers an issue of shares in itself in exchange for the transfer or cancellation of the existing shares of the other company. However it is not necessary that the new shares should all be allotted to shareholders of the other company, and so if the offeror company underwrites its offer (ie arranges for a merchant bank or financial institution to acquire any new shares for cash from any shareholder of the other company who does not wish to take them), the fact that certain of the new shares are allotted to the underwriter does not make the exception inapplicable. Moreover, it is not necessary that the acquisition by the offeror company of shares in the other company should be the only consideration for the issue of new shares by the offeror.[1] Consequently, the exception applies if the offeror company offers an issue of shares in exchange for the transfer to it of the existing shares and debentures of the other company. If the arrangement provides for the cancellation of existing shares of the other company in return for the allotment of shares in the offeror company, the cancellation will be effected by a reduction of the capital of the other company at the same time as the allotment of the new shares.[2]

A further situation where no valuation is required is where the company which allots the new shares does so in connection with a merger of another company with

---

16 Including a private company which has passed a resolution to be re-registered as a public company (Companies Act 1985, s 116) (see p 63, ante).

17 See footnote 20 on p 163, post, for the circumstances in which such a premium may arise.

18 Companies Act 1985, s 103 (1).

19 If the arrangement is for the acquisition of less than all the shares of the other company, or for less than all the shares of a particular class, it would appear that the arrangement must be available proportionately to all the shareholders (eg an offer for 50 per cent of their individual holdings).

20 That is, subsidiaries of the offeror company, its holding company (if any) and subsidiaries of its holding company (see Chapter 20).

1 Companies Act 1985, s 103 (3), (4) and (7).

2 See p 177, post.

itself, that is, when it acquires all the assets and liabilities of the other company in return for the issue of the new shares or other securities (eg debentures convertible into shares) to the shareholders of the other company, with or without an additional cash payment to them.[3] The definition of a merger is a narrow one, and does not include the acquisition of part of the assets or undertaking of the other company by the company which issues the new shares, nor an acquisition of the whole undertaking of the other company in return for an issue of shares to one or more classes of its shareholders and a cash payment to the remainder of them. In those situations a statutory valuation of the assets or undertaking of the other company which the issuing company acquires would be necessary.

To avoid doubt, it is statutorily declared that it is not necessary to have a valuation when shares are issued as fully or partly paid up by appropriating and capitalising an amount standing to the credit of a company's reserves or profit and loss account (ie an issue of bonus shares).[4]

The valuation procedure

Where a valuation of a non-cash consideration for the allotment of shares is required, it must be made by a person appointed by the company which issues the new shares,[5] and that person must be independent of the company and be qualified at the date of his report to be appointed to be the company's auditor,[6] or if he is already its auditor, to continue to be its auditor.[7] However, if the person so appointed considers it reasonable for the whole or part of the valuation to be made by another person with the requisite knowledge and experience, he may engage such another person to make a valuation of the whole or part of the consideration,[8] but the other person so engaged must not be an officer or employee of the issuing company or any other company in the same group,[9] or a partner or employee of such an officer or employee.[8]

When the valuation has been completed, the person appointed to make it must submit a report to the issuing company stating the nominal value of the shares to be allotted for the non-cash consideration and the amount of any agreed share or issue premium on those shares, the description of the consideration, the methods of valuation employed and an identification of that part of the consideration which he valued personally and those parts of it (if any) which were valued by other persons engaged by him, together with their names and the nature of their relevant knowledge and experience; the report must also state the extent to which the nominal value of the shares and any share or issue premium are to be treated as paid up by the non-cash consideration and by any cash payment made, or to be made, by the allottees or other persons.[10] If the company is to allot shares and also to give some other consideration for the non-cash consideration provided by the allottee (eg if the company is to issue both shares and debentures on the acquisition of a property or business), the person appointed to make the valuation, or another person appointed by him to make part of it, must additionally determine the

---

3 Companies Act 1985, s 103 (5).
4 Ibid, s 103(2). For bonus or capitalisation issues of shares, see p 434, post.
5 The appointment will be made by the company's board of directors if (as is usual) the company's articles delegate its powers to them gradually (see Table A, art 70)).
6 For the qualifications required for appointment as an auditor, see p 711, post.
7 Companies Act 1985, s 108(1). The company's auditor currently holding office may be appointed, and is not disqualified as not being independent, even though he is treated as an officer of the company for certain purposes.
8 Companies Act 1985, s 108 (2).
9 See footnote 20 on p 154, ante.
10 Companies Act 1985, s 108 (4) and (5).

proportion of the non-cash consideration which is properly attributable to the new shares to be allotted,[11] and the report of the person appointed by the company to make the valuation must state what valuations were made for this purpose and the method of valuation employed.[12] The valuation report submitted by the person appointed by the company must finally contain, or be accompanied by a note containing, a statement that it appeared reasonable to him to engage another person or persons to make the whole or part of the valuation (if that was done), that the method of valuation employed was reasonable, that it appears to him that there has been no material change in the value of the non-cash consideration since the valuation was made, and that on the basis of the valuation the non-cash consideration plus any cash paid or to be paid for the shares to be allotted is not less than the aggregate of so much of the nominal value of those shares plus any share or issue premium thereon as is to be treated as paid up thereby.[13] If the company gives any other consideration in addition to the allotment of new shares (eg debentures), the statement made by the person appointed to make the valuation will, of course, relate to that part of the non-cash consideration which is properly attributable to the new shares.[12]

A copy of the valuation report must be delivered to the Registrar of Companies with the return of allotments[14] in respect of the shares allotted[15] and the Registrar publishes the delivery of such a copy in the London Gazette.[16]

Consequences of irregularity

The directors of a public company act wrongfully if they allot shares credited as paid up by a non-cash consideration without first obtaining a report containing the statements mentioned above by the person appointed to value the consideration, accompanied by a note containing the additional statements mentioned above if the report does not contain them, or if they do not send a copy of the report and the accompanying note (if any) to the allottee or allottees before allotment,[17] and directors who allot shares without complying with these requirements are liable to the company for any consequential loss it suffers. If the valuer's report shows that the value attributable to the non-cash consideration is less than the amount proposed to be credited as paid up on the shares to be issued, it would appear to be the directors' duty to reduce the amount credited as paid up accordingly. If they nevertheless allot the shares credited as paid up to a greater extent, they will not breach the rules relating to the statutory valuation,[18] but it would seem that the shares will be deemed to be issued at a discount in breach of the statutory prohibition,[19] and the directors will then be liable to the company for the difference as damages for breach of that prohibition.[20] The obtaining of a statutory report on the value of the non-cash consideration and abstaining from issuing shares for it at

11 This will presumably be done by deducting the market value of the additional consideration to be given by the company (eg the market value of debentures to be issued by it) from the valuation of the consideration in kind to be provided by the allottee.
12 Companies Act 1985, s 108 (7).
13 Ibid, s 108 (6).
14 For the return of allotments, see p 309, post.
15 Companies Act 1985, s 111 (1).
16 Ibid, s 711 (1) (*f*).
17 Ibid, s 103 (1).
18 Except possibly the requirement that before the shares are allotted the person appointed to make the valuation must state that the consideration in kind plus any cash to be paid by the allottee is not less than the amount credited as paid up on the shares plus any issue premium (Companies Act 1985, s 108 (6)). But this statement does not have to be included in the valuation report if it is contained in an accompanying note.
19 Companies Act 1985, s 100 (1) (see p 142, ante).
20 *Hirsche v Sims* [1984] AC 654.

a discount revealed by the valuation in the report would not seem to exhaust the directors' duties, however. It would appear that if they do not make a separate decision of their own that the value of the non-cash consideration equals the amount credited as paid up on the shares which they issue for it, they are guilty of a breach of their duties to the company and are liable for consequential loss suffered by it, although no doubt the availability of a statutory report valuing the consideration as equal to the paid up value of the shares would go far to rebut an allegation that the directors acted unreasonably in deciding that there was such an equivalence. It would also appear that if the person appointed to make the statutory valuation makes it negligently by over-valuing the consideration, and the company allots shares accordingly, the valuer is liable and the company may recover damages from him for its resulting loss by suing him for breach of contract and for the tort of negligence, but that he is not liable to the other shareholders of the company whose shares have fallen in value in consequence.[21]

The allottee of shares issued by a public company for a non-cash consideration is liable to pay to it in cash an amount equal to the nominal value of the shares plus any agreed share or issue premium if he has not received a copy of the report by the person appointed by the company to value the consideration before the shares are allotted, or if there has been any other contravention of the statutory rules about the valuation and he is aware or should be aware of the contravention when the shares are allotted.[1] In those circumstances a subsequent holder of the shares is also liable to pay the company the same amount, unless he purchased the shares for value without notice of the failure of the allottee to receive a copy of the valuation report or of the other contravention, or unless he derives title from such a purchaser.[2] The same uncertainty arises under this provision as to whether the allottee's and holder's liability is substituted for their liability to pay the unpaid issue price of the shares as arises under the corresponding provisions governing the consequences of a public company allotting shares for a consideration which need not be wholly provided within five years.[3] If the statutory liability of the allottee and subsequent holders is substituted for a liability to pay the issue price of the shares in cash, the shares must be treated as paid up by the agreed value of the non-cash consideration notwithstanding the contravention; if not, the statutory liability and the liability of the allottee and subsequent holders under the general law to pay the nominal value of the shares plus any share or issue premium in cash will exist concurrently. If that is so, a subsequent holder of the shares will only escape liability to pay for them in cash if he is both a purchaser for value without notice of a contravention or a person deriving title under such a purchaser (so as to escape the statutory liability), and is also a person who has been induced by the company to acquire the shares in the belief that they are fully paid (so as to escape liability for unpaid capital under the general law).[4] A further uncertainty arises if the allottee actually performs his promise to furnish the non-cash consideration, and so has a claim against the company for its agreed value.[5] It would appear that the allottee could set off that claim against his statutory liability to pay the equivalent of the nominal value of the shares plus any share or issue premium in cash, but it is uncertain whether a subsequent holder of the shares would be entitled to do

21 *Arenson v Casson Beckman Rutley & Co* [1977] AC 405, [1975] 3 All ER 901 (see p 723, post).
1 Companies Act 1985, s 103 (6).
2 Ibid, s 112 (1). For the definition of a subsequent holder, see footnote 3 on p 148.
3 Companies Act 1985, s 112 (1) and (5) (see p 148, ante).
4 *Burkinshaw v Nicolls* (1878) 3 App Cas 1004; *Bloomenthal v Ford* [1897] AC 156.
5 The contract for the provision of the consideration in kind is not invalidated by a contravention of the rules for the statutory valuation; it is enforceable by the company (Companies Act 1985, s 115 (1)), and presumably also by the allottee.

so.[6] Furthermore, it may be that the only way in which an allottee who has performed his promise to furnish the non-cash consideration may assert his claim is by seeking relief from the court from his statutory liability to pay the nominal value of the shares and any agreed share premium in cash.[7]

If the statutory valuation procedure is properly carried out and the copy of the valuation report sent to the allottee shows that in the opinion of the person appointed to make the valuation the non-cash consideration to be provided by the allottee is at least equal to the amount credited as paid up on the shares allotted to him, the allottee can incur no statutory liability to the company, even if the valuation is excessive or the directors of the company have not made their own valuation. The allottee may, nevertheless, still be liable to pay the nominal value of the shares and any share or issue premium in cash if he was aware of such an irregularity, or even if he was not, when the irregularity consists of the directors' failure to make their own estimate of the value of the consideration.[8] It would seem, however, that the allottee will not be liable in this way if he relied in good faith on the copy of the valuation report sent to him before allotment, because the company thereby adopted the report as its own document and impliedly represented to the allottee that the shares allotted would be paid up to the extent stated in the report. If the report showed that the shares would be allotted at a discount, however, the allottee would be aware of the irregularity, and he would be liable to pay the amount of the discount to the company in cash.[9] The position of a subsequent holder of the shares in these circumstances will depend on whether the company has represented to him that the shares are fully paid; if it has done so, for example, by issuing a fully paid share certificate to the allottee or an intermediate holder who transfers the shares to the subsequent holder and the latter relies on that certificate when he acquires the shares, the company will not be able to claim unpaid capital from him.[10] Furthermore, a subsequent holder of the shares will not incur a statutory liability to pay the company an amount equal to their nominal value plus any share or issue premium if he purchases the shares for value and is unaware that the issue was at a discount.[11]

Extension of the valuation procedure

The statutory requirement of a valuation of a non-cash consideration for the allotment of shares is extended to non-cash assets provided for a public company by a subscriber of its memorandum under an agreement made within two years after the company obtains its certificate of entitlement to do business[12] if the consideration to be given by the company is equal to at least one-tenth of the company's issued share capital at the time of the agreement.[13] Non-cash assets are defined more narrowly than a consideration other than cash, however; they comprise any property or interest in property other than cash (including foreign currency) and the creation or extinction of any liability other than a liability to pay a liquidated amount.[14] This extension of the compulsory valuation procedure

---

6 Compare the situation of such a holder where shares are allotted in consideration of a promise which need not be fulfilled within five years (see p 148, ante).

7 *Systems Control plc v Munro Corporate plc* [1990] 6 BCC 386 (see p 161, post).

8 *Re White Star Line Ltd* [1938] Ch 458, [1938] 1 All ER 607; *Tintin Exploration Syndicate Ltd v Sandys* (1947) 177 LT 412.

9 Companies Act 1985, s 100 (2).

10 *Burkinshaw v Nicolls*, supra; *Bloomenthal v Ford*, supra.

11 Companies Act 1985, s 112 (1) and (3) (see p 142, ante).

12 See p 30, ante.

13 Companies Act 1985, s 104 (1) and (2) and s 109 (1) and (2).

14 Ibid, s 739 (1) and (2).

is of little practical importance, because the statutory valuation rules apply anyway if the company allots shares in return for any non-cash consideration, and because if the company acquires non-cash assets for any other consideration than the allotment of shares (eg a cash payment or an issue of debentures) the extension only applies if the consideration in kind is provided by a subscriber of its memorandum, and not by any other person connected with it, such as a promoter or director. Furthermore, the extension does not apply to acquisitions of assets by a company in the ordinary course of its business or under the supervision of the court.[15]

Where the extension does apply, however, the agreement for the acquisition of the non-cash assets must additionally be approved by an ordinary resolution passed by a general meeting of the company;[16] this is not necessary when shares are allotted by a public company for a non-cash consideration to a person other than a subscriber of the company's memorandum. If there is a contravention of the rules requiring a valuation of the non-cash assets and a resolution of approval of the acquisition, and shares are allotted by the company, the consequences are the same as on a contravention of the ordinary rules requiring a valuation on the allotment of shares for a non-cash consideration.[17] If there is a contravention in any other situation, where no allotment of shares is involved, but the other party to the agreement knew or ought to have known of the contravention, the company is entitled to recover any consideration it has given to him or an amount equal to its value, and the agreement for the acquisition of the non-cash assets is void so far as it has not been carried out.[18]

The foregoing requirements also apply if a company which has been re-registered as a public company enters into an agreement to acquire non-cash assets equal to at least one-tenth of its issued share capital from any of its members at the date of its re-registration and the agreement for the acquisition is made within two years after that date.[19] This extension of the valuation and approval requirements is, of course, of greater practical importance than the requirements relating to acquisitions from subscribers. The statutory requirements cannot be evaded by the member at the date of the company's re-registration transferring the shares to a person who was not a member at that date before the company agrees to acquire the non-cash assets from him, but if the acquisition is contemplated but no contract for it is made before the company's re-registration, the requirement will not apply if the member transfers his shares and so ceases to be a member of the company before it is re-registered as a public company.[20]

A company which has received a report on the value of non-cash assets acquired from a subscriber of its memorandum within two years after the company becomes entitled to do business, or on the value of non-cash assets acquired from a member of a company at the time of its re-registration as a public company within two years after its re-registration, must deliver a copy of the report to the Registrar of Companies within 15 days after the acquisition is approved by a resolution of a general meeting of the company.[20] The Registrar must publish the delivery of copies of the reports in the London Gazette.[1]

---

15 Ibid, s 104 (6). An example of an acquisition under the court's supervision is one made under a scheme of arrangement approved by the court under the Companies Act 1985, s 425.
16 Companies Act 1985, s 104 (4).
17 Ibid, s 105 (3).
18 Ibid, s 105 (1) and (2).
19 Ibid, s 104 (3). For the re-registration of a private company as a public company, see p 63, ante.
20 The transfer of the member's shares must be registered by the company in its register of members before it is re-registered as a public company, because the member will otherwise still be a member of it at that time (Companies Act 1985, s 22 (2)).
1 Companies Act 1985, s 711 (1) (*f*). ′

Minimum payment of share capital on allotment

A private company need not require any particular fraction of the nominal value or share or issue premium of shares to be paid up on allotment, and so can make a valid allotment of shares on which the whole or any part of the issue price remains to be paid in the future. A public company,[2] however, is prohibited from allotting shares to be paid for in cash or for a consideration other than cash unless at least one quarter of the nominal value of the shares plus the whole of any share or issue premium is paid up before or concurrently with their allotment.[3] In the case of shares issued for cash, the appropriate amount must be received by the company, but when shares are allotted for a consideration other than cash, the consideration may take the form of a promise to be performed within not more than five years after allotment,[4] and so the shares may be allotted as fully paid even though no part of the promise has yet been performed.

If a public company allots shares on which less than one quarter of their nominal value plus any share premium has been paid up, the shares are deemed to be paid up to that extent.[5] Nevertheless, the allottee of the shares is liable to pay the company in cash the minimum amount which should have been paid up on or before allotment less the amount of any consideration which has actually been given to the company for the shares.[6] Subsequent holders of the shares are liable to the company for the same amount, unless they have purchased the shares for value without actual notice that the minimum amount had not been paid on allotment, or unless they derive title under such a purchaser for value.[7]

The requirement that the minimum amount shall be paid up on allotment does not apply to shares allotted under an employees' share scheme.[8] Such shares may be allotted for payment in cash, but they may be allotted on payment of any fraction of the issue price, or even with nothing paid up.[9]

Power of the court to relieve from liability

The allottee of shares in a public company and subsequent holders of the shares may incur a statutory liability to pay it an amount equal to the nominal value of the shares plus any issue premium in cash because of the contravention of any of the rules dealt with above as to the allotment of shares in consideration of work or services,[10] or for the allotment of shares for a non-cash consideration performed or to be performed more than five years after allotment,[11] or because of the contravention of any rules as to the valuation of a consideration other than cash provided in return for an allotment of shares,[12] or as to the valuation of a non-cash asset which the company agrees to acquire within two years after its incorporation

---

2 Including a private company which has passed a resolution to be re-registered as a public company (Companies Act 1985, s 116) (see p 63, ante).
3 Companies Act 1985, s 101(1).
4 Ibid, s 102 (1) (see p 146, ante).
5 Ibid, s 101 (3).
6 Ibid, s 101 (4). For example, if the allottee has actually conferred benefits on the company under an agreement that the value of the benefits shall be credited against the issue price of the shares, the amount payable by the allottee in cash is correspondingly reduced.
7 Companies Act 1985, s 112 (1) and (3). For the definition of a subsequent holder, see footnote 3 on p 148, ante.
8 Companies Act 1985, s 101 (2). For the definition of an employees' share scheme, see p 247, post.
9 If shares allotted under an employees' share scheme are paid up out of the company's profits, they are fully paid when they are allotted.
10 Companies Act 1985, s 99 (3) and s 112 (1) (see p 146, ante).
11 Ibid, s 102 (2), (5) and (6) and s 112 (5) (see p 148, ante).
12 Ibid, s 103 (6) and s 112 (1) (see p 157, ante).

from subscribers of the memorandum of association or within two years after the company's re-registration as a public company from any of its members at the date of re-registration.[13] On the application of any person liable under those rules the court may exonerate him from his liability in whole or part and on such terms as the court thinks fit,[14] but in deciding whether to give relief and on what terms, the court must have regard to any other liability of the applicant to make payments in respect of the same shares and any payments he has in fact made, to the fact that any other person has made or is likely to make payments in respect of the shares, and to any enforceable undertakings of the applicant to confer benefits on the company in return for the shares and any performance by him of such undertakings.[15] Nevertheless, the court must ensure so far as possible that the company receives value at least equal to the nominal value of the shares plus any share or issue premium from the persons who are liable to make payment in cash or from other sources.[16] The court's primary concern, on an application by an allottee of shares for exoneration from his statutory liability because the non-cash consideration which he agreed to provide in return for the allotment has not been the subject of a proper valuation, is to ensure that the company has received or is certain to receive that consideration in full and that its value to the company is at least equal to the paid up value of the shares allotted and any agreed premium.[17] This may be proved by evidence that the company has resold the whole or the greater part of the property or assets constituting the non-cash consideration and has received a price at least equal to that paid up value and premium.[17]

The court has no power to give relief from liability to make payments in respect of shares allotted at a discount,[18] or in respect of shares allotted by a public company without the minimum amount being paid up on allotment.[19]

ISSUES OF SHARES AT A PREMIUM

If a company's issued shares are saleable on the market for more than their paid up value (ie their nominal value if they are credited as fully paid), they are said to be at a market premium. It follows that if the company issues further shares with the same rights, it should be able to obtain a price from subscribers approximately equal to the price at which its existing shares are selling on the market.[20] This price will be made up of two elements, namely, the paid up value of the share and the share or issue premium, which is the excess of the issue price over the paid up value and is received by the company as part of the issue price, unlike a market premium which is received by the seller of existing shares.

13 Ibid, s 105 (1) and (3) and s 112 (2) (see p 159).
14 Ibid, 113 (1) and (2). Similarly under s 113 (8) relief may be given against liability to repay the value of any consideration given by a public company in a transaction between it and the subscribers of its memorandum within two years after its incorporation, or between it and its existing members within two years after its conversion from a private company.
15 Companies Act 1985, s 113 (3) and (4).
16 Ibid, s 113(5).
17 *Re Ossory Estates plc* [1988] BCLC 213, (1987) 4 BCC 460; *Systems Control plc v Munro Corporate plc* (1990) 6 BCC 386.
18 Companies Act 1985, s 100 (2) and s 112 (1) (see p 142, ante).
19 Ibid, s 101 (4) and s 112 (1) (see p 160, ante).
20 In fact, the issue price will be slightly less than the current market price in order to induce investors to subscribe for the shares rather than buy existing shares on the market. If the new shares are offered to the existing shareholders of the company by way of a rights issue, the issue price is often substantially less than the current market price of existing shares of the same class.

Share premium account

A company is prohibited by law from returning any part of its share capital to its members in the form of a dividend declared on the shares, but at common law it could use the money received by it in respect of share premiums for this purpose, provided that it had sufficient assets left to answer for its share capital after paying the dividend.[1] The payment of dividends out of a company's assets representing share premiums is now prohibited by the Companies Act 1985, which requires the company to credit a sum equal to the premiums obtained on the issue or allotment of shares to an account called its share premium account, and provides that the provisions of the Act relating to the reduction of share capital shall apply to a company's share premium account.[2] It is therefore no longer possible for a company to credit share premiums to profit and loss account so as to make them available for paying dividends. Instead, they are credited to the special statutory reserve, share premium account, in order to keep them distinct from profits and revenue reserves, and the application of the rules governing reductions of capital to share premium account ensures that assets representing share premiums are not distributed among the shareholders without a special resolution being passed by a general meeting of the company and the approval of the court first obtained.[3] There are no inherent restrictions on the court's power to approve the reduction of a company's share premium account, however, and so the fact that the share premiums credited to the account arise under the same transaction as that which occasions the reduction is no obstacle to the court approving it (eg share premiums on the acquisition by the company of shares in another company in exchange for the issue of new shares by the acquiring company, where the amount of the share premiums arising on that new issue is to be cancelled and credited instead to a special capital reserve, which will be used to write off the excess of the value attributed to the acquired shares over the book value of the net assets of the acquired company (consolidation goodwill)).[4]

In a balance sheet in double columnar form share premium account appears on the liabilities side as an item in the company's capital reserves immediately after share capital. Consequently, the company's assets on the other side of the balance sheet represent share capital, share premium account, other capital and revenue reserves and also the total amount of the indebtedness of the company.[5] In the winding up of the company its assets are applied, first in paying its debts and liabilities, and then its share capital is returnable to its shareholders, but assets representing share premium account apparently belong to no-one. In fact, assets representing share premiums, like assets representing all capital reserves, are distributable among all the shareholders who are entitled to the residual assets of the company after satisfying its debts and repaying share capital which has priority for repayment in a winding up and no further rights of participation.[6] Consequently, in a winding up assets which represent share premium account are distributed among all such shareholders rateably, whether or not they have paid premiums on the issue of their own shares.[7]

1 *Drown v Gaumont-British Picture Corpn Ltd* [1937] Ch 402, [1937] 2 All ER 609.
2 Companies Act 1985, s 130 (1) and (3) (re-enacting Companies Act 1948, s 56 (1)).
3 See p 185, post.
4 *Re Ratners Group plc* [1988] BCLC 685, (1988) 4 BCC 293; *Re European Home Products plc* [1988] BCLC 690, (1988) 4 BCC 779; *Re Thorn EMI plc* [1989] BCLC 612, (1988) 4 BCC 698.
5 If the company's balance sheet is in single column form, its assets and liabilities are shown first and the balance (the company's net worth) is then shown as corresponding to its capital plus its capital and revenue reserves.
6 Eg preference shares entitled to prior repayment of capital (see p 212, post).
7 *Re Driffield Gas Light Co* [1898] 1 Ch 451.

In requiring share premiums to be credited to share premium account the Companies Act 1985 contains no qualification that it applies only to premiums paid in cash.[8] Consequently, the Act applies whether premiums are paid in cash or kind, and so if a company issues shares for a non-cash consideration which is worth more than the paid up value of the shares, an amount equal to the excess value of the consideration must be credited to share premium account.[9] The directors should therefore have the consideration valued even if the company is a private one so that a statutory valuation is not required,[10] and the excess value of the consideration over the paid up value of the shares allotted for it should be credited to share premium account forthwith in order to avoid any risk of dividends being paid out of the premium by inadvertence. If such dividends were paid, the directors would be personally liable to restore the amount distributed, and could only escape liability by proving that they honestly and reasonably believed that there was no excess value to be credited to share premium account.[11]

Exceptions to treatment of share premiums as a capital reserve

Before a judicial decision in 1980 to the contrary[12] it was widely assumed by practitioners that the need to credit issue premiums to share premium account could be avoided when shares were issued for a consideration other than cash by the contract for the issue of the shares either not mentioning the market or saleable value of the consideration, or expressly providing that the consideration for the issue should be deemed to have a value equal to the nominal or paid up value of the shares, even though the market value of the consideration for the shares was clearly much greater than their nominal value. This practice was particularly prevalent when a merger was carried out by one company transferring its assets and undertaking to another in consideration of the issue of shares by the transferee company to the transferor company's shareholders. Similarly, a takeover bid by an exchange of shares would be carried out without the offeror company crediting any sum to share premium account if the bid did not specify the value which the offeror company put on the offeree company's shares, for it would then be assumed that the offeror's directors had valued them at the exact equivalent of the nominal value of the offeror's shares issued in exchange.

Share premiums on mergers and takeovers

The Companies Act 1981 dealt with the difficulties raised by the inconsistency between the practice on mergers and takeovers and the law by validating retrospectively the action of any company which issued shares before 4 February 1981 in consideration of the issue, transfer or cancellation of shares in another company which thereby became, or already was, a subsidiary of the first company, even though the first company did not credit to its share premium account a sum equal to the excess of the market value of the issued, transferred or cancelled shares over the nominal value of the shares issued by itself.[13] This provision is continued in force by the recent consolidating legislation,[14] but it applies only where the company in question issued the new shares before 4 February 1981, and

---

8 Companies Act 1985, s 130 (1).
9 *Henry Head & Co Ltd v Ropner Holdings Ltd* [1952] Ch 124, [1951] 2 All ER 994; *Shearer v Bercain Ltd* [1980] 3 All ER 295.
10 Companies Act 1985, s 103 (1).
11 *Re Kingston Cotton Mill Co (No 2)* [1896] 1 Ch 331.
12 *Shearer v Bercain Ltd* [1980] 3 All ER 295.
13 Companies Act 1981, s 39 (1) to (3).
14 Companies (Consequential Provisions) Act 1985, s 12 (1) to (4).

immediately before the new shares were issued the other company was already a subsidiary of the issuing company or its holding company, or the other company became such a subsidiary as the result of the issue, transfer or cancellation of shares in itself in consideration of the issue of the new shares.[15] If the first company's holding after the transaction extended only to 50 per cent or less of the other company's equity share capital and the issuing company did not control the composition of the other company's board of directors, therefore, the issuing company was still obliged to credit its share premium account with the excess of the market value of the acquired or cancelled shares at the date it issued its own new shares. The effect of this would be to diminish the profits or revenue reserves shown in the issuing company's balance sheet, and consequently restrict the amount of dividends which it may distribute.[16]

The Companies Act 1985 makes fewer concessions in respect of share premiums arising on issues of new shares in consideration of the acquisition of shares of another company on or after 4 February 1981. It provides cautiously that if a company holds 90 per cent or more of the issued equity share capital[17] of another company (either directly or through other companies in the same group as the first company) as a result of an arrangement (ie any agreement, scheme or, it would seem, offer) for the issue of equity shares by the first company in consideration of the issue or transfer to it of equity shares of the other company or the cancellation of such shares, any share premiums arising from the excess of the market value of the acquired or cancelled shares of the other company over the nominal value of the shares issued by the first company need not be credited to its share premium account, and the first company's accounts may show the shares acquired by it in the other company at a value (ie cost of acquisition) equal to the nominal value of the shares issued by it in exchange.[18] It should be noted that it suffices that, after the issue of the new equity shares, the first company holds 90 per cent of the issued equity share capital of the other company, either by having acquired sufficient shares of the other company to make its total holding (including shares it already held in the other company before the acquisition) equal or exceed 90 per cent, or by sufficient shares of the other company being cancelled by a reduction of its capital so that the first company, after the reduction, holds at least 90 per cent of the other company's remaining issued equity share capital.

An example of the operation of this provision would be where a bid is made by one company, A plc, which holds already 10 per cent of the issued ordinary shares of another company, B plc, for the remaining ordinary shares of B in consideration of an issue of new fully paid ordinary shares of A on a one for one exchange basis when the market value of the shares bid for exceeds the nominal value of the new shares; if under the bid A acquires 80 per cent or more of B's issued ordinary shares, it may disregard the share premium arising on the issue of its own shares, and take the shares in B acquired by it into its accounts at an acquisition cost equal to the nominal value of the new shares issued by it. If B has two or more classes of equity shares, it will be necessary for A to hold 90 per cent or more of each class of such shares in consequence of its bid in order to disregard share premiums arising from the exchange, and A will have to offer a share exchange for all of those classes of shares, though not necessarily at a premium for each class.[19] If in the example given above, B has issued participating preference shares or preferred ordinary

---

15 For the definition of a subsidiary, see p 730, post.

16 Companies Act 1985, s 228 (1) and Sch 4, para 34 (1) and (3).

17 Equity shares and equity share capital are defined as comprising all issued shares of a company other than shares which neither as respects dividends nor as respects capital carry any right to participate beyond a specified amount in a distribution (Companies Act 1985, s 744).

18 Companies Act 1985, s 131 (1), (2), (4), (6) and (7) and s 133 (1).

19 Ibid, s 131 (5).

shares as well as ordinary shares, all such shares will be comprised in its issued equity share capital, and A will therefore have to make a share exchange offer for the participating preference or preferred ordinary shares as well as for the ordinary shares, and immediately after the conclusion of the bid A will have to hold 90 per cent of B's ordinary shares and 90 per cent of its participating preference or preferred ordinary shares. However, it will be immaterial that the market value of the participating preference shares or the preferred ordinary shares is the exact equivalent of the nominal value of the new shares issued by A in exchange and they are acquired by A without a share premium arising. On the other hand, if A makes a cash offer for the participating preference or preferred ordinary shares, the exemption will not apply, and A will have to treat the share premiums arising on the issue of new shares by it in exchange for B's ordinary shares in the normal way and credit them to its share premium account.

If, under an offer to acquire the outstanding equity shares of B, A acquires sufficient of those shares to be entitled to disregard the share premiums arising on the issue of its own shares, A may by the same offer seek also to acquire non-equity shares of B (eg preference shares with no participation rights in surplus profits or in surplus assets in a liquidation) in exchange for the issue of new shares of A (whether equity shares or not); any share premiums arising on the issue of the new shares by A in exchange for non-equity shares in B may then be disregarded by A, and A need not hold any particular percentage of the non-equity shares of B in consequence of the offer.[20] Consequently, if A initially holds 60 per cent of B's ordinary shares but none of its preference shares, and under its composite share exchange offer A acquires 30 per cent of B's issued ordinary shares and 30 per cent of its issued preference shares, it may disregard any share premiums arising from the excess of the market value of both B's ordinary and preference shares over the nominal value of the shares issued by A in exchange. A may similarly disregard share premiums arising on the issue of shares by it in return for the issue to it of non-equity shares of B or in return for the cancellation of existing non-equity shares of B, provided that the simultaneous offer by A in respect of B's equity shares results in A holding at least 90 per cent of B's issued equity share capital.[20]

If in the above examples, A is to disregard premiums arising on the issue of shares in itself, it is necessary that A should hold 90 per cent or more of the total of B's issued equity shares *in consequence* of its offer to acquire equity shares of B (with or without other classes of B's shares).[1] It therefore appears that if A already holds 90 per cent or more of B's equity shares before it makes a consolidation bid for its remaining equity shares, any share premium arising on the issue of its own shares in exchange must be credited to share premium account in the ordinary way, because it is then not in consequence of its bid that A holds 90 per cent or more of B's equity share capital. The court may nevertheless have primary regard to the general purpose of the statutory exception from the obligation to credit the share premium account, and may hold that the exception applies to a further acquisition of B's equity shares, whether A already holds less or more than 90 per cent of those shares before it makes its offer; this would certainly be more logical.[2]

20 Ibid, s 131 (3).
1 Ibid, s 131 (1) and (4).
2 When a company becomes the holder of as much as 90 per cent of the equity share capital of another company, the market value of the remaining minority holdings in that company inevitably falls considerably, and the first company can usually make a later consolidation bid by offering an exchange of further new shares in itself for the minority holdings without as substantial a share premium arising as under its original offer. However, this provides no good legal or commercial reason for denying the first company exemption from the obligation to credit any share premium which does arise under the consolidation bid to its share premium account, and the obligation to do so may actually depress the value of the exchange offer which it does make.

Share premiums on group reconstructions

The Companies Act 1985 also makes a less radical, but nevertheless important, exception to the rules governing share premiums by permitting assets acquired by a parent or holding company of a group or by any of its subsidiaries to be transferred within the group of companies to which it belongs in consideration of an issue of new shares by the transferee company without any excess of the current market value of the transferred assets over their original cost of acquisition being taken into account for the purpose of computing share premiums.[3] This is so, however, only if the transferor and transferee companies are respectively a parent company and its wholly-owned subsidiary, or two wholly-owned subsidiaries of the same parent company.[4] An example of the operation of this provision is where a company, A plc, or its wholly-owned subsidiary, X Ltd, acquires part of the issued share capital of a third company, S Ltd, in consideration of cash or an issue of its own shares to S Ltd's shareholders, and A plc or X Ltd then transfers the shares it holds in S to Y Ltd, another wholly-owned subsidiary of A, in consideration of an issue of new shares by Y. Under the statutory rule as to share premiums as interpreted by the court,[5] Y would have to treat any excess in the current market value of the shares transferred over the nominal value of the new shares issued by Y to A or to X as a share premium, and would have to credit its share premium account accordingly. However, under the statutory exception Y may instead treat the premium as limited to the excess of the original cost to A or X of the shares in S Ltd over the nominal value of the new shares issued by Y, and in its accounts Y may show the acquisition cost to it of the shares in S as equal to the original acquisition cost to A or X.[6] If in its accounts A or X had written down the value of the shares in S to less than the original acquisition cost to it, the written down value would be taken instead of the original cost as the basis for calculating the share premium in Y's accounts and the value attributed by it to the shares in its accounts.[6]

The Companies Act 1985 prohibits the two last mentioned exceptions from the rules governing share premiums being applied in combination in connection with the same share issue, and if both exceptions would appear to apply, the second exception now under consideration applies to the exclusion of the first.[7] This means that a share premium may arise in a case which appears to fall under both exceptions, even though it would not arise if the first exception alone applied. For example, if X Ltd and Y Ltd are two unrelated companies and X acquires 30 per cent of the equity share capital of S Ltd, a third unrelated company, and Y acquires 60 per cent of S's equity capital, an acquisition of X Ltd's holding by Y Ltd in exchange for an issue of Y's equity shares falls under the first exception, and Y need not treat any part of the excess of the current value of X's holding in S Ltd over the nominal value of the new shares issued by Y as giving rise to a share premium in its accounts.[8] If X Ltd and Y Ltd are both wholly-owned subsidiaries of A, however, the second exception alone applies, and Y will have to credit to its share premium account any excess of the acquisition cost to X of its holding in S Ltd over the nominal value of the shares which Y issues to X.[9] On the other hand, there is nothing to prevent the application of the two statutory exceptions to two separate

3 Companies Act 1985, s 132 (1) to (5).
4 Ibid, s 132 (1).
5 *Shearer v Bercain Ltd* [1980] 3 All ER 295.
6 Companies Act 1985, s 132 (1) to (5) and s 133 (1).
7 Ibid, s 132 (8).
8 Ibid, s 131 (1), (2) and (4).
9 Ibid, s 132 (1) to (5).

acquisitions by companies in the same group. For example, if X Ltd acquires 90 per cent of the equity shares of S Ltd in exchange for an issue of its own equity shares, it may apply the first exception, credit nothing to its share premium account and take the acquired shares into its own accounts at an amount equal to the nominal value of the shares it issues in exchange;[8] X Ltd may then later transfer the shares it holds in S Ltd to its fellow wholly-owned subsidiary, Y Ltd, in exchange for an issue of Y's shares, and Y may treat the acquisition cost to itself as equal to the nominal value of the shares which X issued to S Ltd's shareholders and credit its own share premium account only to the extent (if any) that the nominal value of those shares exceeds the nominal value of the shares which Y issues to X.[9]

Other cases

The exceptions to the rules governing share premiums made by the Companies Act 1985 do not form a logical or consistent system, and it is clear that further exceptions will have to be made in the light of experience. To facilitate this, the Act empowers the Secretary of State for Trade and Industry to make regulations which will relieve companies from their statutory obligation to credit share premiums to share premium account where the premium takes a form other than cash, and also to make regulations restricting or modifying the relief from compliance with that obligation which the Act itself confers.[10] By exercising this power the Secretary of State could make it possible for a company to disregard a premium arising on an issue of shares in exchange for the issue, transfer or cancellation of shares in another company if the other company is or becomes a 51 per cent subsidiary or a 20 per cent associate of it, or to disregard a premium arising on the issue of shares within a group of companies comprising a parent company and its 51 per cent subsidiaries in consideration of an internal transfer of any assets within the group.

Permitted uses of share premium account

Assets representing share premium account, like assets representing paid up share capital, cannot be used to make distributions to a company's members,[11] but the Companies Act 1985 permits three uses to be made of the amount standing to the credit of share premium account.

In the first place, share premium account may be used to pay up unissued shares to be issued to members as fully paid bonus shares.[12] So far as the company's accounts are concerned, this is simply a bookkeeping transaction. Share premium account is debited with the nominal value of the bonus shares, and issued share capital account is credited with the same amount. In the company's balance sheet the amount credited to share premium account suffers a reduction whilst issued share capital is correspondingly increased. No assets of the company change hands; the alterations are confined to the liabilities side of the balance sheet if it is in double columnar form and, of course, the total of the entries on that side is the same as before the issue of bonus shares. The operation does affect the shareholders, however. All the shareholders who are entitled to share in the company's residual assets on a winding up are entitled to the bonus shares in proportion to the nominal values of their existing holdings. This may well affect the distribution of voting power between shareholders in general meetings of the company. Furthermore, the market value of their individual shares will fall, but the total value of their

10 Ibid, s 134 (1).
11 Ibid, s 130 (3).
12 Ibid, s 130 (2).

holdings, original and bonus shares together, will be approximately the same as before.[13] Disregarding factors external to the company, only a change in the company's assets or earnings affects the value of shareholders' total holdings,[14] and a bonus issue does not bring about such a change.

The second permitted use of share premium account is in writing off the preliminary expenses of forming the company, raising its original share and loan capital, and paying professional and other fees in connection with the acquisition of its business, and also in writing off the expenses of issuing any shares or debentures, and the amount of commission paid[15] and discount allowed[16] on any such issue.[11] These items appear as assets in the company's balance sheet, because they were paid or allowed for out of the money raised by the issue of shares or debentures, and therefore still represent share or loan capital. But they are not saleable assets, and so the company will write them off as quickly as possible by crediting the accounts in which they appear as assets[17] and debiting profit and loss account, reserve accounts or share premium account with their amount. In a balance sheet in double columnar form the writing off appears as a deduction of the same sum from both sides, leaving the new lower total of assets and liabilities still in balance. The items written off disappear from the assets side of the balance sheet, and profit and loss account, a reserve account or share premium account on the liabilities side is reduced accordingly.

The third permitted use to which share premium account may be put is in providing the premiums payable or the redemption of debentures,[12] or to a limited extent on the redemption of redeemable shares.[18] When debentures are issued and fully paid, their nominal value will appear on the liabilities side of the balance sheet in double columnar form, and should be represented by assets of an equal amount on the opposite side. If the company has agreed to pay a premium over and above the nominal value of the debentures to their holders on redemption, that is, has agreed to redeem them at a sum greater than their nominal value, the money to pay the redemption premium may be found out of the assets which represent share premium account, in which case the assets so applied will cease to belong to the company, and share premium account will be reduced correspondingly.

Share premium account and shares of no par value

Section 130 of the Companies Act 1985 is one of the few sections of the Act which recognise that the real capital of a company is the price which subscribers pay it for its shares. Carried to its logical conclusion, such a recognition results in the admission of shares of no par value. If such shares were permitted, the capital of

13 If the company issued 100,000 £1 shares at par and later a further 100,000 £1 shares at £1·50, its assets should be worth at least £250,000, and on an assets basis each of its shares should be worth £1·25. If the company then issues 50,000 £1 bonus shares to its shareholders, each shareholder will receive one bonus share for every four shares he already holds, but each share, original or bonus, will now be worth only £1 on an assets basis. But five shares worth £1 each are the exact economic equivalent of four shares worth £1·25 each.
14 If the market value of the company's shares before the bonus issue is disproportionately high, the issue may result in the total holding of original and bonus shares being worth slightly more than the original shares before the issue. The reason for this is that the bonus issue makes the shares more marketable.
15 See p 324, post.
16 Discount may be allowed on the issue of debentures (see p 200, post) and formerly could be allowed on the issue of shares if certain conditions were fulfilled and the court's permission was obtained (Companies Act 1948, s 57, repealed by Companies Act 1980).
17 The cost of these items, like all other assets, will appear as a debit entry in the company's accounts in respect of assets.
18 Companies Act 1985, s 160 (2) (see p 189, post).

the company would simply be the total paid for its shares by subscribers,[19] and the accidental payment of dividends out of capital would automatically be precluded by the company's obligation to keep in hand assets worth at least the amount paid by subscribers plus the amount of the company's outstanding debts and liabilities. Until no par value shares are permitted, however, the law can ensure that assets representing the issue price of shares are not dissipated in paying dividends only by using the inelegant device of the share premium account.

Share premiums not obligatory

The Companies Act 1985 imposes no obligation on a company to issue its shares at a premium when a premium is obtainable. Consequently, the issue of shares at par is valid even though a premium could have been obtained,[20] but directors who fail to require subscribers to pay the full issue price obtainable on the market are guilty of breach of duty to the company, and are liable to pay the premium which could have been obtained as damages.[1] Nevertheless, it is generally accepted that directors are not guilty of a breach of duty if they issue shares at a price substantially below their market value to existing shareholders in pursuance of a rights offer made to all the shareholders of the company in proportion to the nominal value of their existing holdings, or alternatively, to all the ordinary shareholders if preference shareholders have no subscription rights conferred by the company's memorandum or articles or by the Companies Act 1985.[2] The reason for this is that all the shareholders concerned may avail themselves of the offer, and if they do, none of them will suffer a diminution of his proportionate interest in the net assets or earnings of the company, and so none of them will suffer harm. If any shareholder fails to subscribe or to sell his right to do so if the offer is renounceable,[3] his loss is self-inflicted. Similarly, it is generally accepted that directors may legitimately offer shares for subscription by directors, officers or employees of the company at prices below the market value of the shares, provided that the difference can be justified as reasonable remuneration for the services of the officers or employees. If shares are so issued to directors or officers, it may be necessary under the company's articles to obtain the approval of a general meeting of the company.[4]

ALTERATION OF SHARE CAPITAL OTHER THAN REDUCTION

A limited company may, if authorised by its articles, make certain alterations to the provisions of its memorandum with regard to share capital by passing a resolution at a general meeting of the company,[5] and unless the memorandum or

19   This is known in the United States as the company's paid in capital. If the whole of the issue price has not been paid, the total amount paid plus the total amount remaining to be paid is called the company's stated capital.
20   *Hilder v Dexter* [1902] AC 474.
 1   *Lowry v Consolidated African Selection Trust Ltd* [1940] AC 648 at 679, [1940] 2 All ER 545 at 565, per Lord Wright.
 2   *Mutual Life Insurance Co of New York v Rank Organisation Ltd* [1985] BCLC 11. An offer made to existing shareholders except certain of their number who are excluded because the company would be put to disproportionate trouble and expense if the offer were extended to them, may also be made at less than the full market value of the shares.
 3   For renounceable rights offers, see p 240, post.
 4   *Neal v Quinn* [1916] WN 223 (see p 597, post).
 5   Companies Act 1985, s 121 (1) and (2). It is nowadays unusual for the memorandum or articles to require a special resolution. Table A, art 32, permits increases in nominal capital and the redivision of shares into shares with a greater or smaller nominal value to be effected by ordinary resolution.

articles otherwise require, the resolution may be an ordinary one. The alterations which may be made are the following:

(1) An increase in the company's nominal capital by an amount stated in the resolution consisting of additional shares with a nominal value likewise stated.[6] This alteration does not affect the company's issued capital, and existing shareholders cannot be compelled to take the additional shares.[7] The company simply takes power to issue new shares in excess of its former nominal capital to willing subscribers. Notice of the increase of nominal capital and particulars of new shares of which it is to consist (if the rights attached to such shares have been decided upon) must be delivered to the Registrar of Companies within fifteen days after the resolution for the increase is passed,[8] and the Registrar must publish the delivery of the notice in the London Gazette.[9]

(2) The redivision of the company's shares into shares of a greater or smaller nominal value.[10] For example, if the company's original nominal capital was £100,000 divided into 200,000 shares of 50p each, the shares may be consolidated into 100,000 shares of £1 each, or subdivided into 400,000 shares of 25p each. The nominal, issued and paid up capital remain the same as before, and the only effect of the alteration is that shareholders either hold a smaller number of shares of a higher nominal value each, or a greater number of shares of a lower nominal value each. Shares may be consolidated or subdivided either before or after they are issued.[11] The tendency nowadays is toward shares of low nominal values, because they are more marketable, and so a company formed eighty years ago with £10 shares, which were then common, may modernise its capital by subdividing each £10 share into 10 £1 shares. If partly paid shares are subdivided, the proportion between capital already paid and remaining unpaid on the original shares must be maintained,[12] for example, if £1 shares, 40p paid, are each subdivided into four 25p shares, the amount credited as paid up on each subdivided share must be 10p. Notice of an alteration of shares by consolidation or subdivision must be given to the Registrar of Companies within one month after the resolution is passed,[13] and the Registrar must publish the delivery of the notice in the London Gazette.[9]

(3) The conversion of fully paid shares into stock, and the reconversion of stock into fully paid shares of any nominal value.[14] The difference between shares and stock is that shares are transferable only in complete units, so that a transfer of half a share is impossible, whereas stock is expressed in terms of an amount of money (its nominal value) and is transferable in any money fractions. Thus, if the company's issued share capital consists of fully paid £1 shares of which X owns 100, he may transfer one £1 share, but he cannot transfer less. If the shares are converted into stock, however, X will hold £100 stock, and he may transfer 50p, 5p or even 1p's worth of it.[15] The articles of companies which have converted their

---

6 Companies Act 1985, s 121 (1) and (2) (*a*).

7 Ibid, s 16 (1).

8 Ibid, s 123 (1) and (2).

9 Ibid, s 711 (1) (*b*). The increase involves an alteration of the capital clause in the company's memorandum.

10 Companies Act 1985, s 121 (1) and (2) (*b*) and (*d*).

11 Ibid, s 711 (1) (*b*). This is because the consolidation or subdivision involves an alteration of the capital clause in the company's memorandum.

12 Ibid, s 121 (3).

13 Ibid, s 122 (1) (*a*) and (*d*).

14 Companies Act 1985, s 121 (1) and (2) (*c*).

15 If a company created stock before the present decimal currency was introduced in 1971 and the stock was transferable in smaller amounts than the equivalent of 1p (eg in 1*d* or ½*d* units), the minimum amount of stock which may now be transferred is 1p's worth, and transfers of larger amounts must be of multiples of 1p's worth (Decimal Currency Act 1969, s 8 (1) (10 Halsbury's Statutes (4th edn) 174)).

shares into stock usually specify the minimum amounts of stock which may be transferred, and these minimum amounts are known as units of stock or stock units. When this is done the advantage derived from converting shares into stock is diminished, and if the stock units have the same nominal value as the former shares, as they usually do, there is no advantage at all.

There was formerly another advantage derived from converting shares into stock. Shares had to be numbered consecutively[16] whereas stock could not be numbered. The records of shares which the company had to keep were therefore more detailed and troublesome, and it was to avoid this additional work that many companies converted their shares into stock. When all the shares of the company or of a particular class are fully paid and rank equally in all respects, however, the company may now dispense with distinguishing numbers for each share[17] and so that advantage of stock over shares has disappeared.

It should be noted that only fully paid shares may be converted into stock; a resolution converting partly paid shares into stock is void.[18] But if a company issues fully paid stock on a capitalisation of profits in pursuance of an ordinary resolution passed by a general meeting, the company and any shareholder who accepts the stock waive the requirement that shares should first be issued and should then be converted into stock, and the issue of stock is valid.[18]

Notice of the conversion of shares into stock or of their reconversion must be given to the Registrar of Companies within one month of the appropriate resolution being passed.[19]

(4) The classification or re-classification of the company's share capital. The memorandum may divide the company's capital stated in the capital clause into two or more named classes of shares,[20] although this is not obligatory. Any such division and designation is therefore a provision of the memorandum which could have been contained in the company's articles, and it may therefore be altered by the company passing a special resolution[1]. If the company's capital is not divided into different classes originally by the memorandum, a division and designation of the classes of shares in the memorandum may be effected in the same way. The power of a company to classify or re-classify its capital in its memorandum does not enable it to alter the rights attached to different classes of its shares,[2] and for this to be done the appropriate procedure must be followed to alter the class rights.[3]

If a company's articles divide its share capital into different classes or designate them by different names, the division or designation may be changed by the company passing a special resolution altering the articles, and a division or designation of different classes of shares may be introduced into the articles in the same way,[4] but if the division or designation in either class is accompanied by an alteration of the rights attached to a class of shares, the appropriate procedure must be followed for that purpose.

When a company classifies or re-classifies its share capital, it must notify the

---

16 The number of the share is the number appearing in the body of the share certificate and in the register of members, not the serial number of the share certificate, which usually appears in the top left hand corner.
17 Companies Act 1985, s 182 (2).
18 *Re Home and Foreign Investment and Agency Co Ltd* [1912] 1 Ch 72.
19 Companies Act 1985, s 222 (1) (*b*) and (*c*).
20 See p 21, ante.
1 Companies Act 1985, s 17 (1) (see p 73, ante).
2 Ibid, s 17 (2).
3 See p 219, post.
4 Companies Act 1985, s 9 (1).

Registrar of Companies within one month,[5] and the Registrar must publish the notification in the London Gazette.[6]

If a company formed before the currency of the United Kingdom was decimalised alters its share capital in any of the ways described above or reduces its share capital, the expression of the nominal and paid up value of its shares after the alteration or reduction in terms of decimal currency does not itself involve an alteration of the company's memorandum, and so can be effected as part of the alteration without a separate resolution being passed by a general meeting.[7] On the other hand, if the company's nominal capital stated in its memorandum is the nominal value of the shares into which it is divided and is expressed in sterling or any other currency, it would appear not to be possible to alter the currency in which those matters are expressed, even though the amounts expressed in the proposed new currency are the current economic equivalents of the original amounts.

REDUCTIONS OF SHARE CAPITAL WHICH DO NOT REQUIRE THE SANCTION OF THE COURT

The reduction of a company's share capital may obviously affect the interests of its creditors and members far more seriously than any other kind of alteration. Because of this, the law permits a company to reduce its capital only if stringent conditions are complied with. These conditions are designed to ensure that creditors are not prejudiced by the company's assets being distributed amongst its shareholders, or by the company releasing its shareholders from liability for uncalled capital, and also to ensure that the scheme of reduction is fair as between different classes of members. A company cannot evade the prohibition on the irregular reduction of its capital by making payments for assets or services supplied to it which are substantially in excess of the highest value which can reasonably be attributed to them,[8] or by selling assets of the company at prices substantially lower than the minimum value which they must have.[9] Nor can a company evade the prohibition on the irregular reduction of capital remaining to be paid on its shares by accepting surrenders of its partly paid shares,[10] nor by taking power by its articles to forfeit wholly or partly paid shares for the failure of a shareholder to pay debts owed to the company.[11] A company may purchase or redeem its shares if it complies with certain statutory conditions imposed for the protection of its creditors,[12] but in general it may not use its assets to purchase wholly or partly paid shares issued by it, whether they are surrendered to the company[13] or transferred to trustees for it.[14] These prohibitions were originally deduced by the courts from the provisions of the Companies Acts governing the limitation of the liability of members of a limited company, but they have now been enacted specifically.[15] The

5 Ibid, s 128 (4).
6 Ibid, s 711 (1) (*b*).
7 *Re Harris and Sheldon Group Ltd* [1971] 2 All ER 87n, [1971] 1 WLR 899.
8 *Re Halt Garage (1964) Ltd* [1982] 3 All ER 1016.
9 *Aveling Barford Ltd v Perion Ltd* [1989] BCLC 626, 5 BCC 677.
10 *Bellerby v Rowland and Marwood's SS Co Ltd* [1902] 2 Ch 14.
11 *Hopkinson v Mortimer, Harley & Co Ltd* [1917] 1 Ch 646. This is because the debt would be extinguished if the forfeiture were valid, and the company's assets would be correspondingly reduced.
12 See p 188, post.
13 *Trevor v Whitworth* (1887) 12 App Cas 409.
14 *Cree v Somervail* (1879) 4 App CAs 648 at 666; *Re Patent Paper Manufacturing Co, Addison's Case* (1870) 5 Ch App 294.
15 Companies Act 1985, s 143 (1).

only departure from the earlier law in the statutory restatement of the prohibitions is that although a transfer of partly paid shares to a nominee or trustee for the company is ineffective to reduce the company's capital or to confer any title to the shares on it, the nominee or trustee does become the beneficial owner of the shares and is personally liable with the company's directors to pay any amount unpaid of the issue price of the shares.[16]

Despite the prohibition on the informal reduction of capital of a limited company, certain transactions which do result in a temporary or permanent diminution in its capital are permitted without compliance with the conditions normally imposed on reductions of capital. In these cases there is no risk of creditors being defrauded or their claims defeated, and the provisions designed to protect creditors are consequently relaxed.

Cancellation of unissued capital

A limited company may, if authorised by its articles, cancel shares which have not been issued or agreed to be issued, and reduce its nominal capital by the nominal value of such shares.[17] The reduction is effected by a resolution passed by the shareholders in general meeting, and an ordinary resolution suffices unless the memorandum or articles require a special resolution.[18] Notice of the cancellation of unissued shares must be given to the Registrar of Companies within one month thereafter,[19] and the Registrar must publish the delivery of the notice in the London Gazette.[20] The resolution does not affect the company's issued or paid up capital; it merely reduces its nominal capital, so that the number of new shares which it may now issue is fewer than before, or its power to issue new shares is completely taken away. The cancellation does not prevent the company from subsequently increasing its nominal capital in the way already indicated, and a cancellation of unissued capital and an increase of capital by the creation of new unissued shares may also be resolved upon simultaneously.

Forfeiture and surrender in lieu of forfeiture

A company may take power by its articles to forfeit the shares of any shareholder who fails to pay for them in accordance with the contract under which they were allotted, and it may also take power to re-issue such forfeited shares.[1] There is no doubt that such a power is valid[2] and its exercise does not amount to a prohibited acquisition by the company of its own shares.[3] A company which has power to forfeit shares for non-payment of calls or instalments of the issue price may also accept a voluntary surrender of them if the shareholder is unable to pay the calls or instalments and the surrender would be for the company's benefit, and it may then re-issue the surrendered shares.[2]

It is questionable whether a forfeiture or surrender of shares does really reduce the company's capital. At first sight it appears to do so, because the company cannot be treated as having taken a transfer of the shares, and it therefore looks as though

---

16 Ibid, s 144 (1) (see p 334, post).
17 Ibid, s 121 (1) and (2) (*e*).
18 By Table A, art 32 (*d*), an ordinary resolution suffices.
19 Companies Act 1985, s 122 (1) (*f*).
20 Ibid, s 711 (1) (*b*). This is because the cancellation involves an alteration of the capital clause of the company's memorandum.
1 See, for example, Table A, arts 19 and 20.
2 *Trevor v Whitworth* (1887) 12 App 409 at 417–18 per Lord Herschell.
3 Companies Act 1985, s 143 (3) (*d*).

the shares are extinguished.[4] But this is not necessarily the result. The cases show that shares are not cancelled by being forfeited or surrendered, but are merely in abeyance until they are re-issued. No dividend is paid in respect of forfeited or surrendered shares,[5] and no votes can be cast in respect of them at shareholders' meetings if the company is a public one[6] or, presumably, if it is a private company,[7] but that does not mean that the shares cease to exist. When forfeited or surrendered shares are re-issued the full rights attached to them revive. The re-issued shares are the same shares that were forfeited or surrendered, and not new shares issued in place of the forfeited or surrendered ones.[8] Consequently, the company may reissue them at whatever price it can obtain, whether more or less than their nominal or paid up value,[9] and they are paid up in the hands of the person who takes them on re-issue to the same extent as they were paid up immediately before they were forfeited or surrendered.[10] The amount received by a company on the re-issue of forfeited or surrendered shares is not paid up capital of the company, except in so far as it is appropriated by agreement to pay calls or instalments of the issue price which is owing but unpaid.[11]

Other surrenders

A company has always been able to accept a surrender of fully paid shares from a shareholder if it gives no consideration out of its assets in return,[12] and this has been confirmed by statute.[13] The company in this situation does not release any liability for unpaid capital nor return any share capital to the shareholder, so that there is no possibility of creditors being defrauded. Moreover, there is no risk that other shareholders may be prejudiced, for as regards them the surrendered shares are treated as though they had not been issued, and so the company's distributable profits will be apportioned amongst fewer shares, and the remaining shareholders will receive larger dividends than before.

In most of the cases which have come before the courts the surrender has been in consideration of the company issuing new shares with different rights in exchange for the surrendered shares. This has been held permissible, because the company does not then distribute any of its assets as consideration for the surrender.[14] A doubt is raised by the statutory provision confirming the legitimacy of the surrender, however, since it requires that the company should give no 'valuable consideration', and this could be construed as including an issue of new shares.[13] In the context this seems unlikely, but even if a surrender of shares in return for an issue of new shares is still possible, the amount credited as paid up on the new shares must not exceed the amount paid up on the surrendered ones. Consequently, where a company proposed to accept the surrender of fully paid £1 shares in return for

4 *Bellerby v Rowland and Marwood's Steamship Co* [1902] 2 Ch 14 at 32 per Cozens-Hardy LJ.
5 *Trevor v Whitworth*, supra, per Lord Watson at 424.
6 Companies Act 1985, s 146 (4).
7 Only members of the company can vote at a meeting of shareholders, and the company cannot be a member of itself. It has been decided in the United States that directors cannot vote in respect of shares surrendered to the company (*Atterbury v Consolidated Coppermines Corpn* (1940) 20 A 2d 743).
8 *Re Exchange Banking Co Ltd, Ramwell's Case* (1881) 50 LJ Ch 827.
9 *Morrison v Trustees, Executors and Securities Insurance Corpn* (1898) 68 LJ Ch 11.
10 *New Balkis Eersteling Ltd v Randt Gold Mining Co* [1904] AC 165.
11 See p 324, post.
12 *Re County Palatine Loan and Discount Co, Teasdale's Case* (1873) 9 Ch App 54; *Eichbaum v City of Chicago Grain Elevators Ltd* [1891] 3 Ch 459; *Re Denver Hotel Co* [1893] 1 Ch 495; *Rowell v John Rowell & Sons Ltd* [1912] 2 Ch 609. There are obiter dicta to the contrary in *Bellerby v Rowland and Marwood's SS Co*, supra, per Stirling LJ at 29, and Cozens-Hardy LJ at 32.
13 Companies Act 1985, s 143 (3).
14 *Eichbaum v City of Chicago Grain Elevators Ltd*, supra; *Rowell v John Rowell & Sons Ltd* [1912] 2 Ch 609.

the issue of a hundred fully paid £1 shares of a different class for each surrendered share, it was held that the new shares would not be fully paid.[15]

It has been held that partly paid shares, too, may be surrendered in return for new shares,[12] but in view of the general statutory prohibition now imposed on a limited company acquiring its own shares[16] and the absence of an express exception for an exchange of partly paid shares,[17] it would seem that such an exchange would be ineffective and the holder of the original shares would retain them, and would be obliged to pay the nominal value of the new shares to the company in cash.[18] An exchange of partly paid shares may be held by the court to be valid under the present law only if the exchange is considered not to involve the acquisition of the original shares by the company, but as eliminating the old shares and substituting the new shares for them; it has been held, however, that there is no such elimination on an exchange of shares.[19] If notwithstanding these considerations it is still possible for partly paid shares to be surrendered in exchange for new shares, the amount credited as paid up on the new shares may not exceed the amount paid up on the surrendered ones,[15] and the amount unpaid on the new shares must not be less than the amount unpaid on the old ones, although it may be differently apportioned amongst the new shares.[20] Thus, where before the present statutory prohibition was enacted, a company had issued £10 shares, half of which were fully paid, and the other half were paid up to the extent of £2 10s per share, an arrangement was upheld by which the fully paid shares were surrendered in return for twice the number of £10 shares with £5 credited as paid up, and the partly paid shares were surrendered for half the number of £10 shares, again with £5 credited as paid up.[20] The result of this scheme was that the company's paid up capital remained the same as before, and the reduction in the amount unpaid on its original partly paid shares was more than compensated by the newly created unpaid capital on the shares which replaced its original fully paid shares.

The effect of a surrender of shares, as was shown above, is that they go into abeyance, but the full rights and liabilities attached to them revive when the company re-issues them, and the re-issued shares are the same shares as the surrendered ones.[1] If instead the company issues new shares carrying different rights to 'replace' them, the surrendered shares do not cease to exist, and for this reason the company must ensure that its nominal capital is large enough to accommodate both the surrendered and the new shares, for if it is not, some or all of the new shares will be in excess of its nominal capital, and will be void. The company may re-issue surrendered shares provided that the rights attached to them are unaltered, and if the company is a public company, it must re-issue or cancel them within three years after they are surrendered.[2] Surrendered shares may be re-issued at any price[3] and they are paid up in the hands of the person who takes them to the same extent as they were paid up at the date of surrender.[1] If the company wishes to cancel the surrendered shares, so as to prevent their re-issue, it may do so under the provisions dealt with below relating to reduction of capital with the sanction of the court,[4] or if the company is a public company, by a

---

15 *Re Development Co of Central and West Africa* [1902] 1 Ch 547.
16 Companies Act 1985, s 143 (1).
17 Ibid, s 143 (3).
18 It would not be possible to treat the whole transaction as void for mistake, because the mistake would be one of law.
19 *Re Denver Hotel Co* [1893] 1 Ch 495.
20 *Re County Palatine Loan and Discount Co, Teasdale's Case* (1873) 9 Ch App 54.
 1 *New Balkis Eersteling Ltd v Randt Gold Mining Co* [1904] AC 165.
 2 Companies Act 1985, s 146 (1) to (3).
 3 *Morrison v Trustees, Executors and Securities Insurance Corpn* (1898) 68 LJ Ch 11.
 4 *Re Denver Hotel Co* [1893] 1 Ch 495.

resolution of its board of directors without the need for the court's approval;[5] the surrendered shares cannot be eliminated under the provision dealt with above, whereby shares which have never been issued may be cancelled without the court's approval.[6]

Surrenders of shares in exchange for the issue of new shares with different rights are not common nowadays, because the variation of rights can usually be effected under a provision in the articles[7] without an exchange of shares taking place at all.[8] Consequently, the only surrenders likely to be met with in practice are gratuitous surrenders of fully paid shares made in order to increase the market value of the company's other shares. This is not a common practice, but it may usefully be employed when the company's existing shares are saleable only at a price less than their paid up value and the company wishes to raise their market value by eliminating some of them so that it may issue further shares at a price at or above par. Such surrenders must be made voluntarily, however.[9] If any shareholder will not join in the arrangement for surrendering shares, the reduction of the capital by cancelling the capital paid up on the shares can only be effected with the sanction of the court.

Instead of accepting a gratuitous surrender of fully paid shares a company may have them transferred to trustees for itself.[10] Similarly, a bequest to a company of fully paid shares held in it by a testator may be given effect by the testator's personal representatives transferring the shares to trustees nominated by the company, and the company may require the personal representatives to execute such a transfer.[11] The shares are not then in abeyance. Dividends are paid in respect of them in the same way as on other shares, unless waived by the trustees. If dividends are paid, the money will belong beneficially to the company, and will consequently be available to pay an additional dividend on the other shares it has issued. If the company is a private one, votes may be cast at meetings of shareholders in respect of the shares transferred to trustees for the company, and the trustees must vote as the directors instruct them.[10] This increases the voting power which the directors already possess in respect of their own shares, but since the transferred shares belong to the company in equity, the directors must use the voting rights attached to them for the company's benefit, and not in their own private interests. If the company is a public one, however, voting rights cannot be exercised in respect of the shares transferred to trustees for the company, and the shares must be cancelled by a formal reduction of capital confirmed by the court or by a board resolution requiring no such confirmation, unless the company disposes of the shares or its interest in them within three years after the trustees acquire the shares.[12]

Consequential re-registration of a public company

If as a result of the forfeiture or surrender of shares of a public company or their acquisition by trustees for the company and, in either case, the subsequent

5 Companies Act 1985, s 147 (1). The resolution must be notified to the Registrar of Companies within 15 days (Companies Act 1985, s 147 (2) and s 380 (1)).
6 Companies Act 1985, s 121 (1) and (2) (e) (see p 173, ante).
7 See, for example, the Companies Act 1948, Table A, art 4. The present Table A contains no provision for the variation of rights attached to classes of shares. The subject of variation of rights attached to shares is dealt with, p 219 et seq, post.
8 *Carruth v Imperial Chemical Industries Ltd* [1937] AC 707, [1937] 2 All ER 422.
9 *Re County Palatine Loan and Discount Co, Teasdale's Case* (1873) 9 Ch App 54.
10 *Kirby v Wilkins* [1929] 2 Ch 444. Such an acquisition is contemplated as legitimate by the Companies Act 1985, s 146 and s 147 (1).
11 *Re Castiglione's Will Trusts. Hunter v Mackenzie* [1958] Ch 549, [1958] 1 All ER 480.
12 Companies Act 1985, s 135 (1), s 146 (1) to (4) and s 147 (1).

cancellation of the shares, the company's issued share capital is reduced below £50,000, the company must within three years be re-registered as a private company.[13] The application for re-registration may be made by the directors pursuant to a board resolution for the purpose,[14] which may make all necessary alterations to the company's memorandum.[15] If the Registrar of Companies is satisfied that the application for re-registration is justified, he must issue a new certificate of incorporation to the company as a private company, and the certificate is conclusive evidence that the company is a private company and has been properly re-registered as such.[16]

REDUCTION OF SHARE CAPITAL WITH THE SANCTION OF THE COURT

Power to reduce capital

A limited company whose articles authorise it to do so, may by a special resolution confirmed by the court reduce its share capital in any way, and in particular may reduce its capital:[17]

(a) by extinguishing or reducing the liability of its shareholders for unpaid capital in respect of their shares; or

(b) by returning to its shareholders any paid up capital which is in excess of its wants; or

(c) by cancelling any paid up capital which is lost or unrepresented by available assets.

The three kinds of reduction of capital which are particularised above are the commonest, but the permissible modes of reduction are not limited to them. Any scheme of reduction may be sanctioned by the court.[18] Thus, where a company has assets in the United Kingdom and the United States, and its shares were held by shareholders who resided in either country, the court approved a special resolution by which the proceeds of sale of the assets in the United States were applied in repaying the capital on the shares held by the American shareholders.[19] The repayment of these shares was part of a scheme by which the American assets of the company were transferred to a newly formed American company, for whose shares the American shareholders were given a preferential right to subscribe; the British company retained the remaining assets, and intended to confine its activities to the United Kingdom after the scheme was carried out. Again, where a company had issued £1 ordinary shares and 10s deferred shares, both fully paid, and the market value of the deferred shares was a quarter of that of the ordinary shares, the court approved a reduction of the deferred shares to 5s shares fully paid, so that other resolutions passed by the shareholders for converting the deferred shares into ordinary shares, on the basis of one ordinary share to be issued in place of each block of four deferred shares, might be carried out.[20] On the other hand, where shareholders of the same class are not all treated in the same way by the scheme of reduction (eg by the shares of some, but not all, of them being repaid), it has been

13 Companies Act 1985, s 146 (2).
14 Ibid, s 147 (1) and (2).
15 Ibid, s 147 (2).
16 Ibid, s 147 (4). For the effect of the conclusiveness of the certificate, see p 28, ante.
17 Companies Act 1985, s 135 (1) and (2).
18 *Poole v National Bank of China Ltd* [1907] AC 229.
19 *British and American Trustee and Finance Corpn v Couper* [1894] AC 399.
20 *Carruth v Imperial Chemical Industries Ltd* [1937] AC 707, [1937] 2 All ER 422.

held that the reduction should be effected under the provisions of the Companies Act 1985 relating to schemes of arrangement approved by meetings of the interested classes of shareholders and by the court,[1] and not under the provisions of the Act presently under consideration.[2] It would therefore appear that schemes of the kind described above may be effected by reductions of capital only when there is no opposition to them by any member or creditor of the company.

Reduction of liability for unpaid capital

A reduction of the liability of shareholders for unpaid capital is usually effected by reducing the nominal value of their shares. Thus, if the company has issued £1 shares on which 50p has been paid up, the liability of the shareholders for unpaid capital may be reduced to 25p by reducing the nominal value of each share to 75p. If it were desired to extinguish the liability for unpaid capital completely, the nominal value of the shares would be reduced to 50p. The same result might be achieved by leaving the nominal value of the shares as £1 and cancelling one share out of every two held by a shareholder.[3] In this latter case the 50p paid up on the cancelled share would be used to pay up the 50p unpaid on the other share, thus making it fully paid. But liability for unpaid capital cannot be reduced by crediting a partly paid share as paid up to a greater extent than the amount which has in fact been paid up on it.[4] Thus, in the example given above, it is not possible to leave the nominal value of the shares at £1, and resolve that each share shall be deemed paid up to the extent of 75p or £1, as the case may be.

Return of capital to shareholders

A company may wish to return paid up capital which is in excess of its wants when it has sold a part of its undertaking or assets and intends to confine its future activities to running the remaining part of its business. It will then distribute the cash it has received on the sale among its shareholders and reduce the paid up value of their shares to an equivalent extent, or alternatively, an appropriate number of their shares will be cancelled. Reductions of capital in this way occurred on a large scale in the late 1940s and early 1950s when companies which carried on two or more different kinds of businesses were compelled to sell one of them to a public corporation under statutory schemes for nationalisation of the coal, electricity and gas industries. However, a company need not convert any of its assets into cash in order to return capital to shareholders. It may return capital in kind, for example, by distributing securities which it holds in other companies, or government stock which has been issued to it on the nationalisation of part of its undertaking. In such a case it is no objection to the reduction that the value of the assets distributed exceeds the amount by which the paid up value of the shares is reduced, provided that there is no likelihood of present or future creditors or shareholders being defrauded or misled, as they would be if the company thereby made itself insolvent.[5]

Another reason why a company may wish to repay capital to one or more classes of its shareholders is that it can obtain fresh capital more cheaply to replace it. For example, if a company issued 15 per cent preference shares at a time when interest rates were high, it may wish to pay off those shares when interest rates fall and it

---

1 Companies Act 1985, s 425.
2 *Re Robert Stephen Holdings Ltd* [1968] 1 All ER 195n, [1968] 1 WLR 522; secus *Re Rank Radio and Television Ltd* (1963) Times, 19 November.
3 *Re Doloswella Rubber and Tea Estates Ltd* [1917] 1 Ch 213.
4 *Re Development Co of Central and West Africa* [1902] 1 Ch 547.
5 *Ex parte Westburn Sugar Refineries Ltd* [1951] AC 625, [1951] 1 All ER 881.

can raise an equivalent amount of capital by issuing, say, 7 per cent preference shares or debentures. This is a legitimate reason for repaying the original preference shares, and the court will approve a reduction of capital for the purpose.[6] The fact that the market value of the preference shares stands at a premium because their yield is higher than current commercial interest rates, and that the preference shareholders will not be able to obtain as high a yield when they re-invest the capital returned to them, will not induce the court to reject the reduction scheme.[7] To protect preference shareholders against such an uninvited reduction in yield, some companies have provided by their articles or the terms of issue of preference shares that on repayment of capital preference shareholders shall receive the amount paid up on the shares or the average market price of the shares during the preceding six months, whichever is greater.[8] Moreover, when preference capital is reduced by repayment, the company sometimes gives the preference shareholders the option of taking new preference shares or debentures instead of receiving cash for their original shares. The court has even gone so far as to approve a scheme for repayment of the original shares which compelled the shareholders to take the new securities, and gave them no option to receive cash.[9] It may be argued that if a company cannot pay off shares out of its existing resources, but has to raise new capital to do so, the capital represented by the original shares cannot be in excess of the company's wants. This is not the view taken by the court, however, which seems to treat issued capital as being in excess of the company's wants when it does not fit into the capital structure which the company thinks would be best for the carrying on of its business.[10]

Cancellation of capital unrepresented by assets

When the value of a company's net assets, after deducting the total of its liabilities, is less than its paid up capital, the company must either never have had assets equal in value to its paid up capital because its shares were watered,[11] or it must have suffered trading losses or a fall in the market value of its assets. In all such cases the company's paid up capital is unrepresented by available assets, and it may resolve to reduce its paid up capital by the amount of the deficiency. The court is ready to sanction a reduction when the company has suffered a trading loss or a fall in the value of its assets; it is more problematical whether the court would be willing to do so when the deficiency was caused by the assets originally not being worth the paid up value of the shares issued in exchange. The court has made it clear, however, that the assets in question must have ceased to exist or must have fallen permanently in value if paid up capital is to be reduced.[12] The mere fact that an asset is by its nature unsaleable, such as preliminary expenses, underwriting commissions, the costs of research or of planning or developing a project, or the

---

6 *Re St James' Court Estate Ltd* [1944] Ch 6; *Re Holders Investment Trust Ltd* [1971] 2 All ER 289, [1971] 1 WLR 583.
7 *Scottish Insurance Corpn Ltd v Wilsons and Clyde Coal Co Ltd* [1949] AC 462, [1949] 1 All ER 1068; *Prudential Assurance Co Ltd v Chatterley-Whitfield Collieries Ltd* [1949] AC 512, [1949] 1 All ER 1094.
8 This is known as the Spens clause or formula, from the name of its originator. If the shares are redeemable preference shares, the market value formula is usually made applicable only if the shares are paid off before the agreed date for their redemption.
9 *Re Thomas de la Rue & Co Ltd* [1911] 2 Ch 361.
10 See cases cited in footnote 7, ante.
11 See p 149, ante.
12 *Re Jupiter House Investments (Cambridge) Ltd* [1985] BCLC 222, [1985] 1 WLR 975; *Re Grosvenor Press plc* [1985] BCLC 286, [1985] 1 WLR 980. It was held in these cases that if it is uncertain whether a loss is permanent or may be recouped in the future, the court may approve a reduction of capital on condition that any amount recouped is credited to a capital reserve so as to prevent its distribution as a dividend.

cost of a sales promotion campaign, does not entitle the company to write the asset off its balance sheet by reducing its capital.[13]

The court is unwilling to cancel shares completely because of a loss of assets. If the company has issued preference shares with priority for repayment of capital, the loss usually falls on the ordinary shareholders, but however great it is, they may still retain the hope that the company's fortunes will improve, and that the capital cover for their shares will be restored. If their shares were cancelled because the loss exceeded the amount paid up on them, the ordinary shareholders would cease to have any interest in the company, and if its fortunes did afterwards improve, the whole of the improvement would be reflected in an increase in the value of the company's preference shares, which would have become ordinary shares as a result of the cancellation. Consequently, in order to preserve for existing ordinary shareholders the benefit of any improvement which may materialise, the court will only approve a cancellation of their shares if it is proved that there is no prospect of any improvement in the future which will restore the whole or part of their capital cover,[14] and in practice it is almost impossible to prove this unless the company goes into liquidation, when a reduction of capital will no longer be possible.

Reduction of nominal and paid up values of shares

When paid up capital is repaid to shareholders, or is reduced because it is not represented by assets, only the paid up value of the shares need be reduced.[15] If the nominal value of the shares is not also reduced, however, the effect of the reduction is to increase the liability of shareholders for unpaid capital by the amount by which the paid up value is reduced. When a company has suffered a loss of assets, this could be used as a device to compel shareholders to contribute new capital. For example, if a company issued 100,000 £1 shares which are fully paid, and its assets are now worth only £50,000, a reduction which leaves the shares with a nominal value of £1, but credits them as paid up only to the extent of 50p, would make the shareholders liable to contribute a further 50p share. In practice the nominal value of the shares is always reduced by the same amount as the paid up value, so that in the above example the shares would be reduced to 50p shares fully paid. Likewise, when capital is repaid, the shares are either cancelled if the whole of the capital paid up on them is returned to the shareholders, or their nominal value is reduced to the same extent as their paid up value if the repayment is only partial.

If on a reduction of the capital of a public company the amount paid up or credited as paid up on shares is reduced to less than the amount which the law requires to be paid up on them when they are allotted, namely, one quarter of their nominal value,[16] the holders of the shares are under no obligation to pay to the company the difference between one quarter of the nominal value of the shares and their lower paid up value on the reduction taking effect. The difference now merely forms part of the capital unpaid on the shares, and must be paid up only when appropriate calls are made by the board or a general meeting[17] or when the company goes into liquidation.

---

13 *Re Abstainers and General Insurance Co* [1891] 2 Ch 124.
14 *Re Floating Dock of St Thomas Ltd* [1895] 1 Ch 691; *Re London and New York Investment Corpn* [1895] 2 Ch 860.
15 *Re Fore Street Warehouse Ltd* (1888) 59 LT 214; *Neale v City of Birmingham Tramways Co* [1910] 2 Ch 464.
16 Companies Act 1985, s 101 (1) (see p 160, ante).
17 See p 316, post.

Reduction of nominal capital

It has been suggested that if a company's issued share capital is reduced, its nominal capital must be reduced by the same amount, so that its unissued capital is no greater after the reduction than before.[18] Although this is the usual practice, there would seem to be no legal requirement for it, and while stamp duty was payable on a company's nominal capital, it had the disadvantage that if the company subsequently increased its nominal capital, a saving of stamp duty was lost. This consideration is no longer material now that no stamp duty is payable on either the nominal capital of a company or on the issue price (including share premiums) of the shares it issues.[19]

Protection of creditors

When liability for unpaid capital is reduced, or paid up capital is returned

If a reduction of capital resolved upon by a company involves reducing its shareholders' liability for unpaid capital or returning paid up capital to the shareholders, any creditor of the company whose debt or claim would be provable if the company were wound up, may object to the reduction.[20] In Scotland this has been held to include a situation where the company proposes to cancel paid up preference shares and to issue in their place debentures credited as paid up to the same extent.[1] The company may deprive a creditor of his right to object by paying off his debt, but to ensure that creditors have either been paid or have been given a chance to object, the court will direct on a summons for directions issued after the petition for the court's confirmation of the reduction of capital has been presented, that a list of the company's creditors verified by the affidavit of one of its officers must be filed in court, that individual notices must be sent to those creditors, and that notices of the proposed reduction must be published in newspapers directed by the court for the benefit of creditors whose names may have been omitted from the filed list.[2] The court will only proceed to consider the company's petition for its sanction to the reduction when it is satisfied by affidavit of the company's solicitor and one of its officers that all creditors who are named in the filed list, or who have notified their claims, have been paid or have consented to the reduction.[3] If the company disputes any of their claims, the creditors concerned must prove their claims by affidavit, and the company must either secure the amounts claimed to the court's satisfaction, or satisfy the court that the disputed claims are not valid.[4]

The court may dispense with these provisions for the protection of creditors,[5] but it will only do so in special circumstances, and on being satisfied that the company has deposited a sum of money sufficient to satisfy all claims which are likely to be made against it,[6] or that a bank or other responsible person or company (eg an insurance company) has guaranteed the payment of such claims, valuing them in the same way as if the company were being wound up, and that the

---

18 *Re Anglo-French Exploration Co* [1902] 2 Ch 845 at 852, per Buckley J. This dictum was not followed in the Southern Rhodesian case of *Ex p Rattham & Son (Pvt) Ltd* 1959 (2) SA 741.
19 Finance Act 1988, s 141 (1) (41 Halsbury's Statutes (4th Edn) 7).
20 Companies Act 1985, s 136 (2) and (3).
1 *Lawrie and Symington Ltd* 1969 SLT 221.
2 Companies Act 1985, s 136 (4), and RSC Ord 102, rr 6, 7, 9 and 10. Advertisements are always directed to be published in the London Gazette and at least one other London daily newspaper.
3 RSC Ord 102, r 11.
4 Companies Act 1985, s 136 (5) and RSC Ord 102, rr 11 and 12.
5 Ibid, s 136 (6).
6 *Re Antwerp Waterworks Co Ltd* [1931] WN 186.

guarantor has sufficient assets to meet all its liabilities.[7] The effect of such a dispensation is not only to obviate the procedural requirements with regard to creditors, but also to deprive them of their right to object to the reduction on the hearing of the company's petition.

If a creditor who is entitled to object to the reduction is by reason of his ignorance of the proceedings not entered on the list of creditors, and after the court has sanctioned the reduction the company is unable to pay his claim,[8] he may require each member of the company at the date the reduction takes effect[9] to contribute toward payment of his claim an amount not exceeding the difference between the nominal and paid up values of the member's shares immediately before the reduction.[10] The provision applies only in favour of a creditor who was entitled to object to the reduction, and so it will not apply when the court dispenses with the provisions for the protection of creditors set out above.

Other kinds of reduction

The court may direct that the provisions for the protection of creditors shall apply in the case of any other kind of reduction of capital, which does not involve the diminution of shareholders' liability for unpaid capital or the return of paid up capital.[11] In the absence of such a direction a creditor has no right to be heard in opposition to the company's petition for the court's sanction,[12] and there are no statutory provisions to ensure that the creditors are not prejudiced. The commonest kind of reduction where the provisions for the protection of creditors do not apply unless the court so directs, is where paid up capital is reduced because it has been lost or is not represented by available assets. Theoretically, no protection for creditors should be necessary here, because no assets of the company will be distributed and no liability for unpaid capital will be cancelled, so that the creditors' position should be the same after the reduction as before. The danger, however, is that a company may pretend to have sustained a loss of assets which it has not suffered, and may obtain the court's sanction to a reduction of capital equal to the pretended loss. After the reduction the real value of its net assets would exceed its reduced capital, and it might then realise some of its assets at an enhanced price and distribute the excess of the price realised over the written down value of the assets in the company accounts amongst its shareholders as though it were a realised profit, thereby diminishing the assets of the company available to pay its debts. The court is therefore vigilant to ensure that the reduction it sanctions is not greater than the loss of assets actually suffered. In early cases the court required to be satisfied in this respect,[13] but in a case decided by the House of Lords,[14] where the company's liabilities were adequately covered by its assets, remarks were

---

7 *Re Lucania Temperance Billiard Halls (London) Ltd* [1966] Ch 98, [1965] 3 All ER 879.
8 A company is deemed unable to pay the debt in the circumstances specified in the Insolvency Act 1986, s 123 (1) in connection with petitions to wind it up.
9 Ie, when the court order approving the reduction is registered by the Registrar of Companies (Companies Act 1985, s 138 (2) (see p 187)).
10 Companies Act 1985, s 140 (2) to (4). This section is not likely to be relied on much in practice because of the rarity of partly paid shares. It should be noted, however, that, (a) the creditor has a statutory right to sue the shareholder without having the company wound up, and (b) the shareholder appears to be liable both to the creditor to the extent of the former amount unpaid in respect of his shares and to the company for the amount which remains unpaid on his shares after the reduction, so that his total liability may exceed the original nominal value of his shares.
11 Companies Act 1985, s 136 (2) to (5).
12 *Re Meux's Brewery Co* [1919] 1 Ch 28.
13 *Re Barrow Haematite Steel Co* [1900] 2 Ch 846; affd [1901] 2 Ch 746.
14 *Poole v National Bank of China Ltd* [1907] AC 229.

made[15] which indicated that it was for the company, and not for the court, to decide what was the value of the assets which the company had lost, and these remarks were treated in a later case[16] as limiting the scope of the enquiry which the court should make. In a further decision of the House of Lords,[17] however, the danger of reductions of capital in respect of fictitious losses was recognised, and the practice of the courts now is to require at least prima facie proof of the alleged loss, leaving it open to shareholders or creditors of the company who oppose the reduction of capital to show that the alleged loss is excessive or non-existent.

The rights of shareholders

When paid up capital is returned, or capital is reduced because of loss of assets

When capital is reduced by being repaid or because it is unrepresented by assets, the order of repayment, or the order in which different classes of shares are reduced to account for the loss of assets, should follow the order of distribution of assets in a winding up or the order in which losses of capital are borne in a winding up (as the case may be); this is because, in effect, such a reduction of capital is a partial winding up. Consequently, if the company has issued preference shares which carry the right to repayment of capital in a winding up before the ordinary share capital is repaid, a reduction of capital because of a loss of assets must be borne first by the ordinary shares, and only after their paid up value has been extinguished will the preference shares be reduced.[18] If the preference shares have no priority for repayment of capital, however, they will be reduced rateably with the ordinary shares[19] in proportion to their respective nominal values.[20] Conversely, if preference shares have priority for repayment of capital in a winding up, the capital paid up on them must be repaid before the ordinary share capital on a reduction of capital by repayment, but the preference shareholders are only entitled to receive the amount paid up on their shares, unless the terms of the shares otherwise provide. No compensation need be paid to the preference shareholders because the market value of their shares is above par, as it may be if the preference dividend is higher than the prevailing commercial rate of interest for new capital;[1] nor because the shares carry the right to participate in surplus profits after the preference dividend and a specified minimum ordinary share dividend have been paid, and the market value of the preference shares is attributable to that fact;[2] nor because the preference shares entitle their holders to participate in the surplus assets of the company in a winding up after all share capital has been repaid, at least if no immediate winding up is in prospect and the market value of the preference shares consequently does not reflect any additional value attributable to this right to participate.[3]

The principle that the scheme of reduction of capital should follow the order of distribution of the company's assets in a winding up seems, however, to apply only

---

15 Especially per Lord Macnaghten at 239.
16 *Re Louisiana and Southern States Real Estate and Mortgage Co* [1909] 2 Ch 552.
17 *Caldwell v Caldwell & Co (Papermakers) Ltd* [1916] WN 70, per Lord Parker of Waddington.
18 *Re Floating Dock Co of St Thomas Ltd* [1895] 1 Ch 691; *Re London and New York Investment Corpn* [1895] 2 Ch 860.
19 *Re Barrow Haematite Steel Co* (1888) 39 ChD 582; *Re Quebrada Rly, Land and Copper Co* (1889) 40 ChD 363; *Re Union Plate Glass Co* (1889) 42 ChD 513; contra, *Re Barrow Haematite Steel Co* [1900] 2 Ch 846; affd [1901] 2 Ch 746.
20 *Re Credit Assurance and Guarantee Corpn Ltd* [1902] 2 Ch 601.
 1 *Scottish Insurance Corpn, Ltd v Wilsons and Clyde Coal Co Ltd* [1949] AC 462, [1949] 1 All ER 1068; *Prudential Assurance Co v Chatterley-Whitfield Collieries Ltd* [1949] AC 512, [1949] 1 All ER 1094 (see p 179, ante).
 2 *Re Saltdean Estate & Co Ltd* [1968] 3 All ER 829, [1968] 1 WLR 1844.
 3 *Re William Jones & Sons Ltd* [1969] 1 All ER 913, [1969] 1 WLR 146.

as between different classes of shares. So far as shareholders of the same class are concerned, it has been held that a reduction of capital by repayment need not adhere to the distribution which would be made in a winding up, and so more capital may be repaid on some shares of the same class than on others.[4] On the other hand, such a reduction would usually conflict with the principle recently laid down that, unless all shareholders of the same class are treated equally by a scheme of reduction, the scheme cannot be approved by the court under the provisions of the Companies Act 1985, governing reductions of capital, but must be propounded as a scheme of arrangement approved by the court under s 425 of the Act.[5]

The normal order of reduction of capital as between different classes of shares can be varied with the consent of the shareholders who are adversely affected, and if the company's articles enable the rights of any class of shareholders to be altered with the consent of a certain fraction of their number,[6] or if the provisions of the Companies Act 1985 permitting class rights to be varied with the consent of a certain fraction of members of the class are applicable,[7] a consent binding the class may be given to a variation of the normal order of reduction. In cases where class consents have been given, the court has approved reductions because of a loss of assets under which preference shares with priority for repayment of capital in a winding up were reduced rateably with ordinary shares.[8] But where preference shares have no priority for repayment of capital, their reduction rateably with the ordinary shares because of a loss of assets does not require the consent of the preference shareholders, either individually or by way of a resolution binding on the whole class. This is so even though the inevitable result of the reduction is to diminish the amount of the preference dividend, which will still be calculated at the same percentage rate, but on a smaller nominal or paid up value.[9] Indeed, if a scheme of reduction affecting such shares provided for repayment of the capital paid up on them in priority to the ordinary share capital, it would be necessary to obtain the consent of the ordinary shareholders to the postponement of their right to be repaid rateably, either by them consenting unanimously or by a class consent binding on them all being given under the terms of the company's articles or the provisions of the Companies Act 1985.[7]

Other kinds of reduction

It is uncertain whether unpaid ordinary share capital may be reduced if the company has issued preference shares with priority for repayment of capital. The preference shareholders no doubt rely to some extent on the capital unpaid on the ordinary shares as cover for their own capital, and it would seem unfair to deprive them of the protection afforded by it without their consent. In one case[10] the court approved such a reduction when the holders of three-quarters of the preference shares had given their consent under a provision in the articles by which the rights of the whole class might thereby be varied. It is doubtful, however, whether preference shareholders have a right to prevent the capital repaid on the ordinary shares being reduced without their consent, and so the class consent in the case cited may have been unnecessary.

Where capital is reduced otherwise than by repayment or because of a loss of

---

4 *Neale v City of Birmingham Tramways Co* [1910] 2 Ch 464.
5 *Re Robert Stephen Holdings Ltd* [1968] 1 All ER 195n, [1968] 1 WLR 522.
6 See, for example, the Companies Act 1948, Table A, art 4.
7 Companies Act 1985, s 125 (2) to (5) (see p 221, post).
8 *Re Welsbach Incandescent Gas Light Co Ltd* [1904] 1 Ch 87; *Re Showell's Brewery Co* (1914) 30 TLR 428.
9 *Re Mackenzie & Co Ltd* [1916] 2 Ch 450.
10 *Re James Colmer Ltd* [1897] 1 Ch 524.

assets, it may be that the normal order of reduction as between different classes of shareholders does not apply, and that the reduction should be made rateably on shares of all classes without regard to their priority for repayment of capital in a winding up.[11] In that case a reduction which is not made rateably on the shares of each class could only be carried out with the individual consents of the shareholders who are adversely affected, or if the company's memoradnum or articles or the Companies Act 1985 permit their rights to be varied with the consent of a fraction of the members of the class to which they belong, then with the consent of that fraction.[11]

Reduction of reserves

If a company has created reserves by the transfer of retained profits[12] and subsequently suffers a loss of assets, it is the normal practice to write off the loss against the reserves, and to reduce share capital only if the reserves are insufficient to cover the loss. This was held to be the correct way to proceed in one case,[13] but in another[14] it was held that where the assets representing share capital and reserves had been employed as a mixed fund in carrying on the company's business, a loss of assets should be attributed to each in proportion to its amount. The former of these two decisions would seem preferable. On a winding up assets representing reserves will be distributed to all the shareholders, except those who are excluded by the terms of issue of their shares, or who have priority for repayment of their capital and no express rights to participate in surplus assets after all share capital has been repaid.[15] Consequently, if the company has issued preference shares with priority for repayment of capital, it will make no difference as between the ordinary and preference shareholders whether losses of assets are attributed to reserves or to ordinary share capital. The only difference which it will make is in the amount the company may distribute as dividends in the future.[16] Reserves may be distributed if they have not been capitalised, and so if a loss of assets is written off primarily out of reserves, the balance left which may be distributed as dividend in the near future will be smaller than if the loss had been apportioned between reserves and ordinary share capital. A similar problem arises when the company has capital reserves, such as a share premium account or a capital redemption reserve.[17] Here again, the practice is to write off losses against them before reducing share capital, but the court has not yet explicitly stated that this is the correct method. Whilst losses may be written off against revenue reserves merely by

11 *Carruth v Imperial Chemical Industries Ltd* [1937] AC 707 at 742–4, [1937] 2 All ER 422 at 432–3, per Lord Blanesburgh; Companies Act 1985, s 125(1) to (5) (see p 221, post).
12 That is, profits transferred from its profit and loss account to a reserve account. Reserve accounts are variously named. Profits carried to reserve do not cease to be profits, and can at any time be distributed to the shareholders as a dividend, unless they are capitalised by a general meeting passing a resolution to that effect and bonus shares representing the capitalised reserves are issued to members (see Table A, art 110). The transfer of profits to reserve merely indicates that the company does not intend to distribute them for the time being.
13 *Re Barrow Haematite Steel Co* [1900] 2 Ch 846; affd [1901] 2 Ch 746.
14 *Re Hoare & Co* [1904] 2 Ch 208.
15 The reason for this is explained at p 221, post.
16 If, exceptionally, the preference shares carry the right to participate in the surplus profits of the company after paying a minimum dividend on the ordinary shares, the proportion of such surplus profits which the preference shareholders may claim may be affected by the loss being written off against reserves instead of ordinary share capital.
17 See p 161, ante and p 189, post.

adjusting the company's accounts,[18] however, losses may only be written off by reducing share premium account or capital redemption reserve if the same steps are taken as are required for reducing share capital.[19]

The court's functions

In addition to ensuring that the rights of different classes of shareholders are respected, the court's function on approving a reduction of capital is to ensure that the scheme of reduction is fair and equitable (which the court seems ready to assume if the scheme is proposed in good faith),[20] and furthermore, to ensure that the scheme will not unfairly prejudice any present or future shareholders or creditors.[1] If the scheme of reduction involves an alteration of the rights attached to a class of shares and by the memorandum or articles of the company or an applicable provision of the Companies Act 1985[2] the consent of the holders of a certain fraction of the shares of the class or of a meeting of the class is required, the court will not approve the reduction of capital if the class consent has been obtained by the vote of the holders of a majority of the shares of the class who did not act in good faith in the interest of members of the class generally, but who wished to promote some other interest of their own, such as their interest as holders of a different class of shares.[3] Subject to these qualifications, the court leaves it to the shareholders in general meeting to decide whether the reduction is necessary or desirable, and if so, what form it shall take. The fact that a minor error is made as to the number of issued and unisssued shares of the company in the circular accompanying the notice of the general meeting which passes the special resolution for the reduction of capital, will not induce the court to refuse its confirmation of the reduction of capital, if the error does not result in the necessary majority of the votes in favour of the reduction not having been cast, and the court can correct the error in its order confirming the reduction.[4]

Procedure

After the special resolution for a reduction of capital or share premium account or capital redemption reserve fund[5] has been passed, the company presents a petition to the Companies Court[6] to confirm the reduction.[7] A summons for directions is then taken out returnable before the registrar of the Companies Court, and in appropriate cases he will direct the steps to be taken for the protection of creditors which have been dealt with above, and in any case he may direct notices of the

---

18 A balance sheet embodying the alteration will have to be laid before the shareholders in general meeting after the expiration of the company's current financial year (Companies Act 1985, s 241 (1)), and may require the shareholders' approval by ordinary resolution under the terms of the articles. Table A does not require such approval, and so the directors of a company governed by Table A may write off losses against revenue reserves by appropriate entries in the annual accounts.

19 Companies Act 1985, s 130 (3) and s 170 (4).

20 *Carruth v Imperial Chemical Industries Ltd* [1937] AC 707 at 769–70, [1937] 2 All ER 422 at 461–2, per Lord Maugham.

1 *Ex p Westburn Sugar Refineries Ltd* [1951] AC 625 at 635m [1951] 1 All ER 881 at 887, per Lord Radcliffe.

2 Companies Act 1985, s 125 (1) to (5).

3 *Re Holders Investment Trust Ltd* [1971] 2 All ER 289, [1971] 1 WLR 583.

4 *Re Willaire Systems plc* [1987] BCLC 67, 2 BCC 99 at 311, CA.

5 Companies Act 1985, s 130 (3), s 135 (1) and s 170 (4). (For share premiums, see p 162, ante, and for capital redemption reserve see p 189, post).

6 RSC Ord 102, r 4 (1) (*c*), (*d*) and (*e*).

7 Companies Act 1985, s 136 (1).

petition to be published.[8] The steps for the protection of creditors are then taken, if necessary, and a certificate obtained from the registrar as to the result of those proceedings.[9] After the registrar's certificate (if any) has been filed, the petition comes on for hearing, and the court may then confirm the reduction on such terms and conditions as it thinks fit.[10] In particular, the court may order the company to publish the reasons for the reduction, and if the court thinks fit, a statement of the causes which led to it, and also the court may, if for any special reason it thinks fit to do so, require the company to add to its name the words 'and reduced' for such period as the court prescribes.[11] In practice these conditions are not imposed nowadays.

When the court's confirmation of the reduction has been given, a copy of the court's order and a minute approved by the court, showing the new state of the company's capital, must be delivered to the Registrar of Companies, and on the registration of these documents the reduction takes effect.[12] The minute is then deemed to be substituted for the capital clause of the company's memorandum.[13] The Registrar issues a certificate under his signature or official seal that the order and minute have been registered, and his certificate is conclusive evidence that the requirements of the Companies Act 1985 have been complied with.[14] If the company's share premium account or capital redemption reserve is reduced, the registration procedure is the same, except that no minute of the state of the company's capital is delivered to the Registrar of Companies.[15] After the court's order confirming the reduction of capital or of share premium account or capital redemption reserve and the minute (if any) have been registered, the registration must be advertised in such manner as the court directs,[16] and the company should ask the court to give such directions in the order sanctioning the reduction. Additionally, the Registrar must advertise the notification of the reduction of capital to him in the London Gazette if the company's capital is reduced.[17]

Because a reduction of capital does not take effect until the resolution for the reduction has been confirmed by the court, the resolution may be a conditional one (eg that the reduction of capital shall take effect only if an increase in capital which is also resolved on has previously taken effect), and provided that the condition has been fulfilled before the court confirms the reduction of capital, the reduction is valid and effective.[18]

Consequential re-registration of a public company

If as a result of a reduction of capital approved by the court the issued share capital of a public company is less than £50,000, the company must be re-registered as a private company, unless the court otherwise directs.[19] It is not necessary that a

---

8 RSC Ord 102, r 6 (1), (3) and (4). Notice of the date on which the petition will be heard is always required to be advertised in the London Gazette and one other London daily newspaper.
9 RSC Ord 102, rr 7 and 9 to 13.
10 Companies Act 1985, s 137 (1).
11 Ibid, s 137 (2).
12 Ibid, s 138 (1) and (2).
13 Ibid, s 138 (5).
14 Ibid, s 138 (4). For the conclusiveness of the certificate, see p 27, ante.
15 *Re Paringa Mining and Exploration Co Ltd* [1957] 3 All ER 424, [1957] 1 WLR 1143.
16 Companies Act 1985, s 138 (3). Advertisements are always required in the London Gazette and one other London daily newspaper.
17 Companies Act 1985, s 711 (1) (*b*).
18 *Re Tip-Europe Ltd* [1988] BCLC 231, (1987) 3 BCC 647.
19 Companies Act 1985, s 139 (1) and (2). It would seem that the court would only direct that the company shall not be re-registered if it is to be wound up or merged with another company immediately.

general meeting should resolve on re-registration in these circumstances, provided that the court authorises the re-registration by its order confirming the reduction, and specifies in its order the alterations to be made to the company's memorandum and articles which are necessary in order to convert it into a private company.[20] The Registrar of Companies issues a new certificate of incorporation to the company on a copy of the court's order and an application for re-registration[1] being delivered to him,[2] and publishes the re-registration in the London Gazette.[3] The certificate of incorporation is conclusive evidence that the re-registration has been properly effected and that the company is a private company.[2] The sanction to ensure that the company is re-registered as a private company is that the Registrar of Companies will not register the order of the court approving the reduction of capital unless the company is simultaneously re-registered as a private company,[4] and until the court's order is registered the reduction of capital does not take effect.[5]

If, by a reduction of capital, a public company reduces its issued share capital to less than £50,000, but immediately increases it to more than £50,000 by a resolution which takes effect before or at the same time as the reduction resolution, there is no obligation to re-register the company as a private one.[6]

REDEEMABLE SHARES AND PURCHASES OF SHARES BY A COMPANY

Redeemable shares

If the articles of a company limited by shares, whether public or private, or of a company limited by guarantee which has a share capital, so provide,[7] the company may issue any class of its shares on terms that they shall be redeemed at a fixed date, or over a fixed period of time, or on the occurrence of one or more specified contingencies, or that the shares may be redeemed at the option of the company or the holders of the shares on a fixed date or at any time.[8] No redeemable shares may be issued at a time when the company has no non-redeemable capital outstanding (eg immediately after the reduction of its original issued capital to nil in anticipation of the issue of redeemable shares),[9] but redeemable shares may be redeemed even though at the time when redemption takes place the company has no other issued capital, although in practice in that situation the company would simply be wound up. Redeemable shares may not be redeemed unless they are fully paid.[10] The terms on which redemption may or must be carried out are those provided by the company's articles (including the calculation of the amount payable on redemption) but the date on or by which, or the dates between which, the shares will be

---

20 Companies Act 1985, s 139 (3).
 1 The application need be signed by only one director or the secretary of the company, but it would appear necessary for the making of the application to be authorised by the board of directors (see Companies (Forms) Regulations 1985 (SI 1985/854), Form 43 (3) (e)).
 2 Companies Act 1985, s 139 (5).
 3 Ibid, s 711 (1) (a).
 4 Ibid, s 139 (2).
 5 Ibid, s 138 (2).
 6 *Re MB Group Ltd* [1989] BCLC 672, 5 BCC 684.
 7 Table A authorises the issue of shares which are redeemable on such terms as the company's articles provide (Table A, art 3).
 8 Companies Act 1985, s 159 (1).
 9 Ibid, s 159 (2).
10 Ibid, s 159 (3).

redeemed may be fixed by the company's directors before the shares are issued, if the articles so provide.[11] Any desired provision may be made in this respect (eg redemption may be effected over a period by drawings or by successive fractional repayments of capital on all the redeemable shares, or the shares may be redeemed on or after a certain date or occurrence, either in any event or at the option of the company or an individual shareholder or a specified fraction of shareholders). Redemption must be effected by payment in cash,[12] which means that a provision in the articles for redemption in cash or by the issue of new shares at the option of the company or an individual shareholder in respect of his shares, or according to the wishes of a specified fraction of shareholders, would be void.[13] The redemption of shares in accordance with the terms on which they were issued does not involve a breach of the statutory rule prohibiting the acquisition by a company of shares in itself.[14]

The amount required to repay the capital of redeemable shares may be found out of the profits of the company available for distribution or out of the proceeds of a fresh issue of shares.[15] Any premium payable on the redemption of shares must be found out of profits available for distribution, or if the redemption is effected out of the proceeds of a fresh issue of shares, out of those proceeds, but a redemption premium paid out of the proceeds of a fresh issue of shares may not exceed the lesser of the aggregate amount of share premiums received by the company on the issue of the redeemable shares and the amount credited to the company's share premium account at the date of redemption (including share premiums paid as part of the proceeds of the fresh issue of shares).[16] Shares are treated as cancelled when they are redeemed, and so the company's issued and paid up share capital (but not its nominal capital) are correspondingly reduced.[17]

If shares are redeemed out of the proceeds of a fresh issue of shares, the capital issued or paid up on those shares will replace the redeemed capital, and if any part of the proceeds of the fresh issue is used to pay a redemption premium, a corresponding reduction must be made in the company's share premium account, so that it represents the balance of the premiums which the company has received and paid.[18] If, alternatively, redeemable shares are redeemed out of assets representing a company's distributable profits, the amount by which its issued share capital is thereby reduced must be transferred from profits or revenue reserves to a special capital reserve known as capital redemption reserve, which can itself be reduced (eg by a repayment to shareholders) only in the same way as paid up share capital.[19] In effect, the amount credited to capital redemption reserve replaces the aggregate nominal values of the redeemed shares, and the transfer from profits or revenue reserves makes the amount transferred unavailable for distribution as dividends. However, it is possible for the amount credited to capital redemption reserve to be converted into share capital by the company using it to

11 Ibid, s 159A (1) to (5), inserted by Companies Act 1989, ss 133 (2).
12 Companies Act 1985, s 160 (1).
13 However, it is possible that an option for each individual shareholder to have his shares redeemed in cash or by the issue or transfer of shares or debentures of the same or another company would be construed as a provision for redemption in cash coupled with an option to subscribe for or purchase the other shares or debentures, in which case it would be valid.
14 Companies Act 1985, s 143 (1) and (3) (*a*).
15 Ibid, s 160 (1).
16 Ibid, s 160 (2).
17 Ibid, s 160 (4).
18 Ibid, s 160 (1) and (2).
19 Ibid, s 170 (1) and (4).

pay up the nominal value of new fully paid shares to be issued as bonus shares to its shareholders at the time the issue is made.[20]

If the proceeds of a new issue of shares are used to redeem the redeemable shares, but the total nominal value of the new shares is less than that of the redeemable shares (either because they are redeemed at a discount or because the balance of the amount paid on redemption is found out of the company's profits or revenue reserves), the difference between the total nominal values of the new shares and the total nominal values of the redeemable shares must be transferred to capital redemption reserve, and the company's profits or revenue reserves must be reduced accordingly.[1]

Public companies cannot redeem shares by applying their existing capital for the purpose, since the essential condition for redemption is that the capital of the redeemed shares shall be replaced either by additional capital issued for the purpose of the redemption or by a capitalisation of distributable profits. Private companies may, subject to certain conditions, redeem shares out of their existing capital, but their power to do this is really only part of their wider power to purchase their shares out of capital, and is consequently dealt with below in that context.[2]

If redeemable shares are redeemed out of the proceeds of a fresh issue of shares, the company may issue the new shares within the limits of its nominal capital as though the redeemable shares had never been issued,[3] and so unless the aggregate nominal value of the new shares exceeds that of the shares to be redeemed (as it may do if a redemption premium is payable) and the company has insufficient unissued capital to cover the excess, it will not be necessary to increase the company's nominal capital in order to accommodate the issue of the new shares. Any necessary increase in the company's nominal capital should be effected by a general meeting exercising the power to increase capital conferred on it by the company's articles before the redemption is effected.[4]

A company must within one month after redeeming any redeemable shares give notice of the redemption to the Registrar of Companies,[5] who must publish the notification in the London Gazette.[6]

Purchases of shares by a company

In addition to empowering companies to issue shares which are redeemable by their terms, the Companies Act 1985 confers a general power on companies limited by shares, whether public or private, and companies limited by guarantee with a share capital to purchase their own shares (including redeemable shares) at any time if they are authorised to do so by their articles,[7] and purchases in conformity with the Act do not involve a breach of the statutory prohibition on a company acquiring shares in itself.[8] The purchase money must be found in the same way as if the purchase were a redemption of redeemable shares (ie out of distributable profits or the proceeds of a fresh issue of shares), and it would appear that if the purchase price exceeds the nominal value of the shares which are purchased, the excess must be found out of distributable profits or, if it is paid out of the proceeds

---

20 Ibid, s 170 (4).
1 Companies Act 1985, s 170 (2).
2 See p 195, post.
3 Companies Act 1985, s 160 (5).
4 Ibid s 121 (1) and (2).
5 Ibid, s 122 (1) (*e*).
6 Ibid, s 711 (1) (*h*).
7 Companies Act 1985, s 162 (1). Table A, art 35, empowers a company to purchase its own shares in the ways authorised by the Companies Act 1985.
8 Companies Act 1985, s 143 (3) (*a*).

of issuing new shares, it must be limited to the lesser of any share premium paid on the issue of the purchased shares and the amount currently credited to the company's share premium account.[9] No purchase of its own shares may be made by a company under these provisions if at the time of the purchase it has no non-redeemable shares outstanding.[10] This prohibition is imposed because shares purchased by a company are cancelled, and the company's issued and paid up share capital is reduced accordingly;[11] in the absence of such a prohibition, there would be nothing to prevent a company from carrying out an informal liquidation of its assets by purchasing the whole of its share capital. On the other hand, there would appear to be no obstacle to a company purchasing the whole of its outstanding shares if simultaneously it issues new shares; in the case of a public company it would not seem necessary that its issued share capital after the issue of the new shares should be at least £50,000.[12] In addition to the general power to purchase its shares which a private company may exercise in the same way as a public company, a private company may, subject to certain strict conditions, purchase shares in itself by using assets representing its existing share capital.[13] This special power will be dealt with separately below.[14]

Off-market purchases

The general power of a company to purchase its shares out of its distributable profits or the proceeds of a fresh issue of shares may be exercised in three different forms. The company may in the first place effect an off-market purchase by negotiation with the selling shareholder or shareholders under the authority of a special resolution passed by a general meeting of the company, which is effective only if for 15 days beforehand and at the meeting a copy of the proposed contract and particulars of the selling shareholders are made available for inspection by members of the company.[15] An off-market purchase is defined as one which is not effected on a recognised stock exchange, or one which is so effected but where the shares are not subject to marketing arrangements with the exchange as a result of which they may be dealt in without prior permission of the exchange authorities for individual transactions.[16] In other words, shares which are purchased by the issuing company must be the subject of an off-market purchase, unless they are either listed on the Stock Exchange or are admitted to the Unlisted Securities Market or the Third Market of the Stock Exchange[17] and the purchase by the company is effected on the exchange and not by a private sale. It follows that all purchases of its shares by a private company are unavoidably off-market purchases; purchases by a public company may be.

In the case of an off-market purchase by a public company, the special resolution authorising the purchase must specify a date on which the authority expires, being not later than 18 months after the date of the resolution.[18] Whether the company is public or private, the shareholder or shareholders who are selling shares to it

9 Ibid, s 162 (2), substituted by Companies Act 1989, s 133 (4).
10 Companies Act 1985, s 162 (3).
11 Companies Act 1985, s 160 (4) and s 162 (2).
12 See p 199, post.
13 Ibid, s 171 (1).
14 See p 195, post.
15 Companies Act 1985, s 164 (1), (2) and (6).
16 Ibid, s 163 (1). The only stock exchange at present recognised is the Stock Exchange of the United Kingdom and Ireland.
17 For stock exchange listings of shares and debentures, see p 233, post. For the admission of securities to the Unlisted Securities Market, see p 234, post.
18 Companies Act 1985, s 164 (4).

may not vote in respect of those shares on either a show of hands or a poll on the special resolution authorising the purchase, and if he or they do so, the resolution is ineffective if it is passed only by reason of their votes.[19] This does not mean that the improper votes of the selling shareholders must simply be deducted from the number of affirmative votes cast; additionally, a corresponding deduction must be made from the total number of votes cast, and the special resolution will still be valid if the net balance of valid affirmative votes is at least 75 per cent of the net total of valid votes.

Market purchases

A company may alternatively purchase shares in itself by a market purchase if its shares are listed on the Stock Exchange or are admitted to the Unlisted Securities Market or the Third Market of the Stock Exchange, but to be a market purchase, the acquisition must be effected on the exchange by a member of the exchange acting on the company's behalf.[20] A market purchase may be effected only if it has been authorised by a resolution of a general meeting of the company, which, unless its articles otherwise provide, may be an ordinary resolution.[1] The resolution may confer a general authority on the directors to purchase shares, or it may be limited to shares of a particular class or description (eg by reference to the identity or characteristics of their registered holders, or the length of time since the issue of the shares, or the circumstances in which they were issued), and the authority may be unconditional or subject to conditions.[2] The resolution must additionally specify the maximum number of shares which may be acquired, the maximum and minimum prices which may be paid for them and the date when the authority to purchase expires, which may not be later than 18 months after the resolution conferring it is passed.[3]

A market purchase may be completed after the expiration of the period for which the authority is given if the contract for the purchase is entered into before the expiration of that period (ie the company's broker must have agreed to purchase the number of shares from a market maker or another broker), provided that the resolution authorising the purchase expressly permits it to be completed despite the fact that the shares are transferred to the company after the authority expires.[4] The absence of a corresponding provision in the case of off-market purchases does not mean that a transfer of shares to a public company after the expiration of the authority for such a purchase is invalid, however. A resolution authorising an off-market purchase in terms authorises the company to enter into a contract or contracts of purchase,[5] and provided that this is done within the time limit set by the resolution, it is immaterial that the transfer of the shares to the company is made afterwards. In the case of a market purchase, it is the purchase of the shares and not the contract to purchase them which is authorised by the resolution,[6] and the purchase (ie the acquisition of a legal or equitable title to the shares) by the company is not concluded when a contract to purchase them is entered into with a market maker or broker. Bargains on the Stock Exchange are for the sale of a certain number of shares, and not for the sale of particular shares, and so the

19 Ibid, s 164 (5).
20 Ibid, s 163 (3).
 1 Ibid, s 166 (1).
 2 Ibid, s 166 (2).
 3 Ibid, s 166 (3) and (4).
 4 Ibid, s 166 (5).
 5 Ibid, s 164 (2).
 6 Ibid, s 166 (1).

equitable title to the shares purchased passes to the company only when particular shares are appropriated to the contract by the seller,[7] which means nowadays under the TALISMAN system,[8] when bought transfers of those shares are executed by SEPON Ltd.[9] For this reason resolutions authorising market purchases of shares by a company should also expressly authorise the completion of contracts of purchase entered into within the period of the authorisation, even though completion takes place afterwards.

The fact that the authorisation of off-market purchases (unlike market purchases) will relate to the purchase of specific shares from shareholders who are identified at the time the resolution authorising the purchase is passed, results in another legal distinction between the two kinds of purchase. Because a market purchase of shares will not have been negotiated before the resolution authorising it is passed, there is no prohibition on a shareholder voting on the resolution authorising the purchase, even though he later sells shares to the company under the authorisation. This would appear to be so even though the authorisation relates to such a large number of shares that, if it is fully exercised, the shares acquired by the company will inevitably include some of those held by the shareholder who votes on the resolution authorising the purchase. On the other hand, shareholders whose shares are purchased by an off-market purchase are identified in the particulars laid before the general meeting which authorises the purchase, and are expressly prohibited from voting on the resolution for authorisation in respect of the shares which the company is to purchase from them.[10]

Contingent purchase contracts

The third kind of purchase by a company of shares in itself which may be effected is a purchase under a contingent purchase contract. Such a contract is one under which the company may, subject to the fulfilment of conditions, become entitled or obliged to purchase shares in itself, but there is no immediate binding obligation on the company to purchase and on the seller to sell.[11] The simplest example of a contingent purchase contract is a 'put' option given by a company to one of its own shareholders under which the company will become obliged to acquire a certain number of shares from him at an agreed price if the shareholder exercises the option. Similarly, a 'call' option taken by a company will be a contingent purchase contract, since it entitles the company to require the other party to transfer a certain number of shares in the company to it at an agreed price if it chooses to call on him to do so. Contingent purchase contracts include other contracts for the purchase of its shares by a company if they are subject to an express condition (eg if the dealing price of listed shares is rising above or falling below stipulated levels, or if the company's profits or dividends are falling below a stipulated amount).

A contingent purchase contract must be authorised by a special resolution passed by a general meeting of the company in the same way as an off-market purchase, and the same rules apply to it.[12] Because of this, a copy of the proposed contract and particulars of the selling shareholders must be available for inspection by members of the company for 15 days before the meeting at which the resolution is passed and at that meeting,[13] and if the company is a public company, the contract

---

7 *Re London, Hamburg and Continental Exchange, Bank, Ward and Henry's Case* (1867) 2 Ch App 431.
8 For the TALISMAN system, see p 395, post.
9 Stock Exchange Regulations, regs E5.5a and 5.13a.
10 Companies Act 1985, s 164 (5).
11 Ibid, s 165 (1).
12 Ibid, s 165 (2).
13 Ibid, s 164 (6).

must be entered into within 18 months after the resolution is passed.[14] Any payment made by a company to procure a contingent purchase contract (eg a premium paid for a call option) must be found out of its distributable profits.[15]

Supplemental

A company cannot assign its rights under a contract to purchase shares in itself,[16] and its rights under an off-market purchase contract or a contingent purchase contract can only be released if a general meeting of the company consents by passing a special resolution.[17] Within 28 days after it acquires shares in itself under its statutory power, a company must notify the Registrar of Companies, and in the case of a public company the notification must state the aggregate purchase price paid and the maximum and minimum prices paid for shares of each particular class.[18] The company must also keep a copy of each purchase contract entered into by it or a written memorandum of its terms for ten years from the completion of the purchase, and must allow any member of the company and, in the case of a public company, any other person to inspect it.[19]

Stock Exchange requirements

In addition to the rules governing the purchase of shares in itself contained in the Companies Act 1985, a company whose shares are listed on the United Kingdom Stock Exchange must comply with the requirements of the Stock Exchange when purchasing any of its shares on or off the market.[20] If the company seeks authority from a general meeting to purchase shares which will result in the acquisition by the company of 15 per cent or more of its issued share capital, the notice of the meeting called to give the authorisation must be accompanied by a circular setting out certain of the information which the Stock Exchange Rules require to be included in listing particulars published by a company seeking a listing,[1] and copies of the circular accompanied by a letter from a merchant bank verifying the sufficiency of the company's working capital after the purchase has been completed must be supplied to the Stock Exchange so that an announcement may be made in the press.[2] If the company has issued shares or debentures which are convertible into equity shares, or has issued warrants or options entitling their holders to subscribe for equity shares, separate class meetings of the holders of such securities must be held to approve the purchase of shares by the company by resolutions passed by a three-quarters majority, in addition to the authorisation of the purchase by a general meeting.[20] A listed company which intends to purchase so many of its shares that the total of its purchases over a period of 12 months will amount to at least 15 per cent of its issued share capital must effect the purchase either by making a proportionate offer to all the holders of shares of the class it seeks to acquire, or by making a tender offer on the Stock Exchange stating the maximum price it is willing to pay for the shares and acquiring all shares tendered to it at or below that price within the following seven days or, if more shares are tendered than the company seeks to acquire, an equal proportion of the shares tendered by their

14 Ibid, s 164 (4).
15 Ibid, s 168 (1).
16 Ibid, s 167 (1).
17 Ibid, s 167 (2).
18 Ibid, s 169 (1) and (2).
19 Ibid, s 169 (4) and (5).
20 Stock Exchange: *Admission of Securities to Listing*, Section 5, Chapter 2, para 31.4.
 1 Ibid, Section 6, Chapter 1, para 3.6 (see p 251, post).
 2 Ibid, Section 5, Chapter 2, para 3.5 and Section 6, Chapter 1, paras 3.8 and 3.9.

holders at the lowest prices.[20] If purchases of shares do not exceed the 15 per cent limit over a period of 12 months, the company may purchase shares on the market, but the maximum price which the company may pay for them must not exceed 105 per cent of the average middle market price taken from the Stock Exchange Official List of Dealings for the ten days preceding the purchase.[2] Finally, all purchases of shares by listed companies must be notified to the Stock Exchange by the business day next following that on which the contract for the purchase was made.[3]

Redemption and purchase of shares by a private company

In addition to its power to issue redeemable shares and to purchase shares in itself in the same way as a public company, a private company, if authorised by its articles, may redeem or purchase such shares out of assets representing its existing paid up share capital, if certain conditions are fulfilled.[4] This special power to redeem or purchase shares out of capital can be exercised only to the extent that the company does not have distributable profits available and, if it issues new shares to raise part of the redemption or purchase price, only to the extent that the proceeds of the fresh issue (including share premiums) together with the company's distributable profits do not suffice to meet the amount payable on redemption or the purchase price.[5] Apart from the fact that assets representing existing paid up share capital may be used to effect the redemption or purchase of shares, however, the special power is subject to the same conditions as a redemption or purchase out of profits or by issuing new shares, and so any redemption premium or any excess of the purchase price paid over the nominal value of the shares is restricted in the same way as on such a redemption or purchase.[6]Moreover, if the assets representing the company's existing capital which are used to effect a redemption or purchase of its shares plus the proceeds of any new issue of shares made for the purpose are less than the nominal value of the shares, the difference must be credited to capital redemption reserve, so that the company's capital plus capital reserves are not diminished by the redemption or purchase.[7] Correspondingly, if the assets representing capital which are used to effect the redemption or purchase plus the proceeds of any new issue of shares made for the purpose exceed the nominal value of the shares redeemed or purchased, the excess may be deducted from the company's capital redemption reserve or share premium account, or from the reserve created on the revaluation of its assets at their current value,[8] or from its paid up share capital, thus ensuring that the company's capital and capital reserves are not increased by reason of the redemption or purchase.[9]

Procedure

The application of capital for redeeming or purchasing a private company's shares must be authorised by the company's articles, and particular purchases must additionally be authorised by a special resolution passed by a general meeting of the company after a copy or memorandum of the contract for the purchase has been made available for inspection by the members of the company for at least 15

3 Ibid, Section 5, Chapter 2, para 17.1.
4 Companies Act 1985, s 171 (1).
5 Ibid, s 171 (3).
6 Ibid, s 160 (2) and s 162 (2) (see pp 189 and 190, ante).
7 Ibid, s 171 (4) and (6).
8 See p 429, post.
9 Companies Act 1985, s 171 (5) and (6). Table A, art 35 authorises a private company to purchase shares in itself out of assets representing existing paid up share capital.

days beforehand and at the meeting itself.[10] The resolution is ineffective if procured by a shareholder or shareholders whose shares are to be redeemed or purchased voting in respect of those shares, but they are free to vote in respect of other shares held by them.[11] The resolution must be passed within a week after a statutory declaration is made by all the directors of the company setting out the amount of capital which may properly be applied in effecting the redemption or purchase and stating that, having made full inquiry into the affairs and prospects of the company, they are satisfied that immediately after the redemption or purchase there will be no ground on which the company could be found unable to pay its debts and liabilities in full, and that having regard to the directors' intentions in respect of the future management of the company and the financial resources which will be available to it, the company will be able to continue carrying on its business as a going concern for at least a year after the redemption or purchase and to pay its debts and liabilities in full as they fall due during that time.[12] In reaching their conclusions as to the company's future solvency, the directors must take into account the company's actual, prospective and contingent liabilities, including liabilities for unliquidated claims against it.[13] The directors' statutory declaration must be supported by a favourable report by the company's auditors stating that they have inquired into the company's affairs, that the amount of capital proposed to be applied in effecting the redemption or purchase of shares has been properly determined, and that they are unaware of anything which indicates that the directors' opinion about the company's actual and prospective solvency is unreasonable.[14]

Within seven days after the special resolution authorising the redemption or purchase of shares out of capital is passed, the company must publish a notice of it in the London Gazette and also either advertise it in a national newspaper or notify it to each of the company's creditors individually,[15] and not later than the publication of the first of these notices the company must deliver a copy of the statutory declaration made by its directors and the supporting auditors' report to the Registrar of companies.[16] The original statutory declaration and auditors' report must be kept at the company's registered office during the period of five weeks following the publication of the first notice of the special resolution, and must be available for inspection there by any member or creditor of the company without charge.[17] The declaration and auditors' report must also be available for inspection by members at the general meeting at which the special resolution is passed.[18]

Within five weeks after the special resolution authorising the redemption or purchase of shares out of capital is passed, any member of the company who did not consent to it or vote in favour of it and any creditor of the company may apply to the court to cancel the resolution[19] and so prevent the redemption or purchase taking place. An application may be made on behalf of several members or creditors by one or more of their number.[20] On hearing the application the court

10 Companies Act 1985, s 164 (6) and s 173 (1) and (2).
11 Ibid, s 174 (2) and (3).
12 Companies Act 1985, s 173 (3) and s 174 (1).
13 Ibid, s 173 (4).
14 Ibid, s 173 (5).
15 Ibid, s 175 (1) and (2).
16 Ibid, s 175 (5).
17 Ibid, s 175 (6).
18 Ibid, s 174 (4).
19 Ibid, s 176 (1). The application is made to the Companies Court by petition (RSC Ord 102, r 4 (1) (*k*)).
20 Companies Act 1985, s 176 (2).

may cancel or confirm the special resolution on such conditions as it thinks fit, and it may make any other order which it could make on an application to cancel a resolution for the re-registration of a public company as a private one.[1]

A payment out of capital on the redemption or purchase of shares by a private company must be made between five and seven weeks after the special resolution authorising it is passed,[2] but the court may alter or extend the period for payment if it confirms the special resolution on an application made by any member or creditor to cancel it.[3] This means that unless such an application is made to the court, the whole operation must be concentrated into a period of eight weeks between the date when the directors' statutory declaration is made before a general meeting is held to authorise the redemption or purchase and the date when the redemption or purchase is completed. This ensures that a redemption or purchase is not effected on the basis of a statutory declaration as to the company's actual and prospective solvency which may have been justified when it was made, but can no longer be supported. If directors realise or should realise from facts known to them before they effect the redemption or purchase of shares that the statements in their statutory declaration as to the company's solvency are no longer justified, it would seem that they are under a duty to the company to preserve its assets by not carrying out the redemption or purchase. If a winding up petition is presented against the company before the redemption or purchase is effected, it is certainly their duty to do so.[4]

Liabilities of participants

If a company is wound up within a year after a payment out of capital is made for the purpose of redeeming or purchasing its shares, any person to whom the payment was made and any director of the company who joined in making the statutory declaration on which the resolution for the payment out of capital was based, is liable to repay the amount paid to that person so far as necessary to discharge the company's liabilities and the costs and expenses of the winding up, but a director may avoid liability by showing that he had reasonable grounds for his opinion as to the company's solvency expressed in the declaration.[5] If a person or director liable under this provision makes a payment to the liquidator of the company, he may apply to the court for an order that any other person who was liable to make that payment shall contribute toward the amount he has paid.[6] Because of his interest in minimising the amount which he may be called on to pay, any person or director who is contingently liable to repay an amount paid by the company in redeeming or purchasing shares is empowered to present a winding up petition against the company within the year while his contingent liability continues.[7]

The facility for a private company to redeem or purchase its shares out of capital without the need to follow the procedure for a formal reduction of capital with the approval of the court,[8] is useful and inexpensive and is likely to be used extensively. It must be borne in mind, however, that a director who makes a statutory declaration for the purpose of a redemption or purchase of shares and who does not have reasonable grounds for the opinion about the company's actual and

---

1 Ibid, s 177 (1) to (5) (see p 65, ante).
2 Ibid, s 174 (1).
3 Ibid, s 177 (2).
4 Insolvency Act 1986, s 127.
5 Ibid, s 76 (1) to (3).
6 Ibid, s 76 (4).
7 Ibid, ss 79 (1) and 124 (1) and (3).
8 See p 177, ante.

prospective solvency expressed therein, is guilty of a criminal offence punishable on indictment by imprisonment for not more than two years or by an unlimited fine or both, and on summary conviction by imprisonment for not more than six months or a fine not exceeding £1,000 or both.[9] Furthermore, apart from his contingent liability to repay the amount of capital expended if the company is wound up within a year after a redemption or purchase, a director will be liable to the company in damages if he did not exercise reasonable care in making the statutory declaration or carrying out the operation, and the company suffers loss as a result of the application of its capital in redeeming or purchasing shares.[10] The auditors who make a report in support of the directors' declaration will also be liable to the company for the loss it suffers if they do not act with reasonable skill and care.[11] There is also a possibility that the company's directors (but not its auditors) may incur a liability in damages for their negligence toward shareholders whose shares are redeemed or purchased out of capital and who are compelled to repay the amount they received, and also to other shareholders whose shares fall in value in consequence of a redemption or purchase out of capital which should not have been carried out. The directors' duty of care is owed primarily to the company, and shareholders cannot recover damages merely because the company has suffered loss;[12] nevertheless, the directors will have induced them to vote for the special resolution authorising the application of the company's capital to redeem or purchase shares by making the statutory declaration as to the company's financial position, and it may be that this creates a special relationship between them which imposes a duty of care of directors toward the individual shareholders.[13] On the other hand, it would appear that the auditors owe no duty of care to individual shareholders in reporting on the reasonableness of the directors' conclusions in their statutory declaration as to the company's present and future solvency, and so will not be liable to shareholders if they are compelled to repay the amounts paid to them on the redemption or purchase by the company of their shares.[14]

Rights of shareholders to fulfilment of company's obligations

The final provision of the Companies Act 1985 concerning the redemption or purchase by a company of its shares deals with the rights of a shareholder who is entitled to have his shares redeemed under the terms of issue of the shares, or to have them purchased by the company under a valid purchase contract, in the event of the company's default. Such a shareholder may obtain an order of specific performance to compel the company to pay him the redemption or purchase price, unless the company can show that it has insufficient distributable profits for the purpose, or if it is in liquidation, that it has not had sufficient distributable profits at any time between the date when the shares should have been redeemed or the purchase completed and the commencement of the liquidation.[15] Any claim for the redemption or purchase price in a liquidation is postponed to payment of the debts and liabilities of the company to other persons, except debts due to members

---

9 Companies Act 1985, s 173 (6) and s 730 (1) and Sch 24.
10 See p 600, post.
11 *Re Thomas Gerrard & Son Ltd* [1968] Ch 455, [1967] 2 All ER 525.
12 *Prudential Assurance Co Ltd v Newman Industries Ltd (No 2)* [1982] Ch 204, [1082] 1 All ER 354.
13 *Hedley Byrne & Co Ltd v Heller & Partners Ltd* [1964] AC 465, [1963] 2 All ER 575.
14 *Arenson v Casson, Beckman, Rutley & Co* [1977] AC 405, [1075] 3 All ER 901; *JEB Fasteners Ltd v Marks, Bloom & Co* [1981] 3 All ER 289; *Caparo Industries plc v Dickman* [1990] 1 All ER 568, [1990] 2 WLR 358, HL.
15 Companies Act 1985, s 178 (1) and (3) to (5).

as such (eg declared but unpaid dividends), and the claim is also postponed to the prior ranking rights of the holders of other classes of shares (eg preference shareholders with priority over the holders of the shares which should have been redeemed or purchased for repayment of capital and arrears of dividends by the terms of issue of the preference shares).[16] Claims for the redemption or purchase price must be satisfied in a liquidation before the capital of other classes of shares is repaid, but no priority at all is given to the holders of shares if the company is wound up before the date for redemption or completion of the purchase arrives, nor if the company has at no time between the date when the redemption or purchase should have been effected and the commencement of the winding up had sufficient distributable profits to carry it out, and the capital in respect of the shares is then repaid in the normal order as though they were not redeemable or had not been purchased by the company.[17] In these two excepted cases the rights of the holders of the shares to be repaid out of capital are exactly the same as though the resolution for the redemption or purchase had not been passed. Finally, to resolve a debatable question, the Act provides that a company shall not be liable in damages for its failure to redeem any redeemable shares issued by it or to complete the purchase of any of its shares which it agrees to purchase.[18] Consequently, the remedies of the shareholder in that situation are confined to seeking an order of specific performance of his contract with the company, presenting a petition for the company to be wound up[19] or for relief against the company's unfairly prejudicial conduct,[20] or claiming the amount payable on the redemption or purchase of the shares in the winding up of the company if it is already in liquidation.

Redemption or purchase of shares by a public company

When shares are redeemed or purchased by a company, they are cancelled,[1] with the result that the company's issued and paid up share capital is correspondingly reduced. If the company is a public one and the redemption or purchase results in its issued share capital being reduced to less than £50,000, the minimum for a public company on its formation,[2] there is no statutory obligation imposed on it to re-register as a private company, as there is when it reduces its issued capital with the approval of the court,[3] and it therefore retains its status as a public company notwithstanding.

LOAN CAPITAL

Definition

Unlike 'capital' or 'share capital', the expression 'loan capital' is not a legal term of art, but a commercial expression used to indicate the total amount borrowed by a company otherwise than by short and medium term borrowing.[4] Loan capital

---

16 Ibid, s 178 (6).
17 Ibid, s 178 (5).
18 Ibid, s 178 (2).
19 *Re Holders Investment Trust Ltd* [1971] 2 All ER 289, [1971] 1 WLR 583.
20 Companies Act 1985, s 459 (1) (see p 666, post).
 1 Ibid, s 160 (4) and s 162 (2).
 2 Ibid, ss 117 (1) and (3) and 118 (1).
 3 See p 187, ante.
 4 Short- and medium-term borrowing is generally understood to comprise loans repayable within ten years. It consists mainly of fixed term bank loans and overdrafts.

comprises the long-term indebtedness of the company secured by mortgages, debentures, debenture stock, loan stock and notes (collectively known as debt securities), and the law relating to these securities, which is vastly different from that relating to share capital, will be dealt with in Chapter 12. Loan capital appears on the liabilities side of a company's balance sheet in double columnar form,[5] and is entered beneath share capital and reserves, but unlike share capital, it does represent indebtedness by the company, and holders of loan capital have the remedies of creditors to recover what the company owes them.

Every company formed to carry on a trade or business has an implied power to borrow and to give security for loans made to it.[6] The amount which the company may borrow is unlimited, unless its memorandum of association sets a limit on the total amount of the loans it may raise or the indebtedness it may incur. It is not usual for the memoranda of modern companies to limit the amount which they may borrow, but it is not unusual for the articles to limit the amount the directors may borrow without first obtaining the consent of the shareholders in general meeting.[7]

Debentures representing money lent to a company have a nominal value, like shares. They are usually redeemable at a fixed future date, and their nominal value is the amount payable to the holder on redemption, unless by the terms of issue a premium is payable on redemption in addition to the nominal value. The company usually provides for such premiums out of its profits, but money representing the company's share premium account may also be used to pay them.[8] Debentures and other debt securities may be issued at a discount, unlike shares, and it is, in fact, more usual for them to be issued at a discount than at an issue price equal to their nominal value. The interest on debt securities will usually be payable at the current market rate at the date when they are issued, or at a rate which is periodically variable with the current market rate, and a company can make the yield it offers slightly more attractive by giving subscribers a few points of discount.[9] A discount has the further attraction that when the securities are redeemed at par, the amount of the discount is capital in the hands of the debenture holder, and is not subject to income tax,[10] unless the debentures were issued to shareholders of the company on the capitalisation of profits,[11] but in cases where no income tax is payable, the discount is subject to capital gains tax when the securities are redeemed.[12] The tax

5 If the balance sheet is in single columnar form, it is usual to show loan capital as the last deduction to be made from the value of the company's assets to arrive at its net worth (ie its paid up capital and reserves).

6 *General Auction Estate and Monetary Co v Smith* [1891] 3 Ch 432.

7 Table A of the Companies Act 1948 limited the borrowing powers of the board of directors to an amount equal to the company's issued share capital for the time being, but this did not apply to temporary bank loans and the limit could be waived by ordinary resolution of a general meeting (Table A, art 79). There are no restrictions on the board's borrowing powers in the present Table A.

8 Companies Act 1985, s 130 (2).

9 For example, if £100 debentures carrying interest at 10 per cent are issued for £95, the subscriber will receive £10 pa for every £95 he invests, which gives him a yield of 10·526 per cent, and if the debentures are redeemable after 20 years, the yield to redemption (taking into account that the investor will then receive £100 for every £95 invested) will be 10·614 per cent.

10 *Lomax v Peter Dixon & Co Ltd* [1943] KB 671, [1943] 2 All ER 255.

11 Income and Corporation Taxes Act 1988, s 209 (2) (c) (44 Halsbury's Statutes (4th edn) 258). Income tax is payable by the recipient shareholder at the higher rates applicable to him (less the basic rate) on the value of such debentures at the date of their issue, and income tax at the basic and higher rates is also payable on the amount paid on their redemption, but the tax paid on the issue of the debentures is allowed as a deduction from that payable on their redemption (Income and Corporation Taxes Act 1988, s 233 (1) and (2)).

12 Capital Gains Tax Act 1979, s 19 (1) and s 20 (1) (42 Halsbury's Statutes (4th edn) 637 and 638).

position with regard to premiums payable on the redemption of the debentures is exactly the same.

Convertible debentures and debentures with subscription warrants

A form of security which has appeared in increasing volume since the early 1960s is the debenture or other debt security which is convertible at the option of its holder into fully paid ordinary shares at a prescribed rate on certain dates or during a certain period.[13] The exercise of the right of conversion by the security holder at the appropriate time would appear by implication to make the principal of the debt immediately due and payable and to appropriate it in payment of the nominal value of the shares issued in exchange plus any premium in respect of them. The shares are therefore issued for cash,[14] and if the company is a public one there is no need to have a statutory valuation of the consideration given for them.[15] The option to convert the debt security is valuable not only because it may entitle the holder to acquire shares at a price which may be less than their market value when the option becomes exercisable, but also because it ensures that the market value of the security cannot fall below the value of the shares for which it is exchangeable while the option to convert exists. But convertible debentures or other debt securities may not be used as a device to enable shares to be issued at a discount; this was illegal under the rules for the maintenance of capital and is now expressly prohibited by the Companies Act 1985.[16] Consequently, when a company proposed to issue £100 debentures at a discount of £20 and the terms of issue entitled the debenture holders to convert each debenture into 100 fully paid £1 shares at any time after the debentures were issued, the court issued an injunction restraining the issue of the debentures on those terms.[17] In that case the debentures were immediately convertible, and the device for issuing shares at a discount was transparent. Cozens-Hardy LJ reserved for future decision the question whether such an option to convert would be valid if it is not exercisable until some time after the debentures are issued.[18] However, now that the Companies Act 1985 expressly prohibits the issue of shares at a discount in all circumstances,[16] it appears that even if the option to convert is a deferred one, the shares taken by the debenture or debt security holder on conversion will be paid up only to the extent of the amount paid to the company for the security.[19] In practice this question is of little importance, however, for the conversion rate usually requires the security holder to submit to a substantial premium in terms of the nominal value of his securities when he converts them into shares, and it is unlikely that a company whose shares stand at a discount on the market would issue debt securities, since the issue price it would obtain would be no higher than if no conversion rights were conferred.[20] If a conversion premium arises on the conversion of debentures or debt

---

13 The option is usually exercisable on fixed dates in successive years, and is less favourable to the debenture holder in later than in earlier years.
14 See p 143, ante.
15 See p 153, ante.
16 Companies Act 1985, s 100 (1) (see p 142, ante).
17 *Mosely v Koffyfontein Mines Ltd* [1904] 2 Ch 108.
18 Ibid at 120.
19 Companies Act 1985, s 100 (2).
20 The conversion premium is the difference between the nominal value of the debentures or securities surrendered, or the higher amount payable on their redemption, and the nominal or lower paid up values of the shares issued in exchange (eg if £100 of debentures are convertible into 20 £1 ordinary shares credited as fully paid, the conversion premium on each share is £4).

securities, it must be treated as a premium paid on the issue of the shares and must consequently be credited to share premium account.[1]

A variant of the convertible debenture, which first appeared in the United Kingdom in 1966, is the debenture or other debt security issued with a subscription warrant entitling the holder to subscribe for a number of ordinary shares at a fixed issue price on or after a specified future date in proportion to the nominal value of his debentures or securities. The warrant may be separated from the securities unless the terms of issue of the debentures provide otherwise, but if the warrant is held with the debentures, its existence tends to support the market value of the debenture in the same way as an option to convert. The support is not so complete, however, for the security holder has to find the issue price in cash if he wishes to exercise his right to subscribe; since the assumption is that he will sell the security to do this and there is no certainty that the saleable value of the security will not fall, the exact number of shares which may be obtained in place of the debenture cannot be calculated in advance, as it can in the case of a convertible security. From the legal standpoint, a subscription warrant issued with debentures or debt securities has the same quality as a letter of rights sent by a company to the holders of its debt securities; the only difference between the two instruments is that a letter of rights is issued after the debt securities and is not contractually connected with them, whereas a subscription warrant is issued at the same time as the debt securities and as part of the contract for their issue. It is, of course, possible for convertible debentures or debt securities to be issued with subscription warrants conferring rights to subscribe for ordinary shares in addition to, or as an alternative to, exercising the conversion rights conferred by the securities.

The Companies Act 1985 contains no special rules governing convertible debentures or debt securities issued with subscription warrants apart from the provisions conferring preferential subscription rights for such securities on a company's existing equity shareholders.[2] Moreover, a term will not be implied in convertible debentures that the number of shares into which the debentures are convertible shall be altered rateably if after the issue of the debentures a change takes place in the number of shares of the same class issued by the company to other persons or in the nominal or paid up values of such shares.[3] On the other hand, the rules of the Stock Exchange do contain important provisions which must be incorporated in the trust deed covering the issue of listed convertible debentures so as to safeguard the conversion rights of holders of the debentures or securities. Until the last date for exercising the right to convert the securities into shares has passed, the company may not reduce its share capital by repaying capital to shareholders or by cancelling their liability for uncalled capital, unless the Quotations Committee of the Stock Exchange consents or the securities provide for a proportionate adjustment of their holder's conversion rights; and the company may not create or issue a new class of equity shares, unless the right to do so within specified limits is reserved by the terms of issue of the securities.[4] Furthermore, while conversion rights remain exercisable, the issuing company may issue further shares on a capitalisation of profits or reserves only if the bonus shares belong to the same class as those already held by the shareholders to whom they are issued, and after the capitalisation issue a proportionate addition must be made to the

---

1 Companies Act 1985, s 130 (1).
2 Companies Act 1985, see s 89 (1) and s 94 (2) (see p 246, post).
3 *Forsayth Oil and Gas NL v Livia Pty Ltd* [1985] BCLC 378.
4 The Stock Exchange: *Admission of Securities to Listing*, Section 9, Chapter 2, para 2.1 (*a*) and (*b*).

number of shares into which the debentures or debt securities may be converted.[5] Also while conversion rights exist the company may make a rights offer to its shareholders only if it is extended on a pro rata basis to the holders of the debentures or debt securities, or if their conversion rights are correspondingly adjusted.[6] If the company goes into voluntary liquidation (except for the purpose of a reconstruction or amalgamation or if the company is insolvent) the security holders' conversion rights must be made exercisable immediately during a period specified in the terms of issue[7] so that in the liquidation they may claim the amount of the company's net assets attributable to the shares to which they are entitled if it exceeds the amount payable on the redemption of their securities. While conversion rights remain exercisable, the company may not purchase any of its own shares, unless the debenture or debt security holders approve by a resolution passed by a three-quarters' majority at a meeting of debenture holders.[8] Moreover the company must maintain sufficient unissued capital to satisfy the conversion rights of the holders of the debentures or debt securities in full,[9] which means that if shares are issued to existing shareholders or to other persons after the issue of the debentures or securities, the company's nominal capital must be increased at the same time if this is necessary to re-establish the required margin of unissued capital. To ensure that the holders of convertible debentures or debt securities do not overlook their conversion rights, their debentures or the certificates in respect of their debt securities must bear the designation 'convertible', and the company must send them a notice reminding them of their rights between four and eight weeks before each date on which the right to convert may be exercised.[10]

---

5 Ibid, Section 9, Chapter 2, para 2.1 (*c*). Consequently, if the company has issued one million £1 ordinary shares and £500,000 debentures convertible at the rate of twenty ordinary shares for £100 nominal amount of debentures, and the company then makes a bonus issue of one new ordinary share for every two shares already held by its ordinary shareholders, the debenture holders must be enabled to convert £100 nominal amount of debentures into thirty ordinary shares.

6 Ibid, Section 9, Chapter 2, para 2.1 (*d*). Consequently, if in the example in the last footnote the company made a rights offer of one new ordinary share for every two shares already held, instead of a bonus issue, the debenture holders must be given the right to subscribe immediately for ten ordinary shares in respect of each £100 nominal amount of debentures they hold, or must be given the right to convert their debentures into ordinary shares at the rate of thirty ordinary shares for each £100 nominal amount of debentures plus the subscription price under the rights offer for ten shares.

7 Ibid, Section 9, Chapter 2, para 2.1 (*e*).

8 Ibid, Section 9, Chapter 2, para 2.1 (*i*).

9 Ibid, Section 9, Chapter 2, para 2.1 (*f*).

10 Ibid, Section 9, Chapter 2, paras 2.2 and 2.3.

CHAPTER 7

Classes of shares

Small companies and even medium and large companies with a Stock Exchange listing often have only one class of shares, all of the same nominal value and all carrying the same rights in respect of dividend, return of capital in a winding up and voting at shareholders' meetings. On the other hand, many companies, whatever their size, have two or, sometimes, three or more classes of shares. The reasons for this are manifold, but primary amongst them are the following. The original shares of the company, its ordinary shares, may still be held by the persons who started the company's business, and they may be unwilling to issue further ordinary shares to strangers or to sell any of their existing shares to them, because ordinary shares usually carry the majority of the voting rights at shareholders' meetings and entitle their holders to the largest share of profits which are distributed, so that if further ordinary shares were issued to outsiders or existing ordinary shares sold to them, the founders' voting and financial control over the company would be diminished and might be destroyed. In such a case the original ordinary shareholders may seek to ensure that the company raises further capital by issuing preference shares or debentures, or by issuing a hybrid form of shares which has become increasingly common in recent years, namely non-voting ordinary shares. If the company is to obtain a listing on the Stock Exchange for its ordinary shares (or for any other class of its shares), at least 25 per cent of the issued shares of that class must be held by the public (ie persons who are not directors or major shareholders or associated with them) and consequently be available for dealing.[1] An admission of ordinary shares to dealing on the Unlisted Securities Market of the Stock Exchange may be obtained if only 10 per cent of the issued ordinary share capital of the company is held by the public.[2]

Sometimes another reason why companies have two or more classes of shares is that it has proved easier to induce outside investors to subscribe for preference rather than ordinary shares. Such investors may have little knowledge of the company's business and no wish to participate in or supervise its management, and so to them the greater security of preference shares compared with ordinary shares outweighs the advantages of financial and voting control which the latter carry. On the other hand, since the introduction of corporation tax in 1965 companies have been disinclined to issue preference shares since, unlike debenture interest, the cost of paying preference dividends is not deductible in ascertaining the net profits of the company subject to corporation tax.[3]

A third reason for a plurality of classes of shares is that at the times when some companies have needed to raise new capital, the current market price of their existing shares was less than their nominal value, so that the only practicable way of raising new capital, apart from borrowing on the security of debentures, was to issue a new class of shares with preferential rights. With some companies,

1 The Stock Exchange: *Admission of Securities to Listing*, Section 7, Chapter 2, para 8.
2 The Stock Exchange: *Memorandum on the Unlisted Securities Market*, Terms and Conditions for Entry, para 5.
3 Income and Corporation Taxes Act 1988, s 338 (1) to (3) (44 Halsbury's Statutes (4th Edn) 404).

particularly those which suffered in the economic recession of the 1930s, the dates of issue of their preference, pre-preference and prior pre-preference shares mark the financial crises of their careers. The alternative course of issuing additional ordinary shares at a discount with leave of the court which was formerly, but is no longer, available,[4] was not resorted to by many companies in this country.

In the 19th century and the early years of this century public companies favoured extremely complicated capital structures. It was not unusual for a company to have three classes of preference shares, a class of preferred ordinary shares, a class of ordinary shares and a class of deferred shares. Nowadays the tendency is towards simplicity, and a common capital structure is not more than one class of preference shares and one or two classes of ordinary shares, the second class of ordinary shares (if there is one) carrying no voting rights and being labelled 'A' or 'B' ordinary shares to distinguish them from voting ordinary shares.

The rights of different classes of shareholders may be set out in the company's memorandum or articles of association, but often the articles merely empower the directors to issue the company's unissued shares with such rights attached to them as they, or more frequently the shareholders in general meeting, think fit.[5] In this latter case the resolution of the board meeting or the meeting of shareholders must be looked at in order to discover the rights attached to the new shares, but if there is a conflict between the terms set out in the resolution and the rights attached to the shares or another class of shares by the company's memorandum or articles, the resolution is ineffective to the extent of the conflict.[6] If the listing particulars or other document inviting applications for the new shares purport to set out the rights which they will carry, the contract between the subscribers and the company embodies those rights, and the subscriber will be entitled to them in addition to rights conferred by the company's memorandum or articles or by resolutions passed thereunder.[7]

When a company allots shares with rights which are not set out in its memorandum or articles of association or in a special resolution passed by a general meeting[8] and the rights are not in all respects uniform with those attached to shares previously issued, the company must within one month deliver to the Registrar of Companies a statement of the rights attached to the shares allotted.[9] The same requirement applies if a company assigns a name or designation to a class of shares.[10] The Registrar must publish the fact that a statement of class rights or a designation of a class of shares has been delivered to him in the London Gazette.[11] It should therefore always be possible for anyone to ascertain the rights attached to a class of shares by inspecting the company's memorandum or articles or the relevant special resolution or statement of class rights filed at the Companies Registry.

The rights which are normally enjoyed by different classes of shareholders will now be examined. The classes of shares will be dealt with in order of the seniority,

---

4 Under the repealed provisions of the Companies Act 1929, s 47 and the Companies Act 1948, s 57. The present prohibition on the issue of shares at a discount makes no exceptions (Companies Act 1985, s 100 (1) (see p 142, ante).

5 Table A, art 2, provides that the rights attached to new shares shall be determined by the shareholders by ordinary resolution. The rights attached to the different classes of shares of a company listed on the Stock Exchange must be set out in the company's articles of association (The Stock Exchange: *Admission of Securities to Listing*, Section 9, Chapter 1, para 10).

6 *Hogg v Cramphorn Ltd* [1967] Ch 254, [1966] 3 All ER 420.

7 *Jacobs v Batavia and General Plantations Trust Ltd* [1924] 2 Ch 329.

8 A copy of such a resolution must be delivered to the Registrar within 15 days after it is passed (Companies Act 1985, s 380 (1) and (4)).

9 Companies Act 1985, s 128 (1) and (2).

10 Ibid, s 128 (4).

11 Ibid, s 711 (1) (j).

and so preference shares will be examined first, and then ordinary and deferred shares.

PREFERENCE SHARES

Dividends

Source of preference dividends

The distinguishing feature of a preference share is that its holder is entitled to a dividend of a fixed amount, usually expressed as a percentage of the nominal or paid up value of the share, before any dividend is paid on the company's ordinary shares. If there are two or more classes of preference shares, the shareholders of the class which has priority are similarly entitled to their preferential dividend before any dividend is paid in respect of the junior class. But these rights in respect of dividends are essentially negative for two reasons. In the first place, preference shares are part of the company's share capital, and are not loans; consequently, preference dividends can be paid only if the company has earned sufficient profits,[12] because if the dividend were to exceed available profits, the payment of the dividend would be an illegal return of capital to the preference shareholders.[13] Secondly, a dividend normally only becomes payable to shareholders when it is declared in the manner laid down by the company's articles,[14] and so unless the preference dividend for the year or other period is properly declared, preference shareholders cannot claim it or sue the company for it.[15] If the company is able to pay the current year's preference dividend without endangering its business, and the directors or ordinary shareholders prevent it from doing so, the preference shareholders may be entitled to a remedy on the ground that they are being treated unfairly,[16] but they are not entitled to treat the preference dividend as a debt and sue for its payment. Apart from this, the only sanction preference shareholders have for payment of their preference dividend is the inability of the ordinary shareholders (who usually hold a majority of the votes which may be cast at general meetings) to procure a resolution declaring a dividend in respect of the ordinary shares if the appropriate dividend in respect of the preference shares has not first been declared. On the other hand, if the articles specify the way in which the company's profits shall be applied, and this includes payment of the preference dividend for the current year or other specified period, the preference shareholder has a contractual right to its payment if the company has earned sufficient profits.[17]

The terms of issue of preference shares usually provide that the preference dividend shall be paid out of 'profits' or out of 'profits available for dividend'. The meaning of the two expressions is the same, namely, that the dividend may be declared out of the net profits of the company after provision has been made for all

---

12 Ibid, s 263 (1) and (2).

13 *Trevor v Whitworth* (1887) 12 App Cas 409.

14 Table A, art 102, provides that dividends shall be declared by the shareholders in general meeting. By the articles of some companies, however, the directors are empowered to declare preference dividends.

15 *Bond v Barrow Haematite Steel Co* [1902] 1 Ch 353; *Re Accrington Corpn Steam Tramways Co* [1909] 2 Ch 40. It makes no difference if the articles provide that the preference dividend shall become payable without any declaration; this merely dispenses with a declaration by the shareholders in general meeting, and it is still necessary for the dividend to be declared by the directors (*Re Buenos Ayres Great Southern Rly Co Ltd* [1947] Ch 384, [1947] 1 All ER 729.

16 Under the Companies Act 1985, s 459 (1) and s 461 (1) (see p 666, post).

17 *Evling v Israel and Oppenheimer Ltd* [1918] 1 Ch 101.

proper matters as determined by the board of directors and the general meeting of shareholders.[18] Consequently, if the company has suffered trading losses in previous years, it was held in a case decided before it became obligatory to do so[19] that the company could write the losses off against the current year's profits, even though this reduced the residual profits to a level which made it impossible to pay the current year's preference dividend in full.[20] Furthermore, if the directors have power by the articles to transfer any part of the company's profits to reserves before a dividend is declared, they may make such transfers, even though the residual profits will be insufficient to pay the preference dividend.[1] But transfers to reserves cannot be made if they will benefit ordinary shareholders exclusively. Thus, a transfer to reserves cannot be made in order to provide funds to maintain the ordinary share dividend at a certain minimum rate in future years when the profits earned in those years may be small or non-existent.[2] It has also been held that the current year's preference dividend may not be defeated by the company setting aside amounts out of the current year's profits to provide for the replacement of assets which should have been provided for out of the profits of past years during the useful life of the assets,[3] though it may be that providing for the depreciation of assets in former years may now be permissible at the expense of the preference dividend for the current year in view of the statutory obligation imposed on companies to provide for depreciation or diminution in the value of its assets.[4] If the company's articles specify the order in which profits shall be applied, and the payment of the preference dividend precedes the setting aside of reserves or any similar appropriation, the preference shareholders are entitled to be paid their dividend for the current year and the unpaid dividends for earlier years (if any) before other appropriations are made.[5]

Cumulative preference dividends

Preference dividend is usually expressed to be cumulative by the company's articles or the terms of issue of the shares. This means that if the profits available for dividend in one year are insufficient to pay the preference dividend in full, the unpaid balance of the dividend is carried forward and is payable out of the profits of later years; in other words, no dividend may be paid in respect of ordinary shares or junior classes of preference shares until the preference dividends for all past years and the current year have been paid in full. It is common to speak of the unpaid balance of preference dividends as 'arrears', but this is misleading, because it conveys the impression that the unpaid balance is an amount which the company already owes the preference shareholders. A preference dividend only becomes owing when there are profits available to pay it and it has been properly declared in accordance with the articles, unless they dispense with a declaration,[5] and when

---

18 *Re Buenos Ayres Great Southern Rly Co Ltd* [1947] Ch 384, [1947] 1 All ER 729.
19 Companies Act 1985, s 263 (3) see p 422, post).
20 *Long Acre Press Ltd v Odhams Press Ltd* [1930] 2 Ch 196, [1930] All ER Rep 237.
1 *Bond v Barrow Haematite Steel Co* [1902] 1 Ch 353; *Fisher v Black and White Publishing Co* [1901] 1 Ch 174; *Re Buenos Ayres Great Southern Rly Co Ltd* [1947] Ch 384, [1974] 1 All ER 729.
2 *Bond v Barrow Haematite Steel Co*, supra per Farwell J, at 362; *Fisher v Black and White Publishing Co*, supra per Romer LJ, at 183.
3 *Dent v London Tramways Co* (1880) 16 ChD 344. In that case the articles expressly required the company to set aside a sufficient sum out of its profits each year for the depreciation of its assets, but it is clear from the judgment of Jessel MR in that case and in the accompanying case, *Davison v Gillies* (1879) 16 ChD 347n, that the result would have been the same if the company had not been obliged to make provision for depreciation.
4 Companies Act 1985, s 228 (1) and Sch 4, paras 18 and 23 (1).
5 *Evling v Israel and Oppenheimer Ltd*, supra.

there are 'arrears' of preference dividends ex hypothesi one or other of these conditions have not been fulfilled. If the profits available in one year are insufficient to pay that year's dividend in full, or if the preference dividend is not declared (when a declaration is required), the result is simply that the preference dividend for the next year or a later year is augmented by the unpaid balance and is a single larger dividend.[6] The accumulation of unpaid preference dividend may continue over any number of years because it is not a debt which becomes statute barred after the expiration of a limitation period; consequently the accumulation will cease only when the total accumulated dividend has been paid. Moreover, the whole of the augmented dividend is payable to the persons who are entitled to the preference shares when it is declared, and the unpaid balance carried forward from earlier years is not payable to the persons who held the shares during those years, nor is the recipient of the augmented dividend in any way accountable to them.[6] If preference shares of the same class have been issued at different times and the dividend is in arrear in respect of some shares for more years than it is in respect of others, the total arrears must be satisfied rateably when a dividend is eventually paid; this is because each shareholder is entitled to a single dividend proportionate to the total dividends unpaid on his shares for former years, and he cannot claim any priority over other shareholders whose shares were issued after his own for dividends for the years before those other shares were issued.[7]

Preference dividends are presumed to be cumulative even though the terms of issue do not in any way indicate that they shall be. Thus, if the terms of issue of preference shares simply provide that their holders shall be entitled to a preference dividend of x per cent out of the company's profits, the dividend is cumulative.[8] The reason given for this by Lord Cranworth LC, in the case which first laid down the rule,[9] was that if the dividend were treated as non-cumulative, the company might set aside so much to reserves out of one year's profits that it disabled itself from paying the preference dividend for that year, and then might employ the money representing the reserve in its business so as to earn larger profits in later years, out of which it would pay a correspondingly larger ordinary share dividend without compensating the preference shareholders for taking from them the money which made this possible. The rule of construction is independent of the reasons underlying it, however, so that whether the company's failure to pay the preference dividend is attributable to the company failing to declare the dividend, or to the transfer of profits to reserves, or to the fact that sufficient profits have not been earned, or that losses have been sustained, the preference dividend is always presumed to be cumulative.

Non-cumulative preference dividends

The terms of issue of preference shares may, of course, provide that the preference dividend shall be non-cumulative, but this is rare in practice. If the dividend is

---

6 *Re Wakley, Wakley v Vachell* [1920] 2 Ch 205; *Godfrey Phillips Ltd v Investment Trust Corpn Ltd* [1953] Ch 449, [1953] 1 All ER 7.

7 *First Garden City Ltd v Bonham-Carter* [1928] Ch 53. Thus, if a company issues 10,000 £1 4 per cent cum pref shares to X in 1970, and 20,000 £1 8 per cent cum pref shares to Y in 1980 (both issues ranking pari passu), and in 1990 for the first time distributes dividends totalling £12,000 to X and Y, the profit will be distributed between X and Y in the proportion £8,000 (£10,000 × 4 per cent × 20) to £16,000 (£20,000 × 8 per cent × 10), ie X will receive £4,000 and Y £8,000.

8 *Henry v Great Northern Rly Co* (1857) 1 De G & J 606; *Webb v Earle* (1875) LR 20 Eq 556. See also *Stevens v South Devon Rly Co* (1851) 9 Hare 313; *Sturge v Eastern Union Rly Co* (1855) 7 De GM & G 158; *Crawford v North Eastern Rly Co* (1856) 3 K & J 723; *Corry v Londonderry and Enniskillen Rly Co* (1860) 29 Beav 263.

9 *Henry v Great Northern Rly Co* (1857) 1 De G & J 606 at 638.

non-cumulative, it is payable only out of the profits of the year or other period in respect of which the dividend is declared, and so if those profits are for any reason insufficient, the unpaid balance of the dividend for that year or period is not carried forward to be satisfied out of the profits of future years. The terms of issue need not expressly provide that the preference dividend shall be non-cumulative for it to have that character; the court may construe the terms of issue, when read as a whole, to mean that the presumption that the dividend was intended to be cumulative is rebutted. Thus, a preference dividend was held to be non-cumulative where it was expressed to be payable 'out of the net profits each year',[10] and also where the preference shareholders were entitled to a preferential dividend of $7\frac{1}{2}$ per cent and a right to participate in the residual profits, subject to a proviso that the total dividend paid to them *in any one year* should not exceed 9 per cent.[11] Likewise, it was held that the preference dividend was non-cumulative where preference shareholders were entitled to a preferential dividend of 5 per cent by one clause of the articles, and by another clause it was provided that the yearly profits should be applied first in paying the preference dividend of 5 per cent, and then in distributing the balance among the ordinary shareholders.[12]

It would appear that when reserves have been created by transferring profits which would otherwise have been used to pay non-cumulative preference dividends, and those dividends have consequently not been paid, the reserves cannot be used to pay dividends in respect of the ordinary shares or a junior class of preference shares until the unpaid non-cumulative preference dividends have been satisfied. If it were otherwise, the reserves would have been used to maintain the dividend paid in respect of the ordinary shares, which clearly cannot be done at the expense of the preference shareholders.[13] It follows that a company may voluntarily apply such reserves in paying all preference dividends which have gone unpaid because of the transfers to reserves in paying non-cumulative preference dividends which have gone unpaid because of the transfer to reserves.[14] If a company proposes to pay a dividend in respect of its ordinary shares before the preference dividends have been paid, any preference shareholder may obtain an injunction to prevent it from doing so.[15]

Payment of preference dividends out of reserves

A problem which the courts of this country have not yet been called on to solve is whether preference dividends may be paid out of reserves created by the transfer of profits which could have been used to pay dividends or out of undistributed profits carried forward from earlier years. This problem raises two distinct questions, namely, (a) the general question whether reserves can be applied as though they were profits earned during the current financial period, which is dealt with hereafter,[16] and (b) the question whether the terms of issue of the particular preference shares entitle their holders to payment of the current year's dividend out of reserves or out of profits carried forward. Only if both these questions are answered in the affirmative may preference dividends be paid out of reserves.

10 *Staples v Eastman Photographic Materials Co* [1896] 2 Ch 303.
11 *J. I. Thornycroft & Co v Thornycroft* (1927) 44 TLR 9.
12 *Adair v Old Bushmills Distillery Co* [1908] WN 24.
13 See cases cited in note 2 on p 207, ante.
14 See the American case of *Day v United States Cast Iron Pipe and Foundry Co* (1924) 96 NJ Eq 736, contra (1924). The right of preference shareholders to be paid non-cumulative preference dividends out of such reserves is not generally recognised in the United States, however (*Barclay v Wabash Rly Co* 280 US 197 (1930)).
15 *Wood v Odessa Waterworks Co* (1889) 42 Ch D 636.
16 See p 430, post.

The wider question, whether reserves generally or profits carried forward from earlier years may be applied in paying the current year's preference dividend, has not been expressly ruled on by the courts of this country. It is uncertain, for example, whether the current year's preference dividend may be paid out of reserves created or profits earned before the preference shares were issued, or out of reserves created or profits earned in a year when the preference dividend for that year was paid in full. It has been held in the United States that when preference dividends were payable 'out of any and all surplus net profits', the current year's dividend was payable out of such reserves.[17] It would seem unnecessary for the terms of issue to contain an expression of this sort, however, for preference dividends are payable out of profits generally in the absence of a contrary provision in the terms of issue,[18] and so it would seem that unpaid dividends are not only accumulated against future profits, but are also payable out of profits and revenue reserves already in hand.[18A] On the other hand, if by the terms of issue the preference dividend for each year is payable out of the profits of that year alone,[19] or if the company's articles direct the payment of the whole of the residual profits to the ordinary shareholders after paying the preference dividend for the year, or provide that such profits shall belong to the ordinary shareholders,[20] the terms of issue or the articles show that the preference dividend cannot be paid out of reserves or profits carried forward, but it has been held in the United States that the mere fact that the preference dividend is declared to be non-cumulative does not have this effect.[17] In an Irish case[1] where the articles entitled the preference shareholders to a cumulative preferential dividend and provided that arrears of the dividend 'shall be a first charge on the subsequent profits of the company', it was held that this latter provision exhaustively defined the preference shareholders' rights in respect of unpaid dividends, and so they were not entitled to be paid their dividends out of reserves created or profits earned before the dividends fell into arrear. This seems to be a harsh application of the maxim *expressio unius est exclusio alterius*, and it is doubtful whether an English court would follow the decision.

Even if preference dividends are properly payable out of reserves or profits carried forward, this can only be done if the profit reserves exist when the payment is proposed. Consequently, if the profits or reserves have been eliminated by losses suffered by the company since they were created or earned,[2] or if they have been capitalised and bonus shares have been issued,[3] the current year's preference dividend cannot be paid out of them, because they no longer exist.

Participation in residual profits

A preference shareholder as such is entitled only to his fixed preference dividend out of the company's distributed profits, and there is no implication that he is also

---

17 *Bassett v United States Cast Iron Pipe and Foundry Co* (1909) 74 NJ Eq 668, affd 75 NJ Eq 539; *Day v United States Cast Iron Pipe and Foundry Co*, supra.
18 *Crawford v North Eastern Rly Co* (1856) 3 K & J 723 at 744 per Page Wood, VC.
18A It is assumed that the reserves in question are not appropriated by the memorandum or articles to some other purpose.
19 See the American case of *Gallagher v New York Dock Co* (1940) 19 NYS (2d) 789, affd (1941) 32 NYS (2d) 348.
20 *Re Bridgewater Navigation Co* [1891] 1 Ch 155 at 169, per North J.
1 *Re Lafayette Ltd, Lafayette Ltd v Nolan and Lauder* [1950] IR 100 at 108.
2 *Re John Fulton & Co Ltd* [1932] NI 35. See Companies Act 1985, s 263 (3) (p 422, post) and also the American case of *Lich v United States Rubber Co* (1941) 123 F 2d 145 to the same effect.
3 Presumably the ordinary shareholders would not be able to take the whole of the bonus shares if there were amounts of preference dividend unpaid. They could certainly not do so if the company's articles were in the form of Table A, art 110 (see p 435, post).

entitled to a share in the residual or surplus profits of the company left after that dividend has been paid.[4] The law presumes that all shareholders of different classes have equal rights, except where the terms of issue of their shares otherwise provide,[5] but where the terms of issue of a class of shares make specific provision with regard to a particular matter, such as dividends, they are to be construed as defining the shareholders' rights exhaustively in that respect, and the presumption of equality is rebutted.[6] Consequently, where the terms of issue of preference shares provided that they should carry a cumulative preferential dividend of 10 per cent, it was held that the preference shareholders were not entitled to share rateably in distributions of residual profits with the ordinary shareholders, even though the articles provided that 'subject to any priorities that may be given on the issue of any new shares, the profits of the company available for distribution . . . shall be distributed as dividend among the members in accordance with the amounts paid on the shares held by them respectively'.[7] When preference shareholders are expressly given the right to share in distributions of residual or surplus profits after payment of their preference dividend, their shares are known as participating preference shares. The participation may then be limited to the profits of the company remaining after it has paid both the current year's preference dividend and a specified rate of dividend on its ordinary shares, or it may extend to the whole of the residual profits after payment of the fixed preference dividend. Furthermore, the terms of issue may entitle preference and ordinary shareholders to participate in residual profits in proportion to the nominal or the paid up value of their shares, or they may attribute a larger or smaller share of the residual profits to one or other class of shareholders. The determination of the preference and the ordinary shareholders' respective rights then depends on the proper interpretation of the articles or the terms of issue of the shares.

Capital

Preference shareholders are not presumed to be entitled to repayment of their capital in a winding up in priority to ordinary share capital. Indeed, the presumption is the other way, namely, that because all shareholders are to be treated as having equal rights unless the terms of issue of their shares provide otherwise, preference and ordinary shareholders must be repaid the nominal values of their shares rateably in a winding up, so that if the net assets of the company after paying its debts are insufficient to repay the whole of that amount, shareholders must be repaid proportionately to the nominal value of their respective shares after calling up the capital unpaid on any of the shares.[8] However, the terms of issue of preference shares may expressly entitle the preference shareholders to priority for repayment of capital, and in that case they must be repaid the nominal or paid up value of their shares (plus any premium specified in the terms of issue for which they are also given priority) before any capital is returned to the ordinary shareholders. In practice preference shares with priority for repayment of capital are far more common than those without such a right.

When a company is wound up it may have reserves created by the transfer of part of its profits while it was a going concern. The shareholders who would have received the assets represented by the reserves if they had been distributed by way of dividend cannot claim those assets as their own in a winding up for that reason

---

4 *Will v United Lankat Plantations Co* [1914] AC 11.
5 *Birch v Cropper* (1889) 14 App Cas 525.
6 *Will v United Lankat Plantations Co*, supra per Lord Haldane LC, at 17.
7 *Will v United Lankat Plantations Co Ltd*, supra.
8 *Birch v Cropper* (1889) 14 App Cas 525.

alone.[9] Their right to receive assets representing reserves while the company was a going concern was dependent on the company resolving that the reserves should be distributed to them as a dividend, and since the company cannot declare a dividend after it commences to be wound up, they cannot now acquire a title to the assets by anything done in the winding up proceedings.[9] Consequently, a reserve fund created by denying the preference shareholders their dividends while the company was a going concern cannot be used to pay arrears of the preference dividend in a winding up, but must be used like the other assets of the company in repaying the capital on both the preference and the ordinary shares.[9] However, if the articles or terms of issue of preference or ordinary shares provide that profits shall be applied in a certain order, including paying a dividend of a certain amount, and profits have been transferred to reserves instead of being used to pay the dividend directed, that part of the reserves still belongs to the shareholders who should have been paid the dividend, and on the winding up of the company the assets representing that part of the reserves must be paid to those shareholders, whether preference[10] or ordinary,[11] and it cannot be applied in repaying share capital.

If the net assets of a company in liquidation are more than sufficient to repay all classes of its share capital, the surplus remaining after such repayment is divisible between all shareholders, whether preference or ordinary, in proportion to the nominal value of their shares.[12] It was formerly held[13] that this was so even where the preference shareholders were entitled to priority for repayment of their capital, but it has now been held by the House of Lords that the provision giving preference shareholders priority for repayment of their capital in a winding up exhaustively defines their rights in that respect, and they are not entitled to share in the surplus assets, unless the terms of issue of their shares expressly so provide.[14] This is so even though the preference shareholders are entitled by the terms of issue of their shares to participate in distributions of the residual or surplus profits of the company after their preference dividend has been paid.[15] The residual profits which have been retained by the company go to swell its assets when it is wound up, but as was shown above, shareholders have no title to profits which could have been distributed to them while the company was a going concern, unless a dividend was in fact declared, or unless the terms of issue of the shares entitled their holders to the profits automatically without a declaration of dividend.[16] The mere fact that preference shareholders are given rights of participation in distributions of residual or surplus profits while the company is a going concern does not of itself give them rights of participation in surplus assets in a liquidation as well.[15]

The result, therefore, is that preference shareholders who are not entitled to priority for repayment of their capital, share in the net assets of the company rateably with the ordinary shareholders in a winding up, whether the assets are insufficient or more than sufficient to repay the whole of the nominal values of the company's issued shares. On the other hand, preference shareholders who are entitled to priority for repayment of their capital are repaid the nominal value (or

---

9 *Re Odessa Waterworks Co* [1901] 2 Ch 190n; *Re Crichton's Oil Co* [1902] 2 Ch 86; *Re Madame Tussaud & Sons Ltd* [1927] 1 Ch 657.

10 *Bishop v Smyrna and Cassaba Rly Co* [1895] 2 Ch 265, as explained in *Re Odessa Waterworks Co*, supra.

11 *Re Bridgewater Navigation Co* [1891] 2 Ch 317; *Scottish Insurance Corpn v Wilsons and Clyde Coal Co* [1949] AC 462, [1949] 1 All ER 1068.

12 *Birch v Cropper*, supra.

13 *Re William Metcalfe & Sons Ltd* [1933] Ch 142.

14 *Scottish Insurance Corpn v Wilsons and Clyde Coal Co*, supra; *Re Isle of Thanet Electricity Supply Co* [1950] Ch 161, [1949] 2 All ER 1060.

15 *Re Isle of Thanet Electricity Co*, supra.

16 See ante, p 211.

if the terms of issue so provide, the paid up value) of their shares plus any premium to which they are entitled by the terms of issue of their shares before the ordinary shareholders receive anything, but the preference shareholders are entitled to nothing more than this unless the terms of issue expressly so provide.

Arrears of preference dividend in a winding up

Unpaid preference dividends for periods preceding the winding up of a company are not payable out of its assets in a winding up, even though the company has earned sufficient profits to pay them,[17] unless:

(a) The dividends have been declared, in which case they will be debts owing from the company[18] and will be payable in the winding up immediately after all its other debts have been discharged;[19] or

(b) the articles or terms of issue provide that the profits of the company while a going concern shall be applied in making specified payments which include the payment of preference dividends, but in this case the arrears can be paid only if sufficient profits have been earned;[20] or

(c) the articles or terms of issue provide that unpaid preference dividend shall be paid in a winding up.

It is provisions under head (c) which are of particular interest at this point. A typical clause in the terms of issue of preference shares which clearly expresses the rights intended to be conferred, is the following:

'The holders of preference shares shall be entitled to a fixed cumulative preferential dividend at the rate of x per cent per annum upon the amount paid up thereon, and in the event of the winding up of the company, to repayment of the amount paid up thereon together with any arrears of dividend (whether earned or declared or not) calculated to the date of such repayment in priority to the claims of the holders of ordinary shares, but shall have no other right to participate in the assets or profits of the company.'

Under such a clause, if the words in parenthesis are omitted, unpaid preference dividends are nevertheless payable for periods up to the repayment of the preference capital, even though the dividends have not been declared,[1] and even though the company did not earn sufficient profits to pay them while it was a going concern.[2] It is important that the arrears of dividend payable should be expressed to be calculated to the date when the preference capital is repaid; if the preference shareholders are merely entitled to 'unpaid preference dividends' or 'arrears of dividends', the dividends are calculated only down to the commencement of the winding up.[3] The arrears of dividend should not be expressed to be those 'due' at the commencement of the winding up, because this means dividends for which the preference shareholders could then sue, in other words, only dividends which had already been declared, or which have fallen due under terms of issue which made

---

17 *Re London India Rubber Co* (1868) LR 5 Eq 519; *Re Odessa Waterworks Co* [1901] 2 Ch 190n; *Re Crichton's Oil Co* [1902] 2 Ch 86.

18 *Re Severn and Wye and Severn Bridge Rly Co* [1896] 1 Ch 559; *Re Artisans' Land and Mortgage Corpn* [1904] 1 Ch 796. A company cannot declare a dividend for the fraction of its financial year immediately preceding the commencement of its winding up, and so, unless paragraph (b) or (c) applies, the preference shareholders have no claim to their dividend for that period (*Re W Foster & Son Ltd* [1942] 1 All ER 314; *Re Catalinas Warehouses and Mole Co Ltd* [1947] 1 All ER 51).

19 Insolvency Act 1986, s 74 (1) (*f*).

20 *Bishop v Smyrna and Cassaba Rly Co* [1895] 2 Ch 265.

1 *Re New Chinese Antimony Co Ltd* [1916] 2 Ch 115.

2 *Re Springbok Agricultural Estates Ltd* [1920] 1 Ch 563; *Re Wharfedale Brewery Co* [1952] Ch 913, [1952] 2 All ER 635.

3 *Griffith v Paget* (1877) 6 ChD 511; *Re E W Savory Ltd* [1951] 2 All ER 1036.

them immediately payable on the ascertainment of sufficient profits.[4] The preference shareholders' rights should be expressed to have priority over all claims of the ordinary shareholders. If they merely have priority over repayment of ordinary share capital, the ordinary shareholders will still rank for payment of dividends which have been declared but not paid on the ordinary shares before anything is paid to the preference shareholders.[5] It is uncertain whether preference shareholders can claim priority for unpaid dividends over the ordinary shareholders' entitlement to repayment of capital if the terms of issue of the preference shares merely direct that arrears of preference dividends shall be paid when the company is wound up; whether the preference shareholders are given priority for repayment of their capital over ordinary shares or not, it would seem that they are entitled to priority for the unpaid preference dividends under such a provision, for otherwise it would be ineffective to give them any additional benefits at all, unless the company had a surplus of assets after repaying the whole of its share capital.

A group of four cases concerning the construction of terms of issue setting out preference shareholders' rights to arrears of dividends in a winding up must be mentioned here, because, although draftsmen now avoid expressing preference shareholders' rights in the way in which they were expressed in those cases, there are preference shares still outstanding which were issued on similar terms before the cases were decided, and the practitioner may consequently still be called on to advise what rights such terms do confer on the preference shareholders.

In the first of these cases[6] the preference shares were expressed to 'confer the right to a fixed cumulative preferential dividend at the rate of 12 per cent per annum on the capital for the time being paid up thereon ... and [to] rank both as regards dividends and capital in priority to the ordinary shares, but not [to] confer the right to any further participation in profits or assets'. Maugham J held that the preference shareholders were entitled in the winding up of the company to unpaid preference dividends for years preceding the winding up. He construed the second part of the clause as conferring this right, because the priority conferred for repayment of capital and the exclusion of further participation in the assets by the preference shareholders could only apply in a winding up, so that the priority conferred for payment of dividends had to be read in that context and was likewise applicable in a winding up. In the second case[7] the preference shares were expressed to 'confer the right to a fixed cumulative dividend of 6 per cent per annum on the capital paid up thereon and [to] rank both as regards dividends and capital in priority to the ordinary shares'. Cohen J held that the preference shareholders were not entitled to unpaid preference dividends in a winding up, because the absence of any provision at the end of the clause excluding the preference shareholders from participating in the surplus assets in a winding up showed that the second part of the clause did not relate solely to their rights when the company was wound up, and so the provision that the preference shareholders should have priority for dividend could, and should, be read as giving them priority only for dividends declared while the company was a going concern, and not as conferring on them also a right to arrears of dividend in a winding up.

In the third case[8] the terms of issue were substantially the same as in the first, and the Court of Appeal held that the preference shareholders were entitled to unpaid preference dividends in a winding up. The court approved the decisions in

---

4 *Re Roberts and Cooper Ltd* [1929] 2 Ch 383.
5 Insolvency Act 1986, s 74 (1) (*f*). This would happen if the company declared, but did not pay, ordinary share dividends for a year before it first failed to pay a preference dividend.
6 *Re Walter Symons Ltd* [1934] Ch 308, [1933] All ER Rep 163.
7 *Re Wood, Skinner & Co Ltd* [1944] Ch 323.
8 *Re F de Jong & Co Ltd* [1946] Ch 211, [1946] 1 All ER 556.

the first two cases, and distinguished the second case on the additional ground that the earlier part of the clause in that case gave the preference shareholders a right to a 'fixed cumulative dividend', not a 'fixed cumulative *preferential* dividend', so that the provision later in the clause, that the preference shares should rank in priority for dividend, could be read simply as conferring a right of payment of the 'fixed cumulative dividend' in priority to dividends on the ordinary shares while the company was a going concern, and as having no application in a winding up at all. It follows from this that if in the second case the dividend had been expressed to be a 'fixed cumulative *preferential* dividend', the arrears of dividend would have been payable in a winding up, and in the fourth case,[9] where the terms of issue were in that form, the preference shareholders were held entitled to arrears of dividend.

In the fourth case Wynn Parry J also said obiter[10] that since the decision of the House of Lords[11] that preference shareholders who are entitled to repayment of their capital before ordinary share capital is repaid, are not also entitled to share in the surplus assets after all share capital has been repaid, a term to this effect can be read into the terms of issue of all preference shares. If this were so, the decision in the second case dealt with above would be different today, but it is very doubtful whether the House of Lords' decision has brought about this change. The problem in determining the rights of preference shareholders is one of construction, and so only the terms of the contract under which the preference shares were issued may be looked at in order to ascertain those rights. The significance of the express provision in the first and third cases above, that preference shareholders shall not be entitled to participate in surplus assets in a liquidation, is that it creates a context in which the earlier provision, that preference shareholders shall have priority for their fixed dividend, can be read. If the provision precluding participation in surplus assets is absent, the court construes the rights of preference shareholders in respect of capital to be the same as if the provision were expressed, but this is because the court treats the priority given for repayment of preference capital as exhaustively defining the preference shareholders' rights,[11] and not because the court implies a provision precluding participation in surplus assets in the terms of issue. Consequently, there is no reason for implying such a provision in the terms of issue when dealing with the question of arrears of dividend, and it is therefore submitted that the decision in the second case dealt with above would be the same if it were decided afresh at present.

Convertible preference shares

In recent years companies have issued preference shares whose terms of issue include an option for the holders to convert their shares into ordinary shares on or after a certain future date or during certain future periods. If the nominal and paid up values of the shares remain the same after they have been converted, the terms of issue will be construed as enabling the preference shareholders to alter unilaterally the rights attached to their shares so that they henceforth carry the same rights as ordinary shares, but without the original shares being cancelled and new shares being issued in their place. When the conversion option is exercised the company must notify the Registrar of Companies within one month of the alteration in the rights now attached to the converted shares and of their re-designation as ordinary shares.[12]

9 *Re E W Savory Ltd* [1951] 2 All ER 1036.
10 Ibid, at 1039.
11 *Scottish Insurance Corpn Ltd v Wilsons and Clyde Coal Co* [1949] AC 462, [1949] 1 All ER 1068.
12 Companies Act 1985, s 128 (3) and (4).

If the nominal or paid up value of the preference shares is changed on their conversion into ordinary shares, the conversion may be effected in five alternative ways, namely:

(i)   by the company consolidating or subdividing the original shares into ordinary shares with a higher or lower nominal value each, the paid up capital in respect of the original shares being allocated proportionately to the new shares;[13] or

(ii) possibly, by the preference shareholders surrendering their original shares in exchange for new ordinary shares with a total paid-up value not exceeding that of the surrendered shares and an amount remaining to be paid up on the new shares not less than the amount unpaid (if any) on the original ones;[14] or

(iii) by the company reducing its issued share capital by a special resolution approved by the court so as to repay the capital paid up on the preference shares, issuing new ordinary shares to the former preference shareholders in their place and appropriating the amount of the reduction of capital to pay up the nominal value of the new shares;[15] or

(iv) by the company purchasing the preference shares for cash under its statutory power to effect off-market purchases[16] and the preference shareholders subscribing for new ordinary shares and paying for them with the purchase price; or

(v)   by a scheme of arrangement approved by meetings of all interested classes of shareholders and by the court.[17]

If the paid up capital in respect of the ordinary shares resulting from the exercise of conversion rights by preference shareholders is to be greater than the capital paid up on their original shares, the difference may be provided by capitalising the company's undistributed profits or revenue reserves, but this may be done only if the company's articles expressly so provide.[18]

ORDINARY AND DEFERRED SHARES

Ordinary shares

Ordinary shareholders are entitled to be paid a dividend in respect of their shares only after all preference dividends have been paid to date, and if the preference shares by their terms of issue have priority for repayment of capital in a winding up, the ordinary shareholders are entitled to be repaid their capital in a winding up or on a reduction of capital only after the preference capital has been fully repaid. In the eyes of the ordinary shareholder, loan capital and preference capital share the same feature, namely, that their holders have rights which rank in priority to his own. Disregarding the fact that loan capital represents indebtedness of the company whereas preference shares are part of the company's share capital, the ordinary shareholder groups debentures, debenture stock, loan stock and notes and preference shares together and calls them 'prior charges', (ie securities which will absorb a fixed amount of the company's income and a fixed amount of its assets

13 Ibid, s 121 (1) and (2) (see p 170, ante).
14 *Re County Palatine Loan and Discount Co, Teasdale's Case* (1873) 9 Ch App 54 (see p 174, ante).
15 Companies Act 1985, s 135 (1) (see p 179, ante); *Re St James' Court Estate Ltd* [1944] Ch 6.
16 Companies Act 1985, s 162 (1) and s 164 (see p 190, ante).
17 Ibid; s 425 (1) and (2).
18 See p 434, post.

before he has any entitlement). His own shares he knows as equities or 'risk capital'. The expression 'equity' in this context is derived from the equity of redemption of a mortgagor, for the ordinary shareholder regards himself as being in the same position as a mortgagor in that he will receive nothing out of the company's assets and profits until the rights of holders of prior charges have been satisfied.

But although the ordinary shareholder is postponed for payment of his dividend and usually also for repayment of his capital, and although he primarily bears the risk of the company's profits and assets proving insufficient, he has the benefits as well as the disadvantages of being the residuary legatee. The preference dividend is fixed and cannot be increased however large the company's profits may be, unless the preference shares carry an express right to participate in surplus profits; except in that case, therefore, the whole of the residual profits of the company after paying the preference dividend may be paid out as a dividend to the ordinary shareholders, either immediately or in later years. Likewise, in a winding up, when preference shareholders with priority for repayment of capital have been repaid the nominal value of their shares, unless the preference shareholders are expressly entitled to participate in surplus assets, the whole of the remaining assets of the company will be distributed among the ordinary shareholders, and so they may receive back the nominal value of their shares several times over. Furthermore, most of the voting power at general meetings will belong to the ordinary shareholders,[19] and it will be they, and not the preference shareholders or holders of loan capital, who will control the affairs of the company and appoint and remove its directors. Finally, ordinary shareholders are normally entitled to subscribe proportionately for further ordinary shares which the company proposes to issue for cash before such shares may be offered to other persons,[20] and by exercising their subscription rights they may each maintain their fractional interest and voting power in the company. The new shares are usually offered to the ordinary shareholders at a lower issue price than they would be offered to outsiders. Preference shareholders are usually excluded from this benefit, and if preferential subscription rights are conferred on them by the company's articles or the terms of issue of their shares, they are normally confined to further issues of preference shares of the class they already hold and to any preference shares created in the future with rights in respect of dividend or capital which rank in priority to existing preference shares.

Because of the greater risk he takes, the ordinary shareholder expects to receive a higher rate of dividend on his shares than is paid on the preference shares. When the company and business generally are prospering, this usually happens. Investors who prefer the security of loan capital or preference shares then become more numerous because of the general feeling of confidence, and consequently the rate of interest or dividend which has to be offered to them falls. If the capital they subscribe is used profitably by the company, the profits earned by it should be more than sufficient to pay the fixed interest or dividend on their securities, and the excess profits will go to swell the fund out of which dividends on the ordinary shares are paid. On the other hand, in times of recession or when interest rates are high, investors can only be induced to subscribe for loan capital or preference shares if the rate of interest or dividend offered to them is correspondingly high. The interest or dividend payable to them may then absorb more than the profits

19 Preference shares which carry no voting rights at general meetings are not uncommon. If a Stock Exchange listing is to be obtained for any of the company's shares, however, 'adequate' voting rights must be given to preference shareholders (The Stock Exchange: *Admission of Securities Listing*, Section 9, Chapter 1, para 6.1). They appear to have 'adequate' voting rights if they are entitled to vote when their dividend is in arrear, on resolutions for reducing share capital and winding up the company, and on resolutions which affect their class rights.
20 Companies Act 1985, s 89 (see 246, post).

earned by the use of their capital, so that profits earned by the use of the ordinary share capital have to be used to pay loan interest or preference dividends, and in consequence the ordinary shareholders qualify only for a much smaller dividend or no dividend at all. From this it can be seen why the value of ordinary shares can change so much more rapidly and so much more extensively than the value of loan capital and preference shares. It is this volatility of ordinary shares which makes them truly risk capital. The higher the ratio of loan and preference capital to the ordinary share capital of a company,[1] the greater are the ordinary shareholders' expectations of high dividends when the company prospers, and conversely the greater also is the risk of the ordinary shareholders receiving no dividend or sustaining a loss of capital if the company suffers adversities.

Because the rights of ordinary shareholders are essentially residual, apart from voting rights at general meetings, it is unnecessary for them to be set out explicitly in the memorandum or articles of association of a company, and there is a danger in doing so, since a conflict may inadvertently be created, with the express rights of the holders of preference or other prior ranking classes of shares.[2] If special rights are to be conferred on ordinary shareholders (such as preferential subscription rights greater than those conferred by statute[3] or pre-emption rights on the sale of shares), however, they must be set out in the company's memorandum or articles or in some other document containing the terms of issue of the shares.

Sometimes companies issue a class of ordinary shares known as preferred ordinary shares. These are really participating preference shares with no priority for repayment of capital. The usual terms of issue of preferred ordinary shares are that their holders shall be entitled to be paid a dividend of a specified percentage of the nominal or paid up value of the shares before any dividend is paid to the holders of ordinary shares, and after a dividend of the same or a specified higher percentage has been paid in respect of the ordinary shares, the holders of the preferred ordinary shares shall be entitled to an additional equal or proportionate dividend out of the residual profits. The rules which govern preference dividends apply to the preferred dividend in respect of preferred ordinary shares, and so, unless the terms of issue provide otherwise, the dividend is cumulative[4] and the current year's preferred dividend may be declared out of accumulated undistributed profits or reserves of the company.[5] The preferred ordinary share dividend is in practice usually expressed to be non-cumulative, and it is unusual for the terms of issue of preferred ordinary shares to entitle their holders to undeclared arrears of dividend in a winding up.

Deferred shares

Deferred shares by their terms of issue qualify for a dividend only when a specified minimum dividend has been paid to the ordinary shareholders. The relationship between deferred and ordinary shares is, consequently, similar to that between ordinary shares and preference shares. Often deferred shares are also postponed to the ordinary shares for repayment of capital. It is rare, however, that deferred shareholders are entitled to the whole of the surplus profits or assets after the ordinary shareholders have been paid their minimum dividend or repaid the nominal value of their shares in a winding up. The deferred shareholders are usually entitled to a large share of the surplus profits or assets, and this is

1 For an example of such a ratio or gearing of loan to share capital, see p 140, ante.
2 See *Re Duncan Gilmour & Co Ltd* [1952] 2 All ER 871.
3 See p 246, post.
4 *J I Thornycroft & Co v Thornycroft* (1927) 44 TLR 9.
5 See p 209, ante.

understandable in view of the very considerable risk attached to their shares, but some share of the surplus is reserved to the ordinary shareholders. Deferred shareholders also often have disproportionately large voting rights compared with ordinary shareholders. A common arrangement used to be for the ordinary shares to have a nominal value of £1, and the deferred shares one of 1s (now 5p), but for each share in the company to entitle its holder to one vote at shareholders' meetings, thus giving the deferred shareholder twenty times the voting power enjoyed by the holder of ordinary shares of the same total nominal value.

Deferred shares can represent capital genuinely put into the company's business, usually by the founders, but often in the past they have represented no value to the company at all, and were part of the gains made by fraudulent promoters at the expense of the ordinary shareholders. For example, a promoter might sell his business, worth £50,000, to a company formed for the purpose at a price of £100,000, to be paid, as to £80,000 in cash, and as to £20,000 in deferred shares. The £80,000 would be raised by issuing ordinary shares to outsiders, and on receiving it the promoter would make a clear profit of £30,000. He would not therefore be overmuch concerned about the value of his deferred shares. They would have served their purpose as an advertisement of his confidence in the company in order to induce outside investors to subscribe for ordinary shares. If the company were successful despite the heavy watering of its shares, the vendor would take a substantial dividend as a deferred shareholder, and what was more important to him, his shares would give him considerable voting power, probably more than half the total voting power of all the shareholders, and so he would still control the business he had sold to the company. This kind of promotion fraud was not uncommon during the last century, but now owing to the greater strictness of the law in respect of offers of shares to the public for subscription or purchase and because of the conditions which the Stock Exchange requires to be fulfilled before it will admit shares to listing, the practice has wholly disappeared in the case of public companies and is rare in the case of private ones. Investors still incline to be prejudiced against deferred shares, however, unless they were issed for cash and are therefore really ordinary shares with deferred rights. Consequently, to avoid the consequences of this distrust, public companies now rarely issue deferred shares, and most public companies which have issued them in the past have converted them into ordinary shares.[6]

ALTERATION OF RIGHTS

Power to alter rights

The memoranda or articles of association of companies usually contain a provision by which the rights attached to any class of shares may be altered with the consent of the holders of a certain fraction (usually three-quarters) of the issued shares of that class, or with the sanction of a resolution (usually an extraordinary resolution[7]) passed at a separate meeting of the shareholders of that class.[8] Sometimes, the

---

6 See, for example, *Carruth v Imperial Chemical Industries Ltd* [1937] AC 707, [1937] 2 All ER 422.
7 An extraordinary resolution, like a special one, is passed if three-quarters of the votes cast by shareholders are in favour of it (see p 617, post).
8 See, for example, Companies Act 1948, Table A, art 4. The present Table A contains no provision for the alteration of class rights. If any shares of a company are to be listed on the Stock Exchange, its memorandum or articles must permit the variation of class rights only with the consent of shareholders of the class concerned at a class meeting at which at least one-third of the issued shares of the class are represented (Stock Exchange: *Admission of Securities to Listing*, Section 9, Chapter 1, para 6.2).

provision is more elaborate, and requires the consent of the requisite fraction of shareholders if the rights of the class are to be 'affected, modified, varied, dealt with, or abrogated in any manner'.[9] On the other hand, articles of association (particularly of older companies) are sometimes silent on the question of the alteration of class rights, but this does not imply an effective prohibition on their alteration.[10]

If the rights of the class in question are conferred by the articles, or by the terms of issue of the shares resolved upon by the directors or a general meeting of a company under a power in the articles, the provision for the alteration of those rights is effective subject to the statutory restrictions dealt with below. In those cases a shareholder of the class affected may have his rights altered despite his individual dissent, whilst, on the other hand, the company cannot alter the rights of the class without first obtaining the consent required by the articles. But if the rights of the class are conferred by the memorandum, they may not be altered at all unless the memorandum so provides, and subject to what is said below, a provision in the articles permitting their alteration would then be ineffective.[11] If the memorandum provides that the rights conferred by it may be altered in the manner laid down by the articles, however, a provision in the articles for the alteration of those rights is valid, and the alteration may be effected in accordance with the articles,[12] which are deemed to be incorporated in the memorandum by reference.

References in the Companies Act 1985 to the rights attached to a class of shares, or to the rights conferred on members of a company holding a particular class of shares or belonging to a particular class of members, and also similar references in the memorandum or articles of association of a company, are not confined to shares which carry distinct rights or powers which other shares do not carry or to the holders of such shares.[13] Such references also include shares whose holders have distinct rights or powers conferred on them in their capacity as members or shareholders of the company, even though those rights or powers are not annexed to identifiable shares and do not pass to transferees of any of the shares held by them. Consequently, if by the articles of association of a company a named shareholder is given the right to subscribe for a certain fraction of further shares issued by the company in the future, or a right of pre-emption over the shares held by other members, or a power to appoint one or more directors to the board of the company, such rights and powers are rights attached to a class of shares, because the conferment of the rights by the articles establishes the shares held by the shareholder as a separate class. Such rights and powers conferred on a named shareholder, as rights attached to a class of shares, cannot be altered without the consent of that shareholder under the provisions of the company's memorandum or articles or the statutory provisions dealt with below.[13] On the other hand, a mere personal right conferred on a member or shareholder by the memorandum or articles (such as his appointment as president of the company) is not a right attached to his shares, and so can be altered or abrogated without his consent.[14]

9 See, for example, *White v Bristol Aeroplane Co Ltd* [1953] Ch 65, [1953] 1 All ER 40, and *Re John Smith's Tadcaster Brewery Co Ltd* [1953] Ch 308, [1953] 1 All ER 518.
10 *Andrews v Gas Meter Co* [1897] 1 Ch 361.
11 Companies Act 1985, s 2 (7) and s 17 (1) and (2).
12 *Re Welsbach Incandescent Gas Light Co Ltd* [1904] 1 Ch 87.
13 *Cumbrian Newspapers Group Ltd v Cumberland and Westmoreland Herald Newspaper and Printing Co Ltd* [1987] Ch 1, [1986] 2 All ER 816.
14 *Re Blue Arrow plc* [1987] BCLC 585, 3 BCC 318.

Conditions for alteration of class rights

Whatever may be the appropriate method for effecting an alteration of the rights attached to a class of a company's shares, the Companies Act 1985 requires that the alteration shall be preceded by the consent of the existing shareholders of that class being obtained, except, it would seem, where the memorandum (if the rights are conferred by it) or the articles expressly provide that the rights of a class of shareholders may be altered simply by a general meeting of the company so resolving. Where the consent of the class of shareholders is required, the form of that consent depends on whether the class rights in question are conferred by the company's memorandum or otherwise and on the circumstances in which the variation is made. If the class rights are conferred otherwise than by the memorandum (ie they are conferred by the articles or are defined by a resolution of a board or general meeting), and the articles contain no provision for their alteration, the rights may be altered with, but only with, the consent of the holders of three-quarters in nominal value of the issued shares of the class concerned, or with the approval of a separate meeting of that class by an extraordinary resolution passed by a majority of three-quarters of the votes cast.[15] If, on the other hand, the class rights are conferred by the memorandum and neither it nor the articles contain a provision for the alteration of the rights, an alteration may be effected only with the consent of all the existing members of the company,[16] and this is so even though the memorandum does not provide that it may be altered or prohibits any alterations of class rights. Nevertheless, if the class rights are conferred by the memorandum or in any other way and the memorandum or articles provide for their alteration, and the alteration is connected with the grant, variation, revocation or renewal of an authorisation for directors to issue shares[17] or is connected with a reduction of share capital, the class rights may be altered only with the consent of the holders of three-quarters in nominal value of the issued shares of the class or with the approval of a class meeting by extraordinary resolution, and any additional requirements of the memorandum or articles regarding the alteration of class rights must also be complied with (eg a provision in the memorandum or articles requiring the consent of the class of shareholders by a greater majority than three-quarters).[18] Finally, if the class rights are conferred by the memorandum or in any other way and the alteration is not connected with the grant, variation, revocation or renewal of an authorisation for directors to issue shares or with a reduction of share capital, the class rights may be altered if the articles so provide and in the manner there provided, but if the class rights are conferred by the memorandum, they may be altered only if the articles so provided when the company was incorporated.[19]

These statutory provisions are clearly not exhaustive, and so it is still possible for class rights conferred by the memorandum to be altered by complying with the conditions and procedure prescribed by the memorandum itself, or with the corresponding provisions of the articles if it is provided in the memorandum that it may be altered by a method set out in the articles.[20] This is not so, however, if the alteration is connected with an authorisation for directors to issue shares or with a variation, revocation or renewal of such an authorisation or with a reduction of capital, when the statutory conditions must always be fulfilled. Furthermore, where

15 Companies Act 1985, s 125 (2).
16 Ibid, s 125 (5).
17 See p 245, post.
18 Companies Act 1985, s 125 (3).
19 Ibid, s 125 (4).
20 *Re Welsbach Incandescent Gas Light Co Ltd* [1904] 1 Ch 87.

the articles do not authorise the alteration of class rights, it would seem that rights conferred otherwise than by the memorandum may be altered in accordance with a provision for their alteration in the memorandum, whether inserted there when the company was incorporated or subsequently, but this will not be so if the alteration is connected with an authorisation for directors to issue shares, or with a variation, revocation or renewal of such an authorisation, or with a reduction of capital, when the statutory conditions must always be complied with. It could be argued on the other hand that this is a situation which falls within the express statutory provision[1] where the class rights are conferred otherwise than by the memorandum and the articles do not provide for their alteration, with the consequence that the class rights could be altered only in accordance with the statutory provision and not in accordance with the provision in the memorandum.

Anomalies and difficulties

The statutory conditions for the alteration of class rights are needlessly complicated and produce the following curious results:

(a) if class rights are conferred by the memorandum and only the articles provide for their alteration, the provision for their alteration must be included in the articles when the company is incorporated if it is to be relied on, and it is insufficient that it is inserted before shares of the class in question are issued, except where the alteration is connected with an authorisation for directors to issue shares or with a variation, revocation or renewal of such an authorisation, or with a reduction of share capital, when the provision for alteration may be inserted in the articles at any time;

(b) if class rights are conferred by the memorandum and it provides for their alteration, or if class rights are conferred otherwise than by the memorandum and the articles provide for their alteration, the rights can be varied by fulfilling the conditions prescribed by the memorandum or articles respectively (eg with the consent of the holders of a majority in nominal value of the shares of the class, or with the approval of an ordinary resolution of a class meeting, or even with the approval of the board of directors), but if the alteration is connected with an authorisation for directors to issue shares, or with the variation, revocation, or renewal of such an authorisation, or with a reduction of capital, it is necessary to obtain the consent of the holders of at least three-quarters in nominal value of the shares of the class or the approval of an extraordinary resolution of a class meeting;

(c) except where an alteration of rights is effected in connection with an authorisation for directors to issue shares, or with the variation, revocation or renewal of such an authorisation, or with a reduction of capital, the consent of a fraction of shareholders of the class concerned to the alteration of their rights is not mandatory, and so a provision in the memorandum or articles authorising the company to alter class rights without any consent being given by or on behalf of the class of shareholders concerned is fully effective (eg a provision in the memorandum or articles that class rights may be altered by the company passing a special resolution at a general meeting with or without the consent of the shareholders affected);

(d) the alteration of the memorandum or articles to remove a provision authorising the alteration of class rights which has previously applied[2] does not enable the company to alter class rights without the consent of holders of the class of

---

1 Companies Act 1985, s 125 (2).
2 See p 223, post.

shares concerned; this is because the memorandum and articles will now contain no provision for the alteration of class rights, and so the relevant statutory provision will apply, namely, that the alteration must be approved by the appropriate statutory fraction of shareholders of the class concerned, or if the class rights are conferred by the memorandum, by all the members of the company.[3]

The different majorities of holders of shares of the class concerned who must consent to the alteration of class rights depending on whether the alteration is, or is not, connected with an authorisation for directors to issue shares, or with the variation, revocation or renewal of such an authorisation, or with a reduction of capital, are not only illogical, but also give rise to difficulties to determining whether there is such a connection. If the company grants or varies an authorisation for directors to issue unissued shares which are classified in the memorandum or articles as ordinary shares, or as shares which have specified rights attached to them, and the shares are now to be issued as preference shares and not ordinary ones, or are to have rights attached to them in addition to the specified rights, it is clear that the alteration of rights is connected with the authorisation to issue the shares, and the appropriate consent of existing ordinary shareholders or of existing holders of shares conferring the specified rights must be obtained. But such a connection is not apparent in any other situation when an authorisation for a further issue of shares is involved. It would not appear possible to establish such a connection if the alteration is effected before the authorisation for the issue of further shares is given, unless it is to be assumed that if there are any unissued shares of the class in question, any alteration of the rights attached to shares of that class (which has an immediate effect only on existing shares) is also connected with any authorisation subsequently given to issue the remainder. Furthermore, any connection between the renewal or revocation of an authority to issue unissued shares and the alteration of rights attached to existing shares must appear tenuous, unless it is purely a chronological connection, because the renewal or revocation and the alteration of class rights are effected at the same general meeting, or unless the revocation or renewal and the alteration of rights are expressly made interdependent and conditional on both operations being carried out.

A connection between an alteration of class rights and a reduction of capital is less difficult to establish since there can only be such a connection if they are expressly made interdependent and are effected by the same transaction. Such a connection would exist, for example, if capital were reduced on preference and ordinary shares rateably because of losses or because of repayments of capital, despite the fact that the preference shareholders were entitled by the terms of issue of their shares to repayment of the capital on their shares in priority to the ordinary shareholders.

Alteration of class rights clauses

A provision in the articles of a company which prescribes the conditions which must be fulfilled or the procedure which must be followed to alter the rights attached to a class of shares is deemed itself to confer class rights on that class of shareholders,[4] with the consequence that a modification of that provision or its removal from the articles is subject to the same conditions and must be effected by the same procedure as an alteration of the substantive rights of the class. It would appear that the company has no implied contractual right to alter or remove such

3 Companies Act 1985, s 125 (2) and (5).
4 Ibid. s 125 (7).

a provision under the contract entered into by it with the shareholders of the class in question when their shares are issued.[5] Consequently, unless the memorandum or articles (as the case may be) expressly provide that the conditions or procedure thereby prescribed for the alteration of class rights may be altered by a special resolution passed by a general meeting without the consent of any class of shareholders, the provision can be modified only with the consent of the appropriate fraction of shareholders of that class required by the articles or the Companies Act 1985, or, if the modification is connected with an authorisation for directors to issue shares, or the variation, revocation or renewal of such an authorisation, or with a reduction of capital, only with the consent of the appropriate fraction of shareholders of the class required by the Companies Act 1985.[6]

Curiously, the statutory treatment of the modification or variation of rights clauses as equivalent to the alteration of substantive class rights only applies when the clause is contained in the articles, and it does not extend to such clauses in the memorandum. Nevertheless, it would appear that under the contract for the issue of the shares between the company and the shareholders of the class concerned, the company has no implied right to modify or remove such a clause in its memorandum.[5] Consequently, it cannot do so without the consent of the class of shareholders called for by the provision itself, and if there is no provision in the memorandum for the modification of the clause, it can only be modified with the consent of all the members of the company.[7]

Statute also treats the insertion of a provision for the alteration of class rights in the articles as equivalent to an alteration of substantive class rights when there has previously been no such provision.[4] The newly inserted provision then replaces the provision in the Companies Act 1985 that the alteration of substantive class rights may only be effected with the consent of the appropriate fraction of shareholders of the class concerned,[8] and since the inserted provision may be less favourable to them than the statutory one, except where alterations of class rights in connection with authorisations to directors to issue shares, or the renewal, modification or revocation of such an authorisation, or the reduction of capital is involved,[9] the consent of the statutory fraction of shareholders of the class to the substitution of the inserted provision must be obtained. If there is no provision for the alteration of class rights in the memorandum or articles, such a provision can be inserted in the memorandum only with the consent of all the members of the company.[7]

Procedure for effecting an alteration

The consent of a class of shareholders required by the Companies Act 1985, or by the memorandum or articles to the alteration of their class rights is merely a condition precedent to the alteration being carried out, and the alteration does not take effect simply by the consent being given. The way in which the alteration may be carried out, after any preliminary class consent has been obtained, depends on the instrument by which the class rights were conferred. If they were conferred by the memorandum, they may be altered only by the kind of resolution thereby provided, or in the absence of such a provision, with the consent of all the members of the company.[7] If the class rights were conferred by the articles, they may be altered by a special resolution passed by the shareholders entitled to vote at a

---

5 See p 84, ante.
6 Companies Act 1985, s 125 (2) to (4).
7 Ibid, s 125 (5).
8 Ibid, s 125 (2) and (3).
9 For example, the newly inserted provision may enable the company to alter the rights of the class in question with the consent of the holders of a bare majority of the issued shares of that class.

general meeting.[10] If the class rights were defined by a resolution passed by the directors or a general meeting pursuant to a power in the articles, it is uncertain what procedure must be adopted to alter them if neither the memorandum, nor the articles, nor the resolution make any provision in that respect. It is clear that a board resolution cannot effect an alteration, for the articles limit the function of the directors to defining the class rights. It may be argued that the alteration can be effected by an ordinary resolution in general meeting, since all powers of the company which are not delegated to the directors and are not required to be exercised by special or extraordinary resolution, may be exercised in that way. The argument would seem to be sound if the memorandum or the articles contain the usual provision requiring the consent of a certain fraction of the shareholders of the class in question to an alteration of the rights of the class. Such a provision recognises a power for the company to alter those rights, and it would seem that the power may be exercised by ordinary resolution.[11] But if there is no provision for the alteration of class rights in the memorandum or articles, the argument begs the question whether the company has any power at all to alter the contract between itself and the shareholders of the class concerned. In that situation the court would probably hold that the contract must be equated with the one implied by the Companies Act 1985 between the company and its members that they shall adhere to the provisions of the memorandum and articles of association.[12] This could be justified by the fact that the power of the directors or a general meeting to define the class rights was conferred by the memorandum or articles. The court would then read the terms of issue of the class of shares into the memorandum or articles as though they were set out there in extenso, and on that basis the class rights would be alterable only by special resolution if the power to define them originally was conferred by the articles,[10] or with the unanimous agreement of all the members of the company if the power was conferred by the memorandum.[7]

Attendance at class and general meetings

If the consent of a class of shareholders to the alteration of its rights is to be given by a resolution passed at a separate meeting of shareholders of that class, only shareholders of that class may attend and speak and vote, but if the class meeting and a general meeting called to effect the alteration are held together, and no member of the class of shareholders concerned objects, the class of shareholders will be taken to have waived their right to a separate meeting, and the alteration resolved upon and consented to at the joint meeting will be effective.[13] The voting rights of shareholders at the separate class meeting depend on the relevant provisions of the memorandum or articles. Usually they apply the same rules as apply to a general meeting,[14] and if a class consent is given by an extraordinary resolution passed by a meeting of the class under the statutory provisions dealt with above, the corresponding rules governing general meetings apply automatically.[15]

Notification of alterations of class rights

If the rights conferred on a class of shareholders by the memorandum or articles of association are altered, the alteration of the memorandum or articles must be

10 Ibid, s 9 (1).
11 This is the position of a company governed by the Companies Act 1948, Table A, art 4.
12 Companies Act 1985, s 14 (1).
13 *Carruth v Imperial Chemical Industries Ltd* [1937] AC 707, [1937] 2 All ER 422.
14 This is what the Companies Act 1948, Table A, art 4, provided.
15 Companies Act 1985 s 125 (6).

notified to the Registrar of Companies,[16] and the notification must be published by him in the London Gazette in the same way as other alterations of the memorandum or articles.[17] If the rights of the class are varied otherwise than by an alteration of the memorandum or articles, the alteration must be notified to the Registrar within one month,[18] and he must publish the notification in the same way.[19] The same requirements apply to the alteration of the name or designation of a class of shares.[20]

What amounts to an alteration of rights

Substantial alteration

Not every act of a company which adversely affects the interests of a particular class of its shareholders amounts to an alteration of their rights. Class rights are altered only if they are different in substance after the alleged act of alteration from what they were before, and so if they are the same in substance but merely commercially less valuable, there is no alteration. The consent of the class under the Companies Act 1985 or the memorandum or articles is then unnecessary, and an appropriate resolution of a general meeting for altering class rights need not be passed. This is so whether the clause in the articles which provides for the consent of the class requires it only when their rights are 'altered', or requires it also when their rights are 'affected, modified, dealt with or abrogated in any manner'.[1]

In two cases[1] where the clause was in this fuller form, a company had issued preference shares which carried a fixed preferential dividend and the right to repayment of capital in priority to ordinary share capital, but no right to participate in surplus profits or assets in a liquidation; the terms of issue of the shares also entitled their holders to vote at general meetings, but only if the preference dividend was in arrear, or if capital was to be reduced or the company wound up, or if the preference shareholders' rights or privileges were directly affected by the resolution in question; the preference shareholders' rights could be altered only with the consent of the holders of a certain fraction of the preference shares. The company proposed to issue further ordinary shares in both cases,[1] and in one of the cases the company also proposed to issue further preference shares ranking equally with the existing ones;[2] the new shares were to be issued to the existing ordinary shareholders, and were to be credited as fully paid up by capitalising profits available for distribution among them.

The court held that the company did not need the separate class consent of the preference shareholders for the issue of the new shares in either of these cases, and that the preference shareholders were not entitled to vote at the general meeting at which the resolution for the issue of the new shares was to be passed. The effect in each case of the company issuing the further ordinary shares would be that the relative voting strength of the preference shareholders in general meetings would be reduced; and the effect of the company in the one case issuing the further preference shares as well would be that, although the relative voting strength of the preference shareholders would not thereby be adversely affected, the voting

---

16 Ibid, s 380 (1) and (4).
17 Ibid, s 711 (1) (*b*).
18 Ibid, s 128 (3).
19 Ibid, s 711 (1) (*j*).
20 Ibid, s 128 (4). If the alteration of name or designation is part of a variation of rights conferred by the memorandum or articles, it will be notified and published accordingly.
 1 *White v Bristol Aeroplane Co Ltd* [1953] Ch 65, [1953] 1 All ER 40; *Re John Smith's Tadcaster Brewery Co Ltd* [1953] Ch 308, [1953] 1 All ER 518.
 2 *White v Bristol Aeroplane Co Ltd, supra.*

strength of preference shareholders who were also ordinary shareholders would be vastly increased, both at general meetings and class meetings, in comparison with preference shareholders who held no ordinary shares. Neither of these things, however, altered the substance of the rights of the original preference shareholders. In the words of Evershed MR.[3]

'It is necessary, first, to note ... that what must be "affected" are the rights of the preference stockholders. The question then is ... are the rights which I have summarised "affected" by what is proposed? It is said in answer—and I think rightly said—No, they are not; they remain exactly as they were before; each one of the manifestations of the preference stockholders' privileges may be repeated without any change whatever after, as before, the proposed distribution. It is no doubt true that the enjoyment of, and the capacity to make effective, those rights is in a measure affected; for as I have already indicated, the existing preference stockholders will be in a less advantageous position on such occasions as entitle them to register their votes, whether at general meetings of the company or at separate meetings of their own class. But there is to my mind a distinction, and a sensible distinction, between an affecting of the rights and an affecting of the enjoyment of the rights, or of the stockholders' capacity to turn them to account.'

There is a sound practical reason for confining the requirements of class consents to cases where the rights of a class of shareholders are altered in substance, and not merely in value. The argument that class consents are required in the latter event would

'mean that any activity on the part of the directors in pursuance of their powers which may in any way affect or touch the value of any of the privileges attached to preference stockholders, would be rendered ineffective save with the prior sanction of a special meeting of the preference stockholders. Such a conception obviously runs counter to the ordinary conception of the relationship between preference and ordinary stockholders in a company of this character.[4]

In fact, there are few acts done by a company which do not affect the value of its shares to some extent, however small, and also affect the value of its different classes of shares to a different extent, so that the wider interpretation of the requirement of a class consent contended for in the two cases cited would result in the preference shareholders becoming a second board of directors with a power of veto over the decisions of the duly constituted board.

On the other hand, an alteration of the substance of the rights of a class of shareholders is possible only with the consent of the class in accordance with the protective clause in the articles or memorandum or with the provisions of the Companies Act 1985. Thus, where a coal mining company, after the nationalisation of the coal industry, reduced its capital by repaying 10s out of every £1 in nominal value of its issued preference stock, but the resolution for the reduction provided that the preference stockholders 'shall remain entitled to the same adjustment of their interests [ie to a share of the compensation paid by the Government to the company] as if the said reduction of capital had not taken effect', the Court of Appeal held that the company could not further reduce its capital by repaying the remaining 10s on each unit of preference stock, and thus extinguish it, because the preference stockholders' rights to an additional share of the Government compensation would thereby be extinguished too, and the preference stockholders had not given their class consent to this alteration of their rights, as required by the

3 *White v Bristol Aeroplane Co Ltd* [1953] Ch 65 at 74, [1953] 1 all ER at 44.
4 *Re John Smith's Tadcaster Brewery Co Ltd* [1953] Ch 308 at 316, [1953] 1 All ER 518 at 522, per Evershed MR.

articles.[5] This decision is preferable to that of Buckley J in another case[6] in which he held that where preference shareholders were entitled by the articles to repayment of the capital paid up before the ordinary shareholders received their capital back, and were also entitled to participate to a limited extent in surplus assets after all share capital had been repaid, the rights of the preference shareholders were not altered by the company reducing its capital by repaying the whole paid up value of the preference shares, and so extinguishing them and the participation rights attached to them. However, if preference shareholders are entitled to priority for repayment of the capital paid up on their shares but to no further participation in the profits or assets of the company, it has been justifiably held that the repayment of the whole of the capital paid up on the preference shares and their consequent extinction does not involve an alteration of the substance of their class rights.[7] This is because on such a reduction the preference shareholders will receive exactly what the law entitles them to, and the decision to alter the company's capital by making the reduction is therefore one which a general meeting of the company is empowered to make without reference to the wishes of any particular class of its members.[7]

The redistribution of voting or other rights without a literal variation of the memorandum or articles may involve an alteration of class rights and so require the consent of the class of shareholders affected, because their rights are altered in substance. Evershed MR envisaged a situation where class rights might be altered in this way when he said:[8]

'... a resolution aimed at increasing the voting power of the ordinary stockholders by doubling it, so giving them twofold their present power, without altering any other of the privileges or rights attached to any class, might be said to be something so directly touching the position, and therefore the rights, of the preference stockholders ... albeit that there was no variation of their own individual rights.'

In this respect Evershed MR departed from the line followed by the court in certain earlier cases, where it was held that rights of a class of shareholders are altered only if they are altered literally. The cases decided under the earlier literal variation criterion must now be examined, and the objections which may be made to them in the light of the newer substantial variation test must be considered.

Literal alteration

Certain decisions of the courts before Evershed MR's statement of the present principle restricted the operation of a clause in a company's memorandum or articles requiring class consents to alterations of rights far more severely than the cases just mentioned, and the court there held that class rights are altered only if the literal form in which they appear is altered. Thus, where some ordinary shares of a company were issued as 10s shares and others as 2s shares, but each share carried one vote at a general meeting, it was held that the subdivision of each 10s share into five 2s shares, so that the voting rights attached to the original 10s shares were increased by a multiple of five, did not amount to an alteration of the rights of the existing holders of 2s shares.[9] It was conceded, however, that if the company had achieved the same result by altering its articles so as to confer five votes on the

5 *Re Old Silkstone Collieries Ltd* [1954] Ch 169, [1954] 1 All ER 68.
6 *Re William Jones & Sons Ltd* [1969] 1 All ER 913, [1969] 1 WLR 146.
7 *Re Saltdean Estate Co Ltd* [1968] 3 All ER 829, [1968] 1 WLR 1844; *House of Fraser plc v ACGE Investments Ltd* [1987] BCLC 478, (1987) 3 BCC 201.
8 *White v Bristol Aeroplane Co Ltd* [1953] Ch 65 at 76, [1953] 1 All ER 40 at 46.
9 *Greenhalgh v Arderne Cinemas Ltd* [1946] 1 All ER 512.

holder of each 10s share, the rights of the holders of the 2s shares would have been altered, and their consent would have been necessary.[10] Again, it has been said obiter[11] that where a company has power by its articles to issue shares on such terms at it thinks fit, it may issue pre-preference shares ranking in priority to existing preference shares for capital and dividend without obtaining the class consent of the existing preference shareholders. Furthermore, where preference shareholders were entitled to a dividend of 4 per cent per annum 'on the amount of the capital from time to time paid up or credited as paid up' on their shares, it was held that their class consent was not required for a reduction of the paid up value of their shares, even though they would in consequence of the reduction receive a smaller preference dividend in future.[12] These decisions placed a premium on an ingenuity which can devise an alteration in the substance of class rights without varying them literally. It is still open to the House of Lords to review all these cases, and it is to be hoped that when it does, it will prefer the far fairer criterion of variation in substance which the Court of Appeal adopted in the two cases dealt with at the beginning of this section.[13]

Class consents to acts by the company

Because a company may take action which is adverse to the interests of a class of shareholders without altering the rights attached to the shares of the class they hold, it is desirable that the memorandum or articles of association should expressly require the consent of the class of shareholders by the same majority as is required for an alteration of their class rights before specified important acts are done by the company which may have such an adverse effect on them. Such acts may include major acquisitions or disposals of assets, the issue of shares or other securities with rights ranking equally with, or in priority to, the rights of the class in question, the purchase of shares in the company by the company itself and the company going into voluntary liquidation. The requirement of the consent of the class of shareholders to such action is a provision of the memorandum or articles which can be enforced as part of the statutory contract between the company and its members,[14] and so shareholders of the class in question may obtain injunctions to prevent the company from doing any of the specified acts without their consent. Furthermore, the right of shareholders of that class to give or withhold their consent is a right of the class, and consequently it can be taken away or altered only with the consent of the class and by the procedure dealt with above for the alteration of class rights. However, as yet few companies have included protective provisions of this more extensive kind in their memorandum or articles.

Class rights and special rights

Clauses in articles relating to the alteration of class rights usually require the consent of the class of shareholders concerned when any of the rights attached to

---

10 Ibid, at 516.
11 *Underwood v London Music Hall Ltd* [1901] 2 Ch 309 at 313. The Companies Act 1948, Table A, art 5 provided that the issue of shares ranking pari passu with existing shares should not be deemed an alteration of the rights attached to the existing shares; this would seem to imply that the issue of shares ranking in priority to the existing shares does amount to an alteration of the rights attached to them.
12 *Re Mackenzie & Co Ltd* [1916] 2 Ch 450. This point was not dealt with in the House of Lords' decisions cited ante, p 183, on the rights of preference shareholders in connection with a reduction of capital.
13 *White v Bristol Aeroplane Co Ltd* (supra); *Re John Smith's Tadcaster Brewery Co Ltd* (supra).
14 Companies Act 1985, s 14 (1) (see p 53, ante).

their shares are to be altered,[14] and the provisions of the Companies Act 1985 requiring class consents similarly apply when there is a 'variation of the rights attached to any class of shares'.[15] In *Re John Smith's Tadcaster Brewery Co Ltd*, Jenkins LJ appeared to suggest that a class consent is required under such clauses or provisions only when special rights, peculiar to the class in question, are to be altered.[16] This clearly cannot be so, because a right enjoyed by a class of shareholders is nonetheless a right of that class even though an identical right is coincidentally enjoyed by another class of shareholders, or even by all the shareholders of the company. For example, if all shares of a company, preference and ordinary, carry one vote, the right to one vote per share is a class right of the preference shareholders, even though the same right is also enjoyed by the ordinary shareholders, and so an alteration of the articles to give two votes per share to the ordinary shareholders will require the prior class consent of the preference shareholders.

Applications to cancel consent to alteration of rights

If provision is made by the memorandum or articles of a company for the alteration of the rights attached to any class of its shares with the consent of a specified proportion of the holders of shares of that class, or with the sanction of a resolution passed at a separate meeting of that class of shareholders, and the rights of that class are altered, or if the rights attached to any class of shares in a company are altered with the consent of the class or a meeting of the class under the provisions of the Companies Act 1985, where the articles contain no provision for alteration,[17] the holders of not less than 15 per cent of the issued shares of that class, being shareholders who did not consent to or vote for the alteration, may apply to the court to cancel it, and if the court is satisfied that the alteration would unfairly prejudice the shareholders of the class represented by the applicants, it may cancel the alteration.[18]

The application to the court is made by petition,[19] and must be made within 21 days after the consent to the alteration is given on behalf of the class or the resolution of class meeting is passed.[20] When a petition has been presented, the alteration is suspended, and becomes effective only if it is confirmed by the court.[17] The petition may be presented by any one or more of the objecting shareholders appointed by the others in writing to represent them as well,[20] but the written authority of the other shareholders must be given to the applicant before he presents his petition,[1] and must actually be communicated to him before he does so,[2] and so it is not possible for objectors who between them hold more than 15 per cent of the issued shares of the class in question to ratify the presentation of a petition by one of their number who lacked their authority originally and did not himself hold a qualifying 15 per cent.

The court's power on hearing a petition for the cancellation of an alteration of class rights is confined to approving or disallowing the alteration; it cannot amend the alteration or approve it subject to conditions.[3] Furthermore, the court can

---

15 Companies Act 1985, s 125 (1).
16 [1953] Ch 308 at 319, [1953] 1 all ER 518 at 524.
17 Companies Act 1985, s 125 (2) (see p 220, ante).
18 Ibid, s 127 (1) and (2).
19 RSC Ord 102, r 4 (1) (*e*). The petition is presented to the Companies Court.
20 Companies Act 1985, s 127 (3).
 1 *Re Suburban and Provincial Stores Ltd* [1943] Ch 156, [1943] 1 All ER 342.
 2 *Re Sound City (Films) Ltd* [1947] Ch 169, [1946] 2 All ER 521.
 3 Companies Act 1985, s 127 (4).

cancel the alteration only if it would unfairly prejudice the shareholders of the class affected, who are represented by the applicant.[3] Such unfair prejudice is made out if the majority who voted in favour of consenting to the alteration at the class meeting acted in bad faith, or did not act in the interest of the shareholders of the class in question as a whole.[4] The court will also find that unfair prejudice exists if the class consent has been procured by the votes of shareholders who are also shareholders of another class, and who voted for the alteration in order that they might gain from it in that other capacity.[5] For example, if preference shareholders consent to a reduction of their preference dividend by a resolution which is passed by means of the votes of preference shareholders who are also ordinary shareholders, and who vote for the reduced preference dividend so that they may obtain an increased dividend on their ordinary shares, the court will hold that the other preference shareholders are unfairly prejudiced, and that the alteration of their rights will consequently be cancelled.

Proof of bad faith on the part of the consenting majority is not the only way by which minority shareholders of the class in question may show that they will be unfairly prejudiced by the alteration. If they can show that their rights are being reduced or eliminated without any necessity in the interest of all the shareholders, or if they alone are called on to make sacrifices without compensation, or if they are discriminated against, or if the scheme for the alteration of rights is otherwise unfair, minority shareholders may succeed in having the alteration cancelled without showing that the majority's motives were tainted.[4] Nevertheless, it has been held that participating preference shareholders who had priority for repayment of their capital but no right to share in surplus assets in a winding up, were not unfairly prejudiced by the company reducing its capital by repaying the whole amount paid up on the preference shares and cancelling them, even though the principal value of the shares resided in the right to participate in surplus profits, and the amount paid up on the shares in no way reflected their market value; this was so despite the fact that the holders of the majority of the preference shares who voted for the reduction of capital were also holders of ordinary shares.[6] It has also been held that preference shareholders are not unfairly prejudiced by a reduction of capital under which the whole amount paid up on their shares is repaid, even though the right conferred on them by the articles to share in the surplus assets of the company in a winding up was thereby extinguished along with the shares.[7] These last two cases may be regarded as applications of the rule dealt with above,[8] that a company is entitled to have the capital structure it wishes, and can therefore repay preference capital and cancel preference shares at any time by passing a special resolution which the court confirms. If this is accepted, the repayment of preference capital when the shares carry only fixed dividends and the right to prior repayment of capital cannot unfairly prejudice the holders of the shares. But when the shares carry rights to participate in surplus profits or assets as well, it is difficult to see how the uncompensated cancellation of those rights is anything but prejudicial and unfair.

The statutory right to apply to the court to cancel alterations of class rights only exists when the consent of the class of shareholders affected is required for an alteration of their rights by the company's memorandum or articles, or by the Companies Act 1985, because the memorandum and articles contain no provisions

4 *Re Holders Investment Trust Ltd* [1971] 2 All ER 289, [1971] 1 WLR 583.
5 *Re Wedgewood Coal and Iron Co* (1877) 6 ChD 627; *British America Nickel Corpn v O'Brien* [1927] AC 369; *Re Holders Investment Trust Ltd*, supra.
6 *Re Saltdean Estate Co Ltd* [1968] 3 All ER 829, [1968] 1 WLR 1844.
7 *Re William Jones & Sons Ltd* [1969] 1 All ER 913, [1969] 1 WLR 146.
8 See p 179, ante.

in that respect.[9] If such a consent is required because the alteration is connected with the authorisation of an issue of shares, or the variation, revocation or renewal of such an authorisation, or with a reduction of capital, and the consent of the class is obtained[10] but the memorandum and articles do not expressly require it, it appears that no application to the court to cancel the alteration may be made by or on behalf of the holders of at least 15 per cent of the shares of the class concerned.[11] Nevertheless, both in that situation and where the memorandum or articles permit alterations of class rights to be made by a resolution passed by a general meeting without the consent of the class concerned, a member of the class affected may obtain an injunction to prevent the alteration being made or acted on if he can show that it is a fraud upon, or oppressive of, shareholders of his class, and that those shareholders are powerless to prevent it because they do not control enough votes exercisable at a general meeting. It has been suggested[12] that an individual shareholder has the right to an injunction in those circumstances, whether the consent of the class to the alteration is required by the Companies Act 1985,[9] or by the memorandum or articles or not. If such a right to obtain an injunction exists, the advantages of it over the statutory right to petition for cancellation of the alteration are that the shareholder does not have to be supported by other shareholders, however small his shareholding, and his action need not be brought within 21 days after the consent to the alteration of the rights of his class is given. On the other hand, a shareholder who seeks an injunction must prove that the majority shareholders who procured the alteration acted fraudulently, or at least deliberately for an improper purpose, and it would not suffice for him merely to show, as in an application to cancel an alteration of rights under the Companies Act 1985, that the majority did not take proper account of the interests of the shareholders of the class in question, or that the scheme for the alteration produces unfairly prejudicial results for those shareholders.

9 Companies Act 1985, s 127 (1).
10 Ibid, s 125 (3).
11 Ibid, s 127 (1) and (2).
12 *Carruth v Imperial Chemical Industries Ltd* [1937] AC 707 at 765, [1937] 2 All ER 422 at 458, per Lord Maugham.

CHAPTER 8

The marketing of securities

THE METHODS OF RAISING CAPITAL

Before considering the law governing the issue and marketing of shares, debentures and other loan securities, it is necessary to give an account of the various ways in which companies raise money and finance their activities by issuing shares or debentures and by other means. The uniting feature underlying all the different methods of financing a company's business activities is the company's desire to obtain money as quickly and cheaply as possible, both in terms of dividend or interest to be paid to investors, and in terms of the cost of raising the money required. Needless to say, the methods employed by companies to raise money vary, but this is less the result of the preferences of their directors and financial advisers than the dictates of the market. For example, a small company would not attempt to raise money to buy new equipment or premises or to acquire another business by issuing shares or other securities to the public. The investing public of today is a very restricted class, and is unlikely to be attracted by the securities of a small concern; predominantly new capital for investment is provided not by individuals, but by institutional investors, such as insurance companies, pension funds, investment trust companies and unit trusts. Furthermore, the cost of a public issue to a small company would be wholly disproportionate to the amount of money raised. Instead, the small company would probably purchase its equipment by hire-purchase or by means of a loan from its bank, or would take a lease of the plant or machinery at a rent from one of the equipment leasing companies. The cost of purchasing another business would most likely be met by the company raising a loan from its bank repayable over a period of between four and ten years and secured by a mortgage or charge over its whole undertaking, or by a similar loan raised from a specialist financial institution. On the other hand, a very large public company, such as a major oil or chemical company, would probably finance the cost of new equipment, property, investments or concessions (e g oil exploitation licences), or the acquisition of additional businesses by an issue of new shares to its own shareholders or the public, or by raising a long-term loan from a bank or financial institution or from a syndicate of banks, or (though rarely nowadays) by issuing debentures or loan stock to the public.

Although the International Stock Exchange of the United Kingdom and Ireland[1] exists primarily to facilitate the sale and purchase of shares, debentures and other securities issued by British and overseas companies and British and Commonwealth and foreign public bodies, it does also provide a mechanism by which public companies can raise capital by issues of their securities if the Stock Exchange admits the securities to be dealt in on it. This may be done by the company

---

1 The Stock Exchange of the United Kingdom and Ireland was formed in 1973 by the merger of the six regional stock exchanges and a provincial brokers' exchange, which had since 1965 together formed the Federation of Stock Exchanges of Great Britain and Ireland. In 1986 the Stock Exchange was incorporated under the Companies Act 1985, and was re-named the International Stock Exchange of the United Kingdom and Ireland.

obtaining a Stock Exchange official listing for its shares, debentures or other loan securities if it satisfies certain conditions and will have a sufficiently large market capitalisation (ie if the expected market dealing price for the whole of the securities to be listed will be not less than the specified minimum). The advantages of a Stock Exchange listing are that one or more firms of market makers, which are members of the Exchange, will make a continuous market in the listed securities (ie offer buy and sell them at openly quoted prices); the prices at which dealings take place are sold on the Stock Exchange are published officially each day,[2] so that the prices obtainable for listed securities at any time can be are readily ascertained, and the existence of a market on which the securities may be disposed of at those prices is a strong inducement to investors to subscribe for them.

If a company has too small a market capitalisation for its shares or debentures to be officially listed, or if it cannot or does not wish to comply with the conditions for a listing, it may seek to have its shares or debentures admitted to dealings on the Unlisted Securities Market of the Stock Exchange, which was established in 1980.[3] The conditions for admission to this market are far less stringent than those for a listing.[4] The manner in which companies admitted to the Unlisted Securities Market may raise capital by use of the Stock Exchange mechanism are the same as for listed companies, and dealings in their securities are carried out in the same way and dealing prices are published daily by the Stock Exchange.[5]

Finally, if a company is newly established in business or wishes to raise finance without being able to comply with the conditions for admission to the Unlisted Securities Market, it may seek admission of its shares to the Third Market, which was established by the Stock Exchange in 1987. There are nevertheless certain more relaxed conditions with which such a company must comply, and its application for the admission of its shares to the Third Market must be sponsored by a broker/dealer firm which is a member of the Stock Exchange and which accepts responsibility for supervising the conduct of the company.[6] It is planned to merge the Third Market with the Unlisted Securities Market as from 1 January 1991.

The various methods of financing the activities of companies fall into two groups, namely, those which involve a large scale issue of shares, debentures or other loan securities, and those which do not. It is convenient to divide the methods of raising money in this way, because the latter are the methods employed by small companies as well as large ones, whereas the former are employed by large companies alone.

Raising capital without a large scale issue of securities

There are five methods of financing a company's activities without a large scale issue of shares, debentures or loan securities. They are:—internal financing out of profits and reserves; the acquisition of assets under hire-purchase and leasing agreements; the factoring of debts owed to the company; the raising of loans by private negotiation; and the issue of the company's shares, debentures or loan stock by private placing or restricted rights issues.

Internal financing

A company is not bound to distribute the whole of the profits it earns as dividends to its shareholders. It will in the first place retain some part of them toward the cost

2 Rules of the Stock Exchange, r 520–1 and r 520–4.
3 Stock Exchange: *Memorandum on the Unlisted Securities Market*, Introduction.
4 Stock Exchange: *Memorandum on the Unlisted Securities Market*, Terms and Conditions for Entry.
5 Rules of the Stock Exchange, r 525–3.
6 The Stock Exchange: *The Third Market*, Detailed Requirements.

of replacing its buildings, equipment and business facilities with a finite life (such as leases and patent and design rights) when they are no longer usable, or have expired or become obsolescent. This is known as making provision for the depreciation of its assets, and is now compulsory in determining the amount of a company's profits available for distribution as dividends.[7] But in addition to this limited form of saving, a company may retain a substantial part of its profits to finance an expansion of its business. It has several reasons for raising the money it requires in this way. In the first place, the retention of the money requires at most the authority of the shareholders by ordinary resolution at their annual general meeting,[8] and if the articles empower the directors to make transfers to reserves or prohibit the shareholders from declaring higher dividends than the directors recommend,[9] all that is required is a resolution of the board of directors. In either case there is the advantage that no expense is incurred in carrying out the transaction. Secondly, by retaining profits instead of distributing them and raising new capital from its shareholders by inviting them to subscribe for new shares, the company may save them income tax. A company has to pay corporation tax on the whole of its profits, whether it distributes them or not,[10] but the shareholders bear income tax only on distributions[11] which are made to them.[12]

On the other hand, although a substantial part of the new money raised by companies is obtained by retaining profits, the method has its limitations. Shareholders expect to be paid a reasonable dividend, and the value of their shares will fall if they are not. In order to satisfy shareholders while at the same time retaining profits, companies frequently turn the retained profits into fresh, paid up capital and make a capitalisation issue of bonus shares or debentures to their shareholders instead of paying them a cash dividend.[13] If the company's shares or debentures are saleable, a shareholder may sell his bonus shares or debentures, and thus obtain a cash payment to compensate him for his loss of dividend. Capital gains tax is payable by the shareholder on the profit he makes by selling the bonus shares (ie on the difference between the price obtained for them and the part attributable to the bonus shares of the price paid by the shareholder for the original shares when that price is apportioned rateably between the original shares and the bonus shares).[14] The issue of redeemable bonus shares and the issue of bonus debentures additionally attract liability for advance corporation tax on the part of the company and income tax on the part of the shareholder in certain circumstances.[15]

Hire-purchase and equipment leasing

The acquisition of machinery and equipment by way of hire-purchase has expanded considerably during the last 40 years. It is a method of financing used

---

7 Companies Act 1985, s 226 (3) and Sch 4, para 18, substituted by Companies Act 1989, s 4.
8 The authority is given by the shareholders in general meeting approving the annual accounts in which appropriations of profits for expansion are made, or by them expressly resolving that transfers of profits to reserve shall be made for this purpose.
9 See Companies Act 1948, Table A, arts 114 and 117 and the present Table A, art 102. See pp 432 and 435, post.
10 Income and Corporation Taxes Act 1988, s 8 (1) to (3) (44 Halsbury's Statutes (4th edn) 33).
11 Distributions are comprehensively defined by Income and Corporation Taxes Act 1988, s 209, s 210 and s 212.
12 Income and Corporation Taxes Act 1988, s 20. Credit is given for the advance corporation tax paid by the company at the time of making distributions (s 231 (1)).
13 Table A, art 110 provides for the capitalisation of profits and the issue of bonus shares or debentures with the authorisation of an ordinary resolution passed by a general meeting.
14 Capital Gains Tax Act 1979, s 19 (1) and ss 77, 78 and 80 (42 Halsbury's Statutes (4th edn) 637 and 681).
15 Income and Corporation Taxes Act 1988, s 209 (2) and s 210 (1).

principally by smaller companies which cannot raise money by large scale public issues of shares or debentures, and which find it cheaper than purchasing their equipment by means of bank loans.

It is outside the scope of this book to deal with hire-purchase agreements in detail. It suffices to say that the agreement is made between the owner of equipment (usually a hire-purchase finance company which has bought it from the manufacturer or a dealer) and the company which wishes to acquire the equipment. The company takes the equipment on hire for a fixed period in return for a rental payable at intervals (eg monthly or quarterly), and the agreement provides that the company may acquire the ownership of the equipment when the final rental is paid to the finance company. A variant of the hire-purchase agreement is the credit sale agreement, by which the purchaser immediately becomes the owner of the equipment, and pays the purchase price to the finance company by instalments. The instalments are the same in amount as the hire rental payable under a hire-purchase agreement, and the difference between the two kinds of agreements is merely in respect of the date when the ownership of the equipment passes.

Another method of acquiring equipment which has been extensively used by companies during the last 20 years is hiring or leasing. The equipment is let to the company by an equipment leasing company (often a subsidiary of a bank) either for a fairly short period if the equipment is not continuously required by the lessee (eg earth moving machinery used by builders), or for a medium term (eg cars and commercial vehicles), or for a period equal to the useful life of the equipment, when the lease is purely a financial transaction, and does not involve the lessor in providing ancillary services, such as repair and maintenance. The hire rental is, of course, calculated on the cost of the equipment to the equipment leasing company plus a margin of profit, and in the case of long term contracts tends to amount in total to the hire-purchase price which would be charged by a finance company. From the point of view of the lessee company, equipment leases have the same advantages as hire-purchase; they avoid the need for locking up capital immediately in paying cash for equipment.

Privately negotiated loans and advances

Privately negotiated loans are made to companies by banks, primarily to finance current trading, and also by industrial finance companies and institutional investors. Bank advances are by far the most important of these loans. A bank advance often takes the form of an arrangement by which the company is permitted to overdraw its account with the bank up to an agreed limit. The advantage of such an overdraft is that the company pays interest only on the amount which it has from time to time overdrawn, whereas if it borrowed a fixed sum of money, it would have to pay interest from the date of the loan, and since there is always some delay between raising a loan and spending it, the company would pay interest on idle money.

Traditionally bank loans are made to finance self-liquidating transactions, for example, the purchase of raw materials to manufacture goods for sale, the proceeds of sale being paid into the borrowing company's bank account to reduce the amount of its overdraft. Since the length of time it takes to manufacture and sell the goods is calculable, it is possible to foresee when the company draws on its account how long it will be before the overdraft will be correspondingly reduced. The company will be able to use the overdraft facilities as a revolving credit, drawing on it repeatedly to meet manufacturing expenses in the knowledge that if the volume of sales is maintained, it will not exceed the limit to the overdraft fixed by the bank. If the company's volume of sales is expanded, the bank will probably be willing to raise the overdraft limit proportionately to the increase in the proceeds of sale paid into the company's accounts. Companies engaged in wholesale or retail dealing or in providing industrial or other services finance their current operations by overdraft in much the same way. Although traditionally banks make advances by means of overdraft facilities in order to finance current trading, until the advent of the fixed term loan some 20 years ago, banks permitted large and even medium-sized companies to use overdraft facilities to meet the cost of capital expenditure, and this resulted in overdrafts increasing substantially, because capital expenditure is obviously not self-liquidating. When a company's overdraft became uncomfortably large, it may 'fund' it by issuing new shares or debentures and use the proceeds of the issue to reduce the overdraft, so making it possible to use its overdraft facilities fully again.

During the last 20 years banks and their specialised subsidiaries have increasingly made advances to companies to meet capital expenditure and to finance projects and expansion in the form of fixed term loans for periods of up to ten years. The advantage of a fixed term loan to the borrowing company is that, unlike an overdraft, it cannot be called in for repayment until the expiration of the fixed term, unless the company defaults on interest payments or in some other way. Its disadvantage is that the rate of interest charged is usually higher than on an overdraft and is periodically variable with changes in the lending bank's current published minimum lending rates. Also a commitment charge in the form of a percentage of the loan is also payable and is deducted from the amount advanced. The interest charge is mitigated by the loan not being wholly made at one time, but the company is instead given the right to draw it out by instalments of a fixed minimum amount over an agreed period, so that interest is charged only on instalments which have been drawn, and a periodic commission at a much lower percentage rate is charged to the company in respect of the part of the loan which remains undrawn. Usually the banks require fixed term loans to be secured on the company's assets or by a guarantee given by its directors or its parent company (if it is a subsidiary), but often also such loans are made without security if the company is large and well established and its trading and profit record is good.

Factoring

As an alternative or a supplement to financing their current trading by bank overdraft, companies may raise the money they require to meet their current expenses by factoring the debts which are owing to them from their trade customers (ie the distributors or purchasers of their products or the users of their services). Factoring facilities are provided by specialised finance companies, many of which are bank subsidiaries. Factoring companies purchase the trade debts owing to manufacturing and other companies under agreements by which a certain percentage of the amount of invoices sent to the company's customers (usually not less than 70 per cent) is paid by the factor to the company in return for an assignment of the invoiced debts, and the factor collects the debts from the company's customers and credits the company with the excess of the amount collected over the amount already advanced less a commission and an interest charge for the period of credit allowed to the customers. If the risk of invoiced debts not being paid by customers is borne by the factor, the factoring agreement is known as a non-recourse arrangement, and the factor charges a higher rate of commission as an insurance premium for bad debts. If the company financed by the factor guarantees payment of the invoiced debts or agrees to re-purchase unpaid debts from the factor, the arrangements is called recourse factoring. The commercial value of factoring to companies is that they are paid amounts in cash by the factor as soon as they send invoices to their customers, and this ensures an uninterrupted cash flow with which to meet their current expenses.

Private placing of shares and debentures

Shares or debentures are placed privately when they are subscribed for by investors as the result of private negotiations between them and the company, with or without the assistance of an intermediary. In the case of small companies, the negotiations are usually conducted by the directors, but in the case of larger companies, which require more money than any individual or group of individuals would be able to provide, an intermediary, such as a merchant bank, or the corporate finance subsidiary of a commercial bank, or a firm of brokers or broker/dealers, is employed. Additionally, specialised financial institutions and corporate finance or venture capital companies accept the placing, with themselves, of shares and other securities issued by small and medium sized companies and find the issue price out of their own resources, or alternatively place the securities with their clients or associates.

Companies which seek to raise substantial amounts of money usually obtain advice on the best way to do so from a merchant bank or a corporate finance subsidiary of a commercial bank. Merchant banks are often closely linked with investment trust companies, which invest their funds in manufacturing and commercial concerns, and so the merchant bank which advises a company is often able to arrange for its associated investment trust company to provide the money required. Similarly, merchant banks and other intermediaries are often able to place shares or other securities of manufacturing and commercial companies with insurance companies and the trustees of pension funds. Institutional investors of these kinds are often prepared to accept shares or debentures which offer a high yield or growth prospects or a sound security for capital, even though they are not listed or dealt in on the Stock Exchange. More frequently, however, institutional investors insist on a Stock Exchange listing or an admission to the Unlisted Securities Market being obtained for shares or other securities placed with them, so that they will be readily saleable; the merchant bank or other intermediary then takes the necessary steps to obtain an introduction of the securities on the Stock Exchange.

Restricted rights issues

Private companies are prohibited from offering their shares, debentures or other loan securities for subscription by the public,[16] and if they seek to raise further capital otherwise than by placings privately negotiated with individuals or institutions, whether directly or through an intermediary, they must inevitably resort to their existing shareholders or debenture holders. An offer of shares or loan securities to such persons individually is, of course, very similar to the offer which leads to a private placing, and the only real differences are that the persons approached are usually more numerous and qualify for the offer as belonging to a selected class, and that the number of shares or securities offered to them for

16 Companies Act 1985, s 81 (1). This provision will be superseded by the Financial Services Act 1986, s 170 (30 Halsbury's Statutes (4th Edn) 410) when it is brought into force by ministerial order. This section prohibits private companies from issuing or causing to be issued in the United Kingdom any advertisement offering securities to be issued by them (s 170 (1)), but the Secretary of State for Trade and Industry may by order specify advertisements of a private character, or dealing with investments only incidentally, or confined to persons sufficiently expert to understand any risks involved, which private companies will be permitted to issue (s 160 (6) and s 170 (2)).

subscription is usually proportionate to their existing holdings. Such an offer is known as a restricted rights offer because it is made proportionately to existing members or debenture holders, and because the right to subscribe for shares, debentures or other loan securities can only be exercised personally by the share or debenture holders to whom the offer is addressed (in which case it is called a non-renounceable rights offer), or by them personally or by other members of the same class to whom they transfer or renounce their right to subscribe (in which case it is called a restricted rights offer). A rights offer which is restricted in this way may be made by a private company without infringing the prohibition on offering its shares or debentures to the public for subscription.[17] A restricted rights offer can, of course, also be made by a public company, but in practice public companies' rights offers are fully renounceable, as is explained below. In practice it is rare for debentures or other loan securities to be offered by way of a rights offer, unless they are convertible into shares or carry the right to subscribe for shares, in which case they are usually offered to the existing shareholders or ordinary shareholders of the company in proportion to their existing holdings. The commonest kind of rights offer is of ordinary shares when the offer is confined to existing ordinary shareholders, and in the case of a restricted rights offer the recipients of the offer are able to renounce their right to subscribe only to other ordinary shareholders.

Raising capital by a large scale issue of securities

Public companies may raise the money they require by a large scale issue of their shares, debentures or other loan securities to numerous investors as well as by the methods mentioned above. A large scale issue has the obvious advantage that the shares or debentures will be spread among many holders, so that no one investor will be able to exercise a predominant influence over the company's affairs. The advantage has to be paid for, however, by the greater expense incurred in carrying out a large scale issue compared with the expense of raising capital in the ways dealt with above.

Large scale issues take three forms, namely, first, rights issues and open offers, secondly, placings, and thirdly, public offers, either by a prospectus published by the company or by an offer for sale published by a merchant bank, a corporate finance subsidiary of a commercial bank or a firm of brokers or dealers.[18] The rules and requirements of the Stock Exchange and the rules of law which it administers have a considerable influence on the way in which these different methods of marketing are carried out, since a company which makes a large scale issue of securities usually seeks a Stock Exchange listing for them, or at least their admission to the Unlisted Securities Market or the Third Market. Nevertheless, a company may employ any of the methods involving a large scale issue of securities without seeking a Stock Exchange listing for them or their admission to the Unlisted Securities Market or the Third Market, and in that case the company does not have to comply with the Stock Exchange's requirements, although it must, of course, comply with the requirements of the relevant legislation.

Rights issues and open offers

In a rights issue the company invites its existing shareholders or its existing debenture or other loan security holders to subscribe the further capital required. This has for many years been the normal way for public companies to raise capital

17 Companies Act 1985, s 60 (1), (3) and (4).
18 Stock Exchange: *Memorandum on the Admission of Securities to Listing*, Section 1, Chapter 3, paras 1, 2, 4 and 5.

by issuing ordinary shares for cash unless their shareholders were unlikely to respond favourably to a rights offer, and this has been reinforced by the Stock Exchange rule that if a company has or seeks a Stock Exchange listing for any of its securities, and it proposes to issue for cash any ordinary shares or debentures convertible into, or carrying a right to subscribe for, ordinary shares, it must first offer the securities to its existing ordinary shareholders in proportion to their existing shareholders, unless a general meeting otherwise resolves.[19] The normal practice has now been translated into law, and in general both public and private companies must now employ rights offers when making cash issues of ordinary shares or debentures which are either convertible into ordinary shares or which carry the right to subscribe for ordinary shares.[20] In practice it is rare for a public company to make a rights offer of debentures, unless they are convertible into ordinary shares or carry the right to subscribe for ordinary shares. Practice varies with regard to issues of preference shares, which are sometimes offered to existing preference shareholders or to all existing shareholders by rights offers, but are also marketed by placings and public offers. Preference shares which carry the right to participate in surplus profits or in surplus assets in a liquidation are treated in the same way as ordinary shares, and so must generally be made the subject of rights offers when issued for cash.[1]

When a rights issue is made, whether obligatory or not, the company sends to each share or debenture holder of the class or classes concerned a circular, called a letter of rights, inviting him to subscribe for further shares or debentures in proportion to his existing holding. If the rights offers is in respect of a large scale issue of securities, the letter of rights will contain a form of renunciation, which the addressee may sign and so convert the letter into one under which the person to whom he transfers it or the holder of the letter for the time being may exercise the right to subscribe. The modern practice is to embody a rights offer in what is known as a provisional letter of allotment, by which the new securities are actually allotted to the share or debenture holder, subject to his right to reject them if he does not wish to subscribe, or to renounce them in favour of someone else by completing the form of renunciation included in the letter of allotment. If the company has a Stock Exchange listing for its existing shares or debentures, rights offers made by it must normally be in renounceable form.[2]

A variant of the rights issue is the open offer. Here again, the invitation is confined to existing share or debenture holders, but no limit is set on the number of securities for which they may apply, and so the number of shares or debentures which the company actually allots to them when it receives their applications does not necessarily bear any relationship to the size of their existing holdings. Sometimes a rights offer is combined with an open offer of the excess shares or debentures not taken up by shareholders or debenture holders to whom the rights offer is addressed. This ensures that if those of them who do accept the rights offer are prepared to take more shares or debentures than their quota, the whole issue is taken up by the shareholders or debenture holders and there are no shares left on the hands of the underwriters. If the company has a Stock Exchange listing for any of its securities, excess shares not taken up under a rights offer must be sold for the benefit of the shareholders who have not taken up their entitlement, but with the approval of a general meeting of the company and the Quotations Committee of

19 Ibid, Section 5, Chapter 2, para 38 (a). The rights of existing convertible debenture holders to subscribe must also be protected (see p 202, ante).
20 Companies Act 1985, s 89 (1) and s 94 (2) and (5) (see p 246, post).
 1 Ibid, s 89 (1) and s 94 (5).
 2 The Stock Exchange: *Admission of Securities to Listing*, Section 1, Chapter 3, para 4.2.

the Stock Exchange they may alternatively be allotted to other shareholders who have applied for more shares than their entitlement under the rights offer.[3] Since it has become obligatory at law for rights offers to be made when cash subscriptions are invited for ordinary shares, participating preference shares, or debentures which are convertible into ordinary or participating preference shares or carry a right to subscribe for them, open offers of such securities can be made lawfully only if the preferential proportionate subscription rights of the company's existing equity shareholders are waived.[4]

The price at which securities are offered by letters of right is usually below the current market value of similar existing securities of the company, in order to induce shareholders or debenture holders to subscribe. But the benefit thus obtained is not denied to a share or debenture holder who does not wish to take the additional securities himself, for if the rights offer is renounceable, he may sell his right to subscribe for the securities to someone who is willing to pay the market price for it, and the consideration he receives from the purchaser will approximate to the difference between the market price of the new securities after the rights offer and the issue price asked by the company.[5]

Placing or selective marketing

When a company has its shares or debentures placed, it agrees to allot the whole issue of the securities at an agreed price to a merchant bank, the corporate finance subsidiary of a commercial bank or one or more firms of stockbrokers or dealers, and the intermediary or intermediaries then sell the securities to purchasers whom they find, and retain the difference between the issue price which they pay to the company and the price at which they sell the securities (less the expenses of re-sale) as their own margin on the transaction. If the intermediaries cannot sell the securities, they still have to pay the issue price to the company, and undertaking this risk is the consideration which they give for the opportunity of making a profit if they can find purchasers. The company is secure in any event, for whether the intermediaries are able to place the securities or not, someone will have to pay their issue price to the company and thus provide it with the money it requires. If a placing is made of ordinary shares, or participating preference shares, or shares or debentures which are convertible into ordinary or participating preference shares or carry the right to subscribe for them (that is securities with an equity element), the preferential subscription rights of the company's existing equity shareholders must be waived beforehand.[6]

Before issuing houses assumed their present importance in the issue of new securities, placings were carried out by stockbrokers, who merely undertook to use their best efforts to find persons to subscribe for the securities offered, but did not agree to take the securities themselves if subscribers were not forthcoming. Under such an arrangement the company could not allot the securities which were not

3 Ibid, Section 1, Chapter 3, para 4.3.
4 Companies Act 1985, s 89 (1) and s 95 (1) and (2) (see p 249, post).
5 The value of the subscription rights under a rights offer is ascertained by comparing the issue price under the offer with the post-rights value of the shares or debentures offered, and this value is taken to be the market value of the issued shares and debentures of the same class before the rights offer plus the total issue price under the offer, divided by the number of shares or debentures issued and outstanding after the rights offer. For example, if a company which has issued 100,000 £1 ordinary shares whose market price is £3, makes a rights offer of one further ordinary share at an issue price of £2 for every two ordinary shares already held, the post-rights market price of all ordinary shares will be £2·66, ie [(100,000 × £3) + (50,000 × £2)/150,000], and the value of the subscription rights will be 66p per new share.
6 Companies Act 1985, s 89 (1) and s 95 (1) and (2).

taken up to the brokers themselves,[7] and so the company bore the risk of the placing proving a failure. Nowadays, only public utility companies place their shares in this way, probably because they find the commission payable to the broker and the cost of underwriting the issue cheaper than the cost of employing an issuing house or other intermediary.

Intermediaries will place substantial issues of securities only if an application is made to the Stock Exchange for them to be listed or admitted to dealings on the Unlisted Securities Market or the Third Market. The placing of securities is regarded by the Stock Exchange as an appropriate method of marketing only if the size of the issue and the market value of all the securities of the company dealt in on the Stock Exchange does not make a public offer of the securities a preferable method. At present a placing of securities with an equity element for which a listing is sought will be permitted only if the total market value of the securities (ie the price at which they will first be sold on the Stock Exchange) will not exceed £15m, unless the company already has a listing, or, if admission of the securities to the Unlisted Securities Market is sought, only if the total market value of the securities will not exceed £3m.[8]

An intermediary which places securities on the Stock Exchange disposes of them by selling them in part to its own clients and to institutional investors and in part to market makers and broker/dealers who are members of the Stock Exchange, and they later resell the securities sold to them on the market in the usual way.[9] To ensure that securities which are placed are fairly distributed, a company whose equity securities are not already listed and which seeks a listing for securities with an equity element, must satisfy a number of other conditions. These conditions are:[10]

(a) if the market value of the securities exceeds £2m, the marketing arrangements must be designed to ensure that at least one-quarter of the securities are either made available for purchase on the Stock Exchange by investors other than clients of the member firms which are carrying out the marketing, or allotted to another member firm which is independent of the single member firm which is carrying out the marketing, so that the other firm may resell the securities as it thinks fit;

(b) the securities must be allotted, allocated or resold to an adequate number of holders, which in principle means that there must be not less than 100 holders in all, and also not less than 30 holders for each £1m in market value of the securities marketed;

(c) allocations of the securities may not be made by any of the firms which are marketing them (including an independent firm to which a single marketing firm is required to make an allocation) to connected clients of such a firm, that is, to partners in the firm or to directors or employees of it, or to a person who alone or with his associates is entitled to exercise or control at least 15 per cent of the voting power at meetings of the shareholders or partners in the firm, or to persons who are related or connected to such persons;

(d) the firms which are marketing the securities (including an independent firm to which a single marketing firm is required to make an allocation) may not

7 *Re Monarch Insurance Co, Gorrissen's Case* (1873) 8 Ch App 507.
8 Stock Exchange: *Admission of Securities to Listing*, Section 1, Chapter 3, para 2.3; *Memorandum on the Unlisted Securities Market*, Introduction, para E.
9 Market makers and broker/dealers buy the shares or debentures from the intermediary at a higher price than it pays to the company, and they in turn make a profit by re-selling at a still higher price to buyers on the Stock Exchange.
10 The Stock Exchange: *Admission of Securities to Listing*, Section 1, Chapter 3, para 2.5.

retain a material amount of the securities for their own account, and where there is a substantial demand by the public for the securities, a retention by any such firm of more than one-fortieth of its allocation is prohibited;

(e) not more than one-quarter of the total amount of securities may be allocated to discretionary investment funds which are managed by the firms which market the securities.

If a listing is sought by a company for debentures or other debt securities, or if a company which already has a listing for any of its securities seeks a listing for securities with an equity element which it is marketing, at least two market makers who are independent of each other must be offered a participation in a selective marketing of the securities.[11] This ensures that a substantial part of the securities which are available for purchase by the public can be acquired from those market makers by investors other than clients of the marketing firm. The rules relating to placings on the Unlisted Securities Market are simpler but no less exacting in requiring at least one quarter of the securities comprised in the placing to be offered to market makers for re-sale to the public.[12]

Public offers

A public offer is an invitation made to the public generally to subscribe for or purchase securities of a company. Under it anyone may apply for any number of the shares or debentures offered, and consequently, before a public offer may be made of a company's ordinary or participating preference shares or of debentures which are convertible into such shares or carry the right to subscribe for them, the preferential subscription rights of the company's existing equity shareholders conferred by the Companies Act 1985 must first be waived.[13]

A public offer may be made in two ways. The company may either issue listing particulars or a prospectus inviting the public to subscribe for the securities, or it may agree to allot the whole issue to a merchant bank or a corporate finance subsidiary of a commercial bank, which then issues listing particulars or a prospectus inviting the public to buy the securities from it. In the latter case the intermediary obtains a margin by offering the securities to the public at a higher price than it agreed to pay to the company but, of course, it undertakes the risk that the public will not purchase the whole of the issue, in which event it will have to pay for the unsold securities out of its own resources. An offer for sale by an intermediary has the advantage that the listing particulars or prospectus will show that it has made itself responsible for the success of the issue, and its reputation will go far to inspire the public with confidence in the securities it offers and so induce them to buy. A company will only invite subscriptions from the public directly, without the intervention of an established and well-known intermediary, if the company is sufficiently large and well known to inspire public confidence by its own name, or if the issue price is so attractive that all the securities offered are certain to be taken up. Even then it will still employ a merchant bank or a corporate finance subsidiary of a commercial bank to prepare the listing particulars or the prospectus and to make the other arrangements which are incidental to the issue.

A public offer of securities has little chance of success unless they are listed on the Stock Exchange or admitted to dealings on the Unlisted Securities Market or the

---

11 Ibid, Section 1, Chapter 3, para 2.6.
12 Stock Exchange: *Memorandum on the Unlisted Securities Market*, Introduction, para E and Terms and Conditions for Entry, para 4.
13 Companies Act 1985, s 89 (1) and s 95 (1) and (2) (see p 249, post).

Third Market, and so an application is usually made to the Stock Exchange for the securities to be listed or admitted to dealings on one of the other two markets provided by the Stock Exchange. Public offers of securities admitted to the Unlisted Securities Market or the Third Market are rare, because it is usually possible for the company to market its securities by placing them, and this method of raising capital is the one which is usually employed.[14]

Underwriting

In marketing shares and public issues of other securities, companies and intermediaries who agreed to subscribe to the securities with a view to selling them to the public run the risk that the public may not subscribe for or purchase all of the securities which are offered. This may be because of matters over which the companies and the intermediaries have no control, such as international crises or increases in commercial interest rates, which may at the last moment spoil the market for the securities. Consequently, they insure against these risks by underwriting. An underwriting agreement is one by which a person agrees to subscribe for or to purchase securities if the persons initially invited to take them do not do so. In return for thus ensuring the success of the issue, the underwriter is paid a commission. A company need only underwrite an issue of securities when it offers them to its existing shareholders or debenture or debt securities holders by a rights or open offer, or when it issues listing particulars or a prospectus inviting the public to subscribe for its shares or other securities, without the intervention of an intermediary. If the securities are placed or offered for sale by an intermediary or intermediaries, it is they who should underwrite, because they, and not the company, bear the risk of the placing or the offer for sale proving a failure.

Underwriting is always arranged by the intermediaries who advise the company, and they usually employ brokers to contact suitable persons for the purpose. Underwriters are usually institutional investors and banks; only they have sufficient resources to undertake the risk involved. They will usually agree to underwrite an issue of securities without making their own enquiries about the issuing company, because they know that the intermediaries who attend to the marketing will have fully investigated the company's affairs and assured themselves that the issue stands a reasonable chance of success. Consequently, arranging underwriting is not a lengthy process, and is usually carried out only a few days before the securities are offered to the public. It may be that persons requested to underwrite securities wish to acquire them or some of them as an investment in any event, and in that case they underwrite the securities 'firm', that is, they indicate that they wish their underwriting commitment to be treated in whole or part as an application for the allotment of the securities in any event and that their applications shall be treated in the same way as applications made by the public. Firm underwriters are still entitled to their underwriting commission, and consequently they obtain the securities at a lower net price than other applicants. To prevent unfairness in this respect, the Stock Exchange requires its approval of firm underwriting arrangements to be obtained before listing particulars are published in respect of securities for which a listing is sought; permission will only be given if the minimum amount of the securities which must be made available to the investing public is not reduced.[15]

Underwriters may reduce the risk to which they are exposed (ie that the marketing of shares or other securities may prove wholly or partly unsuccessful)

14 Stock Exchange: *Memorandum on the USM*, Introduction, para E and Terms and Conditions for Entry, paras 3 and 6.
15 The Stock Exchange: *Admission of Securities to Listing*, Section 1, Chapter 3, para 1.3.

by sub-underwriting. This is done by an underwriter entering into a contract with another person or company (usually an institutional investor or a bank) under which he or it agrees to sub-underwrite an agreed fraction of the number of shares or securities which the main underwriter has agreed to subscribe for or purchase.[16]

PRE-CONDITIONS FOR THE ISSUE OF SECURITIES

Authorisation to issue securities

The choice of the method to be employed to finance a company's activities is normally made by the board of directors of the company in exercise of the general power to manage its affairs conferred on them by the articles of association.[17] The articles may require the approval of a general meeting of the company for raising share or loan capital in certain circumstances (eg where the company's borrowing or indebtedness will be carried beyond a certain limit) or when certain methods of financing are employed, but the discretion left to the directors is usually a wide one. However, apart from any requirements of the articles, if directors are to exercise a power conferred on them by the articles to allot shares (otherwise than under an employees' share scheme,[18] or to the subscribers of the memorandum of association in satisfaction of their obligation to take up the shares for which they there subscribe), or if directors are to allot securities which consist of, or include, the right to subscribe for shares or to convert other securities into shares (ie subscription options, convertible debentures and debentures with subscription warrants attached), they must be authorised to do so by a currently effective provision of the articles or resolution of a general meeting.[19] Such an authorisation may be given for the issue of shares by the directors when they intend to issue shares or other relevant securities, or it may be given generally so as to authorise the issue of such shares or securities over a period of time, not exceeding five years from the date of the company's incorporation, or from the date when the authorisation is conferred by an alteration of the articles or by a resolution of a general meeting (which may be an ordinary resolution); and the authorisation must state the date when it will expire and the maximum amount of shares which may be issued under it.[20] Moreover, an authorisation cannot be given to issue shares in excess of the company's existing nominal capital, and so if directors are to be authorised to do this, the nominal capital must be increased first and a fresh authorisation given for the issue of the shares comprised in the increased capital. A private company, unlike a public one, may, by passing an elective resolution[1] with the unanimous consent of those of its members who have voting rights at general meetings, extend the duration of an authorisation for its directors to issue a stated maximum amount of its shares or other relevant securities for a period exceeding

---

16 Both underwriting and sub-underwriting contracts commit the underwriters or sub-underwriters to subscribe for or purchase a fixed number of the shares or securities comprised in the issue, but the contracts provide that the shares or securities shall first be allotted to members of the investing public who apply for them, leaving the underwriters and sub-underwriters with responsibility only for their respective fractions of the residue not applied for by the public.
17 See, for example, Table A, art 70.
18 See p 247, post for the definition of an employees' share scheme.
19 Companies Act 1985, s 80 (1) and (2).
20 Ibid, s 80 (3), (4) and (6).
 1 Ibid, s 379A (1) and (2), inserted by Companies Act 1989, s 116 (2). For elective resolutions see p 765, post.

five years or for an indefinite period.[2] All private companies may exercise this option by elective resolution, notwithstanding any contrary provision in their articles.[3]

An authorisation to allot shares or other securities may be renewed by ordinary resolution of a general meeting for further successive periods not exceeding five years each, and the renewal resolution must state the amount of the remaining shares or securities which may be allotted under it and the date when the renewal will expire.[4] A current authorisation (including one given by the articles of the company) may be revoked by ordinary resolution of a general meeting at any time, and it may also be varied by such a resolution,[5] apparently, even so as to increase the amount of shares or securities which may be allotted, provided the additional shares are comprised in the company's nominal capital when the authorisation is varied. An elective resolution passed by a private company extending the authorisation of its directors to issue shares or other relevant securities beyond five years may be revoked by an ordinary resolution at a general meeting, and the current authorisation then takes effect as though it had been given for five years.[6] An elective resolution is terminated with immediate effect if the private company is re-registered as a public company.[7]

If directors allot shares or securities when there is no current authorisation in force, or in excess of the amount of shares or securities currently authorised, they are guilty of a criminal offence,[8] but the issue of the shares or securities is valid.[9] Moreover, directors may lawfully allot shares or securities after the expiration of an authorisation under an offer or agreement made before its expiration, but only if the terms of the authorisation expressly permit them to do so,[10] and they may also, without such express permission in an authorisation, allot shares after its expiration in satisfaction of conversion and subscription rights attached to securities already issued or comprised in options already given.[11]

A resolution giving, varying, revoking or renewing an authorisation to issue shares and an elective resolution passed by a private company extending the duration of such an authorisation beyond five years and a resolution revoking such an elective resolution must be notified to the Registrar of Companies within 15 days after it is passed,[12] and the Registrar must publish the notification in the London Gazette.[13]

Preferential subscription rights of equity shareholders

If a public or private company proposes to allot any equity securities for cash, it must offer them for subscription to the holders of its existing equity shares at a uniform issue price and on uniform terms in proportion to the nominal value of their existing equity shareholdings so far as practicable, and allow them at least 21 days to accept the offer before allotting the shares in any other way.[14] Moreover, the issue price and terms of the proportionate offer made to existing equity

2 Ibid, s 80A (1), (2) and (5), inserted by Companies Act 1989, s 115 (1).
3 Ibid, s 379A (5).
4 Ibid, s 80 (5).
5 Ibid, s 80 (4).
6 Ibid, s 80A (7) and s 379A (3).
7 Ibid, s 80A (7) and s 379A (4).
8 Ibid, s 80 (9).
9 Ibid, s 80 (10).
10 Ibid, s 80 (7).
11 Ibid, s 80 (2).
12 Ibid, s 80 (8) and s 380 (1) and (4) (*bb*) and (*f*), as amended by Companies Act 1989, s 116 (3).
13 Ibid, s 711 (1) (*d*).
14 Ibid, s 89 (1), s 90 (6) and s 94 (5).

shareholders must be no less favourable than those on which the shares, or those of them which are not taken up under the proportionate offer, are offered in any other way.[14] Consequently, if a company offers ordinary shares for subscription by a rights offer made to its equity shareholders at £2 per share, it may allot shares not taken up under the rights offer either to its own shareholders under an open offer or to the public at large at an issue price not less than £2, but if it wishes to make an open offer or an offer to the public at £1·50 per share, it must first make another rights offer to its equity shareholders at that or a lower issue price. The proportionate offer made to existing equity shareholders must be made to the persons who were the holders of the relevant shares on a particular day specified in the offer within 28 days before the day when the offer is made.[15] The offer must be notified to each holder of the relevant shares either personally or by sending it by post to his address in the United Kingdom entered in the register of members,[16] and if the offer is sent by post, it is deemed to be notifed and the period for its acceptance begins to run when it would be delivered in the ordinary course of the post.[17] During the period while the offer is open, none of the equity securities in question may be allotted otherwise than in accordance with the offer to the recipients of the offer or to the persons to whom they renounce their rights, unless the company has received acceptances or refusals in respect of all the securities comprised in the offer.[18]

Equity securities which are subject to compulsory proportionate offers are defined as equity shares (that is all shares other than those which entitle their holders to participate only to a specified extent in a distribution of profits and capital)[19] and also all securities which consist of or comprise a right to subscribe for or to convert any security into equity shares.[20] Consequently, equity securities include ordinary and preferred ordinary shares, participating preference shares, non-equity shares and debentures which are convertible into such equity shares or which carry the right to subscribe for them and subscription options for equity shares. However, when any such rights to subscribe for or convert securities into equity shares are exercised, it is not necessary for the company to make a proportionate offer of the equity shares to its existing equity shareholders,[1] and so although it is necessary to make a proportionate offer to existing equity shareholders when debentures convertible into ordinary shares are issued, it is unnecessary, and would in fact be a breach of contract, for the company to offer the ordinary shares to its equity shareholders when the debenture holders exercise their conversion rights.

Employees' shares schemes

Shares or securities are not required to be offered proportionately to equity shareholders if they are to be allotted under the terms of an employees' share

15 Ibid, s 89 (1) and s 94 (7). This is to enable the original shares to be dealt in *ex* rights (ie without the right to subscribe for the further shares) on the Stock Exchange some days before the offer is issued.

16 If an equity shareholder has a registered address outside the United Kingdom, the offer may be posted to him at an address in the United Kingdom supplied by him for the purpose of giving notices to him. If such a non-resident shareholder has not supplied an address for giving notices to him, or if his shares are represented by a share warrant to bearer, the offer may be notified by a notice in the London Gazette.

17 Companies Act 1985, s 90 (2) and (5); Interpretation Act 1978, s 7 (48 Halsbury's Statutes (3rd edn) 1300).

18 Companies Act 1985, s 89 (1) and (4).

19 The excluded shares are principally preference shares carrying a fixed dividend and the right to prior repayment of capital in a liquidation, but no right to any further participation.

20 Companies Act 1985, s 89 (1) and s 94 (2) and (5).

 1 Ibid, s 94 (3).

scheme.[2] Such a scheme is one under which shares or debentures of a company may be acquired by or on behalf of employees or former employees of the company or any other company in the same group, or by or on behalf of the spouses, widows, widowers or children, adopted children or step-children under 18 of such employees or former employees.[3] Consequently, equity shares or securities may be issued to trustees of an employees' share scheme so that they may be held in trust for or acquired by the beneficiaries of the scheme, and securities may be issued under such a scheme directly to beneficiaries of it, without any need for the shares or securities to be offered first at an equally favourable issue price to all the equity shareholders of a company. On the other hand, beneficiaries of an employees' share scheme who hold equity shares under it are entitled in the same way as other equity shareholders to participate proportionately in an issue of equity shares or securities for cash made otherwise than under the scheme,[4] and this enables them to maintain the percentage of the total of the equity securities the company issues.

Preferential class subscription rights

A company's articles may permit it to make a modified form of proportionate offer of equity securities when it has two or more classes of equity shares already issued and it offers further shares of one of the classes for cash subscription. Normally, such further shares would have to be offered to all the existing equity shareholders in proportion to their holdings, and if they all took up the further shares offered to them, the percentage of the total shares of the class concerned which the original shareholders of the class held would be reduced.[5] However, the company's memorandum or articles may validly provide that the compulsory proportionate offer of the further shares of the class shall in the first instance be made only to existing shareholders of that class[6] in proportion to the nominal value of their existing holdings of shares of that class, and an initial offer must then be made accordingly; any shares which are not taken up by shareholders of the class concerned must then be offered proportionately to all other equity shareholders.[7] It should be noted that the memorandum or articles may reserve preferential class subscription rights in this way only in respect of further issues of equity shares of the class concerned, and not issues of equity securities which are convertible into equity shares of that class.[8] On the other hand, a provision in the articles conferring preferential class subscription rights does protect shareholders of the class concerned against a dilution of the total percentage of shares of the class held by them when further shares of the class are issued under an employees' share scheme.[9]

2 Companies Act 1985, s 89 (5).
3 Ibid, s 743.
4 Ibid, s 89 (1) and s 94 (4).
5 For example, if a company has issued 200,000 £1 ordinary shares and 50,000 £1 participating preference shares and now proposes to issue a further 50,000 participating preference shares, if all the equity shareholders accept the proportionate offer made to them, the original participating preference shareholders will hold only 60 per cent of the 100,000 participating preference shares issued and outstanding after the offer has been taken up.
6 The offer may be made to holders of shares of the class in question on a date within 28 days before the offer is made (Companies Act 1985, s 94 (7)).
7 Companies Act 1985, s 89 (2) and (3).
8 In the example given in footnote 5, above, if the company reserved preferential class subscription rights to its original participating preference shareholders, the company could circumvent them by issuing debentures convertible into participating preference shares. This may be prevented, however, by an appropriate provision in the company's memorandum or articles.
9 This is because the further shares of the class concerned are reserved to existing shareholders of that class by the memorandum or articles. Nevertheless, if existing shareholders of the class have acquired their shares under an employees' share scheme, they are still entitled to avail themselves of the preferential class subscription rights attached to their shares by the memorandum or articles.

Shareholders entitled to preferential rights

The sole beneficiaries of a compulsory proportionate offer of equity securities are the equity shareholders of the company on the date when the offer is made if it so provides, or the equity shareholders of the company on a date within the preceding 28 days specified in the offer.[10] The holders of other equity securities, such as debentures or other loan securities convertible into ordinary shares and debentures carrying subscription rights for ordinary shares, are not entitled to insist on further equity securities being offered to them until they have exercised their rights to convert or subscribe for equity shares under the terms of their original securities. If it is desired to give the holders of equity securities other than shares a right to subscribe for equity securities offered by the company before they exercise their conversion or subscription rights,[11] it must be expressly conferred by the terms of their original securities[12] and at the same time the company must authorise its directors to issue sufficient shares to fulfil those terms and partially waive under the rules dealt with below the preferential subscription rights which the equity shareholders would otherwise have had exclusively.[13]

Exceptions from preferential subscription rights

No statutory preferential subscription rights for equity securities are exercisable by shareholders when shares are allotted as wholly or partly paid up otherwise than in cash, and so equity securities may be issued by a company in connection with a takeover bid in exchange for shares of the acquired company without the new shares first being offered for subscription by the first company's shareholders.[14] For obvious reasons, shares issued to the subscribers of the company's memorandum in satisfaction of their subscription undertaking in the memorandum and bonus shares issued on a capitalisation of profits or reserves[15] are exempted from the statutory obligation of a company to offer equity shares preferentially to its existing equity shareholders for cash.[16]

Moreover, when directors are authorised to allot equity securities by the articles or by a resolution of a general meeting under the statutory requirement for authorisation,[17] the articles or a special resolution of a general meeting passed when the authorisation is given or subsequently may exclude the statutory preferential subscription rights of the existing equity shareholders or modify them in any way.[18] A waiver of the statutory subscription rights continues only as long as the authorisation with which it is connected, but if the authorisation is renewed, the waiver may be renewed for a concurrent period by special resolution.[19] A special resolution to waive statutory subscription rights may only be proposed on the recommendation of the directors of the company, and a statement of their recommendation, the reasons for it, the amount to be paid to the company for the

---

10 Companies Act 1985, s 89 (1) and s 94 (7).
11 Such extended subscription rights may be absolute (which is unusual) or conditional on the original conversion or subscription rights eventually being exercised.
12 For conversion and subscription rights attached to debentures, see p 201, ante.
13 For the requirements of the Stock Exchange in this respect when the debt securities are listed, see p 202, ante.
14 Companies Act 1985, s 89 (4).
15 For bonus or capitalisation issues, see p 434, post. The exception curiously does not extend to bonus issues of equity securities other than shares (eg a bonus issue of debentures convertible into equity shares).
16 Companies Act 1985, s 94 (2).
17 See p 245, ante.
18 Companies Act 1985, s 95 (1) and (2).
19 Ibid, s 95 (3).

equity securities and the basis on which that amount was arrived at must be circulated with the notice of the general meeting at which the waiver resolution is to be proposed.[20] A special resolution waiving or modifying the statutory preferential subscription rights must be notified to the Registrar of Companies within 15 days after it is passed,[1] and he must publish the notification in the London Gazette.[2] A public company can waive or modify statutory subscription rights only in respect of a specific number of shares or other equity securities if the issue of those shares or securities has already been authorised, and the waiver is effective only while the authorisation to issue those shares or securities can be exercised. A private company, on the other hand, may exclude or modify the statutory preferential rights of its equity shareholders in any way by its memorandum or articles of association,[3] and this may be done in general terms so that the waiver may relate, not only to unissued shares comprised in the company's existing nominal capital or to other equity securities whose issue has already been authorised, but also to all future issues of equity shares and securities.

Consequences of contravention

If equity securities are allotted by a company in disregard of the proportionate subscription rights of equity shareholders or any preferential class subscription rights conferred by the company's memorandum or articles, the company and its officers who authorise or permit the contravention are liable to compensate any person who was entitled to avail himself of the subscription rights for any loss he suffers and any expense he incurs in consequence, but an action to recover compensation must be brought within two years after a return of allotments is made to the Registrar in respect of equity shares so issued, or within two years after the date of issue in the case of other equity securities.[4]

Statute gives no remedy to an equity shareholder entitled to preferential subscription rights against the persons to whom the equity securities have been improperly allotted. It would seem, however, that apart from his right to obtain an injunction to prevent the allotment of the securities to those persons, the equity shareholder may claim damages from them for conspiring with the company and its directors to inflict loss on him by breach of the statutory provision designed for the protection of the class of shareholders to which he belongs.[5] On the other hand, it would appear that the equity shareholder cannot impugn the validity of allotments made in disregard of his statutory subscription rights, because he has never had a legal or equitable interest in the securities, except possibly where his preferential subscription rights to shares were expressly reserved by the company's memorandum or articles.[6]

FORMS OF OFFERING DOCUMENTS

The forms and contents of documents which advertise shares, debentures or other loan securities of a company for subscription or for sale, vary according to the

20 Ibid, s 95 (5).
1 Ibid, s 380 (1) and (2) (*a*).
2 Ibid, s 711 (1) (*e*).
3 Ibid, s 91 (1).
4 Ibid, s 92 (1) and (2).
5 *Lonrho Ltd v Shell Petroleum Co Ltd* (No 2) [1982] AC 173, [1981] 2 All ER 456.
6 The claim would then be based on the contractual right of the equity shareholder against the person to whom the shares are issued to have the provisions of the memorandum and articles adhered to (Companies Act 1985, s 14 (1) (see p 52, ante).

kinds of marketing of the securities which are employed. If an application if made to the Stock Exchange for the securities to be officially listed on it, the offering document takes the form of listing particulars or, in certain cases, formal newspaper notices, whose contents must comply with the requirements of the Stock Exchange[7] as a matter of law.[8] This is so whether the listing particulars relate to a rights offer; a placing or selective marketing of the securities; a public offer for sale of securities made by a merchant bank, the corporate finance subsidiary of a commercial bank or a firm of broker/dealers which has agreed to subscribe for and market them; or an introduction of existing securities on the Stock Exchange so that investing members of the public may acquire them.

If, on the other hand, the shares or other securities are to be dealt in on the Unlisted Securities Market or the Third Market of the Stock Exchange, or are to be dealt in on another stock exchange or investment market, or are not to have the benefit of a readily available market where they may be sold (although this is unlikely, except in the case of shares in private companies or small public companies), the document by which the securities are offered or advertised will be a prospectus or similar document (eg an offer document, particulars for information or information memorandum). The law regulates the form and contents of such a document, at present under provisions of the Companies Act 1985 which date from an earlier era and are shortly to be repealed,[9] and in the future under provisions of the Financial Services Act 1986[10] which have still to be brought into force by order of the Secretary of State for Trade and Industry.[11]

In this chapter the legal rules relating to listing particulars and the liabilities of the persons responsible for issuing them or authorising their issue alone will be examined in detail. The contents of other prospectuses and offer documents will eventually be prescribed in rules made by the Secretary of State,[11] and will in all probability closely resemble those required to be included in listing particulars.[12]

LISTING PARTICULARS

The philosophy of disclosure

The purpose of listing particulars

Listing particulars are the document containing information about a company and the shares or other securities it has issued, or is about to issue, which is used as the basis for admitting the securities to official listing on the Stock Exchange and, when published, is relied on by investors in deciding whether to invest in the securities

---

7 Stock Exchange: *Admission of Securities to Listing*, Section 2, Chapter 3, paras 1 and 3.1 to 3.6 and Section 3, Chapter 1, paras 1.1 and 3 to 6 and Chapter 3.

8 Financial Services Act 1986, s 144 (2), s 146 (1) and s 156 (1) to (3) (30 Halsbury's Statutes (4th Edn) 386).

9 Companies Act 1985, ss 56 to 63 and Sch 3 (prospectively repealed by Financial Services Act 1986, s 212 (3) and Sch 17, Part I).

10 Financial Services Act 1986, s 159 (1), s 162 (1) and (3).

11 Ibid, s 211 (1).

12 The rules made by the Secretary of State will have to conform to the prescriptions contained in the Directive issued by the Council of Ministers of the European Communities on 17 April 1989 to co-ordinate the requirements of the laws of the Member States for the drawing up, scrutiny and distribution of prospectuses offering or accompanying offers of securities to the public for subscription or sale (Directive 89/298 EEC (Official Journal of the European Communities for 1989, No L124/8)). The provisions of the Directive are based on an earlier directive under which the Stock Exchange Rules governing the official listing of shares and other securities were made.

for which a listing is sought or has been given. If the securities to which the listing particulars relate are newly created by the company, or have been issued by it to an intermediary who offers them for sale to the public, the listing particulars fulfil the function of a prospectus or offering document in inducing investors to subscribe for or purchase the securities and so, directly or through the intermediary, to provide fresh share or loan capital for the company. On the other hand, if the securities already exist, or have been allotted to a person who wishes to dispose of them immediately (such as a vendor of a business to a company for shares which are sold or placed immediately (a vendor placing), or shareholders of a company for which another company has made a takeover bid under which new shares of the offeror company are issued in exchange for shares of the target company and are immediately disposed of by the allottees or by the institutions who have underwritten the bid), the listing of the securities on the Stock Exchange does not result in fresh capital being provided for the issuer, and the listing particulars are then published simply to induce investors to buy the securities from their existing holders or from other investors.

Whether the operation is intended to raise money for the company or, alternatively, to market securities which have already been issued or which it has been agreed will be issued, the listing particulars must necessarily contain the same information in order that investors may be equipped to make sound and well informed decisions whether to invest in the securities. The contents of listing particulars do differ according to the kind of securities to which they relate (shares, debentures or other debt securities, or debentures or debt securities which are convertible into or carry the right to subscribe for shares) and the manner in which they are offered for subscription or purchase (public offering, placing, rights offer, capitalisation issue, takeover or introduction), but they do not vary according to the use to which the price paid by investors who take them is put.

The general disclosure rule

Because listing particulars are vehicles for the information of investors at the time securities are marketed on the Stock Exchange, and their purpose is to ensure that investors are fully and accurately informed about the company and the securities to which the listing particulars relate, the two key rules are, not surprisingly, that no securities of a company shall be admitted to listing on the Stock Exchange unless listing particulars approved by the Quotations Committee of the Stock Exchange have been published,[13] and that listing particulars must contain not only the items of information specified in detail in the Stock Exchange's manual, *Admission of Securities to Listing*, but also 'all such information as investors and their professional advisers would reasonably require and reasonably expect to find there, for the purpose of making an informed assessment of: (a) the assets and liabilities, financial position, profits and losses, and prospects of the company; and (b) the rights attaching to those securities'.[14] The obligation to ensure that listing particulars contain this information is qualified, however, by its limitation to information 'which is within the knowledge of any person responsible for the listing particulars, or which it would be reasonable for him to acquire by making enquiries'.[14]

In deciding what information is required to be included in listing particulars under this rule, regard must be had to:

(i) the nature of the securities to which the particulars relate and the character of the company;

13 The Stock Exchange: *Admission of Securities to Listing*, Section 2, Chapter 3, para 1.
14 Financial Services Act 1986, s 146 (1) and (2).

(ii) the nature of the persons likely to consider acquiring the securities;

(iii) the fact that certain matters may reasonably be expected to be within the knowledge of professional advisers whom those persons may reasonably be expected to consult; and

(iv) information available to investors and their professional advisers as a result of the listing particulars containing the detailed information required by the listing rules summarised below, and as a result of information which is made available under any other relevant enactments or rules of the Stock Exchange.[15]

Specific disclosure requirements

The general requirement in respect of the contents of listing particulars imposes an obligation on the company and the Quotations Committee of the Stock Exchange (which must approve listing particulars before publication) to ensure, so far as they are able, that approved listing particulars contain all the information which investors need to make informed investment decisions, and that that information is complete and accurate. The Stock Exchange rules are largely taken up with setting out the headings and details of information which all listing particulars relating to the same kind of securities (shares or debentures or other debt securities) must contain, but these headings and details are necessarily general in terms, and are designed to govern the standard or average company which seeks a listing or, rather, the features of issues of securities which are common to most such companies. The peculiarities and special features of each company and its securities cannot be wholly subsumed under such generally applicable rules, and so in addition to the detailed information which listing particulars must give about the features of the company and the securities which would figure in listing particulars published by any company of the same kind, supplemental information must be given about the peculiarities and special features of the issuing company and the securities offered.

Moreover, the obligation to give all the information which investors require is overriding to the extent that, although information of a general character common to all companies which raise capital from the public must be given, the headings under which that information is classified in the Stock Exchange listing rules need not be slavishly followed. Where the headings are inappropriate because of the company's area of activity (business activities or other functions) or its legal form, equivalent information may be given under a different arrangement.[16] Furthermore, the information relevant to the particular company must be given in a form that can be analysed and understood as easily as possible,[16] so that varying emphasis should be given to the items of information included in order to indicate their relative importance. The result of fulfilling the requirements of the Stock Exchange listing rules should be to give a true and fair view of the issuer's financial position and prospects and of the securities which are to be dealt in on the Stock Exchange, in the same way as the annual accounts of a company should give a true and fair view of the state of its affairs and its profit or loss for the year.[17]

Different kinds of listing particulars

The detailed requirements of the Stock Exchange rules differ according to whether the listing particulars are issued in respect of shares or debt securities of a company.

---

15 Ibid, s 146 (3). This refers to the annual accounts and reports which a company is required to publish by law, and the continuing information about itself and its affairs which the Stock Exchange Rules require to be published.

16 The Stock Exchange: *Admission of Securities to Listing*, Section 3, Chapter 1, para 1.3.

17 Companies Act 1985, s 226 (2), as substituted by Companies Act 1989, s 4 (1).

These rules require listing particulars to contain detailed information about a variety of matters listed in the Stock Exchange manual, and the volume of information to be given depends on whether the company already has a listing for any of its securities and the kind of operation in respect of which the listing particulars are published.

The degree of detail in which the information mentioned above is required to be given is very substantial; the itemising of the information required takes up some 30 pages of the Stock Exchange's manual, *Admission of Securities to Listing*, and a full exposition and explanation of the items included would take up considerably more space.[18] Consequently, only a summary is given here of the obligatory contents of full listing particulars required when a company seeks a listing for shares or debt securities issued or to be issued by it, together with some indication of the modifications made when such shares or debt securities are marketed in different ways.

The principal obligatory contents of listing particulars

Listing particulars for share issues

In listing particulars in respect of shares of a company, the principal items which must be included are the following:

(a) Persons responsible for the listing particulars   The name of the company which will issue, or has issued, the shares; its registered office; the name, addresses or registered offices of the directors of the issuer and of the other persons (if any) who are responsible for the whole or parts of the listing particulars, indicating the functions they fulfil (e g marketing intermediary, sponsoring member firm of broker/dealers or reporting accountants or other experts) and the respective parts of the listing particulars for which they are respectively responsible; particulars of the issuer's auditors during the preceding three years; and particulars of the issuer's sponsoring brokers, bankers and solicitors.[19] This must be followed by a declaration by the directors of the company and those other responsible persons that to the best of their knowledge and belief (after taking all reasonable care to verify it) the information given in the listing particulars, or in the parts of it for which they are respectively responsible, is in accordance with the facts and omits nothing likely to affect the import of the particulars.[19]

(b) Details of share issue   A statement that an application has been made to the Stock Exchange for the shares to which the listing particulars relate to be listed, indicating whether the securities are available to the public in whole or part; information in respect of the shares in question, stating whether they have already been issued or will be issued only after the listing has been obtained; the rights attached to the shares; any restrictions on the transferability of the shares; particulars of issues of shares made by the company during the preceding 12 months; any preferential subscription rights for the shares to which the particulars relate and any waiver of such rights; any reservations which will be made of tranches of shares for marketing in another member state or other member states

---

18 See the author's *Stock Exchange Listing: the New Requirements* (1985), pp 56 to 110; R Burgess *Corporate Finance Law* (1985) pp 305 to 329. These works are based on the Stock Exchange manual in the form in which it was issued in November 1984. A few changes of detail, but none of substance, have been made since that date.

19 The Stock Exchange: *Admission of Securities to Listing*, Section 3, Chapter 1, para 3.1 (*a*) and Chapter 2, Part 1.

of the European Communities; the issue price for the shares and the manner in which it will be paid (eg amounts and dates for payment by instalments); particulars of any underwriting arrangements; an estimate of the expenses of the issue; the amount of the net proceeds of issue which the company will receive after meeting issue expenses, underwriting commission, fees etc; a statement by the directors of the company as to the sufficiency of its working capital and the manner in which additional working capital (if any) is to be provided; an indication of the date or dates on which dealings in the shares will commence on the Stock Exchange and on other stock exchanges on which the shares are listed, or will be listed if applications made for admission to listing on such exchanges are successful; particulars of simultaneous private placings of shares for which an admission to listing is sought.[20]

(c) **The company's share and loan capital** Information about the issuer and its share capital, in particular, its issued and paid-up capital and the shares into which its share capital is divided; the amount of unissued capital and any preferential subscription rights in respect of it; particulars of issues of convertible debentures or other loan securities and of debentures or loan securities with subscription warrants attached, and of issues of other options to subscribe for shares; particulars of issues, reductions and conversions of share capital during the preceding three financial years; the names of any persons who can alone or jointly exercise control over the issuing company and the proportion of voting shares held by or on behalf of them, and similar information in respect of persons holding alone or jointly 5 per cent or more of the issuer's share capital; a statement as to relevant clearances, indemnities and outstanding liabilities obtained in respect of taxation; a summary of the principal contents of material contracts (other than contracts entered into in the ordinary course of business) which the company has entered into during the preceding two years.[1]

(d) **The company's business activities and turnover** A statement of the company's principal activities, including the main categories of products or services supplied by it and the relative importance of each activity; a breakdown of the company's turnover for the last three years by its categories of business activity; the location of the company's principal establishments, including all establishments which account for more than 10 per cent of its turnover; exceptional factors affecting the company's turnover; the extent of the company's dependence on patents or licences, commercial or financial contracts or new manufacturing processes; particulars of the company's research and development activities over the preceding three financial years; any legal or arbitration proceedings which have had, or may have, a significant effect on the company's financial position; any interruptions in the company's business during the preceding three financial years which have, or may have, significantly affected its financial position; the average number of the company's employees over the last three financial years, and a breakdown of its employees by the categories of the company's activities; the main investments made by the company during the last three financial years, whether directly or by the acquisition of shares or securities of other undertakings; the company's intended principal future investments; if the listing particulars relate to shares issued or to be issued in connection with a merger, takeover or

20 Ibid, Section 3, Chapters 1, para 3.1 (*a*) and Chapter 2, Part 2.
1 Ibid, Section 3, Chapter 1, para 3.1 (*a*) and Chapter 2, Part 3.

division of the issuer's undertaking, a statement of the aggregate value of the consideration for the issue of the shares and any effect of the transaction on directors' remuneration.[2]

(e) Accountant's report and accounting information   An accountant's report on the balance sheets and profit and loss accounts and (if the company is the parent company of a group) the consolidated group accounts of the company for its last three (formerly five) financial years, the profit or loss of the company and the group to which it belongs (if any) and the dividends per share paid by the company for each of its last three financial years; an interim financial statement in respect of the company and the group to which it belongs (if any) covering the first six months of the company's current financial year if its last financial year ended more than nine months before the listing particulars are published; any significant changes since the end of the company's last financial year or the end of the period for which an interim financial statement is included for its current financial year; a table showing the sources and applications of the company's funds and the funds of the group to which it belongs (if any) over the company's last three financial years; particulars of undertakings in which the company holds shares accounting for 10 per cent or more of its net assets or its net profits; particulars of other undertakings in which the company holds at least 10 per cent of the undertaking's issued capital; if consolidated accounts are included in the listing particulars because the company is the parent company of a group, the basis of consolidation, the names of the undertakings included in the consolidation and the percentage of minority interests (if any); if the company is the parent company of a group, the same information as is required under items (**d**) and (**g**) in respect of the group as a whole, instead of that information in respect of the company alone; the total amount of loan capital issued by the issuer and the group to which it belongs which remains outstanding.[3]

(f) Directors   Particulars of the directors of the company and, if it has existed for less than five years, particulars of its promoters; particulars of the interests of the directors and their husbands, wives and minor children in the share and loan capital of the company, including shares and subscription options held by them; particulars of directors' service contracts with the company and other companies in the group to which the issuing company belongs; the total remuneration of the directors for the company's last financial year; the interests of the directors in transactions entered into by the company during its preceding and current financial years otherwise than in the normal course of business; the total amount of outstanding loans made by the company and its subsidiaries to its directors; particulars of any share subscription and participation schemes for the benefit of the company's employees.[4]

(g) Current business trends and prospects   Information on the trend of the company's business since the end of the latest financial year for which it has published annual accounts; information on the company's prospects, at least for its current financial year; if the listing particulars contain a profit forecast, the principal assumptions (including commercial assumptions) on which it was made.[5]

2 Ibid, Section 3, Chapter 1, para 3.1 (*a*) and Chapter 3, Part 4.
3 Ibid, Section 3, Chapter 1, para 3.1 (*a*) and Chapter 2, Part 5.
4 Ibid, Section 3, Chapter 1, para 3.1 (*a*) and Chapter 2, Part 6.
5 Ibid, Section 3, Chapter 1, para 3.1 (*a*) and Chapter 2, Part 7.

Listing particulars for issues of debentures and other loan securities

Listing particulars in respect of debentures and other loan securities issued by the company must basically contain the same detailed information as listing particulars in respect of shares, but there are the following differences in listing particulars relating to debt securities:

(i) Instead of item (**b**) above in listing particulars in respect of shares, details must be given of the terms of the loan secured by the debt securities to be issued; particulars of mortgages and charges created as security for the loan; any tax or taxes which will be payable or withheld in respect of interest payments; arrangements for the redemption of the loan; the yield of the debt securities; particulars of any guarantees of the debt securities; particulars of the trustees of the trust deed (if any) executed by the company for the benefit of holders of the debt securities; underwriting arrangements and particulars of simultaneous placings of the debt securities; and any reservation of a tranche of the securities for marketing in another Member State or States of the European Communities.[6]

(ii) Only a summary of the information about the company's share capital need be given (corresponding to item (**c**) above in listing particulars in respect of shares), but details of conversion and subscription rights attached to the debt securities and a description of the group of companies to which the issuer belongs (if any) must be included.[7]

(iii) Information corresponding to item (**d**) above in listing particulars for shares may be given in less detail; in particular, information about research and development, interruptions of the issuer's business and the average number of its employees need not be given.[8]

(iv) Accounting information corresponding to (**e**) above in listing particulars for shares may be given in less detail; instead of earnings and dividends on classes of shares, there must be stated the total loan capital of the company currently issued and outstanding (distinguishing guaranteed and secured loan capital), the company's total borrowing and indebtedness other than in respect of loan capital, and the company's total contingent liabilities.[9]

Modification of obligatory contents of listing particulars

Rights offers by a listed company

If an application for a listing of shares on the Stock Exchange relates exclusively to shares offered to existing shareholders of the company in fulfilment of their preferential subscription rights, and shares or debt securities of the company are already listed, the listing particulars may omit certain information which it would normally have to contain, namely:[10]

(i) The information required under item (**c**) above in listing particulars in respect of shares, except particulars of the company's share capital, of controlling and substantial shareholdings in the company and of the group to which the company belongs;

(ii) The information required under item (**d**) above in listing particulars for shares, except information as to the extent to which the company is

6 Ibid, Section 3, Chapter 1, paras 3.2 (*a*) and Chapter 2, Part 8.
7 Ibid, Section 3, Chapter 1, para 3.2 (*a*) and Chapter 2, Part 3.
8 Ibid, Section 3, Chapter 1, para 3.2 (*a*) and Chapter 2, Part 4.
9 Ibid, Section 3, Chapter 1, para 3.2 (*a*) and Chapter 2, Part 5.
10 Ibid, Section 3, Chapter 1, para 3.1 (*b*).

dependent on industrial property rights, particulars of recent litigation and arbitration proceedings and of material interruptions in the company's business, and information about current and future investments by the company;

(iii) The information required under item (**e**) above in listing particulars for shares, except an interim financial statement if the company's most recent last annual accounts were made out at a date more than nine months before the publication of the listing particulars, and if the company is a parent company, information about the group as a whole required under items (**d**) and (**g**) above in listing particulars for shares; and

(iv) The information required under item (**f**) above in listing particulars for shares, except particulars of the company's directors and promoters, the remuneration of its directors, directors' shareholdings and subscription options, the interests of directors in the company's transactions and outstanding loans by it to its directors.

However, the listing particulars must include copies of the issuer's annual accounts and consolidated accounts (if any) for its latest financial year.

Debt securities of listed companies

If an application for the listing of debentures or other debt securities relates to securities which carry no conversion or subscription rights, and shares or debt securities issued by the company are already listed, the listing particulars may omit certain information which listing particulars for debt securities would normally have to contain, namely:[11]

(i) information in respect of the company's share capital, except a statement of its issued and paid up capital and the classes into which it is divided, and a description of the group to which the company belongs (if any);

(ii) information in respect of the company's business activities, except information about recent litigation and arbitration proceedings; and

(iii) information in respect of the company's financial position, except an interim financial statement if the company's most recent annual accounts were made out at a date more than nine months before the publication of the listing particulars; particulars of loan capital issued and outstanding and the company's other indebtedness; and if the company is a parent company, the information required by items (**d**) and (**g**) above in respect of the group as a whole.

However, the listing particulars must include copies of the company's annual accounts and consolidated accounts (if any) for its latest financial year.

Convertible debt securities and debt securities with subscription rights

If an application for a listing relates to debt securities which carry rights of conversion into shares or rights to subscribe for shares, the listing particulars must contain:[12]

(i) the information required by items (**c**) to (**g**) above in listing particulars for shares, in respect of the shares which may be acquired by the holders of the debt securities when they exercise their rights of conversion or subscription;

11 Ibid, Section 3, Chapter 1, para 3.2 (*b*).
12 Ibid, Section 3, Chapter 1, para 3.3 (*a*).

(ii) the information required in listing particulars relating to debt securities in respect of the terms of the loan, guarantees and mortgages or charges securing the loan, redemption arrangements, the trustees of any trust deed for the benefit of holders of the debt securities and underwriting arrangements; and

(iii) the conditions and procedure for the exercise of conversion or subscription rights conferred by the debt securities.

However, if the debt securities are offered to shareholders of the issuing company in fulfilment of preferential subscription rights (rights offers), and the shares in respect of which conversion or subscription rights are exercisable are of a class already listed, the listing particulars need contain only:[13]

(i) the information required in listing particulars relating to shares offered exclusively to existing shareholders of the company in fulfilment of preferential subscription rights, except the information required by item **(b)** above in listing particulars for shares;

(ii) the information required in listing particulars relating to debt securities in respect of the terms of the loan, guarantees and mortgages or charges securing the debt securities, redemption arrangements and the trustees of any covering trust deed;

(iii) the conditions and procedure for the exercise of conversion or subscription rights; and

(iv) the company's annual accounts and consolidated accounts (if any) for its most recent financial year.

Permitted omissions from listing particulars

The Quotations Committee of the Stock Exchange may authorise the omission from listing particulars of information whose inclusion would otherwise be required:[14]

(a) because the disclosure of that information would be contrary to the public interest; or

(b) because the disclosure of the information would be seriously detrimental to the company, but the Committee cannot authorise the omission of information the non-disclosure of which would be likely to mislead or make it impossible for a person considering whether to acquire the securities to make an informed assessment of them; or

(c) in the case of debentures or other debt securities issued by way of a placing on the Eurocurrency market by a company, if the omission is authorised because the disclosure is unnecessary for the protection of persons of the kind who may normally be expected to buy or deal in the securities (professional investors).

Exemptions from publication of listing particulars

The Quotations Committee of the Stock Exchange may in certain circumstances give a conditional exemption from the obligation to publish normal listing particulars before it grants a listing for shares or debentures or other debt securities. These circumstances fall into three categories:

13 Ibid, Section 3, Chapter 2, para 3.3 (*b*).
14 Ibid, Section 3, Chapter 1, para 1.5.

(a) Where the shares or debt securities to be listed have been the subject of a public issue, or have been issued in connection with a takeover offer, or a merger or division, or the acquisition of the whole or part of another company's undertaking, or the acquisition by the issuing company of assets other than cash, and within 12 months before the listing of the shares or debt securities a document has been published containing information equivalent to that required in listing particulars, the Quotations Committee may permit the company to publish that document again, together with shortened listing particulars containing only information about material changes which have occurred since the date when the earlier document was published and any other information which the Committee considers necessary to ensure that the earlier document and the shortened listed particulars together contain all the information required in normal listing particulars.[15] Copies of the earlier document and the shortened listing particulars must be made available to the public.[16]

(b) Where a listing is sought for shares which are issued by a company on a capitalisation of its profits or reserves where the shares are issued to the holders of shares in the company which are already listed, or for shares issued in connection with the exercise of conversion or subscription rights when shares of the company are already listed; or for shares which are issued in substitution for shares of the company which are already listed when the total nominal value of the substituted shares does not exceed that of the original ones; or for shares issued for any reason whatsoever, when the company's existing listed share capital is not increased by more than 10 per cent.[17] In any of these situations the company need not publish any listing particulars, but must make available to the public in the form of a brochure certain of the items of information about the shares for which a listing is sought which would be required in full listing particulars.[17]

LISTING PROCEDURE

The publication of listing particulars

Listing particulars in respect of shares and other securities issued by companies cannot be published until they have been approved in draft form by the Quotations Department of the Stock Exchange,[18] but they must be published or, at least, formal notices must be published in respect of them, before the Quotations Committee may admit the securities to listing.[19]

If securities issued or to be issued by a company are offered generally to the public for subscription or purchase for cash, the approved listing particulars must be published in full in two national daily newspapers, but if the company has a strong regional connection (eg with Scotland or Northern Ireland), publication in one national newspaper and in one newspaper with a circulation in that region suffices, and if the securities are equity securities which could have been marketed on a selective basis because of the size of the issue, the listing particulars may be published in full in one national newspaper together with publication of a formal

---

15 Financial Services Act 1986, s 148 (1) and (2); The Stock Exchange: *Admission of Securities to Listing*, Section 3, Chapter 1, para 1.5 and Section 7, para 6.2.
16 The Stock Exchange, *Admission of Securities to Listing*, Section 3, Chapter 1, para 5.2.
17 Ibid, Section 3, Chapter 1, paras 5.3 and 5.4.
18 Ibid, Section 1, Chapter 2, para 13 and Section 3, Chapter 1, para 2.1.
19 Ibid, Section 2, Chapter 3, para 1.

notice in another national newspaper.[20] If the securities are equity shares or securities which are in fact marketed on a selective basis by a placing and their market value exceeds £2m, and at least one quarter of them will be made available to the public on the Stock Exchange, listing particulars must be published in full in one national newspaper, and a formal notice must be published in another national newspaper.[1] However, if the market value of the securities is £2m or less or, exceptionally, less than one quarter of them will be available to the public, publication of a formal notice in one newspaper alone is sufficient.[1] If the securities are debentures or other debt securities of a company which are to be marketed on a selective basis, only a formal notice need be published in one national daily newspaper, and if the company already has a listing for any of its securities, even this is unnecessary unless the securities belong to a class or series which is not already listed.[2]

The formal notices which are published when a company's shares or securities are offered to the general public or are marketed on a selective basis by a placing, must contain brief prescribed particulars of the company which seeks the listing and of the securities for which a listing is sought; if the securities are to be placed and at least one quarter of them will be made available to the public, a statement to that effect and instructions for making applications for the securities must be included; the addresses where copies of the listing particulars may be obtained during the 14 days following publication of the notice must be given; if the application for listing relates to fixed-interest debentures or debt securities, the total amount of such securities belonging to the same class or series which the company may issue must be stated; finally, the notice must contain the names of the sponsoring member firm of broker/dealers and, if the securities are marketed by a placing, the names of the other member firms which will be involved in distributing them.[3]

If the securities for which a listing is sought have already been issued and are to be introduced on the Stock Exchange as listed securities, a formal notice must be published in one national newspaper, but if the company already has a listing for any of its other securities, this is necessary only if the securities for which a listing is now sought do not belong to a class or series which is already listed.[4] The contents of a formal notice published in connection with an introduction of securities are the same as in connection with a selective marketing, so far as they are relevant.

Supplementary listing particulars

If after the submission of draft listing particulars to the Quotations Department in respect of the shares or other securities of a company but before dealings in the securities in question begin, there occurs a significant change affecting any of the contents of the listing particulars which are required to be included in them, or if a significant new matter arises which would have necessitated information about it being included in the listing particulars if it had arisen before they were prepared, the applicant for the listing must submit supplemental listing particulars incorporating information about the change or the new matter for the approval of the Quotations Department.[5] After its approval has been obtained, the supplemental

20 Ibid, Section 2, Chapter 3, para 3.1.
 1 Ibid, Section 2, Chapter 3, para 3.2.
 2 Ibid, Section 2, Chapter 3, para 3.3.
 3 Ibid, Section 2, Chapter 3, para 3.6.
 4 Ibid, Section 2, Chapter 3, para 3.4.
 5 Financial Services Act 1986, s 142 (1) and s 147 (1) and (2): The Stock Exchange: *Admission of Securities to Listing*, Section 3, Chapter 1, para 2.2.

listing particulars must be published in the same manner as the original listing particulars.[5] The obligation to submit and publish supplemental listing particulars applies only if the applicant for a listing is aware of the change or new matter; but any other person who is responsible for the listing particulars and who becomes aware of the change or new matter is under a duty to notify the applicant so that supplementary particulars may be prepared.[6] However, the fact that the original listing particulars contained a misstatement of fact or omitted information which they should have included, or the discovery by the company or any person responsible for the original particulars that the original particulars did so, does not necessitate the publication of supplementary listing particulars.

The grant or refusal of a listing and the subsequent procedure

The Stock Exchange may admit shares or other securities to official listing only if the requirements of the Exchange's listing rules and any other requirements imposed by the Quotations Committee are complied with.[7] Compliance with these requirements confers no right to a listing, however, and so the grant or refusal of a listing is at the Committee's discretion. In particular, the Committee may refuse to grant a listing if it considers that by reason of any matter relating to the company, it would be detrimental to the interests of investors to grant the application, or if the securities are already listed on a stock exchange in another Member State of the European Communities and the company has failed[8] to comply with an obligation which it is under in consequence of that listing.[8] The Committee must notify its decision to the applicant within six months after the application for a listing is made, or if the Committee requires further information in support of the application, within six months after that information is supplied.[8] If the Committee does not notify the applicant of its decision within this period, it is taken to have refused the application.[9]

The grant of a listing by the Quotations Committee becomes effective only when the Stock Exchange posts a notice of it on the Exchange's trading floor or gives notice of it to member firms in any other way (eg by inclusion in the Daily Official List of Dealings).[10] There are no restrictions on the publication of the listing particulars by the company or any other person before this date, provided that the listing particulars in their final form have been approved by the Quotations Department.[11] The approval of the Quotations Department is also required for the publication or circulation of other advertisements or notices in connection with the listing application, unless the Quotations Committee waives the need for its approval of such other advertisements, which it does in practice in respect of mini-prospectuses or condensed versions of listing particulars which are published in connection with major issues of securities and which, if confined to factual matters, need only be notified to the Quotations Department.[12]

There are no restrictions on the issue of, or dealings in, securities after listing

6 Financial Services Act 1986, s 147 (3).
7 Ibid, s 144 (1).
8 Ibid, s 144 (5).
9 Ibid, s 144 (4) and (5).
10 The Stock Exchange: *Admission of Securities to Listing*, Section 1, Chapter 1, para 8; The Stock Exchange Rules r 520.8.
11 The Stock Exchange: *Admission of Securities to Listing*, Section 1, Chapter 2, para 13 and Section 3, Chapter 1, para 2.1. Drafts of listing particulars marked as such may, nevertheless, be circulated in advance of approval of the final version for the purpose of arranging underwriting and placing contracts.
12 Financial Services Act 1986, s 154 (1); The Stock Exchange: *Admission of Securities to Listing*, Section 1, Chapter 1, para 15.

particulars have been approved by the Quotations Department and published, as there were formerly under the Companies Act 1985, before the repeal of those restrictions by the Financial Services Act 1986 as regards listing particulars.[13] Companies are therefore at liberty to issue securities to which listing particulars relate at any time after the particulars have been lawfully published. When securities are offered to the public generally for subscription or purchase, or for subscription by the existing share or security holders of the company under a rights issue or open offer, it is the normal practice for the listing particulars to provide that any contract resulting from an application or acceptance by an investor shall be conditional on a listing for the securities being granted by a stated date, and that in the meantime application moneys or instalments of the issue or purchase price of the securities shall be held in a separate account, and will be returned to the persons from whom they were received if a listing for the securities is not granted by the stated date. The condition operates automatically if a listing is not granted within the stipulated time; contracts for the issue or purchase of the securities under the listing particulars or offer document then become void, and application and other moneys received are treated as having been held throughout in trust for the persons from whom they were received, who may reclaim them from the company or from the intermediary or other person who has received them.[14] The only restriction on dealings on the Stock Exchange in securities to which published listing particulars relate is that dealings in securities offered by a company to the public, or under an open offer to its shareholders, cannot commence until the basis of allotments or allocations has been announced by the company.[15] Under the Stock Exchange's rules (which in this respect do not form part of the law) dealings in securities of any kind and however marketed may not take place until the listing has become effective, and contracts for the sale of the securities cannot be entered into 'subject to listing', that is, subject to a condition that the contract shall become void if a listing is not granted.[16] For practical reasons, the date when dealings in newly listed securities may begin is always fixed by the Quotations Committee at the time the listing is granted, whatever form of marketing is employed, and whether the securities are newly issued, or are existing securities which are introduced on the Stock Exchange.

DEFECTIVE INVITATIONS TO SUBSCRIBE FOR OR PURCHASE COMPANY SECURITIES

If an invitation to subscribe for or purchase shares, debentures or other loan securities which contains false statements of fact is made by a company, a merchant bank, corporate finance subsidiary of a commercial bank or any other person, an investor who is thereby induced to subscribe for or purchase any of the securities has a variety of remedies at common law and equity, and in the case of invitations contained in listing particulars or prospectuses, under the Financial Services Act 1986. In certain circumstances the investor will or may also have remedies against the persons responsible for the invitation if it omits items of information which it should contain. The various remedies available to investors will be dealt with here in sequence, namely:

---

13 Companies Act 1985, s 82 (1) to (3) and (6), repealed as regards listing particulars by Financial Services Act 1986, s 212 (3) and Sch 17, Part I.
14 *Re Nanwa Gold Mines Ltd* [1955] 3 All ER 219, [1955] 1 WLR 1080.
15 The Stock Exchange: *The Admission of Securities to Listing*, Section 5, Chapter 2, para 13.
16 The Stock Exchange Rules, r 535.5 and r 540.2.

(a) the equitable remedy of rescission of the contract under which the investor acquired the shares or other securities;

(b) the common law remedies of an action for damages on the ground of fraud or deceit, or an action for damages because of the failure of the persons responsible for the invitation to exercise reasonable care to ensure that it was accurate and complete; and

(c) the statutory claim for compensation under the Financial Services Act 1986.

These remedies are cumulative, and so the fact that an investor has rescinded the contract under which he subscribed for or purchased securities does not prevent him from subsequently pursuing a claim for damages at common law or a statutory claim for compensation.[17]

Rescission

If an invitation to subscribe for or purchase shares or other securities contains a false statement of fact which is believed to be true by a person to whom it is addressed, and he contracts with the issuer of the invitation to acquire securities to which the invitation relates because of that belief, he may rescind the contract and recover the money he paid for the securities on discovering that the statement is false.

False statement of fact

The plaintiff's case involves proof of a number of matters. The first of these is that the false statement was one of fact. If what he complains of is a misrepresentation of law, or an opinion about the company's prospects and the profits it is likely to earn which turns out to be unfounded,[18] or a promise held out to subscribers or purchasers which is not fulfilled, he cannot rescind the contract, because no misstatement of fact has been made to him. But a statement in a prospectus issued by a company that its directors entertain a certain opinion of the company's prospects, or that they intend to use the proceeds of the issue of securities for a particular purpose, does at least imply that they honestly have that opinion or intention, so that if they do not, they are guilty of a misrepresentation of fact, and the allottee may rescind.[19] Furthermore, a misstatement in a prospectus of the contents of the company's memorandum,[20] particularly of its objects, is a misrepresentation of fact, not of law, and entitles an allottee to rescind if he is misled thereby.[1]

The court has been particularly strict in insisting that prospectuses and other invitations to invest must not only be free from statements which are literally untrue, but also that the statements which they contain must not be misleading when read together, or when given an interpretation which a reasonable man might put upon them. The classic example of statements which, taken individually, were true, but which read together were misleading, is found in *R v Kylsant*.[2] In that case a prospectus was issued by a shipping company in 1928 at a time when for several years such companies had suffered considerably from a trade depression. The prospectus set out the capital and reserves of the company, observed that the

---

17 *Archer v Brown* [1985] QB 401, [1984] 2 All ER 267.

18 *Bentley & Co Ltd v Black* (1893) 9 TLR 580.

19 *Aaron's Reefs Ltd v Twiss* [1896] AC 273 at 284; *Edgington v Fitzmaurice* (1885) 29 ChD 459 at 483.

20 *Oakes v Turquand and Harding* (1867) LR 2 HL 325.

 1 *Downes v Ship* (1868) LR 3 HL 343; *Re Hop and Malt Exchange and Warehouse Co, ex p Briggs* (1886) LR 1 Eq 483.

 2 [1932] 1 KB 442, [1931] 1 All ER Rep 179.

'average annual balance available' over the last ten years after providing for depreciation and debenture interest was sufficient to pay the interest on the debentures offered by the prospectus more than five times over, and set out the dividends paid on the company's shares from 1911 to 1927. In fact the company had suffered trading losses in each year from 1921 to 1927, and dividends had been paid during those years only by using reserves accumulated during the First World War and reserves for future taxation, and by distributing repayments made by the revenue authorities in respect of excess profits duty paid by the company during the war years. The court held that the prospectus contained a false statement of fact, because it impliedly represented that dividends had been paid out of current trading profits, that the company was in a position to earn such profits in the future, and that the 'average annual balance' available for dividend over the previous ten years was representative of the earnings cover which subscribers for debentures could expect in the future. The prospectus carefully avoided saying any of these things, but when read as a whole, that was the impression which it was clearly intended to convey. The case was in fact a criminal prosecution, but the same test would be applied in a civil action for rescission or damages.

In another case,[3] a prospectus stated that the company had agreed to buy an existing business for a sum which included £500,000 for goodwill, and that the vendors guaranteed the company against the assets of the business proving to be worth less than the price paid or its liabilities proving to be greater than as disclosed in the prospectus. In fact the business was insolvent to the extent of £4 million, and the vendors had privately agreed with the directors of the company that the purchase price should be used as a guarantee fund to keep the business going by discharging its liabilities as they accrued. In substance, therefore, the prospectus invited the public to takes shares in a company which owned a solvent and valuable business, whereas in fact they were subscribing money simply to make it solvent. The court consequently held that the prospectus contained misrepresentations entitling the subscribers to rescind or to sue for damages. Again, where a prospectus stated that contracts which the company had entered into were considerably within the capital it proposed to raise, but in fact fulfilment of those contracts would leave the company with so little working capital that it would be unable to carry out the undertaking for which it was formed, it was held that the prospectus was misleading and subscribers were entitled to rescind or to sue for damages.[4] In yet another case[5] a prospectus issued by a gold mining company was held to be misleading when it described the mine to be acquired by the company as rich and only in need of machinery to begin production at once, when in fact the mine had been worked unsuccessfully by three companies in succession, the reports quoted to show that the mine was rich were all more than three years old, and the purchase price payable for the mine (which was not disclosed) would take up so much of the capital which the company hoped to raise by issuing shares under the prospectus that it would not have sufficient capital left to work the mine.

The other common feature of fraudulent prospectuses, ambiguous expressions and statements, is exemplified by two cases. In the first[6] a company formed to manufacture leather tyred wheels for trolleys issued a prospectus stating that it already had orders from various substantial bodies and trial orders from others with a view to placing large orders later. In fact, all its orders were trial orders, and no customer had yet expressed any intention of buying on a large scale.

3 *Peek v Gurney* (1873) LR 6 HL 377.
4 *Central Rly Co of Venezuela v Kisch* (1867) LR 2 HL 99.
5 *Aaron's Reefs Ltd v Twiss* [1896] AC 273.
6 *Greenwood v Leather Shod Wheel Co* [1900] 1 Ch 421.

Anyone who read the prospectus might well understand it to mean that the company was well established in business, whereas in fact it was only just beginning. Consequently, the prospectus was ambiguous and misleading and subscribers were entitled to rescind allotments made to them. In the other case[7] a prospectus offering debentures stated that the value of the company's assets was a certain amount, but did not add that the amount was the estimated cost of replacing them and not their present value. It was held that anyone who read the prospectus would understand the value of the assets to mean the amount which might be realised if the company's business were sold as a going concern, and consequently the statement was ambiguous and amounted to a misrepresentation.

Apart from the requirements of the Financial Services Act 1986 in respect of listing particulars and prospectuses,[8] however, a company is not obliged to disclose facts about itself or its affairs which an intending investor needs to know in order to form a balanced judgment whether to subscribe for the company's securities or not.[9] Thus, where a prospectus failed to disclose that the company's promoter had made a gift of his own shares to certain of the directors to induce them to accept their directorships and in consideration of their negotiating loans to the company, it was held that there was no misrepresentation, and a subscriber for shares under the prospectus had no right to rescind.[10] Failure to disclose facts in an invitation to invest is only relevant when it makes the facts which are stated false or misleading, as in the examples given above. This is made clear in a passage from a leading case,[11] which has sometimes been erroneously cited as authority for the proposition that full disclosure of all material facts must be made in all investment invitations. In that case Kindersley VC said:

> 'Those who issue a prospectus holding out to the public the great advantages which will accrue to persons who will take shares in a proposed undertaking, and inviting them to take shares on the faith of the representations therein contained, are bound to state everything with strict and scrupulous accuracy, and not only to abstain from stating as facts that which is not so, but to omit no one fact within their knowledge the existence of which might in any degree affect the nature, or extent, or quality of the privileges and advantages *which the prospectus holds out* as inducements to take shares' (emphasis supplied).

It is only when the prospectus or other invitation holds out some feature as an inducement to subscribers that it must tell the whole truth about it. If it omits to mention the feature completely, the subscriber or investor is not entitled to rescind.

The statement must be addressed to the plaintiff by the company or the person who offers the shares or debentures

The plaintiff can rescind a contract to subscribe for or purchase securities only if he was induced to take them by a false statement of fact addressed to him by the company or intermediary or seller which offers them. Consequently, he will not be able to rescind if the statement was addressed by the company or other issuer of the invitation to persons other than himself, nor if it was addressed to him by someone whom the issuer or seller of the securities had not authorised to do so.

A prospectus issued by a company is an invitation to investors to subscribe for securities by taking them from the company, or from the intermediary which issues

---

7   *Clark v Urquhart* [1930] AC 28 at 43.
8   Until Part V of the Financial Services Act 1986 (governing prospectuses) is brought into force by ministerial order, the obligatory contents of prospectuses (other than listing particulars) are prescribed by Companies Act 1985, s 56(1) and Sch 3.
9   *Aaron's Reefs Ltd v Twiss* [1896] AC 273 at 287 per Lord Watson.
10   *Heymann v European Central Rly Co* (1868) LR 7 Eq 154.
11   *New Brunswick and Canada Rly and Land Co v Muggeridge* (1860) 1 Drew & Sm 363 at 381.

the prospectus. The information in the prospectus is addressed to such investors alone. It is not addressed to investors who acquire securities of the same company by buying them from existing holders, and so if an investor is induced to buy securities from an existing holder by reading the prospectus under which they were issued, he cannot rescind his purchase and require the company which issued the prospectus to take the securities from him.[12] This is so even though the subscriber who initially took the securities from the company did so as an undisclosed agent for the transferee who seeks to rescind the allotment.[13] If the agency had been disclosed to the company by the subscriber, of course, the result would be different, because then the allotment of the securities by the company would have been made to the present holder directly, and he would be entitled to rescind.

If a prospectus or other invitation to subscribe for or purchase securities is addressed to a limited class of persons, only persons belonging to that class may rely on it and rescind contracts entered into by them to acquire the securities if statements in the prospectus or invitation are false. Thus, non-renounceable letters of rights addressed by a company to its shareholders can be relied upon only by the share or debenture holders of the company to whom they are addressed, and so if another person reads a letter of rights and applies to the company for securities on the strength of it, he cannot rescind if it contains falsehoods. But if the company knew that that other person relied upon the letter of rights at the time it allotted the securities to him, he can rescind, because the company cannot hold him to a contract which it knows he was induced to enter into by a statement made by it which turns out to be false.[14] If a letter of rights is renounceable, however, it may be construed as an offer to issue securities to the existing share or debenture holders to whom it is addressed or to the persons whom they nominate by renouncing,[15] and in that case, a person to whom the letter of rights is renounced can accept the offer and subscribe for the shares himself. If the letter of rights contains a misstatement, he may then rescind the allotment, because the letter was addressed to him as much as to the share or debenture holders of the company at the time, and he was thereby induced to contract with the company. But if the letter of rights takes the form of a provisional letter of allotment, it is arguable that a person to whom it is renounced cannot rescind, because the contract for the allotment is then made with the original share or debenture holder, and the renouncee is in the position of a purchaser of securities from the original subscriber, who cannot rescind.[16] On the other hand, it can also be argued that a provisional letter of allotment is distinguishable from a renounceable letter of allotment issued in response to an application for shares by a subscriber, and that since it is the company which initiates the offer when it issues a letter of rights or a provisional letter of allotment and so must contemplate that someone other than the person to whom it is addressed may take and pay for the securities offered, any such person, whether the first or a later renouncee, should be treated as within the class of addressees of the rights offer and should be entitled to rescind for misrepresentation. From a practical point of view this is a preferable conclusion, because the differences between letters of right and provisional letters of allotment are only technical, and their functions are the same.

Not only must the false statement complained of be addressed to the plaintiff who seeks to rescind; it must also be addressed to him by someone who has authority

12 *Peek v Gurney* (1873) LR 6 HL 377.
13 *Collins v Associated Greyhound Racecourses Ltd* [1930] 1 Ch 1.
14 *Lynde v Anglo-Italian Hemp Spinning Co* [1896] 1 Ch 178 at 183.
15 See p 240, ante.
16 *Collins v Associated Greyhound Racecourses Ltd*, supra.

to do so on behalf of the company, intermediary or other person responsible for the invitation to subscribe or purchase. An individual director has no implied authority to solicit subscriptions for the company's shares, debentures or loan securities on its behalf without authorisation by the board. Consequently, if he obtains such a subscription by misrepresenting facts to the subscriber, the subscriber cannot rescind,[17] unless he proves that the company was aware that the misrepresentation had been made when it alloted the shares or debentures to him.[18] It used formerly to be common for promoters to obtain subscriptions for shares before the company in question was incorporated, and if they procured subscriptions by misrepresentation, the subscriber who wished to rescind was met with the defence that they were not, and could not be, the company's agents to make representations before it was incorporated, and that nothing the company did after its incorporation could ratify their acts. This reasoning was sound, but the subscriber was nevertheless held entitled to rescind if the company was aware that the representation in question had been made when it allotted the shares.[18] Although it had not made the representation itself, the company could not hold the subscriber to a contract which it knew had been induced by a representation made by another person when the representation turned out to be false.

At one time it was considered that a subscriber could not rescind an allotment of shares, debentures or other loan securities if he was induced to subscribe by a false statement contained in a report by an expert which was quoted in the prospectus or invitation to subscribe.[19] It was argued that the expert who prepared the report for the company had no authority from the company to represent it to subscribers as being accurate, and the directors did not vouch for its accuracy by including it in the prospectus or other invitation, unless they did so expressly or used it to substantiate other statements which they made themselves. This is clearly not the law now. If the expert's report included or quoted in the prospectus or invitation to subscribe or purchase securities contains a misstatement, the subscriber may rescind unless the prospectus or invitation makes it clear that the company or other issuer of the invitation accepts no responsibility for its accuracy.[20] This rule is obviously more just, and is in accord with the principle already refered to, that a company or other issuer of the invitation cannot hold a subscriber or purchaser to his contract when it knows that he has been induced to subscribe or purchase by a statement made by anyone, if the statement is in fact false.[1]

The plaintiff must be induced to subscribe or purchase by the false statement

The plaintiff must prove that the false statement in the prospectus or other invitation induced him to subscribe for or purchase the shares, debentures or loan securities he has taken. When the statement is one which would influence a reasonable man, the court will readily infer that it induced the plaintiff to subscribe or purchase.[2] But the plaintiff's acts may show that he did not in fact rely on the statement. Thus, where the plaintiff subscribed for shares in a mining company under a prospectus which inaccurately described the capacity of the company's

---

17 *Re Royal British Bank, Nicol's Case* (1859) 3 De G & J 387.
18 *Re Metropolitan Coal Consumers' Association, Karberg's Case* [1892] 3 Ch 1; *Lynde v Anglo-Italian Hemp Spinning Co,* supra.
19 *Re Reese River Silver Mining Co, Smith's Case* (1867) 2 Ch App 604; affd sub nom *Reese River Silver Mining Co v Smith* (1869) LR 4 HL 64.
20 *Re Pacaya Rubber and Produce Co Ltd, Burns' Application* [1914] 1 Ch 542; *Mair v Rio Grande Rubber Estates Ltd* [1913] AC 853.
 1 *Re Metropolitan Coal Consumers' Association, Karberg's Case,* supra; *Lynde v Anglo-Italian Hemp Spinning Co,* supra.
 2 *Smith v Chadwick* (1884) 9 App Cas 187 at 196; *Cackett v Keswick* [1902] 2 Ch 456 at 464.

mine, he was held not entitled to rescind, because he had inspected the mine himself, and must therefore have relied on his own observations, and not on the contents of the prospectus.[3]

It is not necessary that the misrepresentation made to the plaintiff should be the sole inducement to him to subscribe or purchase.[4] Thus, where a company issued a prospectus which contained false statements, and the plaintiff applied for debentures under it, partly in reliance on those statements and partly because of his mistaken belief that the debentures would be secured on the company's property, the plaintiff was held entitled to rescind.[5] It would therefore appear that if in the case mentioned in the preceding paragraph the subscriber had placed some reliance on the prospectus, and had relied on his own observations only for other matters than the one dealt with inaccurately in the prospectus, he would nevertheless have been entitled to rescind.

A subscriber or purchaser cannot pretend that he was induced to subscribe for or purchase shares or securities by a false statement of which he was unaware. If the invitation to subscribe or purchase was contained in a prospectus or other advertisement a copy of which was received by him, it is obviously almost impossible to show that he was unaware of the statement, but it is still necessary for him to testify positively that he did rely on it.[6] The mere fact that a prospectus or other invitation has been published in one or more newspapers is not, of course, sufficient to enable a subscriber or purchaser under it to rescind, but if a prospectus or invitation to invest is accompanied by application forms for shares or securities offered by it, the fact that a subscriber or purchaser completed and returned such an application form helps to prove that he relied on the contents of the prospectus or invitation.[7] A subscriber for or purchaser of shares or other securities obviously cannot rescind if he knew that the statement of which he complains was false, because he could not then possibly have been induced by it to subscribe for or purchase them. But a subscriber or purchaser is not deemed to have knowledge of the falsity of a prospectus or invitation to invest merely because it indicates the means by which its accuracy may be verified. Thus, where a prospectus referred to certain contracts entered into by the company without setting out their terms, and an examination of the contracts would have shown that the prospectus was misleading, it was held that a subscriber who did not inspect them could nevertheless rescind.[8] The result would seem to be the same if a prospectus or other advertisement had invited subscribers or purchasers to inspect the contracts, because the company cannot fix them with constructive notice of documents by extending an invitation which they are not obliged to accept. But if a subscriber actually inspects documents relating to the company, and those documents would reveal the falsity of the prospectus or invitation to invest to a reasonably careful reader, the subscriber or purchaser is deemed to know that the prospectus or invitation is false, and he cannot rescind.[9] Whether the subscriber or purchaser has knowledge of the falsity of the prospectus or invitation therefore depends on the enquiries which he chooses to make. He is under no obligation to make any enquiries at all, even when invited

---

3 *Jennings v Broughton* (1853) 5 De GM & G 126.
4 *Re Royal British Bank, Nicol's Case* (1859) 3 De G & J 387.
5 *Edgington v Fitzmaurice* (1885) 29 ChD 459.
6 *Smith v Chadwick* (1884) 9 App Cas 187.
7 Under Companies Act 1985, s 56 (1) and (2), application forms could not be distributed unless accompanied by full copies of the prospectus to which they related. This is no longer so when listing particulars are issued.
8 *Central Rly Co of Venezuela v Kisch* (1867) LR 2 HL 99 at 120, 123; *Aaron's Reefs Ltd v Twiss* [1896] AC 273 at 279.
9 *New Brunswick and Canada Rly and Land Co v Conybeare* (1862) 9 HL Cas 711.

to do so, and so will not be prevented from rescinding, even though he fails to make enquiries which a reasonable man in his position would be expected to make.[10]

Loss of the right to rescind

A person who is induced by a misrepresentation to become a member of a company by subscribing its memorandum of association can never rescind the allotment of shares.[11] The company is incorporated on the assumption that he will be a member of it, and other persons who apply for shares may be persuaded to do so because he is a member. Furthermore, the Companies Act 1985 provides that subscribers of the memorandum 'are deemed to have agreed to become members of the company, and on its registration shall be entered as such in its register of members',[12] so that statute expressly requires them to be treated as members in any event, and they cannot escape from being so treated by showing that the contract by which they agreed to subscribe is defective in some way.

Any other holder of shares, debentures or other securities will lose the right to rescind an allotment of securities if he waives the right. This he may do by delaying for an unreasonable time after having cause to suspect the falsity of the statements which induced him to subscribe. What is a reasonable length of time depends on the enquiries which he has to make to verify his suspicions. If they are lengthy and intricate, he will be allowed a sufficient period to conclude them, and if he rescinds before that period expires, his rescission will be effective.[13] On the other hand, if the company informs him of the falsity of the statements, he has no suspicions to verify, and he must rescind forthwith. A delay of 15 days in such circumstances has been held to amount to waiver of the right to rescind.[14] But the company's communication must make it clear that the prospectus was false, so that if the company sends a circular to its members which contains the correct information but does not point out that the prospectus was false in that respect, the subscriber is not deemed to know of its falsity, and will not be precluded from rescinding later when he does realise that it was false.[15] On the other hand, subscribers for shares should familiarise themselves with the company's memorandum and articles promptly after they become members; if they do not, and consequently fail to discover a misstatement of the contents of those documents in the prospectus, they will be taken to have waived their right to rescind.[16] The same considerations appear to apply if an investor is induced to purchase shares or other securities by an invitation to invest which contains false statements of fact.

A subscriber for shares also waives his right to rescind by acting as a member of the company after discovering, or having reason to suspect, the falsity of the prospectus. Thus, if he speaks and votes at meetings of shareholders,[17] or receives and retains dividends paid by the company,[18] or pays calls on his shares,[19] or contracts to sell his shares or any of them,[20] his right to rescind is gone. Presumably

---

10 *New Brunswick and Canada Rly and Land Co v Muggeridge* (1860) 1 Drew & Sm 363 at 382 per Kindersley VC.
11 *Re Metal Constituents Ltd, Lord Lurgan's Case* [1902] 1 Ch 707.
12 Companies Act 1985, s 22 (1).
13 *Central Rly Co of Venezuela v Kisch* (1867) LR 2 HL 99.
14 *Re Scottish Petroleum Co* (1883) 23 ChD 413.
15 *Scholey v Central Rly Co of Venezuela* (1868) LR 9 Eq 266n; *Arnison v Smith* (1889) 41 ChD 98, 348.
16 *Oakes v Turquand and Harding* (1867) LR 2 HL 325; *Downes v Ship* (1868) LR 3 HL 343.
17 *Sharpley v Louth and East Coast Rly Co* (1876) 2 ChD 663.
17 *Re Royal British Bank, Nicol's Case* (1859) 3 De G & J 387; *Scholey v Central Rly Co of Venezuela* (1868) LR 9 Eq 266n.
19 *Scholey v Central Rly Co of Venezuela*, supra.
20 *Re Royal British Bank, Nicol's Case*, supra.

similar acts by a subscriber for debentures or loan securities or by a purchaser of shares or loan securities will forfeit his right to rescind the contract for allotment or purchase.

On rescinding, a subscriber or purchaser must restore the company to the position it was in before it allotted the shares or debentures to him, or in the case of a purchase of securities, must restore the intermediary or other seller who is responsible for the false invitation addressed to the purchaser to that position. A subscriber who rescinds must therefore be able to surrender the shares or other securities subscribed by him to the company, and he obviously cannot do this if he has sold or transferred them. If he has sold only some of the shares or securities, he may not rescind the allotment of the remainder, because the contract for the allotment must be rescinded as a whole, and this can be done only if all the shares or debentures comprised in it are surrendered.[1] But if a subscriber has entered into several contracts with the company for the issue to him of different amounts of shares or securities, he can rescind the contracts under which he was allotted securities which he still holds, even though he has sold the securities allotted to him under the other contracts.[2] This distinction resting on the formalities attending the subscription by an allottee who has since sold some of his securities is scarcely just, however. In one case it was rejected, and the allottee was allowed to rescind the allotment of the unsold shares subscribed by him and to recover an appropriate proportion of the amount he had paid the company in respect of those shares, despite the fact that all the securities were allotted under a single contract.[3] In another case a purchaser of shares was similarly held entitled as against his seller to rescind the purchase of those he retained after re-selling the others; Page Wood VC reasoned that since the shares originally sold were uniform, and each rose and fell in value in the same way as the others, the court would not be remaking the contract between the parties if it compelled the seller to take back the unsold shares and restore the corresponding fraction of the purchase price to the purchaser.[4] This argument is as applicable to contracts for the allotment of securities as it is to contracts to purchase them.

A subscriber for shares loses his right to rescind, and so escape his obligation to pay any part of the nominal value of the shares which remains unpaid, if the company is ordered to be wound up by the court,[5] or resolves to be wound up voluntarily,[6] or ceases to pay its debts in the ordinary course of its business because it is insolvent.[7] The reason for this is that on a winding up the company's creditors may compel shareholders to pay the unpaid capital in respect of their shares in order to satisfy the company's debts, and if a shareholder were still allowed to rescind, he would prejudice the rights of the company's creditors, who were in no way responsible for the misrepresentation.[8] Furthermore, the obligations of a shareholder in a winding up are governed by the Insolvency Act 1986,[9] and are not merely contractual, as they were when the company was a going concern; it would consequently be impossible for a shareholder to restore the company to its position before the shares were allotted if he were allowed to rescind after the

---

1 *Re Metropolitan Coal Consumers' Association Ltd, Grieb's Case* (1890) 6 TLR 416.
2 Ibid. There would be separate contracts where the subscriber applied for shares on separate application forms.
3 *Re Mount Morgan (West) Gold Mines Ltd* (1887) 3 TLR 556.
4 *Maturin v Tredinnick* (1864) 12 WR 740.
5 *Oakes v Turquand and Harding* (1867) LR 2 HL 325.
6 *Stone v City and County Bank Ltd* (1877) 3 CPD 282; *Re Hull and County Bank Ltd, Burgess's Case* (1880) 15 ChD 507.
7 *Tennet v City of Glasgow Bank* (1879) 4 App Cas 615.
8 *Oakes v Turquand and Harding*, supra.
9 Insolvency Act 1986, s 74 (1) and (2).

company has gone into liquidation.[10] The bar on rescission after the commencement of winding up is primarily for the protection of the company's creditors, but the rule is an absolute one, and rescission is impossible even though the company's assets are sufficient to pay its creditors in full without requiring shareholders to contribute to capital unpaid on their shares.[10] This again is because the shareholders' obligations in a winding up are governed by statute, and although in the case of a solvent company they will not be called on to contribute towards payment of the company's debts, it may still be necessary to call up the capital unpaid on their shares to augment the fund out of which all the company's capital will be repaid. It has never been decided explicitly whether a fully paid shareholder may rescind after the company commences to be wound up. There would be little point in him doing so, however, for he would be unable to claim the return of the money he paid for the shares as a creditor of the company.[11] The rule that rescission is impossible after the commencement of winding up applies equally if the shareholder contends that the misstatement of which he complains was a term of the contract under which he subscribed, or resulted in such a fundamental mistake on his part that his contract to subscribe was void.[11] His position is therefore in no way improved by relying on these grounds instead of treating the misstatement simply as a misrepresentation.

If a subscriber wishes to rescind, it is not sufficient for him merely to notify the company that he repudiates the shares or debentures. On receiving such notification the company should remove the subscriber's name from the register of members or debenture holders, and return to him the money which he paid for the securities.[12] If the company refuses to do these things, however, the subscriber should bring an action for rescission against it, and the allotment will be treated as rescinded only when such an action is begun.[13] Consequently, if the subscriber delays suing for an unreasonable time, or if the company commences to be wound up before the action is brought, the right of rescission will be lost.[13] On the other hand, if an action for rescission is begun before the company commences to be wound up, the court can declare that the rescission is effective, even though judgment is not given until after the successful winding up petition is presented or after the making of a winding up order.[14]

The cases in which the court has decided whether a subscriber has lost his right to rescind have all concerned allotments of shares by the company to the subscriber without the intervention of an intermediary, and in no such cases has a sale of shares been involved. If an intermediary acting on its own behalf, and not on behalf of the company, offers securities for sale by a prospectus or other invitation, investors contract to take them from the seller and not from the company. Consequently, the seller alone is responsible for misstatements in the prospectus or invitation, and the effect of rescission is to leave the securities on its hands. Whether the seller or intermediary can rescind the contract it made with the company to subscribe for and market the securities, and thus leave the company to bear the loss, depends on whether the company itself induced the seller to enter into that contract by misrepresentation. It seems that the sale of the securities by the intermediary will not preclude it from rescinding its contract with the company once the securities have been returned to it by the person to whom it sold them.[15] What is uncertain, however, is whether an investor who purchases securities from

10 *Re Hull and County Bank, Burgess's Case,* supra.
11 *Re Addlestone Linoleum Co* (1887) 37 ChD 191.
12 *Reese River Silver Mining Co v Smith* (1869) LR 4 HL 64.
13 Ibid; *Re Scottish Petroleum Co* (1883) 23 ChD 413.
14 *Henderson v Lacon* (1867) LR 5 Eq 249.
15 *Edinburgh United Breweries Ltd v Mollison* [1894] AC 96 at 113 per Lord Watson.

an intermediary or seller loses his right of rescission in the same circumstances as if he had agreed to take them from the company. Logically, the right to rescind should be governed by the same rules, for acts amounting to waiver in the one case must also amount to waiver in the other, and a transfer of the securities by the investor, or the commencement of the company's winding up, makes it equally impossible in both cases for the parties to the contract to be restored to their original positions. Although there is no judicial decision on the point, it seems reasonable to assume, therefore, that the law is the same in both cases.

This would also seem to be the position if a merchant bank, a corporate finance subsidiary of a bank or a firm of sponsoring brokers places securities on the Stock Exchange and the listing particulars or other notice published in connection with the placing contains a misrepresentation. In practice, however, rescission by an investor who purchases from one of the firms of market makers which deals in the securities will rarely be possible, since it is the merchant bank, commercial bank subsidiary or sponsoring broker which is responsible for the misrepresentation, and not any of the firms of market makers who deal in them. On the other hand, it is arguable that since the market maker must know that the purchaser may have read and relied on the listing particulars or other notice published in connection with the placing, the market maker should not be able to hold the purchaser to his contract.[16] If the purchaser can rescind his purchase in this way, the market maker may also be able to rescind its purchase from the merchant bank, bank subsidiary or sponsoring broker, and the latter in turn may be able to rescind its contract with the company, just as in an offer for sale.

Rescission for non-disclosure

If a prospectus issued by a company governed by the Companies Acts failed to disclose the detailed information about the company (its business undertakings, its liabilities and its promoters and directors) which were required to be disclosed by that legislation, a subscriber for the securities offered by the prospectus could not treat the omission as equivalent to a positive assertion that no disclosure was necessary because the facts or circumstances calling for it did not exist, and so the subscriber could not rescind an allotment of shares or debentures made to him because of the non-disclosure.[17] Nevertheless, in one case the court held that the subscriber could recover damages from the company and the persons responsible for the prospectus if he would not have subscribed for the securities had the omitted information required by the Companies Acts been included, but in a later case the House of Lords expressed the view that no such claim for damages could be brought.[18]

Corresponding questions arise under the Financial Services Act 1986, whether a subscriber or purchaser of securities who relies on listing particulars published in relation to shares or other securities which are to be listed on the Stock Exchange, can rescind the contract under which he acquires the securities if the listing particulars do not contain all the detailed information required by the listing rules made by the Stock Exchange, and if he cannot rescind, whether he can instead claim damages. The Financial Services Act 1986 itself contains no indication whether the remedy of rescission is available, and the only sanction it expressly imposes when draft listing particulars submitted to the Stock Exchange do not

---

16 *Re Metropolitan Coal Consumers' Association, Karberg's Case* [1892] 3 Ch 1; *Lynde v Anglo-Italian Hemp Spinning Co* [1896] 1 Ch 178.

17 *Re Wimbledon Olympia Ltd* [1910] 1 Ch 630; *Re South of England Natural Gas and Petroleum Co Ltd* [1911] 1 Ch 573.

18 *Nash v Lynde* [1929] AC 158.

contain all the information required by the Stock Exchange's listing rules is the power and the obligation of the Quotation Committee to refuse the application for a listing.[19] It would seem, therefore, that the omission from published listing particulars of the detailed information which is required by the listing rules will not, of itself, entitle a person who subscribes for or purchases securities in reliance on listing particulars to rescind his subscription or purchase.

The only exception to this is where the listing rules require an express negative statement to be inserted in listing particulars if there is nothing to be disclosed under a particular item of information which the rules require to be disclosed, namely: changes in the issuing company's capital during the preceding three years,[20] the names of persons who are interested in 5 per cent or more of the company's issued share capital,[1] particulars of any litigation or arbitration proceedings in which the company is involved,[2] the amount of outstanding borrowing by the company and the group to which it belongs,[3] details of the interests of directors of the issuing company in transactions entered into by it which are unusual in nature or terms or which are significant to the company or the group to which it belongs,[4] and details of the interests of directors and their spouses and minor children in listed shares and debt securities of the issuer and other companies in the same group.[5] If a negative statement is included in listing particulars in respect of any of these matters, and there is in fact information which the listing rules require to be disclosed relating to it, the negative statement will be a positive misrepresentation, and the subscriber or purchaser of securities under the listing particulars will, if that information is material, be entitled to rescind his subscription or purchase.

Omission of information necessary for an informed assessment

The Financial Services Act 1986 requires that 'in addition to the information specified by listing rules ... any listing particulars submitted to [the Stock Exchange] ... shall contain such information as investors and their professional advisers would reasonably require, and reasonably expect to find there', for the purpose of making an informed assessment of 'the issuer's financial position and the securities to which the listing particulars relate'.[6] The test of whether information additional to that called for specifically by the listing rules need be included in listing particulars depends on the materiality of the information, and this corresponds exactly to the equity test of whether a misrepresentation is material so as to entitle the person misled by it to rescind the contract he enters into under its influence. By inference it could be argued that the statutory test also implies that the specific detailed information which the listing rules require to be included in listing particulars is also to be treated as material for this purpose, whenever a misrepresentation in respect of such a matter would necessarily be material so as to entitle a subscriber or purchaser of securities who relied on it to rescind. If this argument is accepted, the statutory general addition to the specific information called for by the listing rules would then be treated as a general description of the whole category of matters to be disclosed, and the items to be disclosed under the

19 Financial Services Act 1986, s 144 (1) and (2).
20 The Stock Exchange: *Admission of Securities to Listing* Section 3, Chapter 2, para 3.7.
 1 Ibid, Section 3, Chapter 2, para 3.9.
 2 Ibid, Section 3, Chapter 2, para 3.15.
 3 Ibid, Section 3, Chapter 2, para 5.16.
 4 Ibid, Section 3, Chapter 2, para 6.5.
 5 Ibid, Section 3, Chapter 2, para 6.6.
 6 Financial Services Act 1986, s 146 (1).

general addition would be identified by having the same characteristic of materiality which the law by implication treats all the specific items as having.

This argument goes some way toward the conclusion that the intention underlying the statutory requirements of disclosure is that a subscriber or purchaser of securities who acquires them in reliance on listing particulars which omit any item which statute requires to be disclosed, should have the same right to rescind the contract for the acquisition of the securities as if he had been induced to acquire them by positive misrepresentations. The argument is unrealistic, however, because the omission of some of the specific items of information required by the listing rules could well be material to an investor in the case of one company, but not in the case of others (eg failure to disclose whether a listing is being sought for the securities on other stock exchanges,[7] or failure to disclose the company's principal place of business in the United Kingdom,[8] or the total amount of outstanding loans to the directors of the issuer made by it and other companies in the same group).[9] Moreover, the omission of certain of the items of information required by the listing rules could never be material to an investor in deciding whether to subscribe for or purchase securities (eg the statement of the issuing company's date of incorporation,[10] or of any time limit imposed by the company's articles of association on the enforceability of claims for unpaid dividends).[11]

Although many of the specific items of information called for by the listing rules will normally be material to prospective investors when listing particulars are published, only a few of them will inevitably be material in all cases. Even if the court were inclined, in interpreting the Financial Services Act 1986, not to follow the decisions given under the Companies Acts that the omission of information required by those Acts to be included in prospectuses did not entitle subscribers to rescind allotments of shares or securities made to them, the acceptance by the court of the principle that omissions from listing particulars may under the new law entitle subscribers or purchasers of the securities to rescind would have to be limited to cases where the subscriber or purchaser is able to prove positively that the omission or omissions he complains of were material in his particular circumstances, and that it or they together influenced him in deciding to subscribe for or to purchase the securities. Alternatively, the subscriber or purchaser could rescind if the omission from listing particulars of an item or items called for in the listing rules made statements of fact which were included in the listing particulars either false or misleading when read on the assumption that there was nothing to be added to them under the statutory requirements of disclosure.[12]

Action for damages for deceit

The second remedy available to a person who has been induced to subscribe for or purchase shares, debentures or other securities by an invitation which contains a false statement of fact, is to sue the persons who issued the invitation for damages for deceit.

Matters to be proved

The plaintiff must prove the same matters in an action for deceit as in an action for rescission. Additionally, he must prove that the defendant knew that the statement

7 The Stock Exchange: *Admission of Securities to Listing* Section 3, Chapter 2, para 2.2.
8 Ibid, Section 3, Chapter 2, para 4.6.
9 Ibid, Section 3, Chapter 2, para 6.7.
10 Ibid, Section 3, Chapter 2, para 1.2.
11 Ibid, Section 3, Chapter 2, para 2.10.
12 *New Brunswick and Canada Railway and Land Co v Muggeridge* (1860) 1 Drew & Sm 363.

complained of was false, or at least, that he did not honestly believe it to be true, or that he made it recklessly, not caring whether it was true or false.[13] Consequently, it is insufficient for the plaintiff merely to show that the defendant was careless in not discovering the falsity of the statement, unless the defendant's acts show that he was completely indifferent whether it was true or not.[13] However, the plaintiff's burden of proof is eased a little by the court's readiness to infer that the defendant knew of the falsity of the statement on it being shown that he knew facts from which he must have realised that it was false.[14] The effect of such an inference is to shift the burden of proof to the defendant, not to raise an irrebuttable presumption of fraud. A fraudulent state of mind on the defendant's part is still essential, and so if his statement could be understood in two ways, one of which he admits to be false, but he satisfies the court that he honestly intended it to bear the other, true meaning, he is not guilty of deceit, even though the plaintiff reasonably understood the statement to bear the false meaning.[15] Thus, where the defendant issued a circular inviting subscriptions for shares in cash, and the circular stated that about one third of the company's capital has already been 'subscribed', it was held that, although the normal meaning of 'subscribed' is 'subscribed for payment in cash',[16] the defendant honestly understood the word to include subscriptions for payment in kind, and so was not guilty of deceit when it appeared that the one third of the company's capital referred to had been allotted in consideration of promotion services and the sale of patent rights to the company.[17]

As in an action for rescission, the plaintiff in an action for deceit must show that he was induced to take the shares or securities in question by the false statement. If the company informed him of its falsity in clear and unmistakable terms before he agreed to subscribe, he must have contracted with knowledge of its falsity, and he cannot sue the persons responsible for the statement when the securities turn out to be valueless.[18] Again, as in an action for rescission, the plaintiff must show that the false statement was addressed to him in order to induce him to subscribe. A prospectus is addressed to investors in order to induce them to apply for shares or securities to the company or intermediary which publishes the prospectus. It is not issued to induce investors to buy securities which the company has already issued from their existing holders. Consequently, an investor who makes such a purchase in reliance on the prospectus cannot sue the persons responsible for issuing it, even though they knew that it contained statements which were false.[19] But the issue of a prospectus may be merely part of a larger scheme to create a false market in shares or other securities and to induce investors to buy them from existing holders at prices in excess of their real value. If this is so, anyone who buys the securities in reliance on false statements in the prospectus may sue the persons responsible for its issue, for he has been induced to do the very thing which they intended he should do.[20] For this reason, the persons who are responsible for the publication of the listing particulars or other notices in connection with a Stock Exchange placing may be sued for deceit by investors who buy the securities concerned on the faith of it.

13 Derry v Peek (1889) 14 App Cas 337 at 374 to 5.
14 Ibid, at 375 to 6; Aaron's Reefs Ltd v Twiss [1896] AC 273.
15 Akerhielm v De Mare [1959] AC 789, [1959] 3 All ER 485, not following Arnison v Smith (1889) 41 ChD 98, 348.
16 See, for example, Governments Stock and Other Securities Investment Co Ltd v Christopher [1956] 1 All ER 490, [1956] 1 WLR 237.
17 Akerhielm v De Mare, supra.
18 Derry v Peek, supra.
19 Peek v Gurney (1873) LR 6 HL 377.
20 Ibid, per Lord Cairns at 413; Andrews v Mockford [1896] 1 QB 372.

Persons who may be sued

The persons who issue an invitation to subscribe for shares or other securities, whether directors of the company or not, may be sued for deceit. If the invitation is in a prospectus issued by the company, the directors will be responsible, for it is by their resolution at a board meeting or with their unanimous approval that the prospectus is issued. If a director can show that he did not take part in the relevant board meeting or did not agree to his fellow directors issuing the prospectus,[1] however, he will not be personally liable.[2] If the invitation is issued by an intermediary acting on its own behalf in connection with an offer for sale or a placing, prima facie the intermediary alone is liable in deceit,[3] but if it is proved that the directors of the company whose securities are marketed concurred in the invitation being issued in the form it took (and in practice the concurrence of directors in the issue of a prospectus is inevitable), they too will be liable if they knew that the invitation contained falsehoods. Moreover, if an application has been made for the securities to be listed, the listing particulars published in connection with the application will contain a statement that the directors of the issuing company accept responsibility for its contents, and an application for the admission of securities to the Unlisted Securities Market will be accompanied by a copy of the board resolution authorising the publication of the placing notice.[4] The features should suffice to establish the concurrence of each director.

A company is vicariously liable for the fraud of its agents, and so if its directors are guilty of deceit, the company, too, may be sued. Whether it is liable for false statements made by other persons, such as an intermediary or sponsoring broker employed to market the securities, depends on whether they were acting as the company's agents. In the normal form of an offer for sale or placing, the merchant bank, corporate finance subsidiary of a commercial bank or firm of sponsoring brokers agrees to take the securities itself in order to re-sell them, and consequently does not act as an agent of the company. But since the listing particulars or prospectus issued in connection with an offer for sale or placing will state that the company's directors accept responsibility for it, it will be rare that the company can escape liability.

The fact that a subscriber cannot rescind the allotment of the shares or debentures he has taken will not prevent him from suing for damages for deceit,[5] but formerly a subscriber for shares could not sue the company which allotted them to him without having first rescinded the allotment, and if he had lost his right to rescind he could not sue.[6] This was because the subscriber was still bound by the contract between himself and the company and his fellow shareholders implied from his membership,[7] and one of the implied terms of that contract was that the company's assets should be used only for the purpose of achieving its objects, which did not include the payment of compensation to defrauded subscribers.[8] Consequently,

---

1 For example, by voting against the issue of the prospectus at the board meeting which approved it. It seems unnecessary for the director to publish his dissociation from the issue of the prospectus in the way he may do in order to escape liability under the Financial Services Act 1986, s 151 (3) (see p 290, post).

2 *Re Denham & Co* (1883) 25 ChD 752.

3 *Weir v Barnett* (1877) 3 ExD 32; on appeal sub nom *Weir v Bell* (1878) 3 Ex D 238.

4 The Stock Exchange: *Admission of Securities to Listing*, Section 3, Chapter 2, para 1.7; The Stock Exchange: *Memorandum on the Unlisted Securities Market*, Terms and Conditions for Entry, Section A, para 4 (*ix*).

5 *Peek v Gurney* (1873) LR 6 HL 377.

6 *Houldsworth v City of Glasgow Bank* (1880) 5 App Cas 317.

7 Companies Act 1985, s 14 (1).

8 *Houldsworth v City of Glasgow Bank*, supra, per Lord Cairns at 325 and Lord Selborne at 329.

when a company was wound up, it was too late for its shareholders either to rescind the allotment of their shares or to sue the company for damages for deceit.[6] The preclusion of a subscriber for shares from suing the issuing company for damages for deceit has now been removed by statute.[9] This, of course, does not apply to debentures, nor does it apply to actions for deceit brought against persons other than the company.

Measure of damages

Prima facie, the loss suffered by a subscriber or purchaser of shares or other securities who is induced to acquire them by deceit is the difference between the price he paid for the securities and their real value at the date he took them, and this is the amount which he can recover as damages.[10] The subscriber or purchaser cannot recover additional damages for the company's failure to honour the high expectations which it held out in its prospectus,[10] nor for any diminution in the value of his securities caused by acts of the company since the securities were acquired by him.[11] But if the plaintiff can show that the market value of the securities when he took them was greater than the amount he has paid for them, he will be able to recover the difference as additional damages.[10] An increase in the value of the securities after he took them, however, will not entitle him to additional damages, because such an increase is wholly unconnected with the deceit practised on him.[10] Consequently, evidence of the value of the securities even only a few days after the plaintiff took them is inadmissible in assessing the damages he can recover.[10]

Action for damages for negligence

After the decision of the House of Lords in Derry v Peek[12] it was assumed that an action for damages by a subscriber for shares or other securities lay at common law only if he could prove deceit on the part of the persons who induced him to subscribe,[13] and it was on this assumption that Parliament enacted the Directors' Liability Act 1890, which in substance imposed a statutory liability for negligent misstatements on persons who issued prospectuses, and is now replaced by the even wider provisions of the Financial Services Act 1986. A decision of the House of Lords in 1963[14] and part of a judgment of Viscount Haldane in an earlier case[15] have cast doubt on the accuracy of this assumption, however. In its decision in 1963 the House of Lords held that if there is a special relationship between a person who asks for information or advice and the person who gives it, so that the latter understands or should understand that what he says will be relied upon by the other for a business purpose, the person giving the information or advice must exercise due care to see that it is accurate or sound.[16] Nevertheless, some of their lordships considered that this duty of care is not imposed on directors or others who invite the public generally to subscribe for shares or other securities by means of a prospectus (including listing particulars), because any such duty is pre-empted by

---

9 Companies Act 1985, s 111A, inserted by Companies Act 1989, s 131 (1).
10 *McConnel v Wright* [1903] 1 Ch 546.
11 *Clark v Urquhart* [1930] AC 28.
12 (1889) 14 App Cas 337.
13 Curiously, the possibility that a term should be implied in the contract for allotment warranting the truth of the statements contained in the invitation to subscribe has never been judicially ventilated.
14 *Hedley Byrne & Co Ltd v Heller Partners Ltd* [1964] AC 465, [1963] 2 All ER 575.
15 *Nocton v Lord Ashburton* [1914] AC 932 at 955 and 956.
16 [1964] AC 465 at 486, 502, 514 and 530, [1963] 2 All ER 575 at 583, 594, 601 and 610 to 11.

their statutory liability for negligent misstatements, which is dealt with below.[17] Such a duty might arise if securities are offered for subscription or purchase by an invitation other than a prospectus, however, and all their lordships expressly approved a passage in Viscount Haldane's judgment in the earlier case[15] in which he said that such a duty might be owed by directors who invite existing shareholders of a company to subscribe for further shares under a rights offer. The notion of such a duty to existing shareholders conflicts with the refusal of the courts to recognise special duties of directors to shareholders in all other situations,[18] but if the duty exists, it would usefully fill a gap left in the statutory liability of directors and others for false statements in invitations to subscribe for securities under which a statutory liability to pay compensation for misstatements and omissions does not arise.[19]

The extension by the House of Lords of common law liability for negligent information or advice has been read restrictively in a later decision of the Judicial Committee of the Privy Council.[20] In that case a majority of the members of the Judicial Committee held that generally a duty of care arises only when the informant or adviser carries on a business or profession which involves giving information or advice of the kind in question, so that it is possible for the court to establish an objective standard of skill and care to which practitioners in his field must conform.[1] But the majority opinion did concede that a duty of care may be imposed also where the informant or adviser has a financial interest in the matter on which information or advice is given,[2] and since a company always has a financial interest in subscriptions for its shares or other securities, even if its directors do not, it would appear that under the restricted rule the company, if not its directors, would still be liable in damages for information or advice given negligently by its directors or other agents to intending subscribers where they gave it on the company's behalf. Parallel liability would clearly be imposed on intermediaries in respect of information or advice given in invitations or advertisements relating to company securities for which they are engaged to find subscribers or purchasers.

Another distinguishing feature of recent judicial decisions which have imposed liability for negligence on persons who supply goods, services or advice or carry out construction work for the benefit of others, is that liability has been imposed on them not only towards the persons with whom they deal, but also to other persons whom they should envisage as likely to be affected by their negligence.[3] If such an extension of liability can also be made in respect of information or advice given by directors of a company in negotiating for subscriptions of its shares or securities (otherwise than by means of listing particulars or a prospectus where statutory liability to pay compensation is imposed), the curious result would be that third persons who acquire the securities from the subscribers might have claims for negligence against the directors and the company, whereas if the securities were issued under listing particulars or a prospectus, they would be unable to sue for

---

17 Ibid, per Lords Morris and Devlin [1964] AC 465 at 500–501 and 518–519, [1963] 2 All ER 575 at 592–593 and 604.
18 See p 607, post.
19 This will not apply in the case of listing particulars, but statutory liability will be excluded in respect of investment advertisements other than prospectus (as statutorily defined) when Part V of the Financial Services Act 1986 is brought into force by ministerial order.
20 *Mutual Life and Citizens' Assurance Co Ltd v Evatt* [1971] AC 793, [1971] 1 All ER 150.
1 As an example of this, see *Arenson v Casson Beckman Rutley & Co* [1977] AC 405, [1977] 3 All ER 901.
2 [1971] AC 793 at 809, [1971] 1 All ER 150 at 161.
3 *Dutton v Bognor Regis Urban District Council* [1972] 1 QB 373, [1972] 1 All ER 462; *Anns v Merton London Borough Council* [1978] AC 728, [1977] 2 All ER 492, *Ross v Canuters* [1980] Ch 297, [1979] 3 All ER 580; *Yianni v Edwin Evans & Sons* [1982] QB 438, [1981] 3 All ER 592.

damages for deceit or for statutory compensation under the provisions dealt with below.[4]

If a claim for damages for negligence in respect of an invitation to subscribe for securities lies against a company which is vicariously liable for the acts of its directors or other agents, the claimant will not need to rescind his acquisition of the securities before suing the company, and if the securities are shares, the fact that he cannot rescind because the company has gone into liquidation will not prevent him from suing it.[5]

The statutory claim for compensation in respect of listing particulars

Untrue statements and omissions

The remedy which the Financial Services Act 1986 gives expressly to a subscriber or purchaser who acquires securities in reliance on defective listing particulars is the recovery of compensation from the persons responsible for the particulars. Compensation is recoverable for loss suffered by the plaintiff 'as a result of any untrue or misleading statement in the listing particulars,' or the omission from them of any matter required to be included by the sections of the Act which require listing particulars and supplementary listing particulars to contain all such information (in addition to that required specifically by the listing rules) 'as investors and their professional advisers would reasonably require, and reasonably expect to find there, for the purpose of making an informed assessment of:

(a) the assets and liabilities, financial position, profits and losses and prospects of the issuer and the securities; and

(b) the rights attaching to those securities'.[6]

Additionally, an investor may recover compensation if he suffers loss as a result of the issuer of securities not submitting to the Quotations Department and publishing supplementary listing particulars when the Act requires them.[7] Supplementary listing particulars are required when any significant change occurs affecting a matter required to be disclosed in listing particulars by the statutory provisions mentioned above, or when any significant new matter arises which under those provisions would have been required to be included in the original listing particulars if it had existed at the time they were submitted to the Quotations Department for approval.[8]

To avoid any doubt about the meaning of an untrue statement, the Financial Services Act 1986 provides that where the listing rules require information as to any particular matter to be included in listing particulars or to state (if that is the case) that there is no such matter, the omission of information about that matter shall be treated for the purpose of liability to pay compensation as a statement that there is no such matter.[9] This provision applies only where the listing rules expressly require a negative statement if there is nothing to disclose in respect of an item of information specifically called for; it does not mean that the omission of an item of information which should be included in listing particulars automatically implies a negative statement if none is expressly required by the listing rules. Moreover, a negative statement is implied where information should have been,

---

4 *Peek v Gurney* (1873) LR 6 HL 377; *Collins v Associated Greyhound Racecourses Ltd* [1930] 1 Ch 1. For the limitations on the right of an investor to sue for statutory compensation, see p 288.
5 Companies Act 1985, s 111A, inserted by Companies Act 1989, s 131 (1).
6 Financial Services Act 1986, ss 146 (1) and 150 (1).
7 Ibid, s 150 (3).
8 Ibid, s 147 (1) (see p 261, ante).
9 Ibid, s 150 (2).

but has not been, included in listing particulars only for the purpose of claims for compensation under the Act. A negative statement cannot be implied in order to establish the existence of a false statement of fact in listing particulars so that an investor may rescind his subscription or purchase of securities in reliance on it if it was material to his decision to invest.

The investors who may recover compensation

The persons who may recover compensation for loss suffered in consequence of false or misleading statements in, or omissions from, listing particulars are those who have acquired any of the securities to which the particulars relate.[6] Consequently, potential plaintiffs are not confined to persons who subscribe for the securities offered by the listing particulars, or persons who purchase them directly from an intermediary who is responsible for the particulars, but include purchasers of the securities from such subscribers or direct purchasers and derivative purchasers from them. This contrasts with the inability of persons other than subscribers and purchasers from a responsible intermediary to rescind the contract by which they acquire the securities for misrepresentation, or to sue for damages for deceit.[10]

Nevertheless, although the Act does not set a limit on the period during which a subscriber or purchaser of securities may rely on listing particulars, it cannot be intended that persons acquiring securities may rely on listing particulars, however ancient they may be, and that they may claim compensation if the contents of the particulars were inaccurate or incomplete at the time they were first published, or if they became inaccurate or incomplete by reason of significant changes occurring or significant matters arising before dealings in the securities began after their admission to listing.[11] It is probable that the court will treat the functional life of listing particulars as terminating when a reasonable time has elapsed after the commencement of dealings in the securities to which they relate, and that could well be considered to be when the market price of the securities has settled after the initial sales by the subscribers or first purchasers of them (ie between seven and ten days after dealings commence).

The persons from whom compensation may be claimed

The persons who may be sued for compensation if listing particulars or supplementary listing particulars contain false or misleading statements, or if they omit information which they should contain, are the persons who are responsible for the particulars submitted to the Quotations Department. They are defined as comprising:

(a) the company to which the listing particulars relate;
(b) the directors of the issuing company at the time when the particulars were submitted to the Quotations Department for approval;
(c) every person who has authorised himself to be named, and is named, in the listing particulars as a director of the issuing company or as having agreed to become a director of it immediately or in the future;
(d) every person who accepts, and is stated in the listing particulars as accepting responsibility for the particulars or any part of them (eg a merchant bank, the corporate finance subsidiary of a commercial bank or any other

---

10 *Peek v Gurney* (1873) LR 6 HL 377; *Hyslop v Morel* (1891) 7 TLR 263 *Collins v Associated Greyhound Racecourses Ltd* [1930] 1 Ch 1.
11 Financial Services Act 1986, s 146 (1) and 147 (1).

intermediary who offers securities to the public for subscription or sale, or who places them on the Stock Exchange); and

(e) every person who has authorised the contents of the listing particulars or any part of them.[12]

A person is not responsible for listing particulars as a director of the issuing company if they are published without his knowledge or consent, and on becoming aware of their publication he gives reasonable public notice that they were published without his knowledge or consent.[13]

If a person accepts responsibility for only part of the contents of listing particulars, or authorises the inclusion of only part of those contents (eg an accountant whose report on the financial condition and history of the issuing company is included in the listing particulars in compliance with the listing rules, or a valuer, surveyor, engineer or other expert who authorises the inclusion of a report or opinion by him on particular assets or ventures of the company), that person is responsible only for the part of the listing particulars for which he accepts responsibility or whose inclusion he authorises, and then only if its appears in the particulars in the form, or substantially the form, and in the context which he has agreed.[14]

If listing particulars relate to securities which are to be issued in exchange for existing shares or securities issued by another company, or in exchange for the business undertaking of another company, under an offer made or an agreement entered into by the issuing company or its wholly-owned subsidiary (eg under a takeover offer or an agreed merger), and that other company and the persons who are its directors or who have authorised themselves to be named as its directors at the time the listing particulars are submitted to the Quotations Department, have expressly accepted responsibility in the listing particulars for the part of the particulars which relates to the existing securities or the undertaking of the other company (eg for details of that company's business undertaking or assets or its financial condition or history), they are liable to pay compensation in respect of misstatements in or omissions from that part of the listing particulars, but the issuing company and the other persons who are responsible for the listing particulars generally, as directors or proposed directors of the issuing company, are not responsible for that part of the listing particulars.[15] Where the listing particulars are issued in connection with a merger or an agreed takeover bid, therefore, responsibility for the contents of the listing particulars is divided between the acquiring company and its directors on the one hand and the concurring directors of the acquired company on the other.

Liability for the issuing company's failure to submit for approval and publish supplementary listing particulars if, after the submission of draft listing particulars to the Quotations Department for approval, the company becomes aware of a significant change or a significant new matter which affects the original particulars and would have been required to be included in the original particulars if it had existed at the time they were submitted for approval, is imposed only on the issuing company itself, and not on any of the other persons who are responsible for the original listing particulars.[16] The company's liability depends on it becoming aware of the change or new matter before the commencement of dealings in the securities, but if its lack of awareness is attributable to the failure of any other person or persons who are responsible for the original listing particulars to give

---

12 Ibid, s 152 (1).
13 Ibid, s 152 (2).
14 Ibid, s 152 (3).
15 Ibid, s 152 (4).
16 Ibid, s 147 (1) and (3) and s 150 (3).

notice to it of a significant change or significant new matter of which they become aware before that time, they instead are liable to subscribers and purchasers of securities who relied on the original listing particulars.[16] In these circumstances, where liability depends on awareness, the respective liabilities of the company and the other persons responsible for the original listing particulars are alternative, and not cumulative, as they are for defective original listing particulars.

Responsibility statements and consents

The adherence of the directors of the issuing company to the contents of listing particulars is made manifest by the requirement of the listing rules that the particulars must contain a declaration by the directors (usually at the beginning of the listing particulars) that they accept responsibility for the information contained therein, and that to the best of their knowledge and belief (having taken reasonable care to ensure that such is the case) they confirm that the information contained in the particulars is in accordance with the facts and does not omit anything likely to affect the import of that information.[17] Similarly, if the listing particulars contain a statement or report attributed to an expert, they must also contain a statement that he has given and not withdrawn his consent to the issue of the particulars with the statement or report by him included in it in the form and context in which it appears.[18] It is also possible for similar responsibility or authorisation declarations on the part of other persons to be included in listing particulars in respect of the whole or part of their contents,[17] and if the named persons have in fact accepted the responsibility stated, or have authorised the inclusion of statements or reports by them in the way indicated, they will incur legal liability if the listing particulars are inaccurate or incomplete.

Exemptions from liability

There are three exemptions from the liability normally imposed on the directors of the issuing company and on persons named as directors or as having agreed to become directors of the issuer. The first exemption applies where listing particulars relate to debentures or loan securities issued by a company and the securities are denominated in a currency other than sterling, or the company is otherwise connected with an overseas country, or the securities are likely to be dealt in by bodies incorporated or persons resident overseas, and in any such case the securities are of a class specified in the listing rules as eligible for the Quotations Committee to grant them an exemption from the need for listing particulars to contain the normal detailed information required by the listing rules.[19] In fact, the only categories of debt securities which are specified in the listing rules as eligible for such an exemption from the need to submit and publish full listing particulars are debt securities nearly all of which, because of their nature, are normally bought and traded by a limited number of investors who are particularly knowledgeable on investment matters (eg international bond dealers); exemption is not given automatically, but must be sought on each occasion listing particulars are published in respect of such debt securities.[20]

In addition to the automatic exemption from liability for misstatements in and omission from listing particulars in respect of international debt securities which is conferred on directors and persons named in the particulars as directors or as

17 The Stock Exchange: *Admission of Securities to Listing* Section 3, Chapter 2, para 1.7.
18 Ibid, Section 3, Chapter 2, para 1.8.
19 Financial Services Act 1986, s 152 (5) and (6).
20 The Stock Exchange: *Admission of Securities to Listing* Section 3, Chapter 2, para 5.1.

having agreed to become directors, the Quotations Committee can in its discretion extend the exemption from liability to any such persons in connection with any listing particulars submitted to it if the Committee considers that liability should not attach to them by reason of their having an interest in the matter or by reason of any other circumstances.[1] It would seem that this discretionary power to grant exemptions is intended to benefit non-executive directors and directors who have no, or only a small, personal investment in the company and who take no part, or a negligible part, in the preparation and submission of the listing particulars to the Quotations Department and their publication. The power of the Quotations Department to exonerate directors may, it would appear, be exercised before or after the listing particulars are published, but not after an action for the recovery of compensation in respect of the listing particulars has been commenced.

The third exemption from liability, which benefits directors and persons named as directors or proposed directors of an issuing company, is in respect of listing particulars relating to securities which are to be issued in exchange for the existing securities or the business undertaking of another company under an offer or agreement made by the issuing company or its wholly-owned subsidiary (eg on a takeover or merger). As indicated above, the issuing company and its directors and persons named in the listing particulars as its directors or as having agreed to become its directors are exempted from liability in respect of the contents of the listing particulars which relate to the company or other body whose undertaking or shares are to be acquired by the issuing company or its subsidiary, but only if that company and its directors and persons named as its directors in the particulars have expressly accepted responsibility for that part of the listing particulars and are stated therein to have done so.[2]

The circumstances in which liability arises

The statutory liability imposed on the issuing company, on its directors, on persons who authorise themselves to be named in the particulars as directors or as having agreed to become directors of the issuer, and on other persons who expressly accept responsibility for or authorise the inclusion of statements in listing particulars or supplementary listing particulars, is to pay compensation for loss caused to investors in respect of securities acquired by them as a result of:

(a) any untrue or misleading statements in the particulars; or
(b) the omission from the listing particulars of information known to the persons responsible for them at the time of their submission in draft form to the Quotations Department, or the omission of information obtainable by those persons at that time by making reasonable inquiries, where that information supplements the detailed information called for by the listing rules and is reasonably required by investors and their professional advisers to enable them to make an informed assessment of the issuing company and the securities to which the particulars relate; or
(c) in the case of an issuing company, the failure to submit and publish supplementary listing particulars, or (in the case of persons responsible for the original listing particulars) failure to notify information to the issuing company so as to facilitate the submission and publication of such supplementary particulars, containing information concerning significant

1 Financial Services Act 1986, s 152 (5).
2 Ibid, s 152 (4) and (7).

changes affecting matters contained in the original particulars or concerning significant new matters arising since the original particulars were submitted.[3]

The drafting of these provisions imposing and defining liability gives rise to several problems of interpretation. On a literal interpretation of the provisions, the omission from listing particulars of information which is reasonably required for an assessment of the issuing company and the securities to which the particulars relate, entitles an investor to claim compensation only if that information is additional to the detailed information specifically required to be included in listing particulars by the listing rules, and no claim lies for loss resulting from the omission of any of that detailed information, however material it may be for a proper assessment of the issuing company and the securities. It is likely that the court will disregard this defect of drafting, and will regard the general disclosure requirement as the principal obligation, and the specifications of the detailed information called for by the listing rules as being instances of that general requirement if they are material for an informed assessment. This could be achieved by interpreting the introductory words of s 146 (1) of the Financial Services Act 1986, ie: 'In addition to the information specified by listing rules . . .', as meaning 'In addition to the obligation to disclose the information specified by listing rules . . .', thus leaving the principal obligation imposed by the subsection as an obligation to include in listing particulars 'all such information as investors and their professional advisers would reasonably require . . . for the purpose of making an informed assessment . . .', whether that information is specified in detail in the listing rules or not.

The second problem of interpretation arises from the provision in the Financial Services Act 1986 that information needed for an informed assessment of the issuing company and the securities to which the listing particulars relate need only be included in the particulars if it is 'within the knowledge of any person responsible for the listing particulars or . . . would be reasonable for him to obtain by making enquiries'.[4] Presumably, this means that if any of the persons in the five categories of persons who are responsible for listing particulars[5] is aware of the material information which is omitted, or if he would have discovered it if he had made the enquiries which he should have made, all of the persons responsible for the listing particulars are potentially liable to pay compensation, subject to the availability to them of the statutory defences mentioned below. It is presumably to be implied that the knowledge or imputed knowledge of a person who accepts responsbility for only part of the particulars, or who authorises the inclusion of only part of their contents (eg a reporting accountant as regards his financial report), is not to be treated as shared with the issuing company and the other persons responsible for the listing particulars, if what he knows or could discover does not relate to the part of the listing particulars for which he is responsible. Directors of the issuing company would, for example, not be even potentially liable for an omission from the listing particulars of information about persons indirectly interested in 5 per cent or more of the company's issued share capital, if the information is unknown to them, but is known to the accountant who prepares the financial report on the issuer which is included in the listing particulars.

Finally, and even more ambiguously, liability to pay compensation may be incurred by persons responsible for listing particulars in respect of loss resulting from a failure to submit and publish supplementary listing particulars relating to significant changes in matters contained in the original particulars, or relating to significant new matters arising after the submission of the original particulars to

3 Ibid, ss 146 (1) and (2), 147 (1) to (3) and 150 (1) and (3).
4 Ibid, s 146 (2).
5 Ibid, s 152 (1) (see p 281, ante).

the Quotations Department, but liability is imposed only if the issuing company was aware of the significant change or significant new matter if it is the defendant, or if a person responsible for the original particulars was aware of it and failed to inform the company about it, and that person is the defendant.[6] It is uncertain from this provision whether the issuing company is considered as being aware of significant changes and new matters known to any of its directors under the general principle that knowledge by a director of any matter relating to his functions is imputed to the company, unless the director is acting fraudulently,[7] and whether the company is to be treated as aware of matters known to other persons only if they are acting as its officers or agents at the relevant time and they acquire knowledge of the matter in question in fulfilling their functions in relation to the company.[8] Certainly, no knowledge of a significant change or new matter acquired by a person who is responsible for the original listing particulars because he accepted responsibility for them, or authorised the inclusion of a statement by him in them, will be imputed to the issuing company, unless that person is also a director or agent of the company at the time when he becomes aware of the change or new matter. The Financial Services Act 1986 recognises this by imposing a duty on such a person to notify the company of the significant change or new matter when he becomes aware of it,[9] and until that duty is fulfilled, the company cannot be considered as being aware of the change or new matter.

On the other hand, a person who is responsible for the original listing particulars is liable to compensate an investor who suffers loss as a result of that person's failure to notify the issuer of a significant change or significant new matter which makes supplementary listing particulars necessary and of which he becomes aware.[9] This is a purely individual liability, however, and is not extended to the other persons who are responsible for the listing particulars. Moreover, it would seem that a person who is responsible for only part of the contents of the original listing particulars incurs a liability under this head only if he becomes aware of a significant change in, or a significant new matter affecting, the information in that part, and fails to notify the issuing company of that change or new matter. It would not appear that such a person is required to acquaint himself with the whole of the contents of the original listing particulars, so that if he becomes aware of a significant change or a significant new matter affecting part of its contents for which he is not responsible, he must notify the issuing company of it, nor would it appear that he is liable to pay compensation if he actually becomes aware of such a change or new matter and does not notify the company of it.

The loss for which compensation may be recovered

The loss in respect of which a claim for compensation may be brought against the persons responsible for listing particulars or supplementary listing particulars is the loss suffered by an investor in respect of the securities he has acquired as a result of the untrue or misleading statement in, or the omission from, the particulars of which he complains, or as the result of the issuing company's failure to submit and publish supplementary listing particulars when required, or as the result of the failure of the defendant to inform the company of a matter calling for supplementary listing particulars.[10] The loss suffered by the investor is, of course, not caused

6 Ibid, ss 147 (1) and (3) and 150 (3).
7 *Houghton & Co v Nothard Lowe and Wills Ltd* [1928] AC 1.
8 *Blackburn, Low & Co v Vigors* (1887) 12 App, Cas 531; *Bawden v London, Edinburgh and Glasgow Assurance Co* [1892] 2 QB 534.
9 Financial Services Act 1986, ss 147 (3) and 150 (3).
10 Ibid, s 150 (1) and (3).

directly by the misstatement, omission or failure to inform the issuing company of which he complains, but is loss suffered in consequence of the misstatement in, or omission from, the listing particulars influencing his decision to subscribe for or purchase the securities to which the particulars relate, or of the failure to publish supplementary listing particulars inducing him to do so, or not to exercise any right he has to withdraw an offer or application he has already made to acquire securities to which the original particulars relate. It follows that the misstatement or omission in the original listing particulars or the matter which should have been included in supplementary listing particulars must have been material (ie likely to influence the mind of a reasonable investor), and must in fact have influenced the conduct of the investor who claims compensation.

The quantification of the compensation recoverable will be affected by the seriousness of the misstatement or omission from the listing particulars or the failure to publish supplementary listing particulars. It was held by the court under the similar provisions in the Companies Acts governing compensation claims by subscribers of companies' shares or other securities offered by prospectuses containing untrue statements,[11] that the measure of compensation to be awarded was the same as the damages recoverable in a common law action for fraud or deceit, namely, the difference between the market value of the securities at the time the plaintiff subscribed for them (whether higher or lower than the issue price which he paid) and the real value of the securities at that time, taking into account the seriousness of the untrue statements.[12] The wording of the Financial Services Act 1986 is similar in this respect to the wording of the Companies Acts, and it would appear that the compensation recoverable by an investor under it should be assessed in the same way, namely, by taking the difference between the market value of the securities subscribed for or purchased by the plaintiff on the date when he subscribed for or purchased them (or the opening price anticipated at that time if dealings commenced in the securities only later) and the actual value of the securities on the date when the plaintiff acquired them. The court will, of course, have to reconstruct a hypothetical 'real' market value for the securities on that date in the light of the untruth of statements in, or omissions from, the listing particulars which have since been discovered, but this cannot be done by taking the actual market value of the securities at a later date after the discovery had been made, even if only a few days after the plaintiff's subscription or purchase, because the price on that later date may have been influenced by other extraneous factors as well as the discovery.[12]

The statutory defences to a claim for compensation

A number of statutory defences are available to a person who is liable to pay compensation as a person responsible for listing particulars or supplementary listing particulars.

(i) The defence of reasonable belief   The first group of defences are available to a person who is sued in respect of loss caused by an untrue statement in, or omission from, listing particulars for which he is responsible, and who satisfies the court that:

> 'when the particulars were submitted to [the Quotation Department] he reasonably believed, having made such inquiries (if any) as were reasonable, that the statement was

---

11 Companies Act 1985, s 67 (1) and (2) (re-enacting the Companies Act 1948, s 43 (1), Companies Act 1929, s 37 (1) and Companies (Consolidation) Act 1908, s 84 (1)).
12 *McConnel v Wright* [1903] 1 Ch 546; *Clark v Urquhart* [1930] AC 28.

true and not misleading, or that the matter whose omission caused the loss was properly omitted, and [either]:

(a) that he continued in that belief until the time when the securities were acquired [by the plaintiff]; or

(b) that [the securities] were acquired before it was reasonably practicable to bring a correction to the attention of persons likely to acquire the securities in question; or

(c) that before the securities were acquired, he had taken all such steps as it was reasonable for him to have taken to secure that a correction was brought to the attention of those persons; or

(d) that he continued in [the belief that the statement complained of was true and not misleading, or that the omission complained of was not material] until after the commencement of dealings in the securities following their admission [to listing] and that the securities were acquired [by the plaintiff] after such a lapse of time that he ought in the circumstances to be reasonably excused.[13]

The basic element common to the defences in this group is that the person responsible for the listing particulars or the part of them concerned reasonably believed that the statement complained of was true, or that the omission complained of was permissible.

It was held under the similar provisions of the Companies Acts[11] that the defendant's reasonable belief in the truth of a statement in a prospectus which turned out to be false could be based on assurances or information obtained by him from officers or agents of the issuing company who would normally be in possession of the relevant primary records or documents, or who would normally be likely to know about the matter, provided that the defendant had no reason to mistrust them and was unaware of any interest which they might have in concealing the truth.[14] Whether this is so under the new provisions is uncertain, but it may be that if the reasonable inquiries (if any) which the defendant is required to make[15] would necessarily involve him relying on the statements or opinions of other persons, because for example, of the technical nature of the information or its inaccessibility, he may do so and will not be required to verify the statement or the immateriality of the omission by personal investigation.

Liability can, of course, only be imposed on the defendant for the parts of listing particulars for which he is responsible, and so if he is responsible merely as a person who had expressly accepted responsibility for part of the particulars, or has authorised the inclusion in it of only part of its contents (eg an expert's report or statement), he will not be responsible for untrue statements in other parts of the listing particulars or for omissions from those parts,[16] and consequently, he will not need to prove that he reasonably believed that those other parts were true and not misleading and omitted no information which should have been included.

Presumably a person responsible for listing particulars takes reasonable steps to bring a correction of the untrue statement or omission complained of to the attention of persons likely to acquire the securities (so as to be able to rely on the defence provided in paragraph (c) above) by having the correction published in the newspaper or newspapers in which the listing particulars were published, or by having the correction published by the Stock Exchange. The defence under paragraph (d) may be relied on, it would appear, if the plaintiff acquired the securities in question after the market had settled following the time at which initial sales of securities comprised in the same marketing operation had taken place upon the commencement of dealings.

13 Financial Services Act 1986, s 151 (1).
14 *Stevens v Hoare* (1904) 20 TLR 407; *Adams v Thrift* [1915] 2 Ch 21 at 19.
15 Financial Services Act 1986, s 146 (3).
16 Ibid, s 152 (1) (*d*) and (*e*).

(ii) The defence of reliance on an expert The second group of defences available to a person who is responsible for listing particulars or supplementary listing particulars concerns loss caused by untrue statements contained in the particulars which purport to be made by or with the authority of an expert, and which are included in the particulars with the expert's consent and the particulars state that he has given that consent.[17] An expert is a person, such as an engineer, valuer or accountant, whose professional qualifications or experience give authority to a statement made by him,[18] it being implied, of course, that the statement in the listing particulars which is made by him, or which purports to be made by him, relates to a matter on which he is, or is presented by the listing particulars as being, an expert.

A person who is responsible for the listing particulars (other than the expert himself) may defend a claim by an investor for compensation for loss caused by an untrue statement by an expert (eg an untrue statement in the reporting accountant's report on the company's financial position and prospects) by proving:

'that at the time when the particulars were submitted to [the Quotations Department, the person responsible for the particulars] believed on reasonable grounds that the [expert or pretended expert] was competent to make or authorise the statement, and had consented to its inclusion [in the particulars] in the form and context in which it was included, and [either]:

(a) that he continued in that belief until the time when the securities were acquired [by the plaintiff]; or
(b) that they were acquired before it was reasonably practicable to bring the fact that the expert was not competent, or had not consented, to the attention of persons likely to acquire the securities in question; or
(c) that before the securities were acquired [by the plaintiff, the person responsible for the listing particulars] had taken all such steps as it was reasonable for him to have taken to secure that that fact was brought to the attention of those persons; or
(d) that he continued in that belief until after the commencement of dealings in the securities following their admission [to listing] and that the securities were acquired [by the plaintiff] after such a lapse of time that he ought in the circumstances to be reasonably excused.'[17]

This second group of defences is structurally similar to the first, but the reasonable belief which the defendant must have is a belief in the expert's competence to make the statement which was included or quoted in the listing particulars, and not a belief that the statement was true and not misleading. This imposes a far lighter burden of proof on the defendant than the first group of defences, but it would appear, although the Act does not say so expressly, that to rely on the second group of defences, the defendant must have made reasonable inquiries about the expert's competence before the listing particulars were submitted for approval by the Quotations Committee, if he did not know the expert well enough beforehand to reach a conclusion as to the expert's competence and suitability without making inquiries.

An expert himself cannot, of course, rely on the second group of defences in respect of a statement by him which is included or quoted in listing particulars, but he can rely on the first set of defences, and to succeed in any such defence he must show that an expert in his speciality would have acted reasonably in the circumstances if he had permitted the statement attributed to him to be included or quoted, and that such an expert would also have acted reasonably if he had reached the conclusions as to the relevant facts and made the deductions from them

17 Ibid, s 151 (2).
18 Ibid, s 151 (7).

which were expressed in the defendant's statement, as included or quoted in the listing particulars.

The second group of defences relates to the contents of statements made by experts, and no mention is made of omissions from such statements, as it is in the first group of defences. Nevertheless, if the plaintiff's complaint is that the statement by an expert is defective because of a material omission, even if it is not thereby made misleading but simply incomplete, a person responsible for the listing particulars (other than the expert) can rely on the second group of defences, because the loss for which the plaintiff sues is still 'loss in respect of securities caused by a statement purporting to be made by . . . an expert'.[18]

(iii) The defence of a published correction   The third pair of defences are available to all persons who are responsible in any capacity for listing particulars or supplementary listing particulars. Such a person is not liable for loss caused by a statement in, or omission from, listing particulars if either:

'(a) before the securities were acquired [by the plaintiff] a correction, or where the statement was [one made by or on the authority of an expert], the fact that the expert was not competent or had not consented [to the inclusion or quotation of the statement made by him], had been published in a manner calculated to bring it to the attention of persons likely to acquire the securities in question; or

(b) that [the defendant] took all steps as it was reasonable for him to take to secure such a publication and reasonably believed that it had taken place before the securities were acquired [by the plaintiff].'[19]

The importance of this group of defences, as compared with the first two groups, is that to succeed the defendant does not have to prove that he reasonably believed the statement complained of was true, or that he reasonably believed the expert who made the statement was competent to make it and had consented to its inclusion in the listing particulars, but to succeed the defendant need only prove that he procured or took reasonable steps to procure the publication of a correction or of a denial of the expert's competence or consent.

(iv) The remaining defences   There are three other defences which any person responsible for listing particulars or supplementary listing particulars may rely on to escape liability. The first is that the statement complained of was made by an official person, or was contained in a public official document, and was fairly and accurately reproduced in the listing particulars.[20] The terms 'official person' and 'public official document' are not defined, but they would appear to mean an official of a government or public body, whether British or foreign, and a document prepared by such an official or officials, or by one or more persons appointed by a government or public body to produce it, where the document was prepared after proper inquiry and is open to public inspection.[1] The second alternative defence is one which would be available to the defendant at common law, even if it were not mentioned in the Financial Services Act 1986, namely, that the plaintiff acquired the securities in question with knowledge that the statement complained of was false or misleading, or that the listing particulars or supplementary particulars omitted the matter, or that the plaintiff acquired the securities with knowledge of the significant change or new matter whose omission is complained of.[2]

The final alternative defence may be relied on if the issuing company failed to

19 Ibid, s 151 (3).
20 Ibid, s 151 (4).
 1 *Sturla v Freccia* (1880) 5 App Cas 623.
 2 Financial Services Act 1986, s 151 (5).

submit and publish supplementary listing particulars when it became aware of a significant change affecting any matter contained in the original particulars, or of a significant new matter which arose after the submission of the original particulars to the Quotations Department, and information about that change or new matter would have been required in the original particulars if the matter had arisen before their submission.[3] The defence is also available to a person responsible for listing particulars who becomes aware of such a significant change or new matter arising since the submission of the original listing particulars, but does not fulfil his duty to give notice of it to the issuing company so that it may submit and publish supplementary listing particulars.[3] The defence is that the issuing company or the person responsible for the original particulars reasonably believed that the change or new matter was not such as to call for supplementary listing particulars,[4] in other words, that the defendant reasonably believed that the change or new matter was not significant for the purpose of making an informed assessment of the financial position of the issuing company or of the rights attaching to the securities offered.[5]

Liability of the issuing company

The company which issues securities to which listing particulars relate is liable as a person responsible for the particulars or any supplementary listing particulars to pay compensation to an investor who acquires any of the securities and suffers loss in consequence of any untrue or misleading statement in the particulars or supplementary particulars, or in consequence of the omission from them of any information reasonably required for an investor to make an informed assessment of the financial position of the company and the rights attaching to the securities, or in consequence of the company's failure to submit and publish supplementary listing particulars in respect of any significant change or new matter arising since the publication of the original particulars.[6] The issuing company is responsible for the whole of the contents of the particulars, except any part which relates to another company whose existing securities or undertaking the issuing company or its wholly-owned subsidiary is acquiring in exchange for securities issued by the issuing company under a takeover or merger where the directors of that other company expressly accept responsibility for that part of the listing particulars.[7] An issuing company which is sued for compensation can rely on the same defences as any other person who is responsible for the whole of the contents of the listing particulars, or the whole of them subject to that exception (as the case may be), and so the company may rely on the defences relating to statements by experts which are incorporated in the particulars and defences relating to the company's own reasonable belief in the truth and completeness of the information contained in the listing particulars.[8]

It is not necessary that a person who claims compensation from the issuing company should rescind his subscription or acquisition of securities to which listing particulars relate before suing for compensation, and the fact that rescission is no longer possible because the company has gone into liquidation is no bar to a compensation claim.[9]

3 Ibid, s 147 (1) and (3).
4 Ibid, s 151 (6).
5 Ibid, s 147 (2).
6 Ibid, ss 146 (1), 147 (1) and (2), 150 (1) and (3) and 152 (1) (*a*).
7 Ibid, s 152 (1) and (4) (see p 282, ante).
8 Ibid, s 151 (1) to (6).
9 Companies Act 1985, s 111A, inserted by Companies Act 1989, s 131 (1).

The statutory claim for compensation in respect of prospectuses other than listing particulars

At present the obligatory contents of prospectuses, other than listing particulars published in connection with an application for the official listing of shares or other securities of a company on the Stock Exchange, are still governed by the provisions of the Companies Act 1985, which are prospectively repealed by the Financial Services Act 1986.[10] Correspondingly, the statutory liability of the persons who are responsible for such prospectuses to pay compensation to investors who are thereby induced to subscribe for or purchase the securities to which they relate are at present governed by the provisions of the Companies Act 1985, which will be simultaneously repealed when the new rules governing the contents of such prospectuses come into force.[11] The new statutory rules governing the obligatory contents of prospectuses (including those rules which will be contained in delegated legislation)[12] will come into force on a date to be prescribed by the Secretary of State for Trade and Industry, and on the same date the new rules imposing statutory liability to pay compensation to subscribers for, and purchasers of, securities under defective prospectuses and supplementary prospectuses will be brought into force.[13] The new rules in respect of that liability follow closely the provisions governing liability for the payment of compensation in respect of defective listing particulars, as will be shown below.

The parties to compensation claims

As in the case of listing particulars, the persons who will be able to make statutory claims for compensation in respect of misstatements in, or omissions from, prospectuses or supplementary prospectuses will be any persons who have acquired securities to which the prospectus relates,[14] and claimants will not be confined to persons who subscribe for or acquire securities directly in response to the offer which is made in, or which accompanies, the prospectus. The Financial Services Act 1986, gives no indication of the length of time after the issue or publication of a prospectus during which a person who subscribes for or acquires securities to which the prospectus relates may continue to rely on it and claim compensation if the prospectus is defective, but it would seem likely that the court would treat this period as being limited to a reasonable time after the offer contained in or accompanying the prospectus has expired. Such a reasonable period could vary according to the circumstances of the issue of the prospectus, but would rarely be likely to exceed three months.

The persons from whom compensation for misstatements or omissions in a prospectus or supplementary prospectus may be claimed are the persons who are responsible for it, including the company which issues or has issued the securities to which it relates. Those persons are defined in the same way as in the corresponding provision in respect of listing particulars,[15] save that directors of the company will be liable as responsible persons if they are directors at the time when the prospectus is delivered to the Registrar of Companies for registration,[16] (as the Act requires)

---

10 Companies Act 1985, ss 56 to 65 and Sch 3, prospectively repealed by Financial Services Act 1986, s 212 (3) and Sch 17, Part I. For the obligatory contents of prospectives under the Companies Act 1985, see the fifth edition of this book, pp 273 to 285.

11 Companies Act 1985, ss 67 to 69 and s 71, prospectively repealed by Financial Services Act 1986, s 212 (3) and Sch 17, Part I. For this liability see the fifth edition of this book, pp 316 to 319.

12 Financial Services Act 1986, ss 162 to 165.

13 Ibid, ss 166 to 168.

14 Ibid, s 166 (1) and (3).

15 See p 281, ante.

16 Financial Services Act 1986, s 159 (1) and s 160 (1).

and not when it is submitted to the Stock Exchange for approval.[17] However, the company, its directors and persons who authorise themselves to be named in the prospectus as directors or proposed directors of the company will not be liable as such, unless the company itself makes the offer of securities contained in or accompanying the prospectus, or authorises that offer to be made.[18] Since prospectuses may relate to offers for sale or other disposals of securities by substantial shareholders who acquired them as an investment,[19] this provision protects the company and its directors from liability, unless the company consents to or concurs in the issue of the prospectus when existing investors market securities held by them.

A director or proposed director of the company which issues or has issued the securities to which the prospectus or supplementary prospectus relates will not be liable as such to pay compensation if the prospectus is subject to the rules of an investment exchange approved by the Secretary of State for Trade and Industry, and the Secretary of State has directed that prospectuses in respect of securities which have been admitted to dealings on that exchange, or for which an admission to dealings has been sought, shall be subject to those rules as a matter of law instead of the rules made by the Secretary of State as to the obligatory contents of prospectuses, and the exchange has certified that the director or proposed director should not be liable as such 'by reason of his having an interest, or of any circumstances, making it inappropriate for him to be responsible' for the prospectus because of his directorship.[20] It would seem that the power to confer exemptions from liability will be used by approved investment exchanges in circumstances where the director concerned would have a defence to a claim for compensation if the prospectus had been subject to the rules made by the Secretary of State for prospectuses in general, and also where the director holds a part-time appointment or has no substantial financial interest in the company, and was therefore not in a strong position to determine the form and contents of the prospectus.

The remaining exceptions and modifications to the statutory liability of persons responsible for prospectuses are the same as those in respect of listing particulars, except that there will be no equivalent to the exemption from liability of directors or proposed directors of the company which issues or has issued the securities when they are international debt securities normally dealt in only by persons experienced in transactions in them (ie banks and financial institutions).[1]

Defences to statutory claims for compensation

The defences which may be pleaded to a statutory claim for compensation because of a defective prospectus will be substantially the same as the defences which may be relied on to defeat a statutory claim for compensation for loss resulting from misstatements in, or omissions from, listing particulars. Where the defendant relies on the statutory defence that he reasonably believed that the statement complained of was true and not misleading, or that the matter whose omission is complained of was properly omitted from the prospectus, that belief must have existed at the time when the prospectus or supplementary prospectus was delivered to the Registrar of Companies for registration, and one of the other alternative acts or events necessary to complete the defence must subsequently have occurred.[2] These

---

17 Ibid, s 168 (1).
18 Ibid, s 168 (2).
19 Ibid, s 160 (3).
20 Ibid, s 168 (5).
 1 Ibid, s 152 (5).
 2 Ibid, s 167 (1).

alternative acts or events are the same as when this defence is relied on to defeat a compensation claim made in respect of listing particulars.[3] However, the final alternative event on which the defendant may rely is that the securities were acquired by the claimant after such a lapse of time that the defendant ought reasonably to be excused, but if the securities are dealt in on an approved investment exchange, such a lapse of time cannot be considered as having occurred before the commencement of dealings in those securities on that exchange.[4] This last element of the defence, which depends on the lapse of time since the prospectus was registered, assists to some extent in ascertaining how long after the issue of a prospectus a subscriber or purchaser of securities may rely on it and claim compensation if it was untrue or misleading or omitted material information. It would seem, however, that it is for the defendant to satisfy the court that the lapse of time made the claimant's reliance on the prospectus unreasonable, and the claimant need not prove as part of his case that he acquired the securities within a reasonable time after the prospectus was registered.

The same differences exist between the matters which have to be proved by the defendant who is sued for compensation in respect of misstatements in a prospectus when the defendant relies on the defence that the statement complained of was made by, or on the authority of, an expert and with his consent, that at the time the prospectus was registered the defendant reasonably believed that the expert was competent to make or authorise the statement, and that one of the alternative acts or events mentioned above subsequently occurred, as compared with the same defence when pleaded in respect of listing particulars.[5]

The remaining defences which can be pleaded to a statutory claim for compensation in respect of a prospectus are that:

(a) before the securities were acquired a correction was properly published; or

(b) although an expert to whom a statement in the prospectus was attributed was not competent to make it or had not consented to the inclusion of it in the prospectus, the fact that this was so was properly published before the plaintiff acquired securities under the prospectus, or

(c) the defendant took all reasonable steps to secure such a publication and reasonably believed that publication had taken place; or

(d) the statement complained of was made by an official person, or was contained in a public official document, and was accurately reproduced in the prospectus; or

(e) the plaintiff acquired the securities with knowledge that the statement complained of was false or misleading, or that the plaintiff acquired them with knowledge of the matter omitted, or in the case of a supplementary prospectus, with knowledge of the change or new matter which called for its publication.[6]

These defences are exactly the same as the corresponding defences which may be relied on by a defendant who is responsible for listing particulars which contain misstatements or omit material information.[7] Likewise, if a statutory claim for compensation is brought against a person who fails to procure the issue and delivery of a supplementary prospectus for registration when this is required, he may rely on the defence that he reasonably believed that the change in the matter contained

3   See p 287, ante.
4   Financial Services Act 1986, s 167 (1).
5   Ibid, s 167 (2).
6   Ibid, s 167 (3) to (5).
7   Ibid, s 151 (3) to (5) (see p 290, ante).

in the prospectus, or the new matter which had arisen, was not of such significance as to call for a supplementary prospectus;[8] this corresponds exactly to the similar defence which a person who is responsible for listing particulars may rely on when he is sued for compensation for his failure to deliver supplementary listing particulars, or to supply information to facilitate their registration.[9]

8 Ibid, s 167 (6).
9 Ibid, s 151 (6) (see p 291, ante).

CHAPTER 9

Allotment, payment of the issue price and membership

CONTRACTS TO SUBSCRIBE FOR SHARES, DEBENTURES AND LOAN SECURITIES

The contract by which a subscriber or investor agrees to take a certain number of shares, debentures or other securities of a company, and the company or the merchant bank, corporate finance subsidiary of a commercial bank or other intermediary which attends to marketing the securities agrees that they shall be allotted or sold to him, is subject to the ordinary rules of the law of contract as modified by the Companies Act 1985, as amended.

When the contract is made

Invitation, offer and acceptance

When shares, debentures or loan securities are offered for subscription or sale by listing particulars or a prospectus, the issuer of the document, whether the company or an intermediary merely invites investors to subscribe or purchase the securities. The listing particulars or prospectus do not contain an offer which investors can accept, because it does not contain all the terms of the proposed contract, as an offer must do. The identity of the applicants for the securities is still unknown, and it is not known how many shares or other securities they will apply for. It is the application made by an applicant to the company or to the intermediary who is marketing the securities for a particular number of shares or other securities which is the offer, and a contract is concluded only when the company or intermediary accepts the offer by allotting the shares or securities applied for, and notifies the investor that it has done so.[1]

Lapse and revocation

An application for shares, debentures or other loan securities, like any other offer, lapses unless it is accepted within a reasonable time, and it may be revoked by the applicant at any time before it is accepted.[2] Conversely, the application may be accepted by the company or other intermediary who issues the invitation to make applications for the securities at any time after the invitation is made and before it lapses. But by a statutory provision, which will be repealed when the new statutory

---

1 *Re Oriental Commercial Bank, Alabaster's Case* (1868) LR 7 Eq 273; *Re Peruvian Rlys Co, Robinson's Case* (1869) 4 Ch App 322. *Re Metropolitan Fire Insurance Co, Wallace's Case* [1900] 2 Ch 671. But if the acceptance is communicated by post, it is effective as soon as the letter is posted, and it is immaterial that the letter never reaches the applicant (*Household Fire and Carriage Accident Insurance Co v Grant* (1879) 4 ExD 216).
2 *Ramsgate Victoria Hotel Co v Montefiore* (1866) LR 1 Exch 109.

rules relating to prospectuses comes into force,[3] if a prospectus is issued generally, that is, to persons who are not existing members or debenture holders of the company,[4] applications may not be accepted by the company, or in the case of an offer for sale, by the intermediary who issues the prospectus, and shares or other securities to which the prospectus relates may not be allotted to applicants, until the third day after the day on which the prospectus is first issued, or until such later day as is specified in the prospectus as the date on which the subscription lists for the issue will open. The day on which the prospectus is first issued means the day on which it is first issued to persons who are not existing members or debenture holders of the company.[4] If it is issued as a newspaper advertisement, the prospectus is deemed to be first issued when the first newspaper advertisement containing it is published.[5] If shares or other securities are allotted before the date when the subscription lists should open, the allotment is valid, but the company, or the intermediary who issues the prospectus, and their respective officers who are responsible, are punishable by a fine.[6] This statutory provision compulsorily deferring the earliest date for allotments under a prospectus does not apply when listing particulars are published in connection with an application for the official listing of the securities on the Stock Exchange, the repeal of the relevant statutory provision having already taken effect in relation to them.[7]

Under provisions of the Companies Act 1985, which will be repealed when the new statutory rules relating to prospectuses come into force, an application for shares, debentures or other loan securities made under a prospectus issued generally cannot be revoked until the fourth day after the opening of the subscription lists, unless in the meantime a person who could be sued for compensation for false statements in the prospectus has given public notice that it was issued without his consent or that he withdraws his consent to its issue in order to avoid his liability to pay such compensation.[8] As the company or intermediary who invited applications for securities by publishing the prospectus will have accepted an application long before it becomes revocable under this provision, its practical effect is that applications under prospectuses issued generally are irrevocable in the absence of such a notice published by a person responsible for the prospectus repudiating liability under it. This provision, too, does not apply if applications for securities are made in response to listing particulars published in connection with an application for the official listing of the securities concerned.[7]

The reasons why the Companies Act 1985 established a timetable for opening the subscription lists and revoking applications when a prospectus (other than listing particulars) is issued generally are twofold. The delay between the issue of the prospectus and the opening of the subscription lists is imposed to give investors an opportunity to weigh the merits of the securities offered, to read the often informative comments of financial journalists in the press, and to obtain professional advice from their stockbrokers. The second period of delay, on the revocation of applications made under the prospectus, is imposed to render ineffective, or at least more hazardous, one abuse of a practice known as 'stagging'. A stag is an applicant for securities under a prospectus who does not intend to retain and pay for the

3 Companies Act 1985, s 82 (1) and (2), prospectively repealed by Financial Services Act 1986, s 212 (3) and Sch 17, Part I.
4 Companies Act 1985, s 744.
5 Ibid, s 82 (3).
6 Ibid, s 82 (5).
7 Financial Services Act 1986, s 212 (3) and Sch 17, Part I; Financial Services Act 1986 (Commencement) (No 3) Order 1986 (SI 1986/2246), art 5 and Sch 4.
8 Companies Act 1985, s 82 (7), prospectively repealed by Financial Services Act 1986, s 212 (3) and Sch 17, Part I.

securities he applies for, but intends instead to sell them as soon as they have been allotted to him and to reimburse himself for the amounts paid on application and allotment out of the price paid by the purchaser of the securities. If the securities go to a premium on the market, that is, if the price at which they can be sold there when dealings commence exceeds the amount which applicants have already paid to the company or intermediary, the stag will be able to make a profit by selling. He will only have paid the company or intermediary the amount payable on application and allotment at most, and so he will not be greatly out of pocket.[9] Because of this he may have applied for more of the securities than he could possibly hope to pay for, and he will rely on selling them immediately in order to avoid being called on to do so. A stag's activities are profitable, of course, only if the securities go to a market premium on the market. If the securities go to a market discount, that is, if the price at which dealings in them first take place on the market is lower than the amount so far paid up on them, the stag stands to suffer a loss, but formerly he could protect himself against this by revoking his application for the securities before it was accepted. The opening price on the market (that is, the price at which the securities will be saleable immediately after dealings in the securities begin) is fairly accurately known by the day before allotment takes place, and this gave the stag his opportunity to withdraw if he was likely to suffer a loss.

It was a grave inconvenience for companies to have issues of their securities well subscribed, only to be met with revocations just before the subscription lists opened. This inconvenience was relieved by the Companies Act 1985, making applications irrevocable for a sufficient length of time to enable the company or intermediary to accept them, and so if the securities applied for are allotted as soon as the subscription lists open and letters of allotment are posted to applicants immediately, stag applicants have no opportunity to revoke their applications. This protection is not available to the company or intermediary if the prospectus takes the form of listing particulars, and allotments may then take place lawfully at any time after the listing particulars are published, although the date when the subscription lists will open is always specified in the particulars and the company would be held contractually to that date,[10] despite the fact that applicants would be at liberty to revoke their applications at any time.

Invitation of tenders

It has recently become increasingly common for prospectuses and other offer documents to invite subscriptions for ordinary shares, not at a price fixed by the prospectus or offer document, but at a price tendered by the investor, being not less than a minimum specified in the prospectus or other invitation. The prices tendered by applicants will, of course, differ, and the company will allot the available shares to applicants who tender the highest price, and then to those who tender the next highest, and so on until all the shares are absorbed. The penalty for tendering too low a price, therefore, is exclusion from any allotment, and each investor is encouraged to tender what is likely to be the price at which dealings in the shares will begin on the market, for it is the market's collective estimate of the value of the

9 Often stags sell securities without paying the amount due on allotment, leaving it to the purchaser to pay this. If the company does not clear applicants' cheques for the amounts payable on application until after allotments have been made, and the stag sells immediately after allotment, he can avoid being out of pocket at all by paying the price received from the person to whom he sells the securities into his own bank account before his cheque for the amount payable on application is presented.

10 The reason for this is that the company specifies in the listing particulars the manner in which it will accept offers made by applicants to subscribe for the securities, and it cannot accept those offers in any other way (*Financings Ltd v Stimson* [1962] 3 All ER 386, [1962] 1 WLR 1184, CA).

shares which determines the minimum acceptable tender price. The value to the company of inviting tenders is that it invariably obtains a better issue price than if it were to fix the price itself, and the profit which stags obtain by selling shares at more than the amount paid up on them when dealings begin goes to the company instead.[11] An optimistic investor may, of course, tender too high a price, and he will then find that the market price of his share is lower than the issue price he has to pay the company. Usually, however, any inequality in the issue price payable by different allottees is avoided by the prospectus or offer document providing that all allotments will be made at the same minimum tendered price at which all the shares would be taken up. This is no doubt desirable to ensure equality of treatment, but it has the unfortunate result of encouraging investors to submit multiple applications at inflated tender prices to ensure that they are allotted all the shares they want, and it is left to the institutional investors, who are always conservative in estimating the likely opening price for the shares, to tender the real market value of the shares at which all allotments will actually be made.

To ensure that the arrangements for dealing with tenders invited by a prospectus are fair and that applicants are treated on an equal basis, the Stock Exchange requires such arrangements to be submitted to it for its approval when a listing is sought.[12]

Letters of rights

If shares or debentures are offered to existing members or to existing debenture or debt security holders by a letter of rights, the letter itself is an offer, and the contract is made by the recipient notifying the company that he accepts the securities offered to him.[13] If the letter of rights takes the form of a provisional letter of allotment, no notification of acceptance by the recipient is normally necessary,[14] and as soon as he shows by his acts that he accepts the securities (eg by paying an instalment of the issue price or renouncing the letter of allotment to another person), the contract is complete. If an open offer is made to members or to debenture or debt security holders, the offer is, of course, a mere invitation to them to apply for the securities in question. An open offer, unlike a letter of rights, does not specify how many shares or debt securities each recipient may take, and so an offer is made only when a recipient of the invitation applies for a definite number of the securities, and the contract for allotment is complete only when the company accepts his offer and notifies him of its acceptance.[15]

Unconditional acceptance of applications

An application for shares, debentures or other securities must be accepted unconditionally or not at all. Thus, if an applicant applies for shares which are to be credited as fully paid, the company cannot accept by allotting him shares which

---

11 A J Merrett, M Howe and G D Newbould in their *Equity Issues and the London Capital Market* (1967), pp 113 and 140, calculated that in 1963 the average fraction of the proceeds of marketing ordinary shares by tender which was spent in meeting the costs of the issue amounted to 6·4 per cent as against 7·1 per cent in the case of offers for sale and 7·6 per cent in the case of placings; in 1963 the quoted price of the shares on the day following that on which dealings began was on average 3·5 per cent in excess of the issue price when the issue was by tender, 18·9 per cent in excess when the issue was by offer for sale, and 23·2 per cent in excess when the issue was by placing. These percentages are unlikely to have changed substantially since 1963.
12 The Stock Exchange *Admission of Securities to Listing* Section 1, Chapter 3, para 1.4.
13 *Re New Eberhardt Co, ex p Menzies* (1889) 43 ChD 118 at 126.
14 See p 240, ante.
15 See p 240 and 241, ante.

are only partly paid.[16] If the company allots partly paid shares, it makes a counter-offer which the applicant may accept or reject, but if the applicant keeps the document issued by the company showing him to be the holder of the shares and allows his name to appear on the register of members, he will be deemed to have accepted the counter-offer and will be a member in respect of those shares.[17] Likewise, if an applicant applies for shares on condition that the company agrees to take certain of its supplies from him, the company may only accept the application if it agrees to the condition, and an allotment without agreeing to the condition is ineffective.[18]

If an issue is very successful, it may be over-subscribed several times, and the company or intermediary employed to market the shares will then have to ration the available shares or other securities amongst the applicants. Usually preference is given to existing members and employees of the company, or to existing debenture or debt security holders if the invitation relates to a further issue of such securities, and applicants for small amounts of securities as compared with applicants for larger amounts. The usual scheme is to satisfy applications by members and employees, or in the case of an issue of debentures or other debt securities, applications by existing debenture holders, in full up to a certain amount, to satisfy applications by outsiders in full up to a lesser amount, and then to allot a fraction of the amounts applied for in excess of those maxima, the fraction being larger for members and debenture holders than for outsiders. This has given rise to a practice by some applicants of sending in several applications in the names of their friends and relatives and also in fictitious names for small amounts of the securities offered, in the hope of getting a larger allotment than if they sent in one application for the total amount they want; to discourage multiple minute applications (which are expensive to process), companies and intermediaries often reject applications for securities below a certain minimum when an issue is over-subscribed. The Stock Exchange requires arrangements for the preferential treatment of applications to be submitted for its approval before the publication of the listing particulars or other invitation, and normally such arrangements must be limited to 10 per cent of the securities available for allotment and be exclusively for the benefit of existing shareholders and present or former employees of the company or its subsidiaries.[19]

If on an over-subscription of an issue of shares or debentures, a company or other intermediary allots fewer shares, debentures or other debt securities to an applicant than he has applied for, the allotment is not an unconditional acceptance of his application, and he is entitled to refuse to take the securities actually allotted to him. To overcome this difficulty, the application form issued with listing particulars or other invitation is always framed as an application for the number of shares or securities which the applicant wants, but he expressly agrees 'to accept that number or any smaller number in respect of which this application is accepted', thus enabling his application to be accepted by the allotment of a small number. The wording of the application form in this way also precludes an applicant refusing to accept the number of shares or securities allotted to him on the ground that other applicants for a similar number of securities have been treated preferentially and allotted proportionately more securities than he has. There is no possibility, it would appear, for implying a collateral contract between the company and

---

16 *Re Richmond Hill Hotel Co, Pellatt's Case* (1867) 2 Ch App 527; *Re United Ports and General Insurance Co, Wynne's Case* (1873) 8 Ch App 1002; Ibid, *Beck's Case* (1874) 9 Ch App 392; *Re Barangah Oil Refining Co, Arnot's Case* (1887) 36 ChD 702.
17 *Re Richmond Hill Hotel Co, Elkington's Case* (1867) 2 Ch App 511.
18 *Re Sunken Vessels Recovery Co, Wood's Case* (1858) 3 De G & J 85.
19 The Stock Exchange: *Admission of Securities to Listing.* Section 1, Chapter 3, para 1.2.

applicants that their respective applications shall be dealt with on a basis of equality or otherwise equitably.

Minimum subscription and integral subscription

If a prospectus offering shares is issued generally to persons other than existing members or debenture holders of a company,[20] and the prospectus does not take the form of listing particulars published in connection with an application for a listing on the Stock Exchange,[1] it must state the minimum amount of money which the directors consider must be raised by issuing those shares in order to pay the purchase price of any property which is to be paid out of the proceeds of the issue, the preliminary expenses of forming the company and the costs of the issue and commissions payable in connection with it, and the amounts needed to repay any loans made to the company to meet the foregoing expenses and to provide the company with working capital.[2] This minimum amount is known as the minimum subscription, and if the prospectus contains the first invitation which the company has made to the public to subscribe for its shares under which allotments are actually made,[3] none of the shares may be allotted until applications have been received for shares whose issue price (including any share premium payable) equals the minimum subscription and the amount payable on application for the shares has been received by the company.[4]

The purpose of this provision is to ensure that the company will raise adequate capital by its first issue of shares to give its undertaking some chance of success. Before the requirement of a minimum subscription was introduced by the Companies Act 1900, companies could allot shares offered to the public, even though so few had been subscribed for that the capital raised by issuing them would be sufficient only to pay the expenses of promoting the company, and would leave an inadequate amount with which to carry on its business. The inevitable result of this was either that the company was speedily wound up and its assets sold at a price which resulted in loss to its shareholders, or that the shareholders were compelled to contribute further capital in order to keep the company going. The statutory provision requiring a minimum subscription to be obtained does not necessarily prevent this from happening, but by requiring the company to state the amount of the minimum subscription, it does at least give intending investors an opportunity to judge whether that amount is adequate, and so in order to induce investors to subscribe at all, the company is compelled to fix the minimum subscription at a reasonable figure.

If the minimum subscription is not subscribed within 40 days after the first issue of the prospectus,[5] all money received from applicants for shares must be returned to them forthwith, and if the money is not returned within 48 days after the first

---

20 Companies Act 1985, s 744.
 1 Financial Services Act 1986, s 212 (3) and Sch 17, Part I; Financial Services Act 1986 (Commencement) (No 3) Order 1986 (SI 1986/2246), art 5 and Sch 4.
 2 Companies Act 1985, s 56 (1) and Sch 3, para 2.
 3 If the minimum subscription is not subscribed under the first prospectus issued by the company, and it later issues a second prospectus, the minimum subscription specified in that prospectus (which need not be the same amount as in the first prospectus) must be subscribed before allotments may be made, and it is immaterial that in the meantime the company has raised capital by placing shares by private negotiation.
 4 Companies Act 1985, s 83 (1) and (7).
 5 The date when the prospectus is first deemed to be issued is not defined, as it is for the purpose of the Companies Act 1985, s 82, but presumably it means the date on which it is first shown to anyone (except, possibly, an underwriter) in order to induce him to subscribe (*Nash v Lynde* [1929] AC 158). Normally in practice, the prospectus will first be issued when it appears as a newspaper advertisement.

issue of the prospectus, the directors of the company become personally and jointly and severally liable to repay the amounts received together with interest thereon at 5 per cent per annum, but a director may escape personal liability by showing that the company's failure to repay was not due to any misconduct or negligence on his part.[6] The applicant's right to sue for the return of his money accrues against the company on the fortieth day after the prospectus was issued, and against the directors on the forty-eighth day, and he has six years from those respective dates within which to sue.[7] If the company has wrongfully allotted shares to him despite the fact that the minimum subscription has not been subscribed, however, the applicant must rescind the allotment under the provisions dealt with below before he can sue the company or the directors for the return of his money,[8] and his right to sue will therefore accrue only when he does rescind.

If the company fails to comply with the law by allotting shares under a prospectus which should specify a minimum subscription but does not,[9] or by allotting shares when the specified minimum subscription has not been subscribed, or after 40 days from the first issue of the prospectus when the minimum subscription had not been subscribed by the fortieth day, the allottee may rescind the allotment within one month after it is made, and this is so even though the company has commenced to be wound up.[10] Whether he rescinds or not, the allottee may also sue any director who knowingly committed or authorised the irregularity for any loss which the allottee has suffered in consequence, but the action must be brought within two years after the allotment.[11] This right of action is particularly useful when the time for rescinding has expired, and if the shares are worthless, the result is that the directors will be compelled to repay the amount paid by the allottee to the company. It is curious that in such a situation the allottee has only two years within which to sue, whereas if the company had not allotted any shares to him, he could have sued the directors for the return of his money within six years. The company also may sue a director who knowingly committed or authorised the irregularity for any loss it has suffered, and its action, too, must be brought within two years after the allotment.[11]

The statutory rule requiring a minimum subscription for shares to be specified in the prospectus offering them and requiring that minimum subscription to be subscribed within a limited period will be repealed when the provisions of the Financial Services Act 1986, governing prospectuses other than listing particulars, are brought into force by ministerial order.[12]

The provisions in respect of the minimum subscription, even during the period they will remain in force, are not now of the same practical importance that they were formerly. This is because companies under present practice usually underwrite the whole of an issue of securities offered to the public, whether they are shares or debentures. If an issue of shares is underwritten, the company can confidently fix its minimum subscription as high as it likes, because even if the response from the public is poor, the underwriters may be called to take up the remaining shares, and this will ensure that the minimum subscription is subscribed. The same result follows if shares are offered for sale by a merchant bank, the corporate finance subsidiary of a commercial bank or any other intermediary, or if shares are placed by them or by sponsoring brokers/dealers. In the contract with the company the

---

6 Companies Act 1985, s 83 (4) and (5).
7 Limitation Act 1980, s 9 (1) (24 Halsbury's Statutes (4th Edn) 656).
8 *Burton v Bevan* [1908] 2 Ch 240.
9 *Roussell v Burnham* [1909] 1 Ch 127.
10 Companies Act 1985, s 85 (1).
11 Ibid, s 85 (2) and (3).
12 Financial Services Act 1986, s 212 (3) and Sch 17, Part I.

intermediary will probably agree to take up the shares in any event, so that the subscription of the whole issue is guaranteed before it is even offered to the public. For this reason the provisions of the Companies Act 1985 relating to the minimum subscription can have no practical application to an offer for sale or placing (other than a placing on a best efforts basis), but as a formality it is still necessary to state the minimum subscription in the prospectus.[13]

In addition to its requirement that the minimum subscription must be subscribed before allotment, the Companies Act 1985 contains an additional and quite independent rule that if a public company offers shares for subscription (whether they are to be wholly or partly paid up in cash or otherwise), no allotment may be made unless all the shares offered are subscribed, or unless the offer states expressly that if they are not fully subscribed, the company may nevertheless allot the number of shares which have been subscribed, provided any conditions specified in the offer have been fulfilled (eg as to the minimum number of shares which must be subscribed).[14] This rule differs in several ways from the one calling for a minimum subscription before any shares are allotted. The present rule applies to all offers of shares that are not only offers to the public, and it applies whether the consideration to be given for the shares is a cash or non-cash consideration.[15] Consequently, the rule applies to rights offers made to existing shareholders of the company (whether in fulfilment of their preferential right to subscribe or not); it also applies to takeovers and other bids for the shares of another company in exchange for an issue of shares of the offeror company; and it applies when an application has been made to the Stock Exchange for the shares comprised in the offer to be officially listed.[16] The present rule also differs from the minimum subscription rule in that it can be contracted out of by the offer providing that such number of shares as are in fact subscribed (if less than the number offered) will be allotted.[17]

If a public company allots shares before the whole of the shares offered or such minimum number of them as the offer specifies have been subscribed, or if the whole of the shares or that minimum number of them is not subscribed within 40 days after the offer is made, the company must return all money or other consideration received from applicants, and if it does not do so within 48 days after the offer is made, the directors of the company become personally liable to make restitution with interest at 5 per cent per annum on the amount or value of the consideration received.[18] Furthermore, any allottee of shares in those circumstances may rescind the allotment to him within one month after it takes place, and may do so even if the company has meanwhile gone into liquidation.[19] Any director of the company who knowingly contravenes the prohibition on allotment may be sued by the company or the allottee within two years after the allotment for compensation for any consequential loss.[20]

---

13 Companies Act 1985, s 56 (1) and s 58 (2) and Sch 3, para 2.
14 Ibid, s 84 (1).
15 Ibid, s 84 (1) and (4).
16 This is because the rule is not repealed by the Financial Services Act 1986, s 212 (3) and Sch 17, Part I.
17 The Companies Act 1985, s 84 (6) invalidates waivers of the requirement by the terms of the offer, but this is ineffective, because the requirement can be waived by the offer stating that the number of shares applied for will be allotted in any event.
18 Companies Act 1985, s 84 (2) and (3).
19 Ibid, s 85 (1).
20 Ibid, s 85 (2) and (3).

Listing on a stock exchange

If a prospectus, whether issued generally or not, states that an application has been or will be made for the shares or debentures offered thereby to be admitted to listing on any stock exchange,[1] any allotment made under the prospectus is void if the application is not made to the stock exchange before the third day after the first issue of the prospectus,[2] or if the application is refused within the three weeks following the closing of the subscription lists,[3] or within such longer period, not exceeding six weeks, as the stock exchange notifies to the company.[4] This provision does not apply if the prospectus takes the form of listing particulars in connection with an application for the official listing of the securities on the Stock Exchange.[5] As indicated in the preceding chapter, draft listing particulars must be approved by the Stock Exchange before they are published, and so there is no possibility of an application for a listing being made after publication of the relevant listing particulars.[6] Furthermore, the refusal of a listing does not invalidate allotments made in response to applications made under listing particulars, unless they made it a condition of allotment that a listing shall be obtained. In practice this presents no difficulty, because a listing for securities is usually granted at the same time as, or shortly after, the Stock Exchange approves the draft listing particulars.[6] It would appear that the statutory provision invalidating allotments if a listing is not applied for or is refused does not apply if the prospectus states that an application has or will be made for shares, debentures or other securities offered by it to be admitted to the Unlisted Securities Market or the Third Market, because the application is then not for a listing. Consequently, the statutory provision applies, it would seem, only when a prospectus is issued in respect of securities for which a listing application has been or will be made to an overseas stock exchange.

If an allotment does become void or impossible owing to the company's failure to apply for a stock exchange listing of the securities concerned or owing to the stock exchange's refusal of the company's application, all money received from applicants for the shares, debentures or other securities must forthwith be returned to them, and if it is not returned within eight days after the allotment becomes void or impossible, the directors also become personally and jointly and severally liable to repay it together with interest at 5 per cent from the eighth day, but a director may escape personal liability by proving that the company's failure to repay the money was not due to any misconduct or negligence on his part.[7] While any money received from applicants may have to be returned to them by the company, it must be kept in a separate bank account.[8] Because of this, the applicants' money remains their property and the company holds it as a trustee for them.[9] Consequently, other

---

1 That is, an official listing as distinct from permission for the securities to be dealt in on a stock exchange without being listed on it.
2 See footnote 5, on p 297, ante.
3 A prospectus issued generally must state when the subscription lists will be opened (Companies Act 1985, Sch 3, para 3 (1)), but need not state when they will close (ie the latest time by which applications for the securities offered must reach the company or issuing house). In practice, however, this time is always stated, and is always the same day as the one on which the subscription lists open.
4 Companies Act 1985, s 86 (1) and (2).
5 Financial Services Act 1986, s 212 (3) and Sch 17, Part I; Financial Services Act 1986 (Commencement) (No 3) Order 1986 (SI 1986/2246), art 5 and Sch 4.
6 See p 262, ante.
7 Companies Act 1985, s 86 (4) and (5).
8 Companies Act 1985, s 86 (6).
9 *Re Nanwa Gold Mines Ltd, Ballantyne v Nanwa Gold Mines Ltd* [1955] 3 All ER 219, [1955] 1 WLR 1080.

persons who have claims enforceable against the company's property, such as judgment creditors or mortgagees or debenture or debt security holders, cannot claim the money, but must allow it to be returned to the applicants if they are entitled to demand its repayment by the company.[9]

If a prospectus offering shares or debentures for sale is issued by a merchant bank, the corporate finance subsidiary of a commercial bank or any other intermediary, and it states that an application has been, or will be, made to a stock exchange for the securities concerned to be listed, the same provisions apply as if the prospectus were issued by the company itself, but if the permission is not applied for or is refused, only the contracts between the intermediary and the applicants for the securities are avoided,[10] so that the intermediary still has to take the securities from the company itself,[11] and the intermediary alone becomes liable to repay the money paid by applicants.[12] While there is any possibility of money paid by applicants having to be returned to them, the issuing house or intermediary must keep it in a separate bank account,[13] and it remains the applicants' property.

The foregoing provisions, which already do not apply where an appplication for the listing of the shares, debentures or other securities in question is made to the Stock Exchange, will also cease to apply when made or to be made to any other stock exchange, but this will be so only when the provisions are fully repealed on the making of a ministerial order bringing the provisions of the Financial Services Act 1986 relating to prospectuses into force.[14] When an application for a listing of the securities is made to the Stock Exchange, an intermediary which offers the securities for sale must give an irrevocable authority to the bank employed to receive application moneys empowering it to appropriate the money received from applicants toward satisfying the intermediary's liability for the price which it agreed to pay the company,[15] so that there is no risk in any event of persons having claims against the intermediary being able to resort to the money paid by applicants.[16]

Underwriting

An underwriter agrees for a commission to subscribe for or purchase shares, debentures or other securities offered by a company, a merchant bank, a corporate finance subsidiary of a commercial bank, a firm of broker/dealers or any other intermediary if the public or the persons initially invited to subscribe for or purchase the securities do not do so. If the public or the persons initially invited take all the securities offered, the underwriter's liability is at an end. He cannot be called upon to take up the securities if the allottees fail to pay for them, whether they are forfeited by the company or not. If the public or the persons initially invited to subscribe for or purchase the securities only take up some of them, the underwriter must take up the remainder, but if there are several underwriters for different parts of the issue, their underwriting agreement usually provide that each

10 Companies Act 1985, s 87 (1) and (2).
11 For this reason, the contract between the company and the intermediary is always made conditional on the listing being granted by the appropriate stock exchange in order to avoid the intermediary having unsaleable securities left on its hands.
12 Companies Act 1985, s 87 (3).
13 Ibid, s 87 (4).
14 Financial Services Act 1986, s 212 (3) and Sch 17, Part I.
15 The Stock Exchange: *Admission of Securities to Listing*, Section 2, Chapter 1, para 5.14.
16 Consequently, if an intermediary concurrently offers the securities of two companies for sale, and a stock exchange refuses a listing for the securities of one of the companies, the applicants for those securities cannot obtain repayment of the money they have paid out of the money paid by applicants for securities of the other company.

underwriter shall only be obliged to take up his proportion of the remaining securities.[17]

An underwriting agreement is usually made by the underwriter signing a letter in a standard form addressed to the company or the intermediary engaged to market the securities. In the letter the underwriter agrees to subscribe for a certain number of the shares or other securities which are to be offered to the public or the defined class of prospective subscribers by listing particulars or some other offer document a draft of which he has seen, and the letter goes on to provide that applications received from the public or the class of persons to whom the offer is addressed are to go in relief of the underwriters, that is to say, the underwriters shall only be obliged to take up that part of the issue which the public or the primary invitees do not subscribe or purchase.[18] The letter is an offer by the underwriter, and an underwriting agreement does not come into being until the company or marketing intermediary accepts the offer and notifies the underwriter that it has done so.[1] In certain cases, however, it may not be necessary for the company or the intermediary to notify its acceptance. This is so where the number of shares or other securities underwritten is not subject to variation, and the underwriter intends that the company shall accept his offer by proceeding with the invitation to the public or the primary invitees.[2] But if the underwriter agrees to underwrite a certain number of shares or securities, or such less number as the company thinks fit, the company must notify its acceptance in order that the underwriter shall know the extent of his liability.[3] Even when it is necessary for the company to notify its acceptance, it need not do so before the result of the invitation to the public or primary invitees is known,[3] provided that the notification is sent within a reasonable time thereafter.

An underwriting letter often empowers the company or intermediary to vary the terms of the draft listing particulars or other offer document on which it is based before the offer is issued to the public or the primary invitees. This does not entitle the company or intermediary to alter the terms on which the shares or securities are offered, however, nor to alter the particulars or offer document in any other way which materially increases the risk borne by the underwriter.[4] Thus, where a company altered its draft prospectus by reducing the minimum subscription from £15,000 to £100, and by stating that the company might pay for the business it was acquiring by instalments out of the proceeds of successive issues of shares instead of by a lump sum out of the proceeds of the first issue, as originally provided, it was held that the company had exceeded its rights under a power in the underwriting agreement to vary the terms of the draft prospectus, and so the underwriter was released from his obligations.[4] The safest course when negotiating

17 Underwriters invariably underwrite a particular number of shares or debentures, and not a particular percentage of the whole issue. The fraction of the securities not taken up by the public which each underwriter must take is then obtained by dividing the number of shares or debentures he has underwritten by the total number of shares or debentures underwritten by all the underwriters. If the whole issue has not been underwritten, however, an underwriter cannot be required to take up more securities than he has underwritten.

18 Securities underwritten 'firm' (see p 326, post) are deemed to be taken by the public, so that the securities to be taken up by other underwriters are correspondingly fewer; consequently, when calculating the number of securities to be taken by each underwriter, securities underwritten 'firm' are not included in the total number underwritten (*Sydney Harbour Collieries Ltd v Earl Grey* (1898) 14 TLR 373).

1 *Re Consort Deep Level Gold Mines Ltd, ex p Stark* [1897] 1 Ch 575.

2 *Re Bultfontein Sun Diamond Mines Ltd* (1896) 12 TLR 461.

3 *Re Henry Bentley & Co and Yorkshire Breweries Ltd, ex p Harrison* (1893) 69 LT 204; *Re Hemp, Yarn and Cordage Co, Hindley's Case* [1896] 2 Ch 121 at 135.

4 *Warner International and Overseas Engineering Co Ltd v Kilburn, Brown & Co* (1914) 84 LJKB 365.

underwriting contracts is to specify the variations which may be made in the draft listing particulars or offer document (eg enabling the company or issuing marketing intermediary to fix the issue price of the securities offered within specified limits without having to obtain the underwriters' approval), or to permit variations to be made to the draft only in order to correct or supplement the factual information given there provided the variations are not material, or more restrictively, to permit variations only with the consent of the underwriters.

Under the usual form of underwriting agreement, the company or marketing intermediary is entitled to allot to the underwriter the securities which he is obliged to take up without receiving any further application from him. But the legal position may be that if the underwriter refuses to accept the securities before they are allotted to him, the company or marketing intermediary cannot allot them, and its only remedy is to sue him for damages for breach of contract.[5] For this reason underwriting letters always empower a director or some other agent of the company or marketing intermediary to apply on the underwriter's behalf for the allotment to him of the securities for which he is responsible, and the power to apply and the company's or the intermediary's right to allot is expressed to be irrevocable. It has been held that such a power is irrevocable in law, whether expressed to be so or not, because in reality it is given to the company or to the intermediary itself, even if it is expressed to be given to a director or other agent, and the power is coupled with an interest vested in the company or intermediary, namely, its interest in disposing of all the securities comprised in the issue.[6] Consequently, if an application is made in the underwriter's name by the authorised director or agent, the company or the intermediary may accept it despite the underwriter's refusal to take the securities, and the securities will then be effectively issued to him.

Sometimes instead of taking an authority from the underwriter to apply for shares or debentures in his name, the company or marketing intermediary takes an application form signed by him for the maximum number of shares or other securities which he may be called on to take, or such less number of shares or securities as the company may see fit to allot to him under the terms of the underwriting agreement. If the prospectus offering the shares or securities is issued to the public generally, it may be argued that the application signed by the underwriter is made 'in pursuance' of the prospectus, and is therefore irrevocable until the fourth day after the subscription lists open except where the securities are offered by listing particulars,[7] and that the company and any marketing intermediary are therefore adequately protected while the relevant provision remains unrepealed.[8] It is doubtful, however, whether an underwriter's application is made 'in pursuance' of the prospectus; 'in pursuance' appears to mean 'in response to', and the underwriter's application is not made in response to the prospectus, but before the prospectus is issued or, often, even before its contents are finally settled.

---

5   This raises the general question whether any contract to take shares which have not been allotted at the date of the breach is specifically enforceable. There is no authority on the point, but if the cases decided on the similar situation created by breach of an executory contract to enter into a partnership are followed, specific performance will be refused. However, it would seem that underwriting agreements in respect of debentures are made specifically enforceable by the Companies Act 1985, s 195 (see p 470, post), and so the underwriter could not refuse to accept allotment.
6   *Re Hannan's Empress Gold Mining and Development Co, Carmichael's Case* [1896] 2 Ch 643.
7   Companies Act 1985, s 82 (1) (see p 304, ante).
8   The provision will be repealed when the provisions of the Financial Services Act 1986, brought into force by ministerial order relating to prospectuses are.

Sub-underwriting

Underwriting agreements usually require the underwriter either to take up the securities for which he is responsible himself, or to find some other suitable person or persons who will do so.[9] The underwriter can in practice relieve himself of the whole or part of his liability, therefore, by entering into sub-underwriting agreements with other persons by which, in return for a commission paid by him, they agree to underwrite a certain fraction of the securities which he has agreed to underwrite.[10] If the head underwriter is then called on by the company to take up some of the securities, he may, in turn, require the sub-underwriter to take allotment of his appropriate fraction of them. To protect the head underwriter against the sub-underwriter refusing to take the securities for which he is responsible, the sub-underwriting agreement should authorise the head underwriter to apply to the company in the sub-underwriter's name for the allotment of those securities, and this authority is usually irrevocable, whether expressed to be so or not, because of the head underwriter's interest in escaping from personal liability to pay for the securities, and so the company may effectively allot the securities to the sub-underwriter which he is committed to take despite his refusal to accept them.[11]

Subscribers of the memorandum

The subscribers of the company's memorandum of association are under both a contractual and a statutory obligation to take and pay for the number of shares set opposite their signatures at the end of the memorandum.[12] They must take their shares by allotment from the company,[13] and so it is not sufficient for them to accept a renunciation or transfer of shares which have been allotted to other persons.[14] On the other hand, if in the memorandum they undertake to take shares of a particular class, they may satisfy their statutory obligation by taking shares of another class, because the obligation is merely to take the number of shares written opposite the subscriber's signature, and a provision in the memorandum specifying how that obligation shall be fulfilled is ineffective.[15]

A subscriber of the memorandum of a public company must pay the company the nominal value of the shares for which he subscribes and any agreed issue premium in cash,[16] but it would seem to be possible for him to agree with the company after the incorporation that any amount which becomes due to him from it shall be appropriated in payment of the issue price of the shares. The requirement that the subscribers' shares shall be paid for in cash does not apply to a private

---

9 The suitability of a sub-underwriter depends on his financial soundness, and the company or marketing intermediary is often made the arbiter of this by the underwriting contract. If it is not, the question is one of fact, and the burden of proving that the nominated sub-underwriter is not financially reliable appears to rest on the company or intermediary.

10 Sub-underwriters invariably sub-underwrite a particular number of shares or other securities. Each sub-underwriter is then obliged to take up a fraction of the securities which the head underwriter is compelled to take from the company; the fraction is obtained by dividing the number of securities which the sub-underwriter has sub-underwritten by the total number of securities which the head underwriter has underwritten.

11 *Re Olympic Reinsurance Co* [1920] 2 Ch 341.

12 Companies Act 1985, s 22 (1); *Re F W Jarvis & Co Ltd* [1899] 1 Ch 193.

13 It has been held that on the incorporation of the company the subscribers' shares are automatically issued to them, but it was also accepted that they cannot deal with those shares until they have been allotted to them and their holdings entered in the register of members (*Dalton Time Lock Co v Dalton* (1892) 66 LT 704; *Re F W Jarvis and Co Ltd*, supra).

14 *Re South Blackpool Hotel Co, Migotti's Case* (1867) LR 4 Eq 238.

15 *Re New Buxton Lime Co, Duke's Case* (1876) 1 ChD 620.

16 Companies Act 1985, s 106.

company. Before the statutory rule that subscribers of the memorandum of a public company must pay for their shares in cash was introduced, it was held that such a subscriber who agreed with a company after its incorporation to pay for his shares by transferring property to the company and actually did so, could treat the shares allotted to him as taken in fulfilment of his obligation as a subscriber of the memorandum, and consequently he took them as fully paid shares.[17] Likewise, where a new company was formed to purchase an existing business for shares in the new company to be allotted to shareholders of the existing company, it was held that a shareholder of the existing company who subscribed the new company's memorandum for the number of shares to which he was entitled under the arrangement, satisfied his obligation to pay for them by concurring in the sale of the business which was the consideration for the allotment.[18] These cases are, of course, now relevant only in the case of a private company.

The subscriber of the memorandum remains liable to take his shares throughout the company's existence, and the obligation can be enforced against him even when the company is being wound up. The company cannot release him from his obligation,[19] and any surrender of his right to take the shares is ineffective unless he has already paid their nominal value to the company in full. But if the company issues the whole of its nominal capital to other persons, the subscriber is released from his obligation, because the company now has no shares which it can allot to him.[20] If any of the shares allotted to other persons are forfeited or surrendered for non-payment of calls, the subscriber cannot be compelled to take them up in fulfilment of his obligation, because this would require him to take the shares by way of purchase or re-issue from the company, and his obligation as a subscriber of the memorandum is to take shares from the company as their original holder.[20] On the other hand, if after issuing the whole of its original nominal capital to other persons, the company increases its capital so that it now has shares available for issue, the subscriber's obligation revives, and he can be called upon to take the shares for which he subscribed out of the additional capital.[1]

Return of allotments

Within one month after allotting any of its shares, whether on a first or later issue of capital, a company must make a return to the Registrar of Companies stating the number and nominal value of the shares allotted, the names and addresses of the allottees, the amount paid up on the shares in respect of capital and share premium, and the amount of any calls or instalments of the issue price due but unpaid.[2] If shares are allotted for a consideration other than cash, the return must show the number and nominal value of the shares so allotted, the extent to which they are credited as paid up and the consideration for which they were allotted.[2] There must also be delivered for registration a contract in writing between the company and the allottee providing for the allotment and any contract in writing between them which shows the consideration which the allottee has given, or is to give, for the shares,[2] or, if either of these contracts has been made orally, a notice in writing of the terms of the oral contract.[3] A public company which has allotted shares as wholly or partly paid up by a consideration other than cash must also

17 *Re Heyford Co, Pell's Case* (1869) 5 Ch App 11.
18 *Re China SS and Labuan Coal Co, Drummond's Case* (1869) 4 Ch App 772.
19 *Re London and Provincial Consolidated Coal Co* (1877) 5 ChD 525.
20 *Re Tal y Drws Slate Co, Mackley's Case* (1875) 1 ChD 247.
 1 *Re London, Hamburgh and Continental Exchange Bank, Evans' Case* (1867) 2 Ch App 427.
 2 Usually there is only one contract dealing with both matters.
 3 Companies Act 1985, s 88 (1) and (2).

deliver to the Registrar the report of the valuer appointed to make the statutory valuation of the consideration[4] when it makes a return in respect of the shares allotted.[5] The Registrar must publish in the London Gazette the delivery to him by a public company of a return of allotments and any valuer's report in respect of a consideration in kind for the allotment of the shares.[6]

If renounceable letters of allotment are issued when shares are allotted by a company,[7] or if provisional letters of allotment are issued in connection with a rights offer,[8] the Registrar of Companies will in practice accept a return of allotments made within one month after the date on which the letters of allotment cease to be renounceable, and the return will show as allottees the persons in whose names the shares will first be registered.

LETTERS OF ALLOTMENT AND RENUNCIATION, CALLS AND FORFEITURE

Letters of allotment and renunciation

Private companies often issue share certificates, debentures, or debenture stock or loan stock certificates to subscribers as soon as allotment has taken place, whether the whole of the issue price has been paid or any other consideration in return for issue has been received by the company or not.[9] This practice involves the inconvenience that if the issue price is not paid or satisfied in full on allotment, the share certificates, debentures, or debenture stock or loan stock certificates have to be enfaced with a note that a further instalment of the issue price has been paid each time this is done. Public companies and many private companies avoid this inconvenience by issuing letters of allotment in the first instance, and share certificates, debentures or debenture stock or loan stock certificates are issued only when the whole of the issue price has been paid, which is rarely more than a few months after allotment takes place. When instalments of the issue price are paid the letter of allotment is appropriately receipted, so that the amount paid up is apparent on inspection. The Companies Act 1985 requires share certificates and debentures (including debenture stock or loan stock certificates) to be issued within two months after allotment unless the terms of issue provide otherwise,[10] and so when letters of allotment will remain outstanding for longer than two months, the listing particulars or other offer document must state that share certificates, debentures, or debenture stock or loan stock certificates will not be issued until a later date. If shares or loan securities are allotted to a nominee of the Stock Exchange approved by the Secretary of State for Trade and Industry, however, it is in no case necessary for the company to issue a certificate in respect of the securities within two months, [11] but the nominee may, of course, call for a certificate

---

4 See p 156, ante.
5 Companies Act 1985, s 111 (1).
6 Ibid, s 711 (1)(f) and (m).
7 See next section of this chapter.
8 See p 240, ante.
9 This is because a private company's articles often impose some restriction on the transfer of its shares. If freely transferable letters of allotment were issued, no such restriction could be enforced.
10 Companies Act 1985, s 185 (1).
11 Ibid, s 185 (4).

any time the provisions of the company's articles or of the loan securities or the trust deed executed by the company in connection with them.[12]

Position of the holder of a letter of allotment

A subscriber for shares, debentures or loan securities becomes a shareholder or a holder of the other securities when the securities for which he has subscribed are allotted and issued to him. Allotment takes place when the directors of the company resolve that the amount of securities for which the subscriber has applied (or a less amount if there is an oversubscription) shall be apportioned to the subscriber out of the total number of securities available,[13] and in the case of a rights offer made by provisional letters of allotment this precedes the conclusion of the subscription contract by the subscriber accepting the offer. The issue of the securities occurs when the company sends a document to the subscriber indicating that the securities have been allotted to him and evidencing his title to them.[13] Such a document may be a share certificate, debenture or a certificate in respect of other loan securities (eg debenture or loan stock) or alternatively a letter of allotment, and with one exception, its despatch to the subscriber is effective to constitute the issue of the securities to him only if a subscription contract has already been concluded, or if the contract is concluded simultaneously with the despatch of the document, as it is when a letter of allotment is posted in response to an application under a prospectus.[14] The exception is where a provisional letter of allotment is sent to a shareholder or a holder of debentures or other loan securities in connection with a rights issue. Since the person to whom the provisional letter of allotment is addressed cannot be compelled to take the securities comprised in it, they cannot be treated as issued to him until he shows a clear intention to accept them (eg by paying the first instalment of the issue price or renouncing the letter of allotment), but it would appear that when he does this, the securities must be treated as issued to him at the moment of his acceptance, even though the provisional letter of allotment is not confirmed by the despatch of any later document by the company.

When shares or debentures are offered for sale or placed by a merchant bank, the corporate finance subsidiary of a commercial bank or by a firm of broker/ dealers to whom they have not already been both allotted and issued by the company, the issue of the securities occurs when the marketing intermediary despatches letters of acceptance to applicants for the securities. The contract between the company and the marketing intermediary under which the offer for sale or placing is made normally provides that the company allots or agrees to allot the whole of the securities in question to the intermediary and empowers it to despatch the documents evidencing the title of successful applicants to the securities apportioned to them.

When shares, debentures or other loan securities are issued, the addressee of the document evidencing his title to them becomes a holder of the shares or securities immediately, and has all the rights and is subject to all the liabilities of such a person. Consequently, he can be sued for calls or instalments of the issue price, and

---

12 Securities listed on the Stock Exchange may be vested in its nominee, SEPON Ltd, to facilitate dealings without the legal title to the securities being transferred to the purchaser immediately; the nominee then holds the securities as a bare trustee for the person in whom the beneficial title is vested for the time being (see p 395, post).

13 *Re Imperial Rubber Co, Bush's Case* (1874) 9 Ch App 554; *Re Ambrose Lake Tin and Copper Co, Clarke's Case* (1878) 8 ChD 635; *Mowatt v Castle Steel and Iron Works Co* (1886) 34 ChD 58; *Agricultural Mortgage Corpn v IRC* [1978] 1 All ER 248 at 260, per Goff LJ; *W T Ramsay Ltd v IRC* [1979] 3 All ER 213, [1979] 1 WLR 974.

14 *Household Fire and Carriage Accident Insurance Co v Grant* (1879) 4 ExD 216.

is entitled to be paid dividends or interest in the same way as a person whose name has been entered on the company's register of members or debenture holders.[15] If he has subscribed for debentures or other loan securities, he is also entitled to all the remedies of a debenture or loan security holder to recover the principal of the secured loan and interest thereon. But if he has subscribed for shares, he is not yet a member of the company, because his name has not yet been entered in the register of members,[16] and so he is not able to vote at meetings of members, unless the articles expressly empower him to do so.[17] On the other hand, he will be a contributory in the winding up of the company[18] if at that time it can still enforce its contractual right to payment of the issue price against him.[19]

A subscriber for shares has the right to insist on the company entering his name in the register of members when the date for the issue of his share certificate arrives; and he may enforce this right by applying to the court for an order that the register shall be rectified to include his name.[20] Similarly a subscriber for debentures or other loan securities may compel the company to enter his name on the register of debenture holders,[1] but this is, of course, of less importance to him than the corresponding entry is to a subscriber for shares. Furthermore, subscribers for both shares and debentures may apply to the court for an order requiring the company to deliver their share certificates, debentures or other loan securities to them when delivery becomes due under the terms of issue.[2] Surprisingly, it was held in one case[3] that a company has no corresponding right to insist on the name of a subscriber for shares who has received a renounceable letter of allotment being entered on the register of members, but this is inconsistent with a later decision,[4] and is probably wrong. To avoid doubt, application forms for shares and letters of allotment in respect of shares always authorise the company to enter the subscriber's name on the register of members if he or his renouncee does not apply to be registered. The point is really of little practical importance, for under the system of issuing shares now employed, it is always to the advantage of the holder of a

---

15 *McEuen v West London Wharves and Warehouses Co* (1871) 6 Ch App 655 at 661–2.

16 Companies Act 1985, s 22 (2).

17 Table A confers no right to vote on holders of letters of allotment, and the Companies Act 1985, s 370 (6) implies a term in all articles that only members may vote.

18 By the Insolvency Act 1986, s 79 (1) contributories are defined as 'every person liable to contribute to the assets of a company in the event of it being wound up.'

19 *Re Direct Birmingham, Oxford, Reading and Brighton Rly Co, ex p Capper* (1851) 20 LJ Ch 148 at 151, per Cranworth LC; *Re Pennant and Craigwen Mining Co, Fenn's Case* (1852) 1 Sm & G 26.

20 Companies Act 1985, s 359 (1) (see p 337, post).

 1 The remedy appears to be either a mandatory injunction (see *Re British Sugar Refining Co* (1857) 3 K & J 408), or an order for specific performance of the company's promise to maintain a proper register.

 2 Companies Act 1985, s 185 (6) and (7). The application is made to the Companies Court by originating summons (RSC Ord 102, r 2 (1)). If a company has a Stock Exchange listing for any of its securities, the Stock Exchange rules require its directors to issue certificates for securities within one month after the letters of allotment cease to be renounceable (Stock Exchange: *Admission of Securities to Listing*, Section 5, Chapter 2, para 28).

 3 *Re Asiatic Banking Corpn, ex p Collum* (1869) LR 9 Eq 236. The decision was based on earlier decisions that a company which had issued scrip in respect of shares could not register scripholders as members on its own initiative. Scrip merely gave the holder an option to become a member when he had paid the issue price in full (*McIlwraith v Dublin Trunk Connecting Rly Co* (1871) 7 Ch App 134 at 140), so that he obviously could not be compelled to become a member against his will. An applicant for shares, as distinct from scrip, on the other hand, clearly applies for membership of the company, and if the company issues a renounceable letter of allotment to him, it is difficult to see why it thereby loses its right to put him on the register of members.

 4 *McEuen v West London Wharves and Warehouses Co*, supra. In that case the company had actually entered the subscriber's name in its register of members, but that does not affect the principle involved.

fully paid letter of allotment to be entered in the register of members, and so a company is never likely to make the entry against his wishes.

The Companies Act 1985 contains a definition of the allotment of shares for the purposes of the Act, though not for other purposes. The Act provides that shares shall be taken to be allotted when a person acquires an unconditional right to be included in the company's register of members in respect of them.[5] It would seem that an allottee acquires such a right when the directors of the company resolve to allot shares to him, or if shares have been provisionally allotted to him, when he does an act showing that he accepts the shares, and it would appear to be immaterial that the allottee has not yet paid the whole of the issue price of the shares, unless his right to insist on his name being included in the register of members as holder of the shares is expressly made conditional on the issue price being paid in full. If shares are issued under listing particulars or any other offer document which states that renounceable letters of allotment will be issued, and that when all instalments of the issue price have been paid an application may be made by the person who then holds a letter of allotment to be registered as holder of the shares, the right of the allottee to be registered would appear to be unconditional as soon as the directors resolve to make an allotment to him, because the company could not resist a demand by him to be entered in its register of members immediately as the holder of partly paid shares.

Renunciation

A letter of allotment usually has printed on it a form of letter of renunciation and a registration application form.[6] The letter of renunciation is signed by the original allottee when he sells or disposes of the shares, debentures or other loan securities to which the letter of allotment relates; the letter of renunciation is addressed to the company and informs it that the allottee has renounced his rights in respect of the securities to the person who completes the registration application form which is also included in the letter of allotment. The registration application form, as its name implies, is an application by the person entitled to the letter of allotment when it ceases to be renounceable to have his name entered on the register of members or debenture holders as the registered holder of the securities, and to have a share certificate or debentures or loan security certificate issued to him. The letter of allotment may pass through several hands before the registration application form is completed by the ultimate renouncee and the letter of allotment is surrendered to the company. On the other hand, the original allottee may retain the letter of allotment, in which case he will complete the registration application form himself and surrender the letter of allotment. Although shares and debentures are transferable by renunciation of a letter of allotment, neither the letter nor the form of renunciation is liable to stamp duty if the letter is required to be surrendered for registration not later than six months after it is issued,[7] but stamp duty at the rate of 50p for each £100 or part of £100 of the consideration is payable on the renunciation of a letter of allotment (other than one expressed to be in favour of bearer) to a person who alone or together with persons connected with him controls

5 Companies Act 1985, s 738 (1).
6 For examples of letters of allotment, see 6 *Encyclopaedia of Forms and Precedents* (4th edn) 1439 and *Palmer's Company Precedents* (17th edn), Vol 1, p 157. Companies may alternatively issue letters of allotment to bearer, which are transferable by delivery and are presumably negotiable instruments. In practice this is rarely done.
7 Finance Act 1963, s 59 (1), inserting a new head of charge, 'Bearer Instrument' in the first Schedule to the Stamp Act 1891 and providing exemptions from stamp duty; see Exemptions, para 3 (41 Halsbury's Statutes (4th edn) 149, 176).

the company, or will have control of it when arrangements under which the renunciation is made (eg a takeover bid) are completed.[8] On an agreement being made to sell the securities comprised in a renounceable letter of allotment, however, stamp duty reserve tax at the rate of 50p for each £100 or part of £100 of the consideration is payable by the purchaser,[9] but the first sale of securities by a marketing intermediary who offers the securities for sale to the public is exempt from stamp duty reserve tax if the securities are, or are to be, officially listed on the Stock Exchange.[10]

A renounced letter of allotment is not a negotiable instrument, even though the form of renunciation has been signed by the allottee and the registration application form has not been completed. Clearly a letter of allotment in this condition could physically be delivered to any person, who could then procure his own registration as holder of the shares, and because of this the letter could be recognised by law as negotiable. In fact this has not happened, since the stock market has never treated renounced letters of allotment as negotiable instruments,[11] and the necessary mercantile usage for their recognition by the law as having that characteristic is lacking. On the other hand, letters of allotment in favour of bearer (like the now obsolete scrip in bearer form) probably would be negotiable,[12] but in practice companies do not issue such letters of allotment.

If the original allottee wishes to sell or dispose of only some of the shares, debentures or other loan securities to which the letter of allotment relates, he may renounce his right to those securities by completing the letter of renunication in respect of them, and may surrender it immediately to the company, which will issue two split letters of allotment, one to the renouncee for the securities he has acquired, and the other to the original allottee for the balance of the securities for which he subscribed.[13] Each split letter of allotment may then be further renounced or split, and the holder of an original or split letter of allotment who completes the registration application form which it contains when it ceases to be renounceable will be registered by the company in its register of members or debenture holders.

A letter of allotment always prescribes the latest dates on which it may be split or renounced, and provides that if a completed registration application form is not submitted to the company by a slightly later date, the original allottee will be entered as the registered holder of the securities in the company's register of members or debenture holders, and the share certificate, debentures or certificate for other loan securities will be issued to him.[14] No time limits are imposed on splitting or renunciation by the Stock Exchange, however, and so in theory letters of allotment may be made renounceable for as long as desired. In practice letters of allotment are not made renounceable for more than six months, because if they were renounceable for a longer period, in the case of shares they would be subject to stamp duty at the rate of 1·5 per cent of the issue price of the securities they

---

8　Finance Act 1985, s 81 (1) to (6) (41 Halsbury's Statutes (4th edn) 368).
9　Finance Act 1986, s 87 (1) to (3), s 88 (2) and (3) and s 99 (4) (41 Halsbury's Statutes (4th edn) 408).
10　Ibid, s 89A (2) and (3), inserted by Finance (No 2) Act 1987, s 100 (1).
11　By the Stock Exchange Rules, r 660.1 bearer bonds and share warrants are recognised as negotiable, but by r 660.0 renounceable documents are merely recognised as 'passing by delivery'.
12　*Rumball v Metropolitan Bank* (1877) 2 QBD 194.
13　Renounceable letters of allotment issued by companies listed on the Stock Exchange must provide for the issue of split letters of allotment without charge on the surrender of the original letter of allotment. (Stock Exchange: *Admission of Securities to Listing*, Section 9, Chapter 3, para 4 (*b*)).
14　The last day for splitting letters of allotment must be two days before the last day for renunciation (Stock Exchange: *Admission of Securities to Listing*, section 9, Chapter 3, para 4 (*b*)).

represent,[15] and until May 1976 this was also the position in respect of renounceable letters of allotment for debentures or other loan securities.[16]

The legal relationship between the original allottee and his renouncee is, of course, that of assignor and assignee of a chose in action, and the consequences of the renunciation are the same as those of any other assignment. There is no contractual relationship between the company and the renouncee, but it has been held that if the company accepts the renunciation, a new contract arises between it and the allottee and the renouncee, by which the allottee is released from his liabilities to the company, and his liabilities are taken over by the renouncee.[17] Under present practice a company only accepts the renunciation of the shares, debentures or other loan securities comprised in a letter of allotment when the registration application form is completed and the letter of allotment is surrendered by the renouncee, and since this may not be done until all instalments of the issue price of the securities have been paid, the company throughout retains its right to recover the whole of the issue price from the original allottee. If an allottee renounces some only of the shares, debentures or loan securities comprised in a letter of allotment, on the other hand, the issue of split letters of allotment to the allottee and renouncee respectively entails the substitution of two new contracts for the original contract with the allottee, and under the new contracts the renouncee is contractually liable to the company for the unpaid part of the issue price in respect of the shares he has taken, and the allottee is correspondingly liable only for the unpaid part of the issue price of the shares he retains. Whether an original letter of allotment is split or not, the company is bound by the terms of issue of the securities to accept renunciations, and if it refuses to register the renouncee as holder of the securities he has acquired, the original allottee or the renouncee can sue the company for breach of contract, and the renouncee may obtain an order of the court to compel the company to register him as a member or as the holder of the debentures or other loan securities concerned,[18] and also to deliver a share certificate or the debentures or a certificate in respect of the loan securities to him.[19] On the other hand, the absence of a contractual relationship between the company and the renouncee of all the securities comprised in a letter of allotment precludes it from suing him for unpaid instalments of the issue price, and he cannot be made a contributory when the company is wound up, unless the court orders the rectification of the company's register of members on the application of the liquidator.[20] In practice the company does not rely on this expedient to coerce the renouncee into paying; it relies instead on the power to forfeit the shares, debentures or other securities for non-payment, which is always reserved by the prospectus and is repeated in the letter of allotment itself.[1]

Letters of acceptance

If shares, debentures or other loan securities are offered for sale or are placed (otherwise than on a best efforts basis) by a merchant bank, a corporate finance

15 Stamp Act 1891, s 1 and Sch 1, Bearer Instrument (41 Halsbury's Statutes (4th edn) 176); Finance Act 1963, s 59 (1) and (3) and s 61 (1) (41 Halsbury's Statutes (4th edn) 268, 271); Finance Act 1986, s 64 (41 Halsbury's Statutes (4th edn) 267).
16 Finance Act 1986, s 79(2) (41 Halsbury's Statutes (4th edn) 400).
17 *Re Towns' Drainage and Sewage Utilization Co, Morton's Case* (1873) LR 16 Eq 104; *Collins v Associated Greyhound Racecourses Ltd* [1930] 1 Ch 1 per Hanworth MR, at 30 and Luxmoore J, at 20, but doubted by Lawrence LJ, at 36, and contra Russell LJ, at 37.
18 Companies Act 1985, s 359 (1) (shares); and a mandatory injunction or an order of specific performance (debentures).
19 Companies Act 1985, s 185 (6) and (7).
20 Insolvency Act 1986, s 148 (1).
1 See p 321 et seq, post.

subsidiary of a commercial bank, a firm of broker/dealers or any other marketing intermediary, allottees are sent a letter of acceptance by the intermediary instead of a letter of allotment by the company. The legal consequences are exactly the same, save that the contract of allotment is made between the marketing intermediary and the allottee, so that if he or his renouncees fail to pay the instalments of the issue price, it is for the intermediary and not the company to sue him. Once an allottee or renouncee of shares has been entered on the register of members of the company, however, he is a member of the company, and can be sued for any unpaid instalments of the issue price by the company itself, but in practice this situation is not met with, because the company will not register the renouncee as a member until the issue price of the shares has been paid in full. Letters of acceptance may be split in the same way and with the same consequences as letters of allotment.

Renounceable share certificates and debentures

In recent years some companies have adopted the practice of issuing renounceable share certificates, debentures and loan security certificates instead of letters of allotment. Such certificates are really a combination of a letter of allotment and a normal share certificate, debenture or loan security certificate. Like a letter of allotment they contain a form of renunciation which may be used during a limited period, and they provide that the holder of the document when it ceases to be renounceable may present it to the company so that he may be registered as a member or debenture or loan security holder; he will than receive a share certificate, debenture or loan security certificate, and the securities will be transferable only by a registered instrument of transfer. Renounceable share certificates, debentures or loan security certificates enable the original allottee alternatively to cancel or tear off the renunciation form if he intends to retain the shares or securities himself, in which case he will be registered as the member or debenture or loan security holder in respect of the securities when the period of renunciation expires. The share certificate, debenture or loan security certificate then becomes his permanent evidence of title, and no new certificate need be issued to him. The use of renouncable security certificates results in a considerable saving of clerical work, of course, but it is only a convenient device when the shares or other securities are paid up in full on allotment,[2] and for that reason its commonest use has been in connection with capitalisation issues.[3]

Calls and instalments of the issue price

When shares, debentures or other loan securities are issued, the present practice is to specify in the terms of issue the instalments by which the issue price is payable and the dates on which the instalments are to be paid. The subscriber is then contractually bound to pay those instalments, and the company or marketing intermediary can sue him in debt if he does not. Strictly speaking, these instalments are not calls,[4] although they are often referred to as such. Consequently, if the company's articles of association require certain procedural steps to be taken before calls are made, those steps need not be taken before an instalment in arrear is sued for. Nevertheless, articles frequently provide that instalments of the issue price of shares shall be deemed to be calls duly made and falling due on the dates when the

---

2 If the issue price were paid by calls or instalments, the certificate would have to be enfaced or endorsed with a note each time a call or instalment was paid.
3 See p 434 et seq, post.
4 *Croskey v Bank of Wales* (1863) 4 Giff 314 at 331.

instalments are payable so as to give the company the same remedies for their recovery as are available to recover true calls.[5] The amounts and dates for payment of instalments of the issue price of securities are fixed by the company as part of the terms of issue; the only requirement of the law is that at least one quarter of the nominal value and the whole of the share or issue premium of shares allotted by a public company must be paid up at or before allotment.[6]

Making of calls

A call, in the strict sense, is a demand by the company for payment of part of the issue price of shares, debentures or loan securities which has not been paid, and the date of whose payment was not specified in the terms of the issue.[7] If the articles are silent about the making of calls, they may only be made by an ordinary resolution passed at a general meeting of members. Usually the articles confer the power to make calls on the board of directors, but often subject to restrictions as to the amount of calls and their frequency.[8] A call cannot be made in breach of a contract made with shareholders, debenture or loan security holders, and so if a company issues shares on terms that the issue price shall be paid by fixed instalments, it cannot call up the instalments before they are due in reliance on a general power to make calls conferred by the articles.[9]

The resolution of the board or general meeting making a call must specify its amount and the date on which it is payable.[10] Frequently articles enable calls to be made payable by instalments,[11] in which case the amounts and dates of the instalments must be specified. Usually notice of a call has to be given to each member liable to pay it,[12] in which case he is not liable to make payment until proper notice has been given to him. Any irregularity in the proceedings for making the call will invalidate it. Thus, a call has been held invalid when it was made by directors who had not been properly appointed,[13] or at a board meeting which was not attended by a quorum of directors.[14] However, the Companies Act 1985 provides that the acts of a director are valid notwithstanding any defect which is afterwards discovered in his appointment or qualification,[15] so that if a call is made by directors who appear to have been properly appointed and to have the necessary qualification to hold office, the call will be valid even though their appointment was irregular or they are not qualified to act.[16] An irregularity in

5 See Table A, art 16. The provisions of Table A in respect of calls apply only to calls on shares.
6 Companies Act 1985, s 101 (1) (see p 160, ante).
7 It is most unusual for debentures or other loan securities to be issued on terms that the money secured thereby shall be paid to the company on calls being made. If this were done, however, it seems that the principles governing calls on shares would be equally applicable.
8 Table A, art 12, empowers the directors to make calls for payment of the whole or part of the capital unpaid on shares and of any issue premium. The Companies Act 1948, Table A, art 15, provided that no call must be for more than a quarter of the nominal value of the shares, nor be payable earlier than one month after the last call was payable.
9 *Re Cordova Union Gold Co* [1891] 2 Ch 580 at 583.
10 *Re Cawley & Co* (1889) 42 ChD 209.
11 See Table A, art 12.
12 By Table A, art 12, fourteen days' notice must be given to and received by a shareholder before he may be sued. Because of the wording of the article, art 115 (by which notices are deemed to have been served 48 hours after posting) does not apply, and the company must prove that the shareholder actually received the notice.
13 *Howbeach Coal Co Ltd v Teague* (1860) 5 H & N 151; *Garden Gully United Quartz Mining Co v McLister* (1875) 1 App Cas 39.
14 *Howbeach Coal Co Ltd v Teague*, supra.
15 Companies Act 1985, s 285.
16 *Dawson v African Consolidated Land and Trading Co* [1898] 1 Ch 6. This case was decided on an article to the same effect as the Companies Act 1985, s 285.

proceedings which are not an integral part of the procedure for making the call will not invalidate it. Thus, a call has been held valid when notice of it was sent out in a new name which the company had adopted by special resolution, but which had not yet been approved by the Board of Trade (as the law then required);[17] and it was held to be no defence to an action to recover a call for a shareholder who had been served with proper notice of it, to show that proper notice had not been given to other shareholders, so that they were not immediately liable to pay the call in respect of their shares.[18]

Equality of calls

It has been held that a call must be made equally on all shareholders of the same class,[19] so that a call made on some shareholders but not on others, or a call of a greater amount made on some shareholders than on the others, is void, unless their shares belong to different classes. It has been suggested that in certain circumstances discriminatory calls are permissible, but it was held in the case in which this suggestion was made that if some shareholders have failed to pay previous calls promptly, so that the company has been put to expense in recovering them, the company is not justified in calling up the whole of the unpaid capital on the shares of those shareholders alone, merely because it would be less expensive for the company to exact payment in that way than by calling on them to pay successive fractions of their unpaid capital at the same time as calls are made on the other shareholders.[20] Whatever the position may be once shares have been issued, however, it is possible, if the company's articles so provide, for the terms of issue of shares to make calls or instalments of the issue price payable by different shareholders at different times or in different amounts.[1]

Calls must be made in good faith

The directors may validly exercise their power to make calls and to prescribe the instalments by which the issue price of shares and debentures shall be paid, only if they act in good faith for the benefit of the company, and not for their own private advantage. Thus, where directors had subscribed the company's memorandum of association for a substantial number of shares which were allotted to them but on which they had paid nothing, and they then issued shares to other subscribers who were required to pay certain amounts on application and allotment, it was held that the directors were guilty of a breach of duty in not paying up an equal amount on their own shares, and the call on the other shareholders could consequently not be enforced.[2] Again, where directors deliberately deferred the date on which a call was deemed to made[3] so that they might dispose of their own shares in the meantime in order to avoid liability to pay it, it was held that the call was void.[4]

---

17 *Shackleford Ford & Co v Dangerfield* (1868) LR 3 CP 407.
18 *Newry and Enniskillen Rly Co v Edmunds* (1848) 2 Exch 118; *Shackleford, Ford & Co v Dangerfield*, supra.
19 *Preston v Grand Collier Dock Co* (1840) 11 Sim 327 at 347.
20 *Galloway v Hallé Concerts Society* [1915] 2 Ch 233.
 1 Companies Act 1985, s 119 (*a*). Table A, art 17, so provides.
 2 *Alexander v Automatic Telephone* [1990] 2 Ch 56.
 3 It is possible that a board resolution for a call may be validly passed with a proviso that the call shall be deemed to be made at a future date. By Table A, art 16, the call is deemed to be made when the board resolution is passed.
 4 *Re National Provincial Marine Insurance Co, Gilbert's Case* (1870) 5 Ch App 559.

Recovery of unpaid calls

A company may sue for a call made on its shareholders within 12 years after the date on which it is payable.[5] Usually the articles encourage prompt payment by charging interest on unpaid calls from the date on which they should be paid,[6] and in proceedings to recover unpaid calls, whether the articles provide for the payment of interest or not, the court may order interest to be paid at such rate as it thinks fit (not exceeding the rate of interest currently payable on judgment debts) from the date when the call became payable.[7]

The person who is a member of the company on the date when a call is made is liable to pay it, even though he transfers his shares to another before the date on which it is payable.[8] The transferee on being registered as a member in the transferor's place is also liable to pay the call, whether the transfer to him is made before or after the date on which the call is payable.[9] A member is therefore liable for all calls made in the past, whether before or after he became a member, but he can escape liability for calls made in the future by transferring his shares.[10] Furthermore, when a member agrees to sell his shares, the purchaser impliedly agrees to indemnify him against all calls made after the contract for sale is entered into,[11] and if the purchaser is not registered as a member and the company cannot recover the calls from the seller, the company is subrogated to the seller's right to an indemnity, and may recover the calls from the purchaser direct.[12] Likewise, if a subscriber or purchaser of shares has them vested in a nominee or bare trustee who is registered as a member of the company, the beneficial owner impliedly agrees to indemnify the nominee or trustee against calls made after he is registered,[13] and probably also against calls made beforehand. The company may enforce the nominee's right or trustee's right to indemnity against the subscriber or purchaser by subrogation to the nominee or trustee if it cannot effectively recover an unpaid call from the nominee or trustee himself.[14]

If a member is used for unpaid calls, it is no defence for him to allege that he was induced to subscribe for the shares or debentures by misrepresentations made by the company.[15] He must go further and show that he is entitled to rescind the allotment for that reason, and must seek an order of rescission, either by counterclaiming for it or by commencing a separate action.[15] If his shares have already been forfeited for failure to pay a call, however, he can rely on the misrepresentation as a defence to an action subsequently brought by the company to recover unpaid calls, because it is now immaterial whether he could have

---

5 Companies Act 1985, s 14 (2); Limitation Act 1980, s 8 (1) (24 Halsbury's Statutes (4th Edn) 655).

6 Table A, art 15, enables the directors to charge interest at a rate fixed by the terms of issue of the shares or by the call itself.

7 Supreme Court Act 1981, s 35A, (inserted by Administration of Justice Act 1982, s 15 (1) and Sch 7 (11 Halsbury's Statutes (4th Edn) 789).

8 *Aylesbury Rly Co v Mount* (1844) 7 Man & G 898; *Shaw v Rowley* (1847) 16 M & W 810; *North American Colonial Association of Ireland v Bentley* (1850) 19 LJQB 427; *Re National Bank of Wales, Taylor, Phillips, and Rickards' Cases* [1897] 1 Ch 298.

9 *Herbert Gold Ltd v Haycraft* (1901) Times, 27 March.

10 *Huddersfield Canal Co v Buckley* (1796) 7 Term Rep 36.

11 *Spencer v Ashworth Partington & Co* [1925] 1 KB 589. Rule 650.4 of the Rules of the Stock Exchange is to the same effect, and extends also to calls due after the contract for sale is entered into, even though made beforehand. The indemnity does not appear to extend to calls which fell due before the contract for sale was made and which remain unpaid, but the court might infer a promise to indemnify the vendor against past calls if the contract stated that they were unpaid. Probably the renouncee of a letter of allotment also impliedly agrees to indemnify the allottee against calls.

12 *Re European Society Arbitration Acts* (1878) 8 ChD 679.

13 *James v May* (1873) LR 6 HL 328; *Hardoon v Belilios* [1901] AC 118.

14 *Heritage v Paine* (1876) 2 ChD 594; *Re European Society Arbitration Acts*, supra.

15 *First National Reinsurance Co v Greenfield* [1921] 2 KB 260.

rescinded the allotment previously since the company has put it out of his power to do so by the forfeiture.[16]

Payments in advance of calls

If the company's articles so provide, it may accept payment of any part of the issue price of shares from a member before that part has fallen due for payment or has been called up.[17] Such payments in advance of calls are loans to the company, and so if the articles provide that interest shall be paid thereon by the company,[18] the interest is payable, even though the company's profits are insufficient to meet it and payment has to be made out of assets representing the company's paid up share capital.[19] Furthermore, when the company is wound up, payments in advance of calls are repaid immediately after debts owing to other creditors of the company have been paid,[20] and before share capital is returned to members.[1] On the other hand, the loan is peculiar in that it cannot be repaid while the company is a going concern,[2] but will be automatically appropriated to satisfying calls or instalments of the issue price of the shares when they fall due. It is undecided whether the benefit of payments in advance of calls passes with the shares when they are transferred, and if so, whether the payments must be apportioned when a member who has made payments in respect of all his shares transfers only some of them.

The directors' power to accept payments in advance of calls must be exercised in good faith for the benefit of the company, and not for their own benefit. Thus, when directors of an insolvent company purported to make payments in advance of calls on their own shares, and then used the payments to satisfy arrears of salary owing to them from the company, it was held that the pretended payment in advance of calls was a nullity, as it was merely a device to enable the directors to avoid paying the unpaid capital in respect of their shares when the company was wound up.[3] On the other hand, when directors paid up unpaid capital on their shares in advance of calls to enable the company to discharge a debt which they had guaranteed, it was held that the payment in advance of calls was valid,[4] and an agreement by a company that payments made by a director under such a guarantee should be deemed to be payments in advance of calls on his shares, has also been held good.[5] In both these cases the company benefited as well as the directors, and since their motive in making the payment must be considered to have been to benefit the company and not only themselves, the exercise of their power to accept the payment on the company's behalf was valid.

When the issue price of shares, debentures or loan securities is payable by instalments, the prospectus or other offer document sometimes permits subscribers and their renouncees to pay instalments before the due date and to deduct a certain rate of discount from the payments. This discount is, in effect, interest on the advance payment for the period until it would have fallen due. But in law it is not interest paid by the company, and so is not affected by the rules considered above.

---

16 *Aaron's Reefs Ltd v Twiss* [1896] AC 273.
17 Companies Act 1985, s 119 (*b*). The Companies Act 1948, Table A, art 21, so provides, but the present Table A does not.
18 By The Companies Act 1948, Table A, art 21, the directors may pay interest at a rate not exceeding 5 per cent per annum, or such other rate as the members direct by ordinary resolution.
19 *Lock v Queensland Investment and Land Mortgage Co* [1896] AC 461.
20 Insolvency Act 1986, s 74 (2) (*f*).
 1 *Re Exchange Drapery Co* (1888) 38 ChD 171.
 2 *London and Northern SS Co Ltd v Farmer* [1914] WN 200.
 3 *Re European Central Rly Co, Sykes' Case* (1872) LR 13 Eq 255.
 4 *Re Wincham Shipbuilding Boiler and Salt Co, Poole, Jackson and Whyte's Cases* (1878) 9 ChD 322.
 5 *Re Law Car and General Insurance Corpn* [1912] 1 Ch 405.

The issue price less the discount is the net issue price which the subscriber or renouncee has the option of paying instead of the full issue price by instalments. Such an arrangement is permissible without express provision in the company's articles, provided, in the case of shares, that the net issue price is not less than their nominal value. If it is, the shares are issued at a discount, and the rule prohibiting such an issue will apply.[6]

Forfeiture and surrender

A company's articles usually contain a power for it to forfeit the shares of a member who fails to pay calls or instalments of the issue price of his shares within a certain time after they fall due. Such a power is recognised by the Companies Act 1985, as valid.[7] Likewise, the terms of issue of debentures or other loan securities usually contain a similar power of forfeiture if instalments of the issue price are not duly paid. Such a power is valid, even though in the case of shares it involves a reduction of the company's unpaid share capital.[8]

Procedure on forfeiture

The articles usually require the directors to serve a notice on a shareholder who has failed to pay a call, warning him that unless he pays it within a certain time, his shares may be forfeited.[9] If the call is still unpaid at the end of that time, the articles empower the directors to forfeit the shares by a resolution passed at a board meeting.[10] The procedure prescribed for forfeiture must be strictly followed, so that if the original call is not enforceable against the shareholder,[11] or if the notice threatening forfeiture is defective, for example, by demanding interest on the call from the date it was made, when by the articles interest runs only from the date when the call was payable,[12] the forfeiture will be void. On the other hand, if the company has acted as though the forfeiture were effective, for example, by ceasing to pay dividends to the shareholder, or by not sending him notices of shareholders' meetings, the company will not be able to treat the forfeiture as void against the wishes of the shareholder merely because of a procedural defect for which the directors were responsible[13] The shareholder will always be able to set up procedural defects to invalidate the forfeiture, but the company will be prevented from doing so if the forfeiture was substantially carried out in the proper way.

Forfeiture of shares and debentures or loan securities represented by letters of allotment

Prospectuses or other invitations offering shares or debentures or loan securities whose issue price is payable by instalments and which will be represented by letters of allotment until the issue price is fully paid, usually reserve a power for the company to forfeit the allotment if any instalment is unpaid. This power is usually also conferred by the company's articles.[14] If the prospectus or offer document

---

6 Companies Act 1985, s 100 (1) (see p 142, ante).
7 Ibid, s 143 (3) (*d*).
8 *Trevor v Whitworth* (1887) 12 App Cas 409 at 417 to 8.
9 See Table A, art 18.
10 Ibid, art 19.
11 *Garden Gully United Quartz Mining Co v McLister* (1875) 1 App Cas 39.
12 *Johnson v Lyttle's Iron Agency* (1877) 5 ChD 687.
13 *Re Home Counties and General Life Assurance Co, Woollaston's Case* (1859) 4 De G & J 437.
14 Table A, art 16. The procedure for the forfeiture of shares which are represented by a letter of allotment is the same as if the allottee were a member of the company. Table A, art 18 requires notice of an intended forfeiture to be given 'to the person from whom [the instalment] is due', that is, the allottee, and art 16 equates an instalment of the issue price with a call.

relates to shares, the same procedure must be gone through to effect a forfeiture as if the issue price were payable by calls,[14] unless the company's articles otherwise provide, but it would seem that notice of the intended forfeiture would be sufficiently served if sent to the allottee. If the allottee has renounced the shares comprised in the letter of allotment, the company will not know the identity of the person who is at present entitled to the shares, and so cannot give notice to him. If the prospectus or offer document relates to debentures or other loan securities, it seems that the company may effect the forfeiture as soon as an instalment is in arrear without giving notice to anyone, unless the prospectus or offer document expressly provides for notice. When the company exercises its power of forfeiture, instalments of the issue price of the shares, debentures or loan securities which have already been paid may be retained by it, whether it suffers loss by the allottee or renouncee's default or not.

Forfeiture on offers for sale and placings

When shares, debentures or other loan securities are offered for sale or placed by a merchant bank or other marketing intermediary, a power to forfeit allotments for failure to pay instalments of the price payable by allottees may be reserved to it by the prospectus or other invitation it issues. The power must be considered as the equivalent of one to terminate the contract for breach by the allottee, and since time is of the essence of the contract on sales of marketable securities,[15] no further time need be given for the allottee to remedy his default. After forfeiting the securities, the marketing intermediary has no implied right to retain instalments of the price which have already been paid, however,[16] except possibly the amount paid on application, which may be considered as a deposit,[17] but instead it must return such amounts less any damages it has sustained as a result of the allottee's breach of contract. Nevertheless, the prospectus or offer document may expressly empower the marketing intermediary to forfeiture and retain instalments of the issue price already paid, or may alternatively empower it to re-sell the forfeited shares or securities, and to recover as liquidated damages from the allottee in default the difference between the unpaid part of the issue price of the securities and any lower resale price obtained.

Power of forfeiture must be exercised in good faith

Directors may use their power to forfeit only for the benefit of the company in order to coerce reluctant shareholders into paying their calls or instalments of the issue price, or in order to deprive shareholders of their shares if they clearly cannot pay for them.[18] The power cannot be exercised so that shareholders who can pay the calls or instalments may be released from liability merely because they are unwilling to pay.[19] If shares are forfeited for this reason, the forfeiture is void, and the shareholder continues to be responsible for the unpaid part of the issue price. Furthermore, the power of forfeiture cannot be used to relieve a shareholder of shares which he has a right to repudiate because he was induced to subscribe for them by misrepresentation.[20] The proper course in that case is for the directors to

---

15 *Rankin v Hop and Malt Exchange Co* (1869) 20 LT 207.
16 *Dies v British and International Mining and Finance Corpn Ltd* [1939] 1 KB 724.
17 *Collins v Stimson* (1883) 11 QBD 142 at 143, per Pollock, B.
18 *Spackman v Evans* (1868) LR 3 HL 171 at 186, per Lord Cranworth.
19 *Re Athenaeum Life Assurance Society, Richmond's Case* (1858) 4 K & J 305; *Re Agriculturist Cattle Insurance Co, Stanhope's Case* (1866) 1 Ch App 161; Ibid, *Stewart's Case* (1866) 1 Ch App 511; *Re Esparto Trading Co* (1879) 12 ChD 191.
20 *Re London and Provincial Starch Co, Gower's Case* (1868) LR 6 Eq 77.

remove the shareholder's name from the register of members, thereby recognising that, because he has chosen to rescind, he must be treated as though he had never been a member of the company.[1] It has been held that where a shareholder contends that his contract to subscribe is void for mistake,[2] or that it has never become effective because a condition precedent to its validity has not been fulfilled,[3] the directors may compromise the matter by agreeing to cancel the shares. In form this appears to be a forfeiture, but in reality it is simply a recognition by the company that the shareholder never has been a member of it at any time.

Surrender in lieu of forfeiture

If a company has power to forfeit shares for failure to pay calls or instalments of the issue price, it may accept a voluntary surrender of them by a shareholder, provided that in the circumstances it could exercise its power of forfeiture.[4] Such a power is recognised as valid by the Companies Act 1985.[5] But here again, the surrender may only be accepted if it is in the interest of the company to do so. If the directors' purpose is to relieve the shareholder from liability for unpaid capital which he is able but unwilling to pay, the surrender is void.[6]

Recovery of unpaid calls after forfeiture or surrender

When shares have been validly forfeited or surrendered, the former shareholder may not be sued for unpaid calls or instalments of the issue price, unless the articles or terms of issue so provide.[7] If the company has made two successive calls, neither of which have been paid, and it forfeits for non-payment of the first call, it can sue the former shareholder for both the first and second call under an article which enables it to recover calls 'owing' at the date of forfeiture, because the second call became owing when it was made.[8] But if the articles only enable the company to recover calls payable or due at the date of forfeiture,[9] the company will not be able to recover the second call if the shares are forfeited before the date on which it was due to be paid.

Cancellation of forfeiture and re-issue of forfeited shares

Equity cannot give relief against a forfeiture of shares, debentures or other loan securities by allowing the holder an extended period of time within which to pay the unpaid call or instalment of the issue price.[10] However, articles of association often enable a company to cancel a forfeiture of shares;[11] under such a provision the directors may cancel the forfeiture at the former shareholder's request, but he cannot be compelled to take shares back against his wishes.[12] Usually, the articles empower the company to re-issue forfeited shares on such terms as the directors think fit.[11] The re-issue of forfeited or surrendered shares is really a sale of the shares by the company, with the result that the purchase price belongs to the

1 *Reese River Silver Mining Co v Smith* (1869) LR 4 HL 64.
2 *Re Agriculturist Cattle Insurance Co, Lord Belhaven's Case* (1865) 3 De G J & Sm 41.
3 *Dixon v Evans* (1872) LR 5 HL 606.
4 *Trevor v Whitworth* (1887) 12 App Cas 409.
5 Companies Act 1985, s 143 (3) (*d*).
6 *Bellerby v Rowland and Marwood's SS Co* [1902] 2 Ch 14.
7 *Re Blakely Ordnance Co, Stocken's Case* (1868) 3 Ch App 412.
8 *Re China SS and Labuan Coal Co Ltd, Dawes' Case* (1869) 38 LJ Ch 512.
9 As does Table A, part 21.
10 *Sparks v Liverpool Waterworks Co* (1807) 13 Ves 428.
11 See Table A, art 20.
12 *Re Exchange Trust Ltd, Larkworthy's Case* [1903] 1 Ch 711.

company and not the former holder of the shares, and the shares are paid up in the hands of the purchaser to the same extent as they were at the date of forfeiture.[13] Because a re-issue of shares is really a sale of them, the purchase price received by the company is not part of their paid up value, and a public company which re-issues shares need not exact a re-issue price equal to a quarter of the nominal value of the shares similar to the minimum amount of capital which must be paid up on the allotment of shares.[14] If after shares are forfeited or surrendered the company later recovers unpaid calls or instalments of the issue price from the former shareholder, the shares are credited as paid up by the amount of those calls or instalments for the benefit of the purchaser, and the company cannot recover them from him as well.[15] Conversely, if the purchaser pays the calls or instalments in arrear, the former shareholder is relieved from liability, even though the articles of association expressly preserve his liability for unpaid calls.[16] Furthermore, when the company sues the former shareholder for unpaid calls or instalments, it can only recover the difference between those calls or instalments and the price it has obtained for the shares from the purchaser.[16] This is because the company's claim against the former shareholder is for breach of contract, and so it cannot recover more than the damages or loss which it has actually suffered.

COMMISSIONS

Types of commission

When it issues shares, debentures or other loan securities, a company may find it necessary, according to the way it issues the securities, to pay a commission to persons who agree to subscribe for the securities in any event (that is, to persons who underwrite 'firm'), to persons who agree to subscribe for securities which the public or the persons initially invited to subscribe do not take up (underwriting commission), to persons who agree to use their best efforts to find subscribers (placing commission[17]), and to persons who agree to find underwriters (overriding commission).[18] If securities are issued to a merchant bank or other marketing intermediary to be offered for sale or placed, the intermediary does not normally charge a commission, but obtains its remuneration from the difference between the price at which it sells the securities to the public or to investors or to other intermediaries, and the lower issue price which the intermediary agrees to pay to the company. There is nothing to prevent a marketing intermediary being paid a commission, however, and if it were employed to sell or place shares which could not be sold to the public for more than their nominal value, that would be the only way by which it could be remunerated. Out of the difference or margin which it obtains on an offer for sale or a placing, a marketing intermediary has to pay underwriting and overriding commissions (if any), and usually bears a part of the other expenses of the issue.

13 *New Balkis Eersteling Ltd v Randt Gold Mining Co* [1904] AC 165.
14 See p 160, ante.
15 *Re Randt Gold Mining Co* [1904] 2 Ch 468. There is no contractual relationship between the former shareholder and the purchaser from the company, however, and the former shareholder cannot require the purchaser to indemnify him against calls he is compelled to pay.
16 *Re Bolton, ex p North British Artificial Silk Ltd* [1930] 2 Ch 48.
17 In this kind of placing the recipient of the commission does not agree to take the securities in any event, and so securities which are not placed are left on the company's hands.
18 The brokers to a public offer of securities (who support the application for a Stock Exchange listing or for the admission of the securities to the Unlisted Securities Market or the Third Market) are usually employed to find underwriters.

Commission on issues of shares

In order to prevent shares, in effect, being issued at a discount by the payment of heavy commissions, the Companies Act 1985 prohibits companies from applying their shares[19] or money representing share capital in paying commissions on the issue of shares, unless:[20]

(a) the payment of commissions is authorised by the company's articles; and

(b) the total amount of commissions paid does not exceed 10 per cent of the issue price of the shares or such less amount as the articles prescribe (if any); and

(c) the amount or rate of commissions paid is stated in any prospectus or other written invitation to subscribe for the shares, and if the company makes the invitation otherwise than by a prospectus, or is a private company, the amount or rates of commission paid must also be disclosed in a written statement signed by every director or his agent authorised in writing and delivered to the Registrar of Companies; and

(d) the number of shares which are underwritten firm for a commission is disclosed in the same way.

Requirements (b), (c) and (d) above do not apply when shares are offered for subscription or sale by listing particulars and an application for an official listing of the shares has been made to the Stock Exchange,[1] but the Stock Exchange listing rules require that the amount of underwriting and other commissions paid or to be paid shall be disclosed in the listing particulars.[2] Requirements (c) and (d) will also cease to apply to offers of shares otherwise than by listing particulars when the provisions of the Financial Services Act 1986 relating to prospectuses are brought into force by ministerial order, but the maximum rate of commission which may be paid will be limited to 10 per cent of the issue price or such less amount as is presented by the company's articles.[3]

Commissions for underwriting firm

The Companies Act 1985 permits companies, subject to the above conditions, to pay a commission 'to any person in consideration of his subscribing or agreeing to subscribe ... absolutely ... for any shares'.[4] This provision, read literally, appears to permit the payment of commissions not only to firm underwriters, but also to persons who do nothing more than subscribe for shares in response to an invitation made to them by a prospectus or otherwise. It has been held, however, that if the offer of a commission to such subscribers is merely a colourable device to facilitate the issue of shares at a discount, it will be treated as such, and the commission will not be payable.[5] In the case which so decided, the commission offered was 90 per cent of the issue price of the shares, but it is submitted that it is not the size of the commission which is the determining factor. A commission is a reward paid for a service in connection with a particular offer of shares, and subscribing for shares in

---

19 In practice commissions are paid in cash. Public companies are prohibited from allotting shares credited as paid up by remuneration for underwriting or other services in connection with an issue of its shares, debentures or other loan securities (Companies Act 1985, s 99 (2)).

20 Companies Act 1985, s 97 (1) to (3) and s 98 (1).

1 Financial Services Act 1986, s 212 (3) and Sch 17, Part I; Financial Services Act 1986 (Commencement) (No 3) Order 1986 (SI 1986/2246), art 5 and Sch 4.

2 Stock Exchange: *Admission of Securities to Listing*, Section 3, Chapter 1, para 3.1 and Chapter 2, para 2.18.

3 Financial Services Act 1986, s 212 (3) and Sch 17, Part I.

4 Companies Act 1985, s 97 (1).

5 *Keatinge v Paringa Consolidated Mines Ltd* [1902] WN 15.

pursuance of the offer is not a service at all. Underwriting 'firm' is such a service, because the underwriting contract is made before the shares are offered to the persons who are initially invited to subscribe for them, and the underwriter thereby assures the company that the shares underwritten will be taken up in any event. It is therefore submitted that the offer of a commission to subscribers generally must always be regarded as an offer to issue shares at a discount, however small the commission may be, if the net issue price after deducting the commission is less than the nominal value of the shares.

Payment of commissions out of profits and by options to subscribe; brokerage

There is nothing in the Companies Act 1985 to prevent a company from applying its profits or revenue reserves in paying commissions on the issue of shares without restriction,[6] but moneys representing its shares premium account can only be used if the conditions set out above are complied with.[7] A company may also reward underwriters by giving them options to subscribe for further shares at par when the market value of its existing shares is above par, or by giving them options to subscribe for shares at a lower price than the current market value of similar existing shares.[8] The value of the option is not treated as a commission and is not subject to the conditions set out above.[9] Furthermore, a company may pay brokerage without complying with those conditions.[10] Brokerage is a commission paid to a bank, stockbroker, merchant bank or other marketing intermediary for placing shares on a best efforts basis, and is lawful if reasonable in amount.[11] Brokerage cannot be paid to any other person, and so a placing commission paid to a person other than a bank, stockbroker or marketing intermediary is subject to the restrictions imposed by the Companies Act 1985.[12] Furthermore, brokerage can only be paid for services rendered under a contract with the company. Thus, if a broker has a client who is willing to invest in the company, and he agrees to introduce his client to the company in return for a commission, the broker performs no service under the contract, because he has already found an investor with whom the shares can be placed, and consequently he is not entitled to recover the commission.[13] It, therefore, seems that an offer by a company to pay brokerage to any stockbroker or solicitor whose stamp appears on an application form for shares offered by a prospectus or other offer document, is of doubtful legality, unless the

6 The Companies Act 1985, s 98 (1), merely prohibits the use of a company's shares or share capital to pay commissions if the conditions set out in s 97 (2) and (3) are not complied with.

7 The Companies Act 1985, s 130 (2) allows share premium account to be used to write off commissions which have been paid; it is clearly implied that the commissions must have been lawful. Moreover, it is clear that if commissions have been paid out of profits or revenue reserves, an equivalent amount cannot be transferred from share premium account to revenue reserves. In that situation the commission would not appear as an asset in the company's balance sheet, and there would consequently be nothing which share premium account could be used to write off.

8 If a company has a listing for any of its securities on the Stock Exchange, it must obtain the approval of a general meeting for the creation of such options; even if this approval is given, the Stock Exchange may withdraw the listing if the options extend to a material fraction of the company's ordinary share capital, and for that reason it is advisable to obtain Stock Exchange approval of the options before they are created (Stock Exchange: *Admission of Securities to Listing*, Section 1, Chapter 2, para 17).

9 *Hilder v Dexter* [1902] AC 474.

10 Companies Act 1985, s 98 (3).

11 *Metropolitan Coal Consumers' Association v Scrimgeour* [1985] 2 QB 604.

12 *Andreae v Zinc Mines of Great Britain Ltd* [1918] 2 KB 454.

13 *Re Faure Electric Accumulator Co* (1888) 40 ChD 141, as explained in *Metropolitan Coal Consumers' Association v Scrimgeour*, supra, per Rigby LJ, at 609.

brokerage is paid out of profits, or is treated as an ordinary placing commission and the conditions prescribed by the Companies Act 1985 are complied with.

Payment of commissions by vendors and promoters

A vendor of property to a company and a promoter who receives remuneration for his services may apply any of the money or shares which they receive from the company in paying commissions in connection with the issue of the company's shares, but the aggregate of the commissions paid by them and the company must not exceed 10 per cent of the issue price of the shares or the smaller sum (if any) prescribed by the articles.[14] The reason for this provision is to prevent a company from paying illegal commissions through vendors or promoters by artificially inflating the purchase price or remuneration paid to them. On the other hand, there is no similar limitation on commissions paid by marketing intermediaries which have agreed to take shares from a company in order to place them or to offer them for sale. Such commissions may be of any amount, but the company is partially protected by the fact that the price payable to it by the intermediary under its agreement to subscribe for the shares cannot be less than the nominal value of the shares, and if the shares are saleable by the intermediary at more than par, it should not be necessary for the intermediary to pay exorbitant commissions, which would be reflected in a corresponding diminished issue price paid by it to the company.

Consequences of irregularity

If the conditions governing the payment of commissions are not complied with, the person entitled to the commission cannot sue for it, even though the failure to comply was not his fault.[15] If the improper commission takes the form of an allotment of shares, the allotment cannot be made, and if the company purports to make it, it is void.[16] On the other hand, if the company pays an illegal commission in cash and the recipient is unaware of the irregularity, the company cannot recover the commission from him.[15]

Commission on issues of debentures and loan securities

There are no restrictions on the amount of commission which companies may pay in connection with an issue of debentures or other loan securities. This is because debentures, unlike shares, can be issued at a discount, so that there is no danger to be guarded against of commission being paid improperly out of capital. If debentures or loan securities are offered by a prospectus issued generally (other than listing particulars), the amount or rate of commission payable in respect of the issue must be disclosed in the prospectus,[17] and if the securities are offered by listing particulars, they must disclose the total amount of commission paid or to be

14 Companies Act 1985, s 98 (4).
15 *Andreae v Zinc Mines of Great Britain Ltd* [1918] 2 KB 454. In the United States it has been held that if the statutory conditions for the payment of commission have not been complied with by the company, an underwriter may nevertheless recover his commission (*AC Frost & Co v Coeur d'Alène Mines Corpn* (1941) 312 US 38).
16 *Banking Service Corpn Ltd v Toronto Finance Corpn Ltd* [1928] AC 333.
17 Companies Act 1985, s 56 (1) and Sch 3, para 10 (1). This provision will probably be replaced by a requirement that prospectuses shall disclose the identity of the underwriters and the total amount of commission paid to them when the new statutory rules relating to prospectuses are brought into operation (Financial Services Act 1986, s 212 (3) and Sch 17, Part I).

paid in connection with the issue.[18] These requirements are merely intended to give publicity to the amount of commission paid, not to limit its amount, and so if the requirements are not complied with, the person entitled to the commission may still recover it from the company.

SHARE CERTIFICATES AND SHARE WARRANTS

Hitherto it has been possible to deal with the law and practice relating to the issue of shares and debentures (including all forms of loan securities) together, but they must henceforth be dealt with separately, because the law which governs the remaining stages of the procedure for issuing them and the rules which govern dealings with them are not uniform for both categories. The remainder of this chapter and the two following chapters will therefore be concerned with shares alone.

When the letters of allotment or acceptance in respect of shares cease to be renounceable, the company will issue a share certificate or share warrant to the person who surrenders it, and if a share certificate is issued, will enter his name in its register of members as the holder of the shares. If renounceable share certificates have been issued and an allottee has not renounced his shares,[19] he will simply retain his certificate as permanent evidence of his title to the shares, and thenceforth it will have the same legal qualities as a normal share certificate. In that case, because the attached letter of renunciation has not been signed by the allottee and no-one other than he has surrendered the renounceable certificate to the company, the allottee will be entered in the company's register of members as the registered holder of the shares.

Share certificate

A share certificate is a document issued by a company stating that a named person is the registered holder of a specified number of shares of a certain class (if the company has issued shares of more than one class), and that the shares are fully paid or are paid up to a stated amount. Usually the shares are stated to be held by the registered holder 'subject to the company's memorandum and articles of association', but this is a needless addition, for the rights and obligations of shareholders are governed by the memorandum and articles as a matter of law. The certificate is usually issued under the company's seal if it has one,[20] although there is no legal requirement that it should be.[1] A certificate signed by a director or other authorised officer or agent of the company is equally effective and, whether the company has a common seal or not, it may issue share certificates under the signatures of two of its directors or the signatures of a director and the company's secretary.[2] Certificates often bear a distinguishing number corresponding to the same number in the company's own records; this is a safeguard against forgery. Additionally, a share certificate must state the distinguishing numbers of the shares to which it relates,[3] and the register of members must also show the distinguishing numbers of a member's shares and, if the company's share capital is divided into

---

18 Stock Exchange: *Admission of Securities to Listing*, Section 3, Chapter 1, para 3.2 and Chapter 2, para 2.18.

19 See p 316, ante.

20 A company which has a common seal may also have a separate securities seal, designed as such, for sealing share certificates, debentures and debenture stock certificates. (Companies Act 1985, s 40, as amended by Companies Act 1989, s 130 (7) and Sch 17, para 3).

1 Table A, art 6, requires share certificates to be under the company's seal.

2 Companies Act 1985, s 36A (1) to (4), inserted by Companies Act 1989, s 130 (1).

3 Companies Act 1985, s182 (2).

two or more classes, the class or classes of shares held by the member.[4] But if all the issued shares of a class are fully paid and carry equal rights, they need not have distinguishing numbers in the register of members[4] or in share certificates.[3] This appears to be so even if there are unissued shares of the same class, and when such shares are issued it appears unnecessary to attach distinguishing numbers to the existing shares while the newly issued shares remain only partly paid. If fully paid shares have been converted into stock,[5] a stock certificate is issued to the holder, and the rules applicable to share certificates are equally applicable to it, except the rules with regard to distinguishing numbers.

If shares or stock are listed, the rules of the Stock Exchange require the share or stock certificates to be dated and sealed by the issuing company, to bear a note in the top right hand corner stating the number of shares or amount of stock represented by the certificate and the class to which the shares or stock belong, and to contain a statement that transfers of the shares or stock will not be registered unless the certificate is produced, and, if applicable, that shares or stock may only be transferred in specified minimum amounts or multiples thereof.[6]

Share certificate as evidence of title

A share certificate under the company's seal or securities seal is prima facie evidence of the shareholder's title to the shares specified in it,[7] but is not conclusive evidence. It would seem that share certificates which are merely signed by two of the company's directors, or by a director and the company's secretary, or by any other officer or agent authorised by the company, are also evidence of the shareholder's title, at least as against the company itself. Shares belong to the person who can show a chain of title from the original issue by the company down to the disposition to himself, and if by accident or by fraud a share certificate is issued to a person other than the true owner of the shares to which it relates, the certificate in no way affects the title of the true owner. Likewise, if the register of members shows a person other than the true owner as the proprietor of the shares, the true owner may have the register rectified.[8] It is true that a share certificate which is irregularly issued is not wholly devoid of legal effect, as will be shown in the next chapter, but its issue has no effect on the legal title to the shares.

Statement in share certificate of amount paid up on shares

A share certificate always states how much has been paid up on the shares it represents, and if the issue price of the shares has been paid in full, the share certificate states that the shares are fully paid. If an error is made on a share certificate as to the amount paid up on the shares to which it relates, so that the shares appear to have been paid up to a greater extent than they have in fact, the company's right to recover the unpaid capital from the person to whom the certificate is initially issued is not usually prejudiced, because he will usually know how much has been paid, and will not therefore be able to raise any plea of estoppel against the company. But if the person to whom the certificate is issued sells or mortgages the shares to another person who believes that they are paid up to the extent stated in the certificate and pays a corresponding purchase price or lends a corresponding amount, the company will be estopped from denying that the shares

---

4 Ibid, s 352 (3).
5 See p 170, ante.
6 Stock Exchange: *Admission of Securities to Listing*, Section 9, Chapter 4, para 1.2.
7 Companies Act 1985, s 186, as substituted by Companies Act 1989, s 130 (7) and Sch 17, para 5.
8 Ibid, s 359 (1) and (2).

are paid up to that extent as against the purchaser or mortgagee, and in his hands the shares must be treated as paid up to that extent for all purposes.[9]

It is also possible for the person to whom shares are originally allotted to raise such an estoppel against the company if he was induced by the company's representations to believe that the shares were fully paid when they were allotted. Thus where a contractor who was entitled to be allotted fully paid shares for work done for the company, sold his right to call for some of the shares to the defendant, and the company allotted those shares to the defendant and issued share certificates which stated that they were fully paid, it was held that the defendant was entitled to have the shares treated as fully paid shares, even though, as the law then stood, they were not paid up at all, because the contract for their allotment had not been registered before they were issued.[10] For the same reason, if a person buys shares represented by a letter of allotment which bears receipts by the company for the instalments of the issue price, and the company issues a share certificate to him stating that the shares are fully paid, he will be able to plead an estoppel against the company if the instalments of the issue price have not in fact been paid, but he was induced by the receipts to believe that they had been when he bought the shares. If the purchaser has not received a share certificate, he will still be able to plead an estoppel in reliance on the receipts on the letter of allotment; the estoppel rule is general in application, and is not confined to share certificates.

If a purchaser or mortgagee of partly paid shares is entitled to have them treated as fully paid, any person who derives title under him is entitled to the same rights, even though he knew that the shares were only partly paid when he acquired them.[11] If this were not so, the original purchaser or mortgagee would not get the full benefit of the estoppel, for he would be able to sell the shares only at a price corresponding to the amount actually paid up on them to a purchaser who is aware of that fact. The original allottee of the shares also may rely on the estoppel which his purchaser or mortgagee could plead if the allottee obtains the shares back from the purchaser or mortgagee,[11] but is doubtful whether this is so if the allottee obtains them back merely by redeeming a mortgage created by depositing his original certificate with the mortgagee. If the allottee obtained the irregular share certificate by fraud, however, he will not be able to benefit by his own fraud and treat the shares as fully paid in his hands by obtaining them back from a purchaser or mortgagee who could plead an estoppel against the company.[11]

Share warrants

A company limited by shares may, if authorised by its articles, issue share warrants under its common seal or its securities seal in respect of fully paid shares[12] or stock.[13] A share warrant certifies that the bearer of the warrant is entitled to the shares represented by it, and the legal title to the shares is transferred by mere

---

9 *Burkinshaw v Nicolls* (1878) 3 App Cas 1004; *Bloomenthal v Ford* [1897] AC 156. But the directors who issued the certificate are liable to the company for the unpaid share capital which it cannot now recover (*Hirsche v Sims* [1894] AC 654).

10 *Re Building Estates Brickfields Co, Parbury's Case* [1896] 1 Ch 100.

11 *Re Stapleford Colliery Co, Barrow's Case* (1879) 14 ChD 432. The correctness of this decision was doubted in *Re London Celluloid Co* (1888) 39 ChD 190 at 197. There is justification for the doubt from the theoretical point of view (see the similar question in respect of share certificates issued to persons not entitled to the shares, p 350, post); but there can be no doubt that the decision in *Barrow's Case* is the more just.

12 Companies Act 1985, s 188 (1) and (2), as amended by Companies Act 1989, s 130 (7) and Sch 17, para 6.

13 *Pilkington v United Railways of Havana and Regla Warehouses Ltd* [1930] 2 Ch 108, [1930] All ER Rep 649.

delivery of the warrant from one person to another with the intention of passing the title,[14] so that no entry is made on the register of members when a transfer is effected. While a share warrant is outstanding the register of members must bear a notice that it has been issued, the date of its issue, and the distinguishing numbers of the shares represented by it (if any).[15] Subject to any contrary provision in the company's articles, the bearer of a warrant may surrender it at any time, and have his shares registered in his name in the register of members, and he is then also entitled to have a share certificate issued to him in respect of them.[16] Because a share warrant is transferable by delivery, there is no written instrument of transfer when it is sold which can bear ad valorem stamp duty on the amount of the consideration paid. Consequently, the duty is commuted and is paid in advance by the warrant being stamped at the rate of 1·5 per cent of the issue price of the shares if they are offered for public subscription and the warrant is issued within 12 months of subscription, or in any other case, at the rate of 1·5 per cent of the price of the shares first quoted by a stock exchange within one month of the issue of the warrant, or if the shares are not so quoted, 1·5 per cent of their value immediately after the warrant is issued.[17] A share certificate, on the other hand, bears no stamp duty.

Share warrants, unlike share certificates, are negotiable instruments,[18] and so a person who purchases a share warrant, or advances money on the security of it, will be entitled to it free from any defects in the title of the person who delivered it to him if he took it in good faith and for value and was unaware of any such defects at the date of delivery. Consequently, if a warrant has been stolen, or obtained by fraud from the company or any intermediate holder, a subsequent holder may nevertheless obtain a perfect title to it, and can then enforce all the rights which it purports to embody against the company.[19]

MEMBERSHIP

Members

The members of a company are: (a) the subscribers of its memorandum of association, who became members on its incorporation; and (b) every other person who agrees to become a member and whose name is entered on the register of members.[20]

The second category of members is obviously the more numerous and important. A person cannot become a member in this category unless he agrees to do so. The agreement of a subscriber for shares is always expressed in his application for them, and the agreement of a renouncee of a letter of allotment or acceptance by his completing the registration application form contained in it and submitting the letter of allotment or acceptance to the company so that he may be registered as the holder of the shares. If a person acquired shares from an existing member, the

---

14 Companies Act 1985, s 188 (2).
15 Ibid, s 355 (1).
16 Ibid, s 355 (2).
17 Stamp Act 1891, s 1 and Sch 1, Bearer Instrument (41 Halsbury's Statutes (4th Edn) 149, 176); Finance Act 1963, s 55(1A), and s 59 (1) and s 61 (1) (41 Halsbury's Statutes (4th Edn) 268, 271), as amended by Finance Act 1986, s 64 (2). Presumably the reference to offers of shares for public subscription is intended to include offers for sale to the public.
18 *Webb Hale & Co v Alexandria Water Co* (1905) 21 TLR 572.
19 The negotiability of share warrants is dealt with further in Chapter 10.
20 Companies Act 1985, s 22 (1) and (2).

common form instrument of transfer used to state that he agreed to accept the shares, and his execution of the instrument containing that statement evidenced his agreement to become a member. The modern form of transfer of fully paid shares which is authorised by statute[1] contains no such statement, but it does contain a request by the transferee to the company to register the transfer, from which an agreement by him to become a member of the company must be implied. Although a company will not be compelled to register a transfer which has not been executed by the transferee,[2] except where the simplified form of transfer of fully paid shares now authorised by statute[1] has been used, execution of the transfer is not the only way by which the transferee may signify his agreement to become a member, and he will become one if the company registers the transfer and he either recognises the validity of the registration or acts in the capacity of a member,[3] for example, by attending shareholders' meetings or receiving and retaining dividends. The requirement that a person must agree to become a member of a company in order to be one does not mean that there must be a contract between him and the company for the acquisition of shares by him; it is sufficient that he agrees to become a member in the sense of assenting to shares being registered in his name.[4]

In addition to agreeing to become a member, a shareholder's name must appear in the company's register of members for him to be a member. If his name has not yet been entered in the register of members, he may be the beneficial owner of the shares concerned, but he is not entitled to the full rights of membership. The names of the holder of a letter of allotment or acceptance and the owner of a share warrant do not appear in the register of members, and they are therefore not members of the company. The articles may confer any of the rights of a member on the owners of share warrants and may impose any of the obligations of a member on them,[5] and there seems no reason why the holders of letters of allotment or acceptance should not be similarly treated, although this is not done in practice. If the holder of a share warrant or letter of allotment or acceptance is not expressly put in the position of a member by the articles, he is not a party to the statutory contract between the company and its members, by which they undertake to conform to the provisions of its memorandum and articles of association.[6] But it would seem that a contract to the same effect must be implied between the company and the person to whom the share warrant or letter of allotment or acceptance is issued. The rights implied by such a contract (apart from voting rights) pass to other persons on delivery of the document to them with the intention of transferring the ownership of the shares, and the obligations so implied also pass to them in the form of conditions to which they must conform in order to exercise their rights. For example, if the articles enable any shareholder to insist on his fellow shareholders purchasing his shares in certain circumstances, it would seem that a shareholder whose title is embodied in a share warrant or letter of allotment or acceptance could enforce the option. Similarly, if the articles give other shareholders an option to buy the shares represented by the share warrant or letter of allotment or acceptance in certain circumstances, it would seem that the option would be effective against any holder of the warrant or the letter for the time being.

1 Stock Transfer Act 1963, ss 1 and 2 (1) (30 Halsbury's States (4th Edn) 157) (see p 340, post).
2 *Re Imperial Mercantile Credit Association, Marino's Case* (1867) 2 Ch App 596.
3 *Cuninghame v City of Glasgow Bank* (1879) 4 App Cas 607.
4 *Re Nuneaton Borough Association Football Club Ltd* [1989] BCLC 454, (1989) 5 BCC 792.
5 Companies Act 1985, s 355 (5). This is particularly important in connection with voting rights at meetings of shareholders.
6 Companies Act 1985, s 14 (1).

Capacity

The capacity of a person to become a member of a company is determined by the ordinary rules of the law of contract. Consequently, a minor may become a member, but he may avoid an allotment or transfer of shares to himself before or within a reasonable time after he attains his majority,[7] whereupon he ceases to be a member. If he avoids an allotment of shares made to him by the company, the shares are treated as though they had never been issued, and so the company may re-issue them to another person. If the minor repudiates shares which were transferred to him, the transferor becomes a member of the company again in respect of those shares. A company can refuse to register a transfer of shares to a minor,[8] but whether it can cancel a registration which it has already made in order to make the transferor liable for unpaid calls is questionable.[9] In a winding up, however, the liquidator may cancel the registration of a transfer to a minor, even though the minor wishes to retain his shares; this is so at least when the company is insolvent and there is unpaid capital to be called up for which the liquidator wishes to make the transferor responsible.[10] The law gives the liquidator the power of cancellation in such a case because it is conclusively presumed that it would be in the minor's interests to repudiate the transfer, and the court acts as though he had actually repudiated.[11] If a company discovers that shares have been transferred to a minor, it should apparently notify the transferor that it reserves its rights to recover calls from him,[12] though it is difficult to see what rights the company thereby acquires against the transferor, unless the minor repudiates the shares or the company is wound up. If no such notice is given, the company is said to waive its rights against the transferor, and he cannot then be made a contributory if the company is wound up.[13]

Until a minor repudiates the allotment or transfer of shares to him, he is a member of the company, and is bound by the obligations of a member in the same way as any other member. It is therefore no defence for him to plead his minority if he is sued for calls or instalments of the issue price,[14] but if he repudiates the shares taken by him, he cannot be sued for calls made before or after his repudiation or for unpaid instalments of the issue price.[15] On repudiating shares allotted to him, a minor can recover the issue price he has paid to the company for them only if they have always been completely worthless, and the company therefore gave him no valuable consideration for the money he paid to it.[16] Similarly, it would

---

7 *Re Blakely Ordnance Co, Lumden's Case* (1868) 4 Ch App 31. The few decided cases are not consistent in prescribing how long after attaining his majority the minor has to repudiate. Thus, in one case it was held that it was too late to repudiate fourteen months after he attained his majority (*Re Constantinople and Alexandria Hotel Co, Ebbett's Case* (1870) 5 Ch App 302), yet in another case a minor was allowed to repudiate two and a half years after she had attained her majority (*Re Alexandra Park Co, Hart's Case* (1868) LR 6 Eq 512).

8 *R v Midland Counties and Shannon Junction Rly Co* (1862) 15 ICLR 514.

9 In *Re Contract Corpn, Gooch's Case* (1872) 8 Ch App 266 at 268, Lord Selborne LC assumed that the company could cancel the registration at any time before the minor had, after attaining his majority, affirmed his intention to retain the shares, but such a supposed power would be inconsistent with the minor's right to repudiate or retain the share as he chooses.

10 *Re Continental Bank Corpn, Castello's Case* (1869) LR 8 Eq 504; *Re Asiatic Banking Co, Symon's Case* (1870) 5 Ch App 298.

11 *Re Electric Telegraph Co of Ireland, Reid's Case* (1857) 24 Beav 318 at 320.

12 *Re China SS and Labuan Coal Co, Capper's Case* (1868) 3 Ch App 458.

13 *Re European Central Rly Co, Parson's Case* (1869) LR 8 Eq 656.

14 *Cork and Bandon Rly Co v Cazenove* (1847) 10 QB 935; *North Western Rly Co v M'Michael* (1851) 5 Exch 114.

15 *Newry and Enniskillen Rly Co v Coombe* (1849) 3 Exch 565; *North Western Rly co, M'Michael*, supra, at 125.

16 *Steinberg v Scala (Leeds) Ltd* [1923] 2 Ch 452.

appear that a minor who has purchased shares may repudiate the purchase and recover the price paid only if the shares were worthless when he bought them and have had no realisable value at any time since.

A married woman has full capacity to acquire property and undertake obligations.[17] She may therefore acquire shares and become a member of a company, and if she does so, she has the same rights and is subject to the same liabilities as a male member.

An alien may be a member of a company in the same way as a British subject, and even though all the members of a company are aliens, the law does not treat it differently from a company whose members are British.[18] The fact that a company is controlled by aliens does not affect its nationality, domicil or residence, or its liability for taxation.[19]

Prohibition on company's membership of itself

A company cannot be a member of itself,[20] and cannot subscribe for or acquire any shares[1] in itself, except where statute otherwise provides.[2] If a company allots shares to a nominee for itself, or if such a nominee acquires shares in the company by renunciation, transfer or otherwise, the nominee is for all purposes treated as the owner of the shares and the company is treated as having no interest in them.[3] Consequently, the nominee is personally liable to contribute the capital unpaid on the shares and also any agreed share or issue premium, and he has no right to an indemnity from the company for these amounts, but the court may relieve him from personal liability if he acted honestly and reasonably and ought in the circumstances fairly to be excused from liability.[4] Additionally, the directors of the company at the time the shares were acquired by the nominee are jointly and severally liable with him for payment of the issue price of the shares to the company, or if the nominee subscribed the company's memorandum for the shares, the other subscribers of the memorandum are jointly and severally liable with him for the issue price, but the court may relieve them from liability in the same way as it may relieve the nominee himself.[5]

Register of members

A company must keep a register of its members showing their names and addresses, the number of shares or amounts of stock which each one holds, the class of shares or stock to which each member's holding belongs (if the company has more than one class of shares or stock), the distinguishing numbers of the shares (if they have

---

17 Law Reform (Married Women and Tortfeasors) Act 1935, s 1 (27 Halsbury's Statutes (4th Edn) 573).

18 *Princess Reuss v Bos* (1871) LR 5 HL 176; *R v Arnaud* (1846) 9 QB 806. For cases where alien control of a company has induced the court to disregard the separate legal personality of the company, see p 46, ante. These cases are exceptional however.

19 See p 11, ante.

20 *Trevor v Whitworth* (1887) 12 App Cas 409; *Kirby v Wilkins* [1929] 2 Ch 444.

1 Companies Act 1985, s 143 (1).

2 See p 409, post.

3 Companies Act 1985, s 144 (1).

4 Ibid, s 144 (3). Presumably relief would be given if the nominee was unaware of the company's interest when he acquired the shares, or if he honestly believed that the company was entitled to have an interest in the shares under one of the statutory exceptions.

5 Companies Act 1985, s 144 (2) and (3).

distinguishing numbers),[6] the amount paid up or credited as paid up on the shares, and the dates on which each member became and ceased to be a member.[7]

The register must be kept at the company's registered office, unless the work of making it up is done at another office of the company or at the office of another person or company who undertakes that work,[8] in which case it may be kept at that other office if it is in England or Wales,[9] but the company must then inform the Registrar of Companies where the register is kept and of any change in that place.[10] If the company's members are more than 50 in number, it must keep together with its register of members an index of the members' names showing where the entries in the register in respect of each member may be found.[11] This is not necessary, however, if the register is kept in the form of an index,[12] so that if the register is in the form of a loose leaf ledger or card index with a page or card devoted to each member in alphabetical order,[13] a separate index can be dispensed with. The register may alternatively be kept in a non-legible form (such as magnetised computer tape), but the company's obligations to allow inspection of the register by any person or to provide copies of it must then be satisfied by allowing inspection or providing copies of a legible reproduction of the register.[14] A company may remove entries from its register of members if they relate to a former member who has ceased to be a member for 20 years.[15]

Inspection and copies

Any person may inspect the register of members and index at any time; members are entitled to inspect free of charge, and other persons may be charged a fee not exceeding 5p.[16] The company may close its register for not more than 30 days each year[17] on giving notice of its intention to do so by advertisement in a newspaper circulating in the district of its registered office, and no-one can insist on inspecting the register or index during that time.[18] Any person may require a company to furnish him with a copy of any part of its register of members on payment of a fee not exceeding 10p for each hundred words copied.[19] The charges for inspection of the register of members and for supplying copies of any part of it may be increased by regulations made by the Secretary of State for Trade and Industry.[20] If a company fails to allow inspection of its register or to furnish a copy of it on request, the company and any director or secretary who is responsible are guilty of an

6 But a shareholder is a member even though the distinguishing numbers of his shares are not shown (*East Gloucester Rly Co v Bartholomew* (1867) LR 3 Exch 15).
7 Companies Act 1985, s 352 (1) to (3).
8 The register of members is often made up by a specialist company or firm employed by the company as its registrars and transfer agents or as its secretary.
9 Companies Act 1985, s 353 (1).
10 Ibid, s 353 (2).
11 Ibid, s 354 (1) to (3).
12 Ibid, s 354 (1).
13 This is permitted by Companies Act 1985, s 722 (1), but adequate precautions must be taken to prevent falsification of the register (s 722 (2)).
14 Companies Act 1985, s 723 (1) and (3).
15 Ibid, s 352 (6).
16 Ibid, s 356 (1) and (4).
17 The register is usually closed for a few days immediately before the declaration of dividends to facilitate the preparation of dividend warrants.
18 Companies Act 1985, s 358.
19 Ibid, s 356 (3) and (4). When the applicant wishes to communicate with the members, it has become the practice among the bigger public companies in recent years for them to supply the members' names and addresses by addressing envelopes supplied by the applicant.
20 Companies Act 1985, s 356 (1) and (3), as amended by Companies Act 1989, s 143 (8).

offence,[1] and the person who desires inspection or a copy of the register may apply to the court by originating summons[2] for an order that the company shall comply with his request.[3]

Overseas branch register

A company whose objects comprise the transaction of business in Northern Ireland or certain overseas countries (all of which are or were members of the British Commonwealth) may keep an overseas branch register of the company's members who are resident in such a country in which it does in fact transact business.[4] The overseas branch register is deemed to be part of the principal register kept in Great Britain,[5] and must be kept in the same manner as the principal register.[6] Shares registered in an overseas branch register must be distinguished from shares registered in the register kept in Great Britain;[7] this is usually done by the share certificate bearing a conspicuous note of the country where the overseas branch register is kept. Transfers of shares may only be registered in the overseas branch register itself,[7] but copies of all entries made in the register must be sent to the company's registered office so that the company may keep a duplicate of the overseas branch register with its principal register in Great Britain.[8] The duplicate register is deemed to be part of the principal register,[8] and so it is open to inspection by members and the public at the address where the principal register is kept, and copies of it may be obtained from the company.

The advantage of having an overseas branch register is that shares recorded in it are deemed to be property situate outside the United Kingdom[9] for the purpose of stamp duty, so that if such shares are transferred by an instrument of transfer executed outside the United Kingdom, no United Kingdom stamp duty is payable.[10] Furthermore, since transfers of and dealings with shares registered in an overseas branch register may only be recorded in that register,[7] the shares are deemed to be property situate outside the United Kingdom for tax purposes generally,[11] and so will not be subject to United Kingdom inheritance tax if a person domiciled outside the United Kingdom dies entitled to them beneficially.[12] They are likewise deemed to be situate outside the United Kingdom for the purpose of capital gains tax,[13] which is consequently not payable in the event of a disposal of them by an individual who is domiciled outside the United Kingdom, even though he is resident or ordinarily resident there.[14]

---

1 Ibid, s 356 (5).
2 RSC Ord 102, r 2 (1). The application is made to the Companies Court.
3 Companies Act 1985, s 356 (6).
4 Ibid, s 362 (1). The company must inform the Registrar of Companies where its overseas branch registers are kept (s 362 (3) and Sch 14, para 1 (1)).
5 Companies Act 1985, s 362 (3) and Sch 14, para 2 (1).
6 Ibid, para 2 (2).
7 Ibid, para 5.
8 Ibid, para 4 (1).
9 If an overseas branch register is kept in Northern Ireland, the shares registered in it will not be deemed to be situate outside the United Kingdom.
10 Companies Act 1985, s 362 (3) and Sch 14, para 8.
11 *Brassard v Smith* [1925] AC 371; *R v Williams* [1942] AC 541, [1942] 2 All ER 95; *Ontario Treasurer v Aberdein* [1947] AC 24; *Standard Chartered Bank Ltd v IRC* [1978] 3 All ER 644, [1978] 1 WLR 1160.
12 Inheritance Tax Act 1984, s 6 (1) (43 Halsbury's Statutes (4th Edn) 1080).
13 Capital Gains Tax 1979, s 18 (4) (*e*) (42 Halsbury's Statutes (4th Edn) 635).
14 Ibid, s 14 (1).

Rectification

A company's register of members is prima facie evidence of the matters recorded in it,[15] but it is not conclusive evidence, so that if the register does not show the person who is really entitled to shares as the registered holder of them, or if it contains any other incorrect entry, the company can be compelled to rectify it. Where the error is undoubted, it appears that the company should rectify the register on being requested to do so without waiting for the applicant to obtain an order of the court.[16] Even if the matter is doubtful, the company should make some enquiry before rejecting the request for rectification. If it refuses to rectify without making such an enquiry, it will be ordered to pay the costs of successful proceedings brought to obtain an order of the court for rectification.[17]

An action commenced by writ may be brought against a company in any case where the plaintiff has a right to have its register of members corrected or amended.[18] Also, a company which is in doubt about the validity of rival claims to the same shares may interplead,[19] and if the directors are unwilling to bring interpleader proceedings, any member, whether interested in the shares or not, may sue in a derivative action[20] for the rectification of the register of members.[1] However, rectification is now usually sought by making an application to the court on an originating motion[2] under the Companies Act 1985.[3] This summary procedure may be used by any person aggrieved, or by a member of the company or the company itself, whenever the applicant complains; (a) that the name of any person has, without sufficient cause, been entered in or omitted from the register; or (b) that default has been made, or unnecessary delay has occurred, in noting on the register that a person has ceased to be a member of the company.[3] Applications by the company itself are, of course, in the nature of interpleaders. If the court orders the register to be rectified on any application, it may also award damages against the company.[4] The court may order the applicant or the company to pay the costs of the application, but it cannot award costs against a person whose title to shares has been successfully impeached, but who is not a party to the proceedings.[5]

The summary procedure for rectification may be used if the allotment of shares to the applicant was void,[6] or was voidable because of misrepresentations made by the company to induce him to subscribe.[7] It may also be used where there are rival

---

15 Companies Act 1985, s 361.
16 *Reese River Silver Mining Co v Smith* (1869) LR 4 HL 64; *First National Reinsurance Co Ltd v Greenfield* [1921] 2 KB 260 at 279 per McCardie J. In *Re Derham and Allen Ltd* [1946] Ch 31, however, Cohen J expressed the opinion that a company should not rectify without first obtaining an order of the court.
17 *Re Tahiti Cotton Co, ex p Sargent* (1874) LR 17 Eq 273.
18 *Burns v Siemens Bros Dynamo Works Ltd* [1919] 1 Ch 225. In that case joint shareholders sued successfully to compel the company to reverse the order in which their names stood in the register of members. The application was made because, under the company's articles, only the first named of joint shareholders could vote at meetings of members, and the applicants wanted the second named of them to be able to vote in respect of some of their shares.
19 *Robinson v Jenkins* (1890) 24 QBD 275.
20 For derivative actions, see p 651, post.
 1 *Hunter v Hunter* [1936] AC 222.
 2 RSC Ord 102, r 3 (1). The application is made to the Companies Court.
 3 Companies Act 1985, s 359 (1).
 4 Ibid, s 359 (2).
 5 *Re Tahiti Cotton Co, ex p Sargent* (1874) LR 17 Eq 273.
 6 *Re Derham and Allen Ltd* [1946] Ch 31 (shares improperly issued at a discount); *Re Transatlantic Life Assurance Co Ltd* [1979] 3 All ER 352, [1980] 1 WLR 79 (shares issued without requisite Treasury consent under the Exchange Control Act 1947, s 8 (1)).
 7 *Re Russian (Vyksounsky) Ironworks Co, Stewart's Case* (1866) 1 Ch App 574; *Re Blair Open Hearth Furnace Co* [1914] 1 Ch 390.

claims to the same shares by different persons,[8] and it is here that the company's right to apply to the court is useful in order to determine a dispute to which it is not a party.[9] Again, the procedure may be used where a company wrongfully refuses to register a transferee of shares as a member, and the application may be made by the transferor[10] or the transferee.[11] The court may rectify the register after the company has commenced to be wound up, and may make the rectification effective from a date before the winding up began, so that the person whose name appears in the register after the rectification will become a contributory.[12]

The court may in its discretion refuse to rectify the register on a summary application under the Companies Act 1985. Where the facts are admitted and the question is simply one of law,[13] or where the facts can easily be ascertained,[14] the court will entertain the application, but if the facts are complex and in dispute,[15] or if there is pending litigation about the same question between one of the parties to the application and a third person,[16] the court will always refuse to give a decision, and will leave the applicant to seek rectification in an action commenced by writ. Furthermore, an application for rectification will be rejected if it is made for an improper purpose, (e g to prevent votes being cast in respect of shares contrary to the wishes of the applicant, who claims no beneficial interest in them).[17]

If a company incurs a liability to any person by making or deleting an entry in its register of members or by failing to make or delete any such entry, the liability may not be enforced against it more than 20 years after the entry was made or deleted or, as the case may be, the earliest failure of the company to make or delete the entry, but this does not affect the operation of any shorter period of limitation which may be applicable.[18] This provision appears to relate only to a company's liability to pay damages to a person who suffers loss as a result of a wrongful entry or deletion in the register or a wrongful refusal to make an entry or deletion, and not to affect the right of a person to assert a title to shares or to have the company's register of members rectified.

---

8 *Re Diamond Rock Boring Co, ex p Shaw* (1877) 2 QBD 463; *Re Tahiti Cotton Co, ex p Sargent* (1874) LR 17 Eq 273. This is now expressly sanctioned by the Companies Act 1985, s 359 (3).

9 Companies Act 1985, s 359 (1). See, for example, *Re Indo-China Steam Navigation Co* [1917] 2 Ch 100.

10 *Re Stranton Iron and Steel Co* (1873) LR 16 Eq 559. The Companies Act 1985, s 183 (4) gives the transferor a right to require the transfer to be registered if the transferee can require it to be.

11 *Re Gresham Life Assurance Society, ex p Penney* (1872) 8 Ch App 446.

12 *Re Sussex Brick Co* [1904] 1 Ch 598.

13 *Re Stranton Iron and Steel Co*, supra; *Re Tahiti Cotton Co, ex p Sargent*, supra; *Re Diamond Rock Boring Co*, supra.

14 *Re Russian (Vyksounsky) Ironworks Co, Stewart's Case*, supra.

15 *Re Ruby Consolidated Mining Co, Askew's Case* (1874) 9 Ch App 664; *Re Heaton Steel and Iron Co, Simpson's Case* (1869) LR 9 Eq 91.

16 *Re London, Hamburg and Continental Exchange Bank, Ward and Henry's Case* (1867) 2 Ch App 431.

17 *Re Piccadilly Radio plc* [1989] BCLC 683.

18 Companies Act 1985, s 352 (7). The limitation period normally applicable is 6 years (Limitation Act 1980, ss 2 and 5 (24 Halsbury's Statutes (4th Edn) 650 and 653). It is arguable that it is a breach of a company's articles for it to make an improper entry in its register of members or for it to refuse to make a proper entry, and that the appropriate limitation period is therefore 12 years (Limitation Act 1980, s 8(1)). But it has been held that an action for breach of the articles by the company is not one to enforce a specialty, and the limitation period is therefore six years (*Re Compania de Electricidad de la Provincia de Buenos Aires Ltd* [1980] Ch 146, [1978] 3 All ER 668).

CHAPTER 10

Dealing with shares

TRANSFERS OF THE LEGAL TITLE TO SHARES

Power of shareholders to transfer

Registered shares

A share is a legal chose in action,[1] or rather a bundle of contractual and statutory rights, each one of which is a legal chose in action.[2] The legal title to the share is vested in the person entitled to it either by allotment by the company or by transfer from a former holder, but if all the legal rights in respect of the share are to be enjoyed by that person, the company must have registered him as holder of it in the company's register of members.

Shares of companies formed at common law by deeds of settlement were transferable at law, even though at the time other legal choses in action were not generally transferable.[3] The usual provisions of the deed of settlement were that a shareholder might transfer his share by a deed (or, sometimes, by an instrument in writing), which on presentation to the company was to be registered in its register of share transfers, but that the transferee would become a member of the company, and the transferor cease to be one, only when the transferee executed the deed of settlement, whereupon the transferor would cease to be liable for debts of the company incurred thereafter.[4] The provision that the transferor should cease to be liable for future debts, was valid as between the transferor and other members of the company, and so he could not be called upon to contribute to their payment.[5] On the other hand, the transferee, by executing the deed of settlement, became liable to contribute toward payment of all the debts of the company, whether incurred before or after he became a member.[6] These consequences show the real nature of a transfer of shares at common law. It was not merely an assignment of a legal chose in action; it also involved a novation, by which the company and the transferor and transferee agreed that the transferee should be substituted for the transferor as a member of the company, with the same rights as the transferor possessed and subject to the same obligations as those to which the transferor was subject.

The consequences of a transfer of shares as between the transferor, the transferee and the other members of the company did not, of course, affect the rights of the company's creditors. As far as they were concerned the company was simply a

---

1 *Humble v Mitchell* (1839) 11 Ad & El 205; *Colonial Bank v Whinney* (1886) 11 App Cas 426.
2 See p 57, ante.
3 *Pinkett v Wright* (1842) 2 Hare 120; *Poole v Middleton* (1861) 29 Beav 646.
4 See, for example, the precedent of a deed of settlement in Collyer's *A Practical Treatise on the Law of Partnership* (2nd edn 1840), at pp 879 et seq, particularly clauses 123, 125 and 133.
5 *Jeffreys v Smith* (1827) 3 Russ 158; *Re Pennant and Craigwen Consolidated Lead Mining Co, Mayhew's Case* (1854) 5 De GM & G 837; *Re Mexican and South American Co, Aston's Case* (1859) 27 Beav 474 at 484.
6 *Re Monmouthshire and Glamorganshire Banking Co, Cape's Executor's Case* (1852) 2 De GM & G 562; *Mayhew's Case*, supra; *Re Mexican and South American Co, Grisewood and Smith's Case* (1859) 4 De G & J 544.

large partnership, and so the transferor remained liable to them for debts of the company incurred before he ceased to be a member, and the transferee was liable to them only for debts incurred after he became a member.[7] This position was preserved by the Joint Stock Companies Act of 1844, despite the fact that companies completely registered thereunder were incorporated, but with the coming of limited liability and the disappearance of the creditors' right to exact payment of the company's debts from its members personally, the consequences of a transfer of shares were confined to the purely internal ones between the transferor, the transferee and the company itself.

The Companies Act 1985 now provides that shares registered in the company's register of members are 'transferable in the manner provided by [its] articles',[8] and the transferee becomes a member of the company when he has signified his agreement to do so and has been entered on the register of members,[9] whereupon he is bound by the provisions of the memorandum and articles as if he had convenanted to conform to them,[10] although in fact he does not execute them at all. The substance of the novation which occurred on a transfer of shares at common law is therefore preserved, even though the form of the transaction is changed. It is almost certain, therefore, that a transfer of shares today still brings about a novation. It will be shown below that this is of considerable practical importance.

Procedure on transfers

The procedure for transferring shares registered in the company's register of members is for the transferor to execute a share transfer form by which, for a stated consideration (if any is given), he transfers a particular number of shares (describing them by their nominal value and class, stating how much has been paid up on them if they are partly paid, and setting out their distinguishing numbers if they have any) in the company (naming it) to the transferee subject to the conditions of the company's memorandum and articles of association, and the transferee agrees to accept them subject to those conditions.[11] Unless the company's articles require the transfer to be by deed,[12] a transfer is valid if it is signed by the transferor, and if the simplified form of transfer of fully paid shares now provided by the Stock Transfer Act 1963[13] is used, it is valid notwithstanding anything in the company's articles requiring a special form of transfer, provided it is signed by the transferor.[14] The transfer should state the names, addresses and descriptions of the transferor and transferee, but the transfer is valid even though these particulars are omitted or defectively stated, if the company is able to ascertain who the parties are from what is stated.[15] Furthermore, a transfer is valid if it omits to state the distinguishing numbers of the shares transferred,[16] or states them incorrectly.[17]

7 *Lanyon v Smith* (1863) 8 LT 312 at 313, *per* Blackburn J.
8 Companies Act 1985, s 182 (1) (*b*).
9 Ibid, s 22 (2).
10 Ibid, s 14 (1).
11 For precedents of transfers, see 5 *Encyclopaedia of Forms and Precedents* (4th Edn) 773, and *Palmer's Company Precedents* (17th Edn) Vol 1, p 829.
12 Table A, art 23, permits transfers to be made 'in any usual form', thus dispensing with the need for a deed.
13 Stock Transfer Act 1963, s 1 (1) and (4) and Sch 1 (30 Halsbury's Statutes (4th Edn) 157, 163); The Stock Transfer (Amendment of Forms) Order 1974 (SI 1974/1214), para 3 (1)). The prescribed form of transfer may be varied by an order made by the Treasury by statutory instrument (Stock Transfer Act 1963, s 3 (2)–(5); Stock Exchange (Completion of Bargains) Act 1976, s 6 (1) (30 Halsbury's Statutes (4th Edn) 160, 205)).
14 Stock Transfer Act 1963, s 2 (1).
15 *Re Letheby and Christopher Ltd* [1904] 1 Ch 815.
16 *Re Letheby and Christopher Ltd*, supra; *Re Barned's Banking Co, ex p Contract Corpn* (1867) 3 Ch App 105.
17 *Re International Contract Co, Ind's Case* (1872) 7 Ch App 485.

When he has executed the transfer, the transferor delivers it together with his share certificate to the transferee, who executes the transfer, stamps it,[18] and sends both documents to the company for registration.[19] If the simplified form of transfer of fully paid shares provided by the Stock Transfer Act 1963[20] is used, the transferee need not execute the transfer, and the company cannot refuse to register it because he has not done so,[1] but it is undoubtedly entitled to some other proof of his agreement to become a member. Whichever form of transfer is used, the company ascertains that the documents delivered to it are formally in order, and that the transferor is registered as a member in respect of the shares transferred, and it then enters the transferee in its register of members as a member in respect of those shares and enters a note against the transferor's name that he is no longer a member in respect of them, the date inserted against both these entries being the date on which the entry is made and not the date in the instrument of transfer. The transferor's share certificate and the instrument of transfer are retained by the company, and in their place a new share certificate, showing the transferee as the holder of the shares, is issued to him. The new certificate must be ready for delivery to the transferee within two months after the instrument of transfer was lodged with the company,[2] but the terms of issue of the shares may allow the company a longer period,[3] and a certificate need in no case be issued at all if the shares are transferred to a nominee of the Stock Exchange approved by the Secretary of State for Trade and Industry,[4] or to the nominee of any other recognised investment exchange or clearing house recognised by the Secretary of State.[5] If the company fails to prepare the new certificate, the transferee may apply summarily to the court for an order that it shall do so,[6] and if it fails to make the appropriate entries in its register of members, either the transferor or transferee may apply to the court for an order that the register shall be rectified.[7]

A company cannot register a transfer of shares unless a proper instrument of transfer has been delivered to it.[8] Consequently, a provision in a company's articles by which on the death of a shareholder his shares were automatically to pass to his

18 The transfer must be stamped within thirty days after it is executed by the transferor (Stamp Act 1891, s 15 (2) (41 Halsbury's Statutes (4th Edn) 155), and for this reason the transfer is always dated. Directors who register a transfer which has not been properly stamped are guilty of an offence (Stamp Act 1891, s 17), and it has been suggested that the legal title to shares will not pass to the transferee if the transfer is not properly stamped (*Re Indo-China Steam Navigation Co* [1917] 2 Ch 100 at 106, per Eve J). The rates of stamp duty are given below in connection with the disposition to which they relate.

19 By Table A, art 27, no fee is payable to the company on the registration of a transfer, but such a fee is still payable if the company is governed by Table A of the Companies Act 1948, or of any of the earlier Companies Acts.

20 Stock Transfer Act 1963, s 1 (1) and (4) and Sch 1.

1 Ibid, s 2 (1).

2 It is, apparently, the transferee's duty to obtain delivery of his share certificate, and not the company's to despatch it to him.

3 Companies Act 1985, s 185 (1). If the company has a listing for any of its securities on the Stock Exchange, it must register a transfer and issue a new share certificate without payment of any fee within 14 days after a transfer is presented for registration (*Admission of Securities to Listing*, Section 5, Chapter 2, paras 27 and 28).

4 Companies Act 1985, s 185 (4); Stock Exchange (Designation of Nominee) Order 1985 (SI 1985/ 806), para 2. The nominee is the company, SEPON Ltd, formed by the Stock Exchange to facilitate the settlement of bargains (see p 394, post).

5 Companies Act 1985, s 185 (4), as amended by Financial Services Act 1986, s 194 (5).

6 Companies Act 1985, s 185 (6) and (7). The application is made to the Companies Court by originating summons (RSC Ord 102, r 2 (1)).

7 Companies Act 1985, s 359 (1) (see p 337, ante).

8 Ibid, s 183 (1). There is no requirement that the transferor's share certificate should be delivered to the company, but the directors may refuse to register the transfer unless it is delivered or its loss is accounted for (*Re The East Wheal Martha Mining Co* (1863) 33 Beav 119).

widow, was held to be void, because if the provision were effective, the widow would have the right to be registered as a member of the company without producing a written transfer from her husband.[9] Persons to whom the title to shares has passed by operation of law, such as personal representatives and trustees in bankruptcy, are, however, entitled to be registered as members without producing a written transfer.[10]

Restrictions on transfer

Shares are freely transferable unless the company's articles impose restrictions on their transfer.[11] Where there are no such restrictions, the motive of the transferor in disposing of his shares is immaterial. Thus, if a holder of partly paid shares transfers them to a person of small means,[12] or even to an insolvent person,[13] in order to avoid liability for future calls, the transfer is valid and must be registered by the company. This is so even though the transferor pays the transferee to take the transfer,[14] or agrees to indemnify him against future calls.[15] Moreover, it is immaterial that the transferee has been induced to take the transfer by misrepresentation or undue influence, for this merely entitles the transferee to rescind the transfer if he chooses, but gives the company no right to interfere.[14] If a shareholder transfers partly paid shares to a trustee or nominee for himself, the transfer is effective to pass the legal title, and the company must accept the transferee as a member, but the transferor, as beneficial owner, must indemnify the transferee against future calls,[16] and if the company cannot recover the calls from the transferee, it may enforce this right of indemnity against the transferor by subrogation.[17] Furthermore, the transferor of shares to a trustee or nominee for himself may be made a contributory in the company's winding up so that the liquidator may recover unpaid capital from him directly, whether such capital was called up before or after he transferred the shares to the trustee or nominee, and whether the capital was called up by the directors or by the liquidator himself.[18]

A company's articles may impose any kind of restriction on the transfer of shares, but it would seem that they cannot prohibit transfers completely so as to make the company a kind of incorporated partnership, because the Companies Act 1985 contemplates that shares must be transferable to some extent.[19] The court interprets restrictions on transferability strictly, and if there is an ambiguity or uncertainty, inclines to the interpretation which will give the shareholder the greatest freedom to transfer. Thus, where articles empowered the directors to refuse to register a transfer of shares by a shareholder who was indebted to the company, and imposed a lien in favour of the company on the shares of members for money 'due' from

9 *Re Greene, Greene v Greene* [1949] Ch 333, [1949] 1 All ER 167. The articles themselves were not an instrument of transfer, although they had been signed by the shareholder as a subscriber on the formation of the company. A transfer must identify the transferee so that at the date of its execution the transferee may be distinguished from other persons, and at the date the shareholder subscribed the articles it was impossible to identify the person who would be his widow on his death.

10 Companies Act 1985, s 183 (2).

11 *Re Smith, Knight & Co, Weston's Case* (1868) 4 Ch App 20.

12 *Re European Bank, Master's Case* (1872) 7 Ch App 292; *Re Mexican and South American Co, De Pass's Case* (1859) 4 De G & J 544.

13 *R v Lambourn Valley Rly Co* (1888) 22 QBD 463.

14 *Re Hafod Lead Mining Co, Slater's Case* (1866) 35 Beav 391.

15 *Re Discoverers Finance Corpn Ltd, Lindlar's Case* [1910] 1 Ch 207.

16 *James v May* (1873) LR 6 HL 328; *Hardoon v Belilios* [1901] AC 118.

17 *Heritage v Paine* (1876) 2 ChD 594; *Re European Society Arbitration Acts* (1878) 8 ChD 679.

18 *Re Mexican and South American Co, Hyam's Case* (1859) 1 De GF & J 75; *Re Discoverers Finance Corpn Ltd, Lindlar's Case*, supra.

19 Companies Act 1985, s 182 (1)(*b*).

them to the company, it was held that the power to refuse registration of transfers must be read as ancillary to the lien, and so the directors could only refuse to register a transfer by a member who owed a debt which was immediately due and payable, and not merely a debt payable at a future time.[20] On the other hand, a company is entitled to the protection afforded by restrictions on the transfer of its shares, and so if a member obtains registration of a transfer of shares by making false statements to the directors, or by collusion with the directors, the company may cancel the registration, and treat the transferor as still being a member of it.[1]

If a company exercises its right to refuse to register a transfer under a provision of its memorandum or articles, it must notify the transferee within two months after the transfer is presented for registration.[2] If it fails to notify the transferee within the two months, the company cannot afterwards assert its right of refusal against him, and he may compel it to register him as a member of the company.[3] The company need not notify the transferor that it has refused to register the transfer, however, and its failure to do so does not prevent it from maintaining his name on the register of members and treating him as a contributory when the company is wound up.[4] The company's obligation to notify its refusal to register a transfer only applies if its refusal is because it exercises a discretion vested in it to refuse to register a transfer. If the transferee has no right to be registered at all, because, for example, his title to the shares is defective, the company does not lose its power to refuse to register him as a member, and he acquires no right to be registered, merely because the company delays for more than two months in informing him that it will not register him.

Public companies do not, in practice, impose any restriction on the transfer of their fully paid shares, because they cannot obtain a stock exchange listing for any of their shares, debentures or other loan securities if they do.[5] Private companies, on the other hand, were formerly required by law to impose some restriction on transfers of shares by their articles,[6] and still often do so in practice. Consequently, it will be more appropriate to deal with the types of restrictions on transfers of shares which appear in articles of association when private companies are dealt with later in this book.[7]

Share warrants

Share warrants issued in respect of fully paid shares are transferable by delivery[8] without the execution of any written instrument of transfer and without the transfer being registered by the company. The owner of a share warrant is not a member of the company, and therefore does not enter into the implied statutory covenant to observe the provisions of the company's memorandum and articles.[9] Consequently, there is no novation to which the company is a party when the

---

20 *Re Stockton Malleable Iron Co* (1875) 2 ChD 101.
1 *Re Discoverers Finance Corpn Ltd, Lindlar's Case*, supra.
2 Companies Act 1985, s 183 (5).
3 *Re Swaledale Cleaners Ltd* [1968] 3 All ER 619, [1968] 1 WLR 1710.
4 *Re European Central Rly Co, Gustard's Case* (1869) LR 8 Eq 438.
5 Stock Exchange: *Admission of Securities to Listings*, Section 1, Chapter 2, para 4 and Section 9, Chapter 1, para 1.2. Table A, art 24, empowers directors to refuse to register transfers of shares only if they are partly paid or are subject to a lien in favour of the company.
6 Companies Act 1948, s 28 (1) (repealed by Companies Act 1980, s 88 (2) and Sch 4).
7 See p 752, post.
8 Companies Act 1985, s 188 (2), as substituted by Companies Act 1989, s 130 (7) and Sch 17, para 6.
9 Ibid, s 14 (1). But see p 332, ante as to the implication of a similar contract apart from the Companies Act 1985.

owner of a share warrant transfers it, but the protection which is given to a transferee of registered shares by such a novation is given to the same or a larger extent to the transferee of a share warrant by it being a negotiable instrument.[10] Furthermore, a share warrant must be freely transferable, because the method of transferring it obviously makes it impossible for the company to impose restrictions on transfers.

Transfer of shares free from equities between the company and the original allottee

Legal choses in action can usually only be assigned subject to equities existing between the original parties at the date when the first assignment of them is completed by notification.[11] 'Equities' in this context does not mean equitable interests derived out of the chose in action, but instead means defences which the debtor or obligor could have pleaded if sued by the original creditor or obligee at the date when the transfer of the chose in action is notified to the debtor or obligor. Such defences fall into two groups, namely, defects in the original transaction by which the chose in action was created, and rights of the debtor or obligor to set off against the creditor's or obligee's claim some claim of his own which he has against the creditor or obligee.[12] In the case of shares, however, for various reasons equities which a company could plead against the original allottee of shares cannot be pleaded against his transferee.

Defects on the issue of shares

Mere procedural defects on the issue of shares will not prejudice an allottee who is unaware of them, or his successors in title, because they may rely for their protection on the rule in *Royal British Bank v Turquand*.[13] But the protection of the rule will not be available where an issue of shares is defective in substance, as it is when the directors never allot the shares at all, and the share certificate issued to the subscriber is forged by the company's secretary,[14] or when the contract for allotment is void because of a fundamental mistake,[15] or when a subscriber obtains shares by misrepresentation, or when shares are allotted to directors or their nominees in breach of the directors' fiduciary duties to the company.[16] In these cases the company may treat the allotment as void or voidable against the original allottee, but not invariably against persons to whom he transfers his shares.

If a person takes a transfer of shares whose allotment was defective in substance, and he gives value and has no notice of the defect and is registered as a member of the company, the company is precluded from disputing his title to the shares for the following reasons:

(1) A transfer of shares involves a novation, by which the company enters into a fresh contract with the transferee in terms identical to those of the original contract with the allottee. Because of this, the transferee's title is not vitiated by any defects in the original contract, as it would be if he were a mere assignee of a chose in action.

10 *Webb Hale & Co v Alexandria Water Co* (1905) 21 TLR 572.
11 Law of Property Act 1925, s 136 (1) (37 Halsbury's Statutes (4th Edn) 257).
12 This subject is dealt with more fully in Chapter 12 in connection with debentures where it is of greater practical importance (see pp 477, et seq, post).
13 (1855) 5 E & B 248 (see Chapter 5).
14 *Ruben v Great Fingall Consolidated* [1906] AC 439.
15 *Re International Society of Auctioneers and Valuers, Baillie's Case* [1898] 1 Ch 110.
16 *Piercy v S Mills & Co* [1920] 1 Ch 77.

(2) Shares are transferable by a statutory provision,[17] which does not provide that the transfer will be subject to equities. Where a legal chose in action is assignable at law in this way, the purchaser takes free from equities of which he is unaware, whether they make the chose in action voidable[18] or absolutely void.[19]

(3) By registering the transfer, the company waives any right it may have to raise equities against the transferee.[20]

If a transferee of shares has not yet been registered as a member of the company, and has therefore not yet acquired full legal rights in respect of the shares against the company, the company will be prevented from raising equities against him only if it has estopped itself from doing so by its conduct.[1] It has been suggested that the company estops itself by issuing the shares on terms that they may be transferred, because it thereby induces purchasers to take them on the assumption that they were validly issued, and it cannot then raise equities against a purchaser who is unaware of them when he contracts to buy the shares.[2] There is no direct authority for this, however, but even if it is the law, it certainly does not apply when an unauthorised person has put a forged share certificate into circulation, because in that case the company was not a party to its issue.[3] Moreover, there is probably no estoppel when shares are allotted under a contract which is void for mistake, because the company does not give a real assent to their issue and cannot therefore be taken to make any representation as to their validity. The better view would seem to be that a company is precluded from pleading equities against the transferee only if it has registered the transfer, or at least, if the transferee has an immediately enforceable right to insist on registration because the company has accepted the transfer he has presented for registration, or has ceased to be entitled to reject it by failing to notify the transferee to that effect within two months after the transfer is presented for registration.[4]

Set-off

If a shareholder is indebted to the company for a sum which is immediately due and payable, it may set off the debt against any dividends which are payable to him in respect of his shares.[5] Often the articles contain an express power for the company to do this, but the right is one conferred by law in any event, and is therefore not diminished by an enumeration in the articles of particular debts which may be set off (eg unpaid calls).[6] If capital is repayable to a shareholder on a duly authorised reduction of capital, or on the lawful purchase by a company of shares issued by it, or on the maturity of redeemable shares, the company is similarly entitled to set off debts due to it from the shareholder against the repayment of capital on his shares, or against the purchase price or the amount payable on redemption of the shares. But, for the reasons given above, the

---

17 Companies Act 1985, s 182 (1) (*b*).
18 *Re Romford Canal Co* (1883) 24 ChD 85.
19 *Webb v Herne Bay Comrs* (1870) LR 5 QB 642.
20 *Higgs v Northern Assam Tea Co* (1869) LR 4 Exch 387; *Re Northern Assam Tea Co, ex p Universal Life Assurance Co* (1870) LR 10 Eq 458.
1 *Re Romford Canal Co*, supra; *Higgs v Northern Assam Tea Co*, supra.
2 *Re Romford Canal Co*, supra, per Kay J at 93.
3 *Ruben v Great Fingall Consolidated* [1906] AC 439.
4 Companies Act 1985, s 183 (5); *Re Swaledale Cleaners Ltd* [1968] 3 All ER 619, [1968] 1 WLR 1710.
5 *Re Cannock and Rugely Colliery Co, ex p Harrison* (1885) 28 ChD 363.
6 The Companies Act 1948, Table A, art 119, empowered the directors to set off unpaid calls and instalments of the issue price of shares against dividends. The present Table A omits this provision.

company's right to set off a debt owed to it by a shareholder cannot be exercised against a person to whom he transfers the shares if the transfer has been registered, or if the transferee has an immediately enforceable right against the company to have it registered.

Share warrants

Because a share warrant is a negotiable instrument, a transferee of the warrant who gives value and has no notice of circumstances attending its issue which make its issue voidable, is not affected by those circumstances, and may enforce the rights attached to the shares by their terms of issue without reservation.[7] But a purchaser of a forged share warrant has no rights against the company,[8] unless it has estopped itself by its conduct from asserting that the warrant is a forgery, as it would do if it told the purchaser that it was genuine before he completed his purchase and so induced him to do so.[9] The position where a company has been induced to issue a share warrant by a fundamental mistake appears to be the same.[10]

Rights of set-off exercisable against the holder of a negotiable instrument are not available against a transferee who gives value, even if he is aware that his transferor is indebted to the issuer of the instrument.[11] Consequently, a company which has issued a share warrant can only exercise its right to set off a debt owed to it against dividends and repayments of capital if the debt is owed by the present holder of the warrant or by a person from whom he acquired it gratuitously.

Transfer of shares where the transferor's title is defective

General rule

If a transferor's title to shares registered in the company's register of members is defective, the transferee will generally obtain no better title to them than the transferor has. This is because shares, as a species of property, are subject to the general rule of property law that a disponor of property cannot vest a better title in his disponee than he has himself, with the consequence that the true owner of the shares can therefore enforce his rights in respect of them notwithstanding any pretended dealings by unauthorised persons.[12] Thus, if someone forges a transfer of a member's shares to a transferee who believes the transfer to be genuine, the transfer is a nullity, and the true owner may have the register of members rectified if the transferee has been entered as a member in his place.[13] Likewise, if a shareholder is induced to transfer his shares by a fundamental mistake which vitiates the contract for the transfer,[14] or by a mistake made without negligence as to the effect of the instrument of transfer which he executes,[15] the transfer is void,

---

7 *Webb, Hale & Co v Alexandria Water Co* (1905) 93 LR 339.
8 *Morris v Bethell* (1869) LR 5 CP 47; *M'Kenzie v British Linen Co* (1881) 6 App Cas 82.
9 *Greenwood v Martins Bank Ltd* [1933] AC 51, [1932] All ER Rep 318; *Brown v Westminster Bank Ltd* [1964] 2 Lloyd's Rep 187.
10 *Ayres v Moore* [1940] 1 KB 278 at 285, [1939] 4 All ER 351 at 355.
11 *Oulds v Harrison* (1854) 10 Exch 572; *Re Overend, Gurney & Co, ex p Swan* (1868) LR 6 Eq 344; *Montecchi v Shimco (UK) Ltd* [1979] 1 WLR 1180, [1980] 1 Lloyd's Rep 50.
12 *Poole v Middleton* (1861) 29 Beav 646; *Birkenhead, Lancashire and Cheshire Junction Rly Co v Pilcher* (1851) 5 Exch 114 at 123.
13 *Taylor v Midland Rly Co* (1860) 28 Beav 287; affd sub nom *Midland Rly Co v Taylor* (1862) 8 HL Cas 751; *Barton v London and North Western Rly Co* (1888) 38 ChD 144; *Barton v North Staffordshire Rly Co* (1888) 38 ChD 458.
14 *Hardman v Booth* (1863) 1 H & C 803; *Cundy v Lindsay* (1878) 3 App Cas 459.
15 *Foster v Mackinnon* (1869) LR 4 CP 704; *Saunders v Anglia Building Society* [1971] AC 1004, [1970] 3 All ER 961.

and the transferee obtains no title to the shares despite his good faith or the registration of the transfer. But if a transfer is merely voidable, for example, because of a misrepresentation or the exercise of undue influence by the transferee, the transferor cannot rescind the transfer against a purchaser for value from the transferee who has no notice of the circumstances, and such a purchaser will obtain a good title against the transferor, whether the transfer has been registered or not.[16]

A purchaser for value of a share warrant who takes delivery of it obtains a good title notwithstanding defects in the title of his transferor of which he was unaware.[17] This is because a share warrant is a negotiable instrument.

Where the true owner is estopped from denying the validity of an unauthorised transfer

Even though a transferor has no title or a defective title to shares, the true owner may estop himself by his conduct from challenging the transferee's title; the transferee is then entitled to be entered on the register of members as owner of the shares, and his title to them is good against the true owner and, of course, against all other persons. For this to happen it is essential that the transferee should be unaware of the defect in his transferor's title when he takes a transfer. If he was aware of the defect, he cannot say that the true owner's conduct induced him to take the shares, and so cannot contend that the true owner is in any way estopped.

The commonest case of estoppel has been where the registered holder of shares delivers his share certificate and a transfer executed by him with the name of the transferee left blank to an agent to whom he gives a limited authority to deal with the shares, and the agent completes the blank transfer to effect a transaction which is outside the scope of his authority. Here the registered holder puts the agent in a position where he appears to be entitled to the shares himself, or at least to have full power to deal with them,[18] and the registered holder thereby estops himself from denying that the agent is so entitled or empowered to deal with the shares as against a purchaser who believes that to be the case and acts accordingly.[19]

For an estoppel to arise in this way: (a) there must be an apparently complete chain of title from the registered holder named in the share certificate down to the purchaser from the agent, and (b) the owner of the shares must be responsible for creating that apparent title. Thus, where the executors of a deceased shareholder delivered his share certificate with a blank transfer executed by them to agents for forwarding to the company in order that the executors might be registered as holders of the shares, and the agents wrongfully sold the shares, it was held that the executors were not estopped from showing that the agents had no authority to sell, because the executors had not vested them with an apparent title to the shares, there being a break in the chain of title between the deceased, in whose name the share certificate stood, and the executors who executed the transfer.[20] Presumably, if the executors had also delivered the grant of probate of the deceased shareholder's will to the agents, they would then have vested them with an apparent title or power of disposal, and would have been estopped from denying the title of a purchaser who bought on the strength of all three documents.

Again where a shareholder delivered a share certificate and a blank transfer executed by himself to an agent, and the blank transfer did not specify the shares to be transferred by it, it was held that the shareholder was not estopped from

---

16 *White v Garden* (1851) 10 CB 919; *Babcock v Lawson* (1879) 4 QBD 394.
17 *Webb Hale & Co v Alexandria Water Co* (1905) 93 LT 339.
18 *Colonial Bank v Hepworth* (1887) 36 ChD 36 at 54; *Bentinck v London Joint Stock Bank* [1893] 2 Ch 120.
19 *Colonial Bank v Cady and Williams* (1890) 15 App Cas 267, per Lord Watson at 278; *Rimmer v Webster* [1902] 2 Ch 163, per Farwell LJ at 172–3; *Fuller v Glyn Mills Currie & Co* [1914] 2 KB 168.
20 *Colonial Bank v Cady and Williams*, supra.

denying the title of a purchaser to whom the agent purported to transfer other shares belonging to the shareholder by misappropriating the share certificate relating to the other shares and filling in particulars of them in the blank transfer.[1] Here the agent appeared to be entitled to the shares he transferred, but the true owner was not responsible for creating that appearance. He did not give the agent the share certificate for the shares which the agent sold, but merely a blank transfer in which it was possible for the agent to fill in particulars of those shares. Consequently, even if the true owner were responsible for the particulars which the agent filled in, he was still not responsible for creating the agent's apparent title, which was only complete when the agent misappropriated the relevant share certificate.

In order to raise an estoppel against the true owner, the purchaser of shares must believe that the agent is the beneficial owner of the shares, or at least, that he has full power to deal with them. The purchaser can only do this if the blank transfer has the purchaser's name written in as transferee when it is delivered to him,[2] and the relevant share certificate is delivered to the purchaser at the same time[3] or the transfer has been certificated by the company adding a note to it that the share certificate has been deposited with it.[4] If the agent hands the purchaser a transfer executed by the true owner which still has the transferee's name left blank, the purchaser thereby has notice that the agent may not be the beneficial owner of the shares or may not have full power to deal with them, but may merely have a limited authority to act on the true owner's behalf, and the purchaser is then put on enquiry as to the actual limits of the agent's authority.[5] The same rule applies if the transfer to the purchaser is executed by the agent himself, and the transfer is delivered to the purchaser without his name filled in as transferee. Thus, where an owner of shares mortgaged them as security for a loan by depositing with the mortgagee his share certificate and a transfer in which the mortgagee's name was filled in as transferee, and the mortgagee sub-mortgaged the shares to the defendant for a larger loan by delivering to him those documents and a blank transfer executed by the mortgagee, it was held that the fact that the second transfer was executed by the mortgagee in blank gave the defendant notice that the mortgagee might have merely a limited power of disposition, and as the sub-mortgage for the larger loan was outside his actual powers, the owner of the shares could redeem by paying the defendant what he owed the mortgagee, and he did not have to repay the larger amount which the mortgagee had borrowed from the defendant.[6]

But estoppel is not entirely excluded even where a purchaser has implied notice of an agent's limited authority because the transfer delivered to the purchaser is in blank. If the owner of the shares empowers the agent to sell them, and the agent mortgages them instead by delivering the share certificate and a blank transfer to the mortgagee, the mortgagee acquires no title, because mortgaging the shares is a different kind of transaction from selling them, and the mortgagee is unprotected because his name is not inserted in the transfer as transferee when it is delivered to him.[7] But if the owner empowers the agent to mortgage the shares for not more than a specified amount, and the agent mortgages them for a greater sum, the

---

1 *Swan v North British Australasian Co* (1863) 2 H & C 175.
2 *Ortigosa v Brown* (1878) 47 LJ Ch 168; *France v Clark* (1884) 26 ChD 257; *Hutchison v Colorado United Mining Co* (1886) 3 TLR 265; *Fox v Martin* (1895) 64 LJ Ch 473.
3 *Société Générale de Paris v Walker* (1885) 11 App Cas 20 at 28–29 per Lord Selborne.
4 For the effect of certification of a share transfer, see p 379, post.
5 *Earl of Sheffield v London Joint Stock Bank* (1888) 13 App Cas 333, as explained in *London Joint Stock Bank v Simmons* [1892] AC 201 at 208 per Lord Halsbury.
6 *Ortigosa v Brown*, supra.
7 *Fox v Martin* (1895) 64 LJ Ch 473.

mortgagee is entitled to the shares as security for the greater sum, for although the blank transfer gives him notice that the agent only has authority to borrow, the owner is estopped from alleging that the agent has only a limited borrowing power. This is because the owner's act in putting documents in the agent's hands by the use of which a loan may be raised makes it appear to any prospective lender that the agent has authority to borrow any amount, however large.[8]

The rule which protects a purchaser who buys shares on the faith of a transfer duly completed with his name filled in as transferee, resembles the rule that if a holder in due course acquires a bill of exchange, cheque or promissory note which was originally signed by the drawer in blank or when incomplete in respect of its amount, but the bill has been completed before it reaches the holder in due course, the latter may enforce it against the drawer for the amount filled in by any intermediate holder, who is deemed to have authority from the drawer for the purpose.[9] In origin both rules are the same, being based on estoppel. But it is not correct to infer from this that a blank share transfer accompanied by a share certificate is a negotiable instrument.[10] The courts have not recognised the combination as constituting a negotiable instrument, and it would seem theoretically impossible for two documents to have that character in combination when separately neither of them has it.[11] Consequently, if the title of agent who wrongfully sells shares to a purchaser by means of a blank transfer is defective in some other respect, for example, because the transfer to his principal was void, the purchaser will obtain no better title than the principal had to give.

A less common case of estoppel is where the true owner of shares by his deliberate or negligent act enables another person to dispose of his shares to a purchaser who believes that the other person is the owner of them. For an estoppel to arise in this situation, the true owner's act must be the immediate cause of the unauthorised person executing the transfer and deceiving the purchaser. Thus, where a corporation negligently allowed its clerk to have access to its common seal, and the clerk was thereby enabled to forge a transfer of stock owned by the corporation, it was held that the corporation was not estopped from denying the title of the transferee, because it was not foreseeable that the clerk would misuse the common seal in that way.[12] Again, in the case already cited,[13] where a shareholder delivered a share certificate and a blank transfer to an agent, and the agent sold other shares belonging to the same shareholder by misappropriating the share certificate relating to them and filling in particulars of them in the blank transfer, it was held that it was not foreseeable that the agent would use the blank transfer in that way when the shareholder delivered it to him, and so the shareholder was not estopped from denying the purchaser's title. In the light of these cases it seems unlikely that any act on the part of a shareholder short of an express or implied representation to the purchaser that the person who sells the shares to him has the shareholder's authority or consent to do so, will raise an estoppel in favour of the purchaser.

8 *Fry v Smellie* [1912] 3 KB 282.
9 Bills of Exchange Act 1882, s 20 (5 Halsbury's Statutes (4th Edn) 346).
10 *London and Country Banking Co Ltd v London and River Plate Bank Ltd* (1887) 20 QBD 232; affd (1881) 21 QBD 535; *Colonial Bank v Hepworth* (1887) 36 ChD 36 at 53.
11 Share certificates with indorsed blank transfers or with separate blank transfers are treated as negotiable in the United States, but this is the result of legislation, viz, ss 1, 5 and 7 of the Uniform Stock Transfer Act, which was adopted by all fifty states, and which has been re-enacted by the Uniform Commercial Code, art 8–308 and 311. By the Rules of the Stock Exchange, r 660.0 share certificates in American form with indorsed blank transfers are recognised as 'securities passing by delivery', but are not included in the list of securities recognised as negotiable by r 660.1).
12 *Mayor, Constables and Company of Merchants of the Staple of England v Governors of the Bank of England* (1887) 21 QBD 160.
13 *Swan v North British Australasian Co* (1863) 2 H & C 175.

Where the true owner is estopped from denying the validity of the registration of an irregular transfer

If a purchaser acquires shares from an agent in circumstances which estop the owner of the shares from disputing the agent's authority to dispose of them, the purchaser acquires a title to the shares as against the true owner as soon as he takes delivery of the blank transfer duly completed by the agent together with the owner's share certificate or, alternatively, when he takes delivery of a completed transfer which the company has certificated so as to show that the share certificate has been deposited with it. In those circumstances it is not necessary that the purchaser should also be registered as a member of the company in respect of the shares. It remains to discover whether a similar protection is given to a purchaser whose title to the shares is defective for other reasons, if the true owner allows him to become or remain the registered holder of the shares, and the estoppel he pleads depends on that.

Mere registration of a purchaser as the holder of shares in a company's register of members does not prevent the true owner of the shares from insisting on the restoration of his name to the register, because the true owner is not a party to the act of registration.[14] Even if the company notifies the true owner that a transfer of his shares has been presented to it for registration, he is not prevented from insisting on the restoration of his name to the register if he fails to notify the company that the transfer is a forgery or otherwise invalid, and in consequence the company is induced to register it.[15] This is because the owner of the shares owes no duty to the company or to the purchaser to reveal the real facts to them.[15] But if the true owner approves or ratifies the registration, either expressly, or impliedly by receiving the proceeds of sale on a forged transfer of his shares, or by authorising the forger to deal with the proceeds of sale, he cannot insist on the company rectifying the register,[16] and therefore cannot impeach the purchaser's title. Similarly, the true owner will be estopped from impeaching the purchaser's title if he has assured the purchaser that he had authorised the transfer and its registration, and has thereby induced the purchaser not to pursue a remedy against the forger until it is purposeless to do so.[17] The result would be the same if the transfer to the purchaser were invalid for any other reason than forgery. If the true owner has ratified the registration of an invalid transfer, the company cannot remove the purchaser's name from its register of members,[18] and so he is entitled to be treated as a member of the company for all purposes.

Company's estoppel by registering transfers and issuing share certificates

By issuing a share certificate showing a named person as entitled to certain shares, a company represents that he is so entitled, and if anyone deals with him in reliance on the certificate and suffers a detriment in consequence of his having no title to the shares, the company is estopped from denying the truth of its representation. But the falsity of the share certificate does not of itself give a cause of action against the company, unless the directors issue the false certificate knowingly, so that the company is vicariously liable for their deceit, or possibly unless they issue the

---

14 See the cases cited in note 13 on p 346, ante.
15 *Barton v London and North Western Rly Co* (1889) 24 QBD 77.
16 *Welch v Bank of England* [1955] Ch 508, [1955] 1 All ER 811.
17 *Greenwood v Martins Bank Ltd* [1933] All ER Rep 318; *Brown v Westminster Bank Ltd* [1964] 2 Lloyd's Rep 187.
18 *Davis v Bank of England* (1824) 2 Bing 393.

certificate without taking reasonable care to ensure that it is correct,[19] so that the company is vicariously liable for their negligence. If the certificate is issued innocently by the directors, a person who relies on it can only sue the company if he can show that it would owe him some duty if the certificate were correct, that it has not fulfilled that duty, and that it is estopped from pleading the error in the share certificate as an excuse. In most cases the plaintiff will have bought the shares from the person named in the certificate, or will have taken a mortgage of the shares from him, and the breach of duty which the purchaser or mortgagee alleges will be the company's refusal to register him as holder of the shares in its register of members, or the removal of his name from the register once he has been registered.[20] In such cases the plaintiff may sue the company for damages, and because it issued a share certificate showing the seller or mortgagor as holder of the shares, the company will be estopped from contending that he had no title to them and that it was consequently justified in refusing to register the transfer to the purchaser or mortgagee, or in removing his name from the register.

If a person buys or takes a mortgage of shares without relying on a share certificate showing the seller or mortgagor as the registered holder of them, the company is not estopped from showing that he had no title to the shares merely because it issues a fresh share certificate to the buyer or mortgagee, and in those circumstances it may remove his name from the register of members with impunity. In such a case the share certificate issued to the purchaser or mortgagee does not induce him to buy or lend on the security of the shares, because it is issued to him after the transaction is completed; and even though the company allows the purchaser or mortgagee to continue in the belief that he is entitled to the shares by issuing a new certificate to him, it is not the company's act, but the seller's or mortgagor's lack of title to the shares, which causes his loss.[1] But if the company induces the purchaser or mortgagee to do something which he would not have done if the new share certificate had not been issued to him, and he does it in the belief that he is the real owner of the shares, the company will be estopped from denying the validity of the share certificate. Thus, where the plaintiff took a transfer of shares from a seller who had already sold them to another person, and the company erroneously issued a share certificate showing the plaintiff as entitled to the shares, the company was held estopped from denying the plaintiff's title after he had contracted to re-sell the shares in reliance on the share certificate, and, on the company's refusal to register the transfer to his purchaser, had been compelled to buy similar shares elsewhere to complete his contract.[2] In a similar case where the plaintiff, on receiving the erroneous share certificate showing him to be the registered holder of the shares, had reimbursed his vendor for a call made after the plaintiff had agreed to buy the shares, the company was likewise held to be estopped from denying the validity of the plaintiff's title, for the plaintiff was induced to pay the amount of the call by the company's implied assurance that his title to the shares was valid.[3] Equally, the company is estopped if it induces the plaintiff to believe that he has a title to the shares and thereby prevents him from prosecuting an effective claim against the person who sold or mortgaged them to him. Thus, where the secretary of a company purported to transfer to the plaintiff shares in the company which he did not own, and then deceived the directors into

---

19 Such a duty may rest on them under the rule laid down in *Hedley Byrne & Co Ltd v Heller & Partners Ltd* [1964] AC 465, [1963] 2 All ER 575.

20 *Re Bahia and San Francisco Rly Co* (1868) LR 3 QB 584; *Re Ottos Kopje Diamond Mines Ltd* [1893] 1 Ch 618.

1 *Foster v Tyne Pontoon and Dry Co and Renwick* (1893) 63 LJQB 50.

2 *Balkis Consolidated Co v Tomkinson* [1893] AC 396.

3 *Hart v Frontino and Bolivia South American Gold Mining Co Ltd* (1870) LR 5 Exch 111.

issuing a share certificate to the plaintiff showing her as the registered holder of the shares, it was held that the company was estopped from denying her title to the shares when the secretary subsequently became bankrupt, because by deluding the plaintiff into believing that she had a title, the company induced her not to question the secretary's title to the shares, and so prevented her from claiming back the purchase price she had paid to him before his bankruptcy made it impossible to do so effectively.[4] But if the secretary had been bankrupt or insolvent when the share certificate was issued to the plaintiff, the company would not have been estopped, because then it would not have deprived the plaintiff of any effective remedy, and would not have put her in a worse position than she was already in.[5]

A company may estop itself from denying the title of a person whom it treats as a shareholder, even though it does not issue a share certificate to him and does not register him as a member. But the acts of the company in recognising his title, such as paying him dividends, or offering him further shares under a rights offer, will not of themselves estop the company, unless the plaintiff has acted on the faith of the company's representation and has suffered a detriment in consequence.[5] The mere receipt and retention of a dividend would therefore not be sufficient to raise an estoppel, but the subscription of additional shares under a rights offer would seem to estop the company from disputing the subscriber's title to the original shares in respect of which the rights offer was made, because by subscribing for the additional shares he incurs a liability to the company to pay the issue price of those shares, and so acts on the company's representation to his own detriment. This is so even if the additional shares are equal in value to their issue price or have a greater value, so that the subscriber suffers no immediate financial loss. The detriment which entitles him to treat the company as estopped is his contracting a liability to the company which he was not previously under.

A person who presents a transfer of shares for registration by a company thereby represents that the instrument of transfer is genuine,[6] and if it turns out to be a forgery or have been executed by a person who had no authority from the registered holder to do so, the company is not estopped from denying the title of the transferee to the shares, even though he did not know that the transfer was forged or unauthorised when he presented it for registration.[7] Consequently, even if the company issues a share certificate to the person who presents the transfer, and he relies on it believing that he is entitled to the shares, the company may remove his name from the register of members, and he cannot claim damages for wrongful removal.[7] In this situation the representation impliedly made by the person who presents the forged or unauthorised transfer precludes the possibility of the company making a representation to him in the same terms in return. But it is only the person who presents the forged or unauthorised transfer who is prevented from pleading an estoppel against the company. If a purchaser under a forged or unauthorised transfer re-sells or mortgages the shares to another person who relies on the share certificate in the name of the seller or mortgagor,[8] or on the fact that he is registered as owner of the shares in the company's register of members,[9] the company is estopped from denying the validity of his title to the purchaser or mortgagee, and if the company refuses to register the purchaser or mortgagee, it will be liable to him in damages.

The foregoing may be illustrated by an example. If O is the registered holder

---

4 *Dixon v Kennaway & Co* [1900] 1 Ch 833.
5 *Foster v Tyne Pontoon and Dry Docks Co and Renwick*, supra.
6 *Sheffield Corpn v Barclay* [1905] AC 392 at 403, per Lord Davey.
7 *Johnston v Renton* (1870) LR 9 Eq 181; *Simm v Anglo-American Telegraph Co* (1879) 5 QBD 188.
8 *Re Bahia and San Francisco Rly Co* (1868) LR 3 QB 584.
9 *Foster v Tyne Pontoon and Dry Docks Co and Renwick* (1893) 63 LJQB 50.

and true owner of shares in a company, and T steals his share certificate and forges his signature to a transfer of the shares to P, or T executes a transfer to P purporting to act as O's agent when he has no authority to do so, P cannot acquire any rights against the company by registering the transfer and obtaining a new certificate showing himself as owner of the shares, because he is guilty of misrepresentation as to the genuineness of the transfer when he presents it for registration, and his position is in no way improved if he makes the misrepresentation innocently. On the other hand, if P uses the share certificate which the company issues to him to induce S to take a transfer of the shares for value, S can treat the company as estopped from disputing P's title, because S makes no representation to the company as to the genuineness of the transfer from T to P.[10] Consequently, if the company refuses to register the transfer from P to S, or, having registered it, removes S's name from the register and restores O's name as holder of the shares, S can successfully sue the company for damages.

A person who presents a transfer of shares for registration not only impliedly represents, but also impliedly warrants or promises, that the transfer is genuine, and impliedly agrees to indemnify the company if it is not.[11] This is so whether he acts on his own account, or is merely an agent for a purchaser or mortgagee of the shares.[12] A similar warranty and promise of indemnity is implied on the part of a person who induces the company to register a transfer executed by him under a power of attorney which purports to have been given by the true owner of the shares, but which has, unknown to the transferor, been forged by a third person.[13] Consequently, if the company is put to expense in restoring the name of the true owner of the shares to the register, or in paying damages to the true owner of the shares or to a person who has bought the shares from the transferee under the forged or unauthorised transfer, the company can claim to be indemnified by the transferee or his agent who presented the transfer, or by the person who transferred the shares under the forged power of attorney, as the case may be. Here again, the moral innocence of the defendant is immaterial. Even though he was unaware of the irregularity and could not reasonably be expected to discover it, he is still liable to indemnify the company against the expense to which it is put. It is, however, a defence to an action on the implied warranty that the company was aware that the transfer presented for registration was a forgery or unauthorised, but not that the company was negligent in not verifying the transfer against a specimen signature of the true owner in its possession or otherwise checking on its genuineness.[14]

When a company is estopped from denying the validity of a person's title to shares, he does not thereby acquire a title to them, and he cannot prevent the company from removing his name from its register of members or require the company to issue equivalent shares to him. All that he can do is to treat the company as guilty of a breach of duty owed to him by refusing to register the transfer to him or by removing his name from the register, and he may sue it for damages for this breach of duty, the measure of damages being the value of the shares when registration was refused,[15] or when the removal from the register took

---

10 The representation which S does make, that the transfer from P to S is genuine is, of course, correct, even though that transfer does not vest a good title to the shares in S.
11 *Sheffield Corpn v Barclay* supra, per Lord Davey at 403–405.
12 *Royal Exchange Assurance Co v Moore* (1863) 8 LT 242; *Reynolds v Smith* (1893) 9 TLR 494; *Bank of England v Cutler* [1908] 2 KB 208; *Yeung Kai Yung v Hong Kong and Shanghai Banking Corpn* [1981] AC 787, [1980] 2 All ER 599.
13 *Starkey v Bank of England* [1903] AC 114.
14 *Yeung Kai Yung v Hong Kong and Shanghai Banking Corpn*, supra.
15 *Re Ottos Kopje Diamond Mines Ltd* [1893] 1 Ch 618.

place.[16] The plaintiff's negligence in not discovering the defect in the title of the person who purported to transfer the shares to him affords no defence to the company. Consequently, it was held that a director who negligently signed a share certificate in his own favour in respect of shares which belonged to another person, was nevertheless able to plead an estoppel against the company when he agreed to sell the shares, believing that he was entitled to them in reliance on the share certificate.[17] But since the plaintiff's cause of action is a breach of the company's duty to register transfers or to maintain its register of members accurately[18] and not a breach of a contract between the plaintiff and the company, it would seem possible for the court to reduce the damages awarded to the plaintiff by reference to the degree to which the loss he suffered was caused by his own negligence.[19]

The restricted effect of the estoppel in giving the plaintiff a cause of action for damages but not title to the shares, is illustrated by the fact that if a person entitled to the benefit of an estoppel purports to transfer the shares to someone who knows of his lack of title, the transferee cannot sue the company for damages.[20] Likewise, if a person who could plead an estoppel re-transfers the shares to his vendor who acquired them under a forged transfer, the vendor cannot sue the company for damages, because the warranty which he impliedly gave when the forged transfer was registered precludes him from pleading an estoppel himself.[20] In these cases, if the estoppel which the first holder could plead conferred a real title to the shares on him, the second holder would acquire an equally good title despite his inability to plead an estoppel personally, but because the estoppel confers no title at all, the second holder is precluded from suing the company.

When the legal title to shares is transferred

It has often been assumed in judicial reasoning that the legal title to registered shares does not pass to the transferee until the transfer is registered in the company's register of members.[1] When he has presented his transferor's share certificate and the transfer to himself for registration and has fulfilled any other conditions set out in the company's article of association, the transferee has a legal right against the company to have the transfer registered,[2] but until the transfer is actually

---

16 *Re Bahia and San Francisco Rly Co*, supra; *Hart v Frontino and Bolivia South American Gold Mining Co* (1870) LR 5 Exch 111.
17 *Re Coasters Ltd* [1911] 1 Ch 86. In *Dixon v Kennaway & Co*, supra, Farwell J (at 837) queried whether a director who signed a share certificate in favour of another person would not be estopped from denying that person's title when the shares in question were his own. If a director who signs a certificate is under such a duty to see that it is correct, should he not be precluded from relying on a certificate in his own favour which relates to shares really owned by another person?
18 Companies Act 1985, s 352 (1).
19 Law Reform (Contributory Negligence) Act 1945, s 1 (1) (21 Halsbury's Statutes (4th Edn) 185). In *Lumsden & Co v London Trustee Savings Bank* [1971] 1 Lloyd's Rep 114, it was held that the section applied to claims for financial loss as well as physical damage and to claims arising out of torts other than negligence. This decision is no longer law as regards conversions and other torts in relation to goods (Torts (Interference with Goods) Act 1977, s 11 (1) (45 Halsbury's Statutes (4th Edn) 668), but it still applies to wrongs in connection with things in action, including shares and debentures (s 14 (1)).
20 *Simm v Anglo-American Telegraph Co* (1879) 5 QBD 188.
1 *Société Générale de Paris v Walker* (1885) 11 App Cas 20 at 28–29 per Lord Selborne; *Colonial Bank v Hepworth* (1887) 36 ChD 36 at 54; *Re Copal Varnish Co Ltd* [1917] 2 Ch 349 at 354 per Eve J. In *Sun Alliance Insurance Ltd v IRC* [1972] Ch 133 at 146, [1971] 1 All ER 135, 142, Foster J held that registration of a transfer merely perfects the title which the transferee obtains by delivery to him of an executed instrument of transfer, but he did not express an opinion whether perfecting the transferee's title meant that the legal title thereby passed to him.
2 *Roots v Williamson* (1888) 38 ChD 485 at 495.

registered, it has been assumed judicially that his title to the shares is still inchoate, and that the legal title remains vested in his transferor.[3] This line of reasoning was reinforced by the Companies Act 1948, Table A, art 22, which provided that until the name of the transferee was entered in the register of members, the transferor should be deemed to remain the holder of the shares transferred, thus clearly contemplating that the legal title remained vested in him.

Nevertheless, it is doubtful whether the judicial assumption that the legal title to shares passes on registration of the transfer, and not before, has any real foundation. The purposes of registering the transfer is to notify the company of it, so that the transferee may require the company to pay him future dividends and allow him to vote at shareholder's meetings. On registration, the transferee acquires legal rights against the company, but it does not follow that the legal title to the shares has not already passed from his transferor to him by virtue of the executed share transfer and the transferor's share certificate being delivered to him, so making his right to the shares effective against all interested persons except the company. Historically it appears more likely that the legal title to shares passed at common law by delivery of the executed instrument of transfer. Registration was required by companies as a measure for their own protection, and the requirement was embodied as a contractual condition in deeds of settlement in terms similar to the Companies Act 1948, Table A, art 22. But such requirements seemingly have only a contractual effect, and have no bearing on the question when the legal title passes. The question is fortunately of practical importance only in connection with claims to priority when a registered shareholder creates equitable interests out of his shares, and in connection with claims by a donee of shares when the transfer to him has not been registered. In both these cases the court has devised alternative tests to solve the problems of priority and validity,[4] and so it has never been compelled to face squarely the question when the legal title to shares passes on a transfer.

It is not necessary that the transferor's original share certificate issued by the company should be delivered to the company for the transferee to acquire a legal title to the shares transferred to him. Thus, where a registered shareholder forged a duplicate of his share certificate, and executed a transfer of his shares to a purchaser whom the company entered in its register of members on production of the forged certificate, it was held that the legal title had passed to the purchaser.[5] The result would be the same if the company had registered the purchaser without requiring the transferor's share certificate to be produced at all.

EQUITABLE INTERESTS IN SHARES

Kinds of equitable interests

Equitable interests may be created out of the legal title to shares in the same way as out of the legal title to other property. Thus, the registered shareholder or the bearer of a share warrant may declare himself a trustee of his shares, or may transfer them to another person on trusts directed by him. When a shareholder agrees to sell ascertained shares, the equitable ownership of them passes immediately to the purchaser,[6] and if the shareholder gives another person an option to buy

3 *Colonial Bank v Hepworth*, supra.
4 See pp 358, and 403, post.
5 *Guy v Waterlow Bros and Layton Ltd* (1909) 25 TLR 515.
6 *Hawks v McArthur* [1951] 1 All ER 22 at 26.

them, the option vests an equitable interest in that other person immediately. A shareholder may mortgage his shares equitably, or create an equitable charge over them, as will be shown below.

Protection of equitable interests

If several conflicting interests have been created out of the same chose in action, priority between them is normally determined by the order in which the owners of those interests give notice to the debtor or obligor.[7] In the case of shares, the position of the obligor is occupied by the company, but priority for an equitable interest in shares cannot be obtained by giving notice of it to the company. This is because the Companies Act 1985 prohibits any notice of a trust, expressed, implied or constructive, from being entered on the company's register of members.[8] The Act does not in express terms prevent the company from receiving notice of a trust on which shares are held, but it has been held that this is its effect.[9] Furthermore, although the statutory provision refers only to trusts of shares, it has been held to apply equally to equitable mortgages,[10] and there is no doubt that it applies to all other equitable interests as well.[11]

The only way in which the owner of an equitable interest derived out of registered shares can protect himself is by serving a stop notice on the company. Stop notices were introduced by an amendment of the Rules of the Supreme Court in 1965, and have replaced the former notice in lieu of distringas.[12] They are now governed by the Charging Orders Act 1979.[13] A stop notice may be served by an interested person in respect of 'stock of any body (other than a building society) incorporated within England and Wales' and 'stock' includes shares.[14] The former notice in lieu of distringas could only be issued in respect of shares 'standing in the books of a company', and so was apparently confined to shares which were registered in the company's register of members. It was therefore doubtful whether the notice could be issued in respect of shares represented by renounceable letters of allotment, and it seemed impossible to issue the notice in respect of shares represented by share warrants to bearer. The new rule clearly permits a stop notice to be issued in respect of registered shares and shares represented by renounceable letters of allotment, but it would still appear impossible to issue such a notice in connection with shares in bearer form. It is true that an entry that a share warrant has been issued is made in the register of members,[15] but the feature which militates against the idea of them being subjected to the stop notice procedure is that they are negotiable instruments, and the company consequently has no power to implement the stop notice against purchasers of them. This is not so in the case of renounceable letters of allotment, which are not negotiable instruments and which can be subjected to the stop notice procedure when they cease to be renounceable and the holder of them seeks registration in the company's register of members.

Stop notices are derived through the notice in lieu of distringas from the old writ

---

7 *Dearle v Hall* (1823–28) 3 Russ 1; *Meux v Bell* (1841) 1 Hare 73; *Marchant v Morton Down & Co* [1901] 2 KB 829.

8 Companies Act 1985, s 360.

9 *Société Générale de Paris v Walker* (1885) 11 App Cas 20 at 30, per Lord Selborne.

10 *Société Générale de Paris v Walker*, supra.

11 In *Société Générale de Paris v Tramways Union Co* (1884) 14 QBD 424 (affd sub nom *Société Générale de Paris v Walker*, supra), Lindley LJ (at 455) treated s 360 as precluding any equitable interest from being protected by notice of it being given to the company. Table A, art 5 expressly extends the application of the section to all derivative equitable interests.

12 See former RSC Ord 43, r 3 et seq.

13 22 Halsbury's Statutes (4th Edn) 338.

14 Charging Orders Act 1979, s 2 (1) and (2), s 5 (1) and (2) and s 6 (1); RSC Ord 50, r 11 (1).

15 Companies Act 1985, s 355 (1).

of distringas by which the court directed the sheriff to distrain on the goods of a public company as security to prevent it from registering transfers of shares the title to which was in issue in pending litigation between rival claimants.[16] The present form of stop notice[17] is issued by the Central Office of the High Court or any district registry upon the owner of an equitable interest in the shares filing an affidavit setting out the nature of his interest and submitting copies of the notice addressed to the company and signed by the applicant for sealing.[18] The applicant must serve a sealed copy of the notice on the company together with an office copy of his affidavit.[18] The notice merely informs the company that the equitable owner is entitled to an interest in the shares (specifying them), and that the notice is issued in order to prevent the registration of transfers of the shares, or to do that and also to stop the payment of dividends to the registered shareholder.[19] Thereupon so long as the notice remains in force the company must send a notice by first class ordinary post to the owner of the equitable interest named in the notice at least 14 days before the company registers a transfer of the shares or pays a dividend (if the notice extends to dividends), but unless the court otherwise orders, the company cannot defer registering a transfer or paying a dividend for more than 14 days after the notice of the company's intention to do so is posted.[20] If a transfer of shares is registered without notice first being given to the owner of the equitable interest, and the transfer is in breach of trust, or operates to destroy the equitable interest, the directors will themselves be deemed to have participated in the breach of trust, and will be liable to compensate the owner of the equitable interest.[1] Presumably the company, too, will be liable in damages to the owner of the equitable interest for breach of its statutory duty. A person who has served a stop notice may withdraw it by serving on the company a written notice to that effect attested by a solicitor,[2] and any person who is beneficially interested in shares affected by a stop notice may apply to the court for an order discharging the notice, for example, because the person who served it did not have, or no longer has, the equitable interest in the shares set out in his supporting affidavit.[3]

It should now be possible to determine the rules which govern competing claims to priority between an equitable interest in shares and another interest later created. These rules will depend on whether the later interest arises under a transfer of the shares or not.

Later interest arising under a transfer

When a transfer of shares affected by a stop notice is presented for registration, the company must notify the owner of the equitable interest who has served the stop notice, and he may then apply to the court for an injunction restraining the company from registering the transfer.[4] The application is usually made ex parte

16 The writ was originally issued by the Court of Exchequer as part of its equity jurisdiction, but in 1841 jurisdiction to issue the writ was transferred to the Court of Chancery (Court of Chancery Act 1841, s 5), which continued to do so until the writ was replaced by the notice in lieu of distringas in 1881.
17 For the form of notice RSC, Appendix A, Form 80.
18 RSC Ord 50, r 11 (2).
19 Charging Orders Act 1979, s 5 (5). A stop on dividend payments is imposed only when the person who issues the stop notice claims the beneficial ownership of the shares.
20 RSC Ord 50, r 12. If the shares are represented by letters of allotment, presumably the demand for payment of a dividend can be made either by the allottee or a renouncee who has surrendered the letter of allotment to the company with the registration application form duly completed.
1 *Société Générale de Paris v Tramways Union Co* (1884) 14 QBD 424 at 453 per Lindley LJ.
2 RSC Ord 50, r 14 (1) and (2).
3 Ibid, r 14 (3). The application is made by originating summons (r 14 (4)).
4 RSC Ord 50, r 15 (1). The application is made by originating summons or motion (r 15 (2)).

in the first instance, and on the applicant showing a prima facie case, the court will issue an interim injunction and order the applicant to serve notice of the application on the company and the registered shareholder giving a date on which they may appear before the court and oppose the injunction being made permanent. If the owner of the equitable interest does not apply for an injunction before the expiration of 14 days after notice of the company's intention to register the transfer is posted to him, the company must register the transfer,[5] whereupon the legal right to the shares as regards the company will pass to the transferee, and the stop notice will cease to be effective.[6]

If a transferee of the shares purchases them for value and has no notice of an earlier equitable interest, he will not be bound by it, unless the equitable owner brings it to his notice before he has a right to insist on the company registering his transfer. To be immune from a prior equitable interest it is not necessary that the transferee should have actually been registered as holder of the shares before he has notice of the interest, but the only thing remaining to be done in order to complete his title as against the company must be a mere ministerial act by the company which he can insist on having done immediately.[7] Thus, if the directors have a discretion by the articles to refuse to register transfers, the transferee is not in a position to insist on being registered until the directors have approved the transfer to him, or the statutory two months within which they must inform him of their disapproval have expired,[8] and so he is affected by notice of an equitable interest obtained by him before either of those things happens.[7] Even if the directors have no discretion to refuse registration, they are entitled to a reasonable length of time after the transfer is lodged for registration in which to enquire whether it is genuine and effective,[9] and so if the transferee receives notice of the equitable interest before such a reasonable time has expired, he is bound by it, but not if he receives notice after the expiration of that time.[10]

When a company notifies the owner of an equitable interest who has served a stop notice of the presentation of a transfer for registration, he may preserve priority for his interest over rights arising under the transfer by giving an informal notice of his interest to the transferee, or he may give notice by commencing an action to restrain the transferee from procuring the registration of his transfer and serving the writ on him. The company is a necessary party in such an action, for it cannot refuse to register the transfer merely because it knows that an action has been commenced against the transferee, and unless it is made a party to the action, it will not be bound by a judgment against the transferee in favour of the owner of the equitable interest, even if notice of the judgment is given to it.[11] Alternatively, the owner of the equitable interest may apply to the court for an order prohibiting the company from registering the transfer;[12] the transferee is not a party to the application unless the court orders him to be added as a party, but notice of the

---

5   RSC Ord 50, r 12; *Re Blaksley's Trusts* (1883) 23 ChD 549.
6   *Hobbs v Wayet* (1887) 36 ChD 256 at 260.
7   *Moore v North Western Bank* [1891] 2 Ch 599.
8   Companies Act 1985, s 183 (5); *Re Swaledale Cleaners Ltd* [1968] 3 All ER 619, [1968] 1 WLR 1710.
9   *Ireland v Hart* [1902] 1 Ch 522. The Companies Act 1948, Table A, art 25 (*b*), expressly empowered the directors to require the transferee to produce such evidence as they might reasonably require to show the right of the transferor to make the transfer. There is no similar provision in the present Table A.
10 *Peat v Clayton* [1906] 1 Ch 659. The earlier case of *Dodds v Hills* (1865) 2 Hem & M 424, must be read as one where this was so.
11 The Transfer of Stock Act 1800, s 1 made it unnecessary to join the Bank of England as a party in such an action concerning bank stock. The fact that the statute was enacted shows that joinder of the company is necessary in the case of shares in other companies.
12 RSC Ord 50, r 15 (1).

application should be served on him so that he is affected by the applicants' equitable interest and consequently by any order which the court makes against the company. In practice, the owner of the equitable interest will rarely seek a prohibitory order against the company or sue the transferee for an injunction, but will merely notify the transferee of the equitable interest so as to preserve priority for it. He will seek an order against the company to prevent it from registering the transfer only if it is important to him that it should not be registered (e g because the applicant has an option or a contract to purchase the shares).

Later interest not arising under a transfer

If in a case of conflicting interests derived out of shares where the later interest does not arise under a transfer, that interest is bound to be equitable itself, and will consequently be postponed to the earlier equitable interest, whether the owner of the later interest has a notice of the earlier one or not. Thus, if the registered shareholder is a trustee who lacks power to mortgage the shares by statute or the instrument creating the trust, and he mortgages the shares equitably to a lender who believes him to be the beneficial owner of them, the equitable interests of the beneficiaries of the trust will have priority over the interest of the equitable mortgagee.[13] Likewise, if the registered shareholder creates two equitable mortgages of his shares successively, the second mortgagee will be postponed to the first, even though he was unaware of the first mortgage when the second was created.[14] The owner of the earlier equitable interest will be postponed to one created or arising later only if he has induced the owner of the later interest to believe that the earlier one did not exist,[15] as an earlier equitable mortgagee might do by leaving the share certificate in the mortgagor's hands, thus enabling him to lead the second mortgagee to believe that the shares are unencumbered.[16] But the mere fact that the registered shareholder appears to be the beneficial owner of the shares, and that the person who takes the later equitable interest is thereby led to believe that he is, does not prevent the owner of the earlier equitable interest from setting it up.[17] Thus, the fact that a trustee is in possession of the share certificate and the beneficiaries have not protected themselves by serving stop notices, will not prevent them from claiming priority for their interests over a later equitable mortgage, because they cannot prevent the trustee having possession of the certificate, to which he is entitled as legal owner of the shares.[18]

A person entitled to a later equitable interest cannot obtain priority over an earlier interest by being the first to serve a stop notice on the company.[19] Such a notice preserves priority for him against later transferees, but does not confer priority on him over an interest which has already been created. In this respect a stop notice is different from notice of an equitable assignment or disposition given to a debtor, obligor or trustees of any other chose in action.[20]

---

13 *Shropshire Union Rly and Canal Co v R* (1875) LR 7 HL 496.
14 *Société Générale de Paris v Walker* (1885) 11 App Case 20.
15 *Shropshire Union Rly and Canal Co v R*, supra, per Lord Cairns LC, at 506.
16 *Farrand v Yorkshire Banking Co* (1888) 40 ChD 182. In this situation the earlier mortgagee would not be protected by having served a stop notice on the company, because such notices are not entered on the register of members and so the later mortgagee would not have constructive notice of it. Moreover, the later mortgagee, taking only an equitable mortgage, would not lodge a transfer of the shares with the company for registration, and so he might take his mortgage without discovering the earlier mortgage.
17 *Rimmer v Webster* [1902] 2 Ch 163 at 172, per Farwell J.
18 *Shropshire Union Rly and Canal Co v R* (1875) LR 7 HL 496.
19 *Wilkins v Sibley* (1863) 4 Giff 442.
20 *Dearle v Hall* (1823–28) 3 Russ 1.

The company's position

The provision of the Companies Act 1985, which prohibits a company from entering notices of equitable interests in shares in its register of members, also operates to protect the company from liability to the owners of equitable interests.[1] Because of the prohibition the company is deemed not to have notice of such equitable interests, even though it actually knows of their existence and content.[2] Consequently, the company is not liable to the owners of equitable interests in shares for registering improper dispositions of the shares by the registered shareholder, nor is it bound to see that money which it pays to the registered shareholder in respect of dividends or an authorised return of capital or on a purchase or redemption of his shares by the company, is properly applied by him in satisfying equitable claims. Thus, a company which knew that the registered shareholders were the executors of the will of a deceased member because it had received a copy of the deceased's will, was held not to be liable to the beneficiaries to whom the shares were bequeathed for registering a transfer by the executors to another person.[2] Similarly, a company which registers a transfer of shares by a mortgagee is not bound to enquire whether the mortgagee's power of sale has become exercisable, and will not be liable to the mortgagor if it has not. But the Companies Act 1985 only protects the company when it acts in its capacity as keeper of the register of members in registering transfers and in paying dividends and repaying capital. If a company actively participates in a breach of trust by a trustee of its shares, it will be liable to the beneficiaries in the same way as any other person.

Investigations ordered by the Secretary of State for Trade and Industry

By vesting shares in trustees or nominees who are registered in the company's register of members, it is obviously possible to conceal the identity of the persons who are the real beneficial owners of the shares. Because of the form which registers of debenture and loan security holders usually take,[3] this is equally true of such registers. The real beneficial owners of the shares, debentures and loan securities may be few in number, and one of them, or a group of them acting together, may by giving directions to their trustees or nominees be able to control the voting at members' or debenture or loan security holders' meetings. Some of the beneficial owners may have interests inimical to the company, and may direct their trustees or nominees to vote in a way which will harm it. Some may use the device of a trust in order to make successive purchases of small quantities of the company's shares on the market without attracting attention and so causing sellers to ask for a higher price.[4] None of these uses of the trust device is illegal, but Parliament has considered it desirable that there should be machinery for making public the identity and interests of the beneficial owners of shares and debentures and of persons who by the use of voting power may control or influence the policy of public or private companies. The Secretary of State for Trade and Industry has been given powers of inquiry for the purpose, and persons interested in the issued shares of public companies have been subjected to duties of disclosure to the companies themselves.

1 Companies Act 1985, s 360.
2 *Simpson v Molson's Bank* [1895] AC 270.
3 See pp 470 and 484, post.
4 This is the way in which concealed takeovers were formerly effected, but concealed takeovers of public companies are now made difficult, if not impossible, by the provisions of the Companies Act 1985 (as amended by the Companies Act 1989), as to the compulsory notification to the company of the beneficial interests of substantial shareholders.

The first method of discovering the beneficial ownership of shares in any company, whether public or private, is a formal investigation by an inspector or inspectors appointed by the Secretary of State for Trade and Industry to determine 'the true persons who are or have been financially interested in the success or failure (real or apparent) of the company or able to control or to materially influence the policy of the company'.[5] Such an inspector may be appointed by the Secretary of State on his own initiative, and must be appointed to investigate the ownership or control of particular shares, debentures or loan securities if the Secretary of State is requested to make the appointment by at least 200 members of the company or by the holders of one tenth of the company's issued shares, but the Secretary of State must not appoint inspectors if he considers the request vexatious, and if he does appoint inspectors in response to such a request, he may require the applicants to give security for the costs of the investigation in an amount not exceeding £5,000.[6] The extent of the enquiry which the inspector is directed to make may be very much wider than an investigation of the beneficial ownership of shares, debentures and loan securities for persons may be able to 'control or materially influence' the company's policy by having agreements or arrangements[7] with it, or with the owners of its shares or debentures. The actual scope of the investigation is defined by the Secretary of State, but if an investigation is requisitioned by the statutory fraction of shareholders,[5] the Secretary of State may exclude from its scope any matter which the requisitionists seek to have included only if he considers it unreasonable for that matter to be investigated.[8] The inspector has the same powers to compel testimony and the production of evidence for the purpose of the investigation as an inspector appointed to investigate improprieties in the company's management,[9] and he may require any person who appears to be or to have been financially interested in the company's success or failure or able to control or materially influence its policy, or any other person whom the inspector believes possesses relevant information, to produce relevant documents in their custody or control and to assist the inspector by giving information.[10] When the inspector's report is submitted to the Secretary of State he may send a copy of it to the company, and copies of it may be made available to its members and creditors or to the public generally, but the Secretary of State may refuse to divulge the whole or any part of the report when it thinks that there is good reason for doing so.[11]

The Secretary of State for Trade and Industry may alternatively investigate the beneficial ownership of shares, debentures or loan securities less formally by requiring any person whom he reasonably believes to have, or to be able to obtain, any information as to the present or past interests in shares, debentures or loan securities of a company and as to the identity of the persons entitled to such interests

---

5 Companies Act 1985, s 442 (1).
6 Ibid, s 442 (3), (3A) and (3B), amended and inserted by Companies Act 1989, s 62.
7 By the Companies Act 1985, s 442 (4) the inspector must investigate arrangements or understandings, whether legally binding or not, which are observed or are likely to be observed in practice, and are relevant to the investigation.
8 Companies Act 1985, s 442 (2), (3) and (3A), as amended and inserted by Companies Act 1989, s 62.
9 Ibid, s 443 (1) (see p 688, post). The same privileges from testifying or producing evidence apply to solicitors and bankers as in an investigation into improprieties of management (Companies Act 1985, s 462 (1) (see p 688, post)).
10 Companies Act 1985, s 434 (1) to (3) and s 443 (1) and (2), as amended by Companies Act 1989, s 56 (1) to (4).
11 Companies Act 1985, s 443 (1) and (3).

and of other persons acting on their behalf, to disclose that information.[12] The Secretary of State may exercise this power to require disclosure instead of appointing inspectors to investigate the financial interests in, or control or influence over, the policy of a company when he is requested to appoint such inspectors by the number of members or the fraction of shareholders mentioned in the preceding paragraph.[13] For the purpose of exercising the Secretary of State's power to require disclosure of interests in shares, a person is deemed to be interested in shares, debentures or loan securities if he is entitled to acquire or dispose of any interest in them,[14] or if his consent is required to the exercise by other persons of their rights in the shares, debentures or loan securities, or if he can require such other persons to exercise their rights (eg voting rights attached to shares) in accordance with his wishes, or if they are accustomed to do so.[15] There is no provision for the publication of the results of such informal enquiries by the Secretary of State.

Besides being backed by criminal sanctions, the Secretary of State's powers of investigation, both formal and informal, are reinforced by a power to make shares, debentures, or loan securities temporarily worthless if he encounters difficulty in discovering the relevant facts about their ownership or control.[16] In such a case the Secretary of State may by order: (a) prohibit any transfer of the shares, debentures or loan securities, or if only letters of allotment have been issued, prohibit their transfer and the issue of share certificates, debentures or loan stock certificate in place of them; (b) prohibit any votes being given in respect of the shares, debentures or loan securities; (c) prohibit the issue of further shares, debentures or loan securities to the registered holder or his renouncee under a rights offer or a bonus or capitalisation issue made in respect of the original securities; and (d) prohibit the company from making any payment in respect of the shares, debentures or loan securities by way of dividend, interest, return of capital or repayment, except in a winding up.[17] The effect of the Secretary of State's order is to invalidate any transfer of the shares, debentures or loan securities or any agreement to transfer them, and also to invalidate any further issue of shares, debentures, or loan securities in right of the original securities to which the order relates and any agreement transferring the right to the issue of such further shares or debentures or loan securities, or to receive any payment in respect of the original securities to which the order relates.[18] Any person who is interested in shares or debentures to which the order relates may apply to the court to terminate the order imposing restrictions on them,[19] or may request the Secretary of State to do so.[20] The court or the Secretary of State may terminate the order, however, only if the applicant shows that the relevant facts about the shares, debentures or loan securities to which restrictions relate have been disclosed and no unfair advantage has accrued to any person as a result of failure to make an earlier disclosure, or alternatively that the shares are to be transferred for valuable consideration and the court or the

---

12 Ibid s 444 (1). But a solicitor or his client cannot be required to disclose communications between himself and his client which would be privileged in litigation, and a company's bank cannot be required to disclose information about the affairs of any of its customers unless they consent or the Secretary of State so orders (s 452 (1) (1A) and (1B), as amended by Companies Act 1989, s 69 (1) to (3)).
13 Companies Act 1985, s 442 (3C), inserted by Companies Act 1989, s 62.
14 He is therefore interested in shares or debentures for which he has an option to subscribe, or which he has an option to purchase from existing holders.
15 Companies Act 1985, s 444 (2).
16 Ibid 1985, s 445 (1).
17 Ibid, s 454 (1).
18 Ibid, s 454 (1) to (3).
19 Ibid, s 456 (1). The application is made to the Companies Court by originating motion (RSC Ord 102, r 3 (1)).
20 Companies Act 1985, s 445 (1), as amended by Companies Act 1989, s 145 and Sch 19, para 10 (1).

Secretary of State approves the transaction.[1] Moreover, the court will not terminate the restrictions on shares so as to enable them to be sold or transferred if there is a likelihood that the persons who have failed to disclose their interests in the shares will purchase or acquire other shares in the company to replace those which are sold, and so avoid disclosing their interests in the original shares.[2]

When shares, debentures or loan securities are subject to an order by the Secretary of State imposing prohibitions, the company or the Secretary of State may apply to the court for an order that they shall be sold and that thereupon they shall cease to be subject to the prohibitions, and the court may so order and give consequential directions as to the conduct of the sale, the transfer of the shares or debentures and the disposal of the proceeds of sale paid into court.[3] If the court or the Secretary of State terminates an order imposing prohibitions on shares, debentures or loan securities to enable them to be transferred, the court or the Secretary of State may direct that the prohibition on the issue of further shares, debentures or loan securities in right of the original ones and the prohibition on the making of any payment by the company in respect of the original shares, debentures or loan securities, shall continue to apply to rights acquired or offers made before the transfer is registered (eg a dividend declared or a rights offer made before the transfer of the original securities is registered).[4] Such an extended order can be subsequently terminated by the court or the Secretary of State for any reason, and not merely because of belated disclosure of relevant facts or to facilitate the sale of shares, debentures or loan securities issued under a rights offer.[5] A person who knowingly contravenes the restrictions placed on shares or other securities by an order of the Secretary of State, or who agrees to sell securities which are subject to such an order, is guilty of a criminal offence, as is the company itself if it issues further shares or other securities in right of the original securities in defiance of such restrictions.[6]

The notification of interests in substantial holdings in public companies

The Companies Act 1985 requires a person who has an interest in shares of a public company which carry full voting rights to notify his interest and any increase or decrease in it to the company if the total number of such shares in which he has an interest equals or exceeds a certain percentage of all such issued shares, and the company must keep a register of such notified interests which is open to inspection by members of the company and the public.[7]

The duty to notify

The duty to notify the public company arises when a person to his knowledge acquires or ceases to have an interest in its shares which carry the right to vote in all circumstances at general meetings (even though the right may be suspended

---

1 Ibid, s 456 (3), as amended by Companies Act 1989, s 145 and Sch 19, para 10 (1). A contract to transfer shares, debentures, or loan securities subject to the removal of the prohibition by the court or the Secretary of State is valid notwithstanding the prohibition, and becomes effective when the prohibition is removed (s 454 (2)), as amended by Companies Act 1989, s 145 and Sch 19, para 10 (2)).
2 *Re Geers Gross plc* [1987] 1 WLR 837, [1987] BCLC 253; affd [1988] 1 All ER 224, CA.
3 Companies Act 1985, s 456 (4) and (5).
4 Ibid, s 456 (6).
5 Ibid, s 456 (7).
6 Ibid, s 455 (1) and (2).
7 Companies Act 1985, ss 198 to 220.

temporarily[8]), or when having acquired or ceased to have such an interest, he becomes aware of that fact, but the duty to notify applies only if at that time his interest in those shares extends to at least 3 per cent of all the issued shares of the company, or of all the issued shares of the same class, which carry the right to vote in all circumstances.[9] The duty to notify the company also arises if a person who has an interest in shares of a public company becomes aware of a change of circumstances or of any fact which is relevant to the application of the obligation to notify his interests,[10] for example, the fulfilment of a condition on which full voting rights attach to the shares in which he is interested,[11] or the increase or reduction in the total number of issued shares of the class in question, so that there is a change in the percentage of the shares of that class carrying full voting rights in which he has an interest.[12] It will be noted that increases or reductions in the number of shares of a class in which a person has an interest will call for a notification of the change, but if the percentages of those shares in which he was interested before and after the change are identical when rounded down to the nearest lower percentage point, no notification need be given.[13] This means that if a person acquires an interest in less than 1 per cent of the issued shares of the class in question in addition to his existing interests in not less than 3 per cent of those shares, notification of the acquisition will not be necessary unless the shares in which the interest is acquired plus the shares in which he is already interested in excess of the nearest lower full percentage point amount together to 1 per cent of the issued shares of that class. Moreover, if the total number of issued shares of the class in question is greater after the event calling for notification, the percentages of the shares in which a person has an interest before and after that event are determined by reference to that greater number.[14] Consequently, if a person is interested in a holding of voting shares and the company makes a rights offer in respect of all the shares of the same class, it will usually be necessary for him to notify his interest in shares subscribed under that offer in right of the original holding, even though the rights offer is fully and proportionately accepted by all the holders of shares of that class.

The nature of a notifiable interest

An interest in full voting shares of a public company is notifiable, and is therefore taken into account in determining whether the person who has or ceases to have it must give a notification to the company, whatever the nature of the interest or the conditions or restrictions attached to it may be.[15] In particular, a beneficiary of a trust which comprises shares in the company for the time being is deemed to be

---

8 For example, under the provisions of the company's articles or an order made by the Secretary of State for Trade and Industry under the Companies Act 1985, s 445 (see p 362, ante).

9 Companies Act 1985, s 198 (1) and (2), s 199 (2), (4) and (5), and s 201 (1), as amended by Companies Act 1989, s 134 (2). The percentage may be increased or reduced by regulations made by the Secretary of State for Trade and Industry (Companies Act 1985, s 210A(1), inserted by Companies Act 1989, s 134 (5)).

10 Companies Act 1985, s 198 (3).

11 The condition will be imposed by the company's memorandum or articles, but its fulfilment may be within the personal knowledge of the person under the obligation to notify (eg where the articles provide that shares shall carry voting rights only if they are held by or on behalf of persons of British nationality or persons who have other specified qualifications).

12 This could occur as a result of an increase or reduction of issued capital, the alteration of rights attached to certain shares, the exercise of options to convert shares into shares of a different class or a scheme of arrangement taking effect.

13 Companies Act 1985, s 200 (1).

14 Ibid, s 200 (2).

15 Ibid, s 208 (2).

interested in them;[16] and a person is treated as interested in shares if he contracts to purchase or acquire them for any consideration, or if he is entitled to exercise or control the exercise of any rights attached to shares of which he is not the registered holder (other than as a proxy appointed to vote at one general or class meeting or an adjournment thereof, or as a representative of a corporate shareholder[17]), or if he is entitled to call for the delivery of shares to himself on his order, or if he is entitled or obliged to acquire an interest in shares.[18] Consequently, a person is interested in shares which he is entitled to acquire by exercising an option given to him by the company or another person, or by exercising conversion rights attached to debentures or other loan securities; furthermore, he is interested in shares which he is obliged to acquire in consequence of another person exercising an option to sell them to him; and he is also interested in shares when he may decide how votes shall be cast in respect of them (eg under a voting agreement, or by an irrevocable proxy appointment giving him an unfettered discretion in voting at several general meetings). It has been held that the interest of a mortgagee of shares which had been purchased by the registered holder with a loan made on the security of the mortgage, is a notifiable interest, but not the interest of the guarantor of such a loan, who, on repaying it himself, would be entitled to the benefit of the mortgage by subrogation to the rights of the lender.[19] A joint interest in shares is deemed to be an interest of each of the persons in whom it is vested.[20] It is immaterial in determining whether an interest is notifiable that the shares in which it exists are not identifiable;[1] consequently, the interest of a purchaser of shares on the Stock Exchange is taken as arising when his broker agrees to buy the number of shares in question on his behalf, even though the shares to be transferred to him will not be identified until later.[2]

A person is treated as interested in shares if he or certain other persons connected with him have a notifiable interest in them. These connected persons are his spouse, minor child or adopted or step-child, a company or corporation which is, or whose directors are, accustomed to act in accordance with his directions or instructions, and a company or corporation at whose general meetings he is entitled to exercise or control the exercise of one-third or more of the voting power, either directly or through any other company or corporation at whose general meetings he is entitled to exercise or control the same fraction of voting power.[3] The effect of treating the interests of connected persons as interests of the person whose duty to notify is under consideration, is not only to impose a duty on him to notify those interests to the company on becoming aware of them,[4] but also to aggregate those interests with his own for the purpose of determining whether he has notifiable interests in at least 3 per cent of a class of the company's shares carrying full voting rights and for all other purposes. The most complex provisions relating to such aggregation apply when the person whose duty to notify is being considered is a party to a share acquisition agreement entered into by several persons acting in concert and relating to shares of the company; such agreements are dealt with separately below.[5] In all situations where a person is deemed to be interested in shares in

---

16 Ibid, s 208 (3).
17 Ibid, s 209 (2). For the appointment of proxies, see p 627, post, and for the appointment of the representatives of corporate shareholders, see p 642, post.
18 Companies Act 1985, s 208 (4) and (5).
19 *Re Lonrho plc (No 2)* (1987) 4 BCC 234.
20 Companies Act 1985, s 208 (7).
 1 Ibid, s 208 (8).
 2 See pp 391 and 396, post.
 3 Companies Act 1985, s 203 (1) to (3).
 4 Ibid, s 207 (1) to (4).
 5 See p 367.

which another person has an interest, however, the first person's duty to notify the company of the interest does not absolve the other person of his duty to notify the same interest, and so a company may receive several notifications of the same acquisition or disposal of the same interest. Moreover, the imputation of another person's interest to the person whose duty to notify is under consideration may result in him being under a duty to notify when the other person is not, for example, if an individual member of a public company who has interests in 2 per cent of its shares carrying full voting rights, also has a holding of shares in another company carrying one-third or more of the voting rights at its general meeting and that other company has interests in 2 per cent of the full voting shares of the first company.

Excepted interests

Certain interests in shares of a public company are left out of account in applying the rules governing the duty to notify. This means not only that such interests are not themselves notifiable, but also that the shares in which they subsist are not aggregated with other shares in which the person in question has a notifiable interest in order to determine whether he is interested in at least 3 per cent of a class of shares carrying full voting rights. The interests which are disregarded are as follows:[6]

(a) interests of a bare trustee or a custodian trustee and interests under a trust comprising shares of the company;

(b) interests for life under an irrevocable trust comprising shares of the company where the settlor has no interest in any income arising under or property comprised in the trust;[7]

(c) interests in a unit trust authorised under the Financial Services Act 1986,[8] where the trust comprises shares in the company;

(d) interests in shares of market makers who are members of the Stock Exchange where the interests are held for the purposes of their business as market makers;[9]

(e) interests in shares held by authorised deposit-taking institutions,[10] or by insurance companies authorised to carry on business in the United Kingdom[11] or by trustee savings banks, or by stockbrokers who are members of the Stock Exchange, or by the Bank of England or the Post Office in connection with its banking services, provided that the interests are held by way of security under transactions entered into is the ordinary course of business;[12]

(f) interests of the President of the Family Division of the Supreme Court in shares comprised in the estate of a deceased person and interests in shares held by the Accountant General of the Supreme Court; and

(g) other interests in shares prescribed by regulations made by the Secretary of State for Trade. Such regulations require interests in shares to be disregarded if they are those of a beneficiary under a retirement benefits scheme

6 Companies Act 1985, s 209 (1).
7 Ibid, s 209 (3).
8 The authorisation is given by the Securities and Investments Board under the Financial Services Act 1986, s 78 (1) (30 Halsbury's Statutes (4th Edn) 335).
9 Companies Act 1985, s 209 (4A), inserted by Financial Services Act 1986, s 197 (1).
10 That is authorised to take deposits by the Bank of England under the Banking Act 1987, s 9 (1) (4 Halsbury's Statutes (4th Edn) 538).
11 Insurance Companies Act 1982, s 3 (1) (22 Halsbury's Statutes (4th Edn) 158).
12 Companies Act 1985, s 209 (5), as amended by Banking Act 1987, s 108 (1) and Sch 6, para 18 (1).

approved by the Inland Revenue or established by or under statutory provision;[13] or interests of the Public Trustee or of a bank or insurance company which is a trust corporation and has a place of business in the United Kingdom where he or it holds the interest in his or its capacity as a trustee or personal representative;[14] or interests of an offeror under a bid to acquire all the shares of a company or all the shares of a particular class[15] in shares whose holders have accepted the bid but where the total number of acceptances has not yet attained the percentage at which the bid becomes or may be declared unconditional;[16] or the interests of a person authorised to carry on investment business under the Financial Services Act 1986, or exempted from authorisation in shares listed on the Stock Exchange or admitted to dealing on the Unlisted Securities Market where the interests of that person are confined to the power to dispose of, or to consent to or direct the disposal of, the shares under a written agreement to manage investments for another person or persons.[17]

Share acquisition agreements

For the purpose of the statutory provisions governing the duty of a person to notify a public company of interests he has in its shares carrying full voting rights, a person is deemed to be interested in shares in which another person has a notifiable interest if they are parties to an agreement (other than an underwriting or sub-underwriting agreement) for the acquisition of shares or interests in shares of a particular public company by any of the parties to the agreement, and the agreement imposes obligations or restrictions on one or more of the parties as to the retention or disposal of interests in the company's shares acquired under the agreement, or as to the exercise of voting or other rights or of any control or influence arising from such interests; however, this extension of a person's deemed interest in shares applies only from the time when a notifiable interest is in fact acquired in shares of the company under the agreement.[18]

This provision is designed primarily to ensure the notification to a company of interests in its shares carrying full voting rights held by a group of persons acting in concert to prepare the way for a takeover bid for the company or to support a pending takeover bid, but the provision is general in terms and is not confined to bid situations. Any agreement or arrangement, whether legally binding or not, which involves undertakings, expectations or understandings that interests in shares will be acquired and that they will be subject to relevant restrictions at any time while the agreement or arrangement subsists, will fall within the provision extending the notification requirements,[19] but if the agreement or arrangement is not legally binding on the parties, the undertakings, expectations or understandings between them must be mutual and not be imposed on only some of the

13 See Income and Corporation Taxes Act 1988, ss 590 to 612 (44 Halsbury's Statutes (4th edn) 704 to 725).

14 The exception also extends to subsidiaries of the bank or insurance company and to subsidiaries of its holding company.

15 Except shares already held by the offeror or companies in the same group and shares held by persons who have agreed that the bid shall not extend to their holdings.

16 The Public Companies (Disclosure of Interests in Shares) (Exclusions) Regulations 1982 (SI 1982/677) paras 1 and 2.

17 The Public Companies (Disclosure of Interests in Shares) (Investment Management Exclusion) Regulations 1988 (SI 1988/706).

18 Companies Act 1985, s 204 (1), (2), (3) and (6) and s 205 (1).

19 Ibid, s 204 (5).

parties.[1] An agreement does not fall within the notification requirement, however, if it is an agreement under which shares are acquired (eg contracts for the purchase of shares) as distinct from an agreement in pursuance or execution of which shares are to be acquired in the future under separate transactions, nor do agreements which do not themselves impose restrictions on any party but the conclusion of which produce the consequence that one or more of the parties become subject to restrictions imposed by legislation or rules (eg the City Code on Takeovers and Mergers).[2] Moreover, the provision does not apply to an agreement or arrangement until an interest in shares is acquired under it, and notification is required only of interests acquired by the parties under the agreement or arrangement and not otherwise. Consequently, if persons enter into an agreement mutually restricting their right to vote on the shares they respectively hold as they individually see fit, the agreement will not of itself give rise to notifiable interests, and this is so even if the restrictions extend to shares which the parties acquire individually after the agreement is made, provided that they do not acquire them under the terms of the agreement or as a result of undertakings, expectations or understandings which are given or arise under agreement. If the agreement does provide for the acquisition of shares or interests in shares carrying full voting rights, the notification requirements apply from the time when an interest in any such shares is acquired under the agreement, and they continue to apply until none of the parties to the agreement have any notifiable interest in any shares or interests in shares acquired under it; this is so whether such further acquisitions take place or not, and despite the fact that there are changes in the parties to the agreement or in its terms.[3]

The effect of the statutory provision treating a person as interested in shares in which another party to the acquisition agreement has a notifiable interest is that those interests are added to his own[4] to determine whether he is interested in at least 3 per cent of the shares of the company carrying full voting rights, and furthermore, he is under a duty to notify the company of the acquisition, disposal or any change in the circumstances or facts affecting the application of the notification requirements to those interests, as though they were vested in him.[5] The interests of the other party in question are, of course, interests in shares acquired by the other party otherwise than under the agreement;[6] every party to the agreement has a personal interest in shares acquired under it,[7] and the parallel interests of the other parties in such shares are therefore excluded in applying the statutory provision so as to prevent double or multiple counting.

To ensure that the parties to an acquisition agreement are able to fulfil their obligation to notify the company of the interests they are deemed to have in the other parties' shares, they are each obliged to notify the other parties of the interests they have personally when they first become subject to a duty to notify the company of interests they are deemed to have in the other parties' shares, and they must also notify the other parties of the occurrence of subsequent events which may oblige the other parties to notify the company of matters relating to shares in which they have or had a personal interest (eg the acquisition or disposal of interests in such

1 Ibid, s 204 (6).
2 *Re Ricardo Group plc* [1989] BCLC 566.
3 Ibid, s 204 (1), (2) and (4).
4 Including interests of his spouse, his minor children, companies in which he controls one-third or more of the voting powers, and companies whose directors are accustomed to obey his instructions (see p 365, ante).
5 Companies Act 1982, s 205 (1) and (4).
6 Ibid, s 205 (1) and (2).
7 Ibid, s 208 (2).

shares).[8] Such a notification must be given to the other parties to the agreement within two days after the person who has a personal interest could come under an obligation to notify the company,[9] and the notification must contain a statement of the number of the company's shares carrying full voting rights to which the notification relates and must give particulars of the registered holders of those shares.[10] A separate notification of any changes in those registered holders or of any persons becoming registered holders of those shares (eg on the registration of shares previously represented by letters of allotment) must also be given to the other parties to the agreement.[11] Failure to give any such notifications to other parties to a share acquisition agreement is a criminal offence.[12]

Notification procedure and the register of interests in shares

A person who is under a duty to notify a company of any matter relating to an interest which he has or had in its shares carrying full voting rights, or to an interest which he is deemed to have or to have had in such shares, must give a notification to the company in writing within two days after the duty to notify arises, and the notification must specify the number of such shares in which he was interested or deemed to be interested immediately before and after the occurrence giving rise to the duty to notify, or (where appropriate) the notification must state that he is no longer interested in such shares.[13] If the notification relates to an interest which the person giving it is deemed to have in shares in which another person is interested as a result of them both being parties to a share acquisition agreement, the notification must be given within two days after the person giving it becomes aware of the matter to be notified,[14] and must state that it is given by him as a party to a share acquisition agreement, must specify the other parties to the agreement and the number of shares to which the notification relates, and must state that the shares in question are shares in which he is deemed to be interested under the statutory provisions relating to share acquisition agreements.[15] Additionally, a notification that the person giving it or any other person has ceased to be a party to a share acquisition agreement, with the result that the person giving the notification has ceased to have a deemed interest in the other parties' shares, must contain a statement to that effect and particulars of the person who has ceased to be a party to the agreement.[16]

It is a criminal offence for a person who is obliged to give a notification to a company to fail to do so, or for him knowingly or recklessly to give a notification which is false.[17] If a person is convicted of such an offence the Secretary of State for Trade and Industry may make an order subjecting the shares in respect of which the offence was committed to the same restrictions as may be imposed by an order made in connection with investigations into the beneficial ownership of shares by the Secretary of State or by inspectors appointed by him,[18] and the Secretary of

---

8 Ibid, s 206 (2). The mutual obligation to notify personal interests applies however small the percentage of shares in the company in which the interest exists.
9 Companies Act 1985, s 206 (8), as amended by Companies Act 1989, s 134 (3). No regard is paid to the number of shares in which the interest exists.
10 Companies Act 1985, s 206 (3) and (7).
11 Ibid, s 206 (4).
12 Ibid, s 210 (3).
13 Ibid, s 202 (1) and (2), as amended by Companies Act 1989, s 134 (3).
14 Companies Act 1985, s 207 (1), (2) and (3).
15 Ibid, s 205 (4).
16 Ibid, s 205 (5).
17 Ibid, s 210 (3).
18 See p 362, ante.

State may later revoke such an order on an application being made to him.[19] An appeal lies to the court against such an order or the Secretary of State's refusal to revoke it.[20] In the present context an order by the Secretary of State imposing restrictions on shares is imposed as an additional punishment, and not as a means of inducing disclosure of information about the beneficial ownership of shares; it would therefore have been appropriate for the Secretary of State to have been empowered to make orders imposing restrictions on shares for a fixed period, but it would appear that his powers are in fact confined to making orders of indefinite duration and then revoking them at a later date.

Every public company must keep a register in which it must record the contents of notifications of matters relating to interests in its shares carrying voting rights in the order it receives them; every notification must be recorded within three days after its receipt, and if the notification is that a person has ceased to be a party to a share acquisition agreement, that fact must also be recorded against all entries made in respect of his deemed interests in shares in which other parties to the agreement are interested.[1] Unless the register in which the company records notifications is in the form of an index, the company must also keep an index of the names entered in the register so as to enable such entries to be readily found.[2] The register and any accompanying index must be kept at the same place as the company's register of its directors' interests in its shares and debentures,[3] that is, at its registered office or any other address in England and Wales where the work of making up its register of members is done.[4] A public company may remove an entry in its register of interests in its shares when at least six years have elapsed since the entry was made and the entry either recorded the fact that a person had ceased to have an interest in shares or has been superseded by a later entry.[5]

When a company receives a notification that a person has an indirect or deemed interest in shares in which another person is interested as a result of them both being parties to a share acquisition agreement, the company must within 15 days after receiving the notification inform that other person of the entry which the company has made in consequence in its register of interests in shares, and he may apply to the company to remove the entry from its register on the ground that it is incorrect;[6] if the company will not remove the entry, the other person may apply summarily to the court for an order compelling it to do so.[7] Similarly, a person who ceases to be a party to a share acquisition agreement may apply to the company to insert a note to that effect against all entries in the register made in relation to the interests of himself and other parties to the agreement in consequence of him being a party to it,[8] and if the company does not insert such a note, he may apply to the court for an order compelling it to do so.[7] The court appears to have a summary power to order the rectification of the register of interests in shares only in the circumstances indicated, and to have no general power to rectify other errors, except possibly in an action commenced by writ.

The register of interests in shares kept by a company must be made available for inspection by members of the company or other persons during business hours

---

19 Companies Act 1985, s 210 (5).
20 Ibid, s 456 (1) and (2).
1 Ibid, s 211 (1) to (3).
2 Ibid, s 211 (6).
3 See p 557, post.
4 Companies Act 1985, s 211 (8) and s 325 (5) and Sch 13, para 25.
5 Ibid, s 217 (1).
6 Ibid, s 217 (2) and (3).
7 Ibid, s 217(5). The application is made by originating motion (RSC Ord 102, r 3 (1) (*h*)).
8 Companies Act 1985, s 217 (4).

without charge, and any member or other person may require the company to supply him with a copy of the whole or part of the register on payment of not more than 10p or such other amount as is prescribed for every hundred words copied.[9] If inspection of the register is refused, or if a copy of the whole or part of the register is not supplied within seven days after a request for the purpose, a summary application may be made to the court for an order that inspection shall be allowed or the copies supplied immediately.[10] However, no part of the register or the accompanying index need be made available for inspection, nor apparently need copies of it be supplied on request, insofar as that part contains entries in respect of interests in shares of the company held by its holding or parent company or by another company which holds at least 10 per cent of its equity share capital, if the other company carries on business overseas and the disclosure of the information in question would be seriously prejudicial to the business of either company.[11] A company is not deemed to be affected by notice of any rights of any other person as a result of receiving or recording notifications of interests in its shares under the present provisions.[12] This prevents the company being bound to give effect to equitable interests derived out of its shares carrying full voting rights merely because it has received notification of such interests, and it retains its general right to disregard notices of such interests served on it;[13] the protective provision also ensures that the company is not deferred in respect of any interest it claims itself in such shares merely because it has received notification of other interests in those shares under the statutory rules.[14]

Private companies are not required to keep registers of interests in substantial holdings of their voting shares, but if a public company which has been obliged to keep such a register is converted into a private company, it must retain the register and any accompanying index for six years from the date of its re-registration.[15] The company is, of course, not required to make any further entries in the register, but it seems that it remains under a duty to allow inspection of the register and to supply copies of it on request as long as it retains the register.

Investigation by a company of interests in its shares

A public company may require any person who it knows or reasonably believes to be interested in any of the company's shares carrying full voting rights, or to have been interested in such shares within the preceding three years, to state whether he has, or during that period had, a notifiable interest in those shares, and if so, to give the company information about his notifiable interests in the shares at present and during the preceding three years, about any other notifiable interest in the shares of which he is aware and which exists or existed during that period concurrently with any of his notifiable interests, and about the person who became entitled to any notifiable interest in the shares on his ceasing to have that interest during the preceding three years.[16] The information which must be given in response to the

---

9 Ibid, s 211 (8) and s 219 (1) and (2), as amended by Companies Act 1989, s 143 (5).
10 Companies Act 1985, s 219 (4). The application is made by originating summons (RSC Ord 5, r 3 and Ord 102 r 2 (1)).
11 Companies Act 1985, s 211 (9) and s 231 (3), as amended by Companies Act 1989, s 23 and Sch 10, para 3. In this situation the shareholding company need not disclose its interest in the company which keeps the register in its annual accounts, but the consent of the Secretary of State to the non-disclosure of the interest is necessary.
12 Companies Act 1985, s 211 (4).
13 Ibid, s 360 (see p 360, ante).
14 See p 411, post.
15 Companies Act 1985, s 211 (7).
16 Companies Act 1985, s 212 (1), (2) and (5).

company's requirement includes the identity of the persons entitled to the notifiable interests and particulars of any share acquisition agreement to which any of them are or were parties.[17] The disclosure requirement applies to rights to subscribe for shares carrying full voting rights in the same way as it applies to interests in such shares,[18] and so the person required to make disclosure must inform the company of subscription rights which he has or had, and of such rights which other persons have or had concurrently with him. It will be noted that the disclosure requirement does not extend to rights to convert securities into shares carrying full voting rights, and so a company cannot require a person interested in convertible debentures to disclose his own or other persons' interests in the conversion rights they carry.

The notice by which a company requires a person to inform it of notifiable interests in its shares must specify a reasonable time within which the notice must be complied with,[19] and if the time specified is not sufficient to enable the person concerned to obtain and communicate the information required, the notice is invalid, with the consequence that failure to supply the information cannot be used by the company as grounds for applying to the court to impose restrictions on the shares in question, and this cannot be remedied by the company agreeing to extend the time allowed after the notice has been given.[20] Notice calling for disclosure of notifiable interests in shares may be given by a company to a person or company resident outside Great Britain who has no business or other connection with it.[1]

A public company may be required by its members holding at least one-tenth of its paid up capital carrying voting rights at general meetings to exercise its powers to call on any persons to disclose their own and other persons' present and past notifiable interests in shares of the company carrying full voting rights in the same circumstances and to the same extent as the company could require disclosure on its own initiative.[2] The requisition that the company shall call for such disclosure must be in writing signed by the requisitionists, and may consist of several documents in like form; the requisition must specify how the company is required to exercise its powers and must set out reasonable grounds for requiring the company to act.[3] If the requisition is valid,[4] the company must exercise its power to call for the disclosure of notifiable interests in its shares in accordance with the terms of the requisition,[5] and on the conclusion of the company's investigation, it must prepare a report on the information it has obtained, which must be made available at the company's registered office within 15 days after the investigation is concluded.[6] If the company's investigation is not completed within three months after the requisition is made, the company must prepare an interim report on the information it has so far obtained, and further interim reports must be made at three monthly intervals thereafter until the investigation is concluded; interim reports must be made available at the company's registered office within 15 days after the end of the three month period they cover.[7] The company must notify the requisitionists that a final or interim report is available at the company's registered

---

17 Ibid, s 212 (3).
18 Ibid, s 212 (6).
19 Ibid, s 212 (4).
20 *Re Lonrho plc (No 2)* [1989] BCLC 309, (1988) 5 BCC 68.
1 *Re F L Lloyd Holdings plc* (1985) 1 BCC 402.
2 Companies Act 1985, s 214 (1).
3 Ibid, s 214 (2) and (3).
4 This may depend on whether it sets out reasonable grounds for an investigation; if it does not, the company cannot be compelled to act on it.
5 Companies Act 1985, s 214 (4).
6 Ibid, s 215 (1) and (3).
7 Ibid, s 215 (2) and (3).

office within three days after it becomes available.[8] The report may be inspected without charge by a member of the company or any other person during six years from the date when it first becomes available,[9] and the same rules apply with regard to the inspection of the report and the supply of copies of it as apply to the company's register of interests in shares.[10]

A company which obtains information about the notifiable interests of any person in its shares as a result of an inquiry made by the company on its own initiative or as a result of an investigation following on a requisition by its members, must enter the information in its register of interests in its shares with an indication that the information was obtained in such an inquiry or investigation.[11] This applies, however, only to notifiable interests which still exist at the time information is obtained about them, and the information recorded is confined to that concerning the present holders of such interests.[12] The same rules apply to entries in the register in consequence of an inquiry or investigation by the company as apply to the remainder of the register recording information supplied by persons having or deemed to have notifiable interests,[13] and that part of the register is open to inspection by a member of the company or any other person and copies of it must be supplied on request in the same way as the remainder of the register.[14] Likewise, information about the interests of the company's parent company or another company which holds at least 10 per cent of the company's equity share capital may be omitted from the register,[15] and from an interim or final report of an investigation into interests in its shares conducted by a company as a result of a requisition by its members,[16] if the other company carries on business overseas and disclosure would be harmful to either company.[17]

If a company requires any person to disclose information about his present or past notifiable interests in its shares carrying full voting rights and that person fails to give the information required, the company may apply to the court for an order imposing the same restrictions on the shares in which he is interested as the Secretary of State may impose when information about financial interests or control of a company is withheld from inspectors appointed by him.[18] The court may make such an order whether the company's complaint is that its requirement has been rejected or ignored, or whether the information given in response to it is false or incomplete, and the order made by the court may extend to all shares in the company which were the subject of the company's inquiry, including those in respect of which full information has been given, if there are other shares in respect of which no information, or false or incomplete information, has been tendered.[19] It has been held that if the information given in response to the company's requirement, or to several requirements addressed to different persons in respect of the same shares, when combined with evidence in the company's possession or inferences which can properly be drawn from the responses, shows that the information given is very probably incomplete, the court may treat the furnishing of incomplete information as a failure to comply with the company's requirements,

8 Ibid, s 215 (5).
9 Ibid, s 215 (7).
10 Ibid, s 219 (1), (2) and (4) (see 370, ante).
11 ibid, s 213 (1).
12 Ibid, s 213 (2).
13 Ibid, s 213 (3).
14 ibid, s 211 (8), s 213 (3) and s 219 (1) and (2).
15 Ibid, s 211 (9) and s 213 (3) (see p 371, ante).
16 Ibid, s 215 (4).
17 See p 371, ante.
18 Companies Act 1985, s 216 (1) (see p 362, ante).
19 *Re Lonrho plc* [1988] BCLC 53, (1987) 3 BCC 265; *Re Ricardo Group plc (No 2)* [1989] BCLC 766.

and may impose the statutory restrictions on the shares.[20] The court has a discretion whether to impose the statutory restrictions in respect of shares, however, and it may, instead of making an order imposing them, accept undertakings from the registered holder of the shares and persons interested in them not to dispose of their respective interests, and the court may also allow appropriate exceptions from the undertakings (eg to permit lenders of advances secured on the shares to realise their security).[1] Moreover, if the court considers that the imposition of restrictions is unnecessary, because the company can obtain the information it seeks from another source and the registered holder and other persons interested in the shares would suffer a disproportionate detriment if restrictions were imposed (eg inability to accept a takeover bid which will shortly expire), the court will not make an order imposing restrictions, even though it has jurisdiction to do so.[2] However, the court cannot impose the statutory restrictions on shares subject to an exception for the benefit of a particular person whose interest in the shares has been fully disclosed (eg a mortgagee of the shares whose powers of realisation on the default of the registered holder as mortgagor it is sought to preserve).[3] It should be noted that the court may impose restrictions on shares, even though the company's unanswered request for information relates only to past interests in them, and all interests which exist at present have been disclosed.

If an order imposing restrictions is made by the court, the company or any person interested in the shares may apply to the court to terminate the restrictions.[4] However, the court may order the termination of the restrictions only in the same circumstances as it may order the termination of restrictions imposed by the Secretary of State in connection with an investigation of the beneficial ownership of shares by inspectors appointed by him.[5] Consequently, the court will terminate the restrictions once it is satisfied that the requisite information has been given fully and accurately,[6] but the court will not terminate restrictions in order that the shares may be sold if it is likely that the sale is a device to enable the persons whom the company requires to give information to avoid doing so, and it is also likely that after the sale they will replace the original shares by acquiring other shares on the market.[7]

SALES OF SHARES

Having examined the effect of a transfer of shares and the creation of equitable interests out of them, it is now possible to consider in detail the kinds of transactions in shares which take place in practice, beginning with sales.

Contracts for sale

A contract for the sale of shares need not be in any particular form, and so an oral contract is valid and enforceable. If shares, debentures or loan securities are sold or purchased by a broker/dealer member of the Stock Exchange on behalf of a client, the Stock Exchange Rules require the broker/dealer to send a contract note

20 *Re T R Technology Investment Trust plc* [1988] BCLC 256.
1 *Re Lonrho plc (No 3)* [1989] BCLC 480.
2 *Re Ricardo Group plc*, supra.
3 *Re Lonrho plc (No 2)* [1989] 3 WLR 1106, [1990] BCLC 151.
4 Companies Act 1985, s 456 (1) and (2).
5 Under the Companies Act 1985, s 442, s 444, s 456 (3) (see p 362, ante).
6 *Re Ricardo Group plc*, supra.
7 *Re Geers Gross plc* [1987] 1 WLR 837, [1987] BCLC 253, affd [1988] 1 All ER 224, CA.

recording the terms of the transaction to his client, and a broker/dealer must also send a contract note to a client when he sells securities to, or purchases securities from, the client.[8]

A contract to sell shares need not be for the sale of specific shares identified at the time when the contract is made, and a contract to sell shares which the seller does not yet own is perfectly valid, such a transaction being known as a 'short' sale. In fact, all contracts made on stock exchanges are for the sale of unascertained shares, and the seller fulfils his obligations by delivering a transfer of any shares which conform to the description in the contract. If a contract is made for the sale of specific shares, the equitable title to them passes to the purchaser at once when the contract is made, and until the legal title is transferred, the seller holds the shares as a bare trustee for him;[9] this is so even though the sale is subject to the fulfilment of a condition which the purchaser can waive (eg the seller obtaining a certificate from the revenue authorities as to tax liability, or a third person entering into a business contract with the company).[10] If a contract is made for the sale of shares which are not identified in the contract, the equitable title passes to the purchaser only when the seller appropriates particular shares to fulfilment of the contract, which will usually be when he executes a transfer to the purchaser identifying the shares by number or otherwise.[11]

When the equitable title to the shares has passed to the purchaser, he becomes entitled to all dividends thereafter declared by the company, even though they are declared for a financial year which ended before the contract to sell the shares was entered into.[12] But the purchaser is not entitled to dividends declared before the equitable title passed to him, even though they were still unpaid at that time.[13] However, on a sale of unidentified shares the fact that the price is the current market price may show that the parties intended that the purchaser should be entitled to dividends declared and benefits accruing to shares of the same category at any time after the contract of sale was entered into, as well as benefits accruing after particular shares are appropriated to the contract by the seller,[14] and this will certainly be so if there is a market usage to that effect.[15] The same rules as to entitlement to dividends should logically apply to issues of bonus shares on a capitalisation of profits or reserves resolved upon by the company after the contract of sale is entered into. The purchaser is entitled to the benefit of any rights offer of further shares made to shareholders after the date on which he acquired the equitable title to the original shares,[16] or after the contract for sale was entered into if a term to that effect can be implied from the contract price being the current market price,[14] or from a market usage to that effect.[15]

Conversely, the purchaser must indemnify the seller against all calls made on the shares after he acquires the equitable title, or after the date of the contract of sale if the purchaser is entitled to benefits accruing in respect of the shares

---

8 Rules of the Stock Exchange, r 325.1.
9 *Hawks v McArthur* [1951] 1 All ER 22 at 26.
10 *Wood Preservation Ltd v Prior* [1969] 1 All ER 364, [1969] 1 WLR 1077.
11 *Re London, Hamburg and Continental Exchange Bank, Ward and Henry's Case* (1867) 2 Ch App 431 at 438 per Cairns LJ. It would seem that if a seller holds stock or shares which have no distinguishing numbers and he sells only part of his holding, the equitable title passes to the purchaser only when the company registers the transfer to him.
12 *Black v Homersham* (1878) 4 ExD 24; *Re Wimbush, Richards v Wimbush* [1940] Ch 92, [1940] 1 All ER 229.
13 *Re Kidner, Kidner v Kidner* [1929] 2 Ch 121.
14 *Stewart v Lupton* (1874) 22 WR 855; *Spencer v Ashworth Partington & Co* [1925] 1 KB 589 at 602 per Atkin LJ.
15 *Cunliffe-Owen v Teather and Greenwood* [1967] 3 All ER 561, [1967] 1 WLR 1421.
16 *Rooney v Stanton* (1900) 17 TLR 28.

thereafter, and if the purchaser re-sells the shares without being registered himself, his indemnity obligation extends to all calls made before his sub-purchaser registers and thus terminates the seller's liability to the company for future calls.[17] The same rule would appear to apply to instalments of the issue price of shares which become immediately due and payable after the equitable title to the shares has passed to the purchaser, or after the date when the contract of sale is entered into in cases where the purchaser is entitled to benefits accruing thereafter.

A seller is entitled to vote as he wishes in respect of shares he has sold if the purchase price has not been paid in full, even though the equitable title has passed to the purchaser. Until the purchase price is paid in full the seller has a lien on the shares for the unpaid purchase price, and like a mortgagee, can protect his lien by using his voting rights as he thinks fit.[18] When the purchase price has been paid in full, however, the seller must vote as the purchaser directs.[18] These rules, of course, merely govern the rights and duties of the seller and purchaser as between themselves. As far as the company is concerned, the only person entitled to the shares is the registered holder of the shares, and it is to him that all dividends are paid and rights offers and calls are addressed. The rights of the seller and purchaser are then adjusted in the way described above.

If an option to sell or purchase shares is given and the option holder exercises it, the contract for sale takes effect between the parties as if it had been entered into when the option was given.[19] Consequently, if the purchase price is the current market price at the time when the option was given or if there is a relevant market usage, it may be implied that the purchaser is entitled to all dividends declared and all bonus shares issued and rights conferred in respect of the original shares after the option was given, and conversely, that the purchaser must indemnify the seller against all calls made and instalments of the issue price falling due after the option was given.[19]

On completion of a purchase of shares, the seller's obligation is to deliver his share certificate and a duly executed transfer to the purchaser, and to assist him to be registered as a member of the company.[20] If the seller impedes the purchaser from being registered, he is liable to him in damages.[1] But if the directors of the company have power to refuse to register transfers by its memorandum or articles of association, the seller does not impliedly undertake that they will register the transfer to the purchaser,[2] and if they refuse to do so, the seller is not liable to the purchaser in damages, nor can the purchaser treat the contract for sale as repudiated by the seller, and the seller continues to hold the shares as a bare trustee for the purchaser who is entitled, as between himself and the seller, to all the financial and other benefits resulting from the shares.[3] On the other hand, if the

17 *Spencer v Ashworth Partington & Co* [1925] 1 KB 589.
18 *Musselwhite v C H Musselwhite & Son Ltd* [1962] Ch 964, [1962] 1 All ER 201; *Re Piccadilly Radio plc* [1989] BCLC 683.
19 *Cunliffe-Owen v Teather and Greenwood* [1967] 3 All ER 561, [1967] 1 WLR 1421.
20 *Re East Wheal Martha Mining Co* (1863) 33 Beav 119 at 121; *Skinner v City of London Marine Insurance Corpn* (1885) 14 QBD 882 at 887; *London Founders Association Ltd and Palmer v Clarke* (1888) 20 QBD 576 at 582.
1 *Hooper v Herts* [1906] 1 Ch 549.
2 *Stray v Russell* (1859) 1 E & E 888; affd (1860) 1 E & E 916. See also cases cited in note 20, supra.
3 It has been held in Scotland, however, that if the purchaser was aware of the directors' power to refuse registration when he contracted to purchase the shares, he impliedly agrees to obtain their approval of the transfer to him or to some other person to whom he is able to transfer the shares, and if he cannot obtain such approval the seller may rescind the contract for sale (*Stevenson v Wilson* 1907 SC 445). This would not appear to be the law in England, where restrictions or prohibitions imposed by contract on the transfer of property do not prevent the seller being a bare trustee for the purchaser, and the purchaser's knowledge of the restriction or prohibition is immaterial (*Re Turcan* (1888) 40 ChD 5; *Spellman v Spellman* [1961] 2 All ER 498, [1961] 1 WLR 921).

articles require the seller to obtain the directors' consent before transferring his shares,[4] or if the seller expressly undertakes that the directors will register the transfer,[5] he will be liable in damages to the purchaser if registration is not obtained and the purchaser may treat the contract of sale as repudiated.

If a purchaser of shares re-sells them, it is not necessary that he should be registered as a member of the company himself before he completes the sub-sale. He may deliver to the sub-purchaser the seller's share certificate accompanied by a transfer from the seller to the sub-purchaser duly executed by the seller, or accompanied by two transfers, the first from the seller to the purchaser and the second from the purchaser to the sub-purchaser. However, if the purchaser has received from the seller a blank transfer not naming a transferee, it is an offence for him to deliver it to the sub-purchaser or any other person still in blank.[6] The purpose of this rule is to prevent the avoidance of stamp duty, but it does not affect the validity of the transfer to the sub-purchaser, nor does the rule apply at all if the seller delivers the blank transfer direct to the sub-purchaser. The purchaser's obligation to the seller is to take a transfer of the shares himself, or to find a sub-purchaser who is ready and willing to take a transfer,[7] and to the sub-purchaser the purchaser's obligation is to deliver a transfer executed by himself or by a transferor who is able and willing to transfer.[8] If both the seller and the sub-purchaser are willing to complete, therefore, the purchaser's duties to them both are discharged by him procuring the delivery of a transfer from the seller to the sub-purchaser in return for payment of the price he agreed to pay to the seller.

After completion of the sale, the seller has the right to compel the purchaser to register the transfer.[9] Subject to any power conferred by the articles for the company to refuse to register transfers, the seller may require the company to effect registration of the transfer to the purchaser or a sub-purchaser from him,[10] and if necessary, may apply to the court for an order for the rectification of the register of members to ensure that this is done.[11] Likewise a purchaser or sub-purchaser who has submitted the transfer or transfers of the shares and the seller's share certificate to the company with a request for registration, may obtain an order for the rectification of the company's register of members and requiring it to issue a new share certificate in the purchaser's or sub-purchaser's name, if the company refuses or fails to register the transfer or transfers.[12] Unless the terms of issue of the shares provided for a longer or shorter period, the company must have a new share certificate in the purchaser's or sub-purchaser's name ready for delivery within two months after the presentation of a proper transfer duly stamped to the company for registration.[13] If the company has a Stock Exchange listing for the shares, its

---

4 *Wilkinson v Lloyd* (1845) 7 QB 27, as explained by Fry LJ in *London Founders Association v Clarke*, supra, at 583. This form of restriction on transfers is now obsolete in practice.

5 The term formerly found in contracts for the sale of partly paid shares, 'registration guaranteed', is equivocal. It may mean that the seller undertakes that the company will register the purchaser, or it may mean that the purchaser undertakes to procure his own registration or the registration of another person so as to relieve the seller from liability for future calls (*Cruse v Paine* (1869) 4 Ch App 441).

6 Finance Act 1963, s 67 (1) and (2) (32 Halsbury's Statutes (4th edn) 309).

7 *Coles v Bristowe* (1868) 4 Ch App 3.

8 *Hichens, Harrison, Woolston & Co v Jackson & Sons* [1943] AC 266, [1943] 1 All ER 128.

9 *Re Stranton Iron and Steel Co* (1873) LR 16 Eq 559.

10 Companies Act 1985, s 183 (4).

11 Ibid, s 359 (1). The application is made by originating motion (RSC Ord 102, r 3 (1) (*g*)).

12 Companies Act 1985, s 185 (6) and s 359 (1).

13 Ibid, s 185 (1).

directors must issue a new share certificate within 14 days after a transfer of the shares is lodged for registration.[14]

On completion of a sale of shares represented by a share warrant, the seller's duty is to deliver the warrant to the buyer, whereupon the legal title passes to him. If the buyer has re-sold to a sub-purchaser, the seller may either deliver his share warrant to the sub-purchaser on the purchaser's direction, or may deliver it to the purchaser, so passing the legal title to him, and the purchaser may likewise pass the title to the sub-purchaser by delivering the share warrant to him. If a depositary (such as a bank) holds the share warrant on behalf of the seller, delivery may be effected by the depositary handing the share warrant with the consent of the seller to the purchaser or sub-purchaser or to a depositary acting for him, or the seller's depositary may attorn to the purchaser or sub-purchaser, thereby acknowledging that he holds the share warrant as his bailee and agent.

If either the seller or purchaser fails to complete the sale of the shares, the other party to the contract may recover the loss of his bargain as damages. The loss of bargain is the difference between the purchase price and the real value of the shares on the date when completion of the sale should have taken place.[15] Alternatively, the innocent party may obtain an order of specific performance to compel the other to carry out the contract.[16] But if similar shares can readily be bought on an available market, a seller in default under the contract of sale cannot be compelled to transfer the shares he holds specifically; the buyer will have to resort to the market to purchase equivalent shares, and will be entitled to recover from the seller, as damages, the difference between the contract price and the higher price he has to pay on the market.[17] Similarly, a seller of shares which can be readily re-sold on the market will not be able to obtain an order of specific performance against the purchaser, but if the equitable ownership of the shares has passed to the purchaser and the date for completion of the sale has passed, it would appear that the seller can recover the full purchase price from the purchaser by suing him in debt.[18] Specific performance of a contract for the sale of shares can be ordered even though the directors have power to refuse to register transfers; in that case the court will order the seller to execute and deliver a transfer, or the purchaser to accept a transfer and to pay the purchase price, and it will then be for the purchaser to seek the registration of the transfer.[19]

The stamp duty payable on a transfer of registered shares on a sale is at the rate of 50p per £100 of the purchase price[20] and is payable by the purchaser. If an agreement to transfer shares is not effected by the execution of a duly stamped instrument of transfer within two months after the agreement is made, or after any condition to which it is subject is not fulfilled, the purchaser must pay stamp duty reserve tax at the same rate as the stamp duty payable on a transfer, and when a transfer of the shares is later executed, the tax already paid is credited against the stamp duty payable on it.[1] When shares are sold to a market maker member of the Stock Exchange in the ordinary course of his business as such, stamp duty is not payable on any instrument of transfer of the shares to him, and stamp duty reserve

14 Stock Exchange: *Admission of Securities to Listing*, Section 5, Chapter 2, para 28.
15 *Tempest v Kilner* (1846) 3 CB 249; *Shaw v Holland* (1846) 15 M & W 136; *Jamal v Moola Dawood, Sons & Co* [1916] 1 AC 175.
16 *Duncuft v Albrecht* (1841) 12 Sim 189.
17 *Re Schwabacher* (1908) 98 LT 127.
18 *Atkinson v Bell* (1828) 8 B & C 277; *Elliott v Pybus* (1834) 10 Bing 512.
19 *Poole v Middleton* (1861) 29 Beav 646.
20 Stamp Act 1891, 1st Sch Conveyance or Transfer on Sale (32 Halsbury's Statutes (3rd edn) 178; Finance Act 1963, s 55 (1A), inserted by Finance Act 1986, s 64 (1) (41 Halsbury's Statutes (4th Edn) 267).
 1 Finance Act 1986, s 87 (1) to (6), s 91 (1) and s 92 (1) (41 Halsbury's Statutes (4th Edn) 407, 414).

tax is not payable if there is no such instrument of transfer (eg because the shares are credited to the market maker's account under the TALISMAN system).[2]

Certification of transfers

If a seller of shares contracts to sell all the shares represented by a share certificate, he will deliver it to the purchaser together with an executed instrument of transfer on completion of the sale. If the seller sells only part of his holding represented by a single certificate, however, he will instead send the certificate and the executed transfer of the shares which the purchaser is buying to the company so that the transfer may be certificated. An officer of the company, usually the secretary, or the company's registrars and transfer agents (if it has any),[3] will compare the share certificate and the transfer with the company's register of members, and if it appears that the seller is the owner of the shares mentioned in the certificate and that some of those shares are comprised in the transfer, the officer or transfer agents will write in the margin of the transfer a note that the share certificate has been lodged, and will sign the note on behalf of the company. This is known as certification of the transfer, and the transfer is described as a certified or, more explicitly, as a certificated transfer. The certificated transfer is then returned to the seller and the share certificate is retained by the company or the transfer agents. The seller completes the sale by delivering the certificated transfer to the purchaser, who will accept it as equivalent to delivery of an uncertificated transfer accompanied by the share certificate, which is in the company's possession. The purchaser then lodges the transfer with the company or its transfer agents for registration, and the company issues a new share certificate to him for the shares he has bought, and at the same time the company issues a new share certificate to the seller showing him as the registered holder of the balance of the shares which he retains. The seller's original share certificate for the whole holding is retained by the company, and destroyed after a certain length of time.

At common law a secretary of a company to whom the power to certificate transfers had been delegated by the directors, was deemed to have power to certificate them only when documents which were formally in order had been lodged with the company.[4] The company was not bound by its secretary's certification when no share certificate had been lodged, or when the lodged share certificate did not correspond with the register of members, or when the instrument of transfer comprised different shares from those mentioned in the share certificate. In those circumstances the company was not precluded from refusing to register the certificated transfer when it was presented for registration by a purchaser who had relied on the certification, nor from showing that he had no title to the shares comprised in the transfer if he sued the company for damages for refusal to register it. The same rules appeared to apply if the certification was given by the company's registrars and transfer agents. Now, however, a certification is binding on the company, and it is precluded from denying the truth of the representation implied by the certification, if it is signed by any person authorised to certificate transfers on the company's behalf (such as its transfer agents), or by any officer of the company, and the certificated transfer is returned to the transferor or transferee by

---

2 Ibid, s 81 (1) and (3) and s 89 (1) and (3). For the TALISMAN system, see p 393, post.
3 Registrars and transfer agents are firms who specialise in providing recording services in respect of issues and transfers of shares, debentures and other loan securities. They are often firms who also provide accountancy and secretarial services in general. In recent years the registrars' departments of the commercial banks have increasingly undertaken this kind of work.
4 *George Whitechurch Ltd v Cavanagh* [1902] AC 117; *Kleinwort Sons & Co v Associated Automatic Machine Corpn* [1934] WN 65.

a person authorised to issue certificated transfers on the company's behalf.[5] All that the purchaser need prove now in order to preclude the company from denying the truth of the certification is that the certificated transfer was issued by the duly authorised officer or agent of the company; he need not show, as he had to show at common law, that the officer or agent performed his duties properly.

The representation which a company makes by certificating a transfer is not an absolute one that the transferor is entitled to the shares mentioned in the transfer.[6] It is merely a representation:

'that there have been produced to the company such documents as on the face of them show a prima facie title to the shares . . . in the transferor named in the instrument [of transfer]. However, the certification is not to be taken as a representation that the transferor has any title to the shares . . .[7]

If the documents lodged with the company are formally in order, the company incurs no liability to anyone if the transferor named in the certificated transfer has no title to the shares, because, for example, he has already sold them once and has forged a copy of his original share certificate in order to sell them a second time,[8] or because the transferor obtained the shares by a forged transfer to himself, or by a transfer which was void for a fundamental mistake. On the other hand, if a seller forges a transfer of another person's shares, and the company certificates it without requiring production of the share certificate in respect of the shares, the company is estopped from denying that the proper share certificate has been produced. By certificating the transfer, the company makes it appear that the owner of the shares has authorised the transaction, and so a purchaser who relies on the certificated transfer can sue the company for damages if it refuses to register the transfer to him.[9]

The Companies act 1985[10] provides that:

'where any person acts on the faith of a false certification by a company made negligently, the company is under the same liability to him as if the certification had been made fraudulently.'

This provision contemplates that the remedy of a purchaser who relies on a certificated transfer is to sue the company for damages in a tort action for deceit or negligence, but it is more likely the purchaser will sue the company for wrongful refusal to register the transfer to him, or for the wrongful removal of his name from the register if the transfer has in fact been entered in it and the entry is later cancelled. The purchaser will then use the representation implied in the certification, not as a cause of action, but as creating an estoppel which prevents the company from pleading that it is under no duty to register the purchaser as holder of the shares or to maintain his registration on its register of members. The obvious advantage of suing for wrongful refusal to register or for wrongful removal from the register is that the purchaser does not have to prove any deliberate deception or even negligence on the part of the officer or agent of the company who issued the certificated transfer, it being sufficient for the purchaser to show that the company is bound by the representation implicit in the certification.

A certification of a transfer is not only a representation by the company that the

5 Companies Act 1985, s 184 (3).
6 This contrasts with the absolute representation which the company makes when it issues a share certificate (see p 350, ante).
7 Companies Act 1985, s 184 (1).
8 This resembles the situation in *Guy v Waterlow Bros and Layton Ltd* (1909) 25 TLR 515.
9 In this situation the purchaser's position would be stronger than if he had taken delivery of the share certificate and an uncertificated forged transfer (see p 352, ante).
10 Companies Act 1985, s 184 (2).

seller's share certificate has been produced to it; it also subjects the company to a duty to retain the certificate until the certificated transfer is surrendered to the company or presented for registration. This is because the wording of the certification shows that the share certificate has been lodged with the company or its transfer agents, that is, deposited pending completion of the transfer. The certification only takes effect for the purpose of the Companies Act 1985, mentioned above, if it is an annotation of the transfer that the relevant share certificate has been lodged with the company or an annotation to like effect.[11] The company's duty to retain the share certificate is a qualified one, however, namely to take care that the share certificate does not leave the company's hands, and it is owed only to the transferee named in the certificated transfer.[12] Consequently, if a company certificates a transfer, and then deliberately or negligently returns the share certificate to the seller who fraudulently sells the shares a second time and delivers the share certificate to the second purchaser, the company is liable in damages to the transferee under the certificated transfer if it registers the transfer to the second purchaser, and therefore has later to refuse to register the certificated transfer.[13] But it has been held that the company will not be liable in damages to the second purchaser if it registers the certificated transfer even though the share certificate is still in the seller's hands, and it consequently refuses to register the uncertificated transfer to the second purchaser when it is afterwards presented.[12] Furthermore, it has been held that the second purchaser cannot contend that the company is estopped from showing that the seller was not the owner of the shares represented by the share certificate at the time when the second purchaser agreed to buy them. A share certificate embodies a representation by the company that the shareholder named in it is entitled to the shares to which it relates on the date when the certificate is issued, but it does not involve a continuing representation that he remains entitled to the shares so long as the certificate is in his possession.[12] However, since the decision that a company which has certificated a transfer owes no duty to a second purchaser to retain the relevant share certificate so that he may not be misled by the seller,[12] the courts have expanded the range of persons to whom a person who participates in a transaction owes a duty of care to protect them from loss if the transaction miscarries,[13] and it may be that a company will now be liable in damages to such a second purchaser for its negligence in returning the seller's share certificate to him and so enabling the seller to sell the shares a second time.[14]

The certification of a transfer does not imply a representation that a stop notice has not been served on the company in respect of the shares comprised in the transfer.[15] Consequently, if a purchaser completes his purchase on the delivery to him of a certificated transfer, but is unable to register it because of the successful intervention of the owner of an equitable interest in the shares who has served such a notice, the purchaser cannot sue the company for damages.

The Certification Office of the Stock Exchange may certificate share transfers, and transfers so certificated are accepted as good delivery of the shares comprised

---

11 Ibid, s 184 (3). A note on a transfer that the share certificate had been produced to the company would therefore not appear to be a certification, but a note that the certificate has been deposited with, or received by, the company would suffice.

12 *Longman v Bath Electric Tramways Ltd* [1905] 1 Ch 646.

13 *Arenson v Casson Beckman Rutley & Co* [1977] AC 405, [1975] 3 All ER 901; *Ross v Caunters* [1980] Ch 297, [1979] 3 All ER 580; *Yianni v Edwin Evans & Sons* [1982] QB 438, [1981] 3 All ER 592.

14 It may nevertheless be that the seller's deliberate act in selling the shares a second time would break the chain of causation, because the company's act would not be the effective cause of the second purchaser's loss (*Weld-Blundell v Stephens* [1920] AC 956).

15 *Peat v Clayton* [1906] 1 Ch 659.

in them under contracts made with members of the Stock Exchange.[16] The Certification Office forwards the lodged share certificate to the company, but the Council of the Stock Exchange accepts no responsibility for the Office's acts or omissions, so that if the certificate is never lodged with it, or is returned by it to the seller, or miscarries on its way to the company, the Council cannot be sued.[17] The company is also immune from liability, for the Certification Office is not its agent, but if the company receives a share certificate knowing that the Certification Office has certificated a transfer of shares comprised in it, the company probably comes under the same duty towards the transferee named in the certificated transfer not to part with the certificate as if it had certificated the transfer itself. If a company has a Stock Exchange listing for any of its securities, its directors must certificate transfers on delivery of the certificates for the securities and return the transfer to the registered holder duly certificated on the day it is lodged for certification.[18]

Financial assistance for the acquisition of shares

The Companies Act 1985 recast the restrictions on a public or private company giving financial assistance in connection with the acquisition of shares in itself or its holding or parent company which were formerly contained in the Companies Act 1948 (as amended)[19] so as to clarify the legitimacy or otherwise of certain transactions connected with share acquisitions and to moderate certain over-rigorous judicial interpretations of those restrictions.[20]

The Companies Act 1985 begins by imposing two prohibitions, namely, (a) on a company or any of its subsidiaries giving financial assistance directly or indirectly for the purpose of an acquisition of shares in the company if the assistance is given before or at the time of the acquisition;[1] and (b) on a company or any of its subsidiaries giving financial assistance directly or indirectly for the purpose of discharging or reducing a liability incurred by any person for the purpose of an acquisition of shares in the company by that or any other person.[2] Financial assistance in this context means such assistance by way of gift, guarantee or indemnity, or release or waiver of a right or obligation; or by way of a loan or any other agreement under which the obligations of the person giving the assistance are to be fulfilled when under the agreement any obligation of any other party remains unfulfilled; or by way of novation or the assignment of the rights arising under such a loan or other agreement; or by way of any other financial assistance which results in a material reduction in the net assets of the company or which is given by a company with no net assets.[3] The net assets of a company are taken to be its aggregate assets less its aggregate liabilities.[4] The forms which financial assistance may take are therefore extremely diverse, and include the release or deferment of a debt owed to the company, the release or modification of the security for such a debt, and a loan under the guise of a sale of assets to the company coupled with an obligation to repurchase them at a later date or to hire or lease them back. The final item in the definition of financial assistance, namely, any assistance which results in a diminution of the company's net assets, raises problems of interpretation.

---

16 Rules of the Stock Exchange, r 653.1.
17 Ibid, r 653.3.
18 Stock Exchange: *Admission of Securities to Listing*, Section 5, Chapter 2, para 26.
19 Companies Act 1948, s 54; Companies Act 1980, s 88 (1) and Sch 3, para 10.
20 See in particular *Belmont Finance Corpn Ltd v Williams Furniture (No 2)* [1980] 1 All ER 393 and *Armour Hick Northern Ltd v Armour Trust Ltd* [1980] 3 All ER 833, [1980] 1 WLR 1520.
 1 Companies Act 1985, s 151 (1).
 2 Ibid, s 151 (2).
 3 Ibid, s 152 (1) (a).
 4 Ibid, s 152 (2).

If it means any transaction by which the assets of the company before the transaction are diminished, it would include any disposal of assets, whether financial in character or not (eg an exchange of investments), but if, as is probable, it means a transaction which results in a diminution in the company's assets not being fully counterbalanced by the acquisition of assets of equivalent value (including a claim for a money payment which is likely to be met), it would seem that it adds nothing to the more specific items in the definition which precede it.

Of more practical importance is the restriction of the new prohibitions to the giving of financial assistance 'for the purpose of' an acquisition of shares or the discharge of a liability incurred for the purpose of the acquisition. The former prohibition in the Companies Act 1948 was on the giving of financial assistance 'for the purpose of or in connection with' an acquisition of shares,[5] and it was by reliance on the words 'in connection with' the acquisition that the court was able to hold that a contemporary purchase of an asset by the company from the person who acquired shares in it was an infringement of the prohibition unless the purchase was in the ordinary course of the company's business,[6] and that the payment by a subsidiary of a debt owed by its parent company to the person who contemporaneously purchased shares in the parent company was also such an infringement, although payment of the debt by the parent company in the ordinary course of its business would not have been.[7] If transactions of these kinds were to be impeached under the Companies Act 1985, it would be necessary to prove that they were entered into with the intention of providing funds for the acquisition of shares, and it would not suffice that they were not entered into in the ordinary course of the company's business and were contemporary with the acquisition. Moreover, it is doubtful whether they would come within the definition of financial assistance at all unless, in the first case, the sale to the company was at an overvalue, and in the second, the subsidiary which paid its parent company's debt had no indemnity claim against the parent company; sales and payments of debts are not listed specifically in the definition of financial assistance, and so it would seem that they qualify as financial assistance only if they result in a diminution of the company's net assets.

In deciding whether a company has given financial assistance for the purpose of an acquisition of its shares, the whole of the transaction for the acquisition must be considered. If the company does confer a financial benefit on the seller of shares in it (eg a surrender of tax losses by the company to its holding or parent company, which sells shares in the company)[8] and there is a possibility that the purchase price paid by the purchaser is reduced in consequence, account must also be taken of any financial benefits which are conferred by the seller on the company (eg the cancellation or deferment of indebtedness of the company to the seller or the payment of liabilities of the company by the seller).[9] The company then gives financial assistance for the purpose of the acquisition only if the value of the benefits which it confers exceeds the value of the benefits it receives.[9]

The purpose with which a company gives financial assistance is now the deciding factor in determining whether an infringement of the prohibition on a company giving financial assistance for the acquisition of shares in itself or its holding company has occurred. A further refinement is that if the company has two or

5 Companies Act 1948, s 54 (1).
6 *Belmont Finance Corpn Ltd v Williams Furniture (No 2)*, supra.
7 *Armour Hick Northern Ltd v Armour Trust Ltd*, supra.
8 The surrender is effected under the Income and Corporation Taxes Act 1988, s 402 (1) and (2) (44 Halsbury's Statutes (4th Edn) 486), and enables the parent company to set off the surrendered losses against its own profits for the purpose of corporation tax.
9 *Charterhouse Investment Trust Ltd v Tempest Diesels Ltd* [1986] BCLC 1, (1985) 1 BCC 544.

more purposes in giving the financial assistance, no infringement occurs if the company's principal purpose is not to give assistance for the acquisition of shares or for the discharge of a liability incurred for the purpose of the acquisition, or if the giving of the assistance is merely incidental to a larger purpose of the company, but in either case the assistance must be given in good faith in the interests of the company.[10] The exploration of mixed motives and intentions may well give rise to difficulties in practice, but it would seem safe to say that if the company's primary purpose in dispensing funds is to acquire an asset or benefit, even though it knows that the recipient will use the funds wholly or partly to acquire shares in the company, there will be no infringement of the prohibitions. Consequently, it will be no infringement for a company to acquire for cash a business venture or useful tangible asset or intellectual property rights from another company which already holds shares in it, and to raise the necessary cash by making a rights offer to its shareholders which it knows the vendor company will take up in respect of its holding. Nor will it be an infringement for a company to acquire such assets partly for cash and partly by an issue of shares to the vendor, even though it knows that the vendor will use the cash to buy further shares in the company, or even though it issues further shares to the vendor which are paid up by the repayment of the cash. The assumption is made, however, that the acquisition of assets by the company is a genuine transaction entered into in the company's interests. If it were a facade designed to cover the acquisition of shares in the company without the vendor having to incur a cash outlay, there would, of course, be an infringement if the company's net assets suffered a consequential diminution in value, and the suspicion that this was the real purpose of the transaction will be increased if the fraction of the company's issued share capital held or acquired by the vendor is very substantial.

In applying the statutory prohibition, a distinction must be drawn between the purpose for which a company gives financial assistance which is in fact used to acquire shares in it or its holding company, or to repay indebtedness incurred for that purpose, and the reason or motive which induced the company to give the assistance and which, being merely a reason or motive, cannot be a separate purpose justifying the assistance. For example, if a company gives financial assistance to enable an existing holder of shares in it or a company controlled by him to acquire shares in the first company as part of a scheme to divide the company's undertaking or its subsidiaries between its principal shareholders and directors in order to resolve a deadlock in the management of the company, the resolution of the deadlock is the reason why the assistance is given, but not an independent purpose sought to be achieved by giving it, and consequently the statutory prohibition on giving the assistance applies, because there is no other purpose to be achieved than facilitating the acquisition of shares in the company.[11] Likewise, where under a scheme for transferring exclusive control of two groups of companies to different sections of their shareholders respectively, the transfer of their respective shareholdings in the companies in which they relinquished any interest to the other section of shareholders was accompanied by a payment by one of the groups of companies to the other in order to achieve an equalisation in value between the two groups, it was held that the companies which were to make the payment would thereby give financial assistance for the acquisition of shares in themselves by the section of shareholders who were to have exclusive control over them, and that this was the purpose for which the assistance was given, and not the

10 Companies Act 1985, s 153 (1) and (2).
11 *Brady v Brady* [1989] AC 755, [1988] 2 All ER 617, [1988] BCLC 579.

division of control over the two groups of companies, which was merely the motive or reason for the scheme.[12]

Excepted transactions

Certain acts or transactions are explicitly excluded from the prohibition on a company giving financial assistance for the acquisition of shares, and so even if they do facilitate the acquisition of shares in the company and are designed to do so, no infringement of the prohibition occurs.[13] These excluded transactions comprise the distribution of dividends lawfully declared; the distribution of a company's assets to its creditors or shareholders in a liquidation; the issue of bonus shares on a capitalisation of profits or reserves; anything done under a scheme of arrangement approved by the court,[14] or under an arrangement with the company's creditors taking effect under the Insolvency Act 1986,[15] or under a sale of a company's assets by its liquidator for shares in the purchasing company,[16] the reduction of a company's capital approved by the court,[17] or the redemption or purchase of a company's shares under the provisions of the Companies Act 1985.[18] Logically, the payment of cash by a company in connection with a takeover bid should also have been an excluded transaction so as to cover the situation where the current market value of the offeror company's shares makes it likely that accepting shareholders of the offeree company will re-invest the proceeds of their shares in shares of the offeror company, but the absence of a statutory definition of a takeover bid would have made this difficult. In any case, such a situation would fall outside the new prohibitions unless the bid were a facade, because the principal purpose of a takeover bid for cash is the acquisition of control over the offeree company, and not the funding of alternative investments by its shareholders.

In addition to the excluded acts and transactions, certain other transactions are exempted from the statutory prohibitions. These comprise (a) loans by a company made in the ordinary course of its business, which includes the lending of money as part of its ordinary business; (b) the provision in good faith and in the interests of the company of financial assistance for the purpose of an employees' share scheme;[19] (c) the provision of financial assistance for the purpose of, or in connection with, anything done by the company to facilitate transactions in shares of the company or its holding company, between employees or former employees of the company or another company in the same group, their spouses, widows or widowers and their children, adopted children and step-children under the age of 18, provided that the transactions involve the acquisition of the beneficial ownership of the shares by such persons; and (d) loans by a company to employees of itself or its holding company (other than directors) to enable those employees to acquire fully paid shares in the company or its holding company.[20] However, a public company may give assistance in these exempted cases only out of its profits available for distribution, or if the net assets are not thereby reduced.[1] A private company is not

---

12 *Plaut v Steiner* (1988) 5 BCC 352.
13 Companies Act 1985, s 153 (3).
14 Ibid, s 425 (1) and (2).
15 Insolvency Act 1986, ss 1 to 5.
16 Ibid, s 100.
17 Companies Act 1985, s 135 (1) and s 137 (1) (see p 177, ante).
18 Ibid, ss 159 to 181 (see p 188, ante).
19 An employees' share scheme is defined by the Companies Act 1985, s 473 (see p 247, ante).
20 Companies Act 1985, s 153 (4), as amended by Financial Services Act 1986, s 196 (2) and (3) and Companies Act 1989, s 132 and s 144 (4) and Sch 18, para 33.
1 Ibid, s 154 (1).

subject to this restriction, but it would appear to involve a distinction between public and private companies only when the assistance is given gratuitously under an employees' share scheme or to facilitate transactions between employees or former employees and persons closely related to them. A public company can give such gratuitous assistance only out of distributable profits, but a private company is not so limited. The first and fourth of the exemptions are, of course, almost identical with the exemptions from the prohibition on financial assistance contained in the former legislation,[2] and will no doubt be interpreted in the same way. This will mean that a loan may be made under the first exemption only if one of the main objects of the company is the making of loans for general purposes (though not necessarily to the public at large), and it must not be a condition of the loan that it shall be expended in the acquisition of shares in the company or its holding company.[3] This, of course, does not apply to the fourth exemption.

The statutory provisions prohibiting a company giving financial assistance for the acquisition of shares in itself or its holding company make any contravention by a company or its officers a criminal offence[4] and provide that the giving of the assistance shall not be lawful,[5] but the statutory provisions do not deal in detail with the validity or otherwise of a transaction under which financial assistance is given or related transactions. The wording of the statutory provisions declaring the unlawfulness of the assistance is the same as that of the former legislation,[6] and the decisions of the courts as to the effect of that legislation are therefore relevant in determining the effect of the new prohibitions. Under the former legislation it was held that an agreement for the sale of shares was not made void by the fact that the parties intend that the purchase price shall be borrowed from the company,[7] unless this was made a term of the contract of sale and was not merely a facility for the purchaser which he was free to waive.[8] It was also held that a mortgage of the company's assets was valid even though it is given to secure a loan to the company which the lender knew would be used to assist someone to acquire shares in the company,[9] but this was doubted in one case[10] and held to be wrong in another.[11] On the other hand, in yet another case it was affirmatively held that if a company gives security for a loan made by a third person to finance an acquisition of shares in the company by the borrower, the lender cannot enforce a guarantee of the company's obligation under the security, even if it is given by the borrower himself.[11] It was also held that the court would not enforce an agreement to acquire shares specifically if its terms required an act to be done which would be a breach of the statutory prohibition,[12] and it would seem that no action for damages would lie for breach of such an agreement.[13] Because the court treated the agreement as unenforceable in equity if it had been partly carried out by either or both of the parties, it was held that the court would in exercise of its equitable jurisdiction restore them as far as possible to the position they were in before the agreement was made. However, a company could not sue to recover a loan made in breach of

2 Companies Act 1948, s 54 (1).
3 *Steen v Law* [1964] AC 287, [1963] 3 All ER 770.
4 Companies Act 1985, s 151 (3).
5 Ibid, s 151 (1) and (2).
6 Companies Act 1948, s 54 (1).
7 *Spink (Bournemouth) Ltd v Spink* [1936] Ch 544, [1936] 1 All ER 597.
8 *Carney v Herbert* [1985] AC 301, [1985] 1 All ER 438.
9 *Victor Battery Co Ltd v Curry's Ltd* [1946] Ch 242, [1946] 1 All ER 519.
10 *Selangor United Rubber Estates Ltd v Craddock (No 3)* [1968] 2 All ER 1073 at 1153, [1968] 1 WLR 1555 at 1646.
11 *Heald v O'Connor* [1971] 2 All ER 1105, [1971] 1 WLR 497.
12 *South Western Mineral Water Co Ltd v Ashmore* [1967] 2 All ER 953, [1967] WLR 1110.
13 Ibid, *Heald v O'Connor*, supra.

the statutory prohibition,[14] and it seems that once the money advanced has been paid to the borrower, the company could not seek the equitable remedy of an order for the restitution of the amount lent, though it could sue its own directors and any other persons who knowingly participated in making the loan (including the borrower) for damages in respect of its loss resulting from the directors' breach of duty.[15]

Financial assistance for the acquisition of shares in private companies

Private companies are given an additional special exemption from the prohibitions on giving financial assistance for the purpose of acquiring shares in the company or its holding company, or discharging or reducing a liability incurred for the purpose of such an acquisition.[16] If the assistance is for the acquisition of shares in the private company's holding company, however, that company and all intermediate holding companies (where the private company is a sub-subsidiary) must also be private companies.[17] The special exemption for private companies is given, not by reference to the primary purpose of giving the assistance or the form in which it is given, but to the source from which it comes. The assistance must either be provided out of profits of the company available for distribution as dividends,[18] or the net assets of the company must not be reduced in consequence of the assistance being given.[19] In this context the reduction of the company's net assets can only mean a reduction which remains after taking account of the value of any claim which the company has against another person for repayment, reimbursement or indemnification. Thus, a loan by a private company to facilitate the acquisition of shares in itself would be legitimate if the whole of the principal of the loan is repayable by the borrower or any other person, and the interest and any premium on repayment of the loan will suffice to cover the interest and any premium on any loan which the company has itself contracted for the purpose of making the principal loan. Gratuitous financial assistance can be given by a private company under the special exemption only out of its distributable profits, but this does not, of course, prevent a private company from giving gratuitous assistance under an employees' share scheme, or to facilitate transactions in shares between employees or former employees or persons closely related to them, under the general exemptions from the prohibitions on the giving of financial assistance by any company.[20]

The conditions which a private company must fulfil and the procedure it must follow in order to give financial assistance under the special exemption are designed to ensure that it will not jeopardise its business undertaking or expose its creditors to risk by doing so. The giving of the assistance must be approved by a special resolution passed by a general meeting of the company, except where it is a wholly-owned subsidiary of another private company, when no resolution of approval need be passed by its general meeting.[1] If the shares to be acquired are shares in the company's holding company, the assistance must also be approved by a special

---

14 *Selangor United Rubber Estates Ltd v Cradock (No 3)*, supra at [1968] 2 All ER 1073, 1154, [1968] 1 WLR 1555 at 1653.
15 Ibid, [1968] 2 All ER 1073, 1151 to 1152, [1968] 1 WLR 1555 at 1633 to 1634; *Wallersteiner v Moir* [1974] 3 All ER 217, [1974] 1 WLR 991.
16 Companies Act 1985, s 155 (1).
17 Ibid, s 155 (1) and (3).
18 The profits of a private company available for distribution are defined by the Companies Act 1985, s 263 (see p 421, post).
19 Companies Act 1985, s 155 (2).
20 Companies Act 1985, s 153 (4).
1 Ibid, s 155 (4).

resolution passed by a general meeting of the holding company and every intermediate holding company (if any), but no resolution by an intermediate holding company is required where the company giving the assistance and all intermediate holding companies are wholly-owned subsidiaries of the holding company whose shares are to be acquired.[2]

Procedure

Within one week before the appropriate special resolution approving the financial assistance is passed by the company or its holding company or an intermediate holding company (as the case may be), all the directors of the company which passes the resolution must make a statutory declaration setting out particulars of the assistance and of the persons to whom it is to be given, and stating that having regard to the company's situation immediately after the assistance has been given, in their opinion there will be no ground on which the company of which they are directors could be found unable to pay its debts and liabilities in full (including its prospective and contingent liabilities and liabilities for unliquidated amounts), and also that in their opinion the company will be able to pay its debts and liabilities in full as they fall due during the year following the declaration, or alternatively, if it is intended to wind the company up within that time, that the company will be able to pay its debts and liabilities in full within twelve months after the commencement of the winding up.[3] The statutory declaration must have annexed to it a report by the company's auditors that, having inquired into the company's affairs, they are not aware of anything which makes the directors' opinion about the company's present and future solvency appear unreasonable.[4] Each statutory declaration and annexed auditors' report must be available for inspection by members of the company whose directors made it at the general meeting of that company called to pass a special resolution authorising the financial assistance.[5] This is necessary, whether the company is the one which is to give the financial assistance, or is that company's holding company or an intermediate holding company. Within 15 days after the meeting has been held the statutory declaration and report must be delivered to the Registrar of Companies with a copy of the special resolution.[6]

Within 28 days after a special resolution authorising financial assistance is passed by a general meeting of a company, an application may be made to the court to cancel it by the holders of not less than 10 per cent in nominal value of the company's issued shares or of its issued shares of any class, or if the company is not limited by shares, by at least 10 per cent of its members.[7] An application may be made on behalf of two or more members by one of their number authorised by the others in writing.[8] It will be noted that an application to cancel a special resolution can be made only by members of the company which passed it, so that if it is a resolution passed by a holding company or an intermediate holding company because the financial assistance is to be given by a sub-subsidiary for the acquisition of shares in its ultimate holding company, only members of the holding or intermediate holding company (as the case may be) may apply to the court to

2 Ibid, s 155 (5).
3 Ibid, s 155 (6), s 156 (1) to (3) and s 157 (1).
4 Ibid, s 156 (4).
5 Ibid, s 157 (4).
6 Ibid, s 156 (5) and s 380 (1) and (4) (*a*).
7 Ibid, s 54 (3) and s 157 (2) and (3). The application is made to the Companies Court by petition. RSC Ord 102, r 4 (1) (*k*).
8 Companies Act 1985, s 54 (3) and s 157 (3).

cancel the resolution. The requisite fraction of members of the sub-subsidiary which is to give the assistance may, of course, apply to the court to cancel the special resolution passed by that company, and since the question to be decided by the court is the same, whether the special resolution whose cancellation is sought is one passed by the company, its holding company or an intermediate holding company, the applications should be heard together. On the hearing the court may confirm or cancel the special resolution on such terms and conditions as it thinks fit, and may make any order which it could make on an application to cancel a resolution for the re-registration of a public company as a private one.[9] Where there are several special resolutions because a company proposes to give financial assistance for the acquisition of shares in its holding company, the cancellation by the court of any of the resolutions will prevent the financial assistance being given.

Unless every member of the company entitled to vote at general meetings votes in favour of the special resolution, the financial assistance authorised by the resolution may not be given until four weeks after the special resolution authorising it is passed, or if two or more such resolutions are needed because the shares to be acquired are shares in a holding company, until four weeks after the last of such resolutions is passed, and if an application is made to the court to cancel the resolution or any of the resolutions within that period, the assistance may not be given until the court has confirmed the resolution or resolutions which are attacked.[10] Moreover, the financial assistance may not be given more than eight weeks after the directors of the company which gives the financial assistance make the statutory declaration as to the company's actual and prospective solvency, or if two or more such statutory declarations are made by companies in the same group, more than eight weeks after the earliest statutory declaration is made; the court may extend the period of eight weeks in any case, and will need to do so if it confirms a special resolution on hearing an application to cancel it.[11] The time scale for authorising and completing the giving of financial assistance is therefore calculated differently from that for authorising and completing a private company's purchase of shares in itself out of capital,[12] but overall the operation must be initiated and carried out within the same time limits. The reason for this is the same as in the case of a purchase of shares out of capital, namely, to prevent so long a delay occurring after the directors make a statutory declaration as to the company's actual and prospective solvency that statements made in it which were justified when it was made cease to be by the time when the financial assistance is given.

Liabilities of participants

A director who makes a statutory declaration in connection with the giving of financial assistance by a private company for the acquisition of shares in it or its holding company, is guilty of a criminal offence if he expresses an opinion therein as to a company's actual or prospective solvency without having reasonable ground for doing so, and such a director is punishable, if convicted on indictment, by imprisonment for not more than two years and by a fine of unlimited amount or by both such penalties, or if convicted summarily, by imprisonment for not more than six months or a fine not exceeding £1,000 or by both those penalties.[13]

There are no statutory provisions requiring recipients or directors to reimburse

9 Ibid, s 54 (5) and (6) and s 157 (3) (see p 66, ante).
10 Ibid, s 158 (2) and (3).
11 Companies Act 1985, s 158 (4).
12 See p 196, ante.
13 Companies Act 1985, s 156 (7) and s 730 and Sch 24.

the company for the cost of giving financial assistance for the acquisition of shares if the company is wound up within the following 12 months, as there are when a private company purchases shares in itself out of capital.[14] Nevertheless, there can be no doubt that if directors give financial assistance out of the company's resources or incur obligations or liabilities on its part in connection with the giving of such assistance, and the opinion they express as to the company's solvency in the statutory declaration they make has no reasonable basis, or the assistance is given in circumstances where it is hazardous to do so, the company may recover the amount of any consequential loss it suffers by suing the directors for breach of their duty to exercise reasonable care. Auditors who do not exercise reasonable skill and care in preparing their report supporting the directors' statutory declaration will also be liable to the company for its consequential loss, but not, it would seem, to individual shareholders of the company who are induced by the auditors' report to vote for the special resolution that the company shall give financial assistance.[15]

Sales of shares on stock exchanges

It is outside the scope of this book to deal in detail with the organisation, rules and practice of the Stock Exchange, or to give it its full name, the International Stock Exchange of the United Kingdom and the Republic of Ireland. An outline of Stock Exchange practice in connection with sales of shares and other securities is necessary, however, and mention must be made of some of the points where contracts for the sale of shares on the Stock Exchange differ from contracts governed by the general law.

Members of the Stock Exchange are either broker/dealers or market makers, although some member firms of broker/dealers in practice buy and sell securities only as agency brokers acting on behalf of investment clients. All members of the Stock Exchange are permitted by its rules to buy and sell securities which are listed on the Stock Exchange, or admitted to dealing on the Unlisted Securities Market or the Third Market, or in which dealings are specially permitted by the Council of the Stock Exchange, and they may do so either on behalf of their clients or themselves.[16] Those members who are registered with the Stock Exchange as market makers in respect of securities for which they are prepared to quote dealing prices, are obliged to make a continuous market in those securities by quoting continuously the prices at which they are willing to buy and sell them.[17] Market makers are also bound to deal at the prices they quote in normal marketable quantities of the securities.

A member of the Stock Exchange who asks a market maker for his current prices does not reveal whether the member wishes to buy or to sell securities, and the market maker quotes in response two prices, which are respectively a higher price at which he is willing to sell the securities in question (the offer price) and the lower price at which he is willing to buy them (the bid price). If the member who makes the inquiry finds that the price quoted for the transaction he wishes to enter into (sale or purchase) is satisfactory, he tells the market maker that he sells or buys a stated quantity of the securities at that price. The market maker confirms that he agrees, which he is bound to do if the quantity of the securities involved is a normal one for transactions in them.[18]

If the quantity of the security in which the inquiring member wishes to deal is

14 See p 197, ante.
15 *Caparo Industries plc v Dickman* [1990] 1 All ER 568, [1990] 2 WLR 358.
16 Rules of the Stock Exchange, r 535.1 and r 535.2.
17 Ibid, r 356.1, r 357.1, r 406.1 and r 407.1.
18 Ibid, r 357.1 and r 407.1.

abnormally large or small, the market maker is not required to deal at his quoted prices, but he may adjust his quoted prices to take account of the size of the proposed transaction, and if the adjusted price is satisfactory to the inquiring member, a bargain is then agreed upon.[18] A market maker in equity securities is only bound to deal in quantities larger than the normal marketable quantity if he displays a two-way price for specified larger quantities on the Stock Exchange Automated Quotations (SEAQ) system,[19] and the quantity in which he is requested to deal by another member is such a specified larger quantity.[18]

There are at present 26 Stock Exchange member firms which are registered as market makers in listed equity securities and fixed interest securities, and some 20 member firms which are registered as market makers in fixed interest securities issued by companies. Member firms which are not registered as market makers are known as broker/dealers, and may be registered with the Stock Exchange as accredited dealers if they are prepared to use their best endeavours to effect transactions in the securities in respect of which they are registered, either by dealing themselves or by arranging matching bargains.[20] Broker/dealers, whether accredited dealers or not, may deal on the Stock Exchange with market makers or other firms of broker/dealers either on their own account or on behalf of clients, but unlike market makers, they are under no obligation to buy or sell securities when offers are made to them, even though the offer is in respect of a normal dealing quantity of securities and is made at the current market price.

For the settlement of bargains, the work of the Stock Exchange is divided into dealing periods (commonly called 'Accounts') of two weeks' duration, commencing on the Monday of one week and ending on the Friday of the next following week.[1] All bargains done during this period are completed on Account Day (which falls on the Monday of the next week but one after the close of the Account)[2] by the original seller at the beginning of the Account or his broker (if the seller is not a member firm) delivering to the ultimate purchaser at the end of the Account or his broker (if the purchaser is not a member firm) the original seller's certificate for the shares or securities sold and an executed transfer, or alternatively a certificated transfer, or if the securities are in bearer form, the share warrant or bearer certificate, and by the ultimate purchaser or his broker paying the purchase price.[3] The preceding Wednesday is Ticket Day, on which the brokers acting for the ultimate purchasers of shares used to issue tickets giving their names and particulars of the shares they had bought. These tickets were handed by the brokers for the ultimate purchasers to the brokers for their immediate sellers or to the jobbers (the predecessors of the present market makers and accredited dealers) from whom they had bought the shares; these brokers or the jobber indorsed the tickets and handed them to the brokers acting for the persons from whom they had bought or to the jobber who had sold the shares to them, and so on until the ticket reached the broker for the original seller. On the original seller's broker accepting the ticket, the equitable title to the shares passed to the ultimate purchaser,[4] and the seller's broker proceeded to prepare a transfer to the ultimate purchaser so that he might

---

19 The SEAQ system provides a display of market makers' current prices by an electronic communications system and is subscribed to by member firms of the Stock Exchange, institutional investors, merchant banks and the dealing subsidiaries of commercial banks.
20 Rules of the Stock Exchange, r 358.1, r 359.1, r 408.1 and r 409.1.
 1 Ibid, r 600.1 and r 600.2. The dates of the Accounts are fixed annually in advance by the Council of the Stock Exchange. Two accounts of each year are of three weeks' duration, usually one in the summer and one in December.
 2 Rules of the Stock Exchange, r 600.4.
 3 Ibid, r 653.1 and r 653.2.
 4 *Coles v Bristowe* (1868) 4 Ch App 3; *Loring v Davis* (1886) 32 ChD 625.

complete on the Account Day. Nowadays, however, the bringing together of ultimate purchaser and original seller of all securities which are actively dealt in is done by a centralised clearing carried out by the Settlement Centre of the Stock Exchange under the TALISMAN system, which is explained below. It is possible, however, for the parties to agree to settle a bargain on a date earlier than the Account Day for the Account in which the bargain is made, but no bargain may be settled later than that date, unless it is entered into during the last two days of the Account, when it may be settled not later than the Account Day for the next following Account.[5]

Dividends and rights

The Stock Exchange has its own rules to determine whether, in the absence of express agreement, a purchaser is or is not entitled to an accruing dividend or the benefit of a capitalisation issue of bonus shares or of a rights offer made in respect of the shares he purchases. The purchaser is entitled to dividends declared after the date on which he contracts to buy the shares, unless the shares are quoted 'ex div' in the official list of dealings when he buys. Registered shares are quoted 'ex div' on the first day of the Account whose Account Day immediately follows the date when the company closes its register of members for the purpose of preparing dividend warrants.[6] Consequently, if the company closes its register on the 20th of the month with a view to posting dividend warrants on the 31st and the next Account Day after the 20th is on the 28th of the month, the shares will be quoted 'ex div' on the 7th of the month. Shares represented by share warrants are quoted 'ex div', on the day when the dividend is payable.[7] To enable the purchaser of shares represented by a share warrant to claim a dividend to which he is entitled, the appropriate dividend coupon must be delivered to him on settlement.[8] If a sale of shares represented by a registered share certificate is made with the benefit of a dividend, but the purchaser is unable to obtain the dividend from the company because it has closed its register of members before the settlement of the bargain, the purchaser may deduct the amount of the dividend from the purchase price he pays on settlement.[9]

A purchaser's right to bonus shares issued in right of the shares he has contracted to buy is determined in the same way as his right to claim dividends, and if the company intends to issue bonus shares instead of paying a dividend, the original shares are quoted 'ex capitalisation' on the day on which they would otherwise have become 'ex div'. If the purchaser is entitled to bonus shares which are represented by a renounceable letter of allotment, he may claim delivery of the letter duly renounced, provided he notifies the seller at least two days before the last day for lodging the letter of allotment with the company so that the holder of it may be registered in respect of the bonus shares; if the bonus shares are not represented by a renounceable letter of allotment or if the purchaser fails to call for delivery of the letter of allotment in respect of them in time, the purchaser may require the seller to execute a transfer of them to him.[10]

A purchaser of shares who buys them 'cum rights' is entitled to subscribe for the further shares offered by way of rights in connection with the shares he has bought

---

5 Rules of the Stock Exchange, r 601.3 and r 601.4.
6 Ibid, r 515.1a.
7 Ibid, r 515.1d.
8 Ibid, r 663.1.
9 Ibid, r 605.3d.
10 Ibid, r 615.1.

if the last date for accepting the rights offer is on or after the date on which he contracts to buy the original shares and the rights offer is renounceable.[11] In the case of a rights offer being made by the company issuing renounceable provisional letters of allotment, the purchaser is entitled to the new shares if the latest time for submitting applications for registration of the allottee or renouncee of the letter of allotment as a member of the company in respect of the new shares is on or after the date on which the purchaser contracts to buy the original shares.[11] The purchaser should notify the seller that he wishes to subscribe for or acquire the new shares not later than two days before the last day on which the rights offer may be accepted or registration applications in respect of the new shares may be delivered to the company; the seller must then notify the company that the rights offer is accepted and the new shares should be allotted to the purchaser, or if the purchaser requires the letter of rights to be renounced to him or the rights offer is embodied in a provisional letter of allotment, the seller must renounce the letter of rights or provisional letter of allotment and deliver it to the purchaser.[12] If the purchaser notifies the seller of his wish to acquire the new shares less than two days before the rights offer may be accepted or registration applications delivered to the company but before the time for doing so expires, the seller must take all possible steps to procure the new shares for the purchaser, but any additional expense incurred in doing this[13] must then be borne by the buyer.[12] Where a purchaser is entitled to the benefit of a rights offer, the seller must pay all instalments of the issue price of the new shares which fall due between the date of the contract of sale and the Account Day on which the sale is completed, and the purchaser must reimburse the seller for such instalments which he has paid.[14] However, the purchaser may instruct the seller not to pay an instalment at least two business days before it becomes payable, and the seller must then not do so; the risk of forfeiture of the shares is then borne by the purchaser.[15] Instalments of the issue price which fell due before the contract of sale was entered into must, of course, be paid by the seller on his own account, unless the contract was a special bargain for the sale of shares paid up to the extent of instalments actually paid up on them. If by a Stock Exchange transaction an option is given to an investor to sell or to purchase a certain number of shares[16] and the option holder exercises the option, so that a contract for the sale of the shares then arises, the purchaser of the shares is entitled to the benefit of all rights which are exercisable at any time after the option is granted, and this is so even if the rights were conferred before the option was given.[17]

The settlement of stock exchange bargains

Since 1979 the Stock Exchange of the United Kingdom and Ireland has operated a new system for checking and settling bargains in shares and other securities listed

---

11 Ibid, r 614.1 and r 614.5.
12 Ibid, r 614.5a.
13 The additional expense will be the ad valorem stamp duty charged on an instrument of transfer of the shares to the purchaser if the company registers the seller as a member in respect of the new shares because it has not received an application to register the purchaser by the last date for submitting such applications.
14 Rules of the Stock Exchange, r 614.5d.
15 Ibid, r 614.6.
16 An option to sell shares is called a 'put' option, and an option to buy them is called a 'call' option. Option dealings are permitted on the Stock Exchange, provided the option holder is bound to declare whether he exercises the option not later than the seventh Account Day after the option is given (Rules of the Stock Exchange, r 473.2).
17 *Cunliffe-Owen v Teather and Greenwood* [1967] 3 All ER 561, [1967] 1 WLR 1421.

on it and in shares and other securities admitted to dealing on the Unlisted Securities Market. The new system is known as TALISMAN, which is a contraction of the words Transfer Accounting, Lodgement for Investors and Stock Management for Market Makers and Dealers, the three services which the new system provides. The system is operated partly under the Rules of the Stock Exchange and partly under the provisions of the TALISMAN Reference Manual published by the Stock Exchange to which reference is made in the Rules.

The two keys to the system are that a company formed by The Stock Exchange, SEPON Limited (a contraction for Stock Exchange Pool Nominees), acts as a depositary for securities in the course of settlement of bargains, and that a department of the Stock Exchange, the Settlement Centre, keeps accounts of acquisition and disposals of securities by member firms. The securities for the time being credited to such an account represent the beneficial entitlement of the account holder or, in the case of brokers, of the clients of the account holder, to securities of the relevant description. The system applies only to registered securities listed on the Stock Exchange which are issued by companies incorporated in the United Kingdom or Ireland, and so it is not employed in respect of shares, debentures and loan securities represented by bearer certificates or by renounceable letters of allotment or acceptance, or in respect of securities of foreign companies.[18] It does, however, apply to securities registered in a register kept in the United Kingdom or Ireland, even though the issuing company keeps a duplicate register overseas.

Transfer and settlement procedure

The procedure on the sale of securities within the TALISMAN system must be adhered to by member firms on sales between themselves as principals and also on sales where one or both of the member firms act on behalf of a client.[19] The member firms who sell or purchase securities must both report the bargain to the Stock Exchange Settlement Centre, where the reports will be checked, and if they match, a sale docket in respect of the bargain will be sent by the Centre to the member firms.[20] Unless the sale is by a member firm which already has sufficient of the securities sold credited to its stock account kept by the Centre, the selling firm must then deliver to the Centre a 'sold' transfer of the securities to SEPON Ltd signed by the seller[1] together with the seller's certificate for the securities, or alternatively, if the seller is disposing of only part of a holding represented by a single certificate, a 'sold' transfer to SEPON Ltd accompanied by the certificate and a request to the issuing company for a certificate in the seller's name for the unsold balance of the securities.[2] The Centre sends the 'sold' transfer and the seller's certificate for the securities to the issuing company, which registers SEPON Ltd as holder of the securities, but does not issue a new certificate to it.[3] Under the rules of the Stock

---

18 Exceptionally, the securities of Australian and South African companies are within the TALISMAN system. The securities of companies incorporated in certain other Commonwealth countries are also included if the securities are registered in the United Kingdom.

19 Rules of the Stock Exchange r 690.2 and Stock Exchange Regulations, reg E5.3 and reg E5.4.

20 TALISMAN Reference Manual (hereafter referred to as 'Manual'), Bargain Records and Sale Docket. Sale dockets do not operate to transfer any title nor do they create any obligation; they are issued simply to record the sale of the securities and in anticipation of a transfer by the seller.

1 A TALISMAN sold transfer is in a form authorised by regulations made under the Stock Transfer Act 1963 (Stock Transfer (Addition of Forms) Order 1979 (SI 1979/277), para 2 and Sch 1), and the provisions of that Act apply to it (Stock Exchange (Completion of Bargains) Act 1976, s 6 (1) (30 Halsbury's Statutes (4th Edn) 160)). No stamp duty is chargeable on a sold transfer (Finance Act 1986, s 84 (1)) (41 Halsbury's Statutes (4th Edn) 405)).

2 Manual, Deposit Set, TALISMAN Sold Transfer and Certification—TALISMAN Securities.

3 Companies Act 1985, s 185 (4), as amended by Financial Services Act 1986, s 194 (5).

Exchange the equitable beneficial interest of the selling member firm or its client in the securities it has sold will cease on the deposit at the Settlement Centre of the certificate for the securities he has sold accompanied by a 'sold' transfer, or alternatively a 'sold' transfer accompanied by a request for certification which is not rejected. The beneficial interest in the deposited securities is replaced by a proportionate beneficial interest as a co-owner in all the securities of the same description which are registered in the name of SEPON Ltd or which have been deposited at the Settlement Centre for registration in its name.[4] Until the settlement of the sale of the securities, they will be represented by a credit entry in the selling member firm's stock account kept by the Centre,[5] and if the selling member firm's client has been allotted an operating account number by the Centre, it will issue a document called a stock receipt to evidence this fact.[6]

The settlement of bargains in securities under the TALISMAN system takes place on the date prescribed by the Stock Exchange rules, which will normally be the relevant Account Day.[7] The Settlement Centre effects delivery to buyers by debiting the stock accounts of the selling member firms and crediting the stock account of the buying member firms before the commencement of business on the day when settlement takes place. When this has been done, stock or apportionment schedules are handed to the member firms concerned together with payment statements showing the net amount payable by or to them in respect of all the transactions to be settled on the same day so that payment can be made or to the Centre as a clearing agent later that day.[8] Once securities have been credited to its account, therefore, a member firm who re-sells or who has re-sold them is able to deliver the securities to another member firm which is, or acts for, the purchaser by means of accounting entries notified to the firms involved. The debiting of the selling firm's stock account and the consequential crediting of the stock account of the purchasing firm is known as apportionment.[8] A firm to whom securities are apportioned is entitled to have them transferred to the client on whose behalf it purchased them by SEPON Ltd, and a firm in whose favour an apportionment is made in respect of a purchase made by itself as a principal can call for a similar transfer, but is unlikely to do so since its intention will be to re-sell the securities as quickly as possible and a transfer will then be made directly from SEPON Ltd to the purchaser from it.[9] Usually the firm will have bought and sold the same securities during a single Account; in that case the securities will pass through its account on Account Day as a matter of book-keeping, and it will receive no stock transfers in respect of the securities.

As soon as possible after an apportionment of securities has been made, the Centre will have SEPON Ltd execute a TALISMAN 'bought' transfer[10] to the purchasing firm or its client in accordance with particulars of the transferee

---

4 Stock Exchange Regulations, reg E5.5a, reg E5.6 and reg E5.13a and b.
5 Ibid, reg 5.11b; Manual, Accounting Controls.
6 Manual, Stock Receipt. Operating account numbers are allotted at discretion to investors who have frequent substantial dealings in securities on the Stock Exchange.
7 Stock Exchange Regulations, reg E5.11b; Manual, Accounting Controls.
8 Ibid, reg 5.7a, reg 5.8, reg E5.11a and b, reg E13a, reg 5.22a and c and reg 5.26a and b.
9 Ibid, reg 5.12a.
10 A TALISMAN bought transfer is in a form authorised by regulations made under the Stock Transfer Act 1963 (Stock Transfer (Addition of Forms) Order 1979 (SI 1979/277) para 2 and Sch 2), and the provisions of that Act will apply to it (Stock Exchange (Completion of Bargains) Act 1976, s 6 (1)). Stamp duty is payable in respect of a bought transfer at the rate of 50p for each £100 of the price paid for the securities by the buying firm or its client; the bought transfer will be stamped by the Stock Exchange on behalf of the Revenue authorities on payment of the appropriate amount of stamp duty by the purchasing firm; the Stock Exchange will then account for the duty received to the Revenue authorities (Finance Act 1970, s 33 (1) and (2) (41 Halsbury's Statutes (4th Edn) 302)); Finance Act 1986, s 83 (1) and (2) (41 Halsbury's Statutes (4th Edn) 405).

provided by the firm, and the Centre will then send the bought transfer to the company which issued the securities for registration.[9] The issuing company will register the purchaser as holder of the securities and issue a new certificate in his name, which will be returned to the Settlement Centre for collection by the purchasing member firm. At the same time the issuing company will make an entry in its register that SEPON Ltd has ceased to be the holder of the securities transferred. When a bought transfer has been executed by SEPON Ltd, the purchasing member firm's stock account is debited with the number of securities comprised in the transfer; that member firm or its client ceases to be interested as a beneficial co-owner of the securities of the same description which are registered in the name of SEPON Ltd or deposited at the Centre for registration in its name, and becomes instead the beneficial owner of the securities comprised in the bought transfer.[11]

Securities can only be apportioned to a member firm (whether acting on its own account or as agent for a client) if sufficient securities stand to the credit of the selling member firm's account maintained by the Settlement Centre.[12] Securities will be apportioned from the selling member firm's account according to an established order of priority, apportionments where the selling member firm has guaranteed delivery, and reapportionments where a previous apportionment has been followed by the rejection of a bought transfer by the issuing company, having priority over apportionments under normal transactions.[13] If there are insufficient securities credited to a member firm's account to fulfil a contract of sale completely, the securities which are credited to the account will be apportioned, but a 'bought' transfer of those securities will not be executed by SEPON Ltd and delivered to the issuing company for registration until five days have elapsed, so as to allow time for the balance of the securities to be apportioned as they are acquired by the selling member firm and credited to its account.[14] Normally, this will enable all the securities comprised in one contract of sale to be included in a single bought transfer.

Additionally, there may be a further slight delay in registration of a bought transfer to a buyer because there may not be enough securities registered in the name of SEPON Ltd in the register kept by the issuing company. Bought transfers delivered by the Settlement Centre to the company for registration will then be accumulated by it, and when new sold transfers to SEPON Ltd of securities of the same class are registered, the company will register the accumulated bought transfers correspondingly. The only circumstance in which this situation can occur (apart from fraud) is where the original seller has not delivered to the Centre either a formally correct sold transfer accompanied by a certificate for the securities he has sold, or alternatively a formally correct certificated sold transfer, which in either case the company accepts for registration. In that case the Centre will debit the stock account of the member firm which bought the securities from the original seller with the number of securities in question, and the apportionment of the securities comprised in the bought transfer will be cancelled.[15] If the selling firm does not then replace the defective transfer by an effective one, the purchasing member firm may buy the requisite amount of the class of securities comprised in the contract of sale in the market for delivery to itself or its client, and will claim any loss from the selling member firm.[16].

11 Stock Exchange Regulations, reg E5.5a and reg 5.13a.
12 Ibid, reg 5.7a and b.
13 Manual, Stock Queue, Guaranteed Delivery Bargain Condition and Bad Delivery.
14 Manual, Release for Registration—Part Apportionment Hold.
15 Manual, Bad Delivery—Stock Previously Delivered, Insufficient Stock in SEPON, and Apportionment Reversal.
16 Rules of the Stock Exchange, r 800.1 and r 801.1; Stock Exchange Regulations, reg E5.10.

Certain investors (principally institutional investors) deal with the member firms who act for them on a cash-against-documents basis; this means that they do not settle with the firms on a net basis in respect of all their sales and purchases of securities during an Account, but instead pay the whole purchase price on the receipt of transfers of securities to the investors, and similarly such investors receive the whole of the sale price when they deliver to the member firms which act for them transfers of securities which the firms have sold on their behalf. This procedure may be operated under TALISMAN, but with certain necessary variations; for example, since transfers will not be delivered to a purchasing member firm, but to the Settlement Centre, the Centre will issue documents called stock notes which will be evidence of the apportionment of the relevant securities to the purchasing firm, and the investor whom that firm represents will pay the purchase price to the firm in return for a stock note referring to the securities he has purchased.[17] A stock note is only evidence of the apportionment of securities to the purchasing firm, and the firm or its client acquires only the same proportionate interest in the total amount of securities of the class in question held by SEPON Ltd which he would have had if no stock note had been issued; indeed the Stock Exchange recognises no responsibility to the investor for whom the purchasing firm acts and no entitlement by him to such a proportionate interest until he has paid to that firm the purchase price for the securities bought on his behalf.[18] If an investor who has frequent substantial dealings on the Stock Exchange so requests, he may be allotted an operating account number by the Centre which may be used in the documents relating to sales of securities by the member firm which acts on his behalf so as to ensure that the whole or part of the amount credited to the firm in respect of sales of securities on the investor's behalf is paid directly by the Centre to the investor by means of a Centre cheque.[19]

Dividends and rights offers

Incidental problems arising from TALISMAN are dealt with fully by the scheme for its implementation. Dividends declared and interest falling due on securities while they are registered in the name of SEPON Ltd will be paid to it by the issuing company, and it will be a simple matter for the Settlement Centre to trace the person entitled to receive the dividends or interest from the terms of bargains reported to it by member firms and from its records of their holdings.[20] If there are several successive bargains in the same securities during the same Account, they will all be matched together, and SEPON Ltd will lodge with the issuing company a bought transfer to the ultimate buying member firm or its client after an apportionment has been made in favour of him or it.[1] SEPON Ltd cannot accept transfers of securities represented by renounceable letters of allotment or acceptance, whether issued in connection with public offers of securities for subscription or sale, or in connection with rights or capitalisation issues, and contracts for the sale of securities in that form will be settled by the traditional settlement procedure.[2] But letters of allotment will be issued to SEPON Ltd in connection with rights and capitalisation issues made while the underlying securities are registered in its name; SEPON Ltd and the Settlement Centre can then trace the member firms who, or whose clients, are entitled to the new securities from its records of member firms'

17 Stock Exchange Regulations, reg E5.34; Manual, Stock Note.
18 Ibid, reg E5.35 and reg E5.36a.
19 Ibid, reg 5.32a and reg E39a.
20 Ibid, reg 1.24a. Manual, Dividends.
 1 Manual, Matched Bargain List.
 2 Ibid, Residuals.

entitlements to the beneficial ownership of the underlying securities and from the reports of bargains made to the Settlement Centre, and it will issue claims lists accordingly.[3] Conflicting claims to the new securities will then be settled, and SEPON Ltd will surrender the letters of allotment in its name to the issuing company in exchange for split letters of allotment in favour of the persons entitled. If the person entitled is a member firm and the new securities are to be added to the credit balance of its beneficial entitlement of securities held by SEPON Ltd, the firm must procure the registration of SEPON Ltd as registered holder of the new securities by surrendering the split letter of allotment to the issuing company. Finally, since SEPON Ltd can discover from the records kept by the Settlement Centre the identity of the member firm or other person beneficially entitled to securities registered in the name of SEPON Ltd, or at least, the identity of the member firm which represents that person, SEPON Ltd will accept instructions to vote in respect of such securities from the beneficial owner, provided they are communicated to it through a member firm not later than three days before the meeting is to be held or the vote is to be taken.[4]

Advantages of TALISMAN

The advantages of the TALISMAN system over the arrangements previously employed for the settlement of bargains on the Stock Exchange are:

(a) The delivery to the Settlement Centre of sold transfers to SEPON Ltd can be spread over the period from the issue of the sale docket until Account Day or the other date for the settlement of a bargain, instead of being concentrated in the short time between Ticket Day and Account Day.

(b) Member firms which are, or which act on behalf of, sellers of securities receive payment of the price due to them from the Settlement Centre, and member firms which are, or which act for, purchasers pay the price due from them to the Centre. This avoids the need for the practice which existed before the TALISMAN scheme was introduced of the member firm which was or which represented the ultimate purchaser of securities which had been sold several times over during an Account paying a making-up price to the member firm which was, or which acted for, the original seller, and for differences between the making-up price and prices agreed on the successive sales to be settled personally between the member firms involved.[5]

(c) Sold and bought transfers under the TALISMAN system name the transferee of the securities, and the former practice of delivering transfers with the transferee's name left blank is avoided.

(d) All bargains are recorded when the first step for carrying them out is taken, and all amounts payable and receivable by member firms are calculated by a computer in the Settlement Centre, thus reducing the recording and accounting work which member firms have to undertake themselves.

(e) The number of registrations of transfers of securities is reduced, since dealings in the same securities while registered in the name of SEPON Ltd call for only one initial transfer to SEPON Ltd and one transfer by it to the ultimate transferee.

(f) Finally, while securities are held by a member firm or a succession of

---

3 Stock Exchange Regulations, reg E1.25; Manual, Claim Generation—Cash Distributions.
4 Manual, Voting Rights.
5 The making up price for bargains entered into during an Account is fixed by the Stock Exchange on the Wednesday preceding Account Day, and is approximately the average middle market price of the securities during the Account.

member firms acting on their own account, the securities may remain registered in the name of SEPON Ltd and transfers between member firms are made by accounting entries in the Settlement Centre's computerised records; the same advantages are enjoyed by investors whose holdings of securities are credited to their own operating accounts with the Settlement Centre, and which sell or purchase securities in transactions with other such investors or member firms.[6]

Insider dealing

Dealings in shares, debentures or loan securities by persons in possession of information derived from a company which is not available to investors generally, have long been castigated as unfair, since the price at which the transaction takes place reflects the market's estimation of the value of the securities on the assumption that the special facts known to the person who deals (the so-called 'insider') do not exist. Except where a fiduciary relationship exists between the insider and the other party to the transaction, neither common law nor equity intervene in such a situation so as to enable a person who deals with an insider in ignorance of the special facts to rescind the transaction or to compel the insider to account for the profit obtained by him or to compensate the innocent party for his loss,[7] and the only statutory sanctions against insider dealing are purely criminal ones, so that a criminal prosecution may lie in circumstances where there is no civil remedy.

Transactions by insiders

It is an offence for an individual,[8] who is or has within the preceding six months knowingly been connected with a company to deal as principal or agent on a recognised stock exchange[9] in shares, debentures or loan securities of that company, or in rights to subscribe for or to buy or sell such securities (ie options) if he possesses information which he has acquired by reason of being connected with the company, and it is information which it would be reasonable to expect a person in his position not to disclose otherwise than for the purpose of fulfilling his functions as a person so connected with the company (ie the information is confidential), and he knows that the information is unpublished and price sensitive in relation to the securities.[10] A person is connected with a company if he is a director of it or of another company in the same group, or if he occupies a position as an officer or employee of the company or another company in the same group, or a position involving a business or professional relationship between the company and himself or a person, firm or company of which he is a director or employee, and that position gives him access to unpublished price sensitive information in relation to securities of the company which it would be reasonable to expect a person in his position not to disclose otherwise than for the purpose of performing his functions.[11] A person connected with a company or an 'insider' may therefore be a director, senior executive or junior employee of the company or a solicitor, accountant, stockbroker or an

---

6 Stock Exchange Regulations, reg E5.5a.
7 *Percival v Wright* [1902] 2 Ch 421; *Allen v Hyatt* (1914) 30 TLR 444.
8 Not a company or corporation.
9 That is, a stock exchange recognised by the Secretary of State for Trade and Industry. The recognised stock exchanges are the International Stock Exchange of the United Kingdom and the Republic of Ireland and NASDAQ (an acronym for the National Association of Security Dealers (of the United States) Automated Quotations Association) (Company Securities (Insider Dealing) Act 1985, s 16 (1); Insider Dealing (Recognised Stock Exchange) Order 1989 (SI 1989/2165), art 2).
10 Company Securities (Insider Dealing) Act 1985, s 1 (1), s 10, s 12 and s 13 (1).
11 Ibid, s 9.

employee of such a person whose work for the company gives him access to price sensitive information about the company. The unpublished price sensitive information in question must relate to specific matters concerning the company (eg that it has made unexpectedly high profits or losses in its recently concluded financial year, or that it is about to acquire or dispose of a business undertaking or assets which will materially affect the value of its shares or other securities), and it must be information which is not generally known to persons who are accustomed or likely to deal in the securities in question (ie market makers, broker/dealers, institutional investors and substantial individual investors), but which if it were known by them would be likely to affect dealing prices for the securities materially.[12]

Additionally, it is an offence for an individual who is or has within the preceding six months knowingly been connected with a company to deal as principal or agent on a recognised stock exchange in shares, debentures or loan securities of another company, or in rights to subscribe for such securities or options to buy or sell them, if he possesses information which he knows to be unpublished price sensitive information about an actual or proposed transaction involving both companies, or involving one of those companies and securities of the other (eg a takeover bid), and he acquired that information by virtue of his connection with the first company and it would be reasonable to expect a person in his position not to disclose the information except for the purpose of fulfilling his functions as a person so connected.[13] Consequently, if a director of a company, knowing that it intends to make a takeover bid for another listed company, buys shares, debentures or loan securities of that other company on a recognised stock exchange at the current price (which is less than the intended bid price), he commits an offence, as does a director of the other company who, knowing of the intended but unpublished bid, buys or sells shares, debentures or loan securities of the offeror company on a recognised stock exchange in the expectation that when the bid is published the market price of those securities will rise or fall, as the case may be. In the case of a takeover bid which an individual intends to make in one capacity (eg as a director of the offeror company), it is expressly provided that it is an offence for him to deal in shares, debentures or other securities of the company for which the bid is to be made in another capacity (eg on his own account) if the intention to make the bid is not known to the market, or if the intention is known but he knows of the offeror company's intention not to proceed with it.[14] There is, however, nothing to prevent a director of the intending offeror company acquiring shares, debentures or loan securities of the company for which a bid is to be made if he does so on behalf of the offeror company.

Communication of inside information

The prohibitions on an individual connected with a company dealing in its securities or those of another company on a recognised stock exchange while in possession of unpublished price sensitive information about the company with which he is connected, or about the other company if a transaction affecting both companies is pending, are extended to any other individual who is not connected with the company, but who has knowingly obtained the information directly or indirectly from an individual whom he knows to be so connected, or to have been so connected within the preceding six months; to be guilty of an offence, however,

12 Ibid, s 10.
13 Ibid, s 1 (2) and s 12.
14 Ibid, s 1 (5) and s 14.

such a third person must know when he acquires the information that it originated from an individual connected with the company in question and that he obtained the information by reason of his connection, and the third person must also know that the information is unpublished price sensitive information which it would be reasonable to expect the originator not to disclose except in fulfilment of his functions as a person connected with the company.[15] A person may obtain unpublished price sensitive information so as to be guilty of an offence by dealing in securities, if the information is communicated to him without him requesting it, or, it would seem, if it is communicated to him contrary to his expressed wishes.[16]

This extension of criminal liability is intended to prevent inside information being used by persons to whom insiders pass it on (so called 'tippees') to deal in securities for their own advantage, but an essential ingredient of the offence in this case is that the person concerned should know not only that the information is unpublished and price sensitive, but also that it originated from someone connected with the company to which, or to whose transactions with another company, the information relates. It is not necessary that all persons through whom the information has been passed before reaching the accused should be aware of its source, however, and the accused is guilty of the offence if he is aware of the source and nevertheless deals in securities of the company concerned. The originator of the information, that is the person connected with the company concerned, and any intermediary who receives the information and passes it on having cause to believe that the person to whom he communicates the information or any other person will use it to deal in securities of the company concerned on a recognised stock exchange, is also guilty of an offence.[17]

Finally, any person who would himself commit an offence by dealing in securities on a recognised stock exchange is guilty of an offence if he counsels or procures another person (including a company) to do so.[18] Consequently, a person connected with a company who possesses unpublished price sensitive information about it commits an offence by causing another company of which he is a director or shareholder to deal in securities of the first company on a recognised stock exchange, even though he does not communicate the information to the other company's board of directors.

Defences

There are a number of exemptions from criminal liability for insider dealing. Any person accused of any of the offences dealt with above can avoid conviction by showing that he acted otherwise than with a view to making a profit or avoiding a loss (whether for himself or another person) by using the unpublished price sensitive information;[19] or that he entered into the transaction in question in good faith in carrying out his functions as a liquidator, receiver or trustee in bankruptcy;[20] or that he did the act of which he is accused in good faith in the course of his business as a market maker in the securities concerned who is a member of a recognised stock exchange, or in the course of his employment in

---

15 Ibid, s 1 (3) and (4).
16 *Re AG's Reference (No 1 of 1988)* [1989] AC 971, [1989] 2 All ER 1, HL.
17 Company Securities (Insider Dealing) Act 1985, s 1 (8).
18 Ibid, s 1 (7).
19 Ibid, s 3 (1) (*a*). For example, selling shares in order to satisfy the seller's debts or to meet essential expenses, or exercising an option to subscribe for or purchase shares before it expires (*R v Cross* [1990] 6 CC 237).
20 Company Securities (Insider Dealing) Act 1985, s 3 (1) (*b*). It should be noted that a liquidator, receiver or trustee in bankruptcy cannot rely on this defence if he communicates unpublished price sensitive information or counsels or procures another person to deal in securities in reliance on it.

another person's business as such a market maker in those securities, while in possession of information obtained by him in the course of that business, and the information was of a kind which it would be reasonable to expect him to obtain in the course of that business.[1]

Furthermore, a trustee or personal representative, or an individual acting on its behalf if it is a corporation, who is accused of dealing in securities while in possession of unpublished price sensitive information, or accused of counselling or procuring another person to do so, may show that he acted on the advice of an appropriate person (eg a stockbroker, a solicitor or a bank) and that person did not appear to be prohibited from dealing in the securities himself (ie he or it was not connected with the company concerned); in that case it is presumed that the accused acted otherwise than with a view to making a profit or avoiding a loss for himself or another person, and unless it can be shown that this was not his motive, he will escape conviction.[2]

Off market dealing in advertised securities

Although the offences dealt with above will be committed only if the securities in question are dealt in on a recognised stock exchange (eg listed on the Stock Exchange or admitted to dealing on the Unlisted Securities Market or the Third Market) and the dealing takes place on such an exchange, the statutory provisions also apply to dealings outside such an exchange in advertised securities by or through a person who is authorised to carry on investment business[3] and who makes a market in the securities in question by holding himself out as willing to deal in them otherwise than on a recognised stock exchange.[4] Securities are advertised securities for this purpose if they are listed on a recognised stock exchange, or if information indicating the prices at which persons have dealt, or were willing to deal, in them has been published not more than six months before the offence is committed in order to facilitate dealings.[5] The offences of communicating unpublished price sensitive information for the purpose of dealing, and the offences of counselling or procuring dealing in reliance on such information (as well as the primary offence of dealing while the accused is an insider in possession of unpublished price sensitive information) can be committed in respect of advertised securities in the same way as in respect of securities which are dealt in on a recognised stock exchange.[6]

OTHER TRANSACTIONS AND INCIDENTS

Gifts of shares

The legal title to shares may be transferred by way of gift in the same way as on a sale. If the shares are registered in the company's register of members, the donor executes a transfer to the donee in the same form as a transfer on a sale of the

1 Company Securities (Insider Dealing) Act 1985, s 3 (1) (*c*); Financial Services Act 1986, s 174 (1) and (2).
2 Company Securities (Insider Dealing) Act 1985, s 7 (1) and (2).
3 That is, authorised to carry on investment business under the Financial Services Act 1986 by the Securities and Investments Board or by reason of membership of a self-regulating organisation recognised by the Board.
4 Company Securities (Insider Dealing) Act 1986, s 4 (1) and s 13 (3) and (4); Financial Services Act 1986, s 174 (4).
5 Company Securities (Insider Dealing) Act 1985, s 12 (*c*).
6 Ibid, s 4 (1).

shares,[7] and delivers to him the transfer and the donor's share certificate, and the donee sends these documents to the company so that his name may be entered in the register of members and a new share certificate showing the donee as registered holder may be issued to him. If the donor holds a letter of allotment in respect of the shares, he delivers to the donee the letter of allotment with a letter of renunciation signed by the original allottee, whether the donor or a previous holder, and the donee will be able to procure his own registration in the register of members by completing the registration application form and surrendering the whole document to the company. If the donor delivers a blank transfer to the donee, there is a similar prohibition on the donee delivering the blank transfer to a third party as if the gift were a sale to the donee.[8] If the shares are represented by a share warrant, the donor transfers the legal title to the donee by delivering the warrant to him with the intention of transferring ownership of the shares, and no instrument of transfer or deed of gift is necessary.

The law will not assist a donee to perfect an incomplete gift, and so if a donor of shares has not done everything necessary on his part to vest the legal title in the donee before he revokes the gift or dies, the law will not compel him or his personal representatives to complete the transfer. Thus, where a donor had purported to transfer inscribed stock[9] by a deed of gift which was ineffective to pass any title, it was held that after his death his personal representatives were not bound to transfer the stock to the donee.[10] Again, where an American shareholder executed transfers of shares in an English company to a donee resident in England but died before the consent of the Treasury had been obtained to the transfer, as the law then required,[11] it was held that the donee could not insist on the gift being completed, because the failure to obtain the Treasury's consent prevented the donee from acquiring any interest in the shares.[12] On the other hand, if the only thing necessary to perfect the gift is an act which may be done by the donee himself, such as assenting to the gift or executing or registering the transfer, the gift is complete even though the legal title has not yet passed, and if the donor purports to revoke the gift or dies, the donee may still do what is necessary to acquire the legal title.[13] This is so even if the directors of the company are given a discretion to refuse to register transfers of shares in the company, because it is for the donee, and not the donor, to obtain their consent to registration.[13] Similarly, if the donor holds a letter of allotment, it suffices for him to deliver it to the donee, duly renounced, because the donee can now procure his registration as a member of the company without any further aid from the donor.[14] If the shares are vested in a trustee or nominee

---

7 If the shares are fully paid, the instrument of transfer in the recognised statutory form need only be signed by the donor, and its execution as a deed is unnecessary (Stock Transfer Act 1963, s 1 (1) and (4), s 2 (1) and Sch 1 (30 Halsbury's Statutes (4th Edn) 157)). Stamp duty was formerly charged ad valorem on the value of the property comprised in a gift, but no duty is payable on gifts made on or after 26 March 1985 (Finance Act 1985, s 82 (1) and (6) (41 Halsbury's Statutes (4th Edn) 369)).
8 Finance Act 1963, s 67 (3) (41 Halsbury's Statutes (4th Edn) 274); see p 377, ante.
9 That is, stock transferable only by a form of transfer in a book kept by the company. The decision in this case has been misunderstood largely because of failure to appreciate that the stock involved was inscribed. Inscribed stock is now obsolete in practice, all formerly inscribed stock having been converted into securities transferable by registered instruments of transfer.
10 *Milroy v Lord* (1862) 4 De GF & J 264.
11 This consent was then necessary under the Defence (Finance) Regulations 1939, reg 3A, which was later replaced by the Exchange Control Act 1947, s 9 (1) (30 Halsbury's Statutes (4th Edn) 80). Since November 1979 no specific consent by the Treasury is required for sales or gifts of shares by or to persons resident outside the United Kingdom.
12 *Re Fry* [1946] Ch 312, [1946] 2 All ER 106.
13 *Re Rose* [1949] Ch 78, [1948] 2 All ER 971; *Re Rose* [1952] Ch 499, [1952] 1 All ER 1217; *Re Paradise Motor Co Ltd* [1968] 2 All ER 625, [1968] 1 WLR 1125.
14 *Letts v IRC* [1956] 3 All ER 588, [1957] 1 WLR 201.

for the donor, the execution of a transfer by the nominee or trustee at the donor's direction is sufficient to make the gift effective, and a separate written transfer of the donor's equitable interest[15] is unnecessary.[16]

Mortgages and charges

A mortgage of shares may be legal or equitable. If it is a legal mortgage, the mortgagor transfers the legal title to the mortgagee[17] and the transfer is registered in the company's register of members; this makes the mortgagee personally liable for calls or instalments of the issue price if the shares are only partly paid, even though the company is aware when it registers the transfer to the mortgagee that he is interested in the shares only as a security.[18] If the mortgage is equitable, the mortgagor remains the registered holder of the shares, thereby retaining the legal title, and he normally effects the mortgage by depositing his share certificate with the mortgagee with a form of transfer of the shares executed by the mortgagor with the name of the transferee and the consideration for the transfer left blank. This implies an agreement to create a legal mortgage,[19] and the mortgagee can convert the mortgage into a legal one by completing the blank transfer with his own name as transferee and procuring its registration by the company.[20] Until the mortgagee does so, however, his interest in the shares is merely equitable, and in order to perserve priority for himself over later transferees from the mortgagor, he should serve a stop notice on the company.[1] An equitable mortgage can also be created by the mortgagor agreeing expressly to create a legal mortgage of his shares; the agreement can be oral or in writing, and it is not necessary that the mortgagor's share certificate or a blank transfer should be delivered to the mortgagee. The disadvantage of entering into such an agreement without a deposit of the share certificate and a blank transfer is that the mortgagee cannot by his own unaided act procure the registration of himself as holder of the shares, but must obtain an order of specific performance of the mortgagor's agreement to create a legal mortgage,[2] and in the meantime protect himself by serving a stop notice on the company. As an alternative to agreeing to create a legal mortgage over his shares, the mortgagor may agree merely that the shares shall be security for the debt owing to the mortgagee; this creates an equitable charge over the shares, which does not entitle the mortgagee to be registered as their holder, but does entitle him to realise his security in the same way as a mortgagee[3] apart from foreclosing.[4]

---

15 Under the Law of Property Act 1925, s 53 (1) (c) (37 Halsbury's Statutes (4th Edn) 153).
16 *Vandervell v IRC* [1967] 2 AC 291, [1967] 1 All ER 1.
17 No stamp duty is payable in respect of the mortgage (Finance Act 1971, s 64 (1) and Sch 14, Part VI (41 Halsbury's Statutes (4th Edn) 311).
18 *Re Land Credit Co of Ireland, Weikersheim's Case* (1873) 8 Ch App 831.
19 *Harrold v Plenty* [1901] 2 Ch 314.
20 *Re Tahiti Cotton Co, ex p Sargent* (1874) LR 17 Eq 273. If the articles of the company require transfers to be by deed, however, the mortgagee may not complete the blank transfer in his own favour unless the mortgagor has empowered him to do so by a power of attorney, and if he does complete the transfer and registers it, the mortgagor may have the registration cancelled (*Powell v London and Provincial Bank* [1893] 2 Ch 555). But the mortgagee could then compel the mortgagor to execute a fresh transfer to him in performance of the mortgagor's implied obligation to create a legal mortgage on demand. If the shares are fully paid, the mortgagee may complete the blank transfer without any need for a power of attorney, provided the blank transfer is in the statutory form authorised by statute (Stock Transfer Act 1963, s 1 (1) and (4), s 2 and Sch 1).
1 See p 356, ante.
2 *Eyre v McDowell and Wheatley* (1861) 9 HL Cas 619.
3 *Matthews v Goodday* (1861) 31 LJ Ch 282.
4 *Sampson v Pattison* (1842) 1 Hare 533.

Usually the mortgagor executes a document which sets out the terms of the mortgage transaction, in particular, the date on which the loan secured on the shares is to be repaid, the rate of interest on the loan and the powers of the mortgagee to realise his security if the mortgagor defaults. If the loan is not repaid on the agreed date, the mortgagee may sell the shares or apply to the court for a foreclosure order.[5] If the document containing the terms of the mortgage is a deed executed by the mortgagor, the mortgagee may also sell the shares if the mortgagor fails to repay the secured loan within three months after the mortgagee demands its repayment in writing, or if the mortgagor fails to pay an instalment of mortgage interest for two months after it falls due, or if he breaks any other undertaking on his part in the document.[6] The power of sale may be extended by agreement to apply in other situations.

Sometimes there is no document containing the terms of the mortgage transaction, and the date for repayment of the loan is left uncertain. In this case the mortgagee may make the loan repayable by giving the mortgagor a reasonable length of notice demanding payment,[7] and it would seem that such a notice may be given, even if the mortgagee could exercise the statutory power of sale on giving the mortgagor three months' notice to repay the loan, and a reasonable length of notice would be shorter.[6] It is not necessary that the notice demanding repayment should contain a threat to sell the shares if repayment is not made on the date specified, and the notice is not invalid because it demands payment of a larger sum than is due.[8] What is a reasonable length of notice depends on the facts, but the court will pay particular regard to the kind of shares in question, and it has been held that fourteen days' notice was sufficient when the shares were of a speculative character.[9] When the loan has become immediately repayable by the mortgagee serving a notice demanding payment, the mortgagee may sell the shares or apply for a foreclosure order. When exercising his power of sale, whether conferred on him expressly by the terms of the mortgage or implied by law, the mortgagee must use reasonable care to obtain the best price possible, and he is liable in damages to the mortgagor if he fails to do so; the mortgagor may recover from the mortgagee personally, or set off against his personal liability for the secured debt, any deficiency in the price which the mortgagee obtains to satisfy the amount owing under the mortgage and the mortgagee's costs of realisation, but only to the extent that the price which the mortgagee could have obtained if he had exercised reasonable care exceeds the price which he actually obtained.[10]

A legal mortgagee of shares and an equitable mortgagee who has a blank transfer of the shares executed by the mortgagor and the mortgagor's share certificate, can sell the shares without an order of the court. The legal mortgagee can execute a transfer to the purchaser himself, and the equitable mortgagee can fill in the purchaser's name as transferee on the blank transfer he possesses and complete the sale by delivering the now completed transfer and the mortgagor's share certificate to the purchaser.[11] But an equitable mortgagee who has only taken a deposit of the

5 *Harrold v Plenty* [1901] 2 Ch 314; *Deverges v Sandeman, Clark & Co* [1902] 1 Ch 579.
6 Law of Property Act 1925, ss 101 (1) and 103 (37 Halsbury's Statutes (4th Edn) 222, 227).
7 *Deverges v Sandeman, Clark & Co*, supra, per Cozens-Hardy LJ, at 596.
8 *Stubbs v Slater* [1910] 1 Ch 632, per Cozens-Hardy, MR at 640.
9 *Deverges v Sandeman, Clark & Co*, supra, per Cozens-Hardy LJ at 697.
10 *Cuckmere Brick Co Ltd v Mutual Finance Ltd* [1971] Ch 949, [1971] 2 All ER 633 *Bishop v Bonham* [1988] 1 WLR 742, [1988] BCLC 656, CA. This is so even if the mortgage provides that the mortgagee shall not be liable for any loss, however arising, in connection with the sale of the shares by him.
11 *Stubbs v Slater*, supra. If the articles of the company require transfers to be by deed, it is submitted that it is immaterial that the mortgagee completes the blank transfer without having a power of attorney from the mortgagor, if the purchaser is unaware that he is buying from a mortgagee and the transfer is complete when he receives it. This is because the mortgagor, by giving the mortgagee

mortgagor's share certificate without a blank transfer executed by the mortgagor and who has no express authority from the mortgagor to sell the shares, requires an order of the court to enable him to sell, because he lacks power to transfer a legal title to the shares to a purchaser by himself. This is obviously also the position if the mortgagee has not even taken a deposit of the mortgagor's share certificate.

A mortgagee of shares may sub-mortgage them to secure a loan of any amount by the sub-mortgagee to himself. But the mortgagor may redeem his mortgage and obtain his shares back from the sub-mortgagee on paying him what the mortgagor owes the mortgagee, even though the mortgagee's indebtedness to the sub-mortgagee exceeds this sum. The only occasion when the sub-mortgagee may refuse to allow redemption unless the mortgagor pays the full amount secured by the sub-mortgage, is when the sub-mortgagee was unaware of the mortgagor's interest in the shares when he took his sub-mortgage, and believed that the mortgagee was beneficially entitled to the shares because the legal title was vested in him, or because the mortgagee held the mortgagor's share certificate and an instrument of transfer executed by him. But if the mortgagee held a blank transfer executed by the mortgagor, the sub-mortgagee is only protected if the mortgagee completed the blank transfer by inserting the sub-mortgagee's name as transferee and the consideration for the sub-mortgage before delivering the share certificate and the transfer to him.[12] If the blank transfer still omitted the name of the transferee or the consideration for the transfer when it was delivered to the sub-mortgagee, he would be deemed to have notice that the mortgagee had only a limited authority to deal with the shares, and would obtain no better title to them than the mortgagee had.[12] An equitable sub-mortgagee, like an equitable mortgagee, may convert his mortgage into a legal one by inserting his own name as transferee in the blank transfer deposited with him and procuring the registration of the transfer by the company.[13] The mortgagor is liable to the sub-mortgagee in damages if he impedes him in obtaining registration of the transfer to himself.[14] The sub-mortgagee may use the blank transfer to procure his own registration in order to ensure priority for his sub-mortgage over later dispositions of the shares by the mortgagor or the mortgagee, but he cannot, of course, enhance his entitlement against the mortgagor by doing this, and the mortgagor may therefore still redeem the shares by paying the sub-mortgagee the amount secured by the mortgage if it is less than that secured by the sub-mortgage.[12]

On the redemption of a legal mortgage of shares the mortgagee must re-transfer the shares to the mortgagor, and on the redemption of an equitable mortgage or charge the mortgagee must return the share certificate which the mortgagor has deposited with him together with the blank transfer executed by the mortgagor (if any) so that it may be destroyed.

A legal mortgagee may vote as he wishes in respect of the mortgaged shares, and is not bound to obey the directions of the mortgagor, for he is not a trustee of the voting rights for him until the mortgagor has paid off the debt secured by the mortgage.[15] On the other hand, it would seem that a shareholder who has created an equitable mortgage of his shares is equally at liberty to vote as he wishes, and is

---

a blank transfer, has made it appear that the mortgagee is beneficially entitled to the shares, or, at least that he is able to deal with them in any way, and the mortgagor will therefore be estopped from disputing the validity of the transfer to the purchaser (see p 347, ante). If the shares are fully paid, the transfer to the purchaser will be valid in any event if the blank transfer signed by the mortgagor was in the form authorised by the Stock Transfer Act 1963, Sch 1 (ibid, s 2 (1)).

12 *Ortigosa v Brown* (1878) 47 LJ Ch 168; *France v Clark* (1884) 26 ChD 257.
13 *Re Tahiti Cotton Co, ex p Sargent* (1874) LR 17 Eq 273.
14 *Hooper v Herts* [1906] 1 Ch 549.
15 *Siemens Bros & Co Ltd v Burns* [1918] 2 Ch 324.

not required to vote or abstain from voting in accordance with the directions of the mortgagee, unless the agreement for the mortgage so provides.

Shares represented by share warrants or by letters of allotment containing a letter of renunciation signed by the allottee may be mortgaged by the mortgagor delivering the warrants or renounced letters of allotment to the mortgagee with the intention of passing title to him by way of security. This vests the legal title to the shares in the mortgagee, and enables him to sell the shares when the loan becomes repayable on the stipulated date or by the mortgagee demanding repayment in the way described above. But if there is no document setting out the terms of the transaction which makes it clear that it is a mortgage, or other evidence that a mortgage was intended, it appears that the transaction will be treated as a pledge,[16] and the mortgagee will be able to sell the shares to recover his loan, but will not be able to obtain a foreclosure order.[17]

Trusts

Trusts of shares registered in the company's register of members are created by transferring the shares to trustees upon trusts declared by the settlor in a separate document, or upon trusts declared by the trustees themselves after the transfer has taken place. Until the settlor has done all that is necessary on his part to vest the shares in the trustees, the trust is incompletely constituted, and cannot be enforced by beneficiaries who have not given value for the creation of their interests.[18] Alternatively, the settlor may declare himself to be trustee of the shares for the beneficiaries, and this may be done by an oral or a written declaration of trust.

A beneficiary of a trust of shares may serve a stop notice on the company,[19] but this will merely entitle him to notice of any transfer of the shares which the trustees propose to make, and will not enable him to prevent a transfer on sale or mortgage being carried out which is within the trustees' powers conferred by law[20] or any additional powers conferred by the document creating the trust. If the trustees dispose of the shares in breach of trust, the transferee will only hold them free from the trust if he acquires them for value and has not become aware of the trust by the time he is entitled to insist on the company registering the transfer to him.[1]

Trustees who are the registered holders of partly paid shares are personally liable to pay the capital remaining unpaid in respect of them.[2] This is because the trustees come under the statutory obligation to pay unpaid capital when they are registered as members of the company,[3] and it is impossible for the company to relieve them from that liability by agreement.[4] A bare trustee or nominee of shares is entitled to be indemnified against calls or instalments of the issue price by the person for whom he holds the shares, but this does not entitle the trustee to insist on the company enforcing his right to indemnity against the beneficiary by

---

16 A pledge is a security in the form of possession of a tangible movable, and in the case of a pledge of a share warrant or a renounced letter of allotment, is confined to possession of the document without conferring any proprietary interest in the shares it represents.

17 *Carter v Wake* (1877) 4 ChD 605.

18 *Ellison v Ellison* (1802) 6 Ves 656. See also the cases cited on p 403, ante in connection with gifts of shares.

19 See p 356, ante.

20 In *Hume v Lopes* [1892] AC 112 it was held that trustees have a general power to sell securities comprised in the trust in order to re-invest in other authorised trustee investments.

1 See p 358, ante.

2 *Muir v City of Glasgow City Bank* (1879) 4 App Cas 337; *Re Royal Bank of Australia, ex p Drummond* (1860) 2 Giff 189.

3 *Trevor v Whitworth* (1887) 12 App Cas 409.

4 *Muir v Glasgow City Bank*, supra, per Cairns LC at 359–60.

subrogation to the trustee instead of suing the trustee personally.[5] The liability of an individual trustee for the payment of the amount unpaid on shares, like that of any other registered shareholder,[6] extends only to calls made or instalments of the issue price falling due before or during the time he is a registered holder of the shares comprised in the trust. Additionally a trustee may be liable to contribute the amount unpaid in respect of shares registered in his name when the company is wound up, but only if he has been the registered holder of the shares within 12 months before the commencement of the winding up.[7] When a trustee retires or is discharged from the trust and a transfer of the shares to the new or continuing trustees is registered,[8] the former trustee is not liable for future calls or instalments of the issue price (except where the company is wound up within the following 12 months),[7] and the new or continuing trustees alone are liable for such payments. When a trustee dies, his estate is not liable for calls made or instalments falling due after his death, but it is liable for calls already made or instalments which have already fallen due.[9]

A trust of shares represented by share warrants or letters of allotment which have been renounced by the allottee is created by the settlor delivering the warrants or renounced letters of allotment to the trustees with the intention of passing title to them, and by the settlor or the trustees at the same time executing a document which sets out the trusts on which the shares are to be held. Alternatively the settlor may declare himself a trustee of the shares represented by share warrants or renounceable letters of allotment which he holds, and the declaration of trust may be made orally or in writing. Trustees of an existing trust may invest trust funds in share warrants if the shares they represent are investments authorised by law or the instrument creating the trust.[10] The beneficiaries of a trust fund invested in shares represented by share warrants cannot protect their interests by serving stop notices on the company, although they may do so in respect of shares represented by renounceable letters of allotment; in neither case can the beneficiaries protect their interests by giving the company notice of the trust.[11] Consequently, the beneficiaries of a trust comprising shares represented by share warrants cannot be protected against breaches of trust by taking any action involving the company, and if the trustees sell or mortgage the share warrants to a person who takes delivery of them and has no notice of the trust, he takes the warrants free from the trust as a bona fide purchaser of the legal title. It is unlikely that a breach of trust would be committed by the trustees selling or mortgaging the shares, however, because they now have wide powers to do these things,[12] and when they act under such powers, the purchaser or mortgagee acquires a good title, even though he is fully aware of the trust.

---

5 *Re Borough of St Marylebone Banking Co, Davidson's Case* (1849) 3 De G & Sm 21; *Re Moseley Green Coal and Coke Co, Barrett's Case* (1864) 4 De GJ & Sm 416.

6 See p 319, ante.

7 Insolvency Act 1986, s 74 (1) and (2).

8 The statutory vesting of trust property in the new or continuing trustees in consequence of the execution of a deed of appointment or discharge does not apply to registered shares or debentures (Trustee Act 1925, s 40 (4) (c) (48 Halsbury's Statutes (4th Edn) 272)).

9 The personal representatives of the sole or last surviving trustee become trustees in his place if no other appointment is made and they do not disclaim the trusteeship (Trustee Act 1925, s 18 (2)), but this throws no additional liability on the deceased trustee's estate. If the personal representatives of the sole or last surviving trustee are not registered as members in respect of the trust shares, however, the estate of the trustee continues to be liable for unpaid capital, whether called up or falling due for payment before or after the trustee's death (see p 415, post).

10 Trustee Act 1925, s 7 (1).

11 Companies Act 1985, s 360.

12 *Hume v Lopes* [1892] AC 112, HL; Trustee Act 1925, s 16 (1) (48 Halsbury's Statutes (4th Edn) 236).

Company's interests in shares in itself

It has already been shown that a company cannot be a member of itself and cannot subscribe for or acquire shares in itself, either directly or through a nominee.[13] To the prohibition on a company acquiring shares or interests there are a number of exceptions, namely where:[14]

(a) the acquisition is of fully paid shares and is gratuitous;
(b) shares issued as redeemable shares are redeemed, or redeemable or non-redeemable shares are purchased by the company under the powers conferred by the Companies Act 1985;[15]
(c) shares are acquired by the company pursuant to an order of the court made on a petition for the cancellation of an alteration of its objects,[16] or of a provision in its memorandum which could have been included in its articles,[17] or of a special resolution for the re-registration of a public company as a private one,[18] or of a special resolution authorising a private company to purchase its own shares out of capital[19] or to give financial assistance for the acquisition of shares in itself,[20] or on a petition for relief against the unfairly prejudicial conduct of the company's affairs;[1]
(d) shares are forfeited or surrendered for non-payment of any part of the amounts payable in respect of them;[2]
(e) shares are acquired by a nominee of a company which has no beneficial interest in them, apart from its right to remuneration or an indemnity against its expenses as a trustee of the shares for third persons, or as a personal representative of a shareholder or a person interested in the shares;[3]
(f) the interest of the company is in shares acquired by a third person with financial assistance given by the company[4] (eg a mortgage or charge on the shares to secure a loan made by the company to finance their purchase by the holder);
(g) the interest is a charge or lien on the shares to secure amounts owing to the company, but in the case of a public company the charge or lien must be to secure the amount payable in respect of its partly paid shares (ie the unpaid part of their issue price) or, if the company is a public company whose ordinary business includes the lending of money or the letting of goods under hire purchase agreements, the charge must arise under a transaction entered into by the company in the ordinary course of its business;[5]
(h) the interest is a residuary interest of the company in shares in itself held by its nominees as trustees of an employees' share scheme set up by the company for the benefit of employees of itself or any other companies in the group to

---

13 *Trevor v Whitworth* (1887) 12 App Cas 409; *Kirby v Wilkins* [1929] 2 Ch 444; Companies Act 1985, s 143 (1) and s 144 (1) (see p 340, ante).
14 Companies Act 1985, s 143 (3).
15 See p 188, ante.
16 See p 70, ante.
17 See p 74, ante.
18 See p 66, ante.
19 See p 196, ante.
20 See p 389, ante.
1 See p 666, post.
2 See pp 321 and 323, ante.
3 Companies Act 1985, s 145 (2) and (3) and Sch 2, para 4, as amended by Companies Act 1989, s 129 (2). A company which is a trustee of shares in itself can have them registered in the name of its nominee, but not in its own name.
4 Companies Act 1985, s 145 (1). It is uncertain whether the company has a valid interest if it gives financial assistance in breach of the Companies Act 1985, s 151 (1) and (2) (see p 386, ante).
5 Companies Act 1985, s 150 (1) to (3).

which it belongs,[6] or as trustees of a pension scheme for the benefit of employees or former employees of the company (including directors);[7] the acquisition and retention for an indefinite period by the company of its interest in those shares is permitted so long as the company's interest is merely a residuary one which will vest in possession only when the claims of other persons under the scheme have been satisfied in full, or when the trust property ceases to be subject to the trusts created by the scheme in favour of other persons;[8] moreover, a company is not regarded as having any interest in shares in itself held in trust under an employees' share scheme or a pension scheme for the benefit of employees or former employees if the company's interest is a charge or lien over, or a right of set-off against, any interest of another person under the scheme for the purpose of securing a monetary obligation.[9]

The exceptional cases listed above where a company may hold shares in itself or have an interest in its own shares apply whether the company is a public or private one, but if a public company forfeits or accepts a surrender of shares for non-payment of the issue price, or acquires a beneficial interest in its shares otherwise than under an order of the court or on the purchase or redemption of shares[10] (e g if a public company accepts a gratuitous surrender of full paid shares), then whether the company acquires the interest directly or through a nominee, it must within three years either dispose of the shares or its interest therein, or cancel the shares and reduce its issued share capital correspondingly.[11] If any person acquires shares in a public company with financial assistance given by the company and the company has a beneficial interest therein (e g where the company lends the whole or part of the price paid by a purchaser of shares in the company and takes a mortgage or charge on the shares to secure the loan), the company must within one year either dispose of the shares or its interest therein,[12] or cancel the shares and reduce its issued share capital by their nominal value.[11] Where the company's interest in the shares is a residuary interest under an employees' share scheme or an employees' pension scheme, the periods within which the company must dispose of the shares or its interest or reduce its capital run from the date when the interests of all other persons in the shares cease.[13]

Any reduction of issued share capital made to satisfy these requirements may be effected by resolution to the board of directors without going through the normal procedure for a reduction of capital.[14] The resolution must be notified to the Registrar of Companies within 15 days after it is passed.[15] If a public company cancels shares under these provisions and as a result its issued share capital is reduced to less than £50,000, it must be re-registered as a private company on an application made pursuant to a board resolution, which may make all necessary

---

6 For the definition of an employees' share scheme, see p 247, ante.
7 Companies Act 1985, s 145 (2) and (3) and Sch 2, para 1, as amended by Companies Act 1989, s 129 (2).
8 Ibid, s 145 (3) and Sch 2, para 2 (3).
9 Ibid, s 145 (3) and Sch 2, para 3, as amended by Companies Act 1989, s 129 (2).
10 If shares are purchased or redeemed under the Companies Act 1985, they are automatically cancelled (Companies Act 1985, s 160 (4) and s 162 (2)), as amended by Companies Act 1989, s 133 (2) and s 134 (4) (see p 199, ante).
11 Companies Act 1985, s 146 (1) to (3).
12 The company must either sell the shares in realisation of its security or transfer the mortgage or charge to a third person who may then enforce it according to its terms.
13 Companies Act 1985, s 146 (1) and Sch 2, para 2 (4).
14 Ibid, s 147 (1).
15 Ibid, s 147 (2).

alterations to the company's memorandum.[16] Although the provisions requiring a company to dispose of or cancel the shares do not apply to a private company, they do apply retrospectively if the company is later re-registered as a public company, and the period of one year or three years for the disposal of the shares or the company's interest in them or, alternatively, the cancellation of the shares, then runs from the date on which the company is re-registered.[17] While a public company or its nominee holds shares or an interest therein which must eventually be disposed of under the foregoing rules, neither the company, nor the nominee nor the holder of the shares acquired with financial assistance from the company may vote in respect of the shares at general meetings or meetings of a class of shareholders.[18]

Company's lien

A company has no lien or equitable charge on the shares of its members for sums owed by them to it, unless the lien is expressly conferred by the company's articles.[19] Such a lien conferred by the articles of a public company may be expressed to extend only to capital due but unpaid on the shares, but if the company is a private one, it may extend to any indebtedness of the shareholder to the company.[20] A public company may, nevertheless, impose a valid lien or charge on its shares for indebtedness arising from a loan made by the company or a hire purchase agreement entered into by it in the ordinary course of its business if that business includes the lending of money or the letting of goods under hire purchase agreements.[1] A lien imposed by a company's articles attaches not only to the shares in question, but also to dividends payable in respect of them,[2] and this may extend the right which the company has in any case to set off debts owed by its members against dividends payable to them.[3] The right of set-off applies only if the debt is immediately payable, but the lien can be made to extend to debts which will become payable only at a future date or on fulfilment of a condition, so as to enable the company to retain dividends as security for the payment of such future or conditional debts. If a member holds shares in trust for another person, the lien does not implicitly extend to debts which the beneficiary owes the company,[4] but the articles may expressly extend it to such debts.

The articles usually empower the company to enforce its lien by selling the shares,[5] and probably it has a statutory power of sale if an express one is not conferred.[6] In any case it may apply to the court for an order for the sale of the

---

16 Ibid, s 147 (2) to (4).
17 Ibid, s 148 (1) and (2).
18 Ibid, s 146 (4).
19 *Meliorucchi v Royal Exchange Assurance Co* (1728) 1 Eq Cas Abr 8; *Pinkett v Wright* (1842) 2 Hare 120.
20 Companies Act 1985, s 150 (2). Table A, art 8, creates a lien on partly paid shares for unpaid capital and share premiums, whether immediately payable or not. This conforms to the requirements of the Stock Exchange, which will not list a company's shares, debentures or loan securities if its articles impose a lien on its fully paid shares (Stock Exchange: *Admission of Securities to Listing*, Section 9, Chapter 1, para 1.2).
1 Companies Act 1985, s 150 (3).
2 *Hague v Dandeson* (1848) 2 Exch 741.
3 *Re Cannock and Rugely Colliery Co* (1885) 28 ChD 363.
4 *Re Perkins, ex p Mexican Santa Barbara Mining Co* (1890) 24 QBD 613.
5 Table A, arts 9 and 10, confer a power of sale and empower the directors to appoint a person to execute a transfer of the shares to the purchaser.
6 In *Everitt v Automatic Weighing Machine Co* [1892] 3 Ch 506, it was held that the lien was a 'mortgage' within the meaning of the Law of Property Act 1925, s 205 (1) (37 Halsbury's Statutes (4th Edn) 330), and so the company would appear to have the statutory power of sale conferred by s 101 (1) of that Act.

shares. But the articles cannot empower the company to forfeit the shares, at least, if they are only partly paid, for this would involve an illegal reduction of capital.[7]

The lien attaches to the shares from the moment they are issued, even though the shareholder does not become indebted to the company until a later date.[8] Consequently, the lien antecedes any other equitable interest which is created out of the shares, such as an equitable mortgage or the equitable interests of beneficiaries under a trust, and so the lien has priority over those other interests, even for debts owing to the company which arise after those other interests are created.[9] But if before the lien becomes effective by the holder of the shares becoming indebted to the company, it has notice of an equitable interest which has already been created out of the shares, the company cannot claim priority for its lien.[10] The reason for this is that the company is considered as being in the same position as a mortgagee whose mortgage is expressed to secure a principal sum and further advances made subsequently, or to secure advances to be made after the mortgage is created.[11] If such a mortgagee has notice of a second mortgage when he makes such a further or subsequent advance, he is postponed to the second mortgagee for repayment of it.[12] In the case of a company's lien conferred by its articles, the debt owed to the company by the shareholder is the equivalent of a further or subsequent advance. The earlier interest to which the lien is postponed by the company having notice of it may be a mortgage of the shares,[13] or the equitable interests of beneficiaries under a trust[14] or, presumably, the interest of a person who has agreed to buy the shares or has taken an option to purchase them. The provision of the Companies Act 1985,[15] which precludes a company from receiving notice of equitable interests derived out of shares, does not prevent it from receiving such a notice so as to postpone its lien.[16] The statutory provision is designed to protect the company only when it is acting as keeper of the register of members, and is not intended to give it priority for a beneficial interest which it claims in the shares for itself when it would not have priority under the general rules of property law. Because of this, the company's claim under its lien is postponed if it receives only an informal notice of the competing equitable interest; it is not necessary for the owner of that interest to serve a stop notice on the company. On the other hand, if a director of any company, or a person interested in 3 per cent or more of the issued voting share capital of a public company, gives notice to the company of an equitable interest in any of its shares in fulfilment of his statutory obligation to do so,[17] the company is not thereby affected by notice of that interest or put on inquiry as to its existence or extent.[18] To affect the company with notice so as to postpone its lien, therefore, the person giving notice should serve a separate notice on the company in addition to the statutory one.

---

7 *Hopkinson v Mortimer, Harley & Co Ltd* [1917] 1 Ch 646.
8 *New London and Brazilian Bank v Brocklebank* (1882) 21 ChD 302 at 306, per Jessel MR; *Borland's Trustee v Steel Bros & Co Ltd* [1901] 1 Ch 279 at 289, per Farwell J.
9 *New London and Brazilian Bank v Brocklebank,* supra.
10 *Bradford Banking Co v Briggs & Co* (1886) 12 App Cas 29; *Mackereth v Wigan Coal and Iron Co Ltd* [1916] 2 Ch 293.
11 *Bradford Banking Co v Briggs & Co,* supra.
12 *Hopkinson v Rolt* (1861) 9 HL Cas 514. This is now made statutory by the Law of Property Act 1925, s 94 (1) (*b*) (37 Halsbury's Statutes (4th Edn) 209).
13 *Bradford Banking Co v Briggs & Co,* supra.
14 *Mackereth v Wigan Coal and Iron Co Ltd* [1916] 2 Ch 293.
15 Companies Act 1985, s 360.
16 *Bradford Banking Co v Briggs & Co,* supra, *Mackereth v Wigan Coal and Iron Co Ltd,* supra.
17 Companies Act 1985, s 198 (1), s 201, s 203 (1)–(3) and s 205 (1), as amended by Companies Act 1989, s 134 (2) and (3) (see p 363, ante); ibid, s 324 (1)–(3) and s 328 (1) (see p 556, post).
18 Ibid, s 211 (4) and s 325 (5) and Sch 13, para 24.

In practice articles of association never impose a lien on shares represented by share warrants, and even if a lien were imposed, it is difficult to see how the company could enforce it unless the share warrant came into its possession. Liens are often imposed on shares represented by renounceable or non-renounceable letters of allotment, but usually only for unpaid amounts of the issue price of the shares.[19] The law governing liens on registered shares appears to apply equally to liens on shares represented by letters of allotment. Such liens are rarely enforced, since the company usually has the far more effective sanction of forfeiting and reissuing the shares if instalments of the issue price are not paid when they fall due.

Judgment creditors

A person who has obtained judgment in the High Court or in a county court against a shareholder for an ascertained sum of money may levy execution on his shares registered in the company's register of members by obtaining an order of the court charging the shares with payment of the judgment debt.[20] The application for the charging order is made to the division of the High Court in which the judgment was obtained if it is for more than £5,000,[1] or to a county court if the judgment was given by it or was a judgment given by the High Court for not more than £5,000.[2] An ex parte application is made in the first instance, and the court makes an order calling upon the shareholder to show cause why the order should not be made absolute, and in the meantime restraining the company from registering a transfer of the shares or paying any dividend.[3] Copies of the order to show cause, usually called the order nisi, are then served on the shareholder and the company at least seven days before the date on which the shareholder is called on to show cause against it being made absolute,[4] and on the return day named in the order it is made absolute, unless the shareholder can show that he is not the beneficial owner of the shares or that he has discharged the judgment debt.[5] However, the court may in its discretion refuse to make the order absolute if sufficient reasons are shown for it doing so (such as the shareholder's bankruptcy or insolvency),[5] and to enable other creditors of the shareholder to draw the court's attention to any matters relevant in exercising its discretion, the court may order that they or other interested persons shall be served with copies of the charging order nisi.[6]

The effect of a charging order is to give the judgment creditor an equitable charge on the shares as from the date of the order nisi.[7] No disposition of the shares by the shareholder after the order nisi is made is effective against the judgment creditor,[8] and after that date until the order is made absolute or discharged the company cannot register any transfer of the shares or pay any dividends in respect of them without leave of the court.[9] If the company does either of those things

19 See Table A, art 8.
20 Charging Orders Act 1979, s 1 (1), s 2 (1) and (2), and s 6 (1); (22 Halsbury's Statutes (4th Edn) 337); RSC Ord 50, r 1 (1).
 1 If the applicant has several judgments against the same defendant, their amounts may be aggregated and the application made to the division of the High Court in which any of the judgments was obtained (Charging Orders Act 1979, s 1 (4)). Amounts ordered to be paid as costs may be added to the judgment debt (ibid, s 1 (1)).
 2 Charging Orders Act 1979, s 1 (2); County Court Jurisdiction Order 1981 (SI 1981/1123), para 2.
 3 RSC Ord 50, r 1 (2) and r 5 (2).
 4 Ibid, r 2 (1) and (3).
 5 Ibid, r 3 (1); *Roberts Petroleum Ltd v Bernard Kenny Ltd* [1983] 2 AC 192, [1983] 1 All ER 564.
 6 RSC Ord 50, r 2 (2).
 7 Charging Orders Act 1979, s 3 (4).
 8 RSC Ord 50, r 5 (1).
 9 Ibid, r 5 (2).

without leave of the court after the order nisi is made, the company is liable to the judgment creditor for the lesser of the amount of the judgment debt or the value of the shares or, if it has paid a dividend, the amount paid.[9] When the charging order has been made absolute, a copy of it and a stop notice in the same form as one served in order to protect an equitable interest in shares[10] must be served on the company,[11] and the stop notice will have the effect of preventing the company from registering a transfer of the shares by the shareholder and from paying dividends to him without first giving notice of its intention to the judgment creditor so that he may obtain an order of the court prohibiting it from doing so.[12] At any time after the charging order is made absolute the judgment creditor may apply to the Chancery Division by originating summons for an order that the shares shall be sold and the proceeds of sale applied in payment of his judgment debt,[13] but it seems that he cannot obtain a foreclosure order.[14] A charging order for a total amount not exceeding £30,000 may also be enforced by an order for sale made by a county court on an originating application made by the judgment creditor.[15]

A charging order can only be made in respect of the beneficial interest in shares vested in the judgment debtor.[16] This means that he must be the beneficial as well as the registered owner of the shares, and so if he is a trustee for other persons, no charging order can be made.[17] On the other hand, a charging order can be made in respect of shares held by other persons in trust for the judgment debtor, and the charge then attaches to whatever beneficial interest he has in the shares.[18] In such a case, the charging order does not prevent the trustees from transferring the shares or dealing with them under powers given to them by law or the instrument creating the trust,[19] nor does it prevent the company from paying dividends to the trustees.[20] The order takes effect as though the judgment debtor had charged his equitable interest himself,[1] and so it is to the trustees, and not to the company, that the judgment creditor must look for satisfaction. Despite the rule that a charging order can normally be made only in respect of the beneficial interest of the judgment debtor, it is nevertheless possible for such an order to be made directly against the trustees of a trust comprising the shares charged if either the judgment debt is that of the trustees themselves in consequence of an obligation or liability incurred by them as trustees of the trust,[2] or if the judgment debtor is, or the judgment debtors are, the sole beneficiary or beneficiaries of the trust, and in the case of a plurality of judgment debtors, the charging order is made to enforce the same judgment debt recoverable from all of them.[3]

---

10 See p 356, ante.
11 RSC Ord 50, r 5 (3).
12 Ibid, rr 12 and 15 (1).
13 RSC Ord 88, r 1.
14 *D'Auvergne v Cooper* [1899] WN 256; *Daponte v Schubert* [1939] Ch 958, [1939] 3 All ER 495; But in *Hosack v Robins* [1917] 1 Ch 332 at 336, Cozens-Hardy MR said obiter that a foreclosure order could be made.
15 County Courts Act 1984, s 23; County Court Rules, Ord 31 r 4.
16 Charging Orders Act 1979, s 2 (1) and (2).
17 *Re Blakeley Ordnance Co Ltd, Coates' Case* (1876) 46 LJ Ch 367; *Cooper v Griffin* [1892] 1 QB 740; *Howard v Sadler* [1893] 1 QB 1.
18 Charging Orders Act 1979, s 2 (1) and (2).
19 *Adam v Bank of England* (1908) 52 Sol Jo 682.
20 *Churchill v Bank of England* (1843) 11 M & W 323; 12 LJ Ex 233, 7 Jur 353, 538; sub nom *Fowler v Churchill* (1843) 2 Dowl NS 767, 7 Jur 156.
 1 Charging Orders Act 1979, s 3 (4).
 2 For example, liability for a breach of contract entered into by the trustees in execution of the trust, or for a debt incurred by them in execution of the trust, or for the wrongful appropriation of the property of a third person as assets of the trust.
 3 Charging Orders Act 1979, s 2 (1).

A judgment creditor who obtains a charging order nisi has priority for the amount payable to him under the judgment over all persons who later acquire interests in the shares. But because the charging order gives him merely an equitable interest, his charge is subject to interests created before the charging order nisi is made, and it is immaterial that the owners of those earlier interests have not protected them by serving stop notices on the company. Thus, if the judgment debtor has mortgaged his shares by way of an equitable mortgage,[4] or has agreed to sell them and the purchaser has become the equitable owner of the shares,[5] the judgment creditor is postponed to those interests, and in the latter case the court will not make a charging order if the fact that the judgment debtor is no longer the beneficial owner of the shares is drawn to its attention.[5]

It would appear that charging orders can be made in respect of shares represented by share warrants or renounceable or non-renounceable letters of allotment, despite the fact that the order to show cause and the order absolute are made effective by service on the company in which the shares are held.[6] Nevertheless, even though the service of the order nisi in respect of a share warrant on the company is effective against it, so that it may not pay dividends to the holder of the warrant, the charging order is not binding on a subsequent purchaser for value of the shares who had no notice of the order. This is because the share warrant is a negotiable instrument, and a purchaser of it for value takes it free from all adverse interests in it of which he has no notice. On the other hand, it would seem that a subsequent purchaser of a renounceable letter of allotment would be bound by a charging order made in respect of it; a renounceable letter of allotment is not a negotiable instrument, and a purchaser of it is therefore bound by all equitable interests created or arising before he acquires it. If an application is made for a charging order on shares represented by a share warrant or a letter of allotment, the judgment creditor should also apply for the appointment of a receiver by way of equitable execution so that he may take possession of the document representing the shares and be in a position to prevent the shareholder disposing of it pending an order for the sale of the shares.

Personal representatives and trustees in bankruptcy

On the death of a shareholder his shares vest in his personal representatives, and the company must recognise their title to the shares on production of the grant of probate of the deceased's will or the letters of administration to his estate.[7] The personal representatives are entitled to receive the dividends and any return of capital which would have been payable to the deceased if he were still alive, and it is not necessary that they should be registered as members of the company to enforce their claim.[8] If a rights offer is made by the company after the deceased shareholder's death, the personal representatives must be offered the right to subscribe for the number of shares to which the deceased would have been entitled.[8] Furthermore, if the deceased's shares are partly paid, the personal representatives may be compelled to pay the unpaid capital, whether calls are made or instalments of capital fall due for payment before or after the deceased's death, but unless they are registered as holders of the shares, they are liable only to the extent of the deceased's estate.[9] The personal representatives may transfer shares to purchasers

---

4 *Hulkes v Day* (1840) 10 Sim 41.
5 *Gill v Continental Gas Co* (1872) LR 7 Exch 332; *Hawks v McArthur* [1951] 1 All ER 22.
6 RSC Ord 50, r 2 (1) and r 5 (3).
7 Companies Act 1985, s 187.
8 *James v Buena Ventura Nitrate Grounds Syndicate Ltd* [1896] 1 Ch 456.
9 Ibid, at 464 at 467; *Re Agriculturist Cattle Insurance Co, Baird's Case* (1870) 5 Ch App 725.

or to beneficiaries of the deceased's estate without themselves being first registered as members of the company.[10]

Personal representatives can insist on the company registering them as members in respect of the deceased's shares,[11] unless the articles otherwise provide.[12] On the other hand, the company cannot require personal representatives to be registered.[13] It can only register them if they clearly request to be registered,[14] but no such request can be implied from the personal representatives having received dividends on the shares, because they are entitled to the payment of dividends whether they choose to be registered or not.[15] If personal representatives are registered as members, they become personally liable for capital unpaid on the shares,[14] but on the other hand they are entitled to vote at meetings of members, which they cannot do before they are registered unless the articles expressly so provide.[16]

The beneficiaries of the estate of a deceased member have only equitable interests in his shares until the personal representatives assent to the legal title vesting in them by executing appropriate transfers. In the meantime the beneficiaries may protect their equitable interests by serving stop notices on the company, and they will then be in the same position as beneficiaries of a trust of the shares who have served such notices.[17]

The trustee in bankruptcy of a bankrupt member has the same rights and liabilities as the personal representatives of a deceased member. A trustee in bankruptcy can insist on the company registering him as a member,[18] but this is rarely necessary in practice, for he can sell[19] or disclaim[20] the shares without being registered, and the trustee can compel the bankrupt member to vote at meetings of members in accordance with his directions.[1]

If the shares of the deceased or bankrupt shareholder are represented by share warrants or renounceable or non-renounceable letters of allotment, the legal title to the shares vests in the personal representatives or trustee in bankruptcy on the death or adjudication in bankruptcy of the shareholder. Their position is then the same as that of trustees of a trust of share warrants or letters of allotment duly constituted inter vivos.[2] It is important that they should obtain possession of the share warrant or letter of allotment as soon as possible, however, particularly in the case of a share warrant, which is a negotiable instrument and may therefore come into the hands of a bona fide purchaser for value, who may obtain a title good against the personal representatives or trustee. Once possession has been obtained, the personal representatives or trustee in bankruptcy may transfer the shares by delivering to the transferee, as the case may be, either the share warrant or the

---

10 Companies Act 1985, s 183 (3).
11 *Scott v Frank F Scott (London) Ltd* [1940] Ch 794, [1940] 3 All ER 508.
12 By Table A, arts 24 and 30, the directors have the same power to refuse to register personal representatives as holders of partly paid shares as they have to register transferees of such shares.
13 By Table A, art 30, the personal representatives may elect whether to be registered as members, or to transfer the deceased's shares, or to have another person registered as holder of the deceased's shares in place of themselves.
14 *Re City of Glasgow City Bank, Buchan's Case* (1879) 4 App Cas 549.
15 *Re St George's Steam Packet Co, Hamer's Devisees' Case* (1852) 2 De GM & G 366; *Re Herefordshire Banking Co, Bulmer's Case* (1864) 33 Beav 435.
16 *Marks v Financial News Ltd* [1919] WN 237. Table A, art 31, entitles personal representatives who are not registered as members to all the rights of the deceased, except the right to attend and vote at general and class meetings.
17 See p 356, ante.
18 *Re W Key & Sons Ltd* [1902] 1 Ch 467.
19 Insolvency Act 1986, s 314 (1) and Sch 5, para 9.
20 Ibid, s 315 (1) and (2).
1 *Morgan v Gray* [1953] Ch 83, [1953] 1 All ER 213.
2 See p 407, ante.

letter of allotment if it is renounceable. If the deceased or bankrupt shareholder was the original holder of a letter of allotment and he has not signed the letter of renunciation, the personal representatives or trustee may sign it in his place.

If a company is governed by Table A, notices which would have been given by it to a deceased or bankrupt member had he not died or been adjudged bankrupt, must be given instead to his personal representatives or trustee in bankruptcy, but if they have not supplied an address in the United Kingdom for this purpose, the company may give the notice in the same way as if the member had not died or become bankrupt (ie by addressing it to the member himself at his address shown in the register of members).[3]

Loss or destruction of share certificates and share warrants

Articles of association usually enable a member whose share certificate has been lost or destroyed to require the company to issue a new certificate to him on payment of any expenses incurred by the company.[4] In the absence of such a provision, however, the member would not appear to be entitled to a duplicate certificate. If the company issues a new certificate in good faith, whether the articles provide for the issue of duplicates or not, the company will incur no liability to third parties who are injured in consequence of the original certificate not in fact having been lost or destroyed. A share certificate is merely evidence of a title to shares[5] and does not embody the title as does a share warrant, so that if a member improperly procures two successive certificates in respect of the same shares by pretending that the first has been lost or destroyed, and purports to transfer the shares represented by them to different transferees, the transferee who is first to register his transfer, or to become entitled to have it registered, will obtain the legal title,[6] subject, of course, to the equitable rights of an earlier transferee if the later transferee is a donee, or if he is a purchaser with notice of the earlier transfer. The disappointed transferee will not be able to make a claim on the company if it issues the duplicate certificate in good faith, because a share certificate imparts only a representation by the company that the holder named in it is entitled to the shares at the date it is issued; it does not imply any further representation that at the time the claimant takes his transfer the registered holder has not disposed of the beneficial ownership of the shares to another person.[7] Even if the registered holder has already executed an unregistered transfer of his shares before the duplicate certificate is issued, a subsequent purchaser who relies on the duplicate will have no claim against the company on the ground that the registered holder is no longer the owner of the shares. As far as the company is concerned, the first transferee has merely an inchoate interest when the duplicate is issued, and the company is unaffected by that interest.[8] Consequently, the company will only be liable to the subsequent purchaser if he can prove that it has acted deceitfully or, possibly, negligently in issuing the duplicate certificate.

3 Table A, art 116.
4 Table A, art 7, so provides. The company may require an indemnity, but for the reasons given below, it should only extend to its expenses incurred in defending claims by third parties. The articles of companies which have a Stock Exchange listing for any of their securities must provide that new share certificates will be issued without charge to replace certificates which have been worn out, lost or destroyed (Stock Exchange: *Admission of Securities to Listing*, Section 9, Chapter 1, para 2.2).
5 Companies Act 1985, s 186, as substituted by Companies Act 1989, s 130 (7) and Sch 17, para 5 (see p 329, ante).
6 *Guy v Waterlow Bros and Layton Ltd* (1909) 25 TLR 515.
7 *Longman v Bath Electric Tramways Ltd* [1905] 1 Ch 646.
8 Companies Act 1985, s 360 (see p 360, ante).

The loss or destruction of share warrants raises more difficult problems because of the possibility that a warrant which the holder pretends has been lost or destroyed may in fact exist, and may get into the hands of a purchaser in good faith who will have an enforceable claim against the company. At common law the holder of a negotiable instrument at the time of its destruction could sue on it if he proved that it had been destroyed,[9] but not if he merely proved that the instrument had been lost, mislaid or stolen, because of the risk that it might have been acquired by a purchaser for value in good faith, who would have a valid claim against the issuer or the parties bound by the obligations embodied in it.[10] In equity, however, the holder of a negotiable instrument was permitted to sue even in these latter circumstances on offering an acceptable indemnity bond to the party or parties liable on it,[11] and the court may now allow him to sue at law as well.[12] It would therefore appear that the owner of a share warrant may sue for declared dividends even though he has lost his dividend coupons, and may claim the return of his capital when it becomes repayable, even though he cannot produce his warrant. To preserve his rights, it would appear that he may also sue the company for a general declaration that he is entitled to the shares to which the warrant relates. He will have to give the company an indemnity bond with responsible sureties to obtain these remedies, however, and if a subsequent purchaser of the original warrant obtains a good title to it as against the company, the company may enforce the bond so as to compel the former owner and his sureties to reimburse it for all payments it has to make to the purchaser.

The owner of a lost share warrant can rely on his statutory rights only if he is still the owner of the warrant at the time he sues the company. If the company can prove that since the warrant was lost it has been sold to a purchaser in good faith, the purchaser will now be the owner of the shares represented by it, and the original owner's title will have terminated. The owner of a lost or destroyed share warrant has no right to insist on the issue to him of a duplicate warrant unless the company's articles so provide,[13] and so in this respect he appears to be in a worse position than the owner of a lost bearer debenture,[14] and will find himself in practical difficulties when he wishes to sell his shares.

It would seem that the law governing the consequences of the loss or destruction of renounceable letters of allotment is the same as that governing lost share certificates.[15] Although they are transferable by delivery once the allottee has signed the latter of renunciation, they are not negotiable instruments like share warrants, and a company which issues a duplicate does not appear to run the risk of having to pay damages to a subsequent purchaser of the original letter of allotment who acquires it in good faith.

---

9 *Wright v Lord Maidstone* (1855) 24 LJ Ch 623. If the holder deliberately destroyed the instrument himself, he could not sue on it, because he thereby cancelled the obligation which the instrument embodied.
10 *Hansard v Robinson* (1827) 7 B & C 90; *Crowe v Clay* (1854) 9 Exch 604.
11 *Hansard v Robinson*, supra; *Macartney v Graham* (1828) 2 Sim 285.
12 Common Law Procedure Act 1854, s 87 (5 Halsbury's Statutes (4th Edn) 333).
13 Table A does not so provide. If a company has a Stock Exchange listing for any of its securities and its articles empower it to issue duplicate share warrants, the articles must expressly provide that the company may issue duplicates only if it is satisfied beyond reasonable doubt that the originals have been destroyed (Stock Exchange: *Admission of Securities to Listing*, Section 9, Chapter 1, para 2.3).
14 See p 490, post.
15 Table A does not provide for the issue of duplicate letters of allotment.

CHAPTER 11

Profits and dividends

It is a commonplace that companies may only pay dividends on their shares out of the profits they earn, but in seeking to define the funds which may lawfully be distributed, it is preferable to begin with the negative proposition that dividends may not be paid out of capital.[1] This means that a company cannot use money which it has raised by the issue of shares[2] or by borrowing[3] to pay dividends. The use of funds representing share capital would constitute an unlawful return of capital to shareholders, and the use of borrowed money would be a fraud on the company's creditors by making the company so much the less able to pay its debts in full.[4] It follows from this negative proposition that all funds of the company, other than capital and borrowed money and funds which by law must be treated in the same way as capital,[5] may be used to pay dividends, and in the broadest sense all such other funds may be called profits. Sometimes, however, a company's articles of association contain provisions which define or limit the profits which may be distributed by way of dividend,[6] in which case it would be unlawful for the company to distribute profits which do not come within the limits.[7] In this chapter it will be assumed, unless otherwise stated, that the company's articles contain no special provisions, and that it may distribute its profits up to the limits set by the general law.

The rules governing the calculation of profits available for the distribution of dividends to shareholders are now statutory, and they differ slightly as between public and private companies.[8] Additionally, an alternative method of calculating profits available for distribution is provided for public companies which are investment companies.[9] The profits of any company are calculated by reference to its most recent annual accounts (that is, balance sheet and profit and loss account) which have been audited and laid before its members in general meeting, but in

1 In *Verner v General and Commercial Investment Trust* [1894] 2 Ch 239, 266 Lindley LJ, remarked (at p. 266): 'It has been already said that dividends presuppose profits of some sort, and this is unquestionably true. But the word profits is by no means free from ambiguity. The law is much more accurately expressed by saying that dividends cannot be paid out of capital, than by saying that they can only be paid out of profits.'
2 *Macdougall v Jersey Imperial Hotel Co Ltd* (1864) 2 Hem & M 528; *Verner v General and Commercial Investment Trust* (supra).
3 *Re George Newman & Co* [1895] 1 Ch 674 at 686.
4 Borrowed money may be used to pay dividends if the company has earned profits equal to the amount borrowed, but has used the profits to buy further assets for its business or to meet the expenses of carrying it on (*Re Mercantile Trading Co* (1869) 4 Ch App 475; *Mills v Northern Railway of Buenos Ayres Co* (1870) 5 Ch App 621; *Thomas Fattorini (Lancashire) Ltd v IRC* [1942] AC 643 at 652, per Viscount Simon LC).
5 That is, funds credited to capital reserves, such as share premium account and capital redemption reserve (see pp 162 and 189, ante).
6 For example, the not infrequent provision that dividends shall be paid 'out of profits arising from the business of the company', which probably restricts distributable profits to the net revenue earned by carrying on of the business for which the company was formed.
7 Companies Act 1985, s 281.
8 Ibid, ss 263 and 264.
9 Ibid, s 265.

the case of a public company, reference may also be made to later interim accounts of which a copy has been delivered to the Registrar of Companies if that would justify the distribution of a greater amount of profits.[10] The accounts relied on must be prepared in accordance with the detailed rules contained in the Companies Act 1985, as amended by the Companies Act 1989, and the auditor's report on them must either be unqualified (ie it must certify that the accounts need no modification to comply with the requirements of the Companies Act 1985, as amended, or to give a true and fair view of the company's financial position and profit or loss), or must be accompanied by the auditor's certificate that no qualifications in it are material in determining the legality of the proposed distribution.[11] Consequently, the rules which now govern the form and contents of annual accounts and the valuation or calculation of their constituent items also apply in determining the amount of the resulting profit out of which dividends may be paid. This was not formerly so; before the present statutory rules for the calculation of profits and for the construction of annual accounts were enacted in 1981, the judge-made rules limiting a company's freedom to calculate its profits as it wished were unrelated to, and independent of, the statutory rules which prescribed the form and contents of companies' annual accounts.

THE COMPUTATION OF PROFITS

Choice of method

In calculating the amount of profits which a company may distribute under any system of law, a choice has to be made between the available accounting methods which may be used as a basis for the calculation. There are three possible methods of calculating the profits of a particular period for the purpose of dividends.

(1) *The current earnings method.* By this method the profit is taken to be the gross earnings of the financial period less the expenses incurred in carrying on the business activities which produced such gross earnings during the period. No regard is paid to losses suffered in earlier periods, but on the other hand, amounts received or receivable by the company in respect of matters unconnected with the trade which it was formed to carry on do not go to swell the distributable fund. The current earnings method was the one employed by English law before the relevant law was put in statutory form. Companies were free to distribute the current net earnings of a financial period without taking account of losses suffered in earlier periods,[12] and they were under no obligation to provide for the depreciation or diminution in value of the fixed assets (eg buildings, machinery, equipment) with which the company's business was carried on,[13] but, inconsistently with the current earnings method, they were free to distribute profits realised from the disposal of fixed assets provided that losses resulting from such disposals and trading losses (if any) during the same financial period were first deducted.[14]

(2) *The earned surplus method.* This is similar to the first method, except that trading losses suffered in earlier financial periods are carried forward and are set off against

---

10 Companies Act 1985, s 270 (2) to (4) and ss 271 and 272.
11 Ibid, s 271 (2) to (4) and s 272 (2) and (3). The rules governing the form and contents of annual accounts are dealt with in Chapter 17.
12 *Ammonia Soda Co v Chamberlain* [1918] 1 Ch 266 at 289.
13 *Verner v General and Commercial Investment Trust* [1894] 2 Ch 239 at 265; *re Kingston Cotton Mill Co (No 2)* [1896] 1 Ch 331; *Bishop v Smyrna and Cassaba Rly Co (No 2)* [1895] 2 Ch 596.
14 *Lubbock v British Bank of South America* [1892] 2 Ch 198; *Bishop v Smyrna and Cassaba Rly Co (No 2)*, supra, *Foster v New Trinidad Lake Asphalt Co Ltd* [1901] 1 Ch 208.

the earnings of the current period, so that only the balance is distributable as dividend. The method has the virtue of treating the company's trading as a continuous process, and not as one artificially split into successive, insulated periods, but it also has the disadvantage of inhibiting a company which has suffered past trading losses from paying dividends commensurate with its current earnings, and this may depress the market value of the company's shares. This method has in the past been used as a legal basis in a number of the states of the United States, usually with the modification that in calculating profits for the purpose of paying preference dividends (and sometimes ordinary share dividends as well) a company might exceptionally employ the current earnings method so as to leave past trading losses out of account.

(3) *The balance sheet surplus method.* By this method the surplus of the company's assets over its liabilities, share capital and capital reserves at the end of the financial period for which accounts are prepared is treated as the profit distributable for that period. Such a surplus will include not only the trading profit earned during the period, but also accumulated profits carried forward from earlier financial periods, and profits obtained on the sale of the company's fixed assets for more than their cost price or written down value. On the other hand, if in earlier financial periods the company has suffered trading losses or losses on the realisation of its fixed assets, this method prevents the company from paying a dividend until its current profits are sufficient to write off those losses. The method ensures that the company must retain net assets at least equal in value to its share capital and capital reserves after it has paid the dividend it proposes, and this affords some protection to its creditors. But the method can work unfairly when the company issues preference shares with priority for repayment of capital, because the preference shareholders qualify for a dividend only if the company has sufficient resources to pay off both its preference and ordinary share capital, and this in effect makes the preference shareholders guarantors that the ordinary share capital will be kept intact, a reversal of the position usually envisaged by the terms of issue of preference shares.

The statutory rules now in force in Great Britain for the calculation of profits available for dividends involve a combination of the earned surplus and the balance sheet surplus methods. They are derived from traditional western European accounting practice as embodied in national legislation, and both these rules and the statutory rules governing the form and contents of accounts have been enacted in consequence of harmonisation directives issued by the Council of Ministers of the European Communities.[15] The statutory rules mark a substantial change in English law, but in their detailed application it is still legitimate to take the earlier case law into account where the statutory rules are not explicit, on the assumption that the earlier judicial rulings on points of detail remain the law if they are consistent with the principles underlying the statutory rules.

The statutory rules for the calculation of profits

Basic rules applicable to all companies

The first set of statutory rules applies to distributions made by all companies, whether public or private. The rules begin by prohibiting distributions to shareholders except out of profits available for the purpose.[16] Distributions are defined as all distributions of a company's assets to its members, whether in cash or

---

15 Second Council Directive of 13 December 1976 (Official Journal for 1977, No L 261/1); Fourth Council Directive of 25 July 1978 (Official Journal for 1978, No L 222/1).
16 Companies Act 1985, s 263 (1).

in any other form,[17] but as not including the issue of fully or partly paid bonus shares,[18] the redemption of redeemable shares or the purchase by a company of shares in itself under the relevant statutory provisions,[19] the reduction of capital by repayment or by the cancellation of capital not paid up on shares,[20] or the distribution of assets in a winding up.[1] Profits available for distribution are defined as the company's accumulated realised profits from the time of its incorporation (so far as not previously distributed or capitalised on issues of bonus shares) less the company's accumulated realised losses from the time of its incorporation (so far as not written off on a reduction or reorganisation of capital).[2] Profits and losses themselves are defined as both revenue and capital profits and losses.[3] The result of these rules is that, subject to the qualifications made below in the case of a public company, a company's distributable profits are based on its total accumulated earnings less its total accumulated revenue losses, plus or minus the net balance of its accumulated profits and losses on the disposal of its fixed assets; and to arrive at its net profits currently available for distribution a deduction must be made from this amount of the total of its distributions and capitalisations of profits to date and an addition must be made for losses which have been written off against capital. In other words, the method employed to calculate the company's distributable profits is a modified version of the earned surplus method, which also takes into account the net accumulated profits and losses on the disposal of the company's fixed assets.

It is notable that only realised profits and losses are taken into account in calculating profits available for distribution. Unrealised profits cannot be used to inflate distributions, as they could under the previous law.[4] No precise definition is given of realised and unrealised profits and losses,[5] but presumably a profit is realised as soon as the company has a legal and unconditional right to recover money or an asset with a readily realisable and ascertainable value[6] from a third party under a transaction which has involved the company in expenditure or an accrued and quantifiable liability of a smaller amount or value; and a loss is realised either when an asset of the company is lost to it or deteriorates so substantially that it can no longer be used or it has no value, or when a transaction entered into by the company results in expenditure or an accrued and quantifiable liability on its part which exceeds any payment or asset with a readily realisable and ascertainable value to which the company is entitled. However, realised losses are deemed to include provisions made by a company, other than provisions for diminution in value or additional depreciation on the revaluation of all the company's fixed assets (including or omitting goodwill), or provisions for the depreciation of fixed assets on their upward revaluation to the extent that the

---

17 Ibid, s 263 (2).
18 The issue of bonus shares involves an increase in the company's issued share capital but not a disposal of its assets (see p 434, post).
19 See p 188 et seq, ante.
20 See p 177, ante.
 1 No distinction is made in a winding up between distributions of assets representing profits and distributions of assets representing capital.
 2 Companies Act 1985, s 263 (3).
 3 Ibid, s 280 (3).
 4 *Dimbula Valley (Ceylon) Tea Co Ltd v Laurie* [1961] Ch 353, [1961] 1 All ER 769.
 5 The Companies Act 1985, s 226 (3) (as substituted by Companies Act 1989, s 4 (1)) and Sch 4, para 91, merely provide that profits may be shown in a company's annual accounts as realised profits if it is 'in accordance with principles generally accepted . . . for accounting purposes . . . at the time when those accounts are prepared.'
 6 For example, short term securities which can be sold or discounted immediately and securities immediately saleable on a stock exchange.

provisions exceed those which would be made if there were no revaluation.[7] Consequently, normal provisions made by a company in its annual accounts for the depreciation or diminution in value of fixed or current assets, and provisions made to meet liabilities or losses which are likely to be incurred, or which are certain to be incurred but are uncertain in amount or as to the date of their occurrence, must be treated as realised losses.[8] It follows that the unrealised profits and losses which are not taken into account in calculating profits available for distribution are profits and losses which are estimated, or which are the result of the valuation or revaluation of particular assets, and that losses are also unrealised if they take the form of liabilities which have not accrued and for which no provision has been made. The confinement of profits available for distribution to the balance of realised profits and losses means not only that unrealised profits cannot be distributed, but also that they cannot be used to write off realised losses and so increase the balance of realised profits. On the other hand, under the statutory rules applicable to all companies, realised profits are not diminished by unrealised losses, although for the reasons given below such losses must be taken into account in the case of public companies.

Basic rules applicable to public companies

In addition to the restrictions on distributions imposed on all companies, a public company is subject to the further restriction that it may not make a distribution if the amount of its net assets is less than the aggregate of its called up share capital and its undistributable reserves, or if the amount of its net assets after the proposed distribution would be less than its called up share capital plus its undistributable reserves.[9] The amount of the net assets of a company is the total value of its assets as shown in the balance sheet which is used for calculating the distributable profits[10] less the total amount of liabilities and provisions shown by that balance sheet.[11] Called up share capital is the total of the paid up capital of the company, plus capital which has been called but not paid up, plus unpaid capital which is payable in specified amounts at fixed future dates.[12] Undistributable reserves are share premium account, capital redemption reserve, the excess of the company's accumulated unrealised profits (so far as not already capitalised on the issue of bonus shares) over its accumulated unrealised losses (so far as not previously written off by a reduction or reorganisation of capital) and any other reserve which the company is prohibited from distributing by law or by its memorandum or articles.[13] The capital of a public company which is taken into account is its called up (not its paid up) capital, and this includes the part of the issue price for its issued shares which it has not yet received. Nevertheless called up capital which has not been paid up is treated as though it were an asset in the balance sheet,[14] and it is therefore

---

7 Companies Act 1985, s 275 (1) and (2) (see p 429, post). A revaluation of all the company's fixed assets is deemed to take place if the directors assess the current value of all of them, even though some of them are not revalued at a different amount; in that case the notes to the accounts must contain a statement to that effect (Companies Act 1985, s 275 (4) and (5)).
8 Companies Act 1985, s 226 (3) (as substituted by Companies Act 1989, s 4 (1)) and Sch 4, paras 88 and 89.
9 Ibid, s 264 (1).
10 See p 419, ante.
11 Companies Act 1985, s 264 (2).
12 Ibid, s 737.
13 Ibid, s 264 (3).
14 Companies Act 1985, s 226 (3) (as substituted by Companies Act 1989, s 4 (1)) and Sch 4, para 1 (1) and Balance Sheet Formats.

the difference between net assets and paid up capital plus capital reserves which gives the figure for distributable profits.

The additional restrictions imposed on distributions by a public company result in its distributable profits being calculated by the balance sheet surplus method. In a balance sheet the difference between total assets on the one side and the sum of capital, capital (i e undistributable) reserves, liabilities and provisions on the other represents the total accumulated profits (less accumulated losses) of the company. In reality the balance sheet surplus method employed for public companies closely resembles the modified earned surplus method of calculating distributable profits which applies to all companies, and the only substantial differences between them are that:

(a) the treatment of the excess of the accumulated unrealised profits of a public company over its accumulated unrealised losses as a capital reserve prevents it from distributing the excess in the same way as the modified earned surplus method applicable to all companies prevents any unrealised profits from being distributed; additionally, however, the balance sheet surplus method requires any excess of accumulated unrealised losses over accumulated unrealised profits to be taken into account in calculating the distributable profits of a public company, which is not so under the modified earned surplus rules applicable to all companies;

(b) under the balance sheet surplus method all provisions made in the public company's balance sheet must be deducted in arriving at its distributable profits, whereas under the modified earned surplus method applicable to all companies provisions made for diminutions in the value of assets on a revaluation of all the company's fixed assets and provisions for additional depreciation on the upward revaluation of fixed assets do not have to be taken into account;[15] this is the consequence of (a) above, because provisions for diminutions in value and additional depreciation on a revaluation merely reflect unrealised losses.

Investment companies

An alternative method of calculating the profits of an investment company may be employed if it would yield a higher figure for distributable profits than the combination of the earned surplus and balance sheet surplus methods applicable to other public companies. An investment company for this purpose is a public company which has notified the Registrar of Companies of its intention to be treated as an investment company, and which has since the date of the notice complied with certain conditions, namely:[16] (a) the business of the company consists of investing its funds mainly in securities with the aim of spreading the investment risk and managing its investments for the benefit of its members; (b) the investments of the company in any other company or single group of companies (other than securities of another investment company) do not account for more than 15 per cent in value of the company's total investments at the time an investment in the other company or single group is acquired (including that investment); (c) the company is prohibited by its memorandum or articles from distributing capital profits on the realisation of its investments or other fixed assets; (d) the company distributes at least 85 per cent of the income it derives from

---

15 Ibid, s 263 (3) and s 275 (1) and (2).
16 Ibid, s 265 (4) to (6) and s 266 (1) and (2), as amended by Financial Services Act 1986, s 212 (2) and Sch 16, para 19.

securities held by it;[17] (e) the company has a listing for its shares on the Stock Exchange or on any other investment exchange in the United Kingdom, recognised by the Secretary of State for Trade and Industry for the purposes of the Financial Services Act 1986; and (f) the company has not during the financial year or other period[18] whose distributable profits are in question distributed a capital profit or applied unrealised profits or realised capital profits in paying up the issue price of any of its issued shares or its debentures.[19]

The alternative way in which an investment company may calculate its distributable profits is by taking the difference between its accumulated realised revenue profits, that is, its accumulated investment income (so far as not previously distributed or otherwise applied), and its realised and unrealised revenue losses (so far as not previously written off by a reduction or reorganisation of capital), but the difference may be distributed to the members of the company only if the value of the company's total assets shown by the audited accounts used for calculating its profits (but not including uncalled capital) amount to at least 150 per cent of its liabilities and provisions for liabilities and losses of uncertain amount, and a distribution may be made only to the extent that it does not reduce the company's assets to less than that proportion.[20] The method of calculating the company's profits available for distribution is the earned surplus method (taking only realised profits, but both realised and unrealised losses into account), but a limit is placed on distributions, not by reference to the company's balance sheet surplus, but to its solvency margin.[20]

Calculation of revenue profits

Current earnings or revenue profits of a company are the amounts accruing due to it from persons with whom it deals in carrying on its business during the accounting period in question, less the expenses incurred in earning such amounts accruing during that period. Whether such an accrued amount arises from the business which the company was formed to carry on, or is a merely fortuitous gain unconnected with its business, raises a question of construction of its objects, but it seems that unless the company's articles impose restrictions on the kind of profits which may be distributed as dividends, profits arising fortuitously or even from ultra vires activities may be distributed, as well as profits resulting from carrying on the company's legitimate business. Profits must be taken into account in the financial year or accounting period in which they are realised or accrue, and expenses and liabilities must be debited in the same way, without regard to the date when payment is made by or to the company.[1] Prospective profits, that is, profits resulting from payments to which the company will be entitled in the future when it has done work or supplied goods or services over an extended period part of which has already expired, may not be shown in the profit and loss account as profits,[2] and for this reason the anticipated profit may not be apportioned over the accounting periods during which it is being earned. For example, if the company

---

17 The company's income from securities is presumably the total income received by the company from its investments (including the tax credits given to the company in connection with distributions and interest payments) less the corporation tax payable in respect of that income.
18 That is, financial period for which annual or interim accounts are prepared (see p 696, post).
19 There is no restriction on the company capitalising realised or unrealised profits in order to make an issue of bonus shares, but only realised revenue profits may be used to pay up the nominal value of bonus debentures.
20 Companies Act 1985, s 265 (1) to (3).
1 Ibid, s 226 (3) (as substituted by Companies Act 1989, s 4 (1)) and Sch 4, para 13.
2 Companies Act 1985, s 226 (3) (as substituted by Companies Act 1989, s 4) and Sch 4, para 12 (a).

has undertaken construction work which will take three years to complete, it cannot at the end of the first year treat itself as entitled to one-third or any other fraction of the amount which will be payable for the work on its completion. Nevertheless, it would seem legitimate to show an anticipated profit or a fraction of it as an unrealised profit in a company's balance sheet, but it will not be available for distribution until payment under the transaction from which the profit arises has become a debt owing to the company.[3]

In arriving at a company's net profits, questions often arise whether an expense incurred by the company is attributable to carrying on its business, so that it must be debited to the company's trading account, or whether the expense may be treated as a capital expense and be met out of share capital or borrowed money. Directors' remuneration,[4] the wages and salaries of the company's employees,[5] the rent of premises occupied by it,[5] its office and administrative expenses,[6] taxes accrued due or calculable although payable only at a future date,[7] and the cost of selling and advertising the company's products, must all be treated as current expenses and be debited to the company's trading account. So must the cost of raw materials bought by a manufacturing company, and stock in trade bought by a company which deals in goods,[8] but if a company buys raw materials or stock in trade to meet its needs during several accounting periods, it may apportion the cost among those periods, and debit only part of the cost to its trading account for the period in which the goods were bought.[9] Generally, interest paid by a company on money borrowed by it must be treated as an expense of its business and be debited to its trading account,[10] but if money is borrowed to meet the cost of constructing fixed assets, such as a tramway[11] or a reservoir,[12] the interest may be treated as part of the cost of construction, and may be shown as an addition to the cost of the fixed asset.[13] If a company will become indebted in the future for trade debts of an ascertainable amount, provision must be made for meeting them by debiting at least a fraction of their amount to the account for the current financial period.[14] Thus, it has been held that, wholly apart from statutory provisions, an insurance company is not entitled to treat the whole of the premiums which it receives during one financial year as profits without first making provision for its prospective liabilities under policies it had issued.[14] Furthermore, if trade debts owed to the company prove irrecoverable, they must be excluded from the trading account and must not appear as part of the company's earnings.[15] If such debts have already been credited to the company in its trading accounts for earlier periods, they must be deducted before arriving at the profit for the current period.[15]

---

3 Ibid, s 263 (1) and (3). The previous law was the same in this respect (*J P Hall & Co Ltd v IRC* [1921] 3 KB 152; *Willingale v International Commercial Bank Ltd* [1978] AC 834, [1978] 1 All ER 754).
4 *Ashton & Co Ltd v Honey* (1907) 23 TLR 253.
5 *Re County Marine Insurance Co, Rance's Case* (1870) 6 Ch App 104.
6 *Bloxam v Metropolitan Rly Co* (1868) 3 Ch App 337.
7 *Peter Buchanan Ltd and Macharg v McVey* [1955] AC 516n at 521 to 2. But taxes on a company's capital or fixed assets, such as corporation tax paid by it on its capital gains, probably need not be debited against earnings.
8 *Ammonia Soda Co v Chamberlain* [1918] 1 Ch 266 at 286 to 287, per Swinfen Eady LJ.
9 *Jamaica Rly Co v A-G of Jamaica* [1893] AC 127 at 136. This is achieved in practice by debiting the whole cost of the raw materials and stock in the trading account of the period in which they are purchased and crediting the value of the unused or undisposed of raw materials or stock at the end of the period.
10 *Ashton & Co Ltd v Honey* (1907) 23 TLR 253.
11 *Hinds v Buenos Ayres Grand National Tramways Co* [1906] 2 Ch 654.
12 *Bardwell v Sheffield Waterworks Co* (1872) LR 14 Eq 517.
13 Companies Act 1985, s 226 (3) (as substituted by Companies Act 1989, s 4 (1)) and Sch 4, para 26 (3).
14 *Re County Marine Insurance Co, Rance's Case* (1870) 6 Ch App 104.
15 *Re National Bank of Wales Ltd* [1899] 2 Ch 629; affd sub nom *Dovey v Cory* [1901] AC 477.

In practice a company's trading account prepared as a basis for its profit and loss account does more than set off earnings or accruals against trading expenses of the period in question. It recognises that the carrying on of the company's business is a continuous process, and therefore introduces as items in the account the value of the company's raw materials or stock in trade brought forward at the beginning of the current financial period from the last period, and also the value of such assets at the end of the current period so that they may be carried forward to the next period.[16] Consequently, if a company has purchased more raw materials or stock than it has consumed or sold during the current period, its earnings will not be artificially depressed thereby, whilst if its earnings have been artificially inflated by running down its stocks, the balance of earnings distributable as dividend will be correspondingly reduced. This practice is in accordance with the law governing the legitimacy of dividends. Any diminution in the value of the company's raw materials or stocks during the current financial period is to be taken into account in calculating its profits,[17] and this is so even if the volume of raw materials or stocks has not fallen, but their realisable value is less than their cost of acquisition or production.[18] On the other hand, since the cost of raw materials or stocks may be apportioned between the financial periods in which they are consumed or sold,[19] it is permissible to treat an increase in their value during the current period due to an increase in volume as augmenting the profits of that period. However, an increase in the value of raw materials or stocks due to an increase in the level of prices may not be taken into account so as to augment the company's profit.[20] This is so even if the company exercises the option to prepare its annual accounts on the basis of current replacement cost,[1] when stocks and raw materials will be shown in the company's accounts at their current value at the date as at which the accounts are prepared; the excess of their current value over their cost of acquisition or production will be credited to a revaluation reserve, and may only be treated as a profit when the goods are sold at the current value or a higher price.[2]

Because companies acquire raw materials and stock in trade more or less continuously, though inevitably at different prices depending on market conditions, it is obviously a convenience if for accounting purposes a company may treat its raw materials or stock in trade as acquired in a certain order, so that the items it has in hand at the beginning or end of a financial period are assumed to have been acquired at corresponding prices. For example, if the company assumes that the earliest acquired raw materials or stock were the first to be consumed or sold (first in–first out or FIFO), the raw materials or stock on hand at the end of a financial

---

16 For example, if during a financial period a manufacturing company sells £150,000's worth of its products, and incurs £100,000 in manufacturing and other expenses, and its stock of raw materials at the beginning of the period is worth £20,000, and at the end £40,000, its trading profits would be £70,000 not £50,000. In skeleton form its trading account would be as follows:

Raw materials at beginning		Sales	£150,000
of period	£20,000	Raw materials at end	
Expenses	£100,000	of period	40,000
Profit	70,000		
	£190,000		£190,000

17 *Verner v General and Commercial Investment Trust* [1894] 2 Ch 239, 266.
18 Companies Act 1985, s 226 (3) (as substituted by Companies Act 1989, s 4 (1)) and Sch 4, para 23 (1).
19 *Jamaica Rly Co v A-G of Jamaica* [1893] AC 127.
20 Companies Act 1985, s 226 (3) (as substituted by Companies Act 1989, s 4 (1)) and Sch 4, para 22.
 1 Ibid, Sch 4, para 30 (see p 704, post). Current replacement cost may be calculated by applying an appropriate inflation index to the original cost of acquisition or production.
 2 Companies Act 1985, s 226 (3) (as substituted by Companies Act 1989, s 4 (1)) and Sch 4, para 31 (5) and para 34 (1).

period will be considered to consist of those items most recently acquired, and their cost will be calculated accordingly. On the other hand, if prices are rising because of inflation, the company may prefer to treat the items most recently acquired as being consumed first (last in–first out or LIFO), and so treat the value of items on hand at the end of the financial period as equal to the cost of the earliest acquisitions, thus restricting the profits shown for the period. Either the FIFO or LIFO methods of valuation may lawfully be used by a company in calculating its profits,[3] or it may use an average or standard cost method of valuation which treats acquisitions of raw materials or stock during the financial year as having been made at the average of the actual prices paid.[4] Work in progress or stock produced by the company must be valued by adding to the cost of raw materials and consumables (eg energy supplies) used all other direct costs of production, and a reasonable proportion of indirect costs incurred during the period of production (ie general overheads, staff salaries, administration expenses, and advertising and promotion expenses, but not distribution costs) may also be added.[5]

Depreciation and appreciation of fixed assets

If a company's trading and profit and loss accounts are prepared on the basis that profits are calculated according to the current earnings method, the only purchases made by the company which are debited to the accounts will be purchases of raw materials or stock in trade and comparatively small items of equipment for the carrying on of the company's business, such as tools and office equipment. Large items of equipment and fixed assets generally (such as the premises where the company's business is carried on, machinery in a factory, and vehicles for transporting the company's goods) will usually be paid for initially out of the proceeds of the issue of the company's shares, debentures or loan securities[6] (ie out of capital), and will not figure in the trading or profit and loss account at all. But such fixed assets eventually wear out or become obsolete or unusable, and it is now obligatory for the company to set aside a fraction of its current profits each year to provide a fund out of which all fixed assets which have a limited useful economic life can be replaced at the end of their useful life.[7] This must be done by debiting the trading account each year with a fraction of the cost to the company of each fixed asset,[8] and by crediting the same amount against the cost of the asset, which appears as a debit made in the accounting records of the company against the original cost incurred when the asset was acquired or constructed.[7] At the end of

---

3 Companies Act 1985, s 226 (3) (as substituted by Companies Act 1989, s 4 (1)) and Sch 4, para 27 (1) and (2). This was also permissible under the previous law (*Minister of Natural Revenue v Anaconda American Brass Ltd* [1956] AC 85, [1956] 1 All ER 20).
4 Companies Act 1985, s 226 (3) (as substituted by Companies Act 1989, s 4 (1)) and Sch 4, para 27 (1) and (2). This was also permissible under the previous law (*Patrick v Broadstone Mills Ltd* [1954] 1 All ER 163, [1954] 1 WLR 158).
5 Companies Act 1985, s 226 (3) (as substituted by Companies Act 1989, s 4 (1)) and Sch 4, para 26 (2) to (4).
6 They may also be paid for out of profits retained for the purpose or out of short term loans borrowing (eg bank overdrafts) when the intention is to capitalise the profits eventually, or to fund the borrowing by issuing new shares, debentures or loan securities and to discharge the loans out of the proceeds.
7 Companies Act 1985, s 226 (3) (as substituted by Companies Act 1989, s 4 (1)) and Sch 4, para 18.
8 The fraction is usually the reciprocal of the number of years which the asset is expected to last from the time when the company acquires it. This is known as the 'straight line' method of depreciation. An alternative method, known as the 'reducing balance' method, depreciates the written down value of the asset by a standard percentage in each year of its expected useful life. Since the written down value is falling each year, the amounts set aside for depreciation are greater in the early years of the asset's life than in the later.

the useful life of each fixed asset its value in the company's books will then appear as nil or the value of the asset as scrap or its value for a different use. In addition to providing systematically for the depreciation of fixed assets which have a limited useful economic life, a company must provide for every diminution in value of its fixed assets which is expected to be permanent (eg destruction of uninsured buildings or equipment, or equipment falling in value because of technological improvements); this must be done by writing off the diminution in value against profits.[9]

Fixed assets must be shown in a company's accounts at their cost of acquisition or production, and the aggregate amount so far provided for the depreciation or diminution in value of those assets must be shown separately.[10] It follows that until a fixed asset is sold or otherwise disposed of for an amount in excess of its cost of acquisition or production less provisions for depreciation or diminution in value, no profit is realised and no distribution of a profit may be made, even if the saleable value of the asset is indisputably higher than its net balance sheet value.[11] On the other hand, if the company exercises the option to show its assets in its balance sheet at their current value (ie their current replacement cost),[12] it will revalue its fixed assets at the cost of replacing them at the date at which the balance sheet is made out,[13] and in inflationary conditions this will be a greater amount than their acquisition or production cost less depreciation based on it. The excess is not a realised profit, however, and so it must be credited to a special revaluation reserve in the company's accounts, and may only be transferred to profit and loss account and made available for distribution when the fixed asset is disposed of for a sum at least equal to the latest revaluation of the asset less the total provision for depreciation made in respect of it, unless the reserve has meanwhile been capitalised.[14]

When a fixed asset is revalued at current replacement cost, future provisions for its depreciation will be made on the basis of the revaluation figure,[15] and additional provision for depreciation of the asset will be necessary to augment the provision made in earlier accounting periods when the value of the asset was taken at a lower figure.[16] However, the additional provision so made may be treated as a realised profit and so affect the amount which the company may distribute,[17] but with the consequence, it would seem, of obliging the company to increase its provision for depreciation of the asset in future years so as to write down the revaluation figure to the residual or scrap value of the asset by the end of its useful economic life.[18]

9 Companies Act 1985, s 226 (3) (as substituted by Companies Act 1989, s 4 (1)) and Sch 4, para 19 (2). If the provision turns out to be unnecessary, it must be cancelled and profits credited accordingly (Ibid, Sch 4, para 19 (3)).

10 Companies Act 1985, s 226 (3) (as substituted by Companies Act 1989, s 4 (1)) and Sch 4, paras 17 and 42 (3).

11 Ibid, s 263 (1) and (3).

12 Ibid, s 226 (3) (as substituted by Companies Act 1989, s 4 (1)) and Sch 4, para 30.

13 Ibid, Sch 4, para 31 (1), (2) and (3).

14 Ibid, Sch 4, para 34 (1) and (3), as substituted by Companies Act 1989, s 4 (2) and Sch 7, para 6.

15 Ibid, Sch 4, para 32 (1). But the company may alternatively continue to make provisions for depreciation on the basis of the historical cost of the asset (para 32 (3)).

16 For example, if an asset purchased in 1985 for £10,000 has an expected useful life of 10 years and an expected residual value of £2,000, and is revalued in 1990 at a current replacement cost of £20,000, provision for depreciation will be made in 1990 and subsequent years on a straight line basis at the yearly rate of £1,800, and because between 1985 and 1990 provision has been made at the rate of only £800 a year, additional provision for depreciation for those years will be made in 1990 amounting to £5,000.

17 Companies Act 1985, s 275 (2). The effect of treating the additional provision as a realised profit is to reduce the net amount of provisions which are deducted in arriving at distributable profits.

18 In the example given in footnote 16, the company would have to make provision for depreciation between 1990 and 1995 at the yearly rate of £2,800.

Reserves

A company is not bound to distribute the whole of its distributable profits among its shareholders, unless its articles so provide. It is usual for a substantial part of the profits of each accounting period, whether distributable or not, to be carried forward to the next and subsequent periods, when they may be dealt with as if they were profits of the same character earned during those periods. It is also common for a company's articles to provide that the board of directors may transfer any part of its profits to reserves before recommending a dividend, thus diminishing the fund out of which the shareholders may declare a dividend.[19] Under such an article the board may transfer profits to reserves for specific purposes, such as the replacement of fixed assets or the payment of future taxation, but a company's largest reserve is usually its general reserve, which may be used for any purpose, such as the expansion of the company's business by the acquisition of new fixed assets.

Reserves are applicable for the same purposes as profits of the same character earned or credited during the current accounting period if the articles so provide,[20] or if they do not prohibit such an application.[1] Consequently, if the reserves represent realised profits, they may be added to the company's accumulated balance of realised profits and distributed as a dividend.[2] But if the articles require a reserve fund of a certain amount to be set aside for a particular purpose before any dividend is declared, no part of that fund can be distributed as dividend unless the articles are altered.[3] Unless the way in which reserves are to be applied is specified in the articles, the use to which they are put is decided on either by a general meeting or, if the articles so provide, by the directors, and the use of the reserves may be changed from time to time in like manner. Consequently, even though in the company's accounts realised profits have been transferred to reserves for specific purposes, such as the replacement of fixed assets or future tax payments, any part of the reserves may be re-transferred in order to pay dividends.[4]

If a company has retained profits or transferred profits to reserves and subsequently suffers a loss, it has been held that the loss must be written off against the retained profits or reserves before a dividend is paid to the shareholders,[5] and this accords with the statutory rule that dividends may be paid only out of the surplus of the company's accumulated realised profits over its accumulated losses at the date the dividend is declared,[2] or in the case of a public company, out of the surplus of its realised profits over its realised and unrealised losses at that date on the assumption that its net assets are sufficient to cover its called up share capital and its undistributable reserves.[6] For this reason the ruling of the court that a company which reduces its capital because of a loss must first cancel its reserves before reducing capital,[7] is preferable to its decision in another case that the loss

---

19 The Companies Act 1948, Table A, art 117, contained such a power. The present Table A makes no provision for directors to make transfers to reserves.
20 The Companies Act 1948, Table A, art 117, empowered the directors to set aside reserves out of profits and to apply them for any purpose for which profits could be applied, and pending such application, to employ them in the company's business or invest them.
1 *Re Bridgewater Navigation Co* [1891] 2 Ch 317.
2 Companies Act 1985, s 263 (1) and (3).
3 *Re Eastern and Australian SS Co* [1893] WN 31; Companies Act 1985, s 281.
4 With regard to preference shareholders' claims on reserves which are distributed as dividends, see p 209, ante.
5 *Re John Fulton & Co Ltd* [1932] NI 35. See also the American case of *Lich v United States Rubber Co* (1941) 123 F 2d 145.
6 Companies Act 1985, s 264 (1) and (2) and s 280 (3).
7 *Re Barrow Haematite Steel Co* [1900] 2 Ch 846; affd [1901] 2 Ch 746 (see p 185, ante).

must be thrown on capital and reserves rateably.[8] If the latter decision were correct, a company which had suffered a loss could retain its power to pay dividends out of reserves by reducing its capital, and this would be inconsistent with the statutory rules restricting distributions. However, as between different reserves or a single reserve representing both realised and unrealised profits, it would seem to be permissible to cancel reserves representing unrealised profits, except where the losses are realised revenue or capital losses, when they must be set off against accumulated realised profits.[9]

THE PAYMENT OF DIVIDENDS

Declaration and accrual of dividends

A dividend becomes payable only when its amount has been ascertained and any conditions for its payment which are specified in the company's articles have been complied with. If the articles provide that the company's profits shall be applied in paying dividends in a certain order, the dividend is payable as soon as the requisite distributable profits are ascertained.[10] In this connection it has been held that a dividend is payable on ordinary shares as soon as the profits are ascertained if the terms of issue provide that the profits 'shall be divisible' among the ordinary shareholders, because in this context the imperative 'shall' results in the word 'divisible' having the same meaning as 'divided'.[11] But this is not so if the articles also authorise the company to issue preference shares which carry the right to share in the surplus assets left in a winding up after paying the company's debts and repaying its share capital, but only entitle their holders to a fixed preference dividend while the company is a going concern; the automatic division of the company's profits among its shareholders in this case would mean that the ordinary shareholders would be entitled to all the profits left after paying the current year's and any accumulated but unpaid preference dividends, and in a winding up there would be no surplus assets representing undistributed profits in which the preference shareholders could share, which would conflict with the intention of the articles.[12] This reasoning applies also in the converse case where the articles provide that the company's profits shall be applied in paying a preference dividend, then an equivalent ordinary share dividend and finally a further dividend in which both preference and ordinary shares participate, but that on the winding up of the company any surplus assets left after repaying preference and ordinary share capital shall belong to the ordinary shareholders alone; if the preference and ordinary shareholders were automatically entitled to their participating dividend while the company was a going concern, there would be no surplus assets in a liquidation, and so the entitlement to the participating dividend must be construed as being conditional upon the dividend being declared.[13]

Unless the articles make dividends payable automatically on the ascertainment of sufficient distributable profits to meet them, dividends do not become payable unless and until an authorised organ of the company declares them.[14] It is usual for

8 *Re Hoare & Co* [1904] 2 Ch 208.
9 Companies Act 1985, s 263 (3) and s 280 (3).
10 *Evling v Israel and Oppenheimer Ltd* [1918] 1 Ch 101.
11 *Scottish Insurance Corpn Ltd v Wilsons and Clyde Coal Co Ltd* [1949] AC 462, [1949] 1 All ER 1068.
12 *Dimbula Valley (Ceylon) Tea Co Ltd v Laurie* [1961] Ch 353, [1961] 1 All ER 769.
13 *Re Saltdean Estate Co Ltd* [1968] 3 All ER 829 at 833, [1968] 1 WLR 1844 at 1850, per Buckley J.
14 *Bond v Barrow Haematite Steel Co* [1902] 1 Ch 353; *Re Accrington Corpn Steam Tramways Co* [1909] 2 Ch 40.

the articles to provide that dividends shall be declared by a general meeting of the company's members, but sometimes the directors are given power to declare dividends to the exclusion of general meetings. A provision that such part of the profits as the directors determine shall be distributed is construed as conferring an exclusive power on the directors to declare dividends.[15] If the articles are silent as to the payment of dividends, they are payable only when declared by an ordinary resolution passed by a general meeting.[14] When dividends are declared by a general meeting, the articles frequently prevent the members from being too generous to themselves at the expense of the company's future needs by limiting the maximum dividend which they may declare to that recommended by the directors.[16] Dividends are normally declared at the company's annual general meeting, but to enable dividends to be paid in anticipation of the dividend which will eventually be declared, directors are usually given power to pay interim dividends between annual general meetings.[17] Such a power can then only be exercised by the board, and a declaration of an interim dividend by a general meeting will be void, unless a concurrent power to declare such a dividend is expressly conferred on it by the articles.[18] An important difference between final and interim dividends is that once a final dividend has been declared, it is a debt payable to the shareholders and cannot be revoked or reduced by any subsequent action of the company; but where directors have power to pay interim dividends, their decision to do so is not a declaration of a dividend, and so can be rescinded or varied at any time before the dividend is paid.[19]

Unless the company's articles otherwise provide, dividends are payable to the persons who are registered in its register of members, or who are the bearers of its share warrants, on the date when the dividend is declared, or when it becomes payable if the articles dispense with a declaration.[20] To enable the administrative work involved in the payment of dividends to be done before the dividend is declared, the company will usually close its register of members some little while before the dividend becomes payable,[1] so that transfers of shares may not be registered during the interval, and the dividend will be paid to members registered on the date when the register is closed.[2]

Dividends are paid to members by means of dividend warrants, which are in effect cheques drawn by the company on its bank in favour of the member concerned. The dividend warrant must be accompanied by a statement in writing showing the amount of the dividend and the amount of the tax credit for advance corporation tax paid by the company in respect of the dividend,[3] which the shareholder is entitled to set off against his own liability for income tax on the

---

15 *Re Saltdean Estate Co Ltd* [1968] 3 All ER 829 at 832, [1968] 1 WLR 1844 at 1849.
16 Table A, art 102, so provides.
17 Table A, art 103, contains such a power.
18 *Scott v Scott* [1943] 1 All ER 582.
19 *Lagunas Nitrate Co v Schroeder & Co and Schmidt* (1901) 85 LT 22.
20 *Re Wakley, Wakley v Vachell* [1902] 2 Ch 205; *Godfrey Phillips Ltd v Investment Trust Corpn Ltd* [1953] Ch 449, [1953] 1 All ER 7.
 1 The Companies Act 1985, s 358, enables the register to be closed for not more than thirty days each year; the company must advertise its intention to close the register in a newspaper circulating in the district where it has its registered office (see p 335, ante).
 2 The inconvenience of share transfers not being registrable during the few days before declarations of dividends could be avoided by adopting the American practice of the company being empowered by its articles to resolve that dividends shall be paid to shareholders registered on a particular date.
 3 On paying a dividend the company must also pay to the revenue authorities as advance corporation tax an amount equal to the current basic rate of income tax calculated on the dividend paid plus the tax payable in respect of it (Income and Corporation Taxes Act 1988, s 14 (1) to (3) (44 Halsbury's Statutes (4th Edn) 41)). The amount so paid is credited against the company's liability to corporation tax on the whole of its profits for the same accounting period.

dividend plus the advance corporation tax paid in respect of it.[4] On receiving the dividend warrant the shareholder may either pay it into his own bank account for collection by his bank, or may endorse it and transfer it to another person in the same way as a cheque.

It is a simple matter for a company to prepare dividend warrants in respect of shares registered in its register of members. The warrant is simply made payable to the person who is registered as holder of those shares on the date when the dividend is declared or any earlier date on which the register of members is closed. When shares are represented by share warrants, however, it is impossible for the company to know who are the bearers of the warrants on the date the dividend is declared. Consequently, when share warrants are issued, sheets of dividend coupons are issued with them for dividends payable in future years,[5] and when the company is ready to declare a dividend, it publishes newspaper advertisements inviting bearers of share warrants to surrender the appropriate coupon with a note of their name and address so that the company may send them dividend warrants in return. The advertisement is inserted in a newspaper specified in the company's articles or in the terms of issue of the shares represented by share warrants.

When shares are temporarily represented by renounceable letters of allotment, it is usual to provide by the terms of issue that any dividend accruing while a letter of allotment is outstanding shall be paid to the person who surrenders it to the company when it ceases to be renounceable and has his name inserted in the register of members as the first registered holder of the shares. If the company is governed by Table A, provisions to this effect may be made in the terms of issue.[6]

It has been held that a dividend which has become payable by a company is a speciality debt,[7] and that a shareholder may therefore sue to recover it within twelve years after it becomes payable.[8] On the other hand, it has been held that the fact that the memorandum and articles of a company are deemed to have been executed under seal by all its members[9] does not result in amounts owing by the company to its members, whether in respect of dividend or capital, being speciality debts, and so the limitation period applicable to actions for their recovery is six years from the date when payment becomes due.[10] Sometimes articles empower directors to forfeit dividends which have not been claimed or collected within a certain period,[11] but if the company wishes to obtain a Stock Exchange listing for any of its shares or debentures, the power to forfeit must not be exercisable until twelve years after the dividend becomes payable.[12]

If a distribution of dividends is made when a company has no profits or insufficient profits available for distribution, or if a distribution is made without proper annual or interim accounts being prepared and, in the case of annual accounts, if these are not accompanied by the appropriate report by the company's

---

4 Income and Corporation Taxes Act 1988, s 231 (1) and s 234 (1) and (3).
5 The Companies Act 1985, s 188 (3) (as substituted by Companies Act 1989, s 130 (7) and Sch 17, para 6), authorises the issue of such dividend coupons. Dividend coupons are always numbered serially so as to ensure that not more than one coupon is presented for payment of a particular dividend, and they are accompanied by a renewal coupon entitling the bearer of the share warrant to a new set of dividend coupons when the original ones have been used up.
6 Table A, arts 2, 102 and 104.
7 *Re Artisans' Land and Mortgage Corpn* [1904] 1 Ch 796.
8 Limitation Act 1980, s 8 (1) (24 Halsbury's Statutes (4th Edn) 655).
9 Companies Act 1985, s 14 (1).
10 Limitation Act 1980, s 5; *Re Compania de Electricidad de la Provincia de Buenos Aires Ltd* [1980] Ch 146, [1978] 3 All ER 668.
11 Table A, art 108, empowers the board of directors to forfeit dividends which have remained unclaimed for twelve years.
12 The Stock Exchange: *Admission of Securities to Listing*, Section 9, Chapter 1, para 3.2.

auditor,[13] the distribution is unlawful, and the company may recover the amount wrongfully distributed either from its directors who were aware or who should have been aware of the irregularity,[14] or from members of the company who knew or had reasonable grounds for believing that the dividend was paid in contravention of the statutory rules governing the amount available for distribution.[15] If directors are compelled to restore the amount wrongfully distributed, they may seek an indemnity from members who received dividends knowing that they were paid irregularly to the extent of the amount paid to them individually,[16] and possibly from other members as well.[17]

Equality of dividends

A dividend must be declared at a uniform rate on all shares of the same class, and so it is not possible for the holders of a majority of the shares to pass a resolution that a larger dividend shall be paid on their shares than on the shares of other members. Furthermore, dividends must be paid proportionately to the nominal value of the shares, not their paid up value, so that if some of the shares of a class are fully paid and others partly paid, they all qualify for the same amount of dividend.[18] Nevertheless, a company's articles may provide that dividends shall be paid in proportion to the amounts paid up on its respective shares;[19] if they do so provide without stating on what date the paid up values of the shares is to be taken, presumably the dividend must be paid in proportion to their respective paid up values on the date it is declared or, if the dividend becomes payable without a declaration, on the date when it becomes due. Table A provides that dividends shall be paid proportionately to the amount paid up on shares from time to time during the period for which the dividend is paid, so that if shares have been paid up progressively by calls or instalments during a financial year, the dividend in respect of them is calculated on the average amount paid up on them throughout the year, and not on the amount paid up when the dividend is declared.[20] Table A also provides that shares may be issued on terms that they shall rank for dividend as from a particular date,[20] and if this is done the holders of the shares are entitled to be paid the same full dividend as other shareholders if it is declared on or after the specified date.

Capitalisations, bonus issues and dividends in specie

If a company has power by its articles simply to pay dividends, or if its articles are silent on the matter of dividends, it may distribute dividends only in the form of cash. It cannot declare a dividend of so much per share and resolve that the dividend shall be satisfied by the allotment of further shares[1] or debentures[2] of a corresponding nominal value credited as fully or partly paid.

It is common, however, for articles to contain a power for the company by

---

13 *Precision Dippings Ltd v Precision Dippings Marketing Ltd* [1986] Ch 447, [1985] BCLC 385, CA.
14 *Re Exchange Banking Co, Flitcroft's Case* (1882) 21 ChD 519; *Re Kingston Cotton Mill Co (No 2)* [1896] 1 Ch 331.
15 Companies Act 1985, s 277 (1).
16 *Moxham v Grant* [1899] 1 QB 480.
17 Ibid, [1900] 1 QB 88; *Re Mercantile Trading Co, Stringer's Case* (1869) 4 Ch App 475; contra *Re Denham & Co* (1883) 25 ChD 752.
18 *Oakbank Oil Co Ltd v Crum* (1882) 8 App Cas 65.
19 Companies Act 1985, s 119 (c).
20 Table A, art 104.
1 *Hoole v Great Western Rly Co* (1867) 3 Ch App 262.
2 *Wood v Odessa Waterworks Co* (1889) 42 ChD 636.

ordinary resolution in general meeting on the recommendation of its directors (a) to set free for distribution any part of its distributable profits or reserves and to apply them in paying up in whole or part the issue price of partly paid shares held by members, or in paying in full the nominal value of new shares, debentures or loan securities to be issued to members in the same manner and proportions as a cash dividend of the same amount would have been distributed; and (b) to capitalise any part of the amounts standing to the credit of the company's profit and loss accounts or to its reserves which are not available for distribution (ie capital reserves and unrealised profits) and to apply the amount so capitalised in paying in full the nominal value of new shares to be issued to members in the same manner and proportions as a cash dividend of the same amount would have been distributed.[3] Under such provisions in the articles it is possible for a company to capitalise the net amount of its realised and unrealised profits or the amount of its capital or revenue reserves in order to issue bonus shares,[4] but only the company's accumulated balance of realised profits may be used to issue bonus debentures or loan securities or to pay up any unpaid part of the issue price of shares which have already been issued.[5] New shares, debentures or loan securities issued in this way on a capitalisation of profits or reserves are known as bonus shares or debentures, but the name is misleading in that it implies that they are a gift from the company. If they were issued gratuitously, they would not be paid up at all, and in the case of bonus shares, the company could call on their holders to pay for them in cash. In fact bonus shares or debentures are not issued gratuitously, because their nominal value is paid in full or in part by the capitalised profits or reserves which could otherwise have been distributed to the shareholders as a cash dividend, or in the case of unrealised profits, retained as reserve. On the other hand, since no cash dividend is declared, bonus shares are not paid for in cash by each shareholder to whom they are alloted, because there is at no point of time any debt owing to him by the company which he can set off against his liability to pay for the shares. Consequently, an issue of bonus shares must be treated as an issue for a consideration other than cash, and an appropriate return and written contract for the allotment must be delivered to the Registrar of Companies.[6] To overcome the difficulty of having to have a written contract signed by all the shareholders to whom bonus shares are allotted, the articles invariably provide that the directors may authorise some person to enter into the contract on the shareholders' behalf.[7]

An article authorising a capitalisation or bonus issue usually provides that the bonus shares, debentures or loan securities shall be issued to the shareholders in the same proportions as the capitalised profits or reserves could have been distributed as a dividend of the same amount paid in cash.[8] This often results in shareholders being entitled to fractions of bonus shares or debentures, but of course, fractions of shares or debentures cannot be issued.[9] To meet this difficulty, the articles usually provide that the directors may issue fractional certificates which carry in proportion to their respective face values the same financial rights as shares or debentures;[9]

3 See Table A, art 110 (a) and (b), which authorise the issue of bonus shares, but not bonus debentures or loan securities.
4 Companies Act 1985, s 263 (2) (a). Because an issue of bonus shares is not a distribution for the purposes of the Act, it is not subject to the restrictions imposed by ss 264 and 265 (see p 421, ante). Existing companies whose articles authorised the issue of bonus shares are expressly empowered to apply unrealised profits in paying up the nominal value of bonus shares, whenever issued (Companies Act 1985, s 278).
5 Companies Act 1985, s 263 (4).
6 Companies Act 1985, s 88 (2) (see p 309, ante).
7 See Table A, art 110 (d).
8 See Table A, art 110 (b).
9 See Table A, art 110 (c).

such certificates are transferable, but in the case of a bonus issue of shares, do not entitle transferees to membership of the company. If several fractional certificates with a total face value equal to the nominal value of one or more of the company's shares or debentures are surrendered to it, the articles usually oblige the company to issue the appropriate number of shares or debentures in place of them. Articles also usually empower the directors to deal with fractional rights by paying a cash dividend in lieu of them, or by grouping them into whole units of shares or debentures and issuing such shares or debentures to one or more of the shareholders entitled to participate in the bonus distribution in return for a cash price fixed by the directors, the cash so received then being distributed among the other shareholders who are entitled to participate.[9]

Articles authorising capitalisation issues usually leave the company free to determine what rights shall be conferred by bonus shares, debentures or loan securities. In that event the bonus shares may either carry the same rights as shares already issued, or may be of an entirely new class, in which case the provisions of the articles governing the creation of a new class of shares[10] and the provisions of the Companies Act 1985 governing any consequential alteration of any rights attached to an existing class of shares must be adhered to.[11] There is in general no reason why the holders of one class of shares should not be allotted bonus shares of another class which carry superior rights in respect of dividends or capital, and of itself this does not amount to an alteration of the rights of existing holders of shares of the other class[11]. Consequently, if a company has issued preference and ordinary shares, a bonus issue to the ordinary shareholders may be made in the form of preference shares.[11]

The mechanics of issuing bonus shares, debentures or loan securities are similar to those of issuing shares, debentures or loan securities subscribed for in cash. After the necessary resolution for the capitalisation of profits or reserves has been passed, certificates in respect of the bonus shares, debentures or loan securities are issued to the members entitled to them, and appropriate entries are made in the company's register of members or debenture holders. Alternatively, if the bonus shares are to be renounceable for a period, letters of allotment or renounceable certificates are issued in the first instance. Where the articles of association of private companies place restrictions on the free transferability of their shares,[12] it would seem that they may not issue renounceable letters of allotment or renounceable certificates in respect of bonus shares, but there is nothing to prevent them from issuing such documents in respect of bonus debentures or loan securities.

The practical advantages of bonus issues are:

(a) They enable the company to retain money required for its business which it would otherwise have to raise by issuing new shares, debentures or loan securities on the market or by borrowing;

(b) The market value of the company's shares is reduced to a figure nearer their nominal value by a bonus issue, and this makes them more saleable. But the issue increases the total market value of a shareholder's holding only marginally; he merely has more shares of a correspondingly lower value each;[13]

---

10 See, for example, Table A, art 2.

11 *White v Bristol Aeroplane Co* [1953] Ch 65, [1953] 1 All ER 40; *Re John Smith's Tadcaster Brewery Co* [1953] Ch 308, [1953] 1 All ER 518.

12 See p 753, post.

13 If a company has an issued capital of £100,000 in ordinary shares of £1 each, and reserves of £50,000, and the market value of its shares is £1·50, a capitalisation of the reserves on the basis of one bonus share for each two shares already held will reduce the market value of each share to £1 or a few pence more. Each shareholder will now have three shares worth about £1 each instead of two shares worth £1·50 each. These observations are true, of course, only if the bonus shares are ordinary shares.

(c) Formerly bonus shares were not treated as income in the hands of the recipient shareholder, and he did not have to pay income tax on their value.[14] This was so even if the resolution to capitalise profits gave shareholders an option to take a cash dividend instead.[15] But income tax at the higher (but not the basic) rates is now payable if a company issues redeemable preference shares or debentures as a bonus issue,[16] whether on a capitalisation of profits or reserves or otherwise, but not to the extent that the nominal value of the new shares is provided out of share premium account.[17] Moreover, when the shares or debentures are redeemed, the company is treated as though it were paying a cash dividend equal to the amount paid on redemption (except any amount paid up on the securities out of share premium account), and so the company pays advance corporation tax on the redemption payment, and it is treated as part of the income of the holders of the bonus securities for income tax, but the tax which has already been paid on the issue of the bonus shares is allowed as a credit against the income tax payable on redemption.[18]

Income tax is not payable in respect of a bonus issue of irredeemable shares, but if a company issues irredeemable bonus shares and within the following ten years reduces its capital by repayment of the whole or part of the amount paid up on shares of the same class, it is treated as primarily repaying the capital paid up on the bonus shares, and has to pay advance corporation tax on the amount repaid, which is treated as a distribution and is subject to income tax in the recipient's hands.[19] Similarly, if this order of operation is reversed, and a reduction of capital by repayment is followed within ten years by an issue of irredeemable bonus shares, the amount credited as paid up on them is deemed to be a distribution insofar as it does not exceed the amount of the reduction, and it is taxable accordingly.[20]

If a company gives its members the option of taking an issue of bonus shares or a dividend in cash, a member who chooses the cash dividend has always been liable for income tax on it,[1] but since 1975 a member who chooses to take the bonus shares instead also suffers taxation. The company does not have to pay advance corporation tax on the sum which the member could have taken in cash instead of taking the bonus shares, but the member is treated, for the purpose of his income tax liability, as having received that sum plus tax on it at the basic income tax rate, and he is liable to pay tax on it at the higher rate applicable to him by reason of the total amount of his taxable income, but not tax at the basic rate.[2]

In addition to authorising the capitalisation of profits and the issue of bonus shares, it is also common for articles to authorise a company to distribute dividends

---

14 *IRC v Blott* [1921] 2 AC 171; *IRC v Fisher's Executors* [1926] AC 395.
15 *IRC v Wright* [1927] 1 KB 333.
16 Income and Corporation Taxes Act 1988, s 20 (1) and s 233 (1) (44 Halsbury's Statutes (4th Edn) 61 and 283).
17 Ibid, s 254 (5).
18 Ibid, s 233 (2).
19 Ibid, s 211 (1) and (2). The shareholder is entitled to a tax credit equal to the amount of advance corporation tax paid by the company (see footnote 3 on p 432, ante).
20 Ibid, s 210 (1) and (3).
 1 *IRC v Wright* [1927] 1 KB 333.
 2 Income and Corporation Taxes Act 1988, s 230, s 249 (4) and s 251 (2). If the market value of the shares is substantially greater or less than the alternative cash dividend, the market value of the shares is taken instead of the dividend as the amount on which tax is payable.

in the form of specific assets of the company, such as shares, debentures or loan securities which the company holds in other concerns.[3] Dividends in the form of assets are distributions for statutory purposes in the same way as cash dividends,[4] and may therefore be distributed only if their value does not exceed the accumulated balance of the company's realised profits.[5] Nevertheless, if the assets distributed in specie are shown in the company's accounts at their current value for the purpose of the distribution, and that amount exceeds the value at which they are shown as assets of the company in its latest balance sheet immediately before the distribution (eg shares in another company worth £3 each and treated as a distribution of that amount, but shown in the company's balance sheet previously at their acquisition cost of £1 each), the difference may be treated as a realised profit of the company,[6] with the consequence that the company may treat its total realised profits as diminished by the distribution only to the extent of the balance sheet value of the distributed assets. The power to distribute dividends in specie can obviously only be made use of in practice when the assets to be distributed are investments, but there is little point in distributing them if the company can sell them for cash and thus put itself in funds to pay a cash dividend.[7] There is, moreover, no tax advantage to be gained by distributing a dividend in specie instead of in cash, for the company has to pay advance corporation tax on the distribution, and the recipient is liable for income tax on the value of the investments or other assets distributed.[8] Furthermore, if a dividend in specie takes the form of redeemable bonus shares or debentures issued to the company by another company, income tax is payable by the members of the first company to whom the shares are transferred, both when they are transferred and when they are redeemed, in the same way as though they were redeemable bonus securities issued by the first company itself.[9]

GUARANTEES OF MINIMUM DIVIDENDS

When a vendor sells a business to a company he may assist it to raise its initial share capital out of which it pays the purchase price by guaranteeing that a certain minimum dividend will be paid on its shares during a certain period, so that if the company's profits are insufficient to pay the minimum dividend, the difference will be paid by the vendor himself. Such a guarantee is usually contained in the agreement for the sale of the business made between the vendor and the company, and the contractual right to enforce it belongs to the company. But the company will hold its contractual right as a trustee for its shareholders, even though no trusteeship is expressed, and when the company is wound up money payable under the guarantee will be paid to the shareholders, and will not be available to satisfy

3 See Table A, art 105.
4 Companies Act 1985, s 263 (2).
5 Ibid, s 263 (1) and (3).
6 Ibid, s 276.
7 There is no saving on tax on capital gains by the company distributing assets in specie to its shareholders instead of selling them, realising any capital gain on the assets in cash and distributing the whole of the proceeds to its shareholders. The distribution of assets in specie is deemed to be a disposal of them for a consideration equal to their market value at the time of the distribution (Capital Gains Tax Act 1979, s 19 (1) and s 29A (1)) (42 Halsbury's Statutes (4th Edn) 637, 646); consequently, the company is deemed to realise a capital gain equal to the difference between the cost of acquisition of the assets and that market value.
8 Income and Corporation Taxes Act 1988, s 14 (1) and s 209 (2) (b).
9 Ibid, s 20 and s 233 (1) and (2) (see p 437, ante).

the company's debts.[10] Guarantees of minimum dividends may also be given by individuals or other companies (eg the holding or parent company of a group) in order to induce investors to subscribe for or purchase the shares of a company which is already established.

Although guarantees of minimum dividends are legitimate, they may not be used as a device to enable a company to pay dividends out of its capital. If there is evidence that the price of a business or property purchased by a company and paid for out of its capital has been artificially increased in order to put the vendor in funds to meet his prospective liability under a guarantee of minimum dividends which he had given, the part of the purchase price which is excessive is treated as money which still belongs to the company, and the vendor may be ordered to repay it.[11] But the burden of proving that such an artificial increase has been made in the purchase price rests on the person who makes the allegation, and the court will not readily infer that it has, especially when the purchase price approximates to the market value of the business or property.[12]

A guarantor of a minimum dividend who has had to honour his guarantee is subrogated to the rights of the shareholders to whom he has made payments, and may obtain an indemnity from the company to the extent that the shareholders' own claims against it are reduced.[13] Thus, a guarantor of a cumulative preference dividend may claim an indemnity out of the future profits of the company available for dividend, for if he had not honoured his guarantee, the preference dividend to be paid out of future profits would be correspondingly larger, and the residue of profits available to pay an ordinary share dividend correspondingly smaller.[14] On the other hand, if the guaranteed preference dividend were non-cumulative, the guarantor would have no right to an indemnity out of future profits, because if the guarantee had not been honoured, the preference shareholders would have no claim against future profits for their unpaid dividend. The rights of a guarantor of a minimum ordinary share dividend are similar to those of a guarantor of a cumulative preference dividend. When the guaranteed ordinary share dividend for any year financial has been paid, the surplus profits must be applied in indemnifying the guarantor for payments made by him in the past before any dividend in excess of the rate guaranteed for the current year is paid on the ordinary shares. In no case, however, is it permissible for a company to indemnify a guarantor unless it has earned sufficient profits to enable it to do so; if it were to indemnify the guarantor despite an insufficiency of profits, the indemnity would be met out of the company's capital, and it would thus indirectly be using its capital to pay dividends.[15]

The whole or any part of a minimum dividend paid by a guarantor is income in the hands of the recipient for tax purposes,[16] and the guarantor must deduct income tax at the current basic rate when making the payment and account for it to the Revenue.[17] Shareholders who receive payments in respect of guaranteed dividends

---

10 *Re South Llanharran Colliery Co, ex p Jegon* (1879) 12 ChD 503; *Richardson v English Crown Spelter Co* [1885] WN 31; *Re Menell et Cie* [1915] 1 Ch 759; contra *Re Stuart's Trusts* (1876) 4 ChD 213.

11 *Re Menell et Cie Ltd* [1915] 1 Ch 759.

12 *Re South Llanharran Colliery Co, ex p Jegon* (1879) 12 ChD 503.

13 *Re Walters' Deed of Guarantee* [1933] Ch 321, [1933] All ER Rep 430.

14 If a company is able to pay a dividend of only 5 per cent on its 15 per cent cumulative preference shares in one year, and the deficiency is paid by the guarantor, the profits of the following year will be applied, first in paying the 15 per cent preference dividend for that year, secondly in indemnifying the guarantor for the 10 per cent dividend he paid the previous year, and finally in paying an ordinary share dividend.

15 *Re Walters' Deed of Guarantee*, supra.

16 *IRC v Black* [1940] 4 All ER 445.

17 Income and Corporation Taxes Act 1988, s 348 (1) and s 349 (1) (44 Halsbury's Statutes (4th Edn) 419 and 422).

are credited with the income tax deducted by the guarantor when calculating their individual income tax liability for the year in which the payment is made,[18] but since it is the guarantor and not the company which has made the payment, the company cannot treat the tax deducted as though it were advance corporation tax paid in respect of the dividend, and so cannot claim to credit it against its own liability for corporation tax.

18 Ibid, s 348 (1).

CHAPTER 12

Loan and debt securities

THE POWER OF A COMPANY TO GIVE SECURITY FOR ITS DEBTS

The power of a company to borrow has been dealt with in Chapter 6. In this chapter the company's power to give security for loans contracted by it and for its other debts, and the rights and interests which may be conferred on its secured creditors will be considered.

Property over which security may be given

It is normal for the power of a company to mortgage or charge its assets to be set out in the objects clause of its memorandum of association, but in the absence of an express power, a trading company (ie one formed with a view to making a profit) has an implied power to give security over any of its property for debts properly contracted by it.[1]

There is, however, one resource which no company has an implied power to mortgage or charge, namely, its uncalled capital, and an express power to charge it must be given by the company's memorandum if a valid mortgage or charge of it is to be created. In an early case it was held that a power in the company's memorandum to charge its 'funds and property' did not enable it to mortgage its uncalled capital, which ex hypothesi was not its property when the mortgage was created, but was merely money which would become the company's property in the future when it made calls on its shareholders.[2] Despite the invention of the floating charge, by which a company's future assets may be mortgaged or charged since that case was decided, this is still the law, but the courts have shown greater liberality in more recent cases in construing the company's memorandum as giving it the requisite express power to charge uncalled capital. Thus a company has been held to have power to mortgage or charge its uncalled capital when its memorandum authorised it to borrow on the security of a 'mortgage or charge of any property of the company . . . or *any other security* of the company';[3] likewise when the company had power 'to receive money on loan . . . and upon *any security* of the company, or upon the security of any property of the company';[4] and again when the company's memorandum authorised the issue of 'securities founded or based upon all or any of the real and personal assets, or on the credit of the company', and the articles added that the directors might mortgage uncalled capital.[5] On the other hand, a company was held not to have mortgaged its

---

1 *Re Patent File Co, ex p Birmingham Banking Co* (1870) 6 Ch App 83; *Re International Life Assurance Society, Gibbs and West's Case* (1870) LR 10 Eq 312; *General Auction Estate and Monetary Co v Smith* [1891] 3 Ch 432.
2 *Re British Provident Life and Fire Assurance Society, Stanley's Case* (1864) 4 De GJ & Sm 407; contra *Re Colonial and General Gas Co Ltd, Lishman's Claim* (1870) 23 LT 759.
3 *Re Phoenix Bessemer Steel Co* (1875) 44 LJ Ch 683.
4 *Newton v Anglo-Australian Investment Co's Debenture-holders* [1895] AC 244.
5 *Re Pyle Works (No. 2)* [1891] 1 Ch 173.

uncalled capital when the mortgage executed by it merely charged its 'real and personal estate',[6] or its 'undertaking and property, both present and future'.[7] This special treatment of mortgages and charges over uncalled capital is logically unjustifiable. It does not extend to any other debts which may become owing to the company after the creation of the charge, nor even to calls which have been made but not paid at the date of the mortgage,[8] and it would appear not to apply to unpaid instalments of the issue price of shares payable in accordance with their terms of issue after the date on which the charge over them is created.

Forms of securities: debentures, debenture stock, loan stock and loan notes

Companies have always been able to create legal and equitable mortgages and charges over their property in the same form and with the same effect as mortgages and charges created by individuals. The distinctive form of security which may be created by companies, however, is the debenture and its derivatives, namely, debenture stock, loan stock and loan notes.

Debentures first appeared during the 1860s in a form closely resembling the bonds which companies had previously issued in order to raise loans.[9] Their principal difference from bonds was that, in addition to containing a covenant by the company to repay the loan, they charged the company's property or assets or its whole assets and undertaking with repayment; a general charge of this character created a security which later became identified as a floating charge.[10] Gradually the form of debentures changed from that of the bond with greater emphasis on the security given to debenture holders, but like bonds, debentures were still arranged in two parts. The main part contained the company's covenant for payment of principal and interest on the loan and a legal mortgage of the company's fixed assets and a floating charge over its other assets; the other part comprised the endorsed conditions which dealt with the detailed terms of the loan, and conferred remedies on the lender for its recovery out of the security created by the debenture or otherwise.[11]

By the end of the last century public companies found that their issues of debentures were being subscribed for by so great a number of investors that it was inconvenient to employ the form of debenture currently in use. If the company mortgaged its assets to a great number of persons to secure a single collective loan contributed by them in varying amounts, the company gave each of them a security over its assets for the amount contributed by them respectively plus interest, and such securities were uniform and ranked equally as between the individual lenders. This meant that if the company wished to modify the security in the slightest degree or to depart from the terms of its covenants with the individual lenders, it could do so only with the consent of all of them, and this was also necessary if the company wished to dispose of any of its assets which were specifically mortgaged or charged to secure the collective loan. The problem was solved by the introduction of the trust deed by which trustees were appointed to represent the interests of the

---

6 *Re Colonial Trusts Corpn, ex p Bradshaw* (1879) 15 ChD 465.
7 *Re Streatham and General Estates Co* [1897] 1 Ch 15.
8 *Re International Life Assurance Society, Gibbs and West's Case* (1870) LR 10 Eq 312.
9 For examples of early forms of debentures, see *Re Hercules Insurance Co, Brunton's Claim* (1874) LR 19 Eq 302 at 303, and *Re Colonial Trusts Corpn, ex p Bradshaw* (1879) 15 ChD 465 at 466.
10 *Re Panama, New Zealand, and Australian Royal Mail Co* (1870) 5 Ch App 318.
11 For examples, see 6 *Encyclopaedia of Forms and Precedents* (4th Edn) 1187, and *Palmer's Company Precedents* (16th Edn) Vol 3, p 229.

debenture holders. A legal mortgage of the company's fixed assets and a floating charge over its other assets and its undertaking were created by the company in favour of the trustees, and they were empowered to consent on the debenture holders' behalf to minor departures by the company from the terms of the debentures and to minor variations in the security for the debenture debt, and were authorised to call meetings of debenture holders to decide whether the trustees should enforce the security given by the trust deed when a case arose for doing so, or whether the debenture holders should agree to a modification of their rights or their securities when the company was unable to meet its obligations in full. Debentures in the old form were still issued to the debenture holders, but they were always expressed to be subject to the provisions of the trust deed, and although they contained a covenant by the company with the holder to repay the amount of his contribution to the collective loan and interest thereon, they did not vest any security for that amount in the debenture holder individually and left him to rely on the security given to the trustees by the trust deed. By virtue of the covenant to pay principal and interest made with the individual debenture holder, however, he was a creditor of the company, even if the debentures were payable to bearer, and consequently he could exercise all the legal remedies available to a creditor to recover what was individually owed to him.[12]

In the early years of the present century the trust deed underwent a change and assumed its present form. In a modern trust deed the company covenants with the trustees to repay the total amount of the loan secured by an issue of debentures to the subscribers in proportion to their individual subscriptions. They, in turn, are provided with debenture stock certificates issued by the company,[13] which evidence their respective rights to a proportionate share of the total amount of the loan equal to the amount they have individually subscribed, but there is no covenant by the company with them to repay the amounts which they have advanced. Debenture stockholders, unlike debenture holders, are not creditors of the company.[14] The trustees are the creditors of the company for the whole amount of the loan plus interest and the cost of performing their functions which the company agrees to defray, and the debenture stockholders are equitable beneficiaries of the trust on which they hold that entitlement. Consequently, a debenture stockholder's remedies are primarily against the trustees, but by suing them to compel them to enforce their contractual rights against the company and to realise the security vested in them, a debenture stockholder can indirectly enforce the same remedies against the company as a debenture holder can enforce directly.[15] Despite this difference between debentures and debenture stock, however, the law relating to them is basically the same.

A later development in large scale issues of loan securities by leading public companies which have unimpeachable records of financial soundness and stability has been the diminution of the security given by the trust deed securing the issue. Legal mortgages are now rarely given over land or fixed assets, except by property investment companies, and sometimes there is not even a floating charge over the generality of the company's assets and its undertaking. If no security at all is given and the debentures or units of debenture stock are to be dealt in on the Stock Exchange, they must be denominated 'unsecured',[16] and they are commonly known

---

12 *Re Olathe Silver Mining Co* (1884) 27 ChD 278.
13 For examples of trust deeds and debenture stock certificates, see 6 *Encyclopaedia of Forms and Precedents* (4th Edn) pp 1221 and 1240, and *Palmer's Company Precedents* (16th Edn) Vol 3, pp 227 and 273.
14 *Re Dunderland Iron Ore Co Ltd* [1909] 1 Ch 446.
15 *Mortgage Insurance Corpn Ltd v Canadian Agricultural, Coal and Colonization Co Ltd* [1901] 2 Ch 377.
16 Stock Exchange: *Admission of Securities to Listing*, Section 9, Chapter 2, para 6.1.

as unsecured loan stock or, if the loan is a short or medium-term one for a period of up to ten years, unsecured loan notes. It is usual for trust deeds covering such stock or notes to contain a 'negative pledge' clause, by which the company undertakes not to mortgage or charge its property or assets, or not to secure its indebtedness to its creditors for more than a specified total sum. This clause ensures that if the company becomes insolvent and has adhered to its undertaking, the loan stockholders or noteholders will not suffer by the company's assets being consumed in paying secured creditors. The clause does not give the loan stockholders or noteholders any priority over the company's other unsecured creditors, however, and so if the company does become insolvent, loan stockholders or noteholders and other unsecured creditors alike will be paid an equal fraction of their debts. For this reason it is the usual practice for the trust deed also to limit the amount of indebtedness which the company may incur to its trade creditors or by unsecured borrowing, and to require it to discharge promptly any unsecured indebtedness which would rank as preferential in its liquidation.[17]

Bank lending and security

During the last century and the first half of the present century, large and medium-sized companies raised long-term loans predominantly by offering series of debentures, debenture stock or loan stock to the public for subscription or for purchase from an intermediary who had agreed to subscribe for the whole of the series with a view to offering it for sale. Occasionally, issues of such loan securities were placed on the Stock Exchange, or alternatively by private negotiation with several individuals or institutions, who were often represented by one of their number acting as an agent for them all. Bank borrowing by companies was at that time confined to raising short-term loans or using overdraft facilities to finance current trading, but not to meet the cost of large scale capital spending or the cost of acquiring other businesses.

During the last 25 years the prevailing high interest rates have made long-term borrowing at fixed interest rates unattractive to companies, and issues of debenture or loan stock under prospectuses or by placings on the Stock Exchange have been rare. At the same time, the commercial banks and their capital finance subsidiaries have extended both the volume and the duration of the loans which they have made to large and medium-sized companies, and even to small companies which are soundly managed and have good business records or prospects. Such loans have usually been made for between five and 15 years, and interest has usually been charged at a variable rate for successive quarterly or half-yearly periods, and has been fixed at an agreed number of percentage points above the rates at which the lending banks have currently been able to borrow on the money market. The security taken by lending banks has usually been a combination of fixed mortgages or charges over the borrowing company's land, buildings and other fixed assets and a floating charge over its remaining assets, but sometimes the bank loan has been unsecured or only partly secured. The documentation used in connection with long and medium-term bank loans is different from that formerly employed when debentures or debenture or loan stock were issued in series to the public. The terms of the loan (ie amount, fees chargeable by the bank, arrangements for the borrowing company to draw on the loan facility, interest rates, dates for payment of interest and repayments of principal and events of default) are set out in detail in a loan agreement executed by the company and the bank, and the security for

17 Preferential debts which must be paid in priority to a company's other unsecured debts are listed exhaustively in the Insolvency Act 1986, s 175 (1) and s 386 (1) and Sch 6.

the loan is created in favour of the bank or its nominated subsidiary either by the loan agreement or by one or more separate instruments. It is rare for a trust deed to be executed, except where the loan is a very large one made collectively by a syndicate of banks, and often in that situation, instead of a trust deed, a single loan and security agreement is entered into by the company and the leading bank which arranged for participations in the loan facility to be taken by the other banks.

The vast increase in the provision of long and medium-term loans for companies by the commercial banks and their subsidiaries in recent years has had a substantial influence on the forms of security taken in connection with such loans to companies and on the style, contents and nomenclature of the relevant documentation. In particular, the terms 'loan' and 'security agreements' are now widely used in place of the terms 'secured' and 'unsecured debentures', and in order to embrace the whole range of loan and debt securities with which this chapter is concerned, it has become usual to refer to them simply as loan securities, or in a more expanded form, as debentures, debenture stock, loan stock and notes and other loan securities. Despite this broad range of variant terms, the subject of this chapter is a single one, namely, the nature and distinctive features of securities given by companies for loans and other indebtedness.

Legal definition of debentures

From the foregoing it is apparent that the commercial meaning of the term debenture and related terms covers many different forms of investment. The legal definition of a debenture is even wider. In one case, Chitty J said:[18]

'In my opinion a debenture means a document which either creates a debt or acknowledges it, and any document which fulfils either of these conditions is a "debenture". I cannot find any precise legal definition of the term, it is not either in law or commerce a strictly technical term, or what is called a term of art.'

Chitty J was concerned in that case with the meaning of 'debenture' in the Bills of Sale Act 1882. The definition section of the Companies Act 1985[19] is expressed in equally wide terms:

'"debenture" includes debenture stock, bonds and other securities of a company whether constituting a charge on the assets of the company or not.'

Thus, the following widely different kinds of documents have been held to be debentures: a legal mortgage of freehold and leasehold land;[20] a series of income bonds by which a loan to the company was repayable only out of its profits;[1] a note by which the company undertook to repay a loan but gave no security;[2] and a receipt or a certificate for a deposit made with a company (other than a bank) when the deposit was repayable at a fixed period after it was made.[3]

Fortunately, it is not necessary to have a precise legal definition of debentures in order to understand the law relating to them. The law is less concerned with whether a transaction creates a debenture than with the security given to the lender by it (if any). The question which usually has to be answered is not whether a document is a debenture, but whether it creates a mortgage, charge or other

18 *Levy v Abercorris Slate and Slab Co* (1887) 37 ChD 260 at 264.
19 Companies Act 1985, s 744.
20 *Knightsbridge Estates Trust Ltd v Byrne* [1940] AC 613, [1940] 2 All ER 401.
1 *Lemon v Austin Friars Investment Trust Ltd* [1926] Ch 1.
2 *British India Steam Navigation Co v IRC* (1881) 7 QBD 165.
3 *United Dominions Trust Ltd v Kirkwood* [1966] 2 QB 431 at 468, [1966] 1 All ER 968 at 988, per Diplock LJ.

security, and if so whether the security is a specific or floating charge over the company's property, and to what assets of the company does it attach?

SPECIFIC AND FLOATING CHARGES

Definition

A specific charge attaches to a particular piece of property which is identified when the charge is created, and the identity of the property does not change (though it may be extended) during the subsistence of the charge. Examples are the common form legal and equitable mortgages of land owned by the company when the mortgage is created. It is not necessary that the property should exist when the charge is created or that the company should then own it, however, provided that the property or the class of assets to which it belongs is sufficiently defined in the instrument creating the charge that there can be no doubt whether the property is caught by the charge when it does come into existence or when the company does acquire it.[4] Thus, a mortgage of a building, a ship or an aircraft or a piece of machinery which has not yet been constructed is a specific mortgage, as is a charge given over the debts owed to the company at the time when the charge is created or at any subsequent time.[5]

A floating charge, on the other hand, is an equitable charge on property which is constantly changing, for example, the stock in trade from time to time of a company's business or the book or trading debts from time to time owing to a company by its customers, or the whole assets and undertaking for the time being of a company. When an item is sold out of the stock in trade or the company's undertaking, or when a book debt is paid to the company by a customer and the money paid is mixed with the company's other funds, the charge ceases to attach to it, and so the buyer cannot be called on to pay the mortgage debt secured by the charge and the chargee cannot trace the proceeds of sale or the money paid to discharge the book debt into the company's cash resources with which they have been mixed. When a new item is added to the company's stock in trade or business undertaking, or if a further book debt becomes owing to the company, the charge automatically extends to it without any supplemental instrument of charge being executed, but the charge will, of course, continue to attach only so long as the company retains the item or, in the case of a book debt, until it is paid to or disposed of by the company. A floating charge over the whole of a company's assets and undertaking extends to all its assets from time to time, whatever form they may take, and so if stock in trade is sold or book debts are paid, the floating charge automatically shifts to the proceeds and any assets which are acquired with them.

A floating charge would be valueless if the lender or creditor secured by it could not convert it into a specific charge. In certain circumstances he can do this; the process is called 'crystallisation'. When a floating charge crystallises it attaches specifically to all the items of the class of assets charged which the company owns at the date of crystallisation or which it acquires thereafter.[6] Thenceforth the company can only sell or dispose of those assets subject to the charge.

---

4 *Tailby v Official Receiver* (1888) 13 App Cas 523 at 533, per Lord Watson; *Re Yorkshire Woolcombers Association Ltd* [1903] 2 Ch 284 at 294 per Vaughan Williams LJ; affd sub nom *Illingworth v Houldsworth* [1904] AC 355.
5 *Siebe Gorman & Co Ltd v Barclays Bank Ltd* [1979] 2 Lloyd's Rep 142.
6 *N W Robbie & Co Ltd v Witney Warehouse Co Ltd* [1963] 3 All ER 613, [1963] 1 WLR 1324; *Business Computers Ltd v Anglo-African Leasing Ltd* [1977] 2 All ER 741, [1977] 1 WLR 578.

Judicial exposition of the nature of floating charges has usually been couched in the language of metaphor. An example is the description given by Lord Macnaghten:[7]

'A specific charge, I think, is one that without more fastens on ascertained and definite property or property capable of being ascertained and defined; a floating charge, on the other hand, is ambulatory and shifting in its nature, hovering over and so to speak floating with the property which it is intended to affect, until some event occurs or some act is done which causes it to settle and fasten on the subject of the charge within its reach and grasp.'

The description given by Buckley LJ in another case is less figurative:[8]

'A floating security is not a future security; it is a present security, which presently affects all the assets of the company expressed to be included in it. On the other hand, it is not a specific security; the holder cannot affirm that the assets are specifically mortgaged to him. The assets are mortgaged in such a way that the mortgagor can deal with them without the concurrence of the mortgagee. A floating security is not a specific mortgage of the assets, plus a licence to the mortgagor to dispose of them in the course of his business, but is a floating mortgage applying to every item comprised in the security, but not specifically affecting any item until some event occurs or some act on the part of the mortgagee is done which causes it to crystallise into a fixed security.'

A floating charge may crystallise in any of the following three ways:

(1) It will crystallise in the first place if an event occurs upon which, by the terms of the instrument creating the charge, the lender's or creditor's security is to attach specifically to the company's assets generally (ie when the floating charge is given over the company's whole assets and undertaking) or over the company's assets of the class comprised in the charge. Such an event may be one over which the lender or creditor has no control (such as the company's assets falling below a certain amount, or its debts exceeding a certain amount, or the ratio of the company's current debts to current assets exceeding a specified figure, or the company's secured or judgment creditors taking steps to realise any of the company's assets), or it may be an event occurring on the lender or creditor taking action to cause his floating charge to crystallise (eg by giving notice to the company converting it into a fixed charge under a power to do so conferred on him by the instrument creating the charge).[9] Usually such a power to convert a floating charge into a fixed charge is given to the lender or creditor only if specified adverse events occur, such as those mentioned above, but there is no reason why the power should not be unconditional, so that the lender or creditor may convert the floating charge into a fixed charge attaching to the company's assets specifically at the time when the power is exercised. The occurrence of the relevant event causes crystallisation without the lender or creditor or the court appointing a receiver or taking any other steps to realise the security.[10] However, if the instrument creating the charge merely empowers the lender or creditor to appoint a receiver if the relevant event occurs, the floating charge does not crystallise until a receiver is appointed.[11]

7 *Illingworth v Houldsworth* [1904] AC 355 at 358.
8 *Evans v Rival Granite Quarries Ltd* [1910] 2 KB 979 at 999.
9 *Re Woodroffes (Musical Instruments) Ltd* [1986] Ch 366, [1985] 2 All ER 908; *Re Brightlife Ltd* [1987] Ch 200, [1986] 3 All ER 673, [1986] BCLC 418; *Re Permanent Houses (Holdings) Ltd* [1988] BCLC 563, 5 BCC 151.
10 *Re Horne and Hellard* (1885) 29 ChD 736; *Davey & Co v Williamson & Sons Ltd* [1898] 2 QB 194, as explained by Buckley LJ, in *Evans v Rival Granite Quarries Ltd* [1910] 2 KB 979 at 1000; *Re Woodroffes (Musical Instruments) Ltd*, supra; *Re Brightlife Ltd*, supra; *Re Manurewa Transport Ltd* [1971] NZLR 909; contra *R v Churchill Consolidated Copper Corpn* [1978] 5 WWR 652.
11 *Governments Stock and Other Securities Investment Co v Manila Rly Co* [1897] AC 81.

(2) A floating charge also crystallises if a receiver is appointed by the court, or by the lender or creditor under a power contained in the instrument creating the floating charge.[12] If the court appoints the receiver and requires him to give security for his proper conduct before he may act, his appointment is not effective until he has done so, and the floating charge does not crystallise until then;[13] but if the court appoints a receiver with liberty to act immediately and orders him to give security by a certain date, the appointment takes effect forthwith and the floating charge crystallises on the date of the appointment, even though the receiver fails to give security within the time limit.[14]

(3) A floating charge crystallises finally upon the commencement of the company's winding up.[15] This ensures that the lender or creditor secured by the floating charge is paid out of his security before the company's unsecured creditors, other than preferential creditors.[16]

It has been suggested[17] that a floating charge crystallises automatically if the company which created it ceases to carry on business. This suggestion is supported by only two of the ten decisions which are cited in support of it, and in neither of those decisions was the matter material to resolve the questions there in issue[18]. The suggestion was nevertheless adopted by Nourse J in a more recent case,[19] although again the decision in that case would have been the same even if the court had not adopted it. It is submitted that in the absence of clear judicial authority for the suggestion, it cannot be safely assumed that a company ceasing to carry on business does anything more than entitle the lender or creditor secured by a floating charge to apply to the court to appoint a receiver, and it will then be the appointment of the receiver which causes the floating charge to crystallise.

Where several events occur, each of which would cause a floating charge to crystallise, it is the occurrence of the first of those events which causes crystallisation, and the occurrence of the later events makes no change, because the now crystallised floating charge already attaches specifically to the assets of the company of the class charged, or its assets generally if the floating charge was given over its whole assets and undertaking, including assets acquired after the date of crystallisation.[20]

Creation of specific and floating charges

The creation of a specific mortgage or charge over an asset or property of a company requires no particular form of words, beyond observance of the rule that a legal mortgage of land must be effected by demise or sub-demise and a legal mortgage of movables must be by assignment.[1] What is essential, however, is that the mortgage or charge must identify the asset or property which is comprised in the security, and that asset must not change or be susceptible to disposal by the

---

12 *Re Panama, New Zealand and Australian Royal Mail Co* (1870) 5 Ch App 318; *Re Florence Land and Public Works Co, ex p Moor* (1878) 10 ChD 530.
13 *Re Roundwood Colliery* [1897] 1 Ch 373.
14 *Re Sims and Wood Ltd* [1916] WN 223.
15 *Re Panama New Zealand and Australian Royal Mail Co*, supra.
16 See p 452, post.
17 Picarda, *The Law Relating to Receivers and Managers*, pp 16–18; Lingard, *Bank Security Documents*, p 109.
18 *Re Victoria Steamboats Ltd* [1897] 1 Ch 158 at 161 per Kekwich J; *Edward Nelson & Co v Faber & Co* [1903] 2 KB 367 at 376–7 per Joyce J.
19 *Re Woodroffes (Musical Instruments) Ltd* [1986] Ch 366 at 376–8, [1985] 2 All ER 908 at 913–14, [1985] BCLC 227 at 233.
20 See cases cited in footnote 6 on p 446, ante.
 1 Law of Property Act 1925, s 85 (1) and s 86 (1) (37 Halsbury's Statutes (4th Edn) 194, 196). Legal mortgages of land and tangible movables must be executed as deeds, but legal mortgages of intangibles by way of assignment may be executed in writing signed by or on behalf of the company (Law of Property Act 1925, s 136 (1)).

company free from mortgage or charge during the time that the mortgage or charge continues to exist. In particular, if a specific charge over present and future debts payable to the company is to be created, contractual arrangements must be made to ensure that the debts are paid to the lender or his nominee (which may include the company), and that the company will have no power to use payments made by its debtors for its own general purposes, or to dispose of the right to receive the debts free from the charge.[2]

There is no prescribed formula for the creation of a floating charge, and the court has to interpret each debenture or loan security which comes before it to discover whether the parties intended to create a specific or a floating charge. Some guidance in this respect was given by Romer LJ in *Re Yorkshire Woolcombers Association Ltd*:[3]

'... I certainly think that if a charge has three characteristics that I am about to mention it is a floating charge. (1) If it is a charge on a class of assets of a company present and future; (2) if that class is one which, in the ordinary course of the business of the company, would be changing from time to time; and (3) if you find that by the charge it is contemplated that, until some future step is taken by or on behalf of those interested in the charge, the company may carry on its business in the usual way as far as concerns the particular class of assets I am dealing with.'

Thus, a floating charge is created by debentures which charge the company's 'undertaking',[4] or its 'estate, property and effects',[5] or its 'real and personal estate'.[6] In these cases the fact that the whole of the company's assets was charged indicates that a floating charge was intended, because if the charge were specific, the company's business would have been paralysed by its inability to sell a single chattel, and the parties clearly did not intend that.[7] But it is not necessary that the charge should extend to all the company's assets for it to be construed as a floating charge. Thus, a mortgage of a cinema and of the chattels 'which now are or may from time to time be placed upon or used in or about the ... premises' was held to be a floating charge as to the chattels.[8] Likewise a floating charge was created by a mortgage of 'book and other debts now owing [to the company] and also book and other debts which shall become owing during the continuance of this security'.[9] Furthermore, where a seller of goods to a company expressly retained the equitable beneficial ownership of the goods until the price for them was paid in full, but agreed that the company might dispose of the goods or convert them into other products and dispose of such products (in which event the seller would be entitled to the equitable ownership of the proceeds of sale, but the buyer would not have to account for them in specie to the unpaid seller), it was held that the reservation to the seller created a floating charge in his favour over the goods, the resulting products and the proceeds of sale.[10] But a charge will not be a floating charge if the instrument creating it shows that an immediate and irremovable security is intended over the property in question; consequently, a charge over present and future book debts of a company was held to be a specific charge when the charge was stated to be a 'fixed charge' and the company was prohibited from assigning or

2 *Siebe Gorman & Co Ltd v Barclays Bank Ltd* [1979] 2 Lloyd's Rep 142; *Re Armagh Shoes Ltd* [1982] NI 59; *Re Keenan Bros Ltd* [1985] IR 401 at 416 (Irish Supreme Court).
3 *Re Yorkshire Woolcombers Association Ltd* [1903] 2 Ch 284 at 295.
4 *Re Panama New Zealand and Australian Royal Mail Co* (1870) 5 Ch App 318.
5 *Re Florence Land and Public Works Co, ex p Moor* (1878) 10 ChD 530.
6 *Re Colonial Trusts Corpn, ex p Bradshaw* (1879) 15 ChD 465.
7 Ibid, at 472.
8 *National Provincial Bank of England Ltd v United Electric Theatres Ltd* [1916] 1 Ch 132.
9 *Re Yorkshire Woolcombers Association Ltd*, supra; see also *Tailby v Official Receiver* (1888) 13 App Cas 523.
10 *Re Bond Worth Ltd* [1980] Ch 228, [1979] 3 All ER 919.

dealing with the book debts and was required to collect them as the lender's agent and to pay them to the lender immediately on receipt.[11]

Two theories as to floating charges

Throughout the cases concerning floating charges there have run the threads of two different theories about their nature. The older theory, which can conveniently be called the 'licence' theory, explains the company's power to sell and mortgage its assets despite a floating charge which it has already created over them by implying that the lender gives it a licence to do so.[12] The newer theory, the 'mortgage of future assets' theory, explains the company's power to deal with its assets by the fact that the charge does not attach specifically to any of its assets until crystallisation and there is meanwhile no impediment to the company disposing of its assets free from the charge.[13]

These theories are not merely of academic interest; they can produce different practical consequences. Under the 'licence' theory, some limits must obviously be set to what the lender is assumed to license; he must be taken to permit the company to carry on its business in a proper way, but not to engage in ultra vires activities, or to close down its business and sell its assets or to dispose of the whole of its undertaking by a single transaction. If the company attempts to do any of these things, a court which adopts the licence theory will issue an injunction to restrain it, and it will be immaterial that the floating charge has not yet crystallised.[14] On the other hand, a court which adopts the 'mortgage of future assets' theory will refuse to intervene, because the lender has no right to complain until property in which he has a specific interest is being wrongfully disposed of, and the lender has no such specific interest until the floating charge has crystallised.[15] Again, under the 'licence' theory, the company's licence to carry on its business terminates when it commences to be wound up, and a provision in the debenture or loan security agreement that the lender's security shall not become enforceable if the winding up is merely for the purpose of reconstruction or amalgamation will not prevent the floating charge from crystallising if the company is wound up for one of those purposes.[16] On the other hand, if the court adopts the 'mortgage of future assets' theory, it will permit the company and the lender to make what bargain they wish as to the events which shall bring about crystallisation,[17] and if the debenture or loan security agreement makes appropriate provision for the modification of the lender's rights in the event of a reconstruction or amalgamation, he will be compelled to take securities in the new company resulting therefrom instead of realising the assets of the original company.[18] Furthermore, according to the 'licence' theory, the company is merely empowered by the licence to carry on its

---

11 *Siebe Gorman & Co Ltd v Barclays Bank Ltd* [1979] 2 Lloyd's Rep 142 followed by the Irish Supreme Court in *Re Keenan Bros Ltd* [1986] BCLC 242, [1985] IR 401 at 416.

12 *Re Florence Land and Public Works Co*, supra, at 541; *Davey & Co v Williamson & Sons Ltd* [1898] 2 QB 194 at 200; *Re Borax Co, Foster v Borax Co* [1901] 1 Ch 326; *Re Bond Worth Ltd* [1980] Ch 228, [1979] 3 All ER 919.

13 *Evans v Rival Granite Quarries Ltd* [1910] 2 KB 979; *Biggerstaff v Rowatt's Wharf Ltd* [1896] 2 Ch 93 at 105 per Kay LJ.

14 *Re Borax Co, Foster v Borax Co* [1899] 2 Ch 130; *Re Borax Co, Foster v Borax Co* [1901] 1 Ch 326; *Hubbuck v Helms* (1887) 56 LJ Ch 536.

15 *Lawrence v West Somerset Mineral Rly Co* [1918] 2 Ch 250; *Cross v Imperial Continental Gas Association* [1923] 2 Ch 553.

16 *Re Crompton & Co Ltd, Player v Crompton & Co Ltd* [1914] 1 Ch 954.

17 *Davey & Co v Williamson & Sons Ltd* [1898] 2 QB 194, as explained by Buckley LJ in *Evans v Rival Granite Quarries Ltd* [1910] 2 KB 979 at 1000; *Re Brightlife Ltd* [1987] Ch 200, [1986] 3 All ER 673, [1986] BCLC 418.

18 *Sneath v Valley Gold Ltd* [1893] 1 Ch 477; *Re W H Hutchinson & Sons Ltd* (1915) 31 TLR 324.

business in the ordinary way until the licence terminates, so that although it may pay its debts as they fall due, it is not within the terms of the licence for a judgment creditor to compel payment of his debt by levying execution against the company's assets,[19] and debtors of the company may only set off debts which the company owes them against their own liabilities to it if such debts become due while the licence subsists.[20] But if the 'mortgage of future assets' theory is accepted, all executions against the company's property completed before the floating charge crystallises are valid against the debenture or loan security holder,[1] and on crystallisation he takes the company's claims against third persons subject to all rights of set-off which they could plead against it.[2] Moreover, under the latter theory no transactions entered into by the company before crystallisation can be invalidated because they were not entered into for the purpose of carrying on the company's business in the ordinary way, and the only ground on which the holder of the floating charge can impugn them is that they were intended to defraud him by depriving him of a substantial part of his security.[3] On the other hand, in a recent case[4] the licence theory has been applied to lead to the conclusion that the appropriate date to test whether an unregistered mortgage was void against a debenture holder secured by a floating charge created after the mortgage, was the date when the floating charge was created, not when it crystallised.[5] Normally, the rules governing the registration of mortgages and charges created by a company[6] do produce this very result, but in the circumstances of the case in question this could only be so if the licence rather than the mortgage of future assets theory were employed.

It is impossible in the present state of the authorities, to say which theory as to the nature of floating charges is the correct one, although the preponderance of modern judicial opinion is undoubtedly in favour of the 'mortgage of future assets' theory. In this chapter and the next no attempt is made to segregate decisions which rested on one of the theories from those which rested on the other; the decisions are simply given with the conflict inherent in them left unresolved.

PRIORITIES BETWEEN FLOATING CHARGES AND OTHER CLAIMS AGAINST THE COMPANY

A person who lends on the security of a specific mortgage of a company's property is always entitled to repayment on his loan out of the proceeds of sale of the mortgaged property before any other creditor of the company, except a creditor who has a mortgage or charge over the same property which ranks in priority to the lender's mortgage or charge. A person who takes a floating charge is not in as secure a position. In some cases he has to relinquish assets to which his charge would otherwise attach on crystallisation so that they may be used to pay other creditors. The rules which govern competing claims by lenders or creditors secured by floating charges and other classes of creditors of a company must now be examined.

19 *Davey & Co v Williamson & Sons Ltd,* supra.
20 *H Wilkins and Elkington Ltd v Milton* (1916) 32 TLR 618.
1 See p 457, post.
2 *Parsons v Sovereign Bank of Canada* [1913] AC 160; *Rother Iron Works Ltd v Canterbury Precision Engineers Ltd* [1974] QB 1, [1973] 1 All ER 394.
3 *Hamer v London City and Midland Bank Ltd* (1918) 87 LJKB 973.
4 *Watson v Duff Morgan and Vermont (Holdings) Ltd* [1974] 1 All ER 794, [1974] 1 WLR 450. This case would now be decided differently under the rules introduced by the Companies Act 1989.
5 [1974] 1 All ER 794 at 799, [1974] 1 WLR 450 at 456.
6 See p 517, post.

Unsecured creditors

Lenders or creditors secured by a floating charge cannot prevent the company from using its assets to pay its unsecured creditors while their charge continues to float, but as soon as it crystallises they are entitled to repayment of their loan out of the assets to which it attaches before the company's unsecured creditors. To this there is one statutory exception. When a floating charge crystallises by a receiver being appointed by or on behalf of debenture holders or loan security holders or by the court, the receiver must pay claims against the company which are preferential payments out of the assets to which the charge attaches before the debt secured by the floating charge, and if this results in the assets being insufficient to pay that debt, the debenture holders or loan security holders are entitled to payment out of the other assets of the company, if there are any.[7] The statutory reversal of the normal order of priority between debts secured by floating charges and unsecured claims against the company applies whether the floating charge extends to the whole assets and undertaking of the company, or to only a class of those assets, such as stock in trade or book debts.[7] Formerly, preferential claims had priority for payment out of assets subject to a floating charge when a receiver was appointed or the debenture holders took possession of the assets, but only if the floating charge had not crystallised and become a specific charge on the assets beforehand (eg by the debenture or loan security holders exercising a right conferred on them to convert the floating charge into a specific charge, or by an event occurring which by the terms of the debenture or loan security agreement would cause the debenture to crystallise).[8] Now, however, the preferential debt has priority in a receivership if the floating charge was created as such, even though the charge has become a specific charge before the receiver is appointed.[9] If the debenture holders take possession of the assets instead of a receiver being appointed on their behalf, no priority is now given to preferential debts.[9]

The unsecured debts and claims which are preferential payments in a receivership are set out in the Insolvency Act 1986, and are the same debts and claims as are preferential in the winding up of a company, and which are therefore paid in full before other claims against the company.[10] Most of them are related to a period of time preceding the relevant date, namely the date on which the receiver is appointed by the debenture or loan security holders or, it would seem, by the court.[11] For example, the Crown has a preferential claim for unpaid value added tax referable to the six months preceding the relevant date, and employees of the company have preferential claims for wages and salaries in respect of services rendered during the four months immediately preceding that date.[12]

If a company is wound up without a receiver having been appointed to realise a floating charge created by it, the liquidator is directed to pay the preferential claims against the company out of property subject to a charge created as a floating charge before repaying the loan secured by the charge.[13] In this case the relevant periods for quantifying preferential claims are calculated from the date of the order of the court that the company shall be wound up, or the date when the

---

7 Insolvency Act 1986, s 40 (1) to (3). If the floating charge extends to the whole of the company's assets and undertaking, there will, of course, be no such other assets.

8 *Re Woodroffes (Musical Instruments) Ltd* [1986] Ch 366, [1985] 2 All ER 908; *Re Brightlife Ltd* [1987] Ch 200, [1986] 3 All ER 673, [1986] BCLC 418. The former statutory provision was contained in Companies Act 1985, s 196 (1) to (3) (now repealed).

9 Insolvency Act 1986, s 40 (1).

10 Ibid, s 175 (1) and (2), s 386 (1) and Sch 6.

11 Ibid, s 387 (4).

12 Ibid, s 386 (1) and Sch 6, paras 3 and 9.

13 Ibid, s 175 (2) and s 251.

resolution for voluntary winding up is passed, or from the date of the winding up resolution if the company is subsequently ordered to be wound up by the court, or from the date when an administration order is made in respect of the company under the Insolvency Act 1986, if the court has ordered the company to be wound up immediately after it discharged the administration order.[14] This provision formerly applied only if the floating charge had not crystallised and become a fixed charge before the winding up; because it had already crystallised, it was no longer a floating charge, but a specific charge, when the winding up supervened.[15] However, statute now provides that the preferential claims shall be paid in priority if the floating charge was created as such, even though it has crystallised before the company goes into liquidation.[13] In consequence it is notionally possible to have two sets of preferential claims calculated from different dates, and for both sets of claims to rank for payment before the amount secured by a floating charge over the company's assets. In practice it is unlikely that both sets of preferential claims could be asserted. If the holders of the floating charge appoint a receiver of the assets subject to it, the receiver's appointments and powers will not be affected by the company subsequently being wound up, and the liquidator will therefore have no assets of the company subject to the floating charge out of which to pay the preferential debts in a liquidation. If a receiver is appointed after the winding up of the company has begun, the receiver must apply the assets subject to the floating charge in the appropriate order for a receivership, not for a liquidation, and unless the liquidator has already paid the claims which are preferential in the liquidation out of assets subject to the floating charge, there will be no addition to the set of preferential claims which the receiver must satisfy out of those assets to the detriment of the holders of the floating charge.

A receiver appointed by or on behalf of the holders of a floating charge is personally liable to creditors of whose preferential claims he has notice if he has at any time assets in his hands which should be applied to meet their claims in full, but if the assets would have sufficed to discharge only part of their claims, he is personally liable to preferential creditors only for the fraction of their respective claims which could have been paid out of those assets.[16] If the receiver pays the debt secured by the floating charge without first discharging preferential claims, and so makes himself personally liable to pay them, he is entitled to an indemnity from the persons who are entitled to the benefit of the charge and are aware of the preferential claims and the fact that they have not been paid when they receive payment of the debt secured by the charge out of the company's assets,[17] but it seems that the receiver's indemnity is limited to the amounts which he pays to the holders of the debenture or loan security. Moreover, such a holder is personally liable to each creditor who has a preferential claim on the ground that he knowingly concurred in the receiver's breach of duty, but it would seem that his total liability is limited to the value of the assets he has received.[18]

When a debenture or loan security contains a specific mortgage or charge over some of the company's assets and a floating charge over the remainder, creditors who have preferential claims in a receivership or a winding up are entitled to prior payment of their claims only out of the assets subject to the floating charge, so that if the debenture debt can be satisfied out of the assets which are specifically

---

14 Insolvency Act 1986, s 387 (3). If a provisional liquidator is appointed before a winding up order is made, the relevant periods are calculated from the date of his appointment (ibid).
15 *Re Griffin Hotel Co Ltd* [1941] Ch 129, [1940] 4 All ER 324.
16 *Woods v Winskill* [1913] 2 Ch 303; *Westminster Corpn v Haste* [1950] Ch 442, [1950] 2 All ER 65; *IRC v Goldblatt* [1972] Ch 498, [1972] 2 All ER 202.
17 *Westminster City Council v Treby* [1936] 2 All ER 21.
18 *IRC v Goldblatt*, supra.

mortgaged, the debenture holders' claim will not be deferred at all.[19] If the company is in liquidation, the result of this is that the residue of the preferential claims which is not satisfied out of the company's assets subject to the floating charge must be met out of the company's general assets which are subject to neither the floating charge nor to the specific mortgage, if there are such assets. Any surplus proceeds of realisation of assets subject to the specific mortgage after discharging the amount secured by the debentures or loan security and the expenses of realisation are payable to the company or its liquidator, and not to the preferential creditors, because the floating charge does not extend to that surplus.[20] Nevertheless, if the company is in liquidation, the liquidator will be bound to apply those surplus proceeds together with the company's other assets in his hands in paying preferential claims in the liquidation after meeting the costs of the liquidation.[13]

It has been held that since the costs and expenses of winding up a company have to be paid out of its assets before debts which are preferential payments,[1] these costs and expenses also take priority over a debt secured by a floating charge which is deferred to the preferential claims for payment in the company's liquidation.[2] Consequently, the proceeds of sale of assets subject to the floating charge can be applied in the liquidation of the company to discharge the debt secured by the floating charge only when both the costs of the winding up and the preferential payments have been fully satisfied.[2] This is the case, however, only if the assets subject to the floating charge are realised in the liquidation of the company.[3] In the converse situation where those assets are sold or realised by a receiver appointed by or on behalf of the holders of the floating charge, payment of the amount secured by the charge is deferred only to the payment of preferential claims which have accrued at the date when the receiver is appointed,[4] and so neither preferential payments subsequently arising nor the costs and expenses of a liquidation subsequently ordered or resolved upon rank before the debt secured by the floating charge.[5]

Mortgagees and secured creditors

When a company creates a floating charge over its undertaking, it retains power not only to sell, but also to mortgage or charge, the assets which it owns from time to time, and mortgages and charges subsequently created by the company, whether legal or equitable, rank for payment out of the assets over which they are created in priority to the amount secured by the floating charge.[6] But a company cannot create mortgages ranking in priority to the floating charge after it has crystallised, because on crystallisation the floating charge becomes a specific charge over the assets which the company then owns and which it thereafter acquires, and the normal rules of priority apply between the crystallised charge and mortgages and charges which the company later creates. Furthermore, while a floating charge still floats, the company cannot create a second floating charge over its undertaking ranking before the first, even though the debenture or security agreement creating the first floating charge expressly empowers the company to 'deal with its property

19 *Re Lewis Merthyr Consolidated Collieries Ltd* [1929] 1 Ch 498.
20 *Re G L Saunders Ltd* [1986] 1 WLR 215, [1986] BCLC 40.
 1 Insolvency Act 1986, s 175 (2).
 2 *Re Barleycorn Enterprises Ltd* [1970] Ch 465, [1970] 2 All ER 155.
 3 *Re Christonette International Ltd* [1982] 3 All ER 225, [1982] 1 WLR 1245.
 4 Insolvency Act 1986, s 40 (1) and (2), s 386 (1) and s 387 (4).
 5 *Re Christonette International Ltd*, supra.
 6 *Moor v Anglo-Italian Bank* (1879) 10 ChD 681; *Re Hamilton's Windsor Ironworks Co, ex p Pitman and Edwards* (1879) 12 ChD 707; *Wheatley v Silkstone and Haigh Moor Coal Co* (1885) 29 ChD 715.

as it may think fit, and in particular [to] mortgage and sell the same or any part thereof'.[7] If the company is to have power to create a second floating charge over its undertaking ranking before the first, the instrument securing the first charge must so provide expressly.[8] On the other hand, the creation of a first floating charge over a company's undertaking does not prevent it from creating a second floating charge over part of its assets which will rank in priority to the first (eg a charge over its present and future book debts),[8] but if the part of the company's assets charged by the second floating charge were so extensive as to amount to substantially the whole of the company's undertaking, there can be little doubt that the court would give priority to the first floating charge.

It is usual for debentures secured by a floating charge and loan security agreements to prohibit the company from creating specific mortgages or floating charges which would rank for repayment before the debt secured by the floating charge, or would rank equally with it. Such a provision is not only an agreement by the company not to create such mortgages or charges, but also an equitable restriction on its power to do so,[9] and so a lender or creditor of the company who later takes a mortgage or charge over its assets with notice of the provision will be postponed for payment of the amount secured to the prior payment of the amount secured by the floating charge.[10] This consequence, of course, follows a fortiori if the mortgage or charge is expressed to be subject to the floating charge and the amount secured by it.[11] But a later mortgagee who takes a legal mortgage and has no notice of the restriction at the time when that mortgage is created will not be affected by the prohibitory provision; this is because of the general rule that a legal purchaser for value is not bound by prior equitable interests of which he has no notice, and so his mortgage will rank before the floating charge.[12] An equitable mortgagee or chargee who has no notice of the restrictive provision will also rank before the holders of the floating charge if his equitable claim to priority is stronger than that of those holders,[13] which it will be if the debenture holders left the title deeds or documents to the mortgaged property in the company's possession, so making it appear to the later mortgagee or chargee that the property was not encumbered by a prior charge, and the equitable mortgagee or chargee honestly believed that he was taking a first mortgage or charge.[13]

It has been held that a later mortgagee or chargee does not have constructive notice of the prohibition in a debenture on the creation of later mortgages merely because he knows of the existence of the debenture, or has constructive notice of its existence because it is registered at the Companies Registry; this is because knowledge or notice of the existence of a debenture does not necessarily imply knowledge or notice that any security created by it affects the property or assets mortgaged or charged to him, and he is not bound at his peril to examine the

---

7 *Smith v English and Scottish Mercantile Investment Trust Ltd* [1896] WN 86; *Re Benjamin Cope & Sons Ltd* [1914] 1 Ch 800.
8 *Re Automatic Bottle Makers Ltd, Osborne v Automatic Bottle Makers Ltd* [1926] Ch 412 at 423, per Warrington LJ.
9 *Rother Iron Works Ltd v Canterbury Precision Engineers Ltd* [1974] QB 1 at 6, [1973] 1 All ER 394 at 396, per Russell LJ; *Siebe Gorman & Co Ltd v Barclays Bank Ltd* [1979] 2 Lloyd's Rep 142 at 164, per Slade J.
10 *English and Scottish Mercantile Investment Co v Brunton* [1892] 2 QB 700 at 707; *G & T Earle Ltd v Hemsworth RDC* (1928) 44 TLR 605.
11 *Re Robert Stephenson & Co Ltd* [1913] 2 Ch 201.
12 *English and Scottish Mercantile Investment Co v Brunton*, supra; *Re Standard Rotary Machine Co Ltd* (1906) 95 LT 829.
13 *Re Castell and Brown Ltd* [1898] 1 Ch 315; *Re Valletort Sanitary Steam Laundry Co Ltd* [1903] 2 Ch 654.

debenture in case it does.[14] Furthermore, the registration of the debenture at the Companies Registry gives merely constructive notice of its existence to persons dealing with the company; they do not thereby also have constructive notice of the restrictive provision contained in it.[14] There is, in fact, no means under the present law by which the holder of a floating charge may ensure conclusively that all later mortgagees and chargees have notice of the contractual provision prohibiting the company from creating prior or equal ranking mortgages or charges, but when the Secretary of State for Trade and Industry makes regulations to give effect to the new system for registering charges created by companies under the Companies Act 1989,[15] he may require that the particulars of a charge delivered for registration shall include particulars of any restriction imposed by the instrument creating the charge on the company's power to create later mortgages or charges ranking in priority to or equally with it,[16] and any later mortgagee or chargee will be deemed to have notice of such a restriction included in the filed registration particulars.[17]

A restriction in a debenture or loan security agreement on a company's power to create later prior ranking mortgages or charges does not affect the priority of a mortgage or a charge over property to secure a loan with which the purchase price of the property is paid. This is so whether the mortgage is in favour of the vendor,[18] or a third party,[19] and in both cases the mortgagee or chargee is unaffected by the restriction even though he knows of it. The formal reason given by the court why the mortgagee or chargee is given priority is that his equitable rights under the contract to make the mortgage advance attach to the property before the company acquires the legal ownership of it on completion of the purchase, and so such rights have priority in point of time over the equitable rights of the holder of the floating charge under the restriction in the debenture or loan security agreement.[20] Nevertheless, the real reason why the courts have refused to give effect to the restriction in these cases appears to be that the holder of the floating charge would not benefit if it were applied. If the mortgagee or chargee of the purchased property did not have priority over the floating charge, notwithstanding his knowledge of its existence, he would undoubtedly refuse to advance the whole or part of the purchase price, and the company would then probably not be able to buy the property, in which case the holder of the floating charge would have no security over the property at all. The holder of the floating charge is in any case safeguarded against the mortgagee of the purchased property advancing more than the value of the property and taking additional security from the company for the excess. As regards additional security for the advance he makes, the mortgagee is in the same position as any other mortgagee or chargee who takes a mortgage or charge with knowledge of the restrictive provision in the debenture or other instrument creating the floating charge, and so his additional security will rank after that conferred by the floating charge.

If a charge, lien or other security attaches to any property of a company by operation of law and not by the voluntary act of the company, it ranks before a floating charge created over the company's assets and undertaking which has not yet crystallised, whether the debenture or other instrument creating the floating charge does or does not prohibit the company from creating charges ranking in

---

14 *Re Standard Rotary Machine Co*, supra. *Wilson v Kelland* [1910] 2 Ch 306; *Siebe Gorman & Co Ltd v Barclays Bank Ltd* [1979] 2 Lloyd's Rep 142.
15 See p 505, post.
16 Companies Act 1985, s 415 (1) and (2), inserted by Companies Act 1989, s 103.
17 Ibid, s 416 (1), inserted by Companies Act 1989, s 103.
18 *Wilson v Kelland*, supra; contra *Capital Finance Co Ltd v Stokes* [1969] 1 Ch 261, [1968] 3 All ER 625.
19 *Re Connolly Bros Ltd (No 2)* [1912] 2 Ch 25.
20 *Security Trust Co v Royal Bank of Canada* [1976] AC 503, [1976] 1 All ER 381.

priority to it.[1] Furthermore, it has been held that if under a contract with the company such a lien arises after crystallisation of the floating charge, the lien still has priority, and this is so even if the contract confers an express power of sale on the holder of the lien in addition to the mere right of retention which he has at common law.[2] This decision, of course, goes a long way to impair the security afforded by a floating charge, and its correctness is questionable.

There have been no decisions on the effect of a clause in a trust deed executed in connection with an issue of unsecured loan stock or notes, or in the terms of the loan stock or notes themselves, by which the company's power to mortgage or charge its assets is not to be exercised or is subjected to restrictions while the loan stock or notes are outstanding. The purpose of the clause is similar to that of the restriction on the creation of later mortgages and charges in an instrument creating a floating charge, but it may be that its effect is only contractual in view of the fact that the loan stockholders or noteholders have no interest in the company's property apart from the restriction itself. If that is so, the clause would be ineffective to take away the priority gained by later mortgagees or chargees under the general law, even if they were aware of the clause when their mortgages or charges were created. It might be possible in such a situation for equity to make them account to the loan stockholders or noteholders for the proceeds of realisation of their security, or to compel them to share their security rateably with the loan stockholders, but it is far from certain that the court would accord them tracing rights of this character in the absence of fraud.

Judgment creditors

The rules governing competing claims to priority between judgment creditors and debenture holders and other creditors of a company secured by a floating charge are somewhat vague, and contrast unfavourably with the precise statutory rules applicable in a winding up.[3] In one case where the 'licence' theory was rigorously applied,[4] Russell LCJ held that judgment creditors who issue execution against the company's assets have no better title to them than the company, and their rights are therefore subject to the claim of the holders of a floating charge which later crystallises. He added:[4]

'We cannot assent to the view . . . that a seizure under an execution on a judgment against the company is a dealing by the company in the ordinary course of business. . . . It is not in the ordinary course of business that the debts of a going business firm or company shall be liquidated by seizure of their assets under legal process.'

Read literally this statement goes too far. It would mean that on the crystallisation of a floating charge the persons entitled to it could compel judgment creditors who had satisfied their debts by levying execution at any time beforehand to hand over what they have received, whereas creditors who had been paid debts voluntarily by the company could keep the payments made to them. The real problem is not whether judgment creditors may ever retain the proceeds of execution, because clearly they must be entitled to do so, unless the holders of floating charges which have not crystallised are to be recognised as having an exotic right to prevent the company from paying the debts it incurs in connection with its business undertaking. The problem is instead to discover what stage an execution must

---

1 *Brunton v Electrical Engineering Corpn* [1892] 1 Ch 434.
2 *George Barker (Transport) Ltd v Eynon* [1974] 1 All ER 900, [1974] 1 WLR 462.
3 Insolvency Act 1986, ss 183 and 184.
4 *Davey & Co v Williamson & Sons Ltd* [1898] 2 QB 194 at 200.

reach before the floating charge crystallises if the judgment creditor is to benefit by it. The answer to this requires an examination of the different modes of execution.

If the judgment creditor issues a writ of fieri facias against the company's goods, he cannot proceed with his execution if all that has happened before the floating charge crystallises is that the sheriff has taken possession of the goods.[5] But if on seizure the company has paid the whole[6] or part[7] of the judgment debt to prevent a sale, the judgment creditor is entitled to recover the amount paid, even though the money is still in the sheriff's hands when the floating charge crystallises. It is uncertain whether the judgment creditor is entitled to the proceeds of sale if the sheriff sells the goods before crystallisation,[8] although by analogy with the corresponding provision in a winding up,[9] it would seem reasonable to conclude that he is. On the other hand, it has been held at first instance that the judgment creditor can retain the proceeds of sale only if the sheriff has paid them to him before crystallisation, and that the holders of the crystallised floating charge are entitled to the proceeds if they are still in the sheriff's hands at that time,[10] but this is questionable.

If the judgment creditor obtains a garnishee order against a debtor of the company, he is entitled to the debt thus attached only if the garnishee order has been made absolute and the debtor has paid the debt to him before the floating charge crystallises.[11] A garnishee order nisi gives the judgment creditor a charge on the debt owed to the company when it has been served on the company's debtor, and one would therefore expect that the order nisi alone would give the judgment creditor priority over a floating charge which later crystallises. The reason why this is not so has been variously explained by reference to the 'licence' theory[12] and by analogy to execution against goods, where the execution is complete only when the sheriff has both seized and sold them.[13]

Execution against shares, debentures and other loan securities held by the company in other companies and against land owned by the company is effected by the court making a charging order on the application of the judgment creditor, and at any time after the charging order is made, the court may order the sale of the assets charged.[14] The charging order takes effect as if the company had created a mortgage or charge in writing in favour of the judgment creditor over the land or securities comprised in the order at the date the charging order nisi is made.[15] It follows that if the charging order is made before the floating charge crystallises, the judgment creditor may retain the benefit of his execution.[16]

There is a conflict of opinion whether a judgment creditor who obtains the appointment of a receiver of property owned by the company by way of equitable execution acquires a specific charge on it. In one case it was held that he does

---

5 Re Standard Manufacturing Co [1891] 1 Ch 627; Re Opera Ltd [1891] 3 Ch 260.
6 Heaton and Dugard Ltd v Cutting Bros Ltd [1925] 1 KB 655.
7 Robinson v Burnell's Vienna Bakery Co [1904] 2 KB 624.
8 Re Opera Ltd, supra.
9 Insolvency Act 1986, s 183 (1) and (3).
10 Taunton v Sheriff of Warwickshire [1895] 2 Ch 319.
11 Norton v Yates [1906] 1 KB 112; Cairney v Back [1906] 2 KB 746.
12 Norton v Yates, supra at 124.
13 Cairney v Back, supra at 752.
14 Charging Orders Act 1979, s 1 (1), s 2 (1) and (2) and s 6 (1) (22 Halsbury's Statutes (4th Edn) 337; RSC Ord 88, r 1).
15 Charging Orders Act 1979, s 3 (4).
16 The decision in Re Overseas Aviation Engineering (GB) Ltd [1963] Ch 24, [1962] 3 All ER 12, does not militate against this conclusion, for in that case the charging order was held invalid under a provision of the Companies Act 1948, which applied only in a winding up.

acquire a charge on the property when the receiver is appointed,[17] but in another case it was held that a charge arises only when the receiver himself obtains an order against the person in control of the property directing him to account to the receiver and not to the company.[18] Whichever decision is correct, the charge in favour of the judgment creditor will prevail against the holders of the floating charge only if it is obtained before the floating charge crystallises.

Injunctions restraining a company from removing its assets out of the jurisdiction[19] and sequestration orders appointing persons to take possession of a company's assets to constrain it to obey an order of the court[20] are not forms of execution, and in any case operate only against the company and not directly against its assets. If a floating charge created by the company crystallises after any such order is made by the court, therefore, the order does not prevent the holders of the floating charge from enforcing their rights against the company's assets.[19]

Hire-purchase and hiring agreements; sellers' retention of title

If a company acquires goods under a hire-purchase agreement, it does not become the owner of them until the last instalment of the rental has been paid to the supplier or the financing institution (the owner) and the option to acquire the title to the goods conferred on the company by the agreement has been exercised. Holders of specific or floating charges created by the company have no better title to the goods than the company, and the owner may therefore recover the goods from a receiver appointed by the holders of such a specific or floating charge whenever the owner could recover them from the company, and also, if the terms of the hire-purchase agreement so provide, upon the company being wound up or a receiver of its undertaking being appointed. Whether secured creditors of a company have a specific mortgage or a floating charge makes no difference in this respect. Complications arise, however, when goods in the company's possession under hire-purchase agreement are affixed to land which the company owns and which is comprised in the security. On affixation the goods become part of the land, and there may be competing claims by the holders of a mortgage or charge over it to retain the fixtures as part of their security and by the owner of the goods to remove them under the terms of the hire-purchase agreement. The resolution of these claims depends on whether the goods were affixed before or after the security was created and also on the nature of the security.

If the goods were affixed to the land before the security over it was created, the owner may generally retake the goods on the termination of the hire purchase agreement, even though the holders of the security have entered into possession of the land, or have appointed or obtained the appointment of a receiver. This is because the owner's right of removal conferred by the hire-purchase agreement operates as a licence coupled with an interest in the land, and is therefore binding in equity on persons deriving title under the company, including later mortgagees and chargees.[21] However, if the security is a legal mortgage of the land, and the holders of it had no notice of the hire-purchase agreement when the mortgage was created, they are not bound by the owner's equitable right of removal, and can treat the affixed goods as part of their security.[21] Equitable mortgagees and chargees, including debenture holders secured by a floating charge, have no such right of retention, because the owner's equitable right to remove the affixed goods

17 *Levasseur v Mason and Barry Ltd* [1891] 2 QB 73.
18 *Croshaw v Lyndhurst Ship Co* [1897] 2 Ch 154.
19 *Cretanor Maritime Co Ltd v Irish Marine Management Ltd* [1978] 3 All ER 164, [1978] 1 WLR 966.
20 *Eckman v Midland Bank Ltd* [1973] QB 519, [1973] 1 All ER 609.
21 *Hobson v Gorringe* [1897] 1 Ch 182.

on the termination of the hire purchase agreement existed before their equitable mortgage or charge was created, and their interests are therefore subject to the right of removal, which has priority over their claim whether they were aware of the hire-purchase agreement when their security was created or not.[1] A specific mortgagee of land, whether legal or equitable, is entitled as part of his security to fixtures brought on to the land after his mortgage is created.[2] Consequently, if a company affixes goods acquired under a hire-purchase agreement to its land after it has created a specific mortgage over it, the mortgagee may retain the fixtures as part of his security, even though he knew of the hire-purchase agreement when the mortgage was created and even though he also knew of the company's intention to affix the goods. But if the company has created a floating charge, it does not attach specifically to the land until crystallisation, and until that time the holders of the floating charge cannot prevent the owner from removing affixed goods under the terms of the hire-purchase agreement, and if he does so, the floating charge never attaches to the goods at all.[1] On the other hand, if the goods are still affixed to the land when the floating charge crystallises, the holders of the charge can prevent the owner from removing them, because their own equitable charge has now attached specifically to the goods as part of the land to which they are affixed.[1]

Mortgagees or holders of floating charges can, of course, agree to forgo their strict rights, and when the mortgaged premises are used for business purposes the court is ready to imply an agreement by them that the company may remove trade fixtures installed before or after the mortgages were created or the floating charges crystallised.[3] Such an agreement would enure for the benefit of an owner of goods comprised in a hire-purchase agreement which the company affixes to its land. But no such agreement can be implied if the instruments creating the mortgage or charge expressly require the consent of the mortgagee or holders of the charge for the removal of fixtures, and in any case, if the mortgagee or such holders enter into possession of the land, or appoint or procure the appointment of a receiver of the land, any power of removal which the company had is automatically terminated, and so also would be any derivative right of removal vested in the owner of goods which had been affixed.[4]

The rules relating to the affixation of goods owned by a third person to land owned by a company are general in character, and affect owners of goods other than those who have entered into hire-purchase agreements. Consequently, a person who has let goods on hire to a company, or who has sold goods to the company on terms that the seller shall remain the owner of the goods until they are paid for,[5] or whose goods have been wrongfully appropriated or converted by the company, occupies the same legal position as an owner who has delivered goods to the company under a hire-purchase agreement. If any such owner cannot recover goods because they have been affixed to the company's land, he has at most an action in damages against the company for breach of contract or tort, and this will, of course, rank after the rights of mortgagees or of holders of floating charges which have crystallised.

Landlord

The rights of a company's lessor or landlord are unaffected by the crystallisation of a floating charge, and he can employ the same remedies against the company for

1 *Re Morrison, Jones and Taylor Ltd* [1914] 1 Ch 50.
2 *Longbottom v Berry* (1869) LR 5 QB 123; *Meux v Jacobs* (1875) LR 7 HL 481.
3 *Gough v Wood & Co* [1894] 1 QB 713.
4 *Ellis v Glover and Hobson Ltd* [1908] 1 KB 388.
5 *Hendy Lennox (Industrial Engines) Ltd v Grahame Puttick Ltd* [1984] 2 All ER 152, [1984] 1 WLR 485; *Clough Mill Ltd v Martin* [1984] 3 All ER 982, [1985] 1 WLR 111; see further pp 498 and 502, post.

the recovery of rent and for breach of the lessee's covenants as previously including forfeiture of the lease. If he has distrained on the company's goods for arrears of rent before crystallisation, he may sell the goods thereafter, and the holders of the floating charge cannot require him to account for the proceeds of sale.[6] The lessor or landlord can also distrain on goods in the possession of the holder of a floating charge for rent accruing after crystallisation, even though the charge has now attached specifically to those goods.[7] If a receiver appointed by the court is in possession of the company's goods, however, the landlord must apply to the court for leave to distrain, which will always be given if there is rent owing.[7] Moreover, a landlord who has been compelled to return distrained goods to an underlessee or undertenant to whom they belong on the latter undertaking to pay his rent in future to the landlord, or who has served a notice on an underlessee or undertenant requiring him to pay his rent in future directly to the landlord until the arrears of rent owing a landlord by the company under its head lease have been discharged,[8] is entitled to the rent so paid by the underlessee or undertenant, even though the floating charge created by the company had already crystallised before the goods were distrained and a receiver has been appointed of the company's assets, including the head lease.[9] On the other hand, the landlord has no personal claim against the debenture holders or their receiver for arrears of rent, as there is no privity of estate between them and himself, nor can he compel them to apply the company's assets in paying such arrears.[10]

Avoidance of floating charges on a winding up

By statute, in the winding up of a company a floating charge created by it within one year (or in the case of charges in favour of persons then connected with the company, within two years) before the commencement of the company's winding up or the presentation of a petition on which an administration order is made against the company (if that is earlier) or after such a petition has been presented, is void as a security for any amount other than for the repayment of money paid to the company, or for the price of goods or services supplied to it, in consideration of the charge at the time the charge was created or thereafter, or for so much of the consideration for the charge as consists in the discharge or reduction of any debt of the company at or after the time when the charge was created, or for interest at the agreed rate on any amount for which the charge is valid, or for any combination of such validly secured amounts.[11] A person is connected with the company for the purpose of this provision if he is a director or shadow director of the company, or is an associate of such a director or shadow director (ie spouse, relative, partner, employer, employee, trustee of a trust under which that person or an associate of his is a beneficiary or potential beneficiary (other than a pension or employee share scheme trust) or a company which is controlled by that person and his associates), or if he is an associate of the company.[12] When the statutory provision applies, it

---

6 *Re Roundwood Colliery Co* [1897] 1 Ch 373.
7 *General Share and Trust Co v Wetley Brick and Pottery Co* (1882) 20 ChD 260 at 263. But possibly this is so only if the floating charge extends to both the leasehold land and the goods distrained, so that the holder of the charge takes the land subject to the landlord's right to distrain on the goods. If the charge applies only to the goods, it is difficult to see why the landlord should have a right to distrain on them after crystallisation.
8 Law of Distress Amendment Act 1908, ss 1, 3 and 6 (13 Halsbury's Statutes (4th Edn) 584, 586 and 588).
9 *Rhodes v Allied Dunbar Pension Services Ltd* [1989] 1 All ER 1161, [1989] BCLC 318.
10 *Hand v Blow* [1901] 2 Ch 721.
11 Insolvency Act 1986, s 245(2), (3) and (5).
12 Ibid, s 249 and s 435 (1) to (6).

merely invalidates a floating charge as a security for any amount other than the items mentioned above; it does not avoid the liability of the company for the amount ineffectively secured, and so the holder of the invalid floating charge can still prove in the company's winding up as an unsecured creditor for that amount.

The court has construed liberally the requirement that an amount should be paid to the company on or after the date when the floating charge is created so as to uphold the floating charge as validly securing it when the company is wound up. If a person makes a loan to the company on the understanding that he will be given a floating charge as security, the charge is taken as being created when the loan is made, even though the instrument creating the floating charge is not executed until some time after the lender advances the amount of the loan.[13] But this is so only if the company's promise to create the floating charge is unconditional. If the promise is conditional, the floating charge is treated as being created when the instrument creating it is executed, and not at the earlier date when the company made the conditional promise or when the condition was fulfilled.[13] Thus, when a company agreed to give a floating charge to the guarantor of its bank overdraft if the bank called on him to honour his guarantee, and the company did so after the guarantor paid the amount of the overdraft, it was held that the charge could not be treated as having been created at the time when the guarantor discharged the overdraft and the charge was therefore invalidated by the company going into liquidation shortly afterwards.[14] Moreover, a payment made by a guarantor to discharge a debt owed by the company is not treated as money paid to the company itself, because even if the money passes through its hands, the company does not have the right to use it as it wishes; consequently, even if the floating charge is created in favour of the guarantor at the time he discharges the debt, whether pursuant to a prior agreement or not, it will be invalidated if the company is wound up within the appropriate period.[15] Furthermore, money cannot be considered as paid to the company contemporaneously with the creating of a floating charge if the lender has already made a loan to the company on it agreeing to create a fixed charge over certain assets, and that agreement is superseded by a subsequent agreement under which the floating charge is created by the company instead of the fixed charge.[16]

A floating charge is valid as a security for advances made after it is created, even though the lender does not promise to make such loans, and the floating charge is merely expressed to extend to such advances as the lender chooses to make in the future.[17] Admittedly, the statutory provision treats the floating charge as a valid security for advances only if they were made in consideration of the floating charge,[18] and an uncovenanted loan would not at first sight appear to be made in consideration of an existing charge. The court has rejected such a narrow interpretation, however, and reads the statutory words 'in consideration for' the creation of the charge as meaning merely that the lender must make the loan because of his expectation that the charge will secure it, or in other words, that he would not have made the loan if he had been told that the charge would not secure

13 *Re Columbian Fireproofing Co Ltd* [1910] 2 Ch 120; *Re F & E Stanton Ltd* [1929] 1 Ch 180.
14 *Re Gregory Love & Co* [1916] 1 Ch 203.
15 *Re Orleans Motor Co Ltd* [1911] 2 Ch 41.
16 *Re G T Whyte & Co Ltd* [1983] BCLC 311.
17 *Re Yeovil Glove Co Ltd* [1965] Ch 148, [1964] 2 All ER 849. The instrument creating the floating charge must, of course, expressly secure uncovenanted loans; if it does not, the lender has no security for advances which he chooses to make after the floating charge is created, and if the floating charge is extended by agreement to cover such a later loan at the time it is made, the extension will be considered to be an entirely separate floating charge for the purpose of the statutory provisions.
18 Insolvency Act 1986, s 245 (1).

it.[17] Consequently, advances made to an insolvent company by its bank on an overdraft account during the year before it is wound up are validly secured in the winding up by a floating charge given to secure the overdraft before the advances were made, even though the bank was under no obligation to make the advances.[17]

The period of one year (or two years if the charge is given to a connected person) from the creation of the floating charge within which the company must commence to be wound up, or have a successful petition for an administration order presented against it, if the floating charge is to be invalidated, is calculated from the time when the instrument creating the charge is executed, and not from the date when the debentures entitling their holders to the benefit of the charge are issued. Consequently, if more than a year before it commences to be wound up (or more than two years beforehand if the lenders are connected persons), a company executes a trust deed creating a floating charge over its undertaking to secure a series of debentures or an issue of debenture stock, and the company issues some of the debentures or stock as security for its existing debts within that year, the debenture holders or stockholders are nevertheless entitled to the benefit of the charge, and the statutory provision does not apply.[19] On the other hand, if the floating charge is created within the one or two year period before the company goes into liquidation or before a successful petition for an administration order is presented against it, the fact that the advances secured by the floating charge were made more than a year or two years before the commencement of the liquidation or the administration order proceedings does not validate the charge, unless the advances were made in response to an unconditional promise to create the charge to secure them.[13]

Except where a floating charge is created in favour of a person connected with the company, the statutory provision does not invalidate a floating charge given to secure existing indebtedness of a company if it was solvent immediately after the charge was created and did not subsequently become insolvent in consequence of the transaction under which the charge was created.[20] A company is not solvent at that time unless it is then able to pay its debts as they fall due,[1] or if it otherwise proved to be unable at that time to pay its debts for the purpose of winding up proceedings against it.[2] The ways in which a company insolvency may be proved for the purpose of obtaining an order by the court that it shall be wound up include:

(a) proof of the failure of the company to comply with a written demand that it shall pay a debt exceeding £750 within three weeks after service of the demand on it by the creditor;

(b) proof that execution has been levied on the company's assets by a judgment creditor and has been returned unsatisfied in whole or part; and

(c) proof that the value of the company's assets is less than the total of its liabilities,[3] taking into account the realisable value of assets which can only be converted into money over an extended period and the company's prospective and contingent liabilities, however deferred or remote the date on which they may accrue is likely to be.

A floating charge will consequently be invalidated if no new consideration was given for it and no existing debt of the company was discharged or reduced in consideration of the charge, and either the company was insolvent at the time the

---

19 *Transport and General Credit Corpn Ltd v Morgan* [1939] Ch 531, [1939] 2 All ER 17.
20 Companies Act 1985, s 617 (1) and (2).
1 *Re Patrick and Lyon Ltd* [1933] Ch 786, [1933] All ER Rep 590.
2 Insolvency Act 1986, s 123 (1) and (2) and s 245 (4).
3 Ibid, s 123 (1) and (2).

charge was created, or the company was solvent at that time but became insolvent in consequence of the creation of the charge.[4] This latter alternative applies where the company is able to discharge its existing indebtedness in full out of its assets immediately before it creates the floating charge, but the charge is given to secure part of that indebtedness owed to the person who takes the charge together with further advances which do not result in a corresponding increase in the company's assets (eg because the advances are to be paid to another company in the same group or to an associated company and the company guarantees their repayment) with the result that immediately after the creation of the charge the company's assets are less than its total liabilities.

The validation of floating charges created by solvent companies makes clear the purpose of the Act, namely, to prevent a company which is unable to pay its debts from preferring some of its existing unsecured creditors to the others by giving some of its creditors a floating charge over its assets, which will give them priority if the company is wound up or has an administration order made against it, but will not impede the company carrying on business in the meantime. A transparent device to enable such a charge to be given would be for an unsecured creditor to make a new loan to the company on the security of a floating charge on the understanding that the loan shall be applied immediately in paying off his existing unsecured debt. The court refused to countenance this device under the former legislation invalidating floating charges, and held that a charge given in those circumstances was in reality given to secure the existing debt, so that the floating charge was invalid, unless the company was solvent at the time.[5] This was so even if the original debt was a loan made to the company by the lender's wholly-owned subsidiary under an indemnity given by the lender, and the lender's subsequent advance made on the security of the floating charge was made solely for the purpose of discharging the company's debt to the lender's subsidiary.[6] On the other hand, the fact that a condition was attached to the new loan that it should be applied in paying an existing debt owing to the lender, did not invalidate the floating charge under the former legislation if the new loan was made in good faith to enable the company to continue carrying on its business, and not merely to secure the existing debt;[7] whether this was so depended on the proportion of the new loan which was retained by the lender to satisfy his existing debt and the likelihood that the balance of the loan plus any other finance available to the company would keep it solvent for a reasonable time. Thus, where an unsecured creditor allowed the company to pay its other creditors without insisting on payment of any part of his debt, and a new loan by that creditor put the company sufficiently in funds to enable it to continue carrying on its business, which would otherwise have closed down for lack of ready money, it was held that a floating charge given to the creditor to secure his new loan was valid, even though the company undertook to discharge his existing debt out of it.[7] The law in this respect may have been modified by the present statutory provision in favour of a lender who requires any part of a loan made by him to be applied in discharging the company's indebtedness to him. Under the present legislation a floating charge is a valid security in the company's subsequent liquidation or in its administration under a court order if the charge is given in consideration of fresh advances or supplies of goods or services, or in consideration of 'the discharge or reduction . . . of any debt of the company'.[8] This appears to mean that if the person who takes the floating charge agrees to cancel

4 Ibid, s 245 (2) and (4).
5 *Re Destone Fabrics Ltd* [1941] Ch 319, [1941] 1 All ER 545.
6 *Re G T Whyte & Co Ltd* [1983] BCLC 311.
7 *Re Matthew Ellis Ltd* [1933] Ch 458, [1933] All ER Rep 583.
8 Insolvency Act 1986, s 245 (2) (*b*).

the company's existing indebtedness to him, in whole or part, in consideration of the charge being given, the charge is a valid security for an amount equal to the company's existing indebtedness which is cancelled. If this arrangement is embodied in a transaction by which a lender makes a fresh advance to the company, on condition that the whole or part of the advance shall be used to pay the company's indebtedness to the lender, it would consequently appear that a floating charge created to secure the fresh advance would always be immune from invalidation under the statutory provision.

If a floating charge is created as security for amounts owing under the company's current bank account which is already overdrawn, payments subsequently made into the account by the company will, unless otherwise agreed, be applied in discharging the debit items in the account in the order they arose.[9] Consequently the floating charge will, under the statutory provision, be a valid security in the company's liquidation primarily for the amounts more recently advanced to it by the bank, the earlier advances before the charge was created being repaid out of payments subsequently made into the account. This leaves the charge as a valid security for a larger balance of advances made by the bank after the date when the charge was created than if the subsequent payments into the account were credited primarily against drawings made after the charge was created.[10] If drawings were made after the date of the charge simply to enable the company to make payments into the account to discharge the earlier debit items, however, there would be an obvious attempt to evade the statutory provision, and under the former statutory provision the court held that the fresh advances would be considered as not having been made, and the charge would not secure them.[10] It is doubtful whether this would be so under the present statutory provision, however, because the bank would be entitled to treat drawings made subsequently to the creation of the floating charge as being applied to discharge or reduce the existing indebtedness of the company to the bank, and for the reasons given above, the present statutory provision appears not to invalidate the floating charge as a security for the equivalent of the company's indebtedness which is discharged.

Floating charges are invalidated by the statutory provision only when the company is wound up or when an administration order is made against it, and so if before this happens the company redeems a floating charge which would have been invalid in its liquidation or in the administration proceedings,[11] or if the creditor pays himself the amount secured by his floating charge by exercising his powers of realisation,[12] the liquidator or adminstrator cannot require the creditor secured by the charge to repay what he has received. If the redemption or realisation of the charge takes place within six months before the winding up commences, however, it may be a preference of the creditor, in which case the liquidator or administrator can recover the amount paid from him under another statutory provision, if it can be shown that the redemption or realisation put the creditor in a more advantageous position in the company's liquidation or insolvent administration than he would otherwise have occupied and that the company was influenced by a desire to produce that result,[12] which will be the situation only when the creditor realises his floating charge with the concurrence of the directors of the company.[13] When a floating charge is invalidated under the statutory provision relating to floating charges, it is not necessarily the company's unsecured

---

9 *Devaynes v Noble, Clayton's Case* (1816) 1 Mer 572; *Re Hayman, Christy and Lilley Ltd* [1917] 1 Ch 283.
10 *Re Yeovil Glove Co Ltd* [1965] Ch 148, [1964] 2 All ER 849.
11 *Re Parkes Garage (Swadlincote) Ltd* [1929] 1 Ch 139; *Mace Builders (Glasgow) Ltd v Lunn* [1985] 3 WLR 465, [1985] BCLC 154.
12 *Mace Builders (Glasgow) Ltd v Lunn* [1986] Ch 459, [1985] BCLC 154, affd [1987] Ch 191, [1987] BCLC 55.
13 Insolvency Act 1986, s 239 (2) to (5) and s 240 (1).

creditors who benefit thereby. The charge is then invalidated for all purposes, and so mortgagees, judgment creditors, or the owners of goods held by the company under hire-purchase or hiring agreements may assert any rights they have against assets subject to the charge, and thereby prevent the liquidator or administrator from taking them for the benefit of the unsecured creditors of the company.[14] This is so even though those rights would not have been enforceable against the holder of the floating charge if it had not been invalidated under the statutory provision.

Floating charges over foreign assets

Although the laws of England, Ireland and, as a result of legislation, Scotland[15] recognise the floating charge as a valid security, the laws of most other countries do not, and under the rule of private international law that the validity of securities is determined by the law of the country where the subject matter of the security is situate, United Kingdom courts are often constrained to treat floating charges as ineffective to give proprietary interests to holders of such charges over foreign assets. The charge is nevertheless effective under United Kingdom law against the company which created it, and can therefore be enforced against the company and its liquidator by personal remedies. The court may therefore order that the company shall appropriate the proceeds of sale of the foreign assets expressed to be included in a floating charge toward paying the debt secured by the charge;[16] or that the company shall appoint an agent nominated by the holders of debentures or loan securities entitled to the benefit of a floating charge, or an agent nominated by the trustees of such a charge, so that the agent may realise foreign assets comprised in the charge for the benefit of those persons; or that their trustees may realise such assets;[17] or that the liquidator shall give effect to rights of the holders of a floating charge or that the persons entitled to the benefit of it shall be paid before unsecured creditors in the winding up of the company.[18]

PROVISIONS AS TO REDEMPTION

The date on which the principal of the debt secured by debentures or loan securities becomes repayable is fixed as a matter of contract by the terms of issue of the debentures, or by the loan agreement or by the covering trust deed, if there is one. However, debentures and other loan securities which are secured on a company's property are a species of mortgage, and as such appear to be subject to the rules of equity by which provisions in them which clog or fetter the company's right of redemption are void. One of these equitable rules is that the contractual date for redemption of a mortgage must not be postponed for an excessive length of time. This rule does not apply to debentures, debenture stock, loan stock or notes, or other loan securities, however, the Companies Act 1985 providing that:[19]

'A condition contained in any debentures ... is not invalid by reason only that the debentures are thereby made irredeemable or redeemable only on the happening of a

---

14 *Capital Finance Co Ltd v Stokes* [1968] 1 All ER 573 at 578, [1968] 1 WLR 1158 at 1165.
15 Companies (Floating Charges and Receivers) (Scotland) Act 1972 (superseding the Companies (Floating Charges) Scotland) Act 1961). See now Companies Act 1985, ss 462 to 466, as amended by Companies Act 1989, s 140.
16 *Mercantile Investment and General Trust Co v River Plate Trust, Loan and Agency Co* [1892] 2 Ch 303.
17 *Re Huinac Copper Mines Co Ltd* [1910] WN 218.
18 *Re Anchor Line (Henderson Bros) Ltd* [1937] Ch 483, [1937] 2 All ER 823.
19 Companies Act 1985, s 193.

contingency (however remote), or on the expiration of a period (however long), any rule of equity to the contrary notwithstanding.'

Since by definition legal mortgages of a company's land are debentures, the contractual date for their redemption can be postponed for any length of time, even though similar mortgages by individuals would be subject to the equitable rule.[20] Although companies are empowered by the Companies Act 1985 to issue irredeemable debentures, there is no such thing as a debenture which will never be redeemed. Irredeemable debentures always empower the debenture holders to enforce their security if the company fails to pay interest on the loan or if it defaults in various other ways or if any of several specified events occurs, and the enforcement of the security will result in the repayment of the debenture debt. Furthermore, if the company is wound up the holders of irredeemable debentures are entitled to immediate repayment of their loan, and the liquidator is entitled to discharge it.[1] An irredeemable debenture is therefore merely a debenture which provides no fixed date for its redemption and which expressly prevents the debenture holders demanding repayment, or the company making repayment, on a specified date or whenever they wish; the debenture holders consequently have no contractual right to insist on redemption, unless the company defaults or goes into liquidation or unless one of the events specified in the debentures occurs which makes the debentures immediately repayable.

Sometimes debenture trust deeds or loan security agreements contain an undertaking by the company to set aside a fixed sum of money each year as a sinking fund for the repayment of the principal of the debenture debt or the loan. The company may promise to apply this money in redeeming a certain number of the debentures or repaying a fraction of the principal of the loan each year, and if a series of debentures is issued, the debentures which are to be redeemed are usually drawn by lot. But if the trust deed merely provides that debentures issued in a series shall be redeemable by annual drawings without obliging the company to redeem them in that way, the provision means that the company may redeem by drawings at its option, and the debenture holders cannot insist on their debentures being redeemed until the latest date by which the company has promised to repay the principal of the debenture debt.[2] On the other hand, if the trust deed provides that the debentures shall be redeemable on or after a certain date by drawings made by the company, and no drawings are made, all the debentures are treated as falling due for repayment of the amount secured on the specified date.[3] Another common provision which is often combined with a provision for annual drawings is one by which the company can satisfy its obligation to make payments into a sinking fund by purchasing debentures or loan securities comprised in the issue on the market and surrendering them to the trustees of the covering trust deed, whereupon they will be credited to the sinking fund at their nominal value or at the price at which the company bought them, whichever is the less. Sometimes trust deeds empower or require the company to expend a certain sum annually in purchasing debentures or loan securities which are tendered for redemption by their holders, and the trust deed then usually provides that such purchases will be credited to any sinking fund established under the trust deed. If such a provision for tenders is included, the Stock Exchange will not list any of the company's securities, unless all holders of

---

20 *Knightsbridge Estates Trust Ltd v Byrne* [1940] AC 613, [1940] 2 All ER 401.
1 *Wallace v Universal Automatic Machines Co* [1894] 2 Ch 547.
2 *Re Chicago and North West Granaries Co Ltd* [1898] 1 Ch 263.
3 *Re Tewkesbury Gas Co* [1911] 2 Ch 279; affd [1912] 1 Ch 1. The provision for drawings is treated as a suspensive condition, and if it is not fulfilled, the original date for payment becomes operative.

securities of the series are given an opportunity to tender and are treated on a basis of equality.[4]

The Companies Act 1985 does not prevent the application to debentures and loan securities of the equitable rules designed to preserve a mortgagor's right of redemption, other than the rule which prohibits the undue postponement of the earliest date on which the company may redeem. Thus, if a debenture or loan security agreement provides for some advantage to be given to a holder of the security in addition to the payment of the principal of the secured loan or debt and interest thereon, the provision will be void if it is harsh and unconscionable, or if it prevents the company from getting back its property on redemption in substantially the same form and condition as before the security was created.[5] On the other hand, if the collateral advantage given to the holder of the debentures or loan securities is not harsh or unconscionable, but a reasonable commercial consideration to induce the security holders to make the loan (such as a concession to develop part of the company's land or a pre-emption right over its produce at current market prices), the provision for the advantage will be valid and it will not terminate automatically on redemption of the securities.[5] Companies in straitened circumstances have sometimes been compelled to promise to pay a substantial bonus or premium on redemption to induce investors to lend to them, and have charged their undertakings with payment of both the loan and the bonus or premium. It was held in one case[6] that such a bonus or premium is a clog on the company's right of redemption, and that the company can therefore redeem on repaying the loan and interest only. It is doubtful whether this decision is correct. In the first place, it conflicts with a decision of the Court of Appeal[7] that where a payment in addition to the mortgage loan and interest is secured on the mortgaged property, it forms part of the mortgage debt, and unless equity can set the bargain aside because it is harsh and unconscionable, the mortgagor cannot redeem at all unless he pays the whole amount secured on his property. In the second place, it is clearly contemplated by the Companies Act 1985 that premiums may be paid on the redemptions of debentures,[8] and bonuses are indistinguishable from premiums. By contrast, in another case[9] the court held valid a provision in debentures by which the debenture holders were entitled to one third of the company's surplus assets in a winding up; this was so, even though the debentures did not charge the company's property with payment of the share of surplus assets and even though the debentures were redeemed before the company was wound up.

ISSUES OF DEBENTURES AND CREATION OF LOAN SECURITIES

Allotment of debentures, debenture stock and notes and registration by the company

The way in which a company issues debentures, units of debenture stock, or loan stock or notes depends on whether they are subscribed for by one or a few persons,

4 Stock Exchange: *Admission of Securities to Listing*, Section 9, Chapter 2, para 1.1. The maximum purchase price which may be paid by the company for listed debentures, debenture stock, or loan stock or notes is the average middle market price for dealings during the preceding 10 days, or the current market price, not exceeding 105 per cent of that average (ibid).
5 *De Beers Consolidated Mines Ltd v British South Africa Co* [1912] AC 52; *Kreglinger v New Patagonia Meat and Cold Storage Co Ltd* [1914] AC 25.
6 *Re Rainbow Syndicate Ltd* [1916] WN 178.
7 *Santley v Wilde* [1899] 2 Ch 474.
8 Companies Act 1985, s 130 (2) (see p 168, ante).
9 *Re Cuban Land Co* [1921] 2 Ch 147.

or by a larger number of subscribers. If the debenture or loan security holders are few in number, the negotiations will be private, and will be conducted between the directors or an intermediary acting for the company and the lenders. The simplest instance of this kind is where a bank grants a company overdraft facilities or makes a fixed term loan, and takes a combination of specific and floating charges over the company's assets and undertaking as a security. If the debentures or loan securities are to be issued to a large number of persons, the company will either issue a prospectus or listing particulars inviting the public to subscribe for them, or will arrange for a marketing intermediary (such as a merchant bank, the corporate finance subsidiary of a commercial bank or a firm of broker/dealers) to place the securities or to offer them for sale, or the company will offer them for subscription to its own shareholders or existing debenture or loan security holders by letters of rights or provisional letters of allotment. These different methods of large scale issues have been fully described in Chapters 8 and 9. If in connection with a large scale issue of debentures or loan securities, letters of allotment or acceptance are issued, the persons who hold them when they cease to be renounceable will complete the registration application forms included in them and surrender the letters of allotment or acceptance to the company in return for debentures, debenture stock certificates or other loan security certificates in registered or bearer form. These documents must be issued to the persons entitled to the debentures or other securities within two months after allotment, unless the terms of issue otherwise provide,[10] but if debentures or other loan securities are issued to a nominee of the Stock Exchange approved by the Secretary of State for Trade and Industry, the documents need not be issued within the two month period, and the company need only issue them when the nominee requests.[11]

A contract to subscribe for or to purchase a debenture secured by a fixed or floating charge on land is a contract for the disposition of an interest in land, and must therefore be in writing incorporating, expressly or by reference to another document or documents, all the terms of the contract and be signed by each party to it or by his agent.[12] The same applies to contracts to subscribe for or purchase debenture stock or other loan securities where the securities or covering trust deed contain a mortgage or charge over land.[13] In the case of an issue to a large number of subscribers, the application forms signed by them and the letters of allotment or acceptance signed on behalf of the company or intermediary concerned with marketing the issue will constitute the necessary written contract.

If a person contracts to lend money on mortgage and refuses to do so, the intending borrower cannot obtain an order of specific performance to compel him to make the loan.[14] The reason for this is that the intending borrower may obtain his loan elsewhere, and he is therefore adequately compensated for the lender's breach of contract by an award of damages. The underlying reason does not hold good, however, when a company is raising a large loan. It invites subscriptions from the public when it thinks that the issue is most likely to succeed, and a deterioration in market conditions over only a few days could turn a potentially successful issue into a hopeless one. Consequently, the Companies Act 1985 provides

---

10 Companies Act 1985, s 185 (1).
11 Ibid, s 185 (4). The nominee is the company formed by the Stock Exchange, SEPON Ltd, to facilitate the settlement of bargains (see p 311 ante).
12 Law of Property (Miscellaneous Provisions) Act 1989, s 2 (1) to (3) Halsbury's Statutes (4th Edn) 8, Real Property); *Driver v Broad* [1893] 1 QB 539.
13 *Toppin v Lomas* (1855) 16 CB 145 (bonds entitling the holder to the benefit of a trust deed which contained a legal mortgage of land to trustees).
14 *Rogers v Challis* (1859) 27 Beav 175; *South African Territories Ltd v Wallington* [1898] AC 309.

that a contract to subscribe for debentures, debenture stock or other loan securities may be enforced by an order of specific performance,[15] and so subscribers who are disappointed by a change in market conditions since they subscribed cannot deprive the company of the money they have agreed to lend to it. But if the terms of issue provide that the company may forfeit debentures, debenture stock or other loan securities on the holder's failure to pay any instalment of the issue price on the due date, and the company exercises its power of forfeiture, it cannot thereafter sue the subscriber for specific performance.[16] Nor in that case can the company sue the subscriber for damages, unless its right to do so is expressly reserved by the terms of issue.[16]

Unless debentures, debenture stock or other loan securities are issued in bearer form, the securities or the covering trust deed will require the company to keep a register of debenture holders or security holders in a form similar to its register of members. Upon the surrender of letters of allotment or acceptance (if any have been issued), the company or its registrars and transfer agents, or the debenture or security holders' trustees acting as the company's agents, will open such a register showing the names and addresses of the holders of the debentures or securities and the amount and distinguishing numbers (if any) of the debentures or units of the security which they hold. When the debentures or securities are transferred appropriate entries will be made in the register showing the date of the registration of each transfer, the amount of the securities held by the transferee, and the amount (if any) retained by the transferor. Although the Companies Act 1985 does not oblige a company to maintain a register of debenture holders, it does provide that if such a register is maintained, it must be kept at one of the places where the company may keep its register of members,[17] and if the register is kept elsewhere than at the company's registered office, the company must notify the Registrar of Companies where it is kept.[18] The register must be open to inspection by debenture holders, other loan security holders and members of the company without charge and to other persons on payment of a fee not exceeding 5p or such other fee as may be prescribed by the Secretary of State for Trade and Industry, but it may be closed for not more than 30 days each year, when neither inspections nor the registration of transfers will be permitted.[19] Any person may at any time require the company to supply him with a copy of the whole or part of the register for a fee not exceeding 10p for each hundred words copied or such other fee as the Secretary of State may prescribe.[20] Furthermore, any debenture holder or loan security holder may require the company to supply him with a copy of the trust deed securing the series of debentures or other loan securities in which he is interested on payment of a fee not exceeding 20p if the trust deed is printed, or 10p for each hundred words copied if it is not, or such other fees as the Secretary of State may prescribe.[1] A register of the holders of debentures or other loan securities may be kept in books or records or in non-legible form (such as magnetised computer tape or disks), and the same rules then apply in respect of it as apply to a register of members kept in non-legible form.[2]

The Companies Act 1985 requires every limited company to keep a register of charges at its registered office in respect of all specific mortgages and charges

15 Companies Act 1985, s 195.
16 *Kuala Pahi Rubber Estates Ltd v Mowbray* (1914) 111 LT 1072.
17 Companies Act 1985, s 190 (3) (see p 335, ante).
18 Ibid, s 190 (5) and (6).
19 Ibid, s 191 (1) and (6), as amended by Companies Act 1989, s 143 (4).
20 Companies Act 1985, s 191 (2), as amended by Companies Act 1989, s 143 (4).
 1 Companies Act 1985, s 191 (3), as amended by Companies Act 1989, s 143 (4).
 2 Companies Act 1985, s 722 (1) and s 723 (see p 335, ante).

secured on its property and of all floating charges secured on its undertaking or on any of its assets.[3] This register shows the sum secured, the property charged and the names of the persons entitled to the charge,[3] and is open to inspection by the company's members and creditors without payment and by other persons on payment of a fee not exceeding 5p or such other fee as the Secretary of State may prescribe.[4] The register is separate from the register of debenture holders and differs from it in two respects: first, the register of charges does not contain particulars of unsecured loan stock or notes which are not secured by a charge on the company's property; and secondly, when a trust deed is employed, the trustees will be shown as the persons entitled to the charge on the company's property, and no particulars of the individual debenture holders or other loan security holders will be given. Failure by the company to register a mortgage or charge in its register of charges does not affect the mortgagee's security or priority, unless the failure to register was procured or connived at by the mortgagee or chargee with the intention of concealing his mortgage or charge from subsequent creditors of the company, and the creditor who seeks to treat the mortgage or charge as ineffective is such a subsequent creditor.[5] In addition to a register of charges a company must keep at its registered office a copy of every instrument creating or evidencing a charge over any of the company's property or assets, whether the charge is required to be registered with the Registrar of Companies under the provisions of the Companies Act 1985 dealt with hereafter or not.[6] Copies of such charges and the register of charges kept by the company must be available for inspection by members and creditors of the company without charge and by other persons for a fee not exceeding 5p or such other amount as the Secretary of State may prescribe.[7] Any person may require the company to supply him with a copy of any instrument creating or evidencing a charge over the company's property or assets, or a copy of any part of the register of charges kept by the company, on payment of a fee of 10p for each 100 words copied, or such other fee as the Secretary of State may prescribe.[8]

No stamp duty is now payable in respect of loan capital raised by the issue of debentures, debenture stock or other loan securities.[9]

Equality betweeen debenture holders

When several debentures are issued in succession and are secured on the same property, they rank for repayment in the order they are created, in accordance with the equitable rules governing the priority of mortgages, unless they contain a contrary provision.[10] But when debentures are issued in a series to a large number of subscribers, it is not intended that they should rank in succession for repayment according to the dates of their respective subscriptions, but that they should have equal rights, so that if their security is insufficient to repay their loans in full, each debenture holder will be repaid a rateable proportion of what is owed to him. Consequently, debentures issued in a series always contain a clause which provides that they shall rank pari passu (ie equally) in point of charge without any

---

3 Ibid, s 411 (2), as substituted by Companies Act 1989, s 101.
4 Companies Act 1985, s 412 (1), as substituted by Companies Act 1989, s 101.
5 *Wright v Horton* (1887) 12 App Cas 371; *Re General South America Co* (1876) 2 ChD 337.
6 Companies Act 1985, s 411 (1), as substituted by Companies Act 1989, s 101. For registration of charges at the Companies Registry, see p 493, et seq, post.
7 Companies Act 1985, s 412 (1), as substituted by Companies Act 1989, s 101.
8 Companies Act 1985, s 412 (2), as substituted by Companies Act 1989, s 101.
9 Finance Act 1973, s 49 (2).
10 *Gartside v Silkstone and Dodworth Coal and Iron Co* (1882) 21 ChD 762.

preference or priority one over another by reason of the order in which they are issued or for any other reason. Alternatively, a clause to the same effect is inserted in the trust deed under which the debentures are issued, and each debenture states that it is issued subject to the terms and conditions of the trust deed. When debenture stock is issued it is not necessary to have such a clause, because the company's assets are charged to the trustees to secure the global loan contributed by the stockholders, and they, as beneficiaries of the trust on which that debt is held, inevitably have equal rights in respect of the fractions of that single debt to which they are respectively entitled. Nevertheless, out of caution a pari passu clause is inserted in the trust deed even in this case, and also in the trust deed covering an issue of loan stock or notes. Unless a pari passu clause otherwise provides, the company may issue debentures or other loan securities of the series at any time before a receiver is appointed under the securities or before the holders of them realise their security in any other way, and a loan security of the series issued after a debenture holders' action is brought but before a receiver is appointed is not excluded from the series.[11]

The terms of debentures or other loan securities forming a series or the trust deed covering them always limit the total amount which the company may raise by issuing securities of the same series.[12] This ensures that if the mortgage or charge given to secure the global amount of the series turns out to be insufficient, there will be only a limited amount of indebtedness to be satisfied out of it, and each security holder will be repaid a larger fraction of his entitlement than if the company had had an unlimited power to issue securities ranking pari passu with his. If the company issues all the debentures or other securities of the series, it can raise further money by issuing a second series, but debenture holders of that series will be repaid out of the security only when the holders of the first series have been repaid in full. Limits are similarly placed on the total amount which may be raised by an issue of unsecured loan stock or notes, not in order to preserve the sufficiency of the security, for there is none, but simply in order to limit the total of the company's unsecured indebtedness which its assets will be called on to satisfy if it is wound up. In the case of loan stock and note issues, it is also desirable to limit the total amount of the company's other current indebtedness and the medium and long term debts the company may incur, for these debts too will rank equally for payment with the loan stock or notes if the company becomes insolvent. Such limits are also often imposed out of caution by trust deeds covering debentures or other loan securities which are secured by a floating charge on the company's undertaking.

The limit on the number of debentures or the amount of debenture or loan stock or notes of the same series which the company may issue sets a limit on the risk undertaken by each security holder. But if the company redeems or repurchases any of the securities of the series before the contractual date for redemption and the company is still solvent, an unredeemed security holder is better secured than he was before, because the property or assets charged by the securities on the company's assets generally will now be called upon to satisfy a smaller total amount

---

11 *Re Hubbard & Co Ltd, Hubbard v Hubbard & Co Ltd* (1898) 68 LJ Ch 54.
12 It used to be the practice to limit the amount raised by issuing securities of the series to a specific sum, such as £5m in nominal value. In recent years it has become more usual to have a floating limit by which further loan securities ranking pari passu with those previously issued may be issued if the interest payable in respect of the old and the new securities will be covered, say, three or four times by the company's earnings (as shown by its last profit and loss acount) or by its average earnings over the last two or three years, and if the principal repayable in respect of the old and new securities will be covered, say, two, three or four times by the company's net assets after deduction of all other indebtedness (as shown by its last balance sheet). Often such a floating limit is accompanied by a specific maximum limit on the total amount of securities of the series which may be issued.

of indebtedness, and he therefore has more chance of being paid his debt in full if the company later becomes insolvent. At common law the improvement in the debenture or other security holder's position was permanent, because the redeemed or repurchased debentures or other securities were extinguished by the company acquiring them, and they could not be re-issued.[13] The Companies Act 1985 now empowers the company to re-issue redeemed debentures, debenture stock or other loan securities, however, with the same rights and priority as though they had not been redeemed.[14] Consequently, a re-issue of debentures or loan securities restores the unredeemed security holder to his former position, but he is not really prejudiced by the re-issue; all that he has lost is the increased security which he temporarily enjoyed by reason of the premature redemption. Since a subscriber of a re-issued debenture or loan security has by statute the same rights and priorities as though it had not been redeemed,[15] the company may not vary these rights on a re-issue, for to do so would be to issue an entirely new security, not to re-issue the old one.[16] The result of the company varying the terms of the security (eg in respect of the rate of interest to be paid, or the date for or method of redemption) is that the security will be treated as not belonging to the original series at all, and in most cases this will mean that any mortgage or charge created by it, or created for the benefit of its holder under the trust deed of the original series referred to in it, will be subordinate to the security to which the remaining security holders of the original series are entitled.[16] A company may not re-issue redeemed debentures or loan securities if its articles or any contract which it has entered into forbid it to do so,[17] and so if the debentures or the trust deed covering the series prohibit re-issue, an attempted re-issue of a redeemed debenture or other security will be ineffective against the remaining security holders of the series; the 're-issued' debenture will form a separate series by itself, and any mortgage or charge which it confers over the company's assets will be subject to the security interests of the holders of unredeemed debentures or securities of the first series. Furthermore, a redeemed or repurchased debenture or other loan security may not be re-issued if the company has cancelled it by resolution of the directors or otherwise,[17] and this is so even if the subscriber of the re-issued debenture or security is unaware of the cancellation.

When a company issues debentures or debenture or loan stock in a series, it need not require each person who subscribes for a debenture or unit of debenture or loan stock to lend the same amount of money on the security of it, unless the debentures are issued on those terms, as they will be if they are issued under a prospectus which stipulates for a uniform issue price. Thus, if the company issues some debentures or loan securities of a series at par, it may issue others to secure a loan of less than their nominal value. In that situation the company's obligation is to repay the actual amount advanced, and the debentures are merely given as collateral security for repayment.[18] If there is a pari passu clause in the debentures or covering trust deed, all the debenture or other security holders will be repaid rateably out of the proceeds of realising a mortgage or charge given to secure the series in proportion to the nominal value of their respective holdings, and so if the proceeds of realisation are insufficient, those subscribers who advanced to the company less than the nominal value of their debentures will receive back a greater fraction of their loans

13 *Re George Routledge & Sons Ltd* [1904] 2 Ch 474.
14 Companies Act 1985, s 194 (1). The power to re-issue redeemed debentures was first conferred by the Companies Act 1907, and has been re-enacted in each major Companies Act since then.
15 Companies Act 1985, s 194 (2).
16 *Re Antofagasta (Chili) and Bolivia Rly Co Ltd's Trust Deed* [1939] Ch 732, [1939] 2 All ER 461.
17 Companies Act 1985, s 194 (1).
18 *Re Regent's Canal Ironworks Co* (1876) 3 ChD 43; *Robinson v Montgomeryshire Brewery Co* [1896] 2 Ch 841.

than the other debenture holders of the series, but they cannot, of course, receive back more than they actually lent.[18] This kind of transaction must be distinguished from the issue of debentures or debenture or loan stock at a discount. There the company's obligation is to repay the nominal value of the debentures, and the discount may be regarded as the price the company has to pay to obtain the money advanced by the debenture holders. If debentures of the same series are issued at different rates of discount (as they may be unless the terms of issue provide otherwise), all the debenture holders will be repaid rateably out of their security in proportion to the nominal value of their holdings, even though this results in some of them recovering more than they advanced to the company while others receive less.

Subordination agreements and arrangements

A company may issue a debenture or loan security or a series of debentures or loan securities which is expressed subordinated to specified existing debts of the company (whether secured or not), or to indebtedness up to a certain maximum amount which the company may incur in the future, or to securities which it may issue in the future. The purpose of such provisions is to ensure that if the company is wound up or if a receiver is appointed to realise the debenture holders' security, the indebtedness of the company will be discharged out of its assets in a different order from that prescribed by law or from the order of priority for discharging secured indebtedness which would normally obtain. This is achieved by the creditor or creditors who would normally rank in priority or pari passu renouncing their priority and so postponing the satisfaction of their claims to those of other creditors. Such provisions for the subordination of indebtedness operate primarily when the company is insolvent, but they may be extended so as to prevent the company paying a subordinated debt while it is a going concern if other debts to which the debt in question is subordinated remain unpaid, and the effect is then to postpone the contractual date for payment of the subordinated debt.

If a debt secured by debentures or other loan securities is expressed to be subordinated to any other indebtedness of the company, whether secured or not, the conditions of subordination form part of the contract between the debenture or security holders or their trustees and the company, but there is no direct contractual relationship between the debenture holders and the creditors of the company to whose claims the debenture holders' rights are subordinated.[19] Nevertheless, it appears that such other creditors may enforce the provision for subordination, and prevent the subordinated debenture or security holders from relying on any priority rights under a mortgage or charge created by the company in their favour, or by relying on any right to equality of treatment which the general law would give them.[20] The other creditors may do this either by showing that the company contracted with the subordinated debenture holders as a trustee for the other creditors, since the conditions of subordination could only benefit the other creditors and not the company itself,[1] or by proving that the company acted as an agent for

19 If the subordination condition is expressed in the form of a covenant between the debenture or security holders or their trustees on the one hand and the company and the creditors who are intended to benefit on the other hand, the creditors (if an existing closed class of persons) may enforce the condition directly as persons with whom the covenant is made (Law of Property Act 1925, s 56 (1)) (37 Halsbury's Statutes (4th Edn) 156).

20 Eg the Insolvency Act 1986, s 107. The company itself may enforce the subordination provision specifically against the debenture holders (*Beswick v Beswick* [1968] AC 58, [1967] 2 All ER 1197).

1 *Tomlinson v Gill* (1756) Amb 330; *Gregory and Parker v Williams* (1817) 3 Mer 582; *Affréteurs Réunis Société Anonyme v Leopold Walford (London) Ltd* [1919] AC 801.

the other creditors in negotiating the subordination, because for example, the other creditors had agreed to defer enforcement of their claims or to release part of the amounts owing to them if the company raised loan capital on subordinated terms. Furthermore, if the other creditors act in reliance on the subordination provision and would be prejudiced if it were repudiated, they may enforce it in a receivership or in the liquidation of the company as a waiver of the debenture holders' normal right to priority, which is binding on them by estoppel.[2]

In the United States, where the courts have frequently been called on to determine the effect of subordination provisions, they have been upheld for various reasons, namely: (a) as valid unilateral contracts binding on the subordinated creditor without any need for the benefited creditors to show that they acted in reliance on the volunteered subordination;[3] (b) as creating an equitable estoppel binding on the subordinated creditor when the benefited creditors act on it (eg by making advances);[4] (c) as implied assignments of, or charges over, the subordinated debt in favour of the benefited creditors, so enabling them to rely on the priority or security which the subordinated creditor would otherwise have as security for their own claims;[5] or (d) as giving rise to a constructive trust in favour of the benefited creditors over the amount recoverable by the subordinated creditor out of the company's assets in the absence of a subordination provision.[6] It is unlikely that English law would validate subordination arrangements as unilateral contracts, because it treats such contracts as coming into existence only when the offeree does the act proposed by the offeror and thereby furnishes consideration;[7] if this requirement were to be applied by English law in the case of subordination provisions, the benefited creditors would be able to enforce the provision only in the same circumstances as they could rely on it as creating an estoppel. It is also unlikely that English law would imply an assignment, charge or trust from a subordination provision which is merely contractual in terms and which lacks any clear indication that an assignment, charge or trust was intended.[8] It would, of course, be possible for a subordination provision to contain an express assignment of, or charge over, the subordinated debt in favour of the benefited creditors or an express trust of it for them, and this is usually done. Whatever form is used, however, it would appear that the assignment, charge or trust would be treated as given by way of security,[9] and so it would take effect as a sub-mortgage of any mortgage or charge held by the subordinated creditor over the company's assets. This would mean that the benefited creditors would be able to rely on any security over the company's assets given to them directly, on any security held by the subordinated creditor over the company's assets and on any preferential personal right of the subordinated creditor to payment out of the company's assets generally[10] in order to obtain payment in full of the amount owed to them by the company.

2 *Blake v Gale* (1886) 32 ChD 571; *Re Wickham* (1917) 34 TLR 158; *Amalgamated Investment and Property Co Ltd v Texas Commerce International Bank Ltd* [1982] QB 84, [1981] 1 All ER 923, affd; [1982] QB 84, [1981] 3 All ER 577; *Re Walker Construction Co Ltd* [1960] NZLR 523; *Horne v Chester and Fein Property Developments Pty Ltd* [1987] ACLC 245.
3 *Re A B Kreuger & Toll* 96 F 2d 768 (1938); *Re Credit Industrial Corpn 366 F 2d 402* (1966).
4 *Londner v Perlman* 113 NYS 420 (1908); *Re Empire Granite Co* 42 F Supp 440 (1942).
5 *Re George P Schinzel & Son Inc* (1926) 16 F 2d 289; *Re Handy-Andy Community Stores Inc* 2 F Supp 97 (1932); *Bird & Sons Sale Corpn v Tobin* (1935) 78 F 2d 371.
6 *Re Dodge-Freedman Poultry Co* 148 F Supp 647 (1956).
7 *Morrison Shipping Co Ltd (in liquidation) v R* (1924) 20 Ll LRep 283; *Luxor (Eastbourne) Ltd v Cooper* [1941] AC 108, [1941] 1 All ER 33.
8 *Rodick v Gandell* (1852) 1 De GM & G 763; *Citizens' Bank of Louisiana v First National Bank of New Orleans* (1873) LR 6 HL 352; *Morgan v Larivière* (1875) LR 7 HL 423; *Palmer v Carey* [1926] AC 703.
9 *Re Bond Worth Ltd* [1980] Ch 228, [1979] 3 All ER 919.
10 For example, the right to claim the subordinated debt as a preferential payment of the company in its liquidation under the Insolvency Act 1986, s 175 (1) and (2) and s 386 (1) and Sch 6.

TRANSFERS OF DEBENTURES AND LOAN SECURITIES

Debentures and loan securities are transferable subject to equities

The debt evidenced by a debenture or loan note issued by a company and containing a promise to pay the holder is a legal chose in action, whether it is secured by a charge on property or not; as such it may be transferred either by a legal[11] or by an equitable assignment. The rights attached to debenture stock and unsecured loan stock are equitable choses in action, because they take effect under a trust upon which the trustees of the covering trust deed hold the company's undertaking to repay the global loan represented by the stock and any security created in respect of it; units of debenture stock and loan stock are therefore transferable only by equitable assignments.

At common law legal choses in action were not transferable unless statute so provided, but equity assisted a person who had taken a transfer for value of a debt or other legal chose in action by compelling the transferor to sue the debtor, promisor or obligor in the common law courts for the transferee's benefit. The common law courts were, of course, not concerned with the transferee, and the debtor, promisor or obligor was therefore able to plead all defences in the transferor's action which he could have pleaded if the transferor had been suing for his own benefit. Equity followed the law in this respect by allowing the debtor or promisor to plead certain equitable defences as well, such as set-off and misrepresentation. Furthermore, when a transferee of a purely equitable chose in action, such as an interest in a trust fund, sued in equity, the trustee or other defendant was allowed to plead all the common law and equitable defences which he could have pleaded in an action by the transferor. Because of their association with the justice administered in the Court of Chancery, these defences became known as 'equities', a misleading expression, because they are not rights or proprietary interests vested in third persons which incumber the title of the transferor, but are merely defences available to the debtor, trustee, promisor, obligor or other defendant against the transferee. Since 1875 legal choses in action have been transferable at law as well as in equity, but still only subject to equities affecting the transferor.[12] The only alteration in the law resulting from this is that a transferee of a legal chose in action can now sue the debtor, promisor or obligor in his own name instead of having to sue circuitously in the name of the original creditor or the person originally entitled to the transferred right. This is a privilege which transferees of equitable choses in action have all along enjoyed.

The defences which a debtor or other defendant may plead when sued by the transferee of a legal or equitable chose in action fall into two groups, and all these defences may be raised by a company which is being sued by a transferee of debentures, debenture stock, loan stock, notes or other loan securities issued by it. The first group comprises defences arising out of the contract which the transferee seeks to enforce, for example, that the debenture or other loan security is a forgery,[13] that the contract to issue the loan security was induced by a fundamental mistake which makes it void,[14] or by a misrepresentation which makes it voidable,[15] or that the loan security was issued in consequence of a breach of fiduciary duty by one of the company's directors.[16] The second group of defences consists of cross-

---

11 Law of Property Act 1925, s 136 (1) (37 Halsbury's Statutes (4th Edn) 257).
12 Judicature Act 1875, s 25 (6), re-enacted by Law of Property Act 1925, s 136 (1).
13 *Ruben v Great Fingall Consolidated* [1906] AC 439.
14 *Graham v Johnson* (1869) LR 8 Eq 36.
15 *Stoddart v Union Trust Ltd* [1912] 1 KB 181.
16 *Athenaeum Life Assurance Society v Pooley* (1858) 3 De G & J 294.

claims by the company against the transferor which may be set off against the transferee's claim. Thus, if the transferor is indebted to the company when the transferee informs the company of the transfer of the loan security, the company may set off the amount owed by the transferor against the debt owed by the company under the loan security, and need pay only the balance to the transferee.[17] The debt owed by the transferor need not arise out of the same transaction as the loan security, but it must be owing when the transferee notifies the company of the transfer, and it must be due for payment by the time the sum payable under the loan security against which set-off is sought also becomes immediately due and payable.[17] However, if a debenture holder who holds partly paid shares in the company transfers his debentures after the commencement of the company's winding up, the liquidator may set off the amount of capital unpaid on the transferor's shares against the debenture debt payable to the transferee, even though the liquidator does not call up the unpaid capital on the shares until after the transferee has notified him of the transfer.[18] The reason for this is that in a winding up capital unpaid on partly paid shares is deemed to become due to the company when the winding up begins, although it is not payable to the liquidator until he calls it up.[19] Consequently, the transferee of a debenture or loan security after the company's winding up has begun takes his transfer at a time when the unpaid capital on the transferor's shares is already notionally due although not immediately payable, and the transferee therefore takes the debentures or loan security subject to the liquidator's right to set off the unpaid capital. But while a company is a going concern unpaid capital becomes owing to the company only when a call is made,[20] and so a transferee of a debenture or loan security from a transferor who is a holder of partly paid shares does not take subject to calls made in respect of the shares after he has notified the company of his transfer.[1] On the other hand, instalments of the issue price of shares fixed by the terms of issue are owing by the allottee from the time of allotment,[2] and it would therefore appear that if the allottee transfers debentures or loan securities he holds in the company, it may set off against the debenture debt any unpaid instalments on the shares, whether already immediately due and payable or not.

On a transfer of a chose in action, not only debts owed by the transferor, but also claims against him for unliquidated damages arising out of the contract sought to be enforced by the transferee[3] or under a closely connected contract,[4] may be set off by the debtor, if such claims arise directly out of the contract and are not merely incidental, so that it would be inequitable for the transferee to enforce the chose in action without making allowance for them. But this does not apply to unliquidated claims arising out of other transactions between the debtor or promisor and the transferor,[5] and so if a company has a claim for unliquidated damages for a tort or breach of another contract committed by a transferor of a debenture or loan security issued by it, it cannot enforce its claim by setting it off against the amount payable to the transferee of the loan security, unless the unliquidated claim has

17 *Watson v Mid Wales Rly Co* (1867) LR 2 CP 593; *Christie v Taunton, Delmard, Lane & Co, Re Taunton Delmard Lane & Co* [1893] 2 Ch 175.
18 *Re China SS Co, ex p Mackenzie* (1869) LR 7 Eq 240.
19 Insolvency Act 1986, s 80.
20 *Re China SS and Labuan Coal Co Ltd, Dawes' Case* (1869) 38 LJ Ch 512.
1 *Re Taunton Delmard Lane & Co*, supra.
2 See p 317, ante.
3 *Re Natal Investment Co, Financial Corpn Claim* (1868) 3 Ch App 355; *Young v Kitchin* (1878) 3 ExD 127.
4 *British Anzani (Felixstowe) Ltd v International Marine Management (UK) Ltd* [1980] QB 137, [1979] 2 All ER 1063.
5 *Stoddart v Union Trust Ltd* [1912] 1 KB 181.

become a liquidated one (eg by the company obtaining judgment against the transferor) before the transferee notifies the company of the transfer.

The rule that equities available to the company against the transferor of debentures or loan securities are also available against the transferee gives way to the rule in *Royal British Bank v Turquand*[6] in situations where the latter rules applies. If the defect or irregularity on the issue of the debentures or other loan securities is one which does not affect the allottee because of the rule,[7] it equally does not affect a transferee from him. Even if the allottee is precluded from relying on the rule in *Turquand's Case* because of his knowledge of the defect, a transferee from him who has no such knowledge may rely on the rule because of his personal reliance on the apparent regularity of the transaction, and the company may not plead the defect against him as an equity.[8] Similarly, if debentures or loan securities contain a receipt for the loan which the allottee is stated to have made to the company or, if the letters of allotment of the loan securities or the debenture or loan stock certificates issued by the company acknowledge that the issue price has been paid in full, the company will be estopped from denying that it received the loan or the issue price of the securities in full as against a transferee for value who has no notice that the loan had not in fact been made or the issue price fully paid.[9] An innocent transferee is also protected in such circumstances if the debentures or debenture or loan stock certificates contain no receipt for the loan, but merely state that the allottee or the person named in the debentures or stock certificates is the registered holder of the debentures or the debenture or loan stock without any qualification indicating that they are not fully paid.[10]

If a chose in action is transferred successively to two or more transferees, no right of set-off which the debtor could plead against any of the intermediate transferees is available against the person at present entitled to the chose in action.[11] Thus, if a company issues a debenture or note for £1,000 to A, who is indebted to the company for £500 when he transfers it to B, and B later transfers the debenture to C when B owes the company £400, the company may set off A's debt of £500 against C's claim, but not B's debt of £400. This is because at common law C would have sued the company in A's name, as though he still owned the debentures or notes, and transactions between the company and B would have been irrelevant to A's rights. Equity has adopted the same rule in respect of successive transfers of equitable choses in action, and so the result would be the same in the above example if the company had allotted debenture stock or loan stock to A and it had been transferred successively by A to B and by B to C.

Exclusion of equities by express provision

If the rule that transfers of choses in action are subject to equities between the debtor and the original creditor were allowed to apply to debentures and other loan securities without modification, they would be practically unmarketable, because a purchaser would always be required to ensure at his peril that no such equities existed between the company and the original holder before the purchaser completed his purchase, and this would clearly be an impossible task, particularly if the purchase were made on the Stock Exchange. Consequently, to make their

6 (1855) 5 E & B 248; affd (1856) 6 E & B 327 (see p 112 et seq, ante).
7 For examples, see *Duck v Tower Galvanising Co* [1901] 2 KB 314 (p 114, ante) and *Gloucester County Bank v Rudry Merthyr Steam and House Coal Colliery Co* [1895] 1 Ch 629 (p 117, ante).
8 *Robinson v Montgomeryshire Brewery Co* [1896] 2 Ch 841.
9 *Bickerton v Walker* (1885) 31 ChD 151.
10 *Robinson v Montgomeryshire Brewery Co*, supra.
11 *Re Milan Tramways Co, ex p Theys* (1884) 25 ChD 587.

debentures and other loan securities as marketable as shares and thus induce investors to subscribe for them, companies always insert a provision in the debentures or in the trust deed covering an issue of debenture stock or loan stock by which the issuing company foregoes its right to raise equities against transferees. A typical provision of this kind is the following:

'The principal moneys and interest hereby secured will be paid without regard to any equities between the company and the original or any intermediate holder hereof, and the receipt of the registered holder for such principal moneys and interest shall be a good discharge to the company for the same.'

Such a clause estops the company from raising equities against transferees, but it has been held[12] that if the clause is in the above form, only a transferee who has been registered by the company in its register of debenture holders or debenture stock holders or its register of loan stock holders or note holders can rely on the estoppel. This is because the latter part of the clause, which entitles the company to accept the receipt of the *registered* holder as a good discharge, modifies the meaning of the word 'holder' in the earlier part of the clause; that word, too, must be taken to mean the *registered* holder, and so only registered transferees are entitled to the benefit of the earlier part of the clause which confers immunity from equities. If the latter part of the clause is omitted, however, the word 'holder' in the earlier part of the clause has been held to include an unregistered transferee, and he as well as a registered transferee is protected against equities which the company could plead against the original holder of the debentures, debenture stock, loan stock or notes.[13] The artificial interpretation given by the court to the word 'holder' when the clause is set out in full is both logically unjustifiable and practically inconvenient, because it means that before completing his purchase a purchaser of the debentures or other loan securities must make the very enquiries as to the existence of equities which the clause was designed to obviate. The modern practice is to add to the clause set out above the following words:

'The holder of this debenture [*or* of any amount of debenture *or* loan stock *or* notes] shall be entitled to transfer it [*or* them] free from equities between the company and the original or any intermediate holder thereof.'

It has been held that this provision protects an unregistered transferee; the company cannot dispute his right to be registered as a transferee holding the debentures or stock free from equities between the company and the original holder.[14] Nevertheless, to reinforce the point that the provision does not operate merely as a contract between the company and the original holder, it is normal practice to preface the clause set out above with the following words:

'As between the company and any person to whom this debenture [*or* any debenture stock *or* loan stock *or* notes] is transferred (whether the transfer is registered or not). . . .'

Wholly apart from express contractual provisions, it has been held in the case of a company empowered by the statute incorporating it to issue transferable debentures, that the company is estopped from disputing the validity of the issue of debentures as against a transferee for value without notice of any defect attending their issue.[15] This is because the company impliedly invites purchasers to acquire the debentures by holding them out as being freely transferable, and it would be inconsistent with that invitation for the company to impugn the purchaser's title.[15]

---

12 *Re Palmer's Decoration and Furnishing Co* [1904] 2 Ch 743.
13 *Re Goy & Co Ltd, Farmer v Goy & Co Ltd* [1900] 2 Ch 149.
14 *Hilger Analytical Ltd v Rank Precision Industries Ltd* [1984] BCLC 301.

The protection extends to a transferee who has not registered his transfer,[16] but it would not seem to prevent the company from pleading rights of set-off against him if they are available against the original holder before the transferee presents his transfer for registration or notifies the company of the transfer.[17] Whether companies incorporated under the Companies Acts are similarly estopped by holding out their debentures, debenture stock or loan stock or notes as transferable (eg, by making provision in the debentures or the covering trust deed for the registration of transfers), has not yet been decided, but there seems no reason why they should not be.

Even if the circumstances in which a debenture or loan security is issued do not prevent the company from raising equities against a transferee, it may estop itself from doing so by its later conduct. If an intending transferee enquires whether the debentures or other security he is acquiring are valid and whether the company has any cross-claim which it intends to set off against the amount payable under the debenture or other security and the company answers in the negative, it will clearly be unable to rely on any defect in the issue of the debentures or securities or to set off any claim against the transferee after he had completed his purchase on the faith of its answer. Furthermore, the company may impliedly waive its right to raise equities against the transferee by registering his transfer,[18] or accepting a notice of the transfer from him without drawing his attention to the defect on which it subsequently relies.[19] But it has been held that a company does not waive its right to raise equities against a transferee if a receiver for debenture stockholders registers the transfer in the register of debenture stockholders and issues a new debenture stock certificate to the transferee, because a receiver is not the company's agent for this purpose.[20] If by the terms of the debentures or trust deed under which he is appointed the receiver is made the company's agent to register transfers of debentures or debenture stock, however, the company will be estopped by his registration of the transfer from raising equities against the transferee.

If the company is estopped from denying that a debenture or loan security was validly issued as against a transferee, the estoppel operates only against the company and not against the holders of other debentures or securities of the same series which rank pari passu. Consequently, when the debenture holders' security is realised, the other debenture holders can insist on the proceeds of sale being applied primarily in discharging debentures of the series which were validly issued,[1] and the transferee of the invalid debenture will be paid only out of any surplus left over. It would seem that if the trustees for debenture or debenture stockholders are entrusted with keeping the register of debenture holders, they do so on behalf of the company, whether they are or are not expressly made the company's agents for the purpose by the trust deed. Consequently, any conduct by the trustees which estops them from pleading the invalidity of the issue of a debenture or debenture stock against a transferee is effective against the company, but not against the other debenture holders or debenture stockholders of the same series, since the trustees have no authority to make binding representations on their behalf.

15 *Webb v Comrs of Herne Bay* (1870) LR 5 QB 642; *Re Romford Canal Co* (1883) 24 ChD 85.
16 *Re Romford Canal Co*, supra.
17 *Watson v Mid Wales Rly Co* (1867) LR 2 CP 593; *Re Taunton Delmard Lane & Co, Christie v Taunton, Delmard, Lane & Co*, [1893] 2 Ch 175.
18 *Higgs v Assam Tea Co* (1869) LR 4 Exch 387; *Re Northern Assam Tea Co, ex p Universal Life Assurance Co* (1870) LR 10 Eq 458.
19 *Re Hercules Insurance Co, Brunton's Claim* (1874) LR 19 Eq 302.
20 *Re Rhodesia Goldfields Ltd* [1910] 1 Ch 239.
 1 *Mowatt v Castle Steel and Iron Works Co* (1886) 34 ChD 58; *Re W Tasker & Sons Ltd, Hoare v Tasker & Sons Ltd* [1905] 2 Ch 587.

Defects of title to debentures or loan securities

If a transferor's title to debentures or other loan securities is defective because of something which has happened since they were issued by the company, the transferee's position is regulated by the same rules as are applicable to a transfer of shares in those circumstances.[2] Consequently, if the chain of transfers from the original allottee down to the present holder of the securities includes a transfer which is void, for example, because it was forged or induced by a fundamental mistake, the present holder has no title to the securities at all. But if any such transfer was merely voidable by the transferor, the present holder's title is unimpeachable if any person, including himself, acquired the securities for value subsequently to the voidable transfer without notice of the transferor's right to avoid it.

In determining the validity of the present holder's title to debentures or other loan securities, there must also be applied the same rules as those which estop the true owner of shares from impeaching the validity of a transfer made in his name,[3] and from impugning the registration of an invalid transfer which he has ratified.[4] Furthermore, if a company issues a debenture or debenture stock certificate or a loan note stating that the person named therein is the registered holder of certain debentures or debenture stock or notes, the company itself is estopped from denying the validity of his title in the same circumstances as it would be estopped from denying the validity of a share certificate similarly issued.[5] If the debenture or debenture stock certificate or note was improperly issued but the company is estopped from denying its validity, the person named in it as registered holder, or persons who deal with him in reliance on the debenture or stock certificate or note, will be able to sue the company for damages when the true owner is restored to the register. When a company is thus made liable to third persons in consequence of registering a forged transfer, it will be entitled to an indemnity for the damages it has to pay and its costs and expenses from the transferee who submitted the transfer for registration, or from his broker or other agent who submitted the transfer on his behalf.[6] To protect a company against liability when it has registered a transfer which is void or voidable or has paid the principal of the debt secured by the debenture or other loan security or interest thereon to the transferee, the following provision is usually inserted in debentures or loan securities or the covering trust deed:

'The registered holder [i e the person who appears to be entitled to the debenture [*or* stock *or* note] from the company's register of debenture holders] will be regarded as exclusively entitled to the benefit of this debenture [*or* loan stock *or* note], and all persons may act accordingly, and the receipt of the registered holder for such principal moneys and interest shall be a good discharge to the company for the same.'

There is no doubt that such a provision is effective between the company and the true owner of the debentures or other loan securities, at least if the company acts in good faith. Consequently, if the company pays the principal of the debt or interest to a transferee under a forged or defective transfer which it has registered, it will not have to pay the true owner a second time. But it is at least questionable whether the invitation to all persons 'to act accordingly' will prevent the true owner from impeaching the title of a registered holder when he could do so under the general

---

2 See p 346, et seq, ante.
3 *Rimmer v Webster* [1902] 2 Ch 163 (see p 347, ante).
4 *Welch v Bank of England* [1955] Ch 508, [1955] 1 All ER 811 (see p 350, ante).
5 *Sheffield Corpn v Barclay* [1905] AC 392 (see p 350, ante).
6 Ibid; *Royal Exchange Assurance v Moore* (1863) 8 LT 242; *Reynolds v Smith* (1893) 9 TLR 494 (see p 352, ante).

law. If the true owner remains entitled to do this, the registered holder has merely a defeasible title, good against the company, but liable to be destroyed by the true owner taking steps to have the register of debenture or security holders rectified.

There is no summary procedure to determine which of several persons claiming the same debentures, debenture or loan stock or loan notes is entitled to be registered as the holder, as there is to determine disputed claims to shares.[7] If the company receives conflicting claims to the same debentures or other loan securities, it may protect itself by interpleading. The company has a statutory right to do so in respect of debentures and loan notes,[8] and as the court will permit an interpleader where there are conflicting claims to an equitable interest by analogy to legal claims,[9] the company may also interplead in respect of debenture or loan stock. It would seem that the company's right to interplead is not taken away by the provision usually inserted in debentures, debenture and loan stock certificates and loan notes and trust deeds covering debenture or loan stock that the registered holder shall be deemed exclusively entitled to the debentures, notes or stock.

If a company incurs liability to any person as a result of making or deleting an entry in its register of debenture or loan security holders or as a result of a failure to make or delete such an entry, the liability may not be enforced against it more than 20 years after the entry was made or deleted, or as the case may be, after the company's earliest failure to make or delete the entry.[10] This provision appears to relate only to claims for damages against the company, and not to affect the right of a person to assert a title to debentures or loan securities. Moreover, the provision does not affect any shorter limitation period which may be applicable.[10]

Bearer debentures

After some conflict of judicial opinion, it was finally established in two cases at the turn of the last century[11] that debentures in which a company undertakes to pay the debenture debt and interest to the bearer of the debentures are negotiable instruments, and the title to them can consequently be transferred by mere delivery of the debentures without notification to the company. The negotiable quality of bearer debentures also makes them transferable free from equities between the company and the original holder and free from defects in the title of previous holders.[12] It follows that the protective clauses inserted in registered debentures are unnecessary in bearer debentures, and they are consequently omitted. Of course, a transferee of a bearer debenture will only take free from equities and defects in his transferor's title if he has no notice of them and gives value for the transfer,[13] but in the case of negotiable instruments, the debtor's right of set-off against the original holder is not considered to be an equity attaching to the instrument, and consequently a transferee of a bearer debenture takes free from such a right belonging to the company whether he knows of it or not.[14] There is no judicial decision that debenture stock and loan stock certificates in favour of bearer and

---

7 Companies Act 1985, s 359 (1) (see p 337, ante).

8 Law of Property Act 1925, s 136 (1) (37 Halsbury's Statutes (4th Edn) 257).

9 *Usher v Martin* (1889) 24 QBD 272.

10 Companies Act 1985, s 191 (7).

11 *Bechuanaland Exploration Co v London Trading Bank* [1898] 2 QB 658; *Edelstein v Schuler & Co* [1902] 2 KB 144.

12 See pp 346 and 347, ante, where the effect of negotiability is dealt with in connection with share warrants.

13 *Venables v Baring Bros & Co* [1892] 3 Ch 527.

14 *Burrough v Moss* (1830) 10 B & C 558; *Oulds v Harrison* (1854) 10 Exch 572; *Montecchi v Shimco (UK) Ltd* [1980] 1 WLR 1180, [1980] 1 Lloyd's Rep 50.

loan notes to bearer which are not promissory notes[15] are similarly negotiable instruments, but they are treated as negotiable by mercantile usage,[16] and there can therefore be no doubt that they are negotiable and that the same rules apply to them as to bearer debentures.

If bearer debentures or bearer debenture stock or loan stock certificates are issued, the company keeps no register of debenture holders in respect of them, but it must enter particulars of the debentures or the covering trust deed in the register of charges it is required to keep if they are secured on any part of its undertaking.[17] Stamp duty was formerly payable on bearer debentures and bearer debenture stock certificates at three times the rate on which stamp duty was charged on transfers of registered debentures for a consideration equal to the issue price.[18] Stamp duty on transfers of registered debentures has now been abolished, except where the debentures are convertible into shares or contain special terms,[19] and consequently no stamp duty is now payable on the issue of bearer debentures or of debenture stock or loan certificates to bearer or of loan notes to bearer, unless they fall into the excepted categories.[20]

EQUITABLE INTERESTS IN DEBENTURES

Equitable interests may be created out of debentures, debenture stock, loan stock and loan notes in the same way and with the same consequences as out of shares.[1] The owner of an equitable interest may preserve priority for it over interests later created by serving a stop notice on the company,[2] or alternatively, by serving a mere written notice on the company, or, in the case of debenture stock, on the trustees of the trust deed, before the owners of other interests derived out of the debentures or other securities do so. This is because debts secured by debentures, debenture stock, loan stock and loan notes are choses in action, and priority between interests created out of choses in action is governed by the order in which the owners of such interests give written notice to the debtor, or if the chose in action is equitable, to the trustees.[3] But the owner of a later interest cannot obtain

---

15 Loan notes are promissory notes, and so are negotiable instruments under the Bills of Exchange Act 1882, ss 29 and 38 (5 Halsbury's Statutes (4th Edn) 351, 356) only if they contain an unconditional promise by the company to pay a sum certain in money at a fixed or determinable future time (s 83 (1) and s 89 (1)).

16 The Rules of the Stock Exchange, r 600–1 recognises 'bonds to bearer [and] bearer scrip' as negotiable instruments, and in practice this is extended to debentures, debenture stock, loan stock and unsecured notes to bearer.

17 Companies Act 1985, s 411 (2), substituted by Companies Act 1989, s 101.

18 Finance Act 1963, ss 59 (1) and 61 (1) (41 Halsbury's Statutes (4th Edn) 176, 271).

19 See p 485, post.

20 In these cases stamp duty is payable at the rate of £1·50 per £100 of the issue price of the debentures or debenture or loan stock (see Stamp Act 1891, s 1 and Sch 1, Bearer Instrument (as amended by Finance Act 1963, s 59 (1)); Finance Act 1963, s 55 (1A) (inserted by Finance Act 1986, s 64 (1) and s 79 (2)) (41 Halsbury's Statutes (4th Edn) 176, 267 and 400).

1 See p 355, et seq, ante.

2 Charging Orders Act 1979, s 2 (1) and (2), s 5 (2) and s 6 (1) (22 Halsbury's Statutes (4th Edn) 339); RSC Ord 50, r 11 (1) (for stop notices, see p 356, ante).

3 *Dearle v Hall* (1823–28) 3 Russ 1; *Meux v Bell* (1841) 1 Hare 73; *Marchant v Morton Down & Co* [1901] 2 KB 829; Law of Property Act 1925, s 137 (3) (27 Halsbury's Statutes (3rd Edn) 560). In *Coleman v London County and Westminster Bank* [1916] 2 Ch 353, Neville J treated the question of priority between an unregistered transfer of debentures and a subsequent equitable mortgage of them as determined by the order in which they were executed, even though the mortgagee had no notice of the transfer when he took his mortgage and immediately gave notice to the trustee of the debenture trust deed. Although seemingly inconsistent with other cases of this kind, the decision may be justified by the fact that the transferee under the unregistered transfer was also the trustee of the debenture trust

priority over an earlier one under this rule if he gives no value for his interest, or if at the time he took his interest he has notice of the earlier one.

Unless there is a contractual provision to the contrary, the company or the trustees of the relevant trust deed are bound to accept written notices of derivative equitable interests created out of debentures, debenture stock, loan stock or loan notes and to give effect to them, so that, for example, if a registered debenture holder or debenture stock holder mortgages his securities by an equitable mortgage, the company must not repay the debt represented by the securities to the registered holder when it has received notice of the mortgage. There is no provision in the Companies Act 1985 corresponding to the section[4] which absolves companies from receiving notices of equitable interests derived out of shares. This situation is, of course, inconvenient to the company, which would prefer to be able to deal with the registered debenture or other security holder without regard to derivative equitable interests. To enable it to do so, debentures, trust deeds covering issues of debenture and loan stock and loan notes always contain the following provision:

> 'The registered holder [ie the person who appears to be entitled to the debentures or other securities from the company's register of security holders] will be regarded as exclusively entitled to the benefit of the debenture [or debenture or loan stock or loan notes], and all persons may act accordingly. The company shall not be bound to enter in the register of debenture [or security] holders notice of any trust, or to recognise any trust or equity affecting the title to the debentures [or securities] or the moneys thereby secured.'

Such a provision is undoubtedly effective, and when it is employed the only way in which the owners of derivative equitable interests may protect themselves is by serving stop notices on the company. It seems that the provision is intended only for the company's benefit, despite the generality of the wording of the first sentence. If this is so, the provision will not enable a transferee of debentures or other loan securities who takes them as a gift, or buys them with notice that his transferor holds them in trust or subject to an equitable mortgage, to disregard such equitable interests, and as between himself and the owner of any competing equitable interests priority will be governed by the ordinary rules of property law, subject to the modification that it will not be possible for the owner of any interest to gain priority merely by giving written notice of his interest to the company otherwise than in the form of a stop notice.

Equitable interests may be created out of bearer debentures and debenture and loan stock and out of loan notes in the same way as such interests may be created out of shares represented by share warrants or share certificates to bearer. Bearer debentures, bearer debenture and loan stock, loan notes to bearer and trust deeds covering debenture or loan stock to bearer, always contain a provision absolving the company from receiving notices of such equitable interests, in which case there seems to be no means by which they may be protected, for it would appear that stop notices can only be served in respect of registered securities and securities represented by letters of allotment, and that the negotiable character of bearer debentures prevents stop notices being served to protect interests in them.[5]

Trust deeds covering issues of debenture stock in practice rarely extend the provision absolving the company from receiving notice of derivative interests to the trustees themselves, and it appears that the ordinary rules of equity governing priority between such interests according to the order in which notices of them are

---

deed, and therefore, as the law then stood, received notice of the transfer in his capacity as trustee by being the transferee (see *Browne v Savage* (1859) 4 Drew 635, now overruled by the Law of Property Act 1925, s 137 (3)).

4   Companies Act 1985, s 360 (see p 356, ante).

given to the trustees, are not effectively excluded by the standard provision protecting the company. In this situation serving a stop notice on the company will not secure priority for an equitable interest over earlier interests, but will merely safeguard the interest in question against later transfers of the debentures presented to the company for registration, the normal function of a stop notice. In the case of debenture or loan stock, unless the covering trust deed otherwise provides, the owner of a derivative equitable interest can preserve or gain priority only by giving written notice to the trustees of the covering trust deed, for it is they in whom legal title to the total debt, represented by the debenture or loan stock, is vested. This is so whether the debenture or loan stock is in registered or bearer form. In the latter case the apparent contradiction between the negotiability of a debenture or loan stock certificate to bearer and the effectiveness of notices given to determine priorities between competing derivative interests is resolved when it is realised that interests derived out of bearer stock are not themselves negotiable, but are subject to the general rules of property law. The negotiable quality of bearer stock only comes into play when the whole title to the stock is transferred, not when derivative interests are created out of it. If debenture or loan stock to bearer is transferred to a purchaser for value who acts in good faith, he of course takes it free from any derivative interest of which he is unaware, because of the character of the stock certificate as a negotiable instrument, and the fact that notice of the interest has been given to the trustees of the covering trust deed is then immaterial.

TRANSACTIONS IN RESPECT OF DEBENTURES AND LOAN SECURITIES

The various transactions which may be carried out in respect of debentures, debenture stock, loan stock, and loan notes are the same as those which may be effected in respect of shares, but the incidents of such transactions differ in certain respects from those of corresponding transactions in shares.

No stamp duty is payable on transfers or other disposals of debentures or other securities in connection with such transactions, whether for value or not, if the securities represent loan capital as statutorily defined.[6] The definition comprises all capital raised by a company which has the character of borrowed money,[7] but the exemption does not apply to loan capital which at the date of the transfer carries an immediate or deferred right to convert into shares or other securities, or to subscribe for or acquire shares or other securities, nor does it apply to loan capital which at the date of the transfer carries interest at a higher rate than a reasonable commercial return or at a rate which depends on the profits of the company or the value of any property, nor to loan capital which carries the right to the payment on redemption of a premium in excess of that which is normal in the case of loan capital listed on the Stock Exchange.[8] In these exceptional cases stamp duty is payable on the transfer of debentures at the same rate as on corresponding transfers of shares.[9]

5 See p 356, ante.
6 Finance Act 1986, s 79 (4) and (12) (41 Halsbury's Statutes (4th Edn) 400).
7 Ibid, s 78 (7).
8 Ibid, s 79 (5) and (6).
9 Stamp Act 1891, Sch 1, Conveyance or Transfer on Sale etc; Finance Act 1963, s 55 (1A), inserted by Finance Act 1986, s 64 (1) (41 Halsbury's Statutes (4th Edn) 266).

Sales

The procedure on the sale of debentures or other loan securities is the same as on the sale of shares.[10] The purchaser is entitled to all interest on the debt to which the loan securities relate if it accrues during the current interest period or is in arrear at the date of the contract of sale, unless the contract otherwise provides.[11] If the contract is governed by the Rules of the Stock Exchange, the purchaser is entitled to accruing interest for the current period, but on the day when a payment of interest becomes due, the debentures or loan securities are quoted ex interest, and so if the contract is made on or after that date, the seller will retain the interest when he receives it.[12] On the other hand, the Rules of the Stock Exchange also provide that if interest is in arrear on loan securities which carry a fixed rate of interest, a purchaser is entitled to the arrears, which are treated as having been taken into account in arriving at the purchase price.[13] This would seem to apply only if interest is not paid within a reasonable period after it falls due,[14] and to substantiate the purchaser's claim to the arrears, it would not seem to be necessary for the company to have defaulted for so long that the loan security holders are entitled to enforce their security. The Stock Exchange Rules require that the contract notes issued by the members of the Stock Exchange who conclude the sale must specify the arrears of interest which are included in the price,[13] but failure to do this would not appear to affect the rights of the purchaser.

The instrument of transfer of a debenture or other loan security is in the same form as a share transfer. If the debenture or loan security is secured by a legal mortgage of the company's property, the transfer should be made by deed in order to pass the legal title to the mortgage.[15] If the loan security is secured by an equitable mortgage or charge, or is unsecured, or if debenture stock or loan stock or loan notes are the subject of the sale, a transfer signed by the seller suffices.[16] However, if the loan security is fully paid, the simplified form of transfer signed by the transferor now provided by the Stock Transfer Act 1963 may be used,[17] even if the loan security carries the benefit of a legal mortgage. Bearer debentures and loan securities in bearer form, and also renounceable letters of allotment or acceptance in respect of debentures or other loan securities are transferred by delivery to the purchaser without any instrument of transfer being required, but in the case of letters of allotment or acceptance it is necessary that the allottee should have signed the accompanying letter of renunciation.

The transfer of registered debentures or loan securities is completed by the purchaser submitting the debentures, debenture stock certificate, loan stock certificate or loan note and the executed transfer to the company, which enters the transfer in its register of debenture or loan security holders and in its register of charges (if necessary), and returns the original document in respect of the loan security to the transferee endorsed with a note of the transfer, or issues a new debenture, debenture stock certificate, loan stock certificate or loan note, in his name to him, as the case may be. No transfer may be registered unless a written

---

10 See p 374, ante.
11 *Cottrell v Finney* (1874) 9 Ch App 541; *Re Kidner, Kidner v Kidner* [1929] 2 Ch 121; *Barclays Bank Ltd v R* [1974] QB 823, [1974] 1 All ER 305.
12 Rules of Stock Exchange, r 515.1*d*.
13 Ibid, r 602.4.
14 This is normally taken to be seven days from the contractual date for payment of the interest.
15 Law of Property Act 1925, s 114 (1) (37 Halsbury's Statutes (4th Edn) 239).
16 Ibid, s 53 (1) (*c*) and s 136 (1) (37 Halsbury's Statutes (4th Edn) 153, 257).
17 Stock Transfer Act 1963, s 1 (1) and (4) and Sch 1 (30 Halsbury's Statutes (4th Edn) 157, 163); The Stock Transfer (Amendment of Forms) Order 1974 (SI 1974/1214) (see p 340, ante).

instrument of transfer is delivered to the company.[18] Transfers of debentures may be certificated by the company in the same way as share transfers and with the same consequences.[19] The company is under a duty to have the original document in respect of the loan security transferred or a new debenture or loan stock certificate or loan note ready for delivery to the transferee within two months after the transfer is presented for registration, unless the terms of issue of the securities otherwise provide, or the transfer is to a nominee of the Stock Exchange approved by the Secretary of State for Trade and Industry.[20] The directors of a company which has a Stock Exchange listing for any of its securities must issue new debentures, debenture or loan stock certificates or loan notes in the name of the transferee within 14 days after the transfer is presented for registration.[1]

If by the terms of issue of the debentures or loan securities the company is entitled to refuse to register transfers, it must notify the transferee that it has exercised its right of refusal within two months after the transfer is presented for registration.[2] If registration of a transfer is improperly refused, either the transferor or the transferee may apply to the court for an order against the company to register the transfer.[3] The summary procedure for this purpose in respect of shares[4] is not available in the case of debentures; the application must therefore be either for a mandatory injunction to compel the company to register the transfer[3] or for an order for specific performance of the company's promise to maintain a proper register. If the trust deed covering debentures or other loan securities delegates the task of keeping the register of debenture or security holders to the trustees appointed under the deed, it appears that transfers of securities may be presented to them for registration as the company's agents, but the company is responsible for the trustees' defaults in carrying out the company's statutory duties to register transfers, and the company should therefore be made a defendant in proceedings for the rectification of the register.

Gifts

A registered debenture or loan may be transferred by way of gift, and the procedure for the transfer to the donee is the same as on a sale. A bearer debenture, a loan security in bearer form or a renounced letter of allotment or acceptance in respect of a debenture or loan security may be transferred to a donee by mere physical delivery. If a registered debenture or loan security holder executes a transfer to a donee and delivers it to him, and then revokes the gift or dies before the transfer is registered, the gift is complete, because the donor has done all he need do to transfer the title, and all that remains to be done is for the donee to present the transfer for registration.[5] The rule is undoubtedly the same in respect of gifts of debenture stock and loan stock, for the court has held that a gift of an equitable, as well as a legal, chose in action is complete as soon as the donor has done all he need do to transfer his title, and the mere fact that the donee has not notified the debtor or the trustee of the transfer of the equitable interests does not make the gift inchoate so as to invalidate it on the donor's death or attempted revocation.[6]

18 Companies Act 1985, s 183 (1) (see p 341, ante).
19 Ibid, s 184 (see p 379, ante).
20 Ibid, s 185 (1) and (4) (see p 341, ante).
 1 Stock Exchange: *Admission of Securities to Listing.* Section 5, Chapter 2, para 28.
 2 Companies Act 1985, s 183 (5).
 3 *Re British Sugar Refining Co* (1857) 3 K & J 408.
 4 Companies Act 1985, s 359 (1); RSC Ord 102, r 3 (1) (application by originating motion) (see p 337, ante).
 5 *Re Rose* [1949] Ch 78, [1948] 2 All ER 971; *Re Rose* [1952] Ch 499, [1952] 1 All ER 1217 (see p 403, ante).
 6 *Letts v IRC* [1956] 3 All ER 588, [1957] 1 WLR 201.

Mortgages and charges

A registered debenture or other loan security may be mortgaged or charged by
either of the same two methods as shares, namely, by a legal mortgage consisting of
a registered transfer of the securities to the lender, with or without an accompanying
agreement setting out the terms of the transaction and containing a provision for
re-transfer on redemption; or alternatively, by an equitable mortgage or charge
created by an express agreement to transfer or charge the securities to the lender,
or by the borrower depositing with the lender the borrower's debenture, loan note
or debenture stock or loan stock certificate with or without a transfer form executed
in blank by the borrower. The differences between these different kinds of
mortgages and charges have already been explained.[7]

If the mortgagor fails to pay the mortgage debt or interest thereon, the mortgagee
or chargee may sell or foreclose in exactly the same way as if the mortgage or
charge were one of shares.[8] If the debentures or loan securities have been transferred
to the mortgagee, he is able to transfer them to the person to whom he sells them
without the concurrence of the mortgagor. On the other hand, an equitable
mortgagee or chargee by express agreement or by deposit of debentures, debenture
or loan stock certificates or loan notes will be able to transfer the securities to a
purchaser only by obtaining an order of the court authorising him to do so, or by
completing a blank transfer executed by the borrower if such a transfer was
deposited with him when the mortgage or charge was created, or by exercising any
express power to sell and transfer the debentures or other loan securities conferred
on him by the agreement setting out the terms of the mortgage or charge.

A mortgage of a debenture or other loan security in bearer form is created, like
a mortgage of shares represented by a share warrant or bearer share certificate, by
delivery of the debentures, debenture stock or loan stock certificates or the loan
notes to the mortgagee or chargee, usually accompanied by an agreement
containing the terms of the loan. Debentures or loan securities represented by a
renounced letter of allotment or acceptance may likewise be mortgaged or charged
by delivering the letter of allotment to the mortgagee or chargee accompanied by
a letter of renunciation signed by the allottee, and it will also usually be
accompanied by an agreement setting out the terms of the mortgage or charge. On
redemption the mortgagee re-transfers the debentures or other securities to the
mortgagor, or the chargee terminates the charge, by re-delivering the documents
deposited with him. If the mortgagor defaults, the mortgagee or chargee can sell
the debentures or loan securities and transfer them to a purchaser by delivering to
him the loan security in bearer form or the renounced letter of allotment or
acceptance, or a mortgagee (but not a chargee) may obtain a foreclosure order
from the court.[9] But if the deposit of the bearer securities or renounced letter of
allotment is not accompanied by an agreement which makes it clear that the
transaction is a mortgage, the court will treat it as a pledge, and although the
lender will be able to sell the securities he will not be able to obtain a foreclosure
order.[9]

Trusts

Trusts of registered debentures and other loan securities are created in the same
way as trusts of shares, and trusts of loan securities in bearer form and renounced
letters of allotment or acceptance in respect of loan securities are created in the

---

7 See p 404, ante.
8 See p 405, ante.
9 *Carter v Wake* (1877) 4 ChD 605.

same way as trusts of share warrants or share certificates to bearer.[10] The rights and priorities of the beneficiaries and persons dealing with the trustees are also the same. The Secretary of State for Trade and Industry may conduct a formal or informal investigation into the beneficial ownership of debentures or loan securities held by trustees or nominees in the same way as into the beneficial ownership of shares,[11] and he has the same power to make orders temporarily depriving the persons interested of all benefits attaching to the debentures or loan securities if he is unable to obtain the information he requires.[12]

Judgment creditors

Charging orders may be made against debentures, debenture stock, loan stock and loan notes in the same way and with the same consequences as against shares.[13] Nevertheless, it would seem that other modes of execution against loan securities are available if the judgment creditor prefers to employ them. He may in the first place obtain a garnishee order against the company requiring it to account to him for the debt owing in respect of debentures or loan notes and interest thereon, and a garnishee order may be made prospectively before the debt or interest or an instalment thereof falls due for payment.[14] A garnishee order may be made in respect of debenture or loan stock as well as debentures and loan notes, despite the fact that a debenture or loan stockholder is only entitled in equity to a fraction of the global debt owed in respect of the securities.[15] It would also seem that the court may alternatively appoint a receiver by way of equitable execution and empower him to sell the debentures, debenture stock or loan notes.[16] The documents representing such securities may furthermore be seized under a writ of fieri facias as securities for money.[17] The sheriff cannot sell the securities, however, whether they are in registered or bearer form; instead he must recover the debt from the company when it falls due and account for it to the judgment creditor.[18]

Personal representatives and trustees in bankruptcy

On the death or bankruptcy of a holder of a debenture, debenture stock, loan stock or loan notes, his personal representatives or trustee in bankruptcy, as the case may be, become entitled to his securities, and may require the company to register them or him as the holder of them.[19] Personal representatives or a trustee in bankruptcy may dispose of the securities in exercise of their powers to administer the deceased's or bankrupt's property, and it is not necessary that they should be registered themselves before they do so.[20] A trustee in bankruptcy takes the bankrupt's property subject to all equities which bound the bankrupt; it would therefore appear that the company may set off a debt owed to it by the bankrupt when it pays the debt represented by his securities to the trustee in bankruptcy,

10 See p 407, ante.
11 Companies Act 1985, ss 442 and 444 (see p 361, ante).
12 Ibid, ss 445 and 454, as amended by Companies Act 1989, s 62 (see p 362, ante).
13 Charging Orders Act 1979, s 1 (1), s 2 (1) and (2) and s 6 (1) (22 Halsbury's Statutes (4th Edn) 337, 339 and 342) (see p 413, ante).
14 RSC Ord 49, r 1 (1); *Hyam v Freeman* (1890) 35 Sol Jo 87.
15 *Wilson v Dundas and Stevenson* [1875] WN 232; *Re Cowans Estate, Rapier v Wright* (1880) 14 ChD 638.
16 RSC Ord 51, r 1.
17 Judgments Act 1838, s 12 (22 Halsbury's Statutes (4th Edn) 261).
18 Ibid, s 12. The sheriff may sue in his own name to recover the debt, but he cannot be compelled to sue unless the judgment creditor gives security for his costs.
19 *Edwards v Ransomes and Rapier Ltd* (1930) 143 LT 594.
20 Companies Act 1985, s 183 (3).

notwithstanding a provision in the terms of issue of the securities that the holder shall not be affected by equities arising between the company and prior holders. It has been held[1] that a trustee under a deed of arrangement for the benefit of a loan security holder's creditors takes subject to the company's right of set-off in such a case, and a trustee in bankruptcy cannot be in any better position.

Loss or destruction of debentures

The holder of a debenture or other loan security can enforce his rights against the company notwithstanding the loss or destruction of his debenture or other document showing him to be entitled to the security. In the case of a debenture, debenture stock or loan stock certificate or a loan note in favour of a registered holder, this is because of the general principle that secondary evidence of a lost or destroyed document is admissible in actions to enforce claims under it.[2] If a bearer debenture or a debenture or loan stock certificate to bearer has been lost, statute provides that the owner of the rights represented by it may enforce those rights if he tenders an acceptable indemnity bond to the company and, where appropriate, the trustees for debenture or loan stockholders,[3] and if the document has been destroyed, he can enforce his rights without tendering such an indemnity.[4] The owner of a lost bearer debenture or loan note, or the owner of a lost debenture or loan stock certificate to bearer can, of course, enforce the rights evidenced by it only if he is still its owner of the security at the time his action is brought. If the company proves that since the bearer document was lost the security represented by it has been acquired by a purchaser for value in good faith, that purchaser would thereupon have become the owner of the security, and the title of the former owner would be extinguished and so would any claim he had against the company.

It is possible for a bearer debenture or loan note to be a promissory note within the Bills of Exchange Act 1882,[5] even though it contains a charge on a company's property as well as a promise to pay the debt and interest secured by it.[6] Consequently, the owner of a lost bearer debenture or loan note may have a statutory right to demand a duplicate from the company on tendering a suitable indemnity bond.[7] The bond is necessary because of the negotiable character of bearer debentures and loan notes. If the original debenture or note were to come into the hands of a subsequent purchaser for value in good faith, he would be able to enforce it against the company, and the company would then enforce the indemnity bond to protect itself against double liability. However, a bearer debenture or loan note is not a promissory note if the debt thereby secured is payable on a date which is not a fixed or determinable at the time when it is issued, or if the debt is payable on a fixed date or on the earlier occurrence of an event which is not certain to happen or which is otherwise unpredictable.[8] Consequently, a bearer debenture or loan note is not a promissory note, and on its loss its holder has no legal right to a duplicate, if the company has the option to redeem the

---

1 *Re Brown and Gregory Ltd* [1904] 1 Ch 627.
2 *Brewster v Sewell* (1820) 3 B & Ald 296.
3 Common Law Procedure Act 1854, s 87 (5 Halsbury's Statutes (4th Edn) 333) (see p 417, ante).
4 *Wright v Lord Maidstone* (1855) 24 LJ Ch 623.
5 Bills of Exchange Act 1882, s 83 (1) (5 Halsbury's Statutes (4th Edn) 380).
6 Ibid, s 83(3).
7 Ibid, s 69. It is uncertain whether this section applies only when the debenture has been mislaid or stolen, or whether it also applies when it has been destroyed.
8 This is because a promissory note must be payable 'at a fixed or determinable future time'. A note which is payable in the alternative on a fixed date or on the occurrence of an indeterminate event is not payable at a fixed or determinable time (*Alexander v Thomas* (1851) 16 QB 333; *Williamson v Rider* [1963] 1 QB 89, [1962] 2 All ER 268).

debenture or to repay the amount of the note before the date fixed for repayment,[9] or presumably, if by its terms the debenture debt or the debt to which the loan security relates will or may become repayable if any of certain events occur which may endanger the holder's security or the company's insolvency.

Debentures, debenture stock certificates loan stock certificates and loan notes in registered form are not within the statutory definition of promissory notes. In the case of registered debentures and loan notes, this is because the debt secured thereby is not payable to the order of the allottee of the security[10] as the Bills of Exchange Act 1882 requires for a promissory note,[11] but is payable instead to the registered holder of the debenture or loan note for the time being. Debenture and loan stock certificates, whether in favour of registered holder or bearer, cannot possibly be promissory notes in favour of the original holder, because the company's promise to pay the global debt subscribed by the allottees of the securities collectively is made, not to the stockholders, but to the trustees for all the stockholders. Consequently, registered debenture holders and loan noteholders, and registered debenture stockholders and loan stockholders whose certificates have been lost or destroyed cannot require duplicates unless the debentures, or the notes, or the covering trust deed expressly so provide.[12]

INTEREST ON THE DEBT SECURED BY LOAN SECURITIES

Interest is payable on the nominal value of debentures, debenture stock, loan stock or loan notes at the rate specified in the debentures, the loan notes or the covering trust deed, and is due at the times there set out, usually yearly or half-yearly. Interest may be payable at a fixed rate for the whole period of the loan until redemption, or interest may be charged at a variable rate (such as x per cent above the London Inter-Bank Offered Rate at the commencement or conclusion of successive three or six monthly periods during the period of the loan, or in the case of a loan by a bank, x per cent above that bank's base rate from day to day). If the debenture secures a bank overdraft, the principal on which the interest is calculated will also vary from day to day as items are credited to the overdrawn account or drawings are made on it. For this reason and the fact that loans by banks are now always made at variable rates of interest, interest is charged by banks by debiting the company's account with interest at its current overdraft rate, or at an agreed rate, on the daily balance overdrawn on the account, but interest is usually charged to the account only at monthly, quarterly or half-yearly intervals.

Interest on a debt secured by debentures or other loan securities is itself a debt owing from the company, and the security holder's entitlement to it is not conditional on the company earning sufficient profits to pay it during the period in which it accrues, or having sufficient accumulated profits in hand to satisfy accrued

---

9 *Crouch v Crédit Foncier of England Ltd* (1873) LR 8 QB 374 at 384, per Blackburn J; *Bechuanaland Exploration Co v London Trading Bank* [1898] 2 QB 658 at 666, per Kennedy J; *Williamson v Rider*, supra.

10 But a renounceable letter of allotment in respect of a debenture or loan note would seem not to be a promissory note payable to the allottee's order, and a letter of allotment which has actually been renounced would appear not to be a promissory note to bearer.

11 Bills of Exchange Act 1882, ss 8 (4) and 83 (1).

12 A company which has a Stock Exchange listing for any of its securities must issue duplicate debentures or debenture or loan stock certificates or loan notes without charge to replace those which are worn out, lost or destroyed (Stock Exchange: *Admission of Securities to Listing*, Section 9, Chapter 2, para 5.1).

interest.[13] In this respect, interest on loan securities differs fundamentally from dividends paid to shareholders, which can be paid only out of the company's profits. Interest on loan securities further differs from dividends in that it accrues due on the date when the company has promised to pay it, and no further act of the company equivalent to the declaration of a dividend is necessary before the security holder may sue for it. It is, of course, possible for a loan security to provide that either principal or interest, or both, shall be payable only out of the company's profits, and the loan security holder's right to sue is then contingent on sufficient profits being earned. This type of security is known as an income bond, and is usually issued by a company in financial difficulties to its unsecured creditors when they are willing that it should continue to carry on its business rather than be wound up immediately.[14] The profits of a company out of which interest on income bonds is payable are ascertained in the same way as profits available for the payment of dividends on its preference shares,[15] and so although the company may and must deduct proper provisions for depreciation from its trading profits, in arriving at the relevant net profit figure it may not make transfers to general reserve at the expense of interest payments owing to bondholders.[16]

Interest is payable at the stipulated rate on the principal secured by debentures or other loan securities until the principal is actually repaid if repayment is made later than the agreed date for redemption. If the loan securities or the covering trust deed contain an undertaking to pay interest until the date of repayment or as long as the principal is outstanding, interest up to the actual date of repayment is recoverable as a contractual obligation.[17] On the other hand, if the company's undertaking is to pay interest only up to the date fixed for redemption, interest at the agreed rate from then until the actual date when the principal is repaid is recoverable as damages for the company's failure to repay on time,[18] unless the rate of interest is excessive,[19] or unless the loan security holders or their trustees have themselves been responsible for the delay.[20] Under whichever head interest until actual repayment of principal is claimed, it is secured by the mortgage or charge over the company's assets created by the loan securities or by the covering trust deed.[1]

Except where the debenture has been issued to a bank and carries a variable rate of interest which is debited periodically to the company's account, interest under debentures and other loan securities is paid periodically by a method similar to that for the payment of dividends. The company closes its register of debenture or loan security holders a short time before the date on which the interest is payable[2] so that transfers cannot be registered while interest warrants are being prepared. It then prepares warrants payable to the holders of loan securities whose names are

---

13 *Bloxam v Metropolitan Rly Co* (1868) 3 Ch App 337 at 350.

14 For examples, see *Lemon v Austin Friars Investment Trust Ltd* [1926] Ch 1, and *Re White Star Line Ltd* [1938] Ch 458, [1938] 1 All ER 607. Notwithstanding the abolition of ad valorem stamp duty on transfers of loan securities, it is still payable at the rate of 50p per £100 of the purchase price paid on the transfer of income bonds (Finance Act 1986, s 79 (6) (41 Halsbury's Statutes (4th Edn) 401) (see p 485, ante).

15 See p 206, ante.

16 *Heslop v Paraguay Central Rly Co Ltd* (1910) 54 Sol Jo 234.

17 *Economic Life Assurance Society v Usborne* [1902] AC 147; *Fowler v Midland Electric Corpn for Power Distribution Ltd* [1917] 1 Ch 527.

18 *Price v Great Western Rly Co* (1847) 16 M & W 244; *Gordillo v Weguelin* (1877) 5 ChD 287.

19 *Cook v Fowler* (1874) LR 7 HL 27.

20 *Fowler v Midland Electric Corpn for Power Distribution Ltd*, supra, at 533.

 1 *Economic Life Assurance Society v Usborne*, supra.

 2 The register may be closed for not more than 30 days each year (Companies Act 1985, s 191 (1) and (6), as amended by Companies Act 1989, s 143 (4)).

on the register on the date when it was closed, and sends the warrants to them on the date when the interest becomes due. An interest warrant, like a dividend warrant, is a negotiable instrument in the form of a cheque drawn by the company on its bank,[3] and on receiving it the holder of the loan security can either pay it into his bank account, or indorse it and transfer it to another person. The issue of an interest warrant is not payment of the interest due until the warrant is presented to the company's bank and honoured by it; consequently, if the warrant is dishonoured on presentation or is not presented at all, the unpaid interest remains secured on the company's assets which are charged with the principal and interest of the debt in respect of the loan securities.[4] Debenture interest is paid net after deduction of income tax at the current basic rate by the company, and to enable each loan security holder to adjust his tax liability with the revenue authorities, a certificate by the company certifying the amount of tax deducted must be sent to the holder with the interest warrant.[5]

When bearer debentures or other loan securities in bearer form are issued, the payment of interest is facilitated by the issue of an accompanying series of interest coupons, each of which is for one of the interest payments which will be made during the life of the security. When the date for a payment of interest arrives, the bearer of the loan security at the time presents the appropriate coupon to the company's bank, which will credit him with the amount of interest less tax at the current basic rate. An interest coupon is not a cheque, even if drawn in the form of one, because the amount expressed in it is not a sum certain, but is instead the gross amount of the instalment of interest less tax at the basic rate current when the instalment falls due, which must be an unknown quantity when the coupon is issued.[6] Nor is an interest coupon a negotiable instrument by mercantile usage, unless it is accompanied by the loan security in connection with which it was issued and a full set of coupons for all unpaid and future instalments of interest.[7] When interest coupons are issued with loan securities to bearer covering a period which will expire before the date of redemption, there is usually also issued a renewal coupon which may be surrendered by the bearer of the loan security when the original interest coupons have been used up, and in exchange the company will issue a new series of interest coupons for the remaining interest payments.

REGISTRATION OF LOAN SECURITIES AT THE COMPANIES REGISTRY

In addition to keeping a register of charges at its registered office,[8] a company must deliver particulars of certain charges created by it over its assets to the Registrar of Companies for registration.[9] This second duty of registration is more important than the first, for whilst the company's failure to keep its own register of charges is punishable only by a fine, its failure to file particulars of a charge at the Companies Registry may result in the invalidity of the charge itself.

The Companies Act 1989 has completely re-organised the system for registering

3 *Thairlwall v Great Northern Rly Co* [1910] 2 KB 509.
4 *Re J Defries & Sons Ltd, Eichholz v J Defries & Sons Ltd* [1909] 2 Ch 423.
5 Income and Corporation Taxes Act 1988, s 352 (1) and (2) (44 Halsbury's Statutes (4th Edn) 428).
6 Bills of Exchange Act 1882, s 3 (1) and 73 (5 Halsbury's Statutes (4th Edn) 338 and 357).
7 *Picker v London and County Banking Co Ltd* (1887) 18 QBD 515.
8 Companies Act 1985, s 411 (2), as substituted by Companies Act 1989, s 101 (see p 470, ante).
9 Ibid, s 396 (1) and s 398 (1), as substituted by Companies Act 1989, ss 93 and 95. A company which fails to deliver particulars of a registrable charge within the permitted time and its directors and secretary who are in default are guilty of an offence punishable by a fine (s 398 (3)).

mortgages and charges created by companies at the Companies Registry, although the categories of mortgages and charges which must be registered have been little changed. Until the new provisions with regard to registration are brought into force by an order made by the Secretary of State for Trade and Industry,[10] the registration of mortgages and charges continues to be governed by the original provisions of the Companies Act 1985, which were dealt with in detail in the fifth edition of this book.[11]

Charges which are registrable

Only charges created by a company over its property or assets, or created by other persons over property or assets subsequently acquired by the company, need be registered at the Companies Registry.[12] Charges imposed on a company's property by operation of law, such as the charge acquired by a judgment creditor on assets which he has seized, or a vendor's lien for unpaid purchase money,[13] or the lien over goods or documents enjoyed by a person who has provided services,[14] are not created by the company, and are therefore not registrable.[15] If a judgment creditor obtains a charging order against shares or land owned by the company, statute gives the order the same effect as if the company had charged the property in question by a written instrument,[16] but it has nevertheless been held that the charging order is not registrable at the Companies Registry, because the company does not in fact create the charge itself, and it arises by operation of law.[17] Mortgages and charges are registrable whether the property or assets over which they are created are situate in Great Britain or elsewhere.[18]

There are nine classes of charges created by a company which must be registered. They comprise most, but not all, of the charges which a company may create over its assets. They will be dealt with here in groups according to their subject matter, and not in the order in which they appear in the Companies Act 1985 (as amended).

(1) Charges on land

The first group comprises charges on the company's land.[19] If a company mortgages or charges any interest it has in land or acquires land or an interest in land which is already subject to a mortgage or charge, whether the interest is legal or equitable,[20] the mortgage or charge must be registered. It is immaterial whether the charge is created by a document or arises by implication from the company depositing title deeds to secure an advance to itself or a third person.[1] However, a charge on a company's land for rent or any other periodical payment is excepted from registration.[19] Thus, a lease reserving rent to the company's landlord or the

---

10 Companies Act 1989, s 215 (2). It is intended that the new provision shall be brought into force by the end of 1990.

11 See pp 521 to 540.

12 Companies Act 1985, s 395 (2) and s 396 (3), inserted by Companies Act 1989, s 93.

13 *Capital Finance Co Ltd v Stokes* [1969] 1 Ch 261, [1963] 3 All ER 625; *London and Cheshire Insurance Co Ltd v Laplagrene Property Co Ltd* [1971] Ch 499, [1971] 1 All ER 766.

14 *Brunton v Electrical Engineering Corpn* [1892] 1 Ch 434.

15 Companies Act 1985, s 395 (2).

16 Charging Orders Act 1979, s 1 (1), s 2 (1) and (2) and s 6 (1) (22 Halsbury's Statutes (4th Edn) 337, 339 and 342) (see pp 413 and 458, ante).

17 *Re Overseas Aviation Engineering (GB) Ltd* [1963] Ch 24, [1962] 3 All ER 12.

18 Companies Act 1985, s 395 (3).

19 Companies Act 1985, s 396 (1) (a).

20 *Capital Finance Co Ltd v Stokes* [1969] 1 Ch 261 at 278, [1968] 3 All ER 625 at 629, per Harman LJ; *Property Discount Corpn Ltd v Lyon Group Ltd* [1980] 1 All ER 379, [1981] 1 WLR 300.

1 *Re Wallis & Simmonds (Builders) Ltd* [1974] QB 94, [1974] 1 All ER 561.

grant of a perpetual or terminable rentcharge payable out of the company's land[2] do not require registration. On the other hand, if the company itself owns a lease, or a reversion on a lease, or a rentcharge, and it mortgages or charges it, the mortgage or charge must be registered.

Furthermore, a sub-mortgage by a company must be registered if the mortgage on the security of which it borrows is itself secured on land.[3] However, if a company mortgages or charges debentures or loan securities forming part of a series which it holds in another company, and those debentures or loan securities are charged on land, the charge created by the first company over the debentures is not deemed to be given over an interest in land.[4] It would appear that to come within this exception the debentures or loan securities issued by the second company need not also be secured on assets in addition to land (eg a charge over the second company's whole assets and undertaking), and so it would not be necessary for a charge to be registered if it is created by a company over debentures issued in a series by a land investment company, where the debentures are secured by specific legal and equitable mortgages over the land investment company's land and buildings and in no other way. The exemption would not apply to an ordinary sub-mortgage of land, however, because even if the principal mortgage is created by a company over its land, the principal mortgage is not part of a series.

If a company acquires land but does not pay the purchase price in full itself, a lien arises in favour of the vendor or, by subrogation to the vendor, in favour of a third person who pays the whole or part of the purchase price to the vendor. As stated above, such a lien does not require registration, because it arises by operation of law, but if the company creates a mortgage over the land to secure the amount to which the lien extended and the mortgage does not expressly preserve the lien in existence, the lien is superseded and extinguished by the mortgage. Consequently, unless the mortgage is registered at the Companies Registry, it is as ineffective as a mortgage which did not replace a lien, and it cannot be argued that the extinguishment of the lien by the mortgage was conditional on the mortgage being made fully effective by the company registering it.[5]

(2) *Charges on goods*

The second group of registrable charges comprises mortgages and charges over goods or any interest in goods belonging to a company, other than a charge under which the chargee is entitled to possession either of the goods or of a document of title to them.[6] Goods are defined as tangible, movable property other than money,[7] and therefore include all property other than land and goods affixed to land so as to be treated as part of it, cash and currency (whether British or foreign and whether in the form of coins, banknotes or credit balances with banks or financial institutions) and choses in action, which are now usually classed as intangible movables. A mortgage or charge over goods created by a company is therefore registrable whether the goods are plant and machinery or equipment, raw materials, semi-finished or finished manufactured goods, stock in trade or commodities in which the company deals, or individual items of such categories of assets.

2 Subject to certain exceptions, rentcharges cannot be created by grants made on or after 22 August 1977 (Rentcharges Act 1977, s 2 (1) to (3) and s 18 (2) (37 Halsbury's Statutes (4th Edn) 795, 810).
3 *Re Molton Finance Ltd* [1968] Ch 325, [1967] 3 All ER 843.
4 Companies Act 1985, s 396 (2) (*a*).
5 *Capital Finance Co Ltd v Stokes* [1969] 1 Ch 261, [1968] 3 All ER 625; *Burston Finance Ltd v Speirway Ltd* [1974] 3 All ER 735, [1974] 1 WLR 1648.
6 Companies Act 1985, s 396 (1) (*b*).
7 Ibid, s 396 (2) (*b*).

A mortgage or charge over goods is not registrable, however, if it is a charge on debentures or loan securities forming part of a series which have been issued by another company where those debentures are secured by a charge on goods.[8] This exception is similar to that mentioned above in respect of mortgages or charges over debentures issued as part of a series by another company and secured on land, and the same comments apply. An ordinary sub-mortgage of goods by a company will be registrable as a charge over an interest in goods, and will not be exempt from registration even if the sub-mortgagor is a company; this is because the mortgage is not part of a series of loan securities.

A charge over goods created by a company is not registrable if the person secured by it is entitled to possession of the goods or a document of title to them, but the exception does not apply if the secured creditor is entitled to possession of the goods or documents of title only on the company's default or on the occurrence of some other event.[9] This clearly excludes a pledge of goods from registration. A pledge is a possessory security under which the pledgee has no proprietary interest in the goods, but does have the exclusive right to possess and retain the goods and to sell them in order to realise the amount secured on the pledgor's failure to pay the debt or to perform the obligation for which the pledge was given.[10] However, a pledge can only be created by the delivery of physical possession of the goods to the creditor, or by a bailee who holds the goods attorning to the creditor and holding them on his behalf.[10] Mere delivery of a document which entitles the holder to obtain possession of the goods, such as a delivery order, a warehouse warrant or a railway delivery warrant or consignment note, is not equivalent to delivery of the goods themselves,[11] unless (i) the document is a bill of lading in respect of goods on board a ship;[12] or (ii) the pledgor is a mercantile agent,[13] whether acting from a principal or on his own account,[14], or (iii) the pledge is by a buyer of goods who has obtained possession of the goods or a document of title to them[15] with the seller's consent, and the pledgee has no notice that the seller has a lien or other rights in respect of the goods as security for the unpaid price.[16] On the other hand, it has been held that even in a case not within these exceptions, if a document entitling its holder to the delivery of goods is handed to a creditor with a

---

8 Ibid, s 396 (2) (*a*).

9 Ibid, s 396 (1) (*b*) and (2) (*c*).

10 *Ryall v Rolle* (1749) 1 Atk 165; *Martin v Reid* (1862) 11 CBNS 730; *Dublin City Distillery Ltd v Doherty* [1914] AC 823.

11 *William M'Ewan & Sons v Smith* (1849) 2 HL Cas 309; *Madras Official Assignee v Mercantile Bank of India Ltd* [1935] AC 53 at 58–60.

12 *Barber v Meyerstein* (1870) LR 4 HL 317.

13 Factors Act 1889, s 3 (1 Halsbury's Statutes (3rd Edn) 98); *Inglis v Robertson and Baxter* [1898] AC 616.

14 *Lloyds Bank Ltd v Bank of America National Trust and Savings Association* [1938] 2 KB 147, [1938] 2 All ER 63.

15 Documents of title to goods are defined, for the purpose of the Sale of Goods Act 1979, as including bills of lading, dock warrants, warehouse keeper's certificates, warrants or orders for the delivery of goods and 'any other document used in the ordinary course of business as proof of the possession or control of goods, or authorising or purporting to authorise, either by endorsement or by delivery, the possessor of the document to transfer or receive goods thereby represented' (Sale of Goods Act 1979, s 61 (1) (39 Halsbury's Statutes (4th Edn) 129).

16 Sale of Goods Act 1979, s 25 (1). The pledge of the document appears to be valid for all purposes, and not merely to defeat the unpaid seller's lien and right of stoppage in transit. But it seems that the buyer cannot pledge the goods by delivering the document of title to the pledgee once the seller's lien and right of stoppage have been extinguished by the purchase price being paid (*Inglis v Robertson and Baxter* [1898] AC 616 at 630, per Lord Herschell). Consequently, a pledge of documents will in practice be within s 25 (1) only when the loan secured is made to enable the pledgor to pay the purchase price to the seller.

view to him obtaining possession of the goods on the debtor's default, there is a pledge of the goods (and not a mortgage or charge over them), whether the document is a delivery order issued by the debtor himself,[17] or a warehouse warrant issued by a warehouse owner to the debtor.[18] In view of a later decision of the House of Lords,[19] however, it would seem that a document charging goods with indebtedness creates a mortgage or charge over them (and not a pledge) despite the contemporaneous delivery of a document to the creditor enabling him to obtain possession of the goods, unless the goods are delivered to the creditor as well. It is therefore advisable that banks and others who make loans to companies on the security of goods or to finance their acquisition should register the loan agreement at the Companies Registry, even though the company also deposits as security a document under which the lender may obtain possession of the goods. However, it cannot be said with certainty that such a transaction must be registered, because the Companies Act 1985 (as amended) exempts from registration not only charges by which the secured creditor is entitled to possession of the goods, but also securities under which he is entitled to possession of a document of title to them.[20] A document of title to the goods is not defined by the Companies Act 1985 (as amended), but it must clearly include all documents which are documents of title for the purpose of the Sale of Goods Act 1979, and would therefore appear to include warehouse warrants, delivery orders, railway consignment notes, lorry or truck consignment notes and air waybills, with the consequence that if the secured creditor takes such a document as his security coupled with a contractual power to realise the goods on the company's default, the security will apparently not be registrable.

The fact that a secured creditor is empowered by the terms of the transaction to seize and sell goods belonging to the company if it defaults under the transaction, or that the secured creditor will be entitled to possession of the goods under the transaction if any one of certain specified events occurs, or if any one of several specified conditions is fulfilled, will not exempt the transaction from registration.[21] Consequently, a mortgage or charge over goods is not exempted from registration by the fact that it contains a power for the secured creditor to realise his security over them, and a contract to pledge goods or the documents of title to them on the occurrence of any of certain events will require to be registered. To avoid the need for registration, possession of the goods or the documents of title to them must be delivered to the secured creditor when the security is created.

If a company sells goods belonging to it and re-acquires them under a genuine hire-purchase agreement, the mere fact that the total hire rental is equal to the sale price with the addition of interest and service charges does not make the transaction one of loan on the security of the company's goods, and so no charge is registrable at the Companies Registry.[1] But if neither the company nor the other party intends a genuine sale and re-hiring, and the substance of the transaction is the creation of security for a loan, the transaction does give rise to a registrable charge.[2] Delivery of the goods to the other party helps to dispel any suspicion that the sale is a sham,[3] but this is not essential, and other evidence, such as the fact that the company first sold the goods to a third party and that he resold them to the person who let them back to the company under the hire-purchase agreement, has the same effect.[1] The same considerations would seem to apply to a sale of goods by a company

17 *Grigg v National Guardian Assurance Co* [1891] 3 Ch 206.
18 *Re Cunningham & Co Ltd, Attenborough's Case* (1884) 28 ChD 682.
19 *Dublin City Distillery Ltd v Doherty*, supra.
20 Companies Act 1985, s 396 (1) (b).
21 Ibid, s 396 (2) (c).
 1 *Stoneleigh Finance Ltd v Phillips* [1965] 2 QB 537, [1965] 1 All ER 513.
 2 *Yorkshire Rly Wagon Co v Maclure* (1882) 21 ChD 309.
 3 *Polsky v S & A Services Ltd* [1951] 1 All ER 185; affd [1951] 1 All ER 1062n.

accompanied by an immediate re-purchase by it, under which the original purchaser retains the ownership of the goods until the company pays the re-purchase price.

A charge is registrable only if created by a company over goods which it owns at the date of the charge or subsequently while the charge subsists.[4] Consequently, if a company purchases goods on terms that the ownership of them shall not pass to the company until the price of those goods, or of other goods as well, has been paid, the seller's security is the retention of the ownership of the goods and not a charge over them created by the company, and so the seller has no charge to register.[5] But if a contract for the sale of goods provides that the legal ownership of them shall vest in the company subject to the retention of the equitable ownership by the seller until the price is paid, the equitable interest of the seller only arises after the legal ownership of the goods vests in the company, and since its purpose is to secure the unpaid price, it is treated as a charge on the goods created by the company and is registrable.[5] Furthermore, if a seller expressly reserves to himself the ownership of goods he supplies to the company and the ownership of any products into which they are manufactured, with or without the addition of other goods, the ownership of the products vests in the company, and the reservation to the seller operates as a charge over them which is registrable at the Companies Registry.[6] Similarly, a finance agreement with a company by which products sold by a company shall be deemed to be sold by it to the provider of finance and re-sold by the company to its customer as the agent of the provider of finance, is in reality a charge over the products if the company guarantees payment of the resale price and is registrable accordingly.[7]

(3) Charges on intangible movables

The third group of registrable charges comprises mortgages and charges over certain kinds of choses in action, or, to use a more modern expression, intangible movables. Such charges are registrable if they are created over book debts (whether originally owed to the company or assigned to it), goodwill, patents, trade marks, service marks, registered designs, copyright, design rights and licences in respect of such intellectual property rights, and charges on uncalled share capital and calls made by the company but not paid.[8]

Mortgages and charges over proprietary rights in inventions are registrable only if they are patented in the United Kingdom or another country, or if they are comprised in a European Community patent, or a European Convention patent,[9] but mortgages and charges over trade marks, service marks or proprietary interests in designs are registrable whether the trade marks, service marks, or designs are themselves registered[10] or not. Mortgages and charges over other forms of

---

4 *Aluminium Industrie Vaassen BV v Romalpa Aluminium Ltd* [1976] 2 All ER 552, [1976] 1 WLR 676; *Clough Mill Ltd v Martin* [1984] 3 All ER 982, [1985] 1 WLR 111; *John Snow & Co Ltd v DBG Woodcroft & Co Ltd* [1985] BCLC 54.

5 *Re Bond Worth Ltd* [1980] Ch 228, [1979] 3 All ER 919.

6 *Borden (UK) Ltd v Scottish Timber Products Ltd* [1981] Ch 25, [1979] 3 All ER 961; *Re Peachdart Ltd* [1984] Ch 131, [1983] 3 All ER 204; *Clough Mill Ltd v Martin*, supra; *Specialist Plant Services Ltd v Braithwaite Ltd* [1987] BCLC 1. But the reservation of ownership of a component supplied by the seller is effective even after it has been embodied in the product if the component is still identifiable and capable of separation (*Hendy Lennox (Industrial Engines) Ltd v Grahame Puttick Ltd* [1984] 2 All ER 152, [1984] 1 WLR 485).

7 *Welsh Development Agency v Export Finance Co Ltd* (1990) 6 BCC 393.

8 Companies Act 1985, s 396 (1) (c) and (2) (d).

9 Patents Act 1977, s 30 (1) to (6), s 77 (1), s 86 (1) and s 130 (1) (33 Halsbury's Statutes (4th Edn) 158, 210, 221 and 249).

10 Trade Marks Act 1938, s 22 (1) and s 25 (48 Halsbury's Statutes (4th Edn) 65, 69); Registered Designs Act 1949, s 19 (1) (33 Halsbury's Statutes (4th Edn) 90); Trade Marks (Amendment) Act

intellectual or industrial property rights, such as 'know how' or exploitable concepts or ideas, which are protected in English law only by equitable remedies for breaches of confidentiality or by common law passing-off actions, are not registrable at the Companies Registry. Mortgages and charges on uncalled share capital or calls made but not paid presumably include charges on unpaid instalments of the issue price of shares which have not fallen due for payment, or which have fallen due but remain unpaid.

Mortgages and charges over book debts are registrable whether they were originally owing to the company, or whether they arose in connection with another business undertaking and were acquired by the company by assignment, including a general transfer of assets on the acquisition of that business undertaking. Book debts are debts owing to a company or other business undertaking which arise out of the normal carrying on of its business.[11] They are not defined by the Companies Act 1985, and the descriptions of them in most of the decided cases have all been in contexts different from the present, and have been uniformly vague. The distinction to be drawn is probably between debts accruing to the company or other undertaking in the course of carrying on the business for which it was formed,[12] and debts which are merely incidental to carrying on that business, or which, although intra vires, are not directly connected with it. The former are book debts, and the latter are not. Even this, however, may be too wide a definition. It is certain, for example, that if a trading company invests its surplus cash in the debentures or unsecured loan stock or notes of another company, the debts secured by the debentures, loan stock or notes will not be book debts. But the position is less certain if the company was formed to invest in the securities of other companies. An investment company does not usually regard a debenture debt, which may not mature for several years, as a book debt. On the other hand, if an unsecured note is a short term one, payable, say, three or six months after its issue, it may very well be regarded in the same light as a bill of exchange, and the debt embodied in it may be considered a book debt. The Companies Act 1985 (as amended) assists in this respect by providing that a charge given by a company over debentures issued as part of a series by another company shall not be treated as a charge over book debts created by the first company,[13] but it does follow that such a charge over a debenture or loan security held by a company, which does not form part of a series, is inevitably a charge over a book debt.

It is not helpful to conclude that a book debt is what businessmen active in the branch of trade or commerce concerned would consider to be a book debt, but it is the only conclusion which can be stated without reservation. In fact case law has done little to clarify the distinguishing features of book debts beyond ruling that a debt owing from a customer to a company does not cease to be a book debt because it is secured by a bill of exchange,[14] and beyond affirming that a charge on a debt or claim belonging to a company requires registration only if the debt or claim is a book debt at the time the charge is created.[15] Thus, registration was held to be unnecessary when a charge was given over an export credit insurance policy belonging to a company, even though a claim under it subsequently arose, and the

---

1984, s 1 (1) (48 Halsbury's Statutes (4th Edn) 156); Copyright, Designs and Patents Act 1988, s 90 (1) and (3) and s 222 (1) (115 Halsbury's Statutes, (4th Edn) 87, Copyright and 335, ibid, 16, Patents and Designs).

11 *Shipley v Marshall* (1863) 14 CB NS 566; *Re Welsh Irish Ferries Ltd* [1986] Ch 471, [1985] BCLC 372.

12 *Tatung (UK) Ltd v Galex Telesure Ltd* (1988) 5 BCC 325, where a charge given by a company which let electrical equipment on hire, over the rentals payable by its customers under hiring agreements entered into by the company was held to be a charge over its book debts.

13 Companies Act 1985, s 396 (2) (*e*).

14 *Re Stevens, Stevens v Keily* [1888] WN 110; *Dawson v Isle* [1906] 1 Ch 633.

15 *Paul and Frank Ltd v Discount Bank (Overseas) Ltd* [1967] Ch 348, [1966] 2 All ER 922.

amount of the claim was settled before the company went into liquidation.[15] The settled claim might be considered a book debt, since it was in effect a substitute for payment of the price of goods supplied by the company in the ordinary course of its business to a buyer who defaulted, but the policy itself could not possibly be considered as embodying book debt at the date the charge was created, for the company's rights under it were then only contingent.[15] Similarly, a purchase price payable to a company under a contract is not a book debt if its amount is to be determined by future events (eg the quantity of mineral extracted from land), or if the price is to be paid only if certain conditions are fulfilled, but it may become a book debt by those events occurring or those contingencies being fulfilled.[16] A charge over the purchase price given by the company before the events happen or the contingencies are fulfilled is not registrable, and it does not become registrable when they do happen or when they are fulfilled. Furthermore, the credit balance on a company's bank account is not a book debt, whatever the nature of the company's business may be.[17] Also a charge in the form of a shipowner's lien over sub-freights is not treated as a charge on book debts of the shipowning company.[18] Such a charge is generally given by a company which takes the hire of a ship from the owner of it to secure the payment for the hire and is imposed as a term of the charter party entered into by them. The charge attaches to the amounts payable to the hiring company or charterer under bills of lading issued by it to third persons whose goods the company agrees to carry in the ship (freight).

A manufacturing or trading company which experiences a temporary cash shortage may borrow from a bank or other financial institution on a short term loan or by way of overdraft, and at the instance of the bank or lending institution the company may direct its customers to pay the amounts they owe the company directly to the bank or lending institution. In this way the company is put in funds at once to meet the expense of manufacturing or buying goods for sale to its customers, and the bank or financial institution is assured that when the customers become indebted to the company for the price of the goods they have bought, the overdraft or short term loan will be discharged or reduced. Such an arrangement with a bank creates an equitable charge on the company's prospective book debts, however, and must therefore be registered.[19] On the other hand, if a company takes a negotiable instrument from its customer in respect of a book debt (for example, a bill of exchange drawn or accepted by the customer and payable at or after the date when the company has promised delivery of the goods), and the company borrows from its bank or another person or institution by depositing the negotiable instrument as security, the charge thereby created is not registrable.[20] It is unusual, however, for companies other than banks and discount houses[1] to borrow on the security of bills of exchange payable to them; the usual practice is for a manufacturing or trading company to discount the bill to its bank (ie to sell the bill outright), and then no question of charging a book debt can arise.

If a company pledges or charges goods as security for a loan by delivering them or the documents of title relating to them to the lender, and the lender then releases the goods or documents so that the company may sell the goods and discharge the loan out of the proceeds of sale, the instrument by which the release is effected does not create a separate charge on the purchase price payable by the buyer to the

16 *Re Brush Aggregates Ltd* (1983) BCLC 320.
17 *Re Permanent Houses (Holdings) Ltd* [1988] BCLC 563, (1988) 5 BCC 151.
18 Companies Act 1985, s 396 (2) (*g*).
19 *Re Kent and Sussex Sawmills Ltd* [1947] Ch 177, [1946] 2 All ER 638.
20 Companies Act 1985, s 396 (2) (*f*).
 1 That is, the discount houses of the City of London, which deal in bills of exchange and borrow from the commercial banks on the security of the deposit of bills.

company, even though the instrument expressly reserves such a charge;[2] consequently there is no charge on a book debt of the company to be registered at the Companies Registry.[3] The reason for this is that in reality the lender is merely employing the company as his agent to sell the goods so as to realise his pledge or charge over them, and no fresh charge on any of the company's assets is created.[3] But if the company has already sold the goods at the time it purports to charge them or their proceeds of sale to the lender, the security given to the lender is a charge on the purchase price payable by the buyer, at least if the lender is aware of the sale,[4] and the charge is registrable at the Companies Registry.[5] It is therefore vital to determine whether the subject matter of the charge is goods or their proceeds of sale, for whilst charges created by a company over goods in which it deals in the ordinary course of its business will not be registrable if the lender is secured by the delivery of possession of the goods or documents of title relating to them,[6] there is no similar exemption for charges on book debts, and all such charges must therefore be registered.[7]

Hire-purchase transactions by a retailer are often financed by the retailer discounting the hire-purchase agreements entered into by his customers to a hire-purchase finance company. This is done by the retailer assigning the benefit of each hire purchase agreement to the finance company in consideration of it paying him the cash price of the goods less a discount or commission, or alternatively paying him a fraction of the total amount payable by the customer under the hire-purchase agreement less a discount calculated by reference to the amount included in the total hire purchase price for interest, but the assignment always contains a proviso that when the customer has paid a certain amount of hire rental to the finance company, the balance of the hire rental shall belong to the retailer. The transaction looks like a loan by the finance company to the retailer, and this is particularly so when, as often happens, the retailer gives a guarantee to the finance company that his customers will pay the hire rental under the discounted agreements. It has been held, however, that the transaction is really a sale of the hire-purchase agreement by the retailer, and not a charge on the hire rental payable to him by the customer, so that if the retailer is a company, there is no charge on its book debts to be registered.[8] But if the amounts payable to a retail company under hire-purchase agreements are expressly charged with repayment of a loan, and are not merely discounted in return for an immediate cash payment, there is a charge on book debts which must be registered.[9] The same considerations apply if a hire-purchase finance company assigns or charges the benefit of hire-purchase agreements entered into by it to another finance company.

If a company purchases goods on terms that they shall remain the property of the seller until the purchase price is paid, and that if the company re-sells the goods, it shall do so as agent for the seller and the re-sale price payable by the sub-purchaser shall belong to the seller as the company's principal, the company does

2 The documents relating to the goods will usually be a bill of lading or other transportation document or a warehouse warrant, and their release to the company will be under a trust receipt or agreement by which the company agrees to hold the goods and the proceeds of selling them in trust for the lender.
3 *Re David Allester Ltd* [1922] 2 Ch 211.
4 If the lender is unaware of the sale and obtains delivery of the goods or the documents of title thereto as security for his loan, he obtains a valid pledge or charge on the goods which overrides the buyer's interests (Sale of Goods Act 1979, s 24 (39 Halsbury's Statutes (4th Edn) 128).
5 *Ladenburg & Co v Goodwin, Ferreira & Co and Garnett* [1912] 3 KB 275.
6 Companies Act 1985, s 396 (1) (*b*).
7 Ibid, s 396 (1) (*c*) (see p 497, ante).
8 *Re George Inglefield Ltd* [1933] Ch 1; *Lloyds and Scottish Finance Ltd v Prentice* (1977) 121 Sol Jo 847.
9 *Independent Automatic Sales Ltd v Knowles and Foster* [1962] 3 All ER 27, [1962] 1 WLR 974.

not thereby create a charge over the re-sale price, and so the arrangement is not registrable as a charge on its book debts.[10] Both the goods and the claim for the re-sale price belong throughout to the original seller, and no security is created over assets belonging to the company. This is so even if the company is entitled to any surplus of the re-sale price over the amount it owes the seller, and even though the seller has agreed to allow the company time for payment of the original sale price. However, if the reservation of the ownership of the goods delivered by the seller is expressed to extend to products into which they are manufactured, with or without the addition of other goods, the resulting products belong to the company and the seller's interest in the products is treated as a charge over them;[11] if the interest is expressed to extend to the proceeds of sale of the products by the company, it will also constitute a charge over book debts of the company, but would not appear to be separately registrable as such, because the charge is derived from the original charge over the products.[12] Moreover, if by the original contract for the sale of goods to the company the ownership of them is to be retained by the seller until payment of the purchase price, but the company is authorised by the contract to re-sell the goods, whereupon the right to the proceeds of re-sale shall vest in or be assigned to the unpaid seller, the company does not re-sell the goods as an agent or fiduciary for the seller, but on its own account, and the seller's interest in the re-sale price is therefore that of an assignee by way of security or a charge.[13] The seller's interest in this situation is a primary one, and not one derived from a charge over the goods, because his interest in the goods until they are re-sold is that of an owner, not that of a mortgagee or chargee. On the sale of the goods by the company, however, the proceeds belong to the company, subject to the right of the unpaid seller to claim them in order to pay the original purchase price owed to him. Even though the right to the proceeds of sale is expressed to vest automatically in the seller, his claim to them is a charge and extends only to so much of the proceeds as is required to discharge the amount owing by the company. Consequently, to preserve the seller's priority for his charge over the proceeds of sale against other creditors of the company, the charge must be registered at the Companies Registry.[13] On the other hand, if the goods are manufactured by the company into other products which the company then re-sells, the seller will acquire a charge over the products when they are made,[11] and his charge over the proceeds of resale of the products will be a derivative charge which need not be registered.[12]

An outright sale or assignment of book debts by a company does not entail registration at the Companies Registry, because no charge over book debts is created. This occurs when a company assigns or agrees to assign all or certain of the debts owing, or to become owing, to it from its customers to a factoring company which makes an immediate cash payment to the company equal to an agreed fraction of the total amount of the debts, and undertakes the invoicing and collection of the debts itself, with or without a right of recourse to the company if any of the debts are not paid. Even though the company may remain liable to the factoring company if the factored debts are not fully paid, the company creates no charge over the debts which calls for registration.[12]

---

10 *Aluminium Industrie Vaassen BV v Romalpa Aluminium Ltd* [1976] 2 All ER 552, [1976] 1 WLR 676; *Clough Mill Ltd v Martin* [1984] 3 All ER 982, [1985] 1 WLR 111.

11 *Borden (UK) Ltd v Scottish Timber Products Ltd* [1981] Ch 25, [1979] 3 All ER 961; *Re Peachdart Ltd* [1984] Ch 131, [1983] 3 All ER 204; *Clough Mill Ltd v Martin*, supra; *Specialist Plant Services Ltd v Braithwaite Ltd* [1987] BCLC 1 (see p 498, ante).

12 *Re David Allester Ltd* [1922] 2 Ch 211.

13 *E Pfeiffer Weinkellerei-Weineinkauf GmbH & Co v Arbuthnot Factors Ltd* [1987] BCLC 522, [1988] 1 WLR 150; *Tatung (UK) Ltd v Galex Telesure Ltd* (1988) 5 BCC 325.

(4) Charges to secure an issue of debentures and floating charges

The registrable charges in the fourth and final group are defined by their inherent nature, not by the property over which they are given. They comprise charges for the purpose of securing an issue of debentures, and floating charges on the undertaking or property of a company.[14] Their importance as a distinct category lies in the fact that they are registrable even though they affect only property outside the scope of the other three groups. Thus, if an investment company whose only assets are shares and debentures of other companies creates a floating charge over its undertaking, the charge will fall into this fourth group and will be registrable, even though it falls into none of the other groups.

There are two unresolved problems in respect of this fourth group of charges. The first problem is whether an issue of debentures for the present purpose means a large scale issue of debentures or other loan securities, such as an issue to the public at large or a rights issue to the existing shareholders and debenture holders of a listed company, or whether it includes the issue of one or a few debentures or loan securities by private negotiation, such as the issue of a single debenture to secure a bank overdraft or the creation of a security over any property of a company in connection with a loan made to it by a consortium of banks. If an issue of debentures in the present context included all methods of issue, whether large scale or by private negotiation with one lender or creditor, the other groups of registrable charges would be otiose; they would merely particularise types of charges which were already registrable under the present head. The Companies Act 1985 (as amended) helps with the problem of interpretation to some extent by providing that an issue of debentures means a group of debentures or an amount of debenture stock secured by the same charge.[15] This makes it clear that the issue of a single debenture, or the creation of a loan security in connection with a debt owed to, or a loan transaction entered into with, a single person (such as a bank), will not involve an issue of debentures and will therefore not be registrable under the present head. On the other hand, if a company enters into a transaction under which two or more persons make a contributory loan, and a charge is created by the borrowing company to the benefit of which they will each be entitled in order to recover the fraction of the loan which they respectively contribute, the charge will apparently be registrable under the present head, whatever the character of the company's assets over which it is given. Nevertheless, the use of the collective terms 'group of debentures' and 'amount of debenture stock' in the statutory definition does raise the question whether merely a plurality of original lenders or loan security holders is sufficient, and in particular whether a security created in connection with a syndicated loan is registrable under the present head when the loan is expressed to be made by a single lead bank, which assigns the benefit of fractions of it to the other participating banks in proportion to their respective contributions, or declares that it holds the loan and the security for it in trust for itself and the other participating banks in proportion to those contributions.

The second problem in connection with this fourth group of charges concerns the meaning of the expression, 'a floating charge on the whole or part of the company's property'. The problem is whether a floating charge is registrable only if it extends to the whole undertaking or to all the assets comprised in a distinct business undertaking owned by a company, or whether it is sufficient that it extends to one or more classes of the company's assets (eg investments). It has been held that to give effect to the disjunctive 'or', the expression must be construed as

---

14 Companies Act 1985, s 396 (1) (*d*) and (*e*).
15 Ibid, s 419 (1), substituted by Companies Act 1989, s 104.

meaning the company's whole undertaking or any part of its business undertakings or any category of its property.[16] Consequently, a floating charge is registrable even if it is confined to the company's goods,[16] or its present and future book debts,[17] or its rights under a certain class of contracts which it enters into in the course of its business.[18] It has also been held that a floating charge is registrable if it arises by an unpaid seller of goods to a company reserving to himself the equitable ownership of the goods, including any products which result from processing or converting them or combining them with other goods, and the proceeds of sale of the goods or such resulting products.[19] On the other hand, a floating charge over sub-freights created by a charter party to secure the shipowner's right to payment of the agreed hire by the chartering company, is expressly exempted from registration, even though it is a floating charge, because the company will be entitled to receive and recover freight payable to it by the consignors of goods carried by the chartered ship until the shipowner intervenes.[20]

Additional and substituted security

If after the creation of a registered charge on a company's property, the company creates a charge over other property by way of additional security or in substitution for the original charge, the second charge must be registered separately if it falls within any of the categories mentioned above, and it will be invalidated in the same way as an original charge if it is not registered.[1] However, if the instrument creating the original charge empowers the company to substitute alternative property as security with the consent of the debenture or loan security holders or their trustees, the subject of the original charge includes the substituted property, and it is not necessary to register the charge on it when the substitution takes place, unless the original charge itself has not been properly registered.[2]

If a mortgage or charge created by a company is not immediately registrable because of the property or assets comprised in it or the character of the charge (eg a fixed charge over shares held by a company in another company), but the charge is later varied so as to make it registrable (eg the charge is extended to book debts of the company giving it, or the fixed charge is converted into a floating charge), the provisions of the Companies Act 1985 (as amended) apply to the varied charge as though it had been created in its varied form at the time when the variation was made.[3]

The duty to register and the consequences of non-registration

It is the company's duty to deliver particulars of a registrable charge and the instrument creating the charge to the Registrar of Companies within 21 days after its creation, or if the company acquires property or assets already subject to a registrable charge, within 21 days after completion of the acquisition, but if the company fails to do so, any other interested person may register within the permitted time.[4] The company and its directors and other officers who are in

16 *Mercantile Bank of India Ltd v Central Bank of India Ltd* [1938] AC 278, [1937] 1 All ER 231.
17 *Re Yorkshire Woolcombers Association Ltd* [1903] 2 Ch 284.
18 *Hoare v British Columbia Development Association* (1912) 107 LT 602.
19 *Re Bond Worth Ltd* [1980] Ch 228, [1979] 3 All ER 919.
20 Companies Act 1985, s 396 (2) (*g*).
 1 *Hoare v British Columbia Development Association* [1912] WN 235.
 2 *Cunard SS Co Ltd v Hopwood* [1908] 2 Ch 564.
 3 Companies Act 1985, s 419 (2), substituted by Companies Act 1989, s 104.
 4 Companies Act 1985, s 398 (1) and s 419 (3), substituted by Companies Act 1989, ss 95 and 104. If someone other than the company registers the charge, he may recover the registration fees paid by him from the company (s 398 (2)).

default are guilty of a criminal offence punishable by a fine if the company fails to deliver particulars of a charge within the 21 day period, unless another person has delivered particulars within that time.[5] The period of 21 days for delivering particulars of a mortgage or charge is not extended because the subject matter of the charge comprises or includes property outside the United Kingdom, and any further proceedings which are necessary to make the charge effectual under the law of the country where the property comprised in it is situate (eg the local registration of a mortgage or charge over land required by the law of countries under a civil law system) are disregarded in calculating the 21 day period.[6] The particulars of a mortgage or charge delivered to the Registrar of Companies must include all the information required by regulations to be made by the Secretary of State for Trade and Industry, and if the company has undertaken not to create other charges ranking in priority to, or equally with, the charge to be registered, the regulations may require that the particulars of the charge shall state the terms of that undertaking.[7] On receiving particulars of a charge, the Registrar of Companies must file them in a separate register of charges which he keeps for each company, together with a note of the date on which the particulars were delivered, and must send a copy of the filed particulars to the company, to the person named in the particulars as the person entitled to exercise the security rights conferred by the charge (the chargee) and to any other person appearing from the particulars to be interested in the charge who delivered the particulars for registration.[8] The Registrar must, on request by any person, provide him with a signed or sealed certificate stating the date on which particulars of a charge were delivered to him, and the certificate is conclusive evidence that the particulars were so delivered not later than the date stated in the certificate, and presumptive evidence that they were not delivered earlier than that date.[9]

For the purpose of the registration requirements, a registrable charge is treated as being created when the instrument in writing creating it (if any) is executed, or if its execution is subject to a condition (eg a deed delivered as an escrow), when that condition is later fulfilled, and in any other case where the charge is not created by a written instrument, it is treated as created when an enforceable agreement is entered into by the company conferring a security interest forthwith or upon the company acquiring an interest in the property charged.[10] Consequently, when a company creates a charge over present and future assets (eg a specific or floating charge over present and future book debts) the 21 day period for registering it runs from the date when the instrument of charge is executed, even though it can only take effect immediately as an agreement to create a charge over book debts which arise in the future.

If particulars of a registrable charge are not delivered to the Registrar of Companies within 21 days after its creation, the charge is void against an administrator or liquidator of the company appointed under an administration order or a winding up order made on a petition presented after the date when the charge is created, and against a liquidator in a voluntary winding up of the company under a winding up resolution passed after the creation of the charge.[11] If particulars are not so delivered to the Registrar, the charge is also void against

10 Ibid, s 414 (1) and (2).
11 Ibid, s 399 (1) and (2) and s 419 (5), substituted by Companies Act 1989, ss 95 and 104.
5 Companies Act 1985, s 398 (3).
6 Ibid, s 414 (4), substituted by Companies Act 1989, s 103.
7 Companies Act 1985, s 415 (1) and (2), substituted by Companies Act 1989, s 103.
8 Companies Act 1985, s 397 (1) and (2), s 398 (4) and (5) and s 419 (1), substituted by Companies Act 1989, ss 94, 95 and 104.
9 Companies Act 1985, s 397 (3) to (5).

any person who completes the acquisition for value of an interest in or right over property or assets which are subject to the charge after it is created.[12] It is immaterial whether the petition for the winding up or administration order against the company, or the passing of the winding up resolution, or the completion of the acquisition of an interest in the property or assets subject to the charge occurs within or after the period of 21 days for registering it.[13] When a registrable charge becomes void against a liquidator, administrator or other person, the amount secured by the charge becomes payable with accrued interest forthwith on demand by the secured creditor, even if he holds other valid and effective security for the same amount.[14]

A registrable charge is valid against the company which created it even though particulars of it have not been duly delivered for registration,[15] and so if the person entitled to an unregistered mortgage or charge sells his security or forecloses before the company is wound up, the purchaser or foreclosing mortgagee obtains a good title against the liquidator and the company's other creditors. The court is disinclined to give retrospective effect to provisions in the Companies Act 1985 which invalidate transactions when a company goes into liquidation or has an administration order made against it,[16] and the legal position of the purchaser or the foreclosing mortgagee must be determined by the rights or title which he has at the commencement of the liquidation or of proceedings for an administration order, that is, as owners of the mortgaged property and not as the proprietors of a mortgage or charge on it.[17]

Although the Companies Act 1985 (as amended) provides that a charge is void against the liquidator or administrator in insolvency proceedings against the company if particulars of it have not been duly delivered for registration, while the company is a going concern only creditors who have a security interest in the property subject to the unregistered charge which arose after the charge was created can contend that the charge is void against them, and that it is therefore deferred to their claims.[13] Unsecured creditors cannot restrain a company from dealing with its property and assets as it wishes while it is a going concern, and therefore cannot prevent it from paying off an unregistered charge, nor prevent the person entitled to the charge from enforcing his security.[18] Unsecured creditors are protected only by the provision that an unregistered charge is void against the liquidator or administrator,[13] which means that when the company is wound up or an administration order is made against it, they are entitled to have its property applied in payment of their debts, subject only to the discharge of mortgages and charges which have been registered or do not require registration, and are therefore valid against the liquidator. Since registrable mortgages and charges are void against the liquidator or administrator if particulars of them have not been duly delivered for registration, the unsecured creditors are entitled to have the company's assets applied rateably in paying their own debts and the amounts secured by registrable but unregistered mortgages and charges as though the mortgages or charges had not been created. An unregistered charge is invalid against the liquidator or administrator and the unsecured creditors in a liquidation or administration proceedings whether the company is insolvent or not, and although

---

12 Companies Act 1985, s 399 (1) and (2) and s 419 (3).
13 Ibid, s 399 (1).
14 Ibid, s 407 (1) and (2), inserted by Companies Act 1989, s 99.
15 *Independent Automatic Sales Ltd v Knowles and Foster* [1962] 3 All ER 27, [1962] 1 WLR 974.
16 *Re Parkes Garage (Swadlincote) Ltd* [1929] 1 Ch 139; *Mace Builders (Glasgow) Ltd v Lunn* [1986] Ch 459, [1985] BCLC 154.
17 Companies Act 1985, s 406 (1), substituted by Companies Act 1989, s 99.
18 *Re Cardiff Workmen's Cottage Co Ltd* [1906] 2 Ch 627.

it is primarily when the company is insolvent that the unsecured creditors will rely on the invalidity, the creditor secured by the charge cannot avoid that consequence by proving that the company is solvent.[19]

In determining which creditors are entitled to treat unregistered mortgages and charges as void against them, it must be borne in mind that not only persons in whose favour the company has created mortgages or charges over its property rank as secured creditors. Persons who have a charge or lien arising by operation of law, such as an unpaid vendor's lien, the lien of a person or goods in respect of which he has done work or provided services and the charge which a judgment creditor obtains on property which he takes in execution, are also secured creditors, but a prior registrable mortgage or charge created by the company over the same property will only be void against them if it has not been registered in circumstances where they have acquired an interest in the subject matter of the unregistered charge for value, which will be so in the case of an unpaid vendor's lien or a lien for work or services, but not in the case of a judgment creditor.[20] Their own charges or liens, however, are not created by the company, and are therefore not registrable.[1] The position of judgment creditors of the company is particularly important in this respect. A judgment creditor obtains a charge on the company's goods as soon as a sheriff seizes them under a writ of fieri facias,[2] and he likewise obtains a charge on a debt owed to the company as soon as a garnishee order nisi is served on the company's debtor.[3] If the company has created a specific mortgage or charge over the goods or debt taken in execution, therefore, the judgment creditor will not have priority over the unregistered mortgage or charge merely by reason of the fact that it has not been registered. If the charge created by the company is a floating charge which crystallises before the execution is completed, the judgment creditor will likewise not have priority for his charge over the assets of the company taken in execution merely because the floating charge has not been registered.[4]

Although a company which acquires property or assets subject to a mortgage or charge must deliver particulars of the charge to the Registrar of Companies within 21 days after the completion of its acquisition,[5] the company's failure to do so does not invalidate the charge as against the liquidator or administrator of the company in subsequent winding up or administration order proceedings, nor as against a person who subsequently acquires an interest for value in property or assets which are subject to the charge. Furthermore, if the person from whom the company acquired the property or assets subject to an existing mortgage or charge was itself a company, the fact that the acquiring company does not deliver particulars of the charge to the Registrar does not invalidate the charge as against the disposing or the acquiring company's liquidator or administrator. On the other hand, the failure of the disposing company to deliver particulars of the charge when it was created will invalidate it as against a person who later acquires an interest in the property comprised in the charge for value from the company which acquired it subject to the unregistered charge, unless that company acquired the whole interest of the disposing company.[6]

If particulars of a charge over a company's property are not delivered for

---

19 *Re Oriel Ltd* [1984] BCLC 241.
20 Companies Act 1985, s 399 (1).
 1 Ibid, s 395 (1).
 2 *Slater v Pinder* (1871) LR 6 Exch 228, affd (1872) LR 7 Exch 95.
 3 *Re National United Investment Corpn* [1901] 1 Ch 950; *Sedgwick Collins & Co v Rossia Insurance Co of Petrograd* [1926] 1 KB 1.
 4 Whether the floating charge were registered or not, the judgment creditor would have priority over it if he completed his execution before the charge crystallised (see p 458, ante).

registration within 21 days after its creation, the company may agree to cancel the charge and replace it with another charge over the same or different property, and if that charge is registered within 21 days after its creation, the registration is fully effective.[7] An agreement by a company to give a succession of charges over the same property at intervals, each succeeding charge replacing that preceding it, is valid despite the fact that the agreement is designed to avoid the need to register any of the charges, and if the last charge to be created is registered in time, the creditor's security is fully protected.[8] This device to postpone registration is not recommended, however, since the charge which is finally registered may be impeachable in the liquidation of the company as a preference,[9] or as a floating charge given by a company within 12 months before the commencement of its liquidation to secure an amount already owing by the company.[10] Moreover, by postponing registration the creditor may lose priority over another creditor who has meanwhile taken a security over the same property,[11] and if the company goes into liquidation without his knowledge, he may find that it is too late to register the most recent charge he has taken, or to have the directors execute a further charge in substitution for it now that their power to dispose of the company's assets has terminated.

Late registration of charges

Under the former law, a registrable mortgage or charge in respect of which particulars had not been delivered to the Registrar of Companies within 21 days after its creation could be registered thereafter only with leave of the court.[12] Leave of the court is no longer necessary for the late registration of charges; particulars of a registrable mortgage or charge may be delivered to the Registrar at any time for registration, and he is required to register them in the same way as if they had been delivered within 21 days of the creation of the charge.[13] The Registrar must note the date when the particulars are delivered on the copy of them which he files, and must send to the company, to the person appearing from the particulars to be entitled to enforce the security rights conferred by the charge, and to any other person interested in the charge who delivered the particulars for registration, a copy of the particulars and a note of the date when they were delivered.[14] Certificates given by the Registrar as to the date when particulars of a charge were delivered to him have the same evidentiary effect as such a certificate given in respect of particulars delivered within 21 days after the creation of a charge.[15]

The effect of delivering particulars of a charge after the expiration of 21 days from its creation is to protect the charge and to preserve priority for it as against persons who later acquire an interest in the property or assets comprised in the charge, but not to validate it against persons who have already completed the acquisition of interests in that property for value.[16] In other words, the late delivery of particulars of a charge secures priority for the charge as from the date when the

---

5 Companies Act 1985, s 398 (1).

6 Ibid, s 399 (1) and s 405 (2).

7 *Re N Defries & Co Ltd* [1904] 1 Ch 37; *Re Cardiff Workmen's Cottage Co Ltd* [1906] 2 Ch 627 at 630 per Buckley J.

8 *Re Renshaw & Co Ltd* [1908] WN 210.

9 Insolvency Act 1986, s 239 (1) to (5) and s 240.

10 Ibid, s 245 (1) to (5) (see p 461, ante).

11 See p 517, post.

12 Companies Act 1985 s 404 (as originally enacted).

13 Ibid, s 397 (2) and s 400 (1), substituted by Companies Act 1989, ss 94 and 95.

14 Companies Act 1985, s 398 (4) and (5).

15 Ibid, s 397 (3) to (5) (see p 505, ante).

16 Ibid, s 399 (1), (2) and (3) and s 400 (1).

particulars are delivered, and not as from the date when the charge was created, which is the normal consquence of particulars being delivered to the Registrar within 21 days after the creation of the charge.

This principle is modified, however, if at the time when particulars of a charge are delivered more than 21 days after its creation the company is unable to pay its debts within the meaning of the Insolvency Act 1986,[17] or becomes unable to pay its debts in consequence of the charge being created.[18] In that situation the late delivery of particulars of the charge does not protect the charge from invalidation as against the company's liquidator or administrator if a winding up order or an administration order is made against the company on a petition presented within a specified time after the delivery of the particulars, or if a winding up resolution is passed by the company within that time.[19] The specified time is a varying period depending on the nature of the charge and the identity of the person in whose favour it is given. If the charge is a floating charge created by the company in favour of a person connected with the company (ie a director or a shadow director of the company, or an associate of such a director or shadow director, or an associate of the company),[20] the specified period is two years from the late delivery of the particulars; if the charge is a floating charge created in favour of any other person, the specified time is one year from that late delivery; and if the charge is a specific charge created in favour of any person, the specified time is six months from that late delivery.[1] The effect of these provisions where insolvency proceedings commence after the late delivery of particulars of a charge to the Registrar is to defer the effective date of the delivery of the particulars for the appropriate specified time.

Defective particulars of charges

If particulars of a registrable mortgage or charge delivered to the Registrar of Companies are incomplete or inaccurate, the charge is void as against the persons against whom it would be invalid if no particulars of it at all had been delivered, but only to the extent that the particulars delivered do not disclose rights (and presumably remedies) which would be disclosed if the particulars were complete and accurate.[2] The obligatory contents of particulars of charges delivered for registration will be prescribed by regulations to be made by the Secretary of State,[3] and will undoubtedly include particulars of the property or assets comprised in the charge, the designation of the charge as a specific charge or a floating charge, the amount secured by the charge and further amounts which may become secured by it (eg on an overdrawn current account), and particulars of the person or persons entitled to the security created by the charge. Also the Secretary of State may by

17 The company is deemed to be unable to pay its debts if a creditor serves a written demand on it requiring it to pay a debt or debts exceeding £750 in total and the company neglects for three weeks to satisfy or to compound for that indebtedness; or if execution against the company's property is returned unsatisfied in whole or part; or if the company is otherwise proved to be unable to pay its debts as they fall due; or if the value of the company's assets is less than the total amount of its liabilities, including future and contingent liabilities (Insolvency Act 1986, s 123 (1) and (2)).
18 This is the situation if the value of the company's assets at the time when the particulars are delivered, other than the value of those assets which are comprised in the charge, is less than the amount required to satisfy in full its debts and liabilities, other than those adequately secured by the charge.
19 Companies Act 1985, s 400 (2) and (3) and s 419 (5).
20 Ibid, s 400 (3) and s 741 (1) and (2); Insolvency Act 1986, ss 249 and 435. For the persons who are associates, see p 461, ante.
1 Companies Act 1985, s 400 (3).
2 Ibid, s 402 (1) and (2), substituted by Companies Act 1989, s 97.
3 Companies Act 1985, s 415 (1).

regulations require any undertaking by the company not to create other charges ranking in priority to, or equally with, the charge to be included in particulars of the charge delivered to the Registrar.[4]

If any of this information is omitted from particulars of a charge delivered for registration, or is incorrectly stated in those particulars (with the exception of the name of the person entitled to enforce the security interest created by the charge),[5] the charge will be invalid to the extent that the particulars fail to disclose that information fully and accurately, as against the liquidator or administrator of the company in winding up or administration order proceedings commenced at a time when the particulars delivered remain defective (ie after defective particulars are delivered to the Registrar and before corrective particulars are filed), and as against a purchaser for value of any interest in or right over property or assets comprised in the charge who completes his acquisition of that right or interest at a time when the particulars delivered remain defective.[6] The Companies Act 1985 (as amended) does not state whether particulars of a charge are to be regarded as complete and accurate if they contain all the information called for by the regulations made by the Secretary of State and that information is accurately stated, or whether, if there is a provision in the charge which may affect subsequent mortgagees, chargees, purchasers or a liquidator or administrator of the company but which is not expressly required to be included in particulars of the charge by the regulations, the particulars actually delivered to the Registrar are to be regarded as inaccurate or incomplete if they do not disclose it fully. The invalidating provisions of the Act could be construed either affirmatively or negatively in this respect.

Notwithstanding the invalidation of rights or remedies conferred by a registered charge which fails to disclose them properly in the particulars of the charge delivered to the Registrar of Companies, the court may in its discretion order that all the rights and remedies conferred by the charge (including those which are incompletely or inaccurately disclosed or not disclosed at all) shall be effective against the company's liquidator or administrator, or against a person who acquires an interest in or right over the subject matter of the charge for value.[7] The court may make such an order as regards a liquidator or administrator of the company only if it is satisfied that the omission or error is not likely to have misled prejudicially any unsecured creditor of the company, or that no person became an unsecured creditor of the company at a time when the particulars of the charge were defective.[8] Correspondingly, the court may make a validating order as regards a person who has completed his acquisition of an interest in or right over the subject matter of the charge only if the court is satisfied that he did not rely in making the acquisition on registered particulars which were inaccurate or incomplete in a material respect when the acquisition was completed.[9]

Further particulars

Further particulars of a mortgage or charge in respect of which particulars have already been delivered to the Registrar of Companies, may at any time be delivered to the Registrar for registration, provided that they are in the prescribed form and are signed by or on behalf of both the company and the person entitled to the

---

4 Ibid, s 415 (2).
5 Ibid, s 402 (6).
6 Ibid, s 399 (2), s 402 (1) and s 419 (6).
7 Ibid, s 402 (2).
8 Ibid, s 402 (4).
9 Ibid, s 402 (5) and s 419 (3).

security created by the charge.[10] However, if either the company or the person entitled to the charge refuses to sign the particulars or to authorise another person to do so, or if the person entitled to the charge cannot be found, the court may authorise the delivery of the further particulars without them being signed by or on behalf of the company or that person.[11] On receiving further particulars of a charge which appears to be duly signed by or on behalf of the company and the chargee, or particulars which are signed by or on behalf of one of them and an office copy of an order of the court dispensing with the signature of the other, the Registrar must file the further particulars and note on them the date when they were delivered; the Registrar must also send copies of the further particulars and the note of that date to the company, to the person appearing from the further particulars to be entitled to the charge and to any other person who delivered the further particulars for registration.[12]

Further particulars of a charge may be delivered to the Registrar either because the original particulars or any previously delivered further particulars in respect of the charge were incomplete or inaccurate, or because the terms of the charge have been varied by agreement, court order or otherwise, so that the particulars previously filed in respect of the charge do not accurately and completely reflect its terms as they now stand.

If further particulars are delivered by way of correction or amplification of original or earlier further particulars, the person entitled to the registered charge is entitled to enforce his rights and remedies against persons who afterwards acquire an interest in the property or assets comprised in the charge, and against a liquidator or administrator appointed in insolvency proceedings which commence after delivery of the further particulars, insofar as those rights and remedies are disclosed by the original and the further particulars read together. The person entitled to the charge can, on the other hand, enforce the rights and remedies conferred by the charge against a person who completed his acquisition for value of an interest in or a right over the property or assets comprised in the charge before the delivery of the further particulars, only to the extent that those rights and remedies were disclosed by the original particulars delivered in respect of the charge read together with any further particulars previously delivered in respect of it.[13] Likewise, the person entitled to the charge can enforce it or rely on it as against a liquidator or administrator appointed under a winding up order or an administration order made on a petition presented before the further particulars are delivered, or against a liquidator appointed in a voluntary winding up resolved upon before that time, only to the extent that the rights and remedies conferred by the charge were disclosed by the original particulars read together with any further particulars previously delivered in respect of the charge.[13] This is, of course, without prejudice to the court's power to order that all the rights and remedies conferred by the charge, even though not adequately disclosed in the original particulars or previously delivered particulars, shall nevertheless be effective, where the relevant conditions for making such an order exist.[14]

It should be noted that the delivery of corrective further particulars of a charge is effective against a liquidator or administrator of the company appointed in insolvency proceedings commenced at any time after the further particulars are delivered, and the effectiveness of the further particulars is not deferred for a period

10 Ibid, s 401 (1) and (2) and s 419 (1).
11 Ibid, s 417 (1).
12 Ibid, s 401 (3) and (4) and s 417 (3).
13 Ibid, s 399 (2), s 402 (1) and (2) and s 419 (5).
14 Ibid, s 402 (4) and (5) (see p 510, ante).

depending on the nature of the charge and the identity of the person entitled to it, in the way that the effectiveness of particulars of the charge which are delivered late is deferred.[15] This is because further particulars of a charge (in respect of which original particulars are delivered late) can be delivered to the Registrar only after original particulars are delivered, and so the delivery of further corrective particulars will not be effective against a liquidator or administrator of the company until the date on which the original particulars are effective against him at the earliest.

The alternative purpose for which further particulars of a charge may be delivered to the Registrar of Companies is to record variations made in the terms of rights (and also, presumably, remedies) conferred by the charge in respect of which original or previous further particulars have already been delivered.[16] Such a variation, whether made by agreement, court order or otherwise, cannot affect the interests or rights of third persons already acquired in the property or assets comprised in the registered charge, unless they consent to the variation or are otherwise bound by it under the general law. On the other hand, persons who acquire interests in the property or assets comprised in the charge after the variation of its terms will, under the general law, take subject to the variation if they take subject to the charge itself. The requirement that a variation in the rights or remedies conferred by a charge should be included in further particulars delivered to the Registrar therefore means that persons who complete acquisitions for value of interests in and rights over the subject matter of the charge after a variation in its terms has taken effect, but before further particulars in respect of the variation are delivered to the Registrar, will be unaffected by the variation.[17] Similarly, the variation will be ineffective against a liquidator or administrator of the company appointed under a winding up order or an administration order made in consequence of a petition presented after the variation is made but before the further particulars of the variation are delivered, and also against a liquidator of the company in a voluntary winding up resolved upon after the variation but before the delivery of further particulars of it. Again, the court may, if the relevant conditions are fulfilled, order that notwithstanding the fact that further particulars have not been delivered in respect of the variation, it shall be binding on a liquidator or administrator of the company, or a person who has acquired an interest in or right over the property or assets subject to the charge.[18]

Supplemental information

If a registrable charge is created to secure an issue of debentures or other loan securities (ie a number of debentures or an amount of debenture stock secured by the same charge and ranking pari passu),[19] the company must deliver to the Registrar of Companies particulars of the date or dates on which debentures or securities comprised in the issue are taken up, and of the amount taken up on each occasion when this occurs; this must be done within 21 days after any such debentures or securities are taken up.[20] If the company fails to deliver the particulars, it and every director and other officer of it who is in default is guilty of a criminal offence punishable by a fine.[1] This obligation to deliver particulars

15 Ibid, s 400 (2) (see p 509, ante).
16 Ibid, s 401 (1).
17 Ibid, s 399 (2), s 402 (1) and (2) and s 419 (3) and (5) (see p 510, ante).
18 Ibid, s 402 (4) and (5) (see p 510, ante).
19 Ibid, s 419 (1).
20 Ibid, s 408 (1).
 1 Ibid, s 408 (3).

applies whether debentures are issued in a series (eg to the investing public generally, following the publication of listing particulars or a prospectus), or whether debentures are issued by way of a placing or private negotiation, and apparently it will also apply when loan securities are issued by a company to a syndicate of banks or financial institutions which each contribute fractions of a collective loan. The company's failure to deliver prescribed particulars of the taking up of debentures comprised in an issue does not invalidate any mortgage or charge which has been created to secure the issue, but particulars of that charge must be delivered separately to the Registrar under the provisions of the Companies Act 1985 (as amended) dealt with above, before or at the same time as particulars of the taking up of debentures comprised in the issue.

Mortgages and charges over a company's property or assets are usually enforced by the appointment of a receiver by the court, or by the person or persons entitled to the mortgage or charge under powers conferred by it. A person who obtains an order of the court appointing a receiver of the whole or any part of a company's property, or who makes such an appointment in exercise of powers conferred by an instrument (eg a debenture trust deed or a loan security agreement), must give notice of the appointment in the prescribed form to the Registrar of Companies within seven days after the order is made or the appointment takes effect.[2] Furthermore, a receiver or manager of a company's property or business undertaking appointed under powers conferred by an instrument must notify the Registrar when he ceases to act.[3] The sanction for a failure to give either of these notifications to the Registrar is a fine imposed on the person who should have given it,[4] but any security created over the company's property is unaffected. These obligations to notify the Registrar of the appointment of a receiver and of a receiver or manager ceasing to act apply whether the mortgage or charge under which he was appointed is registrable at the Companies Registry or not, and whether it has in fact been registered or not.

The Secretary of State for Trade and Industry may make regulations requiring notice in the prescribed form to be given to the Registrar of Companies of the occurrence of such events as are prescribed affecting the nature of the security under a floating charge of which particulars have been delivered to the Registrar (eg the crystallisation of the charge), and of the taking of such action as is prescribed in the exercise of powers conferred by a specific or floating charge of which particulars have been delivered to the Registrar, or in the exercise of powers conferred by the court in relation to a specific or floating charge (eg the conversion of a floating charge into a specific charge by the person entitled to it giving notice to the company on the occurrence of any one or more of certain events, or the extension of a specific or floating charge to property of the company not originally comprised in it).[5] The regulations may provide that the obligation to deliver notice of the event or action shall be imposed on the company or some other person, may specify the period within which notice must be given, and may make failure to give notice punishable by a fine.[6] Also the regulations may provide for the consequences of notice not being given and, in particular, where notice should be given of the crystallisation of a floating charge, the regulations may make the crystallisation ineffective until notice of it is given to the Registrar, and if notice is

2 Ibid, s 409 (1).
3 Ibid, s 409 (2).
4 Ibid, s 409 (3).
5 Ibid, s 410 (1).
6 Ibid, s 410 (2) and (4).

not given within a certain period, may make the crystallisation ineffective against certain persons (e g creditors of the company) until a further period has elapsed.[7]

Memorandum of the cessation of a registered charge

When particulars of a mortgage or charge created by a company, or particulars of an existing mortgage or charge over property or assets which a company acquires, have been delivered to the Registrar of Companies, the fact that the mortgage or charge has ceased to affect the company's property may be notified to the Registrar by delivering to the Registrar a memorandum to that effect in the prescribed form, signed by or on behalf of the company and the person entitled to the charge.[8] On receipt of such a memorandum appearing to be duly signed, the Registrar must note the date on which the memorandum was delivered and file it in the register of charges kept by him in respect of the company; the Registrar must then send a copy of the memorandum together with a note of the date when it was delivered to the company and to the person who appears from the memorandum to have been entitled to the charge, and if the memorandum was delivered by a person interested in the charge other than the company and the person entitled to it, also to that person.[9] If a signature of the memorandum cannot be obtained because the company or the person entitled to the charge refuses to sign the memorandum or to authorise someone else to do so, or because the person entitled to the charge cannot be found, the court may authorise the delivery of the memorandum without that signature, and the Registrar must then file the memorandum on delivery of it to him signed by the other party together with an office copy of the court's order.[10] The court will, of course, make such an order only on being satisfied that the obligation secured by the charge has been satisfied or otherwise discharged.

The commonest reason for the delivery of a memorandum that a registered charge has ceased to affect a company's property is that the company has paid the debt or discharged the obligation secured by the charge to the person entitled to it, but such a memorandum may also be delivered because the person entitled to the charge has released it, or has accepted the substitution of other property as security for the debt or obligation in respect of which the charge was given, or because the court has declared the security created by the charge to be invalid or to have been discharged.

The delivery to the Registrar of a memorandum that a registered charge has ceased to affect a company's property does not of itself terminate the charge; the memorandum merely records the fact that the charge has been discharged by payment or otherwise. Consequently, if the memorandum states that the charge has ceased to affect the company's property when it has not, the charge continues to exist. Nevertheless, the charge ceases to be effective as against any person who acquires for value an interest in or right over property subject to the charge after the time when the memorandum is delivered to the Registrar, and it is also ineffective as against a liquidator or administrator of the company appointed under a winding up or administration order made in consequence of a petition presented to the court after the memorandum is delivered, and as against a liquidator in a voluntary winding up of the company resolved upon after delivery of the memorandum.[11]

The reason why protection is given to a person who acquires an interest for

7 Ibid, s 410 (2) and (3).
8 Ibid, s 403 (1) and (2).
9 Ibid, s 403 (3) and (4).
10 Ibid, s 417 (1) and (3).
11 Ibid, s 399 (2), s 403 (5) and s 419 (3) and (5).

value in the property subject to a registered charge, after a memorandum that the charge has ceased to affect the property has been delivered to the Registrar, is that such a person will have relied on the memorandum in completing his acquisition, and he would be prejudiced if the person entitled to the charge were able to assert the continued existence of the charge against him, despite the fact that he has signed the memorandum, or is at least bound by the court's finding that the charge has ceased to exist if it has dispensed with his signature. The reason for the ineffectiveness of the charge against the liquidator or administrator in insolvency proceedings commenced against the company after the delivery to the Registrar of a memorandum that the charge has ceased to affect the property subject to it, is rather less obvious. It does not follow from the delivery of such a memorandum that any creditor of the company will have allowed the company to become indebted to him on the assumption that the charge has ceased to exist, or will have agreed to postpone the payment of a debt owed to him on that assumption. It is therefore surprising that there is no power given to the court to declare that the charge is still effective in the insolvency proceedings on the ground that no unsecured creditor of the company has been misled by the memorandum being delivered, or that no person became an unsecured creditor of the company after the memorandum was delivered, in parallel to the discretion which the court has to declare a charge to be fully effective despite the delivery of inaccurate or incomplete particulars of it to the Registrar.[12]

Enforcement of unregistered and defectively registered charges

Despite the invalidation of a registrable charge which has not been registered as against a person who for value acquires an interest in the property or assets subject to the charge, and as against a liquidator or administrator of the company in insolvency proceedings in respect of the company which are commenced after the creation of the charge, the person entitled to the security created by the unregistered charge, or a receiver appointed by him, may exercise a power of sale vested in him by the charge or the general law, and may effectively dispose of property or assets subject to the charge to a purchaser, who is not concerned to inquire whether the charge has become void.[13] The result of such a sale is that the purchaser acquires the property or assets free from the interests of persons against whom the unregistered charge is void (such as later mortgagees and chargees of the same property), and also free from the claims of a liquidator or administrator in insolvency proceedings commenced after the creation of the charge.

In this situation, the proceeds of sale of the property or assets must be held by the person entitled to the unregistered charge in trust to discharge: first, all mortgages, charges and other incumbrances ranking in priority to his own charge under the rules discussed below; secondly, the costs, charges and expenses of the sale and any previous attempted sale; thirdly, the amount secured by the unregistered charge and other charges ranking equally or pari passu with it; and finally, if the proceeds suffice, the amount secured by other charges which rank for priority after the unregistered charge.[14] For this purpose, charges created after the unregistered charge against whose holders it is void for lack of registration, are treated as charges ranking in priority to the unregistered charge, and so the amount secured by such charges must be paid out of the proceeds of sale before the costs of the sale and the amount secured by the unregistered charge.[15] If the company has gone into

12 Ibid, s 402 (4) (see p 510, ante).
13 Ibid, s 406 (1) and (4).
14 Ibid, s 406 (2).
15 Ibid, s 406 (3).

liquidation or has had an administration order made against it since the creation of the unregistered charge, the proceeds of sale must be paid by the person entitled to the charge or his receiver to the liquidator or administrator after payment of the amount secured by other charges on the property which have priority over the charge (because they have been registered), and the person entitled to the unregistered charge or his receiver cannot retain any part of the proceeds to discharge the amount secured by his own charge or the costs and expenses of the sale.[14]

The foregoing provisions apply equally when a person entitled to a registrable but unregistered charge or his receiver exercises any other power to dispose of the property subject to the charge, or to create an interest out of that property where he does so for the purpose of enforcing the charge (eg a mortgagee of land exercising a statutory or other power to lease it, or a chargee exercising a contractual power to exchange the assets comprised in his security for other assets).[16] The rules dealt with above as to the application of the proceeds of sale then apply to whatever consideration is given for the disposal.[16] A disposal by a person entitled to an unregistered charge or his receiver is effective, however, only if it is made for the purpose of enforcing the charge. Consequently, it is questionable whether a mortgage or charge created by the person entitled to an unregistered charge, or his receiver (eg a charge given over particular property or assets of the company by a receiver appointed by the holder of an unregistered floating charge over the company's whole assets and undertaking), would be effective against the company's liquidator or administrator.

The foregoing provisions as to the realisation of an unregistered charge apply also when a person entitled to a registrable charge, or a receiver appointed by him, exercises a power of sale or disposal of property or assets comprised in the charge if the charge is ineffective, or ineffective to some extent, because it was registered more than 21 days after its creation, or because the particulars delivered to the Registrar of Companies in respect of the charge were inaccurate or incomplete.[13] Consequently, if the person entitled to a charge which was registered late or his receiver exercises his power to sell the property comprised in the charge, the amounts secured by other mortgages or charges over the same property which were created after the realised charge but before its late registration, and which rank in priority to the realised charge under the rules considered below, must be paid out of the proceeds of sale before the costs and expenses of sale and the amount secured by the first charge. Similarly, if the registered particulars of the first charge do not disclose all the property or assets of the company over which it is secured, or the total indebtedness for which the charge is given, the proceeds of sale of the omitted property will be applied in paying the amounts secured by other charges which rank for priority under the rules dealt with below, or if the amount secured by the first charge is understated in the registered particulars of it, the proceeds of sale of all the property comprised in it will be applied in paying only the amount of indebtedness disclosed in those registration particulars, and the balance of that indebtedness will be deferred for payment until the amount secured by the later created charges has been discharged.

In a situation where particulars of a charge are delivered late, or are inaccurate or incomplete, the charge is wholly or partly ineffective against a liquidator or administrator appointed in insolvency proceedings which are commenced before the charge becomes fully effective by the delivery of particulars or further particulars of it, and in the case of particulars delivered late, the charge is ineffective against a liquidator or administrator in insolvency proceedings commenced before

16 Ibid, s 406 (4) to (6).

the expiration of the appropriate period of two years, one year or six months since their late delivery.[17] The proceeds of sale or disposal in the hands of the person entitled to the charge or his receiver must therefore in such a situation be applied in discharging other mortgages or charges over the property or assets in question which are effective against the liquidator or administrators (eg because they have been properly registered), and also in paying the amount secured by the charge itself to the extent that it is partially effective against the liquidator or administrator together with the costs of realisation, and the balance of the proceeds must then be accounted for to the liquidator or administrator.[18]

The statutory confirmation of a chargee's power to realise the property or assets subject to the charge even though it is wholly or partly ineffective against a liquidator or administrator of the company, does not absolve the chargee from the need to obtain the permission of the court to sell or otherwise dispose of those assets under the rules relating to insolvency proceedings in situations where the court's permission would be required even if complete and accurate particulars of the charge had been delivered to the Registrar of Companies within 21 days after its creation. Consequently, if the chargee or his receiver seeks to realise the charge after the commencement of the winding up of the company by the court, he must first obtain leave of the court to effect a disposition of the company's property,[19] but permission will readily be given.[20] If the realisation is to be effected after a petition has been presented for the court to make an administration order in respect of the company, or after such an order has been made, the chargee may realise his security only with leave of the court or the consent of the administrator.[1]

Priorities between registrable mortgages and charges

Provisions of the Companies Act 1985 (as amended)

The Companies Act 1985 (as amended) contains only three rules as to the order of priorities between registrable charges to which different persons are entitled over the same property of a company when, on the realisation of the charges, the proceeds are insufficient to pay the amount secured by all of the charges in full. The statutory rules are essentially negative in character, and do not resolve all the problems which may arise.

The first rule is that a registrable charge which has not been registered, or which is registered late, or in respect of which inaccurate or incomplete particulars are delivered to the Registrar of Companies, is not void to the extent described earlier in this chapter as against the person entitled to the subsequent chargee, unless complete and accurate particulars of that charge are delivered to the Registrar within 21 days after its creation, or at a later time before complete and accurate particulars of the first charge are so delivered (whichever is the later).[2] If incomplete or inaccurate particulars of the subsequent charge are delivered to the Registrar, the earlier charge is void against it only to the extent that rights or remedies conferred by the subsequent charge are disclosed by particulars of it delivered before the corresponding particulars of the earlier charge are delivered.[3] This latter rule can apply only where the inaccurate or incomplete particulars delivered in respect of both charges relate to matters which are prescribed by regulations to

---

17 Ibid, s 400 (1) to (3) and s 419 (5).
18 Ibid, s 406 (2) to (4) and (6).
19 Insolvency Act 1986, s 127.
20 *Re David Lloyd & Co* (1877) 6 ChD 339; *Re Joshua Stubbs Ltd* [1891] 1 Ch 187, on appeal [1891] 1 Ch 475; *The Zafiro* [1960] PI, [1959] 2 All ER 537.
1 Insolvency Act 1986, s 10 (1) (*b*) and s 11 (3) (*c*).
2 Companies Act 1985, s 404 (1), inserted by Companies Act 1989, s 99.
3 Companies Act 1985, s 404 (2).

be made by the Secretary of State, and concern rights or remedies in respect of which the two charges contain inconsistent provisions.[4]

The effect of this rule is that where a term of two successive mortgages or charges created by a company over the same property will determine which of the mortgages or charges has priority, the person entitled to the later charge can claim priority only if particulars of that term in the later charge are delivered to the Registrar before corresponding particulars of that term in the first charge are so delivered, but the later chargee will also have priority if he delivers complete and accurate particulars of his charge within 21 days after its creation and at the time of its creation particulars of the term in the first charge which would confer priority on the person entitled to it, had not been delivered to the Registrar. For example, if a first charge over a company's land is created to secure a larger amount than is disclosed by the particulars delivered in respect of it and the charge extends to particular land which is not mentioned in those particulars, a person entitled to a second charge over the same land who delivers correct particulars of the amount secured by that charge and of all the land comprised in it, will, first gain priority for payment of the amount secured by his charge over the undisclosed excess of the amount secured by the first charge out of the proceeds of sale of the land mentioned in the particulars delivered in respect of the first charge; and secondly, will also have priority for the whole amount secured by the second charge over the amount secured by the first charge on the distribution of the proceeds of sale of the land not mentioned in the particulars delivered in respect of the first charge. However, the second chargee will have priority in those two situations only if:

(i) he delivers complete and accurate particulars of his own charge to the Registrar within 21 days after its creation, and further particulars of the first charge covering the two matters omitted from the original particulars of it have not been delivered to the Registrar before the second charge is created; or

(ii) if particulars of the second charge relating to the amount secured by it and the land to which it extends (as the case may be) are delivered to the Registrar before further particulars of the first charge covering the matter omitted from the original particulars of it are delivered.

The second rule as to priority contained in the Companies Act 1985 (as amended) is that any acquisition of property of a company (including a mortgage or charge over it) takes effect subject to an existing registrable but unregistered or defectively registered charge if the terms of the acquisition expressly so provide.[5] For example, if a company mortgages its land or creates floating charges over its undertaking and assets successively to two banks to secure loans made by them, and the instrument creating the second mortgage or charge provides that it shall take effect subject to the first, it is immaterial as between the two banks that particulars of the first mortgage or charge have not been delivered to the Registrar of Companies or are delivered late, or that particulars of the first mortgage or charge which have been delivered are inaccurate or incomplete. However, the subordination of the second mortgage or charge to the first in this situation is effective only as between the persons respectively entitled to them, and does not affect the rights of other secured creditors. Consequently, if a first charge given by a company is registrable but unregistered, and is followed by two further charges created over the same property, the earlier of which is expressed to be subject to the first charge but the

4 Ibid, s 404 (3).
5 Ibid, s 405 (1).

later of which is not, and both the further charges are properly registered within 21 days after they are respectively created, the amount secured by the first charge (so far as it does not exceed the amount secured by the second) will have first priority for payment out of the proceeds of sale of the property, then any excess of the amount secured by the second charge over the amount secured by the first will be paid to the second chargee (although it is unlikely that there will be such an excess), and this will be followed by payment of the amount secured by the third charge, and finally (if the proceeds have not already been exhausted) by payment of an amount equal to that part of the debt secured by the second charge which has been paid to the first chargee. This order of payment will respect the rights of priority of the first and second chargees, the second and third chargees and the third and first chargees as between themselves.

The third rule governing priorities in the Companies Act 1985 (as amended) is that a charge created by a company is not avoided in consequence of an acquisition for value of an interest in or right over property or assets subject to the charge, or in consequence of insolvency proceedings being commenced in respect of the company, if the acquisition or initiation of the insolvency proceedings occurs after the company has disposed of the whole of its interest in the property or assets.[6] An example of the application of this rule is where a company creates a registrable charge, particulars of which are either not delivered to the Registrar of Companies or are delivered in an inaccurate or incomplete form, and the company then transfers the property comprised in the charge gratuitously to another person or company (eg another company in the same group), and that person or company creates a further charge over the same property, of which complete and accurate particulars are delivered to the Registrar within 21 days after its creation if it is created by a company. The invalidity of the first charge against any person who takes a second charge over the same property from the original company does not extend to invalidating the first charge as against a person who takes a second charge from the person who, or the company which, acquires the property from the original company. The first charge therefore has priority over the second charge for the amount secured by the first charge, notwithstanding that the first charge is not registered or is registered defectively. Another example of the operation of the rule is where, after disposing gratuitously to another company of the property or assets comprised in a registrable but unregistered or defectively registered charge, a winding up order or an administration order is made against the company which created the charge on a petition presented after the gratuitous disposition, or after that disposition the company which created the charge resolves to go into voluntary liquidation. The unregistered or defectively registered charge can nevertheless be enforced according to its terms against the other company to which the property or assets are gratuitously transferred, and against any person to whom it mortgages or charges the property or assets comprised in the earlier charge. The rationale for this is that the total or partial invalidation of the earlier unregistered or defectively registered charge would not result in an increase in the assets of the original company available to its liquidator or administrator. It would seem that even if the gratuitous disposal of the property or assets to the other company can be avoided in the liquidation or administration of the original company,[7] the unregistered or defectively registered charge created by that company will still be enforceable according to its terms by reason of the intervening disposal of the original company's entire interest in the property comprised in it.

---

6 Ibid, s 399 (2) and s 405 (2).
7 Under the Insolvency Act 1986, s 238 (1) to (4) and s 423 (1) to (3).

The operation of other priority rules

The ordering of priorities between successive mortgages or charges created by a company over the same property or assets is not governed exclusively by the Companies Act 1985 (as amended). In the first place, where the mortgages or charges are not registrable at the Companies Registry (eg specific charges over shares, debentures or loan securities held by a company in another company), priority between the charges is obviously governed by other rules because the priority rules dealt with above cannot apply.[8] Secondly, even if a mortgage or charge is registrable under the Companies Act 1985 (as amended), and has been properly registered at the Companies Registry, it may also be registrable at another registry under other legislation because of the character of the property comprised in it, and it may lose priority over another mortgage or charge of the same property because it is not so registered. The other statutes calling for registration of mortgages or charges by reason of the property or assets comprised in them are:

  (i)   the Land Charges Act 1972, in respect of unregistered land;[9]
  (ii)   the Land Registration Act 1925, in respect of registered land;[10]
  (iii)   the Patents Act 1977, the Trade Marks Act 1938, the Trade Marks (Amendment) Act 1984 and the Registered Designs Act 1949, in respect of patents, trade marks, service marks and designs;[11]
  (iv)   the Merchant Shipping Act 1984, in respect of British registered ships;[12] and
  (v)   the Civil Aviation Act 1982 and the Mortgaging of Aircraft Order 1972, in respect of British registered aircraft.[13]

It is outside the scope of this book to deal with these other statutory registration requirements and their interaction with the registration requirements of the Companies Act 1985 (as amended), beyond observing that when under these other statutes priority for a mortgage or charge created by a company is forfeited because it has not been registered, or registered before a later mortgage or charge over the same subject matter has either been registered or protected by a priority notice (where such notices may be employed), priority for the earlier mortgage or charge is not preserved by it having been registered at the Companies Registry.[14]

The equity rule was, and in the absence of statutory registration requirements still is, that priority between successive mortgages or charges over the same property is determined by the chronological order in which they are created, subject to the two exceptions that a later legal mortgage takes priority over an earlier equitable mortgage or charge if the legal mortgagee had no notice of it when his mortgage was created, and secondly, that a later mortgage or charge takes priority over an earlier one if the person entitled to the earlier mortgage or charge has by his conduct led the later mortgagee or chargee to believe that there was no earlier mortgage or charge. In respect of registrable mortgages and charges

---

8   For the rules governing priorities between successive mortgages or charges over shares, debentures or loan securities, see pp 356 and 483, ante.
9   Land Charges Act 1972, s 2 (4) (37 Halsbury's Statutes (4th Edn) 405).
10   Land Registration Act 1925, s 25 (1), s 59 (2), s 66 (2) and s 106 (2) (37 Halsbury's Statutes (4th Edn) 544, 568 and 606).
11   Patents Act 1977, s 32 (2) (37 Halsbury's Statutes (4th Edn) 160) and Patent Rules 1982 (SI 1982/717), r 46; Trade Marks Act 1938, s 25 (1) and Trade Marks (Amendment) Act 1984, s 1 (1) (48 Halsbury's Statutes (4th Edn) 90) and Registered Designs Rules 1989 (SI 1989/1105), r 42 (1).
12   Merchant Shipping Act 1894, s 31 (1) and (2) (39 Halsbury's Statutes (4th Edn) 453).
13   Civil Aviation Act 1982, s 86 (1) and (2) (4 Halsbury's Statutes (4th Edn) 213) and Mortgaging of Aircraft Order 600972 (SI 1972/1268), arts 2, 5 and 14.
14   For a detailed treatment of the other statutory registration requirements, see the fifth edition of this book, pp 540 to 546.

created by a company, however, these rules have been superseded by the provisions of the Companies Act 1985 (as amended) dealt with above. Moreover, the possibility of applying the exceptions to the equity priority rules is excluded by the provision enacted by the Companies Act 1989, that a person taking a charge over a company's property shall be deemed to have notice of any matter requiring registration in the register of charges kept in respect of the company by the Registrar of Companies if the matter is disclosed in original or further particulars or other obligatory entries (eg memoranda that charges have ceased to affect a company's property included in the register).[15] It will only be where a matter is discoverable from an inspection of the contents of the register of charges but is not required to be recorded there by the Companies Act 1985 (as amended) and the regulations made under it (ie information included gratuitously in registration particulars) that a person taking a charge over a company's property will not be deemed to have notice of it by reason of its disclosure in the register, or by reason of the chargee having failed to search the register.[16]

Public inspection of the register of charges

The register of charges kept by the Registrar of Companies in respect of a company, like the other records kept in respect of the company at the Companies Registry, may be inspected by anyone on payment of a fee prescribed by regulations, and anyone may on payment of such a fee require the Registrar to supply him with a certified copy of any document included in the register of charges or a copy of any information included in it.[17] However, there is no provision for the Registrar to provide official certificates of the result of a search of the register of charges, nor is any protection provided for intending mortgagees or chargees during a limited period following the making of searches by them so that they may complete their mortgages or charges secure in the knowledge that they will not be affected by entries made in the register since the date when their searches were made.

---

15 Companies Act 1985, s 416 (1), substituted by Companies Act 1989, s 103.
16 Companies Act 1985, s 416 (2).
17 Ibid, s 709 (1) and (2) and s 710A (1), substituted and inserted by Companies Act 1989, s 126 (2).

PART III

Management and control

CHAPTER 13

Promoters

This and the following three chapters are concerned with the legal attributes of the persons who may control or influence the conduct of a company's affairs, namely, its promoters, its directors, its members or shareholders acting collectively by passing resolutions, and its controlling and other shareholders who influence the conduct of the company's affairs. This will call for a definition of the legal relationships of such persons to the company and their obligations to it, to one another and to other persons interested in the company, and an examination of the means by which those duties are enforced.

Chronologically, the first persons who control or influence a company's affairs are its promoters. It is they who conceive the idea of forming the company, and it is they who take the necessary steps to incorporate it, to provide it with the share and loan capital and other financial resources it needs, and to acquire the business which the company is to conduct or the property or assets from which it is to derive its profits. When these things have been done, the promoters hand over the control of the company to its directors, who are often themselves under a different name.

During the last century, a class of professional company promoters grew up, and it was in consequence of their often unscrupulous methods of raising capital from the investing public that the duties dealt with in this chapter were imposed on promoters by the courts. In the wake of the courts' decisions the detailed rules about the contents of prospectuses and the issue of shares, debentures and other loan securities now contained in the Companies Act 1985 and the Financial Services Act 1986 were enacted. But the day of the professional promoter came to an end with the first world war. Higher taxation reduced the private resources available for investment, and an increasing percentage of new investments came to be made by institutional investors, who were interested only in sound and tried companies. The fabulous railway, mining, oil and produce companies of an earlier generation, on which the professional promoter thrived, were now unable to arouse the interest of substantial investors. But this does not mean that promoters are not met with today. Every company which is formed must be promoted by someone. The usual pattern today, however, is for the company to be formed as a private one by the persons who will be its directors, and who, unlike the professional promoter, will continue to be interested in the company's fortunes long after the promotion has been completed. If the company's business later expands sufficiently to warrant an appeal to the public or to institutional investors for further capital, the company will be converted into a public one, and the capital will be raised by one of the methods described in Chapter 8, none of which, it will be noted, requires the services of a professional promoter, although they may require the services of a merchant bank, the corporate finance subsidiary of a commercial bank or a firm of brokers or dealers in securities.

The word 'promoter' is not defined by the Companies Act 1985, even though it appears in the Act in a number of places.[1] The courts have declined to give a precise definition of a promoter,[2] and perhaps the nearest judicial approach to a definition is the description of a promoter as 'one who undertakes to form a company with reference to a given project, and to set it going, and who takes the necessary steps to accomplish that purpose'.[3] A promoter need not undertake the whole of the work involved in forming a company, procuring share or loan capital for it and acquiring a business undertaking or asset for it; the work involved in doing these things may be divided among the members of a group, and each one of them will be a promoter. But a person will be a promoter only if he is concerned in some way with the management or preparations for the management of the company's affairs, in other words, if his functions are analogous to those of a director.[4] If he is employed merely in a professional or technical capacity, such as a solicitor, accountant, valuer or business consultant,[5] he will not be a promoter.[4]

Promoters of a company are not partners, and so in the absence of express agreement are not jointly or vicariously liable upon contracts made by one or more of their number for the purpose of forming the company, or acquiring any property or business for it,[6] or carrying on a business already acquired until the company is ready to take it over.[7] For the same reason promoters are not bound to contribute towards expenses incurred by one of their number for the purpose of forming the company, unless they expressly agree to share such expenses.[8]

If the court makes a disqualification order against a person in consequence of his responsibility for criminal offence, fraud, fraudulent or wrongful trading, breach of duty or default in connection with the management of a company or its property, or because his conduct makes him unfit to be concerned in such management, that person may not during the disqualification period be directly or indirectly concerned or take part in the promotion or formation of any other company without leave of the court, and if he does so he commits a criminal offence.[9]

THE DUTIES OF A PROMOTER

The court has elaborated equitable fiduciary duties which are imposed on promoters similar to those which have been imposed on agents, and it appears that promoters' duties at common law, too, are substantially the same. But a promoter is not a

---

1   The word was defined by s 67 (3) of the Companies Act 1985 (which is prospectively repealed by the Financial Services Act 1986, s 212 (3) and Sch 17, Part I) for the purpose of imposing liability to pay compensation for false statements in prospectuses on the persons responsible for issuing them, but the definition merely excludes persons who provide professional services in connection with the formation of a company from the category of promoters. The Financial Services Act 1986, s 152 (1) and 168 (1) do not impose liability for false statements in or omissions from listing particulars and prospectuses on promoters as such, but they may be liable for such statements or omissions as persons who expressly accept responsibility for the contents of listing particulars or prospectuses or who authorise their issue (see pp 280 and 292, ante).

2   *Emma Silver Mining Co v Lewis & Son* (1879) 4 CPD 396 at 407, per Lindley J.

3   *Twycross v Grant* (1877) 2 CPD 469 at 541, per Cockburn CJ.

4   *Re Great Wheal Polgooth Co Ltd* (1883) 53 LJ Ch 42.

5   But such persons may be experts for the purpose of the rules relating to listing particulars and prospectuses, so as to be personally liable for false statements in, or omissions from, statements made by them which are included in listing particulars or a prospectus.

6   *Wood v Duke of Argyll* (1844) 6 Man & G 928.

7   *Keith Spicer Ltd v Mansell* [1970] 1 All ER 462, [1970] 1 WLR 333.

8   *Hamilton v Smith* (1859) 28 LJ Ch 404.

9   Company Directors Disqualification Act 1986, ss 1 to 4, 6, 8, 10 and 13 (see p 535, post).

trustee for the company he promotes, and so there is no absolute prohibition on his making a profit out of a promotion in which he participates.[10]

The two fiduciary duties imposed on a promoter are: (a) not to make any secret profit out of the promotion of the company without the company's consent; and (b) to disclose to the company any interest which he has in a transaction entered into by it.

Secret profits

The commonest way in which professional promoters used to make a secret profit was by purchasing a property or business themselves and reselling it to the company at an enhanced price. But the difference between the two prices in such a case is a secret profit only if the promoter has begun to promote the company at the time when he purchases the property or business, so that he owes a duty to the company at that time not to profit on a resale to it.[11] If the promoter purchases the property or business at a time when he merely has an intention of promoting a company to acquire it in the future, he owes no fiduciary duty to the company when it is formed,[12] nor is any duty imposed on him by the fact that the contract with his vendor provides that the promoter shall incorporate a company to which the property or business shall be transferred,[13] even if completion of the purchase is delayed until the company is formed and has raised sufficient capital for the promoter to pay the purchase price to the vendor.[14] Since one of the first acts in promoting a company is the negotiation of contracts with vendors, the court's reluctance to hold that the conclusion of a contract of purchase itself implies that the promotion has begun, has deprived this aspect of the rule about secret profits of much practical value. But if the promoters have invited the public or prospective investors to subscribe for shares before they purchase the property or business which they resell to the company, the promotion of the company will have begun before the date of the purchase, and they will be accountable for the profit they obtain on the resale.[15]

Promoters may obtain secret profits by other methods than reselling property to the company, and here the law is stricter on them. Thus, where a promoter negotiated the sale of a business from the vendor to the company which the promoter intended to form, and the vendor agreed to pay a share of the profit he obtained from the sale to the promoter, it was held that the promoter was accountable to the company for that share.[16] Again, where promoters purchased the business of a moribund company and resold it to a new company promoted by themselves, it was held that the promoters were accountable to the new company for the profit they made by buying the old company's debentures cheaply on the market before the promotion of the new company began, and then paying the amount owing under the debentures (including arrears of interest) in full out of the purchase price paid by the new company.[17]

A promoter is permitted to make a profit out of a promotion with the consent of the company, in the same way as an agent may retain a profit obtained through his

10 *Omnium Electric Palaces Ltd v Baines* [1914] 1 Ch 332.
11 *Re Cape Breton Co* (1885) 29 ChD 795 at 804, 805, per Cotton LJ; *Jacobus Marler Estates Ltd v Marler* (1913) 85 LJPC 167 n.
12 *Erlanger v New Sombrero Phosphate Co* (1878) 3 App Cas 1218 at 1234, per Lord Cairns LC; *Ladywell Mining Co v Brookes* (1887) 35 ChD 400 at 409, per Cotton LJ.
13 *Re Coal Economising Gas Co, Gover's Case* (1875) 1 ChD 182.
14 *Re Leeds and Hanley Theatres of Varieties Ltd* [1902] 2 Ch 809.
15 *Ladywell Mining Co v Brookes* (1887) 35 ChD 400 at 411, per Cotton LJ.
16 *Whaley Bridge Calico Printing Co v Green* (1880) 5 QBD 109.
17 *Gluckstein v Barnes* [1900] AC 240.

agency with his principal's consent. The problem is to discover who may give the necessary consent on behalf of the company. If the company has been established with a board of directors which is independent of the promoters, the consent may be given by the board,[18] but if the directors are in any way under the influence of the promoters, or the promoters are represented on it by one or more of their number, it is not sufficient for the board to consent,[19] and the promoter must obtain the consent of the persons who provide the company with its initial share capital,[20] either by such persons all giving their individual consents, or by them approving the retention of the promoter's profit by passing an ordinary resolution to that effect at a general meeting. Consent to the retention of a promotion profit can only be given by the board of directors or by the shareholders (as the case may be) if the promoter makes full disclosure to them of the nature and amount of the profit he has made,[20] and it is insufficient for him to give them information from which they could deduce that he has obtained a profit by making enquiries.[1] If the company issues a prospectus, disclosure to shareholders may be made in it,[2] and each shareholder's subscription for shares on the basis of the prospectus would then be deemed to indicate his consent to the retention of the profit disclosed by the promoter.

Disclosure of interest

In addition to his duty to account for secret profits, a promoter must disclose to the company any interest he has in a transaction entered into by it or proposed to be entered into by it. This is so even where the promoter sells property of his own to the company, but does not have to account for the profit he makes from the sale because he acquired the property before the promotion began.[3] Disclosure must be made in the same way as though the promoter were seeking the company's consent to his retaining a profit for which he is accountable, and must be equally as full.[3]

Remedies for breach of fiduciary duties

If a promoter is accountable for a secret profit, the company may recover it from him by suing him in its corporate name, even though the events giving rise to the duty to account occurred before it was incorporated. The promoter is entitled to deduct the expenses he has incurred in connection with the promotion from the amount he pays to the company,[4] but he is not entitled to any allowance for the fact that the company has recovered damages from another promoter for his breach of duty in respect of the same transaction.[5] If the promoter has made a

---

18 *Erlanger v New Sombrero Phosphate Co* (1878) 3 App Cas 1218 at 1236, per Lord Cairns LC.
19 *Gluckstein v Barnes*, supra.
20 *Lagunas Nitrate Co v Lagunas Syndicate Ltd* [1899] 2 Ch 392; *Re Olympia Ltd* [1898] 2 Ch 153; affd sub nom, *Gluckstein v Barnes*, supra.
1 *Whaley Bridge Calico Printing Co v Green* (1879) 5 QBD 109.
2 Disclosure of promoters' interests were formerly required in a prospectus issued generally by the Companies Act 1985, s 56 (1) and Sch 3, para 7. The International Stock Exchange merely requires the identity of a company's promoters to be disclosed in listing particulars if the issuing company was incorporated less than five years previously (Stock Exchange: *Admission of Securities to Listing*, Section 3, Chapter 2, para 6.7 (a). The identity of a company's promoters and payments made and other benefits conferred on them and the consideration for such payments and benefits must be disclosed in the statutory declaration by a director or secretary of the company which must be filed by a company formed as a public company in order to obtain a certificate of its entitlement to do business from the Registrar of Companies (Companies Act 1985, s 117 (1) to (3)).
3 *Re Lady Forest (Murchison) Gold Mine Co Ltd* [1901] 1 Ch 582.
4 *Bagnall v Carlton* (1877) 6 ChD 371; *Lydney and Wigpool Iron Ore Co v Bird* (1886) 33 ChD 85.
5 *Bagnall v Carlton*, supra.

secret profit by selling his own property to the company in return for an allotment of shares in it, and the promoter has since sold the shares, the company may recover from him the difference between the price at which he sold the shares and the price at which he bought the property.[6]

If a promoter has broken either of his two fiduciary duties, the company may rescind any contract made with him or his nominee in consequence, and may recover any consideration which it has given under the contract. The company is not precluded from rescinding by the fact that property has been transferred to it under the contract,[7] nor by the fact that the promoter has been allotted shares under the contract which he has since sold, and in this latter case the company may recover the price which the promoter obtained for his shares.[8] But the company may rescind only if it can restore to the promoter what he gave under the contract in substantially the same condition as when he gave it. Thus, a company may not rescind a contract to purchase property from a promoter if the company has sold the property,[9] or if the property is leasehold land and the landlord has forfeited the lease.[10] The right to rescind will also be lost if the company delays for an unreasonable time in exercising it. If the board of directors is controlled by the promoters and the directors fail to disclose the promoter's breach of duty to the shareholders, the period of such control will not run against the company so as to bar it from rescinding,[11] but if substantially all the shareholders become aware of the breach of duty and fail to take action within a reasonable time, the company will lose its right to rescind.[12] The company may waive its right to rescind by an ordinary resolution passed by a general meeting of its shareholders,[13] but if the resolution is passed only by means of the votes of the promoters themselves as shareholders, the resolution is ineffective and it is still possible for the company to rescind.[14]

It has been held that a company may sue its promoters for damages for breach of either of their fiduciary duties.[15] This at first sight appears to be inconsistent with principle, because damages are not an appropriate remedy for breaches of equitable duties, except where statute so provides, which it does not do here. It is submitted, however, that the decision is fully justifiable, because the breach of fiduciary duty involved, namely, selling the promoter's own property to the company without disclosing his interest, also involved a breach of the promoter's common law duty of care, which is dealt with below, and so damages were an appropriate remedy. It has been suggested that a company may not recover compensation from a promoter who sells property which he acquired before the promotion begins, unless the property has an ascertainable market value at the date when the company acquires it;[16] but in saying this the court was probably merely intending to state the company's equitable remedies in those circumstances, and was overlooking its right to sue for damages. Moreover, it is questionable

6 *Emma Silver Mining Co v Grant* (1879) 11 ChD 918; *Re Jubilee Cotton Mills Ltd* [1922] 1 Ch 100, revsd sub nom *Jubilee Cotton Mills Ltd v Lewis* [1924] AC 958.
7 *Armstrong v Jackson* [1917] 2 KB 822.
8 *Emma Silver Mining Co v Grant*, supra; *Lagunas Nitrate Co v Lagunas Syndicate Ltd* [1899] 2 Ch 392 at 433, per Lindley MR.
9 *Re Cape Breton Co* (1885) 29 ChD 795.
10 *Ladywell Mining Co v Brookes* (1887) 35 ChD 400.
11 *Lagunas Nitrate Co v Lagunas Syndicate Ltd*, supra.
12 *Erlanger v New Sombrero Phosphate Co* (1878) 3 App Cas 1218.
13 Ibid; *Re Cape Breton Co* (1885) 29 ChD 795 at 812, per Fry LJ.
14 *Atwool v Merryweather* (1867) LR 5 Eq 464 n.
15 *Re Leeds and Hanley Theatres of Varieties* [1902] 2 Ch 809.
16 *Re Cape Breton Co* (1885) 29 ChD 795 at 805, per Cotton LJ (contra Bowen LJ at 810); *Jacobus Marler Estates Ltd v Marler* (1913) 85 LJPC 167 n.

whether the company may not recover compensation in equity from a promoter for breach of his fiduciary duties, wholly apart from any claim for damages which it may have at common law. In equity compensation for loss suffered by beneficiaries of a trust is recoverable from trustees who have broken their fiduciary duties, and the claim for compensation is quite distinct from a claim for the restitution of misapplied trust funds.[17] There seems to be no reason why similar compensation claims may not be made by a company against its promoters for loss resulting from breaches of their fiduciary duties.

A promoter's common law duties

A promoter's duties to his company at common law have not been worked out by the courts in any detail. They cannot depend on contract, because at the time when a promotion begins the company is not incorporated, and so cannot contract with its promoters. It seems, therefore, that the promoter's duties to the company at common law must be the same as those of a person who acts on behalf of another without a contract being entered into between them, namely, to abstain from deception and to exercise reasonable skill and care. Thus, it has been held that a promoter who negligently allows the company to purchase property, including his own, for more than its real value, is liable to the company for the loss it suffers,[18] and the case already cited[15] where damages were awarded against a promoter, ostensibly for breach of a fiduciary duty, may be justified on the ground that his acts amounted to a negligent failure to protect the company's interests. A promoter has also been held liable in damages to the company for issuing a prospectus which contained statements which he knew to be false.[15] Although the promoter's acts were castigated by the court as fraudulent in that case, it is clear that the company's cause of action against him was for breach of his duty to protect its interests, and not for the tort of deceit, because the company did not act on the faith of the false statements, as a plaintiff must have done to succeed in an action for deceit. Instead the company had suffered loss because subscribers for its shares were misled by the false statements, and had exercised their rights to rescind their subscriptions and to sue the company itself in deceit. It has also been held[19] that a promoter is liable in damages if he takes an allotment of a company's shares in payment for property which he has sold to the company at a price in excess of its real value, because the promoter thereby deprives the company of the opportunity of issuing the shares to the public for cash. In all these cases the promoter was in fact also guilty of a breach of fiduciary duty, but it is easy to envisage situations where he might be guilty of negligence alone. If such cases do arise, the court may be as reluctant to require a rigorous standard of care to be shown by promoters as it has been to impose such a standard on directors, and if that is so, the fiduciary duties of promoters will remain the only onerous ones imposed on them.

Termination of a promoter's duties

A promoter's duties do not come to an end on the incorporation of the company which he assists in forming, or even when a board of directors of the company is appointed. The promoter's duties continue until the company has acquired the

---

17 *Fenwick v Greenwell* (1847) 10 Beav 412; *Devaynes v Robinson* (1857) 24 Beav 86; *Sculthorpe v Tipper* (1871) LR 13 Eq 232; *Bartlett v Barclays Bank Trust Co Ltd (No 2)* [1980] Ch 515, [1980] 2 All ER 92.
18 *Jacobus Marler Estates Ltd v Marler,* supra.
19 *Re Jubilee Cotton Mills Ltd* [1922] 1 Ch 100; revsd sub nom *Jubilee Cotton Mills Ltd v Lewis* [1924] AC 958.

property or business which it was formed to acquire and has raised its initial share capital,[20] and the board of directors has taken over the management of the company's affairs from the promoters.[1] When these things have been done, the promoter's fiduciary and common law duties cease, and he is thereafter subject to no more extensive duties in dealing with the company than a third person who is unconnected with it. Thus, where a promoter disclosed the profit which he made out of a company's promotion to the persons who provided it with the share capital with which it commenced business, it was held that he was under no further duty to disclose the profit to persons who were invited to subscribe further capital a year later, and so the company could not recover the profit from him for his failure to do so.[2] Nevertheless, a promoter will continue to be subject to fiduciary and other duties to the company if he becomes or acts as a director or agent of it on or after ceasing to be a promoter, but the duties are then owed by him only in that other capacity.

Actions to enforce a promoter's duties

A promoter owes his fiduciary and common law duties to the company, and the company alone has a right of action against him for breach of those duties. The company's right to enforce these duties is absolute, however, and cannot be taken away by a provision in the articles exonerating the promoters from the duties which they would normally owe or from liability for the breach of such duties.[3] The promoter's duties may be enforced in an action commenced by writ, or by misfeasance proceedings in the company's winding up,[4] or by a derivative action brought by one shareholder suing on behalf of all the shareholders of the company.[5] The derivative action is useful when the promoters are also directors of the company, and are therefore in a position to prevent an action from being brought by the company in its own name.

It seems that a promoter owes no duties to shareholders individually, and is not liable to them if their shares turn out to be valueless because of his breaches of duty owed to the company. Apparently, the only occasion when a shareholder may sue a promoter for loss suffered by the shareholder personally is when the promoter induces him to subscribe for shares by making false statements about the company and its prospects to him individually or to persons invited to subscribe for shares in the company (including him).[6] But it has been suggested that if a promoter sells his own property to the company for shares which it allots to him, and the promoter then sells the shares without disclosing to the purchaser the profit he obtained by the sale of the property, the purchaser may sue the promoter for damages for impliedly representing that the property which he sold to the company was at least worth the nominal value of the shares and that the shares consequently are worth at least their nominal value.[7] It has also been suggested that in those circumstances, the purchaser might rescind the purchase of the shares and recover the amount which he paid for them from the promoter.[8] If these suggestions are correct, a purchaser of shares from a promoter would have remedies against him for breaches

---

20 *Lagunas Nitrate Co v Lagunas Syndicate Ltd* [1899] 2 Ch 392.
1 *Twycross v Grant* (1877) 2 CPD 469.
2 *Re British Seamless Paper Box Co* (1881) 17 ChD 467.
3 *Omnium Electric Palaces Ltd v Baines* [1914] 1 Ch 332 at 347, per Sargant J.
4 Insolvency Act 1986, s 212 (1) to (3) (see p 683, post).
5 *Hichens v Congreve* (1828) 4 Russ 562; *Atwool v Merryweather* (1867) LR 5 Eq 464n. For derivative actions by shareholders, see Chapter 18.
6 See p 275 et seq, ante.
7 *Re Ambrose Lake Tin and Copper Co* (1880) 14 ChD 390 at 397, per Brett LJ.
8 *Jubilee Cotton Mills Ltd v Lewis* [1924] AC 958 at 970, per Lord Dunedin.

of his fiduciary duties which seem to be denied to subscribers for shares from the company.

Promoters owe no duties to creditors of the company. Consequently, if they make full disclosure of their interests to the shareholders, the company cannot recover any profits they have made from the promotion merely because they have not made a similar disclosure to trade creditors[9] or debenture holders,[10] and this is so even though the loan capital subscribed by debenture holders is used to pay the purchase price of property which the promoters have sold to the company.[11] But if when the company is wound up it is found that the promoters did not make proper disclosure to the shareholders, the liquidator may recover secret profits, compensation and damages from them, even if the company is insolvent and the money recovered will be wholly consumed in paying the company's debts.

REMUNERATION AND EXPENSES

The inability of a company to contract before its incorporation makes it impossible for its promoters to obtain contractual rights to remuneration for their services rendered before incorporation and an indemnity for their expenses incurred before that time. A provision in the company's memorandum or articles of association directing that promoters shall be remunerated for their services and indemnified against promotion expenses does not constitute a contract which they can enforce, even if they are members of the company, because it does not relate to their rights as members or shareholders of the company.[12] Whether promoters are entitled to remuneration and an indemnity on equitable grounds, apart from contract, is extremely doubtful.[13] The best provision they can usually make is to include a power in the company's articles for the directors to pay them the value of their promotion services and to reimburse them for the expenses incurred by them in connection with the promotion.[14] This imposes no legal obligations on the company towards the promoters, but as they or their nominees will usually be the first directors of the company, there is little risk of the power not being exercised in their favour. If the company contracts to pay promoters' remuneration or to indemnify them against expenses in connection with services they render before the company's incorporation or before the contract is entered into, the contract is enforceable only if made under the company's common seal or as a deed, because the services and expenditure are then past consideration for the company's promise, and are therefore insufficient to support a simple contract.

9 *Salomon v A Salomon & Co Ltd* [1897] AC 22 at 39, per Lord Watson and Lord Davey at 57.
10 *A-G for Canada v Standard Trust Co of New York* [1911] AC 498.
11 *Re Darby, ex p Brougham* [1911] 1 KB 95.
12 *Re Rotherham Alum and Chemical Co* (1883) 25 ChD 103; *Re English and Colonial Produce Co Ltd* [1906] 2 Ch 435.
13 See p 89, ante.
14 The Companies Act 1948, Table A, art 80, empowered directors to pay all expenses incurred in promoting and registering the company. There is no corresponding provision in the present Table A.

CHAPTER 14

Directors and secretaries

APPOINTMENT OF DIRECTORS

The Companies Act 1985 does not define the term 'director', but merely provides that it shall include any person occupying the position of a director by whatever name called.[1] The articles of a company may therefore designate its directors as members of the governing council or the board of management of the company, or as governors, trustees or administrators, or may give them any other title, but so far as the law is concerned they are simply directors. It is their function and not their name which matters. For certain purposes the Companies Act 1985, the Insolvency Act 1986, and the Company Directors Disqualification Act 1986, treat in the same way as directors any person in accordance with whose directions or instructions the directors of a company are accustomed to act, and such persons are called 'shadow directors'.[2] However, a person is not deemed to be a shadow director merely because the directors of a company act on advice given by him in a professional capacity.[3] The Companies Act 1985 merely uses the category of shadow director to impose certain duties, liabilities or prohibitions on persons who would not otherwise be classed as directors, and such persons do not thereby acquire any rights or powers in connection with the management of the company, nor are they subject to the common law or equitable duties of directors.

The board of directors of a company conducts its business and affairs subject to

1 Companies Act 1985, s 741 (1).
2 Ibid, s 741 (2). The relevant provisions of the Companies Act 1985 are the following—those relating to the register of directors and secretaries and the inclusion of directors' names in business letters (s 288 (6) and s 305 (7), substituted by Companies Act 1989, s 145 and Sch 19, para 4) (see p 553, post); the duty of directors to have regard to the interests of employees as well as members (s 309 (3)) (see p 584, post); the disclosure of directors' interests in contracts and transactions with the company (s 317 (8)); publicity in respect of directors' service contracts (s 318 (6)) (see p 596, post); the need for the duration of directors' contracts of employment and the terms of contracts for the acquisition of substantial amounts of assets by or from them to be approved by a general meeting (s 319 (7) and s 320 (3)) (see pp 540 and 599, post); the prohibition on directors buying options to purchase or sell shares, debentures or other loan securities issued by the company or companies in the same group (s 323 (4)) (see p 595, post); the duty of directors to report the acquisition or disposal of interests in shares, debentures or loan securities of the company or of other companies in the same group and the entry of such interests and disposals of them in a register of directors' holding's (s 324 (6) and s 325 (6)) (see p 556, post); the restrictions imposed on loans and quasi-loans and credit transactions for the benefit of directors and persons connected with them and the reporting of such transactions in the company's annual accounts (s 330 (5)) (see p 565, post); and those relating to the annual return of the company (s 365 (3), substituted by Companies Act 1989, s 139). The relevant provisions of the Insolvency Act 1986 are the following—those relating to criminal offences committed before a company goes into liquidation (s 206 (6)) or during the liquidation (s 208 (3), s 210 (3) and s 211 (3); wrongful trading by a company which goes into an insolvent liquidation (s 214 (7) (see p 44, ante)); and persons connected with a company subject to insolvency proceedings (s 249) (see p 461, ante). The relevant provisions of the Company Directors Disqualification Act 1986 are the following—disqualification for fraudulent trading (s 4 (2)) and the disqualification of unfit directors of insolvent companies (s 6 (3)).
3 Companies Act 1985, s 741 (2).

such control or supervision by its shareholders as is provided for by its memorandum and articles of association and by the Companies Act 1985 (as amended).

Every company must have a board of directors, and the minimum number of directors who must hold office at any time is two in the case of a public company incorporated on or after 1 November 1929, and one in the case of a private company or a public company incorporated before that date.[4] A sole director of a public company incorporated since 1 November 1929 cannot act in its name or on its behalf in relation to outsiders, or even in relation to members (eg he cannot call general meetings or authorise the registration of share transfers). Outsiders who deal with a public company unaware that it has only one director may nevertheless be able to treat the company as bound by his acts under the rule in *Royal Bank v Turquand*.[5]

Power to appoint directors

The power to appoint directors is a corporate one, and is exercisable in the manner laid down in the company's memorandum or article of association. The law imposes no restrictions on what the memorandum or articles may provide in this respect, and although it is usual for the power of appointment to be vested in the shareholders in general meeting, a provision by which the directors themselves, or even an outsider,[6] may appoint directors is valid. Consequently, the memorandum or articles may provide for the representation of the employees of the company on its board of directors, either by direct election by the employees or on the nomination of trade unions or other associations to which the employees belong. If the articles are silent on the appointment of directors, however, and Table A is inapplicable, the power to appoint directors is exercisable by the members of the company in general meeting by ordinary resolution.

First directors

The first directors of a company are usually named in its articles of association or the articles provide that the first directors shall be appointed by the subscribers of the memorandum and articles. The first directors of the company are conclusively the persons named in the statement containing their names and other particulars in respect of them which must be delivered with the company's memorandum and articles in order to obtain the company's incorporation.[7] This statement must be signed by the subscribers and must contain the consent of the persons named as the first directors to act as such; the appointment, by the articles, of any person to be a director is void unless he is named as a director in the statement of first directors.[8]

Effectively therefore, the statement of the company's first directors signed by the subscribers is an instrument of appointment, and not merely a return of the names of directors who have been appointed by other means. Nevertheless, it would seem that the subscribers are bound by the provisions of the articles which they will already have subscribed, so that any one of them can compel the others to sign a statement of the first directors which names as such directors the persons who are nominated in the articles, or who have been chosen in accordance with the procedure prescribed by the articles. If the company is governed in this respect by Table A of the Companies Act 1948, or the earlier Companies Acts, the first

4   Companies Act 1985, s 282 (1) to (3).
5   (1855) 5 E & B 248; affd (1856) 6 E & B 327 (see Chapter 5).
6   *British Murac Syndicate Ltd v Alperton Rubber Co Ltd* [1915] 2 Ch 186.
7   Companies Act 1985, s 10 (2) (see p 27, ante).
8   Ibid, s 10 (3) and (5).

directors are chosen by a majority in number of the subscribers if they cannot make a unanimous appointment.[9]

Subsequent directors

The power to appoint subsequent directors is usually exercisable by the members of the company in general meeting by ordinary resolution.[10] If the articles prescribe the maximum number of directors who may be appointed, appointments in excess of the maximum are void. Usually, however, the members are empowered to increase or reduce the maximum number of directors by ordinary resolution,[11] and then an appointment of a director in excess of the former maximum is taken to be an exercise of the power to increase the number of directors, and is valid.[12] On the other hand, the power to reduce the maximum number of directors cannot be exercised so as to remove an existing director before the expiration of his current term of office;[13] a reduction of the number of directors will therefore only operate in the future by preventing the appointment of new directors in place of those who vacate office until the number of directors has fallen below the new maximum.

When directors of a public company are appointed or re-appointed by the members in general meeting, their appointments must be made individually by separate resolutions, unless the meeting first resolves, without a dissenting vote, that a composite resolution appointing two or more directors shall be put to the vote.[14] An appointment of a director in contravention of this rule is void.[15] The purpose of the rule is to prevent members being coerced into accepting candidates for directorships whom they do not want by the nomination of such candidates being combined with the nomination of other candidates whom the members do want. There is nothing to prevent the members of a private company appointing or re-appointing two or more directors, or even the whole board, by a single resolution, and it is common practice to do this on the re-appointment of the existing directors on the expiration of their current term of office.

There is no legal requirement that any director must enter into a formal service agreement with the company on whose board he serves. If such an agreement is entered into with a company governed by Table A, and the director is to be remunerated, however, the contract must be approved by an ordinary resolution passed by a general meeting,[16] unless the director is appointed by the board to be a managing director, in which case the terms of his service contract are determined by the board.[17]

---

9 Companies Act 1948, Table A, art 75. The present Table A makes no provision for the appointment of the first directors, and so the subscribers, as the only members of the company, may appoint the first directors by an ordinary resolution.
10 See Table A, arts 78 and 80.
11 See Table A, art 64.
12 *Worcester Corsetry Ltd v Witting* [1936] Ch 640.
13 *Foster v Greenwich Ferry Co Ltd* (1888) 5 TLR 16; *Worcester Corsetry Ltd v Witting*, supra, per Lawrence LJ at 650.
14 Companies Act 1985, s 292 (1).
15 Ibid, s 292 (2). If such a void resolution is passed and any of the persons to whom it relates is a director who has completed his period of office and is presenting himself for re-appointment, no provision in the company's articles that he shall be automatically re-appointed if no other person is appointed in his place takes effect so as to result in his re-appointment (Companies Act 1985, s 292 (2)).
16 Table A, art 82.
17 Ibid, art 84.

Casual vacancies and additional directors

The board of directors is usually empowered to fill casual vacancies on the board and to appoint additional directors up to the maximum permissible for the time being, but directors appointed by the board usually hold office only until the next annual general meeting so that the members may then decide whether they wish them to continue in office.[18] An alternative provision, which is sometimes found, is that a person appointed by the board to fill a casual vacancy shall hold office until the director whom he replaces would otherwise have completed his current term of office. A casual vacancy on the board is one which occurs otherwise than by a director's term of office expiring,[19] and so there will be a casual vacancy if a director dies, or resigns, or is removed, or becomes disqualified from holding office.

Usually the members are given a concurrent power with the board to fill casual vacancies and to appoint additional directors,[20] but even when the members are given no such power expressly by the articles, it is presumed that they have such a concurrent power.[21] In the absence of an express provision to that effect, the power of the board to appoint will be construed as exclusive only if the board can fill vacancies and appoint additional directors for the same period and on the same terms as the members may appoint new directors on normal retirements,[1] which will not be the case if the articles provide that the board's appointees only hold office until the next annual general meeting. If the board of directors and the members in general meeting have concurrent powers to fill casual vacancies on the board or to appoint additional directors, an appointment is made effectively by whichever of them acts first, and there is then no vacancy which the other can fill by purporting to revoke or supersede the first appointment.

Contractual rights to appoint directors

If by a company's articles directors are to be appointed by the members in general meeting, the board cannot make a valid contract by which an outsider is empowered to appoint directors.[2] But if the company is governed by Table A, it seems that the board may delegate its power to appoint additional directors by a power of attorney,[3] and this may prove useful when the board wishes to raise a loan from persons who are only willing to lend if they can nominate a certain number of directors to the board to protect their interests. If the articles expressly authorise the appointment of directors by outsiders, their power to do so is undoubtedly valid, and if the company refuses to accept the outsiders' nominee, the court will compel it to do so by injunction, unless the nominee is unfit to act.[4] It has been suggested, however, that if the outsider had power to appoint a majority of the directors, the court would refuse to issue an injunction, because the control

---

18 See Table A, art 79. The Stock Exchange requires the articles of listed companies to contain a provision to this effect (Stock Exchange *Admission of Securities to Listing*, Section 9, Chapter 1, para 4.2).

19 *Munster v Cammell Co* (1882) 21 ChD 183 at 187.

20 See Table A, art 78.

21 *Worcester Corsetry Ltd v Witting*, supra, per Hanworth MR at 647 and Lawrence LJ at 650.

 1 *Blair Open Hearth Furnace Co Ltd v Reigart* (1913) 108 LT 665, as explained in *Worcester Corsetry Ltd v Witting*, supra.

 2 *James v Eve* (1875) LR 6 HL 335.

 3 Table A, art 71.

 4 *British Murac Syndicate Ltd v Alperton Rubber Co Ltd* [1915] 2 Ch 186. In *Plantations Trust Ltd v Bila (Sumatra) Rubber Lands Ltd* (1916) 85 LJ Ch 801, Eve J held that if the outsider has merely a contractual right to nominate a director and the company undertakes to appoint him, the outsider cannot obtain an injunction to restrain the company from preventing his nominee from acting as a director if the company has not formally appointed him to the board, nor an order of specific performance to compel the company to make the appointment. The correctness of this second conclusion is very questionable.

of the company's affairs would then be taken away from its members.[5] Although one can understand the court's reluctance to force outside control on a company in this way, it is difficult to see how the court could logically refuse an injunction to an outsider merely because he has the right to appoint several directors instead of one or a few.

It used formerly to be common in the case of private companies for the articles and directors' service agreements to empower directors or some of them to assign their offices to anyone they chose on their retirement or resignation. Such an assignment is now effective only if it is approved by a special resolution passed by a general meeting of members of the company.[6] Because of this, provisions for the assignment of directorships are not now inserted in articles and service agreements. They have been replaced in practice by a power for the retiring or resigning director to nominate one or more directors to the board, not as his assignees or successors, but simply as ordinary members of the board, and such nominations, of course, do not require the approval of the members.

Often a contract for the sale of a substantial holding of shares contains an undertaking by the sellers to procure the appointment of the purchaser or his nominees as directors of the company. Such an undertaking is valid and is enforceable by an order of specific performance against the sellers, and it is immaterial that the court might not order the company itself to allow the purchaser to act as a director.[7] If the arrangement is not consented to by the other shareholders or the company is a public one, however, the court will not compel the seller, or if the arrangement is for the purchaser to procure the continuance of the vendor in office as a director, will not compel the purchaser if to do so would involve the seller or purchaser voting in a particular manner at a board meeting in his capacity as a director of the company, or persuading the other directors to do so.[8]

Disqualifications

Bankruptcy

It is a criminal offence for an undischarged bankrupt to act as a director of a company or to take part in its management without leave of the court which adjudged him bankrupt.[9] But a bankrupt is not disqualified by law from being appointed a director, and although he may not act in that capacity without leave of the court, his appointment would be effective for other purposes, for example, in determining the number of unfilled vacancies on the board. Because of this omission in the law, articles often provide that bankrupts may not be appointed directors, and that any attempted appointment shall be void.[10]

Order of the court

A person may be disqualified by order of the court from being a director, liquidator or administrator of any company whatever, and from being a receiver or manager

5 *British Murac Syndicate Ltd v Alperton Rubber Co Ltd*, supra, at 196.
6 Companies Act 1985, s 308.
7 *C H Giles & Co Ltd v Morris* [1972] 1 All ER 960, [1972] 1 WLR 307.
8 *Wilton Group plc v Abrams* (1990) 6 BCC 310.
9 Company Directors Disqualification Act 1986, s 11 (1) and (2). Leave of the court for a bankrupt to act as a director may not be given unless notice of the application for leave has been served on the official receiver (an official of the Department of Trade and Industry who acts in insolvency proceedings, and he is under a duty to oppose the application if he considers that it would be against the public interest for leave to be granted (ibid, s 11 (3)).
10 By Table A, art 81 (*b*), a director who becomes bankrupt merely vacates office. The article does not prevent the appointment of a director who is already bankrupt.

of the undertaking or assets or any property of any such company, and from being directly or indirectly concerned in or taking part in the promotion, formation or management of any such company,[11] if:

(a)   he has been/convicted of an indictable offence) (whether on indictment or summarily) in connection with the promotion, formation, management or liquidation of a company or with the receivership or management of the property of a company;[12] or

(b)   in the winding up of a company, it is found in civil or criminal proceedings that he has been guilty of fraudulent trading,[13] or that while an officer[14] or liquidator of a company, or while a receiver manager of any of its property, he has been guilty of any fraud in relation to the company or of a breach of duty toward it;[15] or

(c)   he is or has been a director or shadow director of a company which has at any time become insolvent (whether while he was a director or shadow director of it or subsequently) and his conduct as a director or shadow director of that company (either taken alone or together with his conduct as a director or shadow director of any other company or companies) makes him unfit to be concerned in the management of a company; a company becomes insolvent for this purpose if it goes into liquidation at a time when its assets are insufficient to discharge its debts and liabilities in full together with the expenses of the liquidation; in deciding whether a director's or shadow director's conduct makes him unfit to be concerned in the management of a company, the court must take into account in particular any breach of fiduciary or other duty, or wrongful application or retention of money or other assets by him, his responsibility for any transactions which may be set aside in the company's insolvency, his failure to comply with the accounting and other requirements of the Companies Act 1985 (as amended) and the extent of his responsibility for the causes of the company's insolvency, or its failure to fulfil contracts entered into by it for which it received pre-payment or to call a meeting of the company's creditors in connection with the company going into voluntary liquidation;[16] or

(d)   he is or has been a director or shadow director of a company whose affairs have been investigated by inspectors appointed by the Secretary of State for Trade and Industry[17] or about whose affairs the Secretary of State has exercised his powers to obtain information or documents,[18] and his conduct in relation to that company as revealed by the inspector's report or the Secretary of State's enquiries shows that he is unfit to be concerned in the management of a company;[19] in deciding whether this is so, the court must take into account in particular the same matters as if the company had gone into an insolvent liquidation (apart from the director's or shadow director's responsibility for the insolvency of the company where it is not insolvent);[20]

11 Company Directors Disqualification Act 1986, s 1 (1).
12 Ibid, s 2 (1).
13 Fraudulent trading is defined by the Companies Act 1985, s 458 as a criminal offence and by Insolvency Act 1986, s 213 (1) for the purpose of civil proceedings (see p 41, ante).
14 The expression 'officer' includes a person in accordance with whose directions or instructions the directors of the company have been accustomed to act (ie a shadow director) (Company Directors Disqualification Act 1986, s 4 (2)).
15 Company Directors Disqualification Act 1986, s 4 (1).
16 Ibid, s 6 (1) and (2), s 9 (1) and Sch 1.
17 See p 686, post.
18 See p 692, post.
19 Company Directors Disqualification Act 1986, s 8 (1) and (2).
20 Ibid, s 9 (1) and Sch 1.

(e) he has persistently defaulted as a director or secretary of any company or companies in making returns, delivering accounts or other documents or giving notifications required by the Companies Act 1985 (as amended) to the Registrar of Companies; for this purpose a person is conclusively deemed to be in persistent default if he has been convicted of a default, or required by a court to make good a default,[1] on at least three occasions during the five years before an application for a disqualification order is made,[2] but it is not necessary that the court should have previously convicted a director or made a default order against him on even a single occasion if he is shown to have failed to comply with his obligation to deliver documents or returns to the Registrar of Companies on numerous occasions, so that his defaults can be categorised as persistent;[3] or

(f) the court has made an order under the Insolvency Act 1986[4] that he shall contribute such amount to the assets of a company in liquidation as the court directs on the ground that he has been guilty of fraudulent or wrongful trading.[5]

An application for a disqualification order on grounds (a), (b) or (e) may be made to any court which has jurisdiction to order the company to be wound up, and the application may be by the Secretary of State for Trade and Industry or the official receiver, or by the liquidator or any past or present member or creditor of any company in relation to which an offence or default has been, or is alleged to have been, committed.[6] An application on ground (c) may be made by the Secretary of State or, if the Secretary of State so directs, by the official receiver if the company is being wound up by the court, but the application cannot be made without leave of the court more than two years after the company goes into an insolvent liquidation, or has an administration order made against it, or an administrative receiver of its assets is appointed by a debenture or loan security holder secured by a floating charge over the whole or substantially the whole of its assets.[7] An application on ground (d) must be made by the Secretary of State.[8] A disqualification on grounds (a), (b) or (e) may be imposed by the court which has jurisdiction to wind up the company, whether it is in liquidation or not, or by the court which convicts the disqualified person of an offence under (a) above.[9] A disqualification on ground (c) may be imposed on a present or former director or shadow director of a company by the court which has made a winding up or administration order in respect of the company or, if it is being wound up voluntarily, by the court which would have jurisdiction to make a winding up order against it; the disqualification of any other person on ground (c) may be imposed by the High Court.[10] A disqualification on ground (d) may be imposed by

---

1 By an order under the Companies Act 1985, s 713 (1).
2 Company Directors Disqualification Act 1986, s 3 (1) to (3).
3 *Re Arctic Engineering Co Ltd (No 2)* [1986] 2 All ER 346, [1986] BCLC 253.
4 Insolvency Act 1986, ss 213 and 214 (see pp 41 and 44, ante).
5 Company Directors Disqualification Act 1986, s 10 (1).
6 Ibid, s 16 (2).
7 Ibid, s 6 (2) and s 7 (1) and (2). If the company has an administrative receiver of its assets appointed and is later ordered to be wound up by the court or resolves to be wound up voluntarily, the two year period for making an application runs from the date on which the administrative receiver was appointed (*Re Tasbian Ltd* [1989] BCLC 720, (1989) 5 BCC 729 affirmed (1990) 6 BCC 518).
8 Company Directors Disqualification Act 1986, s 8 (1).
9 Ibid, s 2 (2), s 3 (4) and s 4 (1).
10 Ibid, s 6 (3).

the High Court,[11] and on ground (f) by the court which makes the order for payment of a contribution to the assets of the company.[12]

A disqualification imposed by the court continues for such period as the court directs, not exceeding 15 years from the date of the court's order,[13] but if the disqualification is imposed for persistent default in delivering returns, accounts or other documents to the Registrar of Companies, or if the disqualification is imposed by a magistrates' court on summary conviction for an indictable offence, the disqualification period cannot exceed five years.[14] A disqualification imposed on ground (c) must be for not less than two years.[15] The period of disqualification imposed by the court is proportionate to the seriousness of the offence, breach of duty or default, and will not necessarily be for the maximum period.[16] The court which makes a disqualification order must notify it to the Secretary of State for Trade and Industry, who keeps a register of such orders which is open to public inspection.[17] The variation and termination of such an order and any leave granted by a court under it must likewise be notified and entered in the register.[17]

The court will exercise its jurisdiction to disqualify a person from being a director, liquidator, receiver, administrator or manager of any company and from participating in the formation or management of any company because his conduct as a director or shadow director makes him unfit to be concerned in the management of any company whatsoever, only if the director or shadow director has been guilty of conduct showing a disregard for commercial morality or probity on more than isolated occasions,[18] or if he has been guilty of reckless mismanagement without regard to the company's ability to satisfy the debts and liabilities it has incurred,[19] or if he has manifested gross incompetence.[20] (The purpose of disqualification proceedings is to protect the public and not to punish the respondent director for misconduct.) Consequently, a disqualification order will not be made merely because the director's company has gone into an insolvent liquidation as the result of adverse trading conditions,[2] but disqualification orders will be made if the company's insolvency has been aggravated by its directors taking substantial salaries despite the company's precarious condition,[3] or by the directors selling the company's assets to a new company formed by themselves at a substantially lower price than the company paid for the assets.[4] If the company's insolvency has been caused by the directors following the advice of an apparently competent professional adviser,[5] or by the company's financial and accounting responsibilities

11 Ibid, s 8 (3).
12 Ibid, s 10 (1).
13 Not from the expiration of a term of imprisonment imposed by the court (R v Bradley [1961] 1 All ER 669, [1961] 1 WLR 398).
14 Company Directors Disqualification Act 1986, s 2 (3), s 3 (5), s 4 (3), s 5 (5), s 6 (4), s 8 (4) and s 10 (2).
15 Ibid, s 6 (4).
16 Re Civica Investments Ltd [1983] BCLC 456.
17 Company Directors Disqualification Act 1986, s 18 (1) and (2).
18 Re Dawson Print Group plc [1987] BCLC 601, (1986) 3 BCC 322; Re Bath Glass Ltd [1988] BCLC 329, (1987) 4 BCC 130; Re McNulty's Interchange Ltd [1989] BCLC 709, (1988) 4 BCC 533, Re Lo-Line Electric Motors Ltd [1988] Ch 477, [1988] BCLC 698.
19 Re Stanford Services Ltd [1987] BCLC 607.
20 Re Dawson Print Group plc, supra; Re Rolus Properties Ltd (1988) 4 BCC 446; Re Lo-Line Electric Motors Ltd, supra.
 1 Re Churchill Hotel (Plymouth) Ltd [1988] BCLC 341, (1987) 4 BCC 112; Re Rolus Properties Ltd, supra; Re D J Matthews (Joinery Design) Ltd (1988) 4 BCC 513.
 2 Re Douglas Construction Services Ltd [1988] BCLC 397, (1988) 4 BCC 553; Re C U Fittings Ltd (1988) 5 BCC 210.
 3 Re McNulty's Interchange Ltd, supra; Re Ipcon Fashion Ltd (1989) 5 BCC 773.
 4 Re Keypak Homecare Ltd (No 2) (1990) 6 BCC 117.
 5 Re Douglas Construction Services Ltd, supra.

being attended to by a professionally qualified accountant appointed to the board for that purpose,[6] the court will not disqualify the other directors if they relied in good faith on the adviser or the accountant) But directors cannot absolve themselves from all financial responsibility by employing a qualified accountant or appointing him to be the company's finance director, and so directors were disqualified when they had employed deductions made from employees' wages and salaries for income tax under the PAYE system and for national insurance contributions, and also amounts charged to the company's customers for value added tax, as cash available to meet the company's business expenses, despite the fact that it was the finance director's concern to see that these amounts were paid to the Inland Revenue and the Commissioners of Customs and Excise respectively.[7] The court has, in fact, regarded the improper employment of such amounts as working capital as a particularly serious breach of duty by directors, and has been readier to make disqualification orders for that reason than because directors have failed to satisfy other debts and liabilities of their companies.[8]

Any contravention of a disqualification order is itself a criminal offence,[9] and since the disqualification prevents the disqualified person from being a director as well as from acting as one, his appointment as a director of any company during the disqualification period without leave of the court would be void. A disqualification order prohibits the person against whom it is made both from being a director and 'in any way, whether directly or indirectly, [being] concerned or [taking] part in the promotion, formation or management of a company'; this includes taking any part in the central management and direction of a company's affairs, even though this is done in an advisory role, if it extends to most aspects of management and lasts for a substantial time.[10] On the application of the disqualified person, however, the court which has jurisdiction to wind up the relevant company may give him leave to do anything prohibited by the order imposing the disqualification, either generally, so as to bring the disqualification to an end, or in a particular instance[11] and when making the order imposing a disqualification the court may except from its operation a directorship which the director holds in a particular company.[12]

Age limit

A person may not be appointed to be a director of a public company, or of a private company which is a subsidiary of a public company, if he is seventy years old or more, unless his appointment is made or approved[13] by the members in general meeting by a resolution of which special notice[14] is given specifying the candidate's age.[15] However, the company's articles may exclude this limitation on the appointment of directors because of their age, or may prescribe a higher or lower age limit, in which case the statutory provision takes effect with the substitution of that higher or lower age. If the company was incorporated before 1947, the

6 *Re Cladrose Ltd* [1990] BCLC 204, (1990) 6 BCC 11.
7 *Re Majestic Recording Studios Ltd* [1989] BCLC 1, (1988) 4 BCC 519.
8 *Re Stanford Services Ltd*, supra; *Re Churchill Hotel (Plymouth) Ltd*, supra; *Re Lo-Line Electric Motors Ltd*, supra; secus *Re Dawson Print Group Ltd*, supra.
9 Company Directors Disqualification Act 1986, s 13.
10 *R v Campbell* [1984] BCLC 83.
11 Company Directors Disqualification Act 1986, s 17 (1).
12 *Re Majestic Recording Studios Ltd*, supra.
13 Approval would be necessary where the director is appointed by someone other than the members of the company in general meeting.
14 'Special notice' is defined by the Companies Act 1985, s 379 (1) and (2) (see p 625, post).
15 Companies Act 1985, s 293 (1), (2) and (5).

disqualification does not apply to its directors at all if it had a provision in its articles preventing or restricting the appointment of directors over a given age at the beginning of that year.[16] To ensure that the disqualification is observed, a person must give notice of his age to the company if to his knowledge he is proposed for appointment as a director when he has attained seventy or any greater or less age prescribed by the articles for the retirement of directors.[17]

Articles of association

In addition to the foregoing disqualifications imposed by law on the appointment of persons as directors, further disqualifications may be imposed by a company's articles. Table A, however, imposes no such disqualifications.[18] But subject to such express provisions, a person is not disqualified from appointment merely because he is a minor or an alien, and a company may be a director of another company.[19]

Approval of duration of directors' appointment

A company may not include in a director's service contract or any other agreement a term by which the director will be employed by the company or any of its subsidiaries, whether as a director or in any other capacity, for a period exceeding five years which cannot be terminated by the company giving him notice of termination for any reason whatsoever, unless the term is first approved by a general meeting by ordinary resolution or such other resolution of a general meeting as the articles provide.[20] If the director is already employed or is to be employed by the company or any of its subsidiaries under a contract which the company cannot terminate by giving notice for any reason whatsoever, no further contract for the director's continued employment may be entered into without the approval of a general meeting of the company if the aggregate remaining period of employment under the original and the further contracts exceeds five years from the date of the further contract, and employment under the further contract cannot be terminated by the company giving notice for any reason.[1] This is not so, however, if the further contract is entered into during the last six months of the director's employment under the original contract,[2] and so in that situation the approval of a general meeting is necessary only if the employment under the further contract will last for more than five years.

If the approval of a general meeting is required for a term governing the duration of a contract to employ a director, a written memorandum setting out the whole of the proposed contract must be made available for inspection by the members of the company for 15 days before the general meeting called to approve the contract and at the meeting itself.[3] If a contract of employment is entered into without the requisite approval of a general meeting, it is valid except as to its duration, and it is deemed to contain a term entitling the company to terminate it any time on giving reasonable notice.[4] It is clear that such a contract cannot be

---

16 Ibid, s 293 (7).
17 Ibid, s 294 (1).
18 Table A, art 81 merely specified the grounds on which directors will vacate office.
19 *Re Bulawayo Market and Offices Co Ltd* [1907] 2 Ch 458.
20 Companies Act 1985, s 319 (1) and (3).
 1 Ibid, s 319 (2).
 2 Ibid, s 319 (2). Consequently, if a director enters into two successive contracts of employment for consecutive periods of five years and the second contract is entered into six months before the expiration of the first, the approval of a general meeting is unnecessary, even though at the time the second contract is made the company is obliged to employ the director for a further five years and six months.
 3 Companies Act 1985, s 319 (5).
 4 Ibid, s 319 (6).

validated according to its original terms by a resolution passed by a general meeting after the contract has been entered into, but it would seem that since the term for the duration of the director's employment alone is invalidated if prior approval of a general meeting is not given, the director too may terminate the contract by giving reasonable notice to the company, and that until the contract is terminated by the company or the director, its other terms are enforceable by both parties.

Share qualification

A company's articles of association may require each of its directors to hold a certain minimum number of shares in the company to ensure that they have a material stake in its success, and will consequently devote their best endeavours in its service, if only to preserve the value of their own investments. This minimum number of shares is known as the directors' share qualification.[5] The amount of the share qualification may be specified in the articles, but if the company is governed by Table A of the Companies Act 1948, it may be fixed by ordinary resolution in general meeting, and until it is fixed, no share qualification is required of directors.[6]

Unless the company's articles so require, a director need not obtain his qualification shares before he is appointed, nor need he obtain them by allotment from the company,[7] but unless he obtains shares at least equal to the share qualification by allotment or transfer within two months after his appointment or such shorter time as is fixed by the articles, he ceases to be a director, and is guilty of an offence if he continues to act as such, and he cannot be re-appointed until he has obtained his share qualification.[8]

Before it was first enacted that the failure of a director to obtain his qualification shares should cause him to vacate office,[9] it was held that a director impliedly authorised the company to allot his qualification shares to him if he did not obtain them elsewhere within the time fixed by the articles, or if no time was fixed, within a reasonable time after his appointment,[10] which was interpreted to mean, before he first acted as a director.[11] But the director merely gave an implied authority to the company by not obtaining his qualification shares elsewhere; he did not impliedly contract to take an allotment from it.[12] Consequently, he only became a shareholder if the company allotted his qualification shares to him before he revoked its authority to do so, and he impliedly did this by ceasing to be a director.[13] It is uncertain how far these cases are still law today. It would seem that if the company's articles fix a time within which the director must obtain his qualification shares, it can never allot shares to him so as to make him a shareholder and qualify him as a director, unless he expressly applies to it for them. This is because the company's authority to allot only arises at the expiration of the fixed time, and at the moment when it arises the director vacates office under the provisions of the

---

5 The Rules of the Stock Exchange formerly required the directors of a listed company to hold a share qualification which was not merely nominal, but no share qualification at all is now required by the rules of the International Stock Exchange of the United Kingdom and Ireland.
6 Companies Act 1948, Table A, art 77. There is no share qualification required of directors under the present Table A.
7 *Re Metropolitan Public Carriage and Repository Co, Brown's Case* (1873) 9 Ch App 102.
8 Companies Act 1985, s 291 (1), (3) and (4).
9 By the Companies Act 1900, s 3.
10 *Re Metropolitan Public Carriage and Repository Co, Brown's Case* (1873) 9 Ch App 102; *Re Portuguese Consolidated Copper Mines Ltd, Lord Inchiquin's Case* [1891] 3 Ch 28.
11 *Inchiquin's Case*, supra, per Lindley LJ, at 35.
12 *Brown's Case*, supra; *Re Wheal Buller Consols* (1888) 38 ChD 42.
13 *Re Printing Telegraph and Construction Co of the Agence Havas, ex p Cammell* [1894] 2 Ch 392.

Companies Act 1985,[14] thus revoking the authority. But if no time is fixed by the articles, the company may allot shares to the director equal to the qualification after a reasonable time, and if a reasonable time in the circumstances is less than two months, the company may allot the shares and qualify its director before the statutory provision for the vacation of his directorship takes effect. The only thing which militates against this, however, is the fact that the Companies Act 1985 makes it the duty of a director to obtain his qualification shares within two months of his appointment if the articles do not specify a shorter period,[15] and this may be read as a statutory interpretation of what is a reasonable time for acquiring them. If this is so, the company could not allot the shares and qualify the director at any time, because he would cease to hold office at the very moment when its authority to allot arose.

If a company's articles merely require directors to hold a certain number of shares as their qualification, they may hold them in any capacity, and need not own them beneficially. But they must be registered as members of the company in respect of the shares, and it is not sufficient for them merely to be the holders of letters of allotment, or to have the shares registered in the name of nominees for themselves,[16] and a director is not qualified by holding shares represented by share warrants.[17]

Sometimes articles require directors to hold their qualification shares 'in their own right'.[18] This merely means that a director must be registered as the holder of the shares in such a way that the company can safely deal with him as the owner of them, and it does not mean that he must be the unincumbered beneficial owner.[19] Thus, a director has been held qualified under such a provision when he had created an equitable mortgage of his shares,[20] and when he held the shares jointly with other persons as the personal representatives of a deceased member.[1] But if an entry is made on the register of members showing that the director holds the shares in a fiduciary capacity, he ceases to hold them 'in his own right', even though the entry ought not to be made and the company is entitled to disregard it.[2] Furthermore, it seems that if under the articles another person is entitled to insist on being registered as a member in respect of the director's qualification shares, and has notified his claim to the company, the director ceases to hold the shares 'in his own right', because the company can only disregard the claim at the risk of having to pay damages to the claimant if it is well founded, and the company cannot therefore safely deal with the director as owner of the shares.[3] In the case which so decided,[3] the claimant was the director's trustee in bankruptcy,[4] but the principle would seem equally applicable where the claimant is a purchaser or mortgagee of the shares.

---

14 Companies Act 1985, s 291 (3).
15 Ibid, s 291 (1).
16 *Spencer v Kennedy* [1926] Ch 125; *Holmes v Keyes* [1958] Ch 670, [1958] 1 All ER 721; reversed on another ground [1959] Ch 199, [1958] 2 All ER 129.
17 Companies Act 1985, s 291 (2).
18 The Companies Act 1948, Table A contains no such requirement.
19 *Pulbrook v Richmond Consolidated Mining Co* (1878) 9 ChD 610; *Bainbridge v Smith* (1889) 41 ChD 462 at 475; *Howard v Sadler* [1893] 1 QB 1.
20 *Pulbrook v Richmond Consolidated Mining Co*, supra.
 1 *Grundy v Briggs* [1910] 1 Ch 444.
 2 *Boschoek Proprietary Co Ltd v Fuke* [1906] 1 Ch 148. The entry of trusts of shares in the register of members is forbidden by Companies Act 1985, s 360, p 356, ante.
 3 *Sutton v English and Colonial Produce Co* [1902] 2 Ch 502.
 4 The case was decided before the law first disqualified bankrupts from acting as directors of companies.

VACATION OF THE OFFICE OF DIRECTOR

Termination of period of office

The articles of a company may authorise the appointment of a director for any period, however long or short, and the appointment is valid if made consistently with the articles. Thus, a director may hold office at will, and be removable under the articles at any time by the other directors or by members of the company in general meeting, or he may hold office for a term of years or for life, whether subject to removal during that time or not. Whatever the duration of the director's appointment may be, he ceases to be a director automatically when his period of office expires.

A common provision, found especially in the articles of public companies, is one by which a fraction of the directors retire each year by rotation, and the members are empowered to fill the vacancies at the annual general meeting. Table A contains such a provision. By it all the directors retire at the first annual general meeting of the company,[5] and at the annual general meeting in every subsequent year one-third of them retire, or if their number is not three or a multiple of three, the number of them nearest to one-third retire.[6] Under such an article, if there are only two directors, one will retire each year.[7] If no annual general meeting is held, the appropriate number of directors will retire at the end of the calendar year in which it should have been held.[8] Table A goes on to provide that the directors who retire at the annual general meeting shall be those who have longest held office, but if two directors were appointed on the same day and only one of them is to retire, the one to retire shall be selected by lot.[9]

Retiring directors are made eligible for re-election by Table A,[10] and they may also offer themselves for re-election if the articles are silent on the matter and do not expressly prohibit their re-election. If a retiring director offers himself for re-election, and the members neither elect someone else in his place, nor resolve that the vacancy shall not be filled, nor reject the resolution for his re-election,[11] Table A provides that he is automatically re-elected.[12] This does not apply, of course, if the company is not governed by Table A and its articles made no equivalent provision for automatic re-election.

Disqualification and vacation of office

If a director becomes disqualified by law or by the articles from continuing to be a director, he automatically vacates office.

Bankruptcy and disqualification by the court

The disqualification of a bankrupt from acting as a director, and the power of the court to disqualify persons who have been guilty of various acts or defaults as

---

5 This is because the first directors are appointed by the subscribers of the memorandum (see p 532, ante), and this provision in Table A enables the members who have voting rights at general meetings to decide whether they shall continue in office.
6 Table A, art 73.
7 *Re David Moseley & Sons Ltd* [1939] Ch 719, [1939] 2 All ER 791.
8 *Morris v Kanssen* [1946] AC 459, [1946] 1 All ER 586; *Re Consolidated Nickel Mines Ltd* [1914] 1 Ch 883.
9 Table A, art 74.
10 Ibid, art 80.
11 The omission of this last proviso in the articles led in *Grundt v Greater Boulder Proprietary Mines Ltd* [1948] Ch 145, [1948] 1 All ER 21, to the automatic re-election of a retiring director, even though a resolution for his re-election was defeated at the annual general meeting.
12 Table A, art 75.

directors, promoters, liquidators and receivers of any company from being or acting as the directors of any company and from participation in the management of any company, have already been dealt with.[13] A person against whom the court makes a disqualification order vacates all directorships which he currently holds and cannot be re-appointed to any of them without leave of the court.[14] A director who becomes bankrupt does not vacate office, however, unless the articles so provide.[15]

Age limit

In the case of companies to whose boards of directors a person of seventy years of age or more can only be appointed a director by resolution of the members in general meeting of which special notice has been given,[16] a director who is already in office when he attains seventy vacates office at the annual general meeting next following his seventieth birthday, but he may be re-appointed by an ordinary resolution in general meeting of which special notice is given in the same way as a new candidate for office who is over seventy may be elected for the first time.[17] A director who vacates office at an annual general meeting because he has attained seventy years of age is not automatically re-elected for a further period under a provision in the articles that a director who ceases to hold office shall be deemed to be re-elected if no one else is elected in his place, and the vacancy caused by the director not being expressly re-elected may be filled as a casual vacancy.[18] If the company's articles prescribe a retirement age for directors which is greater or less than seventy years, these rules for the retirement and re-appointment of directors take effect with the substitution of the prescribed retirement age.[19]

Loss of share qualification

A director who ceases to hold his share qualification automatically vacates office.[20] There is no period of grace within which he may re-acquire qualification shares so as to prevent his vacation of office, and he cannot be re-appointed a director until he has acquired his qualification shares again.[1] If the share qualification of directors is increased by an alteration of the articles or otherwise, the directors in office do not cease to hold office immediately if they do not already hold the increased share qualification, but if they do not obtain the additional shares within a reasonable time, it has been held that they impliedly authorise the company to allot the additional shares to them.[2] It has further been held that at the end of such a reasonable time, the directors impliedly agree to subscribe for the additional shares by not resigning.[2] This is inconsistent with the many cases where it has been held that a newly appointed director does not impliedly agree to subscribe for his qualification shares, but merely authorises the company to allot them to him,[3] and is therefore probably wrong. The sounder conclusion would appear to be that if

13 See p 535, ante.
14 Company Directors Disqualification Act 1986, s 1 (1).
15 Table A, art 81 (*b*) does so provide.
16 See p 539, ante.
17 Companies Act 1985, s 293 (3) and (5).
18 Ibid, s 293 (4).
19 Ibid, s 293 (7).
20 Ibid, s 291 (3).
 1 Ibid, s 291 (4).
 2 *Molineaux v London, Birmingham and Manchester Insurance Co Ltd* [1902] 2 KB 589.
 3 See p 541, ante.

the director does not obtain the additional shares within a reasonable time and the company does not exercise its power to allot them to him, he ceases to be a director.

Provisions of the articles

A company's articles may specify additional grounds on which directors will become disqualified or vacate office. Table A[4] provides that a director ceases to hold office if he ceases to be a director or is prohibited from continuing to be a director by law;[5] or if he becomes bankrupt, or makes an arrangement or composition with his creditors generally; or if he is or may be suffering from a mental disorder and either is admitted to hospital under the appropriate statutory provisions, or has a court order made for his detention or for the appointment of a receiver to administer his assets or affairs; or if he resigns his office by notice in writing to the company; or if he is absent for more than six months from meetings of directors held during that period and the board of directors resolves that he shall vacate office.

Where articles provided that a director should vacate office if he 'absents himself from the meetings of the directors during a period of three calendar months', it was held that the expression 'absents himself' implied a voluntary absence, and that a director did not vacate office when he was unavoidably prevented from attending board meetings by illness.[6] It has also been held that under such a provision the period of three months runs from the date of the first board meeting which the director failed to attend, and not from the last meeting which he did attend.[7] It is doubtful whether either of these decisions is applicable to the provision in Table A. By it a director vacates office if he 'shall for more than six consecutive months have been absent' from board meetings, and a director is absent from a board meeting whether the cause of his absence is voluntary or not. Furthermore, the disqualifying absence is 'from meetings of the directors held during that period', which implies that there may be a gap between the beginning of the period and the first meeting held during it, in other words, that the six months begins to run from the last meeting which the director did attend, and not from the first meeting which he failed to attend.

Sometimes articles provide that a director shall vacate office if he is directly or indirectly interested in any contract entered into by the company.[8] Such a disqualification lasts only while the contract is executory, so that if the director is re-appointed after the contract has been fully carried out, his re-appointment is valid.[9]

Vacation of office under provisions in the articles is automatic. It does not require confirmation by the board or a meeting of members to become effective unless the articles expressly so provide, and the board has no power to waive it so that the director concerned may continue to hold office.[9] But where the ground on which office is vacated is the happening of one event, such as becoming bankrupt or being convicted of an indictable offence, the disqualification operates once and for all by vacating the directorship which the director holds at the time when the event occurs, and it does not prevent his immediate re-election.[10] If the disqualification is

---

4 Table A, art 81.
5 See pp 535 and 541, ante. This provision is otiose since the termination of existing directorships is automatic.
6 *Re London and Northern Bank, Mack's Claim* [1900] WN 114.
7 Ibid, *Re London and Northern Bank, McConnell's Claim* [1901] 1 Ch 728.
8 There is no such provision in Table A.
9 *Re Bodega Co Ltd* [1904] 1 Ch 276.
10 *Dawson v African Consolidated Land and Trading Co* [1898] 1 Ch 6.

of a continuing character, however, such as being a bankrupt or of unsound mind, or having been convicted of an indictable offence within the five preceding years, it operates not only to vacate the directorship which the director holds at the time the disqualification commences, but also to prevent his re-election until after the period of disqualification has come to an end.

Claims for wrongful dismissal

A company cannot contract to employ a director on terms which conflict with its articles at the time when he is appointed,[11] and so if a director enters into a service contract with the company which fails to provide that he shall vacate office on the grounds set out in the articles when the contract is entered into, the director cannot claim damages from the company for wrongful dismissal if he subsequently vacates office on one of those grounds. Furthermore, if a company's articles are altered to introduce a new ground on which directors will vacate office, the new ground will apply to directors who are already in office, and may operate to terminate their directorships immediately.[12] But if such a director has a service contract which is not terminable by the company on this new ground by its express terms, he may sue the company for damages for wrongful dismissal, because there is no term implied in the contract that the company may alter its contents by altering its own articles.[12] If the director's service contract incorporates the terms of the articles, however, either by providing expressly that he shall be employed on those terms, or because the contract has arisen from the conduct of the parties by the director serving as a director and the company accepting his services, it is implied that the contract shall embody the terms of the articles as they stand from time to time; consequently, if the articles are altered to introduce a new ground upon which directors shall vacate office, the director will vacate office on that ground in accordance with, and not in breach of, his service contract, and he will have no redress against the company in damages.[13]

Removal

Neither the members nor the board of directors of a company have an inherent power to remove directors before the normal expiration of their period of office in the absence of a power to do so in the articles.[14] If the articles do not specify the duration of a director's appointment, however, he holds office at will, and may be dismissed by an ordinary resolution passed by the members at any time. But if he is employed under a service contract not entered into for a fixed period, he is entitled to reasonable notice of dismissal, and if he is dismissed without such notice, he may sue the company for damages.[15] If the articles empower a director's fellow directors to remove him from the board by a notice given to him by them all or by a board resolution, or if the articles empower them to call on him to resign and provide that he shall cease to hold office if he does not, the other directors must exercise their power in good faith in the interest of the company.[16] Nevertheless even if their motive for the removal of the director is an improper one, the notice removing him from office or calling on him to resign, or the board resolution of removal, is

---

11 *Bluett v Stutchbury's Ltd* (1908) 24 TLR 469.
12 *Southern Foundries (1926) Ltd v Shirlaw* [1940] AC 701, [1940] 2 All ER 445.
13 *Shuttleworth v Cox & Co (Maidenhead) Ltd* [1927] 2 KB 9.
14 *Imperial Hydropathic Hotel Co, Blackpool v Hampson* (1882) 23 ChD 1.
15 *James v Thomas H Kent & Co Ltd* [1951] 1 KB 551, [1950] 2 All ER 1099.
16 This applies to all the powers conferred on directors by the articles (see p 591, post).

effective to terminate his appointment.[17] It would appear, however, that a director who is removed for an improper cause may seek a declaration by the court to that effect, but whether he can then claim damages from his fellow directors or seek a court order for his restoration to the board is uncertain.

By the Companies Act 1985, every company has a statutory power to remove any director before the expiration of his period of office notwithstanding anything in its articles or the director's service contract.[18] But the provision does not enable a private company to remove a director who held office for life on 18 July 1945,[19] and so such a director can only be removed if the articles so provide. The removal of a director under the statutory power is effected by an ordinary resolution at a general meeting of which special notice has been given.[20] The Act does not define an ordinary resolution for this purpose, and it has been construed as having the same meaning as in any other context,[1] namely, a resolution passed by a simple majority of the votes cast in accordance with the rules governing the voting rights attached to shares which are laid down by the company's articles.[2] Consequently, if by the company's articles the shares held by the director whose removal is sought carry additional or multiple voting rights as compared with the shares of other members, the director may use those rights to defeat the resolution for his removal, and the attribution of additional or multiple voting rights to the director by the articles is valid even though its effect is to take away the power which the other members would have otherwise had to remove him from office.[2] This is so even if the articles attribute additional or multiple voting rights to the director only when a resolution for his removal is voted on, and not generally in respect of all resolutions before a general meeting.[2]

When the company is notified that a member intends to move a resolution for the removal of a director, it must inform the director concerned, and he may require the company to circulate a statement by him in his defence to members when notice of the meeting is sent to them, but if the director's statement is received by the company too late for circulation with notice of the meeting, or if the company fails to circulate the statement, the director may have it read out at the meeting.[3] The director's statement must be confined to a reasonable length, and the Companies Court may, on the application of the company or any aggrieved person, order that it shall not be circulated or read out at the meeting if the court considers that the director is abusing his rights to secure needless publicity for defamatory matter.[4] In addition to defending himself by having a statement circulated, the director is entitled to address the meeting at which the resolution is considered, whether he is a member of the company or not.[5] It would appear that he cannot be restrained in advance from making defamatory statements at the meeting, and that the only protection which is available against such statements being made is the power of the chairman of the meeting to confine the director's

---

17 *Lee v Chou Wen Hsien* [1985] BCLC 45. Presumably this is because the act of the other directors, if improperly motivated, is voidable, not void.
18 Companies Act 1985, s 303 (1).
19 Companies Consolidation (Consequential Provision) Act 1985, s 14. This was the date when the Report of the Committee on Company Law Amendment (the Cohen Committee Report) (Cmd 6659) was laid before Parliament.
20 Companies Act 1985, s 303 (1) and (2). For special notice, see p 625, post.
1 See p 617, post.
2 *Bushell v Faith* [1970] AC 1099, [1969] 1 All ER 53.
3 Companies Act 1948, s 304 (1), (2) and (3).
4 Ibid, s 304 (2) and (4). The application is made to the Companies Court by originating summons (RSC Ord 102, r 2 (1)).
5 Companies Act 1985, s 304 (1).

remarks to matters which are relevant.[6] If a director is removed under the statutory power, the vacancy thereby caused may be filled as a casual vacancy,[7] but if it is to be filled at the meeting of members at which the director is removed, special notice of the resolution to fill the vacancy must be given.[8] The person appointed to fill the vacancy holds office for the unexpired part of the period for which the director who has been removed was appointed.[9]

The removal of a director under the statutory power may be costly to the company, because his removal does not prejudice any right which he has to compensation for loss of office or to damages for wrongful dismissal in respect of his directorship or any other appointment which terminates with it.[10] Consequently, if the removal involves a breach of the director's service contract, whether an express contract or a contract which impliedly incorporates the terms of the articles, he may sue the company for damages. If instead a director is removed under a power in the articles, however, whether the power was contained in the articles when the director was appointed or was subsequently inserted therein, he may sue for damages for wrongful dismissal only if he has an express service contract which does not empower the company to dismiss him in that way.[11] The reasons for this are the same as those given above in connection with the automatic vacation of directorships under the provisions of the articles. It may therefore be more economical for a company to remove a director who has no service contract by passing a special resolution altering its articles appropriately than by passing an ordinary resolution for his removal under the statutory power.

If by contract with the company or by its memorandum or articles of association one or more persons have the right to appoint a director or directors to its board, it would appear that the members may remove such a director under the statutory power notwithstanding any contrary provision in the contract or in the memorandum or articles. But it would also seem that the casual vacancies caused thereby may be filled by the persons who made the original appointment, and not by a general meeting or by the board of directors. To remove any possibility of doubt, however, the document conferring the power of appointment and the company's articles should provide expressly to this effect. It is preferable, nevertheless, to ensure that the nominee of the person who enjoys the special right of appointment cannot be removed without his consent. This may be done by a few shares being allotted to that person and the articles of the company providing that those shares shall carry one more vote on a resolution for the removal of a director appointed by him than all the other issued shares of the company together.[12]

Resignation

Articles of association usually provide that a director vacates office if he resigns by giving written notice to the company.[13] Even though there is no such provision in the articles, a director may resign unless the articles forbid him to do so,[14] or unless he has contracted to serve the company for a fixed period; in such cases his resignation is effective in that he cannot be compelled to serve as a director, but if

---

6 Nevertheless, this power may be effective if the director's removal is sought by the other directors and the chairman of the meeting is himself a director, which is usually the case.
7 Companies Act 1985, s 303 (3).
8 Ibid, s 303 (2).
9 Ibid, s 303 (4).
10 Ibid, s 303 (5).
11 *Southern Foundries* (1926) *Ltd v Shirlaw* [1940] AC 701, [1940] 2 All ER 445 (see p 546, ante).
12 *Bushell v Faith* [1970] AC 1099, [1969] 1 All ER 53.
13 See Table A, art 81 (*d*).
14 *Glossop v Glossop* [1907] 2 Ch 370.

he has contracted to serve the company for a fixed period, he will be liable to it for the loss which it suffers in consequence of the premature termination of his services. A resignation is effective as soon as it is notified to the company, and cannot then be withdrawn without the consent of the persons entitled to appoint a new director; but if by the articles a director may resign only if the board consents, the resignation is not effective until the board's consent is given, and the resignation may be withdrawn in the meantime.[14] If a director is authorised by the articles to resign by giving a certain length of notice during a stated period (eg within one year after control of the company passes to an outsider), the resignation is effective so as to preserve consequential rights to the director (eg compensation for loss of office) if notice of it is given within the stated period, even though the notice does not expire until after the end of that period.[15] If the articles require resignations to be in writing, they are nevertheless effective if made orally at a general meeting of the company.[16]

Receiverships and winding up

The appointment of a receiver in a debenture holders' action operates as a dismissal of the company's directors, because the management of the company's business is then taken over by an outsider, and the consequences are the same as if the company had closed its business down or sold it.[17] The appointment of a receiver by debenture or other loan security holders or their trustees under a power conferred by the debentures or the covering trust deed or by a loan security agreement operates to dismiss directors only if the continued exercise of their powers would conflict with the exercise of the receiver's powers, which is not necessarily so, even in the case of a managing director.[18] If directors retain office despite the appointment of the receiver, they can continue to exercise their powers, even though the receiver has equivalent powers under the instrument appointing him, provided that they do not thereby impede the proper conduct of the receivership.[19]

If a company is ordered to be wound up by the court, its directors are thereby dismissed, apparently for the same reasons as in the case of a receivership ordered by the court.[20] It has also been held obiter that directors are dismissed by a general meeting passing a resolution to wind the company up voluntarily,[1] at least if it is insolvent.[2] On the other hand, it has been held[3] that where a solvent company was wound up voluntarily for the purpose of an amalgamation, the company's officers were not dismissed by the passing of the winding up resolution. Moreover, the Insolvency Act 1986[4] appears to contemplate that no voluntary winding up resolution operates to dismiss directors, for it provides that if certain permissions are given, they may continue to exercise their powers during the liquidation. But whether directors are dismissed by the company passing a winding up resolution

---

15 *Taupo Totara Timber Co Ltd v Rowe* [1978] AC 537, [1977] 3 All ER 123.
16 *Latchford Premier Cinema Ltd v Ennion* [1931] 2 Ch 409.
17 *Reid v Explosives Co* (1887) 19 QBD 264.
18 *Re Foster Clark Ltd's Indenture Trusts* [1966] 1 All ER 43, [1966] 1 WLR 125; *Griffiths v Secretary of State for Social Services* [1974] QB 468, [1973] 3 All ER 1184.
19 *Newhart Developments Ltd v Co-operative Commercial Bank Ltd* [1978] QB 814, [1978] 2 All ER 896.
20 *Measures Bros Ltd v Measures* [1910] 2 Ch 248 at 261, per Kennedy LJ.
 1 *Reigate v Union Manufacturing Co (Ramsbottom) Ltd* [1918] 1 KB 592 at 606 per Scrutton LJ.
 2 *Fowler v Commercial Timber Co Ltd* [1930] 2 KB 1 at 6, [1930] All ER Rep 224 at 226, per Green LJ.
 3 *Midland Counties District Bank Ltd v Attwood* [1905] 1 Ch 357.
 4 Insolvency Act 1986, s 91 (2) and s 103.

or not, the liquidator may dismiss them by excluding them from the management of the company's affairs,[5] or by selling the company's undertaking.[6]

If a director is dismissed in consequence of the company being wound up, and he was employed under a contract which incorporated the terms of the company's articles, he cannot sue the company for damages for wrongful dismissal, because it was an implied term of his service contract that it should terminate on the company being wound up.[7] But if the director has an express service contract for a fixed period, no such condition can be implied, and he will be entitled to damages for wrongful dismissal, for which he can prove as a creditor in the liquidation.[7]

NATURE OF THE OFFICE OF A DIRECTOR

No decision of the courts has yet clearly defined the nature of the office of a director, and it is only rarely that the court has seemed to recognise that directors may occupy two positions regulated by entirely different principles, namely, that of officers of the company appointed under the provisions of its constitution, and that of employees or agents of the company serving under express or implied contracts of service. Perhaps it will assist clarity in examining the decided cases if the position of a director under the company's memorandum and articles is referred to as his status, and his rights and obligations under his contract of service, whether express or arising from him acting as a director, are referred to as his contractual rights and obligations. It is the court's frequent failure to make this distinction and its readiness to treat all questions between the director and his company as soluble by reference to his contract of service which has led to the present unsatisfactory state of the law.

Exclusion of directors and interference with their functions

The courts' decisions have been most unsatisfactory when a director has sued his company to establish his title to be a director, or to restrain the company or his fellow directors from preventing him from exercising the powers of his office. Ideally, if the director's title to office is derived directly from the company's memorandum and articles, for example, if the articles provide that directors shall be elected by the members and shall hold office for three years, the director, if duly elected, should be able to compel both the company and his fellow directors to accept him, because his claim rests upon his status under the company's constitution, and not merely on a contract with the company. On the other hand, if his title to his directorship is derived from a contract of service, for example, if the articles empower the board to appoint a managing director for such period as they think fit, and they negotiate a service contract between the company and the plaintiff under which he is to serve as managing director for a fixed term of years, the director should not be able to compel the company to accept his continued services, because this would, in effect, amount to compelling the company to perform his contract of service specifically. Nor, in such a case, should the director be entitled to an injunction to restrain the board from terminating his service contract, although he should be entitled to an injunction to restrain individual directors from interfering with him in the exercise of his powers until the board has duly repudiated the contract on behalf of the company. The distinction between a

---

5 *Fowler v Commercial Timber Co Ltd*, supra; *Re T N Farrer Ltd* [1937] Ch 352, [1937] 2 All ER 505.
6 *Reigate v Union Manufacturing Co*, supra.
7 *Re T N Farrer Ltd*, supra.

director's status and his rights under a service contract is brought out particularly clearly when the company with which he contracts is not the company of which he is a director, for example, where a holding or parent company enters into a service contract with a person whom it appoints to be a managing director of its subsidiary. Here the director's position is purely contractual, and he has no status as a director of the subsidiary to protect by injunction against his premature removal by the parent company or the subsidiary unless his appointment has been confirmed by a resolution passed by a general meeting of the subsidiary or, if its articles permit, its board of directors to appoint directors of it by a board resolution.

The court, however, has not adopted the approach of distinguishing between a director's status and his contractual position. It will declare whether a director has been duly elected, or whether he is still in office, in an action brought by him against the company, but it will not restrain the company from excluding him from board meetings or from preventing him from exercising the powers of his office, because it considers that this would amount to specific enforcement of this employment by the company.[8] On the other hand, the court will restrain a director's fellow directors from interfering with him in the exercise of his powers; there is no contractual relationship between them, and so the court feels free to use the language of status, and to intervene in order to uphold rights conferred on the plaintiff by the company's constitution.[9] In one such case, Jessel MR said:[10]

'The first question is, whether a director who is improperly and without cause excluded by his brother directors from the board from which they claim the right to exclude him, is entitled to an order restraining his brother directors from so excluding him ... Now, it appears to me that this is an individual wrong, or a wrong that has been done to an individual. It is a deprivation of his legal rights for which the directors are personally and individually liable. He has a right by the constitution of the company to take a part in its management, to be present, and to vote at the meetings of the board of directors.'

Whether such an injunction would be issued when the plaintiff's title to office is wholly contractual is uncertain, and it is perhaps significant that in all cases where a managing director serving under a service contract has been dismissed, his claim has been for damages for wrongful dismissal, and not for an injunction against his fellow directors to enable him to continue to exercise the powers of his office.[11]

A further unsatisfactory element has been introduced by a case[12] where it was held that a director may obtain an injunction against his fellow directors to prevent interference with the exercise of his functions only if he has a proprietary interest in the company, such as holding shares in it, or a right to be paid remuneration for his services as a director, or even an expectation of remuneration, as where the articles empower the members in general meeting to fix the directors' remuneration at the end of each year. This requirement of a proprietary interest in the plaintiff director is deduced from certain remarks by Jessel MR, in the case cited above,[13] but it is clear from his judgment that he did not consider that such an interest was a prerequisite for the plaintiff to be able to sue, and in other cases where an injunction was issued against the plaintiff's fellow directors to restrain them from interfering with the plaintiff director when exercising his functions, no mention was made of the need for such an interest.[9] The requirement of a proprietary

8 *Harben v Phillips* (1883) 23 ChD 14; *Bainbridge v Smith* (1889) 41 ChD 462. But in *Munster v Cammell Co* (1882) 21 ChD 183, an injunction was issued against the company.
9 *Munster v Cammell Co*, supra; *Kyshe v Alturas Gold Co* (1888) 4 TLR 331; *Foster v Greenwich Ferry Co Ltd* (1888) 5 TLR 16; *Grimwade v BPS Syndicate Ltd* (1915) 31 TLR 531.
10 *Pulbrook v Richmond Consolidated Mining Co* (1878) 9 ChD 610 at 612.
11 See p 582, post.
12 *Hayes v Bristol Plant Hire Ltd* [1957] 1 All ER 685, [1957] 1 WLR 499.
13 *Pulbrook v Richmond Consolidated Mining Co* (1878) 9 ChD 610.

interest seems to be derived from certain old cases where the court refused to reinstate expelled members of clubs and trade unions unless they had rights or interests in the association's property. The House of Lords has shown that such an interest is no longer necessary in an action for reinstatement,[14] and there seems no reason why a plaintiff director should need such an interest in order to enforce his right to remain in office.

In two cases[15] the Court of Appeal refused to restrain the plaintiff's fellow directors from excluding him from office until a meeting of members had been held to decide whether they wished to have the plaintiff as a director. In both cases the meetings rejected the plaintiff, and the court refused the injunction he sought. The court's reason for directing meetings of members to be held was that it would not force a director on an unwilling company, and in one of the cases[16] this course was perhaps morally justified by the fact that the resolution by which the plaintiff was originally elected was carried only because the appointment of certain proxies who were to vote against his election was technically void. It is submitted that the court should not delegate its duty to decide whether a director's title to office should be upheld in this way. If a director has been duly elected, the only way the company may get rid of him is by resolving to remove him; a resolution rescinding his appointment is ineffective,[17] and the court should not countenance such a resolution by calling a general meeting to decide whether a properly appointed director shall have his appointment made inoperative.[18]

It is outside the scope of this book to consider whether directors are employees for the purpose of statutes other than the Companies Act 1985, in particular, legislation concerning labour relations and employment protection, such as, for example, under the Trade Union and Labour Relations Act 1974 (as amended), the Employment Protection (Consolidation) Act 1978 and the Employment Acts 1980, 1982 and 1988.

Alternate directors

A director's appointment is personal in character, and therefore he cannot appoint a substitute or delegate to attend board meetings and exercise his functions generally in his place unless the company's memorandum or articles permit this to be done. Table A does now contain provisions empowering a director to appoint a fellow director or some other person approved by the board to be his alternate director to hold that position until the appointing director ceases to hold office or removes or replaces him.[19] The alternate director may attend board meetings and vote in place of his appointor, and may do any other thing which his appointor may do in his capacity as a director, and he is entitled to notice of board meetings in the same way as his appointor.[20] Table A provides that an alternate director shall for all purposes be treated as a director, and shall alone be responsible for his own acts and defaults.[1] An alternate director is not to be considered to be the agent

---

14 *Bonsor v Musicians' Union* [1956] AC 104, [1955] 3 All ER 518.
15 *Harben v Phillips* (1883) 23 ChD 14; *Bainbridge v Smith* (1889) 41 ChD 462; contra, *Catesby v Burnett* [1916] 2 Ch 325.
16 *Harben v Phillips*, supra.
17 *Imperial Hydropathic Hotel Co, Blackpool v Hampson* (1882) 23 ChD 1.
18 In both *Harben v Phillips* and *Bainbridge v Smith* the article empowered the members to remove directors, but only by a resolution passed by a three-quarters majority. The resolutions rejecting the plaintiff directors were ordinary resolutions.
19 Table A, arts 65 and 67. Table A of the Companies Act 1948, and the earlier Companies Acts contained no provision for alternate directors.
20 Table A, art 66.
1 Ibid, art 69.

of his appointor,[1] who is presumably liable only for acts of his alternate which he expressly authorises. It would appear that an alternate director is a director of the company for all the purposes of the Companies Act 1985,[2] and that all its provisions relating to directors apply to him accordingly. Consequently, an alternate director may become disqualified from being or acting as a director in the same way and for the same causes as a director appointed in the normal manner, and he is subject to the same prohibitions and restrictions as are imposed by the Companies Act 1985 on normally appointed directors. It is also certain that the fiduciary and other duties toward their company which are imposed on directors at common law and in equity are also imposed on alternate directors while they are acting in that capacity.

PUBLICITY IN RESPECT OF DIRECTORS

Register of directors and secretaries

Every company must keep at its registered office a register of its directors and secretaries, showing in respect of individual directors, their names (including christian or forenames), any former names which they have used,[3] their usual residential addresses, their nationalities, their business occupations, any other directorships which they hold or have held within the preceding five years,[4] and the date of their births; where a director is a corporation, the register must show its corporate name and the address of its registered or principal office.[5]

Every company must send a return to the Registrar of Companies within fourteen days after any change in its directors or the particulars registered in respect of them.[6] The Registrar must advertise in the London Gazette the delivery to him of a return of any change among a company's directors,[7] and until this has been done the company may not rely on any such change having been made as against any person who at the material time is unaware of the change.[8] Consequently, if any person (including a member of the company) enters into a transaction with the directors whose names appear in the most recently advertised returns, and he is unaware that they have ceased to hold office or have been replaced, he may treat the company as bound by the transaction. On the other hand, the fact that a return of a change in the directors has been advertised by the Registrar in the London Gazette does not mean that persons dealing with the company are deemed to know the present composition of the board of directors if they do not actually know this.[9] Nevertheless, a person may be treated as having

2 Companies Act 1985, s 741 (1).
3 This does not include names disused before the age of 18 years, or names disused for not less than 20 years, nor the name of a married woman before her marriage.
4 Except directorships of companies which are or were during the relevant period dormant so as to be exempt from the obligation to appoint auditors (see p 717, post), and except directorships of companies which are or were during the relevant period wholly-owned subsidiaries of the company in whose register the director's name appears, or of a holding company of which that company is the wholly-owned subsidiary, or of other wholly-owned subsidiaries of such a holding company.
5 Companies Act 1985, s 288 (1) and s 289 (1) to (4), as amended by Companies Act 1989, s 145 and Sch 19, para 2.
6 Companies Act 1985, s 288 (2).
7 Ibid, s 711 (1) (c).
8 Ibid, s 42 (1) (c).
9 Companies Act 1985, s 711A (1), inserted by Companies Act 1989, s 142 (1); *Official Custodian for Charities v Parway Estates Developments Ltd* [1985] Ch 151, [1984] 3 All ER 679.

notice of the composition of the board if he could have discovered its membership by making such enquiries as he ought reasonably to have made.[10]

The register of directors and secretaries must be kept open to inspection by members of the company without charge, and by other members of the public on payment of a fee not exceeding that prescribed by the Secretary of State for Trade and Industry.[11]

Business letters

Every company incorporated on or after 23 November 1916, must in all business letters in which the name of any of its directors is stated (otherwise than in the text of the letter or as its signatory), also state in legible characters the name (including christian or forenames, or recognised abbreviations of christian or forenames, or initials) of each of its directors and shadow directors who are individuals, and the corporate names of each of its directors and shadow directors which are companies or other corporations.[12]

Directors' service contracts

Every company must keep a copy of each of its directors' service contracts with the company and its subsidiaries at the company's registered office or at its principal place of business in England, Wales or Scotland (depending on where it is registered), or at the place where its register of members is kept.[13] If there is no written contract, a written memorandum of the terms on which the director serves must be kept instead.[13] The copy or memorandum must show all changes in the terms of the contract made since it was entered into.[14] The company must notify the Registrar of Companies where the copies or memoranda of its directors' service contracts are kept, unless they are kept at its registered office.[15] There is no need for a copy or memorandum to be kept if the contract has less than twelve months to run, or if it is terminable by the company within that time without payment of compensation.[16] If the contract requires the director to work wholly or mainly outside the United Kingdom, the company need not keep a copy of the director's service contract, but it must keep a memorandum showing the name of the director and the duration of the contract, and if the contract is made with the company's subsidiary, the name of that subsidiary.[17] Members of the company may inspect such copies or memoranda of directors' service contracts without charge,[18] and if inspection is refused the court may order it to be allowed on a summary application being made for the purpose.[19]

Register of directors' interests in shares and debentures

Every company must keep a register showing the interests of each of its directors in its shares and debentures and in the shares and debentures of its holding and

10 Companies Act 1985, s 711A (2).
11 Ibid, s 288 (3).
12 Ibid, s 305 (1), (2), (4), (5) and (7), as amended by Companies Act 1989, s 145 and Sch 19, para 4.
13 Ibid, s 318 (1) to (3).
14 Ibid, s 318 (10).
15 Ibid, s 318 (4).
16 Ibid, s 318 (11).
17 Ibid, s 318 (5).
18 Ibid, s 318 (7).
19 Ibid, s 318 (9). The application is made by originating summons (RSC Ord 102, r 2 (1)).

subsidiary companies and of other subsidiaries of its holding company (if any).[20] A director is considered as being interested in shares or debentures of any of those companies if he has an interest of any kind in them, whether subject to restrictions or not,[1] and in particular if he has an interest of any of the following kinds: (a) an interest in a trust which comprises the shares or debentures;[2] (b) an interest under a contract to purchase shares or debentures or to acquire them for valuable consideration;[3] (c) a right or obligation, whether absolute or conditional, to acquire shares or debentures or an interest in them, other than a right or obligation to subscribe for shares or debentures;[4] and (d) a power to exercise or control the exercise of any rights attached to shares or debentures.[5] Furthermore, a director is considered as having an interest in shares or debentures in which another company or body corporate is interested if[6]: (i) it or its directors are accustomed to act in accordance with the instructions of the director in question, or (ii) the director is entitled to exercise or control the exercise of one-third or more of the voting power at general meetings of the other company or body corporate; in applying (ii) the voting power of any third company or body corporate at general meetings of the other company must also be treated as controlled by the director if he is entitled to exercise or control the exercise of one-third or more of the voting power at general meetings of the third company or body corporate.[7] On the other hand, a director or other person is not deemed to be interested in shares or debentures merely because he has been appointed a proxy to vote in respect of them at any one meeting or an adjournment of it, or as the representative of a corporate share or debenture holder authorised by it to vote at any number of meetings.[8] Furthermore, a director is not deemed to be interested in shares or debentures comprised in a trust under which the income is payable to another person for life and the director's interest is only reversionary,[9] or in an authorised unit trust,[10] or in a trust in which his only interest is that of a bare trustee for another person or persons.[11]

For the purpose of the register of directors' holdings, a director is considered as being interested in shares or debentures in which his spouse or minor child has an interest as though the interest were his own, except where the spouse or minor child is a director of the company.[12] This extension of the interests of a director to include family interests applies primarily to interests in shares and debentures of the company which keeps the register of directors' interests and in shares and debentures of companies in the same group.[12] It also applies so as to require family interests in shares or debentures held by other companies in the original company and companies in the same group and interests in such shares vested in other

---

20 Companies Act 1985, s 325 (1) and (2).
 1 Ibid, s 324 (1) and (3) and Sch 13, para 1.
 2 Ibid, Sch 13, para 2.
 3 Ibid, Sch 13, para 3 (1).
 4 Ibid, Sch 13, para 6 (1) and (2).
 5 Ibid, Sch 13, para 3 (1) and (2).
 6 Ibid, Sch 13, paras 4 and 5.
 7 For example, if a director holds 20 per cent of the voting shares of A Ltd which holds shares in the company in question and the director also holds 40 per cent of the voting shares of B Ltd which holds 20 per cent of the voting shares of A Ltd, the two 20 per cent holdings are aggregated, with the result that the director is treated as interested in the shares held by A Ltd in the company in question.
 8 Companies Act 1985, Sch 13, para 7 (3).
 9 Ibid, Sch 13, para 9.
10 Ibid, Sch. 13., para 11 (a). The unit trust must be authorised by the Securities and Investments Board under the Financial Services Act 1986, s 78 (1) (30 Halsbury's Statutes (4th Edn) 335).
11 Companies Act 1985, Sch 13, para 10.
12 Ibid, s 328 (1).

companies, to be entered in the register of directors' interests kept by it, if those other companies are accustomed to act in accordance with directions or instructions given by the director's spouse or minor children, or by the director and any of those persons jointly, or if the director and his spouse and minor children, or some of them, are together entitled to exercise or control the exercise of one-third or more of the voting power at general meetings of those other companies.[13] In applying these provisions attributing interests of his family to a director, contracts to acquire interests in shares or debentures entered into by a director's spouse or minor children are treated as though they had been entered into by the director himself, and rights held by or obligations undertaken by any of them will likewise be attributed to the director to whom they are related.[14]

The Secretary of State for Trade and Industry has power by statutory instrument to except categories of interests of directors and their spouses and children from registration.[15] The Secretary of State has made regulations excepting interests in shares or debentures held by any such person as a trustee or personal representative jointly with the Public Trustee; interests in shares or debentures of a society registered under the Industrial and Provident Societies Act 1965;[16] interests arising out of restrictions on the transferability of shares imposed by the memorandum or articles of the company which issued them (such as pre-emption rights affecting the shares of another member); interests in shares or debentures of a company held by a director, his spouse or child as a trustee or beneficiary of a retirement benefit scheme or a superannuation fund approved for tax purposes;[17] interests in shares or debentures of a holding company or its wholly-owned subsidiary held by a person who is a director of both companies or by his spouse or minor child, but this exception only applies so far as concerns registration by the subsidiary company;[18] and interests in a holding company or any of its subsidiaries, if the holding company was incorporated outside Great Britain and the interest is held by a director of a wholly-owned British subsidiary of the holding company or by his spouse or minor child.[19].

If at the time of his appointment a director, or his spouse or minor child, holds an interest in shares or debentures which is required to be registered, or if any such person at any time during the director's tenure of office becomes or ceases to be interested in such shares or debentures, or contracts to sell any such shares or debentures, or assigns a right to subscribe for any such shares or debentures, or is granted a right to subscribe for shares or debentures of any company in the same group as the company which keeps the register, the director must notify the company within five days after becoming aware of the interest or event, giving particulars of the matter or transaction,[20] and the company must register it within

---

13 Ibid, s 324 (1) and (3), s 328 (1) and Sch 13, para 4.
14 Ibid, s 328 (2).
15 Ibid, s 324 (3).
16 Such societies are usually co-operatives. The exemption is made because they may be the subsidiaries of companies, and companies may be their subsidiaries.
17 Exemption is also given where the trustee of the scheme or fund is a company whose directors are accustomed to act in accordance with the instructions of a director or his spouse or minor children, or is a company in which they control one-third or more of the voting power at general meetings.
18 The reason for the exception is that the interest will have to be registered by the holding company and, since there are no other shareholders of the subsidiary than the holding company and its nominees, no benefit is conferred by having the registration duplicated by the subsidiary.
19 Companies (Disclosure of Directors' Interests) (Exceptions) Regulations 1985 (SI 1985/802), paras 2 and 3.
20 Companies Act 1985, s 324 (1) and (2) and s 328 (1) and (5) and Sch 13, para 15. If the interest is that of the director himself and exists at the time of his appointment, he must notify it within five days after his appointment (ibid, Sch 13, para 14).

three days after receiving the notification.[1] If the company grants a right to subscribe for its shares or debentures to the director, it must register the right within three days after it is created, and must also register the exercise of the right by the director within three days after he avails himself of it.[2] To ensure that rights to subscribe which the company grants to a director's wife or minor child are not missed, the director is under a duty to notify the company that such rights have been created within five days after he becomes aware of it, and the company must register the fact within three days after notification; the same applies to the exercise of such rights to subscribe by a director's wife or minor child.[3] If the shares or debentures in relation to which a director gives his company a notification under the foregoing provisions are listed on the Stock Exchange,[4] the company must inform the Stock Exchange of the contents of the notification by the end of the day following that on which it receives it from the director, and the Stock Exchange may publish the information given to it by the company as it thinks fit.[5] A company is not affected by notice of a derivative interest in shares or debentures by reason of receiving a notification of it from a director or keeping the register of directors' interests;[6] consequently, it is not liable to the person entitled to such an interest if it takes no steps to protect it, and it would appear that the company's own interests in the shares or debentures concerned (eg a lien for amounts owing to it from the registered holder) will not be affected or postponed by a statutory notice of a derivative interest being received by it.

Entries in the register in respect of each director must be made chronologically,[7] and unless the register is kept in the form of an alphabetical index, such an index must also be kept to enable entries to be readily found.[8] The register must be kept at the same place as the company's register of members.[9] Any member of the company and any other person may inspect the register or require the company to supply him with copies of the whole or any part of it in the same way as they may inspect and require copies of the register of members.[10] If the company refuses to allow inspection or to supply copies of the register, the applicant may apply summarily to the court for an order compelling it to do so.[11] The register must also be produced at the company's annual general meeting and be open to inspection during the meeting by members or their proxies who attend.[12]

If the Secretary of State for Trade and Industry suspects that a director has not disclosed a matter which he is required to notify to his company under the foregoing provisions, the Secretary of State may appoint an inspector to investigate the matter, and he has the same powers to obtain information as an inspector appointed to investigate the mismanagement of a company's affairs.[13]

If a director or his spouse or minor child has an interest in the shares of a public

1 Companies Act 1985, s 325 (2) and (5) and Sch 13, para 22.
2 Ibid, s 325 (3) to (5) and Sch 13, para 22.
3 Ibid, s 325 (2) and (5), s 328 (3) and (5) and Sch 13, para 22.
4 At present the International Stock Exchange of the United Kingdom and Ireland is the only stock exchange prescribed under this provision.
5 Companies Act 1985, s 329 (1). The Stock Exchange requires listed companies to notify it immediately they receive notification from directors (Stock Exchange, *Admission of Securities to Listing*, Section 5, Chapter 2 para 16 (*b*)).
6 Companies Act 1985, s 325 (5) and Sch 13, para 24.
7 Ibid, s 325 (5) and Sch 13, para 21.
8 Ibid, Sch 13, para 28.
9 Ibid, Sch 13, para 25.
10 Ibid, Sch 13, paras 25 and 26, as amended by Companies Act 1989, s 143 (10) (see p 335, ante).
11 Companies Act 1985, s 326 (6). The application is made by originating summons (RSC Ord 102, r 2 (1)).
12 Companies Act 1985, Sch 13, para 29.
13 Ibid, s 446 (1) and (3), as amended by Financial Services Act 1986, s 182 and Sch 13, para 8.

company carrying unrestricted voting rights, it is necessary for separate notifications of that interest to be given to the company under the rules relating to the register of directors' holdings and the rules relating to the register of substantial shareholdings,[14] and for entries to be made accordingly in both those registers. In no circumstances is entry of an interest in one of the registers deemed to be registration in the other as well.

REMUNERATION AND LOANS TO DIRECTORS

Remuneration

The remuneration paid to directors may take any form, and its amount will depend on the terms of the articles and the directors' service contracts (if any). Directors who have agreed to devote their whole time to the company's service are usually remunerated by a salary with or without a percentage of the company's profits as an addition. Part-time directors who attend board meetings but take no part in the day-to-day running of the company's affairs are usually paid fees, which are often fixed at a specific annual sum, but are sometimes paid in respect of each board meeting which the director attends or in proportion to the time he devotes to the company's affairs. Table A leaves the form of directors' remuneration open by providing that it shall be determined from time to time by the members in general meeting.[15] Under such an article the members may resolve that the directors shall be paid a salary, fees, or a percentage of the company's profits, but the members retain the power to vary the form or rate of remuneration and to increase or reduce it at any time. The amount or rate of remuneration resolved upon by a general meeting under such an article is for the members to decide, and provided the award is made in good faith, the fact that the company has not received equivalent value in services from the directors, or that the payment of the remuneration has not been for the company's benefit, is no ground for invalidating the resolution and requiring the directors to repay any amounts paid to them.[16] On the other hand, if the remuneration resolved upon is so unreasonably large that it cannot be considered as payment for the director's services but must include an element of gift, the excess over the highest amount reasonably allowable as remuneration will be recoverable from the directors, since the general meeting will have acted beyond its powers in making such a gift.[16]

Directors are not entitled to be paid remuneration for their services unless the articles so provide,[17] and if they pay themselves remuneration out of the company's funds when there is no such provision, they may be compelled to restore the amounts paid, even though they acted in good faith and honestly believed that the payment was permissible.[18] This rule cannot be evaded by the directors appointing one of their number to a salaried position under the company; the appointment is valid, but the director is not entitled to the salary attached to the post.[19] Moreover, the board cannot use a power given to it by the articles to pay additional remuneration to a director who performs special or professional services for the company so as to pay additional remuneration to a director who is professionally

14 See p 363, ante.
15 Table A, art 82.
16 *Re Halt Garage (1964) Ltd* [1982] 3 All ER 1016.
17 *Hutton v West Cork Rly Co* (1883) 23 ChD 654 at 671, per Bowen LJ; *Re George Newman & Co* [1895] 1 Ch 674 at 686.
18 *Brown and Green Ltd v Hays* (1920) 36 TLR 330; *Guinness plc v Saunders* [1990] 1 All ER 652, [1990] 2 WLR 324.
19 *Kerr v Marine Products Ltd* (1928) 44 TLR 292.

qualified in respect of services which may have benefited the company and were of an unusual character, but were neither professional services nor services which called for endeavours beyond those to be expected of a director acting to promote or protect the interests of his company.[20] If directors are not entitled to remuneration by the terms of the articles, they cannot be awarded it by an ordinary resolution passed by the members of the company; if the members wish to remunerate the directors, they must first alter the articles.[1] Directors who are not remunerated are entitled to be indemnified by the company against expenses incurred in carrying out their functions, but remunerated directors must meet the ordinary expenses of their office out of their remuneration,[2] unless the articles expressly provide that their expenses shall be reimbursed by the company.[3]

If by the articles or his service agreement a director is to be remunerated 'at the rate of £x per annum',[4] or his remuneration is expressed as accruing from day to day, the director is entitled to a proportionate part of a year's remuneration if he ceases to hold office during the course of the year, even if he is dismissed for misconduct.[5] But if a director is entitled to '£x per annum'[6] or '£x each year'[7] as remuneration, the court will not imply a term that he shall be entitled to any part of the annual sum if he does not remain a director until the end of the year. It has been suggested[8] that even though such a term cannot be implied, the remuneration, if in the form of a salary, is deemed to accrue from day to day by the Apportionment Act 1870,[9] so that a director who vacates office is entitled to a proportionate part of his yearly salary calculated up to the date when he ceases to be a director. On the other hand it has been argued[10] that the Apportionment Act 1870 applies only where by an agreement a salary is payable for a certain period, and two or more persons are entitled to it for successive parts of that period, and that the Act does not apply in a case like the present where the question to be decided is whether the salary is payable at all under the agreement. The applicability of the Apportionment Act 1870 is therefore uncertain.[11] Even if it does apply, however, it can only assist a director who is remunerated by a salary or an annual fee; it cannot possibly apply where he is remunerated by a percentage of profits or a sum fixed at the discretion of the members at the end of the year.[12] On the other hand, where directors were remunerated by a salary 'at the rate of £x per annum' and they were also entitled to a share of the company's profits in excess of a certain amount, it was held that the provision for remuneration should be read as a whole, and that a director who ceased to hold office during the year was entitled to share in the profits paid to the directors in proportion to the period he had served.[13] When directors' remuneration is payable by reference to a year, the articles or resolution by which the remuneration is conferred should specify whether the year referred to is the company's financial year, the calendar year or a period of 12 months from the date of the director's appointment or from an anniversary of that date.

20 *Guinness plc v Saunders*, supra.
1 *Re George Newman & Co*, supra.
2 *Young v Naval Military and Civil Service Co-operative Society of South Africa* [1905] 1 KB 687.
3 Table A, art 83, so provides.
4 *Inman v Ackroyd and Best Ltd* [1901] 1 KB 613; *Moriarty v Regents' Garage Co* [1921] 2 KB 766.
5 *Healey v Française Rubastic SA* [1917] 1 KB 946.
6 *Re Central De Kaap Gold Mines* (1899) 69 LJ Ch 18; *Re London and Northern Bank, McConnell's Claim* [1901] 1 Ch 728; *Inman v Ackroyd and Best Ltd*, supra; *Moriarty v Regents' Garage Co*, supra.
7 *Salton v New Beeston Cycle Co* [1899] 1 Ch 775.
8 *Moriarty v Regents' Garage Co* [1921] 1 KB 423, overruled, but not on this point, [1921] 2 KB 766.
9 Apportionment Act 1870, s 2 (23 Halsbury's Statutes (4th Edn) 42).
10 *Inman v Ackroyd and Best Ltd* [1901] 1 KB 613 at 616.
11 *Moriarty v Regents' Garage Co* [1921] 2 KB 766.
12 Ibid, per McCardie J at [1921] 1 KB 446.
13 *Diamond v English Sewing Cotton Co* [1922] WN 237.

If a director's remuneration consists of a percentage of the company's profits or a commission calculated by reference to its profits, difficulties can arise in determining the amount of the profits on which it is to be based. The terms of the director's service agreement or the company's articles must, of course, be looked to first for a definition of the relevant profits. If they simply provide that the percentage or commission shall be based on the company's 'profits' or 'net profits'[14] for a certain period, the sum to be taken is the gross trading income of that period less the expenses incurred in earning it.[15] If the company provides for the depreciation of its fixed assets out of its profits, as it is now obliged to do by law,[16] the amount of depreciation allowed for must be deducted in arriving at the figure on which the percentage or commission is based,[17] but unless the parties have otherwise agreed, depreciation should be calculated by the 'straight line' method and not the 'reducing balance' method.[18] Taxation on the profits of the company, such as excess profits tax[19] or corporation tax must also be deducted, but not, it would seem, advance corporation tax which the company cannot set off against its corporation tax liability for the period in which the profits were earned.[20] Interest paid on loans to the company must be deducted, too, but not an allowance of a notional rate of interest on the company's capital or net worth (ie capital plus reserves),[1] nor the amount of preference dividends paid by it. The share of profits to be received by the director must not itself be deducted as an expense,[2] nor any fixed amount of remuneration payable to him (such as fees or a salary).[3] Any other deductions which the terms of the articles or contract governing the percentage or commission require to be made from profits in calculating the amount payable to a director must, of course, be deducted as well, but such specified deductions are not to be interpreted as exhaustive, and so if items which would be deductible under the general law are omitted from the list of specified deductions, the omitted items must be deducted as well as the specified ones.[4] Whether profits made after the company goes into liquidation have to be taken into account is uncertain. In one case[5] it was held that they do, but in another case[6] Chitty J held that they do not, on the ground that since a director's services to the company terminate when it is wound up,[7] it cannot have been the intention of the parties that he should be entitled to a share of the company's profits thereafter. The statutory rules governing

---

14 These terms are synonymous (*Patent Castings Syndicate Ltd v Etherington* [1919] 2 Ch 254 at 275; *Vulcan Motor and Engineering Co Ltd v Hampson* [1921] 3 KB 597 at 605).

15 *Re Spanish Prospecting Co Ltd* [1911] 1 Ch 92 at 98; *Patent Castings Syndicate Ltd v Etherington*, supra, at 311.

16 Companies Act 1985, s 226 (3) and Sch 4, para 19 (1), substituted by Companies Act 1989, s 4 (1).

17 *Re Spanish Prospecting Co Ltd*, supra.

18 *Edwards v Saunton Hotel Co Ltd* [1943] 1 All ER 176 at 180, per Atkinson J. For the difference between the two methods, see p 428, ante.

19 *Patent Castings Syndicate Ltd v Etherington*, supra; *LC Ltd v GB Ollivant & Co* [1944] 1 All ER 510.

20 *Johnston v Chestergate Hat Manufacturing Co Ltd* [1915] 2 Ch 338 (see Income and Corporation Taxes Act 1988, s 239 (1) to (4) (44 Halsbury's Statutes (4th Edn) 289)).

1 *Rishton v Grissell* (1868) LR 5 Eq 326.

2 *Edwards v Saunton Hotel Co Ltd*, supra. The effect of such a deduction would be to reduce the fraction of profits to which the director was entitled to the next smaller reciprocal. For example, if the director is entitled by his service contract to 20 per cent of the company's profits, the profits after deduction of all expenses other than his share would represent 125 per cent of the profits after deducting his share, and his share would then be 20/125 or 16 per cent of the whole.

3 *Rishton v Grissell*, supra.

4 *Johnston v Chestergate Hat Manufacturing Co Ltd* [1915] 2 Ch 338.

5 *Re Spanish Prospecting Co Ltd*, supra.

6 *Frames v Bultfontein Mining Co* [1891] 1 Ch 140 at 143.

7 This is not necessarily so in a voluntary winding up (see p 549, ante).

the calculation of profits available for distribution as dividends to shareholders[8] do not apply to calculations of the profits as the basis for directors' remuneration, and so if the director's service contract makes the profits of each year the basis on which his remuneration for that year is calculated, it is not necessary or permissible to deduct losses carried forward from earlier years or to deduct unrealised losses in respect of fixed assets.

Remuneration payable to a director is a debt owing from the company, and is not contingent on the company earning sufficient profits to pay it,[9] unless, of course, it is expressly made so contingent by the terms of the director's service agreement or the company's articles, as in the case of remuneration in the form of a percentage of profits. Moreover, remuneration is a debt payable to the director in his capacity as a creditor and not as a member of the company, so that if the company is wound up, directors' remuneration remaining unpaid is payable out of the company's assets rateably with the company's other debts, and is not deferred[10] until after the other debts have been paid.[11]

A company may not pay a director remuneration free of income tax at the basic rate or any higher rate applicable to him with the result that the company bears the tax itself, nor may it pay him remuneration of such an amount as will, after paying income tax at the basic rate, or at the rate personal to the director, leave a stipulated sum in the director's hands.[12] Any provision in the articles, in a service contract, or in any resolution passed by the members or the board of directors, for the payment of such prohibited remuneration is to be construed as a provision for the payment of the stipulated sum to the director, leaving him to pay the income tax in respect of it himself.[13] But a contract for the payment of tax-free remuneration which was in force on 18 July 1945, remains valid, and payments under it are lawful,[14] but if the contract is renewed or extended by implication by the director continuing to serve under it after its expiration date, the statutory prohibition attaches to remuneration accruing after that date. The prohibition on the payment of tax-free remuneration applies to remuneration paid to a director in any capacity (eg as secretary or manager) as well as to remuneration paid to him for his services as a director.[12] There is, however, no prohibition on the payment of tax-free remuneration to other officers or employees of a company who are not directors.

If a director is not properly appointed he cannot claim the remuneration to which a director is entitled, even though he believes himself to have been properly appointed and actually serves the company.[15] Nevertheless, he is entitled to a reasonable sum as a quantum meruit for the services he has already rendered.[16] A quantum meruit can be awarded, however, only when the plaintiff's appointment as a director is invalid, or when there is no valid contract between the company and the plaintiff for his employment as a director. Consequently, where a director was validly appointed on terms that his remuneration should be fixed by the board and the board did not resolve that he should be remunerated, it was held that his claim for a quantum meruit failed.[17] Similarly, where a director's service contract entitled him to remuneration only if he served for a full year and he vacated office

---

8 Companies Act 1985, ss 263 to 265 (see p 421 et seq, ante). The statutory rules apply only for the purpose of 'distributions of a company's assets to its members' (s 263 (2)).
9 *Re Lundy Granite Co, Lewis's Case* (1872) 26 LT 673.
10 See Insolvency Act 1986, s 74 (1) (*f*).
11 *Re New British Iron Co, ex p Beckwith* [1898] 1 Ch 324.
12 Companies Act 1985, s 311 (1).
13 Ibid, s 311 (2).
14 Companies Consolidation (Consequential Provisions) Act 1985, s 15.
15 *Woolf v East Nigel Gold Mining Co* (1905) 21 TLR 660.
16 *Craven-Ellis v Canons Ltd* [1936] 2 KB 403, [1936] 2 All ER 1066.
17 *Re Richmond Gate Property Co Ltd* [1964] 3 All ER 936, [1965] 1 WLR 335.

during the year, it was held that he was entitled neither to remuneration nor a quantum meruit for the period during which he had served.[18] Where a director was irregularly awarded additional remuneration by a committee of the board which by the articles had no power to award it, and in expectation of receiving that remuneration the director performed services for the company which he would not otherwise have done, the House of Lords held that the director was not entitled to payment of the value of his services as a quantum meruit or as an equitable allowance, because such a payment would be remuneration which the articles permitted only if awarded by the board or a general meeting.[19]

If directors agree between themselves not to claim remuneration which they have already earned, none of them may sue the company for his remuneration, because it would be a fraud on the others if any one of them were permitted to do so.[20] Furthermore, directors may agree with each other to accept less remuneration in the future than they are entitled to, and even though the company gives no consideration for the reduction, it is binding on each director because of the mutuality of the directors' agreement between themselves, and no director may recover his full original remuneration from the company.[1] But a mere statement by a director that he will waive his right to the whole or part of his remuneration does not amount to a contract binding him to do so. However, it will prevent the director from claiming remuneration if the company acts on the statement, as it may do by incurring liabilities or extending its business in a way which it would not otherwise have done.[1] Nevertheless, the waiver is revocable by the director at any time, and the director's normal remuneration will be payable to him for periods after he notifies the company that he intends to claim it in the future.[2]

Pensions

Although a company has an implied power to pay pensions to its former employees and their dependants,[3] it cannot pay pensions to its former directors or their dependants, unless its memorandum or articles expressly so provide.[4] It is not sufficient for the articles to empower the board to pay pensions to persons employed by the company, because this is interpreted to mean persons employed as subordinate employees, and directors are not engaged in that capacity.[5] Table A, however, contains an express power for the board to pay pensions and gratuities to directors and their dependants if the directors have held executive office under the company or any of its subsidiaries, or if they have been employed by the company or any such subsidiaries, and the company is empowered to make contributions to pension funds and to pay insurance premiums to procure such pensions.[6] This power, like all other powers of the board, can only be used to promote the company's interests, and not primarily in order to be benevolent toward individual directors or their dependants, whether deserving or not. Consequently, it has been held that if a new service contract is negotiated with a managing director who would normally have continued to serve without such a contract, and the contract is entered into because the director has recently suffered from bad health and its

18 *Re London and Northern Bank, McConnell's Claim* [1901] 1 Ch 728.
19 *Guinness plc v Saunders* [1990] 1 All ER 652, [1990] 2 WLR 324.
20 *West Yorkshire Darracq Agency Ltd v Coleridge* [1911] 2 KB 326.
 1 *Re William Porter & Co Ltd* [1937] 2 All ER 361.
 2 *Re Consolidated Nickel Mines Ltd* [1914] 1 Ch 883.
 3 *Hampson v Price's Patent Candle Co* (1876) 45 LJ Ch 437.
 4 *Re George Newman & Co* [1895] 1 Ch 674 at 686.
 5 *Normandy v Ind, Coope & Co Ltd* [1908] 1 Ch 84; *Re Lee, Behrens & Co Ltd* [1932] 2 Ch 46, [1932] All ER Rep 889.
 6 Table A, art 87.

underlying purpose is to provide for payment of a pension to his dependants in the event of his death, the company may repudiate the contract after his death and refuse to pay the pension.[7] On the other hand, if the payment of pensions to former directors is expressed to be an object of the company in its memorandum and the objects clause provides that each of its paragraphs contains a separate main object, the award of a pension of generous proportions to a director on his retirement cannot be attacked as ultra vires, since the payment of pensions is a legitimate object of the company, and if the award is authorised or ratified by the shareholders in general meeting it cannot be attacked as an abuse of the powers of the board.[8]

Compensation for loss of office

A company may not make a payment to a director who vacates office as compensation for loss of office or as consideration for his retirement, unless the proposed payment is disclosed to all the members of the company, including members who have no voting rights at general meetings,[9] and is approved by a general meeting of the company by ordinary resolution.[10] It seems that this rule applies whether the compensation is paid for loss of the office of director or of any other office under the company, so that if a managing director who remains an ordinary director is compensated for loss of his managing directorship,[11] or if a director is compensated for loss of the secretaryship of the company, the approval of a general meeting is required. A payment is only treated as compensation for loss of office if the company is under no legal obligation to make it, and so if a director is dismissed in breach of his service contract, the payment of damages to him, whether assessed by the court or settled out of court, does not require the members' approval.[12] Likewise an amount payable to a director under the terms of his service contract on his resignation or removal from office is not treated as compensation for loss of office, and so is payable unconditionally when his resignation or removal takes place.[13] Moreover, payment of a pension to a retiring director, whether he has contributed toward the cost of it or not, is not deemed to be compensation for loss of office, and does not require the members' approval.[12] If a payment to a director is compensation for loss of office, it is necessary not only that it should be approved by the company's members, but also that it should be authorised by the articles, as otherwise it will be recoverable by the company.[14]

A director may not receive a payment as compensation for loss of office, or as consideration for his retirement, in connection with the transfer of the whole or part of the company's undertaking or property, unless the payment is disclosed to all the members of the company and is approved by an ordinary resolution passed by a general meeting.[15] Likewise, if such a payment is proposed to be made to a director in connection with a transfer of any of the company's shares resulting from an offer made to all the shareholders, or from an offer made by another company with a view to the company becoming its subsidiary or the subsidiary of its holding company, or from an offer made by an individual with a view to acquiring control

---

7 *Re W and M Roith Ltd* [1967] 1 All ER 427, [1967] 1 WLR 432.
8 *Re Horsley and Weight Ltd* [1982] Ch 442, [1982] 3 All ER 1045.
9 *Re Duomatic Ltd* [1969] 2 Ch 365, [1969] 1 All ER 161.
10 Companies Act 1985, s 312.
11 The contrary has been held in Australia (*Lincoln Mills (Australia) Ltd v Gough* [1964] VR 193), but the statutory provision there only extends to 'compensation for loss of office *as a director of the company*', the italicised words being omitted from the Companies Act 1985, s 311 (1).
12 Companies Act 1985, s 316 (3).
13 *Taupo Totara Timber Co Ltd v Rowe* [1978] AC 537, [1977] 3 All ER 123.
14 *Re George Newman & Co* [1895] 1 Ch 674.
15 Companies Act 1985, s 313 (1).

of at least one third of the voting power at general meetings of the company, or from an offer which is conditional on acceptance by the holders of a stated number of shares,[16] the director must take reasonable steps to ensure that notice of the proposed payment is sent to shareholders with the offer, and he may receive the payment only if a meeting of the shareholders to whose shares the offer relates and the holders of shares of the same class as those shares approves it by ordinary resolution.[17] If the offer relates to two or more classes of shares, separate meetings of the shareholders of each such class must approve the payment.[17] If a director receives a payment of compensation for loss of office without the appropriate approval, he holds it, in the case of a transfer of the company's undertaking or property, in trust for the company,[18] and in the case of a transfer of shares, in trust for the shareholders who have sold their shares as a result of the offer.[19] It would appear that an amount so held in trust for shareholders who have sold their shares is distributable between them in proportion to the nominal values of their shares, and that if the offer related to two or more classes of shares, that amount is distributable only between shareholders of classes which have not approved the payment of compensation to a director.

These more complicated provisions apply when the company's undertaking or virtual control of the company is taken over by an outsider. The consequence of the takeover may be that the present board of directors will have to retire, because if the company's undertaking is sold, they will have no business to manage, whilst if the outsider acquires a controlling interest in the company's shares, he will be able to remove the present directors and appoint his own nominees. The outsider may therefore seek the co-operation and goodwill of the present directors by offering them compensation for loss of office, but he will meet the cost of paying the compensation by offering a correspondingly lower price for the company's undertaking or shares. In the end it is the shareholders who bear the cost, and their approval is therefore required. However, no approval by a general meeting or by a meeting of a class or classes of shareholders is required where the director is entitled by his service contract to resign if the company is taken over by another company and to claim payment of a lump sum on such retirement.[20] Nevertheless, the result of such a payment is that the company's assets are diminished and the outsider will therefore offer less for them or for shares in the company than if the company's contingent liability did not exist, and so the economic consequences will be the same as if the outsider paid the lump sum himself and deducted it from the full value of the company's undertaking or the shares he acquires.

To prevent an evasion of the qualified prohibition on the payment of compensation to directors in connection with a sale of the company's undertaking or shares, it is presumed, until the contrary is proved, that payments made to a director by or on behalf of the company or the purchaser of the company's undertaking or of shares issued by it within one year before or two years after the sale of its undertaking or the offer for its shares were made as compensation for loss of office.[1] Furthermore, if the person who makes an offer to acquire shares in the company purchases a director's shares at a price in excess of that obtainable by holders of like shares, or if the offeror gives any valuable consideration in kind to a

---

16 Takeover bids are always made conditional on acceptance of the bid by the holders of a stated percentage of the shares which the bidder seeks to acquire.
17 Companies Act 1985, s 314 (1) and (2).
18 Ibid, s 313 (2).
19 Ibid, s 315 (1).
20 *Taupo Totara Timber Co Ltd v Rowe* [1978] AC 537, [1977] 3 All ER 123.
1 Companies Act 1985, s 316 (1).

director, the excess of the purchase price or the value of the consideration is deemed to be compensation for loss of office.[2] These provisions apply only if the benefit given to the director is not one to which he is entitled under a contract unconnected with the sale of the company's undertaking or the offer to acquire its shares. If the benefit is provided under an independent contract, even though the contingency on which the benefit accrues is such a sale, the director is entitled to claim it without the prior approval of members of the company.[20]

Loans, quasi-loans and credit transactions

Prohibited transactions

A company, whether public or private, may not make a loan to a director of the company or its holding company.[3] A relevant company (that is, a public company or a company which is a member of a group of companies which includes a public company[4]) may not make a quasi-loan to a director of the company or its holding company, nor may it make a loan or quasi-loan to a person who is connected with such a director.[5] Furthermore, a relevant company may not enter into a credit transaction with a director of the company or its holding company or with a person connected with such a director.[6] These prohibitions extend to loans and quasi-loans to shadow directors and credit transactions entered into with shadow directors as though they were duly appointed directors of the company in question,[7] and in this account of the applicable loan references to directors should be read as including references to shadow directors.

A quasi-loan is a transaction under which one person (the creditor) either pays or agrees to pay a sum of money to a third person for the benefit of another person (the borrower),[8] or reimburses or agrees to reimburse a third person against expenditure incurred for the benefit of another (the borrower),[9] if in either case the borrower agrees to reimburse the creditor or is legally liable to do so.[10] A credit transaction is one under which one person (the creditor) either (a) supplies goods or sells land to another on terms that the purchase price shall be paid by instalments, and ownership will pass to the purchaser only when all the instalments have been paid and any other specified act has been done by the purchaser, or any other specified event has occurred;[11] or (b) leases or hires land or goods to another in return for periodical payments, or (c) otherwise disposes of land or supplies goods or services on the understanding that payment (whether by instalments or not) is to be deferred.[12]

2 Ibid, s 316 (2).
3 Companies Act 1985, s 330 (2).
4 Ibid, s 331 (6). A relevant company is one which is a public company, or is a subsidiary of a public company or of a company which has another subsidiary which is a public company, or has itself a subsidiary which is a public company.
5 Companies Act 1985, s 330 (3).
6 Ibid, s 330 (4).
7 Ibid, s 330 (5).
8 There would be a quasi-loan of this kind if a director contracted to purchase property, and when the contract was made the company paid or agreed to pay the price in return for a promise by the director to reimburse it.
9 There would be a quasi-loan of this kind if a director were already indebted to another person for goods or services, and the company paid or agreed to pay the debt in return for a promise by the director to reimburse it.
10 Companies Act 1985, s 331 (3).
11 This refers to conditional sales and hire-purchase agreements. Under the latter the purchaser acquires the ownership of goods only when he has paid all the instalments of the hire-purchase price and has exercised the option to acquire ownership on paying a further (usually nominal) sum.
12 Companies Act 1985, s 331 (7).

A person is connected with a director if he, she or it is either: (a) the director's spouse, or his child, adopted child or step-child under 18 years of age; or (b) a company or corporation in which the director and persons connected with him together hold or are interested in at least one-fifth in nominal value of the issued equity share capital,[13] or are entitled to exercise or control the exercise of at least one-fifth of the voting power at any general meeting, either directly or through a third company which the director and persons connected with him control; or (c) a person acting as trustee of any trust (other than a trust to give effect to an employees share scheme or a pension scheme) the beneficiaries or potential beneficiaries of which include any of the persons within (a) or (b); or (d) a person acting as a partner of the director or any person connected with him under (a), (b) or (c).[14] The range of persons connected with a director is a wide one, but it is provided by way of exceptions[15] that a company or corporation with which a director is associated under (b) is not for that reason treated as connected with him when determining whether another company or corporation is also connected with the director, unless the director and persons connected with him also control more than half of the voting power at general meetings of the first mentioned company or corporation, or are interested in more than half of its issued share capital;[16] it is also provided that a trustee of a trust is not treated as connected with a director under (c) merely because a company or corporation with which the director is connected under (b) is a beneficiary or potential beneficiary of the trust.[17]

If a company is prohibited from making a loan or quasi-loan to any person or from entering into a credit transaction with him or it, the company may not give a guarantee or provide security for such a loan or quasi-loan made to him or it by a third person, or in connection with a credit transaction entered into with him or it by a third person.[18] Furthermore, a company may not take an assignment of a loan or quasi-loan, or of the indebtedness arising under a credit transaction, or agree to a novation by which it becomes entitled to rights or assumes obligations under a loan, quasi-loan or credit transaction, if it would have been illegal for the company itself to have made the loan or quasi-loan to the other party to it, or to have entered into the credit transaction with him.[19] Finally, a company may not take part in an arrangement by which it or a company in the same group gives or agrees to give a benefit to a third person who makes a loan or quasi-loan or who enters into a credit transaction, if it would have been illegal for the company itself to have made the loan or quasi-loan or to have entered into the credit transaction.[20]

13 For equity share capital, see p 247, ante.
14 Companies Act 1985, s 346 (2) and (3).
15 Ibid, s 346 (4) to (8).
16 Consequently, if a director, his wife and minor children together hold 30 per cent of the equity share capital of X Ltd and 10 per cent of the equity share capital of Y Ltd, Y Ltd is not a person connected with the director merely because X Ltd holds 15 per cent of Y Ltd's equity share capital, unless the director, his wife and minor children acting together control at least one-fifth of the votes which can be cast at a general meeting of Y Ltd, either (i) directly by reason of their own shares in Y Ltd, or (ii) indirectly by reason of those votes and the votes which are exercisable by X Ltd in respect of the shares it holds in Y Ltd, but in this latter situation the director and his wife and minor children must also hold more than half of the issued capital of X Ltd or control more than half the votes which can be cast at its general meetings.
17 Consequently, if a director, his wife and minor children together hold 30 per cent of the equity share capital of X Ltd and also 10 per cent of the equity share capital of Y Ltd, and an additional 10 per cent of the equity share capital of Y Ltd is held by T as trustee of a trust of which X Ltd (but not the director or his wife or children) is a beneficiary or potential beneficiary, Y Ltd is not a person connected with the director merely because the director, his wife and children and T together hold one-fifth of the equity share capital of Y Ltd.
18 Companies Act 1985, s 330 (2) to (4).
19 Ibid, s 330 (6).
20 Ibid, s 330 (7).

Permissible transactions

Despite the general prohibition on companies making loans to their directors, and on relevant companies making quasi-loans to them or loans or quasi-loans to persons connected with them, or entering into credit transactions with such directors or connected persons, or giving guarantees or security in connection with such loans, quasi-loans or credit transactions, certain financing transactions are excepted from the prohibition and may lawfully be entered into by a company. These exceptions are as follows:

(1) a company may make a loan or quasi-loan to its holding company, or enter into a credit transaction with it, or give a guarantee or provide security for such a loan or quasi-loan made by a third person or a credit transaction entered into with him;[1]

(2) a company may make a loan or quasi-loan, or give a guarantee or provide security for such a loan or quasi-loan by a third person, if the purpose of the transaction is to provide a director of the company (but not a director of its holding company) with funds to meet expenditure for the company's purposes, or to enable him to perform his duties as an officer of the company, but the loan or quasi-loan must either be approved by a general meeting of the company before it is made, or must be made on terms that if it is not so approved at or before the next annual general meeting, the loan will be repaid, or the quasi-loan will be reimbursed to the company, within six months thereafter, and if the company is a relevant company, the total amount outstanding under this exception must not at any time exceed £10,000;[2]

(3) a company may make a loan to a director of itself or its holding company for any purpose, provided that the aggregate of such loans outstanding under this exception does not exceed £5,000;[3]

(4) a company may make a loan or quasi-loan to its subsidiary or to its holding company or to a fellow subsidiary of its holding company, or give a guarantee or provide security for such a loan made by a third person, even though the borrowing company is connected with a director of the lending company or its holding company by reason of that director and other persons connected with him holding together at least one-fifth of the issued equity share capital of the borrowing company, or being able together to exercise or control the exercise of at least one-fifth of the voting power at any general meeting of the borrowing company;[4]

(5) a company which is a money-lending company (that is one whose ordinary business includes the making of loans or quasi-loans, or giving guarantees in connection with loans or quasi-loans)[5] may make a loan or quasi-loan, or give a guarantee in connection with a loan or quasi-loan made by a third person, if the transaction is entered into in the ordinary course of the company's business and the terms of the transaction are no more favourable to the director or person connected with him than the terms which it is reasonable to expect the company would have offered to a person of the

1 Ibid, s 336.
2 Ibid, s 337 (1) to (3) and s 339 (1) to (3).
3 Ibid, s 334 and s 339 (1) to (3), amended by Companies Act 1989, s 138 (*b*).
4 Companies Act 1985, s 333. For example, the fact that a director of a subsidiary, X Ltd, of a holding company, Alpha plc, holds 20 per cent of the equity share capital of Alpha or of its other subsidiary, Y Ltd, does not prevent X Ltd making a loan to Alpha or to Y Ltd or to any other subsidiary of Alpha.
5 Companies Act 1985, s 338 (2).

same financial standing who was unconnected with the company, but a relevant company which is not an authorised banking company[6] cannot under this exception enter into a transaction with a person if the amount outstanding under the transaction and similar transactions (including loans aggregable under (6) below) entered into with the director and other persons connected with him (other than companies not controlled by him) by the company and its subsidiaries (and if the other party to the transaction is a director of the company's holding company or a person connected with such a director, by the holding company and its other subsidiaries) exceeds £100,000;[7]

(6) a company which is a money-lending company may make a loan to a director of the company or its holding company to facilitate the purchase or improvement of a dwellinghouse for use as the director's main residence and any land to be occupied therewith, or to facilitate the discharge of a loan made previously for the same purpose, but loans of that description must ordinarily be made by the company to its employees on terms which are no less favourable, and the total amount outstanding under all such loans and (if the company is not an authorised banking company)[6] under loans, quasi-loans and guarantees with (5) above made for the benefit of the director by the company and its subsidiaries (and if the director is a director the company's holding company, by the holding company and its subsidiaries) does not exceed £100,000;[8]

(7) a relevant company may make quasi-loans to a director of itself or its holding company if the director is required to reimburse the company within two months of the quasi-loan being made, and the total amount outstanding under all such quasi-loans made to the director by the company and its subsidiaries (and if the director is a director of the company's holding company, by the holding company and its other subsidiaries) does not exceed £5,000;[9]

(8) a relevant company may enter into a credit transaction with a director of itself or its holding company or with a person connected with such a director,[10] if the transaction is entered into in the ordinary course of the company's business and the value of the transaction is no greater and its terms are no more favourable to the other party than those which it is reasonable to expect the company to have offered to a person of the same financial standing as the other party who is unconnected with the company;[11]

(9) a relevant company may enter into a credit transaction with a director of itself or its holding company or with a person connected with such a director,[10] if the total amount outstanding under the transaction and similar transactions made with the director and persons connected with him by the company and its subsidiaries (and if the other party is, or is connected with, a director of the company's holding company, by the holding company and its other subsidiaries) does not exceed £5,000; in calculating the total

---

6 That is, authorised by the Bank of England for the purposes of the Banking Act 1987 (Companies Act 1985, s 744, as amended by Companies Act 1989, s 23 and Sch 10, para 16).
7 Companies Act 1985, s 338 (1) and (3) to (5) and s 339 (1) to (3), as amended by Companies Act 1989, s 138 (c).
8 Ibid, s 338 (1) and (3) to (6) and s 339 (1) to (4), as amended by Companies Act 1989, s 138 (c).
9 Ibid, s 332(1) and (2), as amended by Companies Act 1989, s 138 (a).
10 Apparently the company may not give a guarantee or provide security for a credit transaction entered into by a third person under this exception.
11 Companies Act 1985, s 335 (2).

amount outstanding transactions falling under (8) are not taken into account.[12]

Civil and criminal sanctions

If a company in contravention of the provisions dealt with above makes a loan or quasi-loan, or enters into a credit transaction with a director or person connected with him, or gives a guarantee or provides security to a third person who makes a loan or quasi-loan to, or enters into a credit transaction with, a director or a person connected with him, or if a company in contravention of those provisions takes an assignment of the rights of such a third person, or enters into a novation by which it acquires the rights or obligations of a third person or confers any benefit on a third person in connection with the loan, quasi-loan or credit transaction in question, the contract or transaction may be rescinded by the company, unless restoration of the parties to their original position is impossible, or unless another person not a party to the contract or transaction has in good faith and for value acquired rights under it without being aware of the contravention, but the company may not rescind if it has been indemnified against any loss it has suffered by the director or persons connected with him.[13] Additionally, the director and the person connected with him (if the transaction is with such a person) are accountable to the company for any gain they have made as a result of the contravening transaction, and they and any other director of the company who authorised the transaction are liable to compensate the company for any resulting loss; but if the transaction was entered into with a person connected with a director, the director may escape liability by showing that he took all reasonable steps to prevent the contravention, and the person connected with a director and any director who authorised the transaction may escape liability by showing that he was unaware of the circumstances constituting the contravention.[14]

The result of these provisions is that the company which has made a loan or quasi-loan or entered into a credit transaction which contravenes the statutory prohibitions may either affirm the transactions and enforce its normal rights (eg sue for repayment of a loan with interest) without being met by the defence that the transaction is illegal and therefore void; or the company may rescind the transaction and recover what it has given under it (eg rescission of a mortgage created by the company to secure a contravening loan made by a third person, or rescission of an assignment of such a contravening loan and recovery of the amount paid by the company for it); or the company may recover any gain made by the other party to the transaction (eg the profit made on the sale of an investment acquired with a contravening loan); or the company can sue the persons responsible for the transaction to recover any loss the company has suffered in consequence.

If a relevant company[15] enters into a transaction which contravenes the statutory provisions dealt with above, the company and its directors who authorise the transaction and also anyone who procures the transaction are guilty of a criminal offence.[16] This is not so, however, in the case of a private company which does not belong to a group of companies comprising a public company, and if it enters into a contravening transaction, only civil sanctions are available.

---

12 Ibid, s 335 (1) and s 339 (1) to (3).
13 Ibid, s 341 (1).
14 Ibid, s 341 (2), (4) and (5).
15 See p 565, ante, footnote 14.
16 Companies Act 1985, s 342 (1) to (3).

Disclosure of remuneration, etc, in accounts

The notes to a company's annual accounts must state the aggregate amount paid or payable as directors' emoluments, the aggregate amount of pensions paid or payable to present or past directors, and the aggregate amount of compensation paid or payable to directors for loss of office during the period to which the accounts relate.[17] Emoluments include the remuneration of directors for their services as directors of the company, as directors of its subsidiary undertakings and for other services in connection with the management of the company's and its subsidiary undertakings' affairs and the aggregate remuneration of the directors falling into each of those three categories must be shown separately.[18] Emoluments also include expense allowances, benefits in kind and contributions paid in respect of directors under pensions schemes and payments and benefits received by directors on accepting office.[19] Pensions include all pensions, superannuation allowances, superannuation gratuities and similar allowances paid or payable to directors and their nominees and dependants (including benefits in kind), except pensions paid under schemes which are adequately maintained by annual contributions; again, the amount of pensions, superannuation allowances and gratuities paid or payable to directors for their services as directors of the company and its subsidiary undertakings must be distinguished from pensions etc paid or payable in respect of services by them in other capacities.[20] Compensation for loss of office includes all payments made or due to directors on their ceasing to hold any office under the company or its subsidiary undertakings (including benefits in kind), and the amounts shown must distinguish between compensation for loss of office as directors of the company, for loss of any other office in connection with the management of the company's affairs and for loss of office as directors of subsidiary undertakings of the company or otherwise in connection with the management of its subsidiary undertakings' affairs.[1] If subsidiary undertakings of the company, or any persons other than the company and its subsidiaries, pay or are liable to pay, emoluments, pensions or compensation for loss of office to directors, such payments must be separately disclosed in the notes to the company's accounts, showing the amounts paid or payable by the subsidiary undertakings and the amounts paid or payable by other persons.[2]

In addition to showing the global amounts payable as directors' emoluments, the notes to a company's annual accounts must give additional information in respect of directors' emoluments if the company is a parent company or subsidiary undertaking, or where the global amount of the directors' remuneration equals or exceeds £60,000.[3] There must first be shown the emoluments of the chairman of the board of directors or the individual remuneration of the persons who have successively been chairmen during the relevant financial year,[4] and if any director or directors receive higher emoluments than those paid to the chairman or the aggregate emoluments of successive chairmen, the emoluments of the highest remunerated one among them must also be shown.[5] The other directors' emoluments

17 Ibid, s 232 (1) and (2) and Sch 6, paras 1 (1), 7 (1) and 8 (1), substituted by Companies Act 1989, s 6 (3) and (4) and Sch 4.
18 Ibid, Sch 6, para 1 (2) and (3). For the definition of parent and subsidiary undertakings, see p 730, post.
19 Companies Act 1985, Sch 6, para 1 (4).
20 Ibid, Sch 6, para 7 (2) to (4) and para 10.
 1 Ibid, Sch 6, para 8 (2) and (3).
 2 Ibid, Sch 6, para 10 (1) and (2).
 3 Ibid, Sch 6, para 2.
 4 Ibid, Sch 6, para 3 (1) to (3).
 5 Ibid, Sch 6, para 4 (1), (3) and (4).

will be shown as an aggregate sum, but the notes to the accounts must also show how many of them (other than directors who perform their duties wholly or mainly outside the United Kingdom) receive emoluments not exceeding £5,000, and how many receive emoluments within successive multiples of that figure.[6]

If directors waive their rights to the whole or part of their emoluments, the number of them who have done so must be stated in the notes to the company's accounts, together with the total amount waived.[7]

The notes to a company's annual accounts must give certain particulars of loans and quasi-loans made to its directors, directors of its holding company and persons connected with them, and of credit transactions entered into with such persons if the loan or quasi-loan or credit was given by the company, or by third persons under guarantees or with the benefit of security provided by the company; particulars must also be given of loans and quasi-loans made by other persons and credit transactions entered into by them if the company has taken assignment of those persons' rights, or has entered into novation arrangements by which the company assumes the rights or obligations of those persons, or has given benefits to those other persons in connection with the transaction.[8] Additionally, the notes to a company's annual accounts must give certain details of agreements to make loans or quasi-loans to directors of the company or its holding company or to persons connected with them or to enter into credit transactions with them, and of any other transactions or arrangements in which any directors of the company or its holding company had a material interest.[8] The directors referred to in these disclosure requirements are all persons who have been directors during the period to which the annual accounts relate.[8] The information to be given includes the names of the persons to whom the loans or quasi-loans were made or with whom the transactions were entered into and (if applicable) the directors with whom they were connected; the names of directors with material interests in any transactions or arrangements other than loans, quasi-loans and credit transactions and the nature of those interests; in the case of loans, guarantees and the provision of security, there must be shown the amount owing to the company or for which the company is responsible under a guarantee or security at the beginning and end of the period to which the annual accounts relate, and in the case of loans the greatest amount owing during that period, any arrears of interest remaining unpaid and any provision made by the company for the loan proving irrecoverable.[9] Certain transactions in which directors are interested need not be disclosed in annual accounts, in particular, directors' service contracts,[10] transactions entered into in the ordinary course of the company's business on normal business terms,[11] transactions between two or more companies in which a director is interested merely because he is a director of both or all the companies concerned[12] and transactions involving less important amounts.[13] Disclosure of loans, quasi-loans

---

6 Ibid, Sch 6, para 4 (1) and (2).
7 Ibid, Sch 6, para 6 (1).
8 Ibid, Sch 6, paras 16 and 19. For the definition of holding company and subsidiary, see p 730, post.
9 Companies Act 1985, Sch 6, para 22.
10 Ibid, Sch 6, para 18 (*b*). This is because copies of service contracts must be kept available for inspection by members at the company's registered office (see p 554, ante).
11 Companies Act 1985, Sch 6, para 20.
12 Ibid, Sch 6, para 18 (*a*).
13 Ibid, Sch 6, paras 24 and 25. Exemption from disclosure is given if the aggregate amount involved in reportable loans, quasi-loans and credit transactions in the case of any person did not exceed £5,000 at any time during the period to which the accounts relate, and also in the case of transactions other than loans, quasi-loans and credit transactions, if the aggregate amount did not exceed the greater of £1,000 or the lesser of 1 per cent of the net assets of the company and £5,000.

and credit transactions must be made whether they are prohibited or not.[14] The disclosure requirements apply equally to private companies, and disclosure is required in respect of loans and quasi-loans to, and credit transactions and other transactions with, shadow directors and persons connected with them in the same way as if they were directors.[15]

In addition to disclosing directors' individual interests, notes to the annual accounts of companies must show the aggregate amounts outstanding at the end of the period to which the accounts relate in respect of loans and quasi-loans made, guaranteed or secured by the company and its subsidiaries to or for the benefit of officers of the company (other than directors and shadow directors) and in respect of credit transactions entered into, guaranteed or secured by the company and its subsidiaries for the benefit of such officers together with the number of persons involved in each category of transactions.[16] The annual accounts of authorised banking companies[17] must give the same information in respect of loans and quasi-loans made to their directors, shadow directors and persons connected with them or to their chief executives or managers, and in respect of credit transactions entered into with such persons; no such disclosure is required in respect of loans and quasi-loans made to other officers of banking companies or in respect of credit transactions entered into with them.[18] The reason for this special provision in relation to banking companies is that they are exempted from the obligation to disclose the particulars about loans and quasi-loans to individual directors and persons connected with them and particulars of credit transactions with such persons which other companies must include in the notes to their annual accounts.[19]

THE POWERS OF DIRECTORS

Division of the company's powers

The board of directors and meetings of members of a company can between them exercise all of the functions and powers of the company. Subject to the provisions of the Companies Act 1985 (as amended), which require certain powers to be exercised by the members in general meeting, the division of powers between the board and the members is determined entirely by the memorandum or articles of association, but the distribution can, of course, be varied from time to time by alterations made to the memorandum or articles. Unlike American law and the laws of most European countries, English law does not regard certain powers as managerial or executive and therefore inalienable by the board. The board's powers can be as broad or as narrow as is desired, but the tendency of modern

14 Companies Act 1985, Sch 6, para 16 (a).
15 Ibid, Sch 6, para 27 (2).
16 Companies Act 1985, s 232 (1) and (2) and Sch 6, paras 28 and 29, substituted by Companies Act 1989, s 6 (3) and Sch 4, para 6. The aggregate amount need not include transactions with individual officers under which the total amount outstanding from the officer does not exceed £2,500 at the end of the financial year.
17 That is, authorised by the Bank of England for the purposes of the Banking Act 1987 (Companies Act 1985, s 744, as amended by Companies Act 1989, s 23 and Sch 10, para 16).
18 Companies Act 1985, s 225B(2) and Sch 9, Part IV, para 3(1), substituted by Companies Act 1989, s 18 (1) and Sch 7, Part IV, para 1.
19 Ibid, Sch 9, Part IV, para 2. Authorised banking companies and their holding companies must instead keep a register containing copies of transactions which would otherwise have to be disclosed in the notes to their annual accounts, and during the 15 days preceding the annual general meeting of the company a summary of the register must be available for inspection by members of the company at its registered office (Companies Act 1985, s 343 (1) to (5), as amended by Companies Act 1989, s 23 and Sch 10, para 10).

articles is to follow the pattern of Table A[20] in conferring on the board all the powers of the company, except those which the Companies Act 1985 and the memorandum or articles require to be exercised by the members in general meeting.[1]

In exercising their powers, the directors do not act as agents for the majority[2] or even all[3] of the members, and so, unless the memorandum or articles so provide, the members cannot by a resolution passed by a majority or even unanimously supersede the directors' powers,[4] or instruct them how they shall exercise their powers. This sovereignty of the directors within the limits of the powers conferred on them by the articles was clearly expressed by Greer LJ in the following words:[5]

'A company is an entity distinct alike from its shareholders and its directors. Some of its powers may, according to its articles, be exercised by directors, certain other powers may be reserved for the shareholders in general meeting. If powers of management are vested in the directors, they and they alone can exercise these powers. The only way in which the general body of the shareholders can control the exercise of the powers vested by the articles in the directors is by altering the articles, or if opportunity arises under the articles, by refusing to re-elect the directors of whose actions they disapprove. They cannot themselves usurp the powers which by the articles are vested in the directors any more than the directors can usurp the powers vested by the articles in the general body of shareholders.'

However, although the members cannot treat the directors as their agents and overrule them in the exercise of their powers, it is quite possible for the articles to vest the same power in members and directors concurrently, in which case in the event of a conflict the members' decision would generally prevail over that of the directors, because the members in general meeting are the superior authority. The court is disinclined to treat managerial and executive powers as concurrent, however, and unless the articles provide otherwise, they are exercisable exclusively by the directors. Thus, the directors' power to sell[6] or to retain[7] any of the company's assets, including its whole undertaking, their power to appoint one of their number to be managing director,[8] their power to declare interim dividends[9] and their power to sue in the company's name[10] have been treated as exclusive to them, and so resolutions passed by the members which conflict with the decision of

---

20 Table A, art 70.
 1 The powers reserved to the members in general meetings by the Companies Act 1985 (as amended) are, principally, to alter the memorandum and articles of association, to alter share capital, to authorise the issue of shares (including redeemable shares), to waive preferential subscription rights for further issues of equity capital, to appoint auditors and to remove directors, to authorise the purchase by the company of shares in itself and to put the company into liquidation. Additionally, Table A reserves to the members powers to fix the rights to be attached to a new issue of shares, to appoint directors and to declare dividends and to capitalise profits and reserves.
 2 *Automatic Self-Cleansing Filter Syndicate Co Ltd v Cunninghame* [1906] 2 Ch 34 at 42–43, per Collins MR.
 3 *Gramophone and Typewriter Ltd v Stanley* [1908] 2 KB 89 at 105–6, per Buckley LJ.
 4 *Scott v Scott* [1943] 1 All ER 582, where a resolution of a general meeting that the company's auditors should investigate the conduct of its affairs by the directors was held void. Compare the similar American case of *Charlestown Boot and Shoe Co v Dunsmore* (1880) 60 NH 85, where a resolution of a general meeting appointing a committee of members to supervise the directors' management of the company's business was held void.
 5 *John Shaw & Sons (Salford) Ltd v Shaw* [1935] 2 KB 113 at 134, [1935] All ER Rep 456 at 464.
 6 *Quin and Axtens Ltd v Salmon* [1909] AC 442.
 7 *Automatic Self-Cleansing Filter Syndicate Co Ltd v Cunninghame*, supra.
 8 *Thomas Logan Ltd v Davis* (1911) 104 LT 914; affd (1911) 105 LT 419.
 9 *Scott v Scott* [1943] 1 All ER 582.
10 *John Shaw & Sons (Salford) Ltd v Shaw*, supra; *Breckland Group Holdings Ltd v London & Suffolk Properties Ltd* [1989] BCLC 100.

the directors in respect of such matters are ineffectual.[11] But powers for directors to appoint additional directors and to fill casual vacancies on the board,[12] or to fix the remuneration of the managing director,[13] will be treated as concurrent powers, unless the articles clearly show that they are to be exclusive, and so resolutions passed by the members in respect of such matters will prevail over the directors' own decision. However, in the case of appointments of additional directors or appointments to fill casual vacancies on the board, it is clear that if the board exercises its power of appointment before a general meeting acts, the board's appointments are effective and cannot be rescinded, and the general meeting can only make appointments to places on the board which still remain unfilled. Although the directors' power to sue in the company's name has been treated as an exclusive power,[14] it has been held that if the board decides not to sue, the members may resolve that the company shall sue.[15] It seems, therefore, that the directors' power to sue in the company's name is exclusive only if they choose to exercise it, and that their power really amounts to nothing more than the right to continue litigation which they have begun despite the members' wishes to the contrary.

Articles frequently provide, following Table A of the Companies Act 1948, and the earlier Companies Acts,[16] that directors shall exercise their powers subject to such regulations, being not inconsistent with the articles themselves, as may be prescribed by the company in general meeting. The meaning of this reservation is far from clear. It certainly does not enable the members in general meeting to instruct the directors how they shall exercise their powers in specific instances,[17] and it does not enable them to take away the powers conferred on the directors by the articles, because then the regulations would be inconsistent with the articles.[18] It has been held obiter that a power conferred on the members in general meeting to prescribe regulations enables them to give the board general or specific directions as to the exercise of the residual powers of the company conferred on the board by the articles which neither the Companies Act 1985 nor the articles specifically require to be exercised by a general meeting,[19] but it is doubtful whether this is correct, for there can be no logical distinction made between specific powers conferred on the board by the articles and powers which are not enumerated there but are nevertheless readily ascertainable. The power to prescribe regulations seems to be the vestigial remains of the power to make bye-laws which used to be

11 In *Mercantile Bank of India Ltd v Central Bank of India Ltd* [1938] AC 287, [1938] 1 All ER 52, it was held that when directors had given a power of attorney sealed with the company's seal to an agent to enable him to borrow on the company's behalf, a lender could treat the power of attorney as binding on the company even though the articles did not enable the directors to delegate the borrowing powers vested in them, because the lender could assume that the power to attorney had been authorised by a general meeting. The case did not decide that the members in general meeting had a concurrent power to borrow, but merely that they could make the directors' borrowing powers effective by authorising a delegation of them. Directors' borrowing powers are undoubtedly exclusive.

12 *Worcester Corsetry Ltd v Witting* [1936] Ch 640.

13 *Foster v Foster* [1916] 1 Ch 532; contra, *Thomas Logan Ltd v Davis* (1911) 104 LT 914; affd (1911) 105 LT 419.

14 *John Shaw & Sons (Salford) Ltd v Shaw*, supra; *Breckland Group Holdings Ltd v London & Suffolk Properties Ltd*, supra.

15 *Marshall's Valve Gear Co Ltd v Manning, Wardle & Co Ltd* [1909] 1 Ch 267; secus *Breckland Group Holdings Ltd v London & Suffolk Properties Ltd*, supra. In the later case there was additionally an agreement between all of the shareholders which provided that decisions whether litigation should be initiated by the company were to be taken by the board of directors.

16 Companies Act 1948, Table A, art 80; Companies Act 1929, Table A, art 67; Companies Consolidation Act 1908, Table A, art 71.

17 *Scott v Scott* [1943] 1 All ER 582.

18 *Quin and Axtens Ltd v Salmon* [1909] AC 442.

19 *Thomas Logan Ltd v Davis* (1911) 104 LT 914 at 916–917, per Warrington LJ.

reserved to members by the deeds of settlement of companies formed at common law. Such bye-laws were usually procedural, and it is probable that regulations made by general meetings, too, must be confined to procedural matters, so that the members might, for example, prescribe when and how board meetings shall be held, but not what shall be done at them.[20]

The present Table A[1] makes the exercise of the directors' powers subject to any directions given by a general meeting by special resolution. This would appear to empower a general meeting to give specific directions as to the manner in which the directors shall exercise their powers, whether generally or in respect of a particular transaction. However, such a direction may not invalidate any act which the directors have previously carried out.[1]

Board meetings

Directors can only exercise their powers collectively by passing resolutions at board meetings, unless the articles otherwise provide.[2] But if all the directors agree informally on a certain matter without a board meeting being held, their unanimity is equivalent to a resolution passed at a board meeting, and is binding on the company.[3] Table A provides expressly that this shall be so if the informal but unanimous resolution is reduced to writing and is signed by all the directors.[4]

Notice of board meetings should be given to all the directors in sufficient time to enable them to attend. What is sufficient notice depends on the facts at the time, and so it has been held that three hours' notice to directors who had other businesses to attend to was insufficient, even though their places of business and the place where the board meeting was to be held were all in the City of London,[5] but on the other hand, five minutes' notice to a director was held sufficient when neither distance nor other engagements prevented him from attending.[6] Notice of a board meeting need not be given to a director whose whereabouts are unknown, because, for example, he is travelling, but the mere fact that he is out of the United Kingdom does not justify notice not being given to him,[7] unless the articles so provide.[8] Notice of a board meeting need only specify when and where it is to be held; it is not necessary for it to set out the business to be transacted.[9]

It has been held that unless proper notice of a board meeting is given to each director, the meeting and all resolutions passed at it are void,[10] but in two other cases[11] it has been held that failure to give proper notice to a director merely entitles him to require a second meeting to be held if he does not attend the first; if he does not require a second meeting to be held within a reasonable time after learning of the first meeting, he waives his right to require it, and resolutions passed

---

20 But articles usually deal with the convening and holding of board meetings in detail, and therefore leave little in respect of which regulations could be made.

1 Table A, art 70.

2 *Re Athenaeum Life Assurance Society, ex p Eagle Insurance Co* (1858) 4 K & J 549 at 558; *D'Arcy v Tamar Kit Hill and Callington Rly Co* (1867) LR 2 Exch 158; *Re Haycraft Gold Reduction and Mining Co* [1900] 2 Ch 230.

3 *Re Bonelli's Telegraph Co, Collie's Claim* (1871) LR 12 Eq 246; *Charterhouse Investment Trust Ltd v Tempest Diesels Ltd* [1986] BCLC 1; *TCB Ltd v Gray* [1986] Ch 621, [1986] 1 All ER 587.

4 Table A, art 93.

5 *Re Homer District Consolidated Gold Mines Ltd, ex p Smith* (1888) 39 ChD 546.

6 *Browne v La Trinidad* (1887) 37 ChD 1.

7 *Halifax Sugar Refining Co Ltd v Francklyn* (1890) 59 LJ Ch 591.

8 Table A, art 88, does so provide.

9 *Compagnie de Mayville v Whitley* [1896] 1 Ch 788.

10 *Re Homer District Consolidated Gold Mines Ltd, ex p Smith* (1888) 39 ChD 546.

11 *Browne v La Trinidad*, supra; *Bentley-Stevens v Jones* [1974] 2 All ER 653, [1974] 1 WLR 638.

at the first meeting them become unassailable. From the practical point of view, the second of these two conclusions is obviously preferable.

Unless the articles otherwise provide, it seems that any director can call a board meeting, and the articles usually so provide explicitly.[12]

A board meeting cannot proceed to business unless a quorum of directors is present. The quorum is usually fixed by the articles,[13] but if it is not, the number of directors who usually attend board meetings constitutes a quorum.[14] If the articles disable a director from voting on a particular matter, for example, because he has a personal interest in it, he does not count toward the quorum, and this may result in there not being a quorum of the other directors competent to transact the business in question, even though there is a quorum able to transact other business at the same meeting.[15] The requirement of a competent quorum cannot be evaded by splitting what is really one item of business into two resolutions. Thus, where the quorum was three, and four directors attended and resolved by separate resolutions to issue debentures ranking pari passu to two of their number to secure loans made by them at the same time, it was held that the two resolutions were really one item of business; the two directors who took the debentures were disqualified from voting by the articles because of their interest, and therefore did not count toward the quorum, so that no competent quorum was present, and the resolutions to issue the debentures were void.[16] An alternate director present at a board meeting in place of the director who appointed him counts toward the quorum,[17] but if he is himself a director it would seem that he can only be counted once.

Unless the articles otherwise provide, each director has one vote at a board meeting, and a resolution is carried only if there are more votes for than against it, so that if there is an equality of votes, the resolution is lost.[18] Usually, however, the articles empower the directors to elect a chairman from their number to preside at board meetings,[19] and he is given a casting vote in the event of a tie.[20] The articles usually disable a director from voting on a resolution in which he is directly or indirectly interested,[1] but he is nevertheless entitled to notice of the meeting at which the resolution is to be passed, and to attend and speak on the resolution.[2] If the articles permit the appointment of an alternate director, they always provide

---

12 Table A, art 88 provides that a director may call a board meeting or require the secretary to do so.
13 Table A, art 89, enables the board to fix its own quorum, but until it is fixed the quorum is two. The articles may validly fix the quorum at one, and it seems that an article in the form of Table A, art 89, enables the board to fix a quorum at one (*Re Fireproof Doors Ltd* [1916] 2 Ch 142).
14 *Re Tavistock Ironworks Co, Lyster's Case* (1867) LR 4 Eq 233.
15 *Re Greymouth-Point Elizabeth Rly and Coal Co Ltd* [1904] 1 Ch 32.
16 *Re North Eastern Insurance Co* [1919] 1 Ch 198.
17 Table A, art 89 expressly so provides.
18 *Re Hackney Pavilion Ltd* [1924] 1 Ch 276; *Shepherd's Trustees v Shepherd* 1950 SC (HL) 60.
19 See Table A, art 91.
20 See Table A, art 88.
 1 Table A, art 94, disables a director from voting in respect of any matter in which he has a material interest which conflicts or may conflict with the interests of the company, except where the resolution relates to giving a guarantee, security or indemnity to a director who has lent money to, or incurred an obligation for the benefit of, the company or any of its subsidiaries, or to a third person in connection with an obligation of the company or any of its subsidiaries for which a director has assumed responsibility; or where the resolution relates to the subscription or underwriting by a director of shares or debentures of the company or any of its subsidiaries; or where the resolution relates to a retirement benefits scheme which has been approved by the Inland Revenue or is conditional on its approval. The Stock Exchange requires listed companies to restrict interested directors' right to vote at board meetings to the exceptional cases specified in the articles of association, which have been approved by the Committee on Quotations of the Stock Exchange (Stock Exchange, *Admission of Securities to Listing*, Section 9, Chapter 1, para 4.1).
 2 *Grimwade v BPS Syndicate Ltd* (1915) 31 TLR 531.

that he may attend and vote at board meetings from which the director who appointed him is absent,[2] and usually the articles also provide that if the alternate director is himself a director, he may cast votes in both capacities.[3]

A company must keep minutes of the proceedings at its board meetings, and if the minutes of a meeting are signed by the chairman of that or the next succeeding meeting, they are evidence of the proceedings at the meeting, and it is presumed, until the contrary is proved, that the meeting was properly convened, and that the resolutions recorded in the minutes were duly passed.[4] Minutes, like all other books and documents of the company, are open to inspection by the directors, but members have no general right of inspection.[5]

Delegation by the board

A board of directors must act collectively or collegiately, and it therefore has no inherent power to delegate any of its powers of decision to one or more of its members or to other persons,[6] although the members in general meeting may apparently authorise such a delegation[7] and it has been held in two cases that the board may have an implied power of delegation as part of its general power to manage the companys affairs.[8] However, modern articles of association usually empower the board to appoint committees consisting of one or more of the directors, and to delegate any of the powers of the board to such committees,[9] and they also usually empower the board to appoint any persons, whether directors or members of the company or not, to be the attorneys or agents of the company for such period as the board thinks fit with authority to exercise any of the directors' powers during that time.[10] Under such provisions the board may appoint a committee of directors merely to make recommendations to it, so that it will take the final decisions itself, or it may empower a committee or an attorney or agent to exercise any of its powers and to bind the company without further reference to it, or the board may constitute a committee of some of its members (eg non-executive directors) to exercise a supervisory or reporting function, such as that of an audit committee, which checks the company's internal accounting and financial controls and the accuracy of its management accounts. But in the absence of a provision in the articles or a valid contract to the contrary, all delegations of power may be revoked either expressly or by the board exercising the delegated powers itself.[11] Furthermore, appointments of members of committees are revocable by the board, even though the person concerned was appointed for a fixed period.[12] It is therefore impossible for a board to divide its powers permanently between itself and its committees in the same way as the articles divide the powers of the company between the members and the board.[13]

2 Table A, art 66 so provides.
3 Table A, art 88 so provides.
4 Companies Act 1985, s 382(1), (2) and (4).
5 *Re v Merchant Tailors' Co* (1831) 2 B & Ad 115.
6 *Re County Palatine Loan and Discount Co, Cartmell's Case* (1874) 9 Ch App 691.
7 *Mercantile Bank of India Ltd v Chartered Bank of India Ltd* [1938] AC 278, [1937] 1 All ER 231.
8 *Freeman and Lockyer (a firm) v Buckhurst Park Properties (Mangal) Ltd* [1964] 2 QB 480, [1964] 1 All ER 630; *Hely-Hutchinson v Brayhead Ltd* [1968] 1 QB 549, [1967] 3 All ER 98 (see pp 130 and 133, ante).
9 See Table A, art 72.
9 See Table A, art 72.
10 See Table A, art 71. The appointment need only be made by deed under the common seal of the company, or be otherwise executed as a deed (see p 105, ante), if the attorney is empowered to execute deeds on the company's behalf.
11 *Huth v Clarke* (1890) 25 QBD 391; *Gordon, Dadds & Co v Morris* [1945] 2 All ER 616.
12 *Manton v Brighton Corpn* [1951] 2 KB 393, [1951] 2 All ER 101.
13 *Horn v Henry Faulder & Co Ltd* (1908) 99 LT 524.

Where the board is unable or unwilling to act

If for some reason the board of directors is unable or unwilling to make a decision on a matter, the members in general meeting may make the decision themselves, even though in doing so they may be exercising powers which are conferred on the directors by the articles.

Acts beyond the board's powers

The first situation where the members in general meeting may intervene is where the directors are unable to act because the transaction which they wish to carry out is outside their own powers, even though it is within the objects of the company or the incidental powers conferred on it by its memorandum of association or by law. Authority for the transaction must then be sought from the members in general meeting, in whom the residual powers of the company are vested, and the authorisation may be given by ordinary resolution. It has been suggested[14] that the members may authorise the directors to act only by ratifying the transaction after the directors have carried it out, because if the members authorised the directors to act in advance, they would be altering the articles of association, and this can only be done by special resolution. This deduction is both impractical and illogical. It is impractical because no outsider would be willing to enter into the transaction with the directors knowing that the company might attempt to evade its obligations by the members simply declining to ratify what the directors had done.[15] It is illogical because it treats the exercise of the powers reserved to the members by the articles as an attempt to extend the directors' own powers, when in reality the members, by authorising the directors to act, are merely appointing them to be the members' agents to exercise powers vested in the members themselves.

The correctness of this can be tested by asking two questions. First, would an alteration of the articles be necessary if the members authorised someone other than the directors, such as some of their own number, to do the act in question on their behalf? Clearly it would not, and logically it should make no difference that the agents chosen by the members happen to be the directors. Secondly, if the members gave authority to the directors to act in their name by a special resolution, would it be necessary to alter the articles before the authority could be revoked? Again, clearly not. If the answer were otherwise, the members would not be able to confer a revocable authority on directors without reserving an express power of revocation, and this would conflict with a fundamental rule of the law of agency. It is therefore submitted that members may authorise directors to do an act which is outside the directors' own powers, but within the company's powers, by passing an ordinary resolution either before or after the directors act;[16] that in acting under such authority the directors act as agents for the members and not as directors of the company, and consequently the members may revoke or vary the authority by ordinary resolution at any time; and that it is only necessary to amend the articles when the members wish to add to the powers of the directors as such.

These considerations are in no way affected by the fact that articles often empower a general meeting of members by special resolution to give directions to

---

14 *Irvine v Union Bank of Australia* (1877) 2 App Cas 366; *Grant v United Kingdom Switchback Rlys Co* (1888) 40 ChD 135 at 138 to 140, per Cotton and Lindley LJJ.

15 The outsider would be protected by the Companies Act 1985, s 35A (1) to (3) (inserted by Companies Act 1989, s 108 (1) (see pp 97 and 99, ante), but if the transaction is a substantial one the outsider would probably not be willing to accept this as a substitute for the certainty that the transaction had been properly authorised in accordance with the company's memorandum and articles.

16 This is supported by the judgment of Bowen LJ in *Grant v United Kingdom Switchback Rlys Co*, supra, at 140, and by *Re London and New York Investment Corpn* [1895] 2 Ch 860 at 869.

the board of directors as to the exercise of its powers.[17] This power relates to the exercise of powers which are already vested in the directors, and not to the authorisation of the directors to act as agents of the members in exercising powers vested in them.

Lack of a quorum at board meetings

Directors may be unable to exercise the powers given to them by the articles because they have become so few in number that they cannot constitute a quorum, or because so many of them are interested in the transaction in question and are consequently disabled from voting by the articles, that a quorum of competent directors cannot be found. In these cases the members in general meeting may exercise the directors' powers. Where the number of directors has fallen to less than a quorum, the articles will usually empower the remaining directors to fill the vacancies so as to make up a quorum,[18] but if there are no directors at all, or if the remaining directors are unwilling to fill the vacancies, the members may exercise their powers until a board is properly constituted.[19]

It has been suggested that where the board cannot act because several of its members are disabled from voting, the members can act only by ratifying what the board has purported to do, and not by authorising the board to act in advance.[20] The reasons given for this are the same as in the situation where the directors wish to do acts beyond the powers conferred on them by the articles, and are, of course, equally untenable. It is submitted that when a quorum of competent directors cannot be found, the board's powers temporarily revert to the members, who may then authorise the remaining directors to act, either in advance of their acting or by ratification afterwards, and the remaining directors then exercise that authority as agents for the members, and not in their capacity of directors. This is so, of course, only when it is not possible to make up a quorum of directors competent to vote at a board meeting. Nevertheless, it has been held in one case[1] that if the transaction in question is within the powers of the directors and it would have been possible for it to be resolved upon by a board meeting attended by a competent quorum of directors, the transaction is nevertheless valid although assented to informally by some of the directors who also hold all the company's issued shares. It is difficult to see the logic of the implicit conclusion in this decision that a unanimous decision of the members of the company is a valid substitute for a resolution of a board meeting when there is no difficulty in holding such a meeting, unless at the same time the principle mentioned above, that the powers of the board of directors are exclusive to them and cannot be exercised by the members in general meeting,[2] is to be disregarded.

Conflict with duties to the company

If directors are unable to exercise lawfully a power conferred on them by the articles in a particular instance because to do so would be a breach of their duty to act in the interests of the members of the company as a whole,[3] the members in general meeting may by ordinary resolution ratify what the directors have in fact

17 See Table A, art 70.
18 See Table A, art 79.
19 *Barron v Potter* [1914] 1 Ch 895; *Foster v Foster* [1916] 1 Ch 532.
20 *Grant v United Kingdom Switchback Rlys Co* (1888) 40 ChD 135.
 1 *Re Horsley and Weight Ltd* [1982] Ch 442, [1982] 3 All ER 1045.
 2 See p 573, ante.
 3 See p 591, post.

done,[4] and they may also authorise the directors in advance to do the act in question.[5] But in this situation it is not possible for the members to abrogate the directors' powers to themselves so as to exercise them on other occasions than the one where the directors are inhibited from acting because of the potential breach of duty. Furthermore, if directors abuse their powers to such an extent that the purpose for which they act is outside and unrelated to the company's objects, or is the achievement of something which is in conflict with those objects, the directors act ultra vires the company and not merely in breach of their duties to it. In that situation a general meeting cannot effectively approve the directors' act in advance nor exercise the company's power for that ultra vires purpose itself,[6] but if the directors have already done the act or entered into the transaction which is unrelated to the company's objects, a general meeting may ratify the act or transaction by passing a special resolution to that effect.[7] Whether the unanimous consent of the members to the act or transaction is to be treated as the equivalent of a ratifying special resolution is undecided.

Dissension between members of the board

If directors are unable to act because of dissension between themselves, the members in general meeting may exercise the board's powers until a board is elected which is able to act. But the dissension must result in deadlock before the members may intervene. Consequently, it must be shown, either that so many directors persistently absent themselves from board meetings that a quorum cannot be formed, or that the dissenting factions have equal voting power at board meetings and no resolutions can therefore be passed.[8] The mere fact that on one occasion the votes for and against a resolution at a board meeting are equal does not justify the members in interfering; in that case the resolution is simply lost, unless the chairman can resolve the tie by exercising a casting vote under the provisions of the articles.

Powers of the court

Where the board is unable to act because the directors are so few that a quorum cannot be formed, or because of dissension between the directors, the court may appoint a receiver of the company's business to manage it until a competent board can be constituted.[9] Furthermore, if the power of the board which the members wish to have exercised is one which the court can conveniently exercise itself, such as a power to approve the transfer of shares, the court may exercise the power and give any decision which the board could have given.[10] The court's power in these respects is discretionary, and it is now likely to exercise them only in exceptional circumstances, because it can instead order that a general meeting of members

---

4 *Bamford v Bamford* [1970] Ch 212, [1969] 1 All ER 969.
5 *Multinational Gas and Petrochemical Co v Multinational Gas and Petrochemical Services Ltd* [1983] Ch 258, [1983] 2 All ER 563; *Regal (Hastings) Ltd v Gulliver* [1967] 2 AC 134n at 150, [1942] 1 All ER 378 at 389, per Lord Russell of Killowen; *Bamford v Bamford* [1970] Ch 212 at 241, [1969] 3 All ER 969 at 975, per Russell LJ.
6 *Rolled Steel Products (Holdings) Ltd v British Steel Corpn* [1982] Ch 478, [1982] 3 All ER 57; affd [1986] Ch 246, [1984] BCLC 466.
7 Companies Act 1985, s 35 (3), substituted by Companies Act 1989, s 108 (1).
8 *Barron v Potter* [1914] 1 Ch 895; *Foster v Foster* [1916] 1 Ch 532.
9 *Trade Auxiliary Co v Vickers* (1873) LR 16 Eq 298, 303; *Stanfield v Gibbon* [1925] WN 11; *Re a Company (No 00596 of 1986)* [1987] BCLC 133.
10 *Re Copal Varnish Co Ltd* [1917] 2 Ch 349.

shall be held to elect additional directors, or to decide whether to remove some or all of the existing directors from office.[11]

MANAGING AND EXECUTIVE DIRECTORS

In some companies (particularly the smaller and medium-sized private companies) all the directors devote their whole time and attention to the company's affairs and often they divide the various sectors of management between themselves with or without a formal appointment of directors with a descriptive character being made (eg financial director, production director, marketing director). In other companies some members of the board of directors do not devote their full time to the company's affairs while others do, and the day-to-day management of the company's business then devolves on the full-time directors, who may divide the sectors of management functionally between themselves and are collectively known as executive directors, to distinguish them from the part-time directors, who are labelled non-executive. In the case of public companies this situation is usually deliberately created by the inclusion on the board of part-time non-executive directors whose main interests lie outside the company (eg directors who are also directors of other companies which have commercial connections with the company in question), or who are skilled or experienced in business generally or in fields which are significant to the company (eg directors who are experienced in finance, marketing, advertising or exporting). Usually an arrangement by which day-to-day management is left in the hands of the full-time or executive directors is given formal effect by one or more of the full-time directors being appointed managing or executive director or directors (or if only one senior appointment is made, as chief executive) and by him or them being given powers of management which are exercisable without reference to the board. If the arrangement is to be legally effective, however, the articles must provide for the appointment to be made.[12]

Modern articles usually follow the pattern of Table A,[13] and empower the board of directors to appoint one or more of their number to the office of managing director or to any other executive office under the company for such period, at such remuneration and with such powers as the board thinks fit. If a managing director or chief executive or other executive is appointed otherwise than by the board (eg by the articles of association or by resolution of a general meeting), the board still has power under Table A[13] to award him remuneration.[14] But however the managing or executive director is appointed, if the board does not exercise its power to award him remuneration, he is entitled to none, and cannot recover an equivalent by claiming a quantum meruit for the value of services he has rendered to the company.[14]

A managing or executive director ceases to hold that office when he ceases to be a director,[15] unless the articles otherwise provide,[16] but the articles cannot, of course, preserve a managing or executive director in office when he has become

11 Companies Act 1985, s 371 (1); *Re Paris Skating Rink Co* (1877) 6 ChD 731.
12 *Boschoek Proprietary Co Ltd v Fuke* [1906] 1 Ch 148.
13 Table A, art 84.
14 *Re Richmond Gate Property Co Ltd* [1964] 3 All ER 936, [1965] 1 WLR 335; *Guinness plc v Saunders* [1990] 1 All ER 652, [1990] 2 WLR 324.
15 *Bluett v Stutchbury's Ltd* (1908) 24 TLR 469, where a managing director who was appointed for four years was held to have retired within that period under a provision in the articles for rotation of directors.
16 Table A, art 84, provides that a managing or executive director shall not retire by rotation, but shall cease to be a managing or executive director if he ceases to be a director for any other reason.

disqualified from being a director or has been removed from office under the provisions of the Companies Act 1985.[17] If the company enters into a service contract with a managing or executive director under which he is to hold office for a certain period, and the articles at the time when the contract is made provide that directors shall cease to hold office in certain events, the provisions of the articles are impliedly incorporated in the service contract, because the board has no power to make a contract which excludes them, and the managing or executive director cannot complain that the company has broken his service contract if he ceases to hold office on the happening of one of those events.[18] But if in such a case the managing or executive director ceases to hold office because the board or a general meeting terminates his appointment under a power contained in the articles, he can sue for breach of his service contract, because the power of termination is subordinate to the board's power to appoint a managing or executive director for such period as it thinks fit, and is therefore excluded when it appoints a managing or executive director for a fixed period.[18] Furthermore, if the company's articles are altered after the managing or executive director's appointment so as to provide a new ground on which he may be dismissed, the alteration is not impliedly incorporated in his service contract, and if he is dismissed on that new ground, he may sue the company for damages for breach of contract.[19] If a managing or executive director is appointed without any period being fixed for his tenure of office, the board may terminate his appointment at any time, whether it has an express power to do so by the articles or not,[20] but if the managing or executive director is employed under a contract with the company, the company commits a breach of contract if it does not give him reasonable notice of dismissal.[1] Moreover, in such a case a general meeting of members may remove the managing or executive director by terminating his directorship under a power reserved to them by the articles, and the managing or executive director cannot then sue the company for damages for breach of his service contract, because the members' power to terminate his directorship is impliedly incorporated in the contract.[2]

In all the foregoing cases the managing director had a service contract with the company, and his rights were therefore largely determined by the provisions of that contract. If a managing or executive director is appointed without a service contract being entered into, he impliedly agrees to serve on the terms of the articles applicable to directors and a managing or executive director as they stand from time to time, and so by altering the articles the company can vary the managing or executive director's contract, but not so as to deprive him of rights which have already accrued (e g remuneration for a period which he has served).[3] However, if a managing or executive director is removed by resolution of a general meeting under the provisions of the Companies Act 1985,[4] and he has no service contract, he has a claim for damages against the company if he was appointed for a period which has not expired.

The articles usually empower the board to confer on a managing or executive director any of the powers exercisable by the directors on such terms and conditions as the board thinks fit, either collaterally with, or to the exclusion of, the board's

17 See pp 543 and 547, ante.
18 *Nelson v James Nelson & Sons Ltd* [1914] 2 KB 770; *Shindler v Northern Raincoat Co* [1960] 2 All ER 239, [1960] 1 WLR 1038.
19 *Southern Foundries (1926) Ltd v Shirlaw* [1940] AC 701, [1940] 2 All ER 445.
20 *Foster v Foster* [1916] 1 Ch 532.
1 *James v Thomas H Kent & Co Ltd* [1951] 1 KB 551, [1950] 2 All ER 1099.
2 *Read v Astoria Garage (Streatham) Ltd* [1952] Ch 637, [1952] 2 All ER 292.
3 *Shuttleworth v Cox Bros & Co (Maidenhead) Ltd* [1927] 2 KB 9, [1926] All ER Rep 498 (see p 83, ante).
4 Companies Act 1985, s 303 (1) (see p 546, ante).

own powers, and to revoke or vary any powers conferred on the managing director at any time.[5] Under such an article the managing or executive director is merely a delegate of the board, and his powers may be withdrawn by the board at will. If he serves under a contract with the company which expresses his functions in the same form as such an article, the company is not guilty of breach of contract if it withdraws his powers from him.[6] Even if his contract provides that he shall have specific powers, the company may effectively withdraw them, and his only remedy will be to sue it for damages.[7] A managing or executive director will only be an independent organ of the company if his powers are expressly conferred by the memorandum or articles; then he may prevent his fellow directors from interfering with the exercise of his powers,[8] and, a fortiori, from excluding him from office completely.

In addition to empowering the board of directors to appoint managing or executive directors, articles of association often also empower the board to enter into agreements or arrangements with any director for his employment by the company, or for the provision by him of any services outside the scope of the ordinary duties of a director.[9] Such a power may be used to appoint a director to a salaried position under the company, or to remunerate him for professional or other services rendered on particular occasions or as part of a continuing arrangement, but not to remunerate him for work done or benefits procured for the company of an unusual or isolated character, if the work or procurement of the benefits is merely in fulfilment of his duty as a director to use his best endeavours to promote the company's interests.[10]

DIRECTORS' DUTIES TO THE COMPANY

In addition to their statutory duties, directors owe their company a number of fiduciary duties similar to those owed by an agent to his principal, and also a common law duty to take reasonable care in the management of a company's affairs. These duties are owed exclusively to the company of which the defendant is a director. The fact that they are owed to the company does not impose parallel duties on a director toward the company's members or creditors,[11] nor, if the company is a parent or holding company, does the director owe similar duties to its subsidiary companies, though if the director is also a director of the subsidiary, he may of course owe it a duty in respect of the same matter, but only in that capacity.[12]

Duty not to exceed powers

Directors must not do any act or enter into any transaction which is illegal or ultra vires the company,[13] nor, without the sanction of the members in general meeting, any act or transaction which is beyond the powers conferred on directors by the articles. If they do any such act or enter into any such transaction and the company

---

5 See Table A, art 72.
6 *Harold Holdsworth & Co (Wakefield) Ltd v Caddies* [1955] 1 All ER 725, [1955] 1 WLR 352.
7 *Montreal Public Service Co v Champagne* (1916) 33 DLR 49 (a Privy Council decision).
8 *John Shaw & Sons (Salford) Ltd v Shaw* [1935] 2 KB 113, [1935] All ER Rep 456.
9 Table A, art 84 so provides.
10 *Guinness plc v Saunders* [1990] 1 All ER 652, [1990] 2 WLR 324.
11 See p 649, post.
12 *Lindgren v L & P Estates Co Ltd* [1968] Ch 572, [1968] 1 All ER 917.
13 *Selangor United Rubber Estates Ltd v Cradock (No 3)* [1968] 2 All ER 1073, [1968] 1 WLR 1555.

suffers loss in consequence, the company can recover the amount of its loss from them, and it is not necessary for it to show that they acted negligently.[14] This liability is preserved by the statutory provisions which validate such acts or transactions when the person who deals with the directors acts in good faith.[15] If the directors are employed under service contracts, they may also be sued for damages for breach of those contracts.[16]

It is unlawful for directors to pay dividends out of funds representing share capital, and they are liable to make good any money expended in that way.[17] But if they honestly and without negligence believe that the company has earned sufficient profits to pay the dividend when in fact it has not, they will not be liable.[18] In this latter case they act under a mistake of fact, and the court regulates the duty imposed on them as though the facts as they supposed them to be were true; consequently, they are liable to the company only if they were careless in not discovering the true facts. But if the directors pay a dividend out of capital because of a mistake of law,[17] or because of a misconstruction of the company's memorandum or articles,[19] they are absolutely liable. It appears that a mistake of fact by directors will not reduce their liability to one only for negligence when they apply the company's funds for any other ultra vires or illegal purpose.

A director is liable to his company for exceeding his powers only if he causes it loss by sanctioning an improper use of its assets or any other improper or illegal act (eg a tortious act exposing the company to liability). If he merely votes for a resolution at a board meeting that the board may make a class of payments which is ultra vires, but does not vote for a later resolution that a specific payment of that class shall be made, he is not liable, because it is the later resolution which results in the loss, and the loss would have been suffered even though the former resolution had not been passed.[20] Again, if a director merely votes in favour of ratifying or confirming improper payments which his fellow directors have already made, he is not liable, because the company's loss would be just the same if he had not assented,[1] and similarly if a director participates in an attempted improper disposal of assets which the company has not in fact acquired, he is not liable to the company for their value because the company has suffered no loss in fact.[2]

Duty to act in the interests of members and employees

In exercising their powers directors must act primarily in the interests of the shareholders as a whole,[3] but they must also have regard to the interests of the company's employees in general,[4] though not, it would seem, the interests of employees of other companies in the same group of companies. The duty to have regard to employees' interests is one of imperfect obligation, first, because it can

---

14 *Cullerne v London and Suburban General Permanent Building Society* (1890) 25 QBD 485 at 490; *Re Sharpe* [1892] 1 Ch 154.
15 Companies Act 1985, s 35A (5), inserted by Companies Act 1989, s 108 (1).
16 *Benson v Heathorn* (1842) 1 Y & C Ch Cas 326.
17 *Re Exchange Banking Co, Flitcroft's Case* (1882) 21 ChD 519; *Re Sharpe* [1892] 1 Ch 154.
18 *Re Kingston Cotton Mill Co (No 2)* [1896] 1 Ch 331; *Lucas v Fitzgerald* (1903) 20 TLR 16.
19 *Re Claridge's Patent Asphalte Co Ltd* [1921] 1 Ch 543.
20 *Cullerne v London and Suburban General Permanent Building Society* (1890) 25 QBD 485.
1 *Ramskill v Edwards* (1885) 31 ChD 100; *Lucas v Fitzgerald,* supra.
2 *Selangor United Rubber Estates Ltd v Cradock (No 3),* [1968] 2 All ER 1073 at 1148 to 1149, [1968] 1 WLR 1555 at 1651 to 1652.
3 *Piercy v S Mills & Co* [1920] 1 Ch 77; *Hogg v Cramphorn Ltd* [1967] Ch 254, [1966] 3 All ER 420; *Bamford v Bamford* [1970] Ch 212, [1969] 1 All ER 969; *Charterbridge Corpn Ltd v Lloyds Bank Ltd* [1970] Ch 62, [1969] 2 All ER 1185.
4 Companies Act 1985, s 309 (1).

only be enforced in the same way as any other fiduciary duty owed by directors,[5] namely by an action brought by the company or by a shareholders' derivative action;[6] and secondly, because directors are not required to give any priority or preference to employees' interests over those of members. It is, furthermore, difficult to determine what enquiries directors must make to ensure that they have a correct view of what is the interest or the prevailing interest of employees in general, particularly when the interests of different groups of employees conflict; to what extent directors may or must accept the arguments or demands of the representatives of employees (eg trade union officials, shop stewards) as reflecting the interests of employees in general; and whether the directors are ever justified in overriding the interest of the members of the company in order to protect an interest of employees. Since the directors' duty is to have regard to employees' interests and not necessarily to give effect to them, it would appear that directors fulfil their duty by considering what the employees' interests are and what weight should be given to them, and that a decision by directors reached in good faith cannot be impugned because employees' interests are not promoted or protected by it, provided that the members' interests are promoted or protected.

In one respect the statutory power of directors to give effect to employees' interests is more specific and practical. Notwithstanding any provision in the memorandum or articles, a company may make provision for the benefit of employees or former employees of the company and its subsidiaries in connection with the cessation or transfer of the whole or part of the company's undertaking, and this is so even though the making of that provision is not in the best interests of the company (presumably this means, not in the interests of the members of the company as a whole).[7] The provision for employees or former employees may take the form of direct cash payments (eg gratuities, voluntary redundancy payments, pensions, retraining or removal grants) or facilities or services (eg retraining schemes, creation of new employment opportunities, providing information about the availability of alternative employment). Normally the statutory power to make provision for employees or former employees will be exercised by the directors under a general delegation of the company's powers to them by the articles, but if the company is in liquidation the power is exercisable by the liquidator, although he may make payments which the directors had decided on before the liquidation began.[8]

There are substantial restrictions on the exercise of the statutory power by the directors or the liquidator. If the company is not in liquidation, payments may be made in exercise of the power only out of the company's profits available for distribution to its members,[9] and the power to make provision can only be exercised if a general meeting so resolves by ordinary resolution or by a resolution passed by any greater majority required by the memorandum or articles, but a resolution of the board of directors alone suffices if the memorandum or articles so provide.[10] If the company is in liquidation, the statutory power to provide for employees may be exercised by the liquidator only after the debts and liabilities of the company have been fully satisfied and provision has been made for the costs of the liquidation, and payments may be made only out of the surplus assets which would otherwise be distributed among the members of the company.[11] Furthermore, the liquidator

5 Ibid, s 309 (2).
6 See pp 649 and 660, post.
7 Companies Act 1985, s 719 (1) and (2).
8 Insolvency Act 1986, s 187 (1).
9 Companies Act 1985, s 719 (4).
10 Ibid, s 719 (3).
11 Insolvency Act 1986, s 187 (3).

may exercise the statutory power only if his proposals are approved by a general meeting of the company by ordinary resolution or by a resolution passed by any greater majority required by the memorandum or articles, and even if this approval is given the court may order the liquidator to modify or abandon his proposals on the application of a creditor or member or former member of the company.[12]

Personal profits obtained by the use of director's powers

A director, like any other agent, must account to the company for any profit he has made without the company's consent by the exercise of his functions as a director. Thus, a director must account for commission paid to him by persons with whom he places orders for goods or services on the company's behalf, and this is so even though the commission is only paid to a limited class of persons, so that the company could not qualify for it itself.[13] Again, a director who agreed to place the shares of a railway company with customers of his own company was held accountable to his company for the commission he received from the railway company, because his power to induce the customers to subscribe arose from the business connection he had established with them on his own company's behalf.[14] And where two companies amalgamated, a director of one of them was held accountable for a share of the remuneration paid to the person who negotiated the amalgamation which he gave to the director as a present.[15]

A director may subscribe for shares in his own company, but he must pay the full market price for them, and must not take advantage of the fact that they are available to only a limited number of subscribers. Thus, if directors subscribe for the company's shares at par when their market value is above par, they must account to the company for the difference, or if they have sold the shares, they must account for the profit they have made on the sale.[16] Furthermore, where a company formed another company to acquire certain property, and the directors of the first company subscribed for all the shares of the second at par (which was their real value at the time), and later sold them at a profit, it was held that the directors must account to the first company for the profit, because they obtained their opportunity to subscribe through their directorships.[17] It follows from this that even if directors subscribe for shares in their own company at a price equal to the current market value, they may still have to account for the profit they obtain if they later sell the shares at an enhanced price. But if they offer the new shares to all the existing members of the company or to the public at large, and do not treat their own applications in any way preferentially, it would seem that they are not liable to account for any profit which they subsequently make by selling the shares, because they did not use their position as directors to obtain the shares. This would appear to be so even if the issue price of the shares is less than their market value (eg on a rights offer to existing shareholders of the company which the directors accept in respect of their own holdings).[18]

The courts have been especially strict in making directors account for money and shares given to them by the company's promoters or the vendors of the property or business which the company was formed to acquire. The reason for

12 Companies Act 1985, s 187 (2) and (4).
13 *Boston Deep Sea Fishing and Ice Co v Ansell* (1888) 39 ChD 339.
14 *Imperial Mercantile Credit Association v Coleman* (1873) LR 6 HL 189.
15 *General Exchange Bank v Horner* (1870) LR 9 Eq 480.
16 *Parker v McKenna* (1874) 10 Ch App 96; *Shaw v Holland* [1900] 2 Ch 305.
17 *Regal (Hastings) Ltd v Gulliver* [1967] 2 AC 134n, [1942] 1 All ER 378.
18 For the extent of the directors' duty to obtain a premium on the issue of shares whose market value exceeds their nominal value, see p 169, ante.

this is that the directors' duty is to negotiate with such persons for the company's benefit, and they cannot do so independently if they are morally indebted to them. Consequently, if directors receive gifts of money or shares from the promoters out of their remuneration for the promotion of the company,[19] or from the vendors of a property or business under arrangements made before the contract for sale to the company is fully carried out,[20] the directors must account to the company for the money or the highest value of the shares since they received them. If the gift is of shares in the company, it may alternatively treat the shares as having been paid up with money which belongs to the company itself, which means that they have not been paid up at all, and the directors, as holders of the shares, may be called on to pay their nominal value in cash.[1] If a director buys shares from a promoter or vendor, the burden is on him to show that he paid the full market value, so that there was no element of gift, and if he cannot discharge that burden, he is accountable to the company for the difference between the price he paid for the shares and the highest market value which they have since attained.[2] If a director purchases his qualification shares from a promoter under an arrangement by which he may require the promoter to re-purchase them at the price paid, the director is guilty of breach of duty to the company, because he has deprived himself of the incentive to manage the company's affairs carefully which a share qualification is intended to give him, and if he does resell the shares to the promoter, he is accountable to the company for the price he receives.[3]

In all the foregoing cases the abuse of the director's powers for his own benefit has been fairly obvious. But one is on less certain ground when seeking to discover how far a director is accountable to his company for profits earned by carrying on a business of his own in competition with the company. Prima facie he is not accountable, unless the terms of his service contract preclude him from competing, because competing with his company does not of itself amount to a breach of duty by a director.[4] But he is accountable if he uses the company's property or trade secrets,[4] or his knowledge of the company's customers,[5] or, possibly, any special skill acquired by him while engaged in the company's business,[6] in order to carry on his own rival concern. His duty not to use any special skill or knowledge of the company's affairs comes to an end, however, when he ceases to be a director of the company.[7]

If a director for his private profit anticipates a business opportunity which the company would otherwise have obtained, he is accountable for the profit he makes thereby.[8] Thus, where a company had received and carried out several orders for a customer, and the customer, at the directors' request, placed a further order with another company formed by them, although the first company was able to fulfil

---

19 *Madrid Bank v Pelly* (1969) LR 7 Eq 442; *Re British Provident Life and Guarantee Association, De Ruvigne's Case* (1877) 5 ChD 306; *Re Englefield Colliery Co* (1878) 8 ChD 388; *Nant-y-glo and Blaina Ironworks Co v Grave* (1878) 12 ChD 738; *Re Carriage Co-operative Supply Association Ltd* (1884) 27 ChD 322.
20 *Re Caerphilly Colliery Co, Pearson's Case* (1876) 4 ChD 222; *Eden v Ridsdale Rly Lamp and Lighting Co Ltd* (1889) 23 QBD 368; *Re London and South Western Canal Ltd* [1911] 1 Ch 346.
1 *Re Carriage Co-operative Supply Association Ltd*, supra.
2 *Re West Jewell Tin Mining Co, Weston's Case* (1879) 10 Ch 579.
3 *Re North Australian Territory Co, Archer's Case* [1892] 1 Ch 322.
4 *Bell v Lever Bros Ltd* [1932] AC 161, [1931] All ER Rep 1; *London and Mashonaland Exploration Co v New Mashonaland Exploration Co* [1891] WN 165.
5 *Measures Bros Ltd v Measures* [1910] 2 Ch 248.
6 *Hivac Ltd v Park Royal Scientific Instruments Ltd* [1946] Ch 169, [1946] 1 All ER 350 (a case of an ordinary employee).
7 *Nordisk Insulinlaboratorium v Gorgate Products Ltd (sued as C L Bencard (1934) Ltd)* [1953] Ch 430, [1953] 1 All ER 986.
8 *Cook v Deeks* [1916] 1 AC 554; *Fine Industrial Commodities Ltd v Powling* (1954) 71 RPC 253; *Thomas Marshall (Exporters) Ltd v Guinle* [1979] Ch 227, [1978] 3 All ER 193.

the order, it was held that the directors and the other company were accountable for the profits which they obtained by executing the order.[9] The same result follows if a director solicits orders from his company's customers for the benefit of a competing company in which he is interested, or obtains supplies for the competing company from the first company's regular suppliers over whom he has acquired influence as a result of his directorship.[10] Similarly, where a company was unable to continue the manufacture of a product, but its plant was suitable for manufacturing an alternative product, it was held that a director who devised an invention which would enable the transformation to be carried out and patented it personally, thereby made himself a trustee of the patent for the company.[11]

Even if a director does not forestall a business opportunity which his company could have exploited, he is accountable for any profit he obtains in consequence of putting himself in a position where his duty to promote the company's affairs and to protect its interests conflicts with his private interests, and this is so even though the company suffers no damage by his conduct. An example of such a situation is where a director obtains a profit by making a contract which the company is legally incapable of making or which it is prohibited from entering into, such as dealing in its own shares.[12] Other examples are where the company lacks the resources to engage in the transaction,[13] where the other party would not in any event have transacted the business in question with the company because of his objection to its character,[14] and, probably, where the company would not have entered into the transaction because of the opposition of a majority of its board.[15] Similarly, a director who negotiates the termination of his appointment in return for compensation paid by the company is guilty of a breach of fiduciary duty if he fails to disclose past breaches of his duties to the company, and the company may then recover the compensation if it is ignorant of those breaches.[16] Nevertheless, it has been held that a rejection of a business opportunity available to a company by its board of directors acting in good faith after full disclosure of relevant information about the opportunity in a director's possession, does make that director free to exploit the opportunity himself and to retain the resulting profit.[17]

It has not yet been decided by the courts whether a director is accountable to his company for profits he makes by dealing in shares or securities issued by it when he has inside information about its affairs or prospects which affects the value of the securities but is not available to investors generally. Such information may be considered as property of the company if it has been produced by the company or its employees[18] (eg preliminary profit figures or profit forecasts, revaluations of assets, schemes for the acquisition of other business undertakings); in any case, directors would appear to be under an equitable duty to the company not to make

9 Cook v Deeks, supra.
10 Thomas Marshall (Exporters) Ltd v Guinle, supra.
11 Fine Industrial Commodities Ltd v Powling, supra.
12 Parker v McKenna (1874) 10 Ch App 96 at 118 and 124, per Cairns and James, LJJ.
13 Regal (Hastings) Ltd v Gulliver (1942) [1967] 2 AC 134 at 153, 154, 158, 159, [1942] 1 All ER 378 at 382, 386, 391, 395, per Viscount Sankey, Lord Russell of Killowen and Lords Macmillan, Wright and Porter; contra Heyting v Dupont [1963] 3 All ER 97, [1963] 1 WLR 1192; affd [1964] 2 All ER 273, [1964] 1 WLR 843, CA.
14 Industrial Development Consultants Ltd v Cooley [1972] 2 All ER 162, [1972] 1 WLR 443.
15 Compare Boardman v Phipps [1967] 2 AC 46, [1966] 3 All ER 721, where the defendants were a trustee and the solicitor to the trustees.
16 Horcal Ltd v Gatland [1983] BCLC 60; affd [1984] BCLC 549.
17 Queensland Mines Ltd v Hudson (1978) 52 ALJR 399 (a decision of the Judicial Committee of the Privy Council); Peso Silver Mines Ltd v Cropper (1966) 58 DLR (2d) 1.
18 Boardman v Phipps [1967] 2 AC 46, [1966] 3 All ER 721. Lord Cohen, however, considered that information cannot be treated as property, ([1972] AC 102–103, [1966] 3 All ER 743).

use of information generated by the company or its employees if they do so for the benefit of themselves or anyone other than the company.[19] Consequently, a director who uses such information to make a profit by dealing in securities issued by the company or any other company to which the information relates, would appear to be accountable to his own company for the amount of the profit. Furthermore, it would seem that the director would be liable in damages to the company for any loss it suffered in consequence of his acts, which would appear to be in breach of his implied obligations under his service contract, or at least negligence in causing the company loss which he should have foreseen.

If a director uses information which he has obtained as a result of his position, or in the course of carrying out his functions, for the purpose of dealing in the shares, debentures or other loan securities of his company, or possibly of any other company, and that information is not generally available to investors, or in the case of a company with a listing on the Stock Exchange, has not been communicated to the Stock Exchange and made available to its members, it would appear that the company may require the director to account to it for any profit he thereby obtains, and it is immaterial that the company could not have engaged in the transaction itself.[20] The liability of the director to account may be based on the fact that the information was given to him confidentially, so that he is under an equitable obligation to use it exclusively for the company's own benefit,[1] or on the treatment of the information as property of the company which the director misappropriates by using it for his own personal advantage;[18] or on the wider fiduciary duty of the director not to allow the company's interests and his own to conflict, and to account to the company for an advantage he obtains by using his powers or position to make a personal profit.[2] It is doubtful whether a similar obligation is imposed on a director to account for a profit made by another person dealing in the company's securities if the director has improperly communicated unpublished information about the company's affairs to that person, and he has used it to his own advantage; nevertheless, in such a case it would appear that the director commits a breach of an implied term of his contract of service with the company or of his duty to exercise care to protect its interests, and that he is liable to it in damages for any loss it suffered in consequence.[3]

It is uncertain whether a director is accountable for profits obtained after his retirement from the board. Since his fiduciary duties come to an end on the termination of his directorship[4] otherwise than as a result of the director's breach of his service contract,[5] it would seem that he is guilty of no breach of duty to the company, even though he obtains the profit by reason of his past association with the company, and he is therefore not accountable to it. However, if a director is

19 *Exchange Telegraph Ltd v Central News Agency Ltd* [1897] 2 Ch 48; *Terrapin Ltd v Builders' Supply Co (Hayes) Ltd* [1960] RPC 128.
20 *Parker v McKenna* (1874) 10 Ch App 96 at 118 and 124, per Cairns and James LJJ; *Canada Safeway Ltd v Thomson* [1951] 3 DLR 295.
1 *Fine Industrial Commodities Ltd v Powling* (1954) 71 RPC 253; *Cranleigh Precision Engineering Co Ltd v Bryant* [1964] 3 All ER 289, [1965] 1 WLR 1293; *Thomas Marshall (Exporters) Ltd v Guinle* [1979] Ch 227, [1978] 3 All ER 193.
2 This is the basis on which companies have been held entitled to recover 'insider dealing' profits from directors in the United States and Canada (*Diamond v Oreamuno* (1969) 24 NY 2d 494; *Zwicker v Stanbury* [1953] 2 SCR 438).
3 *Saltman Engineering Co Ltd v Campbell Engineering Co Ltd* (1948) [1963] 3 All ER 413n, 65 RPC 203; *Terrapin Ltd v Builders Supply Co (Hayes) Ltd* [1960] RPC 128. If the third person was aware that the information was confidential, the company may also recover damages from him (*B O Morris Ltd v F Gilman (BST) Ltd* (1943) 60 RPC 20).
4 *Nordisk Insulinlaboratorium v Gorgate Products Ltd (sued as C L Bencard (1934) Ltd)* [1953] Ch 430, [1953] 1 All ER 986.
5 *Thomas Marshall (Exporters) Ltd v Guinle*, supra.

guilty of a breach of fiduciary duty while an officer of the company, and completes the transaction by which he makes a profit after resigning by doing further acts which would amount to breaches of fiduciary duties if he were still a director, the company may recover the whole profit from him.[6] Thus, a director who had developed an invention on the company's behalf, but had discovered the existence of a patent which might prevent his company from exploiting the development, was held accountable to his company when he resigned his directorship, obtained an exclusive licence under the patent from the patentee, and formed a new company to manufacture the patented product with the development added to it.[7] His breach of fiduciary duty while still a director lay in his failure to reveal the discovery of the existence of the patent to the company and to use his best efforts to obtain a licence under it for the company's benefit. Similarly, a former director is accountable if he makes false representations to his company to obtain its agreement to terminate his directorship, when his purpose in doing so is to obtain a profit or advantage from a transaction he has planned in advance, when he would have been accountable for that profit if he had remained a director, and he in fact obtains the profit after the termination of his directorship.[8] On the other hand, a former director is not liable to account to a company on whose board he served if, after ceasing to be a director, he exploits a business opportunity offered by a customer of the company who has not previously offered the opportunity to the company and the company has not sought to obtain it, nor is the former director accountable merely because he learned of the existence and likely future needs of the customer while he was a director.[9]

A company may consent to its director retaining a personal profit for which he would otherwise be accountable. But consent may not be given on its behalf by the board of directors, because the profit is deemed to be the property of the company,[10] and the board may not make gifts of the company's property to its directors.[11] The consent can only be given by the members of the company unanimously or by the members passing an ordinary resolution in general meeting after the director has made a full disclosure of the nature and amount of his personal profit in the notice calling the meeting or otherwise.[12] If the director controls the voting at the meeting of members because he holds a majority of the shares carrying voting rights,[13] or because he can direct how the votes in respect of those shares shall be given,[14] a resolution authorising him to retain the profit passed in consequence of votes cast or controlled by him is void, and he can still be required to account to the company. It is an open question whether in such a situation the director may retain the profit if he does not vote at the general meeting, and the resolution is passed by a majority of the votes cast by the other shareholders.[15]

The right to recover a profit improperly made by a director belongs to the company, and not to its shareholders, at the time the profit was made or at the time

---

6 *Cranleigh Precision Engineering Ltd v Bryant* [1964] 3 All ER 289, [1965] 1 WLR 1293; *Industrial Development Consultants Ltd v Cooley* [1972] 2 All ER 162, [1972] 1 WLR 443; *Canadian Aero Service v O'Malley* (1973) 40 DLR (3d) 371.

7 *Cranleigh Precision Engineering Ltd v Bryant*, supra.

8 *Industrial Development Consultants Ltd v Cooley*, supra.

9 *Island Export Finance Ltd v Umunna* [1986] BCLC 460.

10 *Cook v Deeks* [1916] 1 AC 554 at 563–4.

11 *Re George Newman & Co* [1895] 1 Ch 674.

12 *Kaye v Croydon Tramways Co* [1898] 1 Ch 358; *Tiessen v Henderson* [1899] 1 Ch 861; *Regal (Hastings) Ltd v Gulliver* (1942) [1967] 2 AC 134n at 150, [1942] 1 All ER 378 at 389, per Lord Russell of Killowen.

13 *Cook v Deeks* [1916] 1 AC 554.

14 *Pavlides v Jensen* [1956] Ch 565, [1956] 2 All ER 518.

15 See pp 661 and 664, post.

the action is brought. Consequently, it has been held that a company is not prevented from recovering a profit made by its directors selling shares in the company or an associated company for which they had improperly subscribed, merely because the persons who now control the company bought those shares from the directors at a price which they knew was higher than the issue price paid by the directors, thereby impliedly consenting, as individuals, to the retention of the profit by the directors.[16] It would be more just in such a case to permit the persons who have suffered a financial loss as the result of the directors' breach of duty (in the present instance the other shareholders at the time the directors improperly obtained the shares) to recover a pro rata share of the profit in proportion to their individual holdings, but as the law stands at present, they cannot do this, because the directors owe no duties to them individually.[17]

Abuse of powers

Directors' powers are given to them to be used for the benefit of the company, that is, for the benefit of the shareholders as a whole,[18] and not for the benefit of the directors themselves, nor for the benefit exclusively of a section of the shareholders or employees of the company,[19] nor for the benefit of the company's parent or holding company or the company's subsidiary,[20] or of outsiders. It has been held in Australia that this is so even if the directors in question are nominated by outsiders (such as debenture holders or trustees for them),[1] or by a particular shareholder or group of shareholders (such as a parent or holding company)[2] to represent their interests, but of course, it does not follow that in protecting those interests a nominated director is guilty of a breach of duty to the company, unless at the same time he disregards the interests of its shareholders as a whole. The interests of the shareholders as a whole, to which the directors must have regard,[18] normally means the collective interests of both present and prospective shareholders, but if a takeover bid is made for a company, the interests of the shareholders which the directors must protect in supporting or opposing the bid are those of the present shareholders, and not those of the person who has made the bid as a prospective shareholder if the bid succeeds.[3]

All the cases where directors have abused their powers in order to make a personal profit for themselves may be brought under this present rule, but the rule is wider than the one relating to personal profits, and renders directors liable to compensate their company for loss caused to it in circumstances where they have enjoyed no corresponding gain at its expense. Thus, directors are guilty of an abuse of their powers if they issue new shares to themselves or their nominees, not because the company needs further capital or because they seek to gain some business advantage for the company,[4] but simply in order to gain or retain voting control

---

16 *Regal (Hastings) Ltd v Gulliver* (1942) [1967] 2 AC 134n, [1942] 1 All ER 378.
17 See p 607, post.
18 Nevertheless, the directors must have regard to the interests of the employees of the company generally (see p 584, ante).
19 *Parke v Daily News Ltd* [1962] Ch 927, [1962] 2 All ER 929.
20 *Charterbridge Corpn Ltd v Lloyds Bank Ltd* [1970] Ch 62, [1969] 2 All ER 1185. But this may not be so if the company is a wholly owned subsidiary of the holding company.
1 *Levin v Clarke* [1962] NSWR 686.
2 *Re Broadcasting Station 2 GB (Proprietary) Ltd* [1964–5] NSWR 1648.
3 *Heron International Ltd v Lord Grade and Associated Communications Corpn plc* [1983] BCLC 244; *Re a Company* [1986] BCLC 382.
4 It has been held in Australia that it is legitimate for directors to issue shares to a major international company in order to obtain its interest and protection (*Harlowe's Nominees Pty Ltd v Woodside (Lake Entrance) Oil Co* (1968) 121 CLR 483). It has also been held in Canada that it is legitimate for directors to issue shares to a company engaged in the same kind of business activities as itself in order

in general meetings of the company,[5] or to deprive a shareholder or group of shareholders who hold a majority of the votes at a general meeting of the control over the company which they have,[6] or to defeat a genuine takeover bid made by an outsider,[7] or to favour one of two competing takeover bids made by existing shareholders or outsiders.[6] It is also an abuse of directors' powers for them to approve a transfer of their own partly paid shares in order to escape liability for a call which they intend to make,[8] or for them to pay up the amount unpaid on their shares in advance of calls at a time when the company is insolvent in order to use the amount they pay up to satisfy arrears of salary which the company owes them,[9] or for them to negotiate a new service agreement between the company and its managing director simply in order to confer additional benefits on him or his dependants.[10] It is a serious breach of duty for directors to abdicate their powers of managing the company's affairs by appointing a manager with full powers to run the company's business free from any control or supervision by them,[11] or by obeying the directions of the majority shareholders of the company implicitly without exercising their own discretion.[12] It follows that it may be a breach of duty for directors of a company habitually to conform to the instructions or directions of a person who is a shadow director of the company,[13] and it would appear to be no defence that the shadow director is able to remove them from office if they do not conform. However, directors of a wholly-owned subsidiary company or of a company all of whose shares are held by persons who also hold all the issued capital of other companies, are not guilty of abusing their powers if they cause the first company to enter into a transaction for the benefit of one or all of the other companies which are in the same group or subject to control by the same persons, provided that the purpose of the transaction is also to confer a real and substantial benefit on the first company.[14] On the other hand, it is an abuse of power for directors of a subsidiary to use their powers exclusively in the interest of its parent or holding company and to the detriment of the minority shareholders of the subsidiary.[15]

It does not inevitably follow because directors benefit from the exercise of their powers that they have abused them. Thus, where directors had a valuation of the company's property prepared by an eminent surveyor in order to increase public confidence in the company's prospects and thereby enable it to raise further capital on favourable terms, it was held that they were not accountable for a profit which

to prevent its majority shareholder, a conglomerate concern, from disposing of the company's fixed assets and closing its business down (*Teck Corpn Ltd v Millar* (1972) 33 DLR (3d) 288). Both these decisions were approved by the Judicial Committee of the Privy Council in *Howard Smith Ltd v Ampol Petroleum Ltd* [1974] AC 821, [1974] 1 All ER 1126.

5 *Fraser v Whalley* (1864) 2 Hem & M 10; *Piercy v S Mills & Co* [1920] 1 Ch 77; *Re Jermyn Street Turkish Baths Ltd* [1970] 3 All ER 57, [1970] 1 WLR 1194.
6 *Howard Smith Ltd v Ampol Petroleum Ltd* [1974] AC 821, [1974] 1 All ER 1126; *Heron International Ltd v Lord Grade*, supra.
7 *Hogg v Cramphorn Ltd* [1967] Ch 254, [1966] 3 All ER 420; *Bamford v Bamford* [1970] Ch 212, [1969] 1 All ER 969.
8 *Re National and Provincial Marine Insurance Co, Gilbert's Case* (1870) 5 Ch App 599.
9 *Re European Central Rly Co, Sykes' Case* (1872) LR 13 Eq 255.
10 *Re W and M Roith Ltd* [1967] 1 All ER 427, [1967] 1 WLR 432.
11 *Horn v Henry Faulder & Co Ltd* (1908) 99 LR 524.
12 *Clark v Workman* [1920] 1 IR 107; *Scottish Co-operative Wholesale Society Ltd v Meyer* [1959] AC 324 at 363, [1958] 3 All ER 66 at 86, per Lord Keith of Avonholm; *Selangor United Rubber Estates Ltd v Cradock (No 3)* [1968] 2 All ER 1073 at 1095, [1968] 1 WLR 1555 at 1585.
13 For shadow directors, see p 531, ante.
14 *Charterbridge Corpn Ltd v Lloyds Bank Ltd* [1970] Ch 62, [1969] 2 All ER 1185.
15 *Scottish Co-operative Wholesale Society Ltd v Meyer* [1959] AC 324, [1958] 3 All ER 66 (see p 675 et seq, post).

they obtained by selling some of their own shares at an enhanced price when the market responded favourably to the valuation.[16] The directors did not have the valuation prepared in order to make a profit by selling their own shares, which would have been an abuse of their powers; they had it prepared to enable the company to raise further capital, and the mere fact that they obtained a personal advantage in consequence did not turn the exercise of their power into abuse of it. The court said:[17]

'If the true effect of the whole evidence is that the defendants truly and reasonably believed at the time that what they did was for the interest of the company, they are not chargeable with dolus malus or breach of trust merely because in promoting the interest of the company they were promoting their own, or because they afterwards sold shares at prices which gave them large profits.'

When directors seek to achieve two or more purposes by exercising their powers, and some of those purposes are proper and others are not, it seems that the exercise of their powers is valid so as to bind the company, unless the proper purposes are a mere sham or pretext for the improper ones.[18] But in such a case it would seem that the directors must account for any personal profit which they obtain,[19] although they would not appear to be liable to compensate the company for any loss it suffers. The accountability of directors for profits obtained by the use of their powers primarily for a proper purpose will be particularly important if the courts hold that directors are accountable for using inside information not available to investors generally to deal in shares or securities of the company.[20] In that case it will be no defence for a director to show that the information was withheld from the public generally in order to protect the company's interests, or that the information was actually used to the company's advantage (eg to exploit a profitable business opportunity). However, it has been held that, notwithstanding a director's liability to account for a profit obtained as a result of exercising or concurring in the exercise of the board's powers for purposes which are wholly or partly improper, a director does not breach his fiduciary duties by concurring in a decision of the board which is intended in part to benefit his fellow directors, if his own purpose in doing so is to promote the interests of the company.[1]

Even if directors do use their powers impartially, so that no section of the members are given a special advantage or subjected to a peculiar disadvantage, the exercise of their powers is invalid if they do not use them for the purposes contemplated by the memorandum or articles. Thus, where directors had power to refuse to register transfers of shares if 'in their opinion it is contrary to the interests of the company that the transferee should be a member thereof',[2] or if they disapproved of the transferee,[3] it was held that they could refuse registration only if they had some personal objection to the transferee, and not if they merely thought that the transferee was a nominee of the transferor and that the transfer was made in order to increase the transferor's voting power in general meetings. In a similar

---

16 *Hirsche v Sims* [1894] AC 654.
17 Ibid, at 660.
18 Compare the local government case of *R v Brighton Corpn, ex p Shoosmith* (1907) 96 LT 762 at 765, per Buckley LJ.
19 *Albion Steel and Wire Co v Martin* (1875) 1 ChD 580 (where a director was held accountable for a profit made by selling his own goods to the company, even though the company knew he was the seller and the goods were necessary to establish the company in business).
20 See p 588, ante.
1 *Jackson v Invicta Plastics Ltd* [1987] BCLC 329 at 344.
2 *Re Bede Steam Shipping Co Ltd* [1917] 1 Ch 123.
3 *Moffat v Farquhar* (1878) 7 ChD 591.

case[4] the approval of a transfer of shares by the directors was held invalid when they exacted a payment to the company from the transferor for their approval; it was held that the directors' duty was to approve transfers only if the transferees were suitable persons to become members of the company, and not to use their power of refusal as a means of augmenting the company's funds. Again, if directors have power to pay brokerage on a placing of the company's shares, they may use it only to reward services genuinely performed for the company, and not to make payments to brokers who demand a commission before giving the names of clients who have all along been willing to invest in the company.[5]

One of the most informative rulings on the invalidity of the exercise of directors' powers when used for improper purposes is contained in the report of Mr E Milner Holland, QC (as he then was), acting as an inspector appointed by the Board of Trade to investigate the affairs of Savoy Hotel Ltd.[6] In that case the directors of Savoy Hotel Ltd knew that certain persons were seeking to acquire sufficient shares in the company to give them control of it so that they might compel the board to convert a hotel owned by one of Savoy's subsidiaries into offices. The conversion would undoubtedly have yielded a greater profit to Savoy's subsidiary, and therefore to Savoy, than the continued use of the premises as a hotel, but Savoy's directors considered that the retention of the hotel was in the best interests of the company, and they devised a scheme by which it was made impossible for the controlling shareholders of Savoy to carry out the conversion. A new company was formed with a share capital consisting of £640,000 in preference shares and £10,000 in ordinary shares which carried most of the voting rights in general meeting. Savoy's subsidiary sold the hotel to this new company in exchange for the preference shares, and the ordinary shares were subscribed for in cash by the trustees of a benevolent fund for Savoy's employees. Savoy's directors knew that the trustees could be relied on to fall in with their wishes in exercising the majority voting rights conferred by the ordinary shares. The new company then leased the hotel back to Savoy's subsidiary, but subject to a covenant that it should be used only as a hotel. It thus became impossible for a controlling shareholder of Savoy to compel its directors to convert the hotel into offices, even if an entirely new board were installed in office.

Mr Milner Holland observed that the transaction was not carried out for the personal benefit of Savoy's directors, or to perpetuate them in office. Then, after stating the effect of the transaction, he said:[7]

'... but by no action on their part could the stockholders [of Savoy] ever thereafter alter the decision of their present Board as to the present or future use of the property of the company. The exercise of the directors' powers was therefore used in order to render irrevocable for all time the policy view of the present board. In my opinion, such a use of directors' powers is in principle not distinguishable from an issue of shares to affect voting power, and, however proper the motive behind it, it is not a purpose for which those powers were conferred on the board. Powers conferred by the shareholders on directors for the purpose of managing the business of the company cannot be used for the purpose of depriving those shareholders of such control as under the regulations of the company they may have over the company's assets.'

This ruling was a welcome re-assertion that the powers given to shareholders by

4 *Re Cameron's Coalbrook Steam Coal and Swansea and Lougher Rly Co, Bennett's Case* (1854) 5 De GM & G 284.
5 *Re Faure Electric Accumulator Co* (1888) 40 ChD 141, as explained in *Metropolitan Coal Consumers' Association v Scrimgeour* [1895] 2 QB 604 at 609.
6 The Savoy Hotel Ltd, and the Berkeley Hotel Co Ltd; Investigation under s 165 (6) of the Companies Act 1948, HM Stationery Office, 1954.
7 Ibid, para 17.

the articles, limited as they often are, cannot be taken away indirectly by the misuse of the board's managerial powers, and that the criterion for testing the propriety of directors' acts, namely, whether they are for the benefit of the company, does not depend on the directors' own views of what will be best for it, but on whether those acts are designed to achieve the objects which the shareholders constitutionally decide the company shall pursue.

If directors abuse their powers, the company may treat the resulting transaction as void, even though this may prejudice an innocent third party.[8] But if the third party gives valuable consideration, such as a loan to the company[9] or abstaining from insisting on payment of a debt of the company which is immediately due and payable,[10] the company can set the transaction aside only if the third party was aware that the directors were abusing their powers, or that they intended to achieve an improper purpose by means of the transaction. If the directors have entered into service contracts, they impliedly contract not to abuse their powers, and the company may sue them for damages for any loss which it suffers in consequence of such an abuse.[11] Probably a company may compel its directors to make good such loss even though they have no service contracts, on the ground that they are under a duty to the company to take proper care to prevent the company suffering loss. Alternatively, the company could rely on the implied contract with its directors which arises from them serving as such, and undoubtedly the same term prohibiting the abuse of their powers would be implied in that contract as in an express service contract. On the other hand, as has already been shown,[12] a general meeting of the company may ratify directors' acts despite an abuse of their powers, and in the absence of fraud the resulting transaction is thereby validated and the directors are absolved from liability to the company, whether for breach of contract or of their fiduciary duties or for negligence.[13]

Option dealings by directors

Directors are prohibited from buying options to acquire or dispose of a specified number of shares, debentures or other loan securities for cash or any other consideration, if the shares or securities are listed on a stock exchange in Great Britain or elsewhere and were issued by the company of which they are directors, or by any of its subsidiaries, or by its parent or holding company, or by any subsidiary of its parent or holding company.[14] The prohibition extends to 'two way' options under which the director may either purchase or sell a specified number of securities, and it would seem that the prohibition applies whether the director acquires an original option created by the person who grants it to him, or whether he buys an option which already exists from a person who is not a director. The prohibition on the acquisition of options by directors means that this particular

---

8 *Re Cameron's Coalbrook Steam Coal and Swansea and Lougher Rly Co, Bennett's Case* (1854) 5 De GM & G 284 (where the directors' approval of the transfer of partly paid shares was held void, and the transferor remained liable for future calls): *Re W & M Roith Ltd* [1967] 1 All ER 427, [1967] 1 WLR 432 (executors of a deceased director were held not entitled to recover a pension provided for his dependants by a service contract not entered into for the benefit of the company). But innocent third parties dealing with the directors may be protected by the rule in *Royal British Bank v Turquand* (see Chapter 5).

9 *Re David Payne & Co Ltd* [1904] 2 Ch 608.

10 *Charterbridge Corpn Ltd v Lloyds Bank Ltd* [1970] Ch 62, [1969] 2 All ER 1185; *Rolled Steel Products (Holdings) Ltd v British Steel Corpn* [1986] Ch 246, [1984] BCLC 466.

11 *Benson v Heathorn* (1842) 1 Y & C Ch Cas 326.

12 See p 579, ante.

13 *Hogg v Cramphorn Ltd* [1967] Ch 254, [1966] 3 All ER 420; *Bamford v Bamford* [1970] Ch 212, [1969] 1 All ER 969.

14 Companies Act 1985, s 323 (1) and (3).

form of speculation on future rises or falls in the market value of a company's securities is closed to directors, but there is no prohibition on a company granting options to its directors to subscribe for shares, debentures or other loan securities or on directors purchasing rights to subscribe for shares or other loan securities, or purchasing debentures or other loan securities carrying conversion or subscription rights, when the company has issued the subscription rights, debentures or other securities to other persons.[15] The spouse or minor child of a director is similarly prohibited from buying options to acquire or dispose of shares, debentures or other loan securities which the director himself would be prohibited from buying, subject to the same exceptions as apply to purchases by the director; however, it is a defence for the spouse or child to prove that he or she had no reason to believe that his or her spouse or parent was a director of the company in question.[16]

A contravention of the foregoing prohibitions is a criminal offence.[17] An option contract or a contract for the purchase of an option which a director is prohibited from entering into is not expressly made void by statute, but it would seem that it is void because of the illegality it involves, although it would also appear that the other party could sue for the price the director agreed to pay for the option if the other party was unaware of the illegality when the option contract was made. If the Secretary of State for Trade and Industry suspects that a director has engaged in a prohibited option transaction, he may appoint an inspector or inspectors to investigate the matter and to report,[18] and he has the same powers to compel testimony as an inspector appointed to enquire into mismanagement of the company's affairs.[19]

Contracts, transactions and arrangements with directors

Every director who has a direct or indirect interest in a contract or proposed contract with his company, or in a transaction or arrangement entered into or proposed to be entered into by it, must disclose his interest at the board meeting at which the contract, transaction or arrangement is first considered, or if his interest does not arise until after that time, at the first board meeting after his interest does arise.[20] This applies also to a loan, quasi-loan or credit transaction made or to be made by the company for the benefit of a director or a person connected with him,[1] whether the transaction is prohibited or not.[2] If the director is interested as a member of another company or firm in contracts and transactions between that company or firm and the company of which he is a director, he may give a general notice[3] to his fellow directors that he is interested in all such contracts and transactions, and he need not then disclose his interest each time such a contract or transaction is proposed.[4] Similarly a director may give such a general notice that he is connected with a named person and is to be regarded as interested in all contracts made with him.[4] A director who fails to make proper disclosure of his

---

15 Companies Act 1985, s 323 (5).
16 Ibid, s 327 (1) and (2).
17 Ibid, s 323 (1) and (2).
18 Ibid, s 446 (1).
19 Ibid, s 446 (3), as amended by Financial Services Act 1986, s 182 and Sch 13, para 8 (see p 688, post).
20 Ibid, s 317 (1) and (2).
1 For the definition of a person connected with a director, see p 565, ante.
2 Companies Act 1985, s 317 (6).
3 If the notice is not given at a board meeting, it must be in writing and must be read out at the next board meeting.
4 Companies Act 1985, s 317 (3) and (4).

interests is liable to a fine,[5] but the contract in which he is interested is not thereby avoided.[6] Nevertheless, in equity the failure to make disclosure under the statutory requirements or under an equivalent provision in the company's articles entitles the company to rescind the contract, transaction or arrangement, notwithstanding a provision in the company's articles that such contracts etc shall be valid and binding on the company.[6] Upon the company rescinding the contract, the director must restore to the company any money or benefits which he has received under it, and he cannot set off against the money which he must restore the amount of a cross-claim which he has against the company for the value of services or benefits which he has given under the contract.[7] The board of directors cannot delegate its statutory function of receiving notification of directors' interests to a committee comprising some but not all of the directors, or to any officers or agents of the company, and notification given by a director to such a committee or to such persons is ineffective.[7]

Because of his fiduciary relationship, a contract made by a director with his company is voidable by it in equity even though the director makes proper disclosure of his interest to the board of directors.[8] This applies not only to contracts made in the course of carrying on the company's business, but also to contracts by a director to subscribe for shares[9] or debentures[10] of the company, or to take remunerated employment under it.[11] Furthermore, if a director is indirectly interested in a contract because it is made between his company and another company of which he is a director or member, the contract is voidable by the first company, unless the second company is unaware of the director's interest when the contract is entered into.[12] The second company should nowadays always be aware of an interest arising from common directorships, because its register of directors and secretaries should show what other directorships its own directors hold,[13] but there is no similar means by which it will automatically have notice of an interest arising from one of its members being a director of the first company.

Except where the approval of the contract by a general meeting is required by the Companies Act 1985,[14] the right of a company to rescind a contract in which one or more of its directors are interested may be waived either by the provisions of the company's articles or, in relation to a particular contract, by the members in general meeting, but it cannot be waived by the board of directors.[15] Modern articles usually follow the pattern of Table A[16] and waive the right of rescission to some extent by permitting directors to hold other remunerated offices under the company and other companies in which the company is interested, to enter into binding contracts, transactions and arrangements with the company and such other companies, to be interested in contracts, transactions or arrangements entered

---

5 Ibid, s 317 (7).
6 *Hely-Hutchinson v Brayhead Ltd* [1968] 1 QB 549, [1967] 3 All ER 98, *Movitex Ltd v Bulfield* [1988] BCLC 104; *Guinness plc v Saunders* [1990] 1 All ER 652 at 665, [1990] 2 WLR 324 at 339 per Lord Goff of Chievely.
7 *Guinness plc v Saunders* [1988] 2 All ER 940, [1988] BCLC 607; affd [1990] 1 All ER 652, [1990] 2 WLR 324.
8 *Aberdeen Rly Co v Blaikie Bros* (1854) 1 Macq 461.
9 *Neal v Quinn* [1916] WN 223.
10 *Re North Eastern Insurance Co* [1919] 1 Ch 198.
11 *Benson v Heathorn*, supra.
12 *Transvaal Lands Co v New Belgium (Transvaal) Land and Development Co* [1914] 2 Ch 488.
13 Companies Act 1985, s 289 (1), (see p 553, ante).
14 Ibid, s 320 (1) and (2) (see p 599, post).
15 *Re Cardiff Preserved Coke and Coal Co* (1862) 32 LJ Ch 154; *North West Transportation Co Ltd and Beatty v Beatty* (1887) 12 App Cas 589 at 600.
16 Table A, arts 84 and 85.

into between the company and any other companies or persons, and by permitting directors to retain any profit obtained by reason of such contracts. Such general permission given by a company's articles is generally subject to the condition that the director has properly disclosed the nature and extent of his interest to the company's board of directors, but disclosure is usually dispensed with if the director has no knowledge of the interest in question and it is not reasonable to expect him to have such knowledge, and directors are empowered to give a general notice of the nature and extent of their interests in any transactions or arrangements in which specified persons are interested.[17] It has been held that a director may be interested in a contract with his company and retain any profit obtained by him thereby, if the articles merely provide that he shall not vacate office as a director because of such an interest, or that he may vote at board meetings on matters in which he is interested.[18] It is difficult to see why a company should, by forgoing such restrictions on its director's activities, be taken to have waived his fiduciary duties toward it. If the company wishes to waive the director's duty to account, it is far more satisfactory for its articles to do so in the explicit language of Table A.

Even if the articles expressly allow directors to be interested in contracts with the company and to retain profits made thereby, it does not follow that they are absolved from their duty to act primarily in the company's interests in entering into such contracts. Consequently, it would seem that if an interested director fails to disclose information in his possession which might influence an impartial board in deciding whether to enter into the contract, or if the contract is clearly unfair or results in the interested director or another company with which he is connected making a much larger profit than his fellow directors had reason to expect, the company may still rescind the contract on the ground that the interested director had abused his position.[19]

If the articles do not waive the company's right to rescission, the members may do so by an ordinary resolution passed in general meeting. The notice calling the meeting must set out the director's interest clearly so that every member may see what profit he will obtain.[20] If the director is a member of the company himself, he may vote in favour of approving the contract at the general meeting, even though he or his nominees control a majority of the votes which may be cast.[1] This is different from the situation where the director obtains a profit in breach of his duty to the company, when a resolution that he may retain it cannot be procured by his controlling vote.[2] It is no breach of duty for a director to enter into a fair contract with his company,[3] and it is therefore not oppressive of the other members that he should be allowed to vote in favour of ratifying the contract. But regard must nevertheless be had to the purpose of the contract. If the contract is for the sale to the company of property which the director acquired on its behalf or in breach of duty toward it, the contract amounts to nothing more than a waiver of the company's right to make the director account for a profit improperly obtained by

---

17 Table A, arts 85 and 86.
18 *Costa Rica Rly Co Ltd v Forwood* [1901] 1 Ch 746.
19 For the comparable situation when a trustee contracts with his cestui que trust, see *Dougan v Macpherson* [1902] AC 197. In the American case of *Globe Woolen Co v Utica Gas and Electric Co* (1918) 224 NY 483, a contract for the supply of electricity by the defendant company to the plaintiff company on terms that were prima facie fair was held to be voidable by the defendant company, because the contract was procured by a director of the plaintiff who was also a director of the defendant, and he failed to disclose to the defendant's board that the way in which it was intended to operate the plaintiff's business would result in the contract being very onerous to the defendant.
20 *Kaye v Croydon Tramways Co* [1898] 1 Ch 358; *Tiessen v Henderson* [1899] 1 Ch 861.
1 *North West Transportation Co Ltd and Beatty v Beatty* (1887) 12 App Cas 589.
2 *Cook v Deeks* [1916] 1 AC 554.
3 *Movitex Ltd v Bulfield* [1988] BCLC 104.

him, and the director cannot then procure a resolution ratifying the contract by the use of his controlling voting power as a member and so absolve himself from having to account for the profit he has made.[4]

A company may avoid a contract with its director only if it can restore to him what he has given under it, but the mere fact that the director has transferred property to the company will not prevent it from rescinding the contract if the property can be returned in substantially the same condition as when it was transferred.[5] If the director has not been guilty of a breach of duty resulting in him obtaining an improper profit, the company cannot waive its right to rescind and at the same time compel him to account for the profit he has obtained under the contract.[6] In that situation, the company's sole claim to the profit is as part of the process of restitution which follows on rescission of the contract, and if there is no rescission, there can be nothing for the director to restore.

Statutory approval of contracts and arrangements by general meetings

A company, whether public or private, may not enter into an arrangement (including a contract) by which a director or shadow director of the company or its parent or holding company or a person connected with him[7] acquires or is to acquire from, or transfers or is to transfer to, the company or its parent or holding company any assets (other than cash) in excess of a certain value, unless the arrangement is first approved by resolution of a general meeting, and if the arrangement is entered into with a director or shadow director of the company's parent or holding company, it must also be approved by a resolution of a general meeting of that company.[8] The approval of a general meeting is required under this provision only if the value of the assets in question exceeds 10 per cent of the net assets of the company as shown by its latest annual balance sheet laid before a general meeting, or if it has not yet laid such an annual balance sheet, 10 per cent of its called up share capital.[9] However, if the value of the assets exceeds £50,000, approval of the arrangement is required even though the assets do not equal 10 per cent of the company's net assets, and conversely if the value of the assets is less than £1,000, approval is not required even though the assets are worth more than 10 per cent of the company's net assets.[9] The requisite approval of a general meeting may be given by an ordinary resolution unless the articles otherwise provide.

Irrespective of the value of the non-cash assets involved, no approval by a general meeting is required when a parent or holding company acquires non-cash assets from its wholly-owned subsidiary, or when such a subsidiary acquires non-cash assets from its parent or holding company or from another wholly-owned subsidiary of the same parent or holding company; nor when the arrangement for the acquisition or disposal is entered into by a company which is in liquidation (other than a member's voluntary winding up); nor when a director or shadow director acquires an asset from a company of which he is a member, and does so in his capacity as such a member (eg on a distribution of a dividend by a company to

---

4 *Cook v Deeks*, supra, at 563 to 564.
5 *Transvaal Lands Co v New Belgium (Transvaal) Land and Development Co* [1914] 2 Ch 488; *Armstrong v Jackson* [1917] 2 KB 822.
6 *Burland v Earle* [1902] AC 83.
7 For the definition of a person connected with a director, see p 565, ante.
8 Companies Act 1985, s 320 (1) and (3).
9 Ibid, s 320 (2).

its members in the form of shares or securities held by the company in another company).[10]

If a company enters into an arrangement with a director or a shadow director, or with a person connected with a director or shadow director, without the requisite approval of a general meeting being first obtained, the company may rescind the arrangement and any acquisition or disposal of assets made under it, unless restitution of any money or asset which was the subject matter of the arrangement is no longer possible;[11] or unless the director or shadow director or the person connected with him with whom the arrangement was made has indemnified the company against any loss it has suffered in consequence of the arrangement; or unless a third person has acquired rights under the arrangement in good faith and for value without being aware that the requisite approval has not been obtained;[12] or unless the requisite approval is given by a general meeting of the company and of its parent or holding company (if the arrangement is entered into with a director or shadow director of that company or with a person connected with him) within a reasonable time after the arrangement is made.[13] A director or a shadow director, or a person connected with him, who enters into an arrangement for which approval is needed and is not obtained beforehand, is liable to account to the company for any gain which he has made from the arrangement being carried out, and is also liable to compensate the company for any consequential loss it has suffered.[14] These liabilities are also incurred vicariously by a director or shadow director if any person connected with him enters into the arrangement, and whether the arrangement is entered into by a director or shadow director, or by a person connected with him, liability is also incurred by all directors of the company who authorise the making or carrying out of the arrangement.[14] However, a director or shadow director who is connected with the person who entered into the arrangement with the company may escape liability by showing that he took all reasonable steps to ensure that the requisite approval of a general meeting was obtained, and the person who entered into the arrangement and any other director may escape liability by showing that he was unaware that that person was connected with any director or shadow director of the company.[15]

Negligence

A director, like any other agent, at common law owes a duty to his company to exercise reasonable care in the management and direction of its affairs, and he is liable to the company in damages if he fails to do so. But while the court has imposed stringent duties of honesty and fair dealing on directors in framing their equitable fiduciary duties, it has been at pains not to make their duty of care so onerous that men of ability would be deterred from serving as directors. Thus, in an early case Lord Hatherley LC said that directors would be liable only if:[16]

'. . . they were cognisant of circumstances of such a character, so plain, so manifest, and so simple of appreciation, that no men with any degree of prudence, acting on their own behalf, would have entered into such a transaction as they entered into.'

10 Ibid, s 321 (1) to (3).
11 For example, because the assets have been consumed, destroyed, disposed of or substantially altered, or the recipient of money has become insolvent.
12 For example, if a third person has purchased or contracted to purchase the assets or has advanced or agreed to advance money on the security of them.
13 Companies Act 1985, s 322 (1) and (2).
14 Companies Act 1985, s 322 (3).
15 Ibid, s 322 (5) and (6).
16 *Overend and Gurney Co v Gibb* (1872) LR 5 HL 480 at 487–8.

In another case Lindley MR said:[17]

'If directors act within their powers, if they act with such care as is reasonably to be expected of them, having regard to their knowledge and experience, and if they act honestly for the benefit of the company they represent, they discharge both their equitable as well as their legal duty to the company. . . . The amount of care to be taken is difficult to define; but it is plain that directors are not liable for all the mistakes they may make, although if they had taken more care they might have avoided them. . . . Their negligence must not be the omission to take all possible care; it must be much more blameable than that; it must be in a business sense culpable or gross.'

In view of the low standard of care which the court has exacted from directors, namely, the care which they would be expected to show if acting on their own behalf, it is not surprising that in most of the decided cases the defendant directors have been acquitted of negligence. Thus, directors have been held not liable for completing a purchase of a business without consulting the shareholders when they discovered that, despite its high reputation and good prospects, the liabilities of the business exceeded the value of its assets,[18] or that its assets did not conform to the contract description and the vendor had not rectified this state of affairs although called on to do so,[19] or that the company had been induced to buy the business by misrepresentations made by the vendor.[20].

Directors are not required to examine the company's accounting records, and may trust the managing director and the company's accountants or employees to keep them properly.[1] Consequently, it has been held that if the directors declare a dividend on the basis of a profit and loss account laid before them by the managing director,[2] or even in reliance on his verbal statement that sufficient profits have been earned,[3] they are not liable if the dividend is in fact paid out of the company's capital. This latter decision is questionable, however, in view of the statutory duty now imposed on directors to approve the company's balance sheet, profit and loss account and group accounts (if any) by a formal resolution passed at a board meeting.[4] If the management of the company's business is entrusted to a managing director, the other directors need not make sure that cheques put before them for signature are really required for purchasing assets for the company or paying the company's debts, nor need they see to it that the assets are in fact purchased or the debts paid, nor, if the assets purchased are investments, need they ensure that the relevant share certificates, debentures or loan stock certificates are placed in safe custody.[5] Again, if the board resolves to make a loan on certain security being given to the company, it has been held the directors are not liable if they make the loan without ensuring that the security is in fact given.[6] However, these decisions can apply only when the carrying out of the transaction is properly entrusted to a managing director or directors. If there is no managing director on whose assurances the other directors rely, all the directors are liable if they allow the company's funds to be used in paying a debt which the company does not owe, or in paying a purchase price for assets without making sure that the assets will be

---

17 *Lagunas Nitrate Co v Lagunas Syndicate* [1899] 2 Ch 392 at 435.
18 *Overend and Gurney Co v Gibb*, supra.
19 *Lagunas Nitrate Co v Lagunas Syndicate*, supra.
20 *Re Brazilian Rubber Plantations and Estates Ltd* [1911] 1 Ch 425.
1 *Dovey v Cory* [1901] AC 477; *Re City Equitable Fire Insurance Co Ltd* [1925] Ch 407.
2 *Re Denham & Co* (1883) 25 ChD 752; *Dovey v Cory* [1901] AC 477.
3 *Lucas v Fitzgerald* (1903) 20 TLR 16.
4 Companies Act 1985, s 233 (1), substituted by Companies Act 1989, s 7.
5 *Re City Equitable Fire Insurance Co Ltd* supra at 452–3, 470 and 475.
6 *Re New Mashonaland Exploration Co* [1892] 3 Ch 577.

transferred to the company,[7] or in making loans out of the company's funds without enquiring about the purposes for which they will be applied or ensuring that they are adequately secured.[8]

It has also been held that directors are negligent if they sign cheques without enquiring why the payment is being made,[9] and it is no excuse that had the defendant director made enquiry, he would have been given a plausible but false reason by his fellow directors, or would not have realised that the payment was improper.[10] Moreover, a director who objects to the propriety of a payment, but nevertheless signs a cheque for it, cannot escape liability by showing that a resolution for the payment was carried by the votes of a majority of the directors, and so the payment would have been made even if he had dissented.[11] Again, although a director may trust his fellow directors and the officers and employees of the company to perform their duties properly,[12] and is not responsible for the wrongful acts of his fellow directors at board meetings which he does not attend,[13] he must inform the members of the company of serious derelictions of duty by such persons when he discovers them, and he is guilty of negligence if he contents himself with a protest to his fellow directors.[14] It is also negligence for directors to allow one of their number to assume exclusive control of a part of the company's business without a proper resolution for the delegation of the board's powers to him being passed in accordance with the company's articles, and they will be liable for any loss caused by the defalcations of the director who thus usurps the board's functions.[15]

Many of the foregoing cases involved part-time directors, and often the loss complained of had been caused by the acts of a managing director to whom full powers of management had been properly committed. The court therefore acted fairly in not imposing too heavy a duty on the other directors, particularly when they were part-time, non-executive directors. But these decisions cannot form a reliable guide to the standard of care expected of full-time executive directors employed under service contracts, especially when they are each employed to manage some department of the company's business as well as to supervise its whole undertaking at board meetings. Such directors will usually be specialists in their own field, be it accountancy, engineering, marketing, finance or anything else, and they will be expected to exhibit the skill and care of a competent practitioner in that field when handling the company's affairs.[16] Whether specialists or not, full-time directors may also be under a positive duty to seize all business opportunities available to the company, even to the extent of abandoning its existing business and embarking on activities of a different character if they are intra vires and the prospects they offer are better.[17] Moreover, the service contracts of full-time executive directors will usually require them to devote their whole time and

7 *Selangor United Rubber Estates Ltd v Cradock (No 3)* [1968] 2 All ER 1073 at 1141, [1968] 1 WLR 1555 at 1644.
8 *Dorchester Finance Co Ltd v Stebbing* [1989] BCLC 498.
9 *Land Credit Co of Ireland v Lord Fermoy* (1869) LR 8 Eq 7; *Re City Equitable Fire Insurance Co*, supra, at 460; *Selangor United Rubber Estates Ltd v Cradock (No 3)*, supra, at 1095 and 1121–3; *Dorchester Finance Ltd v Stebbing*, supra.
10 *Joint Stock Discount Co v Brown* (1869) LR 8 Eq 381 at 405.
11 *Ramskill v Edwards* (1885) 31 ChD 100.
12 *Dovey v Cory* [1901] AC 477 per Lord Halsbury LC at 486 and Lord Davey at 492.
13 *Re Denham & Co* (1883) 25 ChD 752.
14 *Joint Stock Discount Co v Brown*, supra, at 403.
15 *Re City Equitable Fire Insurance Co*, supra, at 467–8.
16 *Re Brazilian Rubber Plantations and Estates Ltd* [1911] 1 Ch 425 at 437, per Neville J; *Jackson Invicta Plastics Ltd* [1987] BCLC 329 at 347 per Peter Pain J.
17 *Fine Industrial Commodities Ltd v Powling* (1954) 71 RPC 253 at 258, per Danckwerts J.

attention to the company's affairs, so that failure to attend board meetings over a long period will certainly be evidence of negligence, which it is not in the case of a part-time director.[18] Likewise, a neglect of the company's affair by a full-time director, whether a managing director or not, will be negligence on his part and will make him liable to the company for the consequent diminution in the value of its business. Probably a full-time executive director may trust the honesty and competence of his colleagues and subordinates outside the department which he manages, but it would be stretching credulity to imagine that he need not supervise the staff of his own department. The displacement of the part-time director by the full-time working director is one aspect of the managerial revolution of the last 50 years, and although the court has not been called on during that time to say whether the altered conditions have brought about a change in the law, it cannot now be assumed that all the old cases are a safe guide to the standard of skill and care required of all kinds of directors today.

Actions against directors

An action against a defaulting director may be brought by the company itself, or in certain circumstances, where the breach of duty complained of is a breach of fiduciary duty, by a member suing in a derivative action on behalf of himself and all other members of the company.[19] A director may also be made liable for a breach of fiduciary duty by misfeasance proceedings in the company's winding up.[20] Whatever the nature of the proceedings, however, they must be brought within six years after the breach of duty complained of,[1] unless the director has executed a service contract under seal, when he may be sued for a breach of that contract within twelve years,[2] or unless the director is guilty of fraud or has misappropriated the company's property, when there is no limit on the time within which he may be sued.[3]

No provision in a company's articles or in a director's contract of employment, or in a resolution passed by a board meeting or a general meeting or in any other form, may exempt a director from the fiduciary duties and duty of care imposed on him by law or from any liability for a breach of such duties, and this applies as much to a provision which purports to define the director's duties less onerously than the general law as to a provision which expressly exempts him from liability for breach of duty.[4] However, it would seem that an exempting provision is invalid only if it is to operate in the future, so that the director might be induced by it not to satisfy the standards of conscientiousness and care which the law exacts in the expectation that he will not be liable to the company if it does so; the statutory invalidation would not appear to affect a resolution passed by a general meeting relieving or releasing a director from liability for breaches of duty already committed which he has fully disclosed, because such a power to release is the necessary corollary of the general meeting's power to decide that no legal proceedings shall be brought against the director for such past breaches.[5]

18 *Re Denham & Co* (1883) 25 ChD 752.
19 See p 660, post.
20 Insolvency Act 1986, s 212 (1) and (3) (see p 683, post).
 1 If the breach of duty is a misapplication of the company's funds, the directors are treated as trustees (*Re Lands Allotment Co* [1894] 1 Ch 616), and must be sued within six years (Limitation Act 1980, s 21 (3) (24 Halsbury's Statutes (4th Edn) 672). The limitation period is the same if the director is charged with negligence or breach of contract (Limitation Act 1980, s 5).
 2 Limitation Act 1980, s 8 (1).
 3 Ibid, s 21 (1).
 4 Companies Act 1985, s 310 (1) and (2).
 5 See p 649, post.

If a director is sued for breach of any of his duties, he may apply to the court for relief from liability, and if the court is satisfied that he acted honestly and reasonably, and that in all the circumstances he ought fairly to be excused, it may relieve him from liability on such terms as it thinks fit.[6] This provision is identically worded to the provision in the Trustee Act 1925,[7] which enables the court to relieve defaulting trustees, and the court's jurisdiction will probably be exercised in the same way as under that Act. The court is reluctant to relieve remunerated trustees, and will only do so if they show that they have taken all reasonable steps to make good their breach of trust;[8] the same criterion has been applied when a defaulting liquidator sought relief,[9] and it would no doubt also be applied in the case of a director. On the other hand, the court can give relief, even though the director has used the company's money for ultra vires purposes,[10] and even though the members oppose relief being given.[11] Relief has also been given to a director who in accordance with established practice drew a monthly sum from the company in the expectation that it would be covered by remuneration voted to him at the next annual general meeting, but relief was refused to a director who made monthly drawings against his salary at a rate in excess of that prescribed by the board, and to directors who paid compensation for loss of office to an incompetent fellow director to induce him to retire, without referring the question of compensation and the possibility of dismissing the fellow director to the shareholders in general meeting.[12] Moreover, relief will not be given to a director who, although not guilty of personal dishonesty, has wrongfully received and still retains money or assets of the company,[13] or who has acted in accordance with the directions of a controlling shareholder or some other person without enquiring into the propriety of the transactions in question.[14]

Under the statutory provision, relief can be given against any of the criminal penalties imposed by the Companies Acts 1985,[15] but not against criminal liability under any other statute, or against civil liability to anyone other than the company, whether the liability arises by statute or otherwise, and so apparently no relief may be given in the rare cases when a member or creditor of a company has a personal right to sue its directors.[16] Furthermore, relief cannot be given against a director's potential liability to contribute to the company's assets such amount as the court directs in the liquidation of the company on the ground that he has been guilty of wrongful trading (ie where he has failed to take every possible step to protect the interests of the company's creditors after he became aware, or should have become aware, that the company could not avoid going into an insolvent liquidation).[17] The reason for the exclusion of the court's power to give relief in this situation is that the strict and specific elements of the director's liability for wrongful trading

---

6 Companies Act 1985, s 727 (1). If the director apprehends that proceedings may be brought against him, he may apply to the Companies Court for relief in anticipation (Companies Act 1985, s 727 (2). The application is made by petition (RSC Ord 102, r 5 (1) (*i*)).
7 Trustee Act 1925, s 61 (48 Halsbury's Statute (4th Edn) 295).
8 *National Trustee Co of Australasia Ltd v General Finance Co of Australasia Ltd* [1905] AC 373.
9 *Re Windsor Steam Coal Co (1901) Ltd* [1929] 1 Ch 151.
10 *Re Claridge's Patent Asphalte Co Ltd* [1921] 1 Ch 543.
11 *Re Gilt Edge Safety Glass Ltd* [1940] Ch 495, [1940] 2 All ER 237.
12 *Re Duomatic Ltd* [1969] 2 Ch 365, [1969] 1 All ER 161.
13 *Guinness plc v Saunders* [1990] 1 All ER 652, [1990] 2 WLR 324.
14 *Selangor United Rubber Estates Ltd v Cradock (No 3)* [1968] 2 All ER 1073 at 1155, [1968] 1 WLR 1555 at 1649.
15 *Re Barry and Staines Linoleum Ltd* [1934] Ch 227.
16 *Customs and Excise Comrs v Hedon Alpha Ltd* [1981] QB 818, [1981] 2 All ER 697.
17 Insolvency Act 1986, s 214 (1) to (5).

are inconsistent with the laxer standard of conduct required of a director who qualifies for discretionary relief under the general statutory provision.[18]

If a company's articles or a director's service contract contain an invalid provision exempting him from liability for breaches of duty, the company may nevertheless reimburse the director for his expenses in successfully defending civil or criminal proceedings for an alleged breach of duty, or in successfully applying to the court for relief.[19]

The amount recoverable in an action against directors who have been guilty of a breach of fiduciary duty will be either the loss they have caused the company or the profit they have obtained by the breach, whichever is greater. But if directors improperly use the company's property for their own purposes, they are liable not only for its value, but also for compound interest thereon at such rate as the court thinks fit from the date of the misapplication until the date judgment is entered against them.[20] If two or more directors are guilty of the same breach of fiduciary duty, they are jointly and severally liable to compensate the company.[1] But if the company calls on them to account for improper profits which they have obtained as the result of a breach of duty in which they all participated, they are only liable to account for what they have each respectively received, although they are all jointly and severally liable for costs of the action brought to compel them to account.[2] This is not of great practical importance, however, for all directors who participate in such a transaction are guilty of a breach of duty and are jointly and severally liable to compensate the company for any loss which it suffers, and since the improper profit obtained by one director is deemed to be the company's property, the measure of the company's loss recoverable from all the directors will be the amount of the secret profit.[3] Directors who are guilty of the same act of negligence are also jointly and severally liable to the company.

If several persons are sued in respect of a breach of duty by a director who holds shares in the plaintiff company and the company is being or is about to be wound up and is solvent, any award of damages must be calculated so that no distribution of damages is made to the director in respect of his own shares, but the costs of the proceedings which the company has to bear itself (ie the excess of its costs actually incurred over the costs ordered to be paid by the defendants) must be deducted from the gross amount of the damages before an apportionment of damages is made for this purpose.[4] Thus, if the total loss suffered by the company is £100,000 and the director in question holds 25 per cent of the company's shares and the company's excess costs amount to £10,000, the amount to be deducted from the damages payable by the other defendants is 25 per cent of the difference, namely £22,500, and judgment should be entered against the other defendants for £77,500.

If judgment is obtained by the company against one of its directors in respect of a breach of duty for which several of them are responsible, the director who was sued may recover such contribution as the court thinks just from the others,[5] either

---

18 *Re Produce Marketing Consortium Ltd* [1989] 3 All ER 1, [1989] 1 WLR 745, [1989] BCLC 513.

19 Companies Act 1985, s 310 (3), substituted by Companies Act 1989, s 137 (1).

20 *Wallersteiner v Moir (No 2)* [1975] QB 373, 508n, [1975] 1 All ER 849 (where the court ordered the payment of compound interest calculated with yearly rests at a rate of 1 per cent above the Bank of England's minimum lending rate from time to time).

1 *Re National Funds Assurance Co* (1878) 10 ChD 118; *Re Carriage Co-operative Supply Association* (1884) 27 ChD 322; *Re Faure Electric Accumulator Co* (1888) 40 ChD 141.

2 *Parker v McKenna* (1874) 10 Ch App 96.

3 *Re Carriage Co-operative Supply Association*, supra; *Gluckstein v Barnes* [1900] AC 240.

4 *Re VGM Holdings Ltd* [1942] Ch 235, [1942] 1 All ER 224; *Selangor United Rubber Estates Ltd v Cradock (No 4)* [1969] 3 All ER 965, [1969] 1 WLR 1773.

5 *Ramskill v Edwards* (1885) 31 ChD 100; *Gluckstein v Barnes*, supra; Civil Liability (Contribution) Act 1978, s 1 (1) and s 2 (1) (13 Halsbury's Statutes (4th Edn) 533).

by bringing a separate action against them or by having them joined as co-defendants or third parties in the company's action. But if the breach of duty was a misapplication of the company's funds for the benefit of the director whom the company has sued, he may not seek a rateable contribution from the other directors who participated in the breach of duty, but must make the breach good out of the company's money in his own hands, and confine his contribution claim to any excess of the amount ordered to be paid by him to the company over the money in his hands.[6] If directors have been compelled to restore money paid as dividends out of the company's capital, they may recover the amounts so paid from shareholders who knew that the dividends came out of capital,[7] and also, it seems, from shareholders who were unaware of their source,[8] unless they have meanwhile changed their position in the belief that the dividends they received were legitimate.[9]

Notwithstanding the invalidation of provisions in a company's articles or a contract or resolution exonerating a director from liability for breaches of the duties imposed on him by law, a company may purchase insurance against any such liability for the benefit of the director and may meet the expense of doing so out of the company's resources.[10] It would seem to be immaterial whether the insurance policy is issued to the company so as to cover it for loss suffered by it in consequence of a director's breaches of duty or to indemnify it against its vicarious liability to third persons for wrongs done by a director, or whether the policy is issued to the director himself so as to indemnify him against his own liability to the company or anyone else. In the latter situation the insurance would be ineffective to indemnify the director against liability for deliberate wrongdoing under the general principles of insurance law.[11]

Actions against third persons for directors' breaches of duty

If a breach of duty by a director results in a tort being committed against the company by a third person (eg a third person taking possession of the company's property under a disposition which is void because wrongful or illegal),[12] the company may sue that person for damages or for the specific return of its property.[13] Moreover, if a director disposes of the company's property in breach of his equitable fiduciary duties, the company can recover the property or its value from any person into whose hands it comes, if he knew of the breach of duty, or if he knew of facts which should have caused him to suspect that a breach had been committed.[14] The company may also recover such property from a person who knew of circumstances which should have suggested to a reasonable man possessing the skill and ability of a competent practitioner in the professional or business field in which the defendant is engaged that a breach of fiduciary duty was being committed.[14]

6 *Walsh v Bardsley* (1931) 47 TLR 564.
7 *Moxham v Grant* [1899] 1 QB 480.
8 *Moxham v Grant* [1900] 1 QB 88; *Re Mercantile Trading Co, Stringer's Case* (1869) 4 Ch App 475; contra, *Re Denham & Co* (1883) 25 ChD 752.
9 *Skyring v Greenwood* (1825) 4 B & C 281.
10 Companies Act 1985, s 310 (3), substituted by Companies Act 1989, s 137 (1).
11 *Gordon v Rimmington* (1807) 1 Camp 123; *Beresford v Royal Insurance Co Ltd* [1938] AC 586, [1938] 2 All ER 602; *Rickards v Forestal Land, Timber and Rlys Co Ltd* [1942] AC 50, [1941] 3 All ER 62.
12 This will not be the situation if the transaction is validated by the Companies Act 1985, s 35 (1) substituted by Companies Act 1989, s 108 (1) (see p 97, ante).
13 *Re Woking UDC (Basingstoke Canal) Act 1911* [1914] 1 Ch 300; *Salomons v Laing* (1850) 12 Beav 377.
14 *Selangor United Rubber Estates Ltd v Cradock (No 3)* [1968] 2 All ER 1073 at 1104, 1137, 1142 and 1144, [1968] 1 WLR 1555 at 1590, 1629, 1633 and 1639; *Karak Rubber Co Ltd v Burden (No 2)* [1972] 1 All ER 1210, [1972] 1 WLR 602; *Belmont Finance Corpn Ltd v Williams Furniture Ltd* [1979] Ch 250, [1979] 1 All ER 118.

Furthermore, the company may recover the property or its value if the circumstances of the transaction which the defendant engaged in with the delinquent director should have excited the suspicions of a reasonable man, and the answers which he received to the enquiries he made about the matter, or the answers which he would have received had he made proper enquiries, would not have set such suspicions aside.[14] The liability of the person into whose hands the company's property comes is that of a constructive trustee. It is therefore unnecessary for the company to trace its property through intermediate hands into the hands of the third person as strictly as if it were seeking to recover it at common law, and it suffices that assets representing the company's property, or assets derived from or substituted for that property, have been received by the defendant, whether directly or as the result of intermediate transactions.[15] A person may also incur liability as a constructive trustee to compensate a company for loss suffered by it as a result of a breach of a director's fiduciary duties if he actively and dishonestly participates in the breach of duty, and this liability is incurred even though the participator receives no property of the company and does not benefit personally from the breach.[16] It is essential, however, that he should either intend to defraud the company or that he should be aware that the act in which he participates is a breach of the director's fiduciary duty, although it would suffice that he knew sufficient of the circumstances to make it obvious to him that a breach of duty was being committed.[16] Despite one opinion to the contrary,[17] a third person who participates in a breach of a director's duties is not personally liable merely because he should have realised that the director was committing such a breach.[16]

DIRECTORS' DUTIES TO MEMBERS AND TO PERSONS DEALING WITH THE COMPANY

Duties to members

Directors owe no general fiduciary or other duties to individual members of their companies when negotiating or carrying out transactions with such members, and this is so whether the directors act on behalf of themselves or the company.[18] Thus, where the plaintiff had an option to subscribe for some of the company's shares, and the directors allotted the whole of its authorised capital to other persons, including themselves, so that the option became worthless, it was held that the directors did not have to satisfy the plaintiff's claim under his option by transferring some of their own shares to him.[19] Again, directors may purchase shares from members of their company, and are under no duty to disclose information in their possession which might induce the members to demand a higher purchase price.[20]

15 *Selangor United Rubber Estates Ltd v Cradock (No 3)* [1968] 2 All ER 1073 at 1124, [1968] 1 WLR 1555 at 1615; *Karak Rubber Co Ltd v Burden (No 2)*, supra.
16 *Barnes v Addy* (1874) 9 Ch App 244 at 251–2; *Belmont Finance Corpn Ltd v Williams Furniture Ltd*, supra; *Baden, Delvaux and Lecuit v Société Générale pour Favoriser le Développment du Commerce et de l'Industrie en France* [1983] BCLC 325.
17 *Selangor United Rubber Estates Ltd v Cradock (No 3)* [1968] 2 All ER 1073 at 115, [1968] 1 WLR 1555 at 1649.
18 *Bell v Lever Bros Ltd* [1932] AC 161 at 228, [1931] All ER Rep 1 at 33 per Lord Atkin; *Multinational Gas and Petrochemical Co v Multinational Gas and Petrochemical Services Ltd* [1983] BCLC 461 at 487, per Dillon LJ.
19 *Ferguson v Wilson* (1866) 2 Ch App 77.
20 *Percival v Wright* [1902] 2 Ch 421. It does not seem just that the directors should profit because of inside information which they have acquired as directors and which is not available to investors generally. In the United States it has been held that if the seller is aware that the purchasers are directors, they must disclose all facts known to them which may seriously affect the value of the

Such a contract is not one uberrimae fidei on the part of the director. But if directors induce members to sell their shares at an undervalue by misleading them as to the value of the shares (e g by submitting inaccurate balance sheets and profit and loss accounts), the members may not only sue the directors at common law for deceit or negligence and rescind the sales of their shares in equity, but may also require the directors to account in equity for the difference between the price paid by them for the shares and their higher real value at the time of the sale.[1] In this situation equity intervenes because of the misrepresentation made by the directors, and not because they owe a fiduciary duty to selling shareholders to protect their interests. Moreover, despite the strong bargaining position occupied by directors by reason of their fuller knowledge of the company's affairs than the selling shareholders possess, they owe the selling shareholders no duty to exercise care to ensure that they are properly advised, unless they voluntarily assume the function of advising them. In that case the voluntary tender of advice creates a special relationship between the selling shareholders and the directors, which results in the latter owing a duty at common law to advise the sellers with reasonable skill and care, and a breach of that duty will involve the directors in liability for the consequential loss suffered by the selling shareholders.[2] The position would appear to be the same when directors sell their own shares in the company to other shareholders. No fiduciary or other duties will arise on a sale or purchase of shares by a director in the absence of a special confidence placed by the other party in the director, and so none will attach when shares are sold on a stock exchange and the seller and ultimate buyer are therefore unknown to each other.

Directors may constitute themselves the agents of individual members of a company to carry out particular transactions, and they then owe the same fiduciary duties to such members as any other agent owes to his principal. Thus, where directors induced shareholders to give them options for the purchase of their shares so that the directors might negotiate a sale of the shares to another company, and the directors used the options to purchase the shares themselves and then resold them at a profit to the other company, it was held that the directors had made themselves agents for the shareholders, and were consequently accountable for the profit which they had improperly obtained.[3] Where shareholders employ the directors to negotiate a sale of their shares, the agency relationship may work to their disadvantage, however, for if the directors fraudulently misrepresent the state of the company's affairs to the purchaser of the shares, the shareholders, as the directors' principals, will be vicariously liable in damages to the purchaser.[4]

Directors owe no fiduciary or other duties to individual members of their company in directing and managing the company's affairs, acquiring or disposing of assets on the company's behalf, entering into transactions on its behalf, or in recommending the adoption by members of proposals made to them collectively. If directors mis-manage the company's affairs, they incur liability to pay damages

shares, such as a prospective sale of the company's undertaking (*Strong v Repide* (1909) 213 US 419), or an offer by an outsider to purchase a quarter of the company's issued shares (*Nichol v Sensenbrenner* (1935) 220 Wis 165). The Jenkins Committee recommended that a director 'who in any transaction relating to the securities of his company or any other company in the same group, makes improper use of a particular piece of confidential information which might be expected materially to affect the value of those securities, should be liable to compensate a person who suffers from his action in so doing, unless that information was known to that person' (Report of the Committee on Company Law (Cmnd 1749), para 99 (b)).

1 *Walsham v Stainton* (1863) 1 De G J & Sm 678.
2 *Hedley Byrne & Co Ltd v Heller & Partners Ltd* [1964] AC 465, [1963] 2 All ER 575; *Arenson v Casson Beckman Rutley & Co* [1977] AC 405, [1975] 3 All ER 901.
3 *Allen v Hyatt* (1914) 30 TLR 444.
4 *Briess v Woolley* [1954] AC 333, [1954] 1 All ER 909.

or compensation to the company or to make restitution to it, but individual members cannot recover compensation for the loss they have respectively suffered by the consequential fall in value of their shares, and they cannot achieve this indirectly by suing the directors for conspiracy to breach the duties which they owed the company.[5] However, there may be certain situations where directors do owe a fiduciary duty and a duty to exercise reasonable skill and care in advising members in connection with a transaction or situation which involves the company or its business undertaking and also the individual holdings of its members. The clearest example of this is where a takeover bid is made for a company and its directors advise its shareholders whether to accept or reject the bid. Here the directors undoubtedly owe the company a duty to give the advice honestly, carefully and impartially,[6] and it has been held by the Court of Appeal of New Zealand that they also owe each shareholder to whom the bid is addressed a corresponding fiduciary duty and duty of skill and care.[7] It is uncertain whether this reasoning can be extended to other situations where directors owe duties to the company but the relevant decision has to be made by its members individually or collectively, and the directors advise them as to the decision they should make. Such situations would include a proposed sale or disposal of the company's assets and undertaking, a proposed merger or division of the company, a proposed reorganisation of the company's share capital affecting existing members and a proposal for the voluntary liquidation of the company.

Duties to persons dealing with the company

Directors owe no fiduciary or contractual duties nor any duty of care to persons who deal with their company, provided that they make it clear to the persons with whom they deal that they are contracting on the company's behalf and not personally.[8] They are therefore not liable to pay debts incurred by the company at a time when they know it to be insolvent,[9] but when the company is wound up they may be made personally liable to contribute toward the payment of all the company's debts by order of the court if they have been guilty of fraudulent or wrongful trading.[10] Directors are not liable if the company breaks its contracts,[11] and the other party to a contract cannot make them indirectly liable by suing them in tort for inducing the company to commit the breach.[12] If directors mismanage the company's affairs deliberately or negligently, so that the company becomes unable to pay its debts,[9] or so that the security of debenture holders secured by a floating charge becomes insufficient,[13] they are not personally liable to the creditors or debenture holders, and in the winding up of the company they can be ordered to contribute toward the payment of the company's debts only if they are found guilty of fraudulent or wrongful trading.[10]

The only circumstances in which creditors can sue directors personally at common law is where they have been guilty of a tort toward the creditors as well

---

5 *Prudential Assurance Co Ltd v Newman Industries Ltd (No 2)* [1982] Ch 204, [1982] 1 All ER 354.
6 *Gething v Kilner* [1972] 1 All ER 1166, [1971] 1 WLR 337; *Re a Company* [1986] BCLC 382.
7 *Coleman v Myers* [1977] 2 NZLR 225; secus *Dawson International plc v Coats Patons plc* [1989] BCLC 233 (a decision of the Scottish Court of Session, Outer House).
8 *Bridges and Salmon Ltd v The Swan (Owner), The Swan* [1968] 1 Lloyd's Rep 5.
9 *Wilson v Lord Bury* (1880) 5 QBD 518, Baggallay LJ strongly dissenting; *Multinational Gas and Petrochemical Co v Multinational Gas and Petrochemical Services Ltd* [1983] BCLC 461 at 487, per Dillon LJ.
10 Insolvency Act 1986, s 213 (1) and (2) and s 214 (1) to (3) (see pp 41 and 44, ante).
11 *Ferguson v Wilson* (1866) 2 Ch App 77.
12 *Said v Butt* [1920] 3 KB 497.
13 *Clark v Urquhart* [1930] AC 28 at 53, per Lord Sumner.

as a breach of duty owed to the company. Consequently, directors are personally liable to persons who lend money to the company if they obtain the loan by fraudulent misrepresentations.[14] Likewise they are liable in tort for negligently causing loss to a person with whom the company has entered into a contract, if the circumstances impose a personal duty on the directors toward that person to act with proper skill or care (eg where the company contracts to provide services which can only be rendered by the exercise of personal skill and care by its directors).[15] But if directors deliberately dispose of their company's assets so as to make them unavailable to pay the company's debts, including judgment debts, it would appear that the creditors affected cannot recover damages from them (ie the value of the assets made unavailable) by suing them for the tort of conspiracy, because the director's purpose is to benefit the company by preserving the assets for its benefit.[16]

If directors exercise their powers in a way which involves a breach of duty to the company, creditors of the company cannot complain. Thus, where directors paid up the capital unpaid on their shares in advance of calls in order to pay a debt of the company which they had guaranteed personally, it was held that, although they had acted partly for their own benefit, creditors of the company could not treat the payment in advance of calls as void and require the directors to pay the unpaid capital again when the company was wound up.[17] But if proceedings are taken against directors in the winding up of the company for breaches of duty owed to it, the amount recovered will augment the company's assets and will be used to discharge its liabilities to its creditors and other persons who have dealt with it.

Although directors are generally immune from liability to creditors of their company, it is possible for the memorandum of association of a company limited by shares or by guarantee to provide that they shall be subject to unlimited liability,[18] in which case they are personally liable without limit in the winding up of the company to contribute such amount as is required to meet the company's debts and liabilities and the costs and expenses of the winding up.[19] Such a provision can only be imposed directly by the company's memorandum of association, and no liability to contribute is imposed on a director by the memorandum providing that the company and the conduct of its affairs shall be subject to the rules of a trade or professional association which make directors personally responsible for the debts of a company incurred under transactions regulated by the association.[20] It will be noted that the imposition of unlimited liability on directors by the memorandum does not make them directly liable to the company's creditors as statutory guarantors of its debts while it is a going concern, and the only way in which the liability can be enforced is in the liquidation of the company by the court or liquidator calling on them to make the necessary contribution.[1] Moreover, persons who have ceased to be directors before the commencement of the liquidation

14 *Edgington v Fitzmaurice* (1885) 29 ChD 459.
15 *Fairline Shipping Corpn v Adamson* [1975] QB 180, [1974] 2 All ER 967.
16 *Allied Arab Bank Ltd v Hajjar (No 2)* [1988] QB 944, [1988] 3 All ER 103; *Metall und Rohstoff AG v Donaldson Lufkin & Jenrette Inc* [1989] 3 All ER 14, [1989] 3 WLR 563.
17 *Re Wincham Shipbuilding, Boiler and Salt Co, Pool Jackson and Whyte's Case* (1878) 9 ChD 322.
18 Companies Act 1985, s 306 (1).
19 Ibid, s 503 (1).
20 *Mitton, Butler, Priest & Co Ltd v Ross* (1976) Times, 22 December. In this case the association was the Stock Exchange, which by its rule 224.2 (*b*) imposed personal liability on directors of a company which is a member of the Stock Exchange for debts and obligations for the company incurred as such a member.
 1 The director is made a contributory by the Insolvency Act 1986, s 75 (1), and his contribution is recovered by the same procedure as that of a shareholder.

are liable to contribute only if they were directors within one year before that time, and they cannot in any case be required to contribute towards debts and liabilities of the company incurred after they ceased to be directors.[2]

Breach of warranty of authority

Although a director is not personally liable for his company's failure to perform a contract which he has made on its behalf, he is liable in damages to a person with whom he purports to make a contract which is not binding on his company at all. When a director or any other person representing a company negotiates a contract he impliedly represents to the other contracting party that he has authority to bind the company as its agent. If he lacks this authority, he is guilty of a breach of warranty of authority, and is liable for the loss which the other party suffers as a result of entering into the contract.

To make the director or other representative liable, however, his implied representation must be one of fact, and not of law. Thus, a director is liable if he negotiates a loan to his company which results in it exceeding the limits of its borrowing powers fixed by its memorandum, for the director impliedly represents to the lender as a matter of fact that the company is not exceeding its borrowing powers by borrowing from him.[3] Likewise, directors are liable if they induce the company's bank to honour cheques signed by one of their number when no resolution has been passed by the board authorising the signatory to issue cheques, for the directors impliedly represent to the bank that such a resolution has been passed.[4] But it has been held that directors of a company incorporated by special Act of Parliament (such as a railway or canal company) are not liable to a person whom they induce to enter into a transaction which is patently beyond the company's statutory powers, because the only implied representation which they make is one of law, namely, that the transaction is within the company's powers as defined by its special Act.[5] It is doubtful whether this reasoning applies in the case of a company incorporated under the Companies Acts. It would seem that a representation as to the contents of its memorandum and articles is a representation of fact, because the memorandum and articles contain a private contract between the members of the company,[6] not an enactment by Parliament, and the fact that the contract is given statutory effect by the company being registered under the Companies Acts would not appear to raise its status to that of an Act of Parliament. Consequently, it appears that if directors or other agents of a company misrepresent the powers of their company or of its board of directors to a person who deals with the company, they will be liable for breach of warranty of authority.[7]

The damages recoverable from directors who are guilty of breach of warranty of authority are calculated so as to represent the difference between the value of the other party's actual rights against the company and the value which those rights would have had if the company had been bound by the transaction. Thus, if directors issue debentures without authority, the measure of damages is the market value of similar valid debentures at the time the invalid debentures are issued,

---

2 Insolvency Act 1986, s 75 (2).
3 *Weeks v Propert* (1873) LR 8 CP 427; *Chapleo v Brunswick Permanent Building Society* (1881) 6 QBD 696; *Firbank's Executors v Humphreys* (1886) 18 QBD 54.
4 *Cherry and M'Dougall v Colonial Bank of Australasia* (1869) LR 3 PC 24.
5 *Rashdale v Ford* (1866) LR 2 Eq 750; *Beattie v Lord Edbury* (1872) 7 Ch App 777.
6 Companies Act 1985, s 14 (1).
7 In *West London Commercial Bank v Kitson* (1883) 12 QBD 157, directors were held personally liable for accepting a bill of exchange in the company's name when the company had no power to do so by its memorandum.

which may be more or less than their nominal value.[8] From such an amount there must, of course, be deducted any amount which the plaintiff has already recovered from the company by way of voluntary repayment or by enforcing the equitable remedies of subrogation or tracing.[9] On the other hand, directors cannot escape liability by showing that the other party could have treated the company as bound by the transaction under the rule in *Royal British Bank v Turquand.* That rule entitles the other party to treat the transaction as binding on the company if he chooses, but it does not make the transaction valid for all purposes so as to enable the company or its directors to rely on it.[10]

The potential liability of directors and other agents of a company for breach of warranty of authority has been much diminished by the recent amendments to the Companies Act 1985, which validate contracts and other transactions to which a company is a party notwithstanding them being entered into for purposes unrelated to the company's objects,[11] or in disregard of limitations imposed by the company's memorandum or articles, or by resolutions passed by general or class meetings, or by agreements between members or shareholders of the company.[12] Where these provisions apply, the contract or transaction in question will be binding on the company, at least in favour of a party acting in good faith, and the directors or other agents who represented the company will incur no liability for breach of warranty of authority. It will only be in situations where the other party is unprotected by the statutory provisions (eg because he is a director of the company or its holding company or is connected with such a director),[13] or where the director or other agent of the company acts beyond the authority conferred on him directly or indirectly by the board or without such authority, or where the contract or transaction can be repudiated by the company because of a breach of the fiduciary duties owed to it by the director or other agent, that the liability of the director or agent to the other party for breach of warranty of authority will still be of practical importance.

If directors borrow outside the limits of their own borrowing powers conferred by the articles, or without authority in the form of a resolution of the board, and they apply the loan in paying the company's debts, the lender can claim to be subrogated to the rights of creditors thus paid off,[14] and it would appear that the lender's claim is not affected by the fact that he can enforce the loan contract against the company. Likewise, it appears that if directors borrow without authority and purchase assets or meet expenses of the company with the loan, the lender is subrogated to any right they have to be indemnified out of the company's funds for money expended by them in carrying out their duties.[15]

---

8 *Firbank's Executors v Humphreys* (1886) 18 QBD 54.
9 Subrogation is a remedy by which a lender who cannot recover a loan from a borrower because he is not bound by the loan contract, may instead recover that part of the loan from the borrower which he has used to pay debts owed by him to third persons. Tracing is a remedy by which a person who has paid money to another under a void contract may recover assets which have been acquired with the money or may claim a charge on the assets for repayment of that part of the money which has been used to acquire them.
10 *Cherry and M'Dougall v Colonial Bank of Australasia* (1869) LR 3 PC 24.
11 Companies Act 1985, s 35 (1), substituted by Companies Act 1989, s 108 (1) (see p 97, ante).
12 Companies Act 1985, s 35A (1) to (3), inserted by Companies Act 1989, s 108 (1) (see p 99, ante).
13 Companies Act 1985, s 322A (1) and (2), inserted by Companies Act 1989, s 109 (1) (see p 102, ante).
14 *B Liggett (Liverpool) Ltd v Barclays Bank Ltd* [1928] 1 KB 48.
15 *Re German Mining Co* (1854) 4 De GM & G 19. In *Re Wrexham Mold and Connah's Quay Rly Co* [1899] 1 Ch 440 at 449, Rigby LJ held that that decision applied only to unlimited (query, unincorporated) companies governed by the law of partnership. There is no good reason why this should be so.

SECRETARIES

Every company must have a secretary, and a sole director cannot also be the secretary.[16] There is nothing to prevent one of two or more directors also being the secretary, but if a company's sole director or its secretary is the sole director of another company, that company cannot be the first company's secretary or sole director, as the case may be.[17] There is nothing to prevent one company from being the secretary of another, and it is common for listed public companies to appoint the companies which are their registrars and transfer agents to be their secretaries as well. Usually companies' articles empower their boards of directors to appoint the secretary of the company for such term, at such remuneration and on such conditions as the board thinks fit and to remove the secretary from office at any time.[18] However, the first secretary of a company is the person named in the statement of the first directors and secretary signed by the subscribers of the memorandum of association, and if the person so named is different from the person appointed by the articles or, seemingly, by the directors under the articles, the former and not the latter person is the first secretary.[19]

The directors of a public (but not a private) company must take reasonable steps to ensure that the secretary of the company is a person who has the requisite knowledge and experience and satisfies one of several alternative qualifications for the appointment.[20] These are that he is either professionally qualified by being a barrister or solicitor or a member of one of seven professional bodies of accountants or secretaries,[1] or that he held the office of secretary or deputy secretary of the company on 22 December 1980,[2] or that for at least three of the five years preceding this appointment he held the office of secretary of a company other than a private company, or that by reason of having held any other position or being a member of any other body he appears to the directors to be capable of discharging the functions of secretary of the company.[3]

The register of directors and secretaries kept by a company must show the names (including christian or forenames) of the secretary or secretaries of the company, any former names used by him or them,[4] and his or their usual address or addresses; if the secretary is a corporation, the register must show its corporate name and its registered or principal office; if all the partners in a firm are joint secretaries, the name and principal office of the firm may be shown in the register instead of details of the individual partners.[5] The same information must also be given in the return of any change in these particulars which must be sent to the Registrar of Companies within 14 days after the change occurs.[6]

The secretary of a company is its administrative officer. It is his function to carry

---

16 Companies Act 1985, s 283 (1) and (2).
17 Ibid, s 283 (4).
18 See Table A, art 99.
19 Companies Act 1985, s 10 (2), (3) and (5).
20 Ibid, s 286 (1).
1 That is, the Institutes of Chartered Accountants of England and Wales, of Scotland and of Ireland, the Association of Certified Accountants, the Institute of Chartered Secretaries and Administrators, the Institute of Cost and Management Accountants and the Chartered Institute of Public Finance and Accountancy.
2 This was the appointed day for this provision to come into operation under the Companies Act 1980.
3 Companies Act 1985, s 286 (1) and (2).
4 The former name of a person need not be shown if it was changed or disused before he attained the age of 18 years, or if it has been changed or disused for 20 years or more, or if it was the name of a woman before her marriage.
5 Companies Act 1985, s 290 (1) to (3), as amended by Companies Act 1989, s 145 and Sch 19, para 3 (see p 553, ante).
6 Companies Act 1985, s 288 (2).

out the decisions of the directors, but he has no power to participate in the management of the company's affairs.[7] Consequently, he cannot negotiate or conclude contracts on the company's behalf,[8] nor register transfers of shares without the board's authority,[9] nor call meetings of members.[10] On the other hand, he can enter into contracts and do acts on the company's behalf for the purpose of carrying on the administration of its organisation,[11] and he owes the same fiduciary duties to the company as its directors.[12]

Most of the documents issued by a company are authenticated by the secretary. Many of the documents which the Companies Act 1985 (as amended) requires to be filed at the Companies Registry must be authenticated by him or by a director, or sometimes by both the secretary and a director. Where by the Companies Act 1985 or the company's memorandum or articles an act is to be done by a director and a secretary, it cannot be done by one person acting in both capacities.[13] If at any time there is no secretary capable of acting, any act required to be done by the secretary, or any notice required to be given to him, may be done by or given to an assistant or deputy secretary, or if none has been appointed, by or to an officer of the company (including a director) who has been authorised by the board.[14]

Although the secretary of a company is treated for civil purposes as a mere administrative assistant of the board with a very limited authority to engage in transactions on the company's behalf, statutes creating new criminal offences often make him responsible for the company's crimes to the same extent as the directors. In this respect criminal law is more in accordance with reality, because the secretary is often a full-time director as well, and he may be as influential in managing the company's affairs as his fellow directors.

---

7 *Barnett v South London Tramways Co* (1887) 18 QBD 815 at 817, per Lord Esher MR.
8 For the secretary's apparent authority, see p 127, ante).
9 *Chida Mines Ltd v Anderson* (1905) 22 TLR 27.
10 *Re Haycraft Gold Reduction and Mining Co* [1900] 2 Ch 230; *Re State of Wyoming Syndicate* [1901] 2 Ch 431.
11 *Panorama Developments (Guildford) Ltd v Fidelis Furnishing Fabrics Ltd* [1971] 2 QB 711, [1971] 3 All ER 16.
12 *Re Morvah Consols Tin Mining Co, McKay's Case* (1875) 2 ChD 1.
13 Companies Act 1985, s 284.
14 Ibid, s 283 (3).

CHAPTER 15

Meetings of members

KINDS OF MEETINGS AND RESOLUTIONS

General meetings and class meetings

Meetings of members of a company fall into two broad divisions, namely, general meetings and meetings of separate classes of members, or class meetings. Class meetings are held to pass resolutions which will bind only the members of the class concerned, and only members of that class may attend[1] such meetings and speak and vote.[2] The purposes for which class meetings are held are to assent to alterations in the rights of the class under provisions to that effect in the memorandum or articles or under the provisions of the Companies Act 1985,[3] to assent to compromises or arrangements which affect the class[4] and, though rarely, to consent to other actions by the company specified in its memorandum or articles where the action does not affect the rights of the class but is nevertheless of importance to its members, and for that reason the memorandum or articles require the consent of the class before the company may act (eg the voluntary winding up of the company, the reduction of its share capital, the disposal of the company's business undertaking). General meetings, on the other hand, may pass resolutions binding on all the members and on the company itself, and unless the memorandum or articles of association of the company or the terms of issue of a class of shares take away or limit the voting rights of members of a particular class at general meetings, all members of the company may attend and vote at them.

The provisions of the Companies Act 1985 governing general meetings also apply to meetings of a class of members unless expressed to apply only to general meetings, and this is true also of the provisions of Table A. The rules of common law in respect of general meetings also apply to class meetings, except so far as they are modified or excluded by statutory provisions or provisions in the memorandum or articles of the company or the terms of issue of the class of shares in question.

Kinds of general meetings

This chapter will be almost wholly concerned with general meetings, of which there are two kinds, namely, annual and extraordinary.

Annual general meetings

Every company must hold an annual general meeting in each calendar[5] year, and although the meeting need not be held on the anniversary of the last annual general

---

1 *Carruth v Imperial Chemical Industries Ltd* [1937] AC 707, [1937] 2 All ER 422.
2 Nevertheless members of the class may be represented at class meetings by proxies appointed by them (Companies Act 1985, s 372 (1) and (7)).
3 Companies Act 1985, s 125 (2) to (4) (see p 220, ante).
4 Such arrangements are effective only if approved by class meetings of each class of shareholders affected and confirmed by the court (Companies Act 1985, s 425 (1) and (2)).
5 The word 'calendar' does not appear in the Act, but it has been held that 'year' means 'calendar year' (*Gibson v Barton* (1875) LR 10 QB 329).

meeting, not more than 15 months must elapse between one annual general meeting and the next.[6] However, the Companies Act 1985 provides that if a company holds its first annual general meeting within 18 months after its incorporation, it need not hold an annual general meeting in the year of its incorporation or in the following year.[7] The meaning of this rather abstruse provision is that a company is deemed to have held annual general meetings in the first and second calendar years of its existence if it holds such a meeting within 18 months after it is incorporated. The meeting may, of course, be held in the third calendar year of the company's existence,[8] in which case it will suffice as an annual general meeting for that year as well.

Extraordinary general meetings

The Companies Act 1985 does not define extraordinary general meetings and mentions them by that name in only three of its provisions,[9] although it does contemplate that general meetings other than annual general meetings may be called at any time and for any purpose. However, companies' articles invariably provide that such other meetings shall be known as extraordinary general meetings.[10]

A public company must hold an extraordinary general meeting if its net assets fall to one half or less of its called-up capital;[11] the directors of the company are under a duty to call such a meeting within 28 days after any of their number becomes aware of that fact, and the meeting must be held not later than 56 days after that time.[12] The purpose of the meeting is to consider whether any measures should be taken to deal with the situation, and if so, what those measures should be,[12] but no matter may be considered at the meeting apart from those measures unless it would have been permissible to do so under the rules applicable to general meetings.[13] It seems, therefore, that if remedial measures are called for which cannot be taken by the board of directors, the general meeting can only express an opinion about what is needed or resolve that a further general meeting shall be held to take remedial action, for example, to resolve on a reduction of capital or to resolve to wind the company up voluntarily.

Kinds of resolutions

There are three kinds of resolutions which may be passed at general meetings, namely, special, extraordinary, and ordinary. Which kind of resolution is appropriate in a particular case depends on the nature of the business to be transacted, and not upon the kind of meeing at which it is passed, and so all three kinds of resolutions may be passed at either of the two kinds of general meetings. The Companies Act 1985 requires certain things to be done by special or extraordinary resolution, and the memorandum or articles cannot validly provide

---

6 Companies Act 1985, s 366 (1) and (3).
7 Ibid, s 366 (2).
8 Thus, if a company is incorporated in December 1988, it may hold its first annual general meeting in April 1990, and that meeting will be deemed to be the annual general meeting for 1988, 1989 and 1990.
9 These are the Companies Act 1985, s 142 (1) (see next paragraph), s 368 (1) (see p 620, post) and s 392A (1) and (2) (inserted by Companies Act 1989, s 122 (1) (see p 714, post)).
10 See Table A, art 36.
11 For the definition of called-up capital, see Companies Act 1985, s 737 (1) (p 137, ante).
12 Companies Act 1985, s 142 (1).
13 Ibid, s 142 (3). For matters which may be considered at a general meeting, even though no specific notice of them is given, see p 635, post.

that they may be done in any other way.[14] All other matters may be resolved upon by ordinary resolution, unless the memorandum or articles require them to be effected by a different procedure.[15] This is so even if the act is one authorised by the Companies Act 1985, so that, for example, a company may increase its nominal capital or convert shares into stock by ordinary resolution, unless its memorandum or articles require a different kind of resolution.

A special resolution is one passed by a majority of not less than three-fourths of the members who are entitled to vote and do vote in person or by proxy at a general meeting of which not less than 21 days' notice specifying the intention to propose the resolution as a special resolution has been duly given.[16] An extraordinary resolution is defined in the same way, save that the notice calling the meeting at which it is passed must state that it is to be proposed as an extraordinary resolution, and unless it is to be passed at an annual general meeting, only 14 days' notice of the general meeting at which it is to be proposed need be given.[17] Although the definition of special and extraordinary resolutions refers to a three-quarters' majority of the members who vote, on a poll the majority is calculated by reference to the votes attached to the shares of those members,[18] and so it would be more correct to define a special or extraordinary resolution as one passed by a three-quarters' majority of the total votes cast by members and their proxies.

An ordinary resolution is not defined by the Companies Act 1985. It is a resolution of which due notice has been given, and which is passed by a simple majority of the votes cast by members and their proxies.[19] In the event of an equality of votes the articles usually give the chairman of the meeting a casting vote.[20]

In ascertaining the majorities required to pass any of the foregoing resolutions, regard is paid only to the members who vote for and against the resolution, and the votes of members who do not attend the meeting or appoint proxies to represent them at it, or who do attend in person or by proxy but do not vote, do not enter into the calculation at all. Thus, however large the membership or capital of a company may be, if four members each holding one share attend a duly convened general meeting, three of them can pass an ordinary, extraordinary or special resolution, subject to any requirement in the articles as to a quorum. These remarks apply equally to resolutions at meetings of a class of members.

Although the definition of special and extraordinary resolutions in the Companies Act 1985 confines them to resolutions passed at a general meeting, the Act itself[1] and Table A of the earlier Companies Acts[2] refer to extraordinary resolutions passed at a meeting of a class of shareholders, and clearly this signifies resolutions passed by the same majority at a class meeting called by the same procedure as an extraordinary resolution passed at a general meeting.

---

14 *Ayre v Skelsey's Adamant Cement Co Ltd* (1904) 20 TLR 587; affd (1905) 21 TLR 464.
15 The memorandum or articles could require such acts to be done by resolutions which are neither ordinary, nor special, nor extraordinary; for example, a resolution passed by a two-thirds or four-fifths majority. But such peculiar resolutions are not met with in practice.
16 Companies Act 1985, s 378 (2).
17 Ibid, s 369 (1) and (2) and s 378 (1).
18 Ibid, s 370 (6) (see p 638, post).
19 *Bushell v Faith* [1970] AC 1099, [1970] 1 All ER 53.
20 See Table A, art 50.
1 Companies Act 1985, s 125 (2).
2 Companies Act 1948, Table A, art 4; Companies Act 1929, Table A, art 3.

THE CONVENING OF GENERAL AND OTHER MEETINGS

Persons who may convene

Directors

The articles of a company usually expressly empower the board of directors to convene general meetings[3] and class meetings,[4] and the board has this power at common law even if it is not expressly conferred on them. If the articles provide that the directors may call meetings, a general meeting may be validly called by directors whose term of office has expired, but who have nevertheless continued to act as directors,[5] or by a board meeting of which proper notice has not been given to all the directors,[6] or at which a quorum of directors is not present.[7] But it seems that if directors improperly exclude some of their number from a board meeting, they cannot validly resolve to call a general meeting of members.[8] If a general meeting is called by someone other than the directors, for example, the secretary, the meeting cannot be held unless the board ratifies what he has done.[9]

Members

The Companies Act 1985 provides that unless the articles provide to the contrary, two or more members holding not less than one-tenth of the company's issued share capital may call a general meeting.[10] This is to enable general meetings to be called when there are no directors, or insufficient directors to constitute a quorum at a board meeting, but the members' power to convene meetings is not confined to such cases, and so even if there is a competent board, the appropriate number of members still have a concurrent power to convene general meetings. The members' power may be taken away or limited by the articles, however, and Table A permits it to be exercised only when there are insufficient directors in the United Kingdom to form a quorum at a board meeting, in which case any director or member may call a general meeting,[11] whether it is an annual or an extraordinary general meeting.[12]

It would seem that one or more members holding not less than one-tenth of the issued capital of a company may call meetings of classes of its shareholders as well as general meetings,[10] and this power is not taken away by Table A. It should be noted that the Companies Act 1985 does not confer power on the holders of a fraction of shares of a particular class to call a meeting of shareholders of that class, nor does Table A.

Time and place of meetings

Directors who call a general meeting or a class meeting may decide when and where it shall be held, but they must exercise their discretion in the interests of the company or the class of shareholders in question, and not for their own purposes.

---

3 Table A, art 37.
4 The Companies Act 1948, Table A, art 4 contained such a power, but the present Table A does not.
5 *Gibson v Barton* (1875) LR 10 QB 329; *Boschoek Proprietary Co Ltd v Fuke* [1906] 1 Ch 148.
6 *Browne v La Trinidad* (1887) 37 ChD 1; *Re State of Wyoming Syndicate* [1901] 2 Ch 431 at 437, per Wright J.
7 *Re State of Wyoming Syndicate*, supra.
8 *Harben v Phillips* (1883) 23 ChD 14 at 34, per Cotton LJ.
9 *Re Haycraft Gold Reduction and Mining Co* [1900] 2 Ch 230; *Re State of Wyoming Syndicate*, supra.
10 Companies Act 1985, s 370 (1) and (3).
11 The article does not require the member to hold any particular fraction of the issued share capital.
12 Table A, art 37.

Consequently, where directors called an annual general meeting at an unusually early date in order to ensure that transfers of shares to certain persons who opposed the board would not be registered before the meeting was held, it was held that the directors had acted in bad faith, because their purpose had been to prevent the transferees from voting, and they were consequently restrained by the court from holding the meeting at the date fixed by them.[13] Once a meeting has been called, directors have no power to postpone it, and the meeting may be held even though they purport to postpone or cancel it.[14] Presumably these rules apply equally when members call a meeting.

Secretary of State for Trade and Industry

If a company fails to hold an annual general meeting within the time limit for doing so, any member may apply to the Secretary of State for Trade and Industry to call the meeting, and the Secretary of State may direct that it shall be held when and where he thinks fit.[15] If the meeting is held after the calendar year in which it should have been held, it is deemed to be the annual general meeting for that calendar year only, unless the meeting resolves by ordinary resolution that it shall also be deemed to be the annual general meeting for the year in which it is actually held.[16]

The court

The court has an inherent power to direct that meetings of members or classes of members shall be held,[17] but it will not direct a meeting merely because the directors have rejected a request by a member that one should be called.[18] The most frequent occasions when the court directs the holding of a meeting are when it is impossible to hold a general meeting because of the persistent absence of a quorum at general meetings, or because of the absence of a quorum at a general meeting called or requisitioned by the applicants,[19] or because an action has been brought in the company's name by a member, and the court needs to ascertain whether a majority of the members wish the action to be continued.[20] The Companies Act 1985 expressly empowers the court to call a general meeting or a class meeting on the application of a director or a member of the company who is entitled to vote at the meeting, when it is impracticable to call it by any other means, or to hold it in the manner prescribed by the articles or the Act.[1] The court may do this on the application of a director or member[2] or on its own motion.[3]

Requisitions in respect of meetings and resolutions

The power to call general meetings vested in the board of directors gives it practically dictatorial powers to decide whether a meeting shall be held or not, and

13 *Cannon v Trask* (1875) LR 20 Eq 669.
14 *Smith v Paringa Mines Ltd* [1906] 2 Ch 193.
15 Companies Act 1985, s 367 (1).
16 Ibid, s 367 (4).
17 *Re Paris Skating Rink Co* (1887) 6 ChD 731.
18 *MacDougall v Gardiner* (1875) 10 Ch App 606; *Pergamon Press Ltd v Maxwell* [1970] 2 All ER 809, [1970] 1 WLR 1167.
19 See p 634, post.
20 See p 650, post.
 1 Companies Act 1985, s 371 (1).
 2 The application is made by originating summons (RSC Ord 102, r 2 (1)).
 3 Although 'the court' is defined as 'the court having jurisdiction to wind up the company' (Companies Act 1985, s 744), it would appear that any court before which an action relating to the company is pending may direct a meeting to be held.

if it is held, what its agenda shall be. Articles of association sometimes empower a fraction of the members to require a meeting to be called, or to require a resolution submitted by them to be included in the agenda of a meeting which the directors are about to call, but the most important safeguards for the rights of members in this respect are three provisions of the Companies Act 1985 which the articles cannot restrict or make inapplicable.

Requisitions of extraordinary general meetings

The holders of not less then one-tenth of the paid up capital of the company carrying voting rights[4] may require the directors to call an extraordinary general meeting forthwith.[5] The requisition must be in writing signed by the requisitionists, and must state the purpose or object of the meeting,[6] though not necessarily in the form of one or more resolutions.[7] Several documents in like form requiring a meeting to be called for the same purpose may together constitute the requisition,[6] but the mere fact that some of them require that the meeting shall also consider 'the company's affairs generally' does not invalidate the requisition, because this addition is not sufficiently precise to be a purpose or object of the meeting, and is therefore treated as an excrescence.[7]

The directors must send out notices calling the meeting forthwith, and at the latest within 21 days after receiving the requisition.[8] Unless the articles otherwise provided, there was formerly no limit on the time within which the meeting had to be held, and so it could be called by the directors to be held on a date several months after it was convened.[9] Now, however, the directors are deemed to have failed to comply with the requisition unless they call a meeting for a date more than 28 days after the notice calling the meeting is sent out.[10] If the directors fail to call the meeting within 21 days after the requisition is deposited with them or call it to be held on a date more than 28 days after notice of the meeting is sent out, any of the requisitionists representing more than one-half of the total voting rights exercisable by them all may call the meeting, but it must then be held not later than three months after the deposit of the requisition.[11]

If the meeting is called by the requisitionists themselves, it may transact the business mentioned in the requisition, even though additional matters are specified in the notice calling the meeting, but business specified in the notice cannot be validly transacted if it was not mentioned in the requisition.[12] The requisitionists' reasonable expenses of calling a meeting on the default of the directors may be recovered from the company, which may reimburse itself out of the directors' remuneration.[13] When a meeting has been requisitioned, it would seem that an

---

4 This means shares on which there has been paid up one-tenth of the total amount paid up on all shares carrying voting rights. Thus, if a company has issued 300,000 £1 ordinary shares 50p paid and 100,000 £1 preference shares fully paid, and all the shares carry voting rights, the requisitionists must have paid up on their shares, whether preference or ordinary or a combination of both, one tenth of £250,000.

5 Companies Act 1985, s 368 (1) and (2).

6 Ibid, s 368 (3).

7 *Fruit and Vegetable Growers Association Ltd v Kekewich* [1912] 2 Ch 52.

8 Companies Act 1985, s 368 (1) and (4).

9 *Re Windward Islands (Enterprises) UK Ltd* [1983] BCLC 293; *McGuinness v Bremner plc* [1988] BCLC 673. Table A, art 37 requires the meeting to be called for a date not later than eight weeks after the requisition is received, but this has now been superseded by the statutory requirement that the meeting must be held, at the latest, seven weeks and two days after that date.

10 Companies Act 1985, s 368 (8), added by Companies Act 1989, s 145 and Sch 19, para 9.

11 Companies Act 1985, s 368 (4).

12 *Patent Wood Keg Syndicate Ltd v Pearse* (1906) 50 Sol Jo 650; *Ball v Metal Industries Ltd* 1957 SC 315.

13 Companies Act 1985, s 368 (6).

application could be made to the court to call it if the directors do not fulfil their statutory duty to call it 'forthwith', even though 21 days has not elapsed since the requisition was deposited.[14] Such an application would be appropriate if the business to be dealt with at the meeting were urgent, or if the directors had called the meeting, but fixed the date for holding it more than 28 days after notice of it was sent out, or at an earlier date which is inappropriate in view of the urgency of the business to be dealt with.[15]

An auditor of a company who resigns may require its directors to call an extraordinary general meeting to consider an explanation by him of his reasons for resigning, and the directors must then call a meeting forthwith, and at the latest within 21 days after receiving the requisition, and the meeting must be held not later than 28 days after the notice convening it is sent out.[15] If the directors do not call the meeting in fulfilment of their statutory obligation, the court may order a general meeting to be held on the application of any member of the company,[16] but curiously not on the application of the auditor who has resigned.

Requisitions in respect of resolutions at annual general meetings and class meetings

The third provision of the Companies Act 1985 designed to protect the rights of members to have matters discussed at general meetings, enables a certain fraction of members to require the directors to give notice of a resolution which the requisitionists intend to move at the next annual general meeting.[17] Such a requisition may be made by members who between them possess one-twentieth of the voting rights exercisable at the annual general meeting,[18] or by not less than one hundred members holding shares on which there has been paid up an average sum, per member, of not less than £100, in other words one hundred members who have paid up a total of £10,000 or more on their shares.[19] The requisition, which may consist of several documents in like form, must be signed by the requisitionists, and must be deposited at the company's registered office not later than six weeks before the next annual general meeting is to be held, but if the meeting is called after the requisition is made, the requisition is valid even though the meeting is to be held less than six weeks afterwards.[20] The directors must send notice of the resolution to members entitled to attend the meeting at the same time as notices of the meeting are sent out or, if this is impracticable, notice of the resolution must be sent to them as soon as possible after the meeting has been called.[1] Notice of the general effect of the resolution must also be given to other members of the company (ie members not entitled to have notice of the meeting sent to them) in any manner permitted for giving them notices of meetings of the company.[2] The requisitionists must deposit a sum of money sufficient to cover the cost of circulating their resolution,[3] but since it can usually be included in the notice calling the annual general meeting, the additional printing costs should be light, and there will be no extra postage to pay.

14 *Re Paris Skating Rink Co* (1877) 6 ChD 731; *McGuinness v Bremner plc*, supra.
15 Companies Act 1985, s 392A (1), (2) and (5), inserted by Companies Act 1989, s 122 (1) (see p 714, post).
16 Companies Act 1985, s 371 (1).
17 Ibid, s 376 (1).
18 The amount paid up on the shares is immaterial, so that in the example given in footnote 4, p 620, ante, if each share carried one vote, the requisition could be made by the holders of 20,000 shares.
19 Companies Act 1985, s 376 (2).
20 Ibid, s 377 (1) and (2). This is to prevent the directors from invalidating the requisition by holding the annual general meeting within the six weeks.
1 Companies Act 1985, s 376 (3) and (5).
2 Ibid, s 376 (4).
3 Ibid, s 377 (1).

A right to have resolutions proposed by shareholders at a meeting of the class to which they belong when the meeting is called to consent to the alteration of the rights of that class[4] is conferred on the same fraction of shareholders of the class and on the same terms as the right to requisition the inclusion of a proposed resolution in the notice of an annual general meeting.[5] The right is less important in the context of a class meeting, which is called for the limited purpose of giving or withholding the consent of the class to the proposed alteration, and any variations proposed in the terms of the consent can be put to the meeting as amendments, for which advance notice is not normally required.

Notice of meetings

To whom notice must be given

A meeting cannot be held unless proper notice of it has been given. Unless the articles otherwise provide, notice of an intention to hold a general meeting must be given to every member, whether he is entitled to attend the meeting and vote or not,[6] but members who have no voting rights need not be summoned to the meeting and have no right to attend it.[7] Unless the articles otherwise provide, notice of general meetings need not be given to the holders of shares represented by letters of allotment or by share warrants or bearer share certificates, because they are not members of the company.[8] Where share warrants have been issued, the articles usually provide that notice of general meetings shall be given to their holders by advertisement in one or more newspapers. Notice of a class meeting called for the purpose of consenting to an alteration of the rights of a class must be given to each shareholder of the class, and the articles cannot dispense with giving such notice.[9] Notice of other class meetings must be given to the persons specified in the articles or terms of issue of the shares concerned, and in any event to all the holders of shares of the class, unless the articles or terms of issue explicitly provide otherwise (eg the substitution of notice by newspaper advertisement in the case of shares represented by share warrants or bearer share certificates).[9] Notice of a general or a class meeting may be given to a member either personally, or by sending it by post to his address entered in the register of members, or if his registered address is outside the United Kingdom, to an address within the United Kingdom which he has supplied for the purpose.[10] Notice may be given to joint shareholders by sending it to the one of them whose name is first entered in the register of members.[11] If a member has died or become bankrupt and his personal representatives or trustee in bankruptcy have not been registered as members in

---

4 It is immaterial whether the class meeting is called under the provisions of the memorandum or articles or under the Companies Act 1985, because of the absence of any provision for the alteration of class rights in the memorandum and articles.

5 Companies Act 1985, s 125 (6) and s 376 (1) and (2).

6 Ibid, s 370 (1) and (2).

7 *Re Mackenzie & Co Ltd* [1916] 2 Ch 450. The distinction between notice of a meeting and a summons to attend it is a fine one, but nevertheless important. The obiter dictum of Cohen J, in *Re Warden and Hotchkiss Ltd* [1945] Ch 270 at 278, [1945] 1 All ER 507 at 512, that members who cannot vote need not be given notice of a meeting, must, it is submitted, be confined to that particular case, where the company's articles merely required 'members', not 'every member', to be given notice.

8 Ibid, s 22 (2). The holders of share warrants may be deemed by the articles to be members of the company either for all purposes or for limited purposes (Companies Act 1985, s 355 (5)). If they are deemed to be members for general purposes, it would appear that notices of general and class meetings must be given to them.

9 Companies Act 1985, s 125 (6) and s 370 (1) and (2).

10 Ibid, s 125 (6) and s 370 (2) and Table A, paras 111 and 112.

11 Companies Act 1985, s 370 (2), incorporating Table A, art 112.

his place, notice of a general meeting must be given to his personal representatives or trustee in bankruptcy at an address in the United Kingdom supplied by them, but if no such address has been supplied, the company must give them notice of the meeting by addressing it to the deceased or bankrupt member in the same way as though he had not died or become bankrupt.[12]

Table A provides that notices of meetings shall conclusively be deemed to have reached members 48 hours after posting.[13] Nevertheless, it has been held that where articles provide that notices of a general meeting shall be deemed to be delivered to members a specified time after they are posted, the provision does not apply if the company must be aware that because of prevailing conditions (e g a strike by postal workers), the notices will probably not be delivered within that time; but instead of enjoining the holding of the meeting, the court may accept an undertaking by the company to have the meeting adjourned to a date which will allow sufficient time for the notices to reach members (e g after the postal strike has ended).[14] Moreover, it has been held[15] that where articles provide that the notice of the meeting shall be deemed to have been given when it would be delivered in the ordinary course of the post, there is no need to give notice to members who reside abroad and who cannot be reached as speedily by post as members resident in the United Kingdom,[16] because if every member had to be notified wherever he might reside, there would be indefinite delay in holding the meeting. However, this reasoning does not apply to the provisions in Table A governing notice of meetings.[17] Table A expressly provides that a company governed by it need not give notice of general meetings to members resident abroad who have not supplied addresses in the United Kingdom to which notices may be sent to them.[18] It is questionable whether the provisions in Table A dealt with in this paragraph are incorporated into the Companies Act 1985, so as to apply to companies which are not expressly or impliedly governed by Table A. The Companies Act 1985 merely provides that notices of meetings of a company shall be served on every member of it in the manner in which notices are required to be served by Table A,[19] which incorporates the positive requirements of Table A, but not necessarily its rules as to when notice is deemed to be given, or as to the occasions when notice need not be given at all.

A meeting cannot be held unless notice of it is given to every member of the company who is entitled to be given notice.[20] However, modern articles usually provide that the accidental omission to give notice to a member, or his failure to receive it, shall not invalidate the proceedings at the meeting.[1] This has been held to include the accidental failure of the company or its agents to put a notice to the member into the post,[2] but not a deliberate omission to send out notices to certain members in consequence of a misinterpretation of the articles of association.[3]

---

12 Ibid, s 370 (2), incorporating Table A, art 116.
13 Table A, art 115 (as amended by The Companies (Tables A to F) (Amendment) Regulations 1985 (SI 1985/1052), para 2).
14 *Bradman v Trinity Estates plc* [1989] BCLC 757, 5 BCC 33.
15 *Re Warden and Hotchkiss Ltd* [1945] Ch 270, [1945] 1 All ER 507.
16 This does not mean that no member resident outside the United Kingdom need be notified. Thus, it may be necessary to give notice to members resident in Western Europe or in other countries to which there is a daily airmail service.
17 *Re Warden and Hotchkiss Ltd* [1945] Ch 270 at 279, [1945] 1 All ER 507 at 512, per Cohen J.
18 Table A, art 112.
19 Companies Act 1985, s 370 (2).
20 *Smyth v Darley* (1849) 2 HL Cas 789.
 1 See Table A, art 39.
 2 *Re West Canadian Collieries Ltd* [1962] Ch 370, [1962] 1 All ER 26.
 3 *Royal Mutual Benefit Building Society v Sharman* [1963] 2 All ER 242, [1963] 1 WLR 581.

Length of notice

A company's articles may not provide for an annual general meeting to be called by less than 21 days' notice, nor for any other general meeting, except one called to pass a special resolution, to be called by less than 14 days' notice; and unless the articles otherwise provide, general meetings may be called by those respective lengths of notice.[4] A general meeting which passes a special resolution must be called by not less than 21 days' notice, and unless the articles require longer notice, 21 days' notice suffices.[5] A class meeting must be called by not less than 14 days' notice; the articles may require longer notice, but they cannot permit shorter notice to be given.[4] This is the case also when a class meeting is called to give the consent of a class of shareholders to an alteration of the rights of the class.[6]

The number of days' notice of a general meeting or class meeting required by the Companies Act 1985 or by the articles is calculated by excluding the day on which the notice is given and the day on which the meeting is held.[7] Consequently, if the company is governed by Table A, and notices are therefore deemed to be received by members 48 hours after they are posted,[8] a general meeting may be held at the earliest seventeen or twenty-four days (as the case may be) after the date on which the notices of the meeting are posted. For example, if notices are posted on 1 January, they are deemed to be received on 3 January, and the meeting may be held at the earliest on 18 January if it is an extraordinary general meeting or a class meeting, or on 25 January if it is an annual general meeting or an extraordinary general meeting called to pass a special resolution.

An annual general meeting may be held even though it is called by less than 21 days' notice, if all the members entitled to attend and vote thereat agree.[9] Any other general meeting, including one called to pass a special resolution, and any class meeting, including one called to consent to an alteration of class rights,[10] may be held even though less than the normal length of notice of it has been given, if the shorter notice is accepted as sufficient by a majority in number of the members entitled to attend and vote at the meeting who between them hold 95 per cent in nominal value of the shares carrying voting rights thereat.[11] It is not necessary for members to attend the meeting to give their consent to short notice of it, and so they may give it beforehand by letter or, apparently, even orally. But their attention must be drawn to the fact that the normal length of notice has not been given; consequently, the mere fact that a resolution is passed at the meeting unanimously or by a majority holding 95 per cent of the shares carrying voting rights (as the case may be) does not imply that those members who vote for the resolution have also consented to short notice of the meeting having been given, and any member may subsequently challenge the validity of the resolution on the ground that the meeting was not properly called.[12]

---

4 Companies Act 1985, s 369 (1) and (2). Table A, art 38 requires an extraordinary general meeting called to appoint a director to be called by at least 21 clear days' notice.
5 Companies Act 1985, s 378 (2).
6 Ibid, s 125 (6) and s 369 (1) and (2).
7 *Re Railway Sleepers Supply Co* (1885) 29 ChD 204; *Re Hector Whaling Ltd* [1936] Ch 208, [1935] All ER Rep 302. Table A, art 38 contains an express provision to this effect.
8 Table A, art 115, as amended by the Companies (Tables A to F) (Amendment) Regulations 1985 (SI 1985/1052), para 2.
9 Companies Act 1985, s 369 (3).
10 Ibid, s 125 (6).
11 Ibid, s 369 (3) and (4) and s 378 (3).
12 *Re Pearce, Duff & Co Ltd* [1960] 3 All ER 222, [1960] 1 WLR 1014.

Special notice and advance availability of contracts for inspection

If a general meeting is called to pass any one of three particular ordinary resolutions[13] special notice of the resolution must be given. This means that the person who moves the resolution must give notice of it to the company at least 28 days before the meeting is held, and the company must give at least 21 days' notice of it to its members at the same time and manner as it gives notice of the meeting, or if that is impracticable, the resolution must either be advertised in a newspaper with an appropriate circulation, or be notified to the members in some other way permitted by the articles, at least 21 days before the meeting.[14] But if the person who moves the resolution gives his notice to the company before the meeting is called, and the meeting is held less than 28 days afterwards, the notice is nevertheless validly given.[15] This elaborate procedure is required in certain cases where advance notice of the resolution is necessary[16] in order to give an officer of the company whose removal or replacement is sought an opportunity to defend himself, and because of this, it is not possible for a fraction of the shareholders to accept shorter notice of the meeting, or for the company's memorandum or articles to vary the statutory procedure.[17] This is also the case when special notice is required for other reasons, where there is no question of giving any person an opportunity to prepare and circulate a defence.

The provision relating to special notice[14] is so worded that it could be read as conferring a right on any member to insist on the board calling a general meeting to consider a resolution of which special notice is necessary. It has been held[17] that the section is purely procedural, however, and that a meeting to pass such a resolution can be requisitioned only by the appropriate fraction of members in the way already described.[18] Moreover, the wording of the provision[14] makes it clear that only members who are entitled to notice of the meeting need be given notice of a resolution of which special notice is required. This is because notice of the resolution is to be given to the members 'in the same manner' as notice of the meeting itself.

A similar impediment to a general meeting being held if shorter notice of it is given than is normally required, is the result of two provisions of the Companies Act 1985, which require copies of certain draft contracts which a general meeting is called to approve to be made available for inspection by members for not less than 15 days before the resolution of approval is passed.[19] The contracts in question, which require approval by an ordinary resolution, are a contract for the purchase of a company's shares by itself otherwise than on the Stock Exchange (including such a purchase by a private company out of assets representing share capital)[20] and a contract for the employment of a director by a company or another company in the same group for a period exceeding five years.[1] Although the Companies Act

---

13 Namely, resolutions: (a) to remove a director (Companies Act 1985, s 303 (2)); (b) to elect or re-elect a director to the board of a public company or its subsidiary if he is 70 years old or has reached the age limit prescribed by the articles (s 293 (5)); and (c) to appoint an auditor in certain cases or to remove an auditor (s 391A (1), inserted by Companies Act 1989, s 122 (1)) (see pp 539, 547 and 715).
14 Companies Act 1985, s 379 (1) and (2).
15 Ibid, s 379 (3).
16 Namely, to remove a director or auditor, or to appoint as auditor a person other than the retiring auditor.
17 *Pedley v Inland Waterways Association Ltd* [1977] 1 All ER 209.
18 Companies Act 1985, s 368 (1) and (2) (see p 620, ante).
19 Ibid, s 164 (6) and s 319 (5).
20 Ibid, s 164 (1) and (2) and s 173 (1) and (2) (see p 191, ante).
1 Ibid, s 319 (1) and (3) (see p 540 ante).

1985 does not expressly require notice of the general meeting called to approve the draft contract to be given to members before the draft contract is made available for their inspection, this seems to be implied, because otherwise the members would not know that there was any draft contract to inspect. Consequently, it would seem that notice of the meeting must be given at least 16 days before it is held, and this precludes shorter notice of the meeting being accepted by a majority in number of the members holding 95 per cent in nominal value of shares carrying voting rights.[2]

Contents of notice

A notice calling a meeting must state the time and place at which it will be held,[3] and if the meeting is an annual general meeting, must describe it as such.[4] If the meeting is called to pass a special or extraordinary resolution, the notice must say so,[5] and the proposed resolution must be set out verbatim,[6] or at least the variation between the terms of the notice and the terms of the resolution proposed at the meeting must be purely formal or grammatical, and there must be no variation of substance or effect, however slight.[7] It is also necessary to set out verbatim in a notice of a general meeting the terms of an ordinary resolution of which special notice is required,[8] and the terms of a resolution which has been put on the agenda of an annual general meeting on the requisition of the appropriate fraction of shareholders;[9] but it may well be that formal or grammatical variations in the resolution actually proposed at the meeting will not invalidate the notice, in the same way as such variations do not invalidate notices of special or extraordinary resolutions. Resolutions for the approval of a proposed alteration of the rights of a class of members must also be set out verbatim in the notice calling a meeting of the class;[10] but again probably formal or grammatical variations in the resolution proposed at the meeting are permissible.

Apart from these special points and any supplementary provisions in the company's articles, it suffices that the notice calling a meeting specifies the nature of the business to be transacted at the meeting in sufficient detail to enable members to decide whether they should attend in person or by proxy in order to protect their interests.[11] Consequently, a notice calling a general meeting to elect directors is valid, even though the persons proposed for election as directors are not named in the notice.[11] Likewise, a notice of a general meeting called to resolve that the company shall be wound up is sufficient to enable the meeting to appoint a liquidator, because this follows as a necessary consequence of the company being wound up.[12] On the other hand, a notice of a general meeting called to resolve on an increase in the company's nominal capital is insufficient if it does not set out the amount of the proposed increase;[13] members need to know how many new shares the company will be able to issue if the resolution is passed, for this may affect the liquidity of the company, the gearing of its loan capital and preference shares to its ordinary shares, its power to expand, and also the distribution of voting power at

2 Ibid, s 369 (3) and (4) (see p 624, ante).
3 Table A, art 38 expressly so requires in the case of general meetings.
4 Companies Act 1985, s 366 (1).
5 Ibid, s 378 (1) and (2).
6 *MacConnell v E Prill & Co Ltd* [1916] 2 Ch 57.
7 *Re Moorgate Mercantile Holdings Ltd* [1980] 1 All ER 40, [1980] 1 WLR 227.
8 Companies Act 1985, s 379 (2).
9 Ibid, s 376 (1) and (3).
10 Ibid, s 125 (2) and (3). This is because the resolution is an extraordinary resolution.
11 *Choppington Collieries Ltd v Johnson* [1944] 1 All ER 762.
12 *Re Trench Tubeless Tyre Co* [1900] 1 Ch 408.
13 *MacConnell v E Prill & Co Ltd*, supra.

general meetings. Again, a notice of a resolution to alter the company's memorandum or articles, or to adopt new ones, must set out all material alterations which will be made; it is not sufficient for the notice to invite inspection of a draft of the new or altered memorandum or articles at the company's registered office.[14] Each case must, of course, be decided on its own facts,[15] but the guiding principle is that the notice must be sufficiently detailed to enable a member who knows nothing of the matter to decide whether he need attend the meeting or appoint a proxy to represent him at it, or whether he can safely let the resolution be passed without further enquiry.

Articles often divide the business transacted at meetings into ordinary and special, ordinary business being certain routine matters at annual general meetings, such as the declaration of dividends, the consideration of the accounts and the directors' and auditors' reports, and the appointment of directors and auditors, and special business being all other matters.[16] The value of this arrangement is that when an annual general meeting is called to transact ordinary business only, the notice calling it need not specify what the business to be transacted comprises, because members will be taken to know what it may include from the articles. Furthermore, members will be entitled to move resolutions in respect of ordinary business without giving notice to the other members, but to avoid the risk of a person being proposed for election as a director at an annual general meeting without any prior warning, articles often provide that such nominations must be notified to the company not later than a specified number of days before the meeting, and the written consent of the person proposed as a director to act must be given at the same time.[17]

If directors have an interest in the passing of a resolution, it must be fully disclosed in the notice calling the meeting; if their interest is not disclosed and the resolution is passed, it is invalid.[18] This rule has been made statutory in the case of meetings of classes of members and creditors called to approve compromises or arrangements subject to the sanction of the court, and has been extended in that case to include the interests of trustees for debenture holders.[19] A resolution which benefits directors must clearly show the extent of the benefit. Consequently, a resolution that the directors' remuneration should in future include a percentage of the profits of the company's subsidiary was held to be void when the notice of the meeting failed to disclose that the subsidiary's recent profits had been exceptionally large.[20]

Proxies

The word proxy has two different meanings. Its first meaning is an agent appointed by a member or by a debenture or other loan security holder to vote on his behalf at a meeting at which he is entitled to vote, and its second meaning is the document by which such an agent is appointed.

Every member of a company who is entitled to attend and vote at any general meeting or meeting of a class of members has the right to appoint a proxy to attend

14 *Young v South African and Australian Exploration and Development Syndicate* [1896] 2 Ch 268; *Normandy v Ind Coope & Co Ltd* [1908] 1 Ch 84.
15 *Normandy v Ind Coope & Co Ltd*, supra.
16 The Companies Act 1948, Table A, art 52 so provided. The present Table A contains no such provision.
17 See Table A, art 76, which requires between 14 and 35 clear days' notice of the nomination, unless the person proposed is recommended by the board of directors or is a director seeking re-election.
18 *Kaye v Croydon Tramways Co* [1898] 1 Ch 358; *Tiessen v Henderson* [1899] 1 Ch 861.
19 Companies Act 1985, s 426 (2) and (4).
20 *Baillie v Oriental Telephone and Electric Co Ltd* [1915] 1 Ch 503.

and vote on his behalf, and if the company is a public one, he may appoint two or more proxies to vote in respect of different shares held by him, or he may appoint two or more proxies in the alternative, so that if the first named proxy fails to attend and vote, the second one may do so, and so on.[1] The proxy need not be a member of the company himself.[2] The notice calling a general or class meeting must inform members of their right to appoint proxies, and that proxies need not themselves be members;[3] if this information is omitted, the directors and secretary of the company are liable to a fine,[4] but it appears that the meeting may nevertheless be validly held. Articles of association frequently set out the form which a document appointing a proxy should take,[5] but if the articles permit a form as near thereto as circumstances allow, it appears that any written appointment which would be effective apart from the articles will suffice.[6] Moreover, if the articles permit proxy appointments in 'the usual form', an appointment form is valid even though it contains an error as to the member's name or the shares he holds or as to any other matter, provided the appointment form could mislead no-one as to the meeting at which the proxy may vote.[7]

It is permissible for the board of directors to circulate proxy forms to members and to meet the expense of doing so out of the company's funds,[8] but if the board sends out proxy forms for general or class meetings with the names of proxies already filled in, or accompanied by an invitation to members to appoint a named person or one or more of a number of named persons as their proxies, the same invitation must be sent to all the members entitled to attend the meeting.[9] The purpose of this latter provision is to prevent directors from soliciting members who are unlikely to oppose the board to appoint one or more of the directors as their proxies, without disclosing this tactic to other members who are likely to oppose the board. But directors may quite lawfully supply a member at his request with the names of persons who are willing to act as proxies, if a list of such persons is available on request to every member.[9]

The right to appoint proxies would be valueless if the board could require the documents appointing them to be lodged with the company a considerable time before the meeting is held. Consequently, the Companies Act 1985 invalidates any requirement in a company's articles that proxy appointments shall be lodged with the company or any other person (such as its registrars and transfer agents) earlier than 48 hours before the meeting or an adjournment thereof.[10] This is the time by which articles usually require appointments to be lodged,[11] but if they require lodgment at an earlier time, it would seem that the whole requirement is void, and that a proxy may then attend and vote if he produces the document appointing him at the meeting.[12] On the other hand, the court may construe the invalidation

---

1 Companies Act 1985, s 372 (1), (2) and (7).
2 Ibid, s 372 (1).
3 Ibid, s 372 (3).
4 Ibid, s 372 (4).
5 See Table A, arts 60 and 61.
6 *Isaacs v Chapman* (1915) 32 TLR 183.
7 *Oliver v Dalgleish* [1963] 3 All ER 330, [1963] 1 WLR 1274 (proxy appointment form giving correct date of meeting, but incorrectly describing it as an annual general meeting).
8 *Peel v London and North Western Rly Co* [1907] 1 Ch 5.
9 Companies Act 1985, s 372 (6).
10 Ibid, s 372 (5).
11 See Table A, art 62.
12 The Companies Act 1929 and earlier Acts contained no provisions with regard to proxies. The articles of companies formed under those Acts often permit the appointment of proxies, but require their appointments to be lodged seven to ten days before the meeting which they are to attend. Unless such articles have been altered to conform to the Companies Act 1985, it seems that lodgment in advance of the meeting cannot be required by the company at all.

of the requirement of earlier lodgment of proxy appointments as reducing the time before the meeting by which they must be lodged to 48 hours.

The appointment of a proxy, like that of any other agent, may be revoked by the member at any time, and it is automatically revoked by the member's death, bankruptcy or becoming of unsound mind, and undoubtedly also by the registration of a transfer of the shares in respect of which the proxy is appointed to vote.[13] The member may revoke the proxy's authority by voting himself before the proxy has done so,[14] but once the proxy has voted, the member cannot retract his vote. If a person is appointed a proxy in order to protect an interest of his own for which he has given value,[15] his power to vote in the member's name will not be revoked by any of the acts or events mentioned above. Furthermore, articles often provide that the powers of a proxy shall be exercisable notwithstanding any of those acts or events, unless the company has been notified of the revocation or termination of the authority before the commencement of the meeting which he was appointed to attend.[16] It is doubtful, however, whether such a provision does more than prevent the proxy's vote being challenged if it is cast; it would not seem to justify the proxy in casting the vote as between himself and the member who appointed him, unless the proxy was appointed in order to protect an interest of his own.

Circulars

The notice calling a general meeting is often accompanied by a circular explaining the views of the board of directors on the agenda, and exhorting members to vote in accordance with the board's views. It is perfectly legitimate for the board to send out such circulars and to meet the expense of doing so out of the company's funds, provided that the directors genuinely intend to benefit the general body of members thereby, and do not merely seek to preserve themselves in office, or to gain some other personal advantage for themselves.[17] Vaughan Williams LJ stated the powers of the directors in the following words:[18]

'Is it to be said that the board of directors of a company ... who have had to adopt a particular policy, when that policy is impeached by others (be the number of those who impeach big or small) have not the positive duty to inform the shareholders what have been the reasons for the policy which has been theretofore adopted, and why they think that the policy should be maintained in the future? I cannot myself understand anyone having a doubt as to the directors having that duty. They are not to abstain from their duty to give such information to the shareholders of the company as they think may be desirable for them in the interests of the company because of the accident that a certain number of shareholders take the view that the policy theretofore exercised by the directors has been a wrong policy.'

---

13 A proxy is appointed to perform a personal service for a member, and so the registered transferee of shares must either make his own appointment of a new proxy, or must confirm that the existing appointment of the transferor's proxy shall continue if he is to be represented by the proxy.
14 *Cousins v International Brick Co Ltd* [1931] 2 Ch 90.
15 For example, a proxy given to an equitable mortgagee or an unregistered transferee of shares.
16 See Table A, art 63.
17 *Peel v London and North Western Rly Co* [1907] 1 Ch 5; *Campbell v Australian Mutual Provident Society* (1908) 77 LJPC 117. The Stock Exchange requires listed companies to send out explanatory circulars with notices of general or class meetings called to transact any business other than routine business at annual general meetings (The Stock Exchange: *Admission of Securities to Listing*, Section 5, Chapter 2, para 32).
18 *Peel v London and North Western Rly Co*, supra at 12.

But the directors are generally under no corresponding duty to send out to members a circular prepared by a group of members who are opposed to the board's policy, and who wish to exhort members to vote against the board.[19] However, the same fraction of members who may require the board to put a resolution framed by the requisitionists on the agenda of an annual general meeting,[20] may require the board to circulate to all members entitled to notice of any general meeting, or of a class meeting called to consent to an alteration of the rights of the class, a written statement by the requisitionists, not exceeding one thousand words in length, in respect of any business to be transacted at the meeting.[1] The requisition for the circulation of the statement may consist of several documents in the same form, but the document or documents containing it must be signed by the requisitionists, and must be deposited at the company's registered office not later than one week before the meeting is held, accompanied by a sum of money reasonably sufficient to meet the expense of circulating copies of the statement.[2] If the directors or any other aggrieved person consider that the requisitionists are abusing their rights in order to give needless publicity to defamatory matter, he or they may apply to the court[3] for an order that the statement need not be circulated.[4] The right conferred on members to have a statement of their views circulated by the company is not likely to be used much in practice because of the limit on the length of the statement, and because the right of the board to apply to the court to be excused from circulating a statement which it considers defamatory in effect subjects the statement to the board's censorship. In practice a group of members who are opposed to the board or to approval being given by a class meeting of a proposed alteration in the rights of a class of shareholders will seek to enlist the support of their fellow members by sending out their circular themselves, and they can obtain the names and addresses of their fellow members for this purpose by inspecting the register of members or by requiring the company to supply them with a copy of it.[5] The statutory provision facilitating the circulation of statements by members in respect of business to be transacted at general meetings does not apply to statements relating to business at class meetings, other than those called to consent to an alteration of class rights.

General meetings of companies whose shares are all held by the directors are usually purely formal since all differences of opinion will have been ventilated at board meetings, and because of this formal general meetings are in practice held only when necessary to comply with the Companies Act 1985 (eg the annual general meeting).[6] If a company has a small but not exclusively directorial membership, however, general meetings can be lively occasions at which the opinions expressed are frequently backed up by a personal knowledge of the company's affairs, particularly when members are employed by the company, or were formerly so employed. On the other hand, the members of such companies who are not directors often do not attend general meetings and are not represented there by proxies, except in situations of crisis. Annual general meetings of public and listed companies are rarely well attended by members, and except where controversial matters are involved, or the board of directors is split into factions, or shares in the company are falling in value and there is a prospect of the company

---

19 *Campbell v Australian Mutual Provident Society*, supra.
20 See p 621, ante.
1 Companies Act 1985, s 125 (6) and s 376 (1) and (2).
2 Ibid, s 377 (1).
3 The application is made by originating summons (RSC Ord 102, r 2 (1)).
4 Companies Act 1985, s 377 (3).
5 Ibid, s 356 (1) and (3) (see p 335, ante).
6 Private companies may now dispense even with holding annual general meetings (see p 767, post).

failing, minority shareholders do not in practice attend other general meetings of public companies or appoint proxies to represent them, unless their individual shareholdings are substantial. It is, therefore, no easy matter for a group of members of a public or listed company who are not represented on the board, to arouse the interest and elicit the support of their fellows in order to defeat the incumbent directors at a general meeting and to replace them on the board with their own candidates. If such support is to be obtained, circulars must be sent out and proxies must be solicited well before the meeting is held, and in all this the incumbent directors have obvious advantages. A board of directors can only be seriously threatened if the complaints about their conduct are so serious, or the likelihood of substantial financial loss is so obvious, that all members of the company will take an interest in the meeting. Nevertheless, if the majority of the company's shares carrying voting rights are held by a small number of persons, such as institutional investors or potential takeover bidders, shareholder interest and activity may be more pronounced. Even in these situations, however, the real debate takes place in the circulars sent out by the directors and the group of members which seeks to unseat them, and the result of the voting at the meeting can usually be forecast beforehand from the number of proxy appointments which each side has been successful in obtaining.

The cost of sending out circulars and soliciting proxies can be considerable. The directors will be able to meet their expenses of soliciting support out of the company's funds,[7] but the court has not yet been called on to decide whether a group of members who succeed in overthrowing the board and securing the election of their nominees as directors, may be similarly reimbursed for their campaign expenses, although there are American decisions holding that they may be reimbursed if the members so resolve.[8] Probably such decisions would be followed by an English court on the ground that the group's compaign expenses have been incurred for the benefit of the majority of the members of the company in helping to obtain for them the board of directors they wish to have.[9]

Stock Exchange requirements on acquisitions and disposals

If a company's shares are listed on the Stock Exchange or have been admitted to the Unlisted Securities Market, it must comply with the Stock Exchange's requirements in respect of the notification to it and the press of substantial acquisitions and disposals of assets by the company or its subsidiaries, the issue of circulars to the company's shareholders in respect of such acquisitions and disposals, and the submission of acquisitions and disposals to the approval of a general meeting of the company by ordinary resolution if the transaction exceeds a certain size, or if the other party to the transaction is a present or past director or substantial

---

7 *Peel v London and North Western Rly Co* [1907] 1 Ch 5; *Campbell v Australian Mutual Provident Society* (1908) 77 LJPC 117.
8 *Steinberg v Adams* 90 F Supp 604 (1950); *Rosenfeld v Fairchild Engine and Airplane Corpn* 309 NY 168 (1955).
9 For examples of the court's deference to the wishes of the majority that action should be taken or expenditure incurred, even though it may conflict with directors' fiduciary duties, see *Hogg v Cramphorn Ltd* [1967] Ch 254, [1966] 3 All ER 420, and *Bamford v Bamford* [1970] Ch 212, [1969] 1 All ER 969. If these cases were correctly decided, it would seem that minority shareholders may only prevent a newly elected board from reimbursing their supports' campaign expenses if the minority will thereby be treated oppressively or a fraud will be perpetrated, which is unlikely.

shareholder[10] of the company or another company in the same group, or the other party is an associate[11] of such a person.[12]

If the transaction is so substantial that it affects the company's assets, capital or revenue position to the extent of 15 per cent or more (25 per cent if the company's shares are dealt in on the Unlisted Securities Market), the Stock Exchange and the press must be informed, and a circular must be sent to shareholders; if the company's assets or revenue position is affected to an extent less than 5 per cent and the acquisition or disposal is wholly for cash, the Stock Exchange and the press need not be informed and no circular is necessary; in all other cases the Stock Exchange must be informed, but shareholders need not be sent circulars.[13] In deciding which category an acquisition falls into, four comparisons must be made, namely, between the value of the assets acquired or disposed of and the total assets of the acquiring or disposing company and its subsidiaries; between the net profits attributable to the assets acquired or disposed of and the net assets of the acquiring or disposing company and its subsidiaries; between the price or consideration given and the net assets of the acquiring or disposing company and its subsidiaries; and if the acquiring company issues equity shares in consideration of the acquisition, the proportion between the amount of those shares and the amount of its equity shares previously issued.[14] If any of these comparisons shows that the first item compared bears to the second a proportion of 15 per cent or more (25 per cent if the company's shares are dealt in on the Unlisted Securities Market), the acquisition falls into the first category indicated above, and the acquisition must be notified to the Stock Exchange, the press and the shareholders; if the first three proportions are less than 5 per cent and the acquisition is for cash, no action need be taken; and in all other cases only the Stock Exchange and the press need be notified.[12]

Moreover, if a comparison of the relevant amounts shows that the first item in either the comparison of assets or the comparison of profits bears to the second a proportion of 25 per cent or more and the company's shares are listed, the transaction must be submitted to a general meeting of the company for approval by ordinary resolution.[15] Furthermore, if a comparison of any of the relevant amounts shows that the first item in any comparison bears to the second a proportion of 100 per cent or more and the company's shares are listed, the transaction must be submitted to a general meeting for approval and the company's listing will meanwhile be suspended; on the approval being given the listing will be cancelled, and will be restored only when the company has published listing particulars giving the same full information as though it were making an issue of shares, debentures or other loan securities.[16] Finally, however large or small the

---

10 A substantial shareholder is defined in the same way as for the statutory obligation of a person interested in 3 per cent or more of any class of shares of a public company carrying full voting rights to notify his interest to the company (see p 363, ante), but the qualifying percentage is 10 per cent instead of 3 per cent (Stock Exchange: *Admission of Securities to Listing*, Section 6, Chapter 1, para 1.2.).

11 An associate is defined in the same way as for the purpose of the statutory notification requirement mentioned in the last footnote (Stock Exchange: *Admission of Securities to Listing*, Section 6, Chapter 1, para 1.2).

12 Stock Exchange: *Admission of Securities to Listing*, Section 6, Chapter 1, para 2; Stock Exchange: *The Unlisted Securities Market*, General undertaking, para 5 (a) and Note 1.

13 Stock Exchange: *Admission of Securities to Listing*, Section 6, Chapter 1, paras 3 to 5; Stock Exchange: *The Unlisted Securities Market*, General Undertaking, Note 1 (a) and (b).

14 Stock Exchange: *Admission of Securities to Listing*, Section 6, Chapter 1, paras 1.3 and 3.1.

15 Stock Exchange: *Admission of Securities to Listing*, Section 6, Chapter 1, para 3.4.

16 Stock Exchange: *Admission of Securities to Listing*, Section 6, Chapter 1, para 7. For listing particulars, see p 251 et seq, ante.

transaction, if a company acquires assets from, or disposes of assets to, a person who is or has within the preceding twelve months been a director or substantial shareholder of itself or its holding or subsidiary company or an associate of such a person, or if the company disposes of assets to such a person or his associate, it must notify the Stock Exchange, which may require a circular to be sent to shareholders or their approval of the transaction to be obtained by ordinary resolution at a general meeting, and the Stock Exchange may direct that the director, substantial shareholder or associate shall not vote at the general meeting.[17]

The contents of circulars sent to shareholders in connection with an acquisition or disposal subject to the Stock Exchange's requirements are the same as certain of the obligatory contents of listing particulars which the company would have to publish on an issue of shares or debentures.[18] The information to be given to the Stock Exchange and the press in respect of acquisitions and disposals need only extend to the nature of the assets in question, the nature of the business acquired or disposed of (if relevant), the aggregate consideration paid or given, the value of the assets and the net profits attributable to them, the benefits expected to result to the company as a result of the transaction and the proposed application of any proceeds of sale.[19] Presumably the same information suffices in circulars relating to disposals.

PROCEEDINGS AT GENERAL AND OTHER MEETINGS

Right of attendance

Unless the articles of association otherwise provide, all members of a company are entitled to attend a general meeting, and all members of a class are entitled to attend a meeting of that class, but members of other classes are not entitled to do so.[20] Shareholders who are not members are not entitled to attend general meetings, and so holders of letters of allotment and acceptance and holders of share warrants cannot do so unless the articles so provide.[1] If the articles permit holders of shares of a particular class to attend a class meeting, or if a class meeting is held under the statutory provisions to consent to a variation of the rights of the class,[2] all shareholders of the class concerned may attend, whether members of the company or not. The current Table A (unlike those of earlier Companies Acts) permits directors to attend and speak at general and class meetings, whether they are members of the company or not.[3]

---

17 Ibid, Section 6, Chapter 1, para 1.2 and para 6.1; *The Unlisted Securities Market*, General Undertaking, Note 1 (*d*).
18 Stock Exchange: *Admission of Securities to Listing*, Section 6, Chapter 1, para 3.6.
19 Ibid, Section 6, Chapter 1, para 4.2.
20 *Carruth v Imperial Chemical Industries Ltd* [1937] AC 707 at 761 and 767, per Lord Russell and Lord Maugham.
1 The Companies Act 1985, s 355 (5) provides that the holders of share warrants may be deemed to be members by express provision in the articles.
2 Companies Act 1985, s 125 (2) and (3) (see p 220, ante).
3 Table A, art 44. To ensure that directors may exercise their right to attend general meetings, Table A, art 38 requires notice of such meetings to be given to them in the same way as to members.

Quorum

A general or class meeting cannnot proceed to business unless a quorum[4] of members is present. Unless the articles otherwise provide, two members personally present constitute a quorum at a general meeting.[5] Members who cannot vote at the meeting do not count toward the quorum.[6] Proxies are not counted toward the quorum for a general meeting unless the articles expressly provide that they shall be counted,[7] but Table A does in fact provide that two members present in person or by proxy at a general meeting shall constitute a quorum.[8] The articles usually provide that if a quorum is not present at a general meeting within half an hour from the time appointed for holding the meeting, it shall stand adjourned until the same time the following week,[9] and they often add that at the adjourned meeting the members actually present shall be a quorum, but if the meeting has been called on the requisition of a fraction of the members in exercise of the right given them by the Companies Act 1985,[10] the articles also often provide that the meeting shall be dissolved without an adjournment if a quorum is not present within half an hour of the time originally fixed for holding the meeting.[11] If a quorum is present when a meeting commences, but so many members withdraw while it is being held that less than a quorum of members is left, it seems that the meeting cannot continue. But if the articles merely require a quorum to be present when the meeting proceeds to business,[12] the meeting may complete the business for which it was called, even though the number of members who remain present does not amount to a quorum; this is because the form of the articles shows that a quorum is only required when the meeting begins, and not throughout the time it is being held.[13] A general meeting may not pass valid resolutions if only one person remains present, however, whether he is a member or a proxy for one or more members.[14] This is the result of the rule dealt with below that one person alone cannot constitute a meeting.

A single member who holds all the shares which carry voting rights cannot constitute a general meeting by himself, even though the articles do not require a quorum to be present,[15] and if shares are held by several members and only one member attends the meeting, he cannot constitute a quorum, even though he holds proxies from all the other members.[16] Furthermore, if the articles dispense with a quorum at an adjourned general meeting, it may not be held if only one member

---

4 The word *quorum* (ie of whom) is taken from the phrasing of government and other commissions issued in former times in Latin, and it introduced a specification of the fraction of members of a larger body who might act in its name, or the identification of individual members whose participation in an act of the body was essential. The word 'quorum' is now used as a noun to mean the minimum fraction of members of a body whose presence at a meeting of the body is necessary for it to act.

5 Companies Act 1985, s 370 (1) and (4).

6 *Young v South African and Australian Exploration and Development Syndicate* [1896] 2 Ch 268 at 277.

7 *M Harris Ltd, Petitioners* 1956 SC 207.

8 Table A, art 40.

9 See Table A, art 41.

10 Companies Act 1985, s 368 (1) and (2) (see p 620, ante).

11 Table A, art 54 of the Companies Act 1948, so provided originally, but the provision for the quorum at the adjourned meeting and the dissolution of a requisitioned meeting was repealed by the Companies Act 1980, s 88 (2) and Sch 4; the original provisions of Table A, art 54 still apply to companies registered before 22 December 1980. The present Table A contains no special provision for requisitioned meetings.

12 The Companies Act 1948, Table A, art 53, so provided in respect of general meetings. The present Table A, art 40 prohibits the transaction of business unless a quorum is present.

13 *Re Hartley Baird Ltd* [1955] Ch 143, [1954] 3 All ER 695.

14 *Re London Flats Ltd* [1969] 2 All ER 744, [1969] 1 WLR 711.

15 *Sharp v Dawes* (1876) 2 QBD 26; *Re London Flats Ltd*, supra.

16 *Re Sanitary Carbon Co* [1877] WN 223.

attends.[17] By parity of reasoning it is clear that one proxy representing two or more members, or even all the members, cannot constitute a general meeting, whatever the articles may provide. But if the Secretary of State for Trade and Industry calls an annual general meeting, or if the court directs any general meeting to be held, the Secretary of State or the court may direct that one member present in person or by proxy shall be a quorum.[18] For this reason successful applications have been made to the court to call an extraordinary general meeting in several cases where a shareholder lodged a valid requisition for the meeting with the directors and they called the meeting, but the other shareholders deliberately absented themselves in order to prevent the meeting being held. In these cases the applicant held a majority of the voting shares and the resolutions he sought to procure would undoubtedly have been passed if a meeting had been held, but he was unable to transfer a few of his shares to nominees for himself so as to establish a quorum, because the articles of the company either provided that the directors (to whom he was opposed) could refuse to register transfers,[19] or contained pre-emption provisions by enforcing which the other shareholders could prevent the applicant's proposed resolution from becoming effective.[20]

At a class meeting called to consent to an alteration of the rights of a class of shareholders, the quorum is two or more members of the class or their proxies representing at least one-third in nominal value of the issued shares of the class, but at an adjourned meeting the quorum is reduced to one member of the class present in person or by proxy and no minimum fraction of the shares of the class need be represented.[1] This provision is mandatory and cannot be varied by the articles. A class meeting of this kind cannot be constituted by one proxy attending on behalf of two or more members, because the provision requires at least two persons to be present.[1] If a quorum is not present at the original meeting, an adjournment of it is obligatory only if the articles so provide in respect of the class meeting or in respect of general meetings.[1] At any other class meeting the quorum is that prescribed by the articles, but if they make no express provision, the quorum is two members of the class personally present[2] and proxies for members are not counted. However, it has been held that a class meeting could be held by one shareholder alone when he held all the shares of the class,[3] but this would not seem to be possible without an order of the court[4] where the class meeting is called to consent to an alteration of the rights of the class.[1]

Chairman

If the articles make no provision for the appointment of a chairman to preside at general or class meetings of members, the members may elect one of their own

---

17 *Daimler Co Ltd v Continental Tyre and Rubber Co (Great Britain) Ltd* [1916] 2 AC 307 at 324–5, per Lord Atkinson.

18 Companies Act 1985, s 367 (2) and s 371 (2) (see p 619, ante).

19 *Re El Sombrero Ltd* [1958] Ch 900, [1958] 3 All ER 1; *Re Opera Photographic Ltd* [1989] 1 WLR 634, [1989] BCLC 763; the applicant's proposed resolution in both these cases was for the removal of the directors, who held the remaining shares, and the appointment of his own nominees.

20 *Re H R Paul & Son Ltd* (1973) 118 Sol Jo 166; the applicant's proposed resolution was to appoint directors since there were no directors holding office, but the articles imposed a substantial share qualification on directors (which the applicant proposed to remove), and if he transferred some of his own shares to his nominees in order to qualify them for appointment as directors, the other shareholders would undoubtedly exercise their pre-emption rights under the articles to prevent the qualification being obtained.

1 Companies Act 1985, s 125 (6).

2 Ibid, s 370 (1) and (4).

3 *East v Bennett Bros Ltd* [1911] 1 Ch 163.

4 Companies Act 1985, s 371 (1) and (2) (see p 619 ante).

number to preside.[5] Usually, however, the articles provide that the chairman of the board of directors shall be the chairman at general meetings, or if he fails to attend or is unwilling to act, that one of the other directors chosen by the directors shall be chairman, or if none of them is present or willing to act, the chairman shall be a member chosen by the members present.[6]

The chairman's function is to preserve order at the meeting, to call on members to speak, and to take the vote at the conclusion of the discussion on a resolution. He has no general power to dissolve or adjourn the meeting without the consent of the members present expressed by ordinary resolution,[7] but if a power to dissolve or adjourn the meeting is given to him by the articles, he may exercise or refuse to exercise it despite the contrary wishes of the majority of the members present.[8] If no express power of adjournment is given to the chairman by the articles, he may adjourn the meeting for a short time in the event of disorder, whether or not accompanied by violence, but only for as long as is needed for order to be restored.[9] A chairman also has power, despite any provisions to the contrary in the company's articles, to adjourn a meeting when it is impossible for it to proceed to business or to continue because of some physical obstacle (eg the inadequacy of the accommodation at the place at which the meeting is held so that some of the members or their proxies who attend cannot participate in the meeting, or the failure of audio-visual equipment used to relay the proceedings in the room where the chairman presides to overflow accommodation provided for members and their proxies in other rooms).[10] In this case, however, the chairman must either adjourn the meeting to another place where it can be held, and must delay the holding of the adjourned meeting sufficiently so that members who cannot attend it may appoint proxies to attend in their place,[11] or he must dissolve the meeting and it must be convened afresh as though the first abortive meeting had not been held.[10]

If a chairman improperly refuses to continue a meeting despite the wish of the members or shareholders present or represented, or if the chairman declares the meeting dissolved or adjourned when he has no power to do so, the members may elect a new chairman in his place.[7] The meeting must then continue from the point it had reached when the former chairman wrongfully discontinued it, so that if the former chairman declared the meeting adjourned as a result of a vote taken on a show of hands, and incorrectly refused to put the adjournment motion to a poll, the new chairman must take the poll before the meeting may proceed.[12]

Moving and discussion of resolutions

Any resolution mentioned in the notice calling a meeting may be moved by a member. If the resolution is one which need not be set out verbatim in the notice, the fact that it is set out verbatim does not prevent a member from moving a resolution in different terms which would have been in order if the notice had

5 Companies Act 1985, s 370 (5).
6 See Table A, arts 42 and 43. This provision also applies to class meetings called to consent to an alteration of the rights of the class (Companies Act 1985, s 125 (6)).
7 *National Dwellings Society Ltd v Sykes* [1894] 3 Ch 159; *Catesby v Burnett* [1916] 2 Ch 325.
8 *Salisbury Gold Mining Co v Hathorn* [1897] AC 268. Table A, art 45, empowers the chairman to adjourn a general meeting at which a quorum is present with the consent of the meeting, and requires him to adjourn if the meeting so resolves.
9 *John v Rees* [1970] Ch 345, [1969] 2 All ER 274.
10 *Byng v London Life Association Ltd* [1989] 1 All ER 560, [1989] 2 WLR 738.
11 Proxy appointments must usually be notified to the company at least 48 hours before the adjourned meeting is held.
12 *MacDougall v Gardiner* (1875) 1 ChD 13 at 26, per Baggallay JA.

merely set out the general nature of the first resolution.[13] Consequently, where a meeting was called to pass a resolution to appoint named persons as directors,[13] or a named person as liquidator of the company,[14] it was held that a member was in order in moving a resolution to appoint other persons as directors or another person as liquidator, because if the notice calling the meeting had merely specified the business to be transacted as the appointment of directors or a liquidator, the alternative resolution would clearly have been in order. On the other hand, if the resolution which the meeting is called to pass is one which must be set out verbatim in the notice, it is not in order for a member to move an alternative resolution, even though it concerns the same subject matter.

When a resolution has been moved any member may speak on it or move an amendment to it. There is no need to give notice of a proposed amendment to the company or to the members entitled to attend the meeting, unless it materially alters the nature or effect of the resolution. Thus, where a meeting is called to elect named persons as directors, it is permissible without notice to move an amendment that they shall not be elected, and that other persons shall be elected instead.[15] But if a meeting is called to resolve that the company's undertaking shall be sold to another company in consideration of shares in it, and that the first company shall then be wound up, it is not permissible without notice to move an amendment that the first company shall simply be wound up, because this would entirely alter the character of the original resolution.[16] It is permissible to move amendments to special resolutions[17] and to all other resolutions which must be set out verbatim in the notice calling the meeting,[18] but the resolution passed will apparently be invalid if the amendment alters its substance or effect, however slightly,[19] and so the scope for moving amendments to such resolutions is narrower than in the case of ordinary resolutions. If the chairman improperly refuses to allow an amendment to any resolution to be discussed and voted upon, and the resolution is put to a vote and carried, the resolution is void.[20]

A proxy cannot move a resolution or an amendment thereto or speak at a general or class meeting of a public company unless its articles so provide, but at a general or class meeting of a private company with a share capital, a proxy has a statutory right to speak which cannot be taken away by the articles, but no right to move resolutions or amendments unless the articles so provide.[1]

Closure, dissolution and adjournment

A meeting may resolve to close discussion on a resolution and to take a vote on it forthwith, but the closure may not be moved until members have had a reasonable opportunity to discuss the substantive resolution, and if the closure is applied in order to stifle discussion, the vote taken on the substantive resolution is void.[2]

Members may resolve to dissolve a meeting or to adjourn it until a later day,

---

13 *Betts & Co Ltd v Macnaghten* [1910] 1 Ch 430; *Catesby v Burnett* [1916] 2 Ch 325; *Choppington Collieries Ltd v Johnson* [1944] 1 All ER 762.
14 *Re Trench Tubeless Tyre Co* [1900] 1 Ch 408.
15 See cases cited in footnote 2, ante. The moving of an amendment in such a case is simply a shorter way of achieving the same result as rejecting the resolution originally proposed and then moving a new resolution to elect the other persons.
16 *Re Teede and Bishop Ltd* (1901) 70 LJ Ch 409.
17 *Torbock v Lord Westbury* [1902] 2 Ch 871.
18 For the situations where this is necessary, see p 626, ante.
19 *Re Moorgate Mercantile Holdings Ltd* [1980] 1 All ER 40, [1980] 1 WLR 227.
20 *Henderson v Bank of Australasia* (1890) 45 ChD 330.
 1 Companies Act 1985, s 372 (1) and (2).
 2 *Wall v London and Northern Assets Corpn* [1898] 2 Ch 469.

unless the chairman is given an exclusive power to dissolve or adjourn by the articles and he refuses to consent to a dissolution or adjournment.[3] It is not necessary to give notice of an adjourned meeting to members unless the articles so provide,[4] or unless the original meeting is adjourned so that amendments may be moved to a resolution which will alter its nature or effect substantially. A member may attend the adjourned meeting, even though he did not attend the original one.[5] Also a member may appoint a proxy to attend the adjourned meeting, even though he did not attend or appoint a proxy to attend the original meeting; the company's articles may not require such proxy appointments to be lodged earlier than 48 hours before the adjourned meeting is held.[6] The only business which an adjourned meeting may transact is that left unfinished at the original meeting, and so no new resolution may be moved if it is not within the scope of the notice calling the original meeting.[7]

Motions for the closure of discussion or the dissolution or adjournment of a meeting may be passed by ordinary resolution unless the articles otherwise provide, and a proxy appointed to vote on the substantive resolutions at a meeting may vote on these motions too.[8]

Voting

Votes on a resolution are usually taken in the first place by a show of hands, on which each member present has one vote irrespective of the number of shares he holds.[9] A proxy cannot vote on a show of hands unless the articles so provide,[10] but if they do empower him to vote, he can only record one vote even though he represents more than one member.[11]

On the declaration of the result of the vote on a show of hands, any member[12] or proxy[13] may demand a poll, unless the articles otherwise provide. Restrictions imposed by the articles on the right to demand a poll are generally effective, but notwithstanding anything in the articles, a poll must be held on any resolution at a general or class meeting (except a resolution at a general meeting for the election of a chairman or the adjournment of the meeting),[14] if it is demanded by not less than five members, or by members who can together cast at least one-tenth of the total number of votes which may be cast on a poll, or by members who hold shares on which there has been paid at least one-tenth of the capital paid up on all the shares which carry the right to vote at the meeting.[15] Again, notwithstanding anything in the articles, a proxy may demand or join in demanding a poll as if the member he represents were making the demand himself,[13] and so a proxy for five members may demand a poll by himself without the support of anyone else. By these provisions the law secures minimum rights for members or their proxies to

---

3 *Salisbury Gold Mining Co v Hathorn*, supra. For the provisions of Table A in this respect, see footnote 8 on p 636, ante.
4 Table A, art 45, requires notice of an adjourned general meeting to be given only if the original meeting is adjourned for fourteen days or more, in which case at least seven clear days' notice of the adjourned meeting must be given.
5 *R v D'Oyly* (1840) 12 Ad & El 139.
6 Companies Act 1985, s 372 (5) (see p 628, ante).
7 *Robert Batcheller & Sons Ltd v Batcheller* [1945] Ch 169, [1945] 1 All ER 522.
8 *Re Waxed Papers Ltd* [1937] 2 All ER 481.
9 See Table A, art 46.
10 Companies Act 1985, s 372 (1). Table A does not so provide.
11 *Ernest v Loma Gold Mines Ltd* [1897] 1 Ch 1.
12 *Campbell v Maund* (1836) 5 Ad & El 865; *R v Wimbledon Local Board* (1882) 8 QBD 459.
13 Companies Act 1985, s 373 (2).
14 Table A, art 46, permits a poll to be demanded on these matters, too.
15 Companies Act 1985, s 373 (1).

demand a poll, and these rights cannot be abridged by the company's articles. Table A follows the mandatory provisions of the Companies Act 1985 in this respect, but in addition to the persons who have a statutory right to demand a poll, Table A enables the chairman of a general meeting or at least two members of the company present in person or by proxy to demand a poll.[16]

If the articles give the chairman of a meeting power to demand a poll, it has been held that the chairman must exercise the power when he has reason to believe that the result of a poll would be different from the result of the vote taken on a show of hands if all the members with voting rights were to vote on the poll.[17] But if the chairman has no right to demand a poll himself, either in his capacity as chairman under the terms of the articles or as a member of the company or as a proxy for a member or members, it appears that he is under no obligation to invite a demand for a poll from the requisite number of members or their proxies merely because he has cause to believe that the result of the vote on a show of hands would be reversed on a poll.

A poll cannot be held unless it is duly demanded by members or their proxies or by the chairman, and in the absence of such a demand, the result of the vote taken on a show of hands will be the decision of the meeting.[18] However, if the articles provide that a poll may be demanded before or on the declaration of the result of a vote on a show of hands,[19] it may be demanded before a vote on a show of hands is taken, and the chairman may then proceed to hold it without taking a vote on a show of hands at all.[20]

Notice need not be given to members of the time and place at which a poll will be taken unless the articles so require.[1]

Votes are cast on a poll according to the scheme established by the memorandum or articles of association or the terms of issue of different classes of shares, but unless the articles otherwise provide,[2] at a general meeting and at a class meeting every member has one vote for each share or each complete £10 of stock he holds.[3] Table A confers one vote for each share held by a member on a poll at both general and class meetings, but the voting rights attached to a class of shares at general meetings may be restricted by the terms of issue[4] (eg no voting rights at all may be conferred on the holders of shares of the class, or only voting rights proportionate to the nominal value of the shares, as compared with the higher nominal value of shares of another class). Moreover, the memorandum or articles of association of a particular company may vary the statutory distribution of voting rights in any way desired, and so it is possible at general meetings for a class or classes of shares to carry no voting rights, or voting rights exercisable only in specified

16 Table A, art 46. If such a provision applies to general meetings of the company, it applies also to a class meeting called to consent to an alteration of the rights of the class (Companies Act 1985, s 125 (6)).

17 *Second Consolidated Trust Ltd v Ceylon Amalgamated Tea and Rubber Estates Ltd* [1943] 2 All ER 567.

18 *Carruth v Imperial Chemical Industries Ltd* [1937] AC 707 at 755, [1937] 2 All ER 422 at 441 per Lord Blanesburgh; *Re Horbury Bridge Coal, Iron and Waggon Co* (1879) 11 ChD 109.

19 See Table A, art 46.

20 *Holmes v Keyes* [1958] Ch 670 at 680, [1958] 2 All ER 129 at 136, per Jenkins LJ.

1 Table A, art 52 requires notice of a poll if the time and place for holding it are not announced at the meeting at which it is demanded, in which case at least seven clear days' notice of the poll must be given.

2 The Companies Act 1985 refers only to articles making other provisions, but this undoubtedly includes other provisions made by the terms of issue of shares which were approved by a general meeting (see Table A, art 2), or which were decided upon by the board of directors under a power conferred by the memorandum or articles.

3 Companies Act 1985, s 370 (1) and (6).

4 Table A, art 54.

circumstances;[5] or for one class of shares to carry multiple voting rights in comparison with other classes;[6] or for shares held by individuals identified by name or description (eg directors) to carry multiple or majority voting rights either in respect of all resolutions, or on resolutions of certain kinds (eg for the election or removal of directors).[7] It is possible for the memorandum or articles to confer differential voting rights at class meetings as well as general meetings, but in practice this is not done and voting rights at class meetings are always made proportionate to the number or total nominal value of the shares of the class which are held by each member. The Stock Exchange requires 'adequate' voting rights to be conferred on the preference shareholders of listed companies,[8] but voting rights at general meetings limited to voting only on alterations of the memorandum and articles and on winding up resolutions are accepted as adequate for this purpose. The Jenkins Committee was not opposed to the issue of shares with no voting rights or limited voting rights at general meetings even by listed companies,[9] but it did propose that notices of general meetings should always be sent to the holders of such shares.[10]

On a poll at a general meeting or a class meeting a member or his proxy may cast some of his votes for the resolution and some against, or he may cast only some, but not all, of the votes to which he is entitled;[11] this provision is useful when a nominee holds a block of shares for two or more beneficial owners who give him different instructions as to the way their votes shall be cast. On a poll proxies have a statutory right to cast the votes of the members they represent, and this right cannot be abridged by the articles.[12] It is obvious that a poll can be a complex proceeding involving the issue of voting papers to members and their proxies, the collection of such papers when completed, and the computation of the total number of votes cast for and against the resolution. Consequently, the articles usually empower the chairman at the meeting to direct how the poll shall be held.[13] The chairman may then defer the holding of the poll until a later day, but he is not bound to defer it, and it may be held forthwith.[14] If the holding of the poll is deferred, the meeting is not deemed to be adjourned, and so, unless the articles otherwise provide, no further proxies may be lodged,[15] and if the articles prohibit the revocation of proxies after the meeting has begun, no appointment of a proxy already made may be revoked.[16] A member may vote on a poll even though he did

---

5 Preference shares often carry voting rights at general meetings only on resolutions to alter the memorandum or articles or the preference shareholders' class rights and on resolutions to wind up the company, but it is also common to confer full voting rights on preference shareholders if the preference dividend is in arrear for a specified length of time.

6 This can be achieved expressly (eg by attributing ten votes to each £1 ordinary share and one vote to each £1 preference share) or implicitly by making the nominal value of shares of one class appropriately smaller than the nominal value of other shares (eg by having 10p ordinary shares and £1 preference shares and conferring one vote in respect of each share).

7 Bushell v Faith [1970] AC 1099, [1970] 1 All ER 53.

8 Stock Exchange: Admission of Securities to Listing, Section 9, Chapter 1, para 6.1.

9 Three members of the Committee dissented from this, and would have required future issues of listed ordinary shares to carry voting rights.

10 Report of the Company Law Committee (Cmnd 1749), para 140.

11 Companies Act 1985, s 374.

12 Ibid, s 372 (1).

13 See Table A, art 49. This article applies only to general meetings and to class meetings called to consent to an alteration of the rights of the class (Companies Act 1985, s 125 (6)).

14 Re Chillington Iron Co (1885) 29 ChD 159, rejecting the doubts expressed in Re Horbury Bridge Coal Iron and Waggon Co (1879) 11 ChD 109 at 114.

15 Jackson v Hamlyn [1953] Ch 577, [1953] 1 All ER 887. Table A, art 62 permits proxies to be lodged for the purpose of voting on a poll not later than 24 hours before the poll is to be taken if it is to be taken more than 48 hours after it is demanded, or immediately in any other case.

16 Shaw v Tati Concessions Ltd [1913] 1 Ch 292.

not attend and was not represented by a proxy at the meeting at which the poll was demanded.[17] A resolution carried on a poll is effective only when the result of the voting is declared, and so when directors are elected on a poll, the two months within which they must acquire their qualification shares runs from that time, and not from the earlier date on which the poll was held.[18] The manner in which particular shareholders or their proxies vote on a poll is not confidential information which the chairman of the meeting or the scrutineers appointed under the company's articles to take the poll may disclose at or after which the poll is taken only with the consent of those shareholders, and so the chairman or scrutineers may inform the company and its members how and by whom particular votes were cast.[19]

It is common practice nowadays for companies to issue 'two way' proxy forms on which a member can indicate whether his proxy is to vote for or against a resolution or resolutions to be moved at the meeting.[20] This is the nearest approach to postal voting that companies have yet come to, but it is not the same as postal voting, because, although the proxy is a mere cipher with authority to vote only one way, the member's vote will not count unless the proxy attends the meeting and casts it. Moreover, a company may not employ postal voting in the true sense unless its articles so provide,[1] and in any case, special and extraordinary resolutions cannot be passed in that way by a majority vote because the Companies Act 1985 requires them to be passed at meetings of members by the appropriate fraction of members voting in person or by proxy.[2] It has not yet been decided whether a company is bound by the terms of a 'two-way' proxy form, so that it cannot count the vote of the proxy if he casts it contrary to his principal's instructions. Nevertheless, it has been held that if a proxy has been given 'two-way' proxy forms by different shareholders, some for and some against the resolution, and he votes for the resolution without specifying how many votes he is casting, his vote is valid only to the extent of the votes in respect of which affirmative proxy forms have been lodged.[3]

Articles frequently provide that no objection may be raised to a vote cast at a meeting except at the meeting itself, and that any vote not disallowed thereat shall be valid for all purposes.[4] This provision is effective to prevent any objection being raised either by the chairman or any other person as to the validity of votes or the appointment of a proxy who cast them at any time after the close of the meeting.[5] The second part of such a provision enables the chairman to determine the validity of challenged votes,[4] and his decision is final unless he is guilty of fraud or misconduct.[6]

17 *R v D'Oyly* (1840) 12 Ad & El 139.
18 *Holmes v Keyes* [1958] Ch 670, [1958] 2 All ER 129.
19 *Haarhaus & Co GmbH v Law Debenture Trust Corpn plc* [1988] BCLC 640.
20 See Table A, art 61. If a company seeks a Stock Exchange listing for any of its securities, its articles of association must not preclude the use of 'two way' proxy forms. (The Stock Exchange: *Admission of Securities to Listing*, Section 9, Chapter 1, para 12.1.), and the company must send out 'two-way' proxy forms with notices calling meetings of shareholders or debenture holders (Ibid, Section 5, Chapter 1, para 37.)
1 *McMillan v Le Roi Mining Co Ltd* [1906] 1 Ch 331. But see p 645, post as to written resolutions signed by members unanimously and p 762, post, as to written resolutions of private companies.
2 Companies Act 1985, s 378 (1) and (2). But see p 645, post as to such resolutions consented to by members unanimously.
3 *Oliver v Dalgleish* [1963] 3 All ER 330, [1963] 1 WLR 1214.
4 See Table A, art 58.
5 *Colonial Gold Reef Ltd v Free State Rand Ltd* [1914] 1 Ch 382; *Marx v Estates and General Investments Ltd* [1975] 3 All ER 1064, [1976] 1 WLR 380.
6 *Wall v London and Northern Assets Corpn* [1899] 1 Ch 550; *Wall v Exchange Investment Corpn* [1926] Ch 143.

Articles usually give the chairman of a meeting a casting vote in the event of an equality of votes on a show of hands or a poll,[7] and they also usually make his decision on the result of a vote taken by a show of hands conclusive.[8] The Companies Act 1985 itself makes the chairman's decision conclusive as to the result of a vote on a special or extraordinary resolution taken on a show of hands at a general meeting when no poll is demanded.[9] These provisions prevent the court from enquiring into the correctness of the chairman's decision,[10] unless he fraudulently misrepresents the total number of votes cast for or against the resolution, or unless his decision is wrong on the face of it, as it would be if he stated the number of votes cast for or against a special resolution, and this shows that the resolution was not in fact carried or defeated as the chairman declared.[11]

Corporate members

A corporation which is a member, creditor or debenture holder of a company may by resolution of its governing body authorise any person to act as its representative at a meeting of members or a class of members, or at a meeting of creditors or debenture holders, of the company.[12] If the corporation is in liquidation, the power to appoint a representative is exercisable by the liquidator.[13] The representative may exercise the same powers at the meeting as the corporation could exercise if it were an individual member, creditor, or debenture holder.[14] The representative is not a proxy; consequently, there is no need to notify his appointment to the company before the meeting is held, he counts toward a quorum in all cases, and unlike a proxy, he can move resolutions and amendments, can speak at a general or class meeting even if the company is a public one, and he can vote on a show of hands.[15] There is nothing to prevent a corporate member of a company from appointing a proxy, of course, and the position and powers of such a proxy are the same as those of a proxy appointed by an individual member.

Limitations on voting rights

A member's freedom to vote as he wishes, or to vote at all, at a meeting may be limited in three ways, namely, by the memorandum or articles of the company or the conditions on which his shares were issued, or by a contract entered into by the member, or by law. Restrictions on voting rights imposed by the memorandum or articles and inequalities in voting rights as between different classes of shareholders have already been dealt with,[16] as has the prohibition on a public company or its nominee voting in respect of shares in itself which it has acquired or in which it has an interest.[17]

---

7 See Table A, art 50. This article applies only to general meetings and to class meetings called to consent to an alteration of the rights of the class (Companies Act 1985, s 125 (6)). The chairman has no casting vote if the articles do not confer it on him (*Re v Chapman* (1704) 6 Mod Rep 152, *Anon* (1773) Lofft 315; *R v Ginever* (1796) 6 Term Rep 732).
8 See Table A, art 47. This article applies only to general meetings and to class meetings called to consent to an alteration of the rights of a class (Companies Act 1985, s 125 (6)).
9 Companies Act 1985, s 378 (4).
10 *Re Hadleigh Castle Gold Mines Ltd* [1900] 2 Ch 419; *Arnot v United African Lands Ltd* [1901] 1 Ch 518; contra, *Young v Smith African and Australian Exploration and Development Syndicate* [1896] 2 Ch 268.
11 *Re Caratal (New) Mines Ltd* [1902] 2 Ch 498.
12 Companies Act 1985, s 375 (1).
13 *Hillman v Crystal Bowl Amusements Ltd* [1973] 1 All ER 379, [1973] 1 WLR 162.
14 Companies Act 1985, s 375 (2).
15 *Re Kelantan Coconut Estates Ltd* [1920] WN 274.
16 See p 639, ante.
17 See p 411, ante.

A member may validly contract with another person to vote in a particular way or as that person directs at a general or a class meeting of a company. The contract can be enforced by an ordinary injunction to prevent the member from voting inconsistently with the contract,[18] or by a mandatory injunction to compel him to vote as the contract or the other person directs.[19] Furthermore, a member may validly contract to give a permanent and irrevocable authority to another to exercise the member's voting rights,[20] and he may therefore enter into a valid agreement with other members to pool their voting rights and to vote on all their shares as the majority of them from time to time decide.[1] In the United Kingdom it is unusual for such contractual arrangements to be reinforced by the participating members transferring their shares to trustees and executing a trust deed by which the trustees are authorised and required to vote in respect of the shares in the manner which the participants or a specified number or a majority of them direct. Such voting trusts are not uncommon in the United States, where they are valid at common law,[2] and if set up in this country they would undoubtedly be valid by English law.

In the absence of contractual restraints, a member may vote as he wishes at a general meeting, and may consult his private interests exclusively, even though they conflict with those of the company.[3] This is so even though the member or a group of members who act in concert can exercise or control a majority of the votes which may be cast.[4] Unlike American law, English law has not developed the principle that a controlling shareholder owes a fiduciary duty to the company or to his fellow shareholders, and that his freedom to consult only his own interests is correspondingly limited.[5] On the other hand, resolutions altering the memorandum or articles of association of a company, and resolutions passed at a meeting of a class of members affecting their class rights, are valid only if passed on good faith in the interests of the members or class of members as a whole.[6] This does not mean that a member who has an interest in conflict with those of the other members of the company, or of the other members of the class in question, is disqualified from voting on such resolutions; it means merely that the court will scrutinise the proceedings to ensure that dissenting members are not treated unfairly, and also to ensure that in the long term the alteration or arrangement will operate in a way that does not discriminate between members of the company or of the class.[7] Moreover, if members who control the majority of the votes which may be cast at a general meeting procure the passing of any resolution which will be oppressive or unfairly prejudicial to other members, whether it involves an alteration of the memorandum or articles or of the rights of a class of members or not, the court will set the resolution aside in exercise of its general equitable power to give relief

18 *Greenwell v Porter* [1902] 1 Ch 530.
19 *Puddephatt v Leith* [1916] 1 Ch 200.
20 The person to whom the authority is given must give consideration for it and must have an interest in exercising the power to vote (*Gaussen v Morton* (1830) 10 B & C 731; *Smart v Sandars* (1884) 5 CB 895, 917 per Wilde CJ).
1 Such agreements are valid under American and Canadian common law (*Ringling Bros-Barnum and Bailey Combined Shows Inc v Ringling* (1947) 29 Del Ch 610; *Ringuet v Bergeron* (1960) 24 DLR 2d 449).
2 *Mackin v Nicollet Hotel Inc* (1928) 25 F 2d 783; affd (1928) 278 US 618.
3 *Pender v Lushington* (1877) 6 ChD 70; *Curruth v ICI Ltd* [1937] AC 707 at 765, [1937] 2 All ER 422 at 458, per Lord Maugham.
4 *North West Transportation Co v Beatty* (1887) 12 App Cas 589; *Dominion Cotton Mills Co Ltd v Amyot* [1912] AC 546.
5 *Phillips v Manufacturers Securities Ltd* (1917) 116 LT 290 at 296, per Cozens-Hardy MR (see p 676, post).
6 *British American Nickel Corpn v O'Brien* [1927] AC 369; *Greenhalgh v Arderne Cinemas Ltd* [1951] Ch 286, [1950] 2 All ER 1120.
7 See pp 75 and 230, ante.

against oppression or its statutory power to relieve minority shareholders from unfairly prejudicial treatment.[8] Apart from this, the only ground on which a resolution of a general meeting which does not alter the company's memorandum or articles may be attacked because of the motives of the members who voted for it, is that the resolution was not passed in good faith; the mere fact that it did not assist in achieving the company's objects (although it did not conflict with them), or that the resolution was not for the benefit of the company or of its members as a whole, does not invalidate the resolution or enable the court to set it aside.[9]

The fact that a member of a company is also a director of it does not prevent him from voting at general meetings in accordance with his personal interests,[10] and if he does so, his vote cannot be set aside because it supports a course of action which is against the company's interests, or which will result in the company breaking an obligation it owes to a third party.[11] The only special limitation on the exercise of a director's voting rights in his capacity as a member is that if he and his fellow directors control a majority of the votes at a general meeting, they cannot by the use of their votes procure the release of any of their number from liability for a breach of the fiduciary duties which they owe to the company, or authorise such a breach in advance.[12]

Minutes

Every company must keep minutes of the proceedings of its general meetings, and if the minutes of a general meeting are signed by the chairman who presides at it or at the next following general meeting, it is presumed, until the contrary is shown, that the meeting was duly convened, and that all proceedings recorded in the minutes were regularly taken.[13] This provision merely raises a presumption of regularity in favour of recorded proceedings; it does not preclude proof that other proceedings which are not recorded took place. Consequently, evidence may be given that a resolution was passed at a meeting, even though it is not recorded in the minutes.[14] But if the articles provide that the minutes shall be conclusive evidence of what business was transacted at a meeting, in the absence of fraud it is not permissible for a member to challenge their accuracy and completeness, at least in connection with a transaction between the company and himself in his capacity as a member.[15]

The minutes of general meetings must be kept at the company's registered office, and members may inspect them without charge.[16] Furthermore, a member may require the company to supply him with a copy of any part of the minutes for a fee not exceeding 2.5p, or such other amount as shall be prescribed by regulations made by the Secretary of State for Trade and Industry, for each hundred words copied.[17] If the company refuses to allow such inspection, or fails to supply such a copy of the minutes, the member may apply to the court[18] for an order that it shall do so forthwith.[19]

8 *Clemens v Clemens Bros Ltd* [1976] 2 All ER 268; Companies Act 1985, s 459 (1) (see p 659, post).
9 *Re Halt Garage (1964) Ltd* [1982] 3 All ER 1016.
10 *North West Transportation Co v Beatty*, supra; *Burland v Earle* [1902] AC 83.
11 *Northern Counties Securities Ltd v Jackson and Steeple Ltd* [1974] 2 All ER 625, [1974] 1 WLR 1133.
12 *Cook v Deeks* [1916] 1 AC 554 (see p 590, ante and p 661, post).
13 Companies Act 1985, s 382 (1) and (4).
14 *Re Fireproof Doors Ltd* [1916] 2 Ch 142.
15 *Kerr v John Mottram Ltd* [1940] Ch 657, [1940] 2 All ER 629.
16 Companies Act 1985, s 383 (1), as amended by Companies Act 1989, s 143 (9).
17 Companies Act 1985, s 383 (3), as amended by Companies Act 1989, s 149 (9).
18 The application is made by originating summons (RSC Ord 102, r 2 (1)).
19 Companies Act 1985, s 383 (5).

Minutes of the proceedings of class meetings must be kept by the directors unless the articles otherwise provide,[20] but none of the rules dealt with in the foregoing paragraphs as to the evidentiary value of minutes and their inspection by members apply to the minutes of class meetings. However, if the articles contain provisions relating to minutes of general meetings, they apply also to minutes of class meetings called to consent to alterations in the rights of the class.[1]

Waiver of irregularities in respect of meetings

If all the members of a company who are entitled to attend a general or class meeting do so and vote unanimously in favour of a resolution,[2] or assent unanimously to the resolution without a meeting being held at all,[3] they are taken to waive any irregularities attending the passing of the resolution, and it is as effective as if it had been properly passed at a duly convened meeting. The same applies if a minority of members who could have prevented a resolution being passed at a meeting attend the meeting in person or by proxy and do not vote against the resolution and all the other members vote in favour of it.[4] This power to waive irregularities has been extended by the Companies Act 1985 to enable a certain fraction of members to assent to a general meeting being held although the proper length of notice of it has not been given.[5] Furthermore, Table A provides that a resolution in writing signed by all the members entitled to vote at general meetings shall be as effective as a resolution passed at a duly convened meeting,[6] and this applies also to class meetings called to consent to an alteration of the rights of the class if the articles contain no contrary provision.[7]

The power to waive irregularities is nevertheless subject to limitations. In the first place, the resolution is effective only if all the members entitled to vote assent to it, or at least, if none of them vote against it;[4] a majority, however large, has no power to waive procedural requirements against the adverse votes of a minority, except where the Companies Act 1985 so provides.[8] Secondly, the transaction in question must be honest and for the benefit of the company, so that a unanimous decision to do an act which will defraud the Revenue authorities is not treated as equivalent to a resolution duly passed.[9] Finally, it was formerly doubted whether a special or extraordinary resolution could be passed informally without a meeting being held, because the definition of these resolutions[10] requires them to be passed at a general meeting.[11] It has now been held, however, that the unanimous consent of the shareholders of a company is equivalent to the passing of a special or

20 Table A, art 100 (*b*). This article applies to all companies limited by shares unless expressly excluded by their own articles of association (Companies Act 1985, s 8 (2)).

1 Companies Act 1985, s 125 (6).

2 *Re Express Engineering Works Ltd* [1920] 1 Ch 466; *Re Oxted Motor Co* [1921] 3 KB 32; *Parker and Cooper Ltd v Reading* [1926] Ch 975.

3 *Ashbury Railway Carriage and Iron Co v Riche* (1875) LR 7 HL 653 at 675, per Lord Cairns LC; *Re Duomatic Ltd* [1969] 2 Ch 365, [1969] 1 All ER 161; *Multinational Gas and Petrochemical Co v Multinational Gas and Petrochemical Services Ltd* [1983] Ch 258, [1983] 2 All ER 563.

4 *Re Bailey Hay & Co Ltd* [1971] 3 All ER 693, [1971] 1 WLR 1357.

5 Companies Act 1985, s 369 (3) and (4) and s 378 (3) (see p 624, ante).

6 Table A, art 53. For the ability of general meetings of private companies to pass written resolutions, see p 762, post.

7 Companies Act 1985, s 125 (6).

8 *Imperial Bank of China India and Japan v Bank of Hindustan, China and Japan* (1868) LR 6 Eq 91; *Re Duomatic Ltd* [1969] 2 Ch 365, [1969] 1 All ER 161.

9 *Peter Buchanan Ltd and Macharg v McVey* [1955] AC 516n.

10 Companies Act 1985, s 378 (1) and (2).

11 *Pacific Coast Coal Mines Ltd v Arbuthnot* [1917] AC 607; but see to the contrary, *Ho Tung v Man On Insurance Co Ltd* [1902] AC 232.

extraordinary resolution and has the same effect.[12] Furthermore, it has been held that if a general meeting is held to pass a special or extraordinary resolution, but there is some defect in convening or holding it, the resolution will be treated as validly passed if all the members entitled to attend the meeting susbsequently agree to treat it as binding.[13] On the other hand, it has been held that when a special resolution is effective under the Companies Act 1985 only if it is confirmed by the court (eg a special resolution for the reduction of capital),[14] the court will not give the necessary confirmation unless the resolution has been passed at a general meeting, and the unanimous consent of the members of the company with voting rights, or a document signed by them expressing their unanimous consent, will not be treated as an adequate substitute for this.[15]

The court has said in some cases that a company may be treated as bound by a resolution, even though it is not shown that it was duly passed at a general meeting or that it was assented to by all the members. Thus, it has been held that a company loses its right to rescind a contract with its promoters if substantially all its members are aware of the right to rescind and fail to act for an unreasonable length of time.[16] It has also been held that a company could not sue its directors for borrowing beyond the powers conferred on them by the articles,[17] nor treat an irregular surrender of partly paid shares as void,[18] when all the members had had an opportunity of discovering the irregularity, and no-one had taken steps to challenge it for several years. Similarly, where members of a company which had gone into voluntary liquidation took an active part in the liquidation proceedings, and were fully aware of a procedural defect in the passing of the resolution to wind the company up, it was held that neither they nor the members who voted for the resolution could challenge its validity.[19] Again, where no properly subscribed articles had been delivered to the Registrar of Companies on the incorporation of a company, but it had acted for many years as though an informal document which it had delivered contained its articles, it was held that the members must be taken to have adopted the informal document as the company's articles.[20] It is submitted that the first three of these cases can be explained by the fact that the company was asserting a right against the other party to the litigation which could be lost by acquiescence, and that when acquiescence by a company is alleged, it is not necessary to show that every member of it expressly or tacitly assented to what was done. The fourth case[19] was one in which the company sought to recover money paid to the members in question as a fraudulent preference, and they relied on the invalidity of the winding up resolution as a defence; clearly, it is right that a member should not be able to challenge the validity of a liquidation when he has acquiesced in the liquidator's acts, or has allowed the liquidation to continue

12 *Cane v Jones* [1981] 1 All ER 533, [1980] 1 WLR 1451.
13 *Re Pearce Duff & Co Ltd* [1960] 3 All ER 222, [1960] 1 WLR 1014; *Re Bailey Hay & Co Ltd*, supra. If the defect is that the meeting has not been called by the proper length of notice, it seems that a majority of the members holding 95 per cent of the shares carrying voting rights may waive the defect and make the resolution binding under the Companies Act 1985, s 369 (3) and (4) or s 378 (3) even after the meeting has been held.
14 Companies Act 1985, s 135 (1) (see p 177, ante).
15 *Re Barry Artist Ltd* [1985] BCLC 283, [1985] 1 WLR 1305.
16 *Erlanger v New Sombrero Phosphate Co* (1878) 3 App Cas 1218.
17 *Re Norwich Yarn Co ex p Bignold* (1856) 22 Beav 143.
18 *Phosphate of Lime Co v Green* (1871) LR 7 CP 43. This case was decided before the House of Lords decided in *Trevor v Whitworth* (1887) 12 App Cas 409, that surrenders of partly paid shares are illegal. As the law stood in 1871 the surrender would have been valid if the members had resolved to accept it.
19 *Re Bailey Hay & Co Ltd* [1971] 3 All ER 693, [1971] 1 WLR 1357.
20 *Ho Tung v Man On Insurance Co Ltd* [1902] AC 232.

without drawing the liquidator's attention to the defect of which he complains, but in the instant case the court merely treated the member as estopped from pleading the invalidity as a defence, and it certainly did not rule that the winding up resolution must be deemed valid against all persons and for all purposes. The fifth case,[20] it is submitted, was merely an application of the principle that the law will presume that acts have been done regularly and properly when they appear to have been, and it is noteworthy that the court said that it was entitled to infer that all, and not merely some, of the members had assented to the adoption of the informal documents as the company's articles.[1] Each of these five cases, therefore, involved a special element which dispensed with the need for the unanimous consent of the members of the company in the context of the case. It cannot be deduced from these cases that in the absence of a special element or in a different context a resolution which lacks the unanimous approval of the members will be treated as binding on all of them or the company.

Registration and publication of resolutions

A company must deliver copies of certain resolutions to the Registrar of Companies within 15 days after they are passed.[2] The copies must either be printed or be in some other form approved by the Registrar.[2] The resolutions in question are the following resolutions passed by a general meeting:— special and extraordinary resolutions, resolutions authorising directors to issue shares[3] or for the company to purchase shares in itself by purchases on the Stock Exchange;[4] ordinary resolutions to wind the company up voluntarily[5] elective resolutions passed by a private company;[6] and resolutions and agreements agreed to by all the members of the company, but which, if not so agreed to, would have been effective only if passed as special or extraordinary resolutions. Resolutions and agreements which bind a class of members, whether unanimously agreed to or not, must also be notified to the Registrar,[7] and additionally resolutions of the board of directors must be so notified if they effect a change of name of the company under the direction of the Secretary of State for Trade and Industry so as to include the terminal word 'limited',[8] or if they alter the memorandum or articles of a public company when it is compelled to re-register as a private company after cancelling shares issued by it in which it has acquired an interest.[9]

A copy of such resolutions and agreements must be annexed to every copy of the company's articles issued after they are passed or entered into.[10]

1 Ibid, at 235.
2 Companies Act 1985, s 380 (1) and (4).
3 See p 245, ante.
4 See p 192, ante.
5 Insolvency Act 1986, s 84 (1).
6 Companies Act 1985, s 380 (4), as amended by Companies Act 1989, s 116 (3). See p 765, post.
7 See p 225, ante.
8 See p 7, ante.
9 See p 410, ante.
10 Companies Act 1985, s 380 (2).

CHAPTER 16

The principle of majority rule

THE RULE IN FOSS v HARBOTTLE

The principle of judicial non-interference

The rule of law known as the rule in *Foss v Harbottle*[1] is one which has resulted from the refusal of the courts to interfere in the management of a company at the instance of a minority of its members who are dissatisfied with the conduct of the company's affairs by the majority or by the board of directors. Insofar as it precludes the court from enquiring into the desirability or wisdom of the acts of those who control or manage the company's affairs, the rule is an obvious necessity, because it cannot be the court's function to take management decisions and to substitute its opinions for those of the directors and the majority of the members. But the rule goes beyond this, and in some cases prevents the court from remedying a wrong which has been done to the company, unless the majority want it to be remedied. The rule has been given its widest expression by Mellish LJ, in the following words.[2]

> 'In my opinion, if the thing complained of is a thing which in substance the majority of the company are entitled to do, or if something has been done irregularly which the majority of the company are entitled to do regularly, or if something has been done illegally which the majority of the company are entitled to do legally, there can be no use in having litigation about it, the ultimate end of which is only that a meeting has to be called, and then ultimately the majority gets its wishes. Is it not better that the rule should be adhered to that if it is a thing which the majority are the masters of, the majority in substance shall be entitled to have their will followed?'

The justification for the rule is the need to preserve the right of the majority to decide how the company's affairs shall be conducted,[3] and the ineffectiveness of any attempt by the court to interfere when its decision could be set aside by a resolution of the members.[2] But the rule applies only where the majority can cure the irregularity or illegality complained of or threatened by passing an ordinary resolution,[4] and the court will interfere at the instance of the minority when this cannot be done. Some of these exceptional cases are self-evident, for example, where the act complained of is ultra vires the company, or can only be authorised by a special or extraordinary resolution, but others are not logically deducible from the principle, and are either the result of historical accident or of a conscious desire by the courts to exclude the rule when it works unfairly.

---

1 (1843) 2 Hare 461.
2 *MacDougall v Gardiner* (1875) 1 ChD 13 at 25.
3 *Lord v Copper Miners Co* (1848) 2 Ph 740 at 751; *Harben v Phillips* (1883) 23 ChD 14 at 39 to 40, per Cotton LJ.
4 *Burland v Earle* [1902] AC 83 at 93; *Baillie v Oriental Telephone and Electric Co Ltd* [1915] 1 Ch 503; *Edwards v Halliwell* [1950] 2 All ER 1064.

Corporate rights of action

One reason which the courts have often given for refusing to interfere in the conduct of a company's affairs by entertaining an action brought by individual members to remedy a wrong done to the company, is that the company alone can sue to enforce rights of action vested in it, and only the directors or a general meeting can decide whether an action shall be brought in the company's name.[5] This is a consequence of the company's separate legal personality, because when the company, as a corporate person, sustains a legal injury, it does not follow that any of its members individually suffer a legal injury too, and unless they do, they have no grounds for suing. There is, of course, no logical connection between this reason for rejecting actions brought by members and the principle of majority rule, which applied equally to unincorporated common law companies, where a wrong done to the company was necessarily a wrong done to each member.[6] The result of applying the two principles is the same, however, and they are treated as alternative ways of expressing the rule in *Foss v Harbottle*.[7] Thus, when the court decides that an individual member cannot sue to compel the directors[8] or an agent[9] of the company to make good a breach of duty, or to recover a debt owed to the company,[10] or to redeem a mortgage on its property,[11] the court may give as its reason, either that the majority of the members may wish to waive the company's right to sue, or that the right to sue belongs to the company and not to the plaintiff member.

Nevertheless, the two principles of majority rule and locus standi to redress a corporate injury do not cover identical ground. Their fields of application interlock, so that the rejection of an individual member's action in some circumstances can be justified by either principle; on the other hand, there are situations where only one principle or the other can be invoked.[7] This observation is particularly important when the exceptional cases are examined in which an individual member is permitted to sue. Some of these exceptions are to the principle of majority rule and others to the principle of locus standi to redress corporate injury. In the first type of case the plaintiff is enforcing the rules for the conduct of the company's affairs against the company (notionally in the interest of all its members); in the second type he is suing a third person who has wronged the company, and he champions it by bringing the action in its interest and for its benefit. It is easy to confuse these two different types of cases, because the form in which the plaintiff sues is the same in both, namely, the representative action brought on behalf of all the company's members, other than those of them who are defendants.

The right of a company itself to bring actions in its own name for wrongs done to it is of little value to an individual member, because he cannot sue in the company's name himself, unless the board of directors,[12] or the members by

---

5 *Gray v Lewis* (1873) 8 Ch App 1035 at 1050; *Russell v Wakefield Waterworks Co* (1875) LR 20 Eq 474 at 479; *Burland v Earle* [1902] AC 83 at 93.

6 *Re Norwich Yarn Co, ex p Bignold* (1856) 22 Beav 143.

7 *Prudential Assurance Co Ltd v Newman Industries (No 2)* [1982] Ch 204 at 210–211, [1982] 1 All ER 354 at 357.

8 *Russell v Wakefield Waterworks Co*, supra.

9 *Duckett v Gover* (1877) 6 ChD 82.

10 *Kent v Jackson* (1852) 2 De GM & G 49.

11 *Morris v Morris* [1877] WN 6.

12 *Danish Mercantile Co Ltd v Beaumont* [1951] Ch 680, [1951] 1 All ER 925.

ordinary resolution,[13] or the liquidator of the company if it is being wound up,[14] authorise him to do so, and if he brings an action in the company's name without such authorisation, the defendant may have it struck out.[15] But an initially unauthorised action brought in the company's name is not inevitably doomed to failure, because the board or a general meeting, or the liquidator if the company is in liquidation, may at any time ratify the institution of the action and authorise its continuance.[16] The court may order that a general meeting shall be held to decide whether this shall be done, and may give relief by an interim injunction until the members' wishes are known.[17] Usually the articles confer the right to sue in the company's name on the directors,[18] but they appear to have the right by law in any event.[19] The directors' power to sue is not exclusive, however, so that although the members cannot prevent them from suing in the company's name,[20] there is nothing to prevent the members from resolving that the company shall sue despite the directors' refusal to bring an action.[1] The fact that a receiver of the company's assets has been appointed under debentures or other loan securities issued by it does not prevent the company from pursuing a claim against the receiver or the debenture or loan security holders if the board of directors or a general meeting so resolves, and so an action cannot be brought against them on the company's behalf by a minority shareholder.[2]

Personal rights of members

Although a member can only exceptionally sue to remedy a wrong done to his company, he can always sue for wrongs done to himself in his capacity as a member.[3] The individual rights of a member arise in part from the contract between the company and himself which is implied on his becoming a member,[4] and in part from the general law. Under the contract implied from his membership, he is entitled to have his name and shareholding entered on the register of members and to prevent unauthorised additions or alterations being made to the entry,[5] to vote at meetings of members,[6] to receive dividends which have been duly declared or which have become due under the terms of the articles,[7] to exercise pre-emption rights over other members' shares which are conferred by the articles,[8] and to have his capital returned in the proper order of priority in the winding up of the company or on a duly authorised reduction of capital.[9] Under the general law he

---

13 *Foss v Harbottle* (1843) 2 Hare 461; *Pender v Lushington* (1877) 6 ChD 70; *Marshall's Valve Gear Co Ltd v Manning Wardle & Co Ltd* [1909] 1 Ch 267.
14 *Alexander Ward & Co Ltd v Samyang Navigation Co Ltd* [1975] 2 All ER 424, [1975] 1 WLR 673.
15 *East Pant Du United Lead Mining Co Ltd v Merryweather* (1864) 2 Hem & M 254.
16 *Danish Mercantile Co Ltd v Beaumont*, supra; *Alexander Ward & Co Ltd v Samyang Navigation Co Ltd*, supra.
17 *Pender v Lushington*, supra; *Lawson v Financial News Ltd* (1917) 34 TLR 52.
18 See Table A, art 70.
19 *Pender v Lushington*, supra.
20 *John Shaw & Sons (Salford) Ltd v Shaw* [1935] 2 KB 113, [1935] All ER Rep 456.
 1 *Marshall's Valve Gear Co Ltd v Manning Wardle & Co Ltd*, supra; secus *Breckland Group Holdings Ltd v London and Suffolk Properties Ltd* [1989] BCLC 100.
 2 *Watts v Midland Bank plc* [1986] BCLC 15.
 3 *Pender v Lushington* (1877) 6 ChD 70; *Edwards v Halliwell* [1950] 2 All ER 1064.
 4 Companies Act 1985, s 14 (1) (see p 52, et seq, ante).
 5 *Re British Sugar Refining Co* (1857) 3 K & J 408.
 6 *Pender v Lushington*, supra.
 7 *Wood v Odessa Waterworks Co* (1889) 42 ChD 636.
 8 *Rayfield v Hands* [1960] Ch 1, [1958] 2 All ER 194.
 9 *Griffith v Paget* (1877) 5 ChD 894.

is entitled to restrain the company from doing acts which are ultra vires;[10] to have a reasonable opportunity to speak at meetings of members[11] and move amendments to resolutions proposed at such meetings;[12] to transfer his shares;[13] not to have his financial obligations to the company increased without his consent;[14] and to exercise the many rights conferred on him by the Companies Act 1985, such as his right to inspect various documents and registers kept by the company, to have a share certificate issued to him in respect of his shares, and to appoint a proxy to vote on his behalf at meetings of members. But wide though these rights are, a member is not invested with a personal right to have all the provisions of the Companies Act 1985, or of the company's memorandum and articles duly observed, and so, for example, he cannot restrain directors from acting after their term of office fixed by the articles has expired,[15] nor can he complain if meetings of members are irregularly convened or conducted,[16] or if the chairman of the meeting wrongfully refuses to put a resolution to a poll,[17] nor can he seek an order that errors or omissions in the company's annual accounts shall be corrected.[18]

The dividing line between personal and corporate rights is very hard to draw, and perhaps the most that can be said is that the court will incline to treat a provision in the memorandum or articles as conferring a personal right on a member only if he has a special interest in its observance distinct from the general interest which every member has in the company adhering to the terms of its constitution. A consequence of the distinction between personal and corporate rights is that a member cannot bring a personal action for the loss he has suffered by the diminution in the value of his shares resulting from breaches by the defendants of provisions of the company's memorandum or articles which do not confer personal rights on members, or from breaches of fiduciary duties owed by the defendants to the company.[19] Even if the member can prove a conspiracy between the defendants to commit the breaches of duty complained of, the diminution in the value of his shares is merely a reflection of the loss suffered by the company, and the proper remedy is for the company to sue the defendants or, in appropriate circumstances, for a derivative action to be brought.[19]

REPRESENTATIVE AND DERIVATIVE ACTIONS

In certain circumstances an individual member may bring an action to remedy a wrong done to his company or to compel his company to conduct its affairs in accordance with its constitution and the rules of law governing it, even though no wrong has been done to him personally, and even though the majority of his fellow members do not wish the action to be brought. The form of his action in these

---

10 *Simpson v Westminster Palace Hotel Co* (1860) 8 HL Cas 712; *Hoole v Great Western Rly Co* (1867) 3 Ch App 262 at 277; *Hutton v West Cork Rly Co* (1833) 23 ChD 654. This right is preserved by Companies Act 1985, s 35 (2), substituted by Companies Act 1989, s 108 (1) (see p 94, ante).

11 *Wall v London and Northern Assets Corpn* [1898] 2 Ch 469.

12 *Henderson v Bank of Australasia* (1890) 45 ChD 330.

13 *Re Smith Knight & Co, Weston's Case* (1868) 4 Ch App 20.

14 *Hole v Garnsey* [1930] AC 472. This is now made statutory by the Companies Act 1985, s 16 (1) (see p 85, ante).

15 *Mozley v Alston* (1847) 1 Ph 790.

16 *Cotter v National Union of Seamen* [1929] 2 Ch 58 at 70; *Bentley-Stevens v Jones* [1974] 2 All ER 653, [1974] 1 WLR 638.

17 *MacDougall v Gardiner* (1875) 1 ChD 13.

18 *Devlin v Slough Estates Ltd* [1983] BCLC 497.

19 *Prudential Assurance Co Ltd v Newman Industries Ltd (No 2)* [1982] Ch 204 at 222–223, 48–50, [1982] 1 All ER 354 at 366–367.

exceptional cases is peculiar, because the plaintiff does not sue in his own right alone, but sues instead on behalf of himself and all his fellow members other than those, if any, against whom relief is sought. If the member sues for relief against the company, it must, of course, be made a defendant; if he seeks to enforce a corporate claim against other persons, the company must still be joined as a co-defendant so that it may be bound by the judgment, and so that it may enforce any order giving relief against the substantive defendants.[20]

The individual member's action in these exceptional cases may be described as representative, because it is brought on behalf of himself and persons other than himself. When relief is sought against third parties for the company's benefit, the action may also be described as derivative, because the individual member sues to enforce a claim which belongs to the company, and his right to sue is derived from it.[1] Representative suits were originally entertained by the Court of Chancery during the 18th century and the early years of the last century to enable an action to be brought when the parties wronged by the defendant had the same or similar interests, but were so numerous that they could not conveniently join in the action as co-plaintiffs.[2] This form of action was particularly appropriate when a wrong was done to an unincorporated company, because the proper plaintiffs to sue at law were its members, who might number several hundreds.[3] But with the passage of time the original reason for allowing an action to be brought in this form was overlooked, and representative actions were allowed to be brought by the members of companies incorporated by special Act of Parliament[4] or under the Companies Acts in respect of wrongs done to the company, even though no action could be brought if the totality of members were joined as individual co-plaintiffs. Representative actions are not confined to those brought by members of a company on behalf of the whole membership, however. Such an action may be brought whenever 'numerous persons have the same interest in any proceedings',[5] and so debenture holders' actions to enforce their security, and actions by a class of members or shareholders to enforce their class rights, may also take this form. But these actions do not fall under the exceptions to the rule in *Foss v Harbottle*; in them the plaintiff sues to enforce personal rights which belong to each of the debenture holders or each of the members of the class of members or shareholders in question, and the company is a substantive defendant against which a remedy is sought in favour of each of the persons on whose behalf the action is brought, and is not merely joined as a party for procedural reasons, as it is in a derivative suit.

The plaintiff in a representative action is not an agent for the persons on whose behalf he sues. Consequently, he can discontinue the action without their consent;[6] the defendant can raise any defences against him which could be raised if he were suing in his own right alone,[7] including his participation or acquiescence in the

20 *Spokes v Grosvenor Hotel Co* [1897] 2 QB 124.
1 The distinction between a derivative action and a purely representative one has long been understood by American lawyers, but has only been recognised in this country during the last forty years.
2 The earliest reported cases are *Biscoe v Land Bank* (1709) 2 Eq Cas Abr 166 and *Chancey v May* (1722) Prec Ch 592.
3 *Carlen v Drury* (1812) 1 Ves & B 154; *Baldwin v Lawrence* (1824) 2 Sim & St 18; *Hichens v Congreve* (1828) 4 Russ 562; *Taylor v Salmon* (1838) 4 My & Cr 134.
4 *Gray v Chaplin* (1825) 2 Sim & St 267; *Colman v Eastern Counties Rly Co* (1846) 10 Beav 1; *Eastern Counties Rly Co v Hawkes* (1855) 5 HL Case 331; *Maunsell v Midland Great Western (Ireland) Rly Co* (1863) 1 Hem & M 130.
5 RSC Ord 15, r 12 (1).
6 *Re Alpha Co Ltd* [1913] 1 Ch 203.
7 *Burt v British Nation Life Assurance Association* (1859) 4 De G & J 158; *Towers v African Tug Co* [1904] 1 Ch 558.

defendant's wrongdoing;[8] and the other persons on whose behalf he sues are not liable for costs if the action is unsuccessful.[9] Furthermore, the plaintiff may join a personal claim of his own in the representative action,[10] unless the two claims arise out of different transactions.[11] On the other hand, all the persons on whose behalf a representative action is brought are bound by the judgment given in it,[12] unless the judgment was procured by fraud or collusion, or unless the plaintiff did not fairly fight the case,[13] and any such person who wishes to appeal from the judgment must first be joined as a defendant in the action with leave of the court.[14] If the judgment is favourable, any person on whose behalf the action was brought may take steps to enforce it, and the plaintiff may not after judgment agree to forgo the benefit of it so as to prevent any of the persons on whose behalf he sued from issuing execution.[15] Moreover, if the plaintiff discontinues the action before judgment, or does not conduct his case properly, the court may substitute one of the other persons on whose behalf the action is brought as plaintiff.[16]

The derivative character of a representative action brought by a member to enforce a right vested in the company is shown by the fact that judgment is given in favour of the company, so that the plaintiff obtains no personal benefit from the judgment directly,[17] and also by the fact that the plaintiff can sue only if the company could sue itself, so that if the company has been dissolved no derivative action may be brought.[18] Moreover, a member may bring a derivative action in respect of wrongs done to the company before he became a member, even if he acquired shares in it for the sole purpose of suing,[19] but if the former holder of the shares could not have brought a derivative action himself because of his acquiescence in the wrong complained of, the present member cannot sue either.[20] On a member's bankruptcy his right to bring or continue a derivative action does not vest in his trustee in bankruptcy, as do his personal rights of action, and so he may initiate or continue such an action himself free from interference by his trustee in bankruptcy.[1] A derivative action commenced by a member may not be continued by him if he ceases to be a member, although the court may allow it to be continued by some other member who is substituted as plaintiff by order of the court, and that member will take up the action from the point it has reached, and will be bound by the pleadings which have been delivered and the interlocutory proceedings which have already taken place.[18] Because the plaintiff in a derivative action seeks to enforce a cause of action which belongs to the company and not to himself personally, the court can in its discretion at any time after the commencement of the action order the company to indemnify him for his costs on

8 *Nurcombe v Nurcombe* [1985] 1 All ER 65, [1985] 1 WLR 370.
9 *Price v Rhondda UDC* [1923] WN 228.
10 *Pender v Lushington* (1877) 6 ChD 70, where a personal action and a derivative action were brought by the same proceedings to a resolution passed at a general meeting declared void because the plaintiff's votes had been wrongly rescission.
11 *Stroud v Lawson* [1898] 2 QB 44, where it was held that a personal action by a subscriber for rescission of the allotment of his shares because of a misrepresentation by the directors that a dividend of a certain amount had been paid out of profits, could not be joined with a derivative action against the directors to compel them to restore the dividend, which had in fact been paid out of capital.
12 RSC Ord 15, r 12 (3); *Re Calgary and Medicine Hat Land Co* [1908] 2 Ch 652.
13 *Sewers Comrs of London v Gellatly* (1876) 3 ChD 610.
14 *Watson v Cave* (1881) 17 ChD 19 & 23.
15 *Re Alpha Co Ltd* [1903] 1 Ch 203.
16 *Re Services Club Estate Syndicate Ltd* [1930] 1 Ch 78.
17 *Spokes v Grosvenor Hotel Co* [1897] 2 QB 124.
18 *Coxon v Gorst* [1891] 2 Ch 73; *Clarkson v Davies* [1923] AC 100.
19 *Seaton v Grant* (1867) 2 Ch App 459.
20 *Ffooks v South Western Rly Co* (1853) 1 Sm & G 142 at 168.
1 *Birch v Sullivan* [1958] 1 All ER 56, [1957] 1 WLR 1247.

a common fund basis (and not merely to meet the party and party costs recoverable by him from the substantive defendants), and this discretion can be exercised in his favour whether the derivative action is successful or not.² The court will make such an order early in a derivative action (eg before discovery or the delivery of pleadings) only after considering affidavit evidence filed by the plaintiff and the company and considering submissions from both sides, but without the plaintiff's evidence and submissions being disclosed to the defendant.³ The court will make an indemnity order in favour of the plaintiff only if it appears that his action stands a reasonable chance of success and that its continuance will be for the benefit of the company, and in this connection the court takes account of the wishes of the shareholders of the company, particularly those who are not committed to either side in the litigation.³

A derivative action may be brought by a person who is the equitable owner of shares, such as an equitable mortgagee or the renouncee of a letter of allotment,⁴ but not by a creditor of the company.⁵ The court will only allow a derivative action to proceed if it is brought for the benefit of the company, and so if the plaintiff's motive is to benefit a rival concern which has encouraged him to sue and has indemnified him against costs, the action will be stayed.⁶ Likewise, if directors have paid dividends out of capital, but the company has since earned sufficient profits to replace the capital expended, it seems that the court will not permit a member to bring a derivative action to compel the directors to repay the dividend out of their own pockets, because the company could immediately use the money received from the directors to pay a further dividend, so that the result would be to benefit not the company, but its members individually.⁷

THE EXCEPTIONS TO FOSS v HARBOTTLE

The exceptional cases where a member may sue by a derivative action to compel a company to conform to its constitution and the rules governing the conduct of its affairs, or to enforce a claim belonging to the company, fall into two groups, namely: (a) cases where the members cannot remedy the defect complained of or forgo the company's right to sue by passing an ordinary resolution in general meeting; and (b) cases where the court has excluded the rule in *Foss v Harbottle* because it would work unfairly. If the plaintiff's action does not fall within one of these exceptional cases, the court will stay the action on its own motion even though the defendant raises no objection, because, for example, he has brought a derivative counterclaim against the plaintiff based on a similar ground.⁸ Moreover, it has been held by the Court of Appeal that if an application is made to the court to strike out a derivative action before it is tried on the merits, the court should allow the action to proceed only if the statement of claim sets out allegations of fact which, if true, would entitle the plaintiff to bring a derivative action, and the

2 *Wallersteiner v Moir (No 2)* [1975] QB 373, 508n, [1975] 1 All ER 849.
3 *Smith v Croft* [1986] 1 WLR 580, [1986] BCLC 207; *Jaybird Group Ltd v Greenwood* [1986] BCLC 319.
4 *Bagshaw v Eastern Union Rly Co* (1849) 7 Hare 114; *Binney v Ince Hall Coal and Channel Co* (1866) 35 LJ Ch 363.
5 *Mills v Northern Rly of Buenos Ayres Co* (1870) 5 Ch App 621.
6 *Forrest v Manchester Sheffield and Lincolnshire Rly Co* (1861) 4 De GF & J 126.
7 *Re Exchange Banking Co, Flitcroft's Case* (1882) 21 ChD 519 at 536, per Cotton LJ.
8 *Heyting v Dupont* [1963] 3 All ER 97, [1963] 1 WLR 1192; affd [1964] 2 All ER 273, [1964] 1 WLR 843.

plaintiff tenders prima facie proof of those facts.[9] The reason for this is to avoid a trial of the merits of the action with all the resulting expense to the parties merely to discover whether the plaintiff was entitled to institute a derivative action.[9] But if the facts alleged in the statement of claim are not disputed or are clear (eg where the issue turns on the meaning or effect of the company's memorandum or articles), the court will allow the derivative action to proceed if the plaintiff has an arguable case in law.[10] The court will not allow a derivative action to be initiated or continued if the company goes into liquidation, because the liquidator then has statutory power to litigate in the company's name,[11] and if he is unwilling to do so any member of the company may apply to the court to order that he shall do so.[12] If no application is made to the court to strike out a derivative action which could have been challenged, the findings of fact and rulings on questions of law by the court after a trial on the merits are binding on the parties, including the company.[13] The defendants against whom judgment is given cannot then escape its enforcement against them on the ground that they could have applied to strike out the action before the trial because the plaintiff could not have shown that the facts disclosed a proper case for bringing a derivative action.[13]

The exceptional cases where the rule in *Foss v Harbottle* will not prevent a member of a company from bringing a representative or derivative action under one or other of the heads mentioned above will now be dealt with in detail.

Situations irremediable by ordinary resolution

The situations where the company cannot prevent one member from suing by passing a resolution that the company itself shall not sue, are six in number.

(1) Where the plaintiff seeks to restrain the commission of an ultra vires act,[14] or to compel the directors to compensate the company for loss suffered by it in consequence of such an act,[15] or to recover property of the company which has been disposed of to a third person by an ultra vires transaction which was not effective against the company.[16] If the action is designed to prevent a threatened ultra vires act, the plaintiff may bring either a personal or a representative action against the company, and the directors may be joined as co-defendants so that an injunction may be made against them too;[9] but if the plaintiff member seeks an order that the company shall recover compensation for an ultra vires act which has already been committed, or shall recover property disposed of by an ultra vires transaction, the action must be a derivative one. A company could not at common law ratify or adopt an act or decision which was ultra vires so as to validate or legitimise it even with the assent of all its members,[17] although it may now

---

9 *Prudential Assurance Co Ltd v Newman Industries Ltd (No 2)* [1982] Ch 204 at 221–222, [1982] 1 All ER 354 at 365–366.

10 *Estmanco (Kilner House) Ltd v Greater London Council* [1982] 1 All ER 437, [1982] 1 WLR 2.

11 Insolvency Act 1986, s 165 (3), s 167 (1) and Sch 4, para 4.

12 *Fargro Ltd v Godfroy* [1986] 3 All ER 279, [1986] BCLC 370. The power of the court to direct the liquidator to sue is conferred by the Insolvency Act 1986, s 112 (1) and s 167 (3).

13 *Prudential Assurance Co Ltd v Newman Industries Ltd (No 2)* [1982] Ch 204 at 216–217, [1982] 1 All ER 354 at 362–363.

14 *Simpson v Westminster Palace Hotel Co* (1860) 8 HL Cas 712; *Hoole v Great Western Rly Co* (1867) 3 Ch App 262; Companies Act 1985, s 35 (2), substituted by Companies Act 1989, s 108 (1).

15 *Spokes v Grosvenor Hotel Co* [1897] 2 QB 124.

16 *Salomons v Laing* (1850) 12 Beav 377. For the effectiveness of ultra vires acts and transactions, see p 96, ante.

17 *Ashbury Railway Carriage and Iron Co Ltd v Riche* (1875) LR 7 HL 653 (see p 93, ante).

do so by special resolution;[18] nevertheless it has been held that a company may effectively resolve by ordinary resolution not to pursue a claim for damages or restitution of property in consequence of an ultra vires act or transaction, and provided the resolution is passed in good faith in the interests of the company and not merely to protect the prospective defendant, the resolution is binding on minority shareholders so as to prevent them from bringing a derivative action for damages or restitution.[19]

(2) Where the plaintiff seeks to restrain a threatened breach of any provision in the memorandum or articles. The cases which have decided that the plaintiff may sue for this purpose have all been concerned with threatened breaches of the articles, and the court has concluded that the plaintiff may sue because the articles can only be altered by special resolution, and so no authorisation of a breach of their provisions given by an ordinary resolution would be effective.[20] It is submitted, however, that a member may also sue to restrain a threatened breach of those parts of the memorandum which may be altered by ordinary resolution, such as the capital clause. This is because an alteration of the memorandum or articles can only operate prospectively and not retrospectively,[1] so that if the threatened breach of the memorandum were committed, it would not be possible to rectify it subsequently by altering the memorandum. For example, an issue of shares in excess of the company's nominal capital is void, and the allottee may recover the issue price he has paid the company as money paid for a consideration which has wholly failed;[2] it would not be possible to validate the allotment after the event and to convert the money paid by the allottee into paid up share capital by passing an ordinary resolution increasing the company's nominal capital. Consequently, a member may bring a representative action to restrain the company and its directors from making the allotment in the first place, unless it increases its nominal capital sufficiently beforehand.

(3) Where the plaintiff seeks a declaration that a resolution altering the memorandum or articles, although passed in proper form, is invalid because the alteration was not made in good faith for the benefit of the members of the company as a whole, and an injunction to restrain the company from giving effect to the altered memorandum or articles.[3] There is no express authority requiring the plaintiff to sue by a representative rather than a personal action in this situation, but in the two cases where the plaintiff's action was successful, the action was a representative one,[4] and logically it should take that form. On the other hand, if the plaintiff claims that his personal rights have been wrongfully interfered with in consequence of the invalid alteration, he can bring a personal action to remedy that wrong, and need not first bring a representative action for a declaration that the alteration was invalid.[5]

---

18 Companies Act 1985, s 35 (3), substituted by Companies Act 1989, s 108 (1).
19 *Smith v Croft (No 2)* [1988] Ch 114, [1987] 3 All ER 909, [1987] BCLC 355.
20 *Boschoek Proprietary Co Ltd v Fuke* [1906] 1 Ch 148; *Salmon v Quin and Axtens Ltd* [1909] 1 Ch 311; affd sub nom *Quin and Axtens Ltd v Salmon* [1909] AC 442; *Mosely v Koffyfontein Mines Ltd* [1911] 1 Ch 73.
 1 *James v Buena Ventura Nitrate Grounds Syndicate Ltd* [1896] 1 Ch 456 at 466, per Rigby LJ.
 2 *Bank of Hindustan China and Japan v Alison* (1871) LR 6 CP 222 (see p 137, ante).
 3 See p 75 et seq, ante.
 4 *Brown v British Abrasive Wheel Co* [1919] 1 Ch 290; *Dafen Tinplate Co Ltd v Llanelly Steel Co (1907) Ltd* [1920] 2 Ch 124.
 5 *Shuttleworth v Cox Bros & Co (Maidenhead) Ltd* [1927] 2 KB 9 (breach of director's service contract); *Allen v Gold Reefs of West Africa Ltd* [1900] 1 Ch 656 (action for declaration that an alteration of the articles had not imposed a lien on plaintiff's shares); *Clemens v Clemens Bros Ltd* [1976] 2 All ER 268 (action to invalidate an increase of capital and an issue of shares resulting in the plaintiff's voting rights being diminished, so that they were no longer sufficient to prevent the passing of a special resolution).

(4) Where the plaintiff seeks to have a resolution of a general meeting declared void and to restrain the company from acting on it, because it should be passed as a special or extraordinary resolution, but has not been passed in that form.[6] The action must be a representative one, unless the personal rights of the plaintiff have already been interfered with by implementing the resolution, in which case he may bring a personal action.[7]

(5) Where the plaintiff seeks by a representative action to restrain the company from doing an act which is contrary to the Companies Act 1985, or the general law. Thus, if an insufficient length of notice is given of a general meeting and proper notice is not waived by the requisite fraction of members, any member entitled to attend and vote may sue to restrain the company and its directors from holding the meeting. Similarly, if the company proposes to issue equity shares or securities without first giving effect to its existing equity shareholders' statutory preferential subscription rights,[8] any equity shareholder may seek an injunction to prevent the proposed issue. Again, if directors make an unequal call on shareholders of the same class when the articles do not empower them to do so, any member may sue to restrain them and the company from collecting the call.[9] But a member cannot seek to have every breach by the company of the Companies Act 1985 remedied by seeking a declaration or a mandatory injunction. Consequently, a member cannot bring a derivative action to have errors or omissions in the company's annual accounts corrected.[10] In the present state of the authorities it is impossible to say which threatened or continuing breaches of the Companies Act 1985 are sufficiently serious for a member to obtain an injunction or mandatory injunction against the company to restrain or remedy them. Derivative actions to recover damages or the restitution of property in consequence of an illegal act or decision of the company or its directors or agents are subject to the same restrictions as derivative actions in respect of ultra vires acts and decisions.[11] Consequently, it has been held that such an action may not be brought or continued if the company passes an ordinary resolution that the company shall not seek the remedy to which it is entitled, provided of course, that the resolution is passed in good faith in the interests of the company.[12]

(6) Where a general meeting has resolved validly that a certain thing shall be done or abstained from, and the plaintiff brings a representative action to restrain the company from taking action which conflicts with the resolution and which, if not restrained, will produce irreversible results without a general meeting having an effective opportunity to reconsider the matter.[13] For example, if a general meeting of a company has lawfully resolved that a dividend of a certain amount shall be paid out of the company's distributable profits, any member may seek an injunction to prevent the company and its directors from applying its distributable profits for a different purpose which will prevent the dividend from being paid.

---

6 See cases cited in note 20, supra, and also *Baillie v Oriental Telephone and Electric Co Ltd* [1915] 1 Ch 503.
7 *Wood v Odessa Waterworks Co* (1889) 42 ChD 636.
8 See p 246, ante.
9 *Preston v Grand Collier Dock Co* (1840) 11 Sim 327.
10 *Devlin v Slough Estates Ltd* [1983] BCLC 497.
11 See paragraph (1) on p 655, ante.
12 *Smith v Croft (No 2)* [1988] Ch 114, [1987] 3 All ER 909, [1987] BCLC 355.
13 *Hodgson v National and Local Government Officers Association* [1972] 1 All ER 15, [1972] 1 WLR 130.

It will be noticed that in these situations where the matter cannot be rectified by a general meeting passing an ordinary resolution (other than the first and the fifth), the plaintiff may sue only for a declaration or for an injunction to restrain a threatened act or to compel the carrying out of an act which should be done; the plaintiff cannot seek an award of damages to remedy an improper or irregular act which has already been done. But past wrongs may be remediable by an award of damages or by restitution at the suit of a member if they come within the exceptions to the principle of majority rule grounded on unfairness, oppression or breach of fiduciary duties, which will now be dealt with. Before leaving this present group of exceptional situations, however, it should be noted that, whilst a member may generally be precluded from complaining of improper or irregular acts which have already been committed by his acquiescence in them,[14] he is not thereby prevented from suing to restrain the commission of similar acts in the future.[15]

Inadequate notice of a resolution passed at a meeting of members

It has been held in four cases that if an insufficiently informative notice is given to members of a resolution to be proposed at a general meeting, any member who does not attend the meeting, or who votes against the resolution, may bring a representative action to restrain the company and its directors from carrying out the resolution. In three of the four cases[16] the resolution was a special one, but it is clear that the dissenting member's right to sue did not depend on that fact, because the court's decision in each case was expressly founded on the inadequacy of the notices of the meetings, and not on the nature of the resolution. Moreover, the same reasoning was applied in the fourth case[17] where the resolution was an ordinary one. Again, in three of the four cases[18] the inadequacy of the notice of the meeting lay in its failure to make full disclosure of an interest of the directors in the subject matter of the resolution, but it is clear from the fourth case,[19] where no such interest was involved, that the resolution may be challenged in a representative action, whether the notice is inadequate for that or any other reason.

In only one case[20] has the rule in *Foss v Harbottle* been applied so as to preclude a member from challenging the validity of a resolution because of the insufficiency of the notice of the general meeting at which it was passed. In that case the application of the rule was particularly harsh, because the resolution was a special one for the adoption of new articles, and the notice of the resolution failed to set out several of the material differences between the original and the proposed new articles. It is submitted that the four cases[1] where a representative action was allowed are preferable to this decision, and so should be followed. If this were not done, the rules which the court has devised to ensure that members have proper warning of the business to be transacted at meetings, would be valueless if members who controlled a majority of the votes at a general meeting wished to sustain a resolution of which inadequate notice was given, and which the minority have consequently not had a proper opportunity to consider and oppose by litigation or otherwise.

14 *Burt v British Nation Life Assurance Association* (1859) 4 De G & J 158.
15 *Mosely v Koffyfontein Mines Ltd* [1911] 1 Ch 73.
16 *Tiessen v Henderson* [1899] 1 Ch 861; *Baillie v Oriental Telephone and Electric Co*, supra; *MacConnell v E Prill & Co Ltd* [1916] 2 Ch 57.
17 *Kaye v Croydon Tramways Co* [1898] 1 Ch 358.
18 *Kaye v Croydon Tramways Co*, supra; *Tiessen v Henderson*, supra; *Baillie v Oriental Telephone and Electric Co*, supra.
19 *McConnell v Prill and Co Ltd*, supra.
20 *Normandy v Ind Coope & Co Ltd* [1908] 1 Ch 84.
 1 *Tiessen v Henderson*, supra; *Baillie v Oriental Telephone and Electric Co*, supra. *MacConnell v E Prill & Co Ltd*, supra; *Kaye v Croydon Tramways Co*, supra.

Fraud or oppression

Where the persons who control a majority of the votes which can be cast at a general meeting use their power of control to defraud or oppress minority shareholders, the court will interfere at the instance of the minority, and will upset the majority's machinations.[2] The fraud or oppression need not amount to a tort at common law, but it must involve an unconscionable use of the majority's power resulting, or likely to result, either in financial loss or in unfair or discriminatory treatment of the minority, and it must certainly be more serious than the failure of the majority to act in the interest of the company as a whole, which will induce the court to annul a resolution altering the company's memorandum or articles.

The leading example of the kind of fraud or oppression of this kind is found in *Menier v Hooper's Telegraph Works Ltd.*[3] In that case a company was formed to lay down a transatlantic telegraph cable which was to be made by Hooper's Telegraph Works Ltd, the majority shareholder. Hooper found that it could make a greater profit by selling the cable to another company which wished to lay it down on the same route, but which would not buy unless it had the necessary government concessions for the undertaking. The first company had obtained such concessions, and so Hooper induced the trustee in whom they were vested to transfer them to the second company, which then bought the cable from Hooper. To prevent the first company from suing to recover the concessions, Hooper procured the passing of a resolution that the first company should be wound up voluntarily, and that a liquidator should be appointed whom Hooper could trust not to pursue the company's claim against Hooper and the trustee. Menier, a minority shareholder of the first company, brought a derivative action against Hooper to compel it to account to the company for the profits it derived from the improper arrangements it had made. It was held that Hooper's machinations amounted to an oppressive expropriation of the minority shareholders, and that a derivative action would therefore lie against it. Sir W M James LJ said:[4]

'The defendants, who have a majority of shares in the company, have made an arrangement by which they have dealt with matters affecting the whole company, the interest in which belongs to the minority as well as to the majority. They have dealt with them in consideration of their obtaining for themselves certain advantages. ... The minority of the shareholders say in effect that the majority has divided the assets of the company, more or less, between themselves, to the exclusion of the minority. I think it would be a shocking thing if that could be done, because if so the majority might divide the whole assets of the company, and pass a resolution that everything must be given to them, and that the minority should have nothing to do with it. Assuming the case to be as alleged in the bill, then the majority have put something into their pockets at the expense of the minority. If so, it appears to me that the minority have a right to have their share of the benefits ascertained for them in the best way in which the court can do it, and given to them.'

Menier v Hooper's Telegraph Works Ltd was a blatant case of both fraud and oppression, but a lesser degree of moral guilt on the part of the majority may also warrant the intervention of the court. Thus, if the majority shareholders deliberately resolve that the company shall sell its undertaking at an undervalue so that their capital may be returned to them in cash without the delay which would be necessary for the company to obtain a full market price, the court will restrain the company and its directors from carrying out the sale.[5] Again, if shareholders who

2 *Burland v Earle* [1902] AC 83 at 93.
3 (1874) 9 Ch App 350.
4 Ibid, at 353.
5 *Dominion Cotton Mills Co Ltd v Amyot* [1912] AC 546.

control a majority of the votes at a general meeting procure resolutions for the issue of further shares to themselves in their capacity as directors under an incentive scheme, when their real purpose is to deprive a minority shareholder, who hitherto has held sufficient voting power to prevent the passing of special resolutions altering the company's memorandum and articles, of her power to block such resolutions in future, the court will set aside the resolutions for the issue of the further shares as being oppressive to the minority shareholders.[6] Furthermore, members who are temporarily or permanently deprived of voting rights by the company's articles may by a representative or derivative action challenge a resolution or action procured by the members who control the voting at general meetings if it will defeat or frustrate the purpose for which the company was formed by disposing of its assets in a way which is intra vires but nevertheless incompatible with achieving the company's main objects.[7]

In another case[8] where the majority shareholders were induced to vote for a resolution that the company should invest its funds in another company, by the promise of a director of that company that the majority shareholders might exchange their existing shares for shares in the other company on very favourable terms, it was held that a minority shareholder, to whom no such offer had been made, could restrain the company and its directors from carrying out the resolution, because the inequality of treatment between the majority and the minority was a fraud upon the latter. This case is interesting because it shows that it is not necessary that either the company or the minority shareholders should be harmed or suffer loss in consequence of the oppression of which they complain. The minority's shares would be worth as much after as before the completion of the transaction with the other company, but the court interfered because it was grossly unfair and oppressive of the minority that a benefit should be denied to the minority which was given to the majority in connection with a transaction affecting the assets of the company. It is easy to argue from this conclusion that majority shareholders owe a fiduciary duty to the minority not to use their power and position improperly for their own benefit, but this is a step which the court has not taken, and there is authority to the contrary.[9] The present case should therefore be regarded simply as an example of unfairness amounting to oppression, and not as an example of a wider fiduciary relationship which is grounded on equitable duties rather than on relief from fraud or oppression.[10]

Breach of directors' and promoters' fiduciary duties

Fiduciary duties

A derivative action may be brought against directors and promoters who have been guilty of a breach of their fiduciary duties to the company, if they are able to prevent the company from suing them in its own name because they control a majority of the votes at a general meeting, or because they are otherwise able to

6 *Clemens v Clemens Bros Ltd* [1976] 2 All ER 268.
7 *Estmanco (Kilner House) Ltd v Greater London Council* [1982] 1 All ER 437, [1982] 1 WLR 2.
8 *Kerry v Maori Dream Gold Mines Ltd* (1898) 14 TLR 402.
9 *Phillips v Manufacturers' Securities Ltd* (1917) 116 LT 290 at 296, per Cozens-Hardy MR.
10 In the United States it has been held that majority shareholders do owe fiduciary duties to the minority, and are therefore liable to compensate the minority for loss suffered in consequence of the majority transferring control of the company to persons whom they know are likely to misapply its assets (*Gerdes v Reynolds* (1941) 28 NYS (2d) 622), and that the majority must share with the minority any premium the majority obtain by selling their controlling shares to a person who pays more than the market value of the shares in order to gain access to the company's assets or advantageous business position (*Perlman v Feldman* 219 F 2d 173 (1955)).

prevent a general meeting from resolving that the company shall sue them. Thus, derivative actions have been permitted against directors who were in control of the company for misappropriating the company's property[11] or misapplying it in breach of prohibitions in the Companies Act,[12] to compel such directors to account to the company for profits made by appropriating for themselves a business opportunity which the company would otherwise have enjoyed,[13] to rescind an allotment of shares made by such directors to themselves and their nominees in order to preserve their majority voting power at general meetings[14] or to deprive the members who controlled the company of their power to control it in the future,[15] and to compel such directors to make a call on their own shares equal to a call which they had made on the shares of the other members.[16] Likewise, derivative actions have been permitted against promoters who were in control of the company to rescind contracts made between them and the company when they had been guilty of misrepresentations,[17] or had failed to disclose a secret profit which they obtained from the transaction,[18] and in those cases the court ordered the promoters to repay to the company all money received by them under the contracts.

It must be remembered, however, that acts by promoters or directors which involve a breach of their fiduciary duties can be ratified, or apparently, authorised in advance, by a general meeting passing an ordinary resolution after proper disclosure of the relevant facts;[19] in the absence of fraud, the ratification or authorisation then validates what would otherwise be an unlawful act or transaction. Moreover, although promoters or directors who are controlling shareholders cannot absolve themselves from liability for breaches of duties owed to the company by using their votes as shareholders,[20] it appears that the other shareholders may ratify or authorise the act in question by a resolution on which the promoters or directors who are alleged to have breached their fiduciary duties do not vote.[1] If such a resolution is effective, the promoters' or directors' liability to the company would cease, and it would not then be possible for a shareholder who opposed the resolution to bring a derivative action to enforce the directors' or promoters' liability. Depending on the facts of the case, however, a shareholder might still be able to bring a derivative action based on fraud or the oppression of a minority of shareholders, for such an action can be brought even though the company itself could not sue.

Negligence

Until recently it has been consistently held by the courts that a derivative action cannot be brought against a promoter or director who has merely been guilty of negligence.[2] It is difficult to understand why this should be so when the damage suffered by the company may be as great as when the defendant has been guilty of

---

11 *Spokes v Grosvenor Hotel Co* [1897] 2 QB 124.
12 *Wallersteiner v Moir* [1974] 3 All ER 217, [1974] 1 WLR 991.
13 *Cook v Deeks* [1916] 1 AC 554.
14 *Piercy v S Mills & Co* [1920] 1 Ch 77.
15 *Howard Smith Ltd v Ampol Petroleum Ltd* [1974] AC 821, [1974] 1 All ER 1126.
16 *Alexander v Automatic Telephone Co* [1900] 2 Ch 56.
17 *Mason v Harris* (1879) 11 ChD 97.
18 *Atwool v Merryweather* (1867) LR 5 Eq 464n.
19 *Lagunas Nitrate Co v Lagunas Syndicate Ltd* [1899] 2 Ch 392; *Regal (Hastings) Ltd v Gulliver* (1942) [1967] 2 AC 134n, [1942] 1 All ER 378; *Bamford v Bamford* [1970] Ch 212, [1969] 1 All ER 969 (see pp 579 and 595, ante).
20 *Atwool v Merryweather*, supra; *Cook v Deeks*, supra.
1 *Smith v Croft (No 2)* [1988] Ch 114, [1987] 3 All ER 909, [1987] BCLC 355.
2 *Pavlides v Jensen* [1956] Ch 565, [1956] 2 All ER 518; *Heyting v Dupont* [1963] 3 All ER 97, [1963] 1 WLR 1192; affd [1964] 2 All ER 273, [1964] 1 WLR 843.

a breach of fiduciary duty. The only plausible explanation is that at the time when the Court of Chancery invented the representative action, an action for negligence had to be brought in the common law courts, and they did not permit representative suits; but since it has become possible to bring representative actions in all divisions of the High Court, there seems no reason why this historical accident of procedure should now prevent a derivative action from being brought to enforce a common law claim.[3] On the other hand, although there is no reported case where a representative suit for negligence was attempted in the Court of Chancery before the fusion of law and equity, it might have been possible to bring such an action, despite the common law nature of the claim, on the ground that the plaintiff was disabled from suing at common law by the common law rules of procedure.[4] If this were so, there would be no shred of a reason left for preventing a derivative action for negligence being brought today.

It has been suggested by Professor LCB Gower[5] that a derivative action may be brought for directors' negligence if the plaintiff first requires the board to call a general meeting to resolve that the company shall sue them, and the directors either decline to call the meeting, or call it and defeat the resolution by the use of their own votes as shareholders. Professor Gower argues that if the directors refuse to call the meeting, the court may infer that they have abused their powers, and may permit the derivative action against them to proceed; alternatively, if they call the meeting, their own votes must not be counted, and an action may be brought against them in the company's name if a majority of the other members so resolve. It is respectfully submitted that neither of these deductions is correct. If the court did hold that the directors had abused their powers in refusing to call a meeting,[6] the only remedy the court could give would be for that particular abuse, namely, by calling the meeting itself, and not by allowing an action to proceed on the desirability of which no meeting had had an opportunity to pronounce. If the meeting were called by the directors, it does not follow that they would not be able to vote against the resolution to sue them. The law is not that directors may not vote on a resolution of the sort,[7] but that a resolution absolving them from liability is void if it is procured by their own controlling votes.[8] Consequently, the result of discounting the directors' votes would not be that the resolution to sue them would be deemed to be passed, but simply that the directors would not be absolved from liability, which takes the matter no further. No doubt it is desirable that derivative actions for negligence should lie against controlling directors, but this would be better achieved by a frank recognition that the historical reasons why it may not have been possible for such actions to be brought before the fusion of law and equity are no longer applicable.

3 In the Federal courts of the United States of America derivative actions to enforce common law claims were formerly not allowed (*United Copper Securities Co v Amalgamated Copper Co* 244 US 261 (1917), but since the adoption in 1939 of a rule of procedure similar to RSC Ord 15, r 12 it has been held that such derivative actions lie (*Fanchon and Marco Inc v Paramount Pictures Inc* 202 F 2d 731 (1953)).

4 In some of the States of the United States of America where common law and equity jurisdictions are still segregated, it is recognised that, whilst an action by the company to enforce a common law claim for negligence must be brought in a common law court, a member of the company can enforce the same claim by a derivative action in equity (*Rettinger v Pierpoint* 15 NW (2d) 393 at 397 (1944)).

5 *The Principles of Modern Company Law* (4th edn), pp 650–651.

6 The finding of abuse presupposes that the charge of negligence is well founded, for directors are not bound to call a meeting because a member wishes to air charges against them (*MacDougall v Gardiner* (1875) 10 Ch App 606).

7 *East Pant Du United Lead Mining Co Ltd v Merryweather* (1864) 2 Hem & M 254; *Breckland Group Holdings Ltd v London & Suffolk Properties Ltd* [1989] BCLC 100, (1988) 4 BCC 542.

8 *Cook v Deeks* [1916] 1 AC 554.

In fact, it may well be that a change of judicial attitude has already begun. In a recent case[9] Templeman J held on an application to strike out a statement of claim in a derivative action brought against controlling directors, that such an action may be brought for any breach of duty by controlling directors, provided the directors or some of them have gained personally by the breach of duty. In the case in question the plaintiff alleged that the directors had sold property of the company to the wife of one of their number at a substantial undervalue, and the allegation could have been read as one of deliberate misconduct or, at least, of a breach of the directors' duty to act in the interest of the company. Nevertheless, Templeman J accepted that the rule he applied, permitting the action to proceed, was wide enough to include negligence on the part of directors; it remains to be seen whether the Court of Appeal will uphold this justifiable extension of the circumstances in which a derivative action may be brought.

The element of control

It has repeatedly been held that a derivative action against directors or promoters for breaches of fiduciary duty may only be brought if they have the power to prevent an action being brought against them in the company's name pursuant to a resolution passed in general meeting. This power may arise from their ownership of shares carrying voting rights, or from such shares being vested in their nominees who vote as they are instructed,[10] or from the directors or promoters also being the directors of another company which owns sufficient shares in the first company to enable them to control the voting at its general meetings by combining the votes which the other company may cast in respect of its shares with the votes which the directors may cast in respect of their own shares.[11] In this latter case the voting rights vested in the other company will, of course, be exercised as its directors think fit, and may therefore be exercised in their own interests as directors or promoters of the first company.[11] It would also seem that directors must be treated as being in control of the company which they have wronged if its memorandum or articles expressly confer the right to sue in its name on its board of directors to the exclusion of a general meeting of members.[12] But the mere fact that a member who institutes a derivative action holds shares of a class which carry no voting rights and that he is powerless to requisition a general meeting, does not mean that the directors must be treated as controlling the company, even though the member has no effective remedy against them, and consequently his derivative action against the directors will be dismissed.[13]

The facts showing that the directors or promoters can prevent the company from suing them in its own name must be alleged in the statement of claim in a derivative action as well as be proved at the trial.[14] If the court is in any doubt as to the ability of the directors or promoters to prevent the company suing them in its own name, the Court of Appeal has held that the court should direct the holding of a general meeting of the company to decide whether the derivative action should be continued.[15] If the meeting resolves that it should not be continued, the burden

9 *Daniels v Daniels* [1978] Ch 406, [1978] 2 All ER 89.
10 *Piercy v S Mills & Co* [1920] 1 Ch 77; *Bamford v Bamford* [1970] Ch 212, [1969] 1 All ER 969.
11 *Pavlides v Jensen* [1956] Ch 565, [1956] 2 All ER 518; *Wallersteiner v Moir* [1974] 3 All ER 217, [1974] 1 WLR 991.
12 *Foss v Harbottle* (1843) 2 Hare 461 at 494.
13 *Pavlides v Jensen*, supra.
14 *Birch v Sullivan* [1958] 1 All ER 56, [1957] 1 WLR 1247.
15 *Prudential Assurance Co Ltd v Newman Industries Ltd (No 2)* [1982] Ch 204 at 222, [1982] 1 All ER 354 at 366.

will then rest on the plaintiff in the derivative action to show that the majority votes were cast by the directors and their associates; if they cast less than a majority of the votes against continuance of the action and the majority therefore necessarily included the votes of independent shareholders, the derivative action should be dismissed.[15] Furthermore, even where the directors and their associates are clearly in control of the company and able to prevent it from suing in its own name, it has been held that a derivative action may not be continued if the persons who can exercise a majority of the votes which can be cast at a general meeting by shareholders of the company (other than the directors and their associates) are opposed to the derivative action proceeding because they consider in good faith that its continuance would be against the interests of the company.[16] This decision restricts the availability of a derivative action even further, but it was held in the same case that the further restriction does not apply if the derivative action is brought to obtain injunctive relief against the commission or repetition of breaches of duty by directors in the future.[16]

In cases where the directors are in control of the company by reason of the act which the plaintiff shareholder impugns (for example, allotting shares to themselves or their nominees to gain or retain voting control at general meetings), a representative or derivative action may be brought, even though the outcome will be to deprive the directors of control if the action is successful.[17] But in this situation the court will refer to the shareholders in general meeting the question whether the transaction by which the directors gained or retained control shall be approved, and if an ordinary resolution is passed approving the transaction (no votes being cast in respect of shares whose allotment is impugned by the action), the court will not allow the action to proceed.[18] This applies whether the plaintiff seeks the annulment of the transaction, the issue of an injunction restraining the directors from carrying it out, or, it would seem, the payment of damages or an account of profits to the company.[19]

Despite the general trend of decisions, in some cases the court has permitted derivative actions to be brought against directors and promoters, even though it was not shown that they controlled the company's power to sue. In two early cases concerning unincorporated common law companies, such an action was permitted against promoters to compel them to account for secret profits;[20] in two other cases a derivative action was permitted against directors who had misapplied the company's assets and procured a resolution of approval from a general meeting by fraudulent misrepresentation,[1] or by voting on shares which they had purchased at depressed prices resulting from their own breaches of fiduciary duty;[2] and in another case a derivative action was permitted against a director to compel him to deal as the company should direct with property which he had acquired on its behalf.[3] In later cases where derivative actions have been brought by the members of incorporated companies, non-controlling directors have been held accountable for profits obtained by allotting shares to themselves at an issue price less than their market value,[4] and a proposed allotment of shares to nominees to give non-

16 *Smith v Croft (No 2)* [1988] Ch 114, [1987] 3 All ER 909, [1987] BCLC 355.
17 *Piercy v S Mills & Co,* supra; *Hogg v Cramphorn Ltd* [1967] Ch 254, [1966] 2 All ER 420; *Bamford v Bamford,* supra.
18 *Hogg v Cramphorn Ltd,* supra.
19 *Regal (Hastings) Ltd v Gulliver* (1942) [1967] 2 AC 134n at 150, [1942] 1 All ER 378 at 389, per Lord Russell of Killowen.
20 *Hichens v Congreve* (1828) 4 Russ 562; *Beeching v Lloyd* (1855) 3 Drew 227.
 1 *Davidson v Tulloch* (1860) 3 Macq 783, HL.
 2 *Apperly v Page* (1847) 1 Ph 779.
 3 *Taylor v Salmon* (1838) 4 My & Cr 134.
 4 *Parker v McKenna* (1874) 10 Ch App 96; *Shaw v Holland* [1900] 2 Ch 305.

controlling directors voting control at general meetings has been restrained.[5] It was also recently held by Vinelott J that a derivative action could be brought by a substantial but non-controlling shareholder against directors whose aggregate holdings were less than the plaintiff's when the directors had caused the company loss by purchasing assets at an excessive price, and had procured the approval of the purchase by a general meeting by means of a tricky and deceptive circular and non-disclosure of material facts.[6] This decision was, however, overruled on appeal, primarily on the facts, but the Court of Appeal also ruled that before trying the action on the merits, the trial judge should have ascertained that the directors were in a position to prevent an action being brought in the company's name, and that in fact they had sought or would seek to prevent such an action being brought.[7] Moreover, there are cases where derivative actions for the misappropriation of the company's property by directors,[8] and for the recovery of secret profits from promoters,[9] have been dismissed in limine on demurrer or on the argument of a preliminary point of law, because the plaintiffs could not prove that the directors and their associates had prevented or would prevent an action being brought by the company in its own name. Under modern procedure the court will entertain an application to strike out a derivative action for this reason, unless there are disputed questions of fact or complex questions of law involved which can be better disposed of after a full trial.[10] Furthermore, in some of the cases mentioned above where derivative actions were allowed without the plaintiff alleging or proving that the directors or promoters could prevent the company from suing in its own name, the rule in *Foss v Harbottle* was not mentioned, and it is therefore tempting to dismiss the decisions as given per incuriam. But in three cases[11] it was expressly held that a derivative action does lie against directors who are not in control of the company, if they are supported by so many other members that the plaintiff member cannot procure the passing of a resolution that the company shall sue them. In yet another case[12] Jessel MR held that proof of control by the directors is merely one of several alternative conditions for bringing a derivative action against them. A derivative action lies, he said:[13]

'... if it can be shewn either that the wrongdoer has command of the majority of the votes, so that it would be absurd to call the meeting; or if it can be shewn that there has been a general meeting substantially approving of what has been done; or if it can be shewn from the acts of the corporation as a corporation, distinguished from the mere acts of the directors of it, that they have approved of what has been done, and have allowed a long time to elapse without interfering, so that they do not intend and are not willing to sue.'

It is therefore unsettled whether a derivative action lies against directors and

---

5 *Fraser v Whalley* (1864) 2 Hem & M 10.

6 *Prudential Assurance Co Ltd v Newman Industries Ltd (No 2)* [1981] Ch 257, [1980] 2 All ER 841.

7 *Ibid,* [1982] Ch 204 at 221–222, [1982] 1 All ER 354 at 366.

8 *Foss v Harbottle* (1843) 2 Hare 461; *Mozley v Alston* (1847) 1 Ph 790; *Lord v Governor & Co of Copper Miners* (1848) 2 Ph 740; *Gray v Lewis* (1878) 8 Ch App 1035.

9 *Re Transvaal Gold Exploration and Land Co Ltd* (1885) 1 TLR 604.

10 *Smith v Croft (No 2)* [1988] Ch 114, [1987] 3 All ER 909, [1987] BCLC 355.

11 *Apperley v Page*, supra; *Davidson v Tulloch*, supra; *Atwool v Merryweather* (1867) LR 5 Eq 464n. In *Prudential Assurance Co Ltd v Newman Industries Ltd (No 2)* [1982] Ch 204 at 216–217, [1982] 1 All ER 354 at 362–363, the Court of Appeal explained away *Atwool v Merryweather* as a case where the inability of the plaintiff shareholders to bring a derivative action was not raised on demurrer, but only as a defence at the trial after the court had already found the defendant directors and promoters guilty of a breach of fiduciary duty. In fact, the trial judge, Page Wood VC ruled that the action would not have been dismissed on demurrer in view of the allegations of fraud and breach of fiduciary duty made against the non-controlling directors.

12 *Russell v Wakefield Waterworks Co* (1875) LR 20 Eq 474.

13 Ibid, at 482.

promoters only when they control the company, or whether it lies in other circumstances as well. The tendency of decisions since the beginning of this century has been to confine the action to cases where the defendants are in control, but there is much to be said for allowing it in other cases too, provided that the plaintiff can show a prima facie case and so avoid the need for a full trial merely in order to ascertain whether he is entitled to sue at all.[14] In practice directors can usually control a company if they can exercise a third or more of the voting rights in general meeting, unless the remaining voting rights are exercisable by one or a few shareholders who act together; if the remaining voting rights are dispersed among numerous shareholders who do not act together, a smaller fraction than one third of the voting rights may suffice for control. Although the courts of this country have not yet tackled the problem of de facto control of general meetings by directors, a Canadian court has taken the first step in the direction of treating the relevant test as being whether it is likely that a general meeting would make an independent decision to sue or not to sue, by holding that where the defendant director and his wife between them held 50 per cent of the voting shares of a company, the plaintiffs, who held the other 50 per cent, could bring a derivative action, because the defendant could effectively prevent a general meeting from passing a resolution to sue.[15] If voting control at general meetings is to remain a condition of the availability of derivative actions against directors and promoters, such a criterion of effective control in the circumstances of the particular company has much to commend it.

STATUTORY PROTECTION OF THE MINORITY

The Companies Act 1985 (as amended), supplements a minority shareholder's power to protect his interests by bringing personal, representative and derivative actions in three ways. It first gives minority shareholders a special remedy in situations where they are treated unfairly and harmfully; secondly, it permits them to enforce certain claims of the company free from the restrictions imposed by the rule in *Foss v Harbottle* when the company is wound up; and finally, it enables them to obtain remedies indirectly through an investigation of the company's affairs by inspectors appointed by the Secretary of State for Trade and Industry, who may follow up the inspectors' report by taking remedial action.

Relief against unfair treatment

Any member of a company may present a petition for relief to any court which could order the company to be wound up[16] on the ground that the affairs of the company are being or have been conducted in a manner which is unfairly prejudicial to the interests of its members generally or of some part of its members (including at least himself), or on the ground that any actual or proposed act or omission of the company or of any persons acting on its behalf is or would be so unfairly prejudicial.[17] Only members of a company may seek relief under this provision, and so a petition may not be presented by a person who is a shareholder

---

14 It was because of the potentially heavy expense of litigation to the company and the defendant directors that the Court of Appeal insisted on clear proof of the inability of the company to sue in its own name in *Prudential Assurance Co Ltd v Newman Industries Ltd (No 2)* [1982] Ch 204, [1982] 1 All ER 354.

15 *Glass v Atkin* (1967) 65 DLR (2d) 501.

16 Companies Act 1985, s 744. In practice all petitions for relief are presented to the Companies Court.

17 Companies Act 1985, s 459 (1), as amended by Companies Act 1989, s 145 and Sch 19, para 11.

but not a member, such as the holder of a letter of allotment in respect of partly paid shares, or a share warrant or share certificate to bearer,[18] but exceptionally, persons to whom shares have been transferred or on whom they have devolved by law (personal representatives and trustees in bankruptcy of shareholders) may petition for relief even though they have not been registered as members.[19] But a person who has agreed to become a member, either by agreeing to subscribe for shares or by agreeing with the member in whose name they are registered to take a transfer from him, cannot petition for relief unless a duly executed transfer of shares to the petitioner has been presented to the company for registration and it can be compelled to register him as a member,[20] or possibly, unless the petitioner has subscribed for shares or holds a letter of allotment of shares and has an immediate, unconditional right to be registered as a member in respect of them. If the court is satisfied that the petition is well founded, that is, presumably, that the petitioner has proved his allegations and they constitute an unfair prejudice of the petitioner himself or of the petitioner and all or some of the other members taken together, the court may make such order as it thinks fit to give relief in respect of the matters complained of, and so may fashion the remedy to suit the circumstances of the particular case.[1] The court's jurisdiction is therefore equitable in character although originating in a statutory provision, and the elements which induce the court to give or withhold equitable remedies are therefore relevant, and the elasticity of the remedies which may be given is as great, if not greater, than that of equitable remedies in general. The fact that the petitioner complains that the persons in control of the company have proposed to do an act which would be unfairly prejudicial to him, but that the particular act has now become impossible (eg the holding of a general meeting to resolve on an unfair alteration of the company's articles of association on a date which has passed without the meeting being held), does not prevent the court from giving injunctive relief to the petitioner if the act complained of is likely to be repeated.[2]

The precursor of the present statutory provision was contained in the Companies Act 1948, by which a member of a company who claimed that its affairs were being conducted in a manner oppressive of some part of its members (including himself) could petition for relief, and if the court was satisfied that that was so and that the facts would justify an order that the company should be wound up because in the circumstances it was just and equitable, but that a winding up order would unfairly prejudice the members who were oppressed, the court could make such order as it thought fit to end the matters complained of.[3] The purpose of the earlier provision was that the court should give relief in a form which would enable the company to survive whilst preserving the rights of the petitioner and other oppressed shareholders, as an alternative to winding the company up on just and equitable grounds in situations where a winding up would be disadvantageous to the oppressed shareholders.[4] This explains the equitable character of the court's jurisdiction under both the original and the present statutory provision. However, it was held, illogically, under the earlier provision that the petitioner also had to show that he would have obtained a winding up order under the law as it stood before the original provision was enacted (ie that the company would have a

---

18 *Re a Company (No 007828 of 1985)* (1985) 2 BCC 951.
19 Companies Act 1985, s 459 (2).
20 *Re a Company* [1986] BCLC 391, (1986) 2 BCC 276.
1 Ibid, s 461 (1).
2 *Re Kenyon Swansea Ltd* [1987] BCLC 514.
3 Companies Act 1948, s 210 (1) and (2).
4 See the Report of the Committee on Company Law Amendment (Cmd 6659) of 1945, para 60, on which the Companies Act 1948, s 210 was based.

surplus of assets after paying its debts if it were liquidated immediately, or that the petitioner would be liable to contribute to its assets if it were wound up).[5] This condition does not appear in the present provision, and so the hypothetical alternative of a winding up order does not have to be considered by the court. Indeed, it would appear that in an appropriate case for relief under the present statutory provision, the court would reject a petition for the winding up of the company, because the availability of alternative relief would make it unreasonable for the petitioner to seek a winding up order.[6]

Until the court has, by a sufficient body of case law, established the conditions for obtaining relief under the present statutory provision even though relief would not have been given formerly, it will be impossible to distinguish between situations which satisfy the new criterion of conduct of the company's affairs in a manner which is unfairly prejudicial to the whole or part of the company's members, or of an act or omission which is or would be so prejudicial, from situations which fell within the old criterion of conduct of the company's affairs in a manner oppressive to some part of the members. The only certainties at this stage are that conduct which the court has held to be oppressive under the former provision will also be unfairly prejudicial under the wider terms of the present provision, and that in no case will it now be necessary for the petitioner to prove a course of conduct on the part of those responsible, since the present provision expressly permits relief to be given when single or isolated acts or omissions are complained of.[7] Whether conduct or acts which would not have been oppressive under the original provision will qualify as unfairly prejudicial under the new one, and what elements of oppression may be absent yet conduct or acts still be unfairly prejudicial, will remain uncertain until an adequate volume of case law has been developed under the new provision.

It was held under the original provision that conduct could be oppressive if it was deliberate, even if it was not intended to harm the interests of the petitioners or other members in their position,[8] and it was sufficient that the conduct complained of was unconscionable or unfair and either seriously impaired the rights of the petitioners or prevented their legitimate expectations from being substantially fulfilled.[9] Such an objective test of oppression would not seem to differ from the usually accepted understanding of conduct or an act which is unfairly prejudicial, unless it is supposed that conduct which is not deliberate, but merely negligent, may be unfairly prejudicial if the consequences are serious. On that supposition the expression 'unfairly prejudicial' would then be interpreted as meaning that it would be unjust for the harm suffered by the petitioner to go unremedied. Perhaps indirect support for such an interpretation can be found in the power of the court to give relief under the present provision by authorising civil proceedings to be brought in the company's name by the petitioner or any other person,[10] because obviously civil proceedings can be brought by the company when it and its members have suffered loss as a result of negligence on the part of persons who owe it a duty of care. It is submitted, however, that an interpretation of the expression 'unfairly prejudicial' which relies on the remedies which the court may give if unfairly prejudicial conduct is proved, begs the question and confuses

5 *Re S A Hawken Ltd* [1950] 2 All ER 408; *Re Bellador Silk Ltd* [1965] 1 All ER 667.
6 Insolvency Act 1986, s 125 (2); *Re Abbey Leisure Ltd* [1989] BCLC 619 (1988) 5 BCC 183; revsd on other grounds (1990) 6 BCC 60.
7 Companies Act 1985, s 459 (1) and s 461 (2) (*b*).
8 *Re H R Harmer Ltd* [1958] 3 All ER 689, [1959] 1 WLR 62.
9 *Scottish Co-operative Wholesale Society Ltd v Meyer* [1959] AC 324, [1958] 3 All ER 66; *Re Westbourne Ltd* [1970] 3 All ER 374, [1970] 1 WLR 1378; revsd on other grounds [1971] Ch 799, [1971] 1 All ER 561.
10 Companies Act 1985, s 461 (2) (*c*).

the company's right to sue with unfair prejudice to the petitioning member. If the petitioner seeks the court's authorisation to bring proceedings in the company's name, he must show that the conduct he complains of is actionable by the company and, quite separately, that it is or would be unfairly prejudicial to its members if an action were not brought; the fact that substantial harm has been caused to members by the wrong done to the company does not suffice by itself. It would seem that the expression unfairly prejudicial must be interpreted independently, in the way a court of equity would use the expression, and that only deliberate acts or omissions which are unconscientious or unfair toward the petitioner and other members of the company in a similar position to the petitioner, or to all the members of the company, will qualify for relief. This does not, of course, preclude the possibility that a decision of the board of directors not to bring an action in the company's name against a person who has caused the company substantial loss by his negligence, may be unfairly prejudicial to members if there are no good business or other reasons for the decision, but it will be the unfairness of the board's decision not to sue, and not the harm caused to members by the negligence of the prospective defendant, which entitles a member to seek relief.

The cases decided by the court under the original statutory provision for relief from oppression are examined below together with the growing body of decided cases under the new statutory provision in order to deduce, at least tentatively, the range of situations in which the new criterion will be satisfied of conduct or an act or omission which is unfairly prejudicial to members of a company, and in order to discover the situations which may be relieved under the present statutory provision although not under the original one.

The meaning of unfairly prejudicial conduct

The kind of oppression which justifies the court in making a winding up order, and therefore justified it in making an order under the original statutory provision, included fraudulent or oppressive conduct by majority shareholders and breaches of fiduciary duty by controlling directors or promoters which would entitle a minority shareholder to bring an action against them under one of the exceptions to the rule in *Foss v Harbottle*. But the court required proof of oppressive conduct over a period of time if it was to make a winding up order,[11] and so under the original statutory provision isolated wrongful acts by controlling directors, such as drawing remuneration from the company in excess of their entitlement, were held insufficient of themselves to amount to oppression, even though they would justify minority shareholders bringing a derivative action for breaches of fiduciary duty.[12] But if the controlling directors used their voting power as shareholders to procure or ratify the payment of unjustifiably high remuneration, or to prevent an action being brought against them in the company's name to recover unauthorised remuneration received by them, a case of oppression remediable under the statutory provision might be made out,[12] and this would be a situation where relief would be given under the present statutory provision. Likewise, relief will be given under the new statutory provision if equity shares are allotted by the directors to themselves or their associates without regard to the petitioner's and other members' statutory right to subscribe for so many of the new shares as are proportionate to their respective existing holdings.[13] Moreover, under the present statutory provision the court may give relief from the unfairly prejudicial conduct of the

11 *Loch v John Blackwood Ltd* [1924] AC 783.
12 *Re Jermyn Street Turkish Baths Ltd* [1971] 3 All ER 184, [1971] 1 WLR 1042.
13 *Re a Company (No 005134 of 1986), ex p Harries* [1989] BCLC 383.

company's affairs or from any actual or proposed unfairly prejudicial act or omission,[14] and so a petition may succeed whether a course of conduct or only isolated acts are complained of.

It was not necessary for a petitioner for relief from oppression under the original provision to show that the persons in control of the company of whose conduct he complained had acted malevolently or with a desire to obtain an improper advantage.[15] This is undoubtedly so under the new statutory provision, because members may clearly be unfairly prejudiced by deliberate conduct which is not designed to cause them harm, but merely to gain some benefit for the person who acts improperly, or to enhance his power or position. Every member of a company is entitled to have its affairs properly conducted according to law, and if those who control the company have persistently disregarded the requirements of the Companies Act, or the provisions of the company's constitution, even with the highest motives, relief was given under the former provision,[15] as it will be under the present legislation if those in control of the company fail to comply with the requirements of the Companies Act 1985, as to the holding of annual general meetings or the annual presentation of the company's accounts to the members,[16] or if they divert a business opportunity from the company to another undertaking which they control.[17] Relief will be given particularly if persons in control of the company act in their own interests, for example, by allotting shares to themselves or their associates so as to enable themselves to control the voting at general meetings,[16] but not if there were good business reasons for their actions, for example, if the company urgently needed money and the other shareholders were unwilling to contribute anything.[12] On the other hand, under the original statutory provision, the persons who were alleged to have conducted the company's affairs oppressively must have brought about the situation complained of intentionally; mere negligence, however damaging its consequences, did not amount to oppression. Consequently, a minority shareholder's petition could not succeed if it was based solely on a lack of business ability or inefficiency and carelessness in conducting the company's business on the part of its directors.[18] This was so, even though the controlling shareholders had refused to remedy the situation by removing the directors or overruling them, and even though the value of the petitioner's shares had fallen in consequence of the directors' negligence and the controlling shareholders' inaction.[18] For the reasons given above, it is submitted that under the new statutory provision negligence or inept management causing the company and its members loss will not of itself be unfairly prejudicial conduct, but the refusal of the directors or controlling shareholders to seek any remedy against the persons responsible for the loss to the company may well be unfairly prejudicial to other members, and may entitle them to seek relief if there are no good business or other reasons for not exercising the company's rights.

The court will not involve itself with questions of business policy on hearing a winding up petition,[19] and therefore would not do so on hearing a petition for relief from oppression under the original provision. For the same reason the court will probably refuse to examine the soundness of business decisions made, or a business policy pursued, by a board or directors or controlling shareholders under the present statutory provision. For this reason the court dismissed a petition presented under the original statutory provision when the alleged oppression

14 Companies Act 1985, s 459 (1).
15 *Re H R Harmer Ltd* [1958] 3 All ER 689, [1959] 1 WLR 62.
16 *Re a Company (No 00789 of 1987)* (1989) 5 BCC 792.
17 *Re London School of Electronics* [1986] Ch 211, [1985] BCLC 273.
18 *Re Five Minute Car Wash Service Ltd* [1966] 1 All ER 242, [1966] 1 WLR 745.
19 *Loch v John Blackwood Ltd* [1924] AC 783.

consisted of the refusal of the shareholders who controlled the company to declare adequate dividends, or any dividends at all, out of the company's profits.[20] Even when the company's profits had been absorbed to a considerable extent in paying generous remuneration to the controlling shareholders as directors of the company, the court took the view that what the minority shareholders had foregone by way of dividend might have been compensated by an increase in the market value of their shares resulting from the retention of profits.[20] Similarly, under the present statutory provision, the court held that relief could not be given when the petitioner's only complaint was that unwise decisions had been made by the board of directors at general meetings as the result of the chairman of the board persistently exercising his casting vote, in particular on a proposal to remove the petitioner from his directorship.[1] The reluctance of the court to pronounce on the merits of business or policy decisions extends also to alterations of the company's memorandum or articles, and so the court refused on a petition for relief from an unfairly prejudicial act to set aside a special resolution altering the articles so as to make the president of the company or its chairman removable by a board resolution, whereas previously he had been removable only by a resolution passed by a general meeting.[2]

Nevertheless, under both the original and the present statutory provisions the court's reluctance to examine business decisions would disappear if it were shown that the directors or controlling shareholders concerned did not make the impugned decisions in good faith in the interests of the members of the company as a whole. In the case of directors the decision or decisions in question could be treated as invalid,[3] and in the case of controlling shareholders their reasons for making or giving effect to the decision could be treated as no justification for them,[4] with the result in either case that the harm inflicted on the petitioner and other members in the same position as himself would be both oppressive and unfairly prejudicial, and would merit relief under both the original and the new statutory provision. Consequently, if directors or controlling shareholders are shown to have refused to recommend or vote for reasonable dividends which would still leave sufficient profits undistributed to meet the company's commercial needs, and their motive for doing so was to extract the available profits in some other form (eg as directors' remuneration),[5] or to induce minority shareholders to sell their holdings at an undervalue,[6] or to attract a favourable offer for the controlling shareholders' shares, particularly a takeover bid offering an exchange of shares,[7] the minority shareholders would be able to prove unfair prejudice and would probably obtain relief.

The court applied the principal that it will interfere with business decisions taken by directors or controlling shareholders only if they are wholly unjustifiable. In another case where the directors and controlling shareholders of a company, which could no longer carry on business itself because of its inability to obtain insurance cover to satisfy regulatory requirements, proposed against the opposition of the petitioning minority shareholder to acquire separate parts of the company's

20　*Re Jermyn Street Turkish Baths Ltd*, supra.
1　*Re a Company (No 003096 of 1987)* (1988) 4 BCC 80.
2　*Re Blue Arrow plc* [1987] BCLC 585, (1987) 3 BCC 595.
3　See p 618.
4　*Scottish Co-operative Wholesale Society v Meyer* [1959] AC 324, [1958] 3 All ER 66.
5　*Re Sam Weller & Sons Ltd* [1990] BCLC 801, (1989) 5 BCC 810.
6　A winding up order would be made in this situation on the ground that it was just and equitable (*Loch v John Blackwood Ltd* [1924] AC 783).
7　In this situation the company making the offer would, if the bid succeeded, obtain control over the offeree company's liquid assets representing its undistributed profits by issuing new shares or debentures of the offeror company, and without incurring expenditure in cash.

business themselves by a series of management buy-outs, the petitioner being precluded from participating in these because of a professional disqualification imposed on him for misconduct.[8] The court refused to give relief to the petitioner on it being shown that the only alternative solution to the company's difficulties was the sale of its business to an outsider, which would involve a substantial tax burden on its shareholders which the management buy-outs would avoid, and that the price to be paid to the company under the management buy-outs was as high, if not higher, than the price obtainable on a sale to any outsider who would be willing to buy; the directors and majority shareholders did not seek to obtain an unfair advantage, and the business decision they intended to carry out was made in good faith to enable the company's business to be continued; the remedy which the petitioner sought, namely, a power to be given to any dissenting shareholders to veto the sale, was not designed to protect the legitimate interests of those shareholders, but to reconstruct the company's constitution exclusively in the petitioner's interest.

If a minority shareholder ceases to act as a director or resigns his directorship as a result of personal differences or difficulties of temperament with the other directors, the minority shareholder is unfairly prejudiced if the controlling shareholders do not make an offer to acquire his shares at a reasonable price, or do not respond favourably to an offer by him to sell his shares to them at a reasonable price.[9] On the other hand, such a minority shareholder is not unfairly prejudiced if the company makes a rights offer to its shareholders to raise capital it needs for its business merely because he cannot afford to take up and pay for the new shares offered to him, and the acceptance of the rights offer by the controlling shareholders will result in a serious dilution in the percentage of the issued shares of the company held by him.[9] Furthermore, if there is an irretrievable breakdown in the relationship between a director who is a minority shareholder and the other directors, one of whom is the majority shareholder, so that clearly the company's business cannot be successfully carried on if both directors remain in office, it is not unfairly prejudicial to the director with the minority shareholding for the director who has the majority holding to use his position and influence to procure the dismissal of the other director by a general meeting of the company if no fraud or deception is practised; nor is it then unfairly prejudicial for the board to invoke an existing provision of the company's articles giving the other shareholders the right to purchase the dismissed director's shares at a fair value fixed by the company's auditors on a director ceasing to hold office.[10]

In most cases of the unfairly prejudicial conduct of a company's affairs the persons responsible control a majority of the votes which may be cast at a general meeting, so that the petitioner cannot remedy the situation himself or with the co-operation of his fellow minority shareholders by reconstituting the board of directors. It has been held in South Africa under a statutory provision identical with the original provision enacted in Great Britain, however, that it is not essential that the respondents should control the voting power at general meetings.[11] Consequently, relief can be sought by a member who could cast exactly one half, but not a majority, of the votes at a general meeting, because any resolution he proposed could be defeated by the respondents casting the other half of the votes against it.[11] Moreover, it has been held by an Australian court under a similar

8 *Re Posgate and Denby (Agencies) Ltd* [1987] BCLC 8.
9 *Re a Company* [1986] BCLC 362.
10 *Re a Company* [1987] 1 WLR 102, [1987] BCLC 94; see also *Re a Company (No 005134 of 1986), ex p Harries* [1989] BCLC 383.
11 *Benjamin v Elysium Investments (Pty) Ltd* 1960 (3) SA 467.

statutory provision[12] that if the respondents control less than half the voting power but are in control of the company's affairs in fact, for example, because they or their nominees are directors of the company, relief can be given to any of the other members if it is unlikely that the other members will unite to remove the existing board and replace them by their own candidates. This is certainly the case under English law if the respondents initially controlled less than half the voting power, but as part of their conduct of the company's affairs procured the allotment of sufficient shares to themselves or their associates to give themselves voting control.[13]

The members who are unfairly prejudiced

To succeed with a petition for relief from the unfairly prejudicial conduct of a company's affairs under the Companies Act 1985, as originally enacted, a petitioner had to show that the conduct he complained of was 'unfairly prejudicial to the interests of some part of the members [of the company] (including at least himself)'.[14] It was held in one case that if the conduct complained of affected all the members of the company in the same way, it could not be unfairly prejudicial to some part of the members, and so could not be the subject of a petition for relief.[15] Consequently, it was held in that case that where a company had not paid reasonable dividends to its ordinary shareholders, despite being able to do so without imperilling its solvency or reducing the resources it required to maintain its level of activity or to expand, minority shareholers could not petition for relief under the statutory provision.[15] This was held to be so, even though some of the other ordinary shareholders who had suffered proportionately the same deprivation of dividends as the petitioner, had been compensated for this to some extent by receiving reasonable, but not excessive, remuneration as directors of the company.[15]

However, in another case where the facts were identical, it was held that a minority shareholder could seek relief under the statutory provision, even though his right to have a dividend declared and paid was the same as the rights of the majority shareholders; this was because his interest in the matter as a minority shareholder, who was unable to procure the passing of a resolution for payment of a reasonable dividend, was different from the interests of the majority shareholders, who had power to grant or withhold such a dividend, and the minority shareholder's interest would therefore be unfairly prejudiced by the determination of the majority to pay no dividend at all, or to pay a dividend which was substantially less than the company could reasonably be expected to pay.[16] This latter decision was preferable to the former, and was supported by earlier rulings by the court, under the earlier statutory provision.[17] including a decision of the House of Lords.[18]

The matter has now been set at rest by the amendment made to the present statutory provision by the Companies Act 1989,[19] which substitutes the new test that the petitioner must show that the company's affairs have been or are being conducted in a manner which is 'unfairly prejudicial to the interests of its members generally or of some part of its members', thus confirming the correctness of the second decision mentioned above.

12 *Re Associated Tool Industries Ltd* (1963) 5 FLR 55.
13 *Re Jermyn Street Turkish Baths Ltd* [1970] 3 All ER 57, [1970] 1 WLR 1194; revsd on other grounds [1971] 3 All ER 184, [1971] 1 WLR 1042.
14 Companies Act 1985, s 459 (1), as originally enacted.
15 *Re a Company (No 00370 of 1987), ex p Glossop* [1988] 1 WLR 1068, [1988] BCLC 570.
16 *Re Sam Weller & Sons Ltd* [1990] BCLC 801, (1989) 5 BCC 810.
17 *Re a Company (No 002612 of 1984)* [1985] BCLC 80, affd sub nom *Re Cumana Ltd* [1986] BCLC 430; *Re a Company (No 007623 of 1986)* [1986] BCLC 362.
18 *Scottish Co-operative Wholesale Society v Meyer* [1950] AC 324, [1958] 3 All ER 56.
19 Companies Act 1989, s 145 and Sch 19, para 11.

The capacities in which the parties act

A member of a company who petitioned for relief under the original statutory provision had to show that he, or a group of members to which he belonged, had been treated oppressively in his or their capacity as members. He could not petition merely because he had been treated harshly in some other capacity, for example, if he had been dismissed from his directorship or employment under the company.[20] This was not so, however, if the dismissal involved a breach of the articles of the company, or was part of a campaign of oppression of which he complained in his capacity as a member of the company.[1] In those situations the oppressive treatment of the petitioner in a capacity other than as a member could be used as evidence to support his contention that over a period he and other minority shareholders had been oppressed in their capacity as members.

The new statutory provision has not altered the law in this respect, and a petitioner still cannot seek relief if he has been or is likely to be harmed by the conduct of the company's affairs in a certain manner, or by an act being done on the company's behalf, but the harm has been or will be suffered by him only in some other capacity than as a member or shareholder of the company.[2] This is emphasised by the requirement of the new statutory provision that the petitioner must prove conduct or an act or omission which is unfairly prejudicial 'to the interests of [the company's] members generally or of some part of its members (including at least himself)', and not merely to the interests of the petitioner.[3] It was in fact held in the first decision of the court under the new statutory provision that the petitioner must prove that he has been or will be unfairly prejudiced in his capacity as a member of the company.[4] Consequently a petition complaining that the company had refused to exercise its statutory power to purchase the petitioner's shares although it had ample profits available for the purpose,[5] was rejected firstly, because the petitioner complained in his capacity as a potential seller of his shares and not as a continuing member of the company, and secondly, because the application of a company's profits involves a matter of business policy which the members of the company must decide in general meeting, and the court will not interfere with its decision in the absence of fraud or bad faith.[4] Again, a petition by minority shareholders was dismissed when their complaint was that the majority shareholders had sold their shares to a third person without giving the petitioners an opportunity to purchase them, and the majority shareholders knew that the purchaser was unwilling to permit the petitioners to continue as directors of the company.[6] This attitude of the court has been confirmed in a latter case[7] where the petition of a minority shareholder was dismissed because the substance of his complaint was that the company had broken a contract to employ him as a consultant at an annual salary. On the other hand, it has been held in another case[8] that the interest of a member in selling his shares under an offer to purchase them, whether by way of a takeover bid or otherwise, is one aspect of his interests as a member of the company, and if the directors of the company impede his acceptance

20 *Elder v Elder and Watson Ltd* 1952 SC 49; *Re H R Harmer Ltd*, supra.
 1 *Re Westbourne Galleries Ltd* [1970] 3 All ER 374, [1970] 1 WLR 1378; revsd on other grounds [1971]
    Ch 799, [1971] 1 All ER 561; *Re London School of Electronics Ltd* [1986] Ch 211, [1985] BCLC 273; *Re*
    a Company [1986] BCLC 376.
 2 This was doubted by Vinelott J, however, in *Re a Company* [1983] BCLC 151 at 158.
 3 Companies Act 1985, s 459 (1), as amended by Companies Act 1989, s 145 and Sch 19, para 11.
 4 *Re a Company* [1983] Ch 178, [1983] 2 All ER 36.
 5 See p 191, ante.
 6 *Re Ringtower Holdings plc* (1988) 5 BCC 82.
 7 *Re a Company* (*No 003843 of 1986*) [1987] BCLC 562.
 8 *Re a Company* [1986] BCLC 382, —1986) 2 BCC 24.

of such an offer, or fail to give impartial advice on the relative merits of the offer and those of a rival offer to acquire his shares made by the directors themselves, or if the directors give him misleading advice as to the possibility of the original offer succeeding, the member's interests as such are unfairly prejudiced by the directors conducting the company's affairs in that way, and the member can petition for relief. Likewise, where the company was formed by its shareholders, who were also its directors, as a quasi-partnership, and the success of the company was envisaged by them as depending on the mutual trust and confidence between them, the removal of one of the directors from the board, either by a board resolution or by a resolution of a general meeting, may amount to an act which is unfairly prejudicial to him as a member of the company, unless his removal is for a reason other than a wish to exclude him from the benefits of his shareholding and directorship and a fair offer is made to him for the purchase of his shares.[9]

Where the shareholders of the company who were responsible for the unfairly prejudicial conduct of the company's business have transferred all their shares to another person, or have otherwise ceased to be members of the company before the petition for relief is presented, the court will nevertheless decide whether the petitioner is entitled to relief, and if so will order such relief as is appropriate in the changed circumstances.[10]

The fact that the oppression complained of by the petitioner resulted from acts of the majority shareholders done in some other capacity than that of members of the company did not prevent the court from giving relief under the original statutory provision, and this is undoubtedly so under the present statutory provision as well. Thus, in the first case under the original provision to reach the House of Lords[11] the minority shareholders successfully contended that they were entitled to relief from oppression caused by the majority shareholder, a co-operative society, managing its own affairs so as deliberately to ruin the company. The majority shareholder formed the company in 1946 with the two minority shareholders, and the company's articles provided that its directors should be the minority shareholders and three persons appointed by the majority shareholder. The business which the company was to engage in was manufacturing, dyeing, printing and finishing rayon cloth for resale. The reason why the co-operative society and the minority shareholders collaborated in forming the company was that in 1946 it was necessary to have a Government licence to manufacture rayon cloth, and one of the minority shareholders held such a licence and the co-operative society did not. It was originally intended that the company should manufacture its own cloth, but in fact it bought unfinished cloth from the society, and finished and marketed it itself. In 1950 Government licensing of rayon manufacture came to an end, and in 1952, as the result of a quarrel between the society and the two minority shareholders, the society refused to supply further cloth to the company except at unreasonably high prices, which the company could not afford. The company was unable to procure supplies elsewhere, because the demand for rayon cloth at the time exceeded the supply available, and suppliers declined to sell to persons other than their established customers. Before these events occurred the society had already set up its own finishing plant, and when it ceased to supply the company with unfinished cloth in 1952, it began finishing and marketing cloth itself. The society's purpose in doing these things was to force the company into liquidation, when the amount returnable to the minority shareholders on the sale of the company's assets would

---

9 *Re O C (Transport) Services Ltd* (1984) 1 BCC 68; *Re a Company (No 00477 of 1986)* (1986) 2 BCC 171; *Re a Company (No 006834 of 1988)* (1988) 5 BCC 218.
10 *Re a Company (No 005287 of 1985)* [1986] 2 All ER 253, [1986] 1 WLR 281, [1986] BCLC 68.
11 *Scottish Co-operative Wholesale Society Ltd v Meyer* [1959] AC 324, [1958] 3 All ER 66.

in no way represent the value of their shares while it was a going concern; moreover, the society would have acquired the goodwill of the company's business for nothing as the result of supplying finished cloth to the company's customers, whom the company was no longer able to supply. Neither the Scottish court of first instance[12] nor the House of Lords was in any doubt that the society's conduct was oppressive, but the courts broke new ground in holding that the company's affairs had been conducted oppressively, even though the society had done nothing to further its scheme in its capacity as a member of the company.

The judgments in the House of Lords reached this conclusion in two ways. The first and narrower ground was that relied on by Lord Morton of Henryton and, in part, by Lord Denning. It was that, since the society appointed three of its own directors to be directors of the company along with the minority shareholders, and the society's appointees implicitly assisted its scheme by doing nothing to help the company to obtain supplies of unfinished cloth after 1952 either from the society or elsewhere, the society had carried out its scheme in part, at least, by interfering with the proper management of the company's business, and so had caused the company's affairs to be conducted oppressively by its directors. The second and wider ground, relied on by Lord Simonds and Lord Keith of Avonholm, was that the society's majority shareholding in, and consequent control of, the company cast an obligation on it to manage its own affairs so as to deal fairly with the company, and any unfair dealing by it must be treated as part of the conduct of the company's affairs, because the company had no power to resist. Lord Simonds said:[13]

'My Lords, it may be that the acts of the society of which complaint is made could not be regarded as conduct of the affairs of the company if the society and the company were bodies wholly independent of each other, competitors in the rayon market, and using against each other such methods of trade warfare as custom permitted. But this is to pursue a false analogy. It is not possible to separate the transactions of the society from those of the company. Every step taken by the latter was determined by the policy of the former. . . . It is just because the society could not only use the ordinary and legitimate weapons of commercial warfare, but could also control from within the operations of the company, that it is illegitimate to regard the conduct of the company's affairs as a matter for which it had no responsibility.'

and then he went on to quote with approval from one of the judgments in the Court of Session:

'The truth is that, whenever a subsidiary is formed as in this case with an independent minority of shareholders, the parent company must, if it is engaged in the same class of business, accept as a result of having formed such a subsidiary an obligation so to conduct what are in a sense its own affairs as to deal fairly with its subsidiary.'

At first reading these passages appear to impose a fiduciary duty on majority shareholders toward the minority, and this impression is strengthened by Lord Keith's judgment in which he equated the duty of the society to the minority shareholders with the duty of good faith which partners owe to one another.[14] It is clear, however, that neither Lord Simonds nor Lord Keith intended to impose a fiduciary duty, and that the references to the duties of partners were merely by way of analogy to assist their lordships in defining what kind of oppression entitled minority shareholders to seek relief under the statutory provision. After referring to the duties of partners to each other, Lord Keith said:[14]

'It may not be possible for the legal remedies that would follow in the case of a partnership

---

12 *Meyer v Scottish Textile and Manufacturing Co Ltd* 1954 SC 381, 1954 SLT 273.
13 [1959] AC 324 at 342, [1958] 3 All ER 66 at 71.
14 [1959] AC 324 at 361, [1958] 3 All ER 66 at 84.

to follow here, but the principle has, I think, valuable application to the circumstances of this case' (ie in determining whether there has been oppression).

It is obvious that relief could be given against oppression of minority shareholders under the original statutory provision in situations where neither they nor the company would have had a right of action against the oppressors at law or in equity, and this is undoubtedly so under the present statutory provision which does not require proof of anything more than that the conduct or act of which the petitioner complains should have prejudiced the interests of all or some of the members of the company unfairly, or should be likely to do so. This was recognised by Lord Denning when he said:[15]

> 'Your Lordships were referred to *Bell v Lever Bros Ltd*,[16] where Lord Blanesburgh said that a director of one company was at liberty to become a director also of a rival company. That may have been so at that time. But it is at the risk now of an application under s 210 [of the Companies Act 1948] if he subordinates the interests of one company to those of the other.'

Consequently, when the court defines oppression or unfair prejudice for the purposes of relief under the statutory provision in terms of the breach of duties owed by the majority shareholders to the minority, it must be remembered that the duties do not necessarily have any existence outside the section, and that an attempt to enforce them by an action commenced by writ might fail because of the rule in *Foss v Harbottle*. A more recent decision of the court[17] that a minority shareholder may obtain relief under the present statutory provision when the directors and controlling shareholders of the company have recommended the minority shareholders to accept an offer made by them to purchase the minority's shares and to reject a higher offer made by another company, must therefore be read in the context of the statutory provision, and not as imposing fiduciary duties on the controlling shareholders toward the minority.

Although the capacity in which the persons alleged to be responsible for the unfairly prejudicial conduct of the company's affairs have acted or proposed to act is subject to no limitations, it is essential that their acts must have related to the conduct of the company's affairs, and not merely their own.[18] Consequently, a petition for relief cannot be presented because a shareholder and director of the company has called for immediate payment of a loan owed to him by the company at a time when it lacks the liquid resources to pay it off, or because such a shareholder and director has taken an assignment of a loan owed by the company to a third person without first informing the company of his intention to so do.[18] A petition presented on such grounds will be struck out, not because the respondent shareholder acted as a creditor or intending creditor of the company, but because what he has done in no way relates to the conduct of the company's business and affairs.[18]

The conditions for obtaining relief

A petition for relief from oppression under the original statutory provision would be dismissed if it was not presented in good faith solely in order to obtain such relief, and because of the equitable and therefore discretionary character of the court's jurisdiction under both the original and the present provision, the requirement of good faith on the part of the petitioner undoubtedly continues. Thus, even if the directors or majority shareholders have been guilty of improper

15 [1959] AC 324 at 368, [1958] 3 All ER 66 at 88.
16 [1932] AC 161 at 195.
17 *Re a Company (No 008699 of 1985)* (1986) 2 BCC 24.
18 *Re a Company (No 001761 of 1986)* [1987] BCLC 141.

or irregular conduct, so that there is a prima facie case for relief, it will be refused if the petitioner's real purpose is to obtain payment of debt owed by the company, or to force the directors to accept his views as to the way in which the company's business should be managed;[19] or if the petitioner has submitted to the conduct complained of without protest and has acquiesced in the improper management of the company affairs.[20] Likewise, delay by the petitioner in initiating proceedings after he must have realised that he was the victim of a scheme of oppression or unfair treatment will induce the court to refuse relief, because this indicates that the petitioner has acquiesced in the respondents' conduct and that his complaint is therefore not made in good faith.[1] On the other hand, the fact that the petitioner has taken retaliatory action of the same kind as that of which he complains on the part of the persons who control the company (eg diverting business opportunities from the company) will not prevent the court from granting relief, although it may have a bearing on the form and extent of the relief which the court gives.[2]

The former statutory requirement that the petitioner must show that he was entitled to a winding up order as an alternative to relief under the statutory provision,[3] does not appear in the present enactment, and the availability or otherwise of a winding up order in the circumstances of the case is therefore now irrelevant. This means that the court can no longer require the petitioner, as it formerly did,[4] to prove that the company was solvent or that he could be called on to contribute to its assets if it were wound up. The omission of this requirement would seem to have no other effect, however, and certainly it does not widen the meaning of conduct which unfairly prejudices the interests of some or all members of the company.

Moreover, because of the equitable character of relief under the statutory provision, it would appear that the court will not make an order under it when a winding up order is a more appropriate remedy, for example, because the company has disposed of all its assets required for carrying on its business, and is merely a shell holding liquid assets which should be applied in discharging its liabilities and making a distribution to its members.[5] On the other hand, it was held under the former statutory provision that the petitioner need not prove that the company can be resuscitated if it is managed properly, and relief could be given even though the company had ceased to carry on business and was not likely to do so again.[6] In such a situation the petitioner does not necessarily seek an administration of its assets as in a winding up, but may ask for a personal remedy against the persons responsible for the oppression or unfairly prejudicial conduct of the company's affairs of which he complains, and where that is so, it is clear that the fact that the company's business cannot be rehabilitated should not be a bar to relief.

The court will not give relief against the unfairly prejudicial conduct of a company's affairs, even though a case for relief is made out, if relief of the kind sought in the petition is more appropriately available under the company memorandum or articles (eg a provision entitling the petitioner to have his shares bought out at a fair price by the other shareholders) or, it would seem, under more

---

19 *Re Bellador Silk Ltd* [1965] 1 All ER 667.
20 *Re R A Noble & Sons (Clothing) Ltd* [1983] BCLC 273.
 1 *Re Jermyn Street Turkish Baths Ltd* [1971] 3 All ER 184, [1971] 1 WLR 1042.
 2 *Re London School of Electronics* [1986] Ch 211, [1985] BCLC 273.
 3 Companies Act 1948, s 210 (2).
 4 *Re S A Hawken Ltd* [1950] 2 All ER 408; *Re Bellador Silk Ltd*, supra.
 5 *Re Abbey Leisure Ltd* (1990) 6 BCC 60.
 6 *Scottish Co-operative Wholesale Society Ltd v Meyer* [1959] AC 324 at 364 and 368–369, [1958] 3 All ER 66 at 86 and 89, per Lord Keith of Avonholm and Lord Denning.

specific provisions of the Companies Act 1985.[7] But this will not prevent the court from giving relief if the alternative course available under the articles would deprive the petitioner of substantive or procedural benefits which he would obtain if relief were given under the present statutory provision, in the present case the benefit of an order by the court that the majority shareholders should purchase his shares at the price decided on by the court based on the net value of the company's assets, instead of availing himself of a provision in the company's articles under which the price would be the fair value of his shares as assessed by the company's auditor.[5]

The remedies available

The remedies which the court could employ in giving relief under the original statutory provision were left to its discretion, and could include orders requiring the persons responsible for the oppression to pay compensation to shareholders who had been oppressed,[8] orders appointing or removing directors,[9] or appointing a receiver to manage the company's business temporarily,[10] and orders altering the voting and other rights of classes of members.[11] The court has an equally wide discretion under the present statutory provision, and the only limitation is that the order it makes must be relevant and appropriate in order to give relief from the matters complained of.[12] The petitioners must state in their petition what orders they wish the court to make, however, and a petition will not be heard if it merely asks the court to make an order regulating the company's affairs, or such order as the court thinks just.[13]

Without affecting the generality of its power to give whatever relief is appropriate in the circumstances, the new statutory provision empowers the court to make any order it thinks fit regulating the conduct of the company's affairs in the future; to require the company not to do or not to continue doing any act complained of, or to require it to do any act when the petitioner has complained of the company's omission to do it in the past (injunctive and mandatory injunctive relief); to authorise any person to bring civil proceedings in the name and on behalf of the company on such terms as the court thinks fit; and to provide for the purchase of the shares of any members of the company or by the company itself, and in the latter case the court may order that the company's capital be reduced in consequence.[14] The value of the court's power to permit anyone (eg a shareholder, debenture holder, loan security holder or trustee for debenture or loan security holders) to sue in the company's name lies in the fact that the authorised person will not be personally liable for costs (as he would be in a representative or derivative action in which he was plaintiff) except to the extent the court so orders, and he may be empowered by the court to use the company's resources for the purpose of the action. The court's power to order that any member's shares shall be

---

7 *Re a Company (No 006834 of 1988)*, *ex p Kremer* [1989] BCLC 365.
8 *Scottish Co-operative Wholesale Society Ltd v Meyer* [1959] AC 324 at 369, [1958] 3 All ER 66 at 89, per Lord Denning.
9 *Re H R Harmer Ltd* [1958] 3 All ER 689, [1959] 1 WLR 62.
10 In *Re Hannetta Ltd* (1953) 216 LT Jo 639 at 641, Roxburgh J, held (wrongly, it would seem) that the court has no power to appoint a receiver or manager of the company's business. In *Re a Company (No 00596 of 1986)* [1987] BCLC 133, the court appointed such a receiver as an interim measure, and there appears to be no reason why it should not do so by its final order.
11 Thus, the court could remedy the oppression of a class of members who have no voting rights by conferring voting rights on them.
12 Companies Act 1985, s 461 (1).
13 *Re Antigen Laboratories Ltd* [1951] 1 All ER 110n.
14 Companies Act 1985, s 461 (2).

purchased by other members may be used to resolve an impasse by requiring the majority shareholders to buy the oppressed minority's shares at their fair value at the time when the unfair treatment of the petitioner began.[15] It has been held by a South African court under a similar statutory provision that the court may also use this power to destroy the majority's control by requiring them to sell some of their shares to the minority,[16] but the court in this country has held that such an order breaking up the majority's control of the company will be made only where the majority shareholders have been guilty of seriously improper conduct, and not merely where the mutual confidence between them and the minority shareholders in a company which was formed as a quasi-partnership company has disappeared.[17] The court may alternatively combine orders for the sale of shares held by the petitioner and the respondents respectively by directing that the petitioner or the respondents shall have an option to buy out the other party's shares at a price acceptable to the court, but that if this option is not exercised within a certain time, the other party may purchase the shares of the party who had the first option.[17] The court's power to order that the company shall purchase a member's shares would seem to be useful when the court decides that the petitioner's or the respondents' shares shall be bought from them, but the other party lacks the resources to pay the price which the court fixes.

If the court orders that the shares of the unfairly treated minority shareholders shall be purchased by the majority shareholders and the company was formed as a quasi-partnership,[18] it has been held that the price directed to be paid for the minority's shares should be calculated as though the company were to go into liquidation immediately, and so the price will correspond to an appropriate proportion of the company's net assets (including goodwill), and an amount will be deducted from this figure because the minority shareholders' holdings do not carry control of the company only if they have been guilty of conduct which in the case of a partnership would itself be a ground on which the partnership could be dissolved.[19] Nevertheless, it has been held in other cases that this is not an invariable rule, and that where the controlling shareholders have treated the petitioner unfairly only by failing to make a reasonable offer for his shares when he ceased to take an active part in managing the company, the proper price at which the controlling shareholders should be required to buy his shares should be their fair value at the date of the hearing,[20] or at the earlier date when the petitioner was unfairly dismissed from his directorship,[1] having regard to the company's assets and prospective earnings at that time, and the value should be duly discounted to take account of the minority percentage of the petitioner's holding of the company's

---

15 This was done in *Meyer v Scottish Textile and Manufacturing Co Ltd* (1957) SC 110, 1957 SLT 20; affd [1959] AC 324, [1958] 3 All ER 66) and in *Re OC (Transport) Services Ltd* [1984] BCLC 251, (1984) 1 BCC 68. It has been held in Canada that when the shares are preference shares redeemable at the option of the company, the fair price is that which the company would have to pay to redeem the shares (*Re British Columbia Electric Co Ltd* (1964) 47 DLR (2d) 754).

16 *Benjamin v Elysium Investments (Pty) Ltd* 1960 (3) SA 467.

17 *Re Jermyn Street Turkish Baths Ltd* [1970] 3 All ER 57, [1970] 1 WLR 1194; revsd on other grounds [1971] 3 All ER 184, [1971] 1 WLR 1042.

18 *Re a Company (No 006834 of 1988), ex p Kremer* [1989] BCLC 365, (1988) 5 BCC 218. A quasi-partnership company is a private company whose members formed it on the basis of personal trust and confidence in each other, similar to that which should exist between partners. The character of the company is usually indicated by the shareholders or most of them being directors of the company and by there being restrictions imposed on the transferability of their shares, particularly by mutual pre-emption provisions in the articles.

19 *Re Bird Precision Bellows Ltd* [1984] Ch 419, [1984] 3 All ER 444, affd [1986] Ch 658, [1985] 3 All ER 523; *Re London School of Electronics Ltd* [1986] Ch 211, [1985] BCLC 273.

20 *Re a Company* [1986] BCLC 362; *Re a Company (No 005134 of 1986), ex p Harries* [1989] BCLC 383.

1 *Re O C Transport Services Ltd* [1984] BCLC 251, (1984) 1 BCC 68.

issued shares. The date at which the minority shareholders' shares should be valued for the purpose of an order that they shall be purchased by the majority shareholders will depend on the facts of each case. If the shares have fallen in value as a result of the unfairly prejudicial conduct of the company's affairs by the controlling shareholders, the minority shareholding will be valued as at the time when the unfairly prejudicial conduct began.[2] In most other cases the valuation will be made as at the date of the presentation of the successful petition, but if the company's business has increased in value since that time (otherwise than as a result of acts or events occurring since the petitioner ceased to have any connection with the company apart from his shareholding), the court will select an appropriate later date so that the increase in value will be reflected in the valuation of the petitioner's shares.[3] On the other hand, if the company's business or shares in it have fallen in value since the date when the successful petition was presented, the court will make no allowance for that fall in value in arriving at the proper price at which the persons responsible for the unfairly prejudicial conduct of the company's business are ordered to purchase the petitioner's shares.[4] Moreover, the facts that those persons will have to sell the shares they are ordered to purchase from the petitioner because they have no other means of raising the price ordered to be paid to him, and that there is no prospect of them being able to sell the shares at the price ordered to be paid to the petitioner, will not induce the court to reduce the price ordered to be paid to him.[4]

If in exercise of its power to regulate the company's affairs in the future,[5] the court orders alterations to be made in the company's memorandum or articles, the alterations take effect as though they had been duly made by resolution of the company,[6] and so are susceptible to further alteration by the normal procedure, unless the court expressly forbids further alterations except with its leave.[7] The court can also order the company not to make any alteration to its memorandum or articles, or any particular kind of alteration (eg to the rights of a class of shareholders set out in the articles) without first obtaining its leave,[7] and this applies to provisions of the memorandum or articles which were originally there or inserted by alterations made by the company itself, as well as to provisions ordered to be included in the memorandum or articles by the court.

The only limitation on the court's inventiveness in devising an appropriate remedy to relieve the unfairly prejudicial conduct of a company's affairs seems to be that it cannot alter rights held by the parties in capacities other than those of members or directors of the company. It has consequently been held by a South African court that controlling shareholders found guilty of oppression could not be compelled to submit to a variation of rights conferred by debentures of the company which they held, even though their oppressive conduct had been facilitated by their also being debenture holders.[8] It would seem that under the Companies Act 1985 the court similarly cannot alter the rights of creditors of the company.

2 *Scottish Co-operative Wholesale Society v Meyer* [1959] AC 324, [1958] 3 All ER 66; *Re Cumana Ltd* [1986] BCLC 430.
3 *Re London School of Electronics Ltd*, supra.
4 *Re Cumana Ltd*, supra.
5 Companies Act 1985, s 461 (2) (*a*).
6 Ibid, s 461 (4).
7 Ibid, s 461 (3). Under the Companies Act 1948, s 210 (3) alterations ordered by the court were automatically incapable of further alteration except with leave of the court, and no direction to this effect in the court's order was necessary.
8 *Irvin and Johnson Ltd v Oelofse Fisheries Ltd* 1954 (1) SA 231.

Procedure

The procedure for the presentation and hearing of petitions for relief under the statutory provision is governed by the rules made by the Lord Chancellor which incorporate the rules and practice of the Supreme Court, except so far as they make other express provision.[9] The petition must be in the form set out in the rules, and after setting out formally the company's name and date of incorporation, the address of the company's registered office and its nominal and paid up capital, the petition must state the number of shares in the company which are held by the petitioner and registered in his name,[10] the principal objects of the company and the grounds on which the petition is presented, setting out in detail the facts and events on which the petitioner relies in seeking relief with a formal conclusion that in the related circumstances the affairs of the company are being conducted in a manner which is unfairly prejudicial to the members of the company or to some part of its members (including the petitioner),[11] and the petition then contains a prayer to the court for the specific relief which the petitioner seeks or 'that such other order may be made as the court thinks fair and just'.[12] The company will be made a respondent to the petition, and all directors and members of the company whose conduct is complained of, or against whom relief is sought, or whose rights would be affected if the relief sought by the petition were granted, must be made additional respondents.[13] The names of all other persons on whom it is intended to serve copies of the petition (eg members of the company who are not made respondents) must be set out at the end of the petition.[12]

The petition is presented to the court with sufficient copies for service on the respondents and the persons on whom it is intended to effect service, and after sealing by the court, sealed copies of the petition must be served on each of the respondents at least 14 days before the date fixed by the court for the preliminary hearing, and an endorsement of the time and place of that hearing must appear on each copy of the petition which is served.[14] On that day the petitioner and the respondents must attend before the registrar in chambers, and he may give directions as to the service of the petition on any persons; as to whether particulars of claim and defence (pleadings) are to be delivered by the parties, and generally as to the procedure on the petition; as to whether the petition is to be advertised; as to the manner in which evidence is to be adduced on the hearing on the merits before the judge, and in particular whether evidence is to be taken wholly or in part by affidavit or orally; as to the cross examination of deponents of affidavits and as to the matters to be dealt with in evidence; and generally as to any other matter affecting the procedure on the petition and its hearing and disposal.[15]

If the court on the hearing of the petition on the merits makes an order giving relief to the petitioner, the petitioner and all other persons who appeared on the hearing must, not later than the following business day, leave at the court all the documents required for drawing up the order, but no appointment need be taken

---

9 The Companies (Unfair Prejudice Applications) Proceedings Rules 1986 (SI 1986/200), para 2 (2).
10 If the petitioner is entitled to shares which have been transferred or transmitted to him by operation of law, but they are not registered in his name, the petition must so state.
11 Alternatively, the petition may complain that the acts or omissions, or proposed acts or omissions, which are specified in it are, or would be, unfairly prejudicial to the members or to some part of its members (including the petitioner).
12 The Companies (Unfair Prejudice Applications) Proceedings Rules 1986, para 3 (1) and (2) and Schedule.
13 *Re a Company (No 007281 of 1986)* [1987] BCLC 593.
14 The Companies (Unfair Prejudice Applications) Proceedings Rules 1986, para 3 (1) and (2) and para 4 (1) and (2) and Schedule.
15 Ibid, para 3 (3) and para 5.

for attendance on the registrar to settle the order unless the court considers this necessary.[16] A copy of the order need only be served by the petitioner on the company or any other respondent if the petitioner intends to enforce it by applying to the court for an order for sequestration or committal for contempt.[17] Additionally, the company must deliver an office copy of the order to the Registrar of Companies, within 14 days after it is made, if the order alters the memorandum or articles of association of the company.[18] An order by the court need be advertised only if it so directs.[19]

When a petition has been presented, the court may appoint a receiver of the assets and undertaking of the company as an interim measure pending the hearing of the petition if there is a substantial risk of the company's assets being dissipated or wrongfully disposed of, or if the directors are not managing the company's business properly.[20] On the other hand, the court has no jurisdiction to give the petitioner interim relief pending the hearing of the petition if this would involve a tacit acceptance of the merits of the petitioner's case (eg a payment of money representing part of the value of the petitioner's shares), because the court's statutory power to give substantive relief is conditional on the petitioner proving the allegations made in the petition, which can only be done when the petition is heard on the merits.[1] Furthermore, the court cannot make an order that the company shall secure or pay the petitioner's costs pending the hearing of the petition, or that it shall pay his costs whether the petition is successful or not, as it can in a derivative action brought by a minority shareholder.[2] This is because a petition under the statutory provision is presented to protect the rights and interests of the petitioner as a member or shareholder, and not to remedy a wrong or threatened wrong to the company as is a derivative action, in which the company therefore has an interest.[2]

Misfeasance proceedings

In the winding up of a company an application may be made to the court[3] by the official receiver, the liquidator or by any creditor or, with leave of the court, by any contributory[4] for an order that any present or past officer of the company, any person who has acted as liquidator, administrator or administrative receiver of the company or any other person who has been concerned or taken part in the promotion, formation or management of the company, and who in the case of any such officer has misapplied or retained or become accountable for any money or property of the company, or has been guilty of any misfeasance or breach of any fiduciary or other duty in relation to the company, shall repay with interest at such rate as the court orders, restore or account for the money or property or any part of it, or shall contribute such sum to the company's assets by way of compensation for the misfeasance or breach of duty as the court thinks just.[5]

16 Ibid, para 6 (1) and (2).
17 RSC Order 45, r 5 (1) and r 7 (2) and (3).
18 Companies Act 1985, s 461 (5).
19 The Companies (Unfair Prejudice Applications) Rules 1986, r 6 (3).
20 *Re a Company (No 00596 of 1986)* [1987] BCLC 133.
 1 *Re a Company (No 004175 of 1986)* [1987] BCLC 574; not followed in *Re Blue Arrow plc* [1987] 1 WLR 585, [1987] BCLC 585.
 2 *Re Sherborne Park Residents Co Ltd* (1986) 2 BCC 528.
 3 The court is the court which has jurisdiction to wind up the company (Companies Act 1985, s 744); Insolvency Act 1986, s 117 (1) and (2) and s 251). The proceedings are initiated by an application or (in a voluntary winding up) by an originating application to the Companies Court or any other court which has jurisdiction to wind up the company (Insolvency Rules 1986, r 7.2 (1)).
 4 That is, a present or past member of the company (Insolvency Act 1986, s 74 (1) and s 79 (1)).
 5 Insolvency Act 1986, s 212 (1), (3) and (5).

Misfeasance proceedings may be brought with leave of the court by a member even though he could not bring a derivative action, because, for example, there has been no fraud or oppression by the majority shareholders, or because the respondent promoters or directors do not control the company. But misfeasance proceedings lie only when the company itself could have sued the respondent in an action commenced by writ,[6] and so a member cannot enforce a right of action vested in himself personally by this means.[7] Moreover, even if an action could be brought by the company itself, it does not always follow that misfeasance proceedings may be resorted to. Not all rights of action vested in a company may be enforced by misfeasance proceedings,[8] and the claims enforceable in this way are limited to those which satisfy certain conditions in respect of their nature and the persons against whom they are made.

The only orders which the court may make in misfeasance proceedings are for the return of property to the company or for the payment of compensation or damages for losses wrongfully inflicted on it.[9] Consequently, the court cannot rescind a contract,[10] or order payment of a debt to the company[11] under a misfeasance summons. Nor can it order a director to make a payment to the company, unless he has misappropriated its property or has caused it loss by failing to perform a duty which he owed to it.[12] Thus, misfeasance proceedings cannot be brought against a director who failed to acquire his share qualification fixed by the articles, because he is under no obligation imposed by law to take them from the company.[12] On the other hand, such proceedings may be brought to recover a secret profit from a director, even though the company has suffered no loss, because the profit belongs to the company, and the director is accountable for it.[13] Under the former legislation which has been replaced by the Insolvency Act 1986, it was held that misfeasance proceedings will not lie against a director or other officer of a company to recover compensation for breach of a duty owed to the company, unless the duty was fiduciary in nature.[14] Consequently, such proceedings were held not to lie against a director for mere negligence in managing the company's affairs,[14] although misfeasance proceedings were permitted to be brought against a liquidator who negligently paid an invalid claim made against the company,[15] and against auditors who were guilty of negligence.[16] The present legislation authorises the issue of misfeasance summonses against present or past officers, liquidators, administrators, administrative receivers and other persons concerned in the promotion or formation of a company now in liquidation for breach of 'any fiduciary or other duty in relation to the company',[17] and so it would appear that misfeasance proceedings may be brought to recover compensation for any loss

---

6 *Re Canadian Land Reclaiming and Colonizing Co, Coventry and Dixon's Case* (1880) 14 ChD 660.
7 *Re Hill's Waterfall Estate and Gold Mining Co* [1896] 1 Ch 947, where a member unsuccessfully claimed compensation from a liquidator who had wrongfully disposed of shares in another company which should have been allotted to the member.
8 *Re Etic Ltd* [1928] Ch 861 at 871, per Maugham J.
9 Insolvency Act 1986, s 212 (3).
10 *Re Centrifugal Butter Co Ltd* [1913] 1 Ch 188.
11 *Re Etic Ltd* [1928] Ch 861.
12 *Re Canadian Land Reclaiming and Colonizing Co, Coventry and Dixon's Case*, supra.
13 *Re North Australian Territory Co, Archer's Case* [1892] 1 Ch 322.
14 *Re B Johnson & Co (Builders) Ltd* [1955] Ch 634, [1955] 2 All ER 775.
15 *Re Windsor Steam Coal Co (1901) Ltd* [1929] 1 Ch 151; *Re Home and Colonial Insurance Co Ltd* [1930] 1 Ch 102. But an unjustifiable payment may also have been a breach of fiduciary duty because the liquidator had misapplied the company's funds, even though unintentionally.
16 *Re London and General Bank* [1895] 2 Ch 166.
17 Insolvency Act 1986, s 212 (1).

suffered by the company, whatever the cause of action may be and whether it arises at common law or in equity.

The only persons who may be made respondents in misfeasance proceedings are those named in the statutory provision.[17] The broadest class of these, 'officers of the company', has given rise to some difficulty of definition. The legislation is unhelpful in this respect, because it merely defines 'officers' as including directors, managers and secretaries, without confining the expression to those persons.[18] It has been held that auditors are officers for the purpose of misfeasance proceedings,[16] and it seems that managers are to be considered as officers if they have authority to carry out or supervise the execution of the company's business policy or the general administration of its business, as distinct from managing a department of that business.[19] However, trustees for debenture or loan security holders[20] and receivers and managers appointed by debenture or loan security holders or by the court[1] are not officers for the purpose of misfeasance proceedings, nor are the company's solicitors[2] or its bank,[3] or presumably, any other agent employed by it. On the other hand, a person who acts as a director, even though not properly appointed or qualified to act, is amenable to misfeasance proceedings,[4] and it would appear that the extension of misfeasance proceedings by the present legislation to persons who are or have been concerned in the promotion, formation or management of a company[17] will make all persons who are concerned in the overall direction of a company's affairs (either by participating in it themselves, or by giving instructions to which the directors habitually conform (i e shadow directors)), amenable to such proceedings. Because the classes of persons who may be made respondents in misfeasance proceedings are limited, however, a respondent to such proceedings may not have a person added as a third party so as to enforce a claim for contribution or an indemnity in connection with the misfeasance alleged to have been committed by him, and this is so even if that other person could have been made one of the original respondents in the proceedings.[5] But if such a person has been made a respondent by the person who initiated the misfeasance proceedings, the court can order him to pay such contribution or indemnity as it thinks fit to the other respondents, and so avoid the need for them to take separate proceedings against him.[6]

If a respondent in misfeasance proceedings is found to be guilty of a breach of duty to the company which has caused it loss, the court has a discretion in fixing the amount of compensation which he is ordered to pay to the company, and it need not require him to make good the whole of the resulting loss. Thus, where a liquidator satisfied a claim against the company on an insurance policy issued by it which was technically void, the court merely ordered him to make good so much of the amount so paid as was necessary to pay the company's debts.[7] This was because the company would have honoured the policy voluntarily if it had continued as a going concern, and because the members had resolved that the company should be wound up on the footing that it was insolvent because of its liability on the policy; it would therefore have been inequitable to require the

18 Companies Act 1985, s 744; Insolvency Act 1986, s 251.
19 *Re a Company* [1980] Ch 138, [1980] 1 All ER 284; revsd on other grounds [1981] AC 374, [1980] 2 All ER 634.
20 *Astley v New Tivoli Ltd* [1899] 1 Ch 151 at 154.
1 *Re B Johnson & Co (Builders) Ltd* [1955] Ch 634, [1955] 2 All ER 775.
2 *Re Great Western Forest of Dean Coal Consumers Co, Carter's Case* (1886) 31 ChD 496.
3 *Re Imperial Land Co of Marseilles, Re, National Bank* (1870) LR 10 Eq 298.
4 *Re Canadian Land Reclaiming and Colonizing Co, Coventry and Dixon's Case* (1880) 14 ChD 660.
5 *Re A Singer & Co (Hat Manufacturers) Ltd* [1943] Ch 121, [1943] 1 All ER 225.
6 *Re Morecambe Bowling Ltd* [1960] 1 All ER 753, [1969] 1 WLR 133.
7 *Re Home and Colonial Insurance Co Ltd* [1930] 1 Ch 102.

liquidator to repay the whole amount he had paid out on the policy when the part of that amount not required to meet the company's debts would then be passed on to the members, who had acquiesced in the policy being honoured.[7] In another case[8] a director was allowed to keep a payment made to him under a voidable contract, because the company had benefited from the contract, and almost all the members wished the director to retain the payment. But if a respondent in misfeasance proceedings has a claim against the company, the court cannot allow him to set it off against the amount which the court orders him to pay to the company as compensation for his breach of duty, even though set off would have been possible if the company had sued him in an action commenced by writ.[9]

A member will be given leave by the court to bring misfeasance proceedings only if he has an interest in the property or compensation claimed being returned or paid to the company.[10] He will have such an interest only if the company is solvent, so that there will be assets divisible amongst its members after its debts and liabilities have been discharged, or if his shares are partly paid, so that the property or compensation recovered in the misfeasance proceedings will help to reduce the amount of unpaid capital which will have to be called up from him. But a fully paid shareholder of an insolvent limited company will not be permitted to bring misfeasance proceedings, because he has no interest to protect, unless of course, the amount likely to be recovered in the misfeasance proceedings is so substantial that it will not only enable the company to discharge its debts and liabilities in full, but will also result in a surplus being available for distribution between the company's shareholders.

If a right of action vested in a company in liquidation cannot be enforced by misfeasance proceedings, it must be enforced by an action brought in the company's name by the liquidator,[11] but it cannot be enforced by a derivative action brought by a member after the commencement of the liquidation without the liquidator's authorisation.[12] If the liquidator declines to sue in the company's name, however, a creditor or present or past member of the company may apply to the court for an order that the liquidator shall do so.[13]

Investigations ordered by the Secretary of State for Trade and Industry

The Secretary of State for Trade and Industry may appoint one or more inspectors[14] to investigate the affairs of a company in the following cases:

(1) on the application of the company or of 200 members of the company or of members holding at least one tenth of the company's issued share capital, but the Secretary of State may require the applicants to produce evidence to show that they have good reason to request an investigation;[15] or

(2) if it appears that the company's affairs are being or have been conducted with intent to defraud its creditors or the creditors of another person, or for

---

8 *Re Sunlight Incandescent Gas Lamp Co* (1900) 16 TLR 535.
9 *Re Anglo-French Co-operative Society, Pelly's Case* (1882) 21 ChD 492; *Re Exchange Banking Co, Fitcroft's Case* (1882) 21 ChD 519.
10 *Cavendish Bentinck v Fenn* (1887) 12 App Cas 652; *Re B Johnson & Co (Builders) Ltd*, supra.
11 Insolvency Act 1986, s 165 (3) and s 167 (1) and Sch 4, para 4.
12 *Fargro Ltd v Godfroy* [1986] 3 All ER 279, [1986] BCLC 370.
13 Insolvency Act 1986, s 112 (1) and s 167 (3).
14 The usual practice is for the Secretary of State to appoint two inspectors, one being a barrister and the other an accountant.
15 Companies Act 1985, s 431 (1) to (3). Before making the appointment the Secretary of State may require the applicants to give security, not exceeding £5,000, for the costs of the investigation (Companies Act 1985, s 431 (4)).

any fraudulent purpose,[16] or for any unlawful purpose, or in a manner which is unfairly prejudicial to any part of its members, or that any actual or proposed act or omission of the company would be so prejudicial, or that the company was formed for any fraudulent or unlawful purpose;[17] or

(3) if it appears that the promoters, directors or persons engaged in the management of the company's affairs have been guilty of fraud, misfeasance or other misconduct towards it or its members;[18] in this context 'other misconduct' means misconduct of the same character as fraud or misfeasance, and the Secretary of State therefore cannot initiate an investigation merely on the strength of an allegation of negligence on the part of promoters or directors,[19] or

(4) if it appears that members of the company have not been given all the information with respect to its affairs which they might reasonably expect.[20]

An inspector or inspectors may be appointed under (2), (3) or (4) above even if the company is being wound up voluntarily.[21]

When the Secretary of State appoints an inspector or inspectors under the foregoing provisions, he need not specify which of the grounds (1) to (4) he relies on, what evidence or information led him to order the investigation, or what were his reasons for so ordering.[1] The company and its directors are not entitled to call for disclosure of these matters under the relevant statutory rules or under the rules of natural justice, nor are they entitled to be given an opportunity to answer any allegations which may have been considered by the Secretary of State as calling for the appointment of an inspector.[1]

The Secretary of State must appoint one or more inspectors to investigate the affairs of a company if the court declares that its affairs ought to be so investigated.[2] Consequently, if an individual member fails to persuade the Secretary of State to appoint an inspector or inspectors in cases (2) to (4) above, or if the requisite fraction of members fails to persuade the Secretary of State to do so in case (1), an application may be made to the court[3] to reverse the Secretary of State's decision.

If two or more inspectors are appointed by the Secretary of State, their functions must be carried out and their powers exercised by them jointly, and references hereafter to inspectors should be taken to refer to both or all of the inspectors acting together, or in the exceptional event of only one inspector being appointed, to that inspector.

The affairs of a company for the purpose of the foregoing provisions include all matters relating to its management, assets, profits or losses, and also the affairs of its subsidiaries and sub-subsidiaries insofar as they may directly or indirectly affect it.[4] Usually an inquiry into the conduct of a company's affairs is concerned with the acts of its directors and controlling shareholders, but an investigation may also be directed into the conduct of the company's affairs by a receiver or manager

---

16 This amounts to fraudulent trading, for which directors may be liable if the company is wound up (see p 41, ante).

17 Companies Act 1985, s 432 (2) (*a*) and (*b*).

18 Ibid, s 432 (2) (*c*).

19 *SBA Properties Ltd v Cradock* [1967] 2 All ER 610, [1967] 1 WLR 716.

20 Companies Act 1985, s 432 (2) (*d*). This appears to authorise an investigation even though the members have been given all the information which the Companies Acts 1985 and 1989 require to be disclosed by the company's annual accounts and the directors' report.

21 Companies Act 1985, s 432 (3).

1 *Norwest Holst Ltd v Secretary of State for Trade* [1978] Ch 201, [1978] 3 All ER 280.

2 Companies Act 1985, s 432 (1).

3 The application is made to the court by originating motion (RSC Ord 102, r 3 (1) (*b*)).

4 Companies Act 1985, s 433 (1).

appointed to realise the security held by its debenture or loan security holders.[5] To enable himself to decide whether to order an investigation of a company's affairs or to take other remedial action, the Secretary of State has a general power to require a company or any other person to produce any documents and information recorded in legible form or in a form capable of being reproduced in legible form, and to require any present or past officer or any employee of the company to explain their contents.[6] Ancillary powers are given to the Secretary of State to discover and seize such books and papers, and restrictions are imposed on the communication of their contents.[7]

So far as necessary for the purpose of the investigation they are appointed to undertake, inspectors appointed by the Secretary of State may investigate the affairs of any related company, that is, any company which has at any relevant time been the holding company or subsidiary of the company under investigation, or a subsidiary of its holding company, or a holding company of its subsidiary.[8] The past and present officers and agents of the company under investigation and of related companies whose affairs are also investigated, and any other persons whom the inspectors consider likely to be in possession of information concerning the company under investigation or any related company, must produce to the inspectors all documents relating to any such company which are in their possession or power, must attend before the inspectors when required to do so, and must give all assistance to the inspectors which they are reasonably able to give.[9] The term 'agents' includes auditors, solicitors and bankers[10] and, it seems, receivers or managers appointed by debenture or loan security holders if they are deemed to be agents of the company by the terms of the debentures or trust deed.[11] The inspectors may examine such officers and agents and such other persons considered by them to be in possession of relevant information, and if they think fit may examine them on oath, and if any officer, agent or other person refuses to attend before the inspectors when required to do so, or to answer any question put to him or to produce any document which he should produce, the inspectors may certify that fact to the court, and the court may punish him as though he were guilty of contempt of court.[12]

Inspectors may not require any person to disclose information or to produce documents which he would be entitled to refuse to disclose or produce on the ground of legal professional privilege in an action brought in the High Court, but if he is a lawyer he may be required to disclose the name and address of his client.[13] Moreover, a person cannot be required to disclose information or to produce documents in respect of which he owes a duty of confidence by virtue of carrying on a banking business (ie a bank or an officer of it), unless the person required to do so is the company under investigation or any related company to which the investigation is extended, or unless the person to whom the obligation of confidence is owed is that company or such a related company, or unless the person to whom the obligation of confidence is owed consents to the disclosure or production of

---

5 *R v Board of Trade, ex p St Martin Preserving Co Ltd* [1965] 1 QB 603, [1964] 2 All ER 561.
6 Companies Act 1985, s 447 (2) and (5), as amended by Companies Act 1989, s 63 (1) to (3).
7 See p 693, post.
8 Companies Act 1985, s 433 (1).
9 Ibid, s 434 (1) and (2), as amended by Companies Act 1989, s 56 (1) to (3).
10 Companies Act 1985, s 434 (4).
11 *R v Board of Trade, ex p St Martin Preserving Co Ltd* [1985] 1 QB 603 at 614, [1964] 2 All ER 561 at 571.
12 Companies Act 1985, s 436 (1) to (3), as amended by Companies Act 1989, s 56 (6).
13 Ibid, s 452 (1).

documents, or unless the inspectors' requirement is authorised by the Secretary of State.[14]

A person under examination by inspectors may not refuse to answer questions because his answers may incriminate him, nor may he refuse to answer incriminating questions or questions the answers to which may expose him to civil liability unless the inspectors undertake to allow him to see the testimony of other persons examined and to cross-examine them if their testimony is adverse.[15] But if questions of an incriminating nature are put to a person under examination, the inspectors must as a matter of natural justice allow him to see adverse testimony by other persons and to cross-examine them,[16] or at least must notify him of the substance of the charges made against him and permit him to answer those charges,[17] and the court may order the inspectors to accord him such rights. However, it is not necessary for the inspectors to show a person whom they have examined the parts of their draft report containing criticisms of that person and to give him a further opportunity to refute the criticisms by evidence or argument.[18] Any answer given on oath by a person in the course of an investigation, or by way of explanation during a preliminary inspection of the company's documents in consequence of a requirement of the Secretary of State,[19] may be used as evidence against him in subsequent civil or criminal proceedings, whether those proceedings relate to the affairs of the company under investigation or not,[20] and it has been held that unsworn statements and supplementary correspondence between the Secretary of State and the deponent may likewise be admitted in evidence against him in later civil or criminal proceedings.[1] However, the admission of such evidence, whether sworn or unsworn, is subject to the court's discretion to exclude it if it is a statement made confidentially to the inspector or the Secretary of State for use only in connection with the investigation or inquiry in question.[1]

Although an investigation bears some resemblance to a judicial inquiry, and although it is the normal practice to allow interested persons to be represented by counsel before the inspectors, an investigation is not a judicial proceeding, and the inspectors cannot admit members of the public to any hearing which they conduct.[2]

The inspectors must report their findings to the Secretary of State on the conclusion of the investigation; they may also make interim reports during the investigation and must do so if directed by the Secretary of State.[3] The inspectors must inform the Secretary of State of any matters which come to their knowledge during the investigation if the Secretary of State requires.[4] If the Secretary of State considers that matters have been discovered during the investigation which suggest that a criminal offence has been committed, and those matters have been referred to the appropriate prosecuting authority, the Secretary of State may direct the inspectors not to continue the investigation, or to continue it only to the extent

---

14 Companies Act 1985, s 452 (1A) and (1B), inserted by Companies Act 1989, s 69 (3).
15 *Re Pergamon Press Ltd* [1970] 2 All ER 449, [1970] 1 WLR 1075; affd [1971] Ch 388, [1970] 3 All ER 535.
16 *McClelland, Pope and Langley Ltd v Howard* [1968] 1 All ER 569n; *Re Pergamon Press Ltd*, supra.
17 *Karak Rubber Co Ltd v Burden* [1971] 3 All ER 1118, [1971] 1 WLR 1748; *Maxwell v Department of Trade and Industry* [1974] QB 523, [1974] 2 All ER 122.
18 *Maxwell v Department of Trade and Industry*, supra.
19 See p 692, post.
20 Companies Act 1985, s 434 (5).
1 *London and County Securities Ltd v Nicholson* [1980] 3 All ER 861, [1980] 1 WLR 948.
2 *Re Gaumont-British Picture Corpn* [1940] Ch 506, [1940] 2 All ER 415.
3 Companies Act 1985, s 437 (1).
4 Companies Act 1985, s 437 (1A), inserted by Financial Services Act 1986, s 182 and Sch 13, para 7.

which he directs.[5] In that situation the inspectors will make a final report to the Secretary of State only if the investigation was ordered by the court or if the Secretary of State directs them to do so.[6]

If the inspector was appointed in consequence of an order of the court declaring that the affairs of the company should be investigated, the Secretary of State must send a copy of the inspector's interim and final reports to the court.[7] The Secretary of State may, if he thinks fit, send a copy of any report by the inspectors to the company whose affairs have been investigated, and may furnish such a copy on request and on payment of a prescribed fee to any member of the company or a related company which has been investigated, to any person whose conduct is referred to in the report, to the auditors of the company or a related company whose affairs have been investigated, to the applicants for the investigation and to any other person whose financial interests appear to be affected by the matters dealt with in the report, whether a creditor of the company or a related company or not.[8] Additionally, the Secretary of State may have the inspector's report printed and published,[9] but is not under a duty to do so. If in his discretion the Secretary of State decides not to publish the report or to postpone doing so until other proceedings (eg criminal proceedings or an investigation with a view to instituting such proceedings) have been completed, his decision can be annulled by the court in judicial review proceedings[10] only if he misdirected himself on questions of law, or took into account irrelevant matters, or failed to take relevant matters into account, or if his decision was not one which could reasonably be reached, or if there was some serious and substantial procedural defect.[11] Moreover, when the Secretary of State appoints inspectors to investigate a company's affairs, he may do so on terms that their report shall not be published, and in that case a copy of the report must be sent to the court if the investigation was ordered by it, but copies will not be available to other persons.[12]

The value of the inspectors' report is that it may reveal information about the company which individual members could not discover for themselves, or it may reveal irregularities in the management of the company's affairs about which its members or creditors were ignorant or had only vague suspicions, but the report obviously does of itself not remedy any irregularities in the conduct of the company's affairs which it discloses. Members may of course, take the proceedings normally open to them for this purpose, (including proceedings under the Company Directors Disqualification Act 1986 for the disqualification of directors and other persons)[13], and in any legal proceedings a copy of the report certified by the Secretary of State to be a true copy is evidence of the inspectors' opinion, but not of the facts found by them.[14] Additionally, the Secretary of State may take any of the following steps in consequence of the report or any information obtained by him as a result of calling for the production of the company's documents:[15]

5 Companies Act 1985, s 437 (1B), inserted by Companies Act 1989, s 57.
6 Companies Act 1985, s 437 (1C), inserted by Companies Act 1989, s 57.
7 Companies Act 1985, s 437 (2).
8 Ibid, s 437 (3) (*a*) and (*b*).
9 Ibid, s 437 (3) (*c*).
10 Supreme Court Act 1981, s 31 (3); RSC Ord 53, r 3.
11 *Lonrho plc v Secretary of State for Trade and Industry* [1989] 2 All ER 609, [1989] 1 WLR 525.
12 Companies Act 1985, s 432 (2A), inserted by Companies Act 1989, s 55.
13 See p 535, ante.
14 Companies Act 1985, s 441 (1), as amended by Insolvency Act 1986, s 439 (1) and Sch 13, Part I. The report may be treated as presumptive proof of the facts found by the inspectors in winding up proceedings, but the report cannot be used as evidence of the facts found by the inspectors in proceeding other than winding up proceedings (*Savings and Investment Bank Ltd v Gasco Investments (Netherlands) BV* [1984] 1 All ER 296, [1984] 1 WLR 271).
15 See p 692, post.

(1) If it appears to him to be in the public interest to do so, the Secretary of State may petition for the company to be wound up by the court, or may petition the court for an order giving relief against any unfairly prejudicial conduct of the company's affairs as regards all or part of its members, or against any actual or proposed act or omission of the company which is or would be so unfairly prejudicial;[16]

(2) If it appears to the Secretary of State that any civil proceedings ought in the public interest be brought by any company or body corporate, he may bring such proceedings in the name of and on behalf of that company or body corporate against any person, either for the recovery of damages by the company or for any other remedy available to it.[17] Formerly such proceedings could be brought only for the recovery of damages in respect of any fraud, misfeasance or other misconduct in connection with the promotion or management of the company under investigation, or for the recovery of any of its property.[18] In this context 'other misconduct' meant misconduct of the same character as fraud or misfeasance, and the Secretary of State could therefore not sue in the company's name for negligence.[19] Furthermore, misconduct was only connected with the promotion or management of the company if the acts complained of were done in connection with setting up or carrying on the company's business.[19] The power of the Secretary of State to sue to recover property of the company was confined to property which was recoverable in specie,[19] or which was traceable at common law or in equity.[20] Debts owed to the company and damages recoverable by it could therefore not be recovered as property of the company in an action brought by the Secretary of State. All these restrictions have now disappeared, and in all the situations mentioned above the Secretary of State would now be able to sue in the name of any company affected in exercise of his power to bring any civil proceedings.

The Secretary of State's powers to petition for winding up or for relief from the unfair conduct of the company's affairs, and to sue delinquent directors and promoters and bring other actions in the company's name, have been used increasingly in recent years, and are of value to individual members who lack the means to pursue these remedies themselves, or who are prevented from doing so by the rule in *Foss v Harbottle*. Also the fact that inspections and consequential litigation may be initiated by the Secretary of State has an important effect in dissuading directors and persons in control of companies from engaging in acts which are illegal or unfair, but for which minority shareholders would be unable or unlikely to bring proceedings. Unfortunately, however, investigations directed by the Secretary of State often take a long time to complete, because inspectors are not engaged on them as a full time activity, and when the inspectors' report is available it is often too late to bring civil proceedings effectively against the persons who are shown to be responsible for wrongdoing.

The costs of an investigation by inspectors appointed by the Secretary of State for Trade and Industry (including the costs of any litigation instituted by him in

---

16 Companies Act 1985, s 460 (1), as amended by Companies Act 1989, s 145 and Sch 19, para 11; Insolvency Act 1986, s 124A, inserted by Companies Act 1989, s 60 (3).
17 Companies Act 1985, s 438 (1), as amended by Companies Act 1989, s 58.
18 Companies Act 1948, s 169 (4).
19 *SBA Properties Ltd v Cradock* [1967] 2 All ER 610, [1967] 1 WLR 716.
20 *Selangor United Rubber Estates Ltd v Cradock* [1967] 2 All ER 1255, [1967] 1 WLR 1168.

consequence)[1] may be recovered by the Secretary of State (i) from any person who is prosecuted or who is sued by the Secretary of State in consequence of the inspector's report, to the extent ordered by the court;[2] (ii) from the company itself to the extent of any damages, sums of money or property recovered by the Secretary of State suing in its name;[3] (iii) from the company itself if the investigation was ordered by the court or requisitioned by the fraction of members mentioned in para (1) on p 686, ante;[4] and (iv) if the investigation was requisitioned by that fraction of members, from the requisitionists themselves to the extent directed by the Secretary of State.[5] The Secretary of State may recover the costs of an investigation from any person who is liable under any of these categories, but if the company or requisitionists are compelled to pay costs under heads (iii) or (iv), they may claim an indemnity from persons who could be made liable for costs under heads (i) or (ii), and similarly a company which is compelled to pay costs under head (ii) is entitled to be indemnified by any person who is ordered to pay the same costs under head (i).[6] Although the court may impose the whole burden of the costs of an investigation and consequent litigation on anyone who is found to be liable to the company, it will in practice compel him to pay the costs of an investigation and action only insofar as they relate to wrongdoing or breaches of duty proved against him in the action, and if other defendants are joined in the action and defend themselves successfully, he will not be compelled to pay their costs or the costs of suing them.

Production of companies' documents and records

The power of the Secretary of State for Trade and Industry to require a company or any other person to produce for inspection any of the company's documents or information recorded in legible form or in a form capable of being reproduced in legible form has already been referred to.[7] The Secretary of State may require the production to be made to himself, or to any officer of the Department of Trade and Industry, or to any other competent person designated by the Secretary of State.[8] The power to require the production of documents and records is not confined to cases where the Secretary of State intends to direct an investigation of the company's affairs, or where he intends to do so if an examination of the company's documents and records shows that an investigation is called for. The Secretary of State may exercise the power of inspection whenever he considers that there is good reason to do so,[9] for example, to clarify or correct the contents of the company's annual return or accounts filed at the Companies Registry. The power is also useful as a means of obtaining and preserving evidence which may subsequently be used in connection with an investigation of another company, or in connection with a prosecution or civil proceedings in any company's name. No provision is made for an appeal to the court against the Secretary of State's requirement that a company's documents and records shall be produced for inspection, and it would seem impossible for the company to which the requirement is issued to seek a judicial review of it on the ground that there has been no irregularity in the conduct of the

1 Companies Act 1985, s 439 (7).
2 Ibid, s 439 (2).
3 Companies Act 1985, s 439 (3).
4 Ibid, s 439 (4).
5 Ibid, s 439 (5), as substituted by Companies Act 1989, s 59 (4).
6 Companies Act 1985, s 439 (8).
7 Companies Act 1985, s 447 (2), as amended by Companies Act 1989, s 63 (1) to (3) (see p 688, ante).
8 Companies Act 1985, s 447 (3) and (4), as amended by Companies Act 1989, s 63 (4).
9 Companies Act 1985, s 447 (1) and (2).

company's affairs, for the Secretary of State's requirement need rest on nothing more than his own opinion that production of the company's documents and records is necessary or desirable. Nevertheless, if a company to which a notice is issued requiring the production of documents and records can show that the demand is unreasonable (because, for example, it is not confined to documents in its possession or under its control), or if the notice is issued to an individual who does not have possession or control of the documents or records or certain of them, the court may declare the notice invalid, and even if the notice is formally correct and not manifestly unreasonable, the court will still treat it as invalid if the officer of the Department of Trade and Industry who issued it on behalf of the Secretary of State did not act in good faith or abused his discretion or used it for an improper purpose.[10]

The Secretary of State may require the company or other person who produces documents or records of the company, or any of the company's present or past officers or employees, to explain their meaning and significance, and if documents or records are not produced, the Secretary of State may require any person who was required to produce them to state where they are to the best of his knowledge and belief.[11] Beyond this, however, the Secretary of State has no powers of interrogation, and if he wishes any person to be examined about the company's affairs generally, he must direct that an investigation shall be conducted by inspectors. Documents produced and information obtained in exercise of the Secretary of State's powers may not be disclosed by the officers of the Department of Trade and Industry or by any other person without the consent of the company or person to whom the documents and records concerned belong, except in connection with a prosecution; proceedings under the Companies Acts 1985 and 1989, the Company Securities (Insider Dealing) Act 1985, the Company Directors Disqualification Act 1986, the Insolvency Act 1986, or the Financial Services Act 1986, an investigation of any company's affairs by inspectors; civil proceedings taken by the Secretary of State in any company's name; or winding up proceedings or proceedings for the relief of the unfairly prejudicial conduct of any company's affairs taken by the Secretary of State.[12]

If documents and records required to be produced by the Secretary of State are not produced, he may obtain a magistrates' warrant authorising any constable together with other named persons (such as officers of the Department of Trade and Industry) to enter premises named in the warrant and to search for and seize any such documents and records which are there or to take copies of them, and to require any person named in the warrant to provide an explantion of them or to state where they may be found.[13]

---

10 *R v Secretary of State for Trade, ex p Perestrello* [1981] QB 19, [1980] 3 All ER 28.
11 Companies Act 1985, s 447 (5), as amended by Companies Act 1989, s 63 (3).
12 Companies Act 1985, s 449 (1), as amended by Companies Act 1989, s 65 (1) and (2).
13 Companies Act 1985, s 448 (1) and (3), substituted by Companies Act 1989, s 64 (1).

CHAPTER 17

Accounts, audit and annual return

ACCOUNTS

Introduction

The requirements of the Companies Act 1985 (as substituted by the Companies Act 1989), that companies shall keep and regularly publish proper accounts showing their assets and liabilities and the results of carrying on their business activities, are undoubtedly fundamental for the protection of the interests of directors, persons involved in the conduct of companies' affairs and companies' shareholders and creditors. If these requirements are complied with, they assist in great measure to safeguard directors and other persons participating in the conduct of companies' affairs from personal liability. The benefits derived from proper accounting may be enumerated, though not exhaustively, as:

(a) affording the directors information as to the company's financial position so that they may the better plan its future activities, and may avoid committing irregularities, such as the payment of dividends out of capital or borrowing beyond the limits set for them by the articles;

(b) enabling shareholders to judge whether the company's affairs are being competently managed, whether the ratio of the company's profits to its turnover and its net assets is adequate, whether the dividends recommended by the directors are sufficient, and whether the amount of the company's indebtedness is acceptable or exposes it to risk of default or insolvency; and also enabling shareholders to ascertain whether the value of their shares is higher or lower than a valuation based on the company's assets, earnings and dividends;[1]

(c) enabling creditors of the company to judge whether it is able to pay its debts, whether they may safely extend further credit to it and to what extent unsecured creditors' claims are put at risk by the company having created securities over its assets; and

(d) when the company is wound up, or an administration order is made in respect of it, or an administrative receiver of its assets is appointed, providing information from which the liquidator, administrator or receiver can see what assets he may realise, and what claims against the company he has to meet.

The provisions of the Companies Act 1985 (as substituted by the Companies Act 1989) require companies to prepare and keep two kinds of accounts, namely, original accounting records in which transactions by the company are entered as they occur, and annual accounts showing the results of the company's business

---

1 The figures shown in recent profit and loss accounts for profits and dividends are safer guides for share valuations than the figures shown in the most recent balance sheet for assets and liabilities. Unless there has been a recent revaluation of fixed assets, or unless assets are shown at current replacement cost less corresponding provisions for replacement, they are likely to be undervalued in the present conditions of inflation, and provisions for depreciation based on their cost of acquisition may be inadequate.

activities during the period to which they relate and the company's assets and liabilities at the end of that period. In the following treatment of the statutory provisions relating to companies' accounts, references will be made to those provisions as they have been substituted in their entirety by the Companies Act 1989, Part I,[2] without reference to the individual sections of the Companies Act 1989 which have substituted the present provisions respectively.

Original accounting records

A company must keep accounting records sufficient to show and explain the company's transactions, to disclose its financial position at any time and to enable its directors to ensure that any annual profit and loss account and balance sheet prepared under the Companies Act 1985 complies with the requirements of the Act.[3] In particular, the company's accounting records must contain daily entries of receipts and expenditure, identifying the matters to which they relate, a record of the company's assets and liabilities, annual statements of stock in trade held by the company (if it deals in goods) together with stocktaking records, and if the company deals in goods otherwise than by retail, statements of all goods bought and sold, identifying the sellers and buyers.[4] The company's accounting records must be kept at its registered office or at some other place selected by the directors, but if any accounting records are kept outside Great Britain, accounts and returns must be sent to Great Britain at intervals not exceeding six months showing sufficient detail to enable the directors to prepare proper annual profit and loss accounts and balance sheets.[5]

The Companies Act 1985 provides that a company's accounting records and the accounts and returns sent to Great Britain in respect of accounting records kept abroad shall at all times be open to inspection by the company's officers (ie directors, secretary and auditors).[6] It has been held that this provision does not confer an absolute statutory right on each director of a company to inspect its accounting records, but that he has a common law right to inspect them, which the court will enforce in its discretion by issuing an appropriate mandatory injunction, unless there are good reasons for not doing so, for example, the likelihood that the director will shortly cease to hold office.[7]

Members of a company have no statutory or common law right to inspect the company's accounting records,[8] and they enjoy such a right only if it is given by the articles of association, which is rare.[9] But a member or anyone else who is a party to litigation with the company or any other person may have its original accounts produced on discovery of documents or upon subpoena, if they are relevant to the proof of his case,[10] and it appears that a member may apply to the court for an order directing the production of such accounts in advance of litigation if he has a specific complaint against the company or its directors, and is not merely seeking information which will afford him ground for complaint.[11]

A company must preserve accounting records which the Companies Act 1985

2 Companies Act 1989, ss 1 to 23 and Sch 10, Part I.
3 Companies Act 1985, s 221 (1).
4 Companies Act 1985, s 221 (2) and (3).
5 Ibid, s 222 (1) to (3).
6 Ibid, s 222 (1) and (2).
7 *Conway v Petronius Clothing Co Ltd* [1978] 1 All ER 185, [1978] 1 WLR 72.
8 *Baldwin v Lawrence* (1824) 2 Sim & St 18; *Burn v London and South Wales Coal Co* [1890] WN 209.
9 Table A, art 109, enables a member to inspect the books and accounts of the company only if the board of directors or a general meeting authorises him to do so.
10 *Cartland v Houston* [1912] WN 110.
11 *R v Merchant Tailors' Co* (1831) 2 B & Ad 115.

requires it to keep for six years from the date when the record was made,[12] or for three years from that time if the company is a private company.[13]

Annual accounts and directors' reports

Obligation to prepare, lay and file annual accounts

Every company must prepare a profit and loss account in respect of each of its financial years and a balance sheet made out as at the expiration of each such financial year.[14] In order to ascertain the dates when a company's financial year begins and ends, it must have an accounting reference date, which may be any date selected by the company and notified by it to the Registrar of Companies within nine months after its incorporation; if the company does not so notify an accounting reference date within that nine months period, its accounting reference date will be the last day in the month in which the anniversary of its incorporation falls, or if the company was incorporated before 1 April 1990 and has not selected another date, its accounting reference date will be 31 March.[15] The company's profit and loss account for its first financial year must relate to the period from the date of the company's incorporation to the first occurrence of its accounting reference date thereafter, or to the second occurrence of that date if the first occurrence is less than six months after the company's incorporation (or to a date not more than seven days earlier nor seven days later). The company's profit and loss account for its subsequent financial years must relate to the period from the day following the end of its immediately preceding financial year to the next occurrence of its accounting reference date (or a date not more then seven days before or after that date).[16] The date as at which the company's balance sheet for its first and subsequent financial years must be made out will coincide with the last day of the period to which its corresponding profit and loss account relates, namely, the appropriate accounting reference date for the profit and loss account or a date not more than seven days before or after that date.[17] The period between two successive accounting reference dates is known as the company's accounting reference period.[18]

A company may change its accounting reference date by giving notice to the Registrar of Companies during the currency of an accounting reference period, and the altered date then becomes its accounting reference date for the accounting reference period during which it was given and subsequent accounting periods until it is further altered.[19] The notice of the change of accounting reference date must state whether the company's current accounting reference period is to be shortened so as to end on the first occasion on which the new accounting reference date occurs or occurred after the commencement of the company's current accounting reference period (it being impossible to give a notice making the current accounting reference period expire on a past date which will result in the company being unable to present and deliver copies of its annual accounts for that

---

12 This presumably means when the relevant entry was made, but in the case of a continuous record it will in practice be necessary for the company to retain the whole record for six years from the last entry made in it.
13 Companies Act 1985, s 222 (5).
14 Ibid, s 226 (1).
15 Companies Act 1985, s 224 (2) and (3). Companies Act 1989 (Commencement No 4 and Transitional and Saving Provisions) Order 1990 (SI 1990/355), art 3 and Sch 1.
16 Companies Act 1985, s 223 (1) to (3) and s 224 (3).
17 Ibid, s 223 (1) to (3) and s 226 (1).
18 Ibid, s 224 (1).
19 Ibid, s 225 (1).

period within the time allowed under the rules dealt with in the following paragraph), or whether the company's current accounting reference period will be extended (it being impossible to give a notice making the company's current accounting period longer than 18 months).[1] A company cannot give a notice altering its accounting reference date so as to cause an extension of its current accounting period if it has previously given such a notice and the extended accounting reference period resulting from the earlier notice expired less than five years beforehand, but the Secretary of State for Trade and Industry may permit such a notice to be given.[2] Exceptions are made from the restrictions on a company's liberty to alter its accounting reference date so as to make its immediately preceding accounting reference period (as well as its current and future accounting reference periods) end on a different date, or so as to extend its current accounting reference period although it has already extended a previous accounting period to expire on a date within the preceding five years, if the company is a parent or subsidiary undertaking and the purpose of the alteration is to make the company's accounting reference date coincide with that of its subsidiary (if it is a parent undertaking) or with that of its parent (if it is a subsidiary undertaking).[3]

The significance of the accounting reference periods and accounting reference dates for a company lies in the obligations imposed on the company and its directors to lay a copy of its profit and loss account and balance sheet for each financial year together with copies of its directors' and auditors' reports before a general meeting and to deliver copies of those accounts and reports to the Registrar of Companies within a certain time after the expiration of the accounting reference period used to determine the financial year to which they relate.[4] If the company is a private company, the time allowed for doing these things is ten months, and if it is a public company the time is seven months from the end of that period,[5] but in either case the time is extended by three months if the company carries on business or has interests outside the United Kingdom, the Channel Islands and the Isle of Man and its directors notify the Registrar of Companies that it claims such an extension before the expiration of the seven or ten months normally allowed.[6] If a company changes its accounting reference date so as to shorten its current accounting reference period, it is allowed a minimum period of three months from the date on which the change is notified to the Registrar of Companies to lay and deliver copies of its accounts and accompanying reports for the financial year to which the shortened accounting reference period relates, even though the normal period for doing so expires before that three month period.[7]

The copies of a company's annual accounts and directors' and auditors' reports which are delivered to the Registrar of Companies are open to inspection by the

---

1 Ibid, s 225 (3), (5) and (6).
2 Ibid, s 225 (4).
3 Ibid, s 225 (2) and (4). For parent and subsidiary undertakings, see p 730, post. A company's current accounting reference period may also be extended despite an earlier extension of a previous accounting reference period to end on a date within the preceding five years if an administration order under the Insolvency Act 1986 has been made in respect of the company and remains in force (s 225 (4)).
4 Companies Act 1985, s 241 (1) and (2), s 242 (1) and (2) and s 244. The Registrar of Companies must advertise the delivery of copies of companies' annual accounts in the London Gazette (Companies Act 1985, s 711 (1) (*k*), as amended by Companies Act 1989, s 23 and Sch 10, para 14).
5 Companies Act 1985, s 244 (1) and (6). If the first accounting reference period of a newly incorporated company exceeds twelve months, the time allowed is ten months or seven months (as the case may be) from the first anniversary of the company's incorporation, or three months from the end of the accounting reference period, whichever expires later (Companies Act 1985, s 244 (2)).
6 Companies Act 1985, s 242 (3).
7 Ibid, s 244 (4).

public.[8] The rules with regard to laying and delivering copies of a company's annual accounts and other documents apply in terms to both limited and unlimited companies. However, unlimited companies do not have to deliver copies of their annual accounts and related documents to the Registrar of Companies, and they are consequently immune from inspection of their accounts by the public, if the company has at no time during the relevant accounting reference period been the parent undertaking or subsidiary undertaking of an undertaking with limited liability for its members (ie a public or private limited company or a limited partnership), and if at no such time two or more undertakings with limited liability for their members have held shares in the company or have been able to exercise powers in relation to it which would have made it a subsidiary undertaking if all those shares or powers had been vested in a single parent undertaking.[9]

The directors of a company which defaults in laying a copy of its annual accounts and directors' and auditors' reports before a general meeting or in delivering a copy of those accounts and reports to the Registrar of Companies within the time allowed are guilty of an offence punishable by a fine and also, if the contravention is continued, they are liable to pay a daily fine for the duration of the default.[10] A company which defaults in delivering a copy of its annual accounts and directors' and auditors' reports to the Registrar is additionally liable to a progressive financial penalty which the Secretary of State for Trade and Industry may recover by civil proceedings.[11] Furthermore, if a company defaults in delivering a copy of its annual accounts and directors' and auditors' reports to the Registrar, any member or creditor of the company or the Registrar himself may serve a notice on the directors of the company requiring them to make good the default within 14 days, and if they fail to do so, any such person (not necessarily the person who served the notice) may apply to the court for an order compelling them to do so.[12] On the other hand, on an application made before the expiration of the normal time for a company to lay its annual accounts and accompanying reports before a general meeting and to deliver copies of them to the Registrar, the Secretary of State may for special reasons extend the time allowed for doing so[13] and the sanctions for defaults then apply only when the extended period has expired.

Before a company's annual balance sheet and profit and loss account are laid before a general meeting they must be approved by its directors, and the balance sheet must be signed by a director.[14] The copy of the balance sheet which is delivered to the Registrar of Companies must also be signed by a director.[15] The directors' report which accompanies the balance sheet and profit and loss account, must likewise be approved by the directors and signed by a director or secretary of the company, and the copy of the directors' report which is delivered to the Registrar of Companies must also be signed by a director or the secretary.[16] Copies of the balance sheet and profit and loss account and the directors' and auditors' reports thereon must be sent to every member and debenture holder of the company and to every person who is entitled to receive notice of general meetings of the company (such as its auditors) at least 21 days before the general meeting at which

8 Ibid, s 709 (1), substituted by Companies Act 1989, s 126 (2).
9 Companies Act 1985, s 254 (1) and (2).
10 Ibid, s 241 (2), s 242 (2), s 730 (1) and Sch 24.
11 Ibid, s 242A (1) to (3).
12 Ibid, s 242 (3).
13 Ibid, s 244 (5).
14 Ibid, s 233 (1) and (2).
15 Ibid, s 233 (4).
16 Ibid, s 234A (1) and (3).

the accounts are to be laid.[17] Every member and debenture holder[18] must be sent a copy of these accounts and reports, whether or not he is entitled to attend the meeting or to have notice of it. However, if the annual accounts and accompanying reports are circulated less than 21 days before the meeting, they will be deemed to have been duly sent out if all the members entitled to attend and vote at the meeting agree.[19] In practice a company's annual accounts are always laid at its annual general meetings, but there is no legal impediment to them being laid at any other general meeting instead,[20] unless the articles specifically require them to be laid at the annual general meeting.[1]

If the company's shares, or any class of them, are listed on the Stock Exchange, the company may, instead of sending copies of its annual accounts and directors' and auditors' reports to its members, send them copies of a summary financial statement containing such information derived from the company's annual accounts and reports as is required by regulations to be made by the Secretary of State for Trade and Industry, but any member may require the company to send him a copy of its full annual accounts and reports.[2] If a listed company sends out a summary financial statement, it must contain an explicit statement state that it is only a summary of the company's annual accounts and reports, and must state whether the auditors consider that the summary is consistent with the company's annual accounts and the auditors' report, and whether the auditors' report was qualifed or unqualified (if the auditors' report was qualified, the summary financial statement must set out the auditors' report in full) ; the summary financial statement must also state whether the auditors' report contained a reservation that the company's accounting records were inadequate, or that its annual accounts did not agree with its accounting records, or that the auditors failed to obtain any necessary information or explanations which they required.[2] In addition to his right to receive a copy of the company's annual accounts before they are laid before a general meeting, or in the case of a listed company, a copy of the summary financial statement which it sends out, a member or debenture holder may at any time require the company to provide him with a copy of its last annual accounts and directors' and auditors' reports.[3]

The accompanying directors' report

When the company's annual accounts are laid before a general meeting there must be attached to them a report by the directors containing a fair review of the development of the business of the company and its subsidiary undertakings (if any) during the financial year to which the annual accounts relate and of the position of the company and its subsidiary undertakings at the end of that period, and the directors' report must also state the amount which they recommend shall be paid as dividend (if any) and the amount which they propose to carry to

---

17 Ibid, s 238 (1).
18 It is uncertain whether the expression 'holder of the company's debentures' extends to every person who is a debenture or loan security holder for other purposes. A person to whom the company has given a written acknowledgment of indebtedness is a debenture holder for general purposes (see p 445, ante), but it seems unnecessary for a company to send copies of its annual accounts to all its trade creditors whose invoices it has acknowledged.
19 Companies Act 1985, s 238 (4).
20 Ibid, s 241 (1).
1 Table A contains no such provision.
2 Companies Act 1985, s 251 (1) to (4). The obligatory contents of summary financial statements are prescribed by the Companies (Summary Financial Statements) Regulations 1990 (SI 1990/515).
3 Companies Act 1985, s 239 (1).

reserves.[4] The report must also give the names of the persons who are or have been directors of the company at any time during the financial year to which the report relates; must set out the principal activities of the company and its subsidiary undertakings in the course of that year, and any significant change in those activities during that period; must reveal significant changes in the nature or value of the fixed assets of the company or any of its subsidiary undertakings during the financial year and any significant divergence between the market and book values of the company's and its subsidiary undertakings' land; must set out the interests of directors and of their spouses and minor children in shares and debentures of the company and of companies in the same group (ie the company's holding and subsidiary companies and other subsidiaries of the company's holding company) at the end of the financial year as shown by the register of directors' holdings which the company is required to keep, together with particulars of options to subscribe for shares or debentures of the company or of other companies in the same group which were granted to, or exercised by, directors of the company or their spouses and minor children during the financial year;[5] and must contain particulars of important events affecting the company or any of its subsidiary undertakings which have occurred since the end of the financial year covered by the report, an indication of likely future developments in the business of the company and its subsidiary undertakings and an indication of the activities of the company and its subsidiary undertakings in respect of research and development.[6]

The directors' report must also give certain particulars of shares in the company which have been purchased or acquired gratuitously by it during the financial year to which the report relates, of shares forfeited by or surrendered to the company in lieu of forfeiture during that period, of shares in the company acquired during that period by a nominee for itself or with financial assistance provided by it, and of shares in the company over which it has acquired a lien or charge during that financial year to secure any unpaid part of the issue price.[7] The particulars to be given of such shares include the number and nominal value of the shares purchased and the aggregate consideration paid for them and the reason for their purchase, the number and nominal value of shares acquired by a nominee for the company or with financial assistance provided by it, the number and nominal value of shares over which the company has acquired a lien or charge and the amounts thereby secured, and the number and nominal value of each such category of shares which the company has disposed of during the financial year and the consideration received for each such disposal.[8] If a company or any of its subsidiaries has made donations for political or charitable purposes exceeding £200 in total amount during the financial year to which the report relates, the directors' report must state the total amount expended, and must identify each recipient of donations for political purposes and each political party to which donations exceeding £200 have been made during the year.[9] A donation is considered to be made for political purposes if it is made to a political party in the United Kingdom or to a person who to the company's knowledge 'is carrying on, or proposing to carry on, any activities which can ... reasonably be regarded as likely to affect public support

---

4 Ibid, s 234 (1) and s 241 (1).
5 See p 554, ante. This information may alternatively be given in notes to the company's annual accounts.
6 Companies Act 1985, s 234 (3) and (4) and Sch 7, paras 1, 2, 2A, 2B and 6, as amended by Companies Act 1989, s 8 (2) and Sch 5, paras 2 and 3.
7 Ibid, s 234 (3) and (4). and Sch 7, para 7.
8 Ibid, Sch 7, para 8.
9 Ibid, s 234(3) and (4) and Sch 7, paras 3 and 4.

for ... a political party'.[10] This broad and vague definition may extend the disclosure requirement to any financial support for one side in a matter of public controversy over which the political parties have adopted different positions.

If the average number of persons employed by the company during the financial year to which the report relates exceeded 250, the directors' report must also state the company's policy applied during that period for giving disabled persons opportunities for employment, for continuing the employment of persons who became disabled while employed by the company and for retraining such persons and for generally assisting the training and career development and promotion of disabled persons employed by the company.[11] Furthermore, the directors' report for companies which are to be prescribed by regulations yet to be made by the Secretary of State for Employment will have to contain information similarly prescribed as to the arrangements in force during the financial year to which the report relates for securing the health, safety and welfare at work of the employees of the company and its subsidiaries and for protecting them against risks to health or safety.[12] Again, if the average number of persons employed by the company and working wholly or mainly in the United Kingdom during the financial year exceeded 250, the directors' report must state what action has been taken by the company during the year to introduce, maintain or develop arrangements for providing information for employees on matters concerning them as employees, for consulting employees or their representatives on a regular basis so as to obtain employees' views on matters affecting their interests on which the company is to make decisions, for encouraging the involvement of employees in the company's performance, whether by means of an employees' share scheme[13] or otherwise, and for making employees aware of the financial and economic factors affecting the company's performance.[14]

Form and contents of the annual accounts

British companies legislation from the introduction of accounting requirements in 1928[15] traditionally abstained from prescribing the manner in which a company's annual accounts must be constructed and the methods to be employed for calculating the amounts to be shown for individual items in the accounts, and contented itself with requiring a certain amount of particularity (so that items had to be shown distinctly and not aggregated) and prescribing the minimum amount of detail which had to be given. The Companies Act 1981 marked a departure from this tradition by adopting the approach of the legislation of the western European countries (particularly Germany) and prescribing the form and layout of annual accounts and the rules to be followed in preparing them and in calculating the amounts to be shown against individual items included in them, as well as the minimum acceptable amount of detail to be given. This is not surprising, because the provisions of the Companies Act 1981 in respect of annual accounts were enacted in order that the United Kingdom should comply with its treaty obligation to give effect to the Fourth Directive for the harmonisation of companies legislation governing annual accounts in the member states of the European Communities, which was issued by the Council of Ministers of the Communities in July 1978.[16]

---

10 Ibid, Sch 7, para 5.
11 Ibid, s 234 (3) and (4) and Sch 7, para 9.
12 Ibid, s 234 (3) and (4) and Sch 7, para 10.
13 For the definition of an employees' share scheme, see p 247, ante.
14 Companies Act 1985, s 234 (3) and (4) and Sch 7, para 11.
15 By the Companies Act 1928, s 39 (3) and (4) and s 40.
16 Official Journal No L 222/1 of 1978.

The Directive was based on French and German law and practice, but both it and the Companies Act 1981 did preserve the paramount British rule that annual accounts must give a true and fair view of a company's financial position and the financial results of its operations, which, as well as emphasising the basic purpose of annual accounts, also permits some degree of flexibility. The provisions of the Companies Act 1981 in respect of companies' annual accounts have been re-enacted by the Companies Act 1985 and amended by the Companies Act 1989.

Format of annual accounts; the 'true and fair view'

The Companies Act 1985 (as amended) requires annual accounts of a company, copies of which are laid before a general meeting and delivered to the Registrar of Companies in fulfilment of its statutory obligations,[17] to comply with the requirements of Schedule 4 of the Act (as amended) as to the form and contents of the balance sheet and profit and loss account and the provision of additional information in the notes to the accounts.[18] The Act prescribes two alternative formats for a balance sheet (double columnar, separating assets and liabilities, or single columnar, relating them to each other according to their long or short term characteristics) and four alternative formats for a profit and loss account (double or single columnar, and in each case with items arranged in relation to the progressive steps of the company's operations or, alternatively, in relation to the sources of the company's income or the nature of its expenditure).[19] The items entered in the accounts must follow the order of the chosen format, but it is permissible to break down items so as to show figures for their component parts, and conversely, items (but not prescribed groupings of items, such as 'Tangible Assets', 'Investments') may be combined if their individual amounts are not material.[20] A company must use the same format for its annual accounts in successive financial years unless there are special reasons for change,[1] and in the accounts for any financial year the corresponding figures for the previous period must be given.[2]

Additionally, the Companies Act 1985 requires every balance sheet to give a true and fair view of the state of the company's affairs at the end of its financial year, and every profit and loss account to give a true and fair view of the company's profit or loss for that year.[3] This means that the accounts must be accurate, and must not represent the company's position as being either better or worse than it really is. This obligation overrides the requirements of Schedule 4 of the Companies Act 1985, and so it is necessary for annual accounts to give more detailed information than is required by the prescribed formats or the rules in Schedule 4 where this is needed to present a true and fair view, and the prescribed formats or rules in Schedule 4 may be departed from to the extent that compliance with them would prevent a true and fair view being given, but any such departures and the reasons for them must be mentioned in the notes to the accounts.[4]

---

17 See p 697, ante.
18 Companies Act 1985, s 226 (3) and Companies Act 1989, s 4 (2) and Sch 1. The references to paragraphs of Sch 4 to the Companies Act 1985 and to their contents are to those contents as amended by the Companies Act 1989, Sch 1, and references to the paragraphs of Sch 1 which effect the amendments are omitted.
19 Companies Act 1985, Sch 4, para 1 (1).
20 Ibid, Sch 4, para 3 (1), (3) and (4).
 1 Ibid, Sch 4, para 2 (1). The reasons for changes must be set out in the notes to the accounts (para 2 (2)).
 2 Companies Act 1985, Sch 4, para 4 (1).
 3 Ibid, s 226 (2).
 4 Ibid, s 226 (4) and (5).

The prescribed formats for a company's balance sheet require assets and liabilities to be shown with a minimum degree of particularity, and the details and figures shown for individual items must be supplemented by further information and detail in the notes to the accounts. Similarly, the prescribed formats for a company's profit and loss account require items of income and expenditure to be shown with a minimum degree of particularity, and these items too must be supplemented by further information in the notes to the accounts. Thus, the balance sheet must show the company's fixed assets under the main headings of intangible assets, tangible assets and investments (all of which are further subdivided) and its current assets under the main headings of stocks, debts owed to the company and investments dealt in by the company (with further subdivisions), and correspondingly the main headings on the liabilities side, namely, capital and reserves, provisions for liabilities and contingencies, and debts and other liabilities of the company, must be subdivided into specified sub-headings. The arrangement of the profit and loss account is similarly based on prescribed headings, but there are no sub-headings; the degree of detail to be given is as great as in the balance sheet, however, since the number of headings is far greater than the number of main headings in the balance sheet.

The rules as to the form of companies' accounts are supplemented by prescribed accounting principles which companies must adhere to, although in certain respects alternative choices are given. Accounts must be prepared on the basis that the company is a going concern, unless it has terminated or it is intended to terminate its business undertaking, or such a termination is unavoidable,[5] and accounting policies must be applied consistently within the same accounts and from one financial year to the next.[6] Subject to the detailed valuation rules dealt with below, the amounts at which items in a company's annual accounts are shown must be arrived at on a prudent basis, and in particular only profits realised by the end of the financial year covered by the accounts may be shown in the profit and loss account, whereas liabilities and losses must be taken into account if they have arisen or are likely to arise in connection with the company's operations in the financial year covered by the accounts or prior years, and this includes liabilities or losses which have only become apparent since the end of the financial year.[7] Profit and loss accounts are to be prepared on an earnings or accrual basis, and not with regard to the dates of receipts or payments (cash basis).[8] These principles may be departed from in special circumstances, but departures and the reasons for them must be dealt with in the notes to the accounts.[9]

The valuation of items in the annual accounts

The rules for valuing items which appear in annual accounts offer a choice of valuation on an historical cost basis, or on the basis of alternative accounting rules which facilitate current or replacement cost accounting.[10] If the historical cost basis is chosen, fixed assets with a limited useful economic life must be shown at their purchase price or cost of production, and provision must be made out of earnings for their depreciation or diminution in value, so that at the end of their useful economic life they will have been written down to their originally estimated

5 Ibid, Sch 4, para 10.
6 Ibid, Sch 4, para 11.
7 Ibid, Sch 4, para 12.
8 Ibid, Sch 4, para 13.
9 Ibid, Sch 4, para 15.
10 Ibid, Sch 4, paras 16, 30 and 31.

residual or scrap value.[11] Similar diminutions in the value of the company's investments in other concerns may be provided for out of earnings and written off the original costs of acquisition, and diminutions in the value of any of the company's fixed assets must be so provided for if the diminution is likely to be permanent.[12] Two particular items of fixed assets receive special attention. Development costs may be shown as a fixed asset in a company's balance sheet only in special circumstances, and if they are so shown, the notes to the accounts must give the reason for doing this, and must state over what period it is proposed to write them off out of profits.[13] If development costs are treated as assets, the amount attributed to them must nevertheless, in the absence of special circumstances, be treated as a realised revenue loss in calculating the profits of the company available for distribution to its shareholders,[14] but any provisions subsequently made to write off that amount out of profits will reduce the amount of this notional loss and so release a corresponding amount of profits for distribution. Purchased goodwill may be shown in a company's balance sheet as an asset at its cost of acquisition, but this amount must be written off over a period not exceeding the useful economic life of the goodwill, and the reasons for showing it as an asset and the period over which it will be written off must be stated in the notes to the accounts.[15]

Current assets must be shown in annual accounts at their purchase price or production cost, but if their net realisable value is less than that figure, the lower realisable value must be shown.[16] The figures shown as the purchase price or production cost of stocks and tangible assets (including investments in the case of an investment holding or dealing company) may be arrived at on the basis of treating items as used or disposed of in the chronological order they are acquired (FIFO), or on the basis of treating items as used or disposed of in the reverse of the order of acquisition (LIFO), or on the basis of weighted average cost or any similar method; however, if there is any material difference between the figures shown and the current replacement cost of current assets or the most recent purchase price paid or production cost incurred before the end of the financial year, the difference will have to be stated in the notes to the accounts.[17] If a company is constantly replacing raw materials or consumables whose overall value is not material in assessing the company's financial position, it may show them at a fixed quantity or value if their quantity, value and composition do not change materially from year to year.[18]

The alternative accounting rules which may be followed instead of the historical cost rules incorporate most of the latter rules, but subject to important modifications in order to accommodate current cost accounting. Under the alternative rules fixed assets may be shown at their current cost (ie replacement cost) or, if they are tangibles, at their latest valuation, but this does not apply to goodwill.[19] Investments which are fixed assets may be shown at their market value when they were last valued, or they may be valued on any other basis which the directors consider appropriate; in either case the notes to the accounts must state the method of valuation adopted and the reasons for it.[20] Investments which are current assets

---

11 Ibid, Sch 4, para 18.
12 Ibid, Sch 4, para 19 (1) and (2).
13 Ibid, Sch 4, para 20.
14 Ibid, s 269 (1).
15 Ibid, Sch 4, para 21.
16 Ibid, Sch 4, para 23 (1).
17 Ibid, Sch 4, para 27 (1) to (5).
18 Ibid, Sch 4, para 25. This is known as the base stock method of valuation.
19 Companies Act 1985, Sch 4, para 31 (1) and (2).
20 Ibid, Sch 4, para 31 (3).

and stocks may be shown at current cost.[1] When these alternative methods of valuation are used, they must be explained in the notes to the accounts, and the difference between the amounts shown in the accounts and the corresponding figures on an historical cost basis must be given.[2] When a company employs current cost valuation for the first time or when it subsequently adjusts current cost valuations which it has made, the excess of the valuation or revaluation over the figures previously attributed to the assets in question must be credited to a revaluation reserve, which must be shown separately in the company's balance sheet.[3] Provision for the depreciation or diminution in value of assets valued or revalued at current or replacement cost must be made on the basis of their adjusted value.[4] This will usually be higher than the original or previous value shown for the assets, and the correspondingly increased provisions for depreciation in the future will be made out of earnings, and not out of revaluation reserve. Consequently, when a revaluation is later made on the basis of these current costs, the amount to be credited on that occasion to the revaluation reserve will be the difference between the later revaluation and the amount previously credited to the revaluation reserve. An amount may be transferred from the revaluation reserve to the profit and loss account if the same amount has previously been charged to that account (ie for depreciation or diminution in the value of the revalued assets), or represents a realised profit (ie on the sale or other realisation of the assets), or if the revaluation reserve is capitalised and bonus shares issued by the company are treated as paid up by an amount transferred from it.[5] Also the revaluation reserve must be reduced if the amount transferred to it is no longer required for the purpose of the current cost valuation method (eg on a later revaluation at lower current prices).[5] These rules, of course, accord with the statutory prohibition on the distribution of unrealised profits.[6]

Notes to annual accounts

Various provisions of the Companies Act 1985 require supplemental financial information to be given in notes to a company's annual accounts, in particular, information relating to directors' remuneration, pensions and compensation for loss of office;[7] to loans and quasi-loans made to, and credit and other transactions entered into with, directors and persons connected with them;[8] and to the company's subsidiaries, associated companies and ultimate holding company.[9] Additionally, the rules governing the contents of a company's annual accounts themselves require the figures given in the body of the accounts to be supplemented by further or more detailed figures given in the notes to the accounts, or by appropriate comments qualifying the entries in the body of the accounts. The following are the more important matters which must be included in notes of this kind: (a) the nominal or authorised capital of the company; the amount and classes of shares and debentures which it has issued during the financial year, the consideration received by the company and the reasons for each issue; the terms

1 Ibid, Sch 4, para 31 (4) and (5).
2 Ibid, Sch 4, para 33.
3 Ibid, Sch 4, para 34 (1) and (2).
4 Ibid, Sch 4, para 32 (1).
5 Companies Act 1985, Sch 4, para 34 (3), (3A) and (3B).
6 Ibid, s 263 (1) and (3) (see p 422, ante).
7 Ibid, s 232 (1) and (2) and Sch 6, paras 1 to 14, substituted by Companies Act 1989, s 6 (3) and Sch 4, para 3 (see p 569, ante).
8 Companies Act 1985, s 232 (1) and (2) and Sch 6, paras 15 to 27 (see p 571, ante).
9 Ibid, s 231 (1) and Sch 5, substituted by Companies Act 1989, s 6 (1) and (2) and Sch 3 (see p 746, post).

and dates for the redemption of redeemable share capital;[10] (b) in respect of each category of fixed assets (other than investments) shown in the accounts, their accounting value at the beginning and end of the financial year, the amount of acquisitions and disposals made during that period, the amount of any revaluations made under the rules governing the adoption or operation of current cost accounting and the amount of provisions made for depreciation or diminution in value during the financial year and cumulatively;[11] (c) the aggregate accounting and market value of the company's listed investments and the market value of individual listed investments if they are less than the accounting value;[12] (d) the amount of the company's reserves and provisions at the beginning and end of the financial year and the amounts transferred to and from reserves and provisions during that period;[13] (e) the aggregate indebtedness of the company falling due within five years after the end of the financial year (distinguishing debts payable by instalments) and its aggregate indebtedness falling due only after that time; the aggregate contingent liabilities of the company not covered by provisions and the aggregate financial commitments of the company (eg under construction or development operations) not so covered;[14] (e) the aggregate amount of interest for the financial year on bank loans and overdrafts and on other loans to the company which are repayable within five years after the end of the financial year (distinguishing interest on loans repayable by instalments) and the aggregate amount of interest for the financial year on other loans; the amount set aside during the period for the redemption of share capital and loans;[15] (f) the basis on which the charge for United Kingdom corporation and income tax is calculated, the amount of that charge, the amount of relief from corporation tax to which the company is entitled for overseas taxation and the amount of overseas tax on profits, income and capital gains;[16] (g) the turnover and profits attributable to each class of the company's business activities;[17] (h) the average number of employees of the company of each category during the financial year, and the aggregate amount of remuneration of employees and the aggregate cost to the company of social security contributions and pension payments and contributions.[18]

Banking and insurance companies

A company may prepare annual accounts which comply with a re-enactment of the original and less exacting provisions of the Companies Act 1948 (and not the provisions of the Companies Act 1985, dealt with above) with certain additions and modifications if it is a company which has been authorised to carry on a deposit taking business by the Bank of England,[19] or a company which is governed by the legislation relating to insurance companies,[20] but the annual accounts must then state that they are prepared in accordance with these provisions.[1] It should be noted that the concession made in respect of banking and insurance companies'

10 Companies Act 1985, Sch 4, paras 37 to 40 and 41.
11 Ibid, Sch 4, para 42.
12 Ibid, Sch 4, para 45.
13 Ibid, Sch 4, para 46.
14 Ibid, Sch 4, paras 48 and 50.
15 Ibid, Sch 4, para 53.
16 Ibid, Sch 4, para 54.
17 Ibid, Sch 4, para 55.
18 Ibid, Sch 4, para 56.
19 Under the Banking Act 1987, s 9 (1) (4 Halsbury's Statutes (4th Edn) 538).
20 Insurance Companies Act 1982, s 15 (22 Halsbury's Statutes (4th Edn) 170).
 1 Companies Act 1985, s 255 (1) and (2) and Sch 9, substituted and amended by Companies Act 1989, s 18 (1) and (3) and Sch 7.

annual accounts apply only if they choose to prepare such accounts under the re-enactment of the original provisions of the Companies Act 1948, as modified and supplemented. If they choose instead to prepare annual accounts under the rules of the Companies Act 1985 applicable to all other companies (as amended by the Companies Act 1989), they will enjoy no special concessions by reason of their status as banking or insurance companies.

Modification of small and medium-sized companies filed accounts

Annual accounts laid before the members of all companies must conform to the requirements of Schedule 4 of the Companies Act 1985 as amended, unless they are the annual accounts of banking or insurance companies which may instead conform to Schedule 9 of the Companies Act 1985 (as amended). Nevertheless, the copies of their annual accounts which small and medium-sized companies deliver to the Registrar of Companies in fulfilment of the obligation to do so imposed by the Companies Act 1985, may be in a modified and less revealing form.[2] A company cannot avail itself of this privilege, however, if at any time during the financial year to which the accounts relate it is a public company, or a banking or insurance company, or is authorised to carry on investment business under the Financial Services Act 1986,[3] or if it is a member of a group of companies which includes another company which is a public company or a corporation which may lawfully offer its shares or debentures to the public, or a banking or insurance company, or a company or corporation which is authorised to carry on investment business under the Financial Services Act 1986.[4]

To qualify as a small company, a company must satisfy at least two of the following three conditions, namely, according to its annual accounts its turnover must not exceed £2m, its gross assets must not exceed £975,000 and the average number of its employees must not exceed 50.[5] Moreover, except for its first financial year, the company must fulfil two of those conditions (not necessarily the same ones) in two successive financial years in order to qualify, but it does not lose its privilege if in the next following year it does not fulfil the conditions.[6] A newly incorporated company qualifies as a small company if it fulfils two of the conditions in its first financial year;[7] thereafter it may lose the privilege or re-qualify for it in the same way as any other company. The privileges from disclosure which a small company enjoys are that it may deliver to the Registrar of Companies a modified balance sheet in summary form, showing aggregated amounts for items listed under the same capital letter or Roman numeral in the format it selects from the two formats set out in Schedule 4 of the Companies Act 1985; moreover, the company need not file a copy of its profit and loss account or its directors' report, or (with a few exceptions) the notes to its accounts, and it need not disclose particulars of its directors' remuneration or pensions and payments to them of compensation for loss of office.[8]

To qualify as a medium-sized company, a company must satisfy at least two of the following three conditions, namely, according to its annual accounts its turnover

2 Companies Act 1985, s 246 (1) and Sch 8, substituted by Companies Act 1989, s 13 (1) and (2) and Sch 6.
3 Financial Services Act 1986, s 7 (1), s 15 (1), s 22, s 23 (1), s 24, s 25 and s 31 (1).
4 Companies Act 1985, s 246 (3) and (4).
5 Ibid, s 247 (3), (5) and (6).
6 Ibid, s 247 (1) and (2). The company may continue to qualify as a small company in the year following that in which it does not satisfy two of the conditions if it satisfies two of the conditions in that following year (s 247 (2)).
7 Companies Act 1985, s 247 (1).
8 Ibid, s 246 (1) and Sch 8, paras 1 to 4.

must not exceed £8m, its gross assets must not exceed £3·9m, and the average number of its employees must not exceed 250.[9] The rules as to satisfying two of the three conditions in two successive years, and not losing the privileges of a medium-sized company if the conditions are not fulfilled in the next following year, are the same as for small companies, and so are the corresponding rules for newly incorporated companies.[10] The privileges which a medium-sized company enjoys when delivering copies of its accounts to the Registrar of Companies are restricted to showing aggregate amounts for certain groups of items making up its gross profit or loss in its profit and loss account (namely, turnover, cost of sales, gross trading profit or loss and other operating income) and not disclosing particulars of its turnover and the resulting profit or loss attributable to each class of its business activities.[11] In all other respects the copies of its annual accounts and annexed documents filed by a medium-sized company will be the same as for a company which does not qualify for special treatment.

The qualification which a group of undertakings must fulfil in order to be a small or medium-sized group are the same as those for a single small or medium-sized company (taking the aggregate turnover, gross assets and average number of employees of all the undertakings comprised in the group instead of those of a single company), but with the modification that the group may qualify if its aggregate turnover and assets do not exceed certain net amounts, or alternatively certain greater gross amounts, which are different from the corresponding amounts for a single small or medium-sized company.[12] These amounts are, for a small group, a net group turnover not exceeding £2m or a gross group turnover not exceeding 2·4m, and net group assets not exceeding £1m or gross group assets not exceeding £1·2m.[12] The corresponding amounts for a medium-sized group are, net group turnover not exceeding £8m or gross group turnover not exceeding £9·6m, and net group assets not exceeding £3·9m or gross group assets not exceeding £4·7m.[12] The difference between the net and gross turnover and assets figures for this purpose is that the net figures are taken from the consolidated accounts which a parent company is normally required to prepare in respect of the group's affairs,[13] whereas the gross figures are the aggregate of the corresponding amounts shown in the parent company's and its subsidiary undertakings' respective annual accounts before those amounts are modified for the purpose of being included in consolidated group accounts.[14] In determining whether a group qualifies as a small or medium-sized group the same requirement applies as to a single company, that the group must qualify as such in the financial year for which the accounts are prepared and the preceding financial year, but with the appropriate relaxations for the parent company's first financial year and for a financial year following two years in which the group was qualified as small or medium-sized and for the next following financial year.[15]

A parent company of a group of undertakings which is a small or medium-sized group is additionally exempted from the obligation normally imposed on parent companies to lay consolidated annual accounts relating to the affairs of itself and its subsidiary undertakings before a general meeting of the parent company each

9 Ibid, s 247 (3), (5) and (6).
10 Ibid, s 247 (1) and (2).
11 Ibid, s 246 (1) and Sch 8, paras 5 and 6.
12 Ibid, s 246 (5) and s 249 (1) to (5). For the definition of subsidiary undertakings, see p 730, post.
13 See p 738, post.
14 See p 742, post.
15 Companies Act 1985, s 249 (1) and (2).

year and to deliver a copy of such consolidated accounts to the Registrar of Companies.[16]

Publication of accounts

If a company publishes its accounts in the full form in which they were laid before a general meeting, or if it is a small or medium-sized company, in the modified form in which a copy of them was delivered to the Registrar of Companies (its statutory accounts), the publication must be accompanied by a full version of the auditors' report on the accounts and, if the company is a parent company, a full version of the group accounts annexed to its own accounts[17] which it has filed at the Companies Registry.[18] If a company publishes an abridged or modified version of its annual accounts, it must state in the publication that they are not full accounts or a modified version of them delivered to the Registrar of Companies, and the publication may not be accompanied by the auditors' report on the accounts (non-statutory accounts), but the publication must include a statement whether the company's auditors have reported on the accounts, whether their report was a qualified one, or contained a statement that the company's accounting records were inadequate, or that its annual accounts did not agree with its accounting records, or that the auditors failed to obtain any necessary information or explanations for the audit, and whether a copy of the company's annual accounts has been delivered to the Registrar of Companies.[19]

If a parent company publishes consolidated accounts in the form in which it laid them before a general meeting, it need not accompany them by a copy of its own annual accounts for the same financial year, but the publication must be accompanied by a full version of the auditors' report on the consolidated accounts.[18] The same rules apply to the publication of an abridged or modified version of consolidated accounts by a parent company as apply to publication of such a version of its own annual accounts.[19]

The foregoing rules relating to the publication of a company's annual accounts, or consolidated accounts, or to abridged or modified versions of them, do not apply to the summary financial statements which a company whose shares are listed on the Stock Exchange sends to its members in place of copies of its annual accounts, consolidated accounts and directors' and auditors' reports.[20]

Revision of a company's annual accounts

If directors of a company consider that any annual accounts of the company or any directors' report approved by them do not comply with the requirements of the Companies Act 1985 (as amended), they may prepare revised annual accounts or a revised directors' report, but if a copy of the original accounts or report has been laid before a general meeting of the company or delivered to the Registrar of Companies, the revised accounts or report must be confined to correcting the original ones so as to make them comply with the Act and to effecting consequential alterations.[1] The manner in which annual accounts and reports may be revised

---

16 Ibid, s 227 (1), s 241 (1), s 242 (1), s 248 (1) and s 262 (1) (see p 739, post).
17 See p 739, post.
18 Companies Act 1985, s 240 (1), (2) and (5).
19 Ibid, s 240 (3) and (5).
20 Ibid, s 251 (7) (see p 699, ante).
 1 Ibid, s 245 (1) and (2).

will be governed by regulations to be made by the Secretary of State for Trade and Industry.[2]

If the Secretary of State considers that there may be a doubt as to whether a company's accounts comply with the requirements of the Companies Act 1985 (as amended) in the form in which copies of them have been sent out to members or laid before a general meeting of the company or delivered to the Registrar of Companies, the Secretary of State may give notice to the directors of the company of the matters in respect of which the doubt arises, and the directors must within the period specified in the notice (being not less than one month) either give the Secretary of State an explanation of the accounts or prepare revised accounts.[3] If the directors do not provide a satisfactory explanation or prepare revised accounts which comply with the Companies Act 1985 (as amended) within the time allowed by the Secretary of State, an application may be made to the court by the Secretary of State, or a person authorised by him, for a declaration that the annual accounts to which the notice relates do not comply with the Act and an order that the directors shall prepare revised annual accounts.[4] If the court orders the preparation of revised accounts, it may give directions that they shall be audited, that the original directors' report or, in the case of a listed company, any summary financial statement sent by the company to its members[5] shall be revised in accordance with the court's directions, and that the making of the court's order shall be publicised so as to bring it to the attention of persons likely to rely on the original accounts.[6] The court may also direct that the costs of the application for its order shall be paid by the directors in default.[7] An office copy of the court's order must be delivered by the successful applicant to the Registrar.[8] The persons who are authorised to apply to the court under these provisions will be specified by orders made by the Secretary of State; they must be persons who have an interest in, and satisfactory procedures for, ensuring compliance by companies with the accounting requirements imposed on them and for investigating complaints about their annual accounts, and they must be fit and proper persons to be so authorised.[9]

AUDIT

Auditors

Appointment of auditors

A company must each year at the general meeting at which copies of its profit and loss account and balance sheet for a financial year are laid appoint an auditor or auditors to hold office until the conclusion of the next general meeting at which such accounts for its next succeeding financial year are laid.[10] If the company's

2 Ibid, s 245 (3) and (4).
3 Ibid, s 245A (1) and (2).
4 Ibid, s 245A (3) and s 245B (1).
5 See p 699, ante.
6 Companies Act 1985, s 245B (3).
7 Ibid, s 245B (4).
8 Ibid, s 245B (6).
9 Ibid, s 245C (1) and (4). The persons who are authorised by the Secretary of State will most probably be professionally qualified accountants proposed by the recognised accountancy bodies.
10 Companies Act 1985, s 384 (1) and s 385 (1) and (2), substituted by the Companies Act 1989, s 119 (1). The provisions of the Companies Act 1985, ss 252, 253 and 384 to 394 relating to auditors, have been replaced by the Companies Act 1989, ss 118 to 124. The new sections of the Companies Act 1985 which have been substituted by the Companies Act 1989, are referred to hereafter by number, but no reference is made to the sections of the Companies Act 1989 which have effected the substitutions respectively.

articles provide that the appointment of auditors by an annual general meeting shall be ordinary business,[11] no specific mention of it need be made in the notice convening the meeting, and, subject to what is said below, when the retiring auditors are able and willing to continue in office, no notice need be given of a resolution to appoint auditors, and candidates for the appointment may be nominated by members at the meeting. The directors may appoint the first auditors on the company's incorporation, and they cease to hold office and may stand for re-appointment at the first general meeting of the company at which copies of its first annual accounts are laid before its members,[12] but if the directors fail to appoint any first auditors, the members may appoint them by ordinary resolution.[13] If the company fails to appoint auditors at any general meeting at which annual accounts are laid, it must notify the Secretary of State for Trade and Industry within one week, and the Secretary of State may fill the vacancy.[14] The board of directors or a general meeting, by passing an ordinary resolution, may fill a casual vacancy in the office of auditor;[15] if conflicting appointments are made by the board and by a general meeting, it appears that the earlier of the appointments is effective and the other is not. If there are two or more auditors and a casual vacancy occurs in the office of one of them, the other or others may continue to act,[16] and when the vacancy is filled, they will act jointly with the person appointed to fill it. Special notice[17] is required for a resolution to be passed by a general meeting to fill a casual vacancy in the office of auditor; on receiving notice of an intention to move such a resolution, the company must send a copy of it to the person proposed to be appointed and, if the casual vacancy has been caused by the resignation of an auditor, to that auditor.[18]

The remuneration of auditors is fixed by an ordinary resolution passed by a general meeting, or in such manner as a general meeting prescribes by ordinary resolution (eg the amount decided on by the board or directors),[19] but the remuneration of auditors appointed by the directors, either to be the first auditors of the company or to fill a casual vacancy, is fixed by them.[20] If an auditor is appointed by the Secretary of State because of the company's failure to make an appointment at a general meeting, the auditor's remuneration is fixed by the Secretary of State.[20] The amount of the auditor's remuneration (including expenses) must be stated in a note to the company's annual accounts, and the Secretary of State may make regulations requiring also the disclosure of remuneration paid or payable to an auditor (including expenses) in respect of services other than those of an auditor (eg for preparing the annual accounts, advice on accounting systems or as a management consultant).[21]

Qualifications and eligibility

Under the law in force before Part II of the Companies Act 1989 came into force on 1 March 1990,[1] a person could not be appointed an auditor of a company, unless

11 The Companies Act 1948, Table A, art 52 so provided. The present Table A contains no such provision.
12 Companies Act 1985, s 385 (3).
13 Ibid, s 385 (4).
14 Ibid, s 387 (1) and (2).
15 Ibid, s 388 (1).
16 Ibid, s 388 (2).
17 See p 625, ante.
18 Companies Act 1985, s 388 (3) and (4).
19 Ibid, s 390A (1).
20 Ibid, s 390A (2).
21 Ibid, s 390A (3) and (4) and s 390B (1) and (2).
1 Companies Act 1989, s 215 (2); Companies Act 1989 (Commencement No 2) Order 1990 (SI 1990/ 142), art 3 and Schedule.

he was a member of one of certain statutorily recognised bodies of accountants[2] or of a body of accountants given similar recognition by regulations made by the Secretary of State for Trade and Industry, or unless he had been specially authorised by the Secretary of State on account of a qualification to practise as an accountant obtained outside the United Kingdom,[3] or unless he held a special authorisation given to him by the Secretary of State or the Department of Trade on account of his experience as an employee of a member of a recognised body of accountants,[4] or the fact that he practised as an accountant before 6 August 1947.[5] By the Companies Act 1989, a person is qualified to be appointed and to act as an auditor of a company only if he was so qualified under the Companies Act 1985 on 1 March 1990,[6] or if he holds a professional qualification conferred by a qualifying body established in the United Kingdom and offering a qualification in accountancy which is recognised by the Secretary of State,[7] or if he holds an overseas professional qualification which qualifies him to audit accounts in the country where it was awarded, or is recognised in that country as a professional qualification in accountancy, and the Secretary of State has declared that overseas professional qualification to be sufficient to qualify holders of it to be appointed auditors of companies.[8] As a transitional measure, a person is qualified to be appointed and act as an auditor of a company if at the end of 1989 he was engaged in an approved course of study or practical training to lead to a professional qualification conferred by a body of accountants recognised by the Secretary of State under the Companies Act 1985, and he obtains that professional qualification before 1 January 1996.[9]

When the relevant provisions of the Companies Act 1989 are brought into force by order of the Secretary of State,[10] a person may be appointed or act as an auditor

2 These bodies are: the Institute of Chartered Accountants in England and Wales; the Association of Certified Accountants; the Institute of Chartered Accountants in Ireland; and the Institute of Chartered Accountants of Scotland.

3 The Secretary of State could refuse an authorisation if the country where the applicant obtained his qualification did not confer corresponding reciprocal rights on accountants qualified in the United Kingdom (Companies Act 1985, s 389 (5)).

4 No authorisation could be given to such an employee after 18 April 1978 (Companies Act 1976, s 13 (4) and Companies Act 1976 (Commencement No 3) Order 1977 (SI 1977/529), para 2 and Schedule).

5 Companies Act 1985, s 389 (1).

6 Persons who were qualified on 1 January 1990 otherwise than by membership of a statutorily recognised body of accountants remain qualified for only one year from the date when the Companies Act 1989, s 25 is brought into force (see text, post) unless they notify the Secretary of State within that period or such extended period as he permits that they wish to retain the benefit of the qualification (Companies Act 1989, s 31 (2)). Persons who were so qualified only by holding a special authorisation granted by reason of their having been the auditors of an exempt private company (ie a private company which conformed to certain conditions and was entitled to certain privileges under the Companies Act 1948), are not qualified to audit the accounts of a company any of whose shares or debentures are, or have been, quoted on a stock exchange in the United Kingdom or elsewhere, or have been offered to the public for subscription or purchase (Ibid, s 34 (1) and (2)).

7 All the statutorily recognised bodies of accountants under the Companies Act 1985 confer qualifications in accountancy which are recognised by the Secretary of State. To obtain recognition for its professional qualification, a body of accountants must have rules and standards for the conferment of the qualification which are approved by the Secretary of State (Companies Act 1989, s 32 (1), (2) and (4) and Sch 12, paras 4 to 9).

8 Companies Act 1989, s 24 (1), s 31 (1) and s 33 (1); Companies Act 1989 (Commencement No 2) Order 1990, art 3 and Schedule.

9 Companies Act 1989, s 31 (4) and (5).

10 Ibid, s 25 (1).

of a company only if he is eligible as well as qualified to be so appointed,[11] and he will be eligible only if he is a member of a supervisory body recognised by the Secretary of State which is established in the United Kingdom and which maintains and enforces rules as to the eligibility of persons to seek appointment as company auditors and as to the conduct of audit work. The existing bodies of accountants which are recognised under the Companies Act 1985 will all be recognised supervisory bodies. The function of the recognised supervisory bodies will be to monitor the professional conduct of its members (as distinct from conferring their professional qualification) and to discipline those who do not conform to the standards set by their rules, if necessary by expulsion, which will entail the immediate ineligibility of the former member to be appointed or to act as an auditor of a company and criminal liability if he knowingly does so.[12]

In addition to the disqualification of persons who are professionally unqualified, the Companies Act 1989 makes a person ineligible to be an auditor of a company if he is an officer or employee of the company, or of its parent or subsidiary undertaking or of a subsidiary undertaking of its parent undertaking of its holding company, or if he is a partner or employee of such an ineligible officer or employee, or if he is a partner of a partnership of which such an ineligible officer or employee is a member.[13]

An individual, a partnership, a company or a body corporate may be appointed to be the auditor of a company.[14] If a partnership is appointed to be the auditor of a company, the appointment is of the firm and not its individual members, unless the contrary intention appears.[15] If there is a change in the membership of the firm, or if the firm's practice is acquired by one of the partners or by another partnership whose members are substantially the same as those of the original firm, the appointment of the firm is treated as continuing.[16] A partnership or a company or body corporate appointed to be the auditor of a company may have members who are not professionally qualified as individuals to be appointed as auditors; nevertheless, but the rules of supervisory bodies recognised by the Secretary of State (membership of which is required to make a person, firm or company eligible for appointment as an auditor),[17] will obligatorily provide that a partnership, company or body corporate will be so eligible to be or act as the auditor of a company only if the individuals responsible for audit work done by it hold appropriate professional qualifications and the partnership, company or body corporate is controlled by partners, members or directors who hold such qualifications.[18]

If a person appointed as a company's auditor was, during the period while the audit was conducted, ineligible for appointment, the Secretary of State may direct the company to have its annual accounts audited again by an eligible person to be appointed by it, or to have the audit by the ineligible appointee reviewed by such an eligible person; if the company fails to comply with the Secretary of State's direction, the Secretary of State may apply to the court for an injunction to enforce it, and the company commits a criminal offence by its non-compliance.[19]

11 Ibid, s 30 (1), (2) and (5) and Sch 11, paras 4 to 16.
12 Companies Act 1989, s 28 (1) to (3).
13 Ibid, s 27 (1) and (3) and s 53 (1). For the definition of parent and subsidiary undertakings, see p 730 et seq, post.
14 Companies Act 1985, s 25 (2).
15 Ibid, s 26 (2).
16 Ibid, s 26 (2) to (4).
17 Ibid, s 30 (1) and (5) and Sch 11, paras 4 and 5.
18 Ibid, s 28 (3).
19 Ibid, s 29 (1) and (4) to (6).

Resignation, removal and termination of appointment

An auditor may resign, either immediately or as from a specified date earlier than the normal expiration of his term of office, by giving the company a written notice of resignation, which must be accompanied by a statement of any circumstances connected with his resignation which he considers should be brought to the notice of members of the company, or a statement that there are no such circumstances; the notice is invalid unless it is accompanied by such a statement.[20] The auditors' resignation takes effect when the notice and statement are delivered to the company at its registered office or at such later time as is specified in the notice.[1] The company must send a copy of the notice of resignation to the Registrar of Companies within 14 days after receiving it,[2] and if the notice sets out circumstances connected with the resignation which the auditor considers should be brought to the attention of members, copies of the notice must also be sent within the 14 days to every member and debenture holder of the company, unless the court otherwise orders on an application made by the company on the ground that the notice gives needless publicity to defamatory matter; the application to the court must be notified to the resigning auditor, who may appear on the hearing, but if no such notification is received by him within 21 days after he delivers his notice of resignation to the company, he must deliver a copy of his statement to the Registrar of Companies.[3] On the hearing of the application, if satisfied of the grounds for it, the court will direct that copies of the auditor's statement need not be sent out by the company, and may order that the company's costs in connection with the application shall be paid in whole or part by the auditor.[4] If the court is not so satisfied as to the grounds of the application, the company must send out copies of it to its members and debenture holders within 14 days after the court's decision.[5]

If an auditor delivers to the company with his notice of resignation a statement of circumstances which he believes should be brought to the notice of members, he may also either require the directors to call an extraordinary general meeting to consider any explanation he wishes to make in connection with his resignation, and he may then require the directors to circulate a statement of a reasonable length by him relating to the circumstances of his resignation with the notice of the extraordinary general meeting which he has required the directors to call or, if he does not require such a meeting to be called, with the notice of the general meeting at which his appointment would have expired if he had not resigned or, if it is held earlier, with the notice of a general meeting called to fill the casual vacancy caused by his resignation.[6] If the auditor requisitions an extraordinary general meeting, the directors must call it within 21 days, and it must be held not later than 28 days after the notice convening it is sent out; the directors of the company are guilty of a criminal offence if they fail to take all reasonable steps to call and hold the general meeting within the prescribed periods.[7] If the auditor requires a statement of his explanation to be circulated with the notice of an extraordinary general meeting requisitioned by the auditor, the directors must in the notice calling the meeting state that the auditor's statement has been made and must send copies of it to all members of the company who are entitled to be sent notice of the general meeting,

20 Ibid, s 392 (1) and s 394 (1) and (2).
 1 Ibid, s 392 (1) and (2).
 2 Ibid, s 392 (3).
 3 Ibid, s 394 (3) to (5). The application is made to the Companies Court by originating summons (RSC Ord 102, r 2 (1)).
 4 Companies Act 1985, s 394 (6).
 5 Ibid, s 394 (7).
 6 Ibid, s 392A (1) to (3).
 7 Ibid, s 392A (3) and (5).

unless the statement is received by the company too late for it to do so, but in that case or if the company is in default in circulating the auditor's statement the auditor may require the statement to be read out at the meeting.[8] Copies of the statement need not be circulated or read out at the meeting, however, if the court so orders on the application of the company or any aggrieved person who alleges that the auditor is abusing his rights in order to give needless publicity to defamatory matter.[9] Similar provisions apply if the auditor requires the directors to circulate a statement about the circumstances of his resignation with notices of the general meeting at which his appointment would otherwise have terminated, or an earlier general meeting called to appoint his successor.[10] Whether the auditor requisitions an extraordinary general meeting or merely requires the directors to circulate a statement about the circumstances of his resignation with notice of such another general meeting, he is entitled to receive notice of the relevant general meeting and to address the meeting orally.[11] It would appear that the auditor cannot be restrained in advance from making defamatory statements at an extraordinary general meeting requisitioned by him or at any other general meeting which he is entitled to address orally about his resignation, and that the only protection which is available against such oral statements being made is the power of the chairman of the meeting to confine the auditor's remarks to matters which are relevant to his resignation.[12]

A company may remove an auditor from office before the expiration of his term of office by an ordinary resolution passed by a general meeting, notwithstanding any provision in the contract between him and the company.[13] This power of removal is exercisable whether the auditor was appointed by a general meeting, by the board of directors on the first appointment of auditors or on a casual vacancy, or by the Secretary of State on the failure of a general meeting at which annual accounts are laid to appoint an auditor. There is no corresponding power for the board or the Secretary of State to remove an auditor whom they have appointed. The exercise by a general meeting of its power to remove an auditor does not disentitle him to compensation or damages to which he would otherwise be entitled in respect of the termination of his appointment as auditor or any other appointment which terminates concurrently.[14] An auditor who has been removed is entitled to receive notice of any general meeting of the company at which his appointment would otherwise have terminated or of any general meeting called to fill the casual vacancy caused by his removal, and he is entitled to attend and speak at such general meetings on any business of the meeting which concerns auditors.[15]

An auditor who ceases to hold office for any reason other than resignation or removal (eg failure to seek re-appointment at the general meeting at which the company's annual accounts are laid, becoming ineligible to act as auditor of the company because he, his partner or employer becomes an officer or employee of it), is required to deliver to the company a statement of any circumstances connected with his ceasing to be an auditor of the company which he considers should be brought to the attention of its members or creditors, or a statement that

---

8 Ibid, s 392A (4) and (6).
9 Ibid, s 392A (7). The application is made to the Companies Court by originating summons (RSC Ord 102, r 2 (1)).
10 Companies Act 1985, s 392A (4) to (7).
11 Ibid, s 392A (8).
12 Nevertheless, this power may be effective, because the chairman of the meeting will usually be a director, and the most likely reason for the auditor's resignation will be a dispute with the board.
13 Companies Act 1985, s 391 (1).
14 Ibid, s 391 (3).
15 Ibid, s 391 (4).

there are no such circumstances; this must be done within 14 days after the auditor ceases to hold office or, if he fails to seek re-appointment, not less than 14 days before the date of the general meeting at which his appointment would normally have terminated.[16] The company must then send copies of the auditor's statement to its members and debenture holders as though it had accompanied a notice of resignation by the auditor, unless the court otherwise orders on the company's application on the same grounds and with the same consequences as though the auditor had given notice of resignation.[17]

The resignation or removal of an auditor causes a casual vacancy in the office, which may accordingly be filled by the board of directors or a general meeting.[18]

Special notice procedure

Special notice is required of a resolution proposed at a general meeting to remove an auditor before the expiration of his term of office, or to appoint as auditor anyone other than the auditor who retires at the meeting, or to fill a casual vacancy in the office of auditor, or to re-appoint a retiring auditor who was appointed by the directors to fill a casual vacancy.[19] The statutory requirement of special notice entails the proposer of the resolution giving the company notice of his intention to move it at least 21 days before the meeting is held at which it will be proposed, and the company giving at least 21 days' notice of the resolution to its members before that meeting.[20]

Although the board of a company is not bound to call an extraordinary general meeting simply because one or more members have given special notice of a resolution they wish to propose,[1] it would seem to be improper for directors to fill a casual vacancy in the office of auditor if an extraordinary general meeting is requisitioned for the purpose by members who are entitled to have it convened,[2] for the meeting would then become purposeless. It would appear that special notice of a resolution to re-appoint an auditor who was appointed to fill a casual vacancy is required only on the first occasion when he is re-appointed, and that it is not necessary when he is later re-appointed by a general meeting.[3] Since special notice is required of a resolution to appoint as auditor anyone other than a retiring auditor, it would not appear possible to move an amendment to a proposed resolution for that purpose nominating someone other than the person thereby proposed for appointment, for no special notice would have been given naming the alternative candidate. On the other hand, when an extraordinary general meeting is held to fill a casual vacancy in the office of auditor, there would seem to be no impediment to any member moving an amendment proposing the appointment of someone other than the person named in the special notice, because the resolution is an ordinary one and the amendment relates to the same subject matter as the original proposal.[4]

When a company receives special notice of a resolution relating to the removal

---

16 Ibid, s 394 (1) and (2).
17 Ibid, s 394 (3) to (7) (see p 714, ante).
18 Ibid, s 388 (1).
19 Ibid, s 388 (3) and s 391A (1).
20 Ibid, s 379 (1) and (2) (see p 625, ante).
1 *Pedley v Inland Waterways Association Ltd* [1977] 1 All ER 209.
2 Companies Act 1985, s 368 (1) and (2) (see p 625, ante).
3 Literally the re-appointment is of an auditor who was originally appointed by the directors to fill a casual vacancy, even if he has since been re-appointed by a general meeting, but the purpose of the provision is to obtain the members' approval of an auditor on whose appointment they have not hitherto pronounced.
4 See p 626, ante.

of an auditor, or the appointment of a person other than an auditor who retires at the general meeting, or the appointment of a person to fill a casual vacancy in the office of auditor, or the re-appointment of a person who was appointed by the directors to fill a casual vacancy, it must send a copy of the proposed resolution to the person whose removal, appointment or re-appointment is sought; it must also send such a copy to a retiring auditor if the resolution proposes the appointment of another person in his place; and if a casual vacancy results from an auditor resigning, a copy of the proposed resolution must be sent to him if it is a resolution to fill the vacancy or to re-appoint a person who has been appointed by the directors to fill it.[5] If a copy of a proposed resolution is sent under these provisions to an auditor whose removal is sought, or to an auditor whom it is proposed to replace by another person on the termination of his appointment, the auditor may make written representations of a reasonable length in respect of the matter, and the company must in the notice calling the general meeting state that such representations have been made and send copies of them to every member of the company to whom notice of the general meeting is sent.[6] The same provisions then apply to the power of the court on the company's application to order that defamatory representations need not be circulated and that the costs of the application shall be borne by the auditor whose removal or replacement is sought, as apply to a statement tendered by a resigning auditor about the circumstances of his resignation.[7] If the auditor's representations are received by the company too late for circulation to members before the general meeting is held, or if the company defaults in circulating representations submitted to it in time, the auditor may require that the representations shall be read out at the general meeting.[8] An auditor who is entitled to make written representations is apparently also entitled to address the general meeting on the question of his removal or not being re-appointed, and this is so whether he makes written representations or not.[9] In any event he must be sent notice of the meeting as if he were a member.[10]

Dormant companies

A private company which is not a banking or insurance company or a person authorised to carry on investment business[11] may, by passing a special resolution for the purpose, make itself exempt from the provisions of the Companies Act 1985 (as amended) relating to the audit of its accounts and the obligation to appoint auditors during a period while it is dormant.[12] A private company may avail itself of these privileges only: (a) if it has been dormant from the time of its incorporation and it passes the necessary special resolution before its first general meeting at which annual accounts are laid; or (b) if it has been dormant since the end of its most recent financial year, and is entitled as a small company to the exemptions conferred on such a company from the obligation to include certain matters in the copy of its annual accounts for that financial year which it delivers to the Registrar of Companies, and it is not required to prepare group accounts for that year; or (c) if it is not required to prepare such group accounts and it would be entitled to

5 Companies Act 1985, s 388 (4) and s 391A (2).
6 Companies Act 1985, s 391A (3) and (4).
7 Ibid, s 391A (5) and (6) (see p 714, ante).
8 Ibid, s 391A (5).
9 The Companies Act 1985, s 390 (1) provides that the auditor is entitled to speak on any business which concerns him as auditor, which would seem to include these matters.
10 Companies Act 1985, s 390 (1).
11 Financial Services Act 1986, s 7 (1), s 15 (1), s 22, s 23 (1), s 24, s 25 and s 31 (1).
12 Companies Act 1985, s 250 (1) and (2) and s 388A (1).

exemption under (b) but for the fact that a member of the group of companies to which it belongs is a public company which may lawfully offer its shares or debentures to the public for subscription or sale, or a banking or insurance company or a person authorised to carry on investment business.[13]

A company is dormant during a period in which it enters into no significant accounting transaction, that is, a transaction in respect of which it is under a legal obligation to make an entry in its accounting records, other than the receipt of the issue price of shares subscribed by the signatories of its memorandum of association.[14] If a company which has passed a special resolution exempting itself from the obligation to appoint auditors qualifies for the exemptions of a dormant company in succeeding financial years and remains continuously dormant throughout those subsequent years, it need not appoint auditors nor comply with the provisions of the Companies Act 1985, relating to the audit of its accounts for those financial years.[15] The privileges in these respects of a company which has resolved to make itself exempt from the statutory provisions relating to the audit of its annual accounts and the appointment of auditors terminates immediately if the company ceases to be dormant, or ceases to qualify for the exemption.[16] The directors may thereupon appoint auditors to hold office until the conclusion of the next general meeting at which accounts are to be laid, and if they fail to appoint such auditors, a general meeting may do so.[17]

Auditors' powers and duties

Statutory powers and duties

The auditors' duty is to examine and verify the original accounting records kept by the company, to discover any inaccuracies or omissions therein, to examine the company's annual balance sheet and profit and loss account to ensure that they agree with the company's original accounting records (as verified), and to report to the members of the company on the original accounting records and the annual accounts and directors' report.[18] It is not part of the auditors' duties to prepare the company's annual accounts, but there is nothing to prevent them from agreeing to do so as a separate professional service as an alternative to the company having its annual accounts prepared by accountants employed by it or by an outside firm of accountants. For the purposes of carrying out their functions the auditors have a right of access at all times to the company's books, accounts and vouchers (ie the company's accounting records and related documents), and may require its officers to give them such information and explanations as they think necessary for the performance of their duties.[19] It is a criminal offence for an officer of the company knowingly or recklessly to make to the company's auditors a written or oral statement which conveys, or purports to convey, any information or explanation which the auditors are entitled to require for the purpose of carrying out their functions and which is materially misleading, false or deceptive.[20] If the company has a subsidiary undertaking incorporated in Great Britain, the subsidiary undertaking and its auditors must give the company's auditors such information and explanations as they reasonably require to enable them to perform their duties,

13 Ibid, s 250 (1).
14 Ibid, s 250 (3).
15 Ibid, s 250 (1) and s 388A (1).
16 Ibid, s 250 (5).
17 Ibid, s 288A (2), (3) and (5).
18 Ibid, s 235 (1).
19 Ibid, s 389A (1).
20 Ibid, s 389A (2).

and if the company has a subsidiary undertaking incorporated outside Great Britain, the company itself must take all measures which its auditors reasonably require to obtain such information and explanations.[1] If the auditors fail to obtain all the information and explanations which to the best of their knowledge and belief are necessary for the purposes of the audit, they must state that fact in their report to the members.[2] Auditors are entitled to attend all general meetings of members and to speak on any business thereat which concerns them as auditors, and the same notice of general meetings must be sent to them as to a member who is entitled to attend them.[3]

Despite these extensive powers, the Court of Appeal ruled in 1912 that under the statutory provisions then in force, which gave auditors similar rights to call on the company's officers to supply information and explanations and to allow auditors access to the company's accounting records,[4] an auditor could not compel the company to permit him to exercise the functions of his office during the period for which he was appointed, and consequently, an auditor could not indirectly achieve the same result by suing to compel the company or its officers to provide him with information or explanations, or to produce the documents required for the purpose of his audit.[5] The court's ruling was based partly on its professed inability to interfere with the internal affairs of the company because any decision given by the court could be overruled by an ordinary resolution passed by a general meeting, and partly on the court's unwillingness to enforce the auditor's contract of employment specifically against the company. It is doubtful whether either of these grounds was well founded. Since an auditor appointed by a general meeting, the board of directors or the Secretary of State holds office by statute, and not merely by virtue of the resolution or order appointing him, it is not possible for a general meeting to take away his statutory powers in defiance of the Companies Act 1985, otherwise than by removing him from office under the appropriate statutory provisions.[6] Consequently, an auditor would seem to be entitled to obtain an injunction to restrain any improper interference with the performance of his functions by the company or its officers, and also a mandatory injunction to compel the company and its officers to produce its accounting records and related documents for his inspection. In practice the Court of Appeal's ruling to the contrary has proved no impediment to auditors, who can always obtain the information, explanation and documents which they require to fulfil their statutory duties by threatening to present a qualified auditor's report to the members or to refuse to report on the company's accounts.

The requirement that the auditors shall report to the members on the company's original accounting records and on its annual accounts[7] is the members' safeguard against inaccurate, misleading or incomplete annual accounts being presented to them. The auditors' report must state whether in their opinion the company's annual balance sheet and profit and loss account have been properly prepared in accordance with the requirements of the Companies Act 1985 (as amended) and whether those accounts respectively give a true and fair view of the company's affairs (ie assets and liabilities) at the end of its financial year and of its profit or loss for the year.[8] The report must extend to the notes to the annual accounts as

---

1 Ibid, s 389A (3) and (4).
2 Ibid, s 237 (3).
3 Ibid, s 390 (1).
4 Companies (Consolidation) Act 1908, s 113 (1).
5 *Cuff of London and County Land and Building Co Ltd* [1912] 1 Ch 440.
6 See p 715, ante.
7 Companies Act 1985, s 235 (1) and (2).
8 Ibid, s 235 (2).

well as to the contents of the accounts themselves.[9] Additionally, the auditors must report any inconsistencies between the information given in the directors' report relating to the company's financial year covered by its annual accounts and the contents of those annual accounts.[10] The auditors' report must state the names of the auditors and must be signed by them or, if the auditor is a partnership, company or body corporate, must state the name of the auditor and be signed by an authorised person on its behalf; and the copy of their report which the company must deliver to the Registrar of Companies[11] with a copy of the company's annual accounts must likewise be signed by or on behalf of the auditors.[12] Copies of the auditors' report must be circulated with the annual accounts in advance of the general meeting at which those accounts and the directors' and auditors' reports are laid before the members,[13] and the report must be read out, and be available for inspection, at that meeting.[14] The auditors comply with their duty to report to the members, however, if they send the audited annual accounts and their report to the directors with a view to those things being done, and the auditors are not responsible if the directors fail to call a general meeting or to lay the auditors' report before it, nor if they suppress or falsify the report.[15] Copies of the auditors' report which are laid before the members' general meeting or which are otherwise circulated, published or issued must state the names of the auditors.[16]

Duty of care

In order to prepare their report on a company's annual accounts auditors must carry out such investigations as will enable them to form an opinion whether proper accounting records have been kept by the company, whether proper and adequate returns have been received by them from the company's branches which they have not visited, and whether the annual accounts are in agreement with the company's accounting records and returns from its branches; if this has not been done the auditors' report must state that fact.[17] The matters which auditors must investigate in carrying out the audit of a company's accounts and the depth of their investigation may be prescribed in more detail by their contract with the company or by the company's articles, which are impliedly incorporated in the auditors' contract with the company in the absence of other express provisions.[18] If neither the auditors' contract nor the company's articles specify the details of the auditors' duties in more detail than the duties imposed on them by the Companies Act 1985,[19] their duty is to exercise reasonable skill and care in ascertaining the accuracy of the company's accounting records, and the accuracy and completeness of its annual accounts.[20] The auditors' contract with the company or the company's articles cannot diminish the standard of care and skill required of them by the general law,[1] but the contract or articles may make their duties more onerous by

---

9 Ibid, s 226 (3) and (4) and s 261 (2).
10 Ibid, s 235 (3).
11 See p 697, ante.
12 Companies Act 1985, s 236 (1), (3) and (5).
13 Ibid, s 238 (1) (see p 697, ante).
14 Ibid, s 241 (1).
15 *Re Allen Craig & Co (London) Ltd* [1934] Ch 483.
16 Companies Act 1985, s 236 (2).
17 Ibid, s 237 (1) and (2).
18 *Re City Equitable Fire Insurance Co Ltd* [1925] Ch 407 at 499.
19 Table A contains no provisions in this respect.
20 *Re London and General Bank (No 2)* [1895] 2 Ch 673 at 682 to 3.
1 Companies Act 1985, s 310 (1) (see p 603, ante).

prescribing a higher standard of investigation or verification to which they must conform than the Companies Act 1985 prescribes.

An auditor is not bound to be suspicious in his approach to the accounting records kept by the company's directors and officers or to the company's annual accounts prepared by them or a person engaged by the company for the purpose,[2] and so he will not be liable for failing to uncover frauds or defalcations which the company's accounting records do not make apparent, or which are not discoverable by the exercise of normal skill and care. Thus, an auditor was held not to be liable for failing to notice from the company's accounting records that it had regularly bought investments shortly before successive annual audits and had disposed of them shortly afterwards, and for failing to enquire what had been done with the money representing the investments during the greater part of each year; such enquiries would have revealed that in fact the managing director had been using the money received from these annual sales for his own purposes.[3] On the other hand, if the contents of the company's accounting records should make a competent accountant suspicious, the auditor must investigate the company's affairs with the thoroughness needed to allay such suspicions, and the extent of the investigation he must undertake is correspondingly increased.[4] Consequently, an auditor was held guilty of negligence when he accepted a managing director's assurance that the dates of invoices for stock purchased by the company during the financial year for which the auditor was reporting had been altered by him to dates in the following financial year because the stock had not yet been delivered by the suppliers; in fact the stock had been delivered, as enquiries made of the suppliers would have shown, and the managing director's alterations of the invoices were part of a scheme which he operated for several years to conceal the fact that the company was suffering losses by showing its current assets at the end of each financial year at an inflated figure and its current indebtedness as less than its real amount.[5]

The court has laid down the following specific rules as to an auditor's duties in the absence of express provisions in his contract with the company or in the company's articles:

(1) An auditor must check the company's own cash records with its bank paying-in books and cheque counterfoils and with a statement of its account obtained from its bank.[6] He is not entitled to assume that the directors, officers or employees of the company who have kept its cash records have done so correctly, and so dispense with verifying them.

(2) An auditor need not check that the company owns or possesses the stock in trade stated in its accounting or stock records, nor need he value its stock in trade, work in progress or finished products.[7] However, he should obtain a certificate as to the amount and value of stock in trade, work in progress or finished products from the officers or employees of the company charged with checking it, and if this certificate agrees with the company's accounting and stock records, the auditor need not investigate the matter further, unless the information in his possession should arouse his suspicions.[7] It would seem, moreover, that an auditor must check that the system employed by the

2 *Re Kingston Cotton Mills Co (No 2)* [1896] 2 Ch 279 at 288, per Lopes LJ.
3 *Re City Equitable Fire Insurance Co Ltd*, supra, at 495.
4 *Henry Squire Cash Chemist Ltd v Ball, Baker & Co* (1911) 106 LT 197.
5 *Re Thomas Gerrard & Son Ltd* [1968] Ch 455, [1967] 2 All ER 525.
6 *Fox & Son v Morrish Grant & Co* (1918) 35 TLR 126.
7 *Re Kingston Cotton Mills Co (No 2)* [1896] 2 Ch 279; *Henry Squire (Cash Chemist) Ltd v Ball Baker & Co* (1911) 106 LT 197. Contrast American law, which requires the auditor to check stock or to qualify his report indicating that he has not done so (*Stanley L Block Inc v Klein* 258 NYS 2d 501 (1965)).

company for keeping records of stock and work in progress is sound, and that the records show real and not fictitious values. The auditor is not expected to have a technical knowledge of the way in which the company's business is managed, and so he is not required to check the company's stock merely because its accounting or stock records show it as worth more than a person experienced in that kind of business would expect, although he would be required to investigate if the company's accounting or stock records show its stock at a figure which is manifestly excessive.[8] Furthermore, it has been held that an auditor may accept a certificate as to the value of the company's stock in trade without enquiry, even though its accounting records show that the price at which it has been selling its products recently is much below the value put by the certificate on the items of stock still in hand,[9] but this ruling is questionable in the light of modern auditing practice. In practice auditors check the valuation of stock in trade and work in progress by ensuring that the company has an efficient system for recording the purchase, sale, storage, consumption and disposal of stock and raw materials and for calculating the cost of each of its manufacturing and handling processes, and also by making a number of checks of items of stock in trade and work in progress at random to ensure that they are correctly entered in the company's stock and progress records.

(3) An auditor must ensure that the company possesses the certificates for all the investments which its accounting records show it as having purchased, but if the certificates have been deposited with a proper person, such as its bank or stockbroker, he may accept a written confirmation by that person that he still holds them.[10] If the company has advanced money with or without security, the auditor must not allow its balance sheet to show the loans as worth the amounts owing by the borrowers without enquiring whether the security given by them (if any) is adequate to cover that amount and the costs of realisation, and whether the borrowers are able and are likely to repay.[11] It would seem that the auditor should make similar enquiries about the company's other investments[12] and about unsecured trade and other debts owed to it.[13]

(4) An auditor must check the invoices received by the company to ensure that there are no trade debts owed by it for which provision has not been made in its accounting records, and if persons with whom the company deals send invoices or statements of account to it at fairly regular intervals, an auditor should enquire of such persons whether there are any outstanding debts owing to them.[14]

(5) An auditor need only examine the accounting records and vouchers kept by the company which a company of its type would normally be expected to keep, together with such other documents as the directors or officers of the company produce to him. Consequently, the auditor is not guilty of a breach of duty if he fails to discover an irregularity which can only be traced from

---

8 *Henry Squire Cash Chemist Ltd v Ball & Baker Co*, supra, at 204.
9 *Re Kingston Cotton Mills Co (No 2)*, supra.
10 *Re City Equitable Fire Insurance Co Ltd* [1925] Ch 407 at 514, per Pollock MR.
11 *Leeds Estate Building and Investment Co v Shepherd* (1887) 36 ChD 787; *Re London and General Bank (No 2)* [1895] 2 Ch 673.
12 Particularly if they are listed on a stock exchange, when the balance sheet must state their market value (Companies Act 1985, Sch 4, para 45 (2)).
13 *Scarborough Harbour Comrs v Robinson Coulson Kirby & Co* (1934) 78 Acct LR 65.
14 *Re Westminster Road Construction and Engineering Co* (1932) 76 Acct LR 38; *Re Thomas Gerrard and Son Ltd* [1968] Ch 455, [1967] 2 All ER 525.

other unusual or informal records kept by the company which are not produced to him.[15]

(6) An auditor is only concerned to report to the members of the company on the accuracy of its accounts. He is not guilty of a breach of duty if he fails to inform them that, although the directors have managed the company's affairs perfectly lawfully, they have done so incompetently or imprudently, for example, by failing to maintain sufficient liquid assets to meet the company's liabilities as they fall due, or by recommending that too large a part of its realised profits should be distributed as a dividend and insufficient profits retained for the company's future needs.[16] Nevertheless, now that a company's annual accounts must make proper provision for the depreciation of its fixed assets and the fall in the market or saleable value of its current assets and investments,[17] the auditor must exercise reasonable care to ensure that this has been done.

Enforcement of auditors' duties

Auditors usually serve under express service contracts, which specify their remuneration, and so they can be sued for breach of contract by the company which employs them if they fail to fulfil their duties properly. If an auditor were to act in reliance on the resolution of an annual general meeting appointing him without entering into a contract with the company, it is doubtful whether a contract could be implied from the conduct of the parties, because by accepting the appointment the auditor undertakes only an auditor's statutory functions, and the duty of skill and care he owes the company in carrying out those functions is then imposed on him by law. This is of no great importance, however, for auditors are officers of the company, and so can be made liable for breaches of duty by actions for negligence, and also by misfeasance proceedings when the company is wound up.[18] In misfeasance proceedings auditors may be called to account for negligence as well as for deliberate breaches of duty.[19]

Whether an auditor is sued for breach of contract or for misfeasance, however, he is only liable for loss which the company has suffered in consequence of his defective audit, for example, when it has been induced to pay a dividend out of capital in reliance on an inaccurate profit and loss account audited by him which showed the company's profits as greater than they really were.[20] If the company has merely been misled by inaccurate accounts which he has audited, but has not acted to its loss in the belief that they were accurate, it will not be able to recover substantial damages from the auditor, and will at most only be able to sue him for nominal damages for breach of contract.

It has already been observed that no provision in the company's articles or in an auditor's service contract may exempt him from liability for breach of any duty imposed on him by law.[1] But if he is guilty of such a breach of duty, he may apply

---

15 *Henry Squire Cash Chemist Ltd v Ball Baker & Co* (1911) 106 LT 197.
16 *Re London and General Bank (No 2)* [1895] 2 Ch 673 at 682, per Lindley LJ.
17 Companies Act 1985, s 226 (3) and Sch 4, paras 18, 19, 23.
18 *Re London and General Bank* [1895] 2 Ch 166. For misfeasance proceedings under the Insolvency Act 1986, s 212 (1) to (3), see p 683, ante. Auditors are also officers of the company for the purpose of the criminal provisions of the Companies Act 1985, and other statutes relating to the publication of false accounts (*R v Shacter* [1960] 2 QB 252, [1960] 1 All ER 61).
19 *Re Windsor Steam Coal Co (1901) Ltd* [1929] 1 Ch 151; *Re Home and Colonial Insurance Co Ltd* [1930] 1 Ch 102.
20 *Leeds Estate Building and Investment Co v Shepherd* (1887) 36 ChD 787; *Re London and General Bank (No 2)*, supra.
1 Companies Act 1985, s 310 (1) and (2).

to the court to relieve him from liability, which the court may do if satisfied that he acted honestly and reasonably and ought fairly to be excused.[2] Furthermore, if the company's articles or the auditor's contract with the company do purport to exempt him from liability for breach of duty, the company may indemnify him against his costs in successfully defending civil or criminal proceedings, or in successfully applying to the court for relief from liability.[3] From these provisions it follows that the duty of care imposed by the court on auditors when their contracts and the company's articles are silent, is inescapably imposed on all auditors, and although such contracts or the company's articles may require an auditor to investigate the company's affairs more meticulously, they cannot permit him to omit any of the enquiries which he should make in order to comply with this general duty of skill and care.

Although an auditor's function is to report to the members of a company, his contractual and statutory duties are owed to the company itself, and he is under no contractual or statutory liability to an individual member for failing to carry out his duties properly. But an auditor or accountant will be liable in tort to a member, creditor, debenture or loan security holder or to a prospective investor in the company or a person who proposes to give credit to it, if the auditor knowingly gives him false information about the company's financial position;[4] or if the auditor negligently gives that other person false information or unsound advice about the company's prospects at his request or in response to his inquiry, and the auditor or accountant knows that the other person intends to act on that information or advice;[5] or if the auditor or accountant gives or verifies information to the company itself in circumstances where he realises, or should realise, that it is likely to be communicated to an intending investor in, or an intending creditor of, the company who will act in reliance on it.[6] The auditor or accountant is, of course, liable only if the member, creditor, loan security holder or investor acts in the belief that the information is correct or that the advice is sound, and he suffers loss as a result of this not being so, for example, by buying or selling shares of the company. Moreover, it seems that to incur liability the auditor or accountant must either communicate the information to the plaintiff individually, or must know that the information will be given to him in order that he may act on it (eg a valuation of shares carried out by an auditor at the request of a company so that pre-emption provisions in its articles may be activated),[7] or the auditor or accountant must have realised from facts known to him that the plaintiff would be likely to rely on the information given or verified by him (eg where an auditor makes an unqualified report on a company's annual accounts knowing that the company is in need of financial assistance and that a person who contemplates giving such assistance will probably rely on the annual accounts in deciding whether to do so).[8]

Except in the special circumstances described in the preceding paragraph, no member of the company or other person may treat an auditors' report on a company's annual accounts laid before a general meeting as an inducement to act thereon by investing in its shares or loan securities or by buying or selling shares or

2   Ibid, s 727 (1) and (2). This provision is dealt with in more detail, p 603, ante.
3   Ibid, s 310 (3), as amended by Companies Act 1989, s 137 (1).
4   *Derry v Peek* (1889) 14 App Cas 337.
5   *Hedley, Byrne & Co Ltd v Heller & Partners Ltd* [1964] AC 465, [1963] 3 All ER 575; *Arenson v Casson Beckman Rutley & Co* [1977] AC 405, [1975] 3 All ER 901.
6   *JEB Fasteners Ltd v Marks, Bloom & Co* (a firm) [1981] 3 All ER 289; on appeal [1983] 1 All ER 583; *Lloyd Cheyham & Co Ltd v Littlejohn & Co* [1987] BCLC 303.
7   *Arenson v Casson Beckman Rutley & Co*, supra
8   *JEB Fasteners Ltd v Marks, Bloom & Co*, supra; *Lloyd Cheyham & Co Ltd v Littlejohn & Co*, supra.

loan securities issued by the company, and the auditors are therefore not liable to such a member or investor in damages for loss suffered by them in consequence of the auditors' report being inaccurate or incomplete.[9] The auditors' report is made to the members of the company, it is true,[10] but it is made to them collectively so that they may be assured that the annual accounts laid before them are accurate and complete and that the company's affairs have been conducted as indicated in the annual accounts and the notes to them, and not so that members or debenture holders to whom the accounts are circulated may take action individually in reliance on the accounts by increasing or reducing their investment in the company.

PERIODICAL REPORTS BY LISTED COMPANIES

A company which has a listing for its shares, debentures or other loan securities on the Stock Exchange is required to supplement the publication of its annual accounts and directors' and auditors' reports by publishing half-yearly reports containing the information called for by the Stock Exchange as a condition for maintaining its listing.[11] Under the Stock Exchange's requirements, a listed company must prepare a report on its activities and its profit or loss during the first six months of each of its financial years, and the company must either send copies of the report to holders of its listed securities within four months after the expiration of that six months period, or must publish the report in two national daily newspapers within those four months, but the Stock Exchange may extend that period for exceptional reasons.[12]

The half-yearly report comprises: (a) a statement of the company's net turnover and profit or loss before tax for the relevant six months, excluding extraordinary (ie non-recurring) items; (b) the amount of any interim dividend paid or proposed; (c) an explanatory statement of the company's activities during the relevant period; (d) the amounts of the company's turnover and profit or loss for the same period of its last preceding financial year; (e) the amount of tax payable in the United Kingdom and overseas on the half-year's profits; (f) the extent of minority interests in the half-year's profits of the company's subsidiaries; (g) any extraordinary items included in the half-year's total profits, net of taxation; (h) the half-year's profit or loss attributable to the company's shareholders; and (i) the earnings for the half-year attributable to each share in the company and the corresponding figures in the half-yearly report for the preceding financial year.[13] The explanatory statement of the company's activities must include any significant information enabling investors to make an informed assessment of the trend of the company's activities and its profits or losses, and must indicate any special factors which have influenced its activities so as to facilitate a comparison with the first six months of the preceding financial year.[14] If the accounting information in the half-yearly report has been audited, the auditors' report, including any qualifications, must be included with the copies of the report sent to members or published in the press; if the half-yearly report has not been audited, it must so state.[15] The Stock

9 *Caparo Industries plc v Dickman* [1990] 2 WLR 358, [1990] 6 BCC 164; *Al Saudi Banque v Clarke Pixley* [1990] BCLC 46, [1990] 2 WLR 344.
10 Companies Act 1985, s 235 (1) and s 238 (1).
11 Financial Services Act 1986, s 153 (1) and (2); The Stock Exchange: *Admission of Securities to Listing*, Section 5, Chapter 2, paras 24 and 25.
12 The Stock Exchange: *Admission of Securities to Listing*, Section 5, Chapter 2, para 24.
13 Ibid, para 25 (*a*) and (*b*).
14 Ibid, para 25 (*c*).
15 Ibid, para 25 (*d*).

Exchange may authorise a company to omit from a periodical report any information whose disclosure would be contrary to the public interest or seriously detrimental to the company, but in the latter case the omission must not be likely to mislead the public.[16]

Unless the report on the results of the first six months of a listed company's financial year is published in a newspaper circulating throughout the United Kingdom, copies of it must be made available to the public at the company's registered office.[17] A copy of each half-yearly report must be sent to the Stock Exchange when it is published.[18]

There are no explicit statutory sanctions for the failure of a listed company to publish proper half-yearly reports, apart from the power of the Council of the Stock Exchange to terminate or suspend the listing of the defaulting company's securities.[19] It would, nevertheless appear that any member of the company could seek a mandatory injunction to compel it to prepare and publish half-yearly reports in order to preserve its listing.[20] However, the Registrar of Companies cannot exercise default powers under the Companies Act 1985,[1] as though the company's failure to publish a half-yearly report were the equivalent of a failure to file copies of its annual accounts and reports at the Companies Registry.

ANNUAL RETURN

Every company must make an annual return to the Registrar of Companies in successive calendar years. Each annual return must be made up to a date not later than the anniversary of the date of the company's incorporation, or if the company's immediately preceding annual return was made up to a different date, to a date not later than the anniversary of that date.[2] Each annual return must be delivered to the Registrar of Companies within 28 days after the date to which it is made up, must be signed by a director or secretary of the company and must be in the form prescribed by regulations made by the Secretary of State for Trade and Industry.[3] Failure to deliver an annual return within the proper time is punishable by a fine imposed on the company and its directors and secretary.[4]

The information which must be contained in an annual return comprises the following:[5]

(a) the address of the company's registered office;

(b) the type of company it is and its principal business activities;

(c) the name and address of the secretary of the company and of each of its directors;

(d) in the case of each individual director, his nationality, date of birth and

---

16 Ibid, para 25.3.
17 Ibid, para 24.
18 Ibid, para 24.
19 Financial Services Act 1986, s 153 (1); The Stock Exchange: *Admission of Securities to Listing*, Section 1, Chapter 4, para 1.
20 The basis of the member's action would be his interest in preventing the company from infringing a legal rule which cannot be waived by an ordinary resolution of a general meeting, and the breach of which endangers a substantial interest of the company (*Jenkin v Pharmaceutical Society of Great Britain* [1921] 1 Ch 392).
1 Companies Act 1985, s 713 (1), as amended by Companies Act 1989, s 127 (4) (see p 698, ante).
2 Companies Act 1985, s 363 (1), substituted by Companies Act 1989, s 139 (1).
3 Companies Act 1985, s 363 (2).
4 Ibid, s 363 (3) and (4).
5 Ibid, s 364 (1) to (4).

business occupation, and the particulars of his other directorships which are required to be contained in the company's register of directors;

(e) in the case of each corporate director of the company, the particulars of his other directorships which are required to be contained in the company's register of directors;

(f) if the company's register of members or its register of debenture holders or a duplicate of that register is kept elsewhere than at the company's registered office, the address of the place where it is kept;

(g) if the company is a private company which has passed an elective resolution to dispense with the laying of its annual accounts before a general meeting each year, or to dispense with holding an annual general meeting each year, a statement to that effect.[6]

In addition to the foregoing information, each annual return must contain the following information if the company has a share capital:[7]

(i) the total number of shares issued by the company and their aggregate nominal value;

(ii) if the company has issued two or more classes of shares, the nature of each class and the aggregate nominal value of the shares comprised in each class which the company has issued;

(iii) the names and addresses of the members of the company and the number of shares of each class which are held by them respectively;

(iv) the names and addresses of persons who have ceased to be members of the company since the date of the company's last annual return, or in the case of its first annual return, since its incorporation;

(v) the number of shares of each class which have been transferred by each person who has ceased to be a member of the company since the date of its last annual return and the respective dates of registration of transfers of shares by him.

If either of the two preceding annual returns delivered by the company has given the full particulars required by items (iii) to (v) above, the annual return may give such particulars only in respect of persons who have become or ceased to be members of the company since the date of the company's last annual return and of shares transferred since that date.[8] If the company has converted any of its shares into stock, the information required by items (i) to (v) above must be given in respect of that stock.[8]

Annual returns may be inspected at the Companies Registry by any member of the public.[9] The annual returns made by a company are useful insofar as they contain a history of its membership and give particulars of its present members and their shareholdings, but it should be remembered that an inspection of the return is no substitute for an inspection of the register of members, because the return may be anything up to 13 months out of date. The annual accounts of a company are no longer filed with its annual return, but copies of them must nevertheless be delivered to the Registrar of Companies within seven or ten months after the end of each accounting reference period of the company depending on whether the company is a public or private company, and this period is extended if the company

---

6 See p 766, post.

7 Companies Act 1985, s 364A (1) to (5). A company will have a share capital unless it is a company limited by guarantee, which cannot now be incorporated with a share capital, or an unlimited company, which may be incorporated without one.

8 Ibid, s 364A (6) and (8).

9 Ibid, s 709 (1), substituted by Companies Act 1989, s 126 (1).

carries on business or has interests outside Great Britain, the Channel Islands and the Isle of Man.[10] The filed copies of a company's accounts and its directors' and auditors' reports are also open to inspection by any member of the public at the Companies Registry,[9] and this is a useful facility for creditors of the company and for other persons who wish to ascertain its financial position. Only members and debenture holders must be sent copies of the annual accounts by the company,[11] and so inspection of the accounts filed at the Companies Registry is often the only way by which other persons may examine them.

The Registrar of Companies or any member or creditor of a company which has not filed an annual return or any other document which it is required to deliver to the Companies Registry may by notice require it to make good its default within 14 days, and if it fails to do so, the Registrar or any member or creditor of the company may apply to the court for an order compelling it to do so.[12] The Registrar is under no duty to a member or creditor to make such an application or to take any other steps to obtain the delivery of the company annual return or any other document which the Companies Act 1985 requires it to deliver to him, and so the court will reject an application by a member or creditor for an order compelling the Registrar to do so.[13] The normal way in which the obligation of a company to file annual accounts, directors' and auditors' reports, annual returns and other documents at the Companies Registry is enforced is by the Registrar instituting proceedings against the company and its directors for the imposition of fines and pecuniary penalties[14] and for a default order compelling the directors to comply.[15]

10 Companies Act 1985, s 242 (1) and s 244 (1) to (3) (see p 697, ante).
11 Ibid, s 238 (1).
12 Ibid, s 713 (1), as amended by Companies Act 1989, s 127 (4).
13 *Re Normandie House (Kensington) Ltd* (1967) 111 Sol Jo 131.
14 Companies Act 1985, s 238 (5), s 242A (1) and (2), s 363 (3) and (4).
15 Ibid, s 242 (3).

CHAPTER 18

Groups of companies

DEFINITION

In a commercial sense one company is considered to be the parent or holding company of another if it controls the composition of the other's board of directors by being able to appoint, or direct the appointment, of a majority of the maximum number of directors who may be appointed, or the appointment of directors who may together exercise a majority of the voting rights exercisable at board meetings of the other company. The other company is then known as the subsidiary of the parent or holding company. Control over the composition of the subsidiary's board is almost invariably derived from the voting rights enjoyed by the parent or holding company by virtue of shares in the subsidiary held by it or its nominees, but such control could also arise from the provisions of the subsidiary's memorandum or articles, or from a contract with the subsidiary which empowers the parent or holding company to appoint directors to the subsidiary's board. It will be noted that a parent or holding company need not hold all the shares of the subsidiary in order to control the composition of its board; there may be other shareholders too, but they are almost always minority shareholders, because in practice the parent or holding company's control results from it holding a majority of the voting shares of the subsidiary. If all the subsidiary's shares, voting and non-voting, are vested in the holding company or its nominees, the subsidiary is said to be a 'wholly-owned' subsidiary of the holding company.[1]

The relationship of parent or holding company and subsidiary may come into existence in any one of three ways. The first of these is when an already large company wishes to split its undertaking or the several different businesses carried on by it into separate divisions managed by separate companies, each of which will be responsible only for the liabilities incurred in connection with the activities of its division. For example, if a manufacturing company wishes to have its own wholesale or retail outlets for its products without making the assets of its manufacturing undertaking available to satisfy liabilities incurred in connection with its marketing activities, it will form separate subsidiary wholesale or retail companies, all of whose shares will be vested in the manufacturing company and its nominees. Sometimes subsidiary companies are formed to carry on different sectors of the parent or holding company's business, or to market its products overseas, or to carry on one or more of the various businesses in which the group is engaged. Tax advantages can be obtained by the parent or holding company doing this instead of carrying on all the activities of the group itself. Whether subsidiaries are incorporated Great Britain or overseas is immaterial in determining their status as subsidiaries of the parent or holding company.

The second way in which a parent or holding company/subsidiary relationship may arise is in consequence of the merger of two or more companies, or the takeover of one company by another. A merger by an acquisition of shares may be carried out in either of two ways. The first is for a new company to be formed to

1 Companies Act 1985, s 736 (2), substituted by Companies Act 1989, s 144 (1).

acquire the shares of the merging companies from their present holders in exchange for the issue of shares of the new company. When the exchange is complete, the existing companies become the subsidiaries of the new company, and carry on their respective business subject to its control. The new company does not carry on any business activity itself, but exists merely as a link between its shareholders and its operating subsidiaries. The other method is for one of the merging companies to acquire the shares, or the voting shares, of the other companies from their present holders in exchange for a further issue of its own shares. This method of acquiring control is also used when a takeover bid is made by one company for the shares or the voting shares of another company or other companies, and the bid is accepted by the holders of all or a majority of the shares involved. Whether the transaction is a merger or a takeover, the acquiring company becomes the parent or holding company of the other company or companies, and if the acquiring company is one of the merging companies and not a newly formed company, it also continues to carry on its original business undertaking itself. In this situation it is not uncommon for the parent or holding company not to acquire the non-voting shares of the subsidiaries, and the holders of such shares are then compelled to remain investors in an enterprise over the conduct of whose affairs they have little or no influence. The result of a merger or takeover, or of successive mergers or takeovers, effected by a parent company may be that the subsidiaries of which it is the parent carry on a variety of businesses which are not commercially or economically related to each other. The group of companies is then known as a conglomerate group. This in no way affects the legal relationships between the companies in the group, however, which remain the same as those of the companies comprised in a vertical group (where one or more of the companies market or distribute the products manufactured, imported or purchased by the others) or a horizontal group (where the companies in the group operate at the same level of the manufacturing, marketing or distributing process).

The final way in which a company may become another's subsidiary is by the other investing its cash resources in the shares of the subsidiary simply because it considers them to be a sound investment. Here the relationship of parent or holding company and subsidiary is not created for some ulterior purpose, but results from the parent or holding company acquiring sufficient shares in the subsidiary to control the voting power exercisable at its general meetings. In practice this rarely happens. Although institutional investors subscribe for and purchase ordinary shares in industrial and commercial companies on an extensive scale, they deliberately refrain from acquiring controlling interests, and even though they may exceptionally acquire as much as 20 per cent of a company's ordinary shares, they do not attempt to influence routine management decisions made by its board, nor do they usually interfere on major policy questions within its directors' competence, although they do maintain a general supervision in order to protect their investments in the company.

Statutory definitions of parent and holding company

The Companies Act 1985[2] (as amended) contains two definitions of the parent or holding company/subsidiary relationship, and employs two sets of terms to describe the companies or undertakings involved in the relationship. For accounting purposes (primarily the obligation of a parent company to prepare and lay consolidated annual accounts for the group to which it belongs before a general meeting of its members, in addition to its own annual accounts), the companies or

---

2 Companies Act 1985, s 258 (1), substituted by Companies Act 1989, s 21 (1).

undertakings belonging to the group are designated as a 'parent undertaking' or a 'parent company' (if it is a company) and 'subsidiary undertakings'. An undertaking is defined for this purpose as a body corporate, partnership, or an unincorporated association carrying on a trade or business with or without a view to profit,[3] but only a parent company (ie a corporate body) is required to prepare and lay consolidated accounts.[4] For all purposes other than accounting, the companies belonging to a group are designated as a 'holding company' and 'subsidiaries',[5] and the group is then taken as comprising only corporate bodies. Despite the differences in terms and functions of the parent undertaking/subsidiary undertaking and the holding company/subsidiary relationship, the definition of a parent undertaking and a subsidiary undertaking and the definition of a holding company and a subsidiary are very similar, apart from the fact that a parent undertaking or a subsidiary undertaking may be a partnership or an unincorporated association, whereas a holding company or a subsidiary must be a company,[6] and that there are three situations where a parent undertaking/subsidiary undertaking relationship may exist where, even if all the participants are companies, a holding company/ subsidiary relationship will not arise. Because of the common features of the two definitions they will here be dealt with together.

For the accounting and non-accounting purposes of the Companies Act 1985,[7] one company is the parent undertaking or holding company of another company or undertaking if it controls it in any one of three ways, namely: (a) by holding more than half of the total voting rights which can be exercised at a general meeting of that other company or undertaking; (b) by being a member of the other company or undertaking and having the right to appoint or remove directors of it who together can exercise more than half of the voting rights exercisable at its board meetings; or (c) by being a member of that other company or undertaking and controlling alone, under an agreement with other shareholders, more than half of the voting rights which can be exercised at a general meeting of that other company or undertaking; or (d) by being the parent or holding company of another company or undertaking which is itself the parent company or parent undertaking of a third company or undertaking (a sub-subsidiary). A parent or subsidiary undertaking may be formed or incorporated in Great Britain or any other country and need not be an incorporated body.[8]

Holding more than half of voting rights in the subsidiary or subsidiary undertaking

A parent undertaking or holding company is treated as holding more than half of the voting rights exercisable at a general meeting of another company or undertaking (the potential subsidiary) if it and its other subsidiaries and its and their nominees and trustees who may vote in respect of shares held by them only in accordance with its or their instructions or with its or their consent, together hold shares in the other company or undertaking (the potential subsidiary) which

3 Companies Act 1985, s 259 (1).
4 Ibid, s 227 (1), s 241 (1) and s 262 (1).
5 Ibid, s 736 (1).
6 A company is defined by the Companies Act 1985, s 736A (12) as a company incorporated under the Act or the earlier Companies Acts which it replaces or any other body corporate. Overseas companies incorporated elsewhere than in Great Britain, which establish a place of business there, are required to prepare and deliver annual accounts and, if they are parent undertakings, they must also prepare and deliver consolidated accounts as though they had been formed and registered under the Companies Act 1985 (Companies Act 1985, s 700 (1) and s 702 (1), substituted by Companies Act 1989, s 23 and Sch 10, para 13).
7 Companies Act 1985, s 258 (1), (2) and (5), substituted by Companies Act 1989, s 21 (1); Companies Act 1985, s 736 (1) and s 736A(2), (3) and (8), substituted by Companies Act 1989, s 144 (1).
8 Companies Act 1985, s 259 (1).

enable them to cast more than half of the total number of votes which can be cast at a general meeting of the potential subsidiary at the time the question of the relationship arises, or where the potential subsidiary does not have a share capital, if they are together able to cast more than half of the total number of votes which may be cast at such a general meeting by virtue of their membership, or where the potential subsidiary does not hold general meetings (eg because it is a partnership), if they together have the right under its constitution to direct its overall policy or to alter the terms of its constitution.[9]

Voting rights which are exercisable only in certain circumstances (eg voting rights attached to preference shares which can be exercised only if the preference dividend has not been declared or paid) are taken into account only if and so long as those circumstances exist, or if those circumstances are within the control of the person who has the voting rights; and voting rights which are normally exercisable but are temporarily incapable of being exercised (eg because the court has made an order prohibiting their exercise until the order is rescinded)[10] are treated as always being exercisable.[11] Voting rights which are attached to shares held by way of security are treated as exercisable by the person who provided the security (and not by the holder of the security) if the rights are exercisable by the latter only in accordance with the former's instructions or for the purposes of preserving the security or its value, or if the loan secured on the shares was made as part of the lender's normal business activities and the voting rights are exercisable by him only in the interests of the person who provided the security;[12] this provision will apply where the parent undertaking or holding company or its subsidiary or a nominee for either of them holds a legal mortgage of shares belonging to another person, or where another person holds a legal mortgage of shares belonging to the parent undertaking or holding company or its subsidiary. Finally, a parent undertaking or holding company or its subsidiary is not treated as holding voting rights attached to shares vested in it only in a fiduciary capacity (ie as a trustee or nominee for a third person).[13]

The Companies Act 1985 in its original form made a company the holding company of another because of its shareholding in that other only if the holding company and its subsidiaries and nominees for it and them together held more than half of the issued equity share capital of the subsidiary (ie the whole of its share capital other than preference shares which carried no right to participate in the subsidiary's surplus profits after payment of a fixed dividend or in its surplus assets after repayment of the whole of its share capital in its liquidation).[14] The voting rights attached to the subsidiary's shares were irrelevant. The new provision substituted by the Companies Act 1989 makes no distinction between the equity and non-equity share capital which the subsidiary has issued, and it attaches no importance to the nominal or paid up value of the subsidiary's shares, but only to the voting rights attached to them.

Controlling composition of the board of the subsidiary undertaking

A company is the parent company or undertaking of another company or undertaking if it or any of its other subsidiary undertakings is a member of that

---

9 Ibid, s 258 (2) (*a*) and (6) and Sch 10A, paras 2, 7 (1) and 9 (1); ibid, s 736A (2), (5), (6) and (8).
10 This would apply where the court has made an order under the Companies Act 1985, s 210 (5), s 216 (1) or s 445 (1) with the consequences provided by s 454 (1) (*b*).
11 Companies Act 1985, s 258 (6) and Sch 10A, para 5; ibid, s 736A (4).
12 Ibid, s 258 (6) and Sch 10A, para 8; ibid, s 736A (7).
13 Ibid, s 258 (6) and Sch 10A, para 6; ibid, s 763A (5).
14 Companies Act 1985, s 736 (1) and s 744 (as originally enacted).

other company or undertaking (the potential subsidiary) and by reason of the shareholdings of the parent company and its other subsidiaries and nominees or trustees for it or them, or by reason of the provisions of the memorandum or articles of association of the potential subsidiary or of a contract with it, or by reason of a combination of those factors the parent company or undertaking and its subsidiaries and nominees and trustees for it and them are together able to appoint or remove directors of the potential subsidiary who together are able to cast a majority of the votes which can be cast at board meetings of the potential subsidiary on all or substantially all matters.[15] A company is the holding company of another company if it is a member of it and by reason of the shareholdings of it and its subsidiaries and nominees or trustees for them in that other company (the potential subsidiary), or by reason of any of the other factors mentioned in the preceding sentence, the holding company and its subsidiaries and nominees and trustees for it and them are together able to appoint or remove directors of the company who are able to cast a majority of the votes which can be cast at board meetings of the potential subsidiary on all or substantially all matters.[16] The only difference between the definitions of a parent company or undertaking and a holding company under this head is that either a parent company or undertaking or any of its subsidiary undertakings may be a member of the potential subsidiary undertaking, whereas a holding company must itself be a member of the potential subsidiary.

Rights to appoint or remove directors which are exercisable only in certain circumstances, or rights to appoint directors which are normally exercisable but are temporarily incapable of being exercised, are left out of account or taken into account for the purposes of the present head of the definition in the same circumstances as voting rights at general meetings for the purpose of the first head.[17] Likewise, rights to appoint or remove directors which are held by way of security (eg for a loan made by or to the parent or undertaking holding company or another of its subsidiaries or by a nominee for it or any of them) are treated as exercisable by the person providing the security if, apart from the right to exercise them in order to preserve the value of the security, they can be exercised only on the instructions of that person, or in a situation where the loan was made as part of the lender's business activities, if the rights are exercisable only in the interests of that person.[18] Finally, a parent undertaking or holding company is not treated as holding a right to appoint or remove directors if it holds the right in a fiduciary capacity for another person.[19]

A parent undertaking or holding company or its subsidiary will be treated as having the right to appoint to a directorship of the potential subsidiary if a person's appointment to it follows necessarily from his appointment as a director of the parent undertaking or holding company or any of its subsidiaries (eg because the potential subsidiary's articles so provide), or if the directorship is held by the parent undertaking or holding company itself or by any of its other subsidiaries.[20] On the other hand, a power for a parent undertaking or holding company or any of its subsidiaries or a nominee or trustee for any of them to appoint or to remove a director of the potential subsidiary is left out of account if the power can be exercised only with the consent or concurrence of another person.[1]

The Companies Act 1985 in its original form made a company the holding

15 Companies Act 1985, s 258 (2) (*b*), (3) and (6) and Sch 10A, paras 3 (1), 7 (1) and 9 (1).
16 Ibid, s 736 (1)(*b*) and s 736A (3), (6) and (8).
17 Ibid, s 258 (6) and Sch 10A, para 5; ibid, s 736A (4) (see p 732, ante).
18 Ibid, s 258 (6) and Sch 10A, para 8; ibid, s 736A (7).
19 Ibid, s 258 (6) and Sch 10A, para 6; ibid, s 736A.
20 Ibid, s 258 (6) and Sch 10A, para 3 (2); ibid, s 736A (3) (*a*).
1 Ibid, s 258 (6) and Sch 10A, para 3 (3); ibid, s 736A (3) (*b*).

company of another if it was a member of the other company and it and its subsidiaries and its and their nominees together could appoint or remove a majority in number of the other company's directors.[2] The new provision substituted by the Companies Act 1989 concentrates on the voting power at board meetings which the directors appointed by the parent undertaking or holding company or its other subsidiaries may exercise, so that if by the potential subsidiary's articles of association differential voting rights are conferred on its various directors, a company which has power to appoint only a numerical minority of the potential subsidiary's directors will nevertheless be the other company's parent undertaking or holding company if the directors appointed by it can cast a majority of the votes at the other company's or undertaking's board meetings.

Controlling a majority of the voting rights by agreement

A company is the parent company or undertaking of another company or undertaking if it or any of its subsidiaries is a member of that company or undertaking (the potential subsidiary) and, pursuant to an agreement with other shareholders or members of the potential subsidiary, the parent company or undertaking alone controls a majority of the voting rights exercisable at its general meetings.[3] A company is the holding company of another company if it is a member of that company (the potential subsidiary) and by agreement with other shareholders or members of it, the holding company controls a majority of the voting rights exercisable at general meetings of the potential subsidiary.[4] The slight difference between the two definitions is that in order to be a parent company or undertaking under this head it is sufficient for a subsidiary undertaking of the parent to be a member of the potential subsidiary, whereas a holding company under this head must itself be a member of the company, the potential subsidiary. The agreement pursuant to which the parent undertaking or holding company controls the voting rights of other shareholders so giving it control over a majority of the voting rights, may take any form, and may therefore be an agreement by those shareholders to vote as the potential parent undertaking or holding company directs, or may be an irrevocable proxy appointment enabling it to exercise those voting rights as it thinks fit, or a trust arrangement by which those voting rights are to be exercised as it decides.

In applying the present qualification for a parent undertaking or a holding company, the same rules apply as under the preceding two heads as regards treating voting rights exercisable by subsidiary undertakings of the parent company or by subsidiaries of the holding company, or by nominees or trustees for any of them as though they were exercisable by the parent undertaking or holding company itself, and as regards the treatment of voting rights attached to shares held by way of security and voting rights which are exercisable only in certain circumstances or which are temporarily incapable of being exercised.[5] It is unclear whether a company is a parent undertaking or holding company of another company or undertaking (the potential subsidiary) under this head if it holds voting shares in the potential subsidiary which do not carry a majority of the voting rights exercisable at its general meetings, but by agreement it also controls the voting rights of other shareholders, so that by combining its own voting rights with those of the other shareholders, it does control a majority of the voting rights. It is submitted that in these circumstances there is a parent undertaking/subsidiary

---

2 Companies Act 1985, s 736 (1), (2) and (4) (as originally enacted).
3 Companies Act 1985, s 258 (2) and (3).
4 Ibid, s 736 (1) (c).
5 Ibid, s 258 (6) and Sch 10A, paras 5 to 9; ibid, s 736A (4) to (9).

undertaking or a holding company/subsidiary relationship, because the potential parent undertaking or holding company does control 'pursuant to an agreement with other shareholders or members [of the potential subsidiary] a majority of the voting rights in it'.[6] The word 'pursuant' should be interpreted as meaning 'in consequence of', and it is only in consequence of the agreement that the potential parent or holding company has control, its own shareholding in the potential subsidiary being insufficient for the purpose. It would seem to be immaterial whether the parent or holding company acquires its voting shares in the potential subsidiary before or after it enters into the agreement with other shareholders by which it controls their voting rights, because in either situation it is only because of the existence of the agreement that it has control of a majority of the voting rights at the subsidiary's general meetings.

Superior parent or holding company

If one company, A, is the parent undertaking or holding company of another company or undertaking, B, which is itself the parent or holding company of a third company or undertaking, C, the first company, A, is automatically the parent undertaking or holding company of the third, C, even though it is not a member of it, holds no shares in it, and has no direct control over the composition of its board of directors.[7] Similarly if C itself has a subsidiary or subsidiary undertaking, D, A is the parent or undertaking holding company of D, and this may be repeated indefinitely through further levels of subsidiaries and sub-subsidiaries of D.[7] Thus, a group of companies or undertakings all of which are subsidiaries of one superior holding company, or subsidiary undertakings of one parent company or undertaking, can be graphically represented as a pyramid with the superior holding company or parent company or undertaking at their apex. The existence of a superior parent undertaking or holding company does not take away the status of a parent or holding company from the intermediate parent or holding companies, however, so that there may be sub-groups within the main group.

The superimposing of superior parent undertakings or holding companies on intermediate parent or holding companies not only produces complicated relationships within the group of companies, but also may be used as a device for the majority shareholders of the superior parent undertaking or holding company to acquire or retain control of subsidiaries in the group, even though their investment in the group is small. This is usually the result of high capital gearing of intermediate parent or holding companies and their subsidiaries. For example, a superior parent or holding company may be formed with a capital of 100,000 £1 shares to acquire 50+ per cent of the voting ordinary capital (200,000 £1 shares) in an intermediate parent of holding company, which has also issued 600,000 £1 non-voting ordinary shares. The intermediate parent or holding company's capital (£800,000) is invested in acquiring 50+ per cent of the subsidiary's ordinary capital (1·6m £1 shares), and the subsidiary has also issued 1m £1 preference shares and £1m debenture stock. The result of this arrangement is that the holders of 50,001 £1 shares in the superior parent or holding company control the use to which £3·6m of share and loan capital is put.

The exercise or right to exercise a dominant influence

In addition to the four alternative qualifications for a company to be a parent undertaking or holding company, a company will be a parent undertaking for

6 Ibid, s 258 (2) (*d*); ibid, s 736 (1) (*c*).
7 Ibid, s 258 (5); ibid, s 736 (1).

accounting purposes (but not a holding company for other purposes) if either : (a) it has the right to exercise a dominant influence over another company or undertaking (its subsidiary undertaking) by virtue of the provisions of the subsidiary's memorandum or articles or by virtue of a control contract (ie a contract in writing authorised by the subsidiary's memorandum or articles under which the parent undertaking is entitled to give directions to the subsidiary in respect of its operating and financial policies) ;[8] or (b) the parent undertaking actually exercises a dominant influence over the potential subsidiary undertaking (presumably in respect of major business decisions taken by its directors) or the parent and the subsidiary undertakings (with or without other subsidiaries) are managed on a unified basis, and in either case the parent undertaking together with its other subsidiary undertakings and its and their nominees together have a participating interest in the potential subsidiary undertaking (ie an interest in its shares held on a long-term basis for the purpose of securing a contribution to the parent undertaking's activities by the exercise of control or influence arising from or related to that interest, it being presumed that a holding of 20 per cent or more of a subsidiary undertaking's issued share capital is a participating interest in it unless the contrary is shown).[9]

These alternative qualifications for parent undertaking/subsidiary undertaking relationships have been imported from German law by way of the Seventh Directive of the Council of Ministers of the European Communities of 13 June 1983 for the harmonisation of the law of the member states governing the consolidated accounts of groups of companies.[10] Control contracts are rarely entered into by British companies, and parent companies usually rely on their own shareholdings in their subsidiaries in order to control them or, at least, they rely on their power to appoint or remove the directors of subsidiaries for that purpose. It is uncertain what degree of influence a parent company must be entitled to exercise, or must actually exercise, over a subsidiary undertaking in order to have a dominating influence over it, and to what extent management of a group of undertakings must be unified for them to be managed on a unified basis. The German terms for these concepts, *beherrschender Einfluss* and *einheitliche Leitung*, cannot easily be translated into English terms with a precise legal meaning.

STATUTORY PROVISIONS APPLICABLE TO PARENT AND HOLDING COMPANIES AND THEIR SUBSIDIARIES

Although the subsidiaries of a parent undertaking or holding company are often managed as though they were merely departments of itself, in law they are distinct legal persons with the consequences indicated in Chapter 2. For certain purposes, however, the Companies Act 1985 treats a parent undertaking or holding company and its subsidiaries as though they were a single company, and for some other purposes the Act artificially treats a holding company as being a director of its subsidiaries although it has never been appointed to that position.

---

8 Ibid, s 258 (2) (*c*) and Sch 10A, para 4 (1) and (2).
9 Ibid, s 258 (4) and s 260 (1), (2), (4) and (5). An interest in shares of the potential subsidiary undertaking includes a right to convert another interest into such an interest (eg an interest in debentures or in loan securities which is by the terms of issue convertible into an interest in shares), or an option to acquire an interest in shares (eg debentures or loan securities with subscription warrants attached entitling the holder to subscribe for shares, or an option to purchase shares) (s 260 (3)).
10 Official Journal of the European Communities for 1983, No L193/1.

Subsidiary's membership of its holding company

A subsidiary or its nominee cannot be a member of its holding company, and any allotment or transfer of shares in the holding company to a subsidiary or its nominee is void.[11] However, a subsidiary which was a member of its holding company on 1 July 1948 may continue to be a member of it, and a company which became a subsidiary under the new provisions of the Companies Act 1989 in July 1990 when the new definitions of holding company and subsidiary were brought into operation, but was not a subsidiary under the previous law, may likewise continue its membership of its holding company, but in either case the subsidiary may not vote at general meetings of the holding company nor at meetings of any class of its members.[12] The same rule applies if the subsidiary's nominee was a member of its holding company on 1 July 1948 or in July 1990 (as the case may be).[12] In both these situations the subsidiary may take and retain allotments of further fully paid shares in its holding company which are allotted on a capitalisation of the holding company's reserves, whether revenue reserves, share premium account or other capital reserves, but the subsidiary cannot vote at meetings of the holding company in respect of such shares.[13] Additionally, a subsidiary may be a member of, or hold shares in, its holding company if it is a market maker, ie a company which holds itself out as willing to buy and sell securities at prices specified by it, and does so in compliance with the rules of an investment exchange in the United Kingdom which is recognised by the Securities and Investments Board under the Financial Services Act 1986, and the subsidiary is recognised as a market maker by that investment exchange.[14]

The restrictions mentioned above do not apply if the subsidiary or its nominee is concerned merely as a personal representative or trustee, and neither the holding company nor the subsidiary is beneficially interested in the shares, but a security interest in shares in the holding company for a loan made by the subsidiary in the ordinary course of its business is disregarded for this purpose.[15] A subsidiary is also treated as not having a beneficial interest for this purpose if either the holding company or the subsidiary has a residual interest in shares of its holding company held by it or its nominees as trustees of an employees' share scheme set up by the holding company or the subsidiary for the benefit of employees of itself or any other companies in the same group,[16] or as trustees of a pension scheme for the benefit of employees or former employees of the subsidiary (including directors).[17] This exception applies only until the subsidiary's residual interest vests in possession on the termination of the interests of all other persons under the scheme;[17] when that occurs the subsidiary may continue to be a member of its holding company,[18] but it may not vote in respect of the shares.[19] Additionally, neither a subsidiary nor its holding company is treated as having a beneficial interest in shares of its holding company comprised in an employees' share scheme or a pension scheme if the

---

11 Ibid, s 23 (1) and (7), substituted by Companies Act 1989, s 129 (1).
12 Companies Act 1985, s 23 (4) and (7).
13 Ibid, s 23 (6).
14 Ibid, s 23 (3).
15 Ibid, s 23 (2).
16 For employees' share schemes, see p 248, ante.
17 Companies Act 1985, s 23 (2) and Sch 2, para 1 (1) to (4).
18 If the shares in the holding company are held by a nominee of the subsidiary, it appears that he, too, may remain a member of it.
19 Companies Act 1985, Sch 2, para 2 (2).

interest is a charge or lien over, or a right of set-off against, any interest of another person under the scheme for the purpose of securing or enforcing a monetary obligation.[20]

If a company acquires shares in another company at a time when it is not a subsidiary of that other company, but it later becomes its subsidiary, it may continue to be a member of the holding company and retain the shares which it has already acquired, but it may not vote in respect of the shares it holds at meetings of the holding company or of any class of its members.[1] The subsidiary may not acquire further shares in its holding company after it becomes its subsidiary, but further fully paid shares may be allotted to it on the capitalisation of capital or revenue reserves of the holding company, and the subsidiary may retain those shares but not vote in respect of them at meetings of the holding company.[2]

Holding company as a director of its subsidiary

A holding company can obviously influence the way in which its subsidiary's affairs are managed, and this influence will amount to complete control when the subsidiary is wholly-owned and its directors are merely appointees of the holding company. But the possession of this power to influence or control the subsidiary does not make the holding company a director of the subsidiary for the purposes of the Companies Act 1985, although the holding company may be appointed a director of the subsidiary unless its articles prohibit the appointment of corporate directors. However, for the purpose of certain provisions of the Companies Act 1985, a holding company will be deemed to be a shadow director of its subsidiary and so it will be regulated by those provisions in the same way as a member of its board of directors, but this is so only if the board of the subsidiary is accustomed to act in accordance with the holding company's directions or instructions.[3] The provisions of the Companies Act 1985 in question are all those in connection with which shadow directors are subject to the same rules and requirements as directors,[4] with the exception of the rule that directors must have regard to the interests of its employees as well as its shareholders,[5] the requirement that contracts for the employment of directors by a company in any capacity for more than five years must be approved by a general meeting of the company,[6] the rule that certain acquisitions of assets by a company from a director or by a director from the company must be approved by a general meeting of the company,[7] and the rules and requirements in respect of loans, quasi-loans and credit transactions which are made or entered into by a company for the benefit of any of its directors or persons connected with them.[8] For the purpose of these excepted provisions a holding company will not be treated as a shadow director of its subsidiary, even though the subsidiary's directors are accustomed to act in accordance with the holding company's instructions or directions.

20 Ibid, s 23 (2) and Sch 2, para 3 (1) and (2).
 1 Ibid, s 23 (5).
 2 Ibid, s 23 (6).
 3 Companies Act 1985, s 741 (2) and (3).
 4 For a list of these provisions see p 531, ante.
 5 Companies Act 1985, s 309 (see p 584, ante).
 6 Ibid, s 319 (see p 540, ante).
 7 Ibid, ss 320 to 322 (see p 599, ante).
 8 Ibid, ss 330 to 346 (see p 565 et seq, ante).

GROUP ACCOUNTS AND GROUP UNDERTAKINGS' ACCOUNTS

The obligation to prepare group accounts

If at the end of its financial year a company is a parent company, it must prepare not only its own annual accounts, but also a set of group accounts (in the form of a consolidated profit and loss account and a consolidated balance sheet) showing the profit earned or loss suffered by the parent company and its subsidiary undertakings collectively during the financial year and their collective assets and liabilities at the end of that year.[9] If the group of undertakings is a small or medium-sized one, however, the parent company is under no obligation to prepare group accounts.[10] The group accounts must give a true and fair view of the state of affairs of the undertakings comprised in the group at the end of the parent company's financial year and the profit or loss of those undertakings for that year, so far as concerns members of the parent company.[11] The group accounts must be approved by the parent company's directors when its own annual accounts are approved,[12] and the group accounts must be reported on by the holding company's auditors.[13] Copies of the group accounts and the auditors' report on them must be circulated with copies of the parent company's own annual accounts to its members and debenture holders in advance of the general meeting at which its annual accounts are to be laid, and a copy of the group accounts must be laid before that meeting.[14] The copy of the parent company's annual accounts which is delivered to the Registrar of Companies in compliance with the company's obligation to do so must be accompanied by a copy of its group accounts.[15]

A parent company is exempted from the obligation to prepare group accounts for a financial year if it is itself a subsidiary undertaking and its immediate parent undertaking is established under the law of a Member State of the European Communities, and either (a) the company is a wholly-owned subsidiary of that parent undertaking, or (b) the parent undertaking and its other wholly-owned subsidiaries and its and their nominees together hold more than 50 per cent of the issued share capital of the company, and no notice requesting the company to prepare group accounts is served on the company within six months after the end of its financial year by other shareholders (whether members of it or not) holding in the aggregate more than half in nominal value of the remaining issued shares of the company, or shareholders holding at least 5 per cent of its total issued share capital.[16] The exemption from preparing group accounts is conferred on a parent company in these circumstances only if all the following conditions are fulfilled: (i) the company is included in audited consolidated accounts for a larger group of companies or undertakings which have been drawn up to a date during the company's financial year or to the end of that year in accordance with the law of a Member State of the European Community which conforms to the Seventh Directive of the Council of Ministers of the Community of 13 June 1983 on the consolidated accounts of groups of companies;[17] (ii) the notes to the annual accounts of the company state that it is exempt from the obligation to prepare

9 Ibid, s 227 (1) and (2) substituted by Companies Act 1989, s 5 (1).
10 Companies Act 1985, s 233 (1) and s 262 (1) (see p 708, ante).
11 Ibid, s 227 (3).
12 Ibid, s 233 (1).
13 Ibid, s 233 (1), s 235 (1) and (2) and s 262 (1).
14 Ibid, s 238 (1), s 241 (1) and s 262 (1).
15 Ibid, s 242 (1) and s 262 (1).
16 Ibid, s 228 (1).
17 See p 736, ante.

group accounts and give the name and country of incorporation of its parent undertaking which prepares such group accounts; (iii) the company delivers to the Registrar of Companies within the same period a copy of its own annual accounts, a copy of the group accounts prepared by its parent undertaking in which it is included, together with an English translation if the original group accounts are in a language other than English.[18] Furthermore, a company will not have exemption from preparing group accounts if any of its shares, stock, debentures or other loan securities, subscription warrants in respect of any of the foregoing securities or depositary certificates in respect of them are listed on a stock exchange in a Member State of the European Community.[1]

The purpose, form and contents of group accounts

The purpose of group accounts is to give members of the parent company a picture of the financial position and results of the parent company and its subsidiary undertakings taken together. The value of shareholdings in the parent company depends on the profits and the values of the net assets of its subsidiary undertakings, and so members of the parent company need to know more about the subsidiary undertakings' affairs than the value of the parent company's investments in them (which are usually shown in the parent company's own accounts at the cost of acquisition) and the amount which the parent company has received from its subsidiary undertakings by way of dividend. But group accounts cannot be used as the basis for conducting the parent company's own affairs, so that, for example, the group profit and loss account cannot be used as the basis for calculating the amount which the parent company may distribute to its own members as a dividend.[2] Group accounts are merely a means of presenting the group's financial position and results; they are not accounts in the normal sense of financial documents on which action may be taken.[3]

Undertakings included in group accounts

Group accounts must take the form of a consolidated balance sheet and a consolidated profit and loss account, dealing with the affairs of the parent company and its subsidiary undertakings as though the parent company and the subsidiary undertakings together were a single company.[4] All the subsidiary undertakings of a parent company must be included in the consolidated accounts which it prepares, but a subsidiary undertaking may be excluded: (a) if its inclusion is not material in order to give a true and fair view of the group's state of affairs at the end of the financial year and its profit or loss for the year; or (b) if severe long-term restrictions substantially hinder the exercise by the parent company of the rights over the assets or management of the subsidiary undertaking by virtue of which it is the subsidiary undertaking's parent company (eg contractual restrictions in an arrangement with

18 Companies Act 1985, s 228 (2).
1 Ibid, s 228 (4) and (6).
2 This has never been explicitly decided by an English court, but the Companies Act 1985, s 270 (2) and (3) provide that a company's distributable profits shall be ascertained from its last annual accounts, which in this context appears to exclude the group accounts for the group of which it is the parent company. There is American authority that group accounts cannot be used as the basis for the parent company's declarations of dividends (*Cintas v American Car and Foundry Co* 131 NJ Eq 419 (1942); affd 132 NJ Eq 460 (1942)).
3 But debenture and loan stock trust deeds often limit the amount which a parent company may borrow on the security of debentures or loan stock of the same series by reference to the net worth and net profits of the group of companies as shown by its latest group accounts.
4 Companies Act 1985, s 227 (2).

the subsidiary undertaking's creditors, government imposed restrictions); or (c) the information necessary for the inclusion of the subsidiary undertaking in the consolidated accounts cannot be obtained without incurring disproportionate expense or undue delay; or (d) the interest of the parent company in the subsidiary undertaking by virtue of which it is the subsidiary undertaking's parent company is held exclusively with a view to subsequent re-sale and the subsidiary undertaking has not previously been included in consolidated accounts prepared by the parent company.[5] A subsidiary undertaking must be excluded from consolidated accounts if its activities are so different from those of the undertakings included that its inclusion would be incompatible with the obligation to give a true and fair view of the financial position and results of the group, but this provision does not apply merely because some of the undertakings comprised in the group are industrial, some commercial and some provide services, nor merely because those undertakings carry on industrial or commercial activities involving different products or provide different services.[6]

Detailed contents of consolidated accounts

In addition to giving a true and fair view of the state of affairs and the profit or loss of the undertakings included in them, consolidated accounts must contain the detailed information and comply with the other particular requirements of the Companies Act 1985 (as amended),[7] but if compliance with those requirements would not be sufficient to give a true and fair view of the group's financial position and results, the necessary additional information must be given in the consolidated accounts and the notes to them,[8] and conversely, if in special circumstances compliance with those requirements would be inconsistent with the overriding requirement that the consolidated accounts must give a true and fair view, the consolidated accounts must depart from the particular requirements so far as is necessary to give a true and fair view.[9]

Consolidated accounts must comply so far as practicable with the requirements of the Companies Act 1985 (as amended) in respect of the form and contents of the accounts of a single company, and must incorporate the information contained in the individual annual accounts of the undertakings included in the consolidation.[10] If the financial year of a subsidiary undertaking included in the consolidated accounts does not coincide with the parent company's financial year, the consolidated accounts must be prepared from the annual accounts of the subsidiary undertaking for its financial year ending last before that of the parent company (provided that it ended not earlier than three months before the end of the parent company's financial year), or otherwise from interim accounts of the subsidiary undertaking which must be prepared and must relate to the period to the end of the parent company's financial year.[11] Where the assets and liabilities of the undertakings included in the consolidated accounts have been valued for the purpose of preparing their respective individual annual accounts in a manner different from that used for preparing the consolidated accounts, appropriate adjustments must be made in those valuations so that in the consolidated accounts

5 Ibid, s 229 (1) to (3).
6 Ibid, s 229 (4).
7 Ibid, s 227 (4).
8 Ibid, s 227 (5).
9 Ibid, s 227 (6).
10 Ibid, s 227 (4) and Sch 4A, para 1 (1) and para 2 (1), inserted by Companies Act 1989, s 5 (2) and Sch 2.
11 Companies Act 1985, Sch 4A, para 2 (2).

all the assets and liabilities of the undertakings included in the consolidation are valued in accordance with the same rules, but the directors of the parent company may depart from this requirement in special circumstances, and if they do so, those circumstances and the reasons for the departure must be stated in a note to the consolidated accounts.[12]

In consolidated accounts, debts, claims and liabilities between undertakings included in the consolidation must be eliminated.[13] Likewise profits and losses resulting from transactions between undertakings comprised in the consolidation must be eliminated if they are included in the book or accounting value of assets in the consolidated accounts (ie the cost of acquiring the assets from another group undertaking incurred by the acquiring group undertaking), but the elimination of the profit or loss may be effected in proportion to the group's interest in the issued share capital of the acquiring and disposing group undertakings (ie proportionately to the fraction of the parent company's direct or indirect shareholdings in those undertakings).[14]

Acquisition and merger methods of accounting

Where an undertaking has become a subsidiary undertaking of a parent company, the consolidated accounts prepared by the parent company must show the identifiable assets and liabilities of the acquired undertaking (ie its assets and liabilities which are capable of being disposed of or charged without disposing of a business of the subsidiary)[15] at their fair value at the date when the undertaking became a subsidiary undertaking of the parent company;[16] there must then be set off against the acquisition cost of the shares of the undertaking acquired by the parent company or its other subsidiary undertaking or by nominees for any of them[17] the interest of the parent company and its other subsidiary undertakings in the capital and reserves of the acquired undertaking (after adjusting them to take account of the fair value of the acquired undertaking's identifiable assets and liabilities) and the difference, if positive, must be treated as group goodwill in the consolidated accounts, and if negative, as a negative consolidation difference (ie an amount which reduces the amount of group reserves in the consolidated accounts (the acquisition method of accounting).[18] The result of applying these rules is usually that the group goodwill in the consolidated accounts is increased by the difference between the price paid for the acquisition of the subsidiary undertaking (in cash or by an issue of shares or loan securities) and the fair value of the subsidiary undertaking's tangible and saleable assets less the total of its liabilities. In connection with the acquisition of a subsidiary undertaking, the income and expenditure of the undertaking which is brought into the consolidated balance

---

12 Ibid, Sch 4A, para 3 (1) and (2).
13 Ibid, Sch 4A, para 6 (1).
14 Ibid, Sch 4A, para 6 (2) and (3).
15 Non-identifiable assets comprise goodwill and intellectual property rights (patents, trade marks, service marks and designs) which by their nature are only saleable with the business in connection with which they are used or exist.
16 The fair value of identifiable assets at the date of acquisition of the subsidiary means their realisable value or their value to the parent company, and this will usually be taken to be the value it put upon them for the purpose of the acquisition.
17 The acquisition cost means the amount of any cash consideration paid to acquire shares in the subsidiary undertaking plus the fair value of any other consideration given for those shares. 'Other consideration' will usually be the issue of shares in the parent company or one of its other subsidiary undertakings, and will normally be taken as equal to the nominal value of the shares issued plus any share or issue premium in respect of them which is credited to the issuing company's share premium account.
18 Companies Act 1985, Sch 4A, para 7, 8 and 9 (1), (2), (4) and (5).

sheet and profit and loss account must be confined to income earned or expenditure incurred by it since the acquisition,[19] with the result that the fair value of the subsidiary undertaking's assets brought into the consolidated balance sheet will be increased or reduced by the appropriate fraction of its net income or expenditure for its financial year current at the date of the acquisition which is attributable to the period before the acquisition.

If certain conditions are fulfilled, a parent company may reflect the acquisition of a subsidiary undertaking in the consolidated accounts prepared by it in an alternative manner (the merger method of accounting). The conditions which must be fulfilled for this option to be available are that: (i) at least 90 per cent of the issued equity share capital[20] of the subsidiary undertaking must be held by or on behalf of the parent company or its other subsidiaries; (ii) the holding of that percentage must be in consequence of an arrangement (including a takeover offer) which provided for the issue of equity shares by the parent company or by one or more of its other subsidiary undertakings; (iii) the fair value of any consideration given by the parent company and its other subsidiary undertakings involved in the transaction (other than the issue of equity shares) did not exceed 10 per cent of the nominal value of the equity shares issued by it or them as consideration; and (iv) the use of the merger method of accounting accords with generally accepted accounting principles or practice.[1]

If the conditions for employing the merger method of accounting are satisfied, the assets and liabilities of the undertaking brought into the parent company's group may be shown in the consolidated accounts prepared by it at the amounts at which they stand in the acquired undertaking's accounts at the date of the acquisition (in respect of assets, that will normally be their acquisition cost less depreciation); there must then be set off against the nominal value of the shares issued by the parent company or any of its other subsidiary undertakings as consideration for the acquisition of shares in the acquired undertaking, plus any share premiums credited in respect of those shares to the parent company's share premium account and the fair value of any other consideration given for the acquisition of the shares of the acquired undertaking, the nominal value of the issued share capital of that undertaking held or acquired by the parent company and its subsidiary undertakings, and the difference must be deducted from group's reserves in the consolidated balance sheet, or added to those reserves if the issued share capital so held or acquired exceeded the nominal value and relevant share premiums of the shares issued in exchange plus any other consideration given for the acquisition.[2] The share premiums in respect of shares issued as consideration for the acquisition will only be taken into account in making this calculation insofar as they are required to be credited to the issuing company's share premium account, and so any such premiums (ie the difference between the nominal and market values of those shares at the date of the acquisition) will not be taken into account to the extent that merger relief and group reconstruction relief is available in relation to them under the rules governing share premium account.[3] The income and expenditure of the acquired subsidiary undertaking for the whole of the financial year in which the acquisition takes place must be brought into the consolidated balance sheet and profit and loss account for the group, and not

19 Ibid, Sch 4A, para 9 (3).
20 Equity shares for this purpose are shares which carry an unrestricted right to participate in distributions of the profits and in the assets of the issuing undertaking on its liquidation.
1 Companies Act 1985, Sch 4A, para 10 (1) and (2).
2 Ibid, Sch 4, para 11 (1), (2), (5) and (6).
3 Ibid, ss 131 and 132 (see pp 163 to 166, ante) and Sch 4A, para 11 (5) and (7).

merely the fraction of those amounts which are attributable to the part of the financial year following the acquisition.[4]

Acquisition of a group of undertakings

If a parent company acquires an existing group of undertakings as its subsidiaries, the parent company's consolidated accounts must be drawn up following the acquisition as though it were the acquisition of the shares of the parent company of the existing group,[5] and this is so whether the acquisition is effected by the existing shares of that parent company being transferred by their holders to the acquiring company or by them being cancelled, or by the shares held by that parent company in all its subsidiaries being transferred directly to the acquiring company or cancelled.

Particulars of acquisitions and disposals

Where during a financial year a parent company or any of its subsidiary undertakings has acquired its first or additional subsidiary undertakings, a note to the consolidated accounts must state the names of each acquired undertaking and whether the acquisition or merger method of accounting has been used in incorporating the assets and liabilities of the acquired undertaking and adjusting group goodwill or group reserves in the consolidated accounts.[6] Also, if an acquisition significantly affects the figures shown in the consolidated accounts, the notes to those accounts must state the composition and fair value of the consideration given for the acquisition by the parent company and its other subsidiary undertakings and the profit or loss of the acquired undertaking (or, as the case may be, the acquired parent undertaking in the case of the acquisition of a group of undertakings) from the beginning of its financial year up to the date of the acquisition and for its last preceding financial year, together with the date on which those financial years commenced.[7]

If the acquisition method of accounting has been used, the notes to the accounts must state the book values immediately before the acquisition and the fair values at the date of the acquisition of each class of the assets and liabilities of the acquired undertaking or acquired group and the amount of goodwill or negative consolidation difference resulting from the acquisition, together with an explanation of any significant adjustments of accounting figures which have been made.[8] If the merger method of accounting has been used, an explanation must be given in the notes to the accounts of significant adjustments made to the amount of assets or liabilities of the acquired undertaking or acquired group, together with a statement of any resulting adjustment to the group reserves in the consolidated balance sheet.[9] There must additionally be stated in the notes to the consolidated accounts the cumulative amount of goodwill resulting from acquisitions of subsidiary undertakings in the financial year and earlier years which has been written off.[10]

If during a financial year there has been a disposal of a subsidiary undertaking or group of subsidiary undertakings by the parent company or of its other

4 Ibid, Sch 4A, para 11 (3).
5 Ibid, Sch 4A, para 12.
6 Ibid, Sch 4A, para 13 (1) and (2).
7 Ibid, Sch 4A, para 13 (2) to (4).
8 Ibid, Sch 4A, para 13 (5).
9 Ibid, Sch 4A, para 13 (6).
10 Ibid, Sch 4A, para 14 (1).

subsidiary undertakings, there must be shown in a note to the consolidated accounts the name of the undertaking or the parent undertaking of the group of undertakings so disposed of and the extent to which the profit or loss shown in the consolidated profit and loss account of the group is attributable to the profit or loss of that undertaking or group;[11] the cumulative amount of goodwill resulting from acquisitions which has been written off as stated in the notes to the consolidated accounts must be adjusted by deducting the amount of goodwill written off in respect of subsidiary undertakings or groups which have been disposed of.[10]

The information required to be included in the notes to the consolidated accounts by the provisions dealt with in the three preceding paragraphs need not be included in respect of a subsidiary undertaking which is established under the law of a country outside the United Kingdom, or which carries on business outside the United Kingdom, if in the opinion of the directors of the parent company the disclosure of that information would be seriously prejudicial to the business of that undertaking or to the business of the parent company or any of its other subsidiary undertakings and the Secretary of State consents to the omission of that information.[12]

Minority interests

Minority interests in subsidiary undertakings must be included in consolidated accounts.[13] Because the format of consolidated accounts must follow the format of the balance sheet and profit and loss account of an individual company,[13] appropriate modifications are made to the standard formats to permit the introduction in a consolidated balance sheet of an entry showing the amount of capital and reserves of the group which are attributable to shareholders of the consolidated subsidiaries other than the parent company and its subsidiary undertakings and its and their nominees, and in a consolidated profit and loss account to permit the introduction of two entries showing respectively the amount of the profit or loss of the group from ordinary activities of group undertakings which are attributable to minority shareholders and the amount of such profit or loss from extraordinary activities which is attributable to them.[14]

Excluded subsidiaries and associated undertakings

The total omission of the amount of the group's interests in subsidiary undertakings excluded from the consolidated accounts because their activities are so different from those of the undertakings which are included that their inclusion would be incompatible with the obligation to give a true and fair view of the group's position and results. Consequently, the amount of such interests, and the amount of profit or loss attributable to them, must be shown in the consolidated balance sheet and the consolidated profit and loss account respectively by the equity method of accounting, that is (by taking the fraction of the subsidiary's capital and reserves (after deducting issued capital in respect of classes of shares not held by the parent company and its subsidiaries) which is held by and on behalf of the parent company and its other subsidiary undertakings or is attributable to them, and by taking the fraction of the subsidiary's profit or loss (after deducting dividends payable in respect of shares of the subsidiary undertaking of a class not held by the parent

11 Ibid, Sch 4A, para 14 (2) and para 15.
12 Ibid, Sch 4A, para 16.
13 Ibid, Sch 4A, para 1 (1).
14 Ibid, Sch 4A, para 17.

company and its other subsidiary undertakings) which is attributable to shares held by or on behalf of the parent company and its other subsidiary undertakings).[15]

If an undertaking included in consolidated accounts has a participating interest in one or more other undertakings which are not subsidiary undertakings of the parent company of the group, and the group undertaking exercises a significant influence over the other undertakings' operating and financial policy (associated undertakings), the interest in the associated undertakings must be included in the consolidated accounts prepared by the parent company and shown separately from other participating interests held by it or its subsidiary undertakings, and likewise the income from such participating interests in associated undertakings must be shown separately from income from other participating interests.[16] Participating interests in associated undertakings are presumed to exist when group undertakings hold 20 per cent or more of the voting rights exercisable on all, or substantially all, matters at general meetings of the other undertakings.[17] The participating interests of group undertakings in associated undertakings and the income from them (ie the appropriate fraction of the profits or losses of those undertakings) must be shown by the equity method of accounting.[18]

Supplemental information about parent undertakings, subsidiaries and associated undertakings

A parent company must in the notes to its annual accounts give the name and country of incorporation of each of its subsidiary undertakings, and must state the proportion of each class of the subsidiary undertaking's shares held by itself and its nominees and by its other subsidiary undertakings and their nominees.[19] If the parent company has numerous subsidiary undertakings, so that the information to be given would be of excessive length, the company may confine the particulars in its accounts to those of its subsidiary undertakings whose results or financial position principally affected the figures shown in the parent company's annual accounts and to those of subsidiary undertakings excluded from consolidation in the group's consolidated accounts; but if this is done, the notes to the parent company's annual accounts must indicate that only those subsidiary undertakings have been included, and it must annex the particulars which have been omitted from its accounts to its next annual return.[20] If a parent company has a subsidiary undertaking incorporated or carrying on business in a country outside the United Kingdom, it need not give particulars of the subsidiary undertaking or of its holding in it in the notes to either its annual accounts if its directors consider that such disclosure would be harmful to the business of any undertaking in the group and the Secretary of State for Trade and Industry consents to the omission, but the fact that those particulars are omitted must be stated.[1]

A subsidiary (including an intermediate parent company) must in a note to its annual accounts disclose the name and country of incorporation of its ultimate parent company, but exemption from this requirement can be given by the

---

15 Ibid, Sch 4A, para 18.
16 Ibid, Sch 4A, para 20 (1) and para 21.
17 Ibid, Sch 4A, para 20 (2).
18 Ibid, Sch 4A, para 22 (1).
19 Ibid, s 231 (1) and Sch 5, paras 1, 2, 6, 15 and 16, substituted by Companies Act 1989, s 6 (1) and Sch 3.
20 Companies Act 1985, s 231 (5) and (6). This applies also to information about associated undertakings and undertakings in which the parent company and its subsidiary undertakings and its and their nominees together have significant shareholdings under the provisions dealt with below.
 1 Companies Act 1985, s 231 (3) and (4). This applies also to information about associated undertakings and undertakings in which the group has significant shareholdings.

Secretary of State in circumstances similar to those in which a holding company may be exempted from identifying an overseas subsidiary.[2]

A parent company must in the notes to its annual accounts state the aggregate amount of the capital and reserves of each of its subsidiary undertakings at the end of the financial year to which the accounts relate and the profit or loss of each subsidiary undertaking for that financial year, but this information need not be given if the parent company holds directly or indirectly through its other subsidiaries and nominees for it or them less than 50 per cent of the subsidiary undertaking's issued share capital, nor if the subsidiary undertaking is included in the consolidated accounts of the parent company.[3] If the parent company does not prepare consolidated accounts for the group, the notes to the parent company's annual accounts must also state the aggregate amount of the total investment of the parent company in its subsidiary undertakings by way of the equity method of valuation; this is not necessary, however, if the directors state in the notes that the aggregate value of the parent company's shareholdings in its subsidiary undertakings plus amounts owing to it from them is not less than the amount at which those assets are stated or included in the parent company's balance sheet.[4] Finally, the notes to the parent company's annual accounts must state the number, description and amount of the shares and debentures of the parent company which are held by or on behalf of its subsidiary undertakings, but shares or debentures held by subsidiary undertakings as trustees or personal representatives are excluded unless the parent company or any of its subsidiary undertakings has a beneficial interest in them otherwise than as security for a loan.[5]

A parent company which prepares consolidated accounts must in the notes to its annual accounts give certain additional information in respect of associated undertakings of the group over whose operating and financial policy the parent company and its subsidiary undertakings together exercise a significant influence,[6] where the assets and liabilities and profits or losses of the associated undertakings are included in the group's consolidated accounts.[3] This information comprises the name of each such associated undertaking, its country of incorporation and the fraction of each class of the associated undertaking's issued share capital which is held by the parent company and by other undertakings in the group.[7]

Every parent company must in a note to its annual accounts give the name and country of incorporation of every other undertaking (not being a subsidiary or an associated undertaking included in the parent's consolidated accounts for the group) in which the parent company and its subsidiaries and nominees for it and them together have a significant holding, that is, one-tenth or more of the issued shares of any class or shares exceeding in value one-tenth of the assets of the parent company, and the accounts must also give particulars of each class of shares so held in the other company, including the proportion they represent of the shares of that class which have been issued.[8] If the significant holding of a parent company and its other subsidiary undertakings in another undertaking amounts to 20 per cent or more of the issued share capital of that undertaking, the notes to the parent

2 Companies Act 1985, s 231 (3) and Sch 5, paras 12 and 31.
3 Ibid, Sch 5, paras 3 and 17.
4 Ibid, Sch 5, para 5 (2).
5 Ibid, Sch 5, paras 6 and 20.
6 This is presumed if the parent company and its subsidiary undertakings together hold 20 per cent or more of the voting rights at general meetings of the associated undertakings (Companies Act 1985, Sch 4A, para 20 (1) and (2) and Sch 5, para 22 (6), inserted by Companies Act 1989, s 5 (2) and s 6 (2)).
7 Companies Act 1985, Sch 5, para 22 (1) to (5).
8 Ibid, Sch 5, paras 7, 8, 23 and 24.

company's accounts must also state the total amount of the capital and reserves of that undertaking at the end of its most recent financial year and its profit or loss for that year, but this information is not required if it is not material.[9]

If a parent company has during a financial year issued shares at a premium in consideration of the issue, transfer or cancellation of shares in another company or body corporate and it is exempted by the exception for mergers from having to credit to its share premium account any excess in the value of the shares in the other company or body corporate over the nominal or paid up value of the shares issued by it in exchange,[10] the notes to its annual accounts for that year must state the name of the other company or body corporate, the number, nominal value and class or classes of shares issued by the parent company as such consideration, the accounting treatment given in the parent company's own accounts and the consolidated accounts which it prepares (if any) to the issue, transfer or cancellation of the shares in the other company or body corporate and particulars of the extent to which and the manner in which the profit or loss of the parent company and its subsidiary undertakings shown in the consolidated profit and loss account for the year have been affected by the profit or loss of the other company or body corporate which arose before the issue of shares by the parent company in exchange took place.[11]

THE GENERAL LAW GOVERNING GROUPS OF COMPANIES

English law has not developed a distinct body of law governing the relationships between parent or holding companies and subsidiaries, and between companies which have substantial shareholdings in other companies not conferring legal powers of control over them.[12] Instead, the ordinary rules of company law are applied to such companies and to transactions between them and to transactions by them with other persons as though no special relationship existed. Consequently, the assets of such companies are treated as owned by them, both legally and beneficially, as distinct legal entities, and except where the circumstances enable the court to discover an agency or trustees relationship between them,[13] a parent or holding company is not treated as the owner of any of its subsidiaries' assets. Conversely, the liabilities of companies which are members of the same group are those of the individual companies which incur them; there is no common group liability imposed by law for the obligations of individual members of the group. A parent or holding company is, therefore, responsible for the debts and obligations of its subsidiaries only if it has guaranteed them, or if it has been the sole member of a subsidiary for more than six months, or if it has participated in the mismanagement of a subsidiary with the intention of defrauding its creditors, or if it is ordered to pay a contribution equal to the whole or part of a subsidiary's debts in its liquidation because the parent company has participated in the management of the subsidiary's affairs with intent to defraud its creditors, or the creditors of another person, or for any other fraudulent purpose, or because the parent

9 Ibid, Sch 5, paras 9 and 25.
10 Ibid, s 130 (1) and s 131 (1) to (7) (see p 163, ante).
11 Ibid, Sch 5, paras 10 and 29.
12 In this respect English law is less advanced than the German legislation governing public companies, the *Aktiengesetz* of 1965, §§15–21 and §§291–338 of which contain a distinct body of rules governing groups of companies.
13 See p 48, ante.

company, as a shadow director of its subsidiary, has been guilty of wrongful trading.[14]

In the same way the rights and obligations of other persons are not affected by the fact that the company with which they deal is a member of a group. The directors of a parent or holding company owe no duties as such to its subsidiaries,[15] and the directors of a subsidiary owe no duties as such to its holding company,[16] and cannot justify transactions entered into by them to the detriment of the subsidiary by showing that its parent company has benefited.[17] In fact, if a subsidiary company enters into a transaction, not for the purpose of promoting its own business or achieving its own objects, but in order to assist its parent or holding company or a fellow subsidiary (eg by guaranteeing or securing the other company's debts), the transaction may be a misuse of the powers of its directors and therefore not binding on the company if the other party was aware of the purpose intended by the directors.[18] Similarly, no special rights or obligations attach to a person who stands in a legal relationship to a subsidiary (eg as a director of it) when he enters into a transaction with its parent company,[16] and in the converse situation this is equally true.[15]

The statutory exceptions to the consequences of the separate legal personalities of parent or holding companies and subsidiaries and of companies which are associated by shareholdings of one in another are few in number,[19] and few further exceptions have been made by the courts in cases not covered by statute. The concept of the group of companies has as yet little significance in English law, except as a means of extending certain prohibitions imposed on companies[20] and their directors[1] and as a framework for extended disclosure of information in parent companies' annual accounts and directors' reports.

---

14 Companies Act 1985, s 24 (see p 39, ante); Insolvency Act 1986, s 213 (1) and (2) and s 214 (1), (2) and (7) (see pp 41 and 44, ante).
15 *Lindgren v L & P Estates Co Ltd* [1968] Ch 572 at 595 and 604, [1968] 1 All ER 917 at 922 and 928.
16 *Bell v Lever Bros Ltd* [1932] AC 161 at 228.
17 *Charterbridge Corpn Ltd v Lloyds Bank Ltd* [1970] Ch 62, [1969] 2 All ER 1185.
18 *Rolled Steel Products (Holdings) Ltd v British Steel Corpn* [1982] Ch 478, [1982] 3 All ER 1057; affd [1986] Ch 246, [1985] 3 All ER 52, [1984] BCLC 466.
19 Companies Act 1985, s 23 (1) and s 24 (1); Insolvency Act 1986, ss 213 and 214.
20 Eg Companies Act 1985, s 151 (1) and (2) (see p 387, ante).
1 Eg ibid, s 330 (2) and (3) (see p 565, ante).

PART IV

Private companies

CHAPTER 19

Private companies limited by shares

A private company is defined by the Companies Act 1985 as a company which is not a public company.[1] It may be a private company limited by shares (the commonest kind of private company),[2] or a company limited by guarantee or an unlimited company.[3] The two last kinds of company are dealt with in the next following chapter, and this chapter is concerned only with the private company limited by shares.

THE CHARACTER OF PRIVATE COMPANIES

The popular conception of a private company is of a small concern with few shareholders, most of whom are actively engaged in managing the company's business, and who regard their shares not merely as an investment but as the source of their livelihood. In other words, a private company is often visualised simply as an incorporated partnership. On the whole, in relation to small private companies this picture is an accurate one. Private companies are far more numerous than public ones, but their total paid up share capital is little more than half of that of public companies. This does not mean that all private companies have small share capitals and possess assets of only a small value, however. There is no legal limit on the amount of share capital which a private company may issue, and some of them have a larger issued capital than many public companies. The choice whether a company shall be a public or private one is determined only in part by the amount of capital which it needs to raise. Far more important is the source from which the capital is to come. If it can be raised from a small group of persons, the company will be a private one, but if it will be necessary to invite the public to subscribe for the company's securities, or to place them with institutional investors who wish to be able to sell them on the market, or to introduce or place them on the Stock Exchange, it will have to be a public company.

A private company was defined by the Companies Act 1948 solely by reference to the contents of its articles of association. A company was a private one if its articles (a) restricted the right to transfer its shares; and (b) with certain exceptions, limited the number of its members to 50; and (c) prohibited the company from issuing any invitation to the public to subscribe for its shares or debentures.[4] The Companies Act 1980 repealed this requirement,[5] and so it is no longer necessary for a private company's articles to contain any of these restrictions, and the penalties for not observing them when they are still contained in a company's

---

1 Companies Act 1985, s 1 (3).
2 At the end of 1989 there were 9,800 public companies registered in Great Britain, and 968,000 private companies (Department of Trade and Industry: *Companies in 1988–89*).
3 Companies Act 1985, s 1 (2).
4 Companies Act 1948, s 28 (1).
5 Companies Act 1980, s 88 (2) and Sch 4, repealing Companies Act 1948, ss 28 to 30.

articles have been abolished.[5] Nevertheless, there are many private companies in existence which were incorporated under the Companies Act 1948, or earlier Companies Acts, and whose articles still contain such restrictions. Moreover, the articles of private companies limited by shares which have been formed since the Companies Act 1980 came into operation[6] usually contain one or more of the restrictions in order to keep the control of the company in the hands of a small number of persons and to ensure that shares are not transferred to strangers who are unacceptable to them. The commonest restrictions in the articles of more recently formed private companies are on the transferability of shares, but sometimes there is also a limitation on the number of members (not necessarily 50 or less) or an implicit limitation by membership being confined to persons who have certain qualifications (eg being or having been directors of the company or being employed by it). It is, of course, now unnecessary for the articles of a private company limited by shares to prohibit it from inviting the public to subscribe for its shares or debentures or other loan securities, because such a prohibition is now imposed by law on all private companies.[7]

The effect of restrictions in a private company's articles which were formerly needed to qualify it as a private company will now be considered in detail, because they are still important in practice and are also met with in the articles of private companies incorporated since the restrictions ceased to be obligatory. The Companies Act 1985 imposes no special sanctions for the observation of such restrictions in the articles of private companies, and so they are enforceable by the company against members and as between members themselves in the same way as other provisions of the articles.[8]

Restrictions on transfers of shares

The Companies Act 1948 required some restriction on the transfer of a private company's shares to be inserted in its articles, but did not require any particular form of restriction or prescribe the maximum extent or scope of the restriction required, and so the restriction imposed could be as severe or as slight as the framers of the articles wished.[9] In practice two common forms of restriction were imposed, either separately or together, by the articles of private companies formed under the Companies Act 1948 or any of the earlier Companies Acts, and such restrictions are often also imposed by the articles of private companies formed since the repeal of the statutory restrictions on private companies took effect.[6]

Powers for directors to refuse to register transfers

The first alternative or cumulative restriction often imposed on transfer of shares in a private company is a provision giving the directors power to refuse to register a transfer of shares either for a specific reason, for example, because they do not approve of the transferee,[10] or for any reason whatsoever, for example, when they are empowered to refuse registration in their absolute discretion and without

6 On 22 December 1980 (Companies Act 1980, s 90 (3) and Companies Act 1980 (Commencement No 2) Order 1980 (SI 1980/1785), para 2).
7 Companies Act 1985, s 81 (1). This provision will be replaced by Financial Services Act 1986, s 170 (1) and (2), as amended by Companies Act 1989, s 199, when Part V of the Financial Services Act 1986 is brought into force by an order made by the Secretary of State for Trade and Industry.
8 Companies Act 1985, s 14 (1) (see p 52, ante).
9 Companies Act 1948, s 28 (1) (a).
10 Table A, art 24, imposes such a restriction on the partly paid shares of any company, whether public or private.

assigning any reason therefor.[11] Shares are presumed to be freely transferable,[12] and restrictions on their transfer are construed strictly, and so when a restriction is capable of two meanings, the less restrictive interpretation will be adopted by the court.[13] Consequently, it has been held that restrictions on the right of a member to transfer his shares do not apply to a personal representative or trustee in bankruptcy of a deceased or bankrupt member who seeks to be registered as the holder of shares which have vested in him,[14] unless the articles expressly apply the restrictions on transfers to such cases as well.[15] Furthermore, unless the articles provide otherwise, restrictions on the right to transfer shares imposed by the articles apply only if the shares are registered in the company's register of members. Consequently, such restrictions do not necessarily apply to the renunciation of letters of allotment issued by the company.[16] However, unless the letter of allotment merely states that the company will issue shares at a future date to the allottee or his renouncee, the letter of allotment embodies a title to shares which already exist, and the issue of such a letter which does not restrict its transfer or renunciation would involve a breach of any provision in the articles that all shares in the company shall be subject to restrictions on transfer, whether the shares are registered in the company's register of members or not.

Where directors have power to refuse to register a transfer of shares, they must exercise the power by passing a resolution at a board meeting,[17] and so if they fail to pass such a resolution because their votes are equally divided, the transferee is entitled to be registered.[18] Furthermore, the power of refusal must be exercised within a reasonable time after the transfer is submitted for registration; this will usually be before the conclusion of the next board meeting, but in any case the power must be exercised before the expiration of the statutory period of two months[19] within which the company is required to notify the transferee if his transfer is not to be registered.[20] If it is impossible for the board to act within the appropriate time, the period for reaching a decision will be extended until it is able to act so, but if the only impediment is that there are too few directors in office to form a quorum, and they have power by the articles to appoint additional directors or to fill casual vacancies, no extension of time will be allowed, because they may overcome the impediment themselves.[20] If the board gives no decision on the application for registration of the transfer of shares within the two months or the extended period allowed, the transferor or transferee may obtain an order of the court requiring the company to register the transfer.[20]

The directors must exercise their power to refuse to register a transfer of shares, like all their other powers, in good faith and for the benefit of the company, and not for some extraneous purpose. Consequently, if they exercise the power in order to prevent the transferor from selling his shares at all,[1] or because of their hostility

---

11 The Companies Act 1948, Table A, Part II, para 3, imposed such a restriction on the shares of a private company, and it may still apply to a private company incorporated before 22 December 1980.
12 *Re Smith Knight & Co, Weston's Case* (1868) 4 Ch App 20.
13 *Delavenne v Broadhurst* [1931] 1 Ch 234; *Greenhalgh v Mallard* [1943] 2 All ER 234.
14 *Re Bentham Mills Spinning Co* (1879) 11 ChD 900.
15 Table A, art 30, so provides. The article applies to both public and private companies.
16 *Re Pool Shipping Co Ltd* [1920] 1 Ch 251; *Systems Control plc v Munro Corporate plc* [1990] 6 BCC 386, at 388, per Hoffmann J.
17 *Moodie v W & J Shepherd (Bookbinders) Ltd* [1949] 2 All ER 1044.
18 *Re Hackney Pavilion Ltd* [1924] 1 Ch 276; *Shepherd's Trustees v Shepherd* 1950 SC (HL) 60. In these cases the articles did not give a casting vote to the chairman at the board meeting.
19 Companies Act 1985, s 183 (5) (see p 343, ante).
20 *Re Swaledale Cleaners Ltd* [1968] 3 All ER 619, [1968] 1 WLR 1710.
1 *Robinson v Chartered Bank of India* (1865) LR 1 Eq 32.

toward him,[2] or because the directors wish to gain control of the company themselves and they consider that the acquisition of the shares by the transferee may prevent them from doing so,[3] the court will order the company to register the transfer. Conversely, if the directors approve a transfer of their own shares in order to escape liability for unpaid capital which will inevitably have to be called up to pay the company's existing debts,[4] or if they approve a transfer of a member's shares to themselves when they have bought the shares in order to stifle an inquiry into irregularities in the management of the company,[5] their approval is inoperative, and the court will order the transferor's name to be restored to the register of members, unless the members of the company in general meeting resolve that the transfer shall be registered, or that a registration of the transfer already effected shall remain undisturbed.[6] But the court will only restore a transferor to the register when he has connived with the directors, or has otherwise been a party to the improper approval of the transfer of his shares.[7] This was so in the case cited above where the directors approved a transfer of shares to themselves in order to prevent an inquiry into irregularities,[5] and also in another case[8] where the transferor paid the directors the amount of money which they demanded as the price of their approval, and the fact that the directors undertook to apply the money toward meeting the company's debts made no difference. If a transferor procures the directors' approval of a transfer of his shares by a misrepresentation made to them, the company may cancel the registration of the transfer, and restore the transferor's name to the register.[9]

The directors must not only use their power to refuse to register transfers in the interests of the company, but must also exercise it specifically only on one or more of the grounds for refusing registration which are set out in the articles, unless the articles permit them to refuse registration for any reason they think fit. Thus, if the articles empower the directors to refuse registration if they do not approve of the transfer or of the transferee, they may do so only if they have some personal objection to the transferee, and it is not sufficient that they consider that the number of shares transferred to him is too small,[10] or that shares should not be transferred to persons who do not belong to the family of the founder of the company,[11] or that the transferee is a nominee for the transferor, and the purpose of the transfer is to increase the transferor's voting power unfairly at general meetings,[12] or that the transferee is a nominee for a third person of whom they disapprove.[13] On the other hand, if the articles permit the directors to reject transfers for any reason whatsoever, their discretion is limited only by the rule that they must act in what

---

2 *Re Ceylon Land and Produce Co Ltd, ex p Anderson* (1891) 7 TLR 692.
3 *Tett v Phoenix Property and Investment Co Ltd* [1984] BCLC 599, revsd on other grounds, [1986] BCLC 149, 2 BCC 140.
4 *Re Accidental Death Insurance Co, Allin's Case* (1873) LR 16 Eq 449.
5 *Re Mitre Assurance Co, Eyre's Case* (1862) 31 Beav 177.
6 *Bamford v Bamford* [1870] Ch 212, [1969] 1 All ER 969.
7 *Re Discoverers Finance Corpn Ltd, Lindlar's Case* [1910] 1 Ch 207; affd [1910] 1 Ch 312.
8 *Re Cameron's Coalbrook Steam Coal and Swansea and Lougher Rly Co, Bennett's Case* (1854) 5 De GM & G 284.
9 *Re Discoverers Finance Corpn Ltd, Lindlar's Case*, supra.
10 *Re Bede Steam Shipping Co Ltd* [1917] 1 Ch 123.
11 Ibid; *Re Bell Bros Ltd* (1891) 7 TLR 689.
12 *Re Stranton Iron and Steel Co* (1873) LR 16 Eq 559; *Moffatt v Farquhar* (1878) 7 ChD 591; *Re Bede Steam Shipping Co Ltd*, supra. In these cases the number of votes a member might cast at general meetings was graduated, and the larger his holding, the fewer votes he could cast for each block of ten or twenty shares. By transferring his shares in blocks of ten or twenty to different nominees, the transferor ensured that he could cast the greatest number of votes possible in respect of each block.
13 *Re Bell Bros Ltd*, supra.

they honestly conceive to be the company's interests, and subject to this, they may refuse registration for whatever reason they think fit.[14]

The burden of proving that directors have wrongfully approved or disapproved transfers of shares rests on the person who makes that allegation.[15] The directors need not give reasons for their decision,[16] and their failure to give their reasons, either in the resolution embodying their decision or in evidence at the trial, will not be construed against them.[17] But if the articles empower the directors to reject transfers on one or more of several specified alternative grounds, they must inform the transferor and transferee on which of those grounds they rejected the transfer to the transferee,[16] unless the articles provide that they shall not be bound to specify the grounds for their decision.[18] In proceedings brought to impeach the directors' decision, the court cannot substitute its own discretion for that of the directors, and so cannot hear an appeal on the merits of their decision.[19] A dissatisfied transferor or transferee can attack the directors' decision only if he can show that they exercised their discretion for an improper purpose or for a reason outside the grounds for rejecting transfers which are specified in the articles. But the court can enquire whether reasons voluntarily given by the directors for their decision were their real reasons, or were merely a sham, and the court may infer from statements made by some of their number what their real motives were.[20]

Other members' right of pre-emption over shares

The other common restriction on the transfer of shares found in the articles of private companies is a provision that a member of the company who wishes to transfer his shares to a transferee who is not already a member, shall first offer them to the other members of the company at a price ascertained in accordance with a formula set out in the articles, or at a fair price at which the shares are valued by the directors or by the company's auditors, and that the member may transfer the shares to his proposed transferee only if the other members do not exercise their right of pre-emption. Sometimes this right of pre-emption is extended to the shares of a member who wishes to transfer them to a fellow member, or to the shares of a member who has died or become bankrupt, or of a director who ceases to hold a directorship;[1] in these cases the purpose of the restriction is to preserve the proportionality of the other members' shareholdings as between themselves. There is no doubt about the validity of a right of pre-emption exercisable in any of the events mentioned above,[2] even though the price payable by the other members for the shares is considerably less than their market value,[3] and even though the exercise of the right will result in the company only having one member.[4] A pre-emption provision in an article of association which is expressed to be binding on members of the company who wish to transfer their shares, is also binding on a

---

14 *Re Smith and Fawcett Ltd* [1942] Ch 304, [1942] 1 All ER 542.
15 *Re Gresham Life Assurance Society, ex p Penney* (1872) 8 Ch App 446; *Re Coalport China Co* [1895] 2 Ch 404.
16 *Duke of Sutherland v British Dominion Land Settlement Corpn* [1926] Ch 746. The reasons here referred to are the findings of fact and deductions from them which lead the directors to decide that they are justified in approving or disapproving a transfer on one or more of the grounds specified in the articles.
17 *Re Coalport China Co*, supra.
18 *Berry and Stewart v Tottenham Hotspur Football and Athletic Co Ltd* [1935] Ch 718.
19 *Re Gresham Life Assurance Society, ex p Penney*, supra.
20 *Re Bell Bros Ltd* (1891) 7 TLR 689.
1 In these events the articles often oblige the other members to purchase the shares.
2 *Borland's Trustee v Steel Bros & Co Ltd* [1901] 1 Ch 279.
3 *Phillips v Manufacturers' Securities Ltd* (1917) 86 LJ Ch 305.
4 *Jarvis Motors (Harrow) Ltd v Carabott* [1964] 3 All ER 89, [1964] 1 WLR 1101.

mortgagee of a member's shares,[5] and on the company itself if it claims a lien on the shares under its articles,[6] and so before exercising any power to sell the shares in order to realise the mortgage or to enforce the lien, the mortgagee or the company must offer the shares for purchase by the other members of the company in accordance with the pre-emption provision.

The articles usually provide machinery to give effect to pre-emption rights by requiring a member who wishes to transfer his shares to notify the secretary of the company of his intention to do so if his fellow members do not exercise their pre-emption rights, and by obliging the secretary to notify the other members of the number of shares available for acquisition by them, the price at which they may purchase them and the date by which they must notify the secretary of the number of shares they wish to acquire at that price or, if the articles so provide, at the price determined in accordance with the articles; the secretary is then required to notify the intending transferor of the outcome within a limited period, whereupon a contract is deemed to be concluded for the sale of those of his shares to his fellow members which they have expressed their wish to purchase. If the articles provide that in the event of the member who wishes to transfer his shares and the members who wish to acquire them under a pre-emption provision not agreeing on a price, the directors or, more usually, the auditors of the company shall certify the fair value of the shares, and that shall be the price to be paid by the acquiring members; a contract for the sale of the shares to them is concluded when they notify their wish to purchase, and it is a term of that contract that the price shall be ascertained in the manner provided by the articles.[7]

Where the articles contain no such provision to give effect to the pre-emption rights created by the articles, the member who wishes to transfer his shares must notify all the other members of his intention to do so if they have not already informed him of their wish to purchase the shares; it is not necessary for him to state the price at which he is willing to sell his shares to them, nor if the articles enable other persons in addition to other members (eg their relatives) to purchase the shares of the selling member, is it necessary for the selling member to notify those persons of his intention to transfer his shares.[8] Having notified the other members of his intention to transfer his shares, the selling member must allow a reasonable time for them and any other persons entitled to do so under the articles to inform him of their wish to purchase his shares, and the selling member may require the directors to register a transfer of those shares to the purchaser to whom he wishes to sell them only when a reasonable time has elapsed without the other members or other persons concerned informing him of their wish to purchase.[8] Whether the articles contain machinery for giving effect to the pre-emption rights of other members or not, the execution of an instrument of transfer of the shares in question to the person to whom the member intends to transfer them before an offer of the shares is made to the other members, is not a nullity, but it will become inoperative if the other members exercise their pre-emption rights.[8]

A member cannot evade a provision for pre-emption in the articles by contracting to sell his shares to a third person, or by executing an instrument of transfer to such a person, with the intention that the purchaser shall not apply for registration as a member, but shall rest content with the vendor holding the legal title to the shares as a bare trustee for him.[9] The vendor evinces his wish to sell his shares by agreeing

5   *Hunter v Hunter* [1936] AC 222.
6   *Champagne Perrier-Jouet SA v H H Finch Ltd* [1982] 3 All ER 713, [1982] 1 WLR 1359.
7   See 9 *Encyclopaedia of Forms and Precedents* (5th Edn) 342–344 and *Palmer's Company Precedents* (17th Edn) Vol 1, pp 714–716.
8   *Tett v Phoenix Property and Investment Co Ltd* [1986] BCLC 149, 2 BCC 140.
9   *Lyle and Scott Ltd v Scott's Trustees* [1959] AC 763, [1959] 2 All ER 661.

to sell them to the third person, and until that agreement is terminated, the company[9] or the other members[10] may compel him to comply with the articles. On the other hand, if a member enters into a conditional agreement to sell his shares (eg where the condition is the passing of a resolution altering the company's articles), the agreement is not effective until the condition is fulfilled, and the pre-emption rights of the other members are not exercisable until that has happened.[11] If the condition is one which can be fulfilled by the intended transferee, however (eg the exercise of an option to purchase a member's shares), it would seem that the selling member will be treated as having agreed to transfer his shares as soon as the agreement is entered into.[11]

An offer of shares made to the other members of the company under a pre-emption provision in the articles is not irrevocable unless the company's articles so provide. If they do not, until one or more of the other members have notified the intending vendor[12] of his or their acceptance of the offer so as to constitute a contract to buy the shares at the stipulated price, the member who offers them can change his mind and decide not to sell his shares to anyone, and his offer to the other members will then be revoked when he notifies them or the company to that effect.[9] However, such a revocation of the member's offer to the other members cannot be effected if he has executed an instrument of transfer of the shares to the person to whom he intended to transfer them, and the instrument is still operative and has not been cancelled by agreement with the transferee.[8] Furthermore, until one or more of the other members have accepted the intending vendor's offer in exercise of their pre-emption rights, the vendor holds the shares as a trustee for any outside purchaser to whom he has agreed to sell them, and like any other beneficiary, the purchaser is entitled to have all financial benefits in respect of the shares passed to him, and when he has paid the purchase price, he may also direct how the voting rights attached to the shares shall be exercised.[13]

Pre-emption provisions in articles are construed as applying only when a member proposes to sell or transfer the legal title to his shares, and as not applying if he or anyone else proposes merely to transfer or create an equitable interest, even though the interest extends to the whole beneficial ownership of the shares.[14] The reason for this is that equitable interests may relate to only part of the beneficial ownership, or they may be contingent or conditional, and the owner of such a partial or conditional interest should not be empowered by disposing of it to actuate a right for other members of the company to acquire the whole legal ownership of the shares. It would seem impossible to overcome this obstacle effectively by express provision in the company's articles, first, because the owners of equitable interests in shares may not be members of the company and so may not be personally bound by its articles,[15] and secondly, because there would appear to be no legal method available to the company or other members who wish to exercise pre-emption

10 *Rayfield v Hands* [1960] Ch 1, [1958] 2 All ER 194.
11 *Re a Company (No 005685 of 1988), ex p Shwarcz* [1989] BCLC 424.
12 If the articles contain procedural provisions in the form outlined in the pre-penultimate preceding paragraph, the notice of acceptance is given to the secretary of the company.
13 *Hawks v McArthur* [1951] 1 All ER 22; *Stevenson v Wilson* 1907 SC 445; *Tett v Phoenix Property and Investment Co Ltd* (supra). In *Lyle and Scott Ltd v Scott's Trustees* 1958 SC 230 at 243, Lord Clyde in the First Division of the Court of Session held that no equitable title passed to the outside purchaser until the vendor had offered his shares to the other members and they had declined to buy them, but this point was left undecided by the House of Lords. In *Hunter v Hunter* [1936] AC 222 at 261, Lord Atkin expressed the same view, but it was not necessary for his decision, and the other law lords did not concur in his opinion.
14 *Safeguard Industrial Investments Ltd v National Westminster Bank Ltd* [1980] 3 All ER 849, [1981] 1 WLR 286; affd [1982] 1 All ER 449, [1982] 1 WLR 589.
15 Companies Act 1985, s 14 (1).

rights to compel the owners of equitable interests to release them to such members if they acquire the legal ownership of the shares.

An intending transferor is not bound to sell his shares to other members of the company under a pre-emption provision in the articles unless one or more of the other members are willing to purchase all shares which he proposes to transfer,[16] but it is, of course, possible for the articles by express provision to entitle the other members to purchase such smaller number of shares as they wish to acquire. Conversely, the transferor cannot be compelled to sell more shares to the other members than he proposes to transfer to his intended transferee, and if the other members submit acceptances which amount in the aggregate to more than that number of shares, the articles usually provide some method of apportioning the available shares among them.

If the pre-emption clause requires the shares which a member wishes to transfer to be offered to the other members at a fair value certified by the directors or the company's auditor, the court cannot enquire into the correctness of the valuation, unless there is evidence that it was not honestly made, or unless the person who made it set out the reasons for his valuation, and those reasons show that he did not apply the proper principles.[17] This is so even if the person who made the valuation acted negligently by not taking relevant factors into account, by giving undue emphasis to one of those factors, or by taking irrelevant factors into account,[18] and in that situation the transferor's only remedy is to sue the person who made the valuation for the difference between the valuation and the real value of the shares as damages in an action for negligence.[19] However, where the error appears in the valuation itself, the fact that the company's articles provide that the valuation shall be final, binding and conclusive, or the fact that the shares in question have already been registered by the company in the names of the other members who have exercised their pre-emption rights on the basis of an erroneous valuation, does not prevent the member whose shares are the subject of the valuation from challenging its validity.[20]

Where under a pre-emption provision the price at which the shares must be offered to the other members is their fair value, they should be valued on the assumption that the company's business could be sold as a going concern, but if the company is insolvent or has liabilities which made an immediate winding up or a sale of its undertaking imperative, the shares should be valued on the assumption that the company's assets will be sold piecemeal, and that nothing will be received for its goodwill.[17] It is uncertain whether any addition should be made to the value of the shares ascertained in the normal way when they carry controlling voting rights at general meetings.[1] It is arguable that the value of the control conferred by the shares is a distinct thing from the value of the shares themselves ascertained by reference to the company's financial condition, but it may equally be contended that since the power of control would not exist unless the shares were held by one person, the power must be inherent in the shares collectively, and must therefore form an element of their value as so ascertained. Each argument is logical, and it rests with the court to decide which shall prevail. The only authority which assists towards a conclusion in this respect is the court's decision in a case where a member

16 *Ocean Coal Co Ltd v Powell Duffryn Steam Coal Co Ltd* [1932] 1 Ch 654, [1932] All ER Rep 844.
17 *Dean v Prince* [1954] Ch 409, [1954] 1 All ER 749; *Burgess v Purchase & Sons (Farms) Ltd* [1983] Ch 216, [1983] 2 All ER 4.
18 *Baber v Kenwood Manufacturing Co Ltd and Whinney Murray & Co* [1978] 1 Lloyd's Rep 175.
19 *Arenson v Casson Beckman Rutley & Co* [1977] AC 405, [1975] 3 All ER 901.
20 *Burgess v Purchase & Sons (Farms) Ltd*, supra.
 1 In *Dean v Prince*, supra, Evershed MR considered that an addition should be made for control, but Denning LJ and Wynn Parry J considered that it should not.

petitioned for relief from the unfair conduct of the company's affairs, and successfully contended that the fact that he could have sold his shares to the other members under a provision in the articles, was no reason for refusing the order he sought for the purchase of his shares by the other members or the company at a price equal to the appropriate fraction of the value of the net assets of the company, because if a sale were effected under the articles, the fact that the shares were a minority holding would result in the price being discounted in order to take account of the fact that they did not carry control of the company.[2] It may be deduced from this that if the shares had carried control, a corresponding addition would have had to be made to the price ascertained on a pro rata basis.

Restriction on the number of members

The second provision which formerly had to be contained in the articles of a private company, and which may still be found in the articles of many private companies, is one which limits the number of its members to 50, but under the former statutory requirement the articles could provide that employees of the company who were members of the company and former employees who became members during their employment and have remained members ever since, should not be counted toward the 50.[3] Since the repeal of the statutory requirement that the articles of a private company must limit the size of its membership,[4] a private company may have any number of members without limit. On the other hand, its articles may impose whatever restriction is desired on the number of its members, and may also impose any qualifications for membership or disqualifications from it.

It is uncertain whether directors may be treated as employees for the purpose of a provision in a company's articles limiting the size of its membership, but making an exception for employees and former employees. It has been held that directors are not employees within the meaning of a provision in a company's memorandum giving the directors power to pay pensions to former employees,[5] but managing directors have been held to be employees for the purpose of wartime legislation restricting the power of certain companies to dismiss their employees,[6] for the purpose of legislation entitling employees to compensation for injuries sustained in the course of their employment,[7] or for unfair dismissal,[8] and for the purpose of a trade union's rules defining the persons who were eligible for membership of it.[9] In the context of company law, however, directors, whether managing, full-time or part-time, are not considered to be employees of the company, despite the fact that they often serve the company under service contracts, and so it would seem that directors who are members of a private company should be counted toward the number of members to which it is restricted by its articles. But if a director is also employed by his company in another capacity, for example, as works manager, sales manager or as the company's secretary, he may be treated as an employee of the company notwithstanding his directorship, and he will not then be counted toward the maximum permitted number of members.

2 *Re Abbey Leisure Ltd* (1990) 6 BCC 60.
3 Companies Act 1948, s 28 (1) (*b*).
4 By the Companies Act 1980, s 88 (2) and Sch 4.
5 *Normandy v Ind Coope & Co Ltd* [1908] 1 Ch 84; *Re Lee Behrens & Co Ltd* [1932] 2 Ch 46, [1932] All ER Rep 889.
6 *Trussed Steel Concrete Co Ltd v Green* [1946] Ch 115.
7 *Lee v Lee's Air Farming Ltd* [1961] AC 12, [1960] 3 All ER 420.
8 *Parsons v Albert J Parsons & Sons Ltd* [1979] ICR 271.
9 *Boulting v Association of Cinematograph Television and Allied Technicians* [1963] 2 QB 606, [1963] 1 All ER 716.

Members who are joint shareholders counted as only one person for the purpose of the former statutory restriction on the number of members of a private company.[10] It would seem that joint shareholders must now each be counted separately as a member in applying any restriction on the size of membership, unless the articles otherwise provide.[11] If the articles do provide that joint shareholders shall be counted as one member, they do so for all purposes, whatever arrangements they make between themselves as to the exercise of the voting rights attached to their shares, but if they divide the shares between themselves and each is registered as the holder of a separate block of shares, they cease to be joint shareholders and each of them must then be counted as one member.

The restriction on the number of members of a private company does not affect the number of persons who may be interested in its shares otherwise than as registered holders. Consequently, shares may be held by trustees, nominees or personal representatives on behalf of any number of persons; only the trustees, nominees or personal representatives will count toward the maximum permitted number of members if they are registered as members, and since they will invariably be joint shareholders, they will be treated as a single member under a provision of the articles counting joint shareholders as one member. Furthermore, any number of persons may be interested in the shares as equitable mortgagees, the holders of contracts or options to purchase them or otherwise, and the registered holder of the shares alone will be taken into account in calculating the number of members.

Prohibition on the issue of prospectuses

A private company's articles had formerly to prohibit it from issuing any invitation to the public to subscribe for its shares or debentures.[12] This requirement has now been repealed, but the same prohibition is now imposed by law on a private company limited by shares, and is extended so as to prohibit such private companies allotting or agreeing to allot shares or debentures or other loan securities to any person (eg a merchant bank, the corporate finance subsidiary of a commercial bank or any other intermediary) with a view to them being offered for sale to the public.[13] Consequently, a private company may not issue a prospectus, nor may it have its shares, debentures or loan securities offered for sale or placed on a stock exchange by a financial intermediary, nor offered for subscription or purchase by an investment advertisement which is published in the press or otherwise, or which is circulated generally. On the other hand, a private company will be able to offer its securities for subscription or sale in such circumstances as will be prescribed in an order to be made by the Secretary of State for Trade and Industry exempting advertisements issued in the circumstances specified in the order if the advertisements appear to him to have a private character, or to deal with investments only incidentally, or if the advertisements are issued only to persons who are sufficiently expert to understand any risks involved.[14] Also a private company will be able to issue investment advertisements in any circumstances if

---

10 Companies Act 1948, s 28 (2).

11 The Companies Act 1948, Table A, Part II, para 2 (*c*) did provide that joint shareholders should count as one member, and this provision will still apply to a private company registered before 22 December 1980 whose articles incorporated Table A, Part II by reference.

12 Companies Act 1948, s 28 (1) (*c*).

13 Companies Act 1985, s 81 (1); Financial Services Act 1986, s 170 (1) and (2), as amended by Companies Act 1989, s 199. The latter provision will supersede the former when it is brought into force by an order made by the Secretary of State for Trade and Industry.

14 Financial Services Act 1986, s 170 (2).

they are individually exempted by order of the Secretary of State, because the securities to which the advertisements relate appear to him to be of a kind which can be expected normally to be bought or dealt in only by persons sufficiently expert to understand any risks involved.[15]

Under the provisions of the Companies Act 1985, which will continue to remain effective until the provisions mentioned in the preceding paragraph are brought into force, a private company may issue an invitation to its members or debenture holders which is not calculated to result in shares or debentures or other loan securities becoming available for subscription by persons other than those members or debenture holders, or an invitation which can properly be regarded as a domestic concern of the company and the persons to whom it is addressed.[16] Thus, a private company may issue unrenounceable letters of right, and even renounceable letters of right, if the class of persons to whom the rights may be renounced is limited so as to make the transaction a domestic one. In particular, a private company may invite its existing members or employees, or members of the families of such persons,[17] to subscribe for shares or debentures or other loan securities of the company, and the right to subscribe may be made renounceable to any such persons.[18] Furthermore, under an employees' share scheme established by a private company it may offer shares or debentures for subscription by persons entitled to participate in the scheme, and the right to subscribe may be made renounceable to any other persons entitled to participate in it.[19] In any case where it may lawfully make a renounceable invitation to subscribe for its shares or debentures or other loan securities, a private company may make the offer by means of a renounceable provisional letter of allotment. In that case the invitation to subscribe is addressed to the original recipient of the letter of allotment, and so cannot possibly be an invitation to the public.[20] The recipient's renunciation of the letter of allotment itself signifies his acceptance of the shares or debentures or loan securities which are offered, but since the recipient thereby immediately becomes the holder of the securities offered to him, in the case of shares any restriction on the transfer of shares imposed by the company's articles will apply to the renunciation and to any further renunciation by the renouncee.[1] A private company is, of course, not restricted under the law at present in force to offering its shares and debentures or loan securities to its existing members and debenture holders, or to members and employees and members of their families, or to persons entitled to subscribe under an employees' share scheme established by the company. It can also invite subscription from other persons, provided that the class of persons invited to subscribe is not so large as to make the invitation a public one.

In one respect the statutory prohibition at present in force on a private company offering its shares or debentures or other loan securities to the public is wider than the former requirement that its articles should prohibit it from offering them to the public for subscription.[2] The former prohibition applied only to offers of shares or debentures for subscription in cash,[3] but the prohibition at present in force extends

---

15 Ibid, s 170 (3).
16 Companies Act 1985, s 60 (1).
17 The family of a member or employee comprises his or her spouse, widow or widower, children (including adopted and step-children) and the issue of such children, and a trustee of a trust the principal beneficiaries of which are the member or employee and such other persons.
18 Ibid, s 60 (3) to (5) and (7).
19 Ibid, s 60 (6) and (7). For the definition of an employees' share scheme, see p 247, ante.
20 See p 299, ante.
 1 See p 753, ante.
 2 Companies Act 1985, s 81 (1).
 3 *Governments Stock and Other Securities Investment Co Ltd v Christopher* [1956] 1 All ER 490, [1956] 1 WLR 237.

to all 'offers to the public (whether for cash or otherwise)'[2] with the consequence that a private company may not offer to issue its shares or debentures or other loan securities to a sector of the public (eg the shareholders of another company, if they are sufficiently numerous to prevent the invitation being a matter of domestic concern[4]) in exchange for a non-cash consideration (eg the transfer to the private company of the existing shares of the other company). This extension of the definition of an offer to the public may inhibit a private company from making a takeover bid for another company by an exchange of shares, and it would seem that the prohibition cannot be avoided by the company first allotting or agreeing to allot the new shares or debentures or loan securities to a financial intermediary with a view to making the formal offer of the new shares to the shareholders of the other company. It is true that the prohibition in terms only prevents such an indirect offer being made to the public if the financial intermediary offers the new shares for sale (ie for a consideration in cash),[5] but an offer which is intended to result in the company (and not the intermediary) taking a transfer of shares in the other company must inevitably be made by the intermediary as an agent for the company, and so must fall within the statutory prohibition.

If in contravention of the prohibition a private company offers it shares or debentures or other loan securities to the public, or allots or agrees to allot such securities to an intermediary with a view to them being offered for sale to the public, an allotment or sale of the securities or any agreement for their allotment or sale is not thereby invalidated, and the title of any allottee or purchaser of the shares is therefore unaffected.[6] The only sanction for the contravention is that the company and any officer of it who is in default is guilty of a criminal offence punishable by a fine.[7]

WRITTEN RESOLUTIONS OF PRIVATE COMPANIES AND THE ELECTIVE REGIME

The Companies Act 1989 introduced two privileges for private companies which public companies do not share, namely first, the facility for passing any resolution which a general meeting or a meeting of a class of shareholders of the company may pass (with a few exceptions) by a written resolution being assented to by all the members of the company with voting rights, and secondly, the elective regime by which a private company may dispense with or modify any one or more of five requirements imposed by the Companies Act 1985 (as amended) by passing appropriate adoptive resolutions by the unanimous votes of the members of the company with voting rights at general meetings.

Written resolutions

Subject to the exceptions mentioned below, any resolution which may be passed at a general meeting of a private company or at a meeting of a class of its members may be passed or agreed to without holding a meeting; this may be done by a resolution being set out in writing and being signed by or on behalf of all the members of the company who would be entitled to attend and vote at the meeting.[8]

4 Companies Act 1985, s 60 (1).
5 Ibid, s 81 (1).
6 Ibid, s 81 (3).
7 Ibid, s 81 (2).
8 Ibid, s 381A (1), inserted by Companies Act 1989, s 113 (1).

The signatures of the members or the persons appointed to represent them may be on a single document containing the resolution, or on several documents (eg copies of the resolution circulated to members for signature) each of which states the resolution accurately,[9] which presumably means without a material variation of content. A written resolution takes effect in the same way as an identical resolution would if it were passed by a general meeting or by a meeting of a class of members (as the case may be) at the time when the written resolution is signed by or on behalf of the last member whose signature is necessary.[10] A written resolution may be agreed to under these provisions if it would otherwise need to be passed as a special or extraordinary resolution, or as an elective resolution under the elective regime for private companies dealt with below,[11] and because the resolution takes effect as though it had been passed by a general or class meeting, it will be effective even though under the Companies Act 1985 it requires the confirmation of the court (eg a resolution for the reduction of capital),[12] or even though it may be cancelled by the court on an application made by a certain fraction or number of members within a limited period after it is passed (eg a resolution altering the company's objects,[13] a class resolution consenting to an alteration of the rights of the class,[14] a resolution that the company shall give financial assistance for the acquisition of shares in it or its holding company out of the company's profits or without reducing its net assets,[15] or a resolution that the company may redeem or purchase shares in itself out of assets representing capital).[16]

Despite its wide availability, a private company cannot by a written resolution assented to by all its voting members exercise the statutory powers of a general meeting to remove a director or auditor from office before the expiration of the period for which he was appointed.[17] Moreover, appropriate procedural modifications are made when certain resolutions which can be effected by written resolution are agreed to in writing; these modifications substitute the supply beforehand to each member who signs the written resolution of copies of documents or information which would be required to be circulated to members, or to be available for inspection for a certain period before the resolution is passed, or to be presented to the meeting at which it is passed, if it were passed in the normal way;[18] the modifications also substitute the treatment of members to whose shares certain of the resolutions relate as being members who are not entitled to vote, for provisions that the resolution, if passed at a general meeting, shall not be

---

9 Companies Act 1985, s 381A (2).
10 Ibid, s 381A (3) and (4).
11 Ibid, s 381A (6).
12 Ibid, s 135 (1) (see p 177, ante).
13 Ibid, s 4 (1) and (2) and s 5 (1) to (4), as amended by Companies Act 1989, s 110 (2) (see p 68, ante).
14 Companies Act 1985, s 127 (1) to (4) (see p 230, ante).
15 Ibid, s 157 (1) to (3) (see p 388, ante).
16 Ibid, s 173 (2), s 176 (1) and (2) and s 177 (2) (see p 196, ante).
17 Ibid, s 381A (7) and Sch 15A, para 1. The statutory powers of removal of directors and auditors are conferred by the Companies Act, ss 303 and 391 (see p 547 and 715, ante).
18 Companies Act 1985, s 381A (7) and Sch 15A, paras 3 (2), 4, 5 (3), 6 (3) and 8. The resolutions in question relate to the waiver of preferential subscription rights (s 95 (5)), the authorisation of financial assistance for the purchase of shares of the company or its holding company (s 157 (4)), the authorisation of off-market purchases of the company's own shares (s 164 (4)), the authorisation of the redemption or purchase of shares in the company out of assets representing its capital (s 174 (4)), the approval of directors' service contracts (s 319 (5)) and the approval of advances by the company to the directors to enable them to meet expenditure for the purpose of performing their duties (s 337 (3) and (4)).

valid if it is procured by the votes of those members in respect of those shares.[19]

Before a written resolution is agreed to by the signature of an appropriate document or documents, a copy of the proposed resolution must be sent to the company's auditors, and if the resolution concerns them as auditors, they may within seven days after they receive the copy of the resolution give notice to the company that in their opinion the resolution should be considered at a general meeting of the company, or (as the case may be) at a meeting of a class of members, and the resolution may then be passed only at such a general or class meeting.[20] If the auditors notify the company that in their opinion the resolution does not concern them as auditors, or that although it does so concern them, it does not need to be considered at a general or class meeting (as the case may be), or if the auditors give no notice of their opinion to the company within the seven days allowed, the resolution may be agreed to in writing without holding a meeting.[1] If a written resolution is signed by or on behalf of all or some of the members of the company who are entitled to vote on it before a copy of the resolution is sent to the auditors, the resolution is not void, but it takes effect only when the auditors notify the company of their opinion that it does not concern them as auditors, or that it does not need to be considered at a meeting, or when seven days have elapsed after the auditors received a copy of the resolution and they have given no notice of their opinion to the company,[2] but in any case the written resolution cannot take effect until it has been signed by or on behalf of all the members who are entitled to vote on it.[3]

When a resolution of a general meeting has been agreed to in the form of a written resolution, the company must keep a record of the resolution and the signatures to it in a book to be kept in the same way as the minutes of proceedings at general meetings; the same rules apply to such a record as apply to the minutes which a company is required to keep of general meetings, namely, that such a record duly signed by a director or the secretary of the company is presumed to be accurate and that the proceedings on the written resolution are presumed to have been properly conducted, and that members of the company have the right to inspect and to call for copies of the record.[4]

A private company may pass written resolutions under these provisions notwithstanding any provision of its memorandum or articles.[5] As regards a private company, the statutory provision would, therefore, appear to make unnecessary the provision often found in the articles of both public and private companies that a written resolution signed by every member of the company entitled to vote on it shall be as effectual as though it had been passed at a general meeting of the company which has been duly convened and held.[6] It could be argued that the statutory provisions do, in fact, supersede such provisions in private companies' articles, with the result that such companies may not use those provisions to pass written resolutions in situations where the statutory written resolution procedure is not available (ie the removal of directors or auditors), or to evade the modified procedural requirements which the statutory provisions impose in respect

---

19 Companies Act 1985, s 381A (7) and Sch 15A, para 5 (2) and 6 (2). The resolutions in question relate to the authorisation of off-market purchases of the company's own shares (s 164 (5)) and the authorisation of the redemption or purchase of shares in the company out of assets representing its capital (s 174 (2)).
20 Companies Act 1985, s 381B (1) to (3).
 1 Ibid, s 381B (3).
 2 Ibid, s 381A (5) and s 381B (4).
 3 Ibid, s 381A (3) and s 381B (4).
 4 Ibid, s 382A (1) to (3) (see pp 644 and 645, ante).
 5 Ibid, s 381C (1).
 6 See Table A, art 53.

of certain other written resolutions. The acceptance of this argument would produce the odd result that public companies which provided for a written resolution procedure in their articles would be able to use that procedure in situations where private companies could not do so, and would be able to dispense with the procedural conditions which are modified in the case of certain written resolutions effected by private companies. If the court were to rule that the written resolution procedure authorised by the articles of any company is not available where the Companies Act 1985 (as amended) requires any procedural step in addition to the convening and holding of a general or class meeting to pass the resolution (such as the notification of a director or auditor whose removal is sought, or the circulation or making available of a document or information in advance of the meeting), there would be no conflict between the availability and conditions of the statutory written resolution procedure for private companies and the availability of written resolutions effected under the provisions of companies' articles, but as yet the court has not so decided.

The elective regime

Notwithstanding anything in its articles of association, a private company may by passing an elective resolution adopt any one or more of five relaxations of the strict requirements of the Companies Act 1985.[7] An elective resolution is one which is passed at a general meeting of which at least 21 clear days' notice in writing setting out the terms of the resolution has been given to members entitled to be sent notices of general meetings, and the resolution must be agreed to at the general meeting by all the members entitled to attend and vote at the meeting, or by proxies attending on their behalf.[8] It would appear that a majority in number of the members entitled to attend a general meeting called to pass an elective resolution who between them hold at least 95 per cent in nominal value of the issued shares of the company carrying the right to vote at that meeting, cannot consent to less than 21 days' notice of the meeting being accepted so as to bind the minority, because the provision which facilitates the acceptance of shorter notice of general meetings than that normally required appears to apply only in respect of extraordinary general meetings called to pass ordinary, special or extraordinary resolutions.[9] However, an elective resolution may be agreed to or effected in written form under the statutory provision enabling private companies to pass written resolutions.[10] When an elective resolution has been passed, it continues in operation for an indefinite period, but it may be revoked at any time by a general meeting passing an ordinary resolution for the purpose, and it ceases to be effective if the company is re-registered as a public company.[11]

The relaxations in the requirements of the Companies Act 1985 of which a private company may avail itself by elective resolution are the following:

(1) A private company may by elective resolution extend the period of five years which is normally the maximum period for which its articles of association or an ordinary resolution passed by a general meeting may confer or renew the authority of its directors to issue a specified amount of unissued shares of the company, or during which they may issue any rights to subscribe for, or to convert other securities into, a specified amount of

---

7 Companies Act 1985, s 379A (1), inserted by Companies Act 1989, s 116 (2).
8 Companies Act 1985, s 379A (2).
9 Ibid, s 369 (3) and (4) and s 378 (3).
10 Ibid, s 381A (6).
11 Ibid, s 379A (3) and (4).

unissued shares;[12] the extension may be for an indefinite period or for a fixed period, in which case the resolution must state the date on which the extension will expire.[13] An authorisation to issue shares during a fixed period exceeding five years under such an extension can be renewed for a further fixed period or indefinitely by an ordinary resolution passed by a general meeting, and an original or renewed authorisation can be revoked or varied by such a resolution.[14] If an elective resolution extending the normal maximum period for which an authorisation to issue shares can be given is revoked or ceases to have effect by the company being re-registered as a public company,[11] an authorisation then in force for an indefinite period or for a period of more than five years takes effect as though it has been given for five years from the most recent date on which it was conferred or renewed.[15]

(2) An elective resolution may be passed by a private company dispensing with the need for its annual accounts (including group accounts) and directors' and auditors' reports to be laid before a general meeting of the company each year.[16] The dispensation then takes effect in relation to the annual accounts and reports for the financial year in which the elective resolution is passed and for subsequent financial years.[17] If the elective resolution is revoked or ceases to have effect, the company's annual accounts and its directors' and auditors' reports for the then current financial year and subsequent financial years must be laid before general meetings held within the appropriate periods after the end of those financial years.[18] While an elective resolution is in force dispensing with the laying of annual accounts before general meetings, the company is also absolved from having to lay other accounts by reference to which distributions of dividends by it are justified, and under which the net assets of the company are ascertained for the purpose of determining whether property transactions between the company and directors of the company or its holding company or persons connected with them need to be approved by a general meeting.[19]

Where an elective resolution to dispense with the laying of annual accounts and reports is in force, copies of the company's annual accounts and reports for each financial year must be sent to members and debenture holders of the company not less than 28 days before the date by which they would normally have to be sent (instead of 21 days), and the copies sent to members must be accompanied by a notice of each member's right to require the laying of the accounts and reports before a general meeting.[20] Within 28 days after copies of the annual accounts and reports are sent out, any member or auditor of the company may by written notice require the company to call a general meeting for the purpose of laying the accounts

12 Ibid, s 80 (1), (2), (4) and (5) (see p 245, ante).
13 Ibid, s 80A (1) and (2), inserted by Companies Act 1989, s 115 (1); Companies Act 1985, s 379A (1) (*a*). Because the expiration date of a fixed period for which the authorisation is given must be stated, it is not possible to give an authorisation for the joint lives of the directors, or for the life of any one or more of them.
14 Companies Act 1985, s 80A (4) and (5).
15 Ibid, s 80A (7).
16 Ibid, s 252 (1), s 22 (1), inserted by Companies Act 1989, ss 16 and 22; Companies Act 1985, s 379A (1) (*b*).
17 Companies Act 1985, s 252 (2).
18 Ibid, s 241 (1), s 244 (1) and s 252 (4) (see p 697, ante).
19 Ibid, s 270 (3) and (4) and s 320 (2) and s 252 (3) (see pp 420 and 599, ante).
20 Ibid, s 244 (1) to (3) and s 253 (1).

and reports before it.[1] The directors must then call such a general meeting and if they do not within 21 days after the notice is delivered to the company, call a general meeting at which the annual accounts are to be laid and which is to be held not later than 28 days after it is convened, the member or auditors who gave the notice may call a general meeting for that purpose to be held not later than three months after the notice was delivered.[2] A member or auditor who calls such a general meeting may recover his reasonable expenses of doing so from the company, which may recoup the amount paid out of fees or remuneration payable to the directors who were in default.[3]

Where a private company has passed an elective resolution dispensing with the laying of annual accounts before a general meeting each year, it must appoint or re-appoint auditors by an ordinary resolution of a general meeting within 28 days after copies of its annual accounts and reports are sent to its members and debenture holders, and those auditors will hold office until the time for appointing or re-appointing auditors in the next following year.[4] If a member gives notice requiring the annual accounts and reports to be laid before a general meeting,[1] the appointment or re-appointment of auditors must be made at that meeting or at another general meeting held not later than 28 days after its conclusion.[4]

(3) A private company may by an elective resolution dispense with the holding of annual general meetings of the company in the year in which the resolution is passed and subsequent years.[5] Nevertheless, in any year in which the resolution is effective, any member may require an annual general meeting to be convened and held by giving written notice to the company not later than three months before the end of the calendar year (ie not later than 30 September).[6] The company must then call an annual general meeting to be held on a date before the end of that calendar year.[7] If the elective resolution dispensing with annual general meetings is revoked or ceases to have effect by the company being re-registered as a public company, the company must call and hold an annual general meeting in the calendar year in which that happens, unless fewer than three months of that year remain unexpired, and an annual general meeting must be called and held in each subsequent year.[8]

(4) By passing an elective resolution, a private company may reduce the percentage of the total nominal value of issued shares of the company carrying voting rights which must be held by a majority in number of the members holding such shares who may decide that an extraordinary general meeting of the company shall be held, even though less than the normally required notice of it has been given to members.[9] The normal length of notice required to call an extraordinary general meeting is 21 clear days' notice if it is called to pass a special resolution, or 14 clear days' notice in

1 Ibid, s 253 (2).
2 Ibid, s 253 (3), (4) and (6).
3 Ibid, s 253 (5).
4 Ibid, s 385A (1) and (2).
5 Ibid, s 366A (1) and (2) inserted by Companies Act 1989, s 115 (2); Companies Act 1985, s 379 (1) (c).
6 Companies Act 1985, s 366A (3).
7 Ibid, s 366A (4).
8 Ibid, s 366A (5).
9 Ibid, s 369 (3) and (4) and s 378 (3), amended by Companies Act 1989, s 115 (3); Companies Act 1985, s 379 (1) (d).

any other case.[10] Normally, shorter notice than this may be accepted by a majority in number of the members with voting rights who hold between them 95 per cent in nominal value of the shares carrying such rights, but by an elective resolution that percentage may be reduced to not less than 90 per cent.[11]

(5) A private company may by an elective resolution dispense with the annual re-appointment of auditors.[12] While the elective resolution is in force the auditors of the company who hold office when the resolution is passed are deemed to be re-appointed annually for successive financial years, without the need for actual re-appointment by resolution of the general meeting at which annual accounts are laid, or if the company has dispensed with holding such general meetings, by a resolution passed within 28 days after the circulation of copies of the annual accounts and reports to members and debenture holders.[13] The deemed successive re-appointments cease, however, if the company becomes a dormant one and passes a special resolution exempting itself from the obligation to appoint auditors.[14]

At any time while an elective resolution dispensing with the annual re-appointment of auditors is in force, any member may deliver a written proposal to the company that the appointment of the company's auditors currently holding office shall be brought to an end, but a member may deliver only one such proposal in any financial year.[15] The directors must call an extraordinary general meeting to be held not later than 28 days after such a proposal is delivered to the company, and must propose a resolution at the meeting which will enable the members to decide whether the appointment of the auditors shall be brought to an end.[16] If the general meeting passes an ordinary resolution that this shall be done, the auditors are deemed not to be re-appointed on the next occasion when they would otherwise have been automatically re-appointed, and if the proposal is delivered to the company within 14 days after the distribution to members and debenture holders of the annual accounts for the last complete financial year, any deemed re-appointment of the auditors for the next following financial year is treated as not having been made.[17] If the directors do not call an extraordinary general meeting within 14 days after the written proposal to terminate the auditors' appointment is delivered to the company, the member who delivered the proposal, or any one such member if the proposal was delivered by two or more members, may call an extraordinary general meeting to consider it; the meeting must be held within three months after delivery of the proposal, and the member who calls it may recover his reasonable expenses of doing so from the company, which may recoup the amount paid out of fees or other remuneration of the directors in default.[18]

A company which resolves to dispense with the annual re-appointment of auditors cannot contract with them not to prevent their re-appointment in the way indicated above, and no compensation or damages are payable to

10 Companies Act 1985, s 369 (1) and (2) and s 378 (2) (see p 624, ante).
11 Ibid, s 369 (3) and (4) and s 378 (3).
12 Ibid, s 379A (1) (e) and s 386 (1), inserted by Companies Act 1989, s 119 (1).
13 Ibid, s 386 (2).
14 Ibid, s 386 (2) (see p 717, ante).
15 Ibid, s 393 (1), inserted by Companies Act 1989, s 122 (1).
16 Companies Act 1985, s 393 (2).
17 Ibid, s 386 (2) and s 393 (3).
18 Ibid, s 393 (4) to (6).

auditors if they are not so re-appointed.[19] The termination of the deemed re-appointment of auditors does not involve their removal from office, because the termination of their appointment takes effect only at the end of the current period of their appointment, and not immediately. Consequently, the procedural steps required to be taken when a resolution is proposed to remove auditors during their term of office[20] do not apply.

If an elective resolution dispensing with the annual re-appointment of auditors is revoked, or ceases to have effect because the company is re-registered as a public company,[1] the auditors then holding office continue to do so until the conclusion of the next general meeting at which annual accounts and reports are laid, or if the company has passed an unrevoked elective resolution not to lay copies of its annual accounts at general meetings, at the end of the time for next appointing or re-appointing auditors.[2] The removal of an auditor or the passing of a resolution that an auditor shall not be deemed to be re-appointed under an elective resolution to dispense with annual re-appointments, does not terminate or cancel the elective resolution itself, but merely creates a vacancy in the office of auditor when the removal or the termination takes effect, and the vacancy must be filled by the appointment of an eligible and qualified person by ordinary resolution of a general meeting or by a unanimous written resolution or, alternatively, if an auditor is removed by resolution of the board of directors, by resolution of the board of directors.[3] The person so appointed will then be deemed to be re-appointed each year under the elective resolution until he is removed, or until his appointment is terminated or until the elective resolution ceases to have effect.

The companies which are likely to make most use of the facilities afforded by the elective regime lie at opposite ends of the company spectrum. The regime is intended primarily for small and medium-sized private companies where directors and persons closely connected with them are the only shareholders, or are at least the holders of a substantial majority of the company's issued share capital (ie three-quarters or more), and the remaining shareholders are few in number. Nevertheless, the regime may also prove useful where a substantial fraction of a private company's issued shares are held by one or two institutional investors who do not seek to influence the management of the company's affairs beyond protecting their interests as investors, and where the remaining shares are held by directors of the company and persons closely connected with them. This is the typical situation where the company has expanded with the aid of venture capital provided by such institutional investors, or where the company was formed to effect a management buy-out of its business undertaking, which was formerly carried on by another enterprise.

At the other extreme, the elective regime will prove useful in respect of private companies which are the wholly-owned subsidiaries of a public or private parent or holding company and which function as the operating companies of the group. Even if a small fraction of the subsidiaries' issued share capital is held by persons other than the parent or holding company and its nominees, the regime could still prove useful by enabling the parent company to economise on administration expenses by dealing with its minority shareholders individually. Finally, the regime may prove useful where a private company is formed to carry out a joint venture

19 Ibid, s 393 (7).
20 Ibid, s 391A (1) to (6) (see p 715, ante).
 1 Ibid, s 379A (3) and (4).
 2 Ibid, s 386 (3). For the time for appointing or re-appointing auditors, see pp 710 and 767, ante.
 3 Companies Act 1985, s 384 (2), s 385 (2) and s 388 (1).

of limited size or duration, whether the participants in the venture are public or private companies of modest or substantial dimensions.

DIFFERENCES BETWEEN PUBLIC AND PRIVATE COMPANIES

The Companies Act 1985 (as amended) and the rules of company law laid down by the courts apply to private companies in the same way as they apply to public companies, subject to a number of exceptions which have already been noted in the foregoing chapters. It may be convenient to gather these exceptions together at this point, and so to catalogue the differences between private and public companies.

(1) A private company need not state the kind of company it is in its memorandum, and its name gives no indication of this beyond the fact that it must terminate with the word 'limited' or the contraction 'ltd' if the liability of its members is limited.[4]

(2) There is no minimum nominal, issued or paid up capital for a private company.[5]

(3) A private company may commence business on its incorporation, and it does not need to obtain a certificate of entitlement to do business and to borrow.[6]

(4) A private company may allot shares offered for subscription even though subscriptions have not been received for all the shares offered.[7]

(5) A private company may by its memorandum or articles exclude or modify the preferential rights conferred by law on its existing equity shareholders to subscribe for new shares or debentures which are equity securities and which it offers for subscription in cash.[8]

(6) A private company may allot shares as fully or partly paid up in consideration of an undertaking to do work or perform services, or in consideration of an undertaking which will or may not be fully performed within five years after allotment.[9]

(7) A private company may allot shares as fully or partly paid up for a consideration other than cash without having the consideration valued by an independent person qualified to be appointed as the company's auditor.[10]

(8) A private company need not have such a valuation made of any non-cash assets acquired within two years of its incorporation from the subscribers of its memorandum, or within two years of its re-registration as a private company from its members at the date of re-registration.[11]

(9) A private company is subject to the same restrictions as a public company on acquiring shares in itself, either directly or through a nominee, but with the same exceptions as a public company may claim;[12] however, if a private company or its nominee acquires shares in which it has a permissible beneficial interest, it need not dispose of them within three years after the

4 Companies Act 1985, s 1 (3) and s 25 (2) (see pp 4 and 10, ante).
5 Ibid, s 11, s 101 (1), s 117 (2) and s 118 (1) (see pp 20 and 30, ante).
6 Ibid, s 117 (1) (see p 30, ante).
7 Ibid, s 84 (1) (see p 303, ante).
8 Ibid, s 91 (1) (see p 250, ante).
9 Ibid, s 99 (2) and s 102 (1) (see pp 146 and 147, ante).
10 Ibid, s 103 (1) (see p 153, ante).
11 Ibid, s 104 (1) and (3) (see p 158, ante).
12 Ibid, s 143 (1) and (3) and s 144 (1) (see p 409, ante).

acquisition, as a public company must, and there is no prohibition on the exercise of voting rights in respect of such shares,[13] unless the private company acquires them by purchase or on redemption, when they are cancelled and the voting rights attached to them are consequently terminated.[14]

(10) There are no restrictions on a private company taking mortgages, charges or liens over shares in itself.[15]

(11) A private company (like a public one) may make distributions to its shareholders only out of the excess of its accumulated realised profits (so far as not already applied) over its realised losses (so far as not written off),[16] but (unlike a public company) it does not have to ensure that a distribution does not result in its net assets being less then its called-up capital plus its undistributable reserves,[17] with the consequence that it does not have to provide for any excess of its unrealised losses over its realised profits before making a distribution.

(12) A private company need have only one director,[18] two or more directors of a private company may be elected by a single resolution at a general meeting;[19] a director of a private company who held office for life on 18 July 1945, cannot be removed by an ordinary resolution at a general meeting unless its articles so provided;[20] and a director of a private company which is not the subsidiary of a public company does not retire by operation of law at the annual general meeting following his seventieth birthday, nor is special notice necessary to elect or re-elect such a director.[21]

(13) A member of a private company may appoint only one proxy to represent him at a general meeting or a meeting of a class of members, unless the articles permit the appointment of more than one proxy;[1] a proxy appointed to vote for a member at a meeting of a private company may speak at the meeting as well as vote.[2]

(14) A private company which is not a member of a group comprising a public company may make quasi-loans to its directors and directors of its holding company and enter into credit transactions within them free from the restrictions which are imposed on public companies; moreover, such a private company is not restricted in making loans and quasi-loans to, or entering into credit transactions with, persons who are connected with its directors or directors of its holding company.[3]

(15) There are no statutory requirements that a secretary of a private company must be qualified for appointment by his membership of a professional body or by experience.[4]

(16) A private company which is not a banking or insurance company and is not authorised to carry on investment business may, if its turnover, gross

13 Ibid, s 146 (2) to (4) (see pp 41 and 411, ante).
14 Ibid, s 160 (1) and s 162 (2), as amended by Companies Act 1989, s 133 (4) (see p 189 and 191, ante).
15 Ibid, s 150 (1) (see p 409, ante).
16 Ibid, s 263 (1) and (3) (see p 421, ante).
17 Ibid, s 264 (1) (see p 423, ante).
18 Ibid, s 282 (3).
19 Ibid, s 292 (1).
20 Ibid, s 303 (1); Companies Consolidation (Consequential Provisions) Act 1985, s 14.
21 Companies Act 1985, s 293 (1) and (3).
 1 Ibid, s 372 (1) and (2).
 2 Ibid, s 372 (1).
 3 Ibid, s 330 (3) and (4) and s 331 (6) (see p 565, ante).
 4 Ibid, s 286 (1) (see p 613, ante).

assets and number or employees do not exceed certain maxima, deliver modified versions of its annual accounts to the Registrar of Companies, and if it is the parent company of a group of such undertakings, whose group turnover, gross or net assets and number of employees do not exceed certain maxima, it is not required to prepare or deliver to the Registrar consolidated accounts for the group.[5]

(17) A private company which is not a a banking or insurance company or a company authorised to carry on investment business may by special resolution exempt itself from the obligation to appoint auditors while it is dormant.[6]

(18) A private company may give financial assistance for the acquisition of shares in itself or in another private company which is its holding company, provided that it does so out of its distributable profits or without reducing its assets.[7]

(19) A private company may purchase any of its shares and may redeem any shares issued as redeemable shares by applying assets representing its capital and non-distributable reserves.[8]

(20) Persons entitled to interests in the shares of a private company carrying full voting rights need not disclose them to the company, and the company is not required to keep a register of such interests;[9] a private company has no statutory power to enquire into the existence of such interests, either on its own initiative or on the requisition of a fraction of its members.[10]

(21) A private company's directors need not call an extraordinary general meeting if its net assets fall to one-half or less of its called-up share capital.[11]

PRIVATE COMPANIES IN PRACTICE

Although the law makes only a limited number of distinctions between public and private companies, the practical effect of the distinctions is considerable. Furthermore, the structural features and the functional operation of public companies and most private companies are very different in practice, despite the application to them all uniformly of most of the provisions of the Companies Act 1985 (as amended). Public companies and private companies (except the largest among them which have many members) serve different needs, their modes of operating and conducting their affairs are unlike, and the provisions of the law on which their members rely for the protection of their investments are not the same. The principal practical differences between them may be summarised as follows:

(a) The directors of a private company usually hold all or a majority of its issued share capital (except where institutional investors have subscribed for its shares by providing venture capital or capital required for a management buy-out), so that broadly speaking the people who manage the company also own it. It is rare for the directors of a public company to hold a majority of its issued share capital, except where the company was originally a private

5 Ibid, s 256 (1) to (4) and s 248 (1) and (2) and Sch 8, substituted by Companies Act 1989, s 13 (1) and (3) and Sch 6 (see pp 707 and 708, ante).
6 Companies Act 1985, s 250 (1) to (3), substituted by Companies Act 1989, s 14 (see p 717, ante).
7 Companies Act 1985, s 155 (1) and (2) (see p 387, ante).
8 Ibis, s 171 (1) (see p 195 et seq, ante).
9 Ibid, s 198 (1) and s 211 (1) (see p 363, ante).
10 Ibid, s 212 (1) and s 214 (1) (see p 371, ante).
11 Ibid, s 142 (1) (see p 616, ante).

one and was converted into a public company and a Stock Exchange listing or quotation on the Unlisted Securities Market was obtained for it in order to float off part of its capital, usually with a view to improving the tax position of its original shareholders.

(b) Shares in a private company are rarely transferred, whereas the shares of a public company which has a Stock Exchange listing or whose shares have been admitted to dealings on the Unlisted Securities Market are traded fairly frequently at readily ascertainable prices. The rarity of transfers of shares in private companies is only partly because of the restrictions on the transferability of shares which their articles usually impose. It is the result principally of the fact mentioned in (a) above, namely, that shareholders will often also be directors of the company, and will therefore part with their shares only when they cease to be directors, and also the fact that no readily available market exists for dealing in the shares of private companies.

(c) Because they are virtually the owners of the company, directors of private companies whose shares are not held by other persons to a substantial extent, often take almost the whole of the company's profits (after transfers to reserve) in the form of directors' remuneration instead of having the companies pay dividends to their shareholders. In a public company the directors' remuneration is always related to the value of their services, even if it takes the form of a share of profits, or is fixed by the board or a committee of the board; the major part of the company's profits is therefore available for distribution as dividends, and a substantial amount of the distributable profits are in fact distributed; the directors receive the same return on any shares they hold in the company as other shareholders who are not directors.

(d) The position of a minority shareholder of a private company who is not a director is much weaker than that of a shareholder in a public company which has a Stock Exchange listing for its shares or whose shares are dealt in on the Unlisted Securities Market. If he is dissatisfied with the management of the company, a minority shareholder of a private company cannot readily sell his shares because of the restrictions on their transfer imposed by the company's articles and the lack of an available market. In fact he usually finds that the only potential purchasers of his shares are the directors themselves or the majority shareholders, who are often the same persons and are, of course, in a position to dictate the price. Nor can the shareholders of a private company effectively oppose the re-election of directors, because the articles usually provide that they shall hold office for life or for a far longer period than the three years which is the usual period at the end of which directors of public companies must submit themselves for re-election. The articles of private companies may also entrench the directors' continuance in office by vesting the majority voting power at general meetings in them, even if they do not hold or control more than half the company's issued capital carrying voting rights.

(e) Takeovers of private companies which are opposed by the incumbent directors are more difficult to engineer than opposed takeovers of public companies. This is first, because the majority of the voting shares are usually in the hands or under the control of the directors or persons connected with them, secondly, because the restrictions imposed by the articles on the transfer of shares (particularly, pre-emption provisions) prevent members who are willing to accept a takeover bid from doing to, and thirdly, because it is difficult to arrive at a satisfactory price for the shares in view of the absence of market dealings.

Protection of shareholders in private companies

Clearly the need of shareholders in private companies for legal protection is great. This is provided in part at present by the court's power to give relief if the company's affairs are being conducted in a manner which is unfairly prejudicial to its minority shareholders,[12] and by the power of the Secretary of State for Trade and Industry to order an investigation into the conduct of the company's affairs if a prima facie case of fraud or mismanagement can be made out.[13] But situations often arise where a shareholder cannot complain of illegal acts or oppression or unfair treatment by the persons who control the company, but he is nevertheless dissatisfied with the management of the company's affairs or the rate of dividend in respect of his shares, so that if the company were a public one with a Stock Exchange listing, he would avoid being locked into the company by selling his holding. The draftsmen of the articles of private companies have dealt with this problem in a variety of ways, sometimes successfully and sometimes not. The device most often used is to insert one or more of the following provisions in the company's articles or in a separate agreement entered into by the shareholders:

(a) That disputes between shareholders and the company or its directors (eg as to the rate of dividend to be paid) shall be submitted to arbitration. It should be made clear that the provision extends to disputes relating to any matter connected with the company and its affairs, whether the dispute affects a shareholder as such or in another capacity (eg as a director of the company who is removed or not re-elected). Unless this is done, the only disputes subject to arbitration under a provision in the articles will be those affecting members' rights and obligations as such.[14]

(b) That voting rights attached to shares shall in specified circumstances be exercised in a certain way, or shall not be exercised at all. Arrangements of this kind are best dealt with in a separate agreement between the shareholders, and not in the company's articles, because attempts to restrain shareholders from passing resolutions expressly authorised by the Companies Act 1985 (eg to alter the memorandum or articles) will be void if inserted in the articles themselves.[15] On the other hand, voting agreements between shareholders are valid, whether they require them to vote or to abstain from voting.[16] By means of voting agreements individual shareholders can be given power to veto particular acts or transactions (eg the sale of the business the company was formed to acquire), or to compel the other shareholders to vote for a course of action to which they are personally opposed. The most important example of this latter type is a power for any shareholder to compel the others to join in passing a special resolution to wind the company up voluntarily if any of certain events specified in the voting agreement occur (eg if the company incurs losses in each of a certain number of consecutive years; if the shareholder in question is removed from office as a director of the company; if the company fails to pay a specified minimum dividend in each of a certain consecutive number of years, even though it has sufficient profits and reserves available to do so; or if a director of the company is guilty of certain acts of misconduct). Stipulations of this sort correspond to the provisions inserted in partnership agreements for the

12 Ibid, ss 459 to 461, as amended by Companies Act 1989, s 145 and Sch 19, para 11.
13 Ibid, s 431 (1) and (2) and s 432 (1) and (2) (see p 686 et seq, ante).
14 *Beattie v E & F Beattie Ltd* [1938] Ch 708, [1938] 3 All ER 214.
15 *Ayre v Skelsey's Adamant Cement Co Ltd* (1904) 20 TLR 587; (1905) 21 TLR 464.
16 *Puddephatt v Leith* [1916] 1 Ch 200 (see p 643, ante).

is unnecessary for the memorandum to state what the company's nominal capital will be if it is to have a share capital. The company must have its own special articles of association,[9] which must state the amount of the share capital which it may issue, if it has a share capital.[10] The company's memorandum and articles must, so far as possible, follow the forms specified in regulations made by the Secretary of State for Trade and Industry if the company has a share capital.[11] The regulations require the memorandum and articles to be in the form set out in Table E of the regulations.[12] If an unlimited company is formed without a share capital, there is no standard form of memorandum and articles to which its own must adhere. If an unlimited company has no share capital, the rights of its members and their obligations as between themselves to contribute toward payment of its debts and liabilities when it is wound up will be governed by the provisions of its memorandum and articles, which will bind all members as a matter of contract, whether they became members when the company was formed or later.[13]

The provisions of the Companies Act 1985 governing the alteration of a company's capital do not apply to unlimited companies. Consequently, the company may alter its capital structure set out in its articles simply by passing a special resolution altering the articles themselves,[14] and if it reduces its capital, it is not necessary to obtain the confirmation of the court. If the company's capital structure is set out in its memorandum as well as in its articles, the special resolution altering the articles must alter the memorandum too,[15] but in that event the holders of 15 per cent in nominal value of the company's issued shares of any class have a statutory right to apply to the court to cancel the alteration.[16] When an unlimited company has altered its capital structure, it must give notice of the alteration to the Registrar of Companies within one month,[17] unless the alteration increases the company's nominal capital, when the notice must be given within 15 days,[18] or unless the alteration effects a reduction of capital, when a copy of the special resolution for the reduction must also be delivered to the Registrar within 15 days.[19] The Registrar must publish the fact that notice of the alteration of capital has been given to him in the London Gazette.[20]

Wholly apart from altering its capital structure, an unlimited company may acquire any of its own shares if its articles authorise it to do so, even though the shares are only partly paid, and even though it uses its own assets representing paid up capital to purchase them;[1] the statutory prohibition on companies acquiring their own shares applies only to companies limited by shares or by guarantee with a share capital.[2] The reason for this relaxation of the normal prohibition on a company acquiring its own shares is that the members of an unlimited company

---

9 Ibid, s 7 (1).
10 Ibid, s 7 (2).
11 Ibid, s 3 (1) and s 8 (4).
12 Companies (Table A to F) Regulations 1985, reg 2 and Schedule.
13 Companies Act 1985, s 14 (1).
14 Ibid, s 9 (1).
15 Ibid, s 17 (1). There is an express provision to this effect with respect to unlimited companies which were registered under the Joint Stock Companies Act 1856 (Companies Act 1985, s 678 (2)), but this provision is clearly not exhaustive.
16 Companies Act 1985, s 17 (3).
17 Ibid, s 122 (1).
18 Ibid, s 123 (1).
19 Ibid, s 380 (1) and (4).
20 Ibid, s 711 (1) (*b*).
 1 *Re Borough Commercial and Building Society* [1893] 2 Ch 242.
 2 Companies Act 1985, s 143 (1) (see p 409, ante). The statutory provisions as to the consequences of a nominee of a company acquiring shares in it (see p 334, ante) also do not apply to an unlimited company (s 144 (1)).

are liable to contribute without limit toward the satisfaction of its debts and liabilities when it is wound up. Consequently, a reduction in the company's unpaid capital or a diminution of its assets resulting from the acquisition of shares in the company by the company itself merely operates to increase the personal liability of its members, and on the company being wound up the fund available to satisfy its liabilities should not be reduced, in theory at least. Because of this an unlimited company need not replace the shares in itself which it purchases by issuing new shares with an equivalent nominal value, nor need it create a capital reserve equal to the nominal value of the purchased shares. But if at the time an unlimited company purchases shares in itself the company knows that its existing assets and the amounts which it would expect to exact from its members on a winding up will not be sufficient to satisfy its liabilities, the acquisition of the shares will be set aside as a fraud on its creditors, and the holders of the shares will be compelled to repay the amounts paid to them by the company.[3] Because of its general power to acquire shares in itself, an unlimited company is not given the limited statutory powers to purchase its own shares which are conferred on limited companies.[4] Likewise, an unlimited company has no statutory power to issue redeemable shares,[5] but since it may purchase any of its shares, there seems to be no reason why it should not issue shares on terms that they will or may be redeemed at a future date, and the statutory restrictions imposed on limited companies as to the manner in which redeemable shares may be redeemed[6] are not applicable.

The personal liability of members of an unlimited company to contribute toward payment of its debts is not an asset of the company, but, like the guarantee undertaken by members of a company limited by guarantee, is a contingent liability of the members which will become effective only when the company is wound up. Consequently, while the company is a going concern, its members cannot be called upon to contribute anything beyond the capital unpaid on their shares (if any), and the company cannot mortgage or charge their personal liability to contribute toward payment of its debts and liabilities when it is wound up so as to give any of the company's creditors priority for payment out of their contributions in a liquidation.[7] Furthermore, creditors of an unlimited company cannot sue its members for the company's debts or levy execution on their property to enforce judgments obtained against the company. In these respects an unlimited company differs from a partnership. The only way by which the company's creditors may compel the members to contribute toward payment of its debts is by petitioning for the company to be wound up by the court.[8] If a winding up order is made, the liquidator may make calls on members to raise sufficient money to pay the company's debts and liabilities in full and also to meet the expenses of the liquidation.[9] Calls must be made on the persons who are members of the company at the commencement of the winding up for the capital unpaid on their shares (if any) in the first place, and if this yields insufficient to discharge the company's liabilities, further calls will be made in proportion to the nominal value of each contributory's shares.[10] If the company has no share capital, calls must be made in the proportions provided by the company's memorandum or articles or, in the

---

3 *Mitchell v City of Glasgow Bank* (1879) 4 App Cas 624; *Re Borough Commercial and Building Society* (supra).
4 Companies Act 1985, s 162 (1) and s 171 (1) (see p 190 et seq, ante).
5 Ibid, s 159 (1).
6 Ibid, s 160 (1) and s 171 (1) (see p 188 et seq, ante).
7 *Re Mayfair Property Co, Bartlett v Mayfair Property Co* [1898] 2 Ch 28 at 36, per Lindley MR.
8 Insolvency Act 1986, s 124 (1).
9 Ibid, s 74 (1) and s 150 (1).
10 *Binney v Mutrie* (1886) 12 App Cas 160. This was a partnership case decided before the rule was altered by the Partnership Act 1890, s 24 (1) (32 Halsbury's Statutes (4th Edn) 649). The common law rule would still appear to apply to unlimited companies.

absence of such provisions, by calls made equally upon all the contributories. However, the failure of any member to pay his due contribution must be made good by the other members in the same proportions as they paid their original contributions as between themselves; this is because the other members are liable without limit to contribute the amount required to satisfy the company's creditors. If the members of the company at the commencement of the winding up cannot collectively contribute sufficient to discharge the company's liabilities, the liquidator may resort to persons who were members of the company within one year before the winding up began, but they are liable to contribute only toward payment of debts and liabilities incurred before they ceased to be members.[11]

An unlimited company is of necessity a private company, whether it has a share capital or not, and it can therefore avail itself of the facility to pass or agree to resolutions which may be passed by general meetings or by meetings of classes of its members in the form of written resolutions signed by or on behalf of all the members entitled to vote; also an unlimited company can by elective resolution adopt the whole or any part of the elective regime for private companies.[12]

COMPARISON WITH COMPANIES LIMITED BY SHARES

The Companies Act 1985 as amended and the rules of company law generally apply to companies limited by guarantee and unlimited companies in the same way as they apply to private companies limited by shares, subject to certain obvious exceptions arising from the difference in their constitutions and subject also to certain special exceptions which are dealt with below. The principal difference between such companies is that companies limited by guarantee and unlimited companies need not have a share capital, whereas private companies limited by shares obviously must. In applying the Companies Act 1985 to a company limited by guarantee or an unlimited company, it must be remembered that references to 'a company' includes all kinds of company registered under the Act, whether public or private, whether limited or unlimited and whether with or without a share capital.[13] Furthermore, a company limited by guarantee with a share capital is treated by the Companies Act 1985 in the same way as a company limited by shares; the same rules apply to it, and they are merely supplemented by the special rules relating to the members' additional liability arising under the guarantee clause in its memorandum. On the other hand, the provisions of the Companies Act 1985, which apply to a company limited by shares but not to all companies, do not apply to an unlimited company with a share capital.

The differences between the various kinds of companies can be best illustrated by setting out first, the statutory privileges which are enjoyed only by companies limited by shares and companies limited by guarantee with a share capital, then the rules which apply only to companies limited by guarantee with no share capital and to unlimited companies, whether they have a share capital or not, and finally, the rules applicable only to companies which have no share capital.

---

11 Insolvency Act 1986, s 74 (2) (*b*) and (*c*).
12 Companies Act 1985, s 80A, s 252, s 366A, s 369 (4), s 378 (3), s 379A, s 381A and s 386, inserted or amended by Companies Act 1989, s 16 (1), s 113 to 115 and s 119 (1) (see pp 762 and 765, ante).
13 Companies Act 1985, s 735 (1).

Statutory privileges of companies limited by shares and companies limited by guarantee with a share capital

These are three in number, namely, to issue redeemable shares,[14] to purchase shares in the company but only if certain conditions are complied with,[15] and to issue share warrants to bearer.[16] As has already been pointed out, however, there appears to be no reason why an unlimited company should not issue shares on terms that they shall be redeemable, nor are there any restrictions on solvent unlimited companies purchasing their own shares.

Rules applicable only to companies limited by guarantee and unlimited companies

A company limited by guarantee has only two rules peculiar to itself. The first is that if it has no share capital, it may under the law at present in force invite the public to subscribe for its debentures, or allot its debentures with a view to them being offered to the public under an offer for sale by an intermediary, even though the company is classified as a private company,[17] but it will not be lawful for it to do so when Part V of the Financial Services Act 1986 has been brought into force by an order made by the Secretary of State for Trade and Industry, except so far as permitted by an order made by him.[18] The second rule is that a company limited by guarantee may be incorporated without the word 'limited' as the last word of its name if its objects are confined to the promotion of commerce, art, science, education, religion, charity or any profession, and its memorandum or articles prohibit the payment of dividends to its members and require its residual assets in its liquidation to be transferred to a similar body.[19]

There are a number of rules which are applicable only to unlimited companies. Although the rules for holding general meetings of an unlimited company with a share capital are the same as for a company limited by shares, no unlimited company, unless its articles otherwise provide, need give more than seven days' notice to its members of an extraordinary general meeting called to pass any resolution other than a special one.[20] Furthermore, an unlimited company with a share capital does not need to make a return of allotments of its shares to the Registrar of Companies.[1] The most important privilege of an unlimited company, however, is that it need not deliver copies of its annual accounts to the Registrar of Companies, but this privilege is not enjoyed by unlimited companies which are subsidiaries of limited companies, or in which two or more limited companies have in the aggregate a controlling interest.[2]

Rules peculiar to companies with no share capital

A company which has no share capital may nevertheless have two or more classes of members and confer different rights (eg as to voting at general meetings) on each class. This may be done by the company's memorandum or articles or by a resolution passed pursuant to their provisions; in the latter case a copy of the

---

14 Ibid, s 159 (1) (see p 188, ante).
15 Ibid, s 143 (1), s 162 (1) and s 171 (1) (see p 190 et seq, ante).
16 Ibid, s 188 (1) (see p 331, ante).
17 Companies Act 1985, s 81 (1).
18 Financial Services Act 1986, s 170 (1) and (2), as amended by Companies Act 1989, s 199.
19 Companies Act 1985, s 30 (1) to (3) (see p 7, ante).
20 Ibid, s 369 (1) and (2).
 1 Ibid, s 88 (1) and (2) (see p 309, ante).
 2 Ibid, s 254 (1) and (2), substituted by Companies Act 1989, s 17.

resolution setting out the rights of the class and any subsequent resolution varying such rights must be delivered to the Registrar of Companies.[3] The copy resolution must be delivered within 15 days after the resolution is passed if it is a special or extraordinary resolution, or a resolution agreed to by all the members of the company but which, if not so agreed to, would have been effective only if passed as a special or extraordinary resolution.[4] Whether the rights of the class of members are created or altered by such a resolution or in any other way, a statement of those rights or of the alteration made to them must be delivered to the Registrar within one month after they are created or altered.[3]

Unless the articles of a company with no share capital otherwise provide, each member has one vote at its general meetings,[5] but is not entitled to appoint a proxy to represent him.[6] The articles may, of course, confer multiple or additional voting rights on certain members of the company, or deprive other members of voting rights completely, as in the case of a company limited by shares. If there are differences between members in respect of voting rights or any other rights, the different categories of members must be distinguished in the company's register of members.[7] Members holding one-tenth of the voting rights at a general meeting may require the directors to call an extraordinary general meeting,[8] and members holding one-twentieth of the voting rights may require the directors to circulate to all the members notice of a resolution which the requisitionists wish to move at the next annual general meeting, or a statement not exceeding one thousand words in length in respect of any business to be transacted at any general meeting.[9] Unless the company's articles otherwise provide, one-twentieth of the members may call a general meeting,[10] but the articles usually make this right exercisable only if there are insufficient directors in the United Kingdom to form a quorum at a board meeting.[11] If the company's annual general meeting is called by less than 21 days' notice, it may be held only if all the members entitled to attend and vote consent, but if less than the normal length of notice of an extraordinary general meeting is given, the meeting may be held with the consent of a majority in number of the members who between them hold 95 per cent of the voting rights exercisable at the meeting.[12]

Although a company with no share capital must lay annual accounts before its members in general meeting, it need not send copies of the accounts or of its auditors' or directors' reports to members or debenture holders who are not entitled to be sent notice of the meeting,[13] but such members or debenture holders may at any time demand a copy of the company's last annual accounts and the auditors' and directors' reports which accompanied the accounts.[14] A company with no share capital must in each calendar year deliver an annual return to the Registrar of Companies within the same time limits as a company with a share capital.[15] The

---

3 Companies Act 1985, s 129 (1) and (2).
4 Ibid, s 350 (1) and (4).
5 Ibid, s 370 (1) and (6).
6 Ibid, s 372 (2). The standard form of articles, Table C, arts 1 and 8 permit members of companies limited by guarantee to appoint proxies, however, and such proxies may vote on a poll.
7 Companies Act 1985, s 352 (4).
8 Ibid, s 368 (1) and (2) (see p 619, ante).
9 Ibid, s 376 (1) and (2) (see pp 621 and 630, ante).
10 Ibid, s 370 (1) and (3).
11 Table C, art 1 (incorporating Table A, art 37) so provides, but the meeting may then be called by any one or more directors or members.
12 Companies Act 1985, s 369 (3) and (4) and s 378 (3).
13 Ibid, s 238 (3), substituted by Companies Act 1989, s 10.
14 Companies Act 1985, s 239 (1), substituted by Companies Act 1989, s 10.
15 Companies Act 1985, s 363 (1), substituted by Companies Act 1989, s 139 (1) (see p 726, ante).

annual return must contain the same information as that supplied by a company with a share capital in respect of the company's registered office, the type of company it is, its principal business activities (if any), particulars of its directors and secretary, the address at which the company's registers of members and debenture holders are kept (if not the company's registered office) and a statement whether the company has elected to dispense with the laying of its annual accounts before a general meeting or with holding annual general meetings.[16] Unlike the annual return of a company limited by shares, however, the annual return of a company with no share capital does not contain a list of its members or particulars of changes in its membership during the past year, unless this information is called for by regulations yet to be made by the Secretary of State for Trade and Industry.[17] Finally, in relation to a company with no share capital, an application to the Secretary of State for Trade and Industry for the appointment of one or more inspectors to investigate the company's affairs may be made by one-fifth of its members, whether they are more or less numerous than the two hundred members who may apply for an investigation into the affairs of a company limited by shares.[18]

16 Companies Act 1985, s 363 (2) and s 364 (1).
17 Companies Act 1985, s 365 (1), substituted by Companies Act 1989, s 139 (1).
18 Companies Act 1985, s 431 (1) and (2) (see p 686, ante).

Index

Unfair treatment—*continued*
 unfairly prejudicial. *See* UNFAIRLY PREJUDICIAL
  CONDUCT
Unfairly prejudicial conduct, 668–683
 alteration of rights in shares, and, 230–232
 appointment of receiver, and, 683
 business policy, 670–672
 capacities in which parties act, 674–677
 conditions for obtaining relief, 677–679
 control of voting power, and, 672–673
 delay in initiating proceedings, and, 678
 deliberate, 668
 entitlement to winding up, and, 678
 equitable character of relief, 678
 fiduciary duty of majority shareholders, 676–
  677
 form of petition, 682
 intention, 670
 interference with proper management, 676
 meaning, 669–673
 members, of, 674
 members who are unfairly prejudiced, 673
 motives, 670
 negligence, 670
 other relief more appropriate, 678–679
 petition, 682–683
 procedure, 682–683
 proof of, 669
 remedies available, 679–681
  alteration of rights, 681
  discretion of court, 679
  future regulation of company affairs, 681
  orders of court, 679–680
  purchase of shares, 680–681
 rule in Foss v Harbottle, and, 676–677
 shareholder ceasing to act as director, 672
 shareholders, of, 674–675
United States
 subordination provisions, 475
Unlimited companies, 778–781
 acquisition of own shares, 779–780
 alteration of capital, 779
 limited companies compared, 781–784
 memorandum of association, 778–779

Unlimited companies—*continued*
 personal liability of members, 780–781
 statutory rules applicable only to, 782
 re-registration as limited, 71–72
 re-registration of limited company as, 70–71
Unregistered charge
 enforcement of, 515–517
Unsecured creditors, 452–454
 floating charge, and, 452–454
 preferential claims, 452–454
Untrue statement
 meaning, 280–281

Valuation
 annual accounts, in 703–705
Vicarious liability
 deceit, and, 277
Voting
 meeting, at, 638–642
Voting rights
 alteration of articles of association, and, 79–81

Wales
 registered office, 10–11
War
 separate legal personality of company, and, 46–
  47
Winding up
 arreas of preference dividend in, 213–215
 avoidance of floating charges on, 461–466
 directors, and, 549–550
 limited liability, and, 58–59
 rescission, and, 271–272
Wrongful dismissal
 director, and, 546
Wrongful trading, 44–46
 awareness of directors, 45–46
 imposition of liability, 44–45
 order for payment of contributions, 44–46
 standards required of director, 45
 statutory offence, 44

Yield, 139–140